THE OXFORD HANDBOOK OF

CRITICAL CONCEPTS IN MUSIC THEORY

THE OXFORD HANDBOOK OF

CRITICAL CONCEPTS IN MUSIC THEORY

Edited by
ALEXANDER REHDING
and
STEVEN RINGS

OXFORD
UNIVERSITY PRESS

OXFORD
UNIVERSITY PRESS

Oxford University Press is a department of the University of Oxford. It furthers
the University's objective of excellence in research, scholarship, and education
by publishing worldwide. Oxford is a registered trade mark of Oxford University
Press in the UK and certain other countries.

Published in the United States of America by Oxford University Press
198 Madison Avenue, New York, NY 10016, United States of America.

Library of Congress Cataloging-in-Publication Data
Names: Rehding, Alexander, editor. | Rings, Steven, editor.
Title: The Oxford handbook of critical concepts in music theory /
edited byAlexander Rehding and Steven Rings.
Description: New York, NY: Oxford University Press, 2019. |
Includes bibliographical references and index.
Identifiers: LCCN 2018046637 | ISBN 9780190454746 (hardcover)
Subjects: LCSH: Music theory.
Classification: LCC MT6.O888 2019 |
DDC 781—dc23 LC record available at https://lccn.loc.gov/2018046637

3 5 7 9 8 6 4 2

Printed by Sheridan Books, Inc., United States of America

CONTENTS

PART III   HORIZONTALS AND VERTICALS

PART IV   THE BIG PICTURE

About the Editors

....

Alexander Rehding teaches music theory at Harvard University. He specializes in the music of the nineteenth century, history of music theory, and media theory. His publications include *Hugo Riemann and the Birth of Modern Musical Thought* (2003), *Music and Monumentality* (2009), and *Beethoven's Ninth Symphony* (2017). He is editor-in-chief of the Oxford Handbooks Online in Music and series editor for a six-volume *Cultural History of Music*. He was awarded the 2014 Edward Dent Medal.

Steven Rings teaches music theory at the University of Chicago. His research ranges from transformational theory to studies of the popular singing voice. His book *Tonality and Transformation* received the Emerging Scholar Award from the Society for Music Theory, and his article "A Foreign Sound to Your Ear: Bob Dylan Performs 'It's Alright, Ma (I'm Only Bleeding),' 1964–2009" received the Outstanding Publication Award from the SMT's Popular Music Interest Group. He is Series Editor of Oxford Studies in Music Theory.

CONTRIBUTORS

David Blake is an independent scholar in Potsdam, NY.

Andrew Bowie is Professor Emeritus of Philosophy and German at Royal Holloway, University of London.

Guilherme Schmidt Câmara is Doctoral Research Fellow at the University of Oslo.

Suzannah Clark is Morton B. Knafel Professor of Music and Harvard College Professor at Harvard University.

Richard Cohn is Battell Professor of Music Theory at Yale University.

Anne Danielsen is Professor in Popular Music Studies at the University of Oslo.

Jonathan De Souza is Associate Professor in the Don Wright Faculty of Music at the University of Western Ontario.

Matthew Gelbart is Associate Professor of Music at Fordham University.

Robert O. Gjerdingen is Professor Emeritus of Music at Northwestern University.

Daniel M. Grimley is Professor of Music at the University of Oxford.

Marion A. Guck is Professor Emerita of Music Theory at the School of Music, Theatre & Dance of The University of Michigan.

Stephan Hammel is Assistant Professor of Musicology at the University of California, Irvine.

Dora A. Hanninen is Professor of Music Theory at the School of Music at the University of Maryland.

Daniel Harrison is Allen Forte Professor of Music Theory at Yale University.

Vijay Iyer is Franklin D. and Florence Rosenblatt Professor of the Arts at Harvard University.

Henry Klumpenhouwer is Professor of Music Theory at the Eastman School of Music.

Elizabeth Hellmuth Margulis is Professor of Music at Princeton University.

Susan McClary is Fynette H. Kulas Professor of Music at Case Western Reserve University.

Mitchell Ohriner is Assistant Professor of Music Theory at the University of Denver.

Bryan Parkhurst is Assistant Professor of Music Theory and Aural Skills at the Oberlin Conservatory of Music and Assistant Professor of Philosophy at Oberlin College.

Ian Quinn is Professor of Music at Yale University.

Alexander Rehding is Fanny Peabody Professor of Music at Harvard University.

Steven Rings is Associate Professor of Music at the University of Chicago.

Martin Scherzinger is Associate Professor of Media, Culture, and Communication at New York University.

Janet Schmalfeldt is Professor Emerita of Music at Tufts University.

Michael Tenzer is Professor of Music at the University of British Columbia.

David Trippett is Senior Lecturer at the Faculty of Music and a Fellow of Christ's College, University of Cambridge.

Naomi Waltham-Smith is Associate Professor in the Center for Interdisciplinary Methodologies at the University of Warwick.

About the Companion Website

WWW.OUP.COM/US/OHCCMT

OXFORD has created a website to accompany *The Oxford Handbook of Critical Concepts in Music Theory*. All audio and video examples referenced in-text with the symbol ⊙ are available there.

INTRODUCTION

....

IF you look up "Phrase" or "Sequence" in *Grove* you will find terse descriptions, no more than a few sentences long. If you open the *Harvard Dictionary of Music* at the term "Tonic," the entry refers you to other terms rather than offering a definition (Randel 2003, 900). Brevity may be a hallmark of dictionary style, but it often conceals the complexities that underlie some of the most fundamental concepts we use in music theory. These critical terms are the bread and butter of every music theory. In fact, in our teaching we regularly introduce them early on in the semester, often with a rudimentary explanation, accompanied by a vague and optimistic promise to return to this point later in the semester once we have covered more ground. This book is an opportunity to examine some of these critical concepts in music theory in greater depth than our daily work as teachers and scholars generally allows. In this volume, our authors return to first principles, thinking and theorizing these concepts afresh.

The word "critical" in the book's title carries two connotations. On the one hand it means essential, fundamental, paramount. The concepts studied in the following chapters are, in this familiar sense, critical to music theorizing: theorists cannot do without them. It might be tempting to call them "fundamental concepts," but the word "fundamental" has a different resonance in the music theory classroom. Courses in "fundamentals" are usually those in which students learn the basic materials of Western music: rhythms, pitches, intervals, scales, chords, etc. But they are also precisely the courses in which those concepts are often minimally defined. In a fundamentals class, one might learn how to notate a quarter note and how to slot it into various time signatures, but one generally will *not* take a deep dive into the phenomenological, conceptual, and cross-cultural complexities of meter and rhythm. Such deep dives are exactly what our authors undertake in the following chapters. A reader picking up this handbook hoping to find a primer on "music fundamentals" will be disappointed—but that reader might also be pleasantly surprised by what is here. Opening a chapter on pitch, tone, and note, she will find not a dry account of these terms as stable perceptual and notational categories, but instead a richly detailed dialectical-materialist narrative that reveals their deep historicity.

This leads us to the second sense of the word "critical," which should by now be obvious. Our authors approach these concepts not as settled knowledge but as sites for critical scrutiny; the chapters that follow exert critical pressure on familiar terms. The kinds of pressure brought to bear vary considerably from chapter to chapter—from philosophical to formalist, political to cognitive scientific—but in all cases the authors have sought to bring a renewed critical perspective to these concepts, casting a wary eye on received wisdom and digging deep into ideas we thought we knew well. The twenty-six essays assembled in this volume thus illuminate some of the complexities and, in some cases, contradictions that emerge when we do more than scratch the surface.

The diversity of viewpoints represented here is not a bug but a feature: it reflects the pluralism that characterizes music theory in the early twenty-first century. As has been widely discussed, the firmly delineated tools and repertories that once epitomized American music theory can no longer be taken for granted. The doors have been cast wide open. Many of the essays use this new freedom to extend traditional concepts into unconventional repertoires. Conversely, some essays discuss critical concepts that may not yet have entered the discourse but that should probably be part of any music theory worth its salt in the twenty-first century.

Moreover, concepts can be difficult to contain. Especially the essays in the last section—zooming out for the big picture—often go beyond the neat single-word focus that we maintain in the rest of the book. At the same time these chapters, which allow space to reflect on recent development in technology, politics, and important trends in disciplinary thinking, form an indispensable part of the overall picture. From this perspective, this collection may be read as a seismograph measuring the ripples and aftershocks of the epistemological shifts of the 1990s, known then as the New Musicology. This collection is a reflection on where we are, how we got here, and where we might go next.

In this new world, we often have to renegotiate some of the fundamental terms with which we operate. This is true whether our object of study is canonical or bracingly new. Let's take an example of the latter first: Peter Ablinger's "A Letter from Schoenberg" from his series *Quadraturen 3* (2008). The composition consists of a synthesized version of a letter that the irate Arnold Schoenberg fired off, performed on a computer-assisted player piano. This piano piece has everything that one should expect in a composition that can be analyzed in fairly straightforward terms: it is restricted to twelve distinct pitch classes, it has an unambiguous rhythmic structure, and is fully notated from beginning to end. And yet, it is not even clear where a theorist might want to begin. Our terse description left out some significant elements: the sounds that the piano reproduces do not constitute music in a conventional sense, but deploy the keys of the piano with microtemporal accuracy to reproduce the complex timbres of the speaking voice. Yet the reproduction is faulty: the piano supplies complex tones for each of the voice's partials, blurring and cluttering the signal with additional instrumental noise. In this musical world, all parameters seem definitionally up for grabs. What is pitch? What is timbre? What is rhythm? And, asking further: where exactly is the piece located? Is it nestled in Schoenberg's voice, whose reading forms the basis of the composition? Is it in the piano that reproduces that voice? Is it in the software that enables the piano to play with super-human accuracy? Is it in the score? We seem to be moving in circles.

But the twenty-first-century theorist faces a similarly bewildering range of possibilities even when analyzing a canonical, common-practice piece, say, a Mozart sonata movement. The days in which a Schenkerian sketch was viewed as the *ne plus ultra* of tonal analysis are long gone. This is not to say that Schenkerian analysis is passé: it remains perhaps the richest method for tonal analysis in the academy. But it is clear that Schenkerian hegemony is a thing of the past. In 2018 an analyst might approach a Mozart movement as a data source for a corpus study, as a repository of galant schemata, as a site for transformational theorizing, as an exemplar in a renewed *Formenlehre*, as an empirical test piece for lab work, and so on. As a result of this pluralism, the foundational concepts that music theorists deploy every day have become exhilaratingly mobile—open once again to critical appraisal and (re-)definition. What is a chord for a Schenkerian? For a schema theorist? For a cognitive scientist?

Because of its embeddedness in this particular discourse, this volume's principal focus is music theory as practiced in the Anglo-American world. To be sure, there is much to be gained from an international perspective, but in many cases it would simply have muddled the issues too much. When a German scholar, for instance, describes a *Kadenz*, she tends to have something different in mind than the Anglo-American cadence. A comparative perspective on different intellectual traditions would be a fascinating project in itself, but such a collection would be headed in a different direction than this volume.[1]

In ordering the concept across the volume we move from the small scale to the large scale. We begin with some fundamental categories of music theory: from individual tones to intervals, then via modes and scales to timbre and texture. The second part examines structures that exist in time, from phrase, groove, and meter, to form and diverse temporalities. The third part examines some more complex interactions between tones, from melody and harmony to specific phenomena such as cadence, sequence, or polyphony. The final group of concepts enters the metalevel of music theory, raising broad discursive questions such as: How do music examples marshal music theoretical evidence? What exactly do we have in mind when we invoke the term "music", particularly in a world that is no longer tethered to the rigid work concept that dominated concert music? How can Black Lives Matter be brought to bear on music-theoretical concerns?

Any collection is invariably a selection. It is easy to take issue with the concepts that have been included and those that have been left out. Comprehensive coverage is a noble idea, but almost unattainable in practice. We tried to keep the range of topics manageable, while covering many of the topics that would speak to a broad readership of music theorists—and hopefully including some that extend the expected range of concepts in interesting ways. If the ideas presented in these essays become a springboard for further explorations along similar lines, our volume will have fulfilled its goal.

If you are holding a copy of this book with a cover image, you will see detail from a lively watercolor. You may be able to guess at the image's representational content, but you might also find that your ways of seeing begin to shift as you look closer. What once seemed iconic representations (say, of vegetation) might begin to take on a more abstract—indeed, one might even say musical—quality. In particular, the rhythmic repetition of the purple shapes is highly suggestive of certain musical phenomena ("verticals," if you will, to draw on one of our section titles). The exercise reminds us that the word "theory" derives from the Greek *theōria*, which refers to the act of viewing. To the extent that such viewing leads to puzzlement and curiosity, it begins to enter into the terrain that our authors map in this book, that is, critical reflection on the act of theorizing itself.

NOTE

1 The German *Handwörterbuch der musikalischen Terminologie* (Eggebrecht and Riethmüller 1971–2005) or the Italian *Storia dei concetti musicali* (Borio and Gentili 2007–) may come close to such a comparative perspective, but both take a *begriffsgeschichtlich* approach, as is often the case in European discourse. Another German reference work dedicated specifically to music theory is in preparation, edited by Jan Philipp Sprick, Oliver Schwab-Felisch, and Christian Thorau.

REFERENCES

Borio, Gianmario, and Carlo Gentili, eds. 2007–. *Storia dei concetti musicali*. Rome: Carocci Editore.

Eggebrecht, Hans Heinrich, and Albrecht Riethmüller, eds. 1971–2005. *Handwörterbuch der musikalischen Terminologie*. Wiesbaden: F. Steiner.

Randel, Don Michael, ed. 2003. *Harvard Dictionary of Music*. 4th edition. Cambridge, MA: Harvard University Press.

PART I

STARTING POINTS

CHAPTER 1

··

PITCH, TONE, AND NOTE

··

BRYAN PARKHURST AND STEPHAN HAMMEL

THE familiarity of the words "pitch," "tone," and "note" belies their conceptual unruliness, which reveals itself as soon they are laid bare to a bit of philosophical cross-examination. Are tones more like qualities that attach to quality-bearers, or are they more like events that have causes? That is, is a tone "rather like the redness to the apple, than it is like the burp to the cider" (Bouwsma 1965, 49), or vice versa? More to the musical point: when a musical instrument vibrates as a "sounding body," to use that venerable Rameauian locution, does it possess a tone or does it produce a tone? Does a tone have a pitch, or is it the other way around? If pitch is a feature of tonal events, is it an essential feature, one that tones cannot lack? Is any given tone associated with one and only one pitch, such that a change in pitch is necessarily also a change in tone? Is the whine of an ambulance siren best described as a single tone with an undulating pitch, or as a gradual oscillation between a high-pitched tone and a low-pitched tone, or something else? Are tones and pitches subjective attributes (experiential properties? mental events?) that are to be distinguished from the physical vibrations that are their extramental basis? And what about notes? Is a note a sonic entity, a written symbol, a cognitive category, something else, all of the above? Are notes to tones (or to pitches?) as numerals are to numbers, or as words are to concepts, or what? Do notes describe tones (and/or pitches?), or prescribe them, or designate them, or stand to them in some other relation of aboutness?

Rather than attempting to manicure the conceptual landscape by offering tight formal definitions of "pitch," "tone," and "note," we prefer to embrace the terminological messiness.[1] Hereafter, we will treat "pitch," "tone," and "note" synecdochically, that is, as adaptable omnibus terms that cover wide-ranging domains of interrelated and overlapping phenomena for which there is no single designation in common use. Let "Pitch" serve as the category heading for the material (physical, quantifiable, causal, naturalistic) space in which music's sonic material has its objective, determinately measurable being;[2] "Tone" for the ideal (cognitive, notional, ideational, perceptual, phenomenological, affective, emotional, normative) space in which this material is sensuously and intellectually present to perceivers and knowers; and "Note" for the symbolic (representational, communicative, interpersonal, semantic, semiotic) space in which informational exchanges about sonic/musical material are transacted by members of epistemic and linguistic communities.[3] (Capitalization of these terms indicates that they are being used in this free-wheeling and encompassing manner, with due apologies for the Hegelian look that this lends to the text.) We must emphatically state at the outset that these three realms are not strictly demarcated from one another. Rather, they are dialectically united—reciprocally determinative, interpenetrating, and mutually presupposing—in ways that it is the task of a historical-materialist theory of music to spell out. In detailing, concretely and *in extenso*, the interrelatedness of Pitch, Tone, and Note as they subsist at a given "politico-historical conjuncture" or "articulation,"[4] one would in effect describe an entire musical "form of life" (*Lebensform*), to borrow a Wittgensteinian term (Wittgenstein 1986, 8). Indeed, it could with some justice be said that a musical practice is nothing other than a network of agents and actions located at a historically and culturally specific confluence of Pitch, Tone, and Note.

Our main purpose is to make plausible the ideas (1) that there is an immanent developmental logic to the way that the domains of Pitch, Tone, and Note have changed over time (such that they have a history, properly so-called, and not merely a past); (2) that this trajectory of development is open to empirical investigation and to explanation anchored in the concrete features of human practices and institutions and their environing natural and social contexts (such that the history in question is a materialist history); and (3) that this developmental dynamic has had, and continues to have, numerous and appreciable consequences for "musicking"—that is, any and every manner of "contributing to the nature of the event that is a musical performance" (Small 1998, 9)—in the broadest possible sense of that purposefully broad word.

The way this task can be carried through, in our view, is by means of a Marxian organology, which is to say a materialist history of musical technology.[5] We shall contend that it is principally by virtue of the directional and progressive historical development of technology, a deep-seated and non-contingent feature of the capitalist mode of production, that "the nature of the event that is a musical performance" gets caught up in the forward procession of history. By thematizing the societal acquisition of technological capabilities under conditions of the capitalistic generalization of the commodity form, we hope to make it seem credible that there is a certain directedness to the way that key aspects of the physical domain of sonic possibilities (Pitch), the historically determined "normative sensory imaginary" (Nolan and McBride 2015, 1073) (Tone), and conventional systems of sonic-musical symbolization and semiosis (Note) have changed over time. Prima facie, it may seem that a technocentric account of Pitch, Tone, and Note would be remote from the analytical and pedagogical concerns of music theory as it is nowadays understood and practiced. Quite to the contrary, we think, a Marxian approach to musical technology reveals much about the historical preconditions for the possibility of having this set of concerns in the first place (and thus about the preconditions for the possibility of modern music theory as such) and also about the ineliminably historical character of certain distinctively music-theoretical objects of concern (such as, for instance, musical works). Historical-materialist organological inquiry, that is to say, provides a means whereby the cultural practice of music theory might attain a judicious self-consciousness about itself as a historically situated human institution.

In the first portion of the paper, we touch on some of Marx's own arguments concerning the "directional dynamic and trajectory of capitalist history" (Postone 1996, 320) and reflect on the applicability of those arguments to technological change within the realms of Pitch, Tone, and Note. In the second, we offer three case studies that attempt to cash the methodological checks we write in the first.

Toward a Marxian Organology

In a footnote to his discussion of machinofacture in the first volume of *Capital*, Marx notes that historical treatments of the industrial revolution had yet to achieve scientific rigor.

> A critical history of technology would show how little any of the inventions of the 18th century are the work of a single individual. . . . Darwin has interested us in the history of nature's technology. . . . Does not the history of the productive organs of humanity, of organs that are the material basis of all social organisation, deserve equal attention?. . . . Technology discloses humanity's mode of dealing with Nature, the process of production by which humankind sustains its own life, and thereby also lays bare the mode of formation of its social relations, and of the mental conceptions that flow from them.
>
> (*MECW*, 35:375n2)[6]

In technology, Marx sees a clue for coming to understand how human life is perpetuated in and through an open-ended, metabolic interaction with nature. And, as Marx makes abundantly clear, by "life" he means more than the maintenance of a heartbeat. "Life" refers, instead, to the whole of our metabolism with nature as social animals, predicated as this communal self-sustenance is on the preservation of an elaborately fashioned social and institutional world. This social world is one that we are compelled to continuously reproduce if we are to sustain a recognizably human, and not merely mammalian, mode of existence. And it is a world in which the "life-process of society" must eventually be "treated as production by freely associated people . . . [and] consciously regulated by them in accordance with a settled plan" (*MECW*, 35:90) if the species is to attain a fully human, and not merely recognizably human, mode of existence.

To the degree that music-making is a pervasive part of the reproduction of "life," understood in Marx's rich and valuative sense, the study of music is implicitly addressed by his programmatic statement about duly scientific (*wissenschaftlich*) inquiry into technology. What Marx says suggests that we ought to turn our gaze toward the music's "productive organs" to see how they might "lay bare the mode of formation" of the social relations and mental conceptions proper to a definite form of musical life. The Marxian wager, then, is that technological, thus organological, inquiry can help pinpoint a mediating link between, on the one hand, specific embodied musical practices and, on the other hand, large-scale socioeconomic processes—notably, for Marx, value production and capital accumulation—that work themselves out in accordance with their own indwelling logic of developmental self-propulsion.

The use of organology to illuminate historical concretizations of Pitch, Tone, and Note necessitates an opening-up of the concept of the musical instrument so that admittance to the category is extended to any enabling device whatsoever that enters into the production of music. "Instrument," in this intentionally indiscriminate usage of the term, thus includes in its referential field many implements that don't get "played" in the conventional sense, such as a score, a baton, a microphone, a sound mixer, a turntable, a metronome, a concert hall. "Instrument" can be stretched even further so as to cover what the radical economics literature dubs "paratechnical relations" (Giddens 1973, 233). These are defined as "patterns of social interaction in the material process of work which emanate from the 'cooperative collectivity' among the employees involved" (Welskopp 2002, 92). Musical paratechnical relations, accordingly, correspond to the totality of norms and conventions, tacit as well as explicit, unreflective as well as consciously applied, that organize the division of labor at the point of musical production.

Bukharin (1925) saw the modern symphony orchestra as a repository of paratechnical relations, relations he regarded as both symptomatic of a particular moment and level of economic development and as inseparable from the instrumental technologies employed by the ensemble:

> The organization of persons is also directly connected with the bases of the social evolution. For instance, the distribution of the members of an orchestra is determined precisely as in the factory, by the instruments and groups of instruments; in other words, the arrangement and organization of these members is here conditioned by musical technique (in our restricted [technological] sense of the word) and, through it, based on the stage in social evolution, on the technique of material production as such. (191–192)

The claim that the makeup of the orchestra is "based on the stage of social evolution, on the technique of material production as such" is in accord with Bukharin's view that musical practices in general reflect a "course of social evolution" (189) as it conducts itself within three precincts corresponding, to a close degree of approximation, to our realms of Pitch, Tone, and Note. The "natural and social object-realm" (Reuten 2014, 244) or "space of causes" that is Pitch is addressed by Buhkarin under the rubric of "the element of *objective material things*: . . . musical instruments and groups of musical instruments . . . [which] may be likened to combinations of machines and tools in factories" (Bukharin 1925, 189). The normative "space of reasons"[7] in which "the object realm of experience [is] reconstructed in thought" (Smith 1990, 8)—Tone, in our lingo—comes into Bukharin's consideration under the guise of "*methods* of uniting the various forms, *principles* of construction, what corresponds to style ... *theory* of musical technique, *theory* of counterpoint, etc." And Bukharin's category of "symbols and tokens: systems of notation, musical scores" (Bukharin 1925, 190) may be likened to the discursive "public sphere" (*Öffentlichkeit*, Habermas 1964, 49) we call Note. In the most condensed terms: the overall technological level of society determines what kind and amount of instrumental forces can be placed at music's disposal, and the socially available technical and paratechnical "instrumentarium" of the artform is either regulative or constitutive of—it either materially constrains and causally determines or, more strongly, grounds the essential nature of—Pitch, Tone, and Note as they appear historically. As Bukharin says, "human society in its technology constitutes an artificial system of organs which also are its direct, immediate and active adaptation to nature" (1925, 116). Some of these "artificial organs," of course, are musical (indeed some are organs in the narrowly musical sense); and the properties of these musical organs exert a bearing on and are also subject to the determining influence of the way music is physically instantiated (Pitch), normatively treated and conceptually carved up (Tone), and symbolically precipitated (Note).

This enlargement and stratification of the category of the instrument to include both "first-order" instruments (equipment and paraphernalia for musical production and performance, appurtenances of musical consumption, architectural contexts, as well as any technology that goes into producing aforesaid) and "higher-order" or "meta" instruments (all the techniques, traditions, routines, and "organization of persons" involved in any form or facet of musicking) comports nicely with the etymological roots of "instrument." These lie in the Latin "instruere," meaning both "to equip" and "to instruct." A musical instrument, on our promiscuous interpretation of what it is to be one, can be both a physical tool of the trade (e.g., the conductor's baton) as well as an inculcated form of organization (e.g., the discipline of the orchestra—imposed, in part, by the conductor's baton). Since it seems desirable, for our explanatory purposes, to hang on to the fertile matter/manner ambiguity built into "instrument," the Marxian term of art "forces of production" (*Produktivkräfte*), with its deliberate catholicity about the manifold technical and paratechnical powers and potentialities (*Kräfte*) that shape and provide impetus to the productive process, should at this point be introduced as a usefully vague piece of vocabulary.[8]

Forces of production are the main dramatis personae in the Marxian historical drama. Marx's is an unabashedly progressivist approach to history: he thinks that the saga of modernity can be read as, first and foremost, a chronicle of constant and cumulative gains in the productivity of human labor, brought about by the singular manner in and extent to which capitalist exploitation and competition "spurs on the development of society's productive forces" (*MECW*, 35:588). In the three volumes of *Capital*, Marx focuses on escalating industrial productivity, or growth in the ratio between units of industrial input to units of industrial output, as an additive, accelerative phenomenon that foundationally conditions social existence. In a nutshell, Marx finds that competition among capitalists incentivizes unremitting technical development. Firms innovate in order to dominate in the marketplace, and must seek to dominate in order to ensure survival in an eat-or-be-eaten struggle. Technologies that provide a competitive edge are inevitably (on pain of extinction) adopted by all firms contending with the innovator. This raises the average productive level of the economic sector in which the innovation occurs and prompts a renewed race for further innovation. Positive feedback loops of this sort are the theoretical crux of Marx's historical progressivism. Forces of production reliably and measurably advance, Marx holds, relative to an abstract standard of productivity according to which the "productiveness of a machine" is "measured by the human labor-power it replaces." Correlatively, "the productiveness of labor" performed with the aid of a machine is proportional to "the difference between the labor a machine costs,[9] and the labor it saves" (*MECW*, 35:394).[10] Famously and controversially, Marx singles out capitalism's congenital propensity to replace humans with machines, in the sphere of production and in the name of productivity, as the motor force of modern history.[11]

References to music are infrequent in Marx's writings, but when they do occur they show his cognizance of the fact that music cannot be disembedded from this evolutionary dynamic. In the *Grundrisse* (a.k.a. *Outlines of a Critique of Political Economy*, 1857–1861), Marx restates a point he makes in his youthful *Economic and Philosophic Manuscripts* (1844), to the effect that musical praxis itself is responsible for the human trait of musicality.[12] The *Grundrisse* adds the proviso that this issue (of the social determinants of individual sensibility) is orthogonal to the matter of whether a musical activity yields surplus value or not.[13]

> Productive labor is only that which produces capital. Is it not crazy ... that the piano-maker should be a productive worker but not the piano-player, although surely the piano would be a nonsensical thing [*Unsinn*] without the piano player? But this is exactly the case. The piano-maker reproduces capital; the pianist only exchanges his labor for revenue. But doesn't the pianist produce music and satisfy our musical ear; doesn't he also produce the latter to a certain degree? In fact, he does so; his labor produces something; but it is not thereby productive labor in the economic sense; as little productive as is the labor of the madman who produces delusions.
>
> (*MECW*, 28:231)[14]

This passage insists on the vital inseparability and co-determination of economic and extra-economic factors (the piano industry and the "musical ear," respectively) and, importantly for our purposes, takes an unambiguous stance on where musicking and value production confront one another most substantively: the for-profit manufacture of musical instruments. Marx's passing remark has great probative value for settling the question of what to regard as an authentically Marxian treatment of musical praxis (as delimited, we hold, by a certain historical triangulation of Pitch, Tone, and Note). Given that Marx's position is that value production is the fundamental determinant of modernity's historical trajectory, his explicit assertion that instrumental manufacture is the nexus where value production and musicking intersect implies that, by Marx's lights, a properly historical-materialist treatment of Pitch, Tone, and Note in the modern era could be nothing other than an investigation of how these realms are conditioned by the capitalist manufacture of musical instruments.

By means of three historical vignettes that take up the second part of this chapter, we hope to instill the conviction that such an investigation is both feasible and promising, and to thereby remove at least one brick from the wall of opposition to Marxian historiography within music studies. The first, on Note, examines the origins of musical printing and the birth of the work concept. The second, on Tone, turns to the industrial manufacture of pianos and the rise of twelve-tone equal temperament. The third, on Pitch, probes the invention of sound synthesis. These vignettes are meant to cast some well-known facts in a new light, by showing how specific developmental patterns of value production, as described by Marx, have made palpable interventions into musical practice. They are also meant to unearth some of the historical precedents and causal antecedents of the present-day conceptual terrain of modern music theory, and also to raise a few questions about the future means and ends of the work of music theorists.

Note and Intangible Property

Print and Privilege

In the summer of 1571, the monarch of France, Charles IX, conferred an authorial privilege on the composer Orlando di Lasso (1532–1594):

> It has pleased the king to grant to Orlande de Lassus, master composer of music, both the privilege and permission to have printed, by such printer of this kingdom as suits him, music composed by him, revised by him and arranged in any way that he chooses; and also to have printed that music that he has not yet made public, so that for a period of ten years no other printer besides the one to whom the said Lassus has entrusted his copies and permission shall be able to undertake either to print or to sell any portion of it if consent has not been granted by one or the other, under threat of punishment contained in these letters.
>
> (Oettinger 2004, 114)

Although Lasso's prerogative represents neither the first granting of a printing monopoly nor the first precursor of formal statutory copyright, it is the first instance of "international" (proto-)copyright for a musician,[15] since Lasso was employed in Munich when the French Crown bestowed the honor. It is also one of the earlier instances of patent copyright vested in the conceiver rather than the publisher of a work. It therefore represents a signal moment in the history of music's transmutation into a form of authorial intellectual property, which is at the same time a history of the jurisprudential rearrangement and rationalization of the domain of Note.

Legal protections and privileges around proprietary content, enforced by state censorship,[16] gave the likes of Lasso unexampled say-so over the fate of their mental creations. This new authorial control is symptomatic of an economic and conceptual metamorphosis that began in the early stages of capitalist modernity. In music, this metamorphosis altered the relations between composer, performer, and audience, which came to be mediated as never before by the privatization of intangibles: Charles IX's edict gave Lasso legal title not to chattel goods, real estate, or metallic currency, but to a numinous "symbolic form that can be . . . copied" (Rigi 2014, 909)—in a word, to a piece of information. According to Jakob Rigi's characterization, information in a political-economic context is "defined as forms of perception or cognition such as codes, concepts, formulas, data, design, images, software, language, etc., that can be . . . reproduced" (Rigi 2014, 909). The economic rights to the music itself ("music composed by him") that accrued to Lasso by dint of royal decree were rights to a reproducible *abstractum*. Implicit in the decree is a conception of music as a form of information-content that exists prior to and separately from the physical documents by which it is recorded and distributed, a form that is created or discovered by means of a composer's act of mental inventiveness or excogitation, which act is regarded as sufficient grounds for an assertion of ownership. The type of control Lasso was afforded by his privilege, then, was control over how and whether his privately owned informational property could be copied or encoded—thus physicalized, materialized, or reified—and thereafter exchanged for money. It was control, one may say, over how tones could be turned into notes, and over how notes could be turned into banknotes.

The historians of copyright Benedict Atkinson and Brian Fitzgerald point out that the emergence of property rights that extend to the information disseminated in published texts (as distinct from the physical texts themselves) is part of a tectonic shift in European social norms. An "obligation-based" society, in which "individuals accepted their unchanging status, and fixed function, within the society," and which "channelled the creative impulse into communal rather than individual expression," is supplanted by an "entitlement-based" society that "repudiates the idea of a fixed social order and substitutes, in place of social obligation, the individual freedom, in a contested environment, to accrue material benefit" (Atkinson and Fitzgerald 2014, 7). As entitlement-based society matures economically, the sources of "material benefit" over which free individuals can assert ownership become more numerous, and it comes to pass that, as Marx says, even "objects that in themselves are no commodities, such as conscience, honour, etc., are capable of being offered for sale by their holders, and of thus acquiring, through their price, the form of commodities" (*MECW*, 35:112). Where even conscience is vendible, authorial intellection cannot abide long in the public domain. This phenomenon is not unfamiliar to music scholars. In her monograph on the invention of compositional authorship in the first century of musical printing, for example, Kate van Orden stresses the normative, socially contingent nature of authorial entitlement—"authorship is a function of discourse rather than a status originating in the act of writing," she reminds us (2013, 5)—and explains how the dominion that composers such as Josquin were able to assert over their mental products stemmed from changes in the cultural norms that governed creation and possession. But although nobody will deny that a new conception of musical authorship, as well as a legal scaffolding for it, in fact arose in the print era, music theorists and historians have been mostly reticent about the exact causal mechanisms that lie behind this change.

At least one such mechanism is literally mechanical: the technological contrivance of moveable type is among the principal instigators of the new cultural modality of private intellectual property. Succinctly, the widespread use of moveable type in the publishing industry motivated a reconceptualization of the in-principle compass of proprietary appropriation and legally recognized ownership. With the advent of for-profit, high-volume printing, an intellectual work, an *opus*, comes to be regarded as a thing ontologically distinct from, and both possessible and alienable independently of, the inscriptions that symbolically represented the work.[17] And within an economic, legal, and ethical setting in which people "categorically recognize property in intangibles" (Atkinson and Fitzgerald 2014, 9), musical notes come to fulfill a new social function. Rather than (solely and simply) acting as an aid to learning or recollecting music, as a means of "assist[ing] musicians in forthcoming performances of a particular piece, or else memorializ[ing] a performance that has already taken place" (Steingo 2014, 84), musical inscriptions are called upon to "attest to" (ibid., 83), and provide a tangible, legible specification of, an intangible asset. For a society whose conception of authorship is conditioned by the commercial ethos of the print industry, notes are more than instructions or reminiscences; they are descriptions of or titles to personal property holdings. In short, capitalism redraws Note.

The Formal and Real Subsumption of Note

Marx holds that social norms in general are responsive to the development of the forces of production: "The hand-mill gives you society with the feudal lord; the steam-mill society with the industrial capitalist" (*MECW*, 6:166). But he also perceives that, as a matter of historical fact, the formal social relations necessary for wage labor and value production were often firmly in place before any real transformation in productive technique took hold. He therefore distinguishes between what he calls "formal subsumption" and "real subsumption" of production by (or "under") capital. In a process of formal subsumption, "capital . . . subsumes under itself a given, existing labor process, such as handicraft labor [or] the mode of agriculture corresponding to small-scale independent peasant farming," without also effecting a change "in the real way in which the labor process is carried on" (*MECW*, 24: 425–426). The point is pretty straightforward: land-owning, self-sufficient peasants can easily be turned into propertyless wage-laborers or sharecropper tenants—all you have to do is violently seize their land and forcibly compel them to pay rent, in cash or in kind—while still tilling the land exactly as they had since time immemorial.

The "dynamic capitalism that stimulated the growth of book trades" in the early modern era, and that engendered "a commensurate demand for abstract property rights" (Atkinson and Fitzgerald 2014, 9), was responsible for, first, the formal and, later, the real subsumption of textual production. In the mid-fifteenth century, the book merchant Vespasiano da Bisticci employed waged copyists to produce texts that he went on to sell to wealthy Florentine clients. In so doing, Bisticci reorganized traditional scribal production as wage labor generative of surplus value. In Marx's terms, he oversaw a primal phase of formal subsumption in which "the labor process becomes the instrument of the valorisation process, of the process of capital's self-valorisation" (*MECW*, 34:424). Bisticci's venture is indicative of a continent-wide trend: in the Europe of Bisticci's day, merchant capitalism begins to give way to a form of productive capitalism in which "the capitalist enters the process as its conductor, its director ... for [whom] it is at the same time directly a process of the exploitation of alien labor" (*MECW*, 34:424). But for scribal laborers in an enterprise like Bisticci's, the "real production process," the nuts and bolts of the fabrication of texts, did not differ in the least from what went on in monastic scriptoria, where, under the same primitive division of labor, monks produced manuscript copies in a non-capitalist, unwaged milieu. Textual production was formally reorganized but not yet procedurally altered in Bisticci's copyshop.

Real subsumption, Marx tells us, occurs when the procedural nature of the production activity, and not just its underlying lattice of property relations, is itself transmogrified so as to conform to demands of profit maximization. Real subsumption "can be witnessed as the perfection of subsumption—capital thoroughly penetrates material reality and moves fluidly through this ground of its own being, shaping material adequate to its content, i.e. the production of surplus-value" (Russel 2015, 43). Gutenberg's innovations within the press workshop in the 1450s are a paradigmatic case of a real subsumption of production in which "the instruments of labor are converted from tools into machines" and in which "implements of a handicraft" are incorporated into "a mechanism that, after being set in motion, performs with its tools the same operations that were formerly done by the workman" (*MECW*, 35:374). The motive for the adoption of the printing press, or any other labor-saving device, is not that it is somehow intrinsically desirable to be able to make more books in less time; the motive is profit, which the capitalist, *qua* capitalist, is bound to regard as the be-all and end-all of production. "Like every other increase in the productiveness of labor, machinery is intended to cheapen commodities ... In short, it is a means for producing surplus-value" (*MECW*, 35:374).

The development of mechanical methods for the bulk production of musical texts is a tributary to the mainstream of technological change that flowed from the book industry. Without denying the very real importance of Edisonian historical figures such as Petrucci and Attaignant, who were early standard-bearers of techno-entrepreneurship in music, we should keep in mind that their technical contributions were (in a nonpejorative sense) highly derivative. Petrucci's multiple-impression methods of printing music, and Attaignant's single-impression method (which cut in half the length and expense of Petrucci's system), are prototypical instances of what technological historian Nathan Rosenberg terms "technological convergence." This refers to a historical sequence in which the need to solve specific technical problems in the introduction of a new product or process in a single industry led to exploratory activity [elsewhere]; the solution to the problem, once achieved, was conceived to have immediate applications in producing other products to which it was closely related on a technical basis; and this solution was transmitted to ... other industries. (1976, 18–19)

Adaptation of Gutenberg's device for the printing of notes rather than letters "involved the extension to a new product of skills and machines not fundamentally different from those which had already been developed" (Rosenberg 1976, 26). Real subsumption in the productive domain of Note, therefore, occurs as a "transectorial migration" (Piatier 1988, 205) of technological improvements endogenous to the more lucrative and therefore (other things being equal) more technologically dynamic sector of literary bookmaking.[18] Although there is no known historical evidence of a process of formal subsumption affecting specifically musical textual production that then propelled major technological advances originating within dedicated musical printing firms,[19] nevertheless, Petrucci's and Attaignant's innovations, and those of countless less well-known technicians, are continuous with wider social currents of subsumption.

To sum up the steps of the historical sequence just outlined: capital's subsumption of inscriptive production drives the improvement of "inscriptive technology" (Tomlinson 2007, 32); print technology foments the development and legal articulation of intellectual property norms; and the regime of intellectual property reconfigures Note by creating a normative environment in which musical symbols play the novel social role of delineating an immaterial but ownable entity, the musical "work." Marx provides us with the theoretical resources, under the heading of "real subsumption," for describing the non-contingent connection between the spread of capitalist social relations and the technologization of textual production. And it is intuitively obvious why the "work concept," as discussed by Lydia Goehr (1992) and others, would be tethered to the masthead of intellectual property: musical works are all the more able to become valuable, venerated things in the popular aesthetic consciousness once their very existence is given legal sanction (in copyright codes) and economic tactility (in work-based revenue streams) in the print era. But what precisely gets us from the economic base of print technology to the legal superstructure of copyright laws?

In her magisterial history of the emergence of the print era in Western Europe, *The Printing Press as an Agent of Change* (1979), Elizabeth Eisenstein identifies "typographical fixity" as the key to understanding a cluster of cultural and ideological changes that coincided with the mechanization of printing. Typographical fixity, she argues, is a fallout of the comparatively easy multiplication of identical printed copies of a text enabled by the Gutenberg press and its technological successors. Textual representations of information take on a permanent, unchanging, authoritative form when a single textual configuration is exemplified by a great number of identical, interchangeable token texts. The "preservative powers of print," unlike those of scribal production, make it so that a single sequence of textual characters can be "arrested and frozen" and thereby

immunized from "textual drift." Thus a technologically facilitated "change from a sequence of corrupted copies to a sequence of improved editions" irrevocably alters the
status of written information (112). The printing press makes it possible to generate,
through repeated printings, a functionally inextinguishable, indistinguishable supply of
an exact textual configuration. And in circumstances where an exact typesetting can
have this kind of stability, and where effective control over the stabilizing of it can be a
source of monetary wealth and other forms of social power, there is a societal need to legally arbitrate contests over who controls what, and to statutorily define what the "what"
is. This is how the work comes into its own as an ownable abstraction. "By 1500, legal
fictions were already being devised to accommodate the patenting of inventions and the
assignment of literary properties . . . A literary 'common' became subject to 'enclosure
movements' and possessive individualism began to characterize the attitude of writers to
their work. The terms plagiarism and copyright did not exist for the minstrel. It was only
after printing that they began to hold significance for the author" (Eisenstein 1979, 121).
Typographical fixity, then, underwrites the origination of intellectual property norms.

Once again, and even more elliptically: the formal subsumption of textual production
begets its real subsumption; real subsumption begets typographical fixity; typographical
fixity begets intellectual property; intellectual property begets the work concept; and
all of the above carves out a new set of social roles for musical notation. Once musical
notation comes to possess the discursive function of denoting a form of disembodied
wealth, which is made possible by the broad-based cultural espousal of the work as an
intangible economic asset, the work concept gains a foothold (some would say a stran-
glehold) in art-receptive practices that it has yet to fully relinquish. What this entrench-
ment has entailed for musical practice has been thoroughly discussed by participants in
the work-concept debate within musicology, though to the neglect, for the most part, of
the phenomenon's enabling economic preconditions.

It goes without saying that a readily reproducible, widely circulated, and generally
available body of printed music is a sine qua non for both the existence and the character of music theory in its modern (post-Medieval) form. Not only has the mechanized
manufacture of musical texts been the literal, material source of music theory's defining
objects of study (scores); score production has also inscribed the most essential ideological and conceptual boundaries within which that study has been enacted.[20] In the
most sweepingly epochal terms: if Marx is right, and if our adaptation of his ideas is apt,
music theory's passage from, very roughly, an a priori, dogmatic, and cosmological paradigm to, again very roughly, an empirical, inductive, and work-centered paradigm is
not a transition whose rationale can be discovered by the researches of a self-sufficient
Ideengeschichte. Instead, the rationale lies in the unfurling of an irreversible economic
sequence, initiated and sustained by capitalist social relations, and in the resultant an-
nexation of print production by capital as "self-expanding value" (MECW, 35:176).
Accordingly, the fact that the principal unit of significance in most music-theoretical
inquiry remains the musical work—an assumption so ubiquitous, and so entwined
in the practical warp and woof of music theory as an institutionalized activity, that
we may forget to see it as an explanandum that stands in need of an explanans—is a

fact that can be understood adequately only if it is recognized as a cultural effect of an economic cause.

TONE AND GENUINE MANUFACTURE

The Material Basis of Key Character

The belief that each of the twenty-four major and minor keys has distinctive affective properties is, by and large, absent from contemporary habits of musical reception. Prior to its swift descent into irrelevance in the industrial era, however, the doctrine was a stable fixture throughout more than a century of the history of Tone, the cognitive and sensory domain of musical awareness. During the long reign of the *Affektenlehre* (roughly 1600–1750), a musical work lived, moved, and had its being within a preordained emotional/expressive ambit laid down by the acoustical physiognomy of its key. Key, as a scalar "musical container" (Hyer 2001) that is structured in relation to a referential pitch class, is prior to any individuating thematic and harmonic characteristics of a piece. Thus is Christian Schubart's *Ideen zu einer Aesthetik der Tonkunst* (1806) able to declare that if a composition is in A minor, no matter what else may be true of it, it is ipso facto stamped with "pious womanliness and tenderness of character" (Steblin 1996, 115). Next door, in B♭ minor, things are a little more *serioso*: "Mocking God and the world; discontented with itself and with everything; preparation for suicide sounds in this key" (Steblin 1996, 116–117). Nearly a century and a half before Schubart weighed in on the matter, Marc-Antoine Charpentier pigeonholed E minor as "effeminate, amorous, plaintive" (Steblin 1996, 33). And as late as the 1870s, Hermann von Helmholtz (1954, 551) could speak with a straight face about the "manly earnestness and deep religious feeling" of C major. "While there has never been a consensus on these associations," Brian Hyer observes, "the material basis for these attributions was at one time quite real: because of inequalities in actual temperament, each mode acquired a unique intonation and thus its own distinctive 'tone,' and the sense that each mode had its own musical characteristics was strong enough to persist even in circumstances in which equal temperament was abstractly assumed" (2001).

More precisely, the "material basis" of these semiotic linkages between key and affect—the basis in Pitch for certain cultural inclinations in the area of Tone, we might say—was the use of temperament schemes that were "circulating" (meaning that no keys were rendered unusable by egregiously wide or narrow intervals) but "non-equal," (meaning that each key possessed a unique profile of interval sizes, owing to microtonal differences in the distance between scale degrees) and thus a noticeably different auditory "flavor." While belief in highly particularized key-mood associations did not evaporate all at once—key quality has enjoyed a long, ghostly afterlife in the era of equal temperament[21]—it had no hope of surviving intact a period in which its material basis was systematically eroded.

Equal temperament's culpability for the demise of key quality as a receptive category (i.e., as a facet of Tonal culture) is widely recognized, even if there is controversy surrounding when exactly the decline began and when it was a fait accompli. However, there is insufficient appreciation for why and how the demise of key characteristics was accelerated and brought to consummation by the developmental dynamics of eighteenth- and nineteenth-century capitalist expansion. During the early stages of the First Industrial Revolution,[22] advances in the mass manufacture of pianos transformed the august and ancient art of tuning into a form of "detail work" (*MECW*, 35:372), that is, a limited, repetitive, highly routinized operation done as part of a determinate sequence of productive moments within the factory.[23] Tuning, formerly one among many aptitudes that the omnicompetent *vollkommener Kapellmeister* was expected to hone, is reconstituted as an "activity now confined in one groove, [which] assumes the form best adapted to the narrowed sphere of action" (*MECW*, 35:341). The manner of tuning that is "best adapted to" the piecewise, serial assembly of keyboards under a complex division of labor, historical sources suggest, turns out to be something approximating equal temperament. Briefly: the exigencies of the industrial division of labor create selection pressure that favors the implementation of equal temperament as an industry standard; and mass distribution to a mass market elevates this industry standard to a societal standard. Concurrently with the piano's achievement of complete market penetration throughout the Western world in the nineteenth century, a flattened-out intonational topography—equal-tempered pitch-space—becomes the assumed sonic landscape of music per se.

This ideological response—or Tonal answer, so to speak—to new material realities is perhaps to be expected: if it is true, as Marx thinks, that "only music awakens in man the sense of music" (*MECW*, 3:301), then it should come as no surprise that omnipresent equal-tempered music-making machines would awaken, at the level of a whole culture, an equally equal-tempered sense of music. By the end of the nineteenth century, music, as heard and cognized by musickers whose faculty of listening was formed at and by the all but inescapable piano, naturally seemed to be, and seemed to naturally be, an equal-tempered affair. And the naturalization of equal temperament both impacted and was impacted by an ever-mutating compositional practice. Pianos inspired the creation of, and came to prominence partly because of their ability to meet the instrumental needs of, an evolving musical repertory that at first accepted, and later ceased even to notice, its confinement within the "ivory cage" (Code 2018) of the piano's maximally regular tuning scheme. Thus does capitalism, through the intermediary of the piano, retune Tone.

Tuning as Detail Labor

The earliest pianos, like other instruments—and, for that matter, all commodities—were artisanal products, fashioned out of unprocessed raw materials by a master handicraftsman and subordinate apprentices and journeymen. But soon piano making—from its inception, a petit bourgeois capitalist enterprise, and therefore not a site of formal subsumption—had its real production process subsumed by "the first kind of genuine manufacture" (*MECW*, 35:347). In "genuine manufacture," specially trained laborers who exclusively perform one circumscribed task—"detail workmen" (*Teilarbeiter*) who perform "detail labor" (*Sonderarbeiten*)—use a slew of specialized tools (*MECW*, 35:347) to make identical, standardized components in large quantities. These parts are then put together into a finished product by laborers whose specialized function is assembly. Marx gives pocket-watch manufacture as an archetypal example of this form of production. "Formerly the individual work of a Nuremberg artificer, the watch has been transformed into the social product of an immense number of detail laborers, such as mainspring makers, dial makers, spiral spring makers, jewelled hole makers, ruby lever makers ... " After rattling off thirty more specializations (some with fancy-sounding French titles that belie the undoubted toilsomeness of the task, such as "*planteur d'échappement*" or "*finisseur de charnière*"), Marx concludes: "last of all [there is] the *repasseur*, who fits together the whole watch and hands it over in a going state. Only a few parts of the watch pass through several hands; and all these membra disjecta come together for the first time in the hand that binds them into one mechanical whole" (*MECW*, 35:347–348). Marx could well have made the same point with the piano instead of the watch.[24] More so than other musical instruments, the piano's material constitution lent itself to industrial assembly. In his classic history of the instrument Arthur Loesser quips: "Any zealot for factory production would have cast a lecherous eye upon the pianoforte's tens of identical wooden keys, its dozens of identical jacks and hammer-shanks, its greater dozens of identical tuning pins and hitch pins, and its yards of identically drawn wire. The pianoforte was the factory's natural prey" (Loesser 1954, 233).

It is well established that piano construction fully assumes the character of genuine manufacture in the early to mid-nineteenth century (Loesser 1954; Roell 1991). Equally uncontroversial is the claim that the "whip of competition" (Mandel 1992, 41) creates an exigent need to increase productivity with labor-saving measures, and that this economic imperative, which reaches full force under conditions of heightened capitalist rivalry in the nineteenth century, is the prime mover behind the "division of labor in manufacture" (*MECW*, 35:356). Marx takes this as read:

> It is, in the first place, clear that a laborer who all his life performs one and the same simple operation, converts his whole body into the automatic, specialized implement of that operation. Consequently, he takes less time in doing it, than the artificer who performs a whole series of operations in succession. But the collective laborer, who constitutes the living mechanism of manufacture, is made up solely of such specialized detail laborers. Hence, in comparison with the independent handicraft, more is produced in a given time, or the productive power of labor is increased.
>
> (*MECW*, 35:344)

Tuning is one musical "handicraft" that the division of labor in piano manufacture places within the remit of the wage-laboring detail workman. Previously, a *Klavierstimmer* who was not also, and primarily, a *Klavierspieler* would have seemed strange: "Prior to the advent of the piano, most musicians tuned their own instruments. This was a necessary part of owning one; to call someone in to tune a harpsichord would have been as preposterous an idea as calling someone in to tune a violin for a professional violinist" (Green 2006). Before keyboard instruments became part of the customary mise en scène of middle-class drawing rooms, ownership of them was for the most part restricted to either the professional stratum of keyboardists, for whom mastery of the art and science of tuning was a vocational prerequisite, or else wealthy aristocrats, who would likely have kept paid musicians on retainer, and would thus have had no reason to seek the professional services of a dedicated tuner (Green 2004). The spread of piano ownership and the ascendant vogue of amateur keyboard playing created an economic niche for the figure of the non-musician piano tuner, as Loesser (1954, 73) relates: "The spread of the instrument among the minimally musical led to the curious consequence that the tuner and the player were more and more rarely the same person. It is hard to imagine the most primitive player of a fiddle or guitar who did not know how to pull up his own strings to their proper pitch, but among clavier tinklers this incompetence became the rule. The complication of the tempered tuning may have added to the difficulty." Green (2004) seconds this assessment, and states: "Equal temperament took over from mean tone tuning, making all keys pleasant to play in rather than a restricted number, but was more difficult for the amateur to tune, and as more and more amateurs were beginning to own instruments, tuning was becoming a task carried out by professionals."

However, it was not so much the advent of a private service of piano tuning, in which professional tuners made house calls to the private residences of piano owners, as much as the incorporation of the labor of piano tuning into the commodity production process itself, that would leave the deepest impression in Tonal consciousness. "Piano tuning was a recognized job in the piano factories by the beginning of the 19th century," and by 1838, the Broadwood firm, England's most sizable piano concern, "had a relatively large tuning department of at least three men" (Green 2004). Later in the century, this temperamental workforce needed to expand exponentially:

> The larger London piano houses produced many pianos, all of which needed to be strung, chipped up and then fine-tuned, and at the height of the 1850s and 60s boom there were between 60,000 and 100,000 pianos made in London alone, so a huge number of tunings was required in the factory alone, long before the instruments reached shops, showrooms and homes.
>
> (Green 2004)

This upsurge in the amount of piano tuning taking place on the premises of piano factories meant that this labor needed to be carried out by wage workers who were obliged to complete an apprenticeship in just a few years (the standard at Broadwood's was five), rather than by expert musicians, whose decades of expensive training would have translated into a prohibitive and pointless labor cost for the piano firm. This comparative deskilling of musical labor had the effect of making equal temperament (or the closest achievable approximation thereof) attractive as the default tuning scheme on the factory floor. Mark Lindley notes that Hummel's *Art of Playing the Pianoforte* (*Anweisung zum Piano-Forte Spiel*, 1828)—published at approximately the same time Broadwood's business was entering a phase of aggressive expansion—advocated forcefully for "ignoring the old, unequal temperaments on the grounds that they presented, particularly for the many novice tuners brought into the trade by the popularity of the piano, greater difficulties than equal temperament and that these difficulties were aggravated critically by the burden of tuning, on modern pianos, three heavy strings for each note instead of two thin ones as on older instruments" (Lindley 2001). So, while it is plausible, as Loesser and Green contend, that the difficulty of tuning in equal temperament created a market for professional tuners, since musical dilettantes were unable to satisfactorily tune their own instruments (other than in, perhaps, the simplest meantone systems), it is also true that the comparative ease of implementing (a rough-and-ready semblance of) equal temperament made this tuning scheme convenient to use at the locus of large-scale manufacture. In the factory, tuners—musically inexpert detail workers, whose limited, mostly on-the-job training could not possibly familiarize them with the mathematical esoterica of innumerable subtly different unequal temperament schemes—needed to tune a very great number of pianos, one after another, in exactly the same way. What was called for was a system that was both conceptually tractable and practically manageable for a worker of no great musical discernment working under the tyranny of efficiency. Equal temperament, as it was then understood, filled the bill.[25] Hummel (1828, 69) seems to have intuited the nature of the case:

> The complicated propositions [about how to tune keyboards] laid down by [Sorge, Fritzen, Marpurg, Kirnberger, Vogler, etc.], cannot be so easily put to practice, and we are compelled to adopt a system of temperament by which tuning is made much more easy and convenient . . . Many who profess to be tuners, can hardly be said to have an ear so acute, as to discriminate with the requisite nicety, the minute deviations in the different chords of the unequal temperaments proposed by the authors.

Hummel goes on to recommend a rather cursory procedure in which the keyboard is tuned by fifths that are all slightly narrowed. No pretense of scientific precision is detectable in his advice:

> No one fifth must be tuned perfectly true . . . but each fifth must be tuned somewhat flatter than perfect . . . To afford the ear some guide respecting these flattened fifths, we may divide them into three species, into bad, good, and absolutely perfect. A fifth is bad when it sounds too flat with regard to the lower note. It is good, when not indeed absolutely perfect, but yet so nearly so as not to sound offensive to the ear. It is perfect, when it coincides in pitch with the fifth produced by the resonance of a deep bass note . . . If [every fifth] sounds good, neither too flat, nor too sharp, nor perfect, we may be assured that the temperament is correct. (1828, 70)

If this is more or less indicative of the accepted benchmark of accuracy in Hummel's day for equal-tempered tuning, it is easy to see why it would be non-coincidental—and, moreover, *not* solely a response to autonomous changes in consumers' aesthetic preferences—that equal temperament was adopted by piano manufacturers en masse: it didn't take any extraordinary aptitude or training for tuners to get proficient at it, which spelled savings for employers; the tidy, symmetrical logic of the scheme made sense to promulgate as an industry standard in an era of industrial standardization; and the presence of an industry standard meant that veteran tuners did not need to be retrained if hired by a new firm (as would have been common during an expansion phase in the industry, when many new enterprises were setting up shop).[26] Equal temperament became the official house style of Broadwood's trend-setting outfit in the 1840s, just as the Victorian piano boom was getting into full swing, and just as the need to maximize productivity under conditions of more vigorous competition would have been felt more keenly, and would have sharply incentivized the streamlining and normalization of tuning operations.

The adoption of equal temperament was not an "innovation" in the sense of a stupendous technical leap forward. The concept of equal temperament, the mathematics underlying it, and the practical possibility of implementing it with at least the coarse degree of precision that Hummel found tolerable were all hundreds of years old. But, as the tuning historian Alexander J. Ellis wrote in 1885, "It is one thing to propose equal temperament, to calculate its ratios, and to have trial instruments approximately tuned in accordance with it, and another thing to use it commercially in all instruments sold. For pianos in England it did not become a trade usage till 1846, at about which time it was introduced into Broadwood's" (Helmholtz 1954, 549).[27] The primary reason equal temperament became a "trade usage," we suggest, was the productive dynamic internal to the trade itself, and the need to innovate for efficiency's sake, as opposed to the exogenous influence of consumer demand.

Material Causes, Ideal Effects

The rest, as they say, is history: the preeminent firm's tuning standard, which had an economic rationale, soon enough became the standard for the industry at large, and thus for the piano as such; and the standard for the piano, the preeminent instrument, soon enough became the standard for all instruments, and thus for music in general. Duffin (2007, 141) explains the spread of equal temperament ratios in the design of wind instruments in the nineteenth century as, likewise, a cost-cutting measure: "The need to manufacture so many instruments quickly for [a] new market forced musical instrument makers to cut corners—to streamline and simplify manufacturing techniques—so that the subtle tuning systems of several nineteenth-century instruments got replaced with basic [equal-tempered] systems. It was so much more convenient and cheaper to make instruments that way."[28] The invisible hand of the market, then, took up a tuning key; or, if you like: dollars determined cents. Admittedly, the introduction of equal temperament was hardly the most significant contributor to the gains in productivity that made pianos more affordable and thus more commonplace. It was mechanization (which, for obvious reasons, could only make a limited incursion into the realm of tuning) that conduced most to the cheapening of the instrument. Improvements in both the instrument itself and in the efficiency of its assembly came quickly over the course of the century, and by 1910, the high point of England's second piano manufacturing renaissance, the nation could boast more than fifty piano manufacturing firms whose total output exceeded one hundred thousand instruments per year—all of them tuned on site to equal temperament.[29]

The inexpensive, indispensable piano provided a primary vehicle of amateur music making in the domicile, took a starring role on the public concert stage as this venue came into full flower across Europe, and became a mainstay of elite salon gatherings. Not only its affordable price, but the piano's unique affordances, too, helped secure it a central place. In addition to serving as the most versatile accompanimental instrument, the piano offered the only means of reproducing and consuming orchestral and operatic repertoire that was otherwise accessible only in live concert. As the piano loomed larger in every aspect of nineteenth-century musical life, especially the musical life of the rising bourgeoisie, its intonational complexion gradually took on the guise of natural law rather than custom. "In tune" and "equal-tempered" verged on synonymy.[30]

Late-eighteenth-century composers did not assume an equal-tempered tonal space. Duffin (2007, 82) cites a passage in the first movement development of Haydn's quartet op. 77, no. 2 (1799) in which Haydn instructs the cello, which is given a D♯ followed by an E♭, to play "*l'istesso tuono.*"[31] This is the exception that proves the rule, in the correct sense of that saying: the need for an explicit directive implies that contemporaneous musicians would have taken for granted the microtonal divergence of enharmonic notes. A century later, collective musical consciousness had so thoroughly internalized the soundscape of equal temperament that Haydn's prescription would have seemed like a curious redundancy. (Tellingly, the indication is omitted from most modern editions.) One sign of the ascent of equal temperament in the intervening years is the increasingly utilitarian musical spelling used in tonally adventurous, later tonally ambiguous, and finally tonality-rejecting music. Notational choices about which of two enharmonic "equivalents"—an appellation that is merited only in an equal-tempered framework— to use started to be dictated purely by considerations of readability. This testifies to the final demise of antiquated intonational sensitivities that were obsolescent well before the fin de siècle. Decades prior, a staunchly equalitarian tonal sensibility was already giving outward signs of itself in the compositional use, and orthographic treatment, of equal divisions of the octave. For instance, the effect Liszt aims at in the opening of his *Faust Symphony* (1857)—a "dissonant prolongation" (Morgan 1976) of quasi-stable augmented triads that are not heard as byproducts of contrapuntal motion, but instead as resolutions of comparatively less stable major and minor triads—is flatly unintelligible and impracticable as a compositional goal outside of the conceptual schema (Tone), and corresponding intonational actuality (Pitch), of equal-tempered tonal space. And, needless to say, this goal is remote from the orthographic scruples that steered Haydn's pen (Note).

All this to say that compositional ideology—the complementary counterpart, in the normative domain of Tone, to reception practice—reflexively tails, but also helps to crystalize and reinforce, the materialities of instrumental production. Enharmonic practice flourished in large part because of the spread of equal-tempered pianos, which facilitated experimentation in this direction, and the equal-tempered piano waxed in popularity partly because of its eminent fitness for producing the kind of enharmonic music that was increasingly "in the air." As Mark Lindley (2001) states, "equal tempera-ment ... is virtually considered an inherent characteristic of the modern concert piano. Indeed the ideals of sonority in the acoustic design of the modern piano and in all but the more radical forms of modern pianism are as intimately bound to the acoustic qual-ities of equal temperament as any previous keyboard style ever was to its contemporary style of intonation." This is a sound insight, and a true description of a musical zeitgeist. The key Marxian addendum is an admonition to remember that the zeitgeist is factu-ally in error: equal temperament is emphatically not an inherent characteristic of the piano. It is an extraneous feature selected for by the dynamics of capitalist value pro-duction, which non-accidentally brought about the proletarianization of the labor of piano tuning. Inasmuch as the piano is to blame for "how equal temperament ruined harmony" (as the title of Duffin 2007 polemically puts it), so too is capitalism.

Pitch and Universal Labor

Luddites and Techno-Utopians

In 1906, John Philip Sousa used the pages of *Appleton's Magazine* to bemoan the rise of "mechanical music." In a philippic against the player piano and the phonograph, which were by then cutting into the market for traditional instruments, Sousa claimed that the recent proliferation of "mechanical device[s] to sing for us a song or play for us a piano, in substitute for human skill, intelligence, and soul" (1906, 278), heralded the end of progress in musical art. "The ingenuity of a phonograph's mechanism," he warned, "may incite the inventive genius to its improvement, but I could not imagine that a per-formance by it would ever inspire embryotic Mendelssohns, Beethovens, Mozarts, and Wagners to the acquirement of technical skill, or to the grasp of human possibilities in the art" (1906, 279). Sousa's high-minded aesthetic worries about a decline in musical quality were wrapped up with bread-and-butter economic concerns. The evacuation of human mental and bodily effort from acts of musical sound production could not fail to have a corrosive effect on domestic music-making, predicted Sousa. And a decline in the recreational cultivation of performative musicianship promised to bring about a corre-sponding contraction in opportunities for the musical professions (of which Sousa was a more than usually prosperous member): "Musical enterprises are given financial support [in the United States] as nowhere else in the universe ... [Americans'] wide love for the art springs from the singing school, secular or sacred; from the village band, and from the study of those instruments that are nearest the people. There are more pianos, violins, guitars, mandolins, and banjos among the working classes of America than in all the rest of the world, and the presence of these instruments in the homes has given employment to enormous numbers of teachers" (280). If "machine-made music" were to spread unchecked, warned Sousa, "under such conditions the tide of amateurism cannot but recede" (281)—and with it, importantly for Sousa's own pocketbook and class interest, the tide of professionalism.

What worried Sousa inspired hope in Rudhyar Chennevière (a.k.a. Dane Rudhyar), who announced in the *Musical Quarterly* in 1920 that

> The ordinary pianola ... marks the extremest limit of the antimusical which humanity has ever witnessed.... But with it there is a feeble glimmer of something in the distant horizon, something which may well be the far away annunciation of a new day. The machine which has slain music, perhaps, in the near future, may become the means of its redemption. (506)

Echoing an accelerationist political position now and then hinted at in Marx's writings,[32] Chennevière championed the expediting of musical mechanization as a means of overcoming social relations in which the "musical executant" (501) was reduced to the status of a "wage-earning proletarian" (506). The musical proletariat, he thought, had nothing to lose but the chains of its constrictive, inhuman paratechnical relations: "The players who make up our orchestras being already machines, in the majority of cases, let us courageously admit the fact; and in place of attempting to retard, let us accelerate the new departure" (507–508). In the brave new musical world envisioned by Chennevière, there was to be absolute technical mastery of Pitch—in other words, total and unqualified control over the physical production of sounds:

> Let us create machines sensitive to the extent of vibrating at the slightest melodic inflection ... let us create machines ... which will thus be able to give us all sounds ... which can give the exact number of vibrations desired ... Instead of the orchestra the future, then, will disclose to us ... great electrical instruments ... which, without any question, will reveal to us a wealth of possible sonority beyond our present concepts ... [and] illimitable combinations possible in number and proportion of harmonic means. (508)

But this is no far-fetched, Verneian science fiction. Chennevière specifically cites Thaddeus Cahill's Telharmonium, an actually existing device for delivering performances of electronically synthesized music across telephone wires, as an example of a new technology proper to musical production as it would transpire in a classless society.

Sousa's anxiety and Chennevière's hopefulness were both reactions to a histor-ical reality: a new and profound "real development of the power of social production" (*MECW*, 28:158) was in the works, one that would destabilize long-standing relations of musical production. As the example of the Telharmonium dramatizes in bold relief, new technology was, all of a sudden, being called into existence ab nihilo by systematic re-search and development activities that were bankrolled, directly or indirectly, by capital-intensive, stock-issuing corporations. In music, newfangled, electrified apparatuses were rolled out with a view to appropriating surplus value from enhanced forms of con-trol over the physical production of sound. In essence, scientific labor, financed and overseen by capital, sets in motion a development toward absolute technical mastery over Pitch.

General Labor

For Marx, as we have seen, one of capitalism's distinguishing features is its incessant cre-ation of new and more productive contexts for the performance of "collective" or "coop-erative" labor (*gemeinschaftliche Arbeit*). In collective labor, workers form a corporate entity that is internally differentiated (according to a division of labor), but unified by a common productive purpose. Collective labor is to be distinguished not only from the kind of labor it supplants, individual handicraft, but also from another form of labor that develops in tandem with it, namely, "universal labor" (*allgemeine Arbeit*).

> A distinction should be made between universal labor and cooperative labor. Both kinds play their role in the process of production, both flow one into the other, but are also differentiated. Universal labor is all scientific labor, all discovery and all invention. This labor depends partly on the utilization of the labors of those who have gone before. Cooperative labor, on the other hand, is the direct cooperation of individuals.
>
> (*MECW*, 37:106)

The universality of universal labor derives from the breadth of its applicability. The products of such labor—universal truths "of mechanics, of chemistry, and of the whole range of the natural sciences" (*MECW*, 37:464)—pertain not simply to the labor pro-cess peculiar to a specific commodity, but, more generally, to an entire sector of pro-duction, or to the entire multi-sector economy of a society, or to the entirety of social labor *überhaupt*. Universal labor is necessarily cumulative in character, since it rests upon the edifice of past scientific discoveries. In the nineteenth century and thereafter, massive amplification of the purview, sophistication, and prestige of systematized sci-entific experimentation (within the surrounding and enabling framework of advanced technocapitalism that stepped onto the historical stage in conjunction with steam-powered machinery) goes hand in hand with massive gains in the productivity of in-dustrial labor.[33] This is because labor-saving technological progress comes increasingly to depend upon "progress in the field of intellectual production, notably natural science and its practical application" (*MECW*, 37:85), and science comes to increasingly depend on the subsidization (through corporate taxes or direct investment) of big capital. As both science and capitalism evolve, it becomes more and more evident that they are locked in a mutually dependent embrace, and that "capitalism is the scientification of production" (Kurz 2014, 31).

Marx was well aware of this. But he did not expressly forecast the extent to which formal scientific investigation and methodical technological development would become primary loci of what Marx calls "capital accumulation and reproduction on an extended scale" (*MECW*, 36:vi) in the twentieth century. As Robert Kurz (2014, 35) states, "the systematic social organization of the process of science and of its technological application and the substructure of qualifications that it requires (schools, specialist schools, the expansion of the universities, the foundation of polytechnics, the amalgamation of science and large-scale capital) only got under way gradually," and were just beginning to make their economic importance felt when Marx died in 1883. A highly symptomatic instance of "the amalgamation of science and large-scale capital" in music is the Telharmonium extolled by Chennevière, which Thaddeus Cahill designed roughly a decade after Marx's death. Along with W. Duddell's Singing Arc (1899) and Melvin Severy's Choralcello (1903), the Telharmonium belongs to the first generation of electric pitch synthesizers. Cahill's instrument utilized an ingenious "tone wheel," basically a cog with evenly spaced teeth that rotates next to an electromagnetic receiver. As the teeth pass by the receiver, they induce a current in the receiver's coil whose frequency is proportional to the speed of the cog's rotation. This current causes a sine tone to be output by a loudspeaker. The same loudspeaker also accepts inputs from other receivers, which means that a fundamental frequency can be combined with select upper partials in order to create sounds with complex timbres. Electrical signals created by a performance on the Telharmonium (whose console contained a double manual keyboard) could be transmitted over telephone lines to speakers at remote locations.

Cahill's research proceeded from Helmholtz's demonstration, a few decades earlier, that it is possible to analytically decompose complex sounds into aggregations of simple waveforms. It also built upon the most up-to-date discoveries in electromagnetism.[34] The quintessentially universal labor of Cahill and his predecessors was a condition for the possibility of a new kind of musical labor. Cahill's Telharmonium created an equipment-centered action context in which a "sound engineer" (a later coinage) could create desired tone-qualities "from scratch," by additively combining the simplest individual acoustical constituents of composite sounds. These mechanically manufactured sounds were "synthetic," both in the sense that they were put together in a bottom-up, part-to-whole, simple-to-complex fashion, and also in the sense that they were meant to serve as an artificial substitute for an already sought-after natural thing ("acoustical" sound), much as was the case with the synthetic dyes that were being formulated, patented, and manufactured at exactly that time (indigo was synthesized in 1880 and commercially viable by 1897). This must be appreciated for the drastic rupture in the history of Pitch that it is. The invention of the Telharmonium marks a historical turning point after which musical sound—which was strongly associated with the irrational and ineffable in the eighteenth- and nineteenth-century European imagination—becomes acquiescent to thoroughgoing rationalization, precise quantification, and the "victory of man over the forces of nature" (*MECW*, 35:444). This was thanks to the unaccustomed way in which musical instruments, like "locomotives, railways, electric telegraphs, self-acting mules, etc.," now came to act as "organs of man's will over Nature, or of man's activity in Nature" (*MECW*, 29:92). Had he lived to see the Telharmonium, Marx would have been the first to recognize that such instruments "show the degree to which society's general science . . . has become an immediate productive force, and hence the degree to which the conditions of the social life process itself have been brought under the control of the universal intellect and remolded according to it" (*MECW*, 29:92). With the intrusion of universal scientific labor into the arena of music, the manipulation of Pitch—control over the material basis of sound production—becomes yet another moment of the productive circuit where "human muscles are replaced, for the purpose of driving the machine, by a mechanical motive power" (*MECW*, 35:463).[35] By harnessing electrical motive power, the Telharmonium dissevers the manipulation of Pitch not only from tactile engagement with the *corps sonore* itself—instead one's proximate contact is with an electronic user interface—but additionally from the expenditure of all but the slightest muscular effort. The manipulation of Pitch thus becomes a matter of the operator's physically effortless, interface-mediated management of the flow of electronic information. One could not ask for a more clear-cut case of "the implements of labor, in the form of machinery, necessitat[ing] the substitution of natural forces for human force, and the conscious application of science, instead of rule of thumb" (*MECW*, 35:389).[36]

Economic Motivations

Contemporary accounts lauded Cahill's instrument for the verisimilitude with which it replicated sounds of a variety of acoustical instruments. Whether or not this praise was warranted, it was in line with the inventor's explicit goal, which was to create a machine that would allow a single performer to do the work of an entire symphony orchestra. An enthusiastic contemporary report about the Telharmonium mentions this labor-replacing capacity en passant: "When a large number of generators and keyboards are installed, as they doubtless will be in due time, there is no reason why the Telharmonium, as the invention is called, should not give the subscribers all the pleasures of a full symphony orchestra whenever they wish to enjoy them" (Anon. 1906, 210). This offhand remark gets straight to the heart of the matter: the entire raison d'être of the Telharmonium was its promise to deliver an already saleable "use value"[37] (the pleasures of a full symphony orchestra) at a fraction of the then-current labor cost. Cahill proposed to make a capitalistic frontal assault on the live music industry by electrifying Pitch.

In 1895, two years before Cahill built the first demonstration model of the Telharmonium, O. T. Crosby and F. C. Todd, venture capitalists (as we would now say) from Washington, DC, established the New York Electric Music Company to fund the research and development of the instrument.[38] They controlled the project's fate, determined what other small enterprises to conglomerate with, and set the strategy for how to raise more startup capital. In written appeals to potential investors, it was argued that demand for telephonic music, as a replacement for live music, was potentially vast. In New York City alone, the company claimed, 37.5 million dollars a year was spent on the services of live musicians (whose wages averaged 5 dollars a day). Another million was spent on mechanical music: pianolas, orchestrions, and the like. The sales of Victor Talking Machines were said to be 7.5 million units. This list of cyclopean figures suggests the size of the company's ambitions. It intended the Telharmonium, whose sound production mechanism occupied the entire basement of a concert hall, to insinuate itself in the telecommunications network of the modern city, much like the telephone system whose method of sound relay the Telharmonium appropriated and whose existing infrastructure it piggy-backed on. Initially, the New York Electric Music Company's ambitious and aggressive courting of investors showed impressive results. In all, 426,000 dollars (ca. 12 million dollars in 2018) in capital stock were issued, and the Telharmonium that was finally installed in Telharmonic Hall in midtown Manhattan was valued at 200,000 dollars (ca. 5.6 million dollars in 2018).[39] The birth of sound synthesis technology, this shows, was a tremendously capital-intensive affair, one that is emblematic of capital's ruthless subsumption of general (scientific) labor in the late nineteenth century and after.

As fate would have it, the capital invested in the New York Electric Music Company did not yield a return. Cahill clashed with the telephone utility over disruptions in service caused by the huge amount of electricity required to run the Telharmonium and by resultant interference with telephone circuits. This required a cessation of operations from which the firm never recovered. An initial popularity that the Telharmonium enjoyed as a concert instrument—audiences were at first titillated by its ethereal strains and, somewhat paradoxically, flocked to Telharmonium Hall, at 32nd Street and Broadway, to hear the instrument live—didn't last. The company couldn't recruit and maintain enough subscribers to come anywhere close to recouping its giant initial outlay. Two subsequent attempts at restructuring the company were non-starters. Even if they hadn't been, radio technology, which was just around the corner, would certainly have rendered the Telharmonium's limited home-delivery/subscription business model obsolete. After Cahill filed for bankruptcy, he had the Telharmonium dismantled and sold for scrap.

Although the Telharmonium was a financial flop, it is impossible to exaggerate the importance for Pitch of the trend it launched and epitomized: viz., the "scientification" of sound production, stimulated by burgeoning levels of capital being funneled into research and innovation, specifically in the area of "electronics ... as the basis not only on which new industries were produced out of thin air, but also on which applied natural sciences for the first time ceased to be merely the technological foundation and general prerequisite of industrial labor processes, and became the driving force of the immediate labor process itself" (Kurz 2014, 36). Directly downstream from Cahill's breakthrough is the wondrous arsenal of (now primarily digital) sound synthesis capabilities that have wholly reworked our "instrumental rationality" (in both senses) in regard to Pitch. In the 1970s, it became possible to display audio waveforms on a digital storage oscilloscope, and to reshape sound waves—in a sense that is barely, if at all, metaphorical—with the aid of a video display terminal. This gave rise to both a new form of control over the physicality of sound (Pitch) and a new mode of presentation of the object of control (Note). By the 1980s, due to the improvement and price depreciation of microprocessors, most of the applications of analog equipment (e.g., multi-track recording) could be carried out with digital equipment on hardware platforms that lay within the budget of the general consumer. The democratization and diversification of these accoutrements of sound production (Pitch), most of which employ a non-traditional manner of graphically presenting sonic parameters (Note), instigated a remarkable attenuation of the social importance and economic relevance of Western forms of musical literacy. This has problematized the normative status of the intoned, determinately pitched, discrete sound as the primary musical "building block" (Tone). Many commercial styles that grew up in tandem with synthesis technologies, such as electronic dance music and hip-hop, would be grossly misportrayed by the image of a "composer" creating "works" by making decisions about relationships between individual, individually denominated pitches. In the 1990s and thereafter, the introduction of "digital audio workstation" (DAW) software for the personal computer accentuated and accelerated the aforementioned trends. User-friendly audio production software has rendered recorded sounds infinitely and easily modifiable, so much so that anyone who has basic computer literacy can have virtually untrammeled control over the manipulation of sonic raw material. In the music industry, the ramifications for labor productivity are mind-boggling: one person with a laptop and a microphone can do what previously would have required tens or hundreds of musicians, a small army of technicians, and a sizable piece of real estate. "Hence all powers of labor are transposed into powers of capital; the productive power of labor into fixed capital (posited as external to labor and as existing independently of it as object [*sachlich*]) ... whose most adequate form is machinery" (*MECW*, 29:87).[40]

To date, music theory as an academic discipline has been curiously standoffish toward sound production technology.[41] One might reasonably expect the major determinants of the contemporary soundworld—computerized sounds—to be privileged recipients of theoretical attention. It is possible that this disconnect between theory and (at this point, fully global and transcultural) technological praxis happens because music theory behaves, in certain respects, as an institutional bulwark against purportedly negative repercussions of the technological developments described above. These include the eclipse of staff notation, the departure from the general auditory culture of ingrained familiarity with common-practice tonal syntax and contrapuntal norms, and the loss of the impulse toward a romantic attitude of pious aesthetic reverence. It is unclear at the moment of writing whether recent technoliterate scholarship that grapples with the ineluctable instrumental mediation of musical activity (the "new organology" of the last decade, e.g. Tresch and Dolan 2013; Rehding 2016) will furnish the conceptual resources for a methodological glasnost in the field of music theory, and also whether such an opening-up, if pursued to its logical conclusion, would be distinguishable from the dissolution of music theory as a separate and self-enclosed research paradigm.

Conclusion

We have seen how selected features of Pitch, Tone, and Note are plausibly construed as robustly historical, in that they are "the product of a long course of development, of a series of revolutions in the modes of production" (*MECW*, 6:486). From the point of view of the present, the past of Pitch, Tone, and Note evinces non-randomness, insofar as technological milestones within these domains of musical practice lie along a historical path that is paved by the developmental dynamics of capitalism.

Transformations continue. Copyright laws are metamorphosing—mostly in the direction of frightening draconianism—as a reflex response to the metamorphosis of digital information distribution technology, which has rendered recorded and notated music infinitely reproducible and shareable at zero cost (Rigi 2014). Intellectual enclosure (in the form of an intellectual property rights movement) is being ramped up in order to preserve the commodity status and salability of essentially costless digital data exchange. The overwhelming majority of pianos sold today are digital; they sound more and more like the real thing—in a sense, they now *are* the real thing—and they never need tuning, in the factory or anywhere else. And perhaps the most socially relevant use for the keyboard now is not as a self-standing instrument but as an appendage to the most important instrument in contemporary musical life, by far—the personal computer. PCs already allow for a manipulation of sonic material that is just this side of godlike, and furtherance of their capacities for audio synthesis and editing, musical data compression and storage, music production, and music information retrieval can be expected to keep pace with improvements in microprocessor and data transmission technology generally. The rapid velocity of contemporary technological change, the essentially capitalistic nature of this change, and the drastic encroachments it continues to make into our shared musical environment make a Marxian organology of Pitch, Tone, and Note timely, even urgent.

Acknowledgments

We would like to offer special thanks to Alex Rehding and Steve Rings, the editors of this volume, for their help with this chapter. Their abundant commentary on and criticism of several earlier drafts had a transformative effect on the project.

Notes

1. O'Callaghan (2007) contains an account of the ontology of sounds that works carefully through the kinds of tricky questions posed in the previous paragraph.

2. Here we deliberately eschew the subjectivist leanings of many characterizations of pitch that show up in the scientific literature, for instance: "Pitch is defined as that subjective quality of a note which enables one to place it on the musical scale" (MacKenzie 1964, 112); "Pitch is that attribute of auditory sensation in terms of which sounds may be ordered on a scale extending from low to high" (American National Standards Institute 1994, 34); "Pitch is the perceptual correlate of periodicity in sounds" (McDermott and Oxenham 2008, 452). The broader sense of pitch that we wish to exploit, and from which the musical sense derives, has to do with the general phenomenon of level or degree or magnitude, and, by extension, with susceptibility to measurement and quantification. Thus does one speak of the pitch of an aircraft (its angle of rotation about a transverse axis), the pitch of a roof (the angle it subtends at its intersection with the ceiling), the pitch of a saw or gear (the distance between its regularly spaced teeth), and so on.

3. As this chapter unfolds it will become obvious, if it isn't already, that our category of (uppercase "P") Pitch—the whole province of sonic materiality writ large—encompasses many phenomena that have little or nothing to do with (lowercase "p") pitch (and likewise, mutatis mutandis, for the categories of Tone and Note). This may call to mind Hegel's habit, primarily in the *Phenomenology*, of using specific historical moments (the Enlightenment, the "Absolute Freedom and Terror" of the French Revolution, the "Enthusiasm" [*Schwärmerei*] typical of German romanticism) as metaphorical representatives of quite general intellectual postures and philosophical positions.

4. For a survey of these Althusserian terms, see Koivisto and Lahtinen (2010).

5. We favor "Marxian," as opposed to "Marxist," as a modifier for "organology." The former adjective is usually reserved for concepts, ideas, explanatory models, arguments, and sociological hypotheses that can be found in the writings of Karl Marx and Friedrich Engels. "Marxist" has a much more flexible application, and is associated in the popular consciousness with a host of political projects and theoretical developments that postdate, and that in certain cases have only a tenuous relationship to, Marx's actual texts.

6. Citations of Marx are from the digitized English edition of Marx's and Engel's complete works, *Marx & Engels Collected Works*, 50 vols. (London: Lawrence and Wishart, 2010), herein abbreviated as *MECW*.

7. The common philosophical distinction between a space of reasons and a space of causes was introduced by Wilfrid Sellars (1956). Observe, however, that Tone, as we conceive of it, is not merely a sphere of rationality but also a sphere of embodiment, and includes within its orbit not just a space of reasons, but also a "fundamentally animal space of affect, desire, need, and feeling" (Sachs 2015, 20).

8. In the Marxian lingo, the "mode of production" is said to be comprised of the "forces of production" and the "relations of production." This can give the impression that forces of production—enabling implements and capacities that figure in the productive process—have nothing to do with relations between human beings. But, self-evidently, the division of labor at the point of production is both a productive force (hence the term "labor force") and a productive relation (as part of a system of formal and informal liaisons and social ligatures between and among those engaged in production). Marx typically uses "relations of production" to refer to such social phenomena as capitalists' legal entitlement, enforced

by state power, to the commodities produced at their behest, as well as workers' correlative alienation from the fruits of their labor, both of which fall under the concept of "property relations." "Forces of production," by contrast, usually denotes machines used to make commodities. But what Marx ultimately adduces is not an exclusive disjunction between, but a dialectical conjunction of, forces and relations: "A certain mode of production, or industrial stage, is always combined with a certain mode of cooperation, or social stage, and this mode of cooperation is itself a 'productive force' " (*MECW*, 5:43).

9. Marx's "labor theory of value," which (to simplify greatly) equates how much a thing is worth with how much labor it takes to make it, leads him to speak of "the labor a machine costs."

10. Note, however, that "improvements" of this sort do not guarantee greater social well-being. Advancement in the efficient production of nuclear warheads is no different from advancement in the efficient production of vaccines, from the point of view of abstract productivity.

11. In coarse outline, since it is not our main concern: Marx argues that a system-wide increase in productivity leads to a system-wide decline in the rate of profit, which leads to economic crisis, which can create the conditions for the revolutionary self-organization of the laboring and otherwise wage-dependent classes.

12. "Just as only music awakens in man the sense of music, and just as the most beautiful music has no sense for the unmusical ear—is no object for it, because my object can only be the confirmation of one of my essential powers—it can therefore only exist for me insofar as my essential power exists for itself as a subjective capacity; because the meaning of an object for me goes only so far as my sense goes (has only a meaning for a sense corresponding to that object)—for this reason the senses of the social man differ from those of the nonsocial man. Only through the objectively unfolded richness of man's essential being is the richness of subjective human sensibility (a musical ear, an eye for beauty of form—in short, senses capable of human gratification, senses affirming themselves as essential powers of man) either cultivated or brought into being … The forming of the five senses is a labor of the entire history of the world down to the present" (*MECW*, 3:301–302).

13. Briefly: according to Marx's theory of exploitation, workers who expend their labor-power for capitalists produce an amount of value that is greater than that required to set their labor in motion. This difference in value magnitude, surplus value, is appropriated by the capitalist as profit.

14. It is worth taking the opportunity to quote some of Marx's other similar remarks about music, since they are obscure and are not likely to be encountered by music theorists otherwise: "It may seem strange that the doctor who prescribes pills is not a productive laborer, but the apothecary who makes them up is. Similarly the instrument maker who makes the fiddle, but not the musician who plays it. But that would only show that 'productive laborers' produce products which have no purpose except to serve as means of production for unproductive laborers" (*MECW*, 31:82). "Use value has only value for use, and its existence for use is only its existence as an object for consumption, its existence in consumption. Drinking champagne, although this may produce a 'hangover,' is as little productive consumption as listening to music, although this may leave behind a 'memory.' If the music is good and if the listener understands music, the consumption of music is more sublime than the consumption of champagne, although the production of the latter is a 'productive labor' and the production of the former is not" (*MECW*, 31:195). "A singer who sells her songs on her own account is an *unproductive worker.* But the same

singer, engaged by an impresario, who has her sing in order to make money, is a *productive worker*. For she produces capital" (*MECW*, 34:136). "A singer who sings like a bird is an unproductive worker. If she sells her singing for money, she is to that extent a wage laborer of a commodity dealer. But the same singer, when engaged by an entrepreneur who has her sing in order to make money, is a productive worker, for she directly *produces* capital" (*MECW*, 34:448). See Lindley (2010) for a fascinating discussion of Marx's and Engels's views on music.

15. We use the term "copyright" loosely to mean any conferral of exclusive economic rights on creators of works (authors), or on those who produce or manage the dissemination of products that embody works (such as publishers), which conferral has the practical effect of causing abstractions (ideas, formulas, etc.) to function as a form of property subject to an individual's (or corporation's) sole control. The first statutes that explicitly defined such a property form were the national copyright codes passed in the United Kingdom in 1710.

16. Lasso's "privilege," as the edict states, is in actuality a "threat of punishment," a rule about what others are forbidden to do lest they face monetary penalties and other coercive measures.

17. Richard Taruskin asserts that "the production of printed music books, and the new music-economy thus ushered in, was a crucial stage in the conceptualizing of a 'piece' or 'work' of music as an objectively existing thing—a tangible, concrete entity that can be placed in one's hands in exchange for money; that can be handled and transported; that can be seen as well as heard . . . . This 'thingifying' of music (or reification, to use the professional philosopher's word for it), leading to its commodification and the creation of commercial middlemen for its dissemination—this was the long-range result of literacy, and the vehicle of its triumph" (2010, 542). Taruskin's claim is puzzling, since handmade manuscripts, just like printed music books, can be (and were) "placed in one's hand in exchange for money," "handled and transported," and "seen as well as heard." What music publishing "thingifies," in our view, is not the score as a "tangible concrete entity" (written music was always tangible and concrete), but rather "the music itself" as a non-tangible, but nevertheless ownable and saleable (pseudo-)object.

18. Owing to the economic peripherality of musical text production, and also to idiosyncratic economic characteristics of musical scores (which in some cases, like that of certain orchestral and opera scores, can generate more earnings when the copyright holder rents out a small number of copies, rather than attempting to sell a large number of copies), the individual scribal production of musical texts persists for centuries after it becomes defunct in the book sector.

19. "No evidence has been uncovered . . . of any copying shops that specialized in music. Music scribes were attached to courts and chapels, such as those at Mechelen or Ferrara; the music they copied was often widely circulated and much used, but their activity is distinct from [capitalist] processes of publication" (Boorman, Selfridge-Field, and Krummel 2001).

20. It is necessary to speak in the past tense here, since digitization has, over the last two decades, upended former schemes of distribution of printed and recorded music, rendering the physical production of scores and recordings nearly obsolete.

21. As James O. Young (1991, 235) notes, "critics still frequently talk of dark and joyful keys."

22. Landes (1969) and other economic historians discriminate two separate industrial revolutions: a spate of mostly British technological innovations in the use of cotton, iron,

and steam between 1780 and 1860, and a more global efflorescence in the last quarter of the nineteenth century of technologies that made use of steel, chemicals, and electricity.

23. Marx traces the increasing, and increasingly injurious, specialization imposed upon detail workers to processes of real subsumption: "While simple cooperation leaves the mode of working by the individual for the most part unchanged, manufacture thoroughly revolutionizes it, and seizes labor power by its very roots. It converts the laborer into a crippled monstrosity, by forcing his detail dexterity at the expense of a world of productive capabilities and instincts; just as in the States of Laplata they butcher a whole beast for the sake of his hide or his tallow. Not only is the detail work distributed to the different individuals, but the individual himself is made the automatic motor of fraction operation" (*MECW*, 35:365–366).

24. Marx uses piano manufacture to illustrate the distinction between "productive" labor, which creates surplus value for a capitalist, and "unproductive" labor, which does not. "The workman employed by a piano maker is a productive laborer. His labor not only replaces the wages that he consumes, but in the product, the piano, the commodity that the piano maker sells, there is a surplus value over and above the value of the wages. But assume on the contrary that I buy all the materials required for a piano (or for all it matters the laborer himself may possess them), and that instead of buying the piano in a shop I have it made for me in my house. The workman who makes the piano is now an unproductive laborer, because his labor is exchanged directly against my revenue" (*MECW*, 31:16).

25. Jorgensen (1977 and 1991) maintains that equal temperament was not a practical reality until the second decade of the twentieth century, since no precise method for tuning in equal temperament appeared in print before then. Sturm (2010b) convincingly dismantles Jorgensen's thesis. "Much of Jorgenson's argument about the impossibility of equal temperament before the twentieth century is based on a very narrow definition of equal temperament, where any deviation of as much as one cent in the temperament is enough to make it something different . . . . Jorgensen assumed that minor deviations from 'precise' equal temperament are significant, and that procedures other than those of the twentieth century could not achieve such precision. Both assumptions are subject to question" (20). Sturm suggests that it is an error to fixate, as Jorgensen does, on trivial physical differences in Pitch to the neglect of more germane normative and social facts about Tone: "Practically speaking there was little evidence that tuners were doing other than attempting to tune equal temperament to the best of their ability, using methods that, while some were not very precise in their instructions, were all clearly aimed at creating an equal temperament with all keys sounding alike" (20).

26. We can get an idea about levels of training and compensation from an 1891 article in *The Musical Courier* (1891, 752). "The pay in the factories for tuning pianos averages $18 or $20 a week . . . Moreover, there is evening work outside which is so much extra for the tuner employed in the factory. A piano can be tuned in an hour and a half at any time in the evening that is convenient after resting from the day's work, and the tuner receives for it $1.50 . . . It is not necessary for a piano tuner to be a fine musician . . . On fair average, in order to get piano tuning down fine, it would require about two years to become proficient, but some can acquire excellence in this line in six months." By comparison, the weekly wage of a skilled carpenter in New York in 1890 was around $20 (United States Bureau of Labor 1900, 766).

27. On the continent, equal temperament seems to have met with approbation earlier than it did in England. In Germany, in particular, "the movement toward equal temperament was

becoming quite strong by 1750." Daniel Gottlob Türk's *Klavierschule*, from 1789, is one of a host of German-language theoretical documents of the period that makes mention of the popularity of equal temperament on keyboard instruments (Sturm 2010a, 26). Our claim is not that equal temperament was nowhere to be found before capital's subsumption of tuning, nor that there were no musical reasons to prefer it. The claim is that the economic event of subsumption (of the labor of tuning) coincides with a point of inflection in European intonational norms, after which non-equal temperament goes into rapid decline.

28. Duffin does not provide an explanation of why it would be more convenient or less expensive to manufacture wind instruments in equal temperament rather than in any other scheme, nor does the source he cites to corroborate his claim, Powell (2002). On the face of it, it is hard to see why the choice of temperament would appreciably affect the cost of manufacturing flutes, since differences in temperament on that instrument come down to small differences in where the toneholes would be drilled, which would presumably have little or no effect on production price. Duffin's thought may be that for a flute to play equally well, and with the same intonational profile, in all keys, but without using the evenly spaced semitones of equal temperament, requires a cumbersome mechanism that permits a division of the octave into more than twelve notes, as on split-key keyboard instruments. This sort of contraption would undoubtedly be more expensive to produce than a run-of-the-mill equally tempered instrument. But this assumes a scenario in which a feature of equal temperament—absence of individuating key quality, equivalent usability of all keys—is antecedently sought. In the case of the piano, as we have tried to demonstrate, there appear to be economic factors over and above a standing preference for the virtues of equal temperament—to wit, the need for large numbers of instruments to be tuned, assembly-line style, in a factory environment—that create selection pressure in favor of equal temperament.

29. Wing (1897, 15) says that the figure of 100,000 instruments annually was reached by the American piano industry by 1897.

30. Powell (2002, 149) provides examples of mid- and late-nineteenth-century writers on music who use "perfect intonation" and "equal temperament" interchangeably.

31. The notes in question are in mm. 92–93, in the first movement's development section. E♭ is $\hat{1}$ within a 12-measure tonicization of E♭ minor. But E♭'s status as local tonic is called into question when it is elaborated by its chromatic upper neighbor, F♭. This half-step motion gives the impression that E♭ is about to be treated as $\hat{5}$ of A♭ minor. Instead, E♭ is respelled as D♯, and is then used as the leading tone within a fully diminished seventh chord that tonicizes E minor. The reason the cello's D♯ must initially be "the same tone" as the preceding E♭ in the violins is simple to deduce: a slight change in intonation (which would be noticeable, given that the cello plays the note unaccompanied) would either sound like a mistake (since someone listening without the score would be unaware of the respelling) or else spoil the harmonic punch line. For although the unaccompanied neighboring motion between E♭ and F♭ is respelled with D♯ and E already in mm. 93–94, the listener should be none the wiser until m. 95, when the real auditory surprise arrives: F♯, C, and A as members of the D♯ fully diminished seventh chord.

32. "But, in general, the protective system of our day is conservative, while the free trade system is destructive. . . . In a word, the free trade system hastens the social revolution. It is in this revolutionary sense alone, gentlemen, that I vote in favor of free trade" (*MECW*, 6:465).

33. "In the first half of the nineteenth century—that is, relatively late in the overall development of the bourgeoisie since the Renaissance—when capitalism first really began to develop by means of steam-powered machinery, this historical leap in the development of productivity was not yet in any way the result of a systematic relationship between science and production. The decisive innovations were initially still made by empirical practitioners (such as the engineer-industrialist and inventor of the spinning frame Arkwright) and not by scientists, and these innovations were made not on the basis of the socialized organization of science and technology, but individually" (Kurz 2014, 35). The "state and social organization of the process of science and its direct connection to material production" (36) becomes a core feature of capital accumulation beginning in the late nineteenth century.

34. Electrodynamism is crucial in the Telharmonium not only for the induction of currents that are homologous to, and that cause the connected speaker to emit, various sine waves, but also for controlling the consistent rotation speed of the tone-wheel.

35. Marx is here referring to steam and water power, not electrical power. The first volume of *Capital* appeared in 1867, several years before the electric motor reached a commercially viable form, and more than a decade before electrodynamism became prevalent in industry.

36. Our account of the Telharmonium as a tool that enables a new manner of sonic construction—a brand-new type of musical action-type, brought into being by a new form of technological mediation—is indebted to the stimulating history of the instrument found in Théberge (1997, chap. 3).

37. "Use value" is Marx's vague term for whatever it is about something that makes people willing to accept it in exchange for something else (e.g., money). Marx uses a musical example to illustrate the elusive, protean nature of use values: "Some services or use values, the results of certain activities or kinds of labor, are incorporated in commodities; others, however, leave behind no tangible result as distinct from the persons themselves: or they do not result in a salable commodity. E.g. the service a singer performs for me satisfies my aesthetic needs, but what I enjoy exists only in an action inseparable from the singer himself, and once his work, singing, has come to an end, my enjoyment is also at an end; I enjoy the activity itself—its reverberation in my ear" (*MECW*, 34:139–40).

38. Much of what is known about the history of the New York Electric Music Company comes from musicologist Stoddard Lincoln (1972), the son of Edwin Stoddard Lincoln, an electrical engineering pioneer who came into possession of much of the original documentation concerning the Telharmonium (Weidenaar 1995, 313).

39. These inflation statistics, which are based on the Consumer Price Index, are of questionable value for giving a sense of the size of large capital investments (which are advanced to purchase capital goods, not consumer goods) from the period. For comparison's sake: in 1876, Thomas Edison's entire laboratory in Menlo Park, NJ, which accommodated sixty employees and was considered to be the most impressive research facility in the United States, cost $2,500 to build and contained $40,000 of machines and equipment. In other words, the Telharmonium was outrageously well funded by contemporary standards.

40. In Marx's work, "fixed capital" refers to assets such as machines and buildings that depreciate slowly and transfer their value to commodities gradually. Fixed capital is a fractional part of "constant capital," which refers to the total cost of means of production (including raw materials). "Variable capital," the mutually exclusive and jointly exhaustive counterpart of constant capital, refers to the wage bill (the money capitalists give to workers). One

of Marx's main tenets is that as capitalism goes from cradle to grave, the average ratio of constant capital to variable capital grows, as human labor is displaced by mechanization and automation.

41. One notable exception is the music-theoretical subdiscipline of tuning and temperament studies, where, in a swing of the historical pendulum, digital audio technology has stimulated renewed experimentation with non-equal and non-twelve-note tuning systems.

WORKS CITED

American National Standards Institute. 1994. *Standards on Acoustical Terminology*. Washington, DC: American National Standards Institute.

Anon. 1891. "Women as Piano Tuners." *The Musical Courier* 23: 752.

Anon. 1906. "The Telharmonium: An Apparatus for the Electrical Generation and Transmission of Music." *Scientific American* 96: 210–211.

Atkinson, Benedict, and Brian Fitzgerald. 2014. *A Short History of Copyright*. New York: Springer.

Boorman, Stanley, Eleanor Selfridge-Field, and Donald W. Krummel. 2001. "Printing and Publishing of Music." *Grove Music Online*. 6 Aug. 2018.http://www.oxfordmusiconline.com/grovemusic/view/10.1093/gmo/9781561592630.001.0001/omo-9781561592630-e-0000040101.

Bouwsma, Oets Kolk 1965. *Philosophical Essays*. Lincoln: University of Nebraska Press.

Bukharin, Nikolai. 1925. *Historical Materialism: A System of Sociology*. New York: International Publishers.

Chennevière, Rudhyar D. 1920. "The Rise of the Musical Proletariat." Translated by Frederick H. Martens. *The Musical Quarterly* 6: 500–509.

Code, David Loberg. "The Piano's Ivory Cage." http://wmich.edu/mus-theo/groven/ivorycage.html.

Duffin, Ross W. 2007. *How Equal Temperament Ruined Harmony (And Why You Should Care)*. New York: Norton.

Eisenstein, Elizabeth. 1979. *The Printing Press as an Agent of Change: Communications and Cultural Transformations in Early Modern Europe*. Cambridge: Cambridge University Press.

Giddens, Anthony. 1973. *The Class Structure of the Advanced Societies*. New York: Barnes and Noble.

Goehr, Lydia. 1992. *The Imaginary Museum of Musical Works*. Oxford: Oxford University Press.

Green, Gil. 2006. "The Piano Tuner in England, 1837–1913." In *The Pianoforte Tuners Association: A History 1913–2005*, edited by Les Sherlock, Appendix 8. Bloomington, IN: Trafford. Unpaginated e-book.

Habermas, Jürgen, Sara Lennox, and Frank Lennox. 1964. "The Public Sphere: An Encyclopedia Article (1964)." *New German Critique* 3: 49–55.

Helmholtz, Hermann von. 1954. *On the Sensations of Tone*. Translated by Alexander J. Ellis. New York: Dover.

Hyer, Brian. 2001. "Key." *Grove Music Online*. http://www.oxfordmusiconline.com/grovemusic/view/10.1093/gmo/9781561592630.001.0001/omo-9781561592630-e-0000014942.

Hummel, Johann Nepomuk. 1828. *A Complete Theoretical and Practical Course of Instructions, on the Art of Playing the Pianoforte, Commencing with the Simplest Elementary Principles, and Including Every Information Requisite to the Most Finished Style of Performance*. London: Boosey.

Jorgensen, Dale. 1977. *Tuning the Historical Temperaments by Ear*. Marquette: Northern Michigan University Press.

Jorgensen, Dale. 1991. *Tuning: Containing the Perfection of Eighteenth-Century Temperament, the Lost Art of Nineteenth-Century Temperament, and the Science of Equal Temperament, Complete with Instructions for Aural and Electronic Tuning*. East Lansing: Michigan State University Press.

Koivisto, Juha, and Mikko Lahtinen. 2010. "Konjunktur, politisch-historische." In *Historisch-kritisches Wörterbuch des Marxismus*, vol. 7, no. 2. Edited by Wolfgang Fritz Haug, 1502–1519. Hamburg: Argument.

Kurz, Robert. 2014. "The Crisis of Exchange Value: Science as Productivity, Productive Labor, and Capitalist Reproduction." In *Marxism and the Critique of Value*, edited by Neil Larsen, Mathias Nilges, Josh Robinson, and Nicholas Brown, 17–76. Chicago: MCM' Publishing.

Landes, David S. 1969. *The Unbound Prometheus: Technological Change and Industrial Development in Western Europe from 1750 to the Present*. Cambridge: Cambridge University Press.

Lincoln, Stoddard. 1972. "The Rise and Fall of the New York Electric Music Company: A Study in Early Musak of the Wonderful Telharmonium." Paper presented at the Annual Meeting of the American Musicological Society, Dallas, TX. http://magneticmusic.ws/mmlincolns. PDF.

Lindley, Mark. 2001. "Temperaments." *Grove Music Online*, edited by Deane Root. http://www.oxfordmusiconline.com/grovemusic/view/10.1093/gmo/9781561592630.001.0001/omo-9781561592630-e-0000027643.

Lindley, Mark. 2010. "Marx and Engels on Music." *Monthly Review Online*, August 18. https://mronline.org/2010/08/18/marx-and-engels-on-music/#_edn45.

Loesser, Arthur. 1954. *Men, Women, and Pianos: A Social History*. New York: Dover.

MacKenzie, G. W. 1964. *Acoustics: The Technique of Sound Reproduction*. London: Focal Press.

Mandel, Ernest. 1992. *Power and Money: A Marxist Theory of Bureaucracy*. London: Verso.

Marx, Karl, and Friedrich Engels. 2010. *Marx & Engels Collected Works*. 50 vols. London: Lawrence and Wishart.

McDermott, Josh H., and Andrew J. Oxenham. 2008. "Music Perception, Pitch, and the Auditory System." *Current Opinion in Neurobiology* 18: 452–463.

Morgan, Robert P. 1976. "Dissonant Prolongation: Theoretical and Compositional Precedents." *Journal of Music Theory* 20: 49–91.

Nolan, Jason, and Melanie McBride. 2015. "Embodied Semiosis: Autistic 'Stimming' as Sensory Practice." In *The International Handbook of Semiotics*, edited by Peter Pericles Trifonas, 1069–1078. New York: Springer.

O'Callaghan, Casey. 2007. *Sounds: A Philosophical Theory*. Oxford: Oxford University Press.

Oettinger, Rebecca Wagner. 2004. "Berg v. Gerlach: Printing and Lasso's Imperial Privilege of 1582." *Fontes Artis Musicae* 51: 111–134.

Piatier, Andre. 1988. "Transectorial Innovations and the Transformation of Firms." *The Information Society* 5: 205–231.

Postone, Moishe. 1996. *Time, Labor and Social Domination*. Chicago: University of Chicago Press.

Powell, Ardall. 2002. *The Flute*. New Haven, CT: Yale University Press.

Rehding, Alexander. 2016. "Instruments of Music Theory." *Music Theory Online* 22, no. 4. http://mtosmt.org/issues/mto.16.22.4/mto.16.22.4.rehding.html.

Reuten, Geert. 2014. "An Outline of the Systematic-Dialectical Method: Scientific and Political Significance." In *Marx's Capital and Hegel's Logic: A Reexamination*, edited by Fred Moseley and Tony Smith, 243–268. Boston: Brill.

Rigi, Jakob. 2014. "Foundations of a Marxist Theory of the Political Economy of Information: Trade Secrets and Intellectual Property, and the Production of Relative Surplus Value and the Extraction of Rent-Tribute." *Communication, Capitalism, and Critique* 12: 909–936.

Roell, Craig H. 1991. *The Piano in America, 1890–1940.* Chapel Hill: University of North Carolina Press.

Rosenberg, Nathan. 1976. *Perspectives on Technology.* Cambridge: Cambridge University Press.

Russel, Eric-John. 2015. "The Logic of Subsumption: an Elective Affinity between Hegel and Marx." *Revista Opinão Filosófica* 6: 28–48.

Sachs, Carl. 2015. "Somatic Impulses in the Space of Reasons: Pragmatist Themes in Adorno's Critical Social Epistemology." Paper delivered at the Summer Institute in American Philosophy, University College Dublin. http://www.academia.edu/12425832/Somatic_ Impulses_in_the_Space_of_Reasons_Pragmatist_Themes_in_Adorno_s_Critical_Social_ Epistemology.

Schubart, Christian Friedrich Daniel. 1806. *Ideen zu einer Aesthetik der Tonkunst.* Vienna: Degen.

Sellars, Wilfrid. 1956. "Empiricism and the Philosophy of Mind." In *Minnesota Studies in the Philosophy of Science*, vol. I, edited by H. Feigl and M. Scriven, 253–329. Minneapolis: University of Minnesota Press.

Small, Christopher. 1998. *Musicking: The Meanings of Performing and Listening.* Middletown, CT: Wesleyan University Press.

Smith, Tony. 1990. *The Logic of Marx's Capital: Replies to Hegelian Criticisms.* Albany: SUNY Press.

Sousa, John Philip. 1906. "The Menace of Mechanical Music." *Appleton's Magazine*: 278–284.

Steblin, Rita. 1996. *A History of Key Characteristics in the Eighteenth and Early Nineteenth Centuries.* Rochester, NY: University of Rochester Press.

Steingo, Gavin. 2014. "The Musical Work Reconsidered, in Hindsight." *Current Musicology* 97: 81–112.

Sturm, Fred. 2010a. "A Clear and Practical Introduction to Temperament History, Part 5: German Irregular Circulating Temperaments." *Piano Technicians Journal* 53: 24–27.

Sturm, Fred. 2010b. "A Clear and Practical Introduction to Temperament History, Part 8: Jorgensen's 'Tuning.'" *Piano Technicians Journal* 53, no. 12: 19–21.

Taruskin, Richard. 2010. *Music from the Earliest Notations to the Sixteenth Century.* New York: Oxford University Press.

Théberge, Paul. 1997. *Any Sound You Can Imagine: Making Music/Consuming Technology.* Hanover, NH: Wesleyan University Press.

Tomlinson, Gary. 2007. *The Singing of the New World: Indigenous Voice in the Era of European Contact.* Cambridge: Cambridge University Press.

Tresch, John, and Emily I. Dolan. 2013. "Toward a New Organology: Instruments of Music and Science." *Osiris* 28: 278–298.

United States Bureau of Labor. 1900. *Bulletin of the United States Bureau of Labor.* Vol. V, no. 29.

Weidenaar, Reynold. 1995. *Magic Music from the Telharmonium.* Metuchen, NJ: Scarecrow Press.

Welskopp, Thomas. 2002. "Class Struggle and the Firm: The Interplay of Workplace and Industrial Relations in Large Capitalist Enterprises." In *Authority and Control in Modern Industry: Theoretical and Empirical Perspectives*, edited by Paul L. Robertson, 73–119. London: Verso.

Wing, Frank L. 1897. *The Book of Complete Information about Pianos.* New York: Wing and Son.

Wittgenstein, Ludwig. 1986. *Philosophical Investigations.* Translated by G. E. M. Anscombe. London: Basil Blackwell.

Young, James O. 1991. "Key, Temperament and Musical Expression." *The Journal of Aesthetics and Art Criticism* 49: 235–242.

CHAPTER 2

··

INTERVAL

··

HENRY KLUMPENHOUWER

THE interval is a basic or foundational music-theoretical construct in Western music theory. By basic or foundational, I mean that intervals are among the first constructs one learns as a musician (and among the first topics covered in theory textbooks); and that other constructs contain or presuppose them. Intervals are also transhistorical constructs, occupying theorists continually from the discipline's classical origins to the present. The history of theorizing intervals corresponds to the history of music theory itself.

As a foundational, transhistorical category, the literature on intervals is immense. Even so, one might assume, considering their foundational position in theoretic systems, that they have a primitive, elementary character (Klein 1988, 6), so that the immense literature about intervals is largely repetitive—in other words, that while vast, the literature is weakly innovative, and that variations in the relevant terminology, although interesting, are nevertheless superficial aspects of the category.

With this mind, I will set aside the task of presenting a thoroughgoing historical survey of intervals in Western music. Instead, I plan to put some pressure on the idea that intervals are, to a great degree, conceptually primitive or elementary. While forgoing a historical examination, I do wish to remember that contemporary thinking about intervals is precipitate of historical process, even though the process seems glacial.

As well as foundational, elementary, and transhistorical, intervals are also systematic, which is to say they create and regulate the musical space in which other, more complex theoretical constructs operate. The systemic aspect of intervals serves as our entry point into the category.

We'll begin with a standard definition, one found in the *Harvard Dictionary of Music*. There, we read that an interval is the "relationship between two pitches. A tradition going back at least to Boethius and still current defines interval as the distance between an upper and lower pitch. This spatial metonymy is convenient for inventories of tempered scales as well as for informal descriptions of intervals. A parallel tradition going back to Greek antiquity defines interval as the ratio between an upper and lower pitch" (Randel 2003, 413).

There's a great deal of information loaded into these four sentences, and we will spend some time unpacking them. We'll start by isolating the idea that intervals measure the relationship between two pitches, that terms like major third, augmented prime, and perfect twelfth describe relationships. What kind of relationship is this? The second sentence of the definition tells us that these relationships are (metaphorically) spatial. The space involved is reflected in the comparatives, "upper" and "lower." This seems very natural to us: we are accustomed to regarding pitches along an axis of height, as being "high" or "low." In this metaphor system, which extends back to the Greeks, the vertical axis represents pitch and the horizontal axis represents time—the Western notational system reflects this idea. There is nothing inevitable about these metaphors: traditional Daoist music theory in China, to choose a radically different example, uses the terms "clear" (*qing* 清) and "muddy" (*zhuo* 濁), drawing on water imagery to describe high and low pitches (Chen 1996, 21; and Park 2017). In other words, our definition of intervals depends on thinking of pitches as if they were points on a grid or plane. Intervals are measurements between these points.

What kind of grid or plane is imagined and what kind of measuring is involved in our interval system? We'll address this by thinking about the traditional names of intervals, starting with four examples: major third, minor third, augmented fourth, and perfect twelfth. The names contain the idea of quantity: three, three, four, and twelve, respectively. The numbers are ordinal rather than cardinal; third, third, fourth, twelfth. And they are qualified in some way: major, minor, augmented, perfect.

The names reflect particular kinds of conceptual work. It is important that we understand the conceptual framework that gives rise to interval names and grasp the associated modes of musical thinking. To get at these modes of musical thinking or conceptual frameworks, we'll examine the mechanics of our current interval system more closely. To begin with, we should point out something that seems obvious but from certain perspectives is highly contentious. Our interval systems are filing systems, which is to say, they are designed to collect different objects into classes and to standardize how to think about each class on its own and in relation to other classes. For instance, the conventional interval system places the relationship between F4 and A4, the relationship between F5 and A5, and the relationship between C5 and E5 in the same category—they are all major thirds—and instructs us to think about them in the same way: F4/A4 = F5/A5 = C5/E5. These equivalencies are worth considering. We might even wish to question whether it's a good idea to regard every appearance of F4 and A4, associated in some way, as conceptually identical. Surely, different musical contexts will cause us to ascribe to them different musical meanings. Yet our interval system asks us to ignore these differences, ascribing the same prepackaged meaning to all instances. We can well imagine, however, that the task of devising an interval system that captures such differences, one that doesn't prescribe a single meaning to all possible appearances of, say, F4/A4 (not to mention to all appearances of what we call "a major third"), poses a great many problems. The lesson here is that our theorizing about intervals can never adequately grasp the complexities involved. Our task, however, is not to point out the impossibility of adequately understanding musical structures or to object to taxonomic schemes in general. Our task is to understand the dynamics of our current interval system.

Let's begin with the notes F4 and A4. We are taught to name the relationship a "major third." What has "three" to do with these two notes? What are we counting? Now, let's imagine the notes F4 and B4. We are taught two names for relationships such as these: "augmented fourth" and "tritone." What has "four" to do with these two notes? And why is there a second name we can also use, which suggests that three, not four, is the basis of the relationship?

To find that out, let's examine how we are taught to assign interval names to pitch relations.[1] First, we are to think of the pitches in question as elements in a notational system. The fact that we require notated pitches is a critical aspect of our interval system that we will address later on.

Figure 2.1 presents F4 and A4 in our conventional notation. We are taught that in order to calculate the interval in question, we are to count inclusively the lines and spaces between the two given pitches. In the case of Figure 2.1, we count the lowest space on the clef (where F4 lies), the second line, and the second space (where A4 lies). Since we count three lines and spaces, we say that the interval is a "third."

What does the counting mean, musically speaking? What do the lines and spaces represent? Consider the notes F♯4 and A♭4. When we set about to calculate the relationship between them, we again count inclusively the lines and spaces between F♯4 and A♭4. Since there are three lines and spaces, we say that the relationship between F♯4 and A♭4, like the relationship between F4 and A4, is a "third." As such, we assert an equivalence between F4 and F♯4 and an equivalence between A4 and A♭4. In turn, we assert an equivalence between the relationship F4-and-A4 and the relationship F♯4-and-A♭4. Both are "thirds." And we could assert many further equivalencies: thinking along the same lines, we can consider F♭4, F4, F♯4, F𝄪4—any F with or without an accidental—to be equivalent; and A♭4, A4, A♯4, A𝄪4—any A with or without an accidental—to be equivalent. The relationship between any F with or without an accidental and any A with or without an accidental is a "third." Take F𝄪4 and A♭♭4: there is a sense in which A♭♭4 is higher than F𝄪4, and another sense in which A♭♭4 is lower than F𝄪4. When we calculate interval relationships in the system of lines and spaces, we are thinking not of single pitches, but families of pitches. Accordingly, "pitch" is irrelevant to the matters at hand. So, in this system of measurements, intervals are relationships, not between pitches, but between letter names, and letter names represent order positions.[2] Order positions, not pitches, are the objects at hand.

What system of musical experiences and concepts is represented by a locus of order positions? As creatures of notation, can order positions engage any musical experiences?

FIGURE 2.1 F4 and A4 in conventional notation.

If a locus of order positions has any genuine musical meaning, if it engages with some class of musical experiences, then the relevant music must be read and not just heard. That's an uncomfortable realization, especially in conceptual contexts that valorize listening as the paradigmatic musical activity. Yet we need to bear in mind that much training in musicianship involves associating aural experiences of music with notation. Among other things, that training allows us to apprehend changes of state as a change from one order position to another or as the persistence of a single order position even when different pitches are involved. Take the successions G4–A♭4 and G4–G♯4. The successions of pitches (at least when played on a piano) are identical. The only way to distinguish the former (as a change of order position) from the latter (as the persistence of order position) is an established tonal context. It doesn't matter which particular theoretical apparatus we marshal to explain or codify the relevant tonal contexts: all will be oriented to distinguishing the two successions with respect to order positions and all will be concerned to provide a logic for making the distinction. Theories of scale degrees interact well with the notion of order positions but one should not simply identify order positions with scale degrees: there are other theories of tonality, not embedded in theories of scale structure, that adequately provide experiential content to order positions.[3]

Before allowing this to go any further, one might protest that we are making far too much of this. The discussion so far is a meditation about a certain aspect (or quirk) of our notational system, not our musical system. Notational systems are practical and expedient, nothing more: we would be foolish to imagine they represent anything very important beyond getting people to play the correct *pitch* (*not* letter name!) on their instruments. If our notational system suggests uncomfortable complexities, we shouldn't make too much of it. Perhaps notation should have been reformed to remove this awkwardness, but it would be unfeasible to change things now. (Think of Klavarskribo, for example.) Besides, everyone knows that we do deal with definite pitches. Look at our keyboard: it is an assembly of concrete pitches, not letter names. We know very well that F♭4, F4, F♯4, and F𝄪4 are not equivalent: they are not played on the same keys. Moreover, the various examples considered above involve a ruse: A♭♭ is *really* G♭, which is the same as F♯; and that F𝄪 is *really* G. And it's simply wrong to say that A♭♭4 is a third above F𝄪4. Moreover, we must consider listening to be the paradigmatic musical activity. Not everyone plays an instrument or composes pieces, the two musical activities that (given the musical traditions we are considering here) depend heavily on notation. Listening is democratic: musical activities concerned with notation are exclusive and restricted musical activities.

There are a number of elements in the objection that should be challenged. To begin with, the objection assumes a binary in which one pole is musical sound and its other pole the notation of musical sound. The objection assumes music purely as a sound management system existing with its own logic, its own styles of thinking, and that its notation contributes nothing. The view is very close to the notion that spoken language is original and self-sufficient and that its written form is only a supplement, capable of conveying only what must already be there in the spoken language.[4] This is not the place to go through this debate in any detail. We can point out that one mustn't assume an opposition between sounded music and its notation, let alone a binary weighted against notation. Sounded and written music form a rich historical system in which the two elements condition each other. Without its particular notational system, music could not have developed in the ways that it has. So, if we do not understand the nature of our notational system, the concepts it embeds, A♭♭ and the changes it has undergone, we cannot hope to develop a rich understanding of the relevant music.[5] The whole point is that we cannot legitimately detach sounded music from its notation, which is an assumption that underwrites our ideas about basic musicianship.

In addition to a reliance on a weighted binary of sounded music and its notation, our objection also leans quite heavily on naturalizing the idea of enharmonicism, which lies behind the idea that A♭♭4 is *really* just G♭4, which is the same as F♯4; and that F×4 is *really* G4. As a musical term, "enharmonic" has an exceptionally long history but in its current usage, enharmonic is a relationship under which musical notes are considered equivalent when they share the same pitch, even though they are notated differently. I've chosen terms with some care, distinguishing between "notes" and "pitches," to avoid a certain awkwardness in some definitions of the term "enharmonic." The definition provided in the *Harvard Dictionary of Music* is instructive in this respect. There, we read that the term covers "pitches that are one and the same even though named or 'spelled' differently. . . . Pitches related in this way are said to be enharmonic equivalents of one another" (Randel 2003, 294–295). By employing the term "musical note," we can suggest a more complex object, one that has both a name and a pitch.[6] So, name-and-pitch combinations (that is, musical notes) that have the same pitch are said to be equivalent. At the very least, that claim provides some clarity.

Even with that adjustment, however, the concept of enharmonic equivalence is obscure. How do we know that given name-pitch combinations involve the same pitch? Typically, one resorts to certain instrumental layouts to answer that question. So, because one plays the same key on a piano or organ keyboard to produce A♭♭4, G♭4, F♯4, E×4, all four involve the same pitch, and all four are thus considered enharmonically equivalent. We shall see that the idea of enharmonic equivalence involves many more complexities (and problems) than this, but for now, it will be sufficient to note that we are talking about an *equivalence* relationship, not an *identity* relationship. A♭♭4, G♭4, F♯4, E×4 are equivalent, not identical, under the enharmonic relationship.[7] We have observed that the definition recognizes the musical notes are complex objects, with (at least) two elements: a letter name designation and a pitch designation.

We'll suspend our discussion of these issues for now and return to the investigation of our interval system, which operates within a musical space notated by the lines and spaces of our staff notation, which in turn represents order positions. Figure 2.2 is a visualization of the space. C4 is represented in our notational system by the line under the G clef, the middle line in the alto C clef, the line above the F clef; D4 is represented in our notational system by the space below the G clef, the second highest space in the alto C clef; E4 is represented in our notation system by the lowest line in the G clef, the second highest line in the alto C clef; and so on. We have already noted that we need to regard

. . .

E5

D5

C5

B4

A4

G4

F4

E4

D4

C4

. . .

FIGURE 2.2 Lines and spaces as letter names.

the musical objects in the space as defined principally by their letter designations, and not by pitch, because the letter names may be altered by accidentals, so that each letter name has several different forms, which do not figure into the calculation of interval. Examining the space, we can see F4 and A4, and observe the sense of three-ness in the relationship we noted earlier in connection with Figure 2.1: we count three objects in the span F4–G4–A4. To calculate the relationship between D4 and C5, we inclusively count the objects in the span D4–E4–F4–G4–A4–B4–C5. Since there are seven such objects, we say the interval between D4 and C5 is a seventh.

Before proceeding any further, we need to examine the nature of the measurements we have just carried out. There are two conventions: the first argues that intervallic measurement involves magnitude alone (for instance, perfect fifth); and another that argues that intervallic measurement involves magnitude extended in a certain direction (for instance, perfect fifth up). Both conventions have long histories. Judging from rudiments textbooks, however, the first convention is by far the most common. There is a third practice that uses both conventions depending on musical contexts or modes of appearance, as harmonic intervals (magnitude only) or melodic intervals (directed magnitude), distinguishing them terminologically: perfect fifth vs. perfect fifth down. Under the first convention, we speak about the interval *between* D4 and C5 (as we have been doing); under the second convention, we speak about the interval *from* D4 *to* C5. The first convention understands intervals as spans or measured-off space; the second convention understands intervals as motions through space. Koch's definition of interval, on the one hand, is representative of the first convention. Interval, he writes, "is the space between two different tones" (Koch 1802). Riedt (1753), on the other hand, is careful to distinguish between "over" and "under" intervals. While the first convention—interval as a span—is more widespread, it is also the case that direction is often assumed or preprogrammed—usually, from lower to higher note and from one note to the following note (namely, onward and upward)—so that the relevant terminology does not reflect a given direction.[8] The use of assumed directions occasionally causes problems, as in the reckoning of descending melodic intervals: one ought to make explicit what one is measuring.

It is not my place here to argue in favor of one convention over the other; I am more interested in the different understandings of measurement associated with each. Even so, the use of both conventions differentiated by context is certainly something one ought to avoid: interval measurement should not depend on modes of appearance, not least because the harmonic/melodic distinction is too restrictive. Since interval is genuinely a foundational theoretical category, one should expect to be able to measure the relationship between any two notes one wishes. Furthermore, using both conventions often leads to some leakage between them. As we'll see, the systematic characteristics of the two conventions of measurement differ considerably and are incommensurate.

Let's summarize what we have learned so far about our interval system. To begin with, the musical space in which it operates, represented here in Figure 2.2, contains complex musical objects designated by letter name (not pitch). And letter names emerge from order positions. Reflecting on the display in Figure 2.2, we can see how strongly it relates to the idea of a musical scale. In that connection, we also become aware of the extent to which scales are theoretical constructions. It is tempting to think of them as facts because it is easy to link the concept of a scale with the physical construction of many musical instruments, a linkage strengthened by the idea of "practicing one's scales."[9]

We'll refer to the interval system described so far, the system whose elements are a unison (or prime), a second, a third, a fourth, and so on, as the Order Position Interval System. We often think in terms of this system on its own, when we say things such as "the melody is harmonized in thirds and sixths," or "the melody moves in seconds," or use terms such as "tertian harmony" or "quartal harmony." In this system, the five intervals shown in Figure 2.3 are all "thirds." We could say from the first to the second in each pair is "a third down," invoking our second convention, in which interval is a measurement of motion. For reasons that will become clear, for now we'll set aside the first convention, the idea that interval is a measured span, and exclusively employ the second convention.

Let's compare the first interval and the fourth interval. While both are the same interval in the Order Position Interval System (a third down), we hear a marked difference. We are taught to regard the difference in sound as a difference of size, so that the first third down—extending from A4 to F4—is "bigger" than the third down from A♭4 to F4. We call interval 1 a "major" third down, and interval 4 a "minor" third down. When we consider interval 5, we see that we have three different sizes of "a third down."

The simple use of comparatives major and minor, or bigger and smaller, is insufficient to register all these differences in sizes. To calculate these differences more precisely, we are taught to make use of a supplementary system, in which we count the number of semitones involved. In particular, we are taught that there are four semitones from A4 to F4, three semitones from A♭4 to F4, and two semitones from A♭4 to F♯4. Our training will have also taught us that thirds containing four semitones are called "major thirds"; thirds containing three semitones are "minor thirds"; and thirds containing two semitones are "diminished thirds." And we are trained to make similar distinctions between the various forms of all the intervals in our scale space. Furthermore, we are often encouraged to assert equivalences among intervals on this basis: we consider, for example, augmented seconds to be equivalent to minor thirds because they both contain three semitones.

The mechanics of this may seem fairly simple and straightforward. But it embeds in a great deal of theorizing. First of all, we regard this semitone system as not simply an auxiliary system to the Order Position Interval System discussed earlier. Rather, it is a fully formed interval system on its own. And as we shall see presently, it is entirely different in character from the Order Position Interval System. To explore these matters further, let's return to the mechanics of counting semitones. How do we figure out that interval 1 in Figure 2.3, a third down from A4 to F4, contains four semitones, while interval 3, for example, contains three semitones? The musical space in Figure 2.2 will be of no help at all. Accordingly, the lines and spaces of our notational system will be of no help, either. They represent the letter name space of the Order Position Interval System.

Typically, we are instructed to carry out our calculations with reference to the keyboard. We are told that the distance from one key to an adjacent key is a semitone. Figure 2.4 abstracts a new musical space from the keyboard. Instead of naming the keys by the letter names, as we did in Figure 2.2, we number the keys in Figure 2.4 from the left. On most pianos, the first key is A0, which we will label as 1; the key corresponding to A1,

A4–F4	B4–G4	C5–A4	A♭4–F4	A♭4–F♯4
1	2	3	4	5

FIGURE 2.3 Thirds.

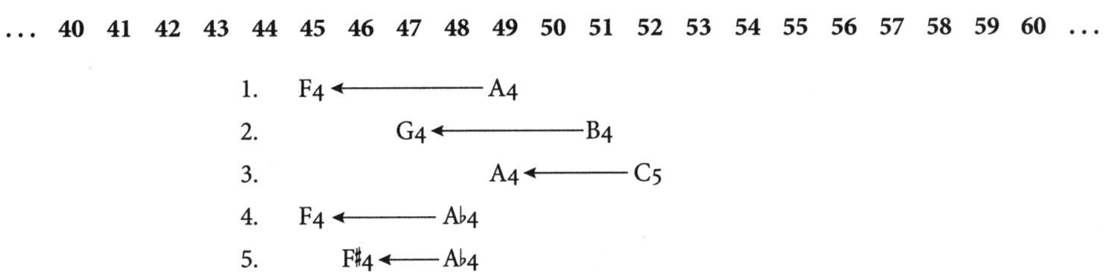

... 40 41 42 43 44 45 46 47 48 49 50 51 52 53 54 55 56 57 58 59 60 ...

1.   F4 ←——————— A4
2.   G4 ←——————— B4
3.   A4 ←——— C5
4.   F4 ←——— A♭4
5.   F♯4 ←——— A♭4

FIGURE 2.4 Keyboard space.

an octave higher, is key 13; A2 is key 25. Figure 2.4 abstracts a segment of the keyboard, extending from key 40 (middle C or C4) to key 60 (A♭5).

Along the bottom, the figure reproduces the five thirds from Figure 2.3 and correlates them with our semitone space. The arrows remind us of the direction in which the interval extends. Examining each interval in turn, we can see the number of semitones they contain. Interval 1, extending from A4 to F4, requires us to move from key 49 to key 45. If we imagine ourselves at key 49, we see that we need to step to the left four times to arrive at key 45. Put arithmetically: 49–45 = 4. Or better, we add –4 (four steps left or down) to key 49 to reach key 45. Interval 2, extending from B4 to G4, requires us to move from key 51 to key 47. If we imagine ourselves at key 51, we see that we need to move to the left four times to arrive at key 47. Put arithmetically: 51–47 = 4. Or better, we add –4 (four steps left or down) to key 51 to reach key 47. Interval 3, extending from C5 to A4, requires us to move from key 52 to key 49. If we imagine ourselves at key 52, we see that we need to step to the left three times to arrive at key 49. Put arithmetically: 52–49 = 3. Or better, we add –3 (three steps left or down) to key 52 to reach key 49. Interval 4, extending from A♭5 to F4, requires us to move from key 48 to key 45. If we imagine ourselves at key 48, we see that we need to step left three times to arrive at key 45. Put arithmetically: 48–45 = 3. Or better, we add –3 (three steps left or down) to key 48 to reach key 45. Interval 5, extending from A♭5 to F♯4, requires a move from key 48 to key 46. If we imagine ourselves at key 48, we see that we need to step to the left twice to arrive at key 46. Put arithmetically: 48–46 = 2. Or better, we add –2 (two steps left or down) to key 48 to reach key 46.

We now turn to an investigation of the systematic nature of Order Position Intervals and Semitone Intervals, and in turn the Common Interval System they combine to form. When we say we are interested in the systematic nature of an interval system, we are chiefly interested with the rules governing how intervals combine with one another. It's not a characteristic of intervals we can safely avoid, because music always presents us with intervals in combination, as melodies or as chords.

We'll begin by investigating the systematic nature of the Semitone Interval System since it's easier to grasp than the Order Position Interval System. Our Semitone Intervals may be represented, as we have been doing in connection with Figure 2.5, by the integers (symbolically $\mathbb{Z}$): $\{ \ldots, -3, -2, -1, 0, 1, 2, 3, \ldots \}$. Positive integers capture the idea of moving some number of semitones up, and negative integers capture the idea of moving some number of semitones down.

We'll represent the idea of combining Semitone Intervals simply by means of addition: $x * y = x + y$. (The symbol $*$ represents the idea of combining x and y: in this

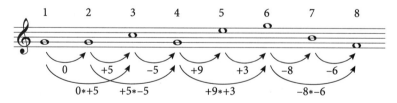

FIGURE 2.5 Combining Semitone Intervals.

case, combination is addition.) In short, we can represent the intervals in the Semitone Interval System by the group of integers under addition.

Figure 2.5 explores interval combination in the Semitone Interval System. The figure provides a melody whose eight pitches are numbered for reference. Underneath the melody, the figure provides the relevant Semitone Intervals, represented by the associated integer: the interval from pitch 1 to pitch 2 (from G4 to G4) is given as "0" for "zero semitones"; the interval from pitch 2 to pitch 3 (from G4 to C5) is given as "+5" for "up five semitones"; the interval from pitch 3 to pitch 4 (from C5 to G4) is given as "–5" for "down five semitones"; the interval from pitch 4 to pitch 5 (from G4 to E5) is given as "+9" for "up nine semitones"; and so on.

The idea of combining intervals is represented by the arrows labeled with some form of $x * y$. So, the idea of combining the interval from pitch 1 to pitch 2 (G4 to G4) and the interval from pitch 2 to pitch 3 (G4 to C5) is represented by the arrow extending from pitch 1 to pitch 3 (G4 to C5) labeled "0 * +5." There is an important systematic feature to note here: we expect that the combination of the intervals 0 and +5, the interval from pitch 1 to pitch 2 and the interval from pitch 2 to pitch 3, respectively, will produce the same result as calculating the interval from pitch 1 to pitch 3. We have that expectation because of our intuitions about our interval systems. According to the rule for combining Semitone Intervals (namely, $x * y = x + y$), the combination $0 * +5 = 0 + +5 = +5$, or up 5 semitones. When we calculate the interval from pitch 1 to pitch 3, we have the same results: up 5 semitones, as expected. Applying the rule for combination to the three arrows labeled "+5 * –5," "+6 * +3," and "–8 * –6," we derive the intervals 0, +9, and –14 (zero semitones, up nine semitones, down fourteen semitones), respectively. In each case, the interval we derive through combination is just what we derive by calculating the interval from pitches at the tail of the relevant arrow to the pitch at its head.

Combining our Order Position Intervals is a different matter entirely. Nevertheless, we can recycle the idea that positive numbers represent some number of letter names moving upward in the musical space in Figure 2.2 and that negative numbers represent some number of letter names moving downward in the musical space of Figure 2.2. Yet, because we are counting inclusively, we cannot use $\mathbb{Z}$, because there is no access under inclusive counting to the integers 0, +1, or –1. So, we will need to employ a different collection of numbers. We'll need to invent that system. We'll define the inclusive integers as $\{ \ldots, -3, -2, 1, 2, 3, \ldots \}$; 1 takes on some but not all the properties of 0 in $\mathbb{Z}$. Inclusive numbers combine idiosyncratically. We cannot simply use the combination protocol of integers as we did in relation to the Semitone Interval System: in the Order Position Interval System, a third up combined with a third up is not a sixth up; or as integers, $3 + 3 \neq 6$. We will need to develop a method for mapping the conventional system of integers under addition onto the system of inclusively counted integers.[10]

Inclusive counting numbers combine according to the following protocols (remember that the symbol $*$ represents combination):

1a. If x or y is 1 or

1b. if x and y are both positive or

1c. if x and y have different signs and $x + y$ is negative, then $x * y = x + y - 1$.

2. Otherwise, $x * y = x + y + 1$.[11]

The protocols adapt the rules for combining integers. So, we will need to read our special inclusive-counting integers as standard integers. There are two rules: we either subtract 1 or add 1 to the conventional combination of inclusive-counting integers read as standard integers depending on the conditions stipulated in the two rules.

Let's see how this works. Figure 2.6 provides the melody given earlier in Figure 2.5, numbering its pitches for reference. Underneath the melody, the figure provides the relevant scale intervals, represented by the associated inclusive counting numbers: the interval from pitch 1 to pitch 2 (from G4 to G4) is given as "1" for "unison" or "prime"; the interval from pitch 2 to pitch 3 (from G4 to C5) is given as "+4" for "a fourth up"; the interval from pitch 3 to pitch 4 (from C5 to G4) is given as "−4" for "a fourth down"; the interval from pitch 4 to pitch 5 (from G4 to E5) is given as "+6" for "a sixth up"; and so on.

Let's combine the interval from pitch 1 to pitch 2 (G4 to G4) in Figure 2.6 and the interval from pitch 2 to pitch 3 (G4 to C5). The figure represents the combination of 1 (prime or unison) and +4 (a fourth up) with the arrow extending from pitch 1 to pitch 3 labeled "1 ∗ +4." Our first task is to determine which line of combination protocol given earlier is appropriate to the present case. We need look no further than the condition described in Rule 1a: If x or y is 1 . . . then $x * y = x + y - 1$. In our case, $x = 1$ and $y = +4$, so $x * y = 1 + 4 - 1 = +4$. Now let's calculate the interval from pitch 1 to pitch 3: the interval from G4 to C5 is "a fourth up" or "+4." So, the Order Position Interval we derive by combining 1 and +4 is just the interval derived by calculating the interval from pitch 1 to pitch 3. The result is just what we expect.

We now combine the interval from pitch 2 to pitch 3 (G4 to C5) and the interval from pitch 3 to pitch 4 (C5 to G4): The figure represents the combination +4 and −4 with the arrow extending from pitch 2 to pitch 4 labeled "+4 ∗ −4." x and y have different signs and $x + y = 0$. None of the three conditions stipulated in Rule 1 apply. Accordingly, we use Rule 2: $x * y = x + y + 1 = +4 - 4 + 1 = 1$. Now let's calculate the interval from pitch 2 to pitch 4: the interval from G4 to G4 is "a prime" or "1." So, again, the interval we derive by combining +4 and −4 is just the interval derived by calculating the interval from pitch 2 to pitch 4, as we expect.

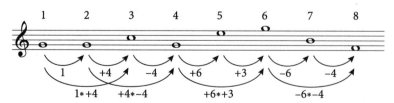

FIGURE 2.6 Combining Order Position Intervals.

We now combine the interval from pitch 4 to pitch 5 (G4 to E5) and the interval from pitch 5 to pitch 6 (E5 to G5): The figure represents the combination with the arrow extending from pitch 4 to pitch 6 labeled "+6 ∗ +3." Again, we begin by determining which of the rules of combination given earlier is appropriate to the present case. We note that +6 and +3 are both positive and so the conditions in Rule 1b apply. Accordingly, $x * y = x + y - 1 : +6 * +3 = 6 + 3 - 1 = 8$, whose terminological correlate is "an octave up."

Finally, we combine the interval from pitch 6 to pitch 7 (G5 to B4) and the interval from pitch 7 to pitch 8 (B4 to F4): The figure represents the combination with the arrow extending from pitch 4 to pitch 6 labeled "−6 ∗ −4." Again, we begin by determining if any of the conditions in Rule 1 applies to the case at hand. None does, so we apply Rule 2. $x * y = x + y + 1$. Accordingly, $-6 * -4 = -6 + -4 + 1 = -9$, or "down a ninth."

Now that we have studied the systematic nature of the Semitone Interval System and Order Position Interval System, we can reflect briefly on the results. As we pointed out, we conventionally use either system on its own. Each is self-sufficient. And as we pointed out earlier, we do easily slip from the Common Interval System to the Order Position Interval Systems. We can talk coherently about major thirds and perfect fifths, but also about thirds and fifths. We are less comfortable with the Semitone Interval System on its own, unless we have studied serial theory or atonal theory, which relies exclusively on the semitone system.

The Common Interval System of minor thirds, major seconds, and so on is thereby a direct product of two distinct interval systems, with two distinct musical spaces, and two distinct ways of moving around in musical space. We have seen that the two systems are completely different in character. In the Order Position Interval System, relationships are determined by inclusively counting its objects, order positions represented by letter names (notated as lines and spaces) similar to the way we measure time in a calendar—January 25 to 27 is three days, not (27 − 25) days—or we count pages in a reading—reading from page 12 to page 17 involves six pages, not (17 − 12) pages; in the Semitone Interval System, relationships are determined by non-inclusively counting objects, or alternatively, similar to the way we measure distance (among other things). From this perspective, combining the two systems, so different in character, into a single system, as we do in our Common Interval System, seems both strange and inefficient. Regarding one interval system (the Semitone Interval System) as a way of refining the other interval system (the Order Position Interval System) distracts us from this strangeness.

It will be useful at this point, I think, to consider the direct product system in connection to the dominant interval system that preceded it, which we will call the Pythagorean Interval System, by contrasting their terminological organizations. The Pythagorean system, which has its origins in antiquity and survives into the early modern age, involves a relatively small catalog: unisonus, semitonus, tonus, semiditonus, ditonus, tritonus, diatessaron, diapente, diapason. (Other intervals are possible through combination: diapente cum tono, for instance.) Surveying the list, we observe that some terms involve inclusive counting: unisonus, diatessaron, diapente, and (although somewhat strained) diapason. The others are elements of what we have called the Semitone Interval System—semitonus, tonus, semiditonus, ditonus, tritonus—and

involve non-inclusive counting.[12] The difference in counting systems is largely registered in language: mostly Greek for names that reflect inclusive counting of objects;[13]
Latin names for non-inclusive counting of a unit of measurement. So, the two systems that define the direct product Common Interval System are both present in the
Pythagorean System, but they stake out different parts of a single interval system. The
objects of the system are strings arranged according to length. The distinction between
the inclusively counted Greek intervals from the non-inclusively counted Latin intervals
registers differences in theoretical function, which in turn is reflected by different orders
of rational simplicity: unisonus, diatessaron, diapente, and diapason are associated with
superparticular ratios formed by whole numbers to 4, directly generated on the monochord; semitonus, tonus, semiditonus, ditonus, and tritonus involve more complex
ratios produced through combinations of simple ratios and differences between them,
and are thus not directly generated on the monochord. The Pythagorean and Common
Interval Systems are structurally and historically related yet are fundamentally conceptually incommensurate.

As a final exercise in understanding the Common Interval System as a direct product
of the Order Position Interval System and the Semitone System, we'll employ a different
notation to replace formulations like major third, minor third, perfect fifth, augmented
fourth, and so on. We will represent the ordered pair notation ⟨α, β⟩, in which α is an
Order Position Interval and β is a Semitone Interval.[14] To explore this further, Figure 2.7
provides another melody. It's worthwhile at this point to sing the melody. As we do, we
may sense some conflicts: after singing the interval from pitch 2 to pitch 3 (F♯ to A), we
are faced with the problem of singing G♭. Do we simply sing the same pitch as pitch 2? Or
do we make a distinction? If so, what kind of distinction? And what about singing from
pitch 5 to pitch 6? If we try to simply match pitch 6 to pitch 5, we'll feel a rupture between
the idea of "descent through a second" and "sing the same pitch." Problems such as these
emerge because the musical objects at hand are not simply pitches: they're letter name/
pitch combinations.

Table 2.1 catalogs the Common Intervals encountered as we sing the melody. The
left column lists the letter name/pitch combinations given in Figure 2.7. The middle
column lists the Common Intervals in our new ⟨α, β⟩ notation, where α is an Order
Position Interval and β is a Semitone Interval. The right column provides the traditional
Common Interval name for the ordered pairs in the middle column.

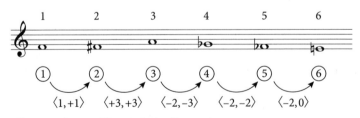

FIGURE 2.7 Common Interval System in ⟨α, β⟩ notation.

Table 2.1. Intervals in Figure 2.7

Letter name / Pitch	$\langle \alpha, \beta \rangle$	Common Interval Name
1 to 2	$\langle 1, +1 \rangle$	augmented prime
2 to 3	$\langle +3, +3 \rangle$	minor third up
3 to 4	$\langle -2, -3 \rangle$	augmented second down
4 to 5	$\langle -2, -2 \rangle$	major second down
5 to 6	$\langle -2, 0 \rangle$	diminished second down

To combine $\langle \alpha, \beta \rangle$ intervals, we invoke the relevant protocols studied earlier. The α-intervals, the Order Position Intervals, combine according to the protocol rules defined above; the β-intervals, the Semitone Intervals, combine according to conventional addition. Therefore, combining the first two $\langle \alpha, \beta \rangle$ intervals, $\langle 1, +1 \rangle$ and $\langle +3, +3 \rangle$, yields $\langle +3, +4 \rangle$, which corresponds to the interval from letter name/pitch object 1 to letter name/pitch object 3. To calculate the combination of the α-intervals 1 and +3, we invoke the Order Position Interval protocols. To calculate the combination of the β-intervals +1 and +3, we add the integers.

The ordered pair format helps us define some musically important relationships. First, letter name/pitch objects related under $\langle x, 0 \rangle$, where x is any member of the inclusive counting numbers other than 1, are enharmonically equivalent.[15] Second, letter name/pitch objects related under $\langle 1, x \rangle$, where x is an integer other than 0, are chromatically equivalent.

We have carried out our work under the convention that understands intervals as measurements of motion, as magnitude extended in a certain direction. It is time to reintroduce into the discussion the convention that understands intervals as spans, as magnitudes alone. We'll begin by adapting the ordered pair notation we introduced to represent intervals as directed magnitudes. To reflect the structure of intervals as magnitudes alone, we need only to replace the number systems involved with both elements in the ordered pair notation. In the Common Interval System as directed magnitudes, the Order Position Intervals, the α-element in the ordered pair format is a member of the inclusive integers, a number system we had to invent: $\{\dots, -3, -2, 1, 2, 3, \dots\}$. The Semitone Intervals, the β-element in the ordered pair notation, is a member of $\{\dots, -2, -1, 0, 1, 2, \dots\}$. In the Common Interval System as magnitudes only, the Order Position Intervals, the α-element in the ordered pair format is a member of the counting numbers, $\{1, 2, 3 \dots\}$. The Semitone Intervals, the β-element in the ordered pair notation, is a member of the whole numbers, $\{0, 1, 2, 3 \dots\}$.

We are using different number systems to represent magnitude intervals, so we need different combination protocols to accommodate the new values for α and β. Figures 2.8 and 2.9 offer some context for thinking about the issues involved. Figure 2.8 provides a short melody: F4–A4–D5. The figure represents magnitude intervals as brackets (rather

FIGURE 2.8 Magnitude Intervals I.

than by arrows) and labels them *j*, *k*, and *l* for reference. The α-values for *j* and *k*, the Order Position Intervals, are 3 and 4, respectively. To determine the combination protocol for magnitude Order Position Intervals, we'll adapt the protocols we developed for directed Order Position Intervals. We note that condition 1b—if both *x* and *y* are positive—applies to magnitudes *j* and *k* in Figure 2.8. Accordingly, we invoke the rule that $x * y = x + y - 1$. So, $3 * 4 = 6$ is the value for α-element of magnitude *l*, as we expect. Before considering the combination protocol for the β-elements, the Semitone Interval, in Figure 2.8, we'll examine the Order Position Intervals in Figure 2.9, which presents another three-note melody along with three brackets, labeled *r*, *s*, and *t* for reference. The values for *r* and s in Figure 2.9 are 3 and 4, the same values for *j* and *k*, respectively, in Figure 2.8. The value for *t* in Figure 2.9, which one expects to correspond to the combination of 3 and 4, is not 6 (the value for *l* in Figure 2.8), but 2. Clearly, we need a different combination protocol. The relevant rule for Figure 2.9 is $x * y = |x - y| + 1$. So, the combination rules for the β-elements, the Semitone Intervals, in Figures 2.8 and 2.9 are $x * y = x + y$ and $x * y = |x - y|$, respectively: $4 + 5 = 9$ and $|4 - 5| = 1$. Accordingly, the direct product interval for *l* in Figure 2.8 is $\langle 6, 9 \rangle$ (major sixth) and for *t* in Figure 2.9 is $\langle 2, 1 \rangle$ (minor second).

While the ordered pair values for *x* and *y* in $x * y$ are identical in the two figures—$\langle 3, 4 \rangle$ and $\langle 4, 5 \rangle$—we require two distinct combinational rules for the figures. $\langle x + y - 1, x + y \rangle$ in Figure 2.8 and $\langle |x - y| + 1, |x - y| \rangle$ in Figure 2.9. We cannot rely on the values for $\langle α, β \rangle$ to know which protocol to apply. We will need to posit an external stipulation, which we'll informally define as follows: if the intervals in question do not intersect, as is the case in Figure 2.8, we combine the intervals using the protocol $\langle x + y - 1, x + y \rangle$. Otherwise, we use the rule $\langle |x - y| + 1, |x - y| \rangle$. The external stipulation works, but it limits the use of the system to concrete situations. When we use directed intervals, we needn't define the notes at hand, so we may deal more abstractly, and define only the intervals. That option is not open to us when we use magnitude-only intervals.

In general, then, the system of magnitude-only intervals, which reflect the idea that intervals are spans, is more awkward than the system of intervals as directed magnitudes, which reflect the idea that intervals are motions. It is particularly disconcerting that we require two distinct protocols to combine intervals as spans. We need both so that intervals combine intuitively. By combining intuitively, we mean that in the case of Figure 2.9, the combination of the interval between F4 and A4 and the interval between A4 and E4 is the same as the interval between F4 and E4. The protocol designed for Figure 2.8—$\langle x + y - 1, x + y \rangle$—fails in that regard. While the protocol does not generate the required equivalency, there is nevertheless a sense in which $\langle x + y - 1, x + y \rangle$

does capture certain combinational aspects of Figure 2.9—in other words, there is a sense in which the bracket labeled t in Figure 2.9 repeats something important about the bracket labeled l in Figure 2.8. We recall that the l in Figure 2.8 is the interval $\langle 6, 9 \rangle$. In Figure 2.9, if we combine the intervals r and s without ensuring that the combination is equivalent to the interval between F4 and E4, in other words if we combine r and s under $\langle x + y - 1, x + y \rangle$, we produce the same result, $\langle 6, 9 \rangle$, we produced in Figure 2.8. In Figure 2.9, however, $\langle 6, 9 \rangle$ represents the accumulated order positions and semitones, but it does not represent the interval between F4 and E4. In other words, in Figure 2.8, l represents two senses of interval combination: the accumulated order positions and semitones; and the combination of the j and k as the interval between the first and the third notes. We'll refer to the former sense of combination as absolute combination and the latter sense of combination as relative combination. In Figure 2.9, the two combinational senses have different values: the accumulated order positions and semitones—absolute combination—is $\langle 6, 9 \rangle$; and the interval between the first and third note—relative combination—is $\langle 2, 1 \rangle$.

Figures 2.10 and 2.11 provide two musical contexts for exploring the different notions of combination that have emerged in connection with Figures 2.8 and 2.9. Figure 2.10 abstracts the first five notes of the first theme of Beethoven's op. 2, no. 1 and represents intervals as brackets, along the lines of Figures 2.8 and 2.9. Figure 2.11 abstracts the first five notes of the first theme of Beethoven's Symphony no. 5 and represents intervals as brackets. The brackets are labeled i1–i6 in Figure 2.10 and j1–j6 in Figure 2.11. The corresponding intervals are given in the ordered pair format in both figures. Examining the melody in Figure 2.10, we note that no adjacent intervals intersect. According to our informal generalization above, we therefore apply the rule $\langle x + y - 1, x + y \rangle$ to all the combinations between i1 and i5 to produce the interval i6: $\langle 4, 5 \rangle * \langle 3, 3 \rangle * \langle 3, 4 \rangle * \langle 4, 5 \rangle * \langle 3, 3 \rangle = \langle 13, 20 \rangle$, or in conventional terminology, minor thirteenth. $\langle 13, 20 \rangle$ is the accumulation of all order positions and semitones spanned

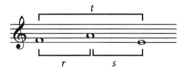

FIGURE 2.9 Magnitude Intervals II.

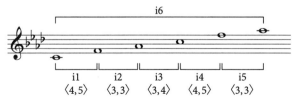

FIGURE 2.10 Beethoven, op. 2, no. 1, First Theme.

from i1 to i5; it is also the appropriate value for i6, the interval spanned between the first note in the melody and the last note. So, in Figure 2.10, the absolute combination of intervals is equivalent to the relative combination of intervals. Examining the melody in Figure 2.11, we note that all adjacent intervals intersect. According to our informal generalization above, we therefore apply the rule $\langle |x-y|+1, |x-y| \rangle$ to all the combinations between j1 and j5 to produce the interval j6: $\langle 3,4 \rangle * \langle 4,5 \rangle * \langle 2,1 \rangle * \langle 6,8 \rangle * \langle 3,3 \rangle = \langle 4,5 \rangle$, or in conventional terminology, perfect fourth. While $\langle 4, 5 \rangle$ is the appropriate value for j6, the interval spanned between the first note in the melody and the last note, it does not reflect the accumulated order positions and semitones, the absolute combination of intervals, from j1 to j5. To quantify that sense of combination, we will need to apply the rule $\langle x+y-1, x+y \rangle$ to the combinations of intervals j1 to j5. So, $\langle 3,4 \rangle * \langle 4,5 \rangle * \langle 2,1 \rangle * \langle 6,8 \rangle * \langle 3,3 \rangle = \langle 14,21 \rangle$, or in conventional terminology, diminished fourteenth. Accordingly, in Figure 2.11 the absolute combination of intervals is not equivalent to the relative combination of intervals. It is close, however, to both the absolute and relative combinations of intervals in Figure 2.10, $\langle 13, 20 \rangle$. The point here is not to claim the analytical importance of the absolute combination of magnitude intervals, which has, as far as I know, no historical or conventional standing.[16] The point is that in the case of intervals as magnitudes, there is a divergence between the two senses of interval combination, while in the case of directed intervals, the two senses of combination fully converge.

For some, the complexities and antinomies we encounter in the combinational workings of magnitude-only intervals have generated a preference for working with intervals as directed magnitudes.[17] In addition to combinational complexities and antinomies, magnitude-only intervals interact awkwardly with the universe of notes (letter name/pitch combinations). Figure 2.12 provides some context. The figure provides three analyses, labeled q, r, and s, of the notes F♯4 and F♭4. q and r are directed intervals: q extends from F♯4 to F♭4 and r extends from F♭4 to F♯4. The arrows are labeled with the appropriate intervals in ordered pair format: $\langle 1, -1 \rangle$ in q and $\langle 1, +1 \rangle$ in r, whose terminological correspondents are diminished prime and augmented prime, respectively. Direction is an issue in q and r. The (directed) Order Position Interval in q and r is unison or prime: it neither ascends nor descends. The (directed) Semitone Interval descends in q and ascends in r. So, we have a conflict between the values for α and β in both q and r. I have followed Riedt's example in assigning the terminological names diminished prime and augmented prime, which resolves the conflict in favor of the Order Position Interval involved (Riedt 1753, 16). If we wish to resolve the conflict in favor of the Semitone

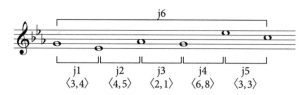

FIGURE 2.11 Beethoven, Symphony no. 5, First Theme.

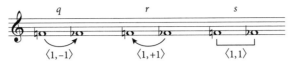

FIGURE 2.12 F♮4 and F♭4.

Intervals involved, we would presumably regard *q* as a descending augmented unison and *r* as an ascending unison; I have not encountered any naming convention that does so. The interval *q* is the inverse of *r*; and *r* is the inverse of *q*. Combining the intervals *q* and *r* produces a perfect unison, $\langle 1, 0 \rangle$, the identity element of the system. In ordered pair format: $\langle 1, -1 \rangle * \langle 1, +1 \rangle = \langle 1, +1 \rangle * \langle 1, -1 \rangle = \langle 1, 0 \rangle$.

The bracket *s* is labeled with the appropriate magnitude-only interval, $\langle 1, 1 \rangle$, whose terminological correspondent is augmented unison. In the magnitude-only interval system, there is no interval whose terminological correspondent is a diminished unison or prime: 0 is the smallest value available for the β-element in the ordered pair format: there are no negative magnitudes. Accordingly, the conflict we encounter when we consider the question of direction in *q* and *r* never arises when we use magnitude-only intervals. We can analyze our current musical context in two ways as directed intervals, but there is only one analysis of the musical context as a magnitude-only interval. The two available directed intervals are inversely related. The question of the inverse of *s* is complicated by the (relative) combinational protocols of magnitude-only intervals: the inverse of any magnitude-only interval is itself and the two intervals in question must intersect to invoke the rule $\langle |x - y| + 1, |x - y| \rangle$. In the present instance, $\langle 1, 1 \rangle * \langle 1, 1 \rangle = \langle 1, 0 \rangle$.[18]

We observed in Figure 2.12 that (among other things), magnitude-only intervals have certain limitations in the way they interact with the universe of letter name/pitch combinations. Yet, so do directed intervals. Figure 2.13 places both conventions in a more stressful context. The figure copies over Figure 2.12 but replaces the F♮4s with E♯4s. The three interval analyses are labeled *u*, *v*, and *w*. *u* and *v* are directed intervals: *u* extends from E♯4 to F♭4 and *v* extends from F♭4 to E♯4. The arrows are labeled with the appropriate intervals in ordered pair format: $\langle +2, -1 \rangle$ in *u* and $\langle -2, +1 \rangle$ in *v*, whose terminological correspondents are ascending doubly diminished second and descending doubly diminished second, respectively. As with *r* and *s* in Figure 2.12, direction is an issue. In *u*, the (directed) Order Position Interval ascends and the (directed) Semitone Interval descends; in *v*, the (directed) Order Position Interval descends and the (directed) Semitone Interval ascends. Our terms take their direction from the Order Position Interval in both instances; it is difficult even to imagine terms that take their direction from the relevant Semitone Interval.

The bracket *w* is meant to be labeled with the appropriate magnitude-only interval. The (magnitude) Order Position Interval, the α-element in the ordered pair format, is clearly 2: the interval is a second. We have surpassed, however, the ability of the (magnitude) Semitone Interval System to register the relationship at hand: we do not have access to negative values for β. I can imagine that, when pressed, some might wish to refer

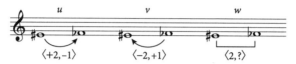

FIGURE 2.13 E♯4 and F♭4.

to *w* as a doubly diminished second, but in the context of magnitude-only intervals, the term is as unavailable as diminished unison is for *s* in Figure 2.12, for precisely the same reason.

Viewed from the perspective of systematics, we observe a degree of awkwardness in the magnitude-only Common Interval System. Its combinational protocols are complicated and (in a sense) contradictory; it is constrained in its ability to analyze many intervals that are available in the universe of musical notes (letter name/pitch combinations). On this score, the directed Common Interval System is a much better-behaved system: it has a reasonably straightforward combinational protocol, and it can deliver an analysis for any pair of musical notes drawn from the universe of musical notes.

Earlier, I claimed that I am not primarily interested in advocating for one convention over the other. Instead my goal has been to survey some of the properties of each system and to catalog the way they each interact and shape musical experience. We can certainly appreciate that those who value systematic behavior will prefer the directed convention. One imagines that would be a compelling attraction. Yet the magnitude-only convention is the majority view. It remains an institutional preference, one imagines, for its conceptual directness and simplicity, which eclipses its awkward and contradictory systematics. And we have seen its complicated and inelegant combinational protocols— its unusual distinction between absolute and relative interval combination—harbor a potential for interesting analytical exercises. Problems only emerge when one slips unconsciously or unannounced from one convention to the next: the two conventions are genuinely incommensurate.

NOTES

1. The process described here corresponds to most contemporary textbooks on musical rudiments. It has a fairly long history: C. P. E. Bach (1762, 11–31) provides the same process.
2. Things are more complicated in the German letter name system.
3. Justin Hofmann (2011) provides very helpful and sophisticated case studies of the central issues.
4. Derrida's (2016) description of logocentrism is worth considering in this connection, even while bearing in mind that language and music are distinct cultural phenomena.
5. Relevant is an important qualifier: clearly, oral musical traditions do not participate in a binary between sounded music and its notation.
6. See also Parkhurst and Hammel's chapter "Pitch, Tone, and Note" in this volume.
7. We're being rather informal in our use of the word "equivalent" in this context. Applying mathematical standards, we note that the enharmonic relation as we commonly discuss it

is symmetrical (for instance, A♭ is enharmonically equivalent to G♯ and G♯ is enharmonically equivalent to A♭) but not reflexive (since we do not commonly consider A♭ to be enharmonically equivalent to A♭), and not transitive (A♭ is enharmonically equivalent to G♯ and G♯ is enharmonically equivalent to A♭, but A♭ is not enharmonically equivalent to A♭). In the context of atonal music, we do indeed form equivalence classes that are reflexive, symmetrical, and transitive, but we probably should be careful to keep our discussions about tonal musics and atonal musics distinct on this issue.

8. Rousseau's definition of interval is representative: "The difference from one sound to another from low to high" (1998, 414).

9. See also Gelbart's chapter "Scale" in this volume.

10. Rousseau (1998, 419) adjusted the counting system to accommodate conventional integers, so that "0" represents "unison" or "prime," "1" represents "a second," and so on. Accordingly, a third up combined with a third up is rendered as 2 + 2. The sum, 4, represents a fifth up. Clough (1979) and Lewin (1987) follow his example.

11. Ivan Suminski provided in conversation a more elegant formulation, which reduces the rules above.

$$\text{sgn}(x) = x/|x|$$
If $x + y = 0$, then $x * y = 1$.
Otherwise, $x * y = x + y - \left[\left(sgn(xy) \, sgn(x + y) \right) \right]$

The protocol makes use of the sign function ($\text{sgn}(x)$), which extracts the sign from integers: the function maps all positive integers to +1 and all negative integers to –1.

12. The terminological system does not reflect certain important complexities: for one thing, the system associates several ratios with the single term "semitonus" and several ratios with the single term "tonus"; moreover, there is no understanding that any of the available semitones are "half" of any of the available whole tones. Indeed, even into the nineteenth century, one could say the same thing about the Semitone Interval System.

13. The exception is unisonus, which is Latin.

14. The ordered pair notation here relates to similar formats used by other theorists. Douthett and Hook (2009) is a particularly interesting use that is marshalled to reform common intervals to resolve what the authors regard as structural ambiguities. The ordered pair notation relates indirectly to Steven Rings's (2011, 41–100) analytical technology. Agmon's (1989) model is also very close to ours, except that he adjusts Order Position Intervals to avoid the combinational idiosyncrasies produced by inclusive counting. As such, his model interacts strongly with Rousseau's (1998, 419) description of intervals as the combination of scale degrees (adjusted for inclusive counting) and tones.

15. Recalling the discussion in note 7, we recognize that the formulation here corresponds to the concept of enharmonicism as a symmetrical relation, rather than a conventional equivalence relation as one encounters in atonal theory.

16. Which is a pity, I think. Examining the distinction between absolute and relative combination strikes me as an engaging idea in connection with many common musical contexts and in a number of theoretical frameworks.

17. Lewin's (1987) great study of interval systems always defines intervals as directed, never as magnitudes alone. He abstracts from the historical interval systems he studies a common

structure. Our directed Common Interval System conforms to this abstracted structure. Our magnitude-only Common Interval System does not.

18. We should not confuse the idea of the inverse of an interval we are using here with the conventional category of interval inversion, under which the inversional cognate to s (F♭4/ F♮4) in Figure 2.12 is the interval F♭5/F♮4, represented in ordered pair format as $\langle 8, 11 \rangle$ and associated with the term diminished octave. Conventional interval inversion comes to us from Rameau's (1722, 6–14) theory of *renversement* (reversal) in which a (magnitude) interval combines with its *renversement* cognate to yield an octave. In the case of s, the *renversement* of $\langle 1, 1 \rangle$ is $\langle 8, 11 \rangle$ because $\langle 1,1 \rangle * \langle 8,11 \rangle = \langle 8,12 \rangle$.

Works Cited

Agmon, Eytan. 1989. "A Mathematical Model of the Diatonic System." *Journal of Music Theory* 33: 1–25.

Bach, C. P. E. 1762. *Versuch über die wahre Art das Clavier zu spielen*. Zweyter Theil. Berlin.

Chen, Cheng Yih. 1996. *Early Chinese Work in Natural Science: A Re-examination of the Physics of Motion, Acoustics, Astronomy and Scientific Thoughts*. Hong Kong: Hong Kong University Press.

Clough, John. 1979. "Aspects of Diatonic Sets." *Journal of Music Theory* 23: 45–61.

Derrida, Jacques. 2016. *Of Grammatology*. Baltimore: Johns Hopkins University Press.

Douthett, Jack, and Julian Hook. 2009. "Formal Diatonic Intervallic Notation." In *Mathematics and Computation in Music*. Edited by Elaine Chew, Adrian Childs, and Ching-Hua Chuan, 104–114. Berlin: Springer.

Hofmann, Justin. 2011. "Listening with Two Ears: Conflicting Perceptions of Space in Tonal Music." PhD diss., Columbia University.

Klein, Rolf. 1988. *Die Intervallenlehre in der deutschen Musiktheorie des 16. Jahrhunderts*. Regensburg: Gustav Bosse Verlag.

Koch, Heinrich Christoph. 1802. "s.v. Intervall." In *Musikalisches Lexikon*. Frankfurt am Main: August Hermann der Jüngere.

Lewin, David. 1987. *Generalized Musical Intervals and Transformations*. New Haven, CT: Yale University Press.

Park, Joon. 2017. "Calligraphy as a Conceptualizing System in Traditional Chinese and Korean Musical Pitches." Paper presented at the Pre-AMS Conference *Instruments of Music Theory* (Rochester, NY, November 8).

Rameau, Jean-Phillipe. 1727. *Traité de L'Harmonie*. Paris: Jean-Baptiste-Christophe Ballard.

Randel, Don Michael. 2003. *The Harvard Dictionary of Music*. 4th edition. Cambridge, MA: Harvard University Press.

Riedt, Friedrich Wilhelm. 1753. *Versuch über die musikalischen Intervalle*. Berlin: A. Haude und J. C. Spener.

Rings, Steven. 2011. *Tonality and Transformation*. New York: Oxford University Press.

Rousseau, Jean-Jacques. 1998. *Essay on the Origin of Language and Writings Related to Music*. Translated by John T. Scott. Hanover, NH: University Press of New England.

CHAPTER 3

···

MODE

···

SUSAN MCCLARY

THE word "mode" has a particularly vexed history in Western music theory. It brought one set of assumptions to a Greek philosopher, others to a medieval scribe or Renaissance polyphonist, and yet others to tonal theorists, Impressionist composers, post-bop jazz artists, and heavy metal guitarists. For each of these musicians, mode has mattered enormously, yet their basic notions and uses of mode differ fundamentally, often in mutually incompatible ways. And these differ still more from the concept of mode in other cultures, including the music of India and elsewhere. I will not deal with non-Western repertories and their theoretical justifications in this entry, although the interested reader may find these easily enough in other sources.[1] My goal here is to set out a history of modes in European musical thought and practice, stretching from Greek antiquity to the present.

Let me begin by dispelling a common misconception. For most of music history, theorists have not defined modes as scales. The word "mode" simply means a way of doing things; we retain this broader sense of the term in expressions such as modus operandi or *la mode*, as in high fashion. Even though the specific details concerning the various categories change radically over time, the concept of mode as a general framework or matrix prevails in most accounts and practices.

Most of us learn to equate modes with scales at the very beginning of our theory training, when we are taught to identify Dorian with the piano's white keys from D to D, with a necessary B♮ to differentiate it from tonal minor. But, as we shall see, the medieval and Renaissance musicians for whom Dorian was the favorite mode would not have recognized such a definition. My years of teaching modal analysis have taught me how very difficult it is for students to eradicate this equation of modes with scales. Yet clinging to the scalar concept greatly hampers our ability to deal intelligently with the thousands of pieces labeled as Dorian.

As soon as modes-as-scales are presented in introductory theory classes, they get pushed aside as primitive and unworkable, leaving only tonal major and minor as viable options. Those Greek labels—painstakingly memorized for the purpose of exams—retreat to the status of trivial information. To be sure, Debussy or Vaughan Williams might seize onto a nonstandard scale later on, but such composers usually intend modal configurations to sound archaic or exotic, as a splash of color gilding an otherwise tonal composition.

Our most frequently cited early account of modes in European history appears in Plato's *Republic* (ca. 380 BCE), where the philosopher famously considers the place and function of music in his utopia. To his credit, Plato acknowledges the power of music, which is precisely why he seeks to control it and to dictate its proper uses (for education, religious ritual, military training, medicine) and to condemn its abuses (for lascivious indulgence). He focuses his discussion of the ethical properties of music on what he calls mode (Plato 1961).

Those who have learned to identify modes with scales like to scoff about how anyone could find the scale from F to F dangerous. But when Plato uses the word, he refers to the entire array of musical practices associated with a particular ethnic group. He—like many people of his time—regards the Lydians, who populated present-day Turkey, as luxury loving; their styles of musicking—instruments and dancing girls included—appealed to the senses and made listeners soft and easily conquered (recall that Troy was a Lydian city). The Phrygians invaded Turkey from the Balkans and brought with them Dionysian rites, and although Plato expresses some misgivings about the wildness of the Phrygians, he advocates allowing their musical practices for specific religious ceremonies and medical purposes. The Dorians, however, were the Spartans: manly, disciplined, rational, superior in military might. Their music instilled such characteristics in citizens and served to ensure the proper working of the Republic. We might productively compare Plato's mapping with the attributes assigned to the societies in *Game of Thrones*, with the Phrygians as Dothrakis, the Lydians as the Qarthi, and the Dorians as the stoic, no-nonsense Starks.

Long after these groups and their sounds had vanished, Plato's labels persisted as nuggets crucial to cultural literacy, even though they became empty signifiers. Boethius, the sixth-century Roman scholar who scrambled to consolidate all the knowledge of antiquity before the barbarians destroyed civilization, reiterates Plato's account of modes and ancient peoples in his *De institutione musica*; he also presents a compressed and somewhat garbled version of Greek theory, repurposing Plato's labels to refer to pitch collections.[2] His contemporary Cassiodorus eliminated altogether the ethnographic dimension of previous accounts and offered a bare intervallic taxonomy of the modes. Yet, although he produces a list of the categories beginning with versions of Dorian, he still defines each as comprising an entire system.[3] In the tenth century, medieval musicians charged with classifying and stabilizing the orally transmitted melodies of their liturgy latched onto aspects of the matrix they had lifted from Boethius and Cassiodorus, their principal sources of classic music theory. In other words, by the time the word "mode" got to Western Europe, it had already passed through several stages of radical misreadings (Taruskin 2005).

The medieval musicians did not impose Greek theory onto their own melodies, but they did borrow the idea that there are four basic types, with four more derived from rearrangement. As they sang through their tunes, they discerned four different ways of distributing whole tones (T) and semitones (s) within the interval of a perfect fifth:

1. TsTT [d to a]
2. sTTT [e to b]
3. TTTs [f to c]
4. TTsT [g to d]

These four species of fifth (diapente) serve as the cornerstones of the system, with a species of fourth (diatessaron) completing the octave (diapason). The scribes also recognized that the final, or principal point of rest, lay at the bottom of the range in some tunes and in the middle of the range for others. Their ancient sources also offered a solution for this: those systems with the species of fifth on bottom counted as "authentic," while those with the fifth on top (and the final in the middle) were "plagal," designated with the prefix "hypo." The musicians then sorted their melodies into these eight groupings:

For the most part, these boundary pitches serve as the principal sites for internal cadences, although exceptions abound. Pieces in the Phrygian modes, for instance, usually circle around A, rather than the unstable fifth degree, B. Similarly, Aeolian and Mixolydian pieces often gravitate toward their fourth rather than fifth degrees. Pieces based on F did maintain the boundary pitches as goals, but they almost always included a B♭, often in the key signature itself; "pure" Lydian, with a B♮, rarely occurred. For the sake of consistency, however, theorists continue to present the species-oriented definitions in Figure 3.1, regardless of the ways these modes operate in practice.

Before proceeding further, I want to mention briefly two other theoretical concepts that entered at about this same time that are often conflated or confused with mode. First, musicians had long sung the multiple verses of the Psalms to formulas called tones. Although numbered in ways that allowed for easy matching of Psalm verses with their associated modal antiphons, they operate very differently, usually comprising little more than an opening gesture, a reciting pitch, and a termination. The psalm tones show

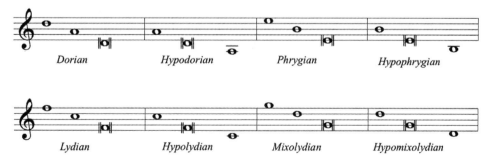

FIGURE 3.1 Eight Modes.

up in musical practice all the way through works such as Monteverdi's *Marian Vespers*: a compendium of polychoral settings of those august formulas. But those have nothing to do with the ways the same composer might manipulate modes in other pieces. Unfortunately, some historical sources, including Cassiodorus and Aron, use the word "tone" when referring to the concept traced here as "mode," although their descriptions make clear which configuration—the matrix of modal species or the formulas of psalm tones—they have in mind.

Second, theorists and musicians learned to sight-sing and conceive of musical space through Guido d'Arezzo's hexachords: the sequence of six pitches starting respectively on C (natural), F (soft, because of its B♭), and G (hard, because of the high B♮). Although the intervallic content is the same in all three, taken together they allow for the negotiation of the entire musical gamut in use at the time. But they coexisted with the modal system and address entirely different needs. Note that one of the hexachords—the one on C—does not even correspond to one of the modal finals.

As often occurs in the meeting of theory and practice, the concept of mode often took precedence, leading some medieval scribes to edit pieces so that they better fit their intellectual grid; recent comparisons among extant manuscript sources demonstrate the ways in which pieces of liturgical chant were altered during the process of standardization. And sometimes scribes awarded an enigmatic piece with one of the extant labels, even if they had to fudge it a bit. For instance, pieces making use of the third species of fifth—or genuine Lydian—almost never appeared in practice. To be sure, medieval musicians designated plenty of pieces as Mode 5. Yet most of these had a signed-in B♭; centuries later, Glareanus would elevate this configuration to the status of Ionian. But in the absence of modal types beginning on C, scribes assigned such pieces to Lydian. They took pains to preserve the eight-mode system (with sanctioned finals only on D, E, F, and G), because it had the weight of tradition backing it up.

Despite occasional discrepancies, this system of modal classification worked quite smoothly for monophonic music, and it allowed for the preservation and relatively accurate transmission of liturgical chant. To see how well this theoretical system accounts for the requisite parameters, take a glance at the *Liber Usualis*, which labels each entry with its modal designation. As burgeoning notation allowed for the recording on paper of new compositions, musicians accustomed to the classifications and melodic types of the various modes produced music that operated much like the music of the church. Modal organization became standard practice.

Modal species manifest themselves in two crucial ways over the course of a monophonic piece, whether liturgical chant or troubadour song. First, they offer a hierarchy of likely cadence points, with the final most common, followed by the fifth degree (or upper boundary of the diapente). What we would call half-cadences involve a halt at the penultimate second degree, the trajectory interrupted just before resolution down to the final. Second, the species provided a framework for calculating a sense of linear direction. This dimension of mode never goes away; it continues to operate in songs and hymns up to the present. Think, for instance, of how Beethoven's "Ode to Joy" animates the diapente that generates it (the leap down to the lower fifth degree on "ge-TEILT" marks the melody as inhabiting the plagal version of its mode).

Not long after the solidification of staff notation at the beginning of the eleventh century, however, musicians began to write down performances that superimposed newly composed voices over the original chant, or cantus firmus. Because early polyphony was based on previously existing material, the resulting complex retained the modal designation of the original piece. The voice part that sang the liturgical line (called the "tenor" since it held on to the chant) also determined many aspects of the new composition, including its cadence points and sense of direction. Whether labeled as duplum and triplum or as contratenor bassus and altus, the added voices took their cues from the generating tenor. For this reason, theorists well into the Renaissance continued to advise musicians simply to attend to the tenor part in judging the mode of a piece.

But polyphonic practice introduced many new complications. Sometimes, a composer of a thirteenth-century motet would choose just a snippet of the original chant, leaving behind the context that might have provided the logical framework. Another composer would set the cantus firmus perversely, harmonizing the chant's cadence points such that they emphasized different pitches and suggested modes other than the one appropriate for the chant ostensibly underlying the new piece. Preoccupied as they were with other issues, such as the refinement of rhythmic notation and developing rules for contrapuntal coordination, theorists did not acknowledge such anomalies. Indeed, the first theorist to mention the issue of mode in polyphony was Johannes Tinctoris in the late fifteenth century, and he just tosses off as an aside in his standard account of monophonic modes that they work the same way in multi-voiced music.[4] But by the time he offered this rather unhelpful tip, musical practice had moved far beyond the stage when composers simply festooned a piece of liturgical chant with additional voices.

In 1525, Pietro Aron assumed the project of determining whether or not polyphonic music operated according to the eight-mode system.[5] Taking advantage of the recent distributions of scores through music printing, Aron works systematically through the pieces in Petrucci's *Odhecaton*. He has no difficulty assigning most of the pieces in this collection—many by Josquin—to one of the traditional modes. But some puzzle him, particularly those that seemed to have finals on C or A. Still loyal to his theoretical matrix, he proposes a variety of ways of placing these revered compositions in his available pigeonholes. Alas, these attempts only produced further inconsistencies within his paradigm.

So glaring were his inconsistencies that the next wave of theorists turned to revising the paradigm itself. They did not do so lightly: the authority of a tradition reaching all the way back to the Greeks was at stake. In 1547, Glareanus published his *Dodecachordon*, in which he proposes expanding the number of modes from eight to twelve in order to include modes on A and C. He too bases his new system on analyses of compositions by Josquin, and full scores of the pieces he discusses were published along with Glareanus's commentary, making it among the most lavish theoretical treatises ever produced.[6] Soon thereafter, Gioseffo Zarlino published his own twelve-mode treatise in *Istitutioni*

Harmoniche (1558), focusing primarily on the works of his own teacher, Adrian Willaert. Whereas Glareanus adds his two new modes on A and C after the standard eight, Zarlino amends this ordering in his *Dimostrationi harmoniche* (1571), starting his on C and then advancing from D to A. He justifies this ordering by replacing the sacrosanct number 4 (the number of modes, the numbers that produced the proportions yielding perfect consonances) with the number 6, which allows him to refer to the hexachord and also to admit into the cluster of mathematically justified consonances the intervals of the major and minor third.[7]

As a result of these modifications, the uniform arrangement of modes that previously had prevailed became confused. The mode starting on D, which medieval musicians and Glareanus would have labeled as mode 1, became mode 3 in Zarlino's system. Yet for all the problems in numbering, all three systems concur in their notions of how modes operate in practice. Whether categorizing liturgical chant or analyzing madrigals by Adrian Willaert, theorists of all three camps define mode in terms of the species of fifth, fourth, and octave that underwrite the unfolding of a composition through cadence points and melodic contour. Because of these inconsistencies in numbering, I will refer to the various modes by their Greek names.

But polyphonic practice had added complications not always acknowledged by sixteenth-century theorists. The first of these—how to decide which line to follow in a four- or five-voice complex—they dispatched quickly by repeating the direction that we focus on the tenor. To a surprising extent, this principle continues to hold in much Renaissance music. Our tonal ears gravitate to the outer voices, and we tend to ignore what we regard as inner parts. But composers at the time still usually built from the tenor, together with the cantus, then fashioned the bass as a means of supporting that two-voice complex.

If we overlook the leading role of the tenor, we often miss important moments and their syntactical implications. In the middle of Jacques Arcadelt's F-Ionian "Il bianco e dolce cigno," for instance, the tenor completes the modal octave to F at the words "ed io moro beato" (and I die blessed), even though the other voices "misunderstand" and harmonize that prematurely transcendent moment as an arrival on D (see Figure 3.2, mm. 19–24). The tenor should ring out with ecstasy on that pitch, making audible Arcadelt's double meanings; the composer makes the paradox of a "happy death" clear at the end of the piece, but presents it here as an audible conundrum. (Note that I have added *musica ficta* to the alto part—the ficta that all Renaissance singers would have added automatically to this standard cadential figure.)

Even Gesualdo's notorious thorny "Moro, lasso" operates from the most transparent of Aeolian species, although the composer harmonizes every pitch of the tenor line in the most bizarre way possible (McClary 2004). To be sure, in many polyphonic pieces, voices other than the tenor sometimes take on the responsibilities of delineating a piece's modal logic, and in densely imitative writing, all parts may participate. If we know how to recognize the contours and behaviors of a mode-bearing voice, however, such

FIGURE 3.2 Arcadelt, "Il bianco e dolce cigno," mm. 19–24.

complexity only contributes to the aesthetic rewards of the composition. It does not in-validate the theorists' basic precepts.

The other complication involves the presence of accidentals, whether notated explic-itly or assumed through the conventions of *musica ficta*: a practice whereby performers inflected their diatonic lines according to taste and somewhat sketchy guidelines. By the fourteenth century, musicians typically added leading tones—sometimes even double leading tones!—at cadence points, and they sought to avoid melodic and har-monic tritones with the judicious corrective of a flat. For those who assume that modes are scales, these impurities would seem to announce the death of modes. Some leading scholars hold this view and regard Glareanus and Zarlino as maintaining old-fashioned concepts concerning mode primarily for the sake of tradition, even in the face of scores riddled with sharps and flats (Powers 1980; Dahlhaus 1990).

Yet I will argue that composers continued to operate within the modal system well into the seventeenth century, and they shaped their strategies in accordance with the particularities of each mode. Let us examine the differences between Dorian and Aeolian, for example. Both share the same species of fifth with respect to interval content—TsTT—and both allow for accidentals at cadences: for leading tones and flat sixth scale degrees. In fact, as long as the piece remains in the area grounded by the final, the two are indistinguishable.

At the structural level, however, the two modes diverge in crucial ways. If composers make use of accidentals, they do not count those altered pitches as eligible for modal construction. Dorian has two available versions of the sixth degree: the B♮ native to its scale and the fictive B♭ that circumscribes the diapente's upper boundary. Because it has a B♮ in its arsenal, Dorian can easily produce perfect authentic cadences on its fifth scale degree, A, which requires the B♮. Aeolian, on the other hand, has access only to its nat-ural sixth degree a half-step above its diapente boundary, making cadences on the fifth degree technically illicit: to cadence on A in D Aeolian would require a B♮ as a real—as opposed to a fictive—pitch (see Figure 3.3).

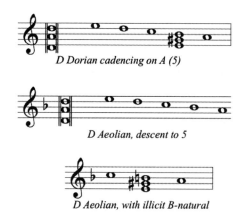

D Dorian cadencing on A (5)

D Aeolian, descent to 5

D Aeolian, with illicit B-natural

FIGURE 3.3 Dorian versus Aeolian.

The ramifications of this difference are enormous. Dorian compositions cadence freely on a whole range of scale degrees, making temporary finals of each by means of cadential leading tones. By contrast, D Aeolian emphasizes the area on the fourth degree, G, which it can establish with no problem, although this creates pieces that tilt toward the sub-dominant region. Given the Picardy third that frequently inflects arrivals, a concluding D-major sonority can sound like V/iv rather than the confirmation of the modal final.

Composers did not regard this characteristic as a liability, however, but rather as an invitation to explore certain affects. Monteverdi situates his "Ah, dolente partita" (Book IV) in Aeolian in order to simulate the speaker's internal divisions (McClary 2004). In the instrumental realm, Dario Castello frequently deploys Aeolian in his violin sonatas to produce much the same effect without any need for lyrics (McClary 2012).

Much later, J. S. Bach constructed his C♯-minor fugue (WTC I) in Aeolian, with imitative answers on the fourth degree and increasing assertion of F♯ minor to the extent that the final sonority functions both as tonic with Picardy third and as dominant to an impending return to F♯ minor (McClary 2012). Following Bach's model, Beethoven composes his C♯-minor string quartet op. 131 as an extended essay in Aeolian. Beethoven's late turn to modes manifests itself most explicitly in the "Heiliger Dankgesang," op. 132, which he labels as being in the Lydian mode. Note that he does not understand Lydian as sporting a spiky B♮ in melodies but rather along the lines just discussed for Aeolian. Genuine Lydian lacks the B♭ it would require for the dominant-seventh to F, leading the movement to sound as if it is actually in C major, with F able only to assert rather than solidify its centrality. The concluding F-major triad implies that it will return to C and instead halts halfway through a plagal "amen" cadence: precisely the inconclusive prayer Beethoven wishes to convey.

Despite such explicit references of later composers to earlier styles, we usually claim that the traditional modes disappeared in the seventeenth century in favor of the major and minor procedures that underlie the tonal composition of the eighteenth and nineteenth centuries and beyond. That claim, however, rests in large part on our collective failure to grasp how modes worked in Renaissance music. Those accidentals that crop up in Dorian or Mixolydian did not spell the corruption and gradual demise of modes, nor were musicians seeking to reach the promised land of tonality. If we accept that sixteenth-century modal practice stands among the most robust and sophisticated ways of putting music together ever devised, then we need to find another explanation for the emergence of major and minor as the only two options.

In 1600, Jacopo Peri presented his *Euridice*, which we celebrate as the first opera: a theatrical work in which all the dialogue is sung. Seven years later, Monteverdi contributed his *Orfeo*, the first acknowledged masterpiece of the new genre. Both composers worked entirely within modal frameworks: *Orfeo*, in fact, presents a complex allegorical structure based on the tensions of Dorian (McClary 2004). Yet both take first steps in the direction that will lead to tonal practice. The changes they implement do not involve pitch relations so much as temporality.

In their attempts at simulating natural speech in music, Peri and Monteverdi experimented with devices that allow for the expansion of the most basic modal pattern—the linear descent through the diapente from the fifth scale degree to the final. This contour conveys movement toward closure in melodies, whether liturgical chant, the generating tenor lines of Renaissance polyphony, or the popular songs of today. So secure was this syntactical unit in the sixteenth century that it had become the basis of improvisation along with its standard harmonizations. Just as any jazz or rock musician can join in immediately with a blues progression, Renaissance players could perform without rehearsal or sheet music on the Passamezzo Antico or Romanesca, the two principal ways of supporting the diapente descent. We all know the most familiar of these: the Passamezzo Antico underwrites the opening strain of "Greensleeves," the Romanesca the second (see Figure 3.4).

In "Greensleeves," the grammar remains resolutely modal. Harmonies matter, of course, but they serve in a secondary capacity. Without the generating diapente descent, the bass lines make no sense. But coupled together, the linear descent plus bass present long-established cadential formulas. Note that the melodic lines in "Greensleeves" do not stick rigidly to the pitches of the diapente. By means of the framework made familiar through thousands of pieces, the singer has the freedom to range in a way that resembles casual speech. As it turns out, Peri had developed exceptional skills as an improviser within these patterns, and the Medici court treasured his ability to deploy them in singing through cantos of epic poetry, accompanying himself on the lute. He brought precisely those well-honed techniques with him when he wrote *Euridice*; Monteverdi modeled his *Orfeo* closely after Peri's composition.

Monteverdi altered the old improvisatory practice in a couple of important ways. Recall that "Greensleeves" moves in lockstep through its background patterns. In the opening speech in Act I of *Orfeo*, seen in Figure 3.5, Monteverdi exerted control over the rate of the descent, expanding some generating units and moving quickly through others for rhetorical effect. The sense of coherence and goal orientation still derive from the modal formula, but the composer now determines the rate of activity.

FIGURE 3.4 Improvisatory Formulas on Diapente Descent; "Greensleeves."

FIGURE 3.5 Monteverdi, *Orfeo*, Act I, Scene i.

Another path to expansion drew on the power of the harmonies associated with the perfect authentic cadence. As we have seen, Renaissance composers made full use of leading tones, though they did so only at the cadence itself. Consequently, the appearance of a leading tone signaled impending closure; so long as the leading tone persists, seventeenth-century listeners would assume they were in a holding pattern for imminent cadence. What Monteverdi does is to harness this expectation in order to sustain a tiny key area for each of the steps along the standard diapente-based formula, as he does in Orfeo's celebratory song that opens Act II (see Figure 3.6). This results in a miniature

FIGURE 3.6 Monteverdi, *Orfeo*, Act II, Scene i.

tonal composition, with cadential harmonies maintaining the integrity of each moment of the background. But the background itself—the modulations from G minor
to B♭ major to F major back to G minor—still owes its coherence to the principal unit of
modal grammar.

In other words, modes did not disappear. They continued to control background
progressions of tonal compositions until this *modus operandi* broke down around 1900.
It is to Heinrich Schenker's credit that he managed to strip away all the middle levels
that had allowed for greater and greater expansion until he arrived back at what he
called the *Urlinie* and what I would call the diapente descent. Recall that Dorian and
Aeolian share the same species of fifth, and Mixolydian and Ionian share another. So
long as composition involves the only expansion of the diapente, Dorian becomes indistinguishable from Aeolian, and Mixolydian from Ionian. And that leaves us with two
options: tonal major and tonal minor.[8] Although Monteverdi and his contemporaries
knew how to produce these small tonal configurations, they still preferred to write extended composites in which some sections made use of tonal expansion but in which
most continued to exercise the complex structural strategies offered by the traditional
modes. The various parts of the composite cohered according to the propensities of the
chosen mode. Carissimi, for instance, favors Mixolydian in oratorios such as *Jefte*, and
composers of sonatas and cantatas treat tonal expansion as one among many options
[McClary 2012].)

Tonal standardization began to consolidate under commercial pressures. The leading
composer of opera in seventeenth-century Venice, Francesco Cavalli, sought ways
of setting an entire play to music in very short amounts of time. If Monteverdi could

indulge in the construction of complex modal allegories in *Orfeo* and *L'incoronazione di Poppea*, Cavalli had to produce complete scores within days. His principal shortcut involved writing arias that adopt more or less the same background structure based on the diapente descent. Similarly, individual sections of sonatas expand to resemble self-contained movements, each operating according to the same principle as Cavalli's arias. Eventually, Arcangelo Corelli fashions his pieces as a series of autonomous tonal movements, thereby reifying the complexity of modal structure into the standard sequence of keys within a cycle:

Minor: i — III (or iv or v) — i — i
Major: I — IV (or vi) — I — I

In the wake of Corelli and his widely circulating publications, compositional practice narrowed to these two available modes. Tonal major descends from the expansion of the diapente with a major third above the final; tonal minor from the diapente with a minor third, though its range of modulatory options resembles that of Dorian far more closely than that of Aeolian (see the discussion above). To anyone who has learned to appreciate the capabilities of the traditional modes in the sixteenth century, this reduction in options may seem not as unqualified progress but as something of an impoverishment. Gone were the highly treasured ambiguities that obtained between cadence points or the open-ended conclusions that refused to decide between competing options. Yet this two-mode system gave rise to the standard concert repertories of the next two hundred years, and it still underwrites much of the music that circulates in popular culture.

Several features made tonality the perfect idiom for eighteenth-century culture. First, the music produced by means of this procedure manifests logic at all levels, the background rendered coherent through the governing modal pattern, the foreground operating according to the harmonies associated with cadential formulas. Composers found ways of expanding this structure radically through what Schenker later theorized as middle-ground manipulations, but the basic premise holds until the late Romantics managed to upend it. Because of this stringent logic, listeners can follow the twists and turns of a particular composition while still trusting in the eventual outcome; they can anticipate future events, even if they experience surprise or suspense along the way. Voltaire's Doctor Pangloss praises his time as the best of possible worlds, and tonality unfailingly delivers a sonic simulation of Pangloss's Enlightenment utopia.

Second, those middle-level strategies of suspense, surprise, and fulfillment allow music to engage in emplotment. The drama we celebrate in Vivaldi or Beethoven depends on tonal syntax to produce its effects. In an age when theater and the novel emerge as reigning literary genres, tonal music parses time in ways that correspond with contemporaneous cultural media. To the extent that we identify a principal theme as a protagonist, we also witness in this music a version of the self revealed through narrative unfolding.

Finally, the binary opposition between major and minor modes encourages an affective dichotomy whereby major registers as positive ("happy") and minor as negative ("sad"). Sixteenth-century modes also carried affective charges, although Dorian—the forerunner of minor—supported plenty of celebratory pieces, and Mixolydian (in part because of conventions associated with tuning) was regarded as harsh and was used in ways that drew on that association. Needless to say, the emotional qualities of tonal pieces range far beyond a simple choice between happy and sad. But not to grasp that convention is not to follow the meanings of the modal vacillations in, say, Schubert songs or Mahler symphonies.

These procedures prevail with scarcely a hitch throughout the eighteenth century: the great period of diatonic tonality. When I teach music history, I treat the period 1700–1800 as a unit rather than breaking it down the middle. No one after Corelli qualifies as Baroque, certainly not Bach and Handel. If the word "Baroque" has any business at all in music history it belongs with the bizarre distortions of early seventeenth-century simulations of divine rapture (McClary 2016). But for all the differences in style introduced by Haydn and Mozart, these composers continue to assume the certainty of the background structures and foreground manipulations already firmly in place in Corelli. The enormous productivity of all these composers stems from those assumptions. As the autograph scores of his cantatas make clear, Bach worked out his material in his opening gambit and then let the standard background progression take it from there. The system worked beautifully to maximize communication between composer and listener, and it greatly facilitated the process of writing vast amounts of music very quickly.

But this best of possible worlds began to entertain doubts in the early nineteenth century. Already in his middle period, Beethoven experimented with alternatives to the time-honored background progression, first substituting the lowered sixth degree for the dominant in sonatas and in his late quartets, exploring a broad range of other key relationships between movements. Such changes required Beethoven to devote much pre-compositional attention to sketches, which often focus on the implications of non-standard backgrounds; they limited the number of works he could produce, and they also bewildered listeners who could no longer follow his idiosyncratic procedures. Schubert also put considerable strain on the conventions he had inherited from his eighteenth-century forebears. Beethoven and Schubert bring to tonality the kinds of critiques leveled against the Enlightenment by philosophers and writers in the nineteenth century, thereby weakening its sense of inevitability from the inside.

Other challenges came from the outside. Expanded trade traffic to and from Asia and the Napoleonic conquest of Egypt made elements from other cultures fashionable. Among the foreign wares now circulating were other modes: the *maqams* of North Africa and the Middle East, the *ragas* of India, the *slendro* of Indonesia. Western musicians latched onto these in part for the sake of exotic color; opera composers particularly deployed such sonorities along with plots that featured oriental temptresses.

But they also turned to these alternatives because of a sense that the major/minor system had been exhausted, and they sought new resources of expressivity. Few exoticists worried about the internal logic of their borrowed scales but rather merely sprinkled in intervals such as the augmented second or effects such as Phrygian cadences.

Occasionally, however, a composer did pursue the implications of other modes more deeply. Grieg, for instance, began his swerve toward nationalism by setting Norwegian folk tunes within entirely tonal settings. But in his late piano works, he experimented with the procedures suggested by the Lydian melodies played by the hardanger fiddle, allowing those idiosyncrasies to shape his harmonic language (McClary 2008). Grieg's experiments influenced Debussy, Ravel, and Bartók, all of whom started to implement other scales—exotic, folkloric, or artificially constructed (e.g., whole-tone, octatonic)— in their music.

Under the weight of such external challenges, as well as those developing from attacks from within the system itself, the two-mode model that had reigned since around 1700 lost its primacy by the beginning of the twentieth century. To be sure, much popular music continues to work within the harmonic language solidified in the eighteenth century. But the double scaffolding of background structure sustained by middle-level expansions collapsed.

Modes continued to show up in twentieth-century music, largely in order to signal exotic or archaic references. Composers of the so-called English Renaissance, such as Ralph Vaughan Williams, sometimes deployed flat seventh degrees at cadences to recall tunes such as "Greensleeves." Even though sixteenth-century singers would have raised that pitch in performance through the common practice of *musica ficta*, the absence of leading tones in most period sources led many modern musicians to identify the sound of the flat seventh degree with earlier eras.

The ramifications of this misreading gave rise to a number of widespread uses of modal configurations. Film-music composers, for example, draw on this convention not only when referring to earlier periods in European history, but also for Bible epics or gladiator movies. Movie audiences have learned to associate the flat seventh degree automatically with bygone eras, and Vaughan Williams's nostalgia for the days of Tudor glory now stands for nostalgia in general.

The folk music revival of the 1960s similarly made use of modal inflections as a means of invoking both nostalgia and authenticity. Simon and Garfunkel's "Parsley, Sage, Rosemary and Thyme" emphasizes that same flat seventh degree at its cadences in ways that recall the lineage that includes "Greensleeves." So does Led Zeppelin's "Stairway to Heaven," buttressed with the faux-medieval images in its enigmatic lyrics. When musicologist Wilfrid Mellers quite correctly labeled such songs as Aeolian, sociologists such as Simon Frith, then beginning to study popular music, jeered at his ridiculously inappropriate terminology.

And musicians themselves took note of such modal labels. The major/minor system that worked for standard popular music and even most rock operated too dependably within the Enlightenment's structures of reason, and many musicians started to explore other idioms. The heavy metal bands that developed in the wake of Led Zeppelin often make the flat seventh degree part of their basic vocabulary. Black Sabbath, for instance, drew on medieval imagery in their lyrics and stagecraft, and they took up residence in Aeolian. As metal musicians labored to push into greater gestures of cultural transgression, some of them have turned to exploring other modal types beyond mere Aeolian.

Metallica and other hard metal groups self-consciously adopt Phrygian for the frame-work of much of their music. They do so for the same reasons Renaissance composers sometimes chose this mode: Phrygian can neither establish its final as stable nor can it escape the gravitational pull of that pitch. The qualities of simultaneous entrapment and futile flailing work perfectly within the ethos of this band. Black metal bands sometimes venture even further to Locrian—the mode based on B with a tritone above the final, which compounds the effect of violent resistance.

The practitioners and fans of heavy metal know how to identify the modes they use or hear. A magazine designed for that community, *Guitar for the Practicing Musician*, used to include a regular column in which Wolf Marshall analyzed in minute detail tunes by Metallica or Black Sabbath or Bach—an indispensable model for metal's heightened rhetoric. When writing his book on metal, *Running with the Devil*, Robert Walser signed up for lessons with Jeff Loven, a long-haired local star, who started by admonishing his student to memorize the materials in his handout titled "Those Crazy Modes": a chart including the very items we distribute in music fundamentals classes (Walser 1993). Just as medieval scribes took up habitation within the empty sets they found in Boethius, these artists have appropriated for their own nefarious purposes the modes displaced by common-practice tonality.

Jazz musicians also resurrected the modes, although they arrived at their experiments through a different and highly unlikely channel. In the 1950s, George Russell—a pi-anist with stars such as Miles Davis and John Coltrane—developed tuberculosis and was confined to a hospital. One of his acquaintances brought him an odd book, Nicolas Slonimsky's *Thesaurus of Scales and Melodic Patterns*: a compilation of every pos-sible scalar type (Slonimsky 1947). Russell and his colleagues had been searching for alternatives to the jazz standards that still structured their improvisations, regardless of the complex harmonic alterations they introduced. As Russell played around with these scales at the hospital's piano, he started to discern in some of them certain qualities that opened up new possibilities. He demonstrated some of these to his friends and soon published a book in 1953 titled *The Lydian Chromatic Concept of Tonal Organization* (Russell 1953).

Russell explained his investment in Lydian by setting it against what he heard as the oppressive demand in tonal music that the fourth scale degree in a dominant-seventh al-ways pulls down, reinforcing a domineering tonic. To his ear, the raised fourth degree of Lydian set the music free to float without performing fealty toward the final. Along with Davis and Coltrane, Russell introduced a practice called modal jazz, which dispensed with tonal-based harmonies as well as the popular tunes bebop had relied upon. The jazz masterpieces of the 1950s and 1960s flowed directly from Russell's fortuitous rediscovery of modes.

The concept of mode has not only worked to account for existing musical practices; as we have seen, it has also been the driving force behind compositional innovations throughout Western music history. The range of inventions afforded by a system of modal classification would have astounded Plato or Cassiodorus or Glareanus. But the mere persistence of this cluster of options has continued to spark creative imaginations and to yield musical practices that galvanize communities of listeners. Plato's ethnography included Dorians, Lydians, Phrygians, and others. Our modal sociology would embrace the fans of Thelonius Monk, Ozzy Osbourne, Vaughan Williams, Adrian Willaert, Josquin, and those nameless scribes who first seized onto surviving manuscripts by Boethius as a way of rationalizing their orally transmitted chant. Despite premature announcements of their demise during the triumph of Enlightenment tonality, modes and their theoretical structures remain among the most fecund sources of new genres. Who can tell what they might engender in centuries to come?

NOTES

1. See Powers (1980).
2. See Boethius, *De istitutione musica*, in Strunk (1998).
3. See Cassiodorus, *Fundamentals of Sacred and Secular Learning*, in Strunk (1998).
4. See Tinctoris, *Liber de natura et proprietate tonorum*, in Strunk (1998).
5. See Aron, *Trattato della natura e cognitione di tuttie gli tuoni*, in Strunk (1998).
6. See Glareanus, *Dodecachordon*, in Strunk (1998).
7. See Zarlino, *Dimostrationi harmoniche*, in Strunk (1998).
8. See Lester (1989) for another account of this transformation.

REFERENCES

Dahlhaus, Carl. 1990. *Studies on the Origins of Harmonic Tonality*. Translated by Robert Gjerdingen. Princeton, NJ: Princeton University Press.

Lester, Joel. 1989. *Between Modes and Keys: German Theory, 1592–1802*. Hillsdale, NY: Pendragon Press.

McClary, Susan. 2004. *Modal Subjectivities: Self-Fashioning in the Italian Madrigal*. Berkeley: University of California Press.

McClary, Susan. 2008. "Playing the Identity Card: Of Grieg, Indians, and Women." *19th-Century Music* 31: 217–227.

McClary, Susan. 2012. *Desire and Pleasure in Seventeenth-Century Music*. Berkeley: University of California Press.

McClary, Susan. 2016. "Doing the Time Warp in Seicento Music." In *Music in Time: Phenomenology, Perception, Performance: A Festschrift in Honor of Christopher Hasty* edited by Suzannah Clark and Alexander Rehding, 237–255. Cambridge, MA: Harvard University Press.

Plato. 1961. *Republic*. In *The Collected Dialogues of Plato*. Edited by Edith Hamilton and Huntington Cairns. New York: Pantheon Books.

Powers, Harold. 2001. "Mode" [1980]. In *The New Grove Dictionary of Music and Musicians*. Edited by Stanley Sadie and John Tyrell. New York: Oxford University Press.

Russell, George. 1953. *The Lydian Chromatic Concept of Tonal Organization*. New York: Concept Publishing.

Slonimsky, Nicolas. 1947. *Thesaurus of Scales and Melodic Patterns*. New York: Scribner.

Strunk, Oliver. 1998. *Source Readings in Music History*. Edited by Leo Treitler. New York: W. W. Norton.

Taruskin, Richard. 2005. *Oxford History of Western Music*. 6 vols. New York: Oxford University Press.

Walser, Robert. 1993. *Running with the Devil: Power, Gender, and Madness in Heavy Metal Music*. Middletown, CT: Wesleyan University Press.

Zarlino, Gioseffo. 1983. *Istitutioni Harmoniche* [1558], Book IV. Translated by Vered Cohen. New Haven, CT: Yale University Press.

CHAPTER 4

···

SCALE

···

MATTHEW GELBART

MUSICIANS tend to encounter and conceive of scales in two ways that can appear only tangentially related. We might call these the performer's idea of scales and the theorist's idea of scales. In the first conception, scales are exercises—finger or vocal patterns intended to develop muscle memory and dexterity—which demonstrate melodic formulas and can be applied toward the execution of "real" music. In the second alternative, scales appear as abstract principles. In this guise they are the sets of available pitches we can draw on to create music that conforms to culturally established expectations, sets organized (for the sake of tidiness, ostensibly) into ascending and/or descending order. As one well-established theory textbook puts it, "A scale in this basic form [starting and ending on the tonic] can be thought of as a symbol of, or abstraction from, the natural flow of music."[1] One might almost envision a scale in this sense as analogous to an alphabet. An alphabet's ordering is a convenience to arrange or memorize the building blocks of a written language (and indeed, we use an alphabetical naming system in English to sequence our scales). Conceived this way—as abstractions and functional enumerations—any number of scales becomes possible: diatonic alongside octatonic, chromatic, and "modal," as well as more idiosyncratic, specially invented sets. Because this handbook is concerned with theory, it is this latter idea of scale, as an abstraction or functional index, that would ostensibly concern us more than the performative exercises we encounter daily. Indeed, some theoretical discussions of scale seem at pains to limit the proper meaning of the word to this sense. For example, the *Oxford Companion to Music* entry on Scale begins: "A scale is not a piece of music, but a theoretical or analytical construct. It consists of all the notes used or usable in the music of a particular period, culture, or repertory, arranged schematically in ascending or descending order of pitch" (Scholes, Nagley, and Temperley 2018).

But how separable are the theoretical and the performative conceptions of scales? Any probing quickly reveals that there is significant mental overlap between scales as abstractions and scales as sounding patterns. Such a tendency to blur the scale as a set of available pitches with the scale as fluid melody or figuration is evident already in much basic terminology and pedagogy. Consider the original introduction of scale in Walter Piston's *Harmony*: "The tones which form [each] interval are drawn from the scale.

Three scales are used as the basis of the music with which we are here concerned—the major scale, the minor scale (with its harmonic and melodic forms), and the chromatic scale" (1941, 3).[2] On the surface, this invocation of scales is entirely theoretical—scales are limited pools of pitches to draw intervals from. But the terminology itself betrays a patterned, melodic element to the theoretical model as soon as it implicates different types of minor, for the melodic minor scale is not an abstracted set of pitches at all. It is a hybrid, an open incursion of scalar melody into the realm of abstractions.[3] The purely abstract "minor" scale, the set of available pitches for composing in minor, sequenced in ascending order, would include both "natural" and raised versions of the sixth and seventh scale degrees. (In A minor, for example, we would have A–B–C–D–E–F–F♯– G–G♯–A, and if the descending direction were even necessary in this conception, it would be identical but in reverse.) The melodic minor instead attempts to capture typ- ical formulas used in ascending and descending figures in minor-key music, while *also*, when taken in its entirety in both directions, showing (albeit with much redundancy) all the pitches that "belong" to a given minor key.[4]

So an analogy to an alphabet breaks down fairly quickly. Although we learn the al- phabet in a particular order to help us remember all the letters and to allow us to organize lists of words or names, that order is semantically arbitrary. Letters don't appear in al- phabetical order in words. When *Sesame Street*'s Big Bird comes across the alphabet and tries to read it phonetically as a word, the result generates laughs. But no one laughs when scales appear whole in a piece of music. We learn scales as exercises not only, or even primarily, to show us all the notes in C minor or A♭ major, or to learn their functions— for if we ordered tonal scales by functional importance, we might learn first tonic, then dominant, then subdominant, and so forth. Rather, we learn scales as exercises precisely

FIGURE 4.1   Mozart, Sonata in C Major, K. 545, first movement, mm. 1–10.

because they present patterns similar or identical to those encountered in melodies generated in each key. We practice scales so that we can play Mozart's "easy" sonata K. 545 "easily" (see Figure 4.1, mm. 5–10). And, when singing such well-known melodies as the first phrase of "Joy to the World," we are just singing scales with distinctive rhythms to mark them. Thus it is perhaps not surprising that another classic textbook, Allen Forte's *Tonal Harmony in Concept and Practice*, plunges right in without defining "scale" at all, introducing the term through its practical aspect: "A scale is more than an exercise for fingers or vocal chords; it can also take the shape of a musical theme."[5]

The fact that scales in recent Western musicking are both exercises (and by extension building blocks of melodies) and abstractions, not clearly separated, raises various chicken-and-egg queries. Does scalar theory derive from practice or vice versa? More specifically: do we like hearing scalar melody because we conceive music as an ordered set, or do we conceive music as drawing on sets ordered in certain ways because we like conjunct motion? Is our conceptual conflation due to the fact that that same word is now used for both conjunct melodic sequences and for potential sets of pitches—in English (and, as it turns out, basically in all European languages)? Or is that vocabulary itself effect rather than cause? And related to this: how much of our conflation of theoretical scales with exercises or melodic scales is the result of strong cultural ideas about how music functions, and how much may it be rooted in human psychology and physiology that affect music in every culture? These are questions I will pursue at least briefly in this chapter.

Before Scales?

Scale and its correlates in other European languages did not always exist, or the terms that did exist did not have the fully conflated meaning we have been examining. In the Middle Ages and Renaissance, European musical education treated modes as self-contained systems. We might think of modes in this sense as representing the "theorist's version" of today's scale: medieval modes were sets of possible pitches used to classify and organize certain chants or sections of chant (and later polyphonic compositions). Medieval modes seem to have begun primarily as classificatory and only gradually to have become more normative, but what remained consistent was that in describing them, theorists stressed certain more heavily weighted, functional pitches, such as cadential points, as well as the ambitus: how the full range of pitches were distributed around those key notes. Like theoretical scales, medieval modes were generally ordered conjunctly in their presentation in written treatises, by virtue of attempts to relate their creation to ancient Greek tetrachordal theories, based on surviving documents—and to relate such tetrachordal theories to octave species.[6] Ordered as they were in the abstract, however, these modal groupings were not generally linked to conjunct practical exercises unfolding the mode in ascending or descending order. While there were psalm tones and other mnemonic or heuristic manifestations for each mode—reinforcing functional elements such as ranges, reciting tones, and finals—these specialized presentations of mode could hardly be considered scales in the modern sense.[7]

Such ordered practical, pedagogical arrangements—akin to scales in the performer's sense—did come to exist too, but *separately*, most notably in the form of the hexachordal system first developed in the early eleventh century by Guido, and then expanded by himself and others soon afterward. This solmization system did not pretend to replace modal theory, but rather allowed singers to negotiate (modal) music in an applied context. They could conceive of its figures either as conjunct motion, or, when they encountered larger melodic intervals, they became more fluently aware of those intervals as leaps of "regular" size, as related to stepwise motion (Guido of Arezzo 1998, 214–218). Arguably, hexachords thus played the role of modern scales as heuristic exercises based on a conjunct presentation (stressed through the visual element of the hand and various charts of the set of pitches commonly in use[8]), while modal theory covered the role of modern scales as abstracted sets of available pitches, including functional hierarchies.[9]

This element of independence of singing pedagogy from modal theory and practice in later medieval and Renaissance Europe appears to indicate that the conflation of the two ways of thinking about scales in modern theory is not a requirement, and that in many cultures it may be absent. Similarly, in a European instrumental context, scales as formalized exercises emerged quite gradually, and surprisingly late. C. P. E. Bach devoted several pages and some plates to scale [*Scala*] fingerings for different keys in his influential 1753 treatise on how to play keyboard instruments, and there were similar explorations for other instruments, such as viola d'amore and guitar, around the same time.[10] But I cannot find full printed sets of exercises called scales (in any language) until a stream of publications beginning in the early to mid-nineteenth century.[11] Again, this might suggest that our current, multivalent Western way of thinking about scales is almost a historical accident. While, as we shall see, there are several indicators that performative and theoretical ideas related to scales were never truly separate in medieval European practice—and likely never can be truly separate in most musical systems—the particularly fluid double sense in which we use "scale" now does seem to be a very specialized development. Indeed, it seems bound to the establishment of functional tonality in Europe.

SCALES AND TONALITY IN EUROPE

We can start to trace our scale concept by looking at the word's European etymology. Here I will put aside attempts to understand ancient Greek words that meant something akin to scale in one or more of its connotations—and that were translated variously in medieval and Renaissance engagements with Greek theory—as they do not shed clear light on the questions at hand.[12] I will start instead with English, not only because this handbook focuses on English theory terms, but because English seems to be fairly typical in its development of a conflated performative-melodic-theoretical scale concept.

The term "scale" itself evidently derives, initially, from the performer's sense of conjunct notes rather than from modal theory, and this is true in various languages. The word seems to have entered English as a musical term in the later sixteenth century. The earliest uses noted in the *Oxford English Dictionary* mark it as a synonym for "gamut."[13] Indeed, Thomas Morley's *Plaine and Easie Introduction to Practicall Muisicke* presents the "Scale of Musicke, which wee [*sic*] terme the *Gam*[ut]" as the very beginning of his discourse on music in general—displaying a chart of notes from the Gamma Ut to ee and the corresponding hexachordal solmizations (1597, 2). That Morley plainly (and easilie) equates "scale" to a performative, vocal phenomenon (rather than to any modal theory at all) is made clear by the content of the following discussion, and is manifest in his insisting there were only six "notes" (i.e., pitch types) in music (ut, re, me, fa, sol, la) and his explanation that there are only twenty notes in the scale overall because that is the compass of most voices.[14]

What is striking about "scale" and "gamut" entering into English as synonyms—and they often remained interchangeable well into the nineteenth century—is that etymologically they are rather different in their implications. Gamut derives, rather singularly, not from a word with a broader meaning in an older language, but from a Latin (or rather hybridized Greek-Latin) term with a specifically musical and very narrow meaning: "Gamma Ut," the lowest pitch in medieval theory as laid out by Pseudo-Odo and Guido. Gamut's etymology thus emphasizes *range*—"gamut" having entered English in the fifteenth and sixteenth centuries to indicate the full array of possible pitches (regardless of mode) that could be drawn upon, as expanded through hexachordal theory. The word has of course preserved its connotations of wide range, now extended to non-musical contexts. "Scale," on the other hand, comes from "scala," the Latin (and then Italian) word for ladder or staircase. The climbing etymology of "scale" emphasizes *ordering* rather than potential or extent. Indeed, the word "scala" had entered Latin treatises on music around 1500, where it suggested, generally through ladder-like visual diagrams, a straightened-out bottom-to-top sense of navigation across the full gamut, becoming linked to the musical staff as well.[15] (These are the sources from which Morley drew his use of scale and gamut as equivalent.) Based on their respective roots, the two words converge on a concept from different sides. "Gamut" abstracts from the practical—the bottom limit represents the scope of possibility—whereas "scale" orders and makes practical the abstract outlines of music. The very fact that "scale" entered English usage by becoming synonymous with gamut, as the full range of potential pitches, but now admixing an emphasis on conjunct patterning, likely set it on its path toward the double meaning we see it hold now.

It is thus not surprising that this etymology is duplicated in the vast majority of European languages, where the modern words for "scale" (carrying our double meaning) are derived either from "scala" or "gamut," or both versions exist simultaneously. We have *escala* in Spanish and Portuguese; *Skala* in German, Swedish, Danish, and so forth; *scala* in Italian; and we have *gamme, gamma,* гамма, *gama* in French, Italian, Russian, and Polish, respectively. Other languages have substituted non-cognate translations of "(note) ladder" or related concepts, such as the Czech *stupnice,* and more literally the

Hungarian *hanglétra* or German *Tonleiter*. The German *Skala* and *Tonleiter* have been, historically, relatively interchangeable, but then again, they both emphasize the ordered aspect (by being either a borrowed word or an autochthonous word for ladder) rather than the range aspect. In Italian, despite variation in etymology, *scala* and *gamma* have often been largely interchangeable.[16] This little linguistic exploration suggests that the use of scale and gamut and their cognates relatively synonymously in various languages (or the choosing between one of the two in other languages to capture essentially the same concept) emerged via the growing identification of the words in Latin treatises. But more relevant to our narrative thread here, it suggests also that words for scale all across Europe were coming to have a double meaning, increasingly signaling a nebulous array of ideas that raised questions about the overall possible range *and* practical disposition of notes available in a piece, or in "music" as a whole.

That the change in connotations of scale accelerated as aspects of common practice tonality were starting to consolidate in music-making, and solidified not long before hexachordal theory was fully replaced by modern major and minor modal theory, is no historical accident either. Tonality brought with it sweeping claims that functional elements of music were natural and universal, and this had a profound impact on the idea of scale. Going beyond Pythagoras and his monochord, theorists from the end of the sixteenth century to the high Enlightenment increasingly sought to justify modal practice with empirical experiment. These developments culminated with Rameau's systematic theory. After a century of practical and numerological arguments, the scale had by now extended from the six notes in hexachordal theory to seven, conceived as repeating by octaves.[17] Although the French scale (*gamme*) had retained the hexachordal solmization names for the first six notes, adding "si" by the later seventeenth century, these syllables themselves were picking up clearly functional roles. At the same time they continued to signal common melodic patterns in and of themselves.

There was thus increasing slippage between scale degrees in functional modal roles and scales as melodies. For example, François Campion (1716), in dealing with the proper harmonization of each scale degree, built clearly upon other recent discussions, but with a new emphasis on conjunct movement along the scale—in this case in bass lines—and the proper voice-leading above such conjunct lines.[18] In Rameau's writing, scales and scale degrees (both in the melody and bass) stand in systematic relation to intervals (and their inversions) generated by acoustic principles that justified the weight and meaning of each pitch class within specific modern keys (*Tons*) (1722, esp. 169–172, 186, and 198–200). In 1723, a year after Rameau's harmony treatise, Marin Marais published an instrumental chamber piece called "La Gamme" that begins with exercise-like octave runs up and down the C major scale, and then playfully expands from there through variations and different keys.

The closer and closer coupling of theory with practical musicianship and pedagogy in one vocabulary word signifying scale is also evident in the fact that Rameau's practical "gammes" came, over the rest of his life, to include not only stepwise unfolding of the octave but, additionally, ordered progressions by thirds and by fifths that would eventually cycle through all seven diatonic scale degrees and/or twelve pitch classes (1760,

2–3). These different configurations could be used both to show generative principles (cycles of overtones that built diatonic and chromatic scales) *and* as exercises to help musicians develop an ear and understand the functional relationships of pitches. In this way, theories of functional tonality became the glue that fully cemented more casual links between scales as patterns and scales as sets. Here we must have the reasons why, as detailed above, it was precisely over the following decades that instrumentalists began publicly to debate scale fingerings and publish exercise books of scales.

SCALES AS SCIENTIFIC INQUIRY INTO THE NATURE OF MUSIC

Rameau's efforts were important to the idea of scale in yet another way. He may have built in many respects upon seventeenth- and early eighteenth-century forbears, notably for instance on the work of Joseph Sauveur.[19] But Rameau's own work is pivotal in that its systematic ambition—its pursuit of a "universal" scientific basis for European tonality—became a driving force in a quest to understand the "scales" Europeans were increasingly encountering from outside their own traditions, in wide-ranging cultures, past and present. By mid-century, bolstered by reports from travelers and missionaries, Europeans were driven to consider scale as a comparative concept. Rameau himself launched a discussion of how the scientific generative processes of musical harmony were used by other cultures, notably by the ancient Greeks and Chinese, but he was not able to reach a satisfactory "universal" answer himself.[20] This cause would soon be taken up by his followers, who made the late eighteenth century the moment when the newly reinforced Western principle of scale became the primary object of analysis in European examinations of music from around the world.

The Enlightenment obsession with scales in fact resulted from attempts at establishing a teleological history of Western harmony and tonality. Mixing Rameau's systematized empirical enquiry with Orientalist historiography, French theorists such as the Abbé Roussier soon found ways to interpret the "scales" of the ancient Egyptians, Chinese, and Greeks, among others, as parts of an evolutionary development—suggesting that there was an ancient and "Oriental" tonal system that was advanced and perfected later in the West. In general, the study of scales beginning in the later Enlightenment drew on philology, which was enjoying a renaissance at the same time. Musicians (and often non-musicians) came to approach scales the way that philologists looked at etymologies, grammar, and other foundations of language: the similarities and differences in global scales were seen as pieces of evidence that could reconstruct migration paths and relationships between musical cultures, or in some cases show a predetermined natural path of development that would even occur *without* direct contact between peoples. The influential work of Charles Burney galvanized thinking along this latter line. Burney took Orientalist conceptions of a generalized "early" pentatonic scale and added in an emerging idea of "primitive" "folk" music within Europe, embedded into the same developmental trajectory. He claimed not only that the ancient Chinese and Greek scales had been identical, but that the Scottish scale—as still found in traditional "national" melodies—was also the same. Most importantly, he ventured a reason: this must indicate that any culture in a certain "primitive" state (whether a long time ago or preserved in its natural simplicity today by separation from cultured, urban "progress") would share a pentatonic foundation that was natural and the basis of all further musical development.[21] His conclusions were soon debated and refined by the many they tantalized. In the generation after Burney, writers even began to term the anhemitonic pentatonic collection the "primary scale of music" and the "national [i.e., folk] scale," and they sought (and found) it in more and more places around the globe (Gelbart 2007, 128–138).

So far, I have been distinguishing between a performative and a theoretical concept of scale, but the discussions of scales from the Enlightenment and later in fact make evident a further cognitive distinction—one within the theoretical category: namely, between, on the one hand, presenting one single scale that lays out *all* the notes available in a particular culture or tuning system and, on the other hand, showing multiple scales that lay out *particular* modes within that tuning system or cultural vocabulary.[22] (In tonal music, the former would be the full chromatic scale and the latter would be various major and minor diatonic scales.)[23] The pentatonic "natural" scale was very frequently seen as the total set of pitches conceivable in many cultures, but it could be arranged with different bass pitches or finals, thus generating permutations—of which certain ones might be favored either by particular nations or for different melodies *within* a given tradition, for instance to set texts with different affects or functions. As more and more theorists began to investigate the scales of different cultures, the relationship between the set of all possible pitches in a theoretical or practical system and the sets used in specific songs or pieces was, directly or indirectly, always at stake, primarily because much speculation about the notes used in ancient music was derived from reconstructing its theoretical principles and organology. So, despite a conceptual separation, the two kinds of theoretical scale were constantly in dialogue.

Furthermore, by seeking explanations of scalar limitations and evolution, these same comparative investigations also contributed further to the increasing conflation of theoretical scales in general with scales as melodic patterns. European theorists commonly suggested one of two reasons for what they saw as the pentatonic scale's "gaps." The first concerned the capabilities of instruments at different historical or geographical junctures. For example, Benjamin Franklin, in a letter that would be reprinted in several editions of *Encyclopaedia Britannica* (Franklin 1968–, 12:158–165; *Encyclopaedia Britannica* 1778–1784 through 1820–1823, s.v. "Music") and was thus widely influential, suggested that if an old harp was strung with a diatonic heptatonic scale, then transposing melodies by a fourth would require skipping certain pitches in order to preserve the intervallic relationship of its notes. This might lead to a cultural predilection for melodies that skipped certain scale degrees in the first place, making possible transposition for different voices. If it were transposition that led to pentatonic melodies, the gapped scale would be a functional preference, a specifically chosen modal scale, rather than representing the total set of pitches "known" or available in a culture. Meanwhile, the other common explanation for "gapped" scales was that certain intervals (particularly half steps) were difficult for untrained or uncultured singers to produce, and gapped scales thus resulted from easy vocal patterns.[24] In this case, practical scalar manifestations are seen (at least partly) as the basis for constructing modal systems. It is assumed that the adjacent notes of a scale were often to be found as consecutive notes at cadences and other crucial melodic points, so that the intervals between them became relevant to defining the full field of potential notes. This type of explanation would suggest that at some point a scale such as the anhemitonic pentatonic scale constituted the entire available set of known pitches (the "one" scale), and if there were modal scales within this system, they varied by which pitch was the modal final rather than whether there were more or different pitches added within the octave. According to these theories, pentatonic scales could be filled out to heptatonic scales over time only by cultural progression that led to more trained ears and larynxes.

Although the explanations for how scales filled out from their ostensibly primal basis varied considerably, such theories of pentatonic scales developing into "modern" heptatonic scales—the latter complemented with tonal harmony—were remarkably tenacious. There were notable exceptions, such as the more racially essentializing theories of François-Joseph Fétis, for whom, despite the fact that his massive *General History of Music* was in large part a history of scales, pentatonicism was more of a dead end preferred by certain "less developed" peoples rather than a jumping-off point (1869, 1:119). Generally, though, theories of a clear evolution of pentatonicism into tonal heptatonicism carried through the nineteenth century and much of the twentieth, with versions propounded by writers across Europe and North America as diverse as Hermann von Helmholtz, Auguste Gevaert, C. H. H. Parry, Cecil Sharp, Hugo Riemann, Erich von Hornbostel, Bence Szabolcsi, and Joseph Yasser.[25]

In the midst of this continuity over time, there were nevertheless also fresh elements introduced into the study and concept of scales, particularly as positivist drives brought new scientific rigor to comparative engagement with music. Helmholtz emerges as a central figure here. His interest in acoustics and the physiology of the ear dovetailed into a curiosity about the production and reception of music, so that he organized part three of his famous *Sensations of Tone as a Physiological Basis for the Theory of Music* around "Scales and Tonality" viewed from a historical (developmental) and cross-cultural standpoint.[26] Extending the inevitable and now multifarious tangled conflations of scale as theory and scale as melodic production, Helmholtz influenced (or was directly involved in) studies of the larynx and of the intersection of vowel quality, timbre, and pitch perception, studies that informed his own theories about intonation.[27]

Indeed, intonation—the precise tuning of notes relative to each other, governed by different culturally and/or acoustically driven concerns—became such a central concern that, following Helmholtz, the accurate measurement of small differences between pitches came for the first time to take up as much place in studies of scales as did their functional "sameness." This aspect of empirical positivism seemed at first to bring confusion and contradiction to the historical line of theories of scalar development framed as a natural phenomenon and leading through milestones marked by cross-cultural similarity. It was Helmholtz's English translator Alexander Ellis who brought the most problematic evidence to light. Having created the precise intervallic measurement system (involving cents) that we still use today, Ellis embarked on an ambitious and influential study "On the Musical Scales of Various Nations"—treating scales primarily as modal or instrumental constructs within each cultural system (Ellis 1885, 486, 491, 496). With more evidence than had previously been used to resist such a theory, Ellis sought to quash the idea that newer scales evolved from a shared pentatonic foundation resulting from the supposed difficulty of having to sing or hear semitones or other intervals smaller than a whole tone (508); he offered multiple examples of semitones and microtones in different so-called "primitive" scales. And, by focusing on the most precise possible pitch measurements of the scales studied, he ultimately moved toward a famous avowal that was potentially devastating in its impact on the many theories about the natural progression of scales outlined across the end of the eighteenth century and the early nineteenth: "The final conclusion is that the musical scale is not one, not 'natural,' nor even founded necessarily on the laws of the constitution of musical sound, so beautifully worked out by Helmholtz, but very diverse, very artificial, and very capricious" (526).

But the earth did not shatter and theories of the natural development of scales persisted, with, if anything, renewed momentum, building on Spencerian evolutionary theory to give them new validity, and ignoring many of the inconvenient implications of Ellis's work even as they took up his measuring tools and examples. Why?

WE HEAR WHAT WE THEORIZE

One problem with so many comparative musical studies, of course, is that we hear what we want or expect to hear; we filter sound through mental frameworks we understand, in particular through scales that we are used to.[28] This psychological proclivity was clearly responsible for both the inaccuracy of many cross-cultural descriptions of scales in the eighteenth and nineteenth centuries, and the sometimes tortuous rationalizations of measurements that found startling results, such as Ellis's. If Helmholtz's data and even Ellis's might still often be compromised by their preconceptions and their need to rely upon reports and intermediaries (alongside more novel means of measurement with tuning forks and the like), there would soon appear a way around this subjectivity. The phonograph presented a sort of "solution" in measuring comparative scales. This new invention seemed to confirm and extend Ellis's assertions about the variety of tunings and scales used around the world; and the cadre of scholars who formed around the new archive of recorded music in Berlin, notably Carl Stumpf, Erich von Hornbostel, and Otto Abraham, seemed determined not to adapt the data to fit their theories, but instead to form their theories (at least to some extent, and though they still sought to universalize as much as they could) to fit the new phonographic data.[29]

But not everyone was on board with this approach. Hugo Riemann railed against the new evidence amassing from phonograph recordings precisely because he felt its vaunted accuracy was a red herring, in that it presented sounds as they existed (often by accident or in error) rather than as they were decoded by and as they signified for human musicians and listeners.[30] Although he was driven to this conclusion by his desire to impose his preconceived and entirely Eurocentric theory of melodic and harmonic development on all the musical data he studied, including preserving a theory of linear evolution from a universal stage of anhemitonic pentatonicism toward the inevitable and perfected modern heptatonic scale [Riemann 1916; Gelbart and Rehding 2011, 148–158], he was nevertheless on to something important as well. Our tendency to hear sounds bent through our expectations is not just something that can be circumvented by "objective" measurement—it is psychologically determinant. In other words, it is itself part of music's meaning. It is how we make sense of music, including scales.[31]

In truth, Riemann's insistence on the subjectivity of hearing was not fully at odds even with the very scholars whose work he seemed to be attacking. Helmholtz had already contended that while physics and physiology formed a certain universal basis for musical taste, these natural outlines might be filled in in very different ways. He emphasized that "The system of Scales, Modes, and Harmonic Tissues does not rest solely upon inalterable natural laws, but is also, at least partly, the result of esthetical principles, which have already changed, and will still further change, with the progressive development of humanity."[32] Both Helmholtz and later Riemann thus played down the ability of acoustics and physiology to determine human scales entirely. Psychology would have to play a role. Where they disagreed was in the younger man's insistence that aesthetics were *not* arbitrary, that psychology tended toward a universal scale as much as acoustics could have.

The question of how universal human hearing might be, viewed from a psychological standpoint, is what effectively made earlier (eighteenth- and earlier nineteenth-century) theories of evolving scales seem as relevant as ever, even alongside new objective measurement techniques. The fallout of various—and often contradictory—attempts to reconcile, on the one hand, acoustics and descriptions of the physiology of the ear (as hard science), and, on the other hand, the much less tangible or measurable aspects of musical psychology and even philosophy, thus became central to ideas of scale beginning in the later nineteenth century. One influential theory balancing "natural" (i.e., universal) outlines of tonal systems with culturally determined elements was put forward by Carl Stumpf's (2012) influential treatise on *The Origins of Music*. Stumpf suggested that certain intervals, especially the octave but also the fifth and fourth, were (for both acoustic and psychological reasons) universal consonances to the extent that they often blended into single pitches in perception. Additionally, due again to a combination of physiological and psychological factors, he noted that "small steps are more suitable for melodic use" (48). Different scales might result from putting those two axioms together: since the smaller intervals were not as clearly linked to universal hearing as were octaves and fifths, the acoustically natural outlines sketched by the larger consonant intervals would be relatively common around the world, but the consequent drive to fill in the smaller intervals could lead to more varied and arbitrary forms (63–64).

Questions about just how universal and how culturally dependent human hearing is remain no less germane today, and definitive answers are not all that much closer than they were a century ago. Experiments in music psychology have certainly progressed. They have even come to form a rapidly expanding discipline in and of themselves (including cognitive musicology, and, with special relevance, the entire field of psychoacoustics). For example, studies of scales have become tied to studies of "scaling," which is our innate way of perceiving by recognizing difference, and the application of this question to how different two frequencies have to be before they are perceived as discrete pitches by listeners.[33] Yet, in addressing the issues discussed above, such studies continue to show that we need to reckon with the malleability of human hearing and the impact of cultural background in describing scales, which clearly go beyond objective measurements of pitch frequency.[34]

VARIABILITY AND DIALECTS IN SCALES

On one level, this disconnect between frequency and scalar cognition presents a dilemma regarding "accuracy" or correctness in describing, and potentially even in playing, scales—and it is not a problem that offers simplistic solutions. Granted, in *cross*-cultural situations, filtering foreign scales through our own cultural expectations without properly studying music within the culture we are describing usually results in something we can label with relative ease as a mishearing or mis-transcription. (Many studies from the eighteenth and nineteenth century are particularly rife with such willful distortions that simply ignore the way non-Europeans listened to music in order to bend their sounds to a preconceived expectation of what their scales would be.) But there are much grayer zones, in which a way of hearing, playing, or transcribing might be judged wrong or inaccurate only in retrospect, or by an outsider for whom different aspects of the sound are semantically important.

Even certain transcriptions that may initially appear ridiculous from our current vantage point might come under this umbrella, seeming less far-fetched if we consider them in their original contexts. Athanasius Kircher famously presented reports that sloths in South America had been observed to intone "the usual intervals of six steps . . . the first elements of music, *Ut, re, mi, fa, sol, la, la, sol, fa, mi, re, ut*" (Clark and Rehding 2001, 4). It would be hard to find a modern claim that sloths sing scales, and Kircher was also in an armchair far away from the tropical rainforests where the sloths lived. But the fact that these observations were apparently duplicated and confirmed by different authors and different Spanish visitors to the New World[35] suggests that at least *perhaps*, within European culture of the time, the sloths could be "accurately" perceived as singing pitches that corresponded to current ideas of a scale, filtered through hexachordal pitch functions and hierarchies.[36] After all—given how varied tuning was in terms of both absolute and relative pitch at the time—Europeans in the mid-seventeenth century needed to be adept in general at adjusting the pitches they heard in practice to a platonic idea of a standard scale.[37] A French visitor to Rome in Kircher's time remarked that the polychoral music of that city depended on supporting the choirs around the church with multiple portative organs that must of course share the same tuning. The visitor marveled, noting that in Paris, "one would hardly be able to find two [such organs] at the same pitch and tuning" (Maugars 2007, 166).

This has broad implications for describing and even defining scales. For example, from a mechanical measurement standpoint, varied tuning systems and base pitches should create different scales. This was part of the thinking that underlay the most "objective" and acoustically oriented systems of measurements from Ellis's time onward. Yet, despite some theoretical engagements from the seventeenth century on scales and temperament, it seems unlikely that many Parisians in 1639 considered all the differently tempered and tuned organs in their city as using semantically different scales.[38] And both temperament and absolute pitch (the tuning of an A) continued to vary wildly across Europe (and often across single countries and cities and even churches) through the first half of the nineteenth century.[39] This suggests, perversely, that the tendency for musicians to hear pitches not as they can be measured by a machine, but rather adjusted into their cultural framework of a scale, is often a necessary and well-honed coping skill for performance and interpretation, rather than a result of poor musicianship or ear training. That scholars such as Ellis, seeking minute measurements of tunings in order to form a cross-cultural idea of scale, emerged from Europe just after a standardized equal-tempered tuning had spread more widely and absolute pitch was homogenizing as well (sometimes even through legal decree) is no accident: the latter circumstance made the very type of enquiry Ellis undertook conceivable. But that situation was not the norm in the history of scales, even in the West. Just as in seventeenth-century Paris, a good degree of variability in pitches perceived, in scalar terms, as the same can be found in most places in the world—as studies of instrumental tunings in Indonesia, India, Central Africa, and many other places have shown.[40] Some scales, such as the nominally equidistant Javanese *slendro* scale, demonstrate particularly high variation from instrument to instrument.[41]

Given the variability of scale degrees in practice at most times and places in the world, it seems that—thinking from a theorist's perspective—a stronger or at least complementary metaphor for a scale, alongside an alphabet (which we have already seen is problematic for other reasons, although it can be helpful), is a series of phonemes.[42] Each phoneme has a distinctive functional meaning (unlike letters, where, for example, *c* and *k* in English can make the same sound), yet there may be variety in the actual sounds, for example between different regional accents pronouncing sounds in what is recognized in the same word. In this sense, I think it is productive to extend the phoneme analogy to cover the idea of musical "allophones": different sounds that are perceived semantically to be versions of the same phoneme.[43] While the transfer of this linguistic concept to music has been adumbrated before,[44] the most well-known example, Bruno Nettl's consideration of raised and lowered versions of the sixth and seventh scale degrees in the minor scale,[45] is somewhat misleading, because the central point of allophones is that semantic meaning does not change when they are substituted for each other.[46] Indeed, with allophones, native speakers are often unaware of the fact that to outsiders they are producing separate sounds. Thus, famously, native speakers of Korean often do not note the difference between *l* and *r*, versions of which are allophones in Korean, and native speakers of English often do not note the difference between aspirated and non-aspirated plosives (such as the *t* in *top* and the *t* in *stop*), which are allophones in English. In most cases, when speaking their own languages, people follow unconscious rules that govern the choice of which sound to use, but when learning or hearing another language, they may have trouble differentiating and reproducing sounds that are allophonic to them.

This allophone metaphor (especially if applied loosely and conceptually) is important in considering scales because it is one factor that often creates a slippage between acoustic accuracy and cultural or semantic accuracy. It may complicate attempted measurements of scales, but it explains why we humans can hear different tunings as conforming to our functional idea of a single scale. And it gets rid of a particularly literalistic definition of scale that some scholars upheld in the wake of positivism and phonograph measurements: that scale in a true sense only existed when it was consistently measurable, as on certain instruments (Hornbostel 1913, 23). If instrumental tunings can be as varied as vocal tunings, but most listeners can ignore these differences semantically, and if, furthermore, the vast majority of scale-like entities in different times and places have a similar and limited number of pitches in them (five to seven, usually) that form the basis of this variation, there is good evidence that scales are quite deep-lying mental constructs governing almost any music-making on some level, and working—once again—at the interface between our feeling for pitch possibility and our feeling for melodic formulas.[47]

That is not to say that minor variation in scale degrees/phonemes is not also often significant. A musician may have a passionate preference for just tuning, for example, or for the resonance of a particular gamelan over another tuned only slightly differently. Seen in light of the above linguistic framework, such tuning variations are akin to accents in different speakers. Different regional (or foreign) accents in language tell us a lot about the people we hear. They may strike us as mellifluous or as ugly; certainly they provide a rich source of the "character" of speech and speakers, and although they seldom become the focus of meaning itself, they can even, indirectly, inflect our semantic interpretation. There are musical equivalents to those moments when variation of a phoneme does become central in language. In many scales (as modes), certain functional pitches are expected to be varied (or bent) by small acoustic intervals. The most well-known examples include blue notes as well as microtonal inflection in Indian classical music. Notably, while for non-linguists, phonemic variation in spoken language (with regional accents, for example) seemingly emerges into the conscious realm most often in moments of social judgment or comedic play, in music the moments when scale degrees are moved or bent can become sublime, perhaps carrying us into a zone where linguistic analogies break down.

Here, we are helped by returning to our opening question of how scales as practical conjunct motion—as performative melodic formulas—relate to the various kinds of theoretically conceived scales. If we assume that theoretical scales are all that matters, then we may be tempted, for example, to fall into the trap of some naïve citations of Indian classical music, which invoke (usually in the name of showing the global diversity of scales) ancient treatises to suggest that musicians are thinking of a 22-note microtonal scale when performing in various *ragas*. But we will not get very far in understanding how this music is produced that way.[48] If we look practically at these musicians, who are largely conceiving of heptatonic pitch collections bearing certain inflections in scale degrees, the relevance of the performative scale becomes important once again. The pitch variations—constrained by typical melodic formulas—can either determine and define the specific mode (and are thus not allophones) or may diverge from performer to performer in the same *raga*, but in consistent ways (and thus might be viewed as allophones), but they are limited in one of these two ways. This would suggest (as more recent Indian theory posits) that as a basis for each *raga* the performer is drawing, rather than on an abstracted theory of all microtonal potential pitches, on a heuristic concept of "scale" that combines theoretical sets (the *thaats* in Hindustani music or *melakartas* in Karnatic music) and practical melodic motion. At least, it would indicate that performative scales are mediating between microtonal theory and heptatonic *raga* theory.[49]

WE THEORIZE WHAT WE HEAR

The evidence piles up, in fact, that we cannot fully separate performative manifestations of scales from theoretical ones if we want to address how humans formulate both modal-theoretical and melodic ideas. There is considerable overlap between melodic formulas, pedagogy, and abstract pitch sets not only when we think about Western scales, but also when we consider related but slightly different concepts such as mode, Indian *raga*, Arabic *maqam*, ancient Greek *systema*, and so many others past and present.

I considered earlier the possibility that the partial separation in medieval Europe of modal theory from heuristic performance practice—and the attendant lack at that time of a word in European languages that encapsulated both sides of our meaning of scale—signaled the prospect that our current use of scale in a conflated (even sometimes confused) sense for both might be arbitrary. Certainly, there are ways in which Western scales have come to be unique. We have marked points in the history of our scale concept: that it was through the introduction of a widespread mnemonic and pedagogical system placed on top of modal theory that the word "scale" (in different languages) entered the European vocabulary in the first place; that it was the solidification of functional tonality that cemented a multivalent meaning around these terms, so that scales became both modal sets and conjunct, practical melodic devices at once; and finally that this multivalent Western conception of scale was soon applied almost obsessively to European studies of non-Western music, raising questions about how transferable the concept might be (and how to address variability in scale tunings in any system). Nevertheless, despite the unique aspects of Western concepts of scale, it has also emerged that most musical cultures have terms partially analogous, and that those terms generally include at least some conflation of performative and theoretical aspects. In light of the interrelated questions of physiology and psychology raised above (ironically, initially, in some of the most ethnocentric studies of scale we have considered), let us end by reconsidering briefly these deeper bonds that go beyond European tonal tradition, and that tie our modern scale into a broader network of modal concepts.

The very names we give to individual pitches often seem to unite the performative and the theoretical sides of scales. While some pedagogical approaches use letter names or "fixed do" systems to teach scales—for example English lettered-pitch terminology for instrumental scales—others highlight the function of pitches within a scale, thus inherently linking scalar melody to modal-functional aspects of scale. In performance contexts, as well as in pedagogical exercises, we seldom use cumbersome, purely theoretical modal-functional names for scale degrees; multi-syllable names such as "dominant" do not lend themselves to singing. But, on the other hand, many musical traditions use "movable do" type solmization systems: single-syllable names for pitches that capture some of the notes' theoretical functionality as scale degrees precisely in order to build awareness of these functions into pedagogical and practical melodic patterns. Chinese *jianpu*-based solmization, Indian *sargam*, Javanese number-based solmization, American shape-note singing: all of these relate to the phonemic importance of scale degrees as concepts discussed above, and all thus unite performative and theoretical aspects of scales. In European music history, the most obviously "functional" movable-do system emerged in Sarah Ann Glover and John Curwen's "tonic sol-fa movement" in nineteenth-century England, when each pitch was given a hand symbol that not only cued the note but also attempted to capture its apparent affective quality within the key, such as "la, the sad or weeping tone," or "ray, the rousing or hopeful tone" (Curwen 1872, iv). Curwen's strong version of the system influenced or formed the basis of most European movable-do solfège systems since (including the Kodály method), systems that integrate the modal-functional aspect of theoretical scales with practical music-making and pedagogy as closely as could be imagined. Singing "do-re-mi-fa-sol-la-ti-do" is truly singing a "scale" in all senses of the word.

Of course the origin of the syllables used here (as with the now standard fixed-do system used for pitch names in France, Italy, and several other countries) was the Guidonian system itself. And so we might turn back and ask again: was hexachordal solmization ever truly divorced from modal theory? As we might anticipate after tracing the above connections, while there was a layer of remove, it never was. Guido's own hexachordal theory is laden with the theoretical background of modal thinking. Even if, as Harold Powers notes, Guido was rather indirect about the connections he drew between modal theory and hexachordal theory, it was in the same letter where he laid out the hexachord as a singing technique that he also hinted at its relation to a modal system, noting modal similarities between pitches a fourth apart, such as

A and D—here meaning the conjunct intervallic structure of semitones and whole tones in the notes surrounding those pitches.[50] Nor, although a primary function of Guido's mnemonic system was to map out the space of the human voice from bottom to top, was it a coincidence that he developed it at almost exactly the same time that an author such as Pseudo-Odo (whose influence on Guido is documented by Guido himself) was pinning down the idea of mode theoretically as based on sequences of conjunct intervals.[51] To some extent, Guido's exercises are a direct outgrowth, an improvement, on modal intonations already common, which persisted alongside the new solmization. And certainly, by the Renaissance, theories of mode themselves had come to meet practical considerations halfway, emphasizing melodic formulas in practice as much or more than octave species.

Solmization may be the obvious case, but it is hard to find heuristic patterns of any kind, when formed into conjunct patterns, that are not inherently linked on some level with theoretical (and quasi-modal) ideas of octave species and related sets of available pitches; and conversely, it is hard to find well-theorized potential sets of pitches that do not manifest themselves often in conjunct, ordered motion as well. Thus, while it seems to be European functional tonality that spurred the fullest fusion of performed scales and theoretical scales into a single vocabulary word for each language (and indeed, while it seems that some aspects of this fusion, such as the existence of scale exercise books for instruments, were dependent not only on the history of tonality but on other specifics of European musical history such as the rise of instrumental virtuosi), similar principles connecting conjunct melodic sequences to available sets of pitches are—if often somewhat looser—extremely widespread.

One practical cause of this connection seems to be the layout of instruments. On any instruments that arrange pitched objects or keys in order of frequency, there will be a visual bridge between pitch and conjunct ordering. Surveying the instruments will give an image of a potential scale or scales. In Europe, the keyboard was likely an important link between pitches and a concrete visualization of a bottom-to-top "scala" diagram of the gamut.[52] But keyboards are only one example. There are several societies with a long tradition of using instruments laid out from bottom to top (such as various metallophones and even lithophones) that also have a long history of theoretical engagement with concepts akin to scales—and, furthermore, with questions of tuning and temperament. China is perhaps the most obvious example here. Arrangements of stone and metal chimes grew over time so that as early as the fifth century BCE, there were huge sets of chime bells arrayed visually from large to small, low to high, and simultaneously, there was extensive theorization of pentatonic modes, with functional properties, related to mathematic tuning systems that provided a fuller array of twelve pitches in an octave.[53] We can, of course move the "why" query to the next level: for some types of instruments, ease of physical construction may be the cause of such ordered layouts. It would, for example, be more difficult to build a wood-framed harp or keyboard instrument strung in a non-conjunct arrangement. On the other hand, such arrangements may in other cases be effect rather than cause: reed pipes, bells, and other objects can be placed in any order. Yet humans seem to prefer conjunct layouts, both visually and sonically, which brings us back to questions of the mind as root cause. Returning one final time to the psychology of music—that mediation between physical sounds and our perception of music that has been so important in studies of scales since Helmholtz and especially Stumpf—we find potential reasons for the close connections between conjunct runs and abstracted sets. Dmitri Tymoczko, in his formulation of "extended tonality" in European music, has noted that "scale-based melodies are easier to remember than non-scalar melodies" (2011, 6). By "scale-based melodies" he means, in context, melodies that draw on the set of notes contained in a theoretical scale. But the slippage implied—since "scale-based melodies" also seems to suggest stepwise motion—either intuitively conflates, or more likely intentionally invokes, another cornerstone of the extended tonality that Tymoczko links partly to basic human physiology and psychology: the "preference for conjunct melodic motion" (5). Many studies both before and after Tymoczko's book have noted as psychological trends the prevalence of conjunct motion in music and our partiality toward such small melodic intervals.[54] (Recall that Stumpf had claimed a century ago that "small steps are more suitable for melodic use.") Indeed, conjunct motion can even at times exert a stronger force in building musical systems than the intervals (such as the octave and fifth) that Stumpf himself and most other Western theorists presumed to be natural consonances, and thus building blocks for all scales. For instance, there appears to be some music built from tuning systems that are additive. Rather than filling in octaves and other larger intervals with small steps, each note is tuned primarily (or only) in relation to the closest pitches (Schneider 2001, 490; Voisin 1994, 89). The psychological pull of conjunct motion seems like a good place to stop when arguing for a basic and widespread connection between scalar runs and theoretical scales: we humans seem to like our abstract sets "ordered," and conversely, to create our theoretical sets from ordered motion.

We might, in conclusion, cement this observation of a general principle with an exception that helps to prove the rule. It is surely *possible* to divorce more fully the reasons why we practice scales as exercises from the sets of notes we draw on within a passage, a piece, or a full cultural system of music. Nevertheless, that something is possible does not imply that it is easy. To really find a strong example of conjunct motion expunged from the presentation of the pitch sets used in a piece, we need to turn to the atonal music of the twentieth century, and most particularly to music built on serial tone rows. These chromatic scales rendered as rows are notable in their attempt to overthrow traditional scalar/modal practice by using sets of pitches *only* as abstractions, by specifically rebuking predictable conjunct motion or formulas. Considered in this light, serial composition—despite initially invoking Beethovenian motivic principles to assert its place in history—was an artistic movement based on negation: in order not to condescend to the listener, as Schoenberg put it, a radically new musical language needed to be forged. If the clearest example we can find of a comprehensive separation between scales as sets of potential pitches and scales as conjunct motion is a reaction to the European theoretical and compositional history that most closely bound together those two ideas of scale in the first place (and a reaction that, speaking with historical hindsight, has not succeeded in subverting that system in the long run), then I would be skeptical of any claim that pitch sets can be *fully* separated from conjunct runs in any musical system. The vicissitudes of European music history have made "scale" a particularly multivalent term, but one that nevertheless overlaps with vocabulary for surprisingly similar ideas shared across most musical systems.

Acknowledgements

I would like to thank Eric Bianchi, Jesse Rodin, and J. Andrew Foster for their very helpful feedback.

Notes

1. Aldwell, Schachter, and Cadwallader 2011, 6. This formulation has been present in all editions of the textbook.
2. In recent editions of the textbook, co-authored by Mark DeVoto, the chromatic scale is introduced first, as the full set of pitches used in Western music, and then diatonic scales are introduced immediately afterward, including all versions of the minor scale (Piston and DeVoto 1978, 1–2).
3. Indeed, as such, it has been resisted in some particularly functional-theory-driven approaches. For example, Alfred Day in his controversial but influential *Treatise on Harmony*, first written in the 1840s, suggested that the only minor scale that should properly exist is the harmonic minor, since it is generated chordally, with all of its degrees provided by the pitches of the tonic, subdominant, and dominant chords (Day 1885, 8). Even Day, however, slides into a discussion of scalar melody, as he goes so far as to suggest that music really ought to proceed melodically from this pure, abstracted notion of scale, so that the stigma attached to augmented seconds should pass.
4. There are similarities to the ascending *arohana* and descending *avarohana* in Indian musical *ragas*, though the concept of a *raga* inherently covers partially different ground than the concept of a "scale." I will return to some cross-cultural considerations below.
5. Forte 1962, 2; the theme of the scherzo of Beethoven's "Archduke" trio is given as an example.
6. For an in-depth consideration of the relationship of medieval modal theory to theoretical (etic) scales (as octave species and fuller sets of potential pitches to draw on—what Cohen calls "background scale system"), see Cohen (2002), Atkinson (2009) and Susan McClary's chapter "Mode" in this volume.
7. Berger (2005, 67–77) discusses a variety of early mnemonic intonation formulas found in tonaries, and other similar aids for memorizing chants.
8. For a discussion of the interrelationship of these visualizations, see Berger (1981).
9. For an argument that hexachordal solmization was a "soft" heuristic device laid over theoretical modal sets (already conceived heptatonically), see Mengozzi (2010). For the strongest version of the claim, see pages 111–113.
10. Bach (1753, 24–33). Although Bach's is the more exhaustive treatment with regard specifically to scale patterns, there is some discussion of the fingering of scales (and its effect on comma differences in accidentals) in J. J. Quantz's well-known flute treatise of the year before as well. See Quantz (1752, 32–39). Fingerings for other instruments were explored at this time too: for instance, one 1760 guitar exposition and tutorial book includes fingering

for two scales (in the basic keys for guitars with special tunings in C and G, respectively). See Oswald (c. 1760). An important case of the term of "scala" labeling a diagram being used to apply hexachordal solmization to keyboard runs appears in Diruta's (1593) seminal organ treatise, *Il Transilvano* (Part I, 2v–3r). Diruta goes on to cover fingering of runs (motion by step [*grado*]), although he is concerned more in that discussion with adapting fingerings to the metrical positions of conjunct pitches than with the starting pitches or other fixed scale fingerings as such (see 6r–9v); in these ways, the eighteenth-century treatises show scale as a broader concept; for Diruta it remained linked to staff-based diagrams of the gamut (see discussion in following section).

11. One of the first most important was a section printing scales in all keys with fingerings in Clementi (c. 1801); Clementi notes that these "ought to be practised daily" (15). An early violin example would be Goodban (1813?), which contains scale-like "exercises on the gamut" (19) as well as scales included in lessons on individual keys (although here they often go beyond the tonic in each direction and circle back). By the 1830s and 1840s, there were more familiar full published books of "scales and exercises" by noted virtuosi for their respective instruments, such as those by the pianists J. B. Cramer and Henri Herz. The timing is similar in other languages. An important early continental collection is Baillot, Rode, and Kreutzer (c. 1803), which includes many exercises on the "gammes" of different keys in different positions. One of the early keyboard scale publications on the Continent was Diabelli (c. 1818).

12. Several different words from ancient Greek have been translated into English as "scale." Take for example the "Harmonic Introduction" treatise of Cleonides, relatively influential later (as it was also translated by Georgio Valla into Latin in 1497). In modern English translations, various words used in this treatise (as in Aristides and other ancient Greek writings) may be rendered as "scale." Thomas Mathiesen's translation in Strunk's *Source Readings* consistently gives as "scale" Cleonides's "σύστημα" (*systema*) (Cleonides 1998, 36ff.), though several other words might indicate similar principles in Greek writing before and during Cleonides's time, such as ἁρμονία (*armonia*), οἱ συνεχεῖς (the *synekis*), and τόνος (*tonos*) (see Solomon 1980, 189, 204, 330; Solomon's own translation of *systema* is "system," 145ff). Exactly which aspects of our term "scale" are embodied in each of these terms and for which writers is subtle, and remains a matter of scholarly debate. (Valla himself translates the Greek *systema* as systema in Latin [Cleonides 1497, unpaginated, first page of translation].) For an in-depth look at the legacy of Greek scale theory in the early Middle Ages, see Atkinson (2009), especially Chapter 1. Meanwhile, the modern Greek word for scale, κλίμακα, draws on a different root (the ladder or step etymology we will see below in English and other languages), and operates more in the double sense we expect today.

13. See O.E.D., s.v. Gamut, esp. this example from 1562: "An easie and moste playne way and rule, of the order of the Notes and Kayes of singing, whiche commonly is called the scale of Musicke, or the Gamma vt" (T. Sternhold & J. Hopkins *Whole Bk. Psalmes* sig. ✠.ii). NB that spellings of "gamut" remained unstandardized for a very long time, probably partly due to the fact that it is a single word that derives from two words in the original Latin theorization.

14. Morley (1597, 3 and 7). "Why then was your Scale deuised of xx notes and no more? . . . Because that compasse was the reach of most voyces: so that vnder *Gam vt* the voice seemed as a kinde of humming, and aboue *E la* a kinde of constrained shrieking," (7). Morley discusses modal theory ("ancient *modi*") only briefly and much later (147–149).

15. For an in-depth discussion of this historical development, see Taddie (1984, 32, 44–115, 136). See also Berger (1981, 112–115).

16. In French, *échelle* and *gamme* have sometimes been interchangeable as well but can have a more fraught relationship: it is counterintuitive (given the etymologies) that in French, gamme most often specifically indicates an ordered collection, whereas échelle can sometimes be applied more to a modal or other pitch-class collection in *un*ordered form.

17. For a brief summary of different versions of this expansion, see Lange (1900, 573–598).

18. Campion here named and solidified his theorizing as the "rule of the octave," versions of which would become common in French and Italian theory at the time. See also Lester (2002, 756–757) and Christensen (1993, 49–51).

19. Sauveur (1701) used the term "système" to indicate ordered collections of possible pitches in different contexts. He also, briefly, considered "the Oriental system" in relation to Western tunings, a type of juxtaposition that would become commonplace among theorists half a century later.

20. Rameau's focus here is on the "triple progression," or stacked pitches whose fundamental frequencies are each three times greater than the previous pitch, generating twelfths (seen as fifths) that build an anhemitonic pentatonic scale with the first five terms, and then might fill in all twelve pitches of a chromatic scale, though with tuning problems. See Rameau (1760, 189–193).

21. Burney (1776–89, 1:37–41). On Roussier, Burney, and this general development, see Gelbart (2007, 120–128).

22. This distinction is noted at the start of the article by Matras (1958–1961, 2:211) on "gamme" as well. Some theorists have sought to disentangle more clearly the two concepts, or similar ones. For example, Dmitri Tymoczko has termed the complete collection of pitches available in a system (or, in his case, more properly within a piece) "macroharmony," distinguishing this from scales that are chosen subsets of this (although they can also be the entire macroharmony in many cases). For Tymoczko, scales proper are subsets of the macroharmony used for choosing melodic notes within specific portions of pieces and in which the stepwise ordering of the pitches, as opposed to acoustic ratios, is the central way of determining their intervallic "distance" from each other. See Tymoczko (2011, 15, 121). A more complex breakdown of types of scale collection can be found in Dowling (1982).

23. Note for example the presentation in the Piston and DeVoto (1978) textbook (see note 2 above).

24. The idea that semitone intervals were hard to sing (and this was the reason why "older" scales had gaps, or flat sevenths, or both) is also found in Burney (1776–1789, 2:21), and in the writing of other early speculative theorists on scale development and singing, for example in Thomson (1822–23, 7).

25. See Gelbart (2007, 147–152); also Gelbart and Rehding (2011, 140–164). Versions of such evolutionary theories (applied to Western scales or beyond) are still in circulation in various reference books; see, for example, Clemens Kühn's article on "Tonleiter" in Metzler (2005, 4:531).

26. Helmholtz (1877, 385–599); translated as Helmholtz (1954, 234–371). On reasons for why scales "expanded" from five-note anhemitonic to the "complete" seven-note scale, see especially Helmholtz (1954, 256–258; 1877, 424–427).

27. On this, see Steege (2012), esp. Chapter 5.

28. A seminal study of this effect is Perlman and Krumhansl (1996).

29. Carl Stumpf had collaborated with the anthropologist Franz Boas and Boas had already noted how transcriptions (even in language) were subject to misperception based on interpretation, an idea that influenced Stumpf's emphasis on an etic, compartmentalized approach to data. See Ellingson (1992, 118–119).

30. See Riemann (1916, v–vi, 112) and Rehding (2003, 179–180). Note that even Stumpf himself had been keenly aware of the psychological aspects of hearing pitch, observing at one point that "hearing complies not with the permanence of instruments, but with that of the instruments of audition" (Stumpf 2012, 53).

31. This is why even the most advanced machine transcriptions can overwhelm with detail and yet fail to capture (at least alone) what is heard in music. On this dilemma, see Ellingson (1992, 134–135).

32. Helmholtz (1954, 235; 1877, 386). Indeed, other earlier writers, such as Fétis, had already considered—or even obsessed about—the "metaphysical" factors that overrode natural laws in determining scales and scale preferences. See Fétis (1834, 27) or much of Fétis (1869).

33. See Burns (1999, 222–226); one well-known application is in Narmour (1990, 78–81, 153–154, 283–325).

34. Arom, Léothaud, and Voisin (1997, 10) seem to echo Riemann in many ways when they point out the problem with digital measurements and assert that "In research into musical scales, it is the concept of *perceived pitch* which should be the aim of all measurement processes, and not the frequency." See also Perlman and Krumhansl (1996), Agmon (1993), and Rytis (2004).

35. Accounts of this phenomenon go back to the sixteenth century, and repeated into a growing legend. See Bianchi (2011, Chapter 5).

36. Clark and Rehding (2001, 2–4) invoke Kircher's claims about the sloth as an example of how our ears hear in the terms they are culturally determined to accept as natural and rudimentary. Bianchi notes that by the time Rousseau was treating the sloth, he had substituted for the hexachord a seven-note scale, showing again the same phenomenon of adapting what we encounter to our cultural understanding of pitch ordering (2011, 218).

37. As Irving (2012) has argued, we should keep this in mind when we consider how Europeans heard and transcribed non-equal-tempered music from beyond their own continent.

38. Seventeenth- and eighteenth-century theorists debated temperaments, and some theorists even considered different temperaments under the rubric of scale, occasionally going so far as to label them different subtypes of diatonic scale on a technical level (see Taddie 1984, 157, 180–182, 196–199, for a good summary here). Nevertheless, these were generally technical adjustments within a shared, determining theoretical system (and adjustments that admittedly pertained only in some settings, primarily with regard to fixed-pitch instruments such as keyboards). This is rather different from nineteenth-century engagements with tunings and microtones as semantically divergent and culturally determined scales.

39. Even after well-tempered tuning had become the standard, it was by no means uncontested. Helmholtz, John Curwen, Alfred Day, and others were all strong proponents of just intonation.

40. See for example Voisin (1994) and Rowell (2000, 153–154). Indeed, in a set of conclusions that have in some ways built on Helmholtz's considerations of timbre and overtones as related to pitch perception, scholars have argued (by using spectral analysis) that conceiving of pitch as single "points" is only one way to understand the sounds we hear, a reductionist approach. See for example Schneider (2001, 496). On the way we learn

psychoacoustically to hear single "virtual" or "residue" pitches from an input of complex tones, see Terhardt (1972) and (1974). This process results in such psychoacoustic phenomena as "stretched" scales as well.

41. This scale has been studied with particular interest by generations of comparative musicologists and ethnomusicologists. On variability, see for example Kunst (1973, 68 and 75–76).

42. This is not a new concept. A famous example positing scale degrees as phonemes is Nicholas Ruwet's (1959) critique of post-Webernian serialism; Ruwet's analogy was partly rebutted in a response by Henri Pousseur (1959, 107). Both articles appeared in English in *Die Reihe* in 1964. A more recent if more abstracted engagement with the pitch as phoneme metaphor can be found in Brown (2001). See also Houghton (1984, 39–40, 76).

43. This section of this article draws on an unpublished response I presented to an AMS panel on transcription in 2012 in New Orleans. I see the idea of allophones in scales as becoming particularly pressing in questions of transcription.

44. See for example Schreuder, Eerten, and Gilbers (2006) for an application of the idea to pitched speech contours. Houghton (1984, 46–53) also considers allophonic pitches and scale degrees.

45. See Nettl (1958, 38–39). See also Bright (1963). These are further discussed and applied in Monelle (1992).

46. See Osmond-Smith (1974, 282–283). It may be more analogous to think of Nettl's example as allomorphic rather than allophonic.

47. One of the likely psychological underpinnings for the preponderance of scales with five to seven pitches is "Miller's law," which suggests that human cognition can hold about seven distinct objects in working memory at a time. See Miller (1956). Miller included pitch perception in his original paper and his findings are invoked in music cognition literature, though most often not to outline new experiments but by way of explanation for existing experimental results and cultural phenomena such as scales.

48. The most influential refutation from the angle of cognitive testing is Jairazbhoy and Stone (1963). See also Kendall and Carterette (1996, 92, 97) for relation of these results to Miller's law (see previous note).

49. Some scholars have gone as far as denying that the old microtonal theory of *srutis* has any relevance in practice; see Powers et al. (2001), "India," §III, 1, (iv) (12:178) in *New Grove* for a brief summary (Richard Widdess revised this section of Powers's original 1980 entry). Others have attempted to consider *srutis* as an addendum justifying or inflecting certain definitions of five-, six-, or seven-note *ragas* and their parent scales (*thaats/melakartas*); see e.g. Mukhopādhyāya (2004, 29, 344–366, 374–375).

50. Powers et al. (2001, 16:790–91 §II, 3, (ii), b and §II, 4, (i)). Frans Wiering revised this section of Powers's original 1980 entry for the 2001 edition.

51. As Cohen notes, this idea can be seen as a further extension of what Hucbald had called "socialitas" (2002, 323, 326, 347).

52. Urquhart (1988, 157–160). I am grateful to Jesse Rodin for drawing my attention to this work.

53. On the early lithophones and metallophones and their tunings, see Tong (1983–1984) and Falkenhausen (1993). Note that Bronze Age Chinese bells evolved to have two different pitches, depending on how they were struck, but the overall ordering by size maintained a scale-like visual arrangement even in these more complicated cases. The mathematical study of tuning and equal temperament reached its greatest heights in

China simultaneously with similar derivations in Europe, around the end of the sixteenth century. See Kuttner (1975).

54. Leonard Meyer (1956, 132–134), for example, considered the idea of "structural gaps," in which melodies may create tension (especially when ascending) by skipping conjunct notes of a scale; the sense of desire formed here is resolved when the gaps are filled in by conjunct motion, especially on the descent. Strikingly, after noting examples from different traditions, he related this phenomenon to historical trends toward filling in "gapped scales"—thus tying the persistent historical narrative we have discussed as a product of the Enlightenment to his psychological approach to music (and even citing Yasser, etc.). The "structural gaps" aspect of Meyer's thesis was used as the basis of more recent experiments by Vos and Troost (1989), who confirmed his beliefs about a drive toward conjunct movement. An interesting corollary (within a clearly tonal setting) is Anta (2013). Other recent studies about proclivities for and perceptions of conjunct movement include Dowling (1984) and Bregman (1990, 461–466); Narmour (1990, 283–325) uses his discussion of scaling to consider reasons why we prefer process continuation (i.e., scale-like melodic motion) when we encounter small intervals.

WORKS CITED

Agmon, Eytan. 1993. "Towards a Theory of Diatonic Intonation." *Interface: Journal of New Music Research* 22: 151–163.

Aldwell, Edward, Carl Schachter, and Allen Cadwallader. 2011. *Harmony and Voice Leading*, 4th edition. Boston: Cengage.

Anta, Juan Fernando. 2013. "Exploring the Influence of Pitch Proximity on Listener's [*sic*] Melodic Expectations." *Psychomusicology* 23: 151–167.

Arom, Simha, Gilles Léothaud, and Frédéric Voisin. 1997. "Experimental Ethnomusicology: An Interactive Approach to the Study of Musical Scales." In *Perception and Cognition of Music*, edited by Irène Deliège and John Sloboda, 3–30. Hove: Psychology Press.

Atkinson, Charles. 2009. *The Critical Nexus: Tone-System, Mode, and Notation in Early Medieval Music*. New York: Oxford University Press.

Bach, Carl Philipp Emanuel. 1753. *Versuch über die wahre Art, das Klavier zu spielen*, part 1. Berlin: Printed for the Author.

Baillot, Pierre, Pierre Rode, and Rodolphe Kreutzer. c. 1803. *Méthode de violon rédigée par le citoyen Baillot. Adoptée par le Conservatoire pour servir à l'étude dans cet établissement.* Paris: Magasin de musique.

Berger, Anna Maria Busse. 2005. *Medieval Music and the Art of Memory*. Berkeley: University of California Press.

Berger, Karol. 1981. "The Hand and the Art of Memory." *Musica Disciplina* 35: 87–120.

Bianchi, Eric. 2011. "Prodigious Sounds: Music and Learning in the World of Athanasius Kircher." PhD diss., Yale University.

Bregman, Albert. 1990. *Auditory Scene Analysis: The Perceptual Organization of Sound*. Cambridge, MA: MIT Press.

Bright, William. 1963. "Language and Music: Areas for Cooperation." *Ethnomusicology* 7: 26–32.

Brown, Steven. 2001. "The 'Musilanguage' Model of Music Evolution." In *The Origins of Music*, edited by Nils L. Wallin et al., 271–300. Cambridge, MA: MIT Press.

Burney, Charles. 1776–1789. *General History of Music*. 4 vols. London: Printed for the Author.

Burns, Edward M. 1999. "Intervals, Scales, and Tuning." In *The Psychology of Music*, edited by Diana Deutsch, 215–264. 2nd edition. San Diego: Academic Press.

Campion, François. 1716. *Traité d'accompagnement et de composition selon la règle des octaves de musique*. Paris: Chez la Veuve Adam, etc.

Christensen, Thomas. 1993. *Rameau and Musical Thought in the Englightenment*. Cambridge: Cambridge University Press.

Clark, Suzannah, and Alexander Rehding. 2001. "Introduction." In *Music Theory and Natural Order from the Renaissance to the Early Twentieth Century*, edited by Suzannah Clark and Alexander Rehding, 1–13. Cambridge: Cambridge University Press.

Clementi, Muzio. c. 1801. *Clementi's Introduction to the Art of Playing on the Piano Forte*. London: Clementi, etc.

Cleonides. 1497. "Harmonicum introductorium." Translated by Georgio Valla. Venice: Simone Bevilacqua.

Cleonides. 1998. "Harmonic Introduction." Translated by Thomas Mathiesen. In *Strunk's Source Readings in Music History*, edited by Oliver Strunk and Leo Treitler, 35–46. New York: Norton.

Cohen, David E. 2002. "Notes, Scales, and Modes in the Earlier Middle Ages." In *The Cambridge History of Western Music Theory*, edited by Thomas Christensen, 305–363. Cambridge: Cambridge University Press.

Curwen, John. 1872. *The Standard Course of Lessons and Exercises in the Tonic Sol-fa Method of Teaching Music*. New ed. London: Tonic Sol-fa Agency.

Day, Alfred. 1885. *Alfred Day's Treatise on Harmony*. Edited by G. A. MacFarren. London: Harrison and Sons.

Diabelli, Anton. c. 1818. *Scalen-Sonate für das Piano-Forte: zur nützlichen und dabey angenehmen Tonleiter-Uebung, so sowohl für angehende, als auch geübtere Clavier-Spieler*. Vienna: Diabelli.

Diruta, Girolamo. 1593. *Il Transilvano: Diolago sopra il vero modo di sonar organi*. Part I. Venice: Giacomo Vincenti.

Dowling, W. Jay. 1982. "Musical Scales and Psychophysical Scales: Their Psychological Reality." In *Cross-Cultural Perspectives on Music*, edited by Timothy Rice and Robert Falck, 20–28. Toronto: University of Toronto Press.

Dowling, W. Jay. 1984. "Musical Experience and Tonal Scales In the Recognition of Octave-Scrambled Melodies." *Psychomusicology* 4: 13–32.

Ellingson, Ter. 1992. "Transcription." In *Ethnomusicology: An Introduction*, edited by Helen Myers, 110–152. New York: Norton.

Ellis, Alexander. 1885. "On the Musical Scales of Various Nations." *Journal of the Society of Arts* 33: 485–527.

Encyclopaedia Britannica. 1778–1784. Second edition. Edinburgh: J. Balfour et al.

Encyclopaedia Britannica. 1820–1823. Sixth edition. Edinburgh: A Constable & Co.

Falkenhausen von, Lothar. 1993. *Suspended Music: Chime Bells in the Culture of Bronze-Age China*. Berkeley: University of California Press.

Fétis, François-Joseph. 1834. *La musique mise à la portée de tout le monde*. Paris: Paulin.

Fétis, François-Joseph. 1869. *Histoire générale de la musique, depuis le temps les plus anciens, jusqu'à nos jous*. Paris: Didot.

Forte, Allen. 1962. *Tonal Harmony*. New York: Holt, Rinehart and Winston.

Franklin, Benjamin. 1968–. *The Papers of Benjamin Franklin*. Edited by Leonard W. Labaree. New Haven, CT: Yale University Press.

Gelbart, Matthew. 2007. *The Invention of "Folk Music" and "Art Music": Emerging Categories from Ossian to Wagner*. Cambridge: Cambridge University Press.

Gelbart, Matthew, and Alexander Rehding. 2011. "Riemann and Melodic Analysis: Studies in Folk-Musical Tonality." In *The Oxford Handbook of Neo-Riemannian Music Theories*, edited by Edward Gollin and Alexander Rehding, 140–164. New York: Oxford University Press.

Goodban, Thomas. 1813?. *A New and Complete Guide to the Art of Playing on the Violin: Containing a Comprehensive Treatise on the* . . . *Formation of the Different Scales &c.* . . . *with Particular Instructions on Bowing, Fingering, & Shifting*. London: Preston.

Guido of Arezzo. 1998. "*Epistola de ignoto cantu*." Translated by Martin Gerbert as "Epistle Concerning an Unknown Chant," in *Strunk's Source Readings in Music History*, edited by Leo Treitler, 214–218. New York: Norton.

Helmholtz, Hermann von. 1877. *Die Lehre von den Tonempfindungen, als physiologische Grundlage für die Theorie der Musik*. 4th edition. Brauschweig: Vieweg and Son.

Helmholtz, Hermann von. 1954. *On the Sensations of Tone as a Physiological Basis for the Theory of Music* [1885]. Translated by Alexander Ellis. 2nd English edition. London: Longmans, Green. Reprint edition. New York: Dover Publications.

Hornbostel, Erich von. 1913. "Melodie und Skala." Publication of the *Jahrbuch der Musikbibliothek Peters*. Leipzig: C. F. Peters.

Houghton, Catherine. 1984. "Structure in Language and Music: A Linguistic Approach." PhD diss., Stanford University.

Irving, David R. M. 2012. "Cross-Cultural Transcriptions and Encounters of Scale Systems in the Eighteenth Century." Paper presented at the Annual Meeting of the American Musicological Society, New Orleans.

Jairazbhoy, Nazir A., and A. W. Stone. 1963. "Intonation in Present-Day North Indian Classical Music." *Bulletin of the School of Oriental and African Studies* 26: 119–132.

Kendall, Roger A., and Edward C. Carterette. 1996. "Music Perception and Cognition." In *Cognitive Ecology*, edited by Morton P. Friedman and Edward C. Carterette, 87–149. San Diego: Academic Press.

Kunst, Jaap. 1973. *Music in Java*. 3rd edition. The Hague: Martinus Nijhoff.

Kuttner, Fritz. 1975. "Prince Chu Tsai-Yü's Life and Work: A Re-Evaluation of His Contribution to Equal Temperament Theory." *Ethnomusicology* 19: 163–206.

Lange, Georg. 1900. "Zur Geschichte der Solmisation." *Sammelbände der Internationalen Musikgesellschaft* 1: 535–622.

Lester, Joel. 2002. "Rameau and Eighteenth-Century Harmonic Theory." In *The Cambridge History of Western Music Theory*, edited by Thomas Christensen, 753–777. Cambridge: Cambridge University Press.

Matras, Jean. 1958–1961. "Gamme." In *Encyclopédie de la musique*. Paris: Fasquelle.

Maugars, André. 2007. *Response faite à un curieux sur le sentiment de la musique d'Italie* [1639], Translated by Walter H. Bishop. In *Music in the Western World: A History in Documents*, edited by Richard Taruskin and Piero Weiss, 165–168. Boston: Cengage.

Mengozzi, Stefano. 2010. *The Renaissance Reform of Medieval Music Theory: Guido of Arezzo between Myth and History*. Cambridge: Cambridge University Press.

Metzler's *Musiklexikon*. 2005. 2nd edition, 4 vols. Stuttgart and Weimar: Metzler.

Meyer, Leonard. 1956. *Emotion and Meaning in Music*. Chicago: University of Chicago Press.

Miller, George A. 1956. "The Magical Number Seven, Plus or Minus Two: Some Limits on Our Capacity for Processing Information." *Psychological Review* 63: 81–97.

Monelle, Raymond. 1992. *Linguistics and Semiotics in Music*. Abingdon: Harwood Academic.

Morley, Thomas. 1597. *Plaine and Easie Introduction to Practicall Muisicke*. London: Peter Short.

Mukhopādhyāya, Prthvīndranātha. 2004. *The Scales of Indian Music: A Cognitive Approach to Thāṭ/Mēḷakartā*. New Delhi: Aryan.

Narmour, Eugene. 1990. *The Analysis and Cognition of Basic Melodic Structures: The Implication-Realization Model*. Chicago: University of Chicago Press.

Nettl, Bruno. 1958. "Some Linguistic Approaches to Musical Analysis." *Journal of the International Folk Music Council* 10: 37–41.

O.E.D. *The Oxford English Dictionary*. oed.com.

Osmond-Smith, David. 1974. "Problems of Terminology and Method in the Semiotics of Music." *Semiotica* 11: 269–294.

Oswald, James. c. 1760. *A Compleat Tutor for the Guittar: With two Scales Shewing the Method of Playing in the Keys of C & G*. London: Oswald.

Perlman, Marc, and Carol L. Krumhansl. 1996. "An Experimental Study of Internal Interval Standards in Javanese and Western Musicians." *Music Perception* 14: 95–116.

Piston, Walter. 1941. *Harmony*. New York: Norton.

Piston, Walter, and Mark DeVoto. 1978. *Harmony*. New York: Norton.

Pousseur, Henri. 1959. "Forme et pratique musicales." *Revue Belge de Musicologie* 13: 98–116.

Powers, Harold, et al. 2001. "Mode [1980]." In *The New Grove Dictionary of Music and Musicians*, edited by Stanley Sadie and John Tyrell. New York: Oxford University Press.

Quantz, Johann Joachim. 1752. *Versuch einer Anweisung die Flöte traversiere zu spielen*. Berlin: Voss.

Rameau, Jean-Philippe. 1722. *Traité de l'harmonie: Reduite à ses principes naturels*. Paris: Ballard.

Rameau, Jean-Philippe. 1760. *Code de musique pratique*. Paris: de l'imprimerie Royale.

Rehding, Alexander. 2003. *Hugo Riemann and the Birth of Modern Musical Thought*. Cambridge: Cambridge University Press.

Riemann, Hugo. 1916. *Folkloristische Tonalitätsstudien*. Leipzig: Breitkopf and Härtel.

Rowell, Lewis. 2000. "Scale and Mode in the Music of the Early Tamils of South India." *Music Theory Spectrum* 22: 135–156.

Ruwet, Nicholas. 1959. "Contradictions du langage sériel." *Revue Belge de Musicologie* 13: 83–97.

Rytis, Ambrazevičius. 2004. "Scales in Traditional Solo Singing." In *Proceedings of the Conference on Interdisciplinary Musicology*, edited by Richard Parncutt, Annekatrin Kessler, and Fränk Zimmer, 1–5. Austria: University of Graz.

Sauveur, Joseph. 1701. *Principes d'acoustique et de musique, ou systême general des intervalles des sons*. Paris: Académie Royale.

Schneider, Albrecht. 2001. "Sound, Pitch, and Scale: From 'Tone Measurements' to Sonological Analysis in Ethnomusicology." *Ethnomusicology* 45: 489–519.

Scholes, Percy, Judith Nagley, and Nicholas Temperley. 2018. "Scale." In *The Oxford Companion to Music*. http://www.oxfordmusiconline.com/subscriber/article/opr/t114/e5921?q=scale&search=quick&pos=2&_start=1#firsthit. Accessed on January 1.

Schreuder, Maartje, Laura van Eerten, and Dicky Gilbers. 2006. "Music as a Method of Identifying Emotional Speech." In *5th International Conference on Language Resources and Evaluation, Workshop Proceedings*, edited by Laurence Devillers, 55–59. Genoa: European Language Resources Association.

Solomon, Jon. 1980. "Cleonides: Εἰσαγωγὴ ἁρμονική; Critical Edition, Translation, and Commentary." PhD diss., University of North Carolina at Chapel Hill.

Steege, Benjamin. 2012. *Helmholtz and the Modern Listener*. Cambridge: Cambridge University Press.

Stumpf, Carl. 2012. *Die Anfänge der Musik* [1911]. Leipzig: Johann Ambosius Barth. Translated by David Trippett as *The Origins of Music*. New York: Oxford University Press.

Taddie, Daniel. 1984. "Scale: An Historical Study of Musical Terminology and Concepts." PhD diss., University of Iowa.

Terhardt, Ernst. 1972. "Zur Tonhöhenwahrnehmung von Klängen," parts I and II. *Acustica* 26: 173–199.

Terhardt, Ernst. 1974. "Pitch, Consonance and Harmony." *Journal of the Acoustical Society of America* 55: 1061–1069.

Thomson, George. 1822–1823. "Dissertation Concerning the National Melodies of Scotland." In *Select Melodies of Scotland, Interspersed with those of Ireland and Wales*. London and Edinburgh: George Thomson.

Tong, Kin-woon. 1983–1984. "Shang Musical Instruments." *Asian Music* 14, no. 2: 17–182; 15, no. 1: 103–184; 15, no. 2: 68–143.

Tymoczko, Dmitiri. 2011. *A Geometry of Music: Harmony and Counterpoint in the Extended Common Practice*. New York: Oxford University Press.

Urquhart, Peter. 1988. "Canon, Partial Signatures, and 'Musica Ficta' in Works by Josquin DesPrez and His Contemporaries." PhD diss., Harvard University.

Voisin, Frédéric. 1994. "Musical Scales in Central Africa and Java: Modeling by Synthesis." *Leonardo Music Journal* 4: 85–90.

Vos, Piet, and Jim Troost. 1989. "Ascending and Descending Melodic Intervals: Statistical Findings and Their Perceptual Relevance." *Music Perception* 6: 383–396.

CHAPTER 5

···

TONIC

···

STEVEN RINGS

CRITERIA FOR TONICITY

BEGIN by listening to ⊙ Audio Example 5.1, a passage for solo cello that lasts about one and a half minutes. Much of the passage consists of the laconic, almost mechanical repetition of a single pitch: the D below middle C (i.e. D3). Its tic-toc reiterations are interrupted by unpredictable gestures that skitter and slide across registers, saturating chromatic space. Then, just as unpredictably, the tic-toc D3 returns. A question arises: Is the repeated D a tonic?

Few readers will likely answer with an unqualified "yes." But it is worth noting that the sheer prevalence of the D—it persists unaccompanied for about one-third of the excerpt's total duration—as well as its extreme salience compared to the other pitches in the excerpt, elevate it to at least *potential* tonic status in certain theories of tonal perception. Carol Krumhansl, for example, writes that

> [t]he means of emphasizing the tonic and organizing the other elements around it vary considerably across musical styles. In most cases, the tonic is emphasized both melodically and rhythmically; it is sounded with relative frequency and with longer duration; and it tends to appear near the beginning and end of major phrase boundaries and at points of rhythmic stress. (1990, 16)

The D3 in our excerpt emphatically satisfies Krumhansl's second criterion: it "sounds with relative frequency and with longer duration" than any other pitch class in the passage.[1] It is also emphasized rhythmically, via its insistent repetition. This repetition arguably lends it "rhythmic stress" as well, though whether it receives any *metric* stress (which Krumhansl might be implying) is an open question: it is not clear if the concept of meter, in any traditional sense, is relevant for this passage.[2] The categories of melody and phrase are similarly problematic, making it difficult to say whether the D receives melodic emphasis or occurs "near the beginning and end of major phrase boundaries."

If anything, it is melodically emphasized through negation: its flat pitch contour stands in stark contrast to the extravagant profiles of the surrounding music (glissandi and all). As for phrase boundaries, the non-sequitur interruptions of the passage problematize the entire concept of phrase, to say nothing of its often-attendant notion of cadence. The returns of D seem to signal boundaries of *some* kind but they have no evident logic, or predictive relationship with what precedes and follows.

Indeed, the music's many jump cuts throw into doubt the relationship between the flush-juxtaposed materials—between the laconically ticking D and the capricious gestures it abuts. The lack of conspicuous tonal threads between the reiterated D and its surroundings may well be the biggest hurdle for listeners who are asked to assign D tonic status.[3] As if to highlight fact, the composer gives the repeated D3 the marking *indifferente* at each of its appearances in the score. Whatever the relationship of a tonic to the other pitches in a passage, surely it cannot be "indifferent." Conversely, non-tonic pitches should not be "indifferent" to it. Rather, the very idea of a tonic seems to assume some sort of heedful relationship between tonic and non-tonic. To be a tonic is to *matter* somehow to non-tonic pitches. Krumhansl suggests as much when she notes that the other pitch elements should be "organized around" the tonic; there is arguably no such organization at work in the passage in question, at least none that is aurally perspicuous upon listening without the score.

The music's radically simplified pitch hierarchy further attenuates any residual tonic effects. D is clearly elevated hierarchically above the other pitch classes in the passage (as a result of its salience and duration), but there are no evident hierarchical distinctions among the remaining 11 pitch classes. As a result, the pitch hierarchy of the passage is like a highly distorted Chicago skyline: a field of low-rise buildings with one soaring Willis Tower (*née* Sears) in their midst. See Figure 5.1. By contrast,

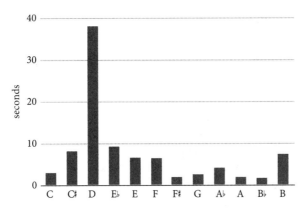

FIGURE 5.1 Pitch-class distribution in ▶ audio example 5.1. Values were determined by measuring pitch durations using Sonic Visualiser, in coordination with the score. Rests are included in the duration of the previous pitch. Glissandi are ignored and microtonal pitches are adjusted to the nearest equal-tempered pitch (per the performer's intonation).

most theories of pitch distribution in tonal music posit pitch hierarchies that look more like the *actual* Chicago skyline, with the twelve pitch classes projecting various building heights based on their statistical prevalence. (We will see examples of such hierarchies later in Figure 5.4.) The Willis Tower in such tonal profiles is still the tallest, but Trump Tower and the Aon Center are a close second and third, not unlike $\hat{3}$ and $\hat{5}$ in traditional common-practice pitch hierarchies. Such a robustly textured hierarchy creates a multitiered sonic environment in which various characteristic relationships can emerge: some pitch classes may be perceived as "close" to the tonic and others "far" (to draw on a familiar distance metaphor); some may seem more "stable" or "at rest" than others (also familiar metaphors); and so on.[4] In addition to the rhetorical disjunctions in the passage, the relative hierarchical "flatness" of the eleven non-D pitch classes[5] frustrates attempts to hear these sorts of characteristic relationships between D and non-D as the passage unfolds. A hierarchical pitch profile would thus seem a necessary condition for the emergence of a tonic, as the absence of such a profile challenges our ability to relate the non-tonic pitch classes to the tonic in a variety of characteristic and meaningful ways.

Finally, some may object to assigning D tonic status on stylistic grounds, arguing that the music that falls between the repeated Ds is clearly coded as "atonal," not only in its pitch content but in its gestural language. These readers may even recognize the piece: it is the opening of Witold Lutosławski's Cello Concerto, composed in 1969–1970.[6] Surely, the argument might go, it is inappropriate to listen for a tonic in such an atonal work. This objection differs from the previous ones. It is based not primarily on a phenomenological argument but on a stylistic one: this is music in which the concept of "tonic" is historically problematic or, to put it more dialectically, in which the idea of tonic continues to exert its influence, but negatively, through a strategic disavowal. Any local tonic effects that remain invite various interpretive responses, among them psychoanalytic readings.[7] Less philosophically inclined interpreters—perhaps of a more music-theoretical bent—might simply assert that, given the surrounding "atonal" pitch structures, any emphasized pitches are not "true" tonics but fleeting epiphenomena.[8] This view is often supported by theoretical commitments regarding what kinds of musical systems can support and sustain tonics in the first place. At one extreme, only art music of the common-practice era and closely related Western vernacular traditions—"tonal music" in the most conventional sense—can contain tonics properly so-called. Some ethnomusicologists may also wish to limit the concepts of "tonic" and "tonality" to these bourgeois European musical traditions but for different reasons: to avoid colonializing discourses and defer to more emic terminology for non-Western musics. At the other extreme—liberal in a different sense—the idea of tonic can be extended to a wide range of world musics in which a single pitch class predominates, from drones in Indian *ragas* to concluding gongs in Javanese gamelan. Indeed, Krumhansl (1990, 16) adduces both of these as examples of world musics that exhibit "tonics," broadly conceived.[9] In such a view, genuine modernist atonality is a singular exception among the musics of the world.

A General Definition

We have seemingly begun at an angle to our main subject, with an oblique example from Lutosławski. But the discussion has in fact brought into focus several primitives about "tonicness." We can even venture a basic definition:

DEFINITION: A *tonic* is

(a) a focal pitch class

(b) with respect to which all remaining pitch classes in some musical passage are hierarchically arranged and perceived

(c) even in its acoustic absence.

If the D in the Lutosławski fails as a tonic, it does so because of (b) and (c), however much it might momentarily satisfy (a).[10]

The adjective "focal" in (a) takes its inspiration from Donald Francis Tovey's memorable simile that a tonic is "like the point of view, or the vanishing point, of a picture" (1949, 134). One often reads of the tonic as a "center," or a "central" pitch class; Tovey's simile captures the spirit of such spatial metaphors but has the additional advantage of indexing an action: the orienting of aural attention in a particular direction.[11] Such an act of aural directing situates the non-tonic pitch classes with respect to the tonic focal point, just as a vanishing point orients peripheral elements in visual perspective. While D in the Lutosławski trivially acts as a focal pitch class during the passages of "indifferent" repetition, its all-but-complete disappearance as orienting presence in the rhapsodic sections vitiates whatever tonic potential it had when sounding alone. We never have an opportunity to fill out the sonic picture, so to speak—to experience the other pitch classes arrayed about the focal D. We instead hear an isolated singularity followed by stochastic scatter.

That the tonic is a *pitch class* might initially seem uncontroversial, but two clarifications are in order. First, the word *tonic* is also a common adjective for chords and keys: we refer to the "tonic chord" within a key, or to the "tonic key" within a musical work that modulates.[12] But it should be clear that these uses depend on and extend the basic pitch-class definition. For one, the tonic pitch class is contained within the tonic chord (as root) and key (as first scale degree). We might say, after Daniel Harrison (1994, 50), that the tonic pitch class "transfers its franchise" to its embedding chord and key. Alternatively, we can observe that the tonic chord and key merit their labels by analogy to the tonic pitch class: they behave in their respective harmonic and modulatory environments more or less as the tonic pitch class does in its local diatonic world. Given the reciprocal part–whole logic of the relationship between tonic pitch class and its eponymous key and chord, we might refer to the latter as "tonics by synecdoche."

Second, the tonic's status as a pitch *class,* rather than a single pitch, should be clear on reflection. If one pitch D acts as a tonic, all Ds, in any register, should as well. Tonicness is thus a perceptual property that inheres in a pitch-class *chroma,* not in a single pitch.[13]

(Again, the pitch specificity of the reiterated D3 in the Lutosławski tells against its tonic potential.) By extension, non-tonics are also pitch classes. Note, however, that part (b) does not refer to the *eleven* remaining pitch classes, for in most notated tonal traditions (especially the common practice) pitch-class spelling matters. The number of non-tonic pitch classes is therefore without theoretical limit.[14]

The qualification "in some musical passage" in part (b) indicates an openness regarding the temporal extent of a tonic's influence. While some theories of monotonality—for example those of Schenker, Schoenberg, and Lerdahl and Jackendoff—assert that a tonic applies for an entire composition, studies in music cognition have challenged the perceptibility of such long-range tonics.[15] This will likely remain a contentious debate, if only because it involves so many variables. These include differences among listeners' capacities (e.g., those with absolute pitch and those without), as well as differences in musical "occasion" (listening with or without a score, playing an instrument or listening to a recording, etc.). There may also be differences in scholarly purpose: a high-flown formal analysis of a tonal work, à la a Schenkerian sketch, need not be read as making the same kinds of perceptual assertions as an empirical study of listener cognition, though both might refer to "tonics."[16] We will return to such distinctions in the next section.

This also relates to part (c) of the definition. For a pitch class to act as a tonic, it must have the capacity to orient our hearing during moments when it is not acoustically present. The Lutosławski again motivates this condition: one reason D is so hard to accept as a tonic is its lack of orienting power when silent. Just how *long* a tonic can remain in effect in absentia is—again—a matter of scholarly debate. But most will agree that even at the most local, phrase level, the tonic typically *will* go silent at some point, at least in common-practice idioms that treat the dominant chord as the tonal lynchpin: the dominant is the harmony that most strongly evokes the tonic, in part *because* it is the only functional pillar that does not contain it as a pitch class. By contrast, consider musics anchored by a drone: the drone is a privileged pitch, to be sure, but is it a tonic? If we take (c) as a necessary condition for tonicness, drones will fall short, as they never have a chance to exert their influence in absentia.

Whether one *wants* to preserve the concept of tonic in non-Western drone-based musics is another matter of course. The definition remains strategically underdetermined in this sense: part (b) does not specify the ways in which the non-tonic pitch classes might be "hierarchically arranged and perceived" with respect to the tonic.[17] As a result, it does not prescribe the range of musical systems within which tonics can operate. This leaves the door open for broad or narrow conceptions of tonality as discussed previously: from an encompassing view that treats tonality in some form as a property of nearly all world musics to a narrow one that considers it a historically contingent feature of bourgeois musical cultures in the West. As Brian Hyer (2002) notes, the concept of tonality in its broadest sense can be considered analogous to *système musical.*[18] The present definition offers flexibility regarding just which *systèmes* one wishes to invoke as capable of sustaining tonics.

A SARABANDE AND ITS TONICS (EMPIRICAL, THEORETICAL, PHENOMENOLOGICAL)

As noted earlier, our broad definition of *tonic* will likely receive subtly differing emphases based on scholars' intellectual commitments. To illustrate the point, let us consider another example for solo cello: the Sarabande from J. S. Bach's fifth cello suite (BWV 1011). Figure 5.2 shows a lightly annotated score of movement. Unlike the Lutosławski, this is a piece from the very heart of the canonical common practice—if any music is tonal, this surely is. Yet it is also an exceptional piece: its sparseness and severity set it apart even from Bach's other movements for solo cello. In this highly reduced texture, local tonal effects speak with particular vividness, making it an especially effective site for exploring the various ways in which tonics can act as objects of perception, theoretical contemplation, and empirical research.

The annotations divide the Sarabande into four phrases. The first three phrases last four measures; the fourth is twice as long, though it is articulated into four-measure subphrases by the quasi-half cadence in m. 16. The contour inversion in mm. 17–18, which mirrors the *recto* statements in mm. 13–14, underscores the sense of subphrase parallelism, especially as a similar inversional relationship obtains between the beginnings of the first two phrases (compare mm. 1–2 and 5–6). Nevertheless, the continuous eighth-note

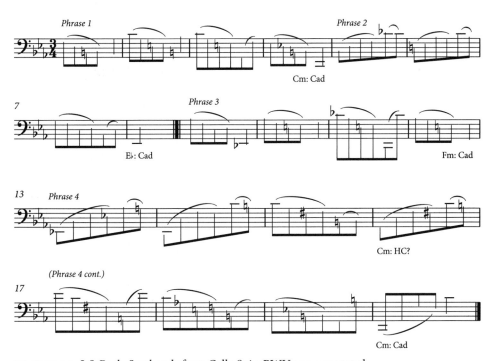

FIGURE 5.2 J. S. Bach, Sarabande from Cello Suite BWV 1011, annotated.

motion in m. 16 attenuates the cadential effect, as does the linear-harmonic continuation: the G bass note of m. 16 can be heard to continue into the first two beats of m. 17, before moving to A♮ on the third beat, thus creating a continuous tonal motion that stitches across any putative cadential seam. The cadential endings in mm. 4, 8, 12, and 20, by contrast, are unmistakable. All are authentic cadences,[19] all bring the eighth-note motion to momentary rest, and all exhibit conventional cadential rhetoric.

Phrases two through four traverse characteristically Bachian tonal trajectories: rather than staking out a key from beginning to end, each phrase traces a tonal motion that leads to cadential confirmation in a new key.[20] No sooner is that goal confirmed than the first measure of the next phrase destabilizes it, setting off for a new tonal station. Only the first phrase exhibits a different logic . . . or does it? There can be little doubt that phrase one projects C minor throughout. The three-note gesture E♭–B♮–C in measure 1 (a highly thematic figure in the movement) points unambiguously to C minor. Moreover, a listener familiar with the tonal conventions of Bach's suites, with their uniform keys across movements, will expect a movement in C minor, the key of the previous three movements. But in the Sarabande the opening and closing tonics in the first phrase differ considerably in effect. The cadential C of m. 4 secures the tonic via the most sonorous means available: the cello's lowest pitch. The effect is almost like the confirmation of an initially tentative hypothesis. The movement begins in C minor and yet the first measure does not seem to sit squarely within the key: it lists to one side.[21] This is due to the striking A♭ on beat three, which seems to nudge the C-minor tonic triad off center. The B♮ at the same location in measure 2 then partially rights the ship, aiming us toward the tonic resolution. Indeed, A♭ and B♮ both sound in this measure, repelling one another and pushing toward their respective resolutions: A♭ down to G, B♮ up to C. As Figure 5.3 illustrates, those resolutions arrive in measures 3 and 4, at the same metric position (beat three). These kinetics of initial destabilization and gradual resolution underlie the sense that the music, though clearly in C minor from the start, only truly stabilizes its tonic with the cadence of m. 4. We are reminded that one of the central roles of a tonic in the common practice is as a *goal* of tonal motion. The effect in the Sarabande is not unlike the "centripetal" tonality that Carl Dahlhaus ascribes to Brahms, though in microcosm: the music begins in a state of tonal imbalance and its "sole ambition is to reach its center" (1980, 74).

This, at least, is how it strikes me. Others' ears may well hang on different details. For example, I suspect that a cellist's experience of the music—when playing *or* listening—would exhibit all manner of somatically mediated texture that mine lacks. Enculturation,

Stemmed notes = beat 3

FIGURE 5.3 The resolution of A♭ and B♮ in phrase one.

embodied practice, temperament, training, mode of musicking (playing, practicing, listening [closely or distractedly], analyzing)—all of these will mediate listeners' phenomenological encounters with the music and its rhetorics of tonic (destabilized, confirmed, on the way, etc.). Scholars of different disciplinary and intellectual commitments nevertheless disagree on how great these experiential differences truly are. Some scholars in music perception and cognition, for example, have tended to downplay them. One such scholar, David Temperley, admits that

> judgments about the kinds of [perceived musical] structure described [in his book] vary greatly among individuals—even among experts (and non-experts). Indeed, one might claim that there is so much subjectivity in these matters that the idea of pursuing a "formal theory of listener's intuitions" is misguided.

But he then continues:

> I do not deny that there are sometimes subjective differences about all the kinds of structure at issue here; however, I believe there is much more agreement than disagreement. The success of the computational tests I present here, where I rely on sources other than myself for "correct" analysis, offers some testimony to the general agreement that is found in these areas.[22]

Temperley's "computational test" regarding the experience of tonics and keys draws on the work of Carol Krumhansl, Edward Kessler, Mark Schmuckler, and others who have sought to map the "tonal hierarchies" that underwrite listeners' experiences of key.[23] Krumhansl and her associates derived these hierarchies from "probe tone" experiments in which listeners were asked to rate the "fit" between the twelve chromatic pitch classes and a previously established key. Figure 5.4 shows Temperley's slightly modified versions of the resulting tonal hierarchies in major and minor. As the comparison in 5.4(c) makes clear, Temperley's major and minor profiles differ only in the values they assign $\hat{3}$ and $\hat{6}$ (here, E♭ vs. E♮ and A♭ versus A♮).[24] Not surprisingly, the tonic is the most hierarchically privileged pitch class in both key profiles.

Krumhansl, Temperley, and other scholars working in this tradition hypothesize that listeners internalize key profiles such as these through statistical exposure to a great deal of music in some tonal idiom.[25] When hearing a musical passage, listeners seek the closest match between the pitch-class distribution in the music and the internalized profiles. What kind of thing is a tonic in this mode of hearing? It is often—but not always—the most statistically prevalent pitch class in the music. The exceptions arise because the pitch-class content of the entire musical texture must approximate one of the key profiles in toto: a statistically prevalent pitch class must be confirmed as tonic by the arrangement of the remaining pitch classes into the peaks and valleys characteristic of its major or minor key profile. In other words, the tonic is ennobled not (only) through its statistical prevalence but through the statistical distribution of the entire field of pitch classes into a familiar, internalized hierarchy, over which it presides as head.

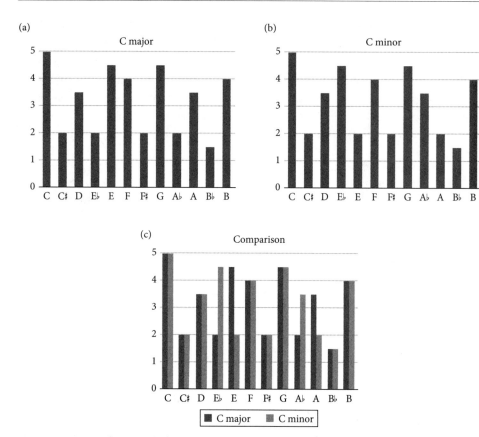

FIGURE 5.4 David Temperley's (2011) key profiles, modified from Krumhansl and Kessler 1982. Color versions of these figures are included in the book's color insert.

To illustrate this template-matching model, Figure 5.5(a) compares the pitch distribution of the entire Sarabande (the "input vector") with the key profile for C minor.[26] Even at sight it is clear that the match is remarkably close. Notably, tonic pitch-class C occurs more than any other in the piece.[27] As Temperley has noted, however, the key profiles are most effective when applied not to pieces in their entirety but to seriated local segments, to better capture the effects of modulation. Figure 5.5(b) thus takes the pitch distribution of the first phrase as its input vector, comparing it with the profile for C minor. It is more difficult to judge the fit visually in this instance, as it is for the first measure alone, as shown in Figures 5.5(c) and 5.5(d): it is not clear at sight if its pitch distribution best fits, say, C minor or A♭ major.

A computational comparison will clearly be more reliable. Temperley employs a "scalar product," which multiplies the values in the input vector with the values for the twelve pitch classes in each of the 24 key profiles. These sums are then totaled, and the highest score reflects the best match between input vector and key profile.[28] Figure 5.6 shows the results for measure 1, which register a tie between C minor, A♭ major, and A♭ minor. A look back at the music makes clear why this is: the measure contains pitches of the complete C minor, A♭ major, and A♭ minor triads and no others. Though pitch-class A♭ lasts twice

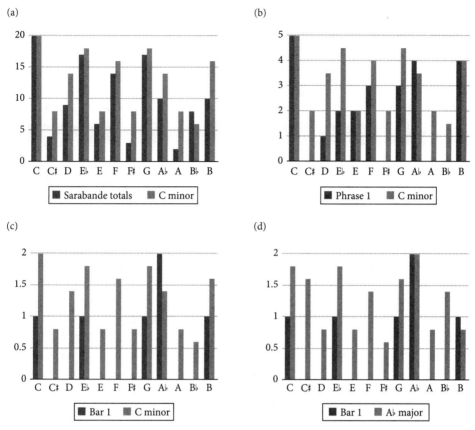

FIGURE 5.5 Pitch distributions in the Bach Sarabande, compared with key profiles. Color versions of these figures are included in the book's color insert.

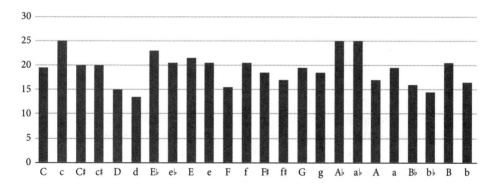

FIGURE 5.6 The scalar product of the input vector for m. 1 in the Sarabande with all twenty-four key profiles. Note the tie between C minor, A♭ major, and A♭ minor.

as long as any other in the measure, and thus might seem to tip the scales in favor of A♭ as tonic, this is balanced out by the fact that either B or C will be chromatic in the A♭ key profiles, but *both* receive high values in the C-minor profile.

To calculate the modulating key structure of an extended passage, Temperley employs a key-finding algorithm that segments the music into measures and determines the best fit between each measure's pitch classes and the key profiles via the scalar product.[29] To reflect the "inertia" of tonal hearing—in which listeners presumably seek to maintain a key unless evidence for a modulation is strong enough to dislodge it—Temperley's algorithm assesses a "penalty" for any change of key from measure to measure. Only when the new key is sufficiently strong to outweigh the persistence of the old does the algorithm register a modulation.

Figure 5.7, a color version of which is included in the book's color insert, shows the results of this algorithm for the entire Sarabande. Yellow and green cells indicate the best and second-best matches (respectively) between each measure's input vector and the twenty-four key profiles; a heavy border indicates the preferred key based on the key-finding algorithm, with the modulation penalty set at −4.[30] If the heavy border encloses a green or white cell, this means that the yellow cell or cells in that column have a score that is not sufficiently strong to motivate a change of key (viz., the score is less than four "points" greater than that in the heavily enclosed cell). A scan of the chart reveals that the algorithm's selected keys match those of a traditional tonal analysis very closely, with modulations to E♭ major and F minor. The key of B♭ major in measures 13 and 14 is more questionable, but a quick glance at the score reveals it as the most plausible choice hereabouts, at least at this level of "resolution" (with single measures as the initial input). One also notes the increasing clarity of the algorithm's results as each phrase comes to a close,[31] a fact that recalls our earlier observations regarding the phrases' Bachian trajectories from tonal destabilization to new tonic confirmation.

We have nevertheless come a long way from the fine-grained phenomenological distinctions with which this section began. Note, for example, that the pitches in the Sarabande could be scrambled within each measure *and* transposed to any register and the results of the key-finding algorithm would be unchanged. The method is thus insensitive both to syntax at the local, note-to-note level and to register. It moreover makes no distinction between bass notes, inner voices, and upper voices—distinctions that are essential in most tonal theories. Other empirical and computational methods address some of these issues. The key-finding approach of Brown, Butler, and Jones (1994; see also Brown and Butler 1984) attends not to pitch-class distributions but to rare intervals and intervallic cues that can signal a key. Such approaches would be sensitive to strong key signals such as the E♭–B♮–C in m. 1. Temperley himself (along with Elizabeth Marvin) has argued that "structural" models such as Brown, Butler, and Jones's likely work in tandem with distributional ones such as his own in listeners' processes of key finding (Marvin and Temperley 2008). Other researchers have developed key-finding models based on harmony rather than key profiles (Winograd 1968; Maxwell 1992), thus showing a sensitivity to chord rather than individual pitch class, while Jamshed Bharucha (1987, 1991) and Fred

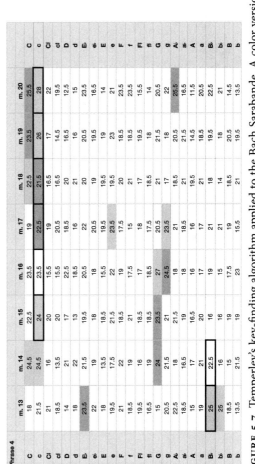

FIGURE 5.7 Temperley's key-finding algorithm applied to the Bach Sarabande. A color version of this figure is included in the book's color insert. (On the present page, light gray cells correspond to yellow in the color version, while darker gray cells correspond to green.)

Lerdahl (2001) have proposed models that take into account the hierarchical interaction of pitches, chords, and keys. Huron (2006) and Aarden (2003) advance key-finding methods that are more sensitive to syntax, proposing that the key-profile model needs to be adjusted to reflect a distinction between *mid-melody* and *phrase-final* contexts.[32] Finally, recent approaches to musical schemata (e.g., Gjerdingen 2007), though not primarily focused on tonal questions, generally model keys and tonics from a more ecological perspective, by tracking stock idioms and gestures that carry their tonal implications along with them, as a snail carries its shell.

For all of their differences, these psychological and empirical studies nevertheless have much in common. They share not only a commitment to certain experimental protocols but also a wariness of adopting any more traditional music theory than necessary (with the possible exception of Lerdahl 2001). If a key-finding model can succeed in identifying the keys in a piece of music through note counting and a few simple algorithmic steps, for example, why invoke sophisticated music-theoretical notions of key, tonic, and modulation? This strategic music-theoretical "thinness" is not merely a casualty of Occam's razor; it also arises from the exigencies of experimental design. It should not be a surprise, then, that the concept of tonic looks quite different when we encounter it within the "thickest" of tonal theories: Schenkerian analysis.

Figure 5.8 shows a generative Schenkerian analysis of the Sarabande, beginning from the minor tonic triad (a), which exfoliates into an *Ursatz* at (b). The middle-ground transformations of (c) and (d) show an initial ascent to the *Kopfton* $\hat{3}$, which is delayed to arrive over V (in a six-four configuration).[33] Figure 5.8(e) shows further prolongations of the subsidiary harmonic stages in this trajectory—III, iv, and V—as the music moves closer to its phenomenal surface. Moving further into the

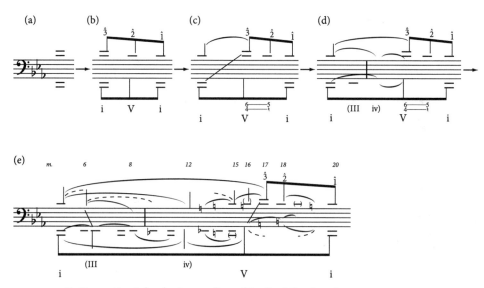

FIGURE 5.8 Generative Schenkerian reading of the Bach Sarabande.

a)

b)

from

FIGURE 5.9 Eric Wen's reading of the Sarabande's first phrase (Wen 1999, 278, Example 3).

foreground, Figure 5.9 presents one analysis, by Eric Wen (1999), of the prolongation of the tonic *Stufe* in the first phrase. Wen reads the striking A♭ bass note in measure 1 as a displaced inner voice. As a result, the opening harmony is implicitly bounded by tonic bass and tonic soprano, an exact reversal of the sounding music, in which tonic C3 falls registrally (and temporally) between the cello's bounding G3 and A♭2, which outline a dissonant major seventh. The cello also traces a dissonant bounding interval in measure 2, now a minor ninth, which is again transformed in Wen's reading to an underlying consonance: an implicit tenth between B♮2 and D4 (as shown in the bottom systems). While some may object to the reading's relegation of the A♭ in measure 1 and G in measure 3 to inner voices,[34] one can also argue that this transformation is partly responsible for the phrase's expressive effect: the sounding music literally turns the underlying structure inside out.

The secure tonic embrace of the outer voices in measure 1 of Wen's reading is emblematic of the role of the tonic in Schenkerian theory. Note the omnipresence of the tonic in Figure 5.8, beginning with the atemporal generative matrix of its triad. As the structure begins to unfurl, tonic manifests itself in two ways: as the harmonic *Stufe* that the composition prolongs and that forms the frame (*Tonraum*) for its temporal unfolding, and as 1̂, the telos of the *Urlinie*. The sketches visually reflect the tonic's theoretical ubiquity: it seems to enfold the entire composition via the beamed outer voices of the *Ursatz*. Within this frame, all tonal phenomena ultimately derive from and are answerable to this encompassing tonic, including the putative *local* tonics of E♭ and F, which are subsumed into the encompassing key, as prolongations of III and iv. Indeed, these *Stufen* are less structurally prominent than the (non-tonicized) dominant (V) that begins in m. 16.

Schenker is well known for his criticism of theories of modulation and his insistence that all ostensible changes of key are in fact only tonicizations of greater or lesser strength. But as an analyst he was highly sensitive to the "illusory keys of the foreground."[35] Indeed, one might argue that tonic as a *perceptual* phenomenon is primarily a foreground effect for Schenker. It is part of what he calls the tonality (*Tonalität*) of the foreground, which is distinct from the austere diatony (*Diatonie*) of the background. The latter prolongs a conceptual tonic triad that may not be easily accessible to hearing, while the former harbors tonics that are the empirically sensible effects of late-middleground prolongation and composing-out.[36] Schenker nevertheless states, in typically Delphic fashion,[37] that "the tonal sparseness of diatony in the background and the fullness of tonality in the foreground are one and the same" (1979, 11). On one reading, Schenker may be asserting that that the process of composing-out mediates *Diatonie* and *Tonalität*, linking the empirically distant tonic of the former with the immediately sensible tonics of the latter via iterative prolongations (which have the potential, among other things, to transform *Stufen* into foreground keys). Another reading would have it that local and global tonics relate dialectically in Schenker's theory: they are phenomenally divergent manifestations of a noumenal singularity.

TONIC AS ORIGIN, TONIC AS GOAL

The Schenker of the 1906 *Harmonielehre* expresses a somewhat different view of tonics and tonicizations. He wonders at our propensity to take any consonant triad heard at the beginning of a piece as a tonic. Faced with examples in which this proves to be false—the finale of Beethoven's Fourth Piano Concerto comes to mind (though Schenker does not cite it)—he wonders:

> Should we conclude from these various possibilities that our assumption was erroneous to begin with? Or is our instinct rooted nevertheless in a natural cause?
>
> It is the latter alternative that is correct. Our inclination to ascribe to any major or minor triad, first of all, the meaning of a tonic fully corresponds to the egotistic drive of the tone itself [*dem Trieb und dem Egoismus des Tones*], which . . . has to be evaluated from a biological point of view. This much is obvious: that the significance of the tonic exceeds that of the other scale steps, and these lose in value the farther they go from the tonic. Thus a scale-step does not aspire to the place of a VI or II in the system, but, on the contrary, it prefers to be a V at least, if not a I, a real tonic.[38]

The animistic language (the "egotistic drive of the tone") is characteristic of Schenker, but here he employs it to describe the tonal effects of local chords rather than the generative processes of prolongation and composing-out, as in his later theories. The idea that all consonant chords aspire to tonic status suggests a view of tonal experience that is more volatile at the moment-to-moment level than his mature monotonal theories suggest.[39]

Schenker is of course not alone in asserting that listeners tend to take opening triads as tonics. Fred Lerdahl, whose cognitive theory is strongly based on Schenker's, similarly argues that a chord or pitch heard in isolation will be taken as a tonic. But he roots the assertion in very different intellectual soil: the *Egoismus des Tones* gives way to the principle of cognitive economy, manifested by the "law of the shortest way":

> In this view, events are interpreted not only in the closest possible relation to one another but also in the closest proximity to a provisional tonic.
>
> It follows that when a single note or chord sounds in isolation, the listener assumes that it is the tonic, for the shortest distance is from an event to itself. In terms of the algebraic pitch-space representation [Lerdahl's "basic space," which hierarchically arranges the twelve pitch classes in a manner resembling the Krumhansl-Kessler key profiles], the listener aligns the basic space to fit the pitch or chord in question, so that the pitch or chord is in the most stable position at the top of the hierarchy.
>
> (Lerdahl 2001, 194)

Richard Cohn presents a similar view, though he is careful to specify its cultural and historical contingency:

> For an acculturated listener, a major or minor triad, sounded in isolation and without prior context, signals the tonic status of its root by default. In a process first described by Gottfried Weber (1846 [1817–1821]), a listener spontaneously imagines an isolated triad housed within a diatonic collection, signifying a tonic that bears its name.
>
> (Cohn 2012, 8)

Cohn is quick to note, however, that such provisional tonics

> require confirmation, weakly through the remaining tones of its associated diatonic collection; more strongly by arranging those tones into a local cadence; more strongly yet by repeating that cadence, perhaps with supplementary rhetorical packaging, at the end of the movement or composition.
>
> (Cohn 2012, 9)

Note that Cohn adduces *closing* gestures as the strongest means of confirming a hypothetical opening tonic. We thus arrive at one of the commonplaces of tonal theory: tonics often *frame* musical trajectories in time, acting as both origin and goal. Daniel Harrison elevates these to basic tenets in the "rhetoric of tonic": "Tonic function ends a composition" and "Tonic begins compositional sections" (1994, 76–80).

That an opening tonic is more provisional than a closing one is also a commonplace of tonal theory. For this reason, some theorists have adopted skeptical positions about opening triads' tonic status. For Schoenberg,

> A triad standing alone is entirely indefinite in its harmonic meaning; it may be the tonic of one tonality or one degree of several others. The addition of one or more other triads can restrict its meaning to a lesser number of tonalities.
>
> (Schoenberg 1954, 1)

Norman Cazden, writing in the same year, agrees:

> [W]e may remark on the strategic logic by which a composition cannot begin on its tonic harmony. The work may be, let us say, in the key of C major, and it may begin with a simple C major chord, but there is no functional relationship as yet that makes us accept that chord as having a tonic role, and the further progress of the composition may easily demonstrate that it is really in another key.
>
> (Cazden 1954, 25; quoted in Brown and Butler 1984, 9)

Few if any theorists have ever argued, however, that closing tonics are similarly provisional.

Though the key of a musical work is often derived by examining its opening and closing tonics, Cohn argues that these bounding tonics do not assure the tonal orientation of the music they bracket:

> We can't just go ⟨B♭ major, Cough, Wheeze, Honk, B♭ major⟩ and pretend that we have made coherent music in B♭ major (Straus 1987). If a tonal theory is to meet its claim of explanatory adequacy, it needs to be able to specify the role, with respect to the tonic, of the harmonies that separate the bounding tonics.
>
> (Cohn 2012, 2)

Cohn is speaking here of enharmonically paradoxical chromatic progressions, but more or less diatonic passages and pieces can occasionally make the point too. Consider Schubert's "Erster Verlust," shown in Figure 5.10. The song opens and closes with an F-minor triad, and it has a key signature of four flats. Any young piano student who has learned a smattering of music theory will tell you that it is in F minor. Yet from the first measure the song wavers between F minor and A♭ major, the two keys taking on conventional semiotic roles: the former representing the desolate present, the latter a halcyon past. The keys infuse one another as the lyric subject broods on the (im)possibility of reanimating first love after it is lost. The singer's tonal gestures point to self-deception: the opening vocal gesture sits more comfortably in A♭ major than in F minor, and the vocal line's only two authentic cadences are in A♭ major (mm. 9 and 21). The piano has the last word, however, following the voice's final cadence by drily reiterating the cadential gesture in F minor—an effect at once matter-of-fact and devastating.

FIGURE 5.10 Schubert, "Erster Verlust" (Goethe), D. 226.

Rather than infusing one another, the two potential tonics now sit side by side, each represented by their most conventional generic signifiers of closure. The fluidly circulating and interpenetrating tonic effects of the song's midsection have hardened and separated, as though we are sonic witness to a nascent dissociative disorder. To appreciate just how dissociative, note that one could remove the piano's F-minor cadence, or replace it with some reiterated version of the A♭ cadence, without doing syntactical damage to the song. The *meaning* would change, to be sure—perhaps tilting toward the more pervasive delusion David Lewin (2006, 137–138) hears at the end of "Ihr Bild"—but the result would not violate tonal propriety. We would confidently analyze the recomposed song in A♭ major throughout, treating its opening F-minor triad not as tonic but as submediant (a role the song's second chord seems to confirm). But now the tonal allegiance of all of the intervening music has shifted.

Of course, this is an exceptional song, perhaps even a limit case: the fact that it admits of such a richly bifocal tonal reading is a testament to Schubert's often-celebrated psychological perspicacity. Yet the exercise should at least raise doubts about the relationship between opening and closing tonics and the music that falls between. This is in part a question of the perceptual status of monotonality, discussed previously. Many Schubert songs begin and end in different keys, after all, without offending listeners' tonal sensibilities.[40] As Brian Hyer has noted, "the dictum that pieces close on the original tonic was an aesthetic rather than a cognitive requirement" (2002, 742). But even in exceptional pieces that open and conclude with the same triad, like "Erster Verlust," monotonality might not be assured.[41] To adopt Cohn's notation, a more accurate representation of the song might be: ⟨F-minor triad, music poised between F minor and A♭ major, A♭-major cadence, F-minor cadence⟩.

It is nevertheless possible to construct a coherent and even compelling Schenkerian sketch of the song in F minor, as Carl Schachter does (1999b, 24, Ex. 1.7). In such a reading the F-minor tonic triad is *prolonged* for the entire song. But, as Schachter notes elsewhere (1987), prolongation and local sense of key can exhibit a certain independence from one another. In other words, to prolong a tonic does not mean to keep it always immediately before the listener's ears. Another exceptional passage from Schubert makes the point vividly. The *Sturm und Drang* episode in mm. 43–60 of the slow movement of the composer's final string quartet, D. 887, begins and ends in G minor. After confirming G minor via its dominant and subdominant in mm. 43–52, the music tumbles down a chain of minor thirds, touching on E minor (fleetingly), C♯ minor, and B♭ minor, before returning to G minor. Figure 5.11 illustrates. This equal-octave division, though tonally paradoxical (Cohn 1996, 2012), is hardly unprecedented: examples are legion not only in Schubert but throughout the nineteenth century. What *is* unprecedented is the alarming reiteration of the bounding G-minor triad's root and third after each intermediate tonal station is reached. Though G-minor is the passage's point of tonic origin and goal, and though Schenkerian analysts would likely read the progression as prolonging G minor,[42] the prolonged chord's *phenomenal* intrusion throughout the progression creates one of the most shocking effects in all of Schubert. Rather than unifying the music as tonic ambassadors, the insistent G–B♭ gestures seem to rip it into two tonal strands, as shown in Figure 5.12: sustained G minor (above) and descending-m3 (below). In mm. 54 and 56, local and bounding tonics enter into direct sonic conflict. While G minor's role as point of origin and goal is beyond dispute, the passage makes palpable the gulf between tonic as theoretically prolonged and as immediately sensible.

FIGURE 5.11 Schubert, String Quartet, D. 887, mvt. ii, mm. 52–60, reduced and annotated.

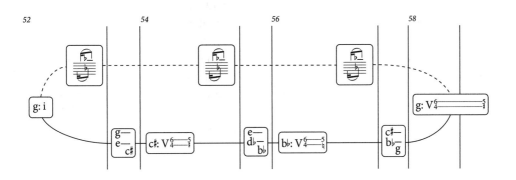

dashed line = sustained g-minor strand
solid line =   descending-m3 strand

FIGURE 5.12 Two tonal strands in Schubert's String Quartet, D. 887, mvt. ii, mm. 52–60.

EPILOGUE: NEGOTIATING POPULAR TONICS

In March 2014 musician Owen Pallett published three articles on Slate.com analyzing songs by Katy Perry, Daft Punk, and Lady Gaga. In his discussion of Daft Punk's 2013 single "Get Lucky," he focuses in part on the four-chord loop that cycles through the entire song: Bm–D–F♯m–E.[43] For Pallett, the loop is tonally ambiguous:

> the song can be heard in two different keys. Most of the time it sounds as if it's in the minor mode of F♯ Aeolian . . .
>
> But the first chord of the progression isn't F♯ minor, it's B minor. The song slides smoothly back to it each time . . . The insistence of the B minor creates the aural illusion that the song could in fact be in the minor mode of B Dorian . . .
>
> So, when the chord cycle comes back around to the beginning, the B minor, each time, the ear is tricked for a moment into thinking that the song is in a different key, a musical Tilt-a-Whirl. I am not going to lie: To my ears the song is clearly identifiable as F♯ minor, but on a Kinsey scale, I'd rate it a 3.
>
> (Pallett 2014)

Pallett's analysis generated considerable discussion in the article's comments section, with many readers casting votes for various tonic candidates in his musical Tilt-a-Whirl. In addition to F♯ minor and B Dorian, several readers argued for A major, despite the A-major triad's sonic absence in the song.[44]

The discussion is noteworthy in part for the various justifications the participants provide for one tonic hearing over another. Some appeal to music-theoretic principles: one poster (writing under the telling name Toccata) argues for an A-major hearing, in part because B minor lacks a leading tone and the quasi-Plagal cadence IV–i (E–Bm) is insufficient to establish a key. Poster Michael Curtis and others argue that Toccata's criteria are too rooted in common-practice harmony: popular music in minor modes often eschews leading tones, and plagal progressions predominate in many pop idioms.[45] As this suggests, the posters tend to base their judgments in their personal listening corpora: while Toccata seems to have a strong background in common-practice art music, others are clearly more literate in pop idioms, and one (Richard Worth) points to his jazz background as a possible reason for his preference to hear the song in B Dorian. Many also make more phenomenological appeals, urging their interlocutors to play the song at the piano, improvise over it, test certain pitches as tonics while listening to the changes, and so forth.

The participants' widely varying subject positions are immediately evident. Some are musicians, some not; some are theoretically trained, others self-taught; some are literate in a wide range of vernacular musics, while others seem to have more parochial listening habits; and so on. The thickness of linguistic mediation is also striking: all of the negotiating and haggling over tonic effects is mediated through discourse, as participants deploy language (along with various illocutionary persuasion tactics) in an attempt to lead others' ears toward their preferred hearings. The attempt to verbalize the progression's sonic effect even seems to change some posters' experience of its potential tonics. The interlocutors' diverse backgrounds and competing discourses challenge any attempt to arrive at a consensus on the progression's "true" tonic.

One might respond that this is clearly an ambiguous harmonic progression—we would not find such a wide variety of opinion in a less ambiguous example. While this is surely true, one final example will nevertheless suggest the extent to which fine-grained experiences of tonicity can vary even in ostensibly clear examples. For his 1999 book *Metal, Rock, and Jazz: Perception and the Phenomenology of Musical Experience*, Harris M. Berger conducted extensive interviews with two musicians about the tonal effects in their own songs, as part of his wide-ranging ethnographic fieldwork. Berger argues persuasively for the integrity, richness, and complexity of individuals' situated musical experiences: "An entire dissertation could be written on one type of musical phenomenon experienced by one player" (1999, 174). As Berger notes, however, it is challenging to articulate that experience via a feedback interview:

> At its best, the process [is] a collaboration, but such collaborations are asymmetrical and complex. The constant goal in the process is to share the participant's experiences. On the one hand, this sharing can never be complete. Because both perceptual experiences and their interpretations are situational and historical, the participant's experience is never the same twice, and its richness always exceeds even the participant's best description. Further, the ethnographer constantly influences both the descriptions and the experiences themselves. On the other hand, partial sharing is possible; the same richness that makes experience exceed its descriptions enables the ethnographer to engage actively in the interpretation and even suggest lines of inquiry. Over time, the ethnographer can learn to engage with the world in ways similar to those of the participants.
>
> (Berger 1999, 175)

The process of collaboration Berger describes is evident in his interviews with Chris Ozimek, guitarist and songwriter for the Akron-based, early 1990s commercial hard rock band Dia Pason. For example, Berger cannot begin to understand Ozimek's experience of the song's tonal character until he introduces some basic music-theoretical concepts and terminology that they can share. Specifically, he describes the tonic as feeling "at rest" and asks Ozimek which chords in the band's song "Turn for the Worse" seem to him to act as tonics.

Ozimek states that the introduction—which is made up of syncopated riffs surrounding an A power chord—is centered on an A tonic. As Berger notes, "given the conventions of Western music theory, this was no great surprise" (1999, 187). But things become more interesting in the verse. When Ozimek sings the song's first line, the harmony shifts to a D power chord. Ozimek *also* hears this as a tonic, despite Berger's repeated attempts to suggest that it might sound like IV:

> Pushing the point further and bringing it back to the question of tonality, I asked again if this D chord feels like the IV chord of a tonic A or if it feels like a I chord on its own. Chris said that on stage, when he has finished singing the first vocal phrase . . . he jumps away from the mike to allow the audience's focus to shift to the guitar; then, when the second vocal phrase of the verse comes up, he moves back to the mike

to sing. As a result, he said, the vocal phrase with the D chord . . . and the guitar part . . . feel very distinct. Given all of this, we concluded that moving into the verse, D was the tonal center while it lasted.

(Berger 1999, 187–188)

Ozimek's response to Berger's prodding is fascinating: his tonal experience of the two chords is inseparable from his somatic experience as a performer. The two tonics correspond to his two positions on stage and to his shifting communicative stances with respect to the audience.

Theorists may well be incredulous reading such an account: perhaps Ozimek simply is not sufficiently attuned to the theoretical distinctions between a I chord and a IV chord to report on a phenomenological difference he must surely experience. Scholars in music cognition and perception might further argue that introspection in such matters is unreliable and should be replaced by more controlled experimentation, with linguistic mediation kept to a minimum.[46] But Berger's ethical injunctions about taking seriously the situated complexity of participants' musical experiences should give us pause, as should the ecological integrity of Ozimek's account. Clearly, whatever these tonic sensations might be for Ozimek, they are inseparable from his somatic, performatively scripted experience as player and singer. We are reminded that our experience of any tonic, however unshakeable or inevitable it might feel, is as subject to the contingencies of culture, history, embodied practice, and musical occasion as is any other musical apperception. A more careful consideration of those contingencies might reveal ways in which they nourish rather than occlude tonal experience in our many daily acts of musicking.

NOTES

1. Other scholars in music cognition have explored the relationship between the statistical prevalence of pitch classes and their tonal status. Marvin and Temperley (2008) provide a valuable survey of this literature. See also Aarden (2003) and Huron (2006) for further discussion of the distributional model and its relationship to tonal hierarchy, syntax, and affect. We explore a distributional key-finding algorithm in Section III.
2. The repeated D3 asserts a *tactus,* to be sure, but no clear metrical hierarchy.
3. In my own listening, I hear such relationships only fleetingly. For example, the very first non-D event—a low tremolo F2—strikes my ear momentarily as a minor $\hat{3}$, though the effect is significantly attenuated by the rhetorical disjunction. And it is difficult for me to hear the scurrying figures immediately following the F2 in relation to the opening D. Only occasional later events carry a similar tonal charge for me; the most notable is the almost cadential tremolo figure on D4 at 1:18. Indeed, this is the closest moment to a phrase ending in the passage (at least to my ears), underscoring Krumhansl's comments.
4. On the richly metaphorical language that often arises in discussions of tonal effects, see Hyer (2002, 728–733). Such metaphors are surprisingly common in the empirical literature (both in experimental prompts and in definitions). David Huron (2006, 422), for example, first defines the tonic straightforwardly as "The first *scale degree* in the Western major and minor scales." But when he reaches in the next sentence for the phenomenological effect of

such tonics, metaphors take over: "The pitch in a scale that sounds most stable or closed." Earlier in the book (145), Huron provides a fascinating account of the poetic and figurative language that theoretically knowledgeable listeners use to characterize the effect of different scale degrees. The metaphoric field for the tonic includes references to stability, pleasure, home, contentment, satisfaction, solidity, and strength.

5. At best, we might note that C♯ and E♭ enjoy a slight edge, with E, F, and B tied for second and the remaining pitch classes trailing in a clump. Compared to the stratospheric D, however, these are negligible distinctions. Six-flat apartment buildings and single-family homes are not all that different in the shadow of a skyscraper.

6. The recorded excerpt is performed by Heinrich Schiff (cello) and the Bavarian Radio Symphony, conducted by the composer (Philips 416 817–811).

7. For examples of psychoanalytical hearings of "uncanny" tonal effects in late Schoenberg, see Cherlin (1993, 2007) and Kurth (2001). See also Straus's (1990) Bloomian interpretation of such effects.

8. For two classic examples of this line of argument, see Forte (1972, 1981). The latter—an analysis of Schoenberg's op. 11, no. 1—appears alongside an explicitly tonal interpretation of the same piece (Ogdon 1981).

9. This liberal extension of the concepts of tonic and tonality to non-Western music is relatively common in the music-cognition literature. See, for example, Castellano, Bharucha, and Krumhansl (1984); Bharucha (1984); and Krumhansl (1990, 253–270, 2004). Such findings have led W. Jay Dowling (1984, 417) to assert that "the musical and psychological phenomenon of tonality as an organizing principle may be all but universal across cultures."

10. For some interpreters it might also fail for the broader historical/stylistic arguments presented previously, but for the moment we will bracket such extra-phenomenological considerations.

11. For further exploration of this idea, which I refer to as "tonal intention," see Rings (2011).

12. Riemann (1990), with his emphasis on harmony and chord, stresses tonic-as-chord in his own definition of "Tonika" in the fifth edition of his *Musik-Lexikon*. After indicating that the word usually refers to "the pitch after which the key is named, that is, C in C major, G in G major, etc.," he adds: "the newer harmonic theory [viz., his own] nevertheless understands by the word tonic the tonic *triad*, that is, the C-major chord in C major, the C-minor chord in C minor" (Riemann 1990, 1151, my translation).

13. "Chroma" is the term music-cognition scholars use for the perceptual property that all octave-related pitches share.

14. David Temperley (2011) refers to such enharmonically distinct pitch classes as "tonal pitch classes," while Julian Hook (2011) uses the term "spelled pitch classes."

15. The most-cited study on this topic is Cook (1987), though Robert Gjerdingen (1999, 164–166) has pointed out significant methodological flaws in Cook's article. For a more experimentally sound study of long-range tonal audition, see Marvin and Brinkman (1999).

16. On the distinction between analyses that seek to model prereflective experience and those that seek to stimulate new experiences, see Temperley (1999).

17. The inclusion of both "arranged" and "perceived" points to both the compositional/performative (or *poietic*) aspects of tonal music-making and their phenomenological (or *esthesic*) results. See Nattiez (1990).

18. Hyer's (2002) seminal article is a definitive account of tonality as a theoretical, historical, discursive, and ideological category. The essay contains much relevant material on tonic as a concept and a phenomenon. In order not to duplicate Hyer's work, I have chosen not

present a detailed historical survey of the term. For more on that history, see Gut (1976) and Beiche (1992).

19. Only the final cadence, which curls up to the tonic with its last note, is an unambiguous perfect authentic cadence. The first three may be perfect or imperfect, depending on how one reads the implied upper voice; thus the neutral label "Cad" in the figure.

20. The following discussion of key interacts productively with Suzannah Clark's chapter on key and modulation in this volume.

21. Here I paraphrase Scott Burnham's (1999) evocative description of Schubert's tonally off-kilter secondary key areas.

22. Temperley (2011, 7); for a similar argument, see Temperley (1999, 79–82). See also Huron (2006, 167): "One important complication of my account [of tonal *qualia*] is that people differ." Huron then discusses differences in individual temperament but also cites psychological studies that argue for certain cross-cultural similarities in statistical learning and tonal experience (168–172).

23. Seminal studies on the perception of key (sometimes called "tonality induction") include Longuet-Higgins and Steedman (1971); Krumhansl and Kessler (1982); Krumhansl (1990, which discusses Schmuckler's contribution); Brown and Butler (1984); and Brown, Butler, and Jones (1994). For a useful overview and literature survey, see Vos (2000), along with the articles that follow in the summer 2000 issue (vol. 17, no. 4) of *Music Perception*.

24. Temperley made his adjustments to Krumhansl's tonal hierarchies in an effort to improve the performance of the Krumhansl-Schmuckler key-finding algorithm. For justification and an explanation of his changes, see Temperley (2011, 176–181). The Krumhansl-Kessler hierarchies and those derived from them (such as Temperley's) do not recognize enharmonic differences in spelling, thus inhabiting a twelve-pc universe. It is possible to add enharmonic distinctions later to the key-finding algorithm—as Temperley does—but I have chosen not to do so for simplicity of demonstration.

25. Huron (2006) presents a sustained argument for statistical learning as foundational to musical experience, though he critiques aspects of the Krumhansl-Kessler key-profile model, as we will see. Huron surveys a wide range of empirical studies that have explored cross-cultural differences and commonalities in the hearing of tonal phenomena (broadly construed) in world musics. He concludes (tentatively) that statistical learning underwrites such processes across cultures. See Huron (2006, 168–172).

26. The values for the pitch profiles in Figure 5.5 were derived by tallying the duration of each pitch class in the Sarabande in eighth notes (the piece's smallest rhythmic subdivision). The key profiles were then adjusted so that their maxima matched those of the input vectors.

27. Some readers may find this surprising, as I did. The tonally off-center first measure, with its emphasized A♭ and fleeting C, can create such a vivid impression—standing as a seal over the entire Sarabande—that one can develop the (mistaken) impression that C is deemphasized throughout the piece. The statistical note-count in Figure 5.5(a) belies this, revealing that one of the means whereby Bach rights the tonal balance by movement's end is by assuring C's statistical dominance as the music progresses.

28. This is a simplification of the formula in the Krumhansl-Schmuckler key-finding algorithm. See Temperley (2011, 175–176).

29. On the justification for using measures as the smallest segments, see Temperley (2011, 189).

30. Temperley (2011, 191) does not provide a method to determine the precise value of the modulation penalty, and he admits to experimenting with various values in his tests and

then selecting the value "which seemed to yield the best performance." I employed the same procedure in this study to arrive at the penalty of –4. For an alternative approach to modulation in a key-finding algorithm, see Huron and Parncutt (1993), which draws on echoic memory.

31. The green cells in measure 8 seem to muddy the cadential clarity here, but this is visually misleading: there are four such cells because the key-finding readings are very coarse in this measure, given that it only includes one pitch. Moreover, the difference between the high scores (30) and the runners-up (27) in this column is greater than in any other measure.

32. Aarden's (2003) research also challenges the validity of the Krumhansl-Kessler profiles as models of statistical distribution, as the most prominent pitch class in many tonal corpora is not the tonic but the dominant. He thus proposes that the Krumhansl-Kessler profiles instead model phrase-final stability (or closure). See also the discussion in Huron (2006, 147–153).

33. On the "controversial" but "characteristically Schenkerian" delay of the *Kopfton* $\hat{3}$ until its arrival over a cadential six-four, see Schmalfeldt (2011, 44). For an instance of such an analysis from Schenker, see *Free Composition* (Schenker 1979, Figure 40, 7).

34. Among other things, one could adduce Bach's arrangement of the Sarabande for lute (BWV 995). In Bach's manuscript, these and the other bass pitches are placed on a separate lower staff, to be played on the lute's ringing, open bass courses (or "bourdons").

35. See Schachter (1987) and Rings (2011, 158n12).

36. But see Schachter (1999a) for a consideration of the ways that a background structure can at times impinge on (or manifest itself *in*) the foreground.

37. Compare Schachter (1999b, 184).

38. Schenker (1954, 252). For the original German, see Schenker (1906, 333).

39. It also prefigures Schoenberg's comments in his own *Harmonielehre* (written five years later) regarding the efforts of nontonic tonal regions to usurp the tonic's control, though here political/military metaphors replace Schenker's animism. See Schoenberg (1978, 150–153) and Hyer (2002, 731).

40. This is also the case with popular songs that involve "truck-driver modulations": wholesale modulations at the end of a song, often up by semitone (like gears shifting). Patrick McCreless (1996, 106) refers to this phenomenon as "Barry Manilow tonality."

41. "Erster Verlust" is arguably a *better* example of "tonal pairing" (Kinderman and Krebs 1996) than some often-cited examples that begin and end in different keys, as Schubert holds F minor and A♭ major in almost perfect equilibrium. For a similar reading of tonal pairing in a Schubert song that begins and ends with the same triad, see Harald Krebs's (1996) discussion of "Meeres Stille."

42. See, e.g., Schenker (1979, Figure 114, 8); and Salzer and Schachter (1969, 215–218, esp. Example 7-71a).

43. In the interest of accessibility, Pallett (2014) transposes the harmonies in his discussion to the white keys: Dm–F–Am–G (much to the consternation of some readers who posted comments). In quotes from Pallett I have substituted the actual, sounding chord names for his transposed ones.

44. The scholarly literature on harmony, tonality, and modality in popular music has grown considerably in recent decades. Several studies are of relevance for the discussion that follows, including Biamonte (2010), de Clercq and Temperley (2011), Doll (2017), Everett

(2004, 2009), Moore (2012), Nobile (2013), Tagg (2009), Temperley (2011), and Tymoczko (2014).

45. A point supported by Tymoczko (2014).

46. Some music cognition scholars nevertheless rely on introspection. David Temperley (1999, 78), for example, describes his working method for his own study of tonality in rock music thus: "I examine my intuitions as to what the tonal center is in many rock songs, assuming that these intuitions are the same as those of most other listeners." Berger's (1999) ethnography serves as a caution against such assumptions.

References

Aarden, Bret. 2003. "Dynamic Melodic Expectancy." PhD diss., Ohio State University.

Beiche, Michael. 1992. "Tonalität." In *Handworterbuch der musikalischen Terminologie,* edited by Hans Heinrich Eggebrecht. Stuttgart: Franz Steiner.

Berger, Harris. 1999. *Metal, Rock, and Jazz: Perception and the Phenomenology of Musical Experience.* Hanover, NH: University Press of New England.

Bharucha, Jamshed. 1984. "Anchoring Effects in Music." *Cognitive Psychology* 16: 485–518.

Bharucha, Jamshed. 1987. "Music Cognition and Perceptual Facilitation: A Connectionist Framework." *Music Perception* 5: 1–30.

Bharucha, Jamshed. 1991. "Pitch, Harmony, and Neural Nets: A Psychological Perspective." In *Music and Connectionism,* edited by Peter M. Todd and D. Gareth Loy, 84–99. Cambridge, MA: MIT Press.

Biamonte, Nicole. 2010. "Triadic Modal and Pentatonic Patterns in Rock Music." *Music Theory Spectrum* 32: 95–110.

Brown, Helen, and David Butler. 1984. "Tonal Structure versus Function: Studies of the Recognition of Harmonic Motion." *Music Perception* 2: 6–24.

Brown, Helen, David Butler, and Mari Riess Jones. 1994. "Musical and Temporal Influences on Key Discovery." *Music Perception* 11: 371–407.

Burnham, Scott. 1999. "The 'Heavenly Length' of Schubert's Music." *Ideas* 6. http://nationalhumanitiescenter.org/ideasv61/burnham.htm, accessed August 7, 2014.

Castellano, Mary, Jamshed Bharucha, and Carol Krumhansl. 1984. "Tonal Hierarchies in the Music of North India." *Journal of Experimental Psychology: General* 113: 394–412.

Cazden, Norman. 1954. "Tonal Function and Sonority in the Study of Harmony." *Journal of Research in Music Education* 2: 21–34.

Cherlin, Michael. 1993. "Schoenberg and *Das Unheimliche*: Spectres of Tonality." *Journal of Musicology* 11: 357–373.

Cherlin, Michael. 2007. *Schoenberg's Musical Imagination.* Cambridge: Cambridge University Press.

Cohn, Richard. 1996. "Maximally Smooth Cycles, Hexatonic Systems, and the Analysis of Late-Romantic Triadic Progressions." *Music Analysis* 15: 9–40.

Cohn, Richard. 2012. *Audacious Euphony: Chromaticism and the Triad's Second Nature.* New York: Oxford University Press.

Cook, Nicholas. 1987. "The Perception of Large-Scale Tonal Closure." *Music Perception* 5: 197–206.

Dahlhaus, Carl. 1980. *Between Romanticism and Modernism: Four Studies in the Music of the Later Nineteenth Century.* Berkeley: University of California Press.

de Clercq, Trevor, and David Temperley. 2011. "A Corpus Analysis of Rock Harmony." *Popular Music* 30: 47–70.

Doll, Christopher. 2017. *Hearing Harmony: Toward a Tonal Theory for the Rock Era.* Ann Arbor: University of Michigan Press.

Dowling, W. Jay. 1984. "Assimilation and Tonal Structure: Comment on Castellano, Bharucha, and Krumhansl." *Journal of Experimental Psychology: General* 113: 417–420.

Everett, Walter. 2004. "Making Sense of Rock's Tonal Systems." *Music Theory Online* 10, no. 4. http://www.mtosmt.org/issues/mto.04.10.4/mto.04.10.4.w_everett.html, accessed August 7, 2014.

Everett, Walter. 2009. *The Foundations of Rock: From Blue Suede Shoes to Suite: Judy Blue Eyes.* New York: Oxford University Press.

Forte, Allen. 1972. "Sets and Nonsets in Schoenberg's Atonal Music." *Perspectives of New Music* 11: 43–64.

Forte, Allen. 1981. "The Magical Kaleidoscope: Schoenberg's First Atonal Masterwork, Opus 11, Number 1." *Journal of the Arnold Schoenberg Institute* 5: 127–168.

Gjerdingen, Robert. 1999. "An Experimental Music Theory?" In *Rethinking Music,* edited by Nicholas Cook and Mark Everist, 161–170. Oxford: Oxford University Press.

Gjerdingen, Robert. 2007. *Music in the Galant Style.* New York: Oxford University Press.

Gut, Serge. 1976. "Dominante—Tonika—Subdominante." In *Handwörterbuch der musikalischen Terminologie,* edited by Hans Heinrich Eggebrecht. Stuttgart: Franz Steiner.

Harrison, Daniel. 1994. *Harmonic Function in Chromatic Music: A Renewed Dualist Perspective and an Account of Its Precedents.* Chicago: University of Chicago Press.

Hook, Julian. 2011. "Spelled Heptachords." In *Mathematics and Computation in Music, Third International Conference,* edited by Carlos Agon, Moreno Andreatta, Gérard Assayag, Emmanuel Amiot, Jean Bresson, and John Mandereau, 84–97. Berlin: Springer.

Huron, David. 2006. *Sweet Anticipation: Music and the Psychology of Expectation.* Cambridge, MA: MIT Press.

Huron, David, and Richard Parncutt. 1993. "An Improved Model of Tonality Perception Incorporating Pitch Salience and Echoic Memory." *Psychomusicology* 12: 154–171.

Hyer, Brian. 2002. "Tonality." In *The Cambridge History of Western Music Theory,* edited by Thomas Christensen, 726–752. Cambridge: Cambridge University Press.

Kinderman, William, and Harald Krebs, eds. 1996. *The Second-Practice of Nineteenth-Century Tonality.* Lincoln: University of Nebraska Press.

Krebs, Harald. 1996. "Some Early Examples of Tonal Pairing: Schubert's 'Meeres Stille' and 'Der Wanderer.'" In *The Second-Practice of Nineteenth-Century Tonality,* edited by William Kinderman and Harald Krebs, 17–33. Lincoln: University of Nebraska Press.

Krumhansl, Carol. 1990. *Cognitive Foundations of Musical Pitch.* Oxford: Oxford University Press.

Krumhansl, Carol. 2004. "The Cognition of Tonality—As We Know It Today." *Journal of New Music Research* 33: 253–268.

Krumhansl, Carol, and Edward Kessler. 1982. "Tracing the Dynamic Changes in Perceived Tonal Organization in a Spatial Representation of Musical Keys." *Psychological Review* 89: 334–368.

Kurth, Richard. 2001. "Suspended Tonalities in Schoenberg's Twelve-Tone Compositions." *Journal of the Arnold Schoenberg Center* 3: 239–266.

Lerdahl, Fred. 2001. *Tonal Pitch Space*. New York: Oxford University Press.

Lewin, David. 2006. *Studies in Music with Text*. New York: Oxford University Press.

Longuet-Higgins, Hugh, and Mark Steedman. 1971. "On Interpreting Bach." *Machine Intelligence* 6: 221–241.

Marvin, Elizabeth West, and Alexander Brinkmann. 1999. "The Effect of Modulation and Formal Manipulation on Perception of Tonic Closure by Expert Listeners." *Music Perception* 16: 389–408.

Marvin, Elizabeth West, and David Temperley. 2008. "Pitch-Class Distribution and the Identification of Key." *Music Perception* 25: 193–212.

Maxwell, H. John. 1992. "An Expert System for Harmonic Analysis of Tonal Music." In *Understanding Music with AI*, edited by Mira Balaban, Kemal Ebcioğlu, and Otto Laske, 335–353. Cambridge, MA: MIT Press.

McCreless, Patrick. 1996. "An Evolutionary Perspective on Nineteenth-Century Semitonal Relations." In *The Second-Practice of Nineteenth-Century Tonality*, edited by William Kinderman and Harald Krebs, 87–113. Lincoln: University of Nebraska Press.

Moore, Allan F. 2012. *Song Means: Analysing and Interpreting Recorded Popular Song*. Burlington, VT: Ashgate.

Nattiez, Jean-Jacques. 1990. *Music and Discourse: Toward a Semiology of Music*. Trans. Carolyn Abbate. Princeton, NJ: Princeton University Press.

Nobile, Drew. 2013. "A Structural Approach to the Analysis of Rock Music." PhD diss., City University of New York.

Ogdon, Will. 1981. "How Tonality Functions in Schoenberg's Opus 11, Number 1." *Journal of the Arnold Schoenberg Institute* 5: 169–181.

Pallett, Owen. 2014. "Ecstatic Melodic Copulation: Explaining the Genius of Daft Punk's 'Get Lucky' with Music Theory." Slate.com, March 28. http://www.slate.com/articles/arts/culturebox/2014/03/daft_punk_s_get_lucky_explained_using_music_theory.html, accessed August 6, 2014.

Riemann, Hugo. 1900. *Musik-Lexikon*. 5th edition. Leipzig: Max Hesse.

Rings, Steven. 2011. *Tonality and Transformation*. New York: Oxford University Press.

Salzer, Felix, and Carl Schachter. 1969. *Counterpoint in Composition*. New York: McGraw-Hill.

Schachter, Carl. 1987. "Analysis by Key." *Music Analysis* 6: 289–318.

Schachter, Carl. 1999a. "Structure as Foreground: 'Das Drama des Ursatzes.'" In *Schenker Studies 2*, edited by Carl Schachter and Hedi Siegel, 298–314. Cambridge: Cambridge University Press.

Schachter, Carl. 1999b. *Unfoldings: Essays in Schenkerian Theory and Analysis*. Edited by Joseph N. Straus. New York: Oxford University Press.

Schenker, Heinrich. 1906. *Harmonielehre*. Vienna: Universal Edition.

Schenker, Heinrich. 1954. *Harmony*. Translated by Elisabeth Mann Borgese, edited by Oswald Jonas. Chicago: University of Chicago Press.

Schenker, Heinrich. 1979. *Free Composition*. Translated and edited by Ernst Oster. New York: Longman.

Schmalfeldt, Janet. 2011. *In the Process of Becoming: Analytic and Philosophical Perspectives on Form in Early Nineteenth-Century Music*. New York: Oxford University Press.

Schoenberg, Arnold. 1954. *Structural Functions of Harmony*. New York: W. W. Norton.

Schoenberg, Arnold. 1978. *Theory of Harmony*. Translated by Roy E. Carter. Berkeley: University of California Press.

Straus, Joseph N. 1987. "The Problem of Prolongation in Post-Tonal Music." *Journal of Music Theory* 31: 1–21.

Straus, Joseph N. 1990. *Remaking the Past: Musical Modernism and the Influence of the Tonal Tradition*. Cambridge, MA: Harvard University Press.

Tagg, Philip. 2009. *Everyday Tonality: Towards a Tonal Theory of What Most People Hear*. New York: Mass Media Music Scholars' Press.

Temperley, David. 1999. "The Question of Purpose in Music Theory: Description, Suggestion, and Explanation." *Current Musicology* 66: 66–85.

Straus, Joseph N. 2001. *The Cognition of Basic Musical Structures*. Cambridge, MA: MIT Press.

Tovey, Donald Francis. 1949. *The Main Stream of Music, and Other Essays*. Oxford: Oxford University Press.

Tymoczko, Dmitri. 2014. "Rock Logic." Keynote paper presented at the 4th Annual Conference of the Royal Musical Association Music and Philosophy Study Group. London, June 28.

Vos, Piet. 2000. "Tonality Induction: Theoretical Problems and Dilemmas." *Music Perception* 17: 403–416.

Weber, Gottfried. 1846. *Attempt at a Systematically Arranged Theory of Musical Composition*, Vol. 1. Translated by James F. Warner. Boston: J. H. Wilkins and R. B. Carter.

Wen, Eric. 1999. "Bass-Line Articulations of the *Urlinie*." In *Schenker Studies 2*, edited by Carl Schachter and Hedi Siegel, 276–297. Cambridge: Cambridge University Press.

Winograd, Terry. 1968. "Linguistics and the Computer Analysis of Tonal Harmony." *Journal of Music Theory* 12: 2–49.

CHAPTER 6

....

TIMBRE

....

DAVID BLAKE

TIMBRE is the distinctive quality of a particular sound. It is how I can tell that I am hearing, for example, a French harpsichord (⊙ Audio Example 6.1) instead of an Italian harpsichord (⊙ Audio Example 6.2), or a virginal (⊙ Audio Example 6.3), or a fortepiano (⊙ Audio Example 6.4), or a musical instrument digital interface (MIDI) keyboard (⊙ Audio Example 6.5), or a player piano (⊙ Audio Example 6.6), or a coffee grinder (⊙ Audio Example 6.7), or a heavy book falling on a carpeted floor (⊙ Audio Example 6.8), or countless other sounds.[1] If this list is slightly ridiculous, it speaks to timbre's power, plasticity, and multidimensionality. Timbre is able to convey enough information about all these things immediately to enable a listener to perceive the source of a sound, sight unseen. At the same time, the manifold shadings of timbre, both caused by individual sound sources and techniques of sonic manipulation and production, provide composers and performers with a virtually unlimited coloristic palette.

The problem with timbre—with *analyzing* timbre—is that it does all its work outside the realm of language. I can hear a French harpsichord and know immediately that it is a French harpsichord, but it is impossible to say directly how I know the instrument sounds, well, "harpsichordy" (see Raffman 1993). Its plectrum-based attack produces an envelope distinct from hammered-string keyboard instruments, and its larger size creates a deeper sound than other plucked-string keyboard instruments. The prosaic fact of owning a French harpsichord also leads me to surmise that if I hear a harpsichord sound at home, the instrument is the likeliest source of the sound that I hear. Yet none of these ex post facto explanations actually identifies the distinctiveness of the harpsichord's sound, nor do they enhance my awareness that I am hearing a French harpsichord. Emily Dolan has pithily stated that "writing about timbre is difficult" (Dolan 2013, 53). This difficulty results not merely from the challenge of describing sonic quality, which is rooted in human cognitive processes discussed later in this chapter, but from the laboriousness of such descriptions and their inadequacy for verbally encapsulating sonic stimuli.

For many years, music theorists were not overly concerned about this problem with timbre. The general equation of a musical work with its written score either excised timbre entirely from analytical consideration or rendered it, in Leonard Meyer's terminology, as a secondary parameter less integral to a work's style and identity than pitch or rhythm (Meyer 1989). Beginning in the 1960s, electronic music composers and analysts of twentieth-century music increasingly recognized the practical and theoretical salience of timbral manipulation in modern composition. Over the past two decades, factors such as the inclusion of popular and non-Western musics in music theory, as well as the broader interest in sonic objects such as performances, recordings, and soundscapes across the humanities, have further intensified the interest in timbre within music scholarship. The increased attention to timbre, though, has only exacerbated its epistemological thorniness. As much as timbre has become part of the contemporary theoretical zeitgeist across musical categories—popular, art, and non-Western—and scholarly disciplines—music theory, musicology, popular music studies, ethnomusicology, anthropology, and philosophy—it remains non-discursive while theoretical analysis remains discursive. Like passengers in London Underground stations, theorists of timbre encounter a gap that needs to be minded.

This chapter focuses on the four main approaches to minding the gaps occasioned by timbral analysis. First, what constitutes timbre? What is the distinctive quality of timbre itself? The inherent interplay between acoustic phenomena and cognitive processes in timbre leads to the second issue: How is timbre perceived? What cognitive, ecological, and social factors shape how it is understood? Third, how does timbre contribute to musical composition? In what ways have theorists approached timbral manipulation? Finally, how can timbre be represented? If timbre "explains as it masks," in Pierre Boulez's eloquent phrase (1987, 170), how can the parameter be unmasked to reinforce a cogent theoretical argument?

These questions have led to a considerable amount of frustration for theorists used to more solid discursive and notational grounding. Notwithstanding the significant debates over the other parameters discussed in this section, it is difficult to imagine an article devoted to any of them that simply asks in exasperation, to paraphrase the title of a 1989 Carol Krumhansl essay, "Why is it so hard to understand?" Yet timbre's affective immediacy and discursive challenges also have stimulated a rich and growing body of interdisciplinary inquiry that increasingly insists on the parameter's centrality in textual and contextual meaning.

WHAT CONSTITUTES TIMBRE?

The final movement of Caroline Shaw's *Partita for 8 Voices*, her *a capella* reimagination of the Baroque genre, is the Passacaglia. Following genre conventions, the piece opens by repeating a harmonic progression (in this case, a ten-bar phrase in D major repeated three times). Unlike Baroque exemplars, which vary the melody or develop accompanimental textures, the progression repeats the exact same note lengths and all but one of the same pitches in all voices.[2] Instead, each iteration opens with a different vowel and vocal technique. The first line (▶ Audio Example 6.9) is on ɔ, the International Phonetic Alphabet

(IPA) sign for the vowel produced in the center-back of the mouth with a semiopen oral cavity (the *au* sound in *cause*).[3] Shaw does not indicate any particular technique, so the singers use a standard chest voice. The second line (⊙ Audio Example 6.10) moves to ɐ, a neutral sound produced by moving forward in the mouth and slightly opening the lips. This time, Shaw specifies that the singers switch between chest and head voice for each harmony, creating pairs of chords. After returning to ɔ for the last two bars, the singers jump to æ, the most forward vowel sound produced with a semiopen mouth (the *a* sound in *at*), for the third iterati on (⊙ Audio Example 6.11). The alternation between chest and head voice intensifies to a belt, punctuated by a "pitched exhale." Accentuating the progression from back to front in vowel sound is an increase in volume for each iteration: *piano* the first time, *mezzoforte* the second, and *fortissimo* the third.

The short analysis given here is intended to demonstrate how Shaw isolates timbre as the most important parameter for the formal development of the Passacaglia's opening. Stipulating that pitch and harmonic rhythm stay constant through each iteration reduces the contribution of those parameters. Demonstrating that the vowel sounds opening each line traverse a smooth progression from back to front of the mouth, a progression apparent on a standard IPA vowel chart (Figure 6.1), suggests Shaw's attention to vocal timbre. The importance of these timbres is seconded by the observation that the vowel progression is augmented by dynamic intensification and framed by contrasting vocal techniques. In this attempt to direct the analytical focus on timbre, though, significant slippage has occurred: I do not discuss timbre qua sound, but instead attend to the vocal techniques and more accessible musical

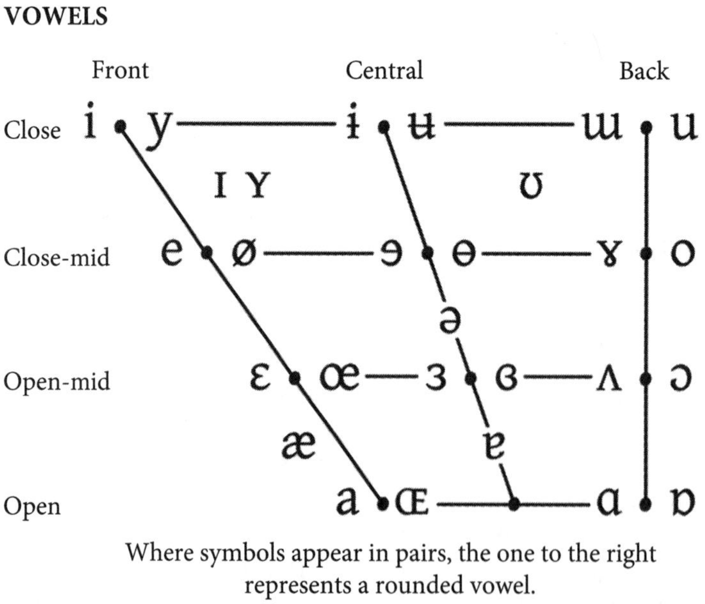

VOWELS

Where symbols appear in pairs, the one to the right represents a rounded vowel.

FIGURE 6.1 IPA vowel chart. The progression ɔ ◊ ɐ ◊ æ moves from the back to the middle to the front of the mouth, with a somewhat open oral cavity.

parameters used to produce particular sounds. Can one actually talk about timbre in and of itself, and if so, how?

As compared with other musical parameters, the analysis of timbre—that is, the theoretical interest in the quality of sound—is in its relative infancy. Such analysis did not begin until the eighteenth century, spurred on by increased refinement and standardization in instrument building, as well as the scientific and taxonomic impulses of Enlightenment philosophy. The earliest exploration of sound in and of itself within the literature on Western music theory is Jean-Jacques Rousseau's entry on "timbre" in Denis Diderot and Jean le Rond d'Alembert's *Encyclopédie* of 1765. Rousseau proposed that differences between sounds are produced from sonic qualities distinct from pitch, rhythm, and dynamics. Yet he resorted to stumbling and vague adjectives when trying to describe those qualities: "An oboe would be difficult to mistake for a flute: it could not soften its sound to the same degree. The sound of a flute would always have a certain *je ne sais quoi* of softness and pleasantness, while that of an oboe would have a certain dryness and harshness, which makes it impossible to confuse the two" (quoted in Dolan 2013, 55). Thus, at the outset of modern timbral analysis, Rousseau recognized that sonic quality was distinctive and describable, but its nature remained quite literally, "I do not know what."

Other early works examining timbre, most notably Hector Berlioz's *Grand traité d'instrumentation et d'orchestration modernes*, continued in Rousseau's direction by describing instrument characteristics through creative yet ultimately vague adjectives. For example, Berlioz characterized the sound of the oboe as a "bittersweet voice" that conveyed "candor, naïve grace, sentimental delight, or the suffering of weaker creatures" (Macdonald 2004, 104)—evocative language that attempts to define sonic quality through emotions and metaphors.

Since timbre is so difficult to describe precisely, it is easier to define it by what it is *not*, rather than by what it is. Parametric negation is the basis of the still-cited definition of timbre set forth in 1960 by the American Standards Association (now the American National Standards Institute): "that attribute of auditory sensation in terms of which a listener can judge that two sounds similarly presented and having the same loudness and pitch are dissimilar" (American Standards Association 1960, 45).[4] This perspective is demonstrated in ▶ Audio Examples 6.9–6.11; timbre distinguishes the three harmonic progressions aside from the difference in volume.

If descriptive precision can occur only via negation, however, the very nature of timbre as an identifiable object is cast into doubt. Is timbre simply residual—that which remains after all other parameters are accounted for (Slawson 1981, 132)? Is it actually an intrinsic sonic quality, or is it the result of an Enlightenment-derived aesthetic and a scientific approach to sound that isolates and measures sonic phenomena apart from its compositional function (Dolan 2013; Steege 2012; Chion 2011)?

The identification and analysis of timbre certainly derive from a particular historical and philosophical context, and yet the parameter has an acoustic mooring. The nineteenth-century physician Hermann von Helmholtz discovered that the quality of a sound was produced by combinations of upper partials, the sine waves above the fundamental pitch produced in a sound. In his pithy summary, "the quality of tone depends on the form of vibration" (Helmholtz 1875, 32). Overtone combinations can be extracted from sounds through Fourier analysis, a mathematical technique based on the French Enlightenment scientist Joseph Fourier's theory that the complex shapes of heat waves can be reduced to pure sinusoidal waves. Following World War II, phonological research in Bell Labs led to computer technologies that could analyze sound waves and synthesize them into visual representations called spectrograms.[5] Spectrograms will be discussed in greater detail in the fourth section of this chapter, but suffice it for now to show those of the harmonies from ⏵ Audio Examples 6.9–6.11 (Figures 6.2–6.4); the

FIGURE 6.2 Spectrogram of Caroline Shaw, Passacaglia from *Partita for 8 Voices* (2012), 0:04–0:18.

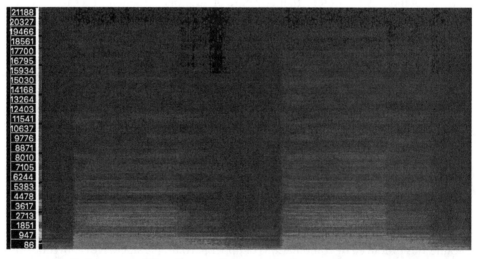

FIGURE 6.3 Spectrogram of Shaw, Passacaglia, 0:39–0:52.

FIGURE 6.4 Spectrogram of Shaw, Passacaglia, 1:12–1:23.

pitches are exactly the same, but the spectrograms show that the chords have progressively increasing combinations of upper partials resulting from changes in vowel and
vocal technique.

HOW IS TIMBRE PERCEIVED?

Acoustic approaches to timbre offer objective physical data that connect tone color
to waveform shape, seemingly sidestepping the seeming vagueness of descriptive
approaches and definitively answering ontological questions. Yet visual representations
of spectra do not account for the other crucial part of timbre: human cognition. Timbre
is not simply acoustical, but *psychoacoustical*; as Brad Osborn (2016, 93) has argued,
"timbre is . . . not so much a musical parameter as a perceptual process of relating
sounds to their sources." These perceptual processes indelibly shape how we understand timbre, how those sonic qualities become meaningful, and why we have trouble
articulating what that meaning is.

Of all musical parameters, timbre is most dependent on human cognitive processes
of sonic stimuli. Ethnomusicologist Cornelia Fales has written that "in a very real
sense, timbre exists only in the mind of the listener" (2005, 163). Timbral perception
is both auditory and embodied; when we hear a voice or an instrument, we can engage

mimetically with the bodily processes that make a particular sound (Heidemann 2014, 2016; Reed 2005; Wallmark 2014; Solís 2015; Schiff 2012, 15–16). It is no accident that the go-to word for expressing timbre is *feel,* because timbre's embodied nature is easier to express than its aural cognition.

Fales's writings on timbre (for instance, Fales 2002, 2005) explain two critical aspects of aural cognition. First, the perception of sound quality, like that of light or temperature, is preattentive, occurring immediately in the subconscious prior to conscious attention. Preattentive perception allows sonic information to contribute instantaneously to reflexive action, which has many advantages. If I hear my toddler crying in the other room, her potential danger or distress is lessened if I am directly compelled to see if she is OK rather than having to catalog the sonic qualities of each item in that room consciously to deduce that my toddler is the most likely source of the sound that I hear.

The preattentive nature of timbral cognition is immeasurably helpful for everyday actions, allowing us to make innumerable snap decisions based strictly on sound. It is also, unfortunately, responsible for the fundamental problem of timbral analysis because unconscious sonic processing precedes and takes place outside of conscious verbalization. This is why students in any college music class can, like Rousseau, readily distinguish between an oboe and a flute but struggle to explain why these instruments sound different aside from using material adjectives (reedy or breathy), metaphors, or personal associations. Our brains are just not wired to describe timbre directly.

Second, perception is a heuristic process geared toward source identification. Consider the complex sound mass that surrounds you right now. At the time that I write this sentence, I hear the clickety-clack of my typing, the humidifier for the aforementioned French harpsichord, the television softly playing in the living room, and cars driving past my window. The way that I describe this sound mass (and you describe yours, I assume) is not as a bunch of waveforms, just as I do not describe my surroundings as a collection of atoms. Rather, I hear and describe a collection of objects.[6] Humans are geared to process and identify what is making a sound through the act of hearing, rather than ruminating on what sonic qualities distinguish one thing from another.

The human brain can identify a remarkable amount of sounds through fine-tuned, subconscious sonic analysis. Yet the sheer wealth of sonic data entering our always-open ears risks overtasking our cognitive processes. As a result, human brains rely on certain tools to help make sense of our sound worlds. Sonic cognition tends to group our cache of known sounds through their associations. The voices of family members are perceived as "my relatives"; guitar, bass guitar, and drums can be perceived as a "rock ensemble"; piano and a classically trained voice singing German as a "Lied"; and so forth.

The strong ties among these various timbres manifest when unanticipated sounds emerge in the contexts where certain categories of sound would be expected to occur, such as the synthesizer melody in the bridge of the Beach Boys' "God Only Knows" (⊙ Audio Example 6.12) or the "kazoo chorus" that Charles Ives added to the penultimate melodic statement in his art song "Son of a Gambolier" (⊙ Audio Example 6.13). New (Beach Boys) and unexpected (Ives) sounds are approached tautologically, drawing on prior experiences to shape interpretation (Fales 2005, 163). The opening verses of "God Only Knows," not to mention the entirety of *Pet Sounds*, use a wider instrumental palette than standard rock songs, so unusual sounds are to be expected. Its electronic timbre is very different than the French horn solo opening the work or the strings swelling up in the second verse, making it hard to describe. In the case of Ives, my knowledge of his repertoire leads me to expect the occasional unusual instrumental insertion, such as the optional flute in the final movement of the *Concord Sonata* and the pianist yodeling in "Charlie Rutlage." The kazoo is a sound that I associate with silliness, which makes its appearance in an art song comic and irreverent to me.

Tautological interpretation is one of the many cognitive tools used to classify and understand sounds. Sound masses with multiple stimuli can also be grouped together according to shared characteristics, a process called perceptual fusion (McAdams, Depalle, and Clarke 2004, 184–185). Many types of perceptual fusion contribute to musical works: shared pitch, harmonic cohesion, or shared attack point, known as onset synchrony. Onset synchrony forms the cognitive basis for the pedagogical aims of Benjamin Britten's *The Young Person's Guide to the Orchestra*. At the opening *tutti* statement of the main theme (⊙ Audio Example 6.14), the listener immediately identifies the full sound as "an orchestra," rather than a combination of a hundred individual instruments that happen to be performing simultaneously. During the concluding double fugue (⊙ Audio Example 6.15), though, the sounds of each instrument are distinguished through their different thematic entrances before coalescing back to the initial "orchestra" sound. The progression from separate onsets to collective performance effectively demonstrates how the orchestra heard at the beginning is a composite of individual instruments.

Other forms of grouping can be more complex. The sound mass of computer keys, passing cars, a humidifier, and television from the previous section includes four quite distinct sounds, but because they are all common and undisruptive sounds within my apartment, I can perceptually group them together as "the usual background noise." (By contrast, the timbre of a toddler's cry is well calibrated to cut through background noise and command immediate attention.)

All these cognitive tools are ultimately directed toward understanding environments. Human cognitive processes have developed over hundreds of thousands of years so that we can better sense, and thus survive in, environments (Tomlinson 2015; Fales 2005, 157–158). James Gibson (1966) argued that senses such as hearing always have an ecological purpose to identify, contextualize, and act upon. Gibson's argument that perception is the process of making sense of environmental stimuli can be adapted to music analysis by considering the role of contextual perception (Clarke 2005). In particular, Gibson's theory of affordances usefully provides an ecological basis for timbral analysis. Affordances are the means of using prior experiences to classify unfamiliar stimuli to make sense of a perceptual environment. The concept of affordance resembles the tautological processes of sonic cognition described by Fales, but it focuses on the practical ways that sounds are created for and understood within given environments, rather than the inner workings of cognitive processes.

The meaning of "environment" from an ecological perspective can be usefully flexible. It can refer to the relationship between sound and a specific place (Osborn and Blake 2017); the site of performance or playback (Clarke 2005); the sound space of a recording (Smalley 2007; Moore 2012; Zagorski-Thomas 2014); and the expectations of a genre, repertoire, or oeuvre (Slater 2011; Gardiner and Lim 2014; Osborn 2016). Each of these elements offers different types of affordances, with composers, record producers, and listeners drawing on the complex web of categorization and disorientation to make timbres meaningful. Brad Osborn's recent book on Radiohead (Osborn 2016), for example, develops a theory of timbre that situates meaning in the sweet spot of recognition and estrangement, which he refers to as *salience*. He suggests that Radiohead's recordings are ecological environments in which the search for familiarity and the exploration of the novel lead to musical satisfaction.

Human cognition is calibrated toward certain sounds more than others. The sound that human sonic cognition is most finely attuned to is the human voice. We use timbre to shape meaning about our identities and our words, and we draw upon it when listening to acquire information about the speaker's identity and his or her words. As Nina Eidsheim (2014, 2) argued, the voice is "an object of knowledge." The timbre of a voice can suggest many things about the person speaking. Who is this person? What are her or his approximate age and gender? What is his or her fluency with the language being used (either linguistic or musical)? Do I recognize him or her? If so, from where? How does this person feel? What are the denotations of what is being said?

Cognition, ecological factors, embodied knowledge, and mimesis allow us to process, understand, produce, and act upon vocal timbre. Collecting and producing this and other information from the voice is so instinctual that it is nearly impossible to conceive of a meaningless voice. Pierre Schaeffer's early *musique concrète* experiments with vocal snippets, for example, grappled with the psychological dimensions of source manipulation. No matter how much vocal sounds were abstracted or distorted, his perception was always directed by the search for identity, producing a sense of estrangement and uncanniness (Kaiser 2015, 169–171).

Early theorists of timbre also began with the voice, exploring the function of vocal timbre in composition (e.g., Cogan 1969; Erickson 1975) and using metaphors drawn from vocal production, such as *openness* or *laxness,* to suggest analytically meaningful timbral factors (Slawson 1985, especially 54–55). Trying to understand sound through our understanding of and experience with the voice first stimulated timbral scholarship. More recent work exploring the relationship between voice and identity has instead deeply unsettled foundational precepts of timbral analysis. Human cognitive processes are geared toward source identification, but vocal timbre can communicate information that differs from desired identities.

For instance, transgender women often grapple with a deep voice coded as "male" as a result of the pubescent processes undergone when growing up in a male body. American academics with accents resulting from birth region or speaking English as a second or third language have to modulate their voice between family and the classroom, especially when that family comes from a less privileged social stratum. Vocal timbre is a space for sonically enacting and negotiating the social politics of identity formation, an observation that has stimulated much recent philosophical work on the affective formation of identity (for instance, Barthes 1977, 1991; Cavarero 2005; Dolar 2006).

Vocal timbre thus always involves a sense of performativity, of social affiliation and disaffiliation, and of power dynamics. Nicholas Harkness's anthropology of South Korean singers of Western classical music identified a perceived link between the supposed cleanliness of classically trained vocal timbre and Protestant narratives of national uplift, one predicated on the debasement of Korean phonemes (Harkness 2013). Nina Eidsheim's work on synthesized voices and vocal pedagogy suggests that techniques and technologies of vocal production reify socioracial differences that have no biological basis (Eidsheim 2009, 2015).

Timbre can be a site to reinforce dominant power structures sonically, but it can also resist and recuperate. In his study of Xhosa choral music, Grant Olwage (2004) scrutinizes the uncomfortable idea that this repertoire, which is primarily sung by black South Africans, somehow "sounds" black. Rather than suggesting that sound itself has racial characteristics, he suggests that the repertoire emphasizes differences between Xhosa phonemes and those of European languages to direct attention to the power of black South African cultural expression. Timbre may arise from acoustic properties, but its production and meaningfulness is profoundly social in orientation.

HOW DOES TIMBRE CONTRIBUTE
TO MUSICAL COMPOSITION?

Timbre is simply too powerful not to have a significant impact on composition throughout Western music history. Yet the aforementioned difficulties with describing it, combined with the problems of representing it (to be discussed in the next section), appear to have rendered it as a subordinate result of genre or ensemble forces rather than an active shaping parameter.[7] It was not until the radical conclusion to Arnold Schoenberg's 1911 treatise *Harmonielehre* that timbre was actively discussed as a primary compositional concern. Upending the traditional focus on pitch in music theory treatises, Schoenberg provocatively suggested that timbre, rendered as *Klangfarbe* or "tone-color," is the most fundamental musical parameter. He wrote that "tone-color is, thus, the main topic, pitch a subdivision. Pitch is nothing else but tone color measured in one direction" (Schoenberg 1978, 421). Imagining the possibility of "tone-color melody," or *Klangfarbenmelodie*, he asserted that the future of musical composition lay in the manipulation and ordering of tone color rather than pitch or harmony. Schoenberg's *Farben*, the third of his *Fünf Orchesterstücke* op. 16 (1909), is seen as the first experiment in tone-color melody.[8]

Schoenberg did not pursue timbral composition systematically after *Farben*, but he rightly predicted that timbre would assume greater prominence as the twentieth century progressed. The scratchy and ineffective recording and playback technologies at the time of Schoenberg's *Harmonielehre* were superseded by improved versions that could circulate sound with increasingly exact fidelity. Electronic instruments were invented that could manufacture specific sonic waveforms, allowing direct acoustic manipulation. Production tools developed the capability of making "any sound you can imagine," in Paul Théberge's phrase (Théberge 1997). At the same time, the experimentalist spirit of twentieth- and twenty-first-century composition has spurred new approaches to sonic materials and formal structures. Schoenberg's concept of *Klangfarbenmelodie* was hardly more than a polemical flight of fancy, but the hundred years since have become, as composer Paul Rudy (2007, 6) put it, the "common timbral period."[9]

Attending to timbre in composition requires exploring its peculiar capabilities. Given its orientation toward identification, timbre can be emphasized through choosing, reimagining, and manipulating sound sources. Simply stated, timbre can emerge when instrumental combinations have thematic importance (Lilly 2005; Lochhead 2005). Composers, especially Edgard Varèse, Anton Webern, and György Ligeti, have more radically reimagined instrumental ensembles as combinations of distinct materials (Thomas 1981; François 1991). Danuta Mirka's analysis of Krzysztof Penderecki's "timbral system" offers an especially thorough methodology on the potential formal centrality of materiality in twentieth-century art music. In her study, Mirka argues that Penderecki's compositions during his 1960s sonorist period exploited timbral difference as a compositional trait through conceiving of the orchestra as a "complex of several different sound generators which reclassify the orchestra based on material purposes" (Mirka 2001, 440). According to Mirka, Penderecki classified the orchestra by three primary types of instrument materials (wood, metal, and leather) and two secondary materials (hair and felt) used to generate sound. She argues that Penderecki's forms arise through the juxtaposition, transformation, isolation, and combination of these distinct material categories. Timbre can also emerge paradoxically through dense polyphonic textures that eradicate individual pitches, rhythms, and instrumental sources, as in micropolyphony (Bauer 2001), spectralism (Murail 1984; Cornicello 2000), and new complexity (Hoffman 2005).

Electronic and electroacoustic music has received a special focus. Electronic manipulation can produce many different timbres, of course, and the recent theoretical interest in timbre was spurred in part by electronic music composers exploring how synthesizers could shape timbre through waveform manipulation (Fennelly 1967; Erickson 1975; Slawson 1981, 1985). Electronic sounds also challenge cognitive processes in interesting ways. Human cognition is attuned to naturally occurring sound worlds comprised of complex combinations of sine waves, but the artificial production of sound through electronics cannot produce the same complexity and irregularity as that of acoustic sources. We lack any affordances to electronic sounds, granting them an estranging, alien quality (Demers 2010; Fales 2005; Leydon 2012). This estrangement intensifies as electronic sounds get simpler and more periodic because we attend to waveform *Gestalten* rather than individual sine waves. Early synthesizers were quite applicable to sci-fi soundtracks because their simple sinusoidal waveforms lacked any natural affordances.

Rebecca Leydon has identified the way that George Crumb's electroacoustic music exploits contrasts between "transparency," or purely electronic sounds, and "turbidity," noisy timbres produced by distortion. She proposes that the palette of string sounds in *Black Angels*—from the purification of the *Der Tod und das Mädchen* viol consort and harmonics of "God Music" to the aggressive, noisy bow pressure in "Devil Music"— represents a modern instantiation of the Enlightenment division between the beautiful and the sublime (Leydon 2012).

Electronically produced sounds may lack natural affordances, but the plasticity of compositional and production tools offers fine-tuned ways to forge timbral meaning. Composers can transform and mimic familiar sounds to exploit ecological affordances in new ways (Smalley 1997). Producers can use distortion, smoothening, compression, and other such techniques to forge connections and distinctions between artists (Moore 2012, 45–46). In popular music in particular, timbre is produced in recognition of the parameter's immediacy for artist and genre identification (Walser 1993; Everett 2000, 278; Berger and Fales 2005; Garrett 2008; Blake 2012).

Finally, because timbre is always shaped by contexts, it is a site for interpreting meaning through source identification and our embodied understanding of those sounds. The terror of Lulu's climactic scream in Berg's eponymous opera comes in part from our knowledge that only traumatic and life-threatening events could cause us to yell with such existential desperation. The intimate nature of crooning or singer-songwriter music results from the unobtrusive amplification of soft, undistorted voices associated with quiet conversation. The extreme distortion of a heavy metal guitar solo magnifies its tactile virtuosity, seeing to reach beyond the terrestrial toward the transcendental.

Returning to the opening of Shaw's Passacaglia, I imagine singing the quiet closed ɔ, in a quiet or solemn setting. By contrast, the loud open æ and pitched exhalation reminds me of the ecstasy and exhaustion of performance.[10] Together, these disparate examples demonstrate how timbral choices always reach toward our stockpile of experiences, emotions, and associations.

How Is Timbre Represented?

The analysis of timbre, or any other musical parameter, requires methodologies to understand its function within a piece or oeuvre. Yet the project of music analysis also necessitates some means of description and visual representation to facilitate the explication of analytic findings. If feelings of frustration over timbral analysis somehow haven't set in yet, they surely will, for not only is timbre sublinguistic and preattentive, making it difficult to describe, it is also multidimensional. The world of possible timbres cannot be scaled quantitatively as pitch (waveform frequency), volume (amplitude), or rhythm (time) can. There is thus no direct way to notate timbre, no straightforward metaphor such as note height for pitch or note shape for duration. Some early theorists of timbre sought to highlight timbral function through augmenting standard notation (for instance, Chou 1979; DeVale 1985). Because timbre involves radically different notational approaches than pitch or rhythm, most scholars instead seek non-score-based means of visual representation that can direct attention to timbre's specific contributions.

Spectrography has emerged as the most common tool for visually representing timbral characteristics.[11] As mentioned at the end of the first section of this chapter, spectrograms depict the overtones of a given sound. Initially developed as a tool for scientific sonic analysis, composer and theorist Robert Cogan has demonstrated their applicability for timbral analysis in a number of foundational studies (for instance, Cogan 1969, 1984; Cogan and Escot 1976). Spectrograms can show the acoustical phenomena comprising distinct timbres empirically, without the mediation of language or notation. Yet they cannot account for psychoacoustical processes, and their interpretation relies on the exegesis of often-obscure spectral configurations to explain immediately perceptible sonic characteristics.

Despite its imperfections, spectrographic exegesis remains the most viable tool for connecting acoustic features with timbral perception. John Latartara, perhaps the leading contemporary proponent of spectrographic analysis, has noted that spectrographic images "do not show us what we hear, but rather provide acoustic reasons for our musical perceptions" (Latartara 2012, 92; see also Brackett 2000, 27).[12] Rather, spectrograms best serve timbral analysis when careful comparisons pinpoint analytically significant acoustic data.

Three examples of comparative analysis in the work of Cornelia Fales, John Latartara, and Daniel Leech-Wilkinson demonstrate the usefulness of spectrography. Fales proposes a theory of "timbral anomaly" (Fales 2002, 66) that involves exaggerating and transforming timbres to produce new effects. Her spectrogram of Tuvan throat singing demonstrates timbral exaggeration by depicting a static overtone framework with shifting formant levels (frequency areas emphasized in a sound through an increased concentration of sine waves), and her excerpt of Inanga Chuchotée singing (a Burundian genre featuring the *inanga*, a zither-like instrument, accompanied by a soft whisper) shows how the whisper sounds amplify the full, noisy overtone structure of the *inanga* (Fales 2002, 68, 71).

Latartara theorizes the fundamental role of the vowel sound ə (a neutral vowel or schwa) in Thai classical singing (*uan*) because of its overtone saturation. His spectrograms of idiomatic melodic fragments show how their partials derive from those of ə, making the vowel sound a plaintive backdrop for sonic transformation (Latartara 2012, 97–105).

Finally, Leech-Wilkinson analyzes Guillaume de Machaut's ballad "Rose, lis, printemps, verdure," arguing that Machaut's poetic structure places vowel sounds adjacent in the mouth next to one another in the text. He shows spectrograms of two performances of the opening text to "Rose, lis," which indicate a gradually rising formant indicative of smooth vowelistic progression (Leech-Wilkinson 2003, 259). All these examples use carefully explained comparisons of spectrograms to extract the precise acoustic data that encapsulate striking timbral features.

Spectrograms and standard notation are imperfect strategies for representing timbral effects, but words are the only available alternative. And since timbre is sublinguistic, verbal language appears to be one of the worst media for understanding the parameter. It is not irredeemable, though, so long as analysts accept that words do different things for timbre than for other musical parameters. In exploring the concept of nuance in rhythmic grooves, philosopher Tiger Roholt distinguishes between direct description, the ability to state something precisely; and indirect description, the recourse to contextual factors when direct description is impossible (Roholt 2014, 29). Like nuance, timbre resists direct description, but indirect description can still be meaningfully and contextually precise. Some forms of description, such as references to materiality (Mirka 2001) or contrasts between opposing characteristics (Cogan 1984; Moore 2012), attempt to harness timbral multidimensionality through relying on commonly accepted descriptors. But if, as the composer Jean-Charles François has argued, "any project that would establish a topography of timbre can only be circumstantial" (François 1991, 49), and if the production and perception of timbre is deeply subjective and environmental, and the expression of timbre can't help but be indirect, why try to fit the square peg of timbre into the round hole of analytic expectations set up for other parameters?

Louise Meintjes's ethnography of a popular music studio devoted to black South African music embraces the use of timbral descriptors as meaningful sites of contentious aesthetic debates rather than impoverished adjectives. She writes "timbre matters because it houses debates that are articulated as a feeling about things—a 'Zulu' guitar, a 'ballsy' drum sound. Because timbral qualities are about feeling, they are deeply invested but never fully defined or finally fixed. That is why timbre is so crucial to the contingent production of meaning" (Meintjes 2003, 254). Theoretical analysis has generally prioritized the objective and transferable, and there is no combination of sounds that is objectively "ballsy," nor can guitars sound precisely "Zulu." Yet Meintjes asserts that terms with localized meaning can hold analytical purchase as well. She thus makes a crucial methodological argument for timbral analysis: scholars can bypass the impossible task of forging objective explanations of sonic phenomena and instead pursue the potential usefulness of situationally powerful description.

CONCLUSION: "100,000 FIREFLIES"

Robert Cogan lamented nearly a half-century ago that "timbre, of all the parameters of music, is the one least considered. It lacks not only an adequate theory, but even an inadequate one" (Cogan 1969, 75). His words still ring true. Timbral theory remains a nascent discipline, as compared with the long-standing work on the other parameters in this section of this handbook. There are very real fundamental questions about what timbre is (if it is even anything) and how to discuss and represent it (if it is even discussible or representable), and only a little more than a few decades of sustained discourse from which to glean answers. As a result, timbral analysis is generally not only concerned with compositional function, but simultaneously with fundamental methodological and ontological questions. The more one reads, the more one finds imperative statements of the need for answers to these questions, followed by lamentations over timbre's resistance to systematization, description, visual representation, or any sort of analytical manageability. Carol Krumhansl's 1989 question referenced at the beginning of this chapter, "Why is musical timbre so hard to understand?," remains pressing.

The gap between timbre's ineffability and the discursive nature of analysis lingers, but timbre scholarship has begun to coalesce into a scholarly field, especially within the past half-decade. Annual meetings of the Society for Music Theory regularly feature panels devoted to timbre. New dissertations have offered provocative new directions for timbre scholarship intersecting cognition, embodiment, ecology, and spectrography (for instance, Wallmark 2014; Heidemann 2014; Lavengood 2017). Two current edited collections are devoted to timbre (Latour, Wallmark, and Fink, 2018; Dolan and Rehding, 2020). Broad theories of music analysis no longer dismiss timbre as a secondary parameter, but rather embrace its potential compositional and analytical usefulness (Hanninen 2012, 25–26; Howland 2015, 71).

As timbre scholarship continues to develop, though, it is important to sound a reminder that timbre entangles concerns that have often been disconnected through the disciplinary divides of music scholarship—cognition, ecology, form, structure, acoustics, identity, and so forth. As a result, timbre scholarship in musicology and ethnomusicology too often focuses on the cultural at the expense of the cognitive, while music theoretical approaches to timbre underemphasize the contextual within the textual. For the field to continue to develop, scholars need to continue to mine interdisciplinary and holistic modes of interrogation that accept timbre's sublinguistic character, multidimensionality, and inherently social orientation.

This chapter concludes by demonstrating such a holistic timbral analysis of the Magnetic Fields' "100,000 Fireflies," written by main songwriter Stephin Merritt for the group's 1991 debut album *Distant Plastic Trees* and self-released under the label name PoPuP Records. Underneath the alto voice of singer Susan Anway, the song uses two primary instrumental textures: a chime-like keyboard sound over cheap bass and snare drum sounds for the two verses and choruses (▶ Audio Example 6.16); and a piano-like sound over the bass drum sound for the lengthy coda (▶ Audio Example 6.17). The chime keyboard and snare are noisier instruments that foreground distortion, while the piano keyboard and bass drum trade upper partials for greater resonance of fundamental pitches. A comparison of the spectrograms (Figures 6.5 and 6.6) bears out the shift from noise to fundamental. The first texture has a formant around 5,000 Hz, while the chime's pulsing eighth-note triads and the snare's distorted smack thickly fill the space up to nearly 18,000 Hz. The second texture fills a similar frequency space—accounting for their similarity—but the upper partials are much thinner.

Notice the adjective "cheap," used to describe the drum sounds in the previous paragraph. Although not an objective sonic descriptor, "cheap" encapsulates both the cognitive and generic aspects of the song's timbres. The sounds are recognizable to anyone

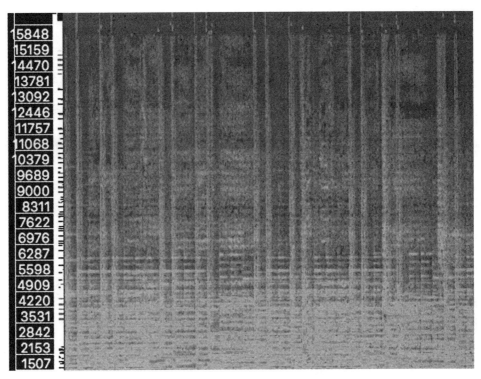

FIGURE 6.5 Spectrogram of the Magnetic Fields' "100,000 Fireflies," 0:00–0:08.

familiar with synthesized pop music as keyboard, bass, and snare drum. They sound scarcely like the real thing, though; the bass drum makes a dull thud and the snare resembles digital distortion. Their sonic recognition partially derives from familiarity with the "boom-chick bass–snare drum" pattern in rock music. Because the sounds are recognizable yet poor facsimiles, the listener can infer that they come from low-end instruments lacking the storage space for the increased overtone capacities necessary for more realistic replications. The cheapness of the recording is partially due to inaccessibility of better instruments and recording equipment, but it is also emphasized for genre identification. The Magnetic Fields was also an indie pop group that valorized lo-fi recording artists on prominent late 1980s independent labels such as K and Sarah Records. Merritt's arrangement thus foregrounds rather than ashamedly hides the grain of cheapness of their instrumental forces.

The instrumental cheapness also grants the timbres hermeneutic interest. The lyrics of the first verse and pre-chorus invoke the emotional power of certain instruments—a mandolin whose serenade is gut-wrenchingly unanswered, a dobro that "sounds like a mountain range in love," and an electric guitar. The sounds referenced in the lyrics are, not coincidentally, absent from the song's instrumental texture. Instead of hearing "a mountain range in love"—a gorgeous, impossible sonic image—the listener hears cheap sounds reiterated in timbral and registral stasis, with beautiful noise receding into resonant emptiness at the end.

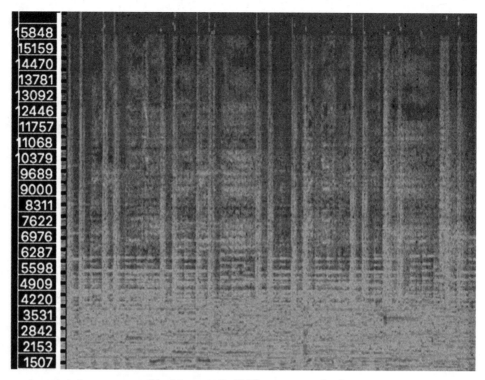

15848	
15159	
14470	
13781	
13092	
12446	
11757	
11068	
10379	
9689	
9000	
8311	
7622	
6976	
6287	
5598	
4909	
4220	
3531	
2842	
2153	
1507	

FIGURE 6.6 Spectrogram of the Magnetic Fields' "100,000 Fireflies," 2:17–2:25.

Given the estranging nature of electronic music—and the fact that "100,000 Fireflies" is resolutely synthetic—the heard timbres pale in comparison to those invoked. The distance between the heard and unheard may reflect the text's description of the depression of lost love. The limited physiology involved in performing the song intensifies the lyrical sense of emptiness. Amway sings with little bodily engagement. She barely completes some of her vocal lines before her breath dies away. The keyboard lines require almost no hand movement to play. Both keyboard sounds stay within a single octave, while the verse's main I–IV–I–V–IV progression uses strict parsimonious voice leading. The drum sounds of the first texture require only two fingers to play, and then only one in the second half. The immobility and estrangement of the song's timbres is thus echoed by that of the song's performance.

This short analysis of "100,000 Fireflies" interweaves cognition, hermeneutics, metaphor, description, embodied knowledge, and spectrography to explore the potential meaningfulness of timbral choices. Timbre analysts have an ever-growing toolbox for understanding its myriad functions. It is incumbent on analysts to combine approaches to provide a fuller understanding of both individual works and of timbre itself without shoehorning it into the methodological expectations of other parameters. Timbre intersects the cognitive and the acoustic, the subjective and the objective, the physical and the psychical, the social and the textual. It is so very difficult to understand, but that is precisely what makes it so compelling.

Audio Examples

Audio Example 6.1. French harpsichord. Recorded by the author, July 2016.

Audio Example 6.2. Italian harpsichord. Recorded by Hayley Roud, July 2016.

Audio Example 6.3. Virginal. Recorded by Hayley Roud, July 2016.

Audio Example 6.4. Fortepiano. Recorded by Hayley Roud, July 2016.

Audio Example 6.5. MIDI keyboard. Recorded by the author, July 2016.

Audio Example 6.6. Player piano, from Scott Joplin, "Maple Leaf Rag" (1916), mm. 1–6.

Audio Example 6.7. Coffee grinder. Recorded by the author, July 2016.

Audio Example 6.8. Heavy book falling on a carpeted floor. Recorded by the author, July 2016.

Audio Example 6.9. Caroline Shaw, Passacaglia from *Partita for 8 Voices,* mm. 1–4. Recorded by Roomful of Teeth, on the album *Roomful of Teeth* (New Amsterdam, 2012).

Audio Example 6.10. Shaw, Passacaglia, mm. 11–14.

Audio Example 6.11. Shaw, Passacaglia, mm. 20–24.

Audio Example 6.12. Beach Boys, "God Only Knows," from *Pet Sounds* (Capitol, 1966), 1:00–1:11.

Audio Example 6.13. Charles Ives, "Son of a Gambolier" (1895), mm. 90–105. Recorded by Paul Sperry (tenor), Irma Vallecillo (piano), Eva Kokoris, Jerrold Seigel, Jeanette Thompson, Albert K. Webster, and Eric Zivian (kazoo) on *The Complete Songs of Charles Ives,* vol. 1 (Albany, 1992).

Audio Example 6.14. Benjamin Britten, *The Young Person's Guide to the Orchestra,* mm. 1–6. Recorded by Orchestre National de France, conducted by Lorin Maazel, on Sergei Prokofiev: *Peter and the Wolf;* and Benjamin Britten: *The Young Person's Guide to the Orchestra* (Deutsche Grammophon, 1990 [1963]).

Audio Example 6.15. Britten, *Young Person's Guide to the Orchestra,* Fugue, beginning nine measures after *con slancio* (*l'istesso tempo*).

Audio Example 6.16. The Magnetic Fields, "100,000 Fireflies," from *Distant Plastic Trees* (PoPuP, 1991), 0:00–0:20.

Audio Example 6.17. The Magnetic Fields, "100,000 Fireflies," 2:17–2:25.

Notes

1. References to listening and human cognitive practices throughout this chapter assume full hearing capabilities. Deaf listeners interact with sound in multisensory ways that relate to the cognitive, ecological, and embodied modes of perception discussed in this chapter, but they are not fully accounted for by these modes. For a summary of deaf hearing, see Holmes (2017).

2. The D major harmony in the third bar of the progression, spelled D3–A3–D4–F♯4 in the first two iterations, switches to A2–A3–D4–F♯4 in the third. In the work's recording on Roomful of Teeth's eponymous 2012 album, one of the basses improvises a drop to D2 for this harmony, as well as for the D major chord that opens the third iteration (also spelled D3–A3–D4–F♯4 in the score). The expanded range also accents the increased volume and forward vowel progression discussed in this paragraph.

3. The mouth placement of vowel-s is taken from Reynolds (2017), and sample words in American English are taken from Dillon (2008). American English IPA dictionaries do not always distinguish between the schwa (ə) and ɐ, and they occupy a similar position in

the IPA vowel chart. The latter can be understood as a neutral vowel sound produced with a slightly more open mouth sound than the schwa.

4. The definition goes on to note that "timbre depends primarily on the spectrum of the stimulus, but is also depends upon the waveform, the sound pressure, the frequency location [i.e., pitch] of the spectrum, and the temporal characteristics [i.e., envelope and duration] of the stimulus." In other words, sonic quality is inextricable from other categories.

5. Latartara (2008b, 68–70) discusses the history of spectrography in greater detail.

6. The concept of hearing objects first, rather than mere sounds, reflects Martin Heidegger's discussion of the motorcycle in *Being and Time* (1927). He argues that when we hear the sounds of a motorcycle, we claim to hear the thing (the motorcycle) rather than its sounds, suggesting our attunement to things over sensations. Heidegger's argument is summarized in Kane (2014, 196–197).

7. Musicologists working with historical soundscapes and the "culture of listening" (Thompson 2002) have become interested in timbre in pre-twentieth-century repertoires. Scholarship on Mahler has been particularly attuned to how his emphasis on orchestration reflects sociocultural contexts and identity politics (Adorno 1992; Painter 1995; Sheinbaum 2006; Dolp 2010), but timbre has also made inroads into works ranging from Machaut (Cogan and Escot 1976; Leech-Wilkinson 2003; Latartara 2008a) to Mozart (Keefe 2009). The growing analytical purchase that timbre has had for music from different time periods suggests that the marginalization of timbre as a secondary parameter has more to do with the inability to experience soundscapes prior to the advent of recording technology combined with modernist analytical schemata, rather than historical compositional priorities.

8. Despite its importance for the history of timbral composition, the analyses of *Farben* in Burkhart (1973) and Cramer (2002) have contended that Schoenberg's conception of *Klangfarben* was primarily harmonic.

9. Some theorists have similarly argued that timbral manipulation is the most central parameter for central compositional practices in art music (Bauer 2001; Lochhead 2016), jazz (Schiff 2012), and popular music (Walser 1993, 41; Blake 2012; Moore 2012).

10. My interpretation here is guided by Shaw's description of the work as "Born of a love … of the human voice, of dancing and tired ligaments" (Shaw 2012).

11. Another method, multidimensional shading (MDS), places sounds on a three-dimensional graph using the axes of overtone distribution, spectral fluctuation, and prominence of fundamental pitch (Grey 1977). Some electronic music composers have employed this system (McAdams 1999; McAdams and Giordano 2009; Malloch 2000), but the notation is mathematically forbidding and is better suited for classifying individual sounds than analyzing compositions.

12. Some scholars have argued more systematically that descriptive terms can be situated in spectrographically visible characteristics in order to mediate the acoustic and perceptual (Howard and Tyrell 1997; Malloch 2000), but this perspective runs the risk of universalizing the contextual and individual nature of sonic perception.

WORKS CITED

Adorno, Theodor W. 1992. *Mahler: A Musical Physiognomy.* Translated by Edmund Jephcott. Chicago: University of Chicago Press.

American Standards Association. 1960. *American Standard Acoustical Terminology (Including Mechanical Shock and Vibration)*. New York: American Standards Association.

Barthes, Roland. 1977. "The Grain of the Voice." In *Image Music Text*. Translated by Stephen Heath, 179–189. New York: Hill and Wang.

Barthes, Roland. 1991. "Listening." In *The Responsibility of Forms*. Translated by Richard Howard, 245–260. Berkeley: University of California Press.

Bauer, Amy. 2001. " 'Composing the Sound Itself': Secondary Parameters and Structure in the Music of Ligeti." *Indiana Theory Review* 22, no. 1: 37–64.

Berger, Harris M., and Cornelia Fales. 2005. " 'Heaviness' in the Perception of Heavy Metal Guitar Timbres: The Match of Perceptual and Acoustic Features over Time." In *Wired for Sound: Engineering and Technologies in Sonic Cultures*. Edited by Paul D. Green and Thomas Porcello, 181–197. Middletown, CT: Wesleyan University Press.

Blake, David K. 2012. "Timbre as Differentiation in Indie Music." *Music Theory Online* 18, no. 2. Available at http://www.mtosmt.org/issues/mto.12.18.2/mto.12.18.2.blake.html.

Boulez, Pierre. 1987. "Timbre and Composition—Timbre and Language." Translated by R. Robertson. *Contemporary Music Review* 2: 161–172.

Brackett, David. 2000. *Interpreting Popular Music*. Berkeley: University of California Press.

Burkhart, Charles. 1973. "Schoenberg's *Farben*: An Analysis of Op. 16, No. 3." *Perspectives of New Music* 12: 141–172.

Cavarero, Adriana. 2005. *For More Than One Voice: Toward a Theory of Vocal Expression*, translated by Paul A. Kottman. Stanford, CA: Stanford University Press.

Chion, Michel. 2011. "Dissolution of the Notion of Timbre." Translated by James A. Steintrager. *Differences: A Journal of Feminist Cultural Studies* 22: 235–239.

Chou, Wen-Chung. 1979. "Ionisation: The Function of Timbre in Its Formal and Temporal Organization." In *The New Worlds of Edgard Varèse: A Symposium*. Edited by Sherman Van Solkema, 27–74. New York: Institute for Studies in American Music.

Clarke, Eric F. 2005. *Ways of Listening: An Ecological Approach to the Perception of Musical Meaning*. New York: Oxford University Press.

Cogan, Robert. 1969. "Toward a Theory of Timbre: Verbal Timbre and Musical Line in Purcell, Sessions, and Stravinsky." *Perspectives of New Music* 8: 75–81.

Cogan, Robert. 1984. *New Images of Musical Sound*. Cambridge, MA: Harvard University Press.

Cogan, Robert, and Pozzi Escot. 1976. *Sonic Design: The Nature of Sound and Music*. Englewood Cliffs, NJ: Prentice Hall.

Cornicello, Anthony. 2000. "Timbral Organization in Tristan Murail's *Désintégrations*." PhD diss., Brandeis University.

Cramer, Alfred. 2002. "Schoenberg's *Klangfarbenmelodie*: A Principle of Early Atonal Harmony." *Music Theory Spectrum* 24: 1–34.

DeVale, Sue Carole. 1985. "Prolegomena to a Study of Harp and Voice Sounds in Uganda: A Graphic System for the Notation of Texture." In *Selected Reports in Ethnomusicology, Volume 5: Music of Africa*. Edited by J. H. Kwabena Nketia and Jacqueline Cogdell DjeDje, 250–281. Berkeley: University of California Press.

Demers, Joanna. 2010. *Listening Through the Noise: The Aesthetics of Experimental Electronic Music*. New York: Oxford University Press.

Dillon, George. 2008. "Symbols for American English Vowel Sounds." University of Washington. Available at http://faculty.washington.edu/dillon/PhonResources/newstart.html.

Dolan, Emily I. 2013. *The Orchestral Revolution: Haydn and the Technologies of Timbre.* Cambridge: Cambridge University Press.

Dolan, Emily I., and Alexander Rehding, eds. 2020. *The Oxford Handbook of Timbre.* New York: Oxford University Press.

Dolar, Mladen. 2006. *A Voice and Nothing More.* Cambridge, MA: MIT Press.

Dolp, Laura. 2010. "Viennese Moderne and Its Spatial Planes, Sounded." *19th-Century Music* 33: 247–269.

Eidsheim, Nina Sun. 2009. "Synthesizing Race: Towards an Analysis of the Performativity of Vocal Timbre." *TRANS* 13. Available at http://www.sibetrans.com/trans/articulo/57/synthesizing-race-towards-an-analysis-of-the-performativity-of-vocal-timbre.

Eidsheim, Nina Sun. 2014. *Sensing Sound: Singing and Listening as Vibrational Practice.* Durham, NC: Duke University Press.

Eidsheim, Nina Sun. 2015. "Race and the Aesthetics of Vocal Timbre." In *Rethinking Difference.* Edited by Olivia Bloechl, Melanie Lowe, and Jeffrey Kallberg, 338–365. Cambridge: Cambridge University Press.

Erickson, Robert. 1975. *Sound Structure in Music.* Berkeley: University of California Press.

Everett, Walter. 2000. "Confessions from Blueberry Hell, or, Pitch Can Be a Sticky Substance." In *Expression in Pop-Rock Music.* Edited by Walter Everett, 269–345. New York: Garland.

Fales, Cornelia. 2002. "The Paradox of Timbre." *Ethnomusicology* 46: 56–95.

Fales, Cornelia. 2005. "Short-Circuiting Perceptual Systems: Timbre in Ambient and Techno Music." In *Wired for Sound: Engineering and Technologies in Sonic Cultures.* Edited by Paul D. Green and Thomas Porcello, 156–180. Middletown, CT: Wesleyan University Press.

Fennelly, Brian. 1967. "A Descriptive Language for the Analysis of Electronic Music." *Perspectives of New Music* 6: 79–95.

François, Jean-Charles. 1991. "Organization of Scattered Timbral Qualities: A Look at Edgard Varèse's *Ionisation.*" *Perspectives of New Music* 29: 48–79.

Gardiner, Michael, and Joyce S. Lim. 2014. "Chromatopes of *Noh*: An Analysis of Timbral Progressions in the Introductions to Three Plays." *Asian Music* 45, no. 2: 84–128.

Garrett, Charles Hiroshi. 2008. "The Musical Tactics of Ani DiFranco." *American Music* 26: 378–397.

Gibson, James J. 1966. *The Senses Considered as Perceptual Systems.* Boston: Houghton Mifflin.

Grey, John M. 1977. "Multidimensional Perceptual Scaling of Musical Timbres." *Journal of the Acoustical Society of America* 61: 1270–1277.

Hanninen, Dora A. 2012. *A Theory of Musical Analysis: On Segmentation and Associative Organization.* Rochester, NY: University of Rochester Press.

Harkness, Nicholas. 2013. *Songs of Seoul: An Ethnography of Voice and Voicing in Christian South Korea.* Berkeley: University of California Press.

Heidemann, Kate. 2014. "Hearing Women's Voices in Popular Song: Analyzing Sound and Identity in Country and Soul." PhD diss., Columbia University.

Heidemann, Kate. 2016. "A System for Describing Vocal Timbre in Popular Song." *Music Theory Online* 22, no. 1. Available at http://www.mtosmt.org/issues/mto.16.22.1/mto.16.22.1.heidemann.html.

Helmholtz, Hermann L. F. 1875. *On the Sensations of Tone as a Physiological Basis for the Theory of Music.* Translated by Alexander Ellis. London: Longmans, Green, and Company.

Hoffman, Elizabeth. 2005. "Textural *Klangfarben* in James Dillon's *La Femme Invisible* (1989): An Explanatory Model." *Perspectives of New Music* 43: 4–33.

Holmes, Jessica A. 2017. "Expert Listening Beyond the Limits of Hearing: Music and Deafness." *Journal of the American Musicological Society* 70: 171–220.

Howard, David, and Andy Tyrell. 1997. "Psychoacoustically Informed Spectrography and Timbre." *Organized Sound* 2, no. 2: 65–76.

Howland, Patricia. 2015. "Formal Structures in Post-Tonal Music." *Music Theory Spectrum* 37: 71–97.

Kaiser, Katherine. 2015. "Listening to Recorded Voices in Modern Music." PhD diss., State University of New York at Stony Brook.

Kane, Brian. 2014. *Sound Unseen: Acousmatic Music in Theory and Practice*. New York: Oxford University Press.

Keefe, Simon P. 2009. "'We Hardly Knew What We Should Pay Attention to First': Mozart the Performer-Composer at Work on the Viennese Piano Concertos." *Journal of the Royal Musical Association* 134: 185–242.

Latartara, John. 2008a. "Machaut's Monophonic Virelai *Tuit mi penser*: Intersections of Language Sound, Pitch Space, Performance, and Meaning." *Journal of Music History Research* 27: 226–253.

Latartara, John. 2008b. "Pedagogic Applications of Fourier Analysis and Spectrographs in the Music Theory Classroom." *Journal of Music Theory Pedagogy* 22: 61–90.

Latartara, John. 2012. "The Timbre of Thai Classical Singing." *Asian Music* 43, no. 2: 88–114.

Latour, Melinda, Zachary Wallmark, and Robert Fink, eds. 2018. *The Relentless Pursuit of Tone: Timbre in Popular Music*. New York: Oxford University Press.

Lavengood, Megan. 2017. "A New Approach to the Analysis of Timbre." PhD diss., City University of New York Graduate Center.

Leech-Wilkinson, Daniel. 2003. "*Rose, lis* Revisited." In *Machaut's Music: New Interpretations*. Edited by Elizabeth Eva Leach, 249–262. Rochester, NY: Boydell & Brewer.

Leydon, Rebecca. 2012. "Clean as a Whistle: Timbral Trajectories and the Modern Musical Sublime." *Music Theory Online* 18, no. 2. Available at http://www.mtosmt.org/issues/mto.12.18.2/mto.12.18.2.leydon.html.

Lilly, Stephen. 2005. "Form as an Outgrowth of Timbre and Rhythm: Wesley Fuller's 'Sherds of Five.'" *Perspectives of New Music* 43: 142–170.

Lochhead, Judith. 2005. "Texture and Timbre in Barbara Kolb's *Millefoglie* for Chamber Orchestra and Computer-Generated Tape." In *Engaging Music: Essays in Music Analysis*, edited by Deborah Stein, 253–272. New York: Oxford University Press.

Lochhead, Judith. 2016. *Reconceiving Structure in Contemporary Music: New Tools in Music Theory and Analysis*. New York: Routledge.

Macdonald, Hugh. 2004. *Berlioz's Orchestration Treatise: A Translation and Commentary*. Cambridge: Cambridge University Press.

Malloch, Stephen. 2000. "Timbre and Technology: An Analytical Partnership." *Contemporary Music Review* 19: 155–172.

McAdams, Stephen. 1999. "Perspectives on the Contribution of Timbre to Musical Structure." *Computer Music Journal* 23, no. 3: 85–102.

McAdams, Stephen, and Bruno L. Giordano. 2009. "The Perception of Musical Timbre." In *Oxford Handbook of Music Psychology*, edited by Susan Hallam, Ian Cross, and Michael Thaut, 72–80. New York: Oxford University Press.

McAdams, Stephen, Philippe Depalle, and Eric Clarke. 2004. "Analyzing Musical Sound." In *Empirical Musicology: Aims, Methods, Prospects*, edited by Eric Clarke and Nicholas Cook, 157–196. New York: Oxford University Press.

Meintjes, Louise. 2003. *Sound of Africa! Making Music Zulu in a South African Studio*. Durham, NC: Duke University Press.

Meyer, Leonard. 1989. *Style and Music: Theory, History, and Ideology*. Chicago: University of Chicago Press.

Mirka, Danuta. 2001. "To Cut the Gordian Knot: The Timbre System of Krzyzstof Penderecki." *Journal of Music Theory* 45: 435–456.

Moore, Allan F. 2012. *Song Means: Analysing and Interpreting Recorded Popular Song*. Burlington, VT: Ashgate.

Murail, Tristan. 1984. "Spectra and Pixies." Translated by Tod Machover. *Contemporary Music Review* 1: 157–170.

Olwage, Grant. 2004. "The Class and Colour of Tone: An Essay on the Social History of Vocal Timbre." *Ethnomusicology Forum* 13: 203–226.

Osborn, Brad. 2016. *Everything in Its Right Place: Analyzing Radiohead*. New York: Oxford University Press.

Osborn, Brad, and David K. Blake. 2017. "Triangulating Timbre in Sigur Rós's Iceland." In *Sounds Icelandic*. Edited by Tony Mitchell, Nicola Dibben, Þorbjörg Daphne Hall, and Árni Heimir Ingólfsson, 208–219. Sheffield, UK: Equinox.

Painter, Karen. 1995. "The Sensuality of Timbre: Responses to Mahler and Modernity at the 'Fin de siècle.'" *19th-Century Music* 18: 236–256.

Raffman, Diana. 1993. *Language, Music, and Mind*. Cambridge, MA: MIT Press.

Reed, S. Alexander. 2005. "The Musical Semiotics of Timbre in the Human Voice and Static Takes Love's Body." PhD diss., University of Pittsburgh.

Reynolds, Amy. 2017. "Understanding the IPA Chart." University of North Carolina Department of Linguistics. Available at http://amyrey.web.unc.edu/classes/ling-101-online/tutorials/understanding-the-ipa/.

Roholt, Tiger. 2014. *Groove: A Phenomenology of Rhythmic Nuance*. London: Bloomsbury.

Rudy, Paul. 2007. "Timbral Praxis: When a Tree Falls in the Forest, Is It Music?" *Organized Sound* 12, no. 1: 5–13.

Shaw, Caroline. 2012. *Partita for 8 Voices*. Available at https://web.archive.org/web/20130419101314/http://carolineshaw.com:80/0/hear/partita/.

Schiff, David. 2012. *The Ellington Century*. Berkeley: University of California Press.

Schoenberg, Arnold. 1978. *Theory of Harmony*. Translated by Roy E. Carter. Berkeley: University of California Press.

Sheinbaum, John J. 2006. "Adorno's Mahler and the Timbral Outsider." *Journal of the Royal Musical Association* 131: 38–82.

Slater, Mark. 2011. "Timbre and Non-Radical Didacticism in the Streets' *A Grand Don't Come for Free*: a Poetic-Ecological Model." *Music Analysis* 30: 360–395.

Slawson, Wayne. 1981. "The Color of Sound: A Theoretical Study in Musical Timbre." *Music Theory Spectrum* 3: 132–141.

Slawson, Wayne. 1985. *Sound Color*. Berkeley: University of California Press.

Smalley, Denis. 1997. "Spectromorphology: Explaining Sound-Shapes." *Organized Sound* 2, no. 2: 107–126.

Smalley, Denis. 2007. "Space-Form and the Acousmatic Image." *Organized Sound* 12, no. 1: 35–58.

Solís, Gabriel. 2015. "Timbral Virtuosity: Pharoah Sanders, Sonic Heterogeneity, and the Jazz Avant-Garde in the 1960s and 70s." *Jazz Perspectives* 9: 45–63.

Steege, Benjamin. 2012. *Helmholtz and the Modern Listener*. Cambridge: Cambridge University Press.

Théberge, Paul. 1997. *Any Sound You Can Imagine: Making Music/Consuming Technology*. Middletown, CT: Wesleyan University Press.

Thomas, Jennifer. 1981. "The Use of Color in Three Chamber Works of the Twentieth Century." *Indiana Theory Review* 4, no. 3: 24–40.

Thompson, Emily. 2002. *The Soundscape of Modernity: Architectural Acoustics and the Culture of Listening in America, 1900–1933*. Cambridge, MA: MIT Press.

Tomlinson, Gary. 2015. *A Million Years of Music: The Emergence of Human Modernity*. Cambridge, MA: Zone Books and MIT Press.

Wallmark, Zachary. 2014. "Appraising Timbre: Embodiment and Affect at the Threshold of Music and Noise." PhD diss., University of California–Los Angeles.

Walser, Robert. 1993. *Running with the Devil: Power, Gender, and Madness in Heavy Metal Music*. Middletown, CT: Wesleyan University Press.

Zagorski-Thomas, Simon. 2014. *The Musicology of Record Production*. Cambridge: Cambridge University Press.

CHAPTER 7

....

TEXTURE

....

JONATHAN DE SOUZA

INTRODUCTION

....

MUSICAL texture is commonly described in terms of four categories: monophony, homophony, polyphony, and heterophony. Yet applying these concepts can be complicated. For example, consider the C-major prelude from the first book of Johann Sebastian Bach's *Well-Tempered Clavier*. Its texture is consistent and seems simple, especially when compared to the following fugue or, say, the Brandenburg Concertos. But how does it fit these textural categories? I imagine three possibilities:

1) Heard as a series of broken chords, the prelude would have a homophonic texture. In this view, the sixteenth notes on the musical surface articulate sustained, underlying harmonies, as represented in Figure 7.1(a). This hearing might be encouraged by performances that let each note ring: when a pianist is generous with the sustain pedal, or when the piece is played on classical guitar or harp. (Performers on these instruments may also *feel* the homophonic texture in the hand positions that are held for each measure.)

2) Alternatively, the prelude could be monophonic. Since each note is attacked separately, it can be conceived as a single, flowing line, as seen in Figure 7.1(b). Monophonic instruments with wide enough ranges can play the piece, with the final chord excepted. The American singer Bobby McFerrin even performs it as a vocal solo. This brings out melodic contour or vertical movement, more than chord-to-chord voice leading.

3) Where homophonic or monophonic hearings fuse the notes into a harmonic or melodic whole, a polyphonic hearing splits them apart. Though this analysis might be less plausible in general, it seems appropriate for Glenn Gould's 1963 recording of the prelude. Here Gould sustains two left-hand voices against an articulated upper part. This somewhat literal interpretation of Bach's notation suggests a form of tiered polyphony, a characteristic Baroque texture in which parts move

at distinct rates (see Figure 7.1(c); see also Auerbach 2008). Performing the piece with hands on different organ manuals might effect a similar separation, using stops instead of touch. An arrangement by the Swingle Singers maximizes the polyphony, with the eight pitches of each measure corresponding to the eight singers in the group.

The sketches in Figure 7.1 share the same pitches and surface rhythm. Yet they imagine different groupings, different relations between parts. All are based in Bach's score, but as the contrast between McFerrin and Gould shows, they are also related to instrumentation, articulation, and so forth—that is, to aspects of performance.

This interplay of notation and performance points to a double meaning. "Texture" does not only refer to the coordination of parts. It also refers to sensual or material qualities of sound, involving timbre, density, and register, that are often described via tactile metaphors. (McFerrin's falsetto, for example, sounds smooth, while Gould's piano sounds a little dry.) The first sense of the word corresponds roughly to certain uses of the German *Satz*, as a technical term in counterpoint; the second sense encompasses the Italian *tessitura*, among other factors; and the Kaluli *dulugu ganalan*—translated by Steven Feld as "lift-up-over sounding"—involves aspects of both ("Texture," *Grove Music Online;* Feld 1988). But none of these foreign words captures the precise meaning of "texture," which as a musical term is unique to English.[1]

This might seem to be an unfortunate terminological ambiguity, and confusion may arise if scholars use one meaning or the other out of context. This chapter, however,

FIGURE 7.1 Three textural interpretations of Johann Sebastian Bach, Prelude in C Major from *Well-Tempered Clavier*, Book I, mm. 1–2. It might be heard as (a) chordal homophony, (b) monophony, or (c) three-part polyphony.

claims that the double meaning is significant. Like "text" and "textile," "texture" derives from the Latin verb for weaving, *texere*. Many authors have exploited this etymology, comparing music's "vertical" and "horizontal" dimensions to the warp and weft threads of woven fabric (Rowell 1984, 158; Bregman 1990, 456; Cai 1997, 63). Here I extend the metaphor by considering a passage from the Bauhaus-trained textile artist Anni Albers:

> The structure of a fabric or its weave—that is, the fastening of its elements of threads to each other—is as much a determining factor in its function as is the choice of the raw material. In fact, the interrelation of the two, the subtle play between them in supporting, impeding, or modifying each other's characteristics, is the essence of weaving. (2010, 29)

Albers distinguishes between a fabric's *structure* and its *material*. Woven structure involves the crossing of horizontal weft threads over and under vertical warp threads. For example, an uneven twill pattern goes over one, under two, over three, then under one (31). Material differences—for example, between silk and wool—may seem more immediate, though harder to quantify. In isolation, though, neither structure nor material accounts for the finished fabric. In other words, its properties are *emergent*.[2]

Mapping structure onto the first meaning of texture and material onto the second, this chapter argues that musical texture involves a similar kind of emergence. Whereas pitch, duration, dynamics, and timbre may, to some degree, be independently adjusted, texture arises from dynamic interactions among these different elements. Texture, then, is not a fully separable musical parameter but an "auxiliary variable" or "superparameter" (Levy 1982, 482; Cohen and Dubnov 1997, 387). Like musical form, it involves high-level wholes. It is made with smaller parts, though irreducible to them.

Moreover, as demonstrated by my textural variations on the C-major Prelude, texture emerges in particular listening experiences. Perceived texture may shift with individual listeners' memories, intentions, or actions. Psychologically it involves both bottom-up and top-down processes, both perception and cognition.

This chapter's organization follows Albers's distinction. The first section investigates "textural structure" in terms of perceptual principles and music-theoretical tools. The second supplements that with timbral and performative aspects of "textural materials," while the third considers some of texture's cultural affordances. Throughout, the chapter offers a critical introduction to foundational research on texture and diverse analytical vignettes. By exploring texture as an emergent phenomenon, I hope to show that the term's two meanings are distinct but also interrelated, that their subtle play is the essence of musical texture.

Textural Structure

"There is always texture," writes Leonard Meyer, "whether it be that of a single melodic line or that of a complex polyphonic web" (1956, 263). Though I agree with Meyer, many writers associate texture with density, richness, and roughness—as in the unsettling intensity of Krzysztof Penderecki's *Threnody for the Victims of Hiroshima* or the intertwined voices of a mass by Josquin des Prez. This opposition of melody and texture appears in music journalism, too. For example, a recent review in *Entertainment Weekly* magazine states that "*LP1* [by British R&B artist FKA twigs] is sparing with its hooks, favoring texture over melody" (Raymer 2014). Literary scholar Renu Bora identifies a similar tendency in discourse on nonmusical textures: "Technically speaking, all materials have texture, though colloquially we often say that only rough things ... do. Smoothness is both a type of texture and texture's other" (1997, 98–99). Like smoothness, then, an unaccompanied melody is both a type of texture and texture's other.

Following Meyer, I claim that hearing a single part *as a single part* already involves textural emergence. Monophony, in this view, is no more self-evident than other kinds of texture. It depends on the same musical conditions, the same principles of perceptual grouping.

This might be clearest in a counterexample: with compound melody, a sequence of notes is perceived in terms of multiple parts. As Meyer notes, "if the over-all articulation is simpler when a piece for a single instrument is understood as implying several 'lines' or voices, then this mode of organization is the one that will probably appear" (1956, 186–187). At the beginning of Steve Reich's *Piano Phase*, for example, the two pianists play a rapid looping figure in unison (see Figure 7.2(a)). At some point, however, my hearing switches from monophony to polyphony; I perceive an upper part, moving between B4 and D5, and a lower one on E4 and F♯4. (This is represented in Figure 7.2(b)). Splitting the notes around a perfect-fourth gap here involves a simpler grouping, even though it involves more streams.

While *Piano Phase* offers an example of "virtual polyphony," the converse—what might be called "virtual monophony"—is also possible. Here notes produced by different musicians would be heard as a single stream. This is primarily associated with the hocket techniques found in various traditions, including many kinds of African drumming and medieval polyphony.[3] Like the Reich example, passages of hocket often afford multistable textural interpretations. Figure 7.3 presents an excerpt from a fourteenth-century Florentine madrigal in which a florid upper part and held lower part lock into hocket to imitate a lamb's bleating. It is possible to hear this as one leaping melody. At faster tempos, though, I have trouble hearing it as a single stream instead of

FIGURE 7.2 Monophonic and polyphonic interpretations of the opening pattern from Steve Reich, *Piano Phase*.

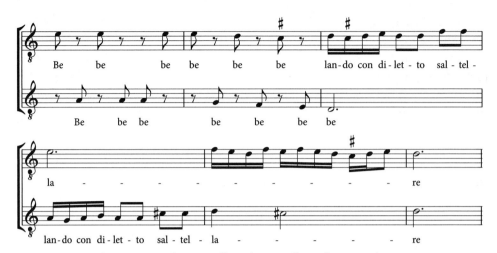

FIGURE 7.3 Hocket in Donato da Cascia, "Lucida pecorella son," Squarcialupi Manuscript.

Adapted from Sanders (1974, 252).

two interlocking parts. (This may be enhanced by the differentiation of parts before and after the hocket.)

In other cases, it may be difficult to perceive any sustained line, and listeners may experience what Bregman (1990, 468) calls "a kind of perceptual granularity." In the pointillistic, varied texture of Pierre Boulez's *Structures 1a* for two pianos, streams flicker in and out without fully coalescing. Notes that are close in pitch and time group together in fragments, though the larger sequence of events may feel discontinuous. For many listeners, this textural instability may be as challenging as the piece's pitch organization. A distinct musical "figure" may emerge only with extensive practice or repeated listening.

These examples suggest that monophony requires a sense of continuity, which can be surprisingly fragile. Empirical research on auditory streaming shows that this integration involves several factors. Greater pitch distances, of course, encourage perceived separation, which helps explain cross-cultural preferences for small melodic intervals (Huron 2001, 25). But as Bregman (1990, 61) notes, tempo is also a central factor: "At slower rates, the listener can integrate the whole sequence even at fairly large frequency separations, but at high speeds, the separation must be less than five semitones." This is to say that melodic integration and segregation, fusing and splitting, emerge from interactions of pitch and rhythm.

Bregman explains this by connecting musical and everyday listening. He argues that auditory streaming processes evolved to track sounding objects and events in the world. Accordingly, sounds that share timing and movement characteristics—and contiguous sequences that repeat or transform such sounds—are streamed together because they are likely produced by the same source.

From this perspective, monophony need not have the minimal density of one note. Thicker events may also form a single stream if they move together in pitch and time.

I distinguish, then, among different kinds of monophony: solo, unison, and doubling. Unison represents a strict form of doubling—that is, a consistent doubling at the same pitch.[4] Other strong doublings might use parallel motion or intervals that promote tonal fusion, such as perfect fifths. Of course, traditional voice-leading rules prohibit such doublings because of their textural effects (Huron 2001, 37). Weaker doublings might use imperfect consonances or dissonances, or similar motion, which would produce varied harmonic intervals.

Thickened monophony requires shared rhythms and shared pitch motion. Yet these conditions for monophony, along with their opposites, account for multipart textural structure in general. A statistical analysis by David Huron arranges a diverse sample along dimensions of onset synchrony and "semblant motion" (Huron 1989; "semblant motion" includes both parallel and similar motion). This generates a square "texture space," reproduced in Figure 7.4. Its corners correspond to the four traditional terms for texture. In strict homophony, parts share attacks but not motion; in heterophony, they

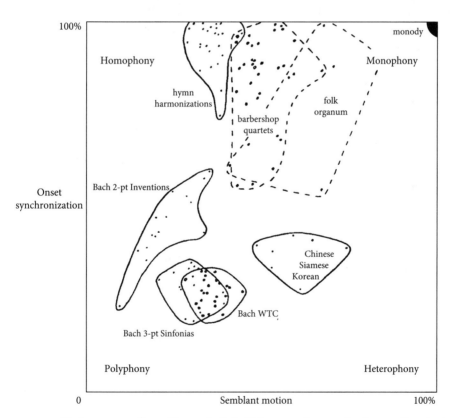

FIGURE 7.4 Texture space from Huron (1989). This space is organized according to two dimensions, onset synchronization and semblant pitch motion (which is also called "pitch comodulation"). Its corners correspond to traditional textural categories, while points on the graph represent individual works from Huron's sample.

Reproduced from Huron (2001, 52).

elaborate the "same" melodic material with asynchronous rhythms; in strict polyphony, parts are doubly independent.[5]

Measurements in both dimensions are percentages that compare two parts.[6] They may be calculated in various ways. Huron's measure of onset synchrony takes the percentage of all onset points that are shared, while Ben Duane's is based on the part with more onsets (Huron 1993, 437; Duane 2013, 51). Likewise, "semblant motion" may be measured in terms of shared contours, though Duane (2013, 51) employs a more sophisticated function that uses logarithms to account for degrees of pitch comodulation. Regardless of such details, these measurements productively "fuzzify" the traditional textural categories. That said, the space's crisp boundaries may still be relevant, since the mind tends to "improve" the perceived organization and to continue it once it is established (Meyer 1956, 92; on experimental consequences of this continuation tendency [which is called "hysteresis"], see Bregman 1990, 55).

I see a couple of ways to extend this model. First, besides summative single points, it is possible to trace dynamic paths here. To illustrate, Figure 7.5(b) charts some upper-voice relations in Bach's three-part Sinfonia in E♭ Major, BWV 791. (The relevant excerpt appears in Figure 7.5(b). The soprano and alto lines start with weak doubling. Then, in mm. 5–8, they become independent, though some small degree of pitch comodulation remains (because of the descending sequence).

Second, this space might be used to plot multiple concurrent streams. This is to say that the basic textural types can be *combined* in a kind of "hyper-polyphony." Just as

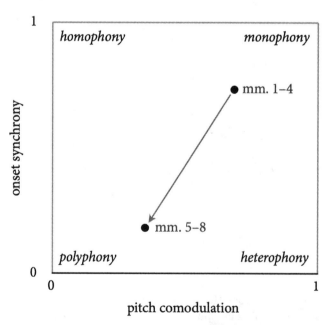

FIGURE 7.5(A) Texture-space analysis of upper voices from Bach's Sinfonia 5 in E♭ Major, BWV 791, mm. 1–8. At m. 5, they become more independent in both pitch and rhythmic dimensions. This moves from the monophonic quadrant of the space to the polyphonic quadrant.

FIGURE 7.5(B)   Bach, Sinfonia 5 in E♭ Major, BWV 791, mm. 1–8.

higher-level polyphony can theoretically be decomposed into several lower-level monophonic voices, a melody-and-accompaniment texture might be conceived as a monophonic stream plus a homophonic or polyphonic stream. Duane's (2013, 48) research
considers how thresholds of synchrony and pitch comodulation might cue such hierarchical streaming. I want to emphasize that this approach might conceive the basic
textural categories as elements to be layered, juxtaposed, and combined. Imitation
may contribute to this hierarchical streaming. On one level, it distinguishes parts. The
alto's entry in Bach's Sinfonia seems less like doubling, because it echoes the opening
melody. But imitation also helps group the upper parts, separating them from the
nonimitative bass.

Like these proposed extensions, Wallace Berry treats texture as fluid and multilayered. In other words, whereas Huron establishes criteria for defining textural structures,
Berry develops a textural energetics. His analysis hinges on this distinction between
larger streams and their components:

> Two lines moving in parallel thirds may in an important sense be said to constitute
> a single *real* textural factor consisting of two *components*. At any point at which dif-
> ferentiation is established—in rhythm, in direction of motion, in the distance of mo-
> tion, or in any other sense—a texture initially consisting of a *single real factor* (of two
> sounding components) becomes a texture of *two real factors* (or at least progresses in
> the direction of such differentiation). (1987, 186)[7]

Berry represents this numerically.[8] Each number stands for a textural stream (or "real
factor"), with its cardinality corresponding to the number of voices (or "sounding
components") that it contains. For example, 2 denotes a single stream with two
components, whereas 1/1 would represent two streams with one component in each.
Berry (1987, 188, 209) uses curves to plot changes in the number of streams and changes
in the overall number of components (which he calls the "density-number").[9] He

illustrates with an excerpt from Darius Milhaud's Six Sonnets for mixed chorus (see Figure 7.6). Four voices enter in imitation, then align homophonically as they approach a cadence. Berry's analysis, reproduced in Figure 7.7, considers this as a pattern of textural progression and recession.

Berry's work on texture is full of analytical insights and proliferating jargon. It is as rich as it is idiosyncratic. Perhaps it is productive, then, to translate his numbers into the more familiar terms of transformational theory. This would model textures as ordered pairs of the form (s, d), where s is the number of streams and d is Berry's "density-number." Both variables involve the group of integers under addition. Some information is initially lost, since this translation does not show how the components in d are divided among the

FIGURE 7.6 Darius Milhaud, Six Sonnets for mixed chorus, no. 3, mm. 1–7.

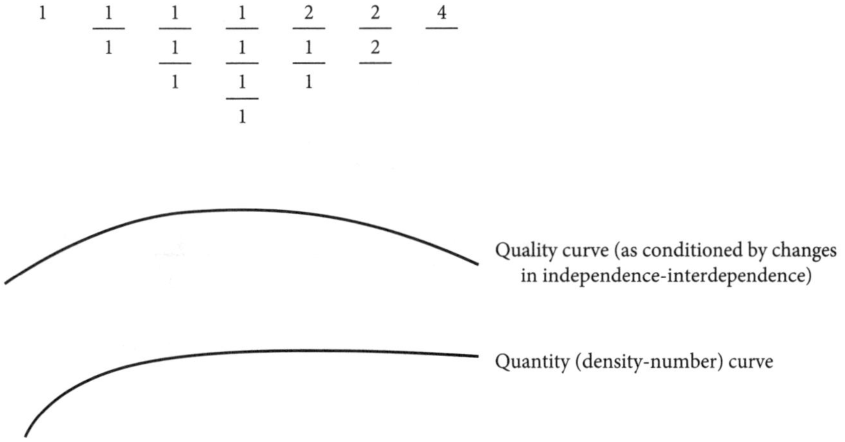

FIGURE 7.7   Analysis of texture in Milhaud's Six Sonnets, no. 3, mm. 1–7 from Berry (1987, 188).

streams in s. (Where this is problematic, sets of textures—as in $((s_1, d_1), \ldots, (s_n, d_n))$—offer a workaround.) More importantly, the transformational approach can clarify both a formal space of possibilities and particular "textural gestures." Figure 7.8 analyzes the Milhaud passage via a transformational network. It includes only two operations: (+1, +1), which corresponds here to the addition of a new, independent voice, and (-1, 0), the fusing of two voices. The inverses of these operations, which are not used in this excerpt, point to other possibilities. (-1, -1) would represent the removal of an independent voice, while (+1, 0) would split a stream without a change in density. Operations of the form (0, +n) and (0, -n) would thicken or thin layers without changing s. It is fairly simple to define other transformations in this space, such as "Split," which would make s equal to d—making every part independent—or "Fuse," which would take s to 1, joining all parts into a single stream.

This transformational model shares a weakness with Berry's approach: the numbers alone cannot specify relations between streams. They do not distinguish, for example, between melody and accompaniment. Here, inspired by Leonard Meyer, I find it useful to supplement measurements of textural structure with terms borrowed from gestalt psychology. For Meyer, "texture has to do with the ways in which the mind groups concurrent musical stimuli into simultaneous figures, a figure and accompaniment (ground), and so forth" (1956, 185).

The visual analogy seems helpful. With dense counterpoint, as in an intricate drawing, people generally perceive an overall image instead of discrete lines.[10] The alternative hearings of Reich's *Piano Phase* pattern recall optical illusions like the well-known picture of the duck/rabbit.[11] And a melody with polyphonic accompaniment suggests a solid figure over a patterned background. It would also be possible to have a polyphonic figure against a monophonic background—say, a drone. It is no coincidence that, in this last example, the background drone is static, since gestalt theory teaches that smaller or more active elements tend to form the figure (Meyer 1956, 185).

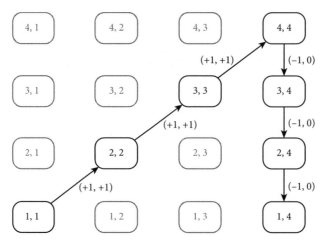

FIGURE 7.8 Transformation network based on Berry's analysis of Milhaud's Six Sonnets, no. 3, mm. 1–7. In the first four operations, the texture increases both in density and in the number of independent streams. The number of streams then decreases, with all the voices fusing at the cadence.

At the same time, auditory figure-ground relationships may differ from visual ones. To begin with, sounds are transparent. As Bregman (1990, 469) notes, "a nearer but softer sound can never occlude from perception a farther but louder one." And Meyer (1956, 186) argues that music may present a figure without any ground. Gestalt theorist Kurt Koffka would disagree. "There exists a ground in the auditory field as well as in the visual field, or in any other sensory field," writes Koffka. "This ground may be 'stillness' or it may be the mixture of street-noises which, in a city, never cease during the day-time" (1992, 554).[12] Aron Gurwitsch's phenomenological refinements to gestalt theory might resolve this dispute. Gurwitsch (1964, 4) distinguishes among "theme" (figure), "thematic field" (a ground that frames the figure), and "margin" (an irrelevant background). This would clarify the difference between accompaniment—which supports and affects the theme, as a thematic field—and underlying silence or noise.

Meyer also notes that it is possible to hear an auditory ground with no figure—an unaccompanied accompaniment. He illustrates with the opening of Ludwig van Beethoven's Symphony no. 9. The rustling perfect fifth seems like a background, even before the first violins' entrance. "All the factors making for a clearly articulated relationship are present," writes Meyer. "Not only is the ground much more uniform than the figure, but it begins before the figure is introduced, thus surrounding it in a temporal sense" (1956, 194). This textural articulation is particularly remarkable, given that the figure and ground use the same two pitch classes! This confirms principles of textural structure discussed above. Onset synchrony and pitch comodulation are low between streams and high within them. The ground is homophonic, though rhythmically activated.[13] Meanwhile, the figure might be conceived as monophony or polyphony, depending on whether the violas and contrabasses are heard to continue or to echo the first violins' motive.[14]

Meyer (1956, 194–195) goes on to show that this initial distinction between parts weakens. Late in the introduction, the figure starts to dissolve into the ground. As the Huron-style measurements of Figure 7.9(a) show, this involves increasing onset synchrony. It creates a slight shift from polyphony toward homophony. (Note that pitch comodulation stays at 0 in mm. 1–16.) At the same time, Berry-style analysis would indicate a substantial growth in density, while maintaining the number of higher-level streams, as seen in Figure 7.9(b). Furthermore, both methods can help chart the momentous textural change following the introduction in m. 17—as an outbreak of strict rhythmic and pitch doubling, or as the fusing of two streams without a change in density, as shown in Figure 7.9(c) and (d).

These approaches, though, also leave something out. Beethoven's symphony—being a symphony—involves orchestration, timbre, and dynamics. And this leads away from textural structure, toward textural materials.

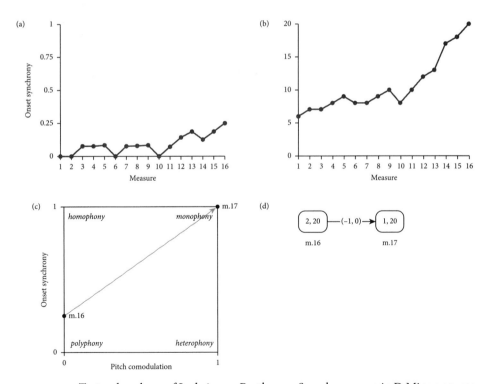

FIGURE 7.9 Textural analyses of Ludwig van Beethoven, Symphony no. 9 in D Minor, op. 125, first movement, mm. 1–17. Both (a) onset synchrony and (b) textural density increase throughout the introduction (mm. 1–16). Following that, the prevailing polyphony switches to (c) a unison, while maintaining (d) the established densit.

TEXTURAL MATERIALS

Just as Anni Albers represents thread-crossing patterns with numbers, I have examined textural structures through functions and transformations. Yet these relatively abstract structures are realized using raw materials, which are less easily measured. Albers illustrates their interplay with the balanced plain weave, a kind of fabric in which the horizontal weft threads alternately pass over and under the vertical warp threads: "The fact that warp and weft appear on the surface in equal amounts and intersect visibly leads to the use of contrasting materials and colors for them, thereby underlining the original structure of the weave" (2010, 30). This example resonates with long-standing conceptions of timbre as sound color (Dolan 2013). If color affects the perception of visual shapes, timbre, articulation, or loudness may emphasize one of two competing musical figures (Wessel 1979; McAdams and Giordano 2008).

This happens often in ensemble arrangements of solo works.[15] Consider the third piece from György Ligeti's *Musica ricercata* for solo piano. It involves Bartók-like counterpoint, passing a motive between the player's hands (see mm. 11–12 in Figure 7.10, which reproduces the music's contours without staff lines). Then, in mm. 13–14, the hands play the motive in synchronized parallel motion, fusing into a single layer.

Ligeti's arrangement of the piece as the first of Six Bagatelles for Wind Quintet adds timbral coloring. The antiphony in mm. 11–12 becomes trading between oboe and horn. The timbral distinction enhances the polyphonic implications of the piano version. In the second, paired part of the passage, however, Ligeti continues the antiphony, now

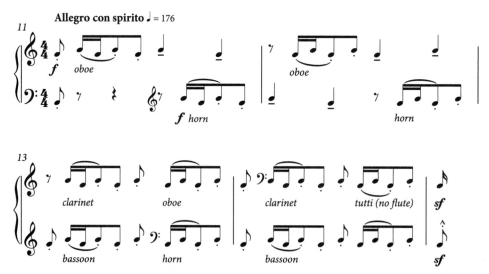

FIGURE 7.10 Schematic representation of György Ligeti, *Musica ricercata*, no. 3, mm. 11–15 (with staff lines removed). The top and bottom staves correspond to the pianist's right and left hands. Instrumental annotations are based on Ligeti's Six Bagatelles for Wind Quintet, no. 1.

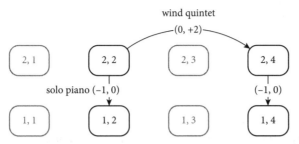

FIGURE 7.11 Transformation network comparing Ligeti's *Musica ricercata*, no. 3, mm. 11–15, with his version for wind quintet. When the pianist's hands unite in m. 13, the winds maintain two streams and double the density. Instead, they fuse later in m. 14.

between a clarinet/bassoon pair and an oboe/horn pair. Figure 7.11 uses my transformational model to bring out the difference. Both versions end with a fusing gesture, modeled via the operation (-1, 0) or the Fuse transformation. But the wind quintet involves an intermediate stage: where the piano's upper and lower parts potentially fuse, the quintet first thickens the polyphony with two new timbral strands.

Here Ligeti amplifies the piano's polyphony, "underlining the original structure of the weave." Yet timbre may also suggest new groupings. Perhaps the best known case of this is Anton Webern's orchestration of the six-part ricercar from Bach's *Musical Offering* (Dethorne 2014, 126–133). Webern divides Bach's lines among various instruments. The initial fugal answer, for example, starts with the flute, then passes to the clarinet, oboe, and harp (mm. 9–16). It still may be followed as a single stream, though the variegation makes this more demanding. Against this wind-based line, the countersubject is presented by muted strings (alternating between the second violin section and a solo viola). In other words, Webern's orchestration presents timbral differentiation *both within and between* layers of Bach's polyphonic texture.

This example suggests that a sense of timbral homogeneity or heterogeneity depends on the context of the ensemble. Still, the distinction seems useful. Instruments with similar timbres—like the members of a string quartet—may fuse into what Eric Clarke (2005, 179) calls an imaginary "multi-instrument."

In larger orchestral works, timbral differences may be used to support the "hyper-polyphony" mentioned in the previous section. *The Unanswered Question* by Charles Ives, for example, involves three distinct streams: the slow-moving string section forms a homophonic background for two alternating figures, a solo trumpet and an increasingly agitated flute quartet. While the trumpet provides a monophonic figure, the flute quartet—though timbrally unified—projects a polyphonic one, which itself involves fusing and splitting. The composer emphasizes the importance of the performance setup in defining the relationships between these layers. "The string quartet or string orchestra (*con sordini*), if possible, should be 'off stage,' or away from the trumpet and flutes. The trumpet should use a mute unless playing in a very large room, or with a larger string orchestra" (1953, 2). In other words, dynamics and even spatial layout, along with timbre, contribute to the separation of streams.

Timbral separation of streams is also prevalent in popular music. For example, mixing practices contribute to the textures of rock music. Especially with stereo recordings, they often isolate instrumental strands, as in the common rock-band setup of two guitars, bass, and drums (Moore 2001, 120–126). At the same time, though, multitrack recording can facilitate thick textures with many layers, creating a wall of sound in which individual strands blend into a larger sonic fabric. That is, timbre can separate but also fuse textural layers. Materials may underline structure—or they may subvert it.

A brief excerpt from "Nun will die Sonn' so hell aufgeh'n"—the first of Gustav Mahler's *Kindertotenlieder*—can serve as an illustration. According to a piano reduction, the phrase at rehearsal number 10 has a straightforward three-part texture. The melody is supported by gently rocking harmonic filler and a sustained bass.[16] Yet Mahler orchestrates this with a series of timbral overlaps: the first violins heterophonically double the voice; the second violins double the harp's upper part; and low strings, then horn, double the harp's bass. Textural material, then, cuts across textural structure. The muted strings color both the voice and harp, softening textural definition. In a sense, this intertwining—in which layers cannot readily be separated—is crucial for experiences of texture as a higher-level phenomenon. Here texture seems to emerge as a whole, with distinct yet connected parts.

That said, textural materials are not only about defining or blurring structural streams. Surely the affect of the Ives and Mahler pieces is related to their *sound quality*. Both use muted strings to create atmosphere. In the Ives, this is set against the brightness of the flutes and the fullness of the trumpet's middle range; in the Mahler, it blends with the decaying plucks of the harp and the expressive voice. From this perspective, timbre does not merely color a preexisting design but is an essential aspect of—or a precondition for—such designs.

But perhaps calling this "sound quality" is still too abstract. Perhaps the very idea of "timbre" isolates sound from performance (Dolan 2013, 56 but also 88). As the examples from Ives and Mahler show, timbre, register, and dynamics are all tied up with each other and with specific *instrumentation*. In *The Unanswered Question*, the flutes end in an extremely high register, where the instrument is particularly shrill. Instead of an absolute measure of pitch height, then, this suggests a more holistic concept of *tessitura*, according to which a part is not simply high or low but also easy or demanding, stable or volatile, smooth or harsh, given a particular context of performed action. Like textural structure, then, textural material would involve a kind of emergence. Sound quality would be produced by several combined elements—register, dynamics, articulation, and so on—that are grounded in interactions between instruments and performers' bodies.[17]

In this view, sonic *materials* may index the *materiality* of performance. This resembles the interplay of vision and tactility in object textures.[18] I can *see* that this mug feels smooth, that the blanket feels soft. So too, musical texture might be intersensory: I *hear* that this voice feels strained; that this drum *sounds* like metal, wood, or plastic.[19] This resonates with research in ecological acoustics that shows how various sonic characteristics relate to their physical production. Dynamics, for example, generally correlate with the force of an interaction, while timbre correlates with material properties of the objects involved (Gaver 1993, 11). Both dynamics and timbre may be affected by spatial location, contributing to the sense of nearness or distance—which contributes to the haunting presence of the muted strings. Like Bregman's perspective on auditory streaming, this ecological view may imply continuity between musical and everyday listening. Many listeners recognize familiar instruments, though admittedly, instrumental identities may also be masked, indistinct, or creatively ignored.[20]

This suggests a different and potentially rich approach: an account starting from raw materials instead of formal structure might view musical texture in terms of embodied practices and cultural meanings.

TEXTURAL SIGNS

Besides structure and material, there is a third element hidden in Albers's definition of weaving: function. The interplay of structure and material affects a fabric's flexibility, its strength, and its potential use for garments or upholstery. In this section, likewise, I am interested less in what texture *is* and more in what texture *does*. How does it mediate other musical features? How does it communicate? Though my answers here are far from exhaustive, I hope they suggest varied functions for texture.

This investigation builds on the work of Janet Levy. In her essay "Texture as a Sign in Classic and Early Romantic Music," Levy distinguishes between contextual and conventionalized signs. Contextual signs involve "particular sets of associations or idiosyncratic relationships between or among textures *within* a given piece" (Levy 1982, 483). She illustrates with the opening movement of Joseph Haydn's String Quartet in C, op. 74, no. 1 (483–487). In the movement's primary theme, the violins and viola form a stream with a high degree of rhythmic synchrony and similar motion, accompanied by a "drum bass" figure in the cello (see Figure 7.12). Later, this theme appears with

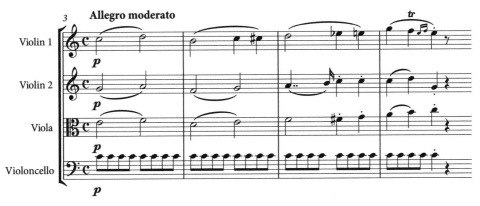

FIGURE 7.12 Joseph Haydn, String Quartet in C Major, op. 74, no. 1, mm. 3–6.

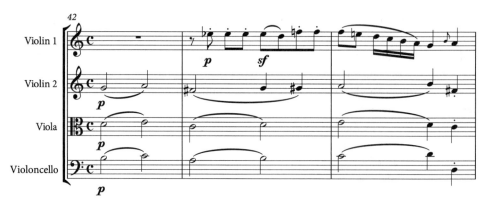

FIGURE 7.13 Haydn, String Quartet in C Major, op. 74, no. 1, mm. 42–44.

different textures. Leading into the exposition's closing material, for example, the three-part stream returns without the bass's rhythmic and harmonic support. Instead, a new, active line is added in the first violin (see Figure 7.13). These streams compete for listeners' attention: one was established earlier in the piece; the other moves more quickly. Levy argues that the change in texture has formal significance. As the new texture destabilizes the theme, it implies that the section at hand is not a straightforward presentation but is more open-ended and developmental.

Other styles—from post-tonal to popular music—also employ contextual signs. Texture articulates form in Witold Lutosławski's 1964 String Quartet, where doubled octaves come to function as a contextual sign that denotes sectional boundaries.[21] For an example in a different style, consider "I Love Rock n' Roll" by Joan Jett and the Blackhearts. In this song, the third presentation of the chorus varies the texture. The guitars rest, and only the drums accompany the singers.[22] Like the "false recapitulation" examples discussed by Levy, this defers closure. Though the song is nearly finished, the new texture signals that this is not yet the final chorus. (This seems to have two further functions: first, varying the texture of repeated material may reengage listeners; second, the simplification in texture may encourage participation.)

Whereas contextual signs involve intra-opus associations, conventionalized signs reflect more general stylistic tendencies. Levy discusses three kinds of conventionalized signs: accompaniment patterns, solos, and unisons.

For Levy, the entrance of a repetitive accompaniment pattern signals stability:

> There is a kind of double psychic economy provided by our recognition of this kind of textural sign. First, we are "told," by the appearance of the Alberti or other familiar pattern, that stability is likely to reign—at least until closure or until other signs contravene this one. Because for the moment there is no question of what the passage *is*, we can relax and simply experience its unfolding. Second, some of the perceptual work is, so to speak, done for us. The Alberti bass (or other regular) pattern provides a kind of palpable motor action that measures or marks off time regularly for us; the

palpability of meter is in inverse proportion to the amount of effort the performer/
listener must expend. (1982, 491–492)

As a ground awaiting a figure, the accompaniment pattern suggests that a melodic
presentation is about to occur. It may even define a figure as such. Figure 7.14 presents
the beginning of Frédéric Chopin's Nocturne in C♯ Minor, op. 27, no. 1. Levy (1982,
494) argues that the left-hand sextuplets indicate that the slow-moving upper part is, in
fact, a melody (see Figure 7.14).

This textural effect may also appear in less conventionalized situations. Arnold
Schoenberg's op. 19, no. 2 begins with a repeated third, staccato and pianissimo (see
Figure 7.15). Establishing this background in mm. 1–2 helps the following melody cohere
as a figure, despite its opening leap of a thirteenth.

Solos, for Levy (1982, 497–501), imply a kind of beginning, a call awaiting a response.
Because of this, they may deny musical closure, as in cadenzas and lead-ins. And
unisons—that is, ensemble unisons—are marked for attention, even if their significance
is ambiguous. They may seem to gather streams together or to dissolve a more complex

FIGURE 7.14 Frédéric Chopin, Nocturne in C♯ Minor, op. 27, no. 1, mm. 1–4.

FIGURE 7.15 Arnold Schoenberg, Little Piano Piece, op. 19, no. 2, mm. 1–3.

texture into a single line (519). While Levy focuses on Western art music from the late eighteenth and early nineteenth centuries, she suggests that some of these principles may be realized in other musical cultures. For example, she notes that classical Indian music distinguishes between an unaccompanied prelude and the beginning marked by the entrance of tabla drums (496).

Like contextual signs, conventionalized signs cue expectations about formal organization. But there is another aspect to Levy's theory that anticipates later research on music and metaphor.[23] She suggests that solos are analogically understood as vocal utterances and unisons as regulated collective action. This reflects texture's capacity to support extramusical references. These mappings, I argue, respond not to individual parameters but to the ways that they are interwoven. Emergent sonic streams make it possible to hear metaphorical bodies, voices, agents, and objects in music (Clarke 2005, 185–187). This might commonly be monophonic or homophonic, though a polyphonic stream could represent the coordination of two independent hands or feet. As Rolf Inge Godøy writes, "it seems that most (or perhaps all) features at different timescales may be correlated with some kind of body movement and/or posture, hence that musical textures, be they instrumental, vocal or electroacoustic, may also be seen as choreographies of sound-related movements" (2010, 58).

If the interplay of figure and ground resembles a body in an environment, music without a singular figure may support kinesthetic metaphors less well. Numerous interlocking streams might more readily suggest the interplay of multiple agents: a flock of birds, conversational partners, and so on. Dense or fluid textures might also imply sonic landscapes, as in depictions of seas and storms.

These textural signs rely on some kind of resemblance. Following Charles Sanders Peirce's trichotomy of sign-object relations, they might be called textural icons. Along these lines, textural indexes would be signs based on co-occurence or association.[24] Like Levy, I suggest that textural signs may involve fairly general principles that are, obviously, realized in particular ways in different cultural groups. As such, I illustrate this distinction between textural icons and indexes through Steven Feld's ethnomusicological work with the Kaluli people of Papua New Guinea. First, Kaluli music theory describes melodic motion in terms of waterfalls (Feld 1981, 30–31). This involves iconic resemblance between musical and aquatic streams. Second, Feld argues that heterophony in Kaluli music reflects social values (Feld 1988, 71–114). These "in sync but out of phase" textures do not simply resemble social relationships; for participants, they indexically embody them as well. As Thomas Turino writes, *"When music makers and dancers are in sync, such signs move beyond felt resemblances to experienced fact of social connections and unity"* (1999, 241, emphasis in the original). Turino argues that dense textures like the heterophony of Kaluli music are common to participatory musics—and that texture typically differentiates participatory and presentational styles of performance (Turino 2008, 44–45).

In various styles of music theater, textural indexes can help depict characters' social relationships. (Again, singing in homophony or unison does not merely resemble coordinated action; it embodies it.) For example, consider a number from the first act of *Don Giovanni*, in which the eponymous rake seduces the peasant girl Zerlina. In "Là ci darem la mano," Giovanni sings the first stanza alone. Zerlina repeats his music with her own words. They then repeat the same material but split into counterpoint, trading lines. The two intertwined voices compete as a polyphonic figure. Giovanni insists. Zerlina hesitates, remembering her poor fiancé. In the duet's final section, however, she assents. In homophonic harmony, they sing "Andiam, andiam, mio bene . . . " ["Let's go, let's go, my love . . . "]. The shift in texture indexes Zerlina's capitulation. This textural strategy is common in theatrical duets: starting with monophony, moving into antiphony, then to some form of rhythmic synchrony. (This recalls the splitting-fusing trajectory of the Milhaud network in Figure 7.8.) In *Don Giovanni*, this textural journey represents seduction. A very similar pattern, culminating in a unison, is used to represent vows of commitment (in the act I finale from Gaetano Donizetti's *Lucia di Lammermoor*) or reconciliation (in the climactic duet "For Good," from Stephen Schwartz's contemporary broadway hit, *Wicked*).

Texture may also refer to musical instruments. For example, the pastoral topic conventionally imitates the texture of small rural bagpipes, with a drone and diatonic pitch collection.[25] Of course, the resemblance is not always exact. The opening of Franz Schubert's Piano Sonata in G Major, D. 894, for example, echoes the pastoral pipes in a more pianistic style. This blend of instrumental textures may reveal the sonata's opening as an instance of what Robert Hatten calls "troping": "the bringing together of two otherwise incompatible style types in a single location to produce a unique expressive meaning from their collision or fusion" (2004, 67). Material and symbolic gaps between the two instruments affect my hearing of Schubert's pastoralism. By transforming pipes into the piano, Schubert seems to take a distinct perspective on the pastoral, mixing rural and urban, peasant and bourgeois, public and private, past and present.

Many musical topics are based on instrumental textures like this, especially those not related to the rhythms of dance (Agawu 1991, 30; Rumph 2012, 83). Chorale textures are similar, based as they are on a style of collective singing. As another case, consider a common jazz rhythm-section texture, in which a walking bass line is distinct from rhythmically irregular homophonic comping. This conventional texture typically supports a melody. But it might also be used to reference the genre (or at least particular styles of jazz).

These diverse textural functions suggest a hermeneutic or semiotic approach to texture that would respond both to stylistic conventions and to contexts of performance and reception. Of course, this would pursue textural effects that are sometimes unstable. Their implications are not always fulfilled, and they are culturally specific. Still, coming to terms with such effects seems important, because they get at texture's apparent immediacy. As Levy puts it, "texture is at once the most surface and most complex" (1982, 482).

CONCLUSIONS

This chapter has argued that musical texture is emergent on several levels. Textural structure and textural materials interact with each other, but both are also produced by multiple factors. Similarly, listeners' experiences of texture combine bottom-up and top-down processes, both basic grouping principles and cultural understanding.

The first section showed how textural structure emerges from the interplay of pitch and rhythm. Following David Huron, it located basic textural categories—monophony, homophony, polyphony, and heterophony—in dimensions of onset synchrony and pitch comodulation. Adapting Wallace Berry's theoretical work added new perspectives on textural change and intensity, while Leonard Meyer's gestalt-based approach helped characterize relationships between streams. The second section, however, claimed that textural structure is supplemented by textural materials. Timbre, articulation, or dynamics might support groupings suggested by pitch and rhythm—or work against them. Moreover, because sound quality is rooted in performance, texture is related to embodied action and instrumental materiality. The third section explored texture's varied functions. Starting from Janet Levy's research on textural signs, this touched on large-scale form, musical metaphor, dramatic meaning, and social values.

The chapter's trajectory might be understood as a series of metaphors. The first section emphasized visual imagery, with its discussion of lines, shapes, and figure-ground relationships. (Indeed, textural structure is often visible in musical notation.) The second section turned from sight to touch. It compared sound quality to the tactile textures of objects, while also indicating the contact of body and instrument in performance. With its semiotic focus, the third section imagined texture as discourse. This suggested similarities between texture and linguistic or gestural communication.

This conceptual variety is matched by the diversity of the chapter's musical examples. Texture's importance in many styles seems to warrant further research involving theoretical formalization or psychological experiments. Yet I also expect important insights to come from sustained investigation of texture in particular repertoires. This might productively engage the statistical and computational methods of corpus studies, or it could be combined with more traditional modes of analysis. Either way, I believe that texture has great interpretive potential. If texture is an emergent phenomenon, it resists reductionism. Attending to texture, then, may help sensitize scholars, students, listeners, and performers to ways that music holds together and ways that it comes apart, to ways that music moves and ways that it moves us.

Notes

1. Jonathan Dunsby (1989, 47) hypothesizes that the term was introduced by discourses of post-tonal music. But though the term may have gained prominence in the early twentieth century, it is much older. For example, it appears throughout Burney (1776–1789).
2. For an introduction to ongoing philosophical debates about emergence, see Gregersen (2008).
3. For example, see Anku (1997) and Sanders (1974).
4. With doubling, it can be interpretively revealing to ask: "Who is doubling whom?" See Sutcliffe (1987, 321).

5. Polyphonic music tends to avoid onset synchrony, according to the analysis in Huron (1993, 435–443).

6. With an n-part texture, these measurements can be arranged in an $n \times n$ matrix that covers all pairs.

7. As this quote suggests, Berry imagined a textural "spectrum" similar to Huron's texture space. This model, however, is overcomplicated, with three dimensions—rhythm, direction, and interval—each of which may be homo-, hetero-, or contra- (1987, 193–194).

8. Berry's notation resembles a shorthand used by Moe (1974).

9. For Berry, changes in the number of streams are "qualitative" (as in a qualitative shift from monophony to polyphony), while changes in density-number are "quantitative."

10. Listeners have difficulty distinguishing more than three parts with the same timbre, as shown by Huron (1989).

11. For a more general treatment of multistability in music, see Karpinski (2012).

12. Koffka further notes that experiments with auditory stimuli do not require complete silence; consistent background noise produces the same results.

13. On textural activation, see Berry (1987, 222).

14. The polyphonic interpretation would involve an imitative "diagonal" relation, according to Berry (1987, 216).

15. It is common, of course, to imagine different layers of a piano piece in terms of orchestral instruments. To some degree, this may reflect a longstanding culture of transcription for piano. But it is still a way of imaginatively adding articulation or clarity to textural layers.

16. This kind of three-part texture, common in nineteenth-century piano music like Felix Mendelssohn's *Songs without Words*, is examined in Cai (1997).

17. For analysis of body-instrument interaction, see De Souza (2017).

18. For an overview of nonmusical texture perception, see Rosenholtz (2015).

19. For further discussion, see Downey (2002, 496).

20. In this respect, I agree with the critique of ecological acoustics in Demers (2010, 36–37).

21. For analytical comments on texture in Lutosławski's quartet, see Reyland (2008, 19–23).

22. I am grateful to Brett Kingsbury for suggesting this example and to Jillian Bracken for her insights about it.

23. For example, see Zbikowski (2002).

24. Levy's conventionalized signs, incidentally, might be a form of textural symbol. For introductions to Peircean semiotics and music, see Turino (1999) and Lidov (2005).

25. On pastoral instruments, see Monelle (2006, 207–215). For a more general discussion of instrumental idioms and topics, see De Souza (2017).

Works Cited

Agawu, Kofi. 1991. *Playing with Signs: A Semiotic Interpretation of Classic Music*. Princeton, NJ: Princeton University Press.

Albers, Anni. 2010. "On Weaving." In *The Craft Reader*. Edited by Glenn Adamson, 29–33. Oxford and New York: Berg.

Anku, Willie. 1997. "Principles of Rhythm Integration in African Drumming." *Black Music Research Journal* 17: 211–238.

Auerbach, Brent. 2008. "Tiered Polyphony and Its Determinative Role in the Piano Music of Johannes Brahms." *Journal of Music Theory* 52: 273–320.

Berry, Wallace. 1987. *Structural Functions in Music*. New York: Dover.

Bora, Renu. 1997. "Outing Texture." In *Novel Gazing: Queer Readings in Fiction*. Edited by Eve Kosofsky Sedgwick, 94–127. Durham, NC: Duke University Press.

Bregman, Albert S. 1990. *Auditory Scene Analysis: The Perceptual Organization of Sound*. Cambridge, MA: MIT Press.

Burney, Charles. 1776–1789. *A General History of Music, from the Earliest Ages to the Present Period*. London.

Cai, Camilla. 1997. "Texture and Gender: New Prisms for Understanding Hensel's and Mendelssohn's Piano Pieces." In *Nineteenth-Century Piano Music: Essays in Performance and Analysis*. Edited by David Witten, 53–93. New York: Garland Publishing.

Clarke, Eric F. 2005. *Ways of Listening: An Ecological Approach to the Perception of Musical Meaning*. New York: Oxford University Press.

Cohen, Dalia, and Shlomo Dubnov. 1997. "Gestalt Phenomena in Musical Texture." In *Music, Gestalt, and Computing: Studies in Cognitive and Systematic Musicology*. Edited by Marc Leman, 386–405. Berlin and New York: Springer.

De Souza, Jonathan. 2017. *Music at Hand: Instruments, Bodies, and Cognition*. New York: Oxford University Press.

De Vale, Sue Carole. 1984. "Prolegomena to a Study of Harp and Voice Sounds in Uganda: A Graphic Notation of Texture." *Selected Reports in Ethnomusicology* 5: 285–315.

Demers, Joanna. 2010. *Listening Through the Noise*. New York: Oxford University Press.

DeThorne, Jefferey. 2014. "Colorful Plasticity and Equalized Transparency: Schoenberg's Orchestrations of Bach and Brahms." *Music Theory Spectrum* 36: 121–145.

Dolan, Emily I. 2013. *The Orchestral Revolution: Haydn and the Technologies of Timbre*. Cambridge: Cambridge University Press.

Downey, Greg. 2002. "Listening to Capoeira: Phenomenology, Embodiment, and the Materiality of Music." *Ethnomusicology* 46: 487–509.

Duane, Ben. 2013. "Auditory Streaming Cues in Eighteenth- and Early Nineteenth-Century String Quartets: A Corpus-Based Study." *Music Perception* 31: 46–58.

Dunsby, Jonathan. 1989. "Considerations of Texture." *Music & Letters* 70: 46–57.

Feld, Steven. 1981. "Flow Like a Waterfall: The Metaphors of Kaluli Musical Theory." *Yearbook for Traditional Music* 13: 30–31.

Feld, Steven. 1988. "Aesthetics as Iconicity of Style, or 'Lift-Up-Over Sounding': Getting into the Kaluli Groove." *Yearbook for Traditional Music* 20: 74–114.

Gaver, William W. 1993. "What in the World Do We Hear? An Ecological Approach to Auditory Event Perception." *Ecological Psychology* 5: 1–29.

Giordano, Bruno L., and Stephen McAdams. 2010. "Sound Source Mechanics and Musical Timbre Perception: Evidence from Previous Studies." *Music Perception* 28: 155–168.

Godøy, Rolf Inge. 2010. "Images of Sonic Objects." *Organised Sound* 15: 54–62.

Gregersen, Niels Henrik. 2008. "Emergence and Complexity." In *The Oxford Handbook of Religion and Science*. Edited by Philip Clayton, 767–783. New York: Oxford University Press.

Gurwitsch, Aron. 1964. *The Field of Consciousness*. Pittsburgh, PA: Duquesne University Press.

Hatten, Robert. 2004. *Interpreting Musical Gestures, Topics, and Tropes: Mozart, Beethoven, Schubert*. Bloomington: Indiana University Press.

Huron, David. 1989. "Characterizing Musical Textures." In *Proceedings of the 1989 International Computer Music Conference*, 131–134. San Francisco: Computer Music Association.

Huron, David. 1989. "Voice Denumerability in Polyphonic Music of Homogeneous Timbres." *Music Perception* 6: 361–382.

Huron, David. 1993. "Note-Onset Synchrony in J. S. Bach's Two-Part Inventions." *Music Perception* 10: 435–443.

Huron, David. 2001. "Tone and Voice: A Derivation of the Rules of Voice-Leading from Perceptual Principles." *Music Perception* 19: 1–64.

Ives, Charles E. 1953. *The Unanswered Question*. New York: Southern Music Publishing.

Karpinski, Gary S. 2012. "Ambiguity: Another Listen." *Music Theory Online* 18, no. 3. http://mtosmt.org/issues/mto.12.18.3/mto.12.18.3.karpinski.php.

Koffka, Kurt. 1992. "Perception: An Introduction to the Gestalt-Theorie." *Psychological Bulletin* 19: 531–585.

Levy, Janet M. 1982. "Texture as a Sign in Classic and Early Romantic Music." *Journal of the American Musicological Society* 35: 482–531.

Lidov, David. 2005. *Is Language a Music? Writings on Musical Form and Signification*. Bloomington: Indiana University Press.

McAdams, Stephen, and Bruno L. Giordano. 2008. "The Perception of Musical Timbre." In *The Oxford Handbook of Music Psychology*. Edited by Ian Cross, Susan Hallam, and Michael Thaut, 72–80. New York: Oxford University Press.

Meyer, Leonard B. 1956. *Emotion and Meaning in Music*. Chicago: University of Chicago Press.

Moe, Orin. 1974. "Texture in Haydn's Early Quartets." *The Music Review* 35: 4–22.

Monelle, Raymond. 2006. *The Musical Topic: Hunt, Military and Pastoral*. Bloomington: Indiana University Press.

Moore, Allen F. 2001. *Rock: The Primary Text: Developing a Musicology of Rock*. 2nd edition. Aldershot, UK: Ashgate.

Raymer, Miles. 2014. "FKA twigs, *LP1*." *Entertainment Weekly*. August 15, 66.

Reyland, Nicholas. 2008. "Notes on the Construction of Lutosławski's Conception of Musical Plot." *Witold Lutosławski Studies* 2: 19–23.

Rosenholtz, Ruth. 2015. "Texture Perception." In *The Oxford Handbook of Perceptual Organization*. Edited by Johan Wagemans, 167–188. New York: Oxford University Press.

Rowell, Lewis. 1984. *Thinking about Music: An Introduction to the Philosophy of Music*. Amherst: University of Massachusetts Press.

Rumph, Stephen C. 2012. *Mozart and Enlightenment Semiotics*. Berkeley: University of California Press.

Sanders, Ernest H. 1974. "The Medieval Hocket in Practice and Theory." *The Musical Quarterly* 60: 246–256.

Sutcliffe, W. Dean. 1987. "Haydn's Piano Trio Textures." *Music Analysis* 6: 319–332.

Turino, Thomas. 2008. *Music as Social Life: The Politics of Participation*. Chicago: University of Chicago Press.

Turino, Thomas. 1999. "Signs of Imagination, Identity, and Experience: A Peircean Semiotic Theory for Music." *Ethnomusicology* 43: 221–255.

Wessel, David L. 1979. "Timbre Space as a Musical Control Structure." *Computer Music Journal* 3: 45–52.

Zbikowski, Lawrence. 2002. *Conceptualizing Music: Cognitive Structure, Theory, and Analysis*. New York: Oxford University Press.

PART II

TIME

CHAPTER 8

REPETITION

ELIZABETH HELLMUTH MARGULIS

REPETITION permeates the practice of music at so many levels and in so many forms that it can elude notice, assuming the invisibility of the truly taken for granted. But it is the specific mandate of this volume to revisit the foundational elements of music and theorize about them head on, rather than as incidentals on the way to some more impressive topic. Accordingly, this chapter aims to journey into the obvious, bypassing many of the complex structures and characteristics that attract more attention in traditional theoretical accounts, and focus squarely on an element that seems so ordinary as to hardly warrant mention.

As is often the case with foundational elements, defining repetition is not a trivial task. An important initial distinction separates acoustic repetition—repetition that is objectively identifiable within an acoustic signal—from perceived repetition, to which a person might be able to explicitly or implicitly respond. In the explicit case, a person might be able to say: yes, I heard a theme repeat a minute and 45 seconds into the track. In the implicit case, a person might be unable to overtly recognize a repetition has taken place, but reveal faster reaction times (Hutchins and Palmer 2008), attentional shifts (Taher, Rusch, and McAdams 2016), fluctuations in aesthetic response (Margulis 2013), or altered duration estimates (Matthews and Gheorghiu 2016), demonstrating the effects of repetition even in the absence of explicit awareness about it.[1]

Musical notation both reflects and encourages the conceptual prioritization of discrete elements, such as pitch and duration, over more continuous elements such as dynamics and tone color. Although performance nuances in pitch inflection and expressive timing can render even pitch and duration as continuous as anything else, these elements tend to be perceived categorically. For example, slight adjustments in pitch height tend to be heard as better or worse exemplars of a particular category (as an intune or a sharp C), but subtle changes in dynamics don't seem like more or less canonic exemplars of mezzoforte in quite the same way (see Patel 2008 for pitch and Desain and Honing 2003 for duration). The centrality of pitch and duration in typical Western notions of what defines a piece of music has been reified by music theory's emphasis on these dimensions, at the expense—some would claim—of other ones, such as timbre and dynamics (see Cogan and Escot, 1976; Slawson 1985). Yet the tendency to conceptualize music in this way influences what kinds of phenomena come to be perceived as repetitions. For example, a theme that's repeated at a different dynamic level tends to get conceptualized as repetitive in a way that a dynamic contour repeated with different pitches and rhythms does not.

These notions of what constitutes sameness depend critically on enculturation. Goehr (1992) traces the history of the concept of the musical work as an entity capable of being repeated. A 1995 review in *Fanfare* magazine complained that the limited, historically informed embellishments and improvisatory variations in Robert Levin's recording of the Schubert piano sonata in A minor, D. 537 (Sony Vivarte, SK53364), should have earned it a "warning label" for failing to count as a performance of the work listed on the album cover (Kagan 1995). Yet in some traditions, much greater variation can occur from performance to performance, with all of them qualifying as repetitions of a single piece. For example, Kofi Agawu chronicles the different musical features that characterize two Akpafu funeral dirges, including one's use of free versus the other's use of strict rhythm. "In spite of what would appear to be unmistakable musical differences between these two dirges, they are perceived as the same by the Akpafu. Asked about the relationship between the two dirges, the Akpafu often respond, 'Ne ame ide ne' ('It is the same thing')" (Agawu 1988, 90). Agawu explains that the Akpafu categorize the dirges primarily based on the meaning and social function of the text. The salient equivalence at this level doesn't argue against divergence at a less prominent one—listeners in the West are accustomed to hearing rondos as repetitive, despite the fact that every time the theme returns it might be notated differently or performed with different expressive inflections. Moreover, technology has played a significant role in shaping current notions of repetition—before the advent of recording technology, what constituted "the same" likely admitted of much more variability than it does now. In fact, recordings have been blamed for standardizing expressive performances of classical music (Philip 2004).

These complexities illustrate that acoustic repetition occupies an endpoint on a spectrum spanning all shades and types of similarity, with perceived repetition failing to map neatly on top. In some uncontroversial cases, such as listening and relistening to the same digital recording, acoustic and perceived repetitions overlay one another closely, but in the majority of cases, the relationship is more complex, with repeating elements in the acoustic signal failing to be registered as such, or percepts of repetition emerging from non-identical acoustic signals.

To think through different kinds of repetition and how they relate to one another, it can be helpful to imagine a three-dimensional map with axes defined by some of the key characteristics: timescale of repeating entity (short to long); precision of replication (exact to varied); and distance between iterations (immediate to delayed). Repetitions that cluster near the origin (immediate, exact, and short repetitions) tend to be more salient, but the examples discussed in this chapter reveal the way that genre, context, and culture can shift this relationship.

More difficult to map is the nature of the repeating entity itself—whether it's a pattern comprised of pitches, intervals, timbres, dynamic levels, articulations, or textures. The opening of Beethoven's Symphony no. 3, for example, contains repetitions that prolif-erate or retreat depending on what kind of lens is applied. The opening E♭ major chords, replicating each other in every aspect susceptible to notation, seem like repetitions in all but the stingiest account (someone strictly opposed to this characterization might cite differences in hypermetric placement, for example, or subtle differences in perfor-mance nuance between the two). The repeated syncopated Gs played by the first violins in mm. 7–8 are similarly clear cut, except that they get progressively louder and the last one is durationally extended. But do these count as repetitions of the Gs that the same instruments played in the opening measures? Those were much louder, and asserted within striking tonic chords; the Gs in mm. 7–8 emerge tentatively on top of a chromatic diminished seventh. If these two episodes of Gs can be considered varied repetitions of one another, can they also be understood to repeat octave-lower Gs played by the second violins in the intervening measures? Arguably, the subsequent varied iterations of the motive played by the lowest strings from the upbeat to m. 5 through the first beat of m. 6—despite that they are tossed back and forth by different instruments, in different registers, within different textures, articulating different harmonies—are more saliently repetitive than any of the Gs.

All of these examples involve a pattern established by some combination of pitch and duration, but a wider lens could take in other sorts of patterns as well. For example, mm. 25–26 and mm. 28–35 repeat a patterned alternation of sforzandi every two notes, and then every three. Nothing about the pitches need repeat for a pattern to recur within parameters like dynamics or texture. In fact, replication of elements like these—especially timbre—can come to define a genre. People are quite good at identifying the type of music they are hearing from exposure to very brief (250 millisecond) segments, likely because individual timbral patterns (the presence or absence of a harmonica or saxophone, for example) evoke particular genres (Gjerdingen and Perrott, 2008).

It might seem like some of these complications could be sorted out by distinguishing between repetitions that occur within the musical materials themselves, repetitions that listeners perceive, and repetitions that arise out of a piece being performed or heard multiple times. Yet even these categories are complicated by misalignments between the notated score and the acoustic signal to which it gives rise—the first two chords in the Eroica might look the same on the page, but be performed with different expres-sive inflections. Additionally, there might be little difference in the case of a short piece replayed three times and the recurrence of a section of equivalent length in a rondo.

It would be hard to talk about repetition if all of these definitional challenges were roped into the inquiry; at the same time, it would be unsatisfying to restrict the discus-sion to the clearest and most extreme cases. Instead, this chapter will adopt a pragmatic approach, focusing on intuitive notions of what constitutes repetition in Western mu-sical culture, and addressing the definitional malleability by acknowledging rather than rectifying it. It will emphasize the role of repetition in people's experiences of listening to music, rather than repetition's role in some more abstract notion of musical structure. In keeping with this emphasis, the next few sections will consider the kinds of experiences repetition tends to encourage. First, repetition can establish the basic parameters for engaging with a piece of music. Second, repetition can choreograph attention. Third, repetition can draw listeners into a participatory relationship with sound.[2]

Repetition Can Establish the Basic Parameters for Engaging with a Piece of Music

Repetition can shape fundamental aspects of how listeners approach a piece, such as whether they hear it tonally, and with what tonic. David Huron proposes this definition of tonality: "a system for interpreting pitches or chords through their relationship to a reference pitch, dubbed the *tonic*" (2006a, 143)—a phenomenon explored more deeply in Steven Rings's chapter "Tonic" in this volume. When a piece establishes a tonic, its pitches snap into a network of perceived relationships that utterly transforms their perceived identity. The probe-tone technique (Krumhansl 1990) provides a picture of this network, producing tone profiles that track how well individual pitches are perceived to fit within a tonal context.

How do these tonal percepts emerge? The earliest computer models tallied the raw frequency and duration of individual pitches and matched these distributional profiles with tone profiles for various keys, hypothesizing that the one with the best match represented the perceived key (Krumhansl 1990). These distributional models of key finding were reinforced by studies that used musical systems unfamiliar to the North American participants (Indian classical music or artificially designed pitch-class distributions) and found that pitches heard more frequently tended to be perceived as tonic (Castellano, Bharucha, and Krumhansl 1984; Oram and Cuddy 1995). Other studies, however, argued for the role of temporal ordering over raw frequency, asserting the importance of which pitch follows which other pitch beyond a simple tally of which pitches are present (Brown 1988; Brown, Butler, and Jones 1994; Matsunaga and Abe 2005). Temperley and Marvin (2008) outline evidence that key perceptions emerge from a combination of distributional and structural mechanisms.

Yet both accounts place repetition at the heart of what drives tonal perception. According to the distributional account, increased repetition of particular pitches across the course of an excerpt draws listeners into the practice of hearing all the notes in relation to a particular tonic. According to the structural account, increased repetition of patterns at the larger-than-note level plays the primary role. Whether it is repetition at the level of individual notes or at the level of larger-scale patterns, the profound perceptual shift referred to as tonal hearing arises because listeners track statistical regularities, storing information about the frequency with which things are repeated even when they aren't explicitly aware of these tallies. At a level that mostly eludes conscious awareness, repetition shapes the phenomenology of pitch (see Huron 2006b), leading one note to sound stable and restful, for example, and another tense and implicative. When Schoenberg sought to prevent the emergence of tonality, he proscribed precisely this sort of repetition, ensuring that no individual pitch class could be restated until all twelve had occurred once. The fact that the effort to suppress tonality relied so predominantly on the effort to suppress repetition underscores repetition's central role in giving rise to tonal hearing, one of the most basic ways of organizing sound. DeBellis (1995) observes that most listeners cannot immediately tell whether the italicized words in this phrase "*Oh*-oh say can you see, by the dawn's early *light*" (⊙ Audio Example 8.1) are sung on the same pitch, and yet tallies of precisely these sorts of recurrences are what enable a listener to experience a sense of arrival at the last note in "twilight's last gleam*ing*." In the absence of any attention or effort, repetition draws listeners into particular relationships with sound—in this case, the experience of tonality.

Sometimes, the expressive impact of a piece depends on tracking the repetition of individual pitches and pitch classes. For example, in the opening of Brahms's Intermezzo in E minor, op. 119, no. 2 (Figure 8.1 and ⊙ Audio Example 8.2), the persistent failure to resolve D♯ plays a critical role in imparting a sense of restless dissatisfaction (see Cadwallader 1988). The first salient example occurs in m. 2, where the top-voice sforzando D♯—the highest pitch yet—emerges and is sustained for twice as long as any previous note. Yet no top-voice ascent to E is forthcoming. When an inner voice moves to D♯ at the end of m. 3, it skips over the anticipated resolution and up to an F♯ on the downbeat of m. 4, despite the fact that the parallel moment at the end of m. 1 reinforced the implication for E. The only other moment at which D♯ progresses to an adjacent pitch is the end of m. 4, where it is spelled as E♭ and resolves down to D. The top voice D♯ in m. 5, again durationally emphasized, is repeated three times before bypassing E on the way to a high F♯ in m. 6, echoing the inner-voice evasion several measures earlier.

When a top voice D♯ finally resolves to E in m. 12, it is harmonized as a dominant leading into the A minor passage, not a point of resolution. This passage articulates E in the top voice, including a sustained, accented iteration (m. 19) that recalls the sforzando in m. 2, but these Es are never preceded by a D♯ that would imbue them with the force of resolution. Instead, the m. 19 E is corrected to a series of D♯s in m. 21, which once more overshoot their target and progress to F♯.[3]

The repeated Fs in the opening phrase of "The Star-Spangled Banner" are just as much acoustic repetitions as the repeated D♯s in the Intermezzo. They might be predicted to function as perceived repetitions more easily than the D♯s, because they are separated by just three measures, and because they are articulated within a simpler texture. Yet as DeBellis observes, the repetitions of the F often fail to make the leap from acoustic to perceived, and the repetitions of the D♯, I would argue, often succeed.[4] Why?

FIGURE 8.1 Johannes Brahms, Intermezzo in E minor, op. 119, no. 2, mm. 1–23.

For one thing, the Fs serve different local tonal functions. The first one serves as the initiator of a descending tonic triad; the second as the goal of a secondary dominant's push to V. In one case, the F is serving as the fifth of the tonic chord, and in the other as the root of the (tonicized) dominant. For another, the Fs serve different formal functions. The first F serves as a beginning, and the second as an end. What's heard by many listeners is not a repetition of F, but rather an initiating, tonic-harmony note and a concluding, dominant-harmony note.

The D♯s, on the other hand, repeatedly occur as components of the dominant harmony, and are often stated saliently in positions that emphasize their implicative nature. In addition to this harmonic and textural similarity, there is a formal similarity, with the D♯s functioning frequently as interruptions toward the end of a segment or phrase. What many listeners might hear is not precisely a repetition of D♯, but rather a repetition of a sustained, interrupting, top-voice, end-of-segment, implicative note. (A smaller subset of listeners might connect the salient D♯s to the more subtle, inner-voice ones.) Perceived repetition tends to be less a function of particular aspects of the acoustic signal and more a function of the way these aspects combine to produce events. When sounds function at the level of perceived musical units—beginnings, interruptions, outbursts, cadences, leaps—they can be heard as repeated interruptions or repeated cadences or repeated leaps, but when the sounds combine with other elements to produce perceived units at some superordinate level, their repetition is less easily perceptible. In the case of the examples raised here, "The Star-Spangled Banner" Fs help construct other, larger-scale events, but the Intermezzo D♯s function more like events themselves, making their repetition more salient.

Repetition beyond the level of the individual pitch can choreograph listening experiences in similarly powerful ways. Consider, for example, the formal functions of repetition in eighteenth-century European art music. Not only do themes tend to start with the immediate (in a typical sentence) or gapped (in a typical period) repetition of a basic idea, but the themes themselves tend to recur in predictable ways across the course of a section, and the sections themselves are often enclosed in repeat signs. For the initiated, these seams serve as landmarks that help orient a listener within the structure (having spotted a repeat sign, how quickly do introductory theory students raise their hands to identify the end of the exposition), and for everyone else, they encourage a kind of conceptualization that can redefine the way a piece is experienced. In a process Rahn (1993) refers to as "thingifying," these repeated elements tend to establish themselves as points of reference—to emerge from the continuous stream of musical elements as a cohesive unit, capable of being referred to and mulled over and conceptualized as a thing.

When a passage gets thingified through repetition, it can on the one hand acquire an atemporal, intellectualized quality—thinking in terms of "that theme" or "that gesture" becomes easier, as does overtly pondering the music's structure. Since music transpires in time, the individual events can seem elusive, occurring and then passing on, but repetition tends to bind the notes together, making them available to memory and capable of being revisited as a stable entity. Repetition thus makes music more conceptually graspable and amenable to verbalization. On the other hand, thingification can take place at a more intuitive level, encouraging a different kind of engagement rather than a different kind of thinking. Because repetition tends to bind the individual events more tightly to each other, the beginning of a thingified passage tends to already imply all the subsequent events. The beginning triggers this attitude of expectation, which tends to manifest as a sense of involvement and participation, or an inclination to feel the continuations before they occur—even to hum or sing along. In this case, the emergent "thing" is less a subject of perceived discourse, and more a special way of experiencing sounds in time.

Indeed, some research suggests that repeated musical passages elicit a stronger urge to move, tap, or sing along than passages that are merely similar (Margulis 2014b). Other research traces the emergence of the expectational attitude. In Wong, Roy, and Margulis (2008), people returned to a lab five times over the course of two weeks. In each session, they listened to Bizet's *L'Arlésienne Suite* no. 1, and afterward moved a slider to continuously rate their perceptions of tension and relaxation from moment to moment as a short excerpt from the piece progressed. This excerpt featured a clear climactic moment, where perceived tension tended to be highest. As shown by the small circle along the solid line in Figure 8.2, participants initially indicated the highest perceived tension just after the climactic moment (represented by the gray circle). The arrow traces the way the perceived tension peak moved back in time across repeated exposures, such that eventually—as illustrated by comparison with the black circle along the dotted line—it actually preceded the climactic moment in the music. Repetition, in other words, drew listeners into an anticipatory mode, such that they perceived more tension in the moments spent anticipating the climactic event than in the moments spent reacting to it. This shift in the dynamics of engagement represents the more tacit, felt aspect of thingification.

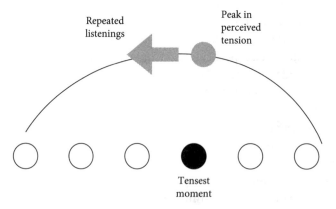

FIGURE 8.2 Across repeated exposures, the perceived tension peak moves earlier until it actually occurs before the precipitating event in the music.

Repetition Can
Choreograph Attention

The end of the last section showed how repetition can funnel attention toward specific expected future events. But it can also choreograph attention in a variety of other subtle yet aesthetically relevant ways. Work in linguistics has shown that the repetition of spoken utterances often functions to draw attention to latent or unexpected meanings. For example, if you say "call your mother," it might take several repetitions for me to understand that you mean that something's really wrong—the repeated statements start to imply that there's more to your imperative than the words convey on the surface. Spoken repetition can ultimately lead to semantic satiation (Severance and Washburn 1907), where the meanings of the words recede, allowing the normally overlooked qualities of the sounds themselves to amplify and become the focus of attention. Work in the psychology of ritual has suggested that repeated gestures can contribute to eliciting a special—and often highly pleasurable—attentional state focused on the lower-level properties of actions (Boyer and Liénard 2006).

Similarly, musical repetition has been shown to shift the time-scale of attention, in this case from relatively lower to higher levels of the musical structure. In Margulis (2012), people detected low-level, short repetitions on their first hearing of a piece, but gradually shifted to detecting higher-level, longer repetitions on subsequent hearings. This shift traces the way listeners zoom out and begin to apprehend structural connections that extend beyond the surface across repeated exposures to a particular work. But in musical styles where the richest content lies not up at the level of hierarchical relationships but down in the marrow of individual sounds—in timbre and microtiming, for example—repetition can shift attention below the surface, into the sonic grain. In an essay on Morton Feldman, Brian Kane describes what he refers to as "the dialectical role of repetition: to enforce remembering by reiteration and to aid forgetting of the immediately past by asserting, and reasserting, the new" (Kane 2016, 26). He chronicles how Feldman's repetitions unshackle listeners from habit and reconnect them to the materiality of the individual sounds.

The key commonality between both these processes—shifting up to hierarchical spans and burrowing down into the sound itself—is that repetition pushes listeners beyond the surface, in one direction or the other. Our restless ears don't seem to be satisfied by attending to the same aspect of a passage again and again; rather, as a general rule, we indulge in attentional redirections that generate variety within apparent stasis. Luis-Manuel Garcia observes the way this active attentional path finding gives rise to a distinct sort of pleasure. His analysis targets looping in electronic dance music, where "a persistently-looping, dense collection of riffs provides a dense layering of textures without pre-determining the listener's path of focus" (Garcia 2005, ¶5.2).

Similar attentional shifts arise when listening to music that features gradual transformation rather than insistent repetition or music in which the repetition is restricted to a single layer, against which other layers vary. In these cases, instead of pushing attention toward new aspects of the repeating sounds, the repetition pushes attention toward the elements that are actually changing. Taher et al. (2016) played people two-part contrapuntal excerpts with one repetitive and one nonrepetitive part and asked them to continually rate the relative prominence of the voices as the excerpts progressed. Participants tended to rate the nonrepetitive part as more prominent, indicating that repetition can shift attention away from itself and toward the more novel or changing aspects of the texture. In a piece like "When I am Laid" (Dido's Lament) from Purcell's *Dido and Aeneas* (▶ Audio Example 8.3), for example, this attentional shift means that many listeners entirely fail to register the presence of the repeated descents of the ground bass. In a piece like Terry Riley's *In C*, it can mean that people find themselves hyper-attuned to tiny fluctuations and changes as the music progresses. Music that merely repeats leaves the attentional path more open to the listener; music that introduces transformation tends to draw attention toward the changes, controlling the attentional choreography more closely and leaving less up to the listener. Thus—paradoxically, perhaps—the varied repetition of *In C* exerts more control on the aspects to which listeners will generally attend than the unvaried baseline of "When I am Laid," against the backdrop of which listener's attention is free to wander.

Repetition Can Draw Listeners into a Participatory Relationship with Sound

Turino (2008) distinguishes between presentational music, such as a classical concert, where performers with special training play and everyone else listens, and participatory music, such as a campfire jam, where everyone is meant to join in the music-making. Participatory music often relies heavily on repetition, because repetition enables newcomers to start playing along as quickly and easily as possible. But even presentational music exploits repetition's affordance for participation; it just tends to shift listeners into a particular kind of perceptual orientation with the sound, rather than into overt music-making. (Although absent the social cues that prohibit such things, many a listener has been known to sing and steering-wheel drum to such presentational classics as Beethoven's Symphony no. 5.) Hearing a passage repeatedly tilts attention forward, such that all the subsequent notes seem to tumble inevitably out of the initial ones. This orientational shift seems quite salient on introspection—it is relatively easy to notice that we tend to mentally sing through a familiar phase as it plays or after it is truncated. Furthermore, several empirical findings tend to support it: after repeated listenings, people anticipate climaxes before they happen (Wong et al. 2008); verbatim repetition elicits reports of an elevated tendency to move along with the music (Margulis 2014b);

and people rate random sequences of tones as more musical when they've previously been exposed to them on loop rather than via a single presentation (Margulis and Simchy-Gross 2016).

People asked to describe their peak experiences with music often refer to a sense of feeling like one with it—as if the boundaries between themselves and the sound had dissolved (Gabrielsson 2011). These types of experiences, and their paler cousin, the highly enjoyable but not transcendent experience of music, tend to occur in response to familiar music—that is, music to which the listener has been repeatedly exposed (Pereira et al. 2011). Even short-term repetition can impact the pleasure people derive from musical listening; people without formal musical training exposed to contemporary art music rated it more enjoyable, more interesting, and more likely to have been crafted by a human artist than randomly generated by a computer when the audio files had been manipulated to introduce literal repetitions of phrase segments (Margulis 2013).

The transcendent experiences Gabrielsson documents can be thought about as powerful illusions of participation—despite the fact that the listener may be slumped in an airline seat with headphones, she feels as if the music is sweeping her away. More ordinary varieties of musical pleasure often seem to involve a similar sensation, if not so all-consuming. Both the milder and more intense kinds can be partially understood by referencing the power of repetition to generate experiences of virtual participation. To a certain extent, composers can manipulate the degree to which listeners partake in this sense of shared subjectivity with the sound—repetition can serve as an implicit invitation to participate, even if only imaginatively.

In a musical experience centered on virtual participation, listeners feel that they are embodying the sounds, and hearing forward into the next notes before they occur. In some ways, this experience is maximally different from a more analytic type of experience, in which a listener thinks explicitly about what she's hearing and makes overt judgments about it. Cone (1977) traces the role of multiple hearings in eliciting these different types of attending. On the first hearing, he explains, the sounds simply wash over the listener. As the listener studies the piece, a certain amount of struggle ensues—her attention darts back and forth from the sounds as they progress to explicit thoughts and ideas about them, as she seeks to integrate her conceptual understanding with her sensory experience. In Cone's ideal "third reading," this integration has been sufficiently completed and the listener is able once more to immerse herself completely in the sound of the music, the analysis having shaped and enriched what she actually hears. Cone's three stages chronicle the progress of a listener devoted to explicit study; for many less studiously minded listeners, the second stage involves not a period of wrestling with analytic notions, but rather of a gradual pulling-in, where the listener becomes increasingly invested in the sounds implied by the current one.

Schubert's Impromptu in A♭ major, op. 142, D. 935, no. 2 (Figure 8.3 and ⊚ Audio Example 8.4) exemplifies the way that presentational music can exploit repetition's capacity to involve. The second eight measures repeat the first, with the right hand transposed up an octave and the last three measures altered to strengthen the cadence.

FIGURE 8.3 Franz Schubert, Impromptu in A♭ major, op. 142, D. 935, no. 2, mm. 1–46.

As if this weren't enough repetition, the whole sixteen-bar section is enclosed in repeat signs. It recurs again in modified form in mm. 31–46, measures that—along with the intervening middle section—are once more enclosed in repeat signs. Finally, a lightly modified version of these initial 46 measures follows a texturally distinct trio. All of this repetition, together with the lilting dance topic, conspires to invite the listener into an especially intimate relationship with the sound. In this mode of listening, the events to come are wrapped into the events that are already sounding, allowing the music to be experienced more subjectively than is typical—as if through listening, the music was being made rather than heard.

Across the course of all these repetitions at the phrase and section level, the tenor voice, with only occasional deviations, persistently repeats a single note—E♭. The octave transposition of the right hand that first occurs with the pickup to m. 9 leaves this E♭ more exposed. Its steady repetition among the harmonic and melodic vagaries of other voices promotes it to an object of attention. The other voices can seem to reveal ever-new aspects of this repeated pitch, sometimes harmonizing it as a tonic, sometimes a dominant; sometimes casting it as a beginning and sometimes as an end. This draws the listener deep into the sound of the E♭, revealing it as something much larger and more complex than a first hearing might have implied. Because the E♭ is couched within an inner voice, it can seem veiled or reluctant to expose itself, increasing the sense of intimacy that arises out of coming to know it so well. By exploring so many aspects of this inner-voice pitch, the impromptu gives the impression of divulging something that could not have been accessible by public proclamation, but can only become knowable via sustained encounters.

VARIETIES OF REPETITION

Although repetition admits of many different types, it can be useful to delineate a few specific oppositions that highlight some of the roles repetition can play in music. Middleton (1990) draws a distinction between musematic repetition, consisting of the unvaried repetition of short units such as riffs, and discursive repetition, consisting of the repetition of longer units such as themes or sections, and often leading to hierarchical discourse structures. This distinction is related to the one Sisman (1993) draws between immediate and gapped repetition. Immediate repetition—often of short units such as those Middleton describes—tends to draw listeners into an affiliative relationship with the sound, manifesting as a kind of feeling or orientation. Listeners may nod along or sing through the riff mentally, attention directed at the sounds about to unfold. Gapped repetition, on the other hand, tends to spark more explicit awareness of structure—a more conceptualized, cognitive kind of response—in parallel with the increased participatory affiliation. This kind of repetition can provide listeners with identifiable landmarks that are easy to think and talk about, generating an impression of "discourse" as Middleton describes it.

This mapping from gapped repetition to impressions of discourse represents just one of the innumerable ways that meaning and expressive resonance can be derived from the use of repeating elements. For example, Rebecca Leydon outlines the way repetition's musematic or discursive character can map onto different types of perceived subjectivity:

> Music that confounds hierarchic listening altogether because of a preponderance of undifferentiated "riffs" may suggest a "will-less" or "automatized" subject. Hierarchies that are shallow, with few levels, may suggest a tentative volitional state. In more highly stratified textures with differentiated levels of musematic and discursive parsing, the subject may be understood as more "willful," provided the strata are perceived as hierarchically interlocked. Particularly deep or complex hierarchies or situations in which metrical relationships between figure and ground are ambiguous may suggest a split subject or a plurality of willful subjects.
>
> (Leydon 2002, 14)

Beyond constructing these broad notions of voice, repetition can connote more specific expressive worlds. Leydon outlines six such resonances in minimalist music, ranging from repetition that seems maternal or soothing, to repetition that seems aphasic, representative of a mental or logical breakdown.

Listeners without formal training can articulate these mappings, and their descriptions show a surprising level of consensus. Margulis (2017) played people ninety-second excerpts from orchestral music. If they reported hearing a story in the music, they were asked to describe it. People who heard the opening of Terry Riley's *In C* tended to describe mechanistic scenes—a construction site, a railroad crossing, an assembly line, an alarm, a train. People who heard the opening of John Adams's *Shaker Loops* tended to describe kinetic episodes featuring people and animals rather than machines—people or horses running, racing, or dashing. Additionally, descriptions of the Riley excerpt tended to be fairly static, whereas descriptions of the Adams emphasized suspense and progress toward a goal. The core repeating element in the Riley involves a series of percussive attacks that people generally experienced in terms of the metaphor of a machine, but the core repeating element in the Adams involves syncopations and a hovering shimmer, which instead elicited a sensation of agential striving.

Fink (2005) explores minimalism in terms of the society of mass consumerism that arose in postwar America, as well as the recording technologies that changed the very concept of what it meant to repeat oneself. The contemporary notion of exact, verbatim repetition, Hunter (1984) has argued, did not exist before systems of notation were developed to compensate for the fallibility of memory. Prior to that, retellings that involved paraphrase and new words might be conceptualized as repetitions of the same story, and performances that involved new notes might be conceptualized as repetitions of the same piece. As exemplified by the debate over Levin's embellishments in the Schubert sonata, what constitutes "the same" remains far from resolved; however, the addition or omission of improvisatory ornamentation is perceptually available in a way Hunter theorizes it was not in ancient times.

In fact, contemporary listeners of Western art music tend to place much stock in small differences in dynamics and microtiming; after all, they are what distinguish a performance that might be considered legendary from one considered merely accurate. This shift in attention from what is the same about many performances to what distinguishes them from each other mirrors the shift in attention that repetition often seems to engender, toward the elements that change—if elements change—or toward different aspects of the sound if they don't. Many varieties of repetition can be understood in terms of this push toward listening for the new. Composers can establish repetition along a particular dimension and count on attention shifting toward the parts that are changing (see Taher et al. 2016) but the same process occurs when nothing actually varies; the drive for novelty, instead of latching on to something new in the acoustic signal, turns inward, and seeks alternative ways of hearing something that is superficially invariant.

As an example of this process, Hasty (1997) demonstrates the way identical repeating events—even the ticks of a car's blinker—come to sound very different from one another simply by the fact of succeeding one another in time. One event might possess the perceived accent of serving as the beginning, and the next the subtly different quality of serving as a continuation. When the repeating element is richer than an individual tick, attention doesn't need to resort to the raw dynamics of temporal succession; instead it can burrow into an inner voice, or zoom out to contemplate deeper hierarchic relationships. Margulis (2012) tracked precisely these kinds of attentional shifts as people listened and relistened to the same musical excerpt.

Indeed, repetition need not occur within a piece to critically influence the way music is heard. Repeated exposures—an aspect of how people interact with music, rather than an aspect of the music itself—have similar effects. Especially now, people tend to listen and relisten to their favorite recording, transforming even the least repetitive music into a recurring experience. Many forms of twentieth-century art music that explicitly eschew overt repetition rely on recording technology to make possible repeated close listenings that over time expose their structures. A long tradition in psychoaesthetics (see Berlyne 1971) traced an inverted-U-shaped curve across repeated exposures, where multiple hearings initially increase what scholars in the 1970s referred to as "hedonic value," but ultimately decrease it. Complexity has long been understood as a factor that modulates the slope of this rise and fall, with more complex music admitting more rehearings before reaching its peak.

This kind of pop radio song cycle aspect of repeated exposures may seem less relevant to the kind of deep listening music theorists often consider. But the fact is that this deep listening depends essentially on repetition. Marion Guck has advocated eloquently for acknowledging the relationship between the analyst and the music in theoretical accounts. "Sounds do not become music until they have entered a person, until they have been heard or imagined and attended to. Music exists only in the interaction between sound and the body-and-mind of an individual. There is paper and ink and there is sound separate from individuals; there is not music" (Guck 1997, 346). By the time analysts are writing about a particular piece, they have very often listened and relistened to it innumerable times. Thus, the "music" they are analyzing is the kind that arises not only out of the intersection of sound and mind, but the intersection of repeated sound and mind. Multiple hearings forge a kind of intimacy and affiliation not different in kind from that sustained between anyone and his favorite piece. All of the forces outlined in this chapter contribute to the kind of experience that a teenager might have with the songs on her favorite playlist as much as the kind of experience a music theorist might have with the pieces she is analyzing.

But a person need not have previously heard a recording of the performance for elements within it to function as repetitions. If I have heard 105 different performances of Chopin's Mazurka in A minor, op. 59, no. 1, my attention might slide to the more idiosyncratic elements of the performance I am hearing—I might notice, for example, the way a trill is sustained a shade longer than usual, or the moment when a finger slips and the pianist plays an F$\sharp$ instead of a G$\sharp$. If I have never heard this mazurka before, but have heard a lot of other mazurkas, the elements that op. 59, no. 1 has in common with this larger set tend to recede, foregrounding what is special to this particular mazurka. On the other hand, if I have never heard a mazurka before, I might find the emphasis on the second beat oddly prominent and halting, with this novelty obscuring the details so salient to the veteran. This same principle fans out to all aspects of the experience—if I have never heard a piano before, for example, the timbre might be more noticeable than anything else. What constitutes repetition recedes into the background, setting forward the aspects that constitute novelty—but since what constitutes repetition can vary dramatically from listener to listener, different people can end up digesting very different aspects of the music.

Borrowing, sampling, and quoting—pointedly repeating some part of a different piece—plays with this divide. Whereas repetition within a piece constructs a shared sense of affiliation among all listeners, as everyone comes to identify more and more with what is happening in the sound, repetition between pieces separates listeners who recognize the quotation from listeners who do not. Whether and in what way Shostakovich quoted other music—such as Stalin's favorite song—can determine whether a piece should be understood as compliant or resistant. And nothing makes you feel quite so much like you have missed the point than to love a song you later discover is a cover. Sharing a cabin in the Ozarks with friends, an avowed secular humanist not from around these parts played his favorite jazz track over the house's speakers—what he took to be an undiscovered gem—and four of the other people started singing along with lyrics prominently centered on Jesus. He had not known that the track was based on a hymn sung in Baptist churches throughout the countryside. The simple act of recognizing something as a repetition can define a community's borders.

A piece's potential to be replayed, at great temporal and geographical distance from the first hearing, relates fundamentally to music's capacity to define not only community but also personal identity. Rehearing a song from adolescence at several decades' remove can bring back the sights and smells of a neighborhood with disconcerting specificity; music is a particularly effective carrier of autobiographical memories (Janata et al. 2007). Across a lifespan, these experiences accrue, such that hearing one of these songs may ultimately trigger not only the memory of teenage summers, but also the memory of rehearing the song and *thinking* of the teenage summers during midlife. Repetition is one of the key elements that enables music to carry such rich and complex social meanings. Every time a passage is reheard, it carries a trace of the previous real-life contexts within which it was heard, weaving a network of associations that contributes essentially to its experience.

REPETITION AND PERCEIVED VARIETY

A person might change between hearings of a work, but this is not the only type of change in context with the power to transform how a passage is heard. Hanninen (2003) explores how repeated elements within a piece are ceaselessly recontextualized, functioning differently each time depending on the surrounding context. For example, in an article about the much-maligned and often-skipped formal repeat, Dunsby (1987) shows how performances that neglect the repeat sign can at times miss out on some of the most significant expressive potential of the piece. He puts forward the opening of Brahms's Waltz, op. 39, no. 9 (Figure 8.4 and ⏵ Audio Example 8.5) as one of these cases. The piece opens with a conventional progression in the home key of D minor, and moves to a half cadence in G minor at m. 8, just before the repeat sign. When the first eight measures are replayed, the opening D-minor chord follows the prominent D-major chord that closed the first phrase, imbuing it with a sense of sly resistance it had lacked in the previous statement. As the F♯ and the F♮ rub against one another (even more so for straddling different voices), it quickly becomes apparent that in addition to this local relationship, there is a more global relationship emerging: namely, the relationship of "repeated phrase" between the first and second performance of the opening eight bars. From the local viewpoint, the F has acquired an agential quality from following the D-major chord; from the global viewpoint, there is no real connection between m. 8 and the restatement of mm. 1–8 concludes the first phrase and m. 1 starts its repetition. They are the end and start point of two parallel strips. Precisely by asking a listener to sustain both viewpoints, the beginning of the repetition adds a touch of paradox and involving complexity to what might have seemed a simple waltz.

Even when the intervening material does not recast the perception of a repeated passage in this special of a way, the second rendition has been recontextualized simply by virtue of following the first. People are able to zoom out across rehearings and contemplate larger-scale relationships, gaining a sense of their position within the larger span of the section. Regardless of whether performers take the repeat, sonata forms tend to recontextualize the first theme when it appears in the recapitulation. What functioned initially as a beginning comes to carry the additional resonance of an ending when it recurs, because it now serves as the culmination of the development in addition to the beginning of the recapitulation.

Repetition's capacity to transform the way passages sound, even when they are acoustically identical, underscores the constructive role of the listener. Perhaps no other musical phenomenon makes it clearer that a listener's prior experiences, within and outside any particular piece, fundamentally shape what they hear. This could be viewed as an

FIGURE 8.4 Johannes Brahms, Waltz in D minor, op. 39, no. 9, mm. 1–13.

invitation for music analysts to study the minds and culture of human listeners as much as the music itself.

AUDIO EXAMPLES

Audio Example 8.1. From "The Star-Spangled Banner," United States Navy Band and Sea Chanters Chorus. From the album *Patriotic Pride*, Coker & McCree, 2004.

Audio Example 8.2. From Intermezzo, op. 119, no. 2 by Johannes Brahms, Julius Katchen, piano. From the album *Brahms: Works for Solo Piano*, Decca Music Group Unlimited, 1997.

Audio Example 8.3. From "When I am Laid" by Henry Purcell, Catherine Bott, soprano with Christopher Hogwood and the Academy of Ancient Music. From the album *Henry Purcell: Dido and Aeneas*, Decca Music Group Unlimited, 1995.

Audio Example 8.4. From Impromptu in A♭ major, op. 142, D. 935, no. 2, Radu Lupu, piano. From the album *Radu Lupu: Schubert Impromptus*, Decca Music Group Unlimited, 1999.

Audio Example 8.5. From Waltz in D minor op. 39, No. 9 by Johannes Brahms, Leon Fleisher, piano. From the album *Brahms, Piano Concertos Nos. 1 & 2, Variations and Fugue on a Theme by Handel, Op. 24, Waltzes, Op. 39*. Sony Music Canada, Inc., 1997.

NOTES

1. For an overview of the notion of implicit learning, see Reber (1989).
2. For a fuller consideration of these potentialities, see Margulis (2014a).
3. See Rings (2011, 129–34) for a fascinating discussion of this piece in general, and of D♯'s reluctance to move to E in particular.
4. Rings (2011, 64) also contains a discussion of a similar effect in the D♯-minor Fugue from Book 1 of Bach's *Well-Tempered Clavier,* where a shift in tonal context obscures a sense of perceived repetition.

WORKS CITED

Agawu, V. Kofi. 1988. "Music in the Funeral Traditions of the Akpafu." *Ethnomusicology* 32: 75–105.

Berlyne, Daniel Ellis. 1971. *Aesthetics and Psychobiology*. New York: Appleton-Century-Crofts.

Boyer, Pascal, and Pierre Liénard. 2006. "Why Ritualized Behavior? Precaution Systems and Action Parsing in Developmental, Pathological and Cultural Rituals." *Behavioral and Brain Sciences* 29: 595–613.

Brown, Helen. 1988. "The Interplay of Set Content and Temporal Context in a Functional Theory of Tonality Perception." *Music Perception* 5: 219–249.

Brown, Helen, David Butler, and Marie Riess Jones. 1994. "Musical and Temporal Influences on Key Discovery." *Music Perception* 11: 371–407.

Cadwallader, Allen. 1988. "Foreground Motivic Ambiguity: Its Clarification at Middleground Levels in Selected Late Piano Pieces of Johannes Brahms." *Music Analysis* 7: 59–91.

Castellano, Mary A., Jamshed J. Bharucha, and Carol L. Krumhansl. 1984. "Tonal Hierarchies in the Music of North India." *Journal of Experimental Psychology: General* 113: 394–412.

Cogan, Robert, and Pozzi Escot. 1976. *Sonic Design: The Nature of Sound and Music*. Englewood Cliffs, NJ: Prentice Hall.

Cone, Edward T. 1977. "Three Ways of Reading a Detective Story—or a Brahms Intermezzo." *Georgia Review* 31: 554–574.

Debellis, Mark. 1995. *Music and Conceptualization*. Cambridge: Cambridge University Press.

Desain, Peter, and Henkjan Honing. 2003. "The Formation of Rhythmic Categories and Metric Priming." *Perception* 32: 341–365.

Dunsby, Jonathan. 1987. "The Formal Repeat." *Journal of the Royal Music Association* 112: 196–207.

Fink, Robert. 2005. *Repeating Ourselves: American Minimal Music as Cultural Practice*. Berkeley: University of California Press.

Gabrielsson, Alf. 2011. *Strong Experiences with Music: Music Is Much More Than Just Music*. Translated by Roy Bradbury. New York: Oxford University Press.

Garcia, Luis-Manuel. 2005. "On and On: Repetition as Process and Pleasure in Electronic Dance Music." *Music Theory Online* 11, no. 4. http://www.mtosmt.org/issues/mto.05.11.4/mto.05.11.4.garcia.html.

Gjerdingen, Robert, and David Perrott. 2008. "Scanning the Dial: The Rapid Recognition of Musical Genres." *Journal of New Music Research* 37: 93–100.

Goehr, Lydia. 1992. *The Imaginary Museum of Musical Works: An Essay in the Philosophy of Music*. Oxford: Clarendon Press.

Guck, Marion. 1997. "Music Loving, or the Relationship with the Piece." *Journal of Musicology* 15: 343–352.

Hanninen, Dora A. 2003. "A Theory of Recontextualization in Music: Analyzing Phenomenal Transformations of Repetition." *Music Theory Spectrum* 25: 59–97.

Hasty, Christopher F. *Meter as Rhythm*. 1997. New York: Oxford University Press.

Hunter, Ian M. L. 1984. "Lengthy Verbatim Recall (LVR) and the Mythical Gift of Tape-Recorder Memory." In *Psychology in the 1990's*. Edited by Kirsti M. J. Lagerspetz and Pekka Niemi, 425–440. Amsterdam: North-Holland Publishing Company.

Huron, David. 2006a. *Sweet Anticipation: Music and the Psychology of Expectation*. Cambridge, MA: MIT Press.

Huron, David. 2006b. "Are Scale Degree Qualia a Consequence of Statistical Learning?" In *Proceedings of the 9th International Conference on Music Perception and Cognition*. Edited by Mario Baroni, Anna Rita Addessi, Roberto Caterina, and Marco Costa, 1675–1680. Bologna, Italy: University of Bologna.

Hutchins, Sean, and Caroline Palmer. 2008. "Repetition Priming in Music." *Journal of Experimental Psychology: Human Perception and Performance* 34: 69–88.

Janata, Peter, Stefan T. Tomic, and Sonja K. Rakowski. 2007. "Characterisation of Music-Evoked Autobiographical Memories." *Memory* 15: 845–860.

Kagan, Susan. 1995. Review of Schubert Piano Sonatas, Robert Levin, Pianoforte. *Fanfare* 19: 362–363.

Kane, Brian. 2016. "Of Repetition, Habit, and Involuntary Memory: An Analysis and Speculation upon Morton Feldman's Final Composition." http://browsebriankane.com/My_Homepage_Files/Download/Feldman%20paper.pdf.

Krumhansl, Carol L. 1990. *Cognitive Foundations of Musical Pitch*. New York: Oxford University Press.

Leydon, Rebecca. 2002. "Towards a Typology of Minimalist Tropes." *Music Theory Online* 8, no. 4. http://www.mtosmt.org/issues/mto.02.8.4/mto.02.8.4.leydon.html.

Margulis, Elizabeth Hellmuth. 2012. "Musical Repetition Detection across Multiple Exposures." *Music Perception* 29: 377–385.

Margulis, Elizabeth Hellmuth. 2013. "Aesthetic Responses to Repetition in Unfamiliar Music." *Empirical Studies of the Arts* 31: 45–57.

Margulis, Elizabeth Hellmuth. 2014a. *On Repeat: How Music Plays the Mind*. New York: Oxford University Press.

Margulis, Elizabeth Hellmuth. 2014b. "Verbatim Repetition and Musical Engagement." *Psychomusicology: Music, Mind, and Brain* 24: 157–163.

Margulis, Elizabeth Hellmuth. 2015. "Perceiving Music Narratively: Who Does It, and When?" Paper presented at the Biennial Meeting of the Society for Music Perception and Cognition, Nashville, TN, August 1–5.

Margulis, Elizabeth Hellmuth, and Rhimmon Simchy-Gross. 2016. "Repetition Enhances the Musicality of Randomly Generated Tone Sequences." *Music Perception* 33: 509–514.

Matthews, W. J., and Ana I. Gheorghiu. 2016. "Repetition, Expectation, and the Perception of Time." *Current Opinion in Behavioral Sciences* 8: 110–116.

Matsunaga, Rie, and Abe, Jun-Ichi. 2005. "Cues for Key Perception of a Melody: Pitch Set Alone?" *Music Perception* 23: 153–164.

Middleton, Richard. 1990. *Studying Popular Music*. Buckingham, UK: Open University Press.

Oram, Nicholas, and Lola L. Cuddy. 1995. "Responsiveness of Western Adults to Pitch-Distributional Information in Melodic Sequences." *Psychological Research* 57: 103–118.

Patel, Aniruddh D. 2008. *Music, Language, and the Brain*. New York: Oxford University Press.

Pereira, Carlos Silva, João Teixeira, Patrícia Figueiredo, João Xavier, São Luís Castro, and Elvira Brattico. 2011. "Music and Emotions in the Brain: Familiarity Matters." *PLOS ONE* 6, no. 11: e27241. doi: 10.1371/journal.pone.0027241.

Philip, Robert. 2004. *Performing Music in the Age of Recording*. New Haven, CT: Yale University Press.

Rahn, John. 1993. "Repetition." *Contemporary Music Review* 7: 49–57.

Reber, Arthur S. 1989. "Implicit Learning and Tacit Knowledge." *Journal of Experimental Psychology: General* 118: 219–235.

Rings, Steven. 2011. *Tonality and Transformation*. New York: Oxford University Press.

Severance, Elisabeth, and Margaret F. Washburn. 1907. "The Loss of Associative Power in Words after Long Fixation." *The American Journal of Psychology* 18: 182–186.

Sisman, Elaine R. 1993. *Haydn and the Classical Variation*. Cambridge, MA: Harvard University Press.

Slawson, Wayne. 1985. *Sound Color*. Berkeley: University of California Press.

Taher, Cecilia, René Rusch, and Stephen McAdams. 2016. "Effects of Repetition on Attention in Two-Part Counterpoint." *Music Perception* 33: 306–318.

Temperley, David, and Elizabeth West Marvin. 2008. "Pitch-Class Distribution and the Identification of Key." *Music Perception* 25: 193–212.

Turino, Thomas R. 2008. *Music as Social Life: The Politics of Participation*. Chicago: University of Chicago Press.

Wong, Patrick C. M., Anil K. Roy, and Elizabeth Hellmuth Margulis. 2008. "The Complex Dynamics of Repeated Musical Exposure." In *Proceedings of the 10th International Conference on Music Perception and Cognition*. Edited by Ken'ichi Miyazaki, Yuzuru Hiraga, Mayumi Adachi, Yoshitaka Nakajima, and Minoru Tsuzaki. Sapporo, Japan.

CHAPTER 9

....

METER

....

RICHARD COHN

When we encounter music, our minds engage with it, seeking patterns. The engagement is spontaneous and involuntary, perhaps preceding awareness that we are in music's presence. The patterns are not always in the sonic stimulus, at least not in the pure form we might imagine them to be. Our minds uncover them, filtering out extraneous noise, smoothing irregularities and perturbations, and manipulating the sonic signal to match it to a library of internalized schemes and prototypes.

Researchers have a particular interest in two mental systems that filter, organize, and regulate music: tonality, which processes pitched sound, and meter, which processes sound in time. As with natural language, aspects of both systems are present from early infancy (Hannon and Trehub 2005), but the systems develop through exposure and thus vary across cultures. Because pitched sounds exist in time, and most musical sounds in time are pitched, the systems interact. They can nonetheless be treated as separable in principle, and researchers find it productive to do so.

Theories of tonality have been of perpetual interest for many centuries. Metric theory is just as venerable, but has suffered from long periods of neglect. After one such period that lasted for most of the twentieth century, interest in meter began to surge during the 1970s, coalescing into two distinct research communities in the fields of music theory and perceptual psychology. After forty years of intensive focus in both fields, we understand meter from a deeper, broader, and richer perspective.

Anyone who wants access to that perspective, however, should not bother to take a course in music theory, or read a textbook on the topic. Tonality has long held the center of music-theory pedagogy, to the extent that curricula treat it as co-extensive with the term "music theory." Modern textbooks typically devote to meter only a single early "rudiments" chapter, the content of which is unchanged from the 1770s (Cohn 2015). Apart from some orthodox strains of theological training, it is difficult to think of any pedagogical practices that have bumbled along in such oblivious relationship to the work of the modern research academy.

The conception of meter that most musicians inherit was developed from eighteenth-century theories of poetic meter, and was customized to a musical culture that had vocal music at its center. That conception was frozen into a notational system and educational curriculum that stabilized in the early nineteenth century, and has been perpetuated by inertia. At the same time, music itself has flowed along, dispersing into, and merging with, countless stylistic arteries—Schumann and Brahms, Bartók and Stravinsky, jazz and minimalism, Afropop and salsa—whose metric properties are foreign to the *Kapellmeister*.[1]

Seeking to honor this plurality, this essay aims to rebuild a model of meter from the ground up, synthesizing forty years of music-theoretic and psychological research for the benefit of the performer, composer, musicologist, music-theory instructor, or musical amateur. What is meter? What are the types of meter? How can those types be represented, using language, symbols, or images? How do meters relate to each other? How can those relationships be mobilized into compositional strategies? How does meter change? How can metric change contribute to a theory of musical form?

The model sketched here aspires to be general, in the sense that it aims to serve as a resource for exploring the properties of, and our responses to, the many metric musics of the world—notated or recorded, composed or improvised, ephemeral or timeless. My generalizing aspiration is shared by psychological approaches, and the model sketched here draws on perceptual and neuro-cognitive research. Yet my aims are nonetheless distinct from psychological models, whose primary focus is on normative and spontaneous human responses to ordinary musical input. What I sketch here is an *analytical* model: a resource for musicians, analysts, and listeners to explore and communicate particular metric properties and strategies, in whatever metric music they wish to understand through a sustained encounter that engages concept as well as percept.

Locating Meter

If we look for meter, where shall we find it? I began by suggesting that meter is a capacity of the mind, in response to music. Most musicians and listeners locate it elsewhere: in the music itself. For a score-based musician, meter is in the signature and the barlines: "the meter of the waltz is 3/4." For a musician in an oral or improvised tradition, or for a listener, meter is located in the sound: "the song is in three." A dancer, by contrast, might locate meter in the body: "I feel it in four."

This proliferation of orientations threatens to destabilize the ground on which a model of meter is mounted. Fortunately, though, three of these four ways of characterizing meter collaborate rather than compete; they are interlocked aspects of a single system of relations. For the listener, the sound provides the stimulus, the mind seeks and identifies patterns in the stimulus, and the body expresses those patterns, representing to the mind what it is recognizing.[2]

The outlier in this scheme is notation, which is proper to a minority of the world's metric music. The metric information made explicit by the musical score often stands in a complex relationship to the metric patterns perceived by the mind and entrained by the body. A meter signature records isochronies, or "beats," at several distinct speeds; a faster counting beat, a slower "down" beat, and often beats of intermediate speed as well. But it is a lazy and occasionally mendacious witness. The mind recognizes, and the body responds to, regularities that are faster than the counting beat and slower than the down-beat. For example, the box-step patterns that waltzers entrain are nowhere recorded in the score of a waltz. The pulses that it does report may not be the ones that listeners project and entrain at a particular musical moment, just as a key signature bears false witness to the local scale and tonic after a modulation.[3]

And here we encounter the central problem: classical musicians have long been trained to equate the meter of a composition with the meter signature at the head of its score. Moreover, due to its historical depth and cultural prestige, classical music tacitly—some might say, insidiously—furnishes much of the conceptual and terminological framework for thinking and talking about jazz, electronic dance music, and all manner of popular music. As a result, even musicians who don't "read music" are inclined by default to describe heard meter using the categories of musical notation. The terms, categories, and concepts of notation are overlaid upon, and often conceal, those of musical experience. This substitution has skewed our understanding of what meter is, and of our metric responses to particular musical input. To achieve a productive understanding of metric experience, at the level of both general capacities and responses to the musically particular, we will need to strip back this heritage, and start at the beginning.

But where shall we begin to access meter, if not from the notation? Shall we enter through the mind, the body, or the sound itself? We conceive of these three domains in different ways, and talk about them using different discourses. It is precarious to try to integrate those discourses from the start, holding them all in balance simultaneously. We'll have a better chance of successfully launching a model if we enter through one of these domains, and tunnel through to the others, translating terms and discourses as we go.

In keeping with the analytical aspirations of this model, I will enter through the portal of sound, where the metric experience is triggered for the listener, and its particularity defined. Because sound can be abstracted from the human subject, it is the easiest of the three domains to represent using the Cartesian terms and images of which models are characteristically composed. The model thus will have many of the outward characteristics of a structural model rather than a phenomenological or behavioral one. Readers should strive to bear in mind that this choice is a manner of speaking, rather than a project of essentializing meter as sound. In most significant respects, the model can be translated into perceptual or neurobiological terms, reframed explicitly around projection or entrainment "in here" rather than time-point and pulse sets "out there," without significantly altering its structure, the claims it makes about general music or musical experience, or its application to a particular instance of music. Sound, mind, and body co-generate meter, but foregrounding them all at once in the representation is a recipe for confusion.[4]

DEFINING METER

Having considered meter as a general human capacity, we address now how that capacity responds to particular musics, as when we say that a composition has, or is in, a meter. The definition offered here is adapted from Yeston (1976), and its essential components underlie modern metric research. Because the definition is distinct from the eighteenth-century one that appears in modern textbooks, it may feel alien. While the definition requires only a few words, its elaboration and historical contextualization require many more.

A meter is a set of pulses. Pulses, in turn, are sets of time points. If they are notionally isochronous, a set of three or more distinct time points qualifies as a pulse. If they are related by inclusion, a set of two or more distinct pulses qualifies as a meter. Consolidating the above into a definition: a meter is an inclusionally related set of distinct, notionally isochronous time-point sets.

Figure 9.1 depicts a meter as an array of points, or dots. Each column represents a time point. Each row represents an even distribution of time points, hence a pulse. Each individual dot thus represents a time point's membership in a pulse. Each column connects continuously to a point on the bottom row, which indicates that the inclusion condition is fulfilled.

Points in time, as in space, lack individuating properties, are undefinable and indivisible, and lack extension: they begin and end "at the same time." Thus no time point is larger or longer than any other. But musical events, such as sounding tones, do have extension. They begin and end at distinct time points, which bound a continuous span of time that has a measurable duration.

Points and spans stand in dual relation (Boone 2000). A pair of time points specifies a unique continuous span; conversely, that span is bounded only by that pair of time points. This suggests an alternative definition of pulse, as a set of adjacent, non-overlapping spans of notionally equal duration. Although the two definitions are equivalent, the definition of pulse as a set of points has two advantages. First, our bodily responses to pulses are more point-like than span-like. Those responses are the visible manifestations of invisible neural oscillations, which imaging technologies depict as bursts of cortical activity "followed by periods of quiesence before the next burst

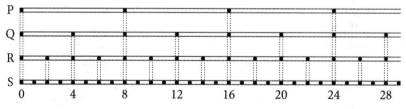

FIGURE 9.1 A 4-deep pure duple meter represented as a dot array. Each dot represents inclusion of a time point in a single pulse.

occurs" (Large and Snyder 2009, 63). Second, analysts talk about many sorts of musical spans, such as phrases, motivic groupings, etc., which often cut across the metric spans. If we discuss both content-segments and abstract meters in terms of spans, we risk conflations that have historically undermined otherwise coherent models of musical meter (for example Cooper and Meyer 1960). Indeed, the birth of modern metric theory can be traced to the moment in the 1970s when music theorists segregated meter from other sorts of musical groupings (Komar 1971, 5; Lerdahl and Jackendoff 1983, 17).

A pulse, as used here, is a series of time points, rather than an individual member of that series; it is equivalent to "pulse stream" and "isochronous series" in other writings. Isochrony refers to constant distance between adjacent time points. That distance, the pulse's period, is measured by psychologists in microseconds, by neuroscientists in Hertz units, and by musicians using durational values, or quantities of notated measures. In principle, there are no limits on the size (or duration) of a period, but in practice, there are physiological thresholds of pulse entrainability at both the fast and slow end of the pulse spectrum. However, the precise position of those thresholds depends on the number of pulses active (Madison 2014), the skill of the musician (Clayton 2000, 85), and other contextual considerations (London 2012, 28). As the context for musicians, analysts, and creative artists is determined by concept as well as by raw percept, it seems best to refrain from imposing such thresholds, independent of any uses to which the model might be put.

Isochrony is notional because human-generated pulses are elastic. Musicians inevitably push and pull "the beat," even when they are not seeking a special expressive effect such as rubato. "Expressive variation" is thus not a special case; it is a ubiquitous property of human musical production and experience (Repp 1998; see also Mitchell Ohriner's chapter in this volume). A pulse is perceived when an incrementally variable series of durations is equalized (quantized, snapped to grid) by the spontaneously regulating brain. In principle, there is no limit to the degree of durational wobble that can be tolerated, but in practice, there are thresholds of irregularity beyond which a pulse will lose its status. As is the case with absolute speed, the precise position of isochrony thresholds depends on context.

A meter is a set of pulses. It is useful to begin by considering exactly two distinct pulses, which I will call a minimal meter. The inclusion condition requires that each time point of the slower pulse is also a time point of the faster one. The periods of the pulses must then be integral; that is, the period of the slower pulse is n times greater than the period of the faster one, where n is an integer greater than 1.

If $n = 2$ or 3, then the pulses are adjacent, forming duple and triple minimal meters. In traditional musics of the West, larger values of n produce gaps that are filled by pulses of intermediate speed. These pulses might be evident in the acoustic signal, or they might be subjectively metricized by the listener (Brochard et al. 2003), as images that spectrally radiate from the faster and slower pulses flanking them on the speed spectrum. If pulses are related by a larger prime such as five or seven, then a quasi-pulse (also known, paradoxically, as a non-isochronous pulse) is spontaneously radiated, a special situation to be studied in the final section, "Expanding Meter." If they bear a composite ratio such as four or six, then listeners imagine at least one intermediate pulse that forms a minimal meter with both surrounding ones (Schachter 1987, 14). Although the tendency to subjectively metricize intermediate pulses varies across cultures (Hannon and Trehub 2005), it may be linked to human capacities for numerosity, as three is the point at which pre-verbal subitization begins to attenuate, eliding into mental systems informed by higher-level mental functions of verbalization and calculation (Repp 2007). It may also be desirable, from a cognitive standpoint, if every weak beat is either preceded or followed by a strong beat, just as scalar tones neighbor at least one tone of the tonic triad.

A meter is deep if it contains three or more distinct pulses, each pair of which forms a minimal meter. To establish that a pulse set qualifies as a meter, it is sufficient to order the pulses from slowest to fastest, and determine that each pair of adjacent pulses forms a minimal meter. (The transitivity of inclusion eliminates the need to compare non-adjacent pulses.) Thus, in traditional and classical musics of the West, a meter can be characterized as a set of adjacent pulse pairs, each of which forms a duple or triple minimal meter. That characterization forms the basis of the classification system proposed below in the section "Representing Meter."

The depth of a meter refers to its number of constituent pulses. A minimal meter is two-deep. Psychological researchers require pulses to fit an envelope of entrainability, and thus cap depth at between four and six simultaneously unfolding pulses (London 2012; Forth 2012). Although this limitation is not incompatible with the model proposed here, it is an optional accessory rather than a defining property. As noted above, an analytical attitude encourages a more flexible view of pulse perceivability at the thresholds of speed, and accordingly I will decline to constrain metric depth, at the level of definition.

The modern research definition of meter is distinct from the one given in current music-theory textbooks, whose central substantive terms— beat, grouping, accent, and pattern—are recombined in some order (Cohn 2015), for example "a grouping of beats into a regular repeating pattern of strong and weak" (Lester 1982). The definition was appropriated in the eighteenth century from poetic meter, whose verse feet are arranged in regular repeating patterns of accented and unaccented syllables (Kirnberger 1982, 391ff).

The historical conception of meter has two defining properties: isochronous time points, and their uniform grouping into accent patterns. This uniform grouping creates a regular spacing of accents, and one might observe that they form a slower isochronous pulse. But this slower pulse is not acknowledged by the definition; it is its accidental by-product. The modern research conception inverts these functions. The isochrony of the slower pulse becomes the defining component, and the repeating accentual pattern its epiphenomenal byproduct. "It is not differentiation of accents which produces meter, it is meter which produces a differentiation of accents" (Zuckerkandl 1956, 169).

This distinction at the definitional core has significant functional consequences. In the modern conception of minimal meter, the fast pulse is comprised of time points, from which the slow pulse isochronously selects. Thus the two defining components are made of the same stuff, but to a different degree of density. Accordingly, the fast pulse of one minimal meter can also serve as the slow pulse of another minimal meter, and vice versa. This ontological equivalence establishes the conditions for infinite recursion, made finite only by the external imposition of physical and mental thresholds at the boundaries of entrainable speed.

By contrast, even though eighteenth-century theorists emphasized a "double uniformity" at the core of meter (Mirka 2009, 4), its two defining uniformities are ontologically distinct. The beat is composed of points, like raindrops; the accents "group" those points. But that group is not itself a point. Meter's recursive potential is blocked; the model is doomed to only ever recognize a single minimal meter.

Of course, the incommensurability of beat and accentual group does not deter eighteenth-century theorists from recognizing that the relation of accent and beat is replicated simultaneously at faster speeds (Mirka 2009); they were, after all, musicians making observations about music and their responses to it. But it did evidently discourage them from building that recognition into their models of meter. Moreover, the theoretical limitations served as a disincentive to making claims about what they were observing at slower speeds. Few eighteenth-century theorists recognized accentual distinctions between beats 1 and 3 in common time (Küster 2012). Yet fewer acknowledged pulse periodicities slower than the notated downbeat, even though contemporaneous composers often wrote suspension-resolution figures (the quintessential marker of metric position since the fifteenth century) across two- and four-bar spans.

Most eighteenth-century theorists were also church composers, whose activities setting liturgical texts would have encouraged a minimal conception of meter. In seeking a model for musical meter, it would have been in any case natural to look to theories of poetic meter, which were not only at hand, but also bore the authoritative stamp of Classical antiquity. But for the liturgical composer, the relation of poetic and musical meter was more than analogical. The metered poetry was folded right into the metered music, and he would have had a hard time thinking about them separately (Küster 2012, 18). Prior to the twentieth century, poetic theorists recognized "only two sorts of syllables, stressed and unstressed" (Holder 1995, 25), and it would have felt natural to assume the same of music, even though this assumption was problematized by every meter signature that indicated four or more beats to the notated bar. It is hardly a coincidence that the earliest post-medieval theorists to propose recursive models of meter were both amateur musicians: the Swiss mathematician Leonhard Euler in 1739, in a spirit of speculative induction (Grant 2013); and the Glasgow potter John Holden in 1770, from a more empirical and cognitive perspective (Raz 2018).

Within educational institutions, the church musician's shallow model of meter survived the remarkable set of events that transpired between the deaths of Mozart in 1791 and of Beethoven in 1827: the waning influence of the *Kapellmeister*, the substitution of instruments for voices at the center of European culture, the decay of the semiotic system known as *tempo giusto*, the rise of the integrated metric shift (Grant 2014), and the increasing recognition of pulse periods longer than the notated downbeat. Meter signatures were functionally repurposed to the practical aims of score reading and ensemble coordination, and were frozen into a stabilizing system of notation and institutional pedagogy. Two centuries later, musical primers at all levels continue to conflate meter with metric notation, and to classify beats into an absolute binary of strong and weak.

CLASSIFYING METER

The six-fold system for classifying meters is older yet. This system, which holds that there are three kinds of meter (duple, triple, and quadruple), each of which come in two varieties, simple or compound, was introduced in 1696 by Étienne Loulié, the musical servant of the Duchesse de Guise (Houle 1987). What the system putatively classifies is meter, a sounding property of a composition or improvisation as organized by the listening mind and entraining body. But what is actually being classified here is that subset of the heard pulses that happen to be made explicit by the meter *signature*, a representation that the performer is seeing, using the notational conventions developed for music of the eighteenth century. The six-fold system serves well as an introduction to conventions of musical notation, and as a resource for historically informed performance of early modern repertories. But when incorporated into a general model of musical meter, Loulié's classification system is a poisonous pill. To see that this is the case, consider the following three propositions.

(1) Two musics are identical if they sound identical, that is, no one can distinguish them from each other on the basis of listening.
(2) Identical musics have identical metric properties.
(3) A classification system that assigns identical musics, with identical properties, to identical classes is superior to one that assigns them to different classes.

These propositions seem uncontroversial, even self-evident. It is difficult to imagine grounds under which one would want to argue against any of them.

Consider now how these propositions apply to the five phrases notated in Figure 9.2. If you're unfamiliar with this piece, you may wish to guess which notation is Beethoven's, for the opening measures of the third movement of his Piano Sonata op. 27, no. 1. When performed at comparable tempi, the phrases sound identical. To test this claim, consider performing one of these notations at the piano, or running its MIDI-file through a synthesizer. Assuming that you know which one is Beethoven's notation, on what grounds would you penalize students who transcribed it using one of the other four, and what principles would you invoke to rectify such "errors"?

Proposition 1 dictates that these notations represent five identical phrases; proposition 2 that the five identical phrases have identical meters; and proposition 3 that a good classification system will assign them to the same metric class. Loulié's system could

FIGURE 9.2 Five equivalent notations, representing five of Loulié's six metric classes, of a single passage from Beethoven's Piano Sonata no. 13, op. 27, no. 1.

FIGURE 9.2 *continued.*

not be a more wretched performer, assigning the five identical phrases to five different metric classes! This suggests that the composer's choice of meter signature can be incidental to the classification of metric experience, perhaps as the choice of font is incidental to the content of a prose essay.

Musicians loyal to Loulié's classification system, as it applies to modern metric experience, often protest that meter signatures instill different ineffable "flavors," which might be realized as incremental variations in volume, attack and release timing, articulation, and so forth. In the eighteenth century, this was certainly the case: signs nominally affiliated with meter also convey supplementary information about other musical characteristics, and eighteenth-century theorists devoted considerable attention to these distinctions. But the mere fact that these supplements were attached to a notational device whose function was allegedly metric does not entail that those characteristics are metric per se. The eighteenth-century meter signature was a portmanteau, communicating information about musical properties (expressive timing, tempo, touch, loudness) that vary independently of meter, and thus are external to a theory of meter. A Swiss army "knife" might contain a magnifying glass and a can opener, but it would be an error to assume that those protrusions will effectively slice a carrot or drive off an intruder. Just so, a "meter signature" might suggest to a performer how loudly to attack a note, how long to sustain it, and how elastically to approach the next onset, but that does not entail that a theory of meter is incomplete if it doesn't subsume a theory of loudness, articulation, tempo, and microtiming.

Honoring proposition 3 requires a classification system based on the metric properties that the five identical phrases share. We can identify those properties by ordering the pulses from slowest to fastest, and documenting the minimal meters formed by adjacent pulse pairs. In the case of Figure 9.2, a performance of each phrase projects four pulses which, ordered from slowest to fastest, form three adjacency pairs.[5] The slower two are duple, and the fastest is triple. This description presents one way to model the equivalence of the five phrases in Figure 9.2: they share a set of pulse relations.

REPRESENTING METER

Since any deep meter is comprised of an ordering of duple and triple meters, it can be compactly represented by an ordered multiset, each element of which is either a 2 or a 3. This reduces "The slower two are duple, and the fastest is triple" by converting it to "⟨2 2 3⟩" (Apel 1949).

More concretely if less economically, a deep meter can be modeled by a dot array, such as was introduced in Figure 9.1.[6] In Figure 9.3(a), {P, Q} and {Q, R} represent minimal duple meters, and {P, R} a quadruple meter. A pulse stack qualifies as a meter if vertical columns of dots are continuous and terminate at the fastest pulse, thus ensuring that every pair of pulses is inclusionally related.

As noted above, subjective metricization dictates that any music that stimulates pulses P and R also radiates spectral Q, even in the absence of any reinforcing stimulus. {P, Q, R} is a deep meter that could be notated as a series of measures in common time, and realized by the duration set {𝅝 𝅗𝅥 𝅘𝅥}. This notation is prototypical for this metric class, but the class can be equally well represented by any set of durational symbols or interonset intervals with the same proportion, including multiples of notated bars. The class is neutral with respect to the many duration sets that it represents, and to the assignment of downbeat and counting status to its constituent pulses.

By adding a fourth pulse, S, Figure 9.3(b) furnishes a dot representation of the metric class of the Beethoven Scherzo, as it is variously notated in Figure 9.2. Realization of this class as any of the five notations presented there involves assigning duration values to the four pulses, and fixing a counting and downbeat pulse. Beethoven's notation, as four bars of 3/4 meter, affixes the values at {4 bars 2 bars 𝅗𝅥. 𝅘𝅥.}.

A third way to represent a meter is as a "ski-hill graph" such as Figure 9.4(a) (Cohn 2001). Each node represents a pulse, and each edge represents an adjacent minimal meter. Duple meters skew down to the left, and triple ones down to the right. Each graphic shape is associated with an abstract metric class. Filling the nodes with specific duration values or interonset periods realizes the abstract graph as a network (Lewin

FIGURE 9.3 Two dot-array representations. (a) Of a 3-deep pure-duple meter. (b) The same, with a fast triple minimal meter added.

1987). Figures 9.4(b) and (c) realize the graph in two different ways: as Beethoven's 3/4 meter (Figure 9.2(b)), and as a series of 12/8 measures (Figure 9.2(c)).

The three modes of representation are useful in different contexts. Dot notation is the most concrete. Its space points represent time points, and it unfolds from left to right in piece time. The advantage of its materiality is offset by the disadvantage of its bulk: the tedium of drawing it, and the space that it consumes, do not always justify the limited returns. The ordered-number representation is compact and discursively compatible; it is easily embedded into a print or spoken sentence. Although the graphic array is neither efficient nor concrete, it positions a meter on a field of possible meters, facilitating comparison between distinct meters, and furnishes a map upon which metric distances can be viewed, syntaxes traced, and metric forms developed. A later section will show some ways how.

METRIC FORM

Despite their equivalent status as systems through which the mind regulates and organizes musical input, in theories of musical form tonality is perpetually a star player, while meter sits quietly on the bench watching. This is a strange state of affairs on the face of it, but it makes sense when we regard it as a consequence of an under-nourished and archaic theory of meter. That theory equates meter with meter signatures, which typically do not change, except occasionally at formal boundaries simultaneously marked by change in other parameters such as tempo, texture, and motive.

As soon as we release meter from metric notation, and link it to music as heard, we license it to enter the arena of musical form, and we can quickly see that it has a vigorous contribution to make. At different moments of a composition, we hear, project, and entrain different pulses at different moments. The conversion of meter from an invariant global attribute to a mutable local one opens up a range of questions of central interest to musical analyst, composer, performer, improviser. How are the meters ordered? What is the rate of change? Is change sudden or gradual, rough or smooth? Is it expected or unexpected? Can we measure the distance between two meters? Can we talk about formal trajectories, for example some progression of states that gradually recedes from or progresses toward an anticipated point?

These analytical questions engage not just "the music itself," but also listener behavior, artistic hypotheses about that behavior, and artistic actions motivated by those hypotheses. This is the moment to usher mind and body onto the stage. Attentive readers will realize that they have been lurking in the wings, and indeed have made explicit cameos in the invocation of notional isochrony and spectral radiation (that is, subjective metricization). We now want to ask not only what mental capacities help us recognize pulses and meters, but also how we experience them as they unfold in time.

The two critical terms here are "projection" and "entrainment." We recognize—or perhaps more accurately, create—a single pulse by comparing the durations between event

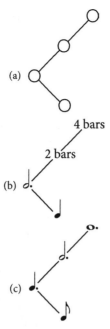

FIGURE 9.4 Three ski-hill representations of Figure 9.2 and 9.3(b). (a) Independent of nota-tion. (b) Realized according to Beethoven's notation, Figure 9.2(b). (c) Realized in 12/8 meter, Figure 9.2(e).

onsets. Matching of consecutive durations triggers projection of future onset points (Hasty 1997), and stimulates neural oscillations that synchronize to those projections (Large and Snyder 2009). The oscillations are the invisible interface between internal rec-ognition and external response, sending back confirmations that direct future projections, while simultaneously directing synchronous motor activities (bobbing, tapping, dancing). Entrainment can be present even in the absence of such external symptoms. In general, the body does not explicitly entrain as many pulses as the mind projects.

The experience of pulse thus involves not only passive recognition of musical events at the moment of presentation, but also active anticipation of events at specified moments in the future. When those expectations are denied, the sense of expectations does not die with it. Pulses, "once established, can persist in the listener's consciousness without special sensory reinforcement. Indeed, they can persist for a time in the face of strongly contradictory signals" (Schachter 1987, 5). A new pulse co-habits the mind along with the inertial expectation of the previous pulse's continuation, establishing a duality between present sensation and past expectation (Krebs 1999). This duality gives meter its entry point into the game of musical form, and engages the strategic attention of composers, performers, improvisers, and analysts.

Relating Meters

A minimal change of meter involves adding or subtracting a pulse to or from the set. These two operations are less frequent and effective in isolation than in collaboration, as substitutions.

Pulses survive their own disarticulation, as spectral images (Volk 2008) that slowly attenuate, or disappear when another pulse replaces it. Conversely, a newly articulated pulse does not add to the set of entrained pulses, if that same pulse is already spectrally present through subjective metricization. We might conceive of spectral pulses as resembling harmonic partials radiating from an acoustic fundamental. Harmonic change occurs not when a frequency already present in the harmonic series is directly articulated, but rather when an articulated tone replaces another tone of similar frequency, whether articulated or inferred. Analogously, meter changes when an articulated pulse substitutes for a pulse of nearby periodicity (we might say: in the same *register*), whether that pulse is directly articulated or subjectively metricized.

Metric substitutions come in two types: either the period of the new pulse is the same (1:1) as the one it is replacing, or they differ by a 3:2 ratio. Theorists refer to these substitutional types respectively as "displacement" and "(re-)grouping" (Kaminsky 1989; Krebs 1999). As these terms are incompatible with aspects of the model developed here, I will instead use theoretically neutral labels that refer instead to the historical prototypes that they respectively generalize: "syncopation" and "hemiola."

Figure 9.5(a) illustrates one of these prototypes, the Renaissance pre-cadential syncope. According to the sixteenth-century conception (DeFord 2015), the B initiated on the fourth beat is displaced from beat 3, where it would have been consonant with the other voices. Beat 3 participates in two pulses of the meter, labeled Q and R. The singer could have used either one to "locate" the time point of the displaced tone's onset. As indicated by the two arrows, she could measure a Q unit later than the G, or an R unit later than the C. Both measurements are easily made, as they match pulse projections that she is already entraining.

The displacement from beat 3 to beat 4 circumscribes the singer's options, since the new onset participates in only a single pulse, R, and she must locate the displaced onset by measuring it an R unit later than beat 3, as modeled in Figure 9.5(b) by the unbroken arrow. But she is not herself articulating the time point at the solid arrow's head. If she were singing her line solo, in the absence of the counterpointing voices, she would need to mark that point, perhaps by a silent motion in her bodily extremities. She might be tempted to measure her onset a Q unit later than her own previous onset, as indicated by the curved broken arrow in Figure 9.5(b). But this is not a measurement that she is tracking, as the pulse in which beats 2 and 4 are adjacent remains as yet unentrained.

Figure 9.5(c) adds that pulse, labeling it Q'. It is the same speed as the Q pulse that she is already entraining, but relates to it by exclusion rather than inclusion, and so the two pulses cannot co-participate in a single meter. In order to entrain Q', the singer will need to embed it in a new meter, relinquishing Q and the meter in which it is embedded

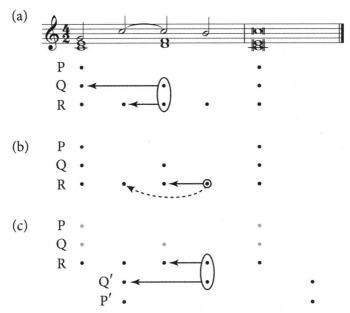

FIGURE 9.5 Renaissance pre-cadential suspension with three dot-array analyses. (a) Two congruent ways to "locate" beat 3 by measuring its distance from some pulse-adjacent point. (b) Two congruent ways to locate beat 4, which seed a metric substitution. (c) Locating beat 4 according to a fully realized metric substitution.

(as modeled by its fading in Figure 9.5(c)). The singer is unlikely to take the bait. She may be aware of this alternative meter as a latent potential. But it is likely that that alternative meter will be over-ridden by, or assimilated to, the ongoing meter, whose pulses she is strongly entraining.

Figure 9.6 presents a more extended syncopation from Saint-Saëns's *Allegro Appassionato*, op. 43. The preceding passage projects a normalized 4/4 meter (notated as 2/4 in duple hypermeter), labeled as meter 1 = {P, Q, R, S}. From m. 1, cellist and orchestra co-articulate the downbeats but otherwise play complementary time points of S. From bar 5, the complementary relation is extended to a four-bar span. For young musicians, passages such as this can be confusing; they easily "lose their place," and often need coaching by a teacher or rehearsal partner in order to stay on track. The cellist has two ways of locating her time points: externally, an S unit later than the immediately preceding time point in the orchestra, preserving the prior meter; or internally, an R unit later than her immediately preceding time point in the cello. As there is no pulse in the prior meter in which those two time points are adjacent, she can only make this latter measurement by positing the existence of a new pulse R′, which is incompatible with the R that was previously entrained. It is the conflict between these two strategies that is confusing. Mature performers are not oblivious to it. They sense the potential for destabilization, and their ability to contain that potential may help them find pleasure or meaning in this music (Fitch and Rosenfeld 2007; Vuust, Gebaeur, and Witek 2014). The listener, who is entraining the pulses alongside the performer, has a similar choice. If the performer or listener measures distances from prior time points internal to a single

FIGURE 9.6 Two metric analyses of the cello part from Saint-Saëns's Allegro Appassionato for Cello and Orchestra, op. 43.

auditory stream, then she is entraining pulse R′ and relinquishing the entrainment of R. The substitution of R′ for R has a ripple effect. R′ does not include slower pulses P and Q, and therefore cannot co-participate in a meter with them. Cut off from the meter like a ruptured vine, these slower pulses also wither. Thus meter 1 is replaced by meter 2 = {P′, Q′, R′, S}, as labeled in Figure 9.6.

The moment when such a substitution occurs seems to be inherently indeterminate. It may vary from performer to performer, from listener to listener, from performer to listener, and from one listening to the next. Following Leong (2011), Figure 9.7 models this variety as a horizontal continuum. The procession from left to right might model an accumulation of time, or of musical features. One end is associated with a "conservative" hearing that assimilates to the ongoing meter; the other with a "radical" hearing that resets to the new meter (Imbrie 1973; Fitch and Rosenfeld 2007). In the middle is a zone of possible time points when the meter might tip or flip (Locke 2010) from one hearing to the other, for some listener on some listening occasion. Imbrie (1973) and Temperley (2008) have both documented the phenomenological complexity and indeterminacy of the tipping process as it applies to the specific case of classical hypermeter but similar processes arise at faster pulses as well. Passages within this zone are associated with perceptual rivalry or "bistability," a general psychological phenomenon better understand in the visual than the auditory domain, and whose prototypes are the duck/rabbit (Jastrow 1899) and the Necker cube. These visual phenomena afford mutually exclusive interpretations, and stimulate oscillations that are sudden, involuntary, random, and inevitable (Pressnitzer and Hupé 2006). Whether all of these attributes are present in the case of auditory bistability is as yet an open question.

In Figure 9.7, the bistability model is placed above an alternative model that posits an intermediate state of coexistence, "the simultaneous perception of two distinct auditory

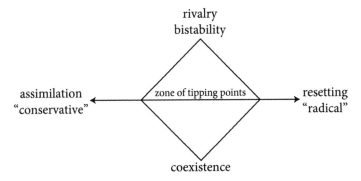

FIGURE 9.7 The syncopation continuum, after Leong (2011). The left terminus represents the secure ongoing meter; the right terminus represents a secure substitution for the ongoing meter; and the middle represents the zone of points where a listener might substitute the new meter, or—according to a different paradigm—within which the two meters are held in balance.

streams, with independent, out-of-phase metrical structures." (Fitch and Rosenfeld 2007, 53). Metric coexistence has analogues in tonal theory, as when a modulation terminates on a chord that is both stable as a local tonic and unstable as a global dominant. The coexistence model remains controversial (London 2012, 67). If it is psychologically real, it is as yet poorly understood. If it is illusory, we are far from understanding why expert musicians are convinced that they possess a mastery that some psychological researchers insist is beyond the capacity of their species.

A hemiola-type substitution engages many of the same phenomenological processes as a syncopation, but its structure is quite distinct, as is the environment in which it can arise. Substitution of period-equivalent pulses is situationally unconstrained; it can apply to a pulse of any speed, in any meter, at any moment. By contrast, the only pulse that can be replaced by a pulse of different periodicity is one that participates in two different classes of adjacent minimal meter, one duple and one triple. The replacing pulse also adjoins a duple and triple meter, but permutes their order, exchanging ⟨3 2⟩ and ⟨2 3⟩.

Figure 9.8(a) presents a Baroque pre-cadential hemiola, the historical prototype for this second class of pulse substitution. The first two bars sustain a robust ongoing duple hypermeter of {P, Q, R, S} = {𝅗𝅥 𝅗𝅥. ♩ ♪𝅘𝅥𝅮}, representing meter class ⟨2 3 2⟩. At the point of hemiola, 𝅗𝅥 replaces 𝅗𝅥. with all other pulses invariant, transforming the initial ⟨2 3⟩ subset to ⟨3 2⟩ as a permutation of its elements, and locally suggesting {P, Q′, R, S} = {𝅗𝅥 ♩♩ ♪𝅘𝅥𝅮} of class ⟨3 2 2⟩. The normative downbeat pulse immediately returns after the tonic arrives at the end of the phrase.

As with the sixteenth-century pre-cadential syncope, a hemiola ruffles the metric surface, activating a potential that would be fulfilled if the substitute pulse were sustained through a continuous series of two-bar spans. If the original intermediate pulse continued to be present throughout such an extension, then the two rival pulses might be

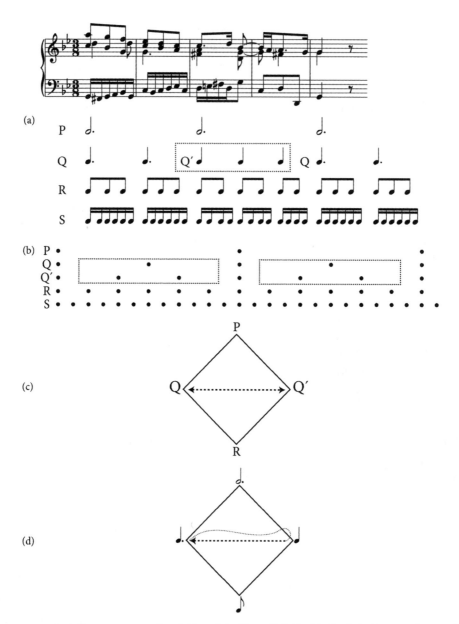

FIGURE 9.8 A Baroque pre-cadential hemiola (from J. S. Bach's English Suite in G minor). (a) Modeled as a dot array, with a temporary substitution of pulse Q′ for Q, and of minimal meter {PQ′RS} ∈ ⟨322⟩, for {PQRS} ∈ ⟨232⟩. (b) Superimposition of Q′ and Q demonstrates that neither is included in the other and thus that {PQRS} and {PQ′RS} are distinct meters. (c) The same meters as two distinct ski-hill paths. (d) The same interpreted as a tension/release scheme.

superposed in equilibrium. The perceptual dynamic along the horizontal axis of Figure 9.7 would then be activated, as would the conceptual dynamic along the vertical axis.

Figure 9.8(b) models the superposition of these two meters using dot notation. The two meters are not directly active at the same moment in Figure 9.8(a), as they are in other compositions, but they suggest an indirect relationship between expectation and presentation (Krebs 1999).

The four-pulse set {P, Q, Q′, R} forms six pairs, five of which form minimal meters. The exception is {Q, Q′}, whose mutual non-inclusion, highlighted by the boxes, unilaterally disqualifies the four pulses from co-participating in a single meter. (The situation is isomorphic with major- or minor-seventh chords, which are classified as dissonances even though five of their six intervals are consonant.)

Figure 9.8(c) represents the pulse set on a ski hill. Meter {P, Q, R} and meter {P, Q′, R} are represented as two distinct paths that connect the slowest P pulse at the top to the fastest R pulse at the bottom. The double-headed arrow, overlaid onto the graph, signifies the non-inclusion of Q and Q′, and the sensation of friction, conflict, or "dissonance" that arises when they are perceived to be directly superimposed. This arrow could be replaced by a single-headed arrow, pointing in either direction, if one meter were perceived to replace the other, however tentatively. A pre-cadential hemiola might be modeled as a spring-loaded rightward arrow, immediately compensated by a restorative leftward arrow representing the moment when metric and tonal "resolutions" are synchronized, as illustrated at Figure 9.8(d).

Whereas a syncopation-type substitution of identical-period pulses triggers pulse substitutions at slower levels, the hemiola type is confined within its diamond. In many cases, though, a hemiola-type substitution stimulates a domino effect. If a set of duple minimal meters combines with a single triple one, then the single triple meter can reel up and down the line of duple meters through a series of adjacency swaps, from slowest to fastest (⟨2 2 [2 3]⟩ to ⟨2 [2 3] 2⟩ to ⟨[2 3] 2 2⟩ to ⟨3 2 2 2⟩), or from fastest to slowest.

Figure 9.9 presents an example from Schumann's *Fantasie* for Piano, op. 17. The five systems in the example correspond to five distinct segments, each roughly four bars in length. The first and last segments project pure duple {𝅝 𝅗𝅥 𝅘𝅥 𝅘𝅥𝅮} = ⟨2 2 2⟩. The second substitutes 𝅘𝅥𝅮 → 𝅘𝅥𝅮₃; the third segment substitutes 𝅘𝅥 → 𝅘𝅥₃, projected initially by the E♭-major arpeggio; and the fourth segment substitutes 𝅗𝅥 → 𝅗𝅥₃ projected by the parallel descending segments. The final system undergoes a wholesale reversal, as each tripleted value is replaced by its corresponding duplets, recuperating the original pure duple state.

The dashed lines connecting the systems embellish this story, indicating that each duplet-to-triplet conversion is foreshadowed in the preceding segment. In the second segment, 𝅗𝅥 → 𝅗𝅥₃ is suggested by the harmonic tones once the melody stops articulating the 𝅘𝅥𝅮 pulse. In the third segment, 𝅗𝅥 → 𝅗𝅥₃ is suggested by the tolling B♭4s. And in the fourth segment, the triplet-to-duplet reversals 𝅗𝅥₃ → 𝅗𝅥 and 𝅗𝅥₃ → 𝅗𝅥 are suggested by boundaries and peaks of the lower voice at measure 59.

The progressive series of adjacency swaps suggests a scripted journey through a series of metric states, executing a departure/return scheme that has analogues in tonal theory. Another script familiar from theories of tonality is a departure/overshoot/

FIGURE 9.9 Five consecutive passages from Schumann's *Fantasie* op. 17, with ski-hill representations.

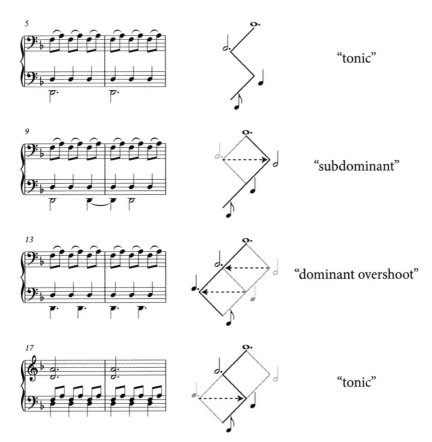

FIGURE 9.10 Four consecutive passages from Glass's Violin Concerto, with ski-hill representations.

return sequence (Lewin 1981; Cohn 2001). Figure 9.10 presents the opening measures of the final movement of Philip Glass's Violin Concerto (1987), which is dominated by a ♪♪ oscillation over a throbbing ♩. Across sets of twelve oscillation/throbs, an added bass projects 𝅗𝅥. (measure 5), which is then gradually abbreviated to 𝅗𝅥, ♩., and finally ♩ at measure 17. A violin open fifth D4/A4 then repeats the same process of compression (measures 17–29). The initial series of meters suggests an initial 𝅗𝅥. → 𝅗𝅥 perturbation; a 𝅗𝅥 → 𝅗𝅥. reversal synchronized with a new ♩ → ♩. perturbation that overshoots the origin; and then a final reversal ♩. → ♩ that parallels the initial 𝅗𝅥. → 𝅗𝅥 perturbation at twice its speed. The script resembles the paradigm of tonic–subdominant–[tonic]–dominant–tonic, where the subdominant acts as "a stretched bow that overshoots the mark" (Riemann 1893, 29).

Another script opens up a disjunctive gap and then fills it. Figure 9.11 presents the beginning portion of "Bawa," a harvest festival dance from the Dagarthi in northwestern Ghana. Anku (1992) transcribes the dance with a 2/4 signature. An audio file is available in Anku (2000), Example 2, in a performance by Collins Kwashie. My adaptation

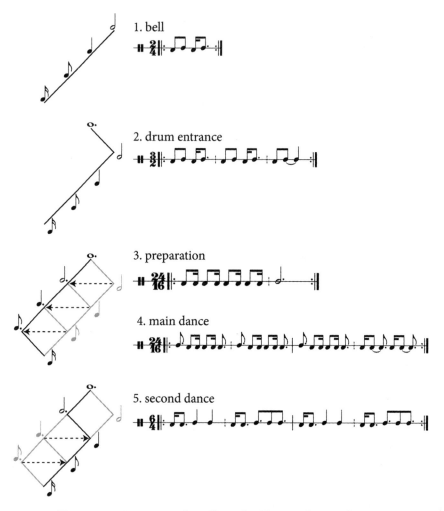

FIGURE 9.11 Five consecutive passages from "Bawa," a Ghanaian harvest dance.

imposes signatures flexibly according to the interpretation suggested by local context. In the first system, the bell pattern projects a pure duple {♩♩♪♩} meter, ⟨2 2 2⟩. In the second system, the drummer triply groups the bell pattern, deepening the meter to {𝅝 ♩♩♪♩} of metric class ⟨3 2 2 2⟩. In the third system, the drummer simultaneously replaces the three intermediate pulses with their dotted equivalents, ♩→♩. with ♩→♩. with ♪→♪. This is a strongly disjunctive triple hemiola that slings the lone triple meter from the slow end ⟨3 2 2 2⟩ to the fast end ⟨2 2 2 3⟩, an inversion of the prior meter (Leong 2007) and of the ongoing meter of the bell cycle. The new rhythm of the main dance, in the fourth system, projects the same pulses and thus sustains the triple hemiola with the bell. In the final system, the faster dotted values are retracted, ♩. → ♩ and ♪. → ♪ producing ⟨2 3 2 2⟩, so that the hemiolic relation only endures in the tension between the ♩. of the drum and the ♩ of the bell.

Together, these three short analyses suggest how successions of meters can project trajectories through sectors of metric space, traverse them incrementally or suddenly, and execute such familiar narrative schemes as departure/return, overshooting, and gap filling, which have a long history of underwriting analytical scripts in the harmonic and modulatory domains of tonal music. The capacity for tonal states and entities to be mapped across a variety of distances, and through a variety of coherent trajectories, is the key to tonality's star status in the game of musical form. The identification of spaces and maps in the metric domain, with comparable properties and physiognomies, shows how meter can be a major player in that game, too.

Expanding Meter

The definition of pulse proposed earlier (in the section "Defining Meter") is flexible, allowing meters to be composed of pulses that are very slow or irregular. I have nonetheless applied it with caution, recognizing only isochronous pulses that fall inside a prototypical range of speed. This final section broadens the model to include meters (or "meters") that have irregular "quasi-pulses" and slow "hyper-pulses." My open definition considers them to be meters, albeit not prototypical ones. A more closed definition that imposes context-free thresholds excludes them, so that they become "meters" whose status as meters is metaphorical (Hasty 1997). Metaphorical extensions underlie some of the most influential concepts in the history of music theory (Cook 1989; Perlman 2004), so their productive potential should not be dismissed, although their value is far from guaranteed.

Before we consider quasi-pulses, we need to first release the requirement that adjacent meters be either duple or triple. Although this requirement was not worked into the definition of meter, I adopted it *de facto* on the empirical grounds that it is "characteristic" of Western musical sensibilities, and on the speculative (and thus possibly specious) grounds that it is consistent with aspects of numerical cognition. Releasing this constraint has potential analytical value on its own. For example, it allows ⟨5 2⟩ to count as a meter, to be mapped equally well on a ski hill, and to be implicated into a formal script. The Mars movement from Holst's *The Planets*, which involves the hemiolic play of ⟨5 2⟩ and ⟨2 5⟩ meters, suggests that such a move can be analytically productive. It also allows the model to be placed into contact with Balkan and south-Asian repertories based on cyclic *aksak* and tala systems of rhythmic organization.

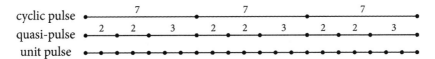

FIGURE 9.12 A dot-array representation of a quasi-pulse, as part of a quasi-meter.

The second expansion treats quasi-pulses, such as 2 + 2 + 3, as if they were literal pulses. Quasi-pulses are constituents of quasi-meters, which are traditionally labeled as mixed or additive meters, and more recently as non-isochronous meters. A quasi-meter sandwiches a quasi-pulse inside a minimal meter comprised of a slow cyclic pulse, which functions as a point of cyclic orientation or renewal, and a faster unit pulse, as illustrated in Figure 9.12. (The unit pulse might be only spectral rather than activated by persistent onsets.) As the number of units per cycle grows, additional pulses or quasi-pulses may also be folded inside a quasi-meter.

London 2012 proposes that a quasi-pulse is well-formed only if the durations of its adjacent time points are limited to two distinct values in a 2:3 proportion, where the longer and shorter durations are distributed maximally evenly in relation to the slower cyclic pulse (Clough and Douthett 1991). Guerra 2018 suggests some persuasive analytical motivations for relinquishing the maximal evenness constraint while continuing to limit local spans to two durations in notional 2:3 relation.

The third and final expansion involves treating very slow hyperpulses as if they were entrainable. A *hypermeter* is a minimal meter one of whose pulses is slower than a notated measure. The term loses meaning when notation is incidental to metric identity (London 2012), so I will redeploy it here to refer to any meter that contains a hyperpulse, defined as a pulse whose period is slow enough as to fall outside of the normal threshold of entrainability, wherever we might set that. Accordingly, many notational hypermeters, such as those analyzed in Temperley (2008), are treated here as meters without qualification.

Analyses of the Scherzo from Beethoven's Symphony no. 9 (Cohn 1992) and of Brahms's "Gypsy" Rondo, op. 25 (Murphy 2007) suggest that it can be productive to posit a seamless continuum that connects fast prototypical pulses to slow hyperpulses. That continuum threads all the way from atomistic periodic durations felt in an instant, to "true" periodic durations inside of which we can be aware of time passing (Clarke 1999), to slower durations whose periodicity can be felt only by subconsciously marking intervening time points, to still slower hyperpulses that may initially be more conceived than perceived. This continuum resembles the number line, which also transgresses boundaries between perceptual registers, threading together imperceptible zero, small numbers subitizable in pre-verbal infancy, mid-range numbers cognizable through verbal counting, and very large numbers present to consciousness only through induction and calculation (Repp 2007).

Hypermeters and quasi-meters generalize complementary features of prototypical meters. Quasi-pulses are entrained, but not isochronous. Hyperpulses are isochronous, but not entrained. They thus flank prototypical meter on two sides, like a subdominant and a dominant flank a tonic.

Suitably adapted, the general model of meter is capable of expanding to encompass both hypermeter and quasi-meter. Does this mean that they "really" are meters, but just not prototypical ones? Or that they are only metric in the "metaphorical" sense? If the expanded model treats them functionally in the same way, and produces the same analytical results for specific cases, then the distinction lacks significance. In either case, an expanded conception of meter along these lines would catalyze an expansion of its domain of application, thereby taking a step toward fulfilling the generalizing ideal outlined in the beginning of this chapter.

NOTES

1. Clayton (2000, 45) sketches a comparable dynamic between historical conception and evolving practice with respect to Indian notions of *tal*.
2. The precedence ordering of mind and body in response to temporal patterns is complex and perhaps intractable. For two contrasting views from neural science, see Patel and Iversen (2014) and Chemin, Moureaux, and Nozaradan (2014).
3. For historical accounts of how heard meter gradually detached from notated meter around 1800, see Grant (2014). Kirnberger signaled this detachment already in the 1770s ([1771–79] 1982, 39), when he suggested that several measures of a Couperin Courante are in 6/4 even though they are notated in 3/2.
4. For a discussion of similar methodological issues, see Câmara and Danielson's chapter in this volume.
5. Schachter (1987) identifies a fifth, slower one, which I omit because it doesn't have time to blossom in the fragments presented here.
6. Dot arrays originate in the eighteenth century (Grant 2013, 252), and were popularized more recently by Lerdahl and Jackendoff (1983).

WORKS CITED

Anku, Willie. 1992. *Structural Set Analysis of African Music*. Vol. 2, *Bawa*. Legon, Ghana: Soundstage Production.

Anku, Willie. 2000. "Circles and Time: A Theory of Structural Organization of Rhythm in African Music." *Music Theory Online* 6, no. 1. http://www.mtosmt.org/issues/mto.00.6.1/mto.00.6.1.anku_frames.html.

Apel, Willi. 1949. *The Notation of Polyphonic Music, 900–1600*. Cambridge, MA: Mediaeval Academy of America.

Boone, Graeme M. 2000. "Marking Mensural Time." *Music Theory Spectrum* 22: 1–43.

Brochard, Renaud, Donna Abecasis, Doug Potter, Richard Ragot, and Carolyn Drake. 2003. "The 'Ticktock' of Our Internal Clock: Direct Brain Evidence of Subjective Accents in Isochronous Sequences." *Psychological Science* 14: 362–366.

Chemin, Baptiste, André Moureaux, and Sylvie Nozaradan. 2014. "Body Movement Selectively Shapes the Neural Representation of Musical Rhythms." *Psychological Science* 25: 2147–2159.

Clarke, Eric F. 1999. "Rhythm and Timing in Music." In *The Psychology of Music*, 2nd ed., edited by Diana Deutsch, 473–500. San Diego: Academic Press.

Clayton, Martin. 2000. *Time in Indian Music: Rhythm, Metre, and Form in North Indian Rāg Performance*. New York: Oxford University Press.

Clough, John, and Jack Douthett. 1991. "Maximally Even Sets." *Journal of Music Theory* 35: 93–173.

Cohn, Richard. 1992. "The Dramatization of Hypermetric Conflicts in the Scherzo of Beethoven's Ninth Symphony." *19th-Century Music* 15: 188–206.

Cohn, Richard. 2001. "Complex Hemiolas, Ski-Hill Graphs and Metric Spaces." *Music Analysis* 20: 295–326.

Cohn, Richard. 2015. "Why We Don't Teach Meter, and Why We Should." *Journal of Music Theory Pedagogy* 29: 1–19.

Cook, Nicholas. 1989. "Music Theory and 'Good Comparison': A Viennese Perspective." *Journal of Music Theory* 33: 117–141.

Cooper, Grosvenor, and Leonard B. Meyer. 1960. *The Rhythmic Structure of Music.* Chicago: University of Chicago Press.

DeFord, Ruth I. 2015. *Tactus, Mensuration and Rhythm in Renaissance Music.* Cambridge: Cambridge University Press.

Fitch, W. Tecumseh, and Andrew Rosenfeld. 2007. "Perception and Production of Syncopated Rhythms." *Music Perception* 25: 43–58.

Forth, James. 2012. "Cognitively-Motivated Geometric Methods of Pattern Discovery and Models of Similarity in Music." PhD diss., Goldsmiths College, University of London.

Grant, Roger Mathew. 2013. "Leonhard Euler's Unfinished Theory of Rhythm." *Journal of Music Theory* 57: 245–286.

Grant, Roger Mathew. 2014. *Beating Time and Measuring Music in the Early Modern Era.* New York: Oxford University Press.

Guerra, Stephen. 2018. "Expanded Meter and Hemiola in Baden Powell's Samba-Jazz." PhD diss., Yale University.

Hannon, Erin E., and Sandra E. Trehub. 2005. "Metrical Categories in Infancy and Adulthood." *Psychological Science* 16: 48–55.

Hasty, Christopher. 1997. *Meter as Rhythm.* New York: Oxford University Press.

Holder, Alan. 1995. *Rethinking Meter: A New Approach to the Verse Line.* Lewisburg, PA: Bucknell University Press.

Houle, George. 1987. *Meter in Music, 1600–1800: Performance, Perception, and Notation.* Bloomington: Indiana University Press.

Imbrie, Andrew. 1973. "'Extra' Measures and Metrical Ambiguity in Beethoven." In *Beethoven Studies*, edited by Alan Tyson, 45–66. New York: W. W. Norton.

Jastrow, Joseph. 1899. "The Mind's Eye." *Popular Science Monthly.*

Kaminsky, Peter Michael. 1989. "Aspects of Harmony, Rhythm, and Form in Schumann's Papillons, Carnaval, and Davidsbündlertänze." PhD diss., University of Rochester.

Kirnberger, Johann Philipp. [1771–1779] 1982. *The Art of Strict Musical Composition.* Edited and translated by David W. Beach and Jürgen Thym. New Haven, CT: Yale University Press.

Komar, Arthur. 1971. *Theory of Suspensions.* Princeton, NJ: Princeton University Press.

Krebs, Harald. 1999. *Fantasy Pieces: Metrical Dissonance in the Music of Robert Schumann.* New York: Oxford University Press.

Küster, Martin. 2012. "Thinking in Song: Prosody, Text Setting and Music Theory in Eighteenth-Century Germany." PhD diss., Cornell University.

Large, Edward W., and Joel S. Snyder. 2009. "Pulse and Meter as Neural Resonance." *Annals of the New York Academy of Sciences* 1169: 46–57.

Leong, Daphne. 2007. "Humperdinck and Wagner: Metric States, Symmetries, and Systems." *Journal of Music Theory* 51: 211–243.

Leong, Daphne. 2011. "Generalizing Syncopation: Contour, Duration, and Weight." *Theory and Practice* 36: 111–150.

Lerdahl, Fred, and Ray Jackendoff. 1983. *A Generative Theory of Tonal Music.* Cambridge, MA: MIT Press.

Lester, Joel. 1982. *Harmony in Tonal Music.* Vol. 1, *Diatonic Practices.* New York: Alfred A. Knopf.

Lewin, David. 1981. "On Harmony and Meter in Brahms's op. 76, no. 8." *19th-Century Music* 4: 261–265.

Lewin, David. 1987. *Generalized Musical Intervals and Transformations*. New Haven, CT: Yale University Press.

Locke, David. 2010. "Yewevu in the Metric Matrix." *Music Theory Online* 16.4. http://www.mtosmt.org/issues/mto.10.16.4/mto.10.16.4.locke.html.

London, Justin. 2012. *Hearing in Time: Psychological Aspects of Musical Meter*. 2nd ed. New York: Oxford University Press.

Madison, Guy. 2014. "Sensori-motor Synchronisation Variability Decreases as the Number of Metrical Levels in the Stimulus Signal Increases." *Acta psychologica* 147: 10–16.

Mirka, Danuta. 2009. *Metric Manipulations in Haydn and Mozart: Chamber Music for Strings, 1787–1791*. New York: Oxford University Press.

Murphy, Scott. 2007. "On Metre in the Rondo of Brahms's Op. 25." *Music Analysis* 26: 323–353.

Patel, Aniruddh D., and John R. Iversen. 2014. "The Evolutionary Neuroscience of Musical Beat Perception: The Action Simulation for Auditory Prediction (ASAP) Hypothesis." *Frontiers in Systems Neuroscience* 8: 57.

Perlman, Marc. 2004. *Unplayed Melodies: Javanese Gamelan and the Genesis of Music Theory*. Berkeley: University of California Press.

Pressnitzer, Daniel, and Jean-Michel Hupé. 2006. "Temporal Dynamics of Auditory and Visual Bistability Reveal Common Principles of Perceptual Organization." *Current Biology* 16: 1351–1357.

Raz, Carmel. 2018. "John Holden's *Essay Toward a Rational System of Music* (1770): An Eighteenth-Century Theory of Musical Cognition." *Journal of Music Theory* 62: 205–248.

Repp, Bruno H. 1998. "Variations on a Theme by Chopin: Relations between Perception and Production of Timing in Music." *Journal of Experimental Psychology: Human Perception and Performance* 24: 791–811.

Repp, Bruno H. 2007. "Perceiving the Numerosity of Rapidly Occurring Auditory Events in Metrical and Nonmetrical Contexts." *Attention, Perception, & Psychophysics* 69: 529–543.

Riemann, Hugo. 1893. *Harmony Simplified*. London: Augener.

Schachter, Carl. 1987. "Rhythm and Linear Analysis: Aspects of Meter." *Music Forum* 6: 1–59. New York: Columbia University Press.

Temperley, David. 2008. "Hypermetrical Transitions." *Music Theory Spectrum* 30: 305–325.

Volk, Anna. 2008. "The Study of Syncopation Using Inner Metric Analysis: Linking Theoretical and Experimental Analysis of Metre in Music." *Journal of New Music Research* 37: 259–273.

Vuust, Peter, Line K. Gebauer, and Maria Witek. 2014. "Neural Underpinnings of Music: The Polyrhythmic Brain." *Neurobiology of Interval Timing*, 339–356. New York: Springer.

Yeston, Maury. 1976. *The Stratification of Musical Rhythm*. New Haven, CT: Yale University Press.

Zuckerkandl, Victor. 1956. *Sound and Symbol*. Princeton, NJ: Princeton University Press.

CHAPTER 10

TEMPORALITIES

MARTIN SCHERZINGER

FORWARD: FROM CARTOGRAPHIES OF EUROPEAN TIME TO EPHEMERA OF AFRICAN TIME

> How do we read the relationship between metropole and colony as conjunctive when our ideological desire is the inscription of their uneven temporality and their inherent heterologies?
>
> (Gikandi 1996, 7)

THIS chapter considers the question of musical temporality in broad historical perspective.[1] Instead of simply reflecting on the various modes of time and timing found in music—rhythm, meter, tempo, tactus, subdivision, texture, grouping, form, and so on—the argument traverses a vast global terrain, intersecting elements of philosophy, history, and geography with elements of music theory and analysis. The chapter only deals with recent history, notably the past 250 years, which it tentatively calls the modern period. In Europe, this was a period when the concept of absolute time gained ascendancy, following prolonged intellectual efforts to locate the correct measure of time in seventeenth-century astronomy. The quest for general historical tendencies is set in relief with specific examples (sometimes fragmentary and ephemeral) concerning practical technics of time-reckoning. As a method, then, one may speak here of Walter Benjamin's notion of constructivism, a kind of burrowing of historical wormholes; placing temporalities on sliding scales, seeking to illuminate an occasional uncanny alliance or a surprising rupture (Benjamin 1968).

The chapter begins by outlining a traditional philosophical engagement with musical temporality, vividly set against, and in critical relation to, a dominant physics and mechanics of time. This tradition registers the relevance of, and paradoxical distinction between, two senses of musical time that are central to contemporary music theory—measured or abstract, on the one hand, and lived or experiential, on the other. The chapter demonstrates the varied attempts to reach outside of the constraints of the abstract, rigidly construed cartographies of time in the European industrial period and traces the emergence of two broad cultures of critique. The first, associated with music theory, is attentive to the alternative temporalities proffered by music, frequently adumbrated in phenomenological, experiential, and semiotic terms. The second, more ethnographic in approach, relativizes industrialized imperatives of measured time by proliferating temporalities in the form of overdetermined assemblages and actor-networks. Both cultures of critique take aim at the period of consolidating a universal theory of time, which was also the great period of European colonial expansion. More precisely speaking, they take aim at modern cartographies of time that graphically amplified time-sequenced phenomena in terms of precisely segmented linear progress.

The chapter argues that the various challenges to this kind of globally projected chronographic template have only inadequately dethroned its coercive constraints. This is because the varied attempts to counterpoint the linear time that characterizes the modern age in the West remain bound up in colonial thought in various complex ways, mostly perpetuating unreconstructed binaries that fragment cultural geographies into plural dimensions. The chapter argues that the value brought to the analyses of global time by new phenomenologies of listening, on the one hand, and by disjunctures and differences of polychronic scale, on the other, are limited in scope. While critical in aspiration, these epistemological shifts are grounded in an ab initio exclusion of certain modes of practice and thought. Attentive to the vexing interplay of power and knowledge as foundational for critique, the chapter nonetheless attempts to theorize an exit from modernity's predicaments. In quest of loci for regenerative critique, the chapter gestures toward dissimilar senses of musical temporality as a site for thinking outside of hegemonic time. Perhaps a superannuated formalism—strategically mobilized in an exponentially post-formalist era—has a role to play in dissecting music's material, sociopolitical, and historical manifestations of temporality in a genuinely global sense. In particular, the analysis of musical ephemera from Africa, in dialogue with facets of Western musical thought, suggests one such opening.

THE QUESTION OF TEMPORALITY: TOWARD A TIME OUTSIDE OF TIME

Theorizations of time have taken up considerable residency in philosophical writings from continental Europe in the previous century. Drawing on a tradition of nineteenth-century thought—ranging from Georg Wilhelm Friedrich Hegel to Arthur Schopenhauer, Karl Marx, Søren Kierkegaard, Friedrich Nietzsche, and others—we find in these writings a general turn toward grasping relations between subjects and objects in temporal terms, with a special emphasis on emergence, fluidity, variation, and becoming. From Edmund Husserl's (1973) genetic phenomenology of experience and Henri Bergson's (2002) account of indivisible time—resistant to mathematical or scientific thought—to Alfred North Whitehead's (1929) diagnosis of reality as a structure of evolving processes and Martin Heidegger's (2010) extensive account of being as irreducibly inflected by time, these writers saturate their research objects with all manner of temporalities, denuding them of either representational or (then) common-sense optics that would index them to the stasis of the present. In the second half of the century, these arguments became methodologically axiomatic. Gilbert Simondon (2017), for example, substituted for ontology the concept of ontogenesis; Jacques Derrida's (1982) concept of *différance* drew attention to the differential structure—the undecidability of differing and deferring—of our naturalized grasp of presence; and Gilles Deleuze and Félix Guattari (1987) located difference at the heart of repetition, later articulated by the philosophers as the virtual ground from which actualization emerges as an effect. For all the variations in the details, these methodological inclinations—dialectics, transcendental reasoning, phenomenology, deconstruction, psychoanalytic and hermeneutic techniques, schizoanalysis, and so on—shared a resistance to dominant modern forms of time, which represent it as linear, teleological, cartographic, calendric, continuous, sequential, standardized, or uniform.

The philosophical avoidance of theories of time that were modeled, on the one hand, on some kind of naturalized perception, or, on the other, as the object of physics, shows no signs of abating in the twenty-first century. Indeed, in the contemporary moment, academic humanists—responsive perhaps to the emergence, in the post-Cold War period, of widespread popular discontent, xenophobia, decontextualized affective orders, dislocations of language, and above all ecological damage and climate change—increasingly contend that human history can only be grasped in the context of a plurality of timescales. As a result, conceptions of temporality have expanded their scope and authority in at least two senses. First, what was once largely a philosophical orientation has increasingly migrated into anthropology, sociology, geography, political science, literary theory, and even musicology; and second, what was once regarded as a fundamentally human-focused inquiry into temporality has expanded to include the production of time by both human and nonhuman mediators, entities, and agents. In other words, the living *anthropos* is constituted by a variety of both commensurate and incommensurate temporalities that exceed the scale of anthropomorphic time: geological time, biological time, cosmological time, technological and financial time, among many others. The challenge for contemporary disciplines of the humanities lies in crafting diagnostic guidelines for how these multiple temporalities are to be represented. If temporal processes multiply across various scales and strata—a thousand plateaus (in Deleuze and Guattari's memorable terms)—how can temporality be thought nonanthropocentrically? How can philosophical inquiry be set adrift from the conceit that humanly organized time is the dominant temporality that bears on, and gets entangled in, human life? This grand reckoning with multiscalar timeframes, from microscopic particle vibration to the grand tectonic shifts of geological time, does not align with the lived experiences of duration, change, and rhythm.

The investigation into nonhuman and quasi-human temporalities—including species extinction, life after humans, slow time, the Long Now, the time of computing, biopolitical time, the rhythms of capitalist production and accumulation, digital temporalities, the nanochronemics of neuromedia, and many more—entails an element of both production and enactment, on the one hand, and hypothesis and conjecture, on the other. First, to the point about production and enactment, we find in Bruno Latour's actor-network theory (2005), for example, or the assemblage theory of Manuel Delanda (2016), the idea that the textural media that shape human life are only partially constituted by pregiven forms of literature, architecture, computer science, molecular biology, or data science. In these philosophical positions, such media are more emphatically enjoined by a ceaseless play of temporal forces, productive pulsions, and variously scaled morphogenetic processes. Second, given that temporal orderings of this sort exist beyond the singular timeframes of human history, their articulation as narrative hypothesis requires an additional element of speculation or conjecture. Quentin Meillassoux's philosophy (2009), for example, engages the question of ancestrality—the time outside of, and indifferent to, the time of human consciousness. The philosopher speculatively resists temporalities that relativize human knowledge to the scale of anthropomorphic logics (such as narrative-bound interpretive communities, situated knowledges, culturally specific enactments, language-games, and the like). For Meillassoux, the apparently healthy skepticism that limits all absolute knowledge claims—by demonstrating their irremediable spatiotemporal limits, for example, or the specificity of their historical and contextual conditioning grounds—is a false humility that de facto constrains the capacities of speculative reason. Considerations of deep time—the retrospective reconstruction of ancestrality, no less than the future-oriented modeling of the Anthropocene—are thereby ceded to the terrain of relativism, fundamentalism, and faith. In the speculative realism of Meillassoux, no less than the new realism of Maurizio Ferraris, for instance, or the object-oriented ontology of Graham Harman (2002) and Levi Bryant (2014), we find a reconsideration of the question of temporality that attempts to allay the conceptual hemorrhaging associated with anthropocentrism. It is as if we witness today the great philosophical return of time outside of human time—a full two centuries after Immanuel Kant conceptually distinguished the phenomenal world from the noumenal on account of its inadequate availability to the subjective forms of time, space, causality, and so on.

THE QUESTION OF MUSICAL TEMPORALITY: WITHIN AND WITHOUT TIME

It is a paradox of musical time that it is at once produced *within* domain- and species-specific habitus and nonetheless said to gesture toward, or to be perceived as, time *outside* of quotidian human time, however broadly construed—as naturalized temporal perception, machinic, or measured time (such as "clock-time"), the time of physics, and so on. In other words, ostensibly at the heart of, and wholly absorbed by, the anthropo-morphic sensorium, music—that *humanly* organized sound (in John Blacking's words [1970, 12])—is also said to temporalize at some remove from ordinary anthropomorphic time. Although their guiding conceptual metaphors vary, this dual inflection of the temporality of music is as true for modern music theories, broadly speaking, as it is for modern philosophies of music. In both spheres, the relation of music to time is frequently construed in a double, if not outright disjunctive, sense. First, time is advanced as a *general* condition of music's possibility: music takes place *in* time. And second, music is advanced as a *particular* case of crafting a unique time: music suspends ordinary time and shapes an (idealized) substitute. Examples of such dual (and dueling) temporalities abound. In the words of Suzannah Clark and Alexander Rehding: "Not only can music be understood as sounds shaped in time but—more radically—as time shaped in sounds" (Clark and Rehding 2016, ix). The distinction between the time a musical piece occupies or takes (usually conceptualized as its real-time or actual duration) and the time it shapes or constructs (variously conceptualized as the time it represents, evokes, and signifies, or as the time of its phenomenological experience or perception) guides a variety of contemporary music-theoretical approaches to musical temporality.

What is less acknowledged in the literature is the paradox that music's particular phenomenological temporality actually creates the conditions for the undermining of its claimed axiomatic persistence *in* time. Basil de Sélincourt, for example, astutely observes that music demands the "absorption of the whole of our time consciousness; our own continuity must be lost in that of the sound to which we listen" (in Langer 1959, 153). On the one hand, Sélincourt hereby gives voice to a then-common trope about music's elevated experiential metaphysics. On the other hand, Sélincourt delicately observes the principle of the excluded middle: the loss of quotidian continuity in the sensuous throes of musical absorption. In other words, in the act of musical close-listening, we witness an irreconcilable delinking of temporalities, a giving-*and*-taking of time itself. This particular substitutive maneuver, the shaping of time removed, marks a historical symptom, a rupture between musical temporalities and a general time-concept that had sedimented throughout the eighteenth and nineteenth centuries into an authoritative norm. For the industrialized global terrain of the early twentieth century, a kind of monochronic time—segmented into a sequence of equidistant basic units—had become the primary mode of time reckoning. (I will return to this concept of absolute time in the next section.) In contrast, according to at least one dominant romantic-modern strain of its reception and interpretation within the very historical period that witnessed the ascendancy of absolute time, music seemed to shape time according to its own distinct—imaginative or autonomous—organizational principles. Against the governing chronological system that structured and managed time in abstract measurable segments, musical time from Beethoven to Boulez by way of Brahms, Wagner, and Schoenberg, seemed, according to this tradition, to also offer an experience of boundlessness and becoming, of developing variation and thematic transformation, of idealized suspension and virtual possibility. Music in the modern-romantic tradition thereby exemplified a temporality that was said to suspend, transform, or otherwise transcend ordinary time.

It is a peculiarity of history that philosophies of music in the modern period frequently invoked an aspect of music's temporality to suggest such a time outside of time. The idea that an irrefutably human sonorous creativity could leverage philosophical insight into the polychronic temporalities of the extra-human world seems counterintuitive, if not outright absurd, on the face of it. And yet, as if haunted by the ancient numerics of sonic frequency, philosophers from the early nineteenth to the late twentieth centuries often turned their attention to just such an intellectual effort. Although this point requires an extensive account of the variety of meanings attributed to sonotropic temporalities in the philosophy of the previous two centuries, two telling examples that bookend this period will suffice here.[2] First, in *The World as Will and Representation*, Schopenhauer leveraged a fundamental distinction between will, on the one hand, and representation, on the other, with reference to music's foundational temporality. First, against the sequential abstraction and stasis of representation, Schopenhauer advanced the temporal flow of music as a striking analogy to the will itself. He writes: "We hear in its language the secret history of our will and of all its stirrings and strivings with their many different delays, postponements, hindrances, and afflictions" (Schopenhauer 1958, 451). Second, wholly set apart from the "world as representation," or indeed any "ideas or grades of the will's objectification," Schopenhauer also detected in music a striking parallelism with the fundamental structure of nature itself (447, 448). He writes: "The four voices or parts of all harmony … correspond to the four grades in the series of existences, hence to the mineral, plant, and animal kingdoms, and to man" (447). In this often-ignored passage, Schopenhauer offers a twist on musical sublimity that is as banal as it is enigmatic. By suggesting some kind of correlation between musical frequencies and the structure of the world, the philosopher actually abbreviated the place of man within that structure. In Friedrich Kittler's words: "If the stones speak in the bass, the plants in the tenor, the animals in the alto, and mankind in the soprano, then music speaks the language of the world and no longer that of the human, who literally shrinks to a fraction" (Kittler 1995, 96). Schopenhauer thereby located in music's apparently auto-generative independence a capacity to register the foundational temporalities of both the internal (subjective) and the external (nonhuman) world. Set against the static propositional nomenclatures that were critically indexed as representation, music exemplified the temporal flux of boundless becoming both before and beyond human time.

Almost two centuries later, Deleuze and Guattari ekphrastically deployed the conceptual and sensual modalities of music for a philosophy similarly targeted at both internal and external temporal processes. In *A Thousand Plateaus: Capitalism and Schizophrenia*, for example, the philosophers creatively adopted modernist serial structures as philosophical leverage for thinking identity across analytic strata—like a rhizome. "The rhizome," they write, "has no beginning or end; it is always in the middle, between things, interbeing, *intermezzo*. … The tree imposes the verb 'to be,' but the fabric of the rhizome is the conjunction 'and … and … and …' " (Deleuze and Guattari 1987, 25). Modernist musical thought was central to Deleuze and Guattari's argument. Their conceptual debt to Pierre Boulez alone extended to their philosophical concepts of the dividual (individuation without identity), the synthesizer (construed in contrast to the dialectical *synthetic apriori*), the concepts of deterritorialization and diagonal (unsubscribed from the spatialized coordinates of vertical and horizontal), and smooth space and smooth time (set against striated space and time).[3] The intersemiotic transposition of music-theoretical terms for philosophical concepts brought a noteworthy temporal dimension to their analytic approach. For example, Boulez's description of smooth time, a technical term concerning the timing of instrumental resonance, morphs in A Thousand Plateaus into a nonmetric temporality of limitless connection and mutation. Against metric time, which one "counts in order to occupy," in smooth time "one occupies without counting" (477). The philosophers wrote: "The smooth is the continuous variation, continuous development of form; it is the fusion of harmony and melody in favor of the production of properly rhythmic values, the pure act of the drawing of a diagonal across the vertical and horizontal" (478).

As it was with Schopenhauer, we find, in Deleuze and Guattari, the idea that music's peculiar temporalities—construed as "continuous variation, continuous development", "properly rhythmic values," "a diagonal," and so on—are set against the striated temporalities of traditional philosophical taxonomies. Furthermore, as it was in Schopenhauer's theoretical scheme, these specifically musical temporalities were leveraged to address both internal *and* external dimensions of life. First, regarding the internal dimension, Deleuze and Guattari regarded productive activity in terms of interactive and interruptive flows, which—against Freud's concept of the Id—they called desiring-machines. Desiring-machines opportunistically seek out "couplings and connections" of "desiring-production" in an "ongoing process of becoming that is the becoming of reality" (1, 35). It is a striking fact that the desiring-machine—a late-twentieth-century incarnation of Schopenhauer's will—was modeled on music's irreducibly alternate temporalities. The conceptual genealogy is particularly noteworthy in the context of theories of affect in the twenty-first century, powerfully elaborated in the work of Brian Massumi (2002), Eve Kosofsky Sedgwick (2003), Eric Shouse (2005), and Nigel Thrift (2008), among many others, which owe a considerable debt to Deleuze and Guattari's concept of the desiring-machine. In other words, the turn to affect in twenty-first-century philosophy, anthropology, geography, literary studies, and political theory is genealogically linked to a tradition of modern thought about musical time. Massumi, for example, regards the anti-intentionalism of affect in explicitly temporal terms, often in microscopic increments of split-seconds. In other words, the twenty-first-century construal of affect as autonomous nonconscious intensity is in fact a post-postmodern reinscription of a traditional question—from will to desiring-machine—addressed to the modern antinomies of musical temporality.

Second, regarding the external dimension, Deleuze and Guattari's concept of the rhizome, exemplified by the "logic of the AND," reached beyond anthropomorphic time toward an assemblage of *multilinear* temporal systems. From black holes to the inner lives of spiders, Deleuze and Guattari's rhizomic analysis assembled both humanly perceptible and imperceptible temporalities—"differential speeds and slownesses in a kind of molecular lapping . . . *seconds, tenths and hundredths of seconds*" (italics in original; Deleuze and Guattari 1987, 267). Again, while ostensibly striking out toward terrain once regarded as *noumenal*, Deleuze and Guattari paradoxically—but directly—deployed musical thought as a portal into nonanthropomorphic spheres. For example, the music of Edgard Varèse, they argued, is arranged "according to variable relations of speed, but also into so many waves or flows of a sonic energy irradiating the entire universe, a headlong line of flight. That is how he populated the Gobi desert with insects and stars constituting a becoming-music of the world, or a diagonal for a cosmos" (309). Likewise, the philosophers invoked the music of Olivier Messiaen in terms of temporal multiplicities—"multiple chromatic durations in coalescence"—which directly engaged the world beyond the Anthropocene: the music alternates durations "between the longest and the shortest . . . the infinitely long duration of the stars and the mountains and the infinitely short ones of the insects and atoms" (309). In keeping with Schopenhauer's parallelism between musical time and the temporality of phenomena beyond human creation, Deleuze and Guattari wrote: "Music is not the privilege of human beings: the universe, the cosmos, is made of refrains; the question in music is that of a power of deterritorialization permeating nature, animals, the elements, and deserts as much as human beings" (309).

Once again, there is a curious conceptual genealogy linking Schopenhauer's various "grades in the series of existences"—mineral, plant, animal, human—with Deleuze and Guattari's "multiple durations in coalescence"—natural, animal, elemental, ecological, human—both of which are arrived at on the terrain of philosophical engagement with musical temporality. As with affect theory, this is striking in the context of theories of twenty-first-century theories addressed to plateaus, assemblages, and actor-networks, which too owe a considerable debt to the work of Deleuze and Guattari. Delanda's realist ontology, for example, insists on the independence of the world from human thought by deploying a kind of Deleuzian model of countless plateaus—assemblages—that are aleatorically linked by "attractors" that are "never actualized" (2016, 23). For Delanda, singularities, or entities (from rocks to corporations), are merely the symptomatic fallout of an inherently temporal multiplicity; they are the "asymptotic stability" of certain "long-term tendencies" of a system of attractors (23). Likewise, for Latour, reality is produced in a proliferated network of planes of immanence, marked by human and nonhuman actants that interact within both continuous and discontinuous temporalities. It should be clear at this point that the above-discussed work of Meillissoux partakes of a similar discourse on time. What is fascinating about these new realist philosophies of the twenty-first century is their historical allegiance—without any demonstrable awareness on the part of their authors—to philosophical thought about temporal multiplicity and polycycles in *music*. For philosophy of the modern period, music provided a kind of speculative microcosm for thinking temporality outside of the taxonomic strata (representations, forms, laws) that guided its scientific and common-sense understandings, offering instead a model for thinking temporality within nontaxonomic strata (gradations, existences, plateaus) that suspended human time in favor of cosmic and microcosmic time. The networks and assemblages of contemporary theory are but the most recent incarnation of these traditions of musical thought.

SPATIAL GEOMETRIES OF COLONIAL TIME

My argument so far suggests an intimate, but uncanny, alliance between the contemporary conceptualization of temporality in general and the specifically *musical* conceptualization of temporality. Again, the conceptual proximity of both theories of will, desire and affect, on the one hand, and inorganic time, plateaus and assemblages, on the other, to the speculative logics associated with theories of musical time seems absurd if viewed in historical isolation. However, grounded in the idea that music occasions a distinct time of its own making (broadly speaking), it is perhaps less surprising that philosophical tropes involving temporality—will, affect, rhizome, assemblage, and so on—gather fluency and currency across musical terrain. Furthermore, historically speaking, both musical and philosophical temporalities emerge in relation to the ascendancy of another kind of time, which they are said to somehow cancel, multiply, annul, or suspend. In other words, musical time is said to unfold in some kind of contrast to the standardized time of the modern era—construed as absolute time—that is measured in mathematical abstraction and said to unfold in a kind of ceaseless, contiguous chronology. This notion of time is variously construed as linear time (or timeline), clock time (measured time), divisible time (points on a spatial trajectory), and so on. It is important to note that both the time inspired by music and the (internally directed) temporalities of affect theory (and its historical antecedents) as well as the (externally directed) temporalities of assemblage theory (and *its* antecedents) lie beyond, outside of, or parallel to this kind of exhaustively inscribed and quasi-mechanical conception of time. Henri Bergson, for example, considered the linear timeline to be an idolatrous interpolation of spatial coordinates into continuous movement.

What is the time projected by motionless line? The historians Daniel Rosenberg and Anthony Grafton (2010) point out that the framework of absolute time, adumbrated most forcefully by Isaac Newton in the late seventeenth century, only fully emerged as a dominant scheme for time-reckoning within the age of modernity itself. Contending with the fact that the rate of the earth's rotations was continually subject to variation, that is, external "forces" that retarded or accelerated its motion, the consolidation of absolute time, regarded as pure duration or the persistence of objective existence, was achieved against considerable empirical, religious, and conceptual odds. Rosenberg and Grafton furthermore argue that, while absolute time was frequently deployed to elucidate a kind of linear narrative of overarching progress (about which more below), its unique temporality was in fact wrapped up in all manner of nontemporal metaphors. In the European seventeenth century, it seems, time was less temporal than it was geometric or (in Rosenberg and Grafton's terms) cartographic.

Likewise, W. J. T. Mitchell argues that modern temporal discourse is frequently bound up in a whole array of spatial logics: "We speak of 'long' and 'short' times, of 'intervals' (literally, 'spaces between') of 'before' and 'after'—all implicitly metaphors which depend upon a mental picture of time as a linear continuum" (2005, 13). Modern time, in short, was primarily grasped through the mediation of *geometric space*; in particular, modern time was visualized as a kind of *line* traced through space. For Rosenberg and Grafton, the art of visualizing temporal chronologies benefited centrally from the "ubiquity, flexibility, and force" of the graphic line (Rosenberg and Grafton 2010, 13). That is, the continuous line could be rendered in multiple ways—as straight, curved, simple, embellished, furrowed, branched, circular, and so on. The mechanical clock, for example—invented in the Middle Ages, but heralded by Lewis Mumford as the "key-machine of the *modern* industrial age"—deploys hour and minute "hands" that track time in space as a *circle* (Mumford 1934, 14; emphasis added). Arguably, this latent spatial metaphor, the equidistantly intercalated circle, persists in digital clocks, even in the absence of an overtly visualized tracking mechanism.

The Newtonian visualization of time as an abstract sequence of points on a line had implications for the way historical chronology came to be understood. Four decades after Newton's death, in 1765, the English scientist Joseph Priestley published a *Chart of Biography* (Rosenberg and Grafton 2010, 18). The chart deployed a simple linear graph: a measured timeline marking an equidistantly arranged sequence of dates on a horizontal axis, and the length of a (famous) person's life marked by horizontal lines of varying length. Rosenberg and Grafton argue that, although the visual vocabulary of the map drew on centuries of conceptual experimentation, Priestley's chart, shown in Figure 10.1, proved to be a watershed moment, displacing competing structures for visualizing chronology. The reason for its success lay not only in its intuitive visualization, the historians argue, but in its effective alignment with a display of scientific progress, thereby underwriting ideologies of industrialization and colonial expansion. The mechanisms of representation, associated with scientific laws of motion, were thus leveraged to chart the actual flow of time (as opposed to the many variations of either sacred time or subjective time), as well as real events (as opposed to the miscellany of haphazardly chronicled incidents). On the one hand, then, the abstract mediation of time by visualized scientific laws secured an optics at once complex and precise. It also reinforced an impression of history as neutral, immediate, and realistic. On the other hand, however, this mechanism for representing time, in turn, shaped the way European Empire conceived of historical, no less than evolutionary, time itself.

Armed with new technologies for tracking time, the history of the world was projected as uniform, directional, and irreversible. During the nineteenth century, new imaging technologies, for example, the chronophotographic devices of Étienne-Jules Marey, and methodological techniques, for example, the tree ring analyses of Andrew Ellicott Douglas, amplified the scope and authority of visualizing temporal phenomena on both microscopic and macroscopic timescales. The precision of these technical devices underscored the notion that history could be graphed and represented as a sequence of objective facts. Of course, to register as a historical subject or object within

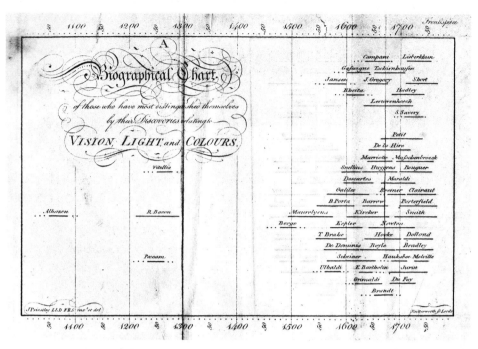

FIGURE 10.1 A small chart from Joseph Priestley's "A Chart of Biography" (1765). The chart appeared in Priestley's *The History and Present State of Discoveries Relating to Vision, Light, and Colours* (1772).

Image taken from Rosenberg and Grafton (2010, 18).

forward-directed templates of time required more than a mere chronological framework for notating significant occurrences. As Hayden White has forcefully argued, every calendar, almanac, graph, chart, chronicle, list, or table entailed a dimension of selection, organization, and hierarchy to make events count within the order of historical meaning (White 1987). Modern chronologies of historical time, while giving the appearance of disinterested, incrementally ordered, geometric spaces, were no different; they excluded phenomena as much as they included them, practically by definition.

Within the standardized graphics of a future-oriented chronology, the objects and subjects of colonial conquest, for example, were increasingly cast in a chronological vacuum, lacking graphic representation, as if to fall outside of historical time itself. This phenomenon was widely diagnosed and studied in the field of postcolonial studies that emerged in the late twentieth century.[4] For instance, in an influential book on how the contemporary discipline of anthropology crafts its research object, Johannes Fabian (1983) demonstrated how the non-Western Other is cast as either less evolved in the deep time of evolution ("primitive," "savage," and so on), or as stable and unchanging ("static," or "cold" cultures, in Claude Lévi-Strauss's terms). The distinction between the dynamic (or modern) time of the ethnographer and the unchanging (or premodern) time of the native interlocutor constituted a projection of temporal difference, or a "denial of coevalness," that conditioned anthropological knowledge in the industrialized world. Visually represented as indifferent chronological sequences (to be passively annotated by historical events), European cartographies of absolute time in fact possessed a structure, an order of discipline, and a set of interpretive axioms that were vested in, and practically oriented toward, a period of military and economic dominance. Indeed, the ability to manage and measure time was critical for the overall coordination required for the nineteenth-century colonization of Asia and Africa.

Fabian attributes the consolidation of absolute time in the Renaissance era to the rediscovery of Classical mathematical scientific treatises, the encounter with diverse populations in the discoveries of colonial conquest, and the technological improvements in oceanic navigation. More strikingly, he also argues that this modern secular projection of time was always already permeated by textures of premodern sacred histories of time. Indeed, the secularization of progressivist time was conceptually allied with the salvational logic of a religious worldview: the promise of redemption in the afterlife; the telos of lying-in-wait. The sacred time of salvation thereby underwent a process of generalization and universalization in the age of colonial expansion. The value of religious striving was sublimated into the secular pursuit of knowledge and improvement. This helps explain how tropes of scientific progress and missionary salvation were frequently allied in the British colonies of the nineteenth century, thereby striking a distinction between the universal forces of permanent progress and the transitory fate of both fragmented colonial territories and past political empires. Of course, the actual emergence of a uniform calendric approach to historical time entailed a much more complicated set of debates, negotiations, struggles, and compromises between Catholics and Protestant Reformers (notably about how events of the Old and New Testaments should be represented) as well as those between astronomers, mathematicians, politicians, scientists, and revolutionaries. The rigid decimalism of the French Revolutionary Calendar, for example, apparently shorn of all traces of religious and royalist influence, indicates some of the practical difficulties involved in overcoming sacred lineages, which themselves partook of both mythic *and* systematic thought. The calendar was abandoned in 1805, having been in use for only twelve years.

Not surprisingly, Benedict Anderson's (2006) diagnosis of modern temporalities is an inversion of the terms of Fabian. Anderson argues that the great sacral culture of pre-revolutionary times (reflecting the Latin hegemony of cosmic orders) gave way to an empty, sequentially ordered homogeneous time in the era of modern nations. New media forms, such as the newspaper, gathered disconnected events under the rubric of calendric coincidence, paradoxically producing perspectivism, fragmentation, and juxtaposition of multiple temporalities. Although Anderson acknowledges the post-revolutionary substitution of religious for secular destiny within various nation-states, the idea that Western modernity is an ideology of linear progress is monolithic and simplified. Even at a minimally conceptual level, the future-directed projection of biblical time (from Creation to Apocalypse) onto nationally imagined secular destiny was simultaneously interwoven with, and encircled by, repeating units of modern time.

Just as the clock subtended a twelve-point circumference, modern historical time was wrapped cyclically around a 365-day solar year. The time of modernity was a temporality simultaneously conceived as directional *and* circular.

Let us recall that the time of music—particularly as it was adumbrated by nineteenth- and twentieth-century philosophies of music—was understood to stand in a critical relation to the relentless, sequential abstraction of modern time. However, as this short historical sweep across the terrain of absolute time actually suggests, there are at least two complicating factors in any assessment of the value of this musicalized critique. First, absolute time was genealogically ensnared in a complex set of premodern temporal systems, not always evident in the critical resistance to it. Second, the critique of absolute time itself frequently recapitulated, instead of resisted, some of the central organizing principles of modern time, properly understood as partaking of both linearity and cyclicity.

From Cyclic Time
to Polychronic Assemblages

By the end of the twentieth century, two overarching temporal frameworks— unilinear developmentalism and cultural relativism—emerged as the symptomatic global antinomies of this cartographic projection of measured time. Although they were marked by the colonial legacy, and leveraged for colonial governance, these frameworks were noteworthy for their capacious stability within the *post* colonial period. Their methodological orientations were projected onto all manner of historical and geographical phenomena, frequently buttressed in the form of institutions. In other words, the dual inflection of time in a global sense was sublimated into the basic structure of natural and cultural phenomena in all their diverse particularity. A few rudimentary examples from the contemporary study of music will need to suffice. First, consider the basic periodization practices of Western music. In standardized popular histories of music, for instance, the music of Romanticism, commonly described as dynamic and generative, characterized by development and transformation, was distinguished from the music of the Classical period, commonly characterized, in contrast, by formal architectures of balance and repose. The point is not only that historical periodization involved an aspect of chronographic linearity, but that the idea of modern progressivism was simultaneously inscribed into the inner workings of musical production itself. Against the forward-directed temporalities of Beethoven's thematic developments, for example, the themes of Mozart's music registered as stable and topheavy. These popular temporal characterizations, pitting temporal *being* against that of *becoming*, inflected the way serious studies marked divisions between premodern and modern musical epochs as well. For example, in a detailed study of the music of Bach and Mozart, Karol Berger (2007) distinguished between the "cycles" found in the music of the premodern Christian (Baroque) composer and the "arrows" of the modern post-Christian (Classical) one. In this case, of course, the temporal conceptions of Mozart's music projected an orientation toward the future (against a cyclic music that simply unfolded "in time"), but this difference served to revise a commonplace dating scheme rather than to upend the symptomatic developmentalist chronologies that enframed musicological discourse itself.[5] In contrast, a period discussion of the role of time in history itself—situating the technics of chronology-making *as* the object of study—would reveal that the idea of successive events simply occurring sequentially (or "in time") was as modern as (if not more modern than) the idea that the past flowed toward the future.

The second temporal framework to emerge within the modern antinomies of time upheld the idea that global cultural patterns were neither uniform nor universal, and could therefore be compartmentalized, and then relativized, according to localized expressive communities. Originating in the anthropological methods of Franz Boas (2014) and Ruth Benedict (1948), this temporal paradigm had, by the mid-twentieth century, risen to prominence in the American discipline of ethnomusicology. Music should be understood as a cultural practice, the argument went, embedded in distinct contexts of belief, meaning, and value. In the 1960s, a new methodological distinction between insider and outsider temporalities was variously expressed and reframed—from what the anthropologist Paul Bohannan dubbed "folk organization" as opposed to "analytic organization" to Marvin Harris's paradoxically more *analytic*-sounding "emic-etic" dichotomy (Bohannan 1963, Harris 1968). This disciplinary effort to understand culture on its own terms frequently entailed a critique of time as understood from a "Western point of view" (Merriam 1982, 447).

Anthropologists of music routinely weighed in on the debate before proceeding to explain, describe, analyze, or thickly describe various differentiated musical contexts. In his work on time-reckoning among the African Nuer, for example, E. E. Evans-Pritchard put it thus: "European time is a continuum. Whatever point we start at, each succeeding generation increases the distance from that point. Our grandfathers were nearer to 1066 than our fathers and our father were nearer to 1066 than we are" (Evans-Pritchard 1939, 212). Evans-Pritchard here outlined the linear and spatial dimensions of modern time-reckoning—marked by points, succession, and distances—which he vividly contrasts with the Nuer who "have no concept of time" (208). For Evans-Pritchard, the Nuer did not coordinate activities within an abstract passage of time: "There are no autonomous points of reference to which activities have to conform with precision" (208). The technological externalization of an abstract passage of time to which events conformed with precision was simply anathema to the Nuer. This relativist insight was frequently generalized two decades later to include most cultures of the world. For example: "Most primitive peoples," wrote Edmund Leach, "can have no feeling that the stars in their courses provide a fixed chronometer by which to measure all the affairs of life" (1961, 133). Paul Bohannan appealed to an argument grounded in technological determinism to amplify the contrast between Western and non-Western time: "We in Western Europe have elicited an idea, or a medium, which we call 'time'—or better 'chronology'—and have calibrated it into a standard gauge against which we associate events or a series of events. The presence of such a time-gauge . . . means that we . . . measure time . . . with the aid of special devices [such as 'metronomes' and 'clocks']" (Bohannan 1963, 125, 262). In contrast to the abstract chronologies of the West, in non-Western time, argued Leach, "there is no sense of going on and on in the same direction, or round and round the same wheel. On the contrary, time is experienced as something discontinuous, a repetition of a repeated reversal, a sequence of oscillations between polar opposites: night and day, winter and summer, drought and flood, age and youth, life and death" (Leach 1961, 126, 133). As any short survey of this sort will attest, modern technocratic time—construed within the relativist paradigm—was the reified antithesis of non-modern temporality, largely construed as organized around recurring natural phenomena, cyclic embodiments, and social activities.

It is a noteworthy fact that the great diversity of temporalities projected by relativist thought upon cultures of the world turned out to be strikingly uniform, persistent, and widespread. Broadly speaking, in contrast to the teleological progressivism of Euro-American time, a timeless—mostly "cyclical"—conception of time was routinely used to describe non-Western temporal concepts in general—capaciously inclusive of Balinese sonic culture, aboriginal Australian spiritual life, traditional Japanese thought, Indian philosophical time, African past time, and so on.[6] For example, for MacGaffey, the African BaKongo people were said to have a "concept of time as spiral in nature," which permitted recurrence without repetition: "BaKongo . . . do not think of history as a record of linear progress in the accumulation of material and moral goods, and indeed do not appear to think historically at all" (MacGaffey 1972, 60). This particular conception of African time reflected a relatively uniform construal in the anthropological literature of the twentieth century. Addressing the issue of African temporality in general, Merriam wrote: "Time-reckoning is thought to be nonlinear . . . it can be reversed, discontinuous, a 'sliding scale,' circular, or spiral. Time-reckoning is carried on in terms of referral to natural phenomena, or particularly, social activity. Time is not reckoned as distance, it is not epochal, and it is not measured with special apparatus" (Merriam 1982, 456). Against the geometrically measured, historical, developmental, and technocratic time of the West, we find in Africa the prevalence of organic, social, embodied, holistic, and natural modes of time-reckoning.

Aside from their curious homogeneities, the relativized temporal patterns projected onto the non-West also frequently freighted a developmental logic into their findings. Strictly speaking, relativism served as a foil to the colonial evolutionism of Western temporality—ostensibly marking on a large scale the mere calendric coincidence of modern cultural diversity—but, like the figure of Baroque music as premodern cycle, we find the world's temporality itself premodernized by metaphors of cycle, spiral, and timelessness. In other words, against the demands of its own logic, the institutionalized production of cultural difference was itself inflected by developmental time. Of course, the richly contextual methods of ethnomusicology rejected the comparative thrust of developmental time, but its ecumenical relativism—marked by an insistence on field-work, a foregrounding of native voices, and so on—actually recapitulated the logic of a separate-but-equal set of cultural differences.[7] This logic of cultural difference ex-tended beyond ethnography. The influential media theorist Marshall McLuhan, for example, routinely deployed the perceived temporalities of a generalized non-West to issue dire warnings about technological developments in the late twentieth century. Writing against a "Western civilization" that had become mesmerized by a false "pic-ture of a universe as a limited container," McLuhan drew on the imagined historical Other—"the caveman, the mountain Greek, the Indian hunter (indeed . . . the latter day Manchu Chinese)"—to describe a world that was "multicentered and reverberating . . . like being inside a sphere" (McLuhan 2004, 68). For McLuhan, the perspectival linearity of Western thought canceled entire sensory modalities; in particular, those asso-ciated with the listening ear. As if to conjure once more the high spirits of speech in the age of Plato, McLuhan wrote: "Acoustic space is a dwelling place for anyone who has not been conquered by the one-at-a-time, uniform ethos of the alphabet" (68). The af-finity here between McLuhan's argument with the traditional European philosophical critique of geometrically projected time—Bergson's divisible time, Deleuze's striated time, and so on—is striking. Once again, we find the resonant, spherical, immersive, and omnidirectional temporalities of musical and sonorous time leveraged against the "infinite, divisible, extensible, and featureless" spatial temporalities of the West (69). The difference is that in McLuhan's more ethnographically inflected relativist account, we find the recruitment of entire continents of non-Western thought to mount a cri-tique of Western oculocentrism: "Acoustic space . . . is the natural space of nature-in-the-raw inhabited by non-literate people" (71). "It exists in the Third World and vast areas of the Middle East, Russia, and the South Pacific . . . India" (69). This kind of homogenized cultural relativism, blending sensory embodiments with distinct cultural epistemologies, became normative for anthropologically oriented knowledge produc-tion in the twentieth century. Furthermore, without spelling out the deep continuities within this tradition, it is clear that sensuous ethnographies of this sort show no signs of abating in the twenty-first century. In other words, a sonorously attuned non-West be-came a placeholder for the holistic organic time that was meant to challenge the linear, uniform, and homogeneous temporalities of the West. While critical in aspiration, the production of homogenized relativisms also constituted the terms of a fundamentally colonial dialectic.

The relativist disavowal of colonial intervention—creating disinterest in the disjunctures of conquest by producing a concomitant fascination with apparently in-tact parallel cultural universes—became the object of anthropological scrutiny in the first decades of the twenty-first century. One attempt to resist the production of ho-mogeneous non-Western temporalities, marked by key terms like nonlinearity, os-cillation, circularity, repetition, discontinuity, reversibility, and so on, emerged with the idea that uniform temporalities were in themselves a kind of myth. In their wake, we find the methodological emergence of multiple temporalities as well as temporal multiplicities—themselves crosshatched with heterogeneity—which traverse numerous scales and enact differential curves of change. The concern for multiple temporal relations and their transformations, already mentioned in the work of Deleuze and Guattari as well as Delanda and Latour, became normative for twenty-first-century anthropological writing. Addressing the "heterochrony of modern time," for example, Laura Baer describes the work of anthropology as an endeavor to bring "incommensurable rhythms and [temporal] representations into synchronicity" (Baer 2014, 18, 20). A new academic language of alternate modernities—Brian Larkin's "pirate modernity" in Nigeria, for example—came to represent a method that was ostensibly imbricated in a plurality of timescales, and thereby set adrift from the dominant colonial chronographics of a bygone industrial era (Larkin 2008). As mentioned above, in its more comprehensive form, these heterogeneous, and partially open, systems get entangled in temporalizations wrought by both human and nonhuman agents and entities.

The turn away from the unifying imperatives of conventional scientific, political, and historical timelines became a hallmark of twenty-first-century approaches to the anthropological study of culture. In "Making Time: Temporality, History, and the Cultural Object," for example, Georgina Born adumbrated the multiple ways that music "temporalizes" history (Born 2015, 371). The first of these temporalities refers back to the idea that music shapes time, or "enlivens musico-social experience and 'entrains' musical attention" (372). This modality of time largely engages the disciplines of music theory and music perception, which in turn ordinarily engage aspects of rhythm and meter, phrasing, and form. Born shows how the academic critique of the "visual and spatial biases of the score-based analyses of time on which these fields had been built"— exemplified in the work of Judith Lochhead (2015), David Lewin (2007), Christopher Hasty (1997), and Jonathan Kramer (1988)—produced new categories for thinking time in music. Kramer's notions of directional linear time, nondirectional linear time, moment time, vertical time, and multiple time, for example, indicated a new time-consciousness that recognized, even at the "first order of intramusical temporality," an inherent multiplicity (Born 2015, 372). For Born, a second order of temporality involves the "dynamics of retention and protention proffered by the musical object as its own past and future (or virtuality)" (372). As with a generation of new theorists concerned with nonhuman agents (mentioned above), Born is particularly interested in the "radically object-centered, post-humanist perspective" that is animated in this temporal conjuncture of music's genre-formation (373). Born describes two further temporalities—a third order, which concerns the "metarhythms of repetition and difference, inertia or change" of genres themselves (construed as "objects distributed in time"), and a fourth order, which engages the matter of human temporal ontologies themselves (373–374). Born argues that this layering of temporal orders is productive, first, because it spotlights "the multiple ways music produces time," and second, because it resists "teleological accounts of music history and musical change, in particular by holding temporal ontology (fourth) up against the temporality of genre (third)" (375).

One problem with this catholic construal of music's temporality is its ease of use in academic parlance. As a general condition for *all* cultural objects, the emphasis on limitless plateaus of time risks losing specific diagnostic capacities. It is instructive therefore to turn to the actual examples provided by scholarly schemas such as this. Born's first example is the Kenyan musical genre known as *kapuka*, which she systematically engages in relation to her four temporal orders. In terms of the first temporality, the music is said to produce a "kind of intramusical time, a vernacular rhythmic field" through blending music from the Congo and Jamaica (376). At the second level, Born includes further elements of style, such as hip-hop and the Nairobi "River Road" sound, which are labelled "retentions," as well as aspirations for forging "affective alliances" among Kenyan youth audiences, which are labelled "protentions" (376). In terms of the third and fourth temporalities, Born amasses evidence for various political, social, technological, and aesthetic transformations—including media liberalization in the late stages of Daniel arap Moi's regime, the emergence of cosmopolitan radio programming, and the influx of digital technologies—to describe the peculiar temporal remixes constituting *kapuka*. She writes: "It is the synergies between these and other trajectories of change, each with distinctive temporalities and pluri-temporalities, that catalysed the Nairobi music scene for genres like *kapuka* that protended, and effected, at once music-and-social-historical change" (377). At first glance, this kind of temporally inflected description of *kapuka* seems unassailable. But there is more here than meets the eye. Born's *kapuka* at once emerges as a constellation shot through with a dizzying array of temporal vectors, that simultaneously—like a subterranean red thread of the narrative—culminates in a productive music effecting social and historical *change*. The multiplication of *temporalities* and *pluri-temporalities*, in other words, are ultimately identified in this text with the liberalization of politics from authoritarian strains.

There are two points to be made here about both this omnitemporalized construal of music and its attendant politics. First, what do we make of the music itself? While Born does not offer a specific example, we can use the genre-defining song "Kapuka" by the hip-hop duo K-South as an analytic reference. The members of K-South were "Bamboo" (Tim Kimani) and "Doobeez" (Jerry Manzekele). The name of the group was an abbreviation of the Nairobi suburb of Kariobangi South; and the title of the song was a derogatory term for overly commercial artists. The song, which circulated widely in Nairobi, appeared on their 2004 album *Nairobizm*, one year before the group disbanded.

Although it is inflected by local Kenyan voices, the song's overarching referent is American hip-hop. Anchored in samples from *Super Mario Bros*, a video game developed and published by the Japanese multinational consumer electronics company Nintendo Entertainment in the mid-1980s, the song's vocal inflections oscillate smoothly between rapping in Swahili and English. Aside from the rhythmic profile of the synth bass and a short hemiola-like interlude (when the rappers repeat the syllables "kapu" in a kind of insistent ternary time), there is little in the song that can plausibly be shown to derive from African practices. In other words, the sonic referents of the song—from the timbre of the actual voices and the particular techno-terroir of its sampling practices to the recurring 3+3+2 rhythm of the clap-track and the rhythm of its rhyming—are recognizably, and self-consciously, American.

While there is no faulting these aesthetics in themselves, they need to be situated in the overarching context of the post-Cold War period. To multiply the temporal vectors attendant to its production and reception; and then, in a complicated rhetorical move, to associate such temporalizing with productive political futures is to disavow the imperatives of global political economy. In other words, the recognition that music is a time-sequenced phenomenon—multiply implicated in temporalities at various scales, and so on—activates a determined disinterest in the emergent sound of global cosmopolitanism in its hegemonic form. It is in this sense that the hyper-postmodernist refusal of uniform temporalities—the impassioned rejection of teleological time, for example—is a disavowal of the highly coordinated rhythmic ordering of multinational industrial production in an international frame. The critical assault on relativism in the generalized turn toward temporal disjuncture and difference resulted not in its supersession, but in its revision. Otherwise put, the polychromic assemblages that emerged at the turn of the twenty-first century were the ideological refinement of the temporalized relativism of the colonial mid-century.

To return, then, to the opening epigraph of this section: "How do we read the relationship between metropole and colony as conjunctive when our ideological desire is the inscription of their uneven temporality and their inherent heterologies?" (Gikandi 1996, 7). To this we may add a second, specifically musical, question: How do we methodologically constitute non-Western music in such a way that it weighs upon the content of what goes as hegemony when our ideological desire is to disavow its specific capacities in the form of multiply fractured temporalities of a heterogeneous non-West?

LEGACIES OF MUSICAL NEWTONIANISM

The methodological turn toward differentiating the world's systems of time-reckoning into discrete pluralities produced certain noteworthy effects for music analysis. First, the interesting assumption that historical, cosmological, lived, and natural times were somehow recapitulated in the temporalities of actual music-making produced a prohibition on the deployment of certain methodological terms for non-Western music. For example, Merriam's assemblage of ethnographies of African music—which argued that the general concept of time in Africa was fundamentally different to that of the West—cast doubt on two "assumptions" about musical time found in analyses of African music: the projection of an "equal pulse base" and a "linear concept of time" (Merriam 1982, 444). On the one hand, his account moved seamlessly between temporal scales, collating a variety of quotidian experiences of time with musical time, as if no act of translation were required between them. This was the antithesis of the European philosophical approach to musical time, which—along with certain prominent strains of music theory—regarded music as uniquely shaping its own time. On the other hand, Merriam's account produced a radical disjuncture between the experiences of musical time on either side of the Mediterranean, as if no act of translation were even possible. As a result, Merriam recoiled from any notion of African music that either calibrated time in standardized basic units, thereby rejecting outright the concomitant "assumption of meter" for all African music, or construed its temporal flow in directional terms, as a "linear system" (457, 448). Merriam therefore systematically debunked a range of ethnographic work that somehow detected a steady time pulse in African music—variously described as an "underlying pulse" (Blacking 1970, 5, 9), "metronome sense" (Waterman 1952, 211), "regulative beat" (Nketia 1963, 64), "regular beat" (Ward 1927, 217), "elementary pulse" (Kubik 1972, 33), and "fastest pulse" (Koetting 1970, 125), among many others (Merriam 1982, 449–450).

To stave off the grids and lines of Western thought, the anthropologist went to great lengths to unearth empirical irregularities of pulse in African music. He recruited Robert Garfias's electronic analysis of a Hukwe (San) bow song which indicated "many minute differences in spacing between . . . bow strokes" (1964, 240), as well as Kubik's observations about Ugandan xylophone music about the "slight rhythmic unevenness on the part of musicians . . . between strokes" (Garfias 1972, 33), before criticizing Garfias and Kubik for assuming a steady pulse in these repertoires (Merriam 1982, 450–451). While resting on scant evidence in Merriam's text, the general interest in demonstrating a special endowment for micro-timing in the musical practices of Africa (and African America)—sublimated in popular concepts like swing, groove, or simply the idea of "amping up the moving beat"—show no signs of abating today (Przybylek 2016). Rainer Polak's recent studies in such phenomena, or what he calls the "patterned non-isochrony of rhythmic feels," in West African drum ensembles were continuous with this methodological turn, but they did not recapitulate the desire to remove all metric considerations from African musical thought (Polak 2010). For Polak, in contrast, different metric schema were even reinforced, or "synchronized to operate in parallel," within these musical systems. Polak furthermore stressed that the precision of beat-production in the live context of African drum ensembles easily eclipsed that of the average European professional orchestra, a point echoed by Kofi Agawu in his critique of ethnographic prohibitions on thinking African temporalities as either unit-based or linear (Polak 2016). Agawu rhetorically asks, "what is one to make of the contrast between an ostensibly casual African sense of time—dictated by sun and shadows ('African time,' which euphemistically denotes perpetual lateness)—and the amazing precision in timing that one finds, say, in xylophone ensemble performances?" (Agawu 2016, 158). Agawu hereby connected Merriam's projected organic temporalities, such as the idea that the "smallest period in African time-reckoning is the division of the day," with a false topos of non-modern tardiness and idleness, and precisely deployed music's unique temporality to challenge the topos (2016, 158). It is no small coincidence that Agawu recruited the very xylophone music that Merriam deployed to debunk isochronous beats in the context of African music to *secure* their high functioning in this context.

We find in Agawu's text, then, a deconstruction of an entire catalogue of ideas advanced by hyper-relativist ethnography of the mid-century. First, he resisted the very homology between the social organization of time and musical time-reckoning, arguing that no musical insight can emerge from such reflections. Second, he rejected the idea that African music was somehow primarily "circular (or spiral)"—as opposed to "linear or goal-oriented"—and that it was not conceived within equidistant units of time, attuned instead to natural temporalities of social life (158). The idea that cyclic temporality can be inflected with linearity, or vice versa, was increasingly given analytic voice as music theory expanded its field of global referents. Michael Tenzer, for example, advanced the concept of "discursive cyclicity," which "suggests a transformative temporality anchored by a permanent cycle" (Tenzer 2010). Agawu's position was aligned with the idea that music's temporality should best be regarded as a dialectic of synchronous and diachronous elements. In Agawu's words, "while there is indeed a circular or cyclical element in dance drumming, there is at the same time a strongly linear or goal-oriented element as well" (Agawu 2016, 158). Tellingly, Agawu's position was also more aligned with the actual account of African time given by Gerhard Kubik, who studied and notated the African xylophone music in question, than with the use to which Kubik had been put in Merriam's account. Kubik acknowledged that from the strict vantage point of ethnography there was indeed no "time" concept in various African cultures, but he argued that this fact alone did not undercut the idea that musicians conceived a "regular series of pulses" as a guiding framework for their performances (Kubik 1972, 451).

Instead of invoking cultural cosmologies of time to explain a musical system, Agawu drew attention to the movements of accompanying dances to explain a basic metric structure for African music. "For cultural insiders," he wrote a decade earlier, "identifying the gross pulse or the 'pieds de danse' ('dance feet') occurs instinctively and spontaneously. Those not familiar with the choreographic supplement, however, sometimes have trouble locating the main beats and expressing them in movement" (Agawu 2003, 73). Asserting the primacy of this choreographic supplement, Agawu demonstrated unambiguously metric schemes in seemingly ambiguous metric environments. In other words, patterns that appeared as polymetric to various theorists of African music—Jones, Nketia, Arom, Locke, and others—were in fact simply metric, in Agawu's view. To grasp this fundamental point, the ethnographer had only to direct attention to the movement of the dancers' feet. For example, the so-called "standard" pattern, often associated with bell patterns in various Ewe dances—*Agbadza, Agbekor,* and *Adzida*—is strikingly adept at maximally facilitating what theorists call "grouping dissonance," or what I would simply term metric modulation. The pattern elaborates a kind of "diatonic" temporality—⟨0, 2, 4, 5, 7, 9, e⟩—depicted with accents above a simple modulo 12-time span (with time points from 0 to e), in Figure 10.2. In other

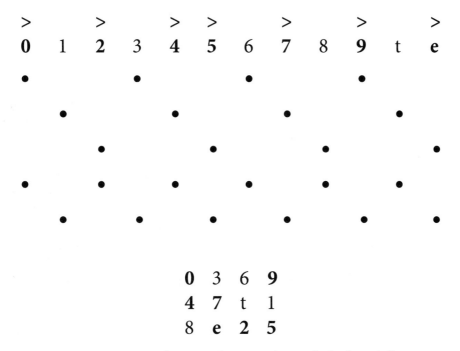

FIGURE 10.2 A representation of metric ambiguity in the standard African bell pattern. Basic forms of ternary and binary meter are indicated by dots below the 12-point time span. These can be rotated to begin at any point within the time span.

words, ternary meter (or "compound time") can be expressed with equal cogency if it were projected from any of the twelve time-points of the pattern. This characteristic is illustrated by differently distributed dots below the numbers in Figure 10.2. Three basic forms of ternary meter are indicated by dots below the 12-point time span—the first begins on t0, the second on t1, and the third on t2. These can be rotated to begin at any point within the time span. The same is true for binary meter (or "simple time"). The two basic forms of binary meter are indicated by dots below the three basic forms of ternary time, beginning on t0 and t1, respectively. Again, these can be rotated to begin at any point within the time span; they can also be subdivided into units of four beats, and then analogously rotated. Below the dots, this property is summed up in a matrix with bold numbers marking coincidences and numbers in plain text marking non-coincidences.[8]

    Patterns such as this have been much discussed in the recent literature on African music. Simha Arom, for instance, detects within it an asymmetrical segmentation of ⟨5 + 7⟩. For Arom, the "resulting rhythmic combinations are remarkable for both their complexity and their subtlety. They follow a rule which may be expressed as 'half–1/half+1' " (Arom 2004, 246). Following Arom's analysis, one might say, asymmetries of this sort may be the sonic outcome of nesting various binary and ternary temporalities, which in turn, inflect its field of metric entrainments. David Locke's concept of the "metric matrix" is similarly oriented toward differentially oriented metric possibilities (Locke 2010). In his discussion of an Ewe instrumental ensemble repertoire of *Yewevu*, for example, Locke includes the surrounding ensemble in his discussion of this phenomenon: "Within a cyclic multipart texture played by an ensemble of drums, bells, rattles and hand claps, structured patterns of accentuation are exchanged among instruments. Rhythmic design can be discussed with precision using what is termed 'the metric matrix,' that is, a set of beats of different duration and location within a fixed time span" (Locke 2010). Locke's analysis puts Polak's investigation of micro-timing in African drum ensembles in relief. In Locke's analysis, the music's unique groove emerges as a phenomenal fallout of a transformational situation—the shifting accentuation patterns within the matrix—rather than as a reflection of inherently non-isochronous African musical pulses. Shifting perceptions of temporal order are wrought on the basis of rhythmic design—"a specific feeling of musical groove will activate when sounded accents coincide with a flow of tacit beats in the metric matrix" (Locke 2010).

Against the idea that patterns such as this are metrically complex—variously described as "rhythmic oddity" (Arom 2004, 246), "maximal metric ambiguity" (Scherzinger 2010), or "simultaneous multidimensionality" (Locke 2010)—Agawu nonetheless claimed an unambiguous four beats (in 12/8) for this kind of pattern. Attentive to the dangers of exoticizing alternate temporalities for African music (as found in Merriam and others), Agawu posited a kind of regulative background (rejected by Merriam and others) to affirm an unambiguous metric grid. It is worth pointing out that the temporal complexity described above (by Locke, Arom, and Scherzinger) is grounded neither in homologies with natural or cosmological time nor in the aprioristic rejection of the seemingly Western "equal pulse base" and "linear concept of time" (Merriam 1982, 444). On the contrary, the former may even count as a condition for the possibility of the latter in these musical ensembles. What is striking, however, is that Agawu's analysis is in fact stridently beholden to axioms found in theories of rhythm and meter that vividly dichotomize their internal temporal tendencies. Within this paradigm, rhythm is regarded as a sequence of musical durations while meter is the abstract grid of equidistant beats—inscribed with an independent set of hierarchies—that encases rhythm. While beats are said to be inferred from sounding rhythmic phenomena, they are themselves regarded as durationless instants—like "geometrical points rather than . . . the lines drawn between them," in Christopher Hasty's skeptical words (1997, 19). Two proponents of this theory, for example, claimed that "even though the two structures [meter and rhythmic grouping] obviously interact, neither is intrinsically implicated in the other; that is to say they are formally (and visually) separate" (Lerdahl and Jackendoff 1983, 26). In support of this construal of music's bifurcated temporalities, Agawu insisted on a "non-alignment between grouping and metrical structure" in African music as well. Held in the conceptual grip of a generative theory of tonal music—its attendant rules for metric preference in particular—Agawu envisaged metric designs for Africa. This rubric for musical time led Agawu to jettison the very idea of "polymeter" as a Western "invention" (Agawu 2003, 78, 84–86).

This kind of impasse raises the question whether concepts such as polymeter—or, say, Locke's more nuanced concept of metric matrix—ought to be abandoned, or perhaps revised, or whether, instead, this particular rubric for organizing musical time itself ought to be revised. After all, the twofold modern construal of musical time was hardly a scientific fait accompli, but rather itself a formulation of limited historical scope and geographical reach. In other words, the theoretical investment in meter construed as a sequence of isochronous beats with a specific cardinality (number of beats in a measure)—in turn hierarchized both internally and at higher levels of organization—reflected an abbreviated mode of engaging and experiencing music that was of extremely recent vintage. In the late twentieth century, these theories ranged from commonsensical pragmatics—simply framing musical timespans in relation to equal divisions of a fixed number of hierarchized pulses—to complex accounts of cognitivism—framing the division of listeners' actual perceptual capacities (by bootlegging cognitive archetypes to hierarchized metric preference rules, for example).[9] Roger Grant has demonstrated how modern conceptions of meter actually fragmented earlier understandings of meter, which were generally more imbricated in multidimensional facets of embodied motion, note duration, character, and tempo. Arguing that "theorists in the eighteenth century shifted the focus of their explanations for the physical act of the beat to the properties of the measure," Grant demonstrates how this development was part of an "elaborate taxonomic project" that sought to standardize the great variety of measurement systems of Western Europe (Grant 2014, 10).

Key technological artifacts for keeping time in music emerged throughout this period, but they did not strictly drive this reconceptualization of time. In other words, because of their archetypal and epistemological composition, physical technologies for measuring time—such as Dietrich Nikolaus Winkel's musical chronometer of 1814 or Johann Nepomuk Maelzel's newly patented metronome of 1816—embodied existing modes of action and thought, which they then came to guide and augment. Indeed, even references to the moving hand of the clock as an analogy for musical notation, for example, occurred intermittently throughout the sixteenth and seventeenth centuries. Instead of construing mechanical devices as themselves agents for rethinking musical time, Grant too contextualizes the modern re-theorizing of musical meter in relation to the broad contemporary reception of Newton. Against Descartes's "plenist" ideas of time, Newton's theory of time—grounded in force and geometry—proffered an abstract measure for locating events (Grant 2014, 98). In his *Principia* of 1687, for example, Newton wrote: "Absolute time and mathematical time, of itself, and from its own nature, flows equably without relation to anything external . . . relative, apparent and common time . . . is some sensible and external (whether accurate or unequable) measure of duration by means of motion" (in Grant 2014, 98). Grant illustrates how Newton's formal separation of absolute time from actual external motions amounted to a "cunning reversal" of previous Scholastic terms, "in which the continuity of motion

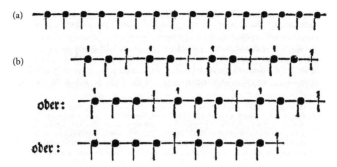

FIGURE 10.3 A fragment from Kirnberger's *Die Kunst des reinen Satzes in der Musik*, facsimile ed. (1771–1779; see Kirnberger 1968, 2: 115). The first image represents an undifferentiated sequence of durations; the second represents their division into metric groups of two, three, and four beats.

explains the continuity of time" (102). He furthermore shows how Newton's basic axioms were codified on nonscientific terrain, in particular the re-conceptualizations of musical meter in the eighteenth century by Johann Philipp Kirnberger and his circle.[10] Grant argues that Kirnberger's *Die Kunst des reinen Satzes in der Musik* marked a kind of watershed moment for imagining and imaging metric division: an undifferentiated flow of a kind of absolute time, which could be divided by accentuations grouped in two, three, and four beats, as depicted in Figure 10.3.

While ubiquitous in music-theoretical writings of the second half of the twentieth century, then, the idea that meter existed as a series of nonexpressive points on a standardized grid—curiously tethered to an autonomously operational graduated hierarchy that was ever-identical within its cardinality—was in fact a monumental historical achievement dating back no more than two hundred and fifty years. Far from crafting systems to facilitate music's ostensible capacity for fashioning alternative temporalities outside of measured time, as was imagined by a specific theoretical and philosophical tradition, then, the dominant turn in eighteenth-century music theory revised the internal division and dynamism of musical meter according to Newton's calculus. A standardized temporal divisionism became tethered to external prosthetics for timekeeping, from metronomes and charts to measures and maps, which in turn proffered feedback loops for disciplinary practices. As historians have shown, Priestley's cartographic representations—so naturalized and commonsensical today—actually marked a new consciousness of historical time in the 1760s, just as Kirnberger's metric divisions—so banal and intuitive today—marked a new consciousness of musical time, also in the 1760s. In other words, both historical time and musical time were standardized in accordance with Newton's revisionary scientific writings on the nature of absolute time. The measure of time thereby converged and expanded: all manner of chronographies swept up in the gravitational force of the Newtonian legacy.

FRAGMENTS FROM AN AFRICAN TIMELINE

I have already argued that this kind of Newtonian temporal framework dialecti-cally produced modern global antinomies of time under the rubrics of unilinear developmentalism (or progressivism), on the one hand, and cultural relativism (or mul-ticulturalism), on the other. These are seemingly disjunctive temporalities: the first (not unlike the modern concept of rhythm itself) is attuned to qualitative differences and tracks the duration of events in a linear temporality; the second (not unlike the modern concept of meter) is indifferent to qualitative differences and tracks patterns of repetition and temporal coincidence. However, as I have shown, both temporalities are conditioned by the practical demands of colonial expansion. It is therefore a consistent symptom of this universalized measure of time—whether developmentalist or relativist—that engagements with perceived non-Western temporal phenomena result in an episte-mology of radical difference. Even the finest postcolonial approaches, explicitly resisting the production of epistemological difference, bear the mark of this deep contradiction.

Let me briefly explain with reference to a specific example already introduced above. Recall that Agawu insisted that the "standard" bell pattern found in *Agbadza, Agbekor, Adzida,* and other dances fell within four main beats in 12/8. He likewise domesticated the starkly off-beat character of the signature highlife pattern into four unambiguous beats in 4/4. Recoiling from the exoticizing tendencies of unfettered relativism, Agawu correctly engaged a universal theory for time-reckoning to reach this conclusion. In particular, he invoked the work of David Temperley, who deployed Lerdahl and Jackendoff's *Generative Theory of Tonal Music,* to clarify "this basic aspect of African rhythm" (Agawu 2003, 77). Citing Temperley at length, Agawu made a point about the politics of current institutional divisions in music studies: "Ethnomusicology is concerned with the production of differences among world musical cultures, while music theorists tend to produce sameness" (2003, 174). Music-theoretical systems, therefore, were put to political work in Agawu's text, ostensibly eschewing the Newtonian antinomies of time. Agawu depicted the "generative process for the highlife *topos*" in a disarmingly simple four-step pro-cess, thereby clinching an argument about cultural sameness across geographical borders. Using the highlife example as a referent, Agawu rejected the widespread idea, articulated by A. M. Jones, that "in African music there is practically al-ways a clash of rhythms: this is the cardinal principle" (Agawu 2003, 78). Far from rehearsing this capacious idea, Agawu argued that accentual differentiations in African music were possible "only as temporary, imagined, or simulated departures from solid ground" (78). The basic outline of this generative process for the highlife pattern is depicted in Figure 10.4.

This analysis is an entirely symptomatic production of radical difference in the paradoxical quest for sameness. While Agawu rhetorically upheld the universal

Step 1: Establish 4/4 metrical cycle

Step 2: Suppress the downbeat

Step 3: Subdivide remaining beats

Step 4: Suppress the on-beats

FIGURE 10.4 Kofi Agawu's (2003, 78) representation of a "generative" process for the Nigerian highlife pattern.

cognitivist terms of Lerdahl and Jackendoff's theory, the four-step analysis actually contradicted those terms. Generative metric preference rules, for example, spelled out the cognitive apparatus that *infers* a metric structure from sonorous morphologies—which, according to the rules, largely support it. In contrast, Agawu's analysis actually *posits* a metric structure that may be identical to the (ethnographically retrieved) choreographic supplement, but does not interact at all with the sounding morphologies—which, according to the rules, largely contradict it. Agawu's interpretation of metric structure in the highlife topos or the standard pattern may be ethnographically accurate, at least in some local expressive communities, but they cannot be said to be generated by the protocols of Lerdahl and Jackendoff's preference rules. A proper application of metric preference rules would proffer a strict 4/4 meter, starting on either the eighth, or possibly the fourth, eighth-note beat in the measure. The point is that Lerdahl and Jackendoff's theoretical scheme can generate neither the desired cognitive universal (toward which its authors aspire) nor the desired political sameness (toward which Agawu aspires). Instead, a properly executed generative procedure proliferates the very polymetric ambiguity between the music's morphology and its choreographic supplement—the maligned clash of rhythms—that is the object of Agawu's strident critique. In other words, a properly executed procedure casts the colonial Other not as *primitive*, but as *different*—the inevitable symptom of a global culture that has been fractured into separate-but-equal relativism. A stridently postcolonial analysis thereby paradoxically attests to an uncanny return of the antinomies of colonial temporality.

An effort in recent music theory to return to the study of meter a kind of plenist aspect—set adrift from the sharp bifurcations of Newtonian time—does little to upend this fundamental antinomy. Exemplified in the work of Christopher Hasty (1997) and Justin London (2012), this kind of theoretical revision departed from earlier paradigms, largely challenging the strict separation of time from motion, as it had become standardized in the age of Kirnberger. London draws on the work of cognitive psychologists—notably Edward Large and Bruno Repp—at once to challenge the theoretical idealizations of musical meter and advance a fundamentally perceptual argument about it. In the more phenomenologically oriented inquiries into meter-formation, in slight contrast, we witness the encroachment of the above-discussed philosophical traditions on music-theoretical thought. Hasty, for example, draws on the work of both Bergson and Edmund Husserl, while the younger scholar

Brian Hulse (2010) draws on the work of Deleuze and Guattari. Departing from spatial representations of notated music, these theories generally direct their attention toward musical performance, perception, embodiment, and phenomenology. Hasty tellingly draws on Bergson's elastic conception of duration: "Nothing that is actual—that is, nothing becoming or having become—is without duration" (Hasty 1997, 69). Hasty reconceptualizes meter in processual, or projective, terms. In triple meter, for example, beats are not subdivided into three isochronous units, but projected in a duple manner (as depicted in Figure 10.5). He writes: "Since projection is essentially binary and requires that the two terms be immediately successive, and since projection results in equality, a projective account of triple, unequal meter is problematic" (67). As a result, Hasty regards the second and third beats of triple meter as a kind of prolongation (and "deferral") of the first beat. Deferral in triple time is therefore intensified in the context of the binary beating of time. The music theorist hereby returns to the analytic scene a kind of motional praxis for guiding metric perception that recalls premodern treatises on meter. Grant, for example, points out that in his *Musica Figuralis Deudsch* (1532), Martin Agricola defines "the beat (*tact*)" as a "motion of the hand," likewise construed as an oscillating down-up gesture (Grant 2014, 68). In short, by reaching across the Newtonian moment, Hasty brings the German construal of embodied "*Paarigkeit*," or pairedness, to bear on a contemporary interpretation of musical perception (Hasty 1997, 135). *Meter as Rhythm*—a reinscription of the tactile *tact*.[11]

This kind of phenomenological reinterpretation of theories of time does less to displace the modern concepts of rhythm and meter than to bestow upon them an aspect of plasticity, motional projection, and embodiment. By focusing not just on the metrics of absolute time but on modes of perception and production, Hasty and others cast doubt on the strictly Newton-centered theory of musical time. However, Hasty did not consider how the sensory mediation of listening and doing is itself not direct or immediate, but shaped by historical socialization and by prevailing cultures of perception. Historical change across cultures is typically uneven and nonsynchronous, enclosing multiple temporalities, and reflexively negotiated as the facts of the past emerge into view. Hasty's project paradoxically naturalizes, in the process of disturbing, certain dominant concepts for understanding musical time. This production of embodied,

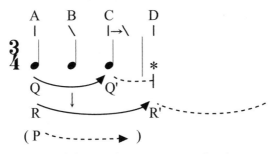

FIGURE 10.5 Christopher Hasty's (1997, 138) representation of triple meter as a case of intensified deferral.

perceptual, and motional time is the functional analogue—within an arguably *intra*-cultural dialectic—for the production of embodied, perceptual, and motional time in Africa—within an arguably *inter*-cultural dialectic. Merriam's natural cycles of time-reckoning in Africa, or the centrality of swing in Polak's representations of African music, therefore march in step with freshly revised temporalities produced by phenomenologically inflected theories of musical time. Perhaps this convergence is not too surprising given the extensive diffusion of print and electronic media throughout the world, which in turn has led to an explosion of creative engagements with under-acknowledged or under-appreciated pasts. Michael Tenzer has observed, for example, that recent studies, such as those of Hasty and London, "come to the table differently, marshaling evidence of universals of perception to theorize Western art music. The goal is finer-grained depictions of musical works and musical perceptions" (Tenzer 2011, 384n1). Are these the new universals mediating the complex and multiple temporalities that intersect within a given medium?

AFTERWORD: ON MUSICAL VENTRILOQUISM

Is not the exact *opposite* approach required today? The temporalizing impulse of contemporary continental philosophies of music (briefly sketched in the first section of this chapter), no less than their counterparts in recent music theory (briefly sketched in the last), appear to disrupt the scope and authority of the rigid and relentless orders of industrial time-reckoning. But they do not displace these orders and they cannot replace them. In Tenzer's words: "What is missing is the complement: an ambition to survey and compare, supra-culturally, species of musical temporality, and to envision relationships and connections *not* constrained by experience or culture" (Tenzer 2011, 384; emphasis in the original). Although he also valorizes "finer-grained depictions" of perception, Tenzer also astutely detects in the very emphasis on experience—perception, embodiment, and the like—the lurking grip of a false relativism (384). To this conundrum, one should add that the human sensorium, a conduit for historical and cultural memory, is but *one* mode of producing musical temporalities. In other words, modes of time-reckoning through musical media frequently defy strict perceptual articulation. Instead, an analysis genuinely attuned to the material feedback loops of actual music-making demands—in addition to perception and experience—an extended meditation on the interiority of the material objects that are leveraged to produce them. In closing, I will briefly gesture toward a simple, and preliminary, sketch for such a meditation, by considering a single rhythmic fragment, less than three seconds in length.

Consider the motional patterns deployed to render simple rhythms recorded and notated by Gerhard Kubik in the Village near Rumi in Central Malawi (then Nyasaland) in 1962, two years before independence. The rhythms notated in Figure 10.6 emerge in one particular section of the *Vimbuza* dance, performed on conical drums with single membranes made of cowhide, called *Mohambu*. The dance, practiced among the Tumbuka people, partakes of a biomedical tradition that involves possession by the *Vimbuza* spirits. Forbidden by missionaries because of its association with local resistance to colonialism, the *Vimbuza* dance intersects the natural and the supernatural world in an effort to overcome social grievances as well as physical and mental illness. Drummers produce a high ("small") and a low ("big") tone depending on how closely to the middle of the membrane they tap the drum (Kubik 1962, 38). These simple motional patterns are striking for the varied ways in which they render their respective rhythmic groupings. Noting particularly the morphology of the second pattern, *Mohambu* II, Kubik makes a distinction between the "musician's hands (motor image)" and the "pattern actually coming out (acoustic image)" (39). A short documentary produced by the Malawi National Commission for UNESCO in 2008 (*Vimbuza* Candidature Video) offers a recent glimpse into the world of the *Vimbuza* healing dance, even though the drumming of *Mohambu* II on this film no longer strictly follows the principles adumbrated by Kubik (UNESCO 2008).

Kubik notates three patterns of the *Vimbuza* dance, marking the sticking patterns of left and right hands with "l" and "r" above and below the notated rhythms of *Mohambu* I and II, respectively (see Figure 10.6). He concerns himself with the disalignment between motor and acoustic images in the music. In other words, motor images, which are clearly grasped by the performing musicians, cannot be instantly registered by the listening dancers. This principle of audiovisual disalignment is a fairly widespread African musical idea. In the *mahume* (sometimes spelled *mheme*) drumming of Wagogo women from the Dodoma region of central Tanzania (then Tanganyika), for example, the motor movements of left and right hands is different, frequently marking *tacet* pulses—"beating into the air"—along with sounding pulses, thereby demarcating embodied temporal patterns that are asynchronous with the concomitant sounding ones associated with them (Kubik 1962, 40). Feathered extensions attached to the upper arms of the women, along with exaggerated shoulder movements, further create visual illusions of temporal patterning at odds with the sounding rhythms of this ritually restricted sacred

FIGURE 10.6 Gerhard Kubik's (1962, 39) representation of sticking patterns for the rhythms of the *Vimbuza* dance. This music and dance is a healing ritual of the Tumbuka people living in the village of Thethe near Rumi in Central Malawi (then Nyasaland).

music. A recent—staged—example of Wagogo women's *"muheme"* drumming, performed by the Nyati group from Nzali village in Dodoma, Tanzania, is available online (Malago Shiro 2012). The lead drummer, along with the backing drummers, frequently beat into the air with their left hands.

A closer analysis of the details of the *Mohambu* II of the Tumbuka *Vimbuza* dance in 1962 is instructive. First, the hands alternate—effectively tapping the membrane in a simple *binary* time—as they simultaneously track back-and-forth between small and big tones—effectively tracing a simple *ternary* time. Although this is a simple two-note monophonic line, the pattern thereby nests two alternate temporalities in its motional vectors. Which of these embodied perceptions of the beat is dominant? Both the standard modern theories of meter *and* the projective analyses of meter associated with the phenomenological turn (including their sixteenth-century forebears) are of little use here. At first glance, one might argue, the way this drumming technique inflects a kind of binary *feel* into a ternary situation resonates with Hasty's embodied *Paarigkeit*. But this is not so—the inflection is produced in an entirely different manner in the African case. First, the "projection" (in Hasty's terms) of binary qualities in the context of 3/4 meter in the *Vimbuza* dance is of *un*equal duration. In other words, the projective deferral in Hasty's recent phenomenological account—no less than the lowering and raising of the hand in Agricola's premodern account—is a motional praxis that discloses binary and ternary qualities within the elastic bounds of *equal* duration, while the African case disrupts the equality of that duration. Second, the peculiar temporality of this *Vimbuza* rhythm additionally encapsulates an inverse projective capacity that the European case does not—a "projection" of ternary qualities in the context of 2/4. In other words, where triple meter was "problematic" for Hasty on account of its "essentially binary" character—no less than it was for premodern theories, where triple meter often garnered special treatment—in the African case, the pattern is wholly suspended between the projection of binary qualities in triple time and the projection of ternary qualities in duple time.

No amount of plasticity wrought by motional praxes of meter formation can quite capture this particular African inflection of musical temporality. To give a sense of this, let us speculatively cast the *Mohambu* II *Vimbuza* pattern of 1962 in terms of Agricola's *Musica Figuralis Deudsch* of 1532. What is at stake is the *separation* of conducting hands, whereby one hand is simultaneously lowered and raised in the tempo of an inverted (triple time) *"proporcien tact,"* while the other is lowered and raised *in between* the arcs of the first hand. The latter could be in the same tempo as the former, or, as is frequently found in southern African music, in the tempo of a (duple time) *"half tact."* The inflection of the musical *tact* with internal temporal tendencies, in other words, cannot reckon with the dual inflections of simultaneous interlocking tactūs; nor can a simple appeal to perception or embodiment suffice. In fact, it would not be an exaggeration to say that the more embodied accounts of metric entrainment *reinforce* the very unit of measured beats that they *flexibly* inflect. This point applies to both pre- and (ostensibly) postmodern European accounts of meter as much as it applies to ethnographic and popular accounts of non-European meter. Colloquially speaking, the feel of African music's swing, one might say, is the true topos of the neo-Newtonian legacy. Stated differently, the phenomenological resistance to absolute time is a kind of constrained resistance, or even a resistance-without-resistance—a resistance that preserves and intensifies its object of critique by paradoxically endowing its disembodied quantities with embodied qualities. The theorist of musical time is thus faced with a conundrum. Disarmed by the Scylla of constrained critical recoil from modern industrial time-reckoning (discussed here), on the one hand, and incapacitated by the Charybdis of globally proliferating temporal assemblages (discussed earlier), on the other, the disciplinary space for counter-theorization might be shrinking.

Kubik draws attention to a different aspect of the short rhythmic fragment recorded in Thethe Village in 1962, namely the sound of the drummer's total rhythmic configuration. This is a third perception—which Kubik calls the "acoustic image"—and it is heard apart from both the ternary and binary embodiments of the drummer's motional arcs. The pattern adds an additional cross-metric relation to the rhythmic line—the dotted note pitch pattern that proffers a four-beat measure in "compound time." This inherent rhythm, is-sued forth by the woven temporalities of two distinct embodied rhythms, carries the un-mistakable microtemporal inflections of a thrown voice—the swing (if swing must be the word) not of perception, but of material musical ventriloquism. The production of disembodied, but inherently salient, rhythms such as this is a central aspect of African musical practices. Inherent rhythms are particularly manifest on material instrumentaria that pre-date the ravages of colonial conquest. Their nanochronemics cannot be collapsed into the embodiments of some kind of biological knowledge, but emerge instead at the technical crossroads between the human perceptual faculty, a precise division of imper-sonal, unedited motor processes, and the interface designs attendant to music's mate-rial media. It is in the sparse conditions of this ephemeral archive that a global theory of musical temporality—genuinely dislocated from the vexing antinomies of the modern measure of time—begins. The inability to find discernible material traces need not lead to lack, but can encourage imagined connections, negotiated presences, and mediated returns. This is the musical ventriloquism, beyond refusal or redemption, that hopes to bring unexamined temporal practices to the ear.

NOTES

1. I would like to thank the editors Alexander Rehding and Steven Rings for their incredible intellectual generosity, encouragement, and patience, so amply expressed throughout the writing of this chapter. Alex's brilliant and erudite input in the final days of writing consid-erably sharpened my central argument. I am deeply grateful.
2. On sonotropism in philosophy from Schopenhauer to Badiou, see the essays by Amy Cimini, James Currie, Michael Gallope, Jennifer Lynn Heuson, Brian Kane, Trent Leipert,

Jairo Moreno and Gavin Steingo, Martin Scherzinger, Stephen Decatur Smith, and Holly Watkins in Scherzinger 2015.

3. For a full account of the interplay between the philosophy of Deleuze and Guattari and the music of Boulez, see Scherzinger 2013.

4. Contributions to the debate on temporality within postcolonial studies included Attwell 2005; Bhabha 1994; Bannerjee 2006; Bevernage and Lorenz 2013; Chakrabarty 2000; Fabian 1983; Harootunian 2005; Jameson 2003; Mbembe 2001; Parry 2009; and Wenzel 2009. See also "The New Metaphysics of Time," a virtual special issue of *History and Theory* (August 2012): http://onlinelibrary.wiley.com/journal/10.1111/%28ISSN%291468-2303/homepage/virtual_issue__the_new_metaphysics_of_time.htm.

5. Berger's twenty-first-century account deploys an erudite contemporary historical method, rich with philosophical resonance, but its central theme is wholly in sync with a hundred-year-old trope about the nonlinearity of the Baroque. In an influential 1915 study demonstrating the development of the classical sonata form out of the Baroque *Fortspinnungstypus*, for example, German music theorist Wilhelm Fischer likewise opposes the cyclical temporalities of premodern/Baroque music with those of the goal-directed modern/Classical (see Fischer 1915).

6. See, for example, Balslev 1983; Edwards 1994, 79; MacGaffey 1978; McGraw, 2008; and Tairako 1996, 101.

7. Without delving into the historical conditions of its emergence, it should be noted that the invention of the disciplinary study of "Ethnomusicology" in the United States in the 1950s was directly pitted against the comparative thrust of German engagements with non-Western music (in the disciplinary form of "*Vergleichende Musikwissenschaft*") some fifty years earlier.

8. I would like to thank Rick Cohn for pointing out the matrix representation to me.

9. Well-known texts that uphold this kind of theory of rhythm and meter include Krebs 1999, Lerdahl and Jackendoff 1983, Schachter 1987, and Temperley 2007.

10. Already in 1975, the German musicologist Wilhelm Seidel similarly pointed to the modernity of Kirnberger's conceptions of musical time, an idea later taken up by Carl Dahlhaus, William Caplin, and Thomas Christensen. See Seidel 1975.

11. Grant points out that, while fundamentally allied with them, Hasty's theory actually reverses the basic duple construction of triple meter found in historical theories. Where we find in Hasty a temporal projection from short to long, the "*proporcien tact*, Agricola's triple meter, consists of two motions, the first a lowering of the hand twice as long as the subsequent raising" (2014, 69).

WORKS CITED

Agawu, Kofi. 2003. *Representing African Music: Postcolonial Notes, Queries, Positions.* New York: Routledge.

Agawu, Kofi. 2016. *The African Imagination in Music.* New York: Oxford University Press.

Anderson, Benedict. 2006. *Imagined Communities: Reflections on the Origin and Spread of Nationalism.* London: Verso.

Arom, Simha. 2004. *African Rhythm and Polyrhythm: Musical Structure and Methodology.* Cambridge: Cambridge University Press.

Attwell, David. 2005. *Rewriting Modernity: Studies in Black South African Literary History.* Athens: Ohio University Press.

Baer, Laura. 2014. "Doubt, Conflict, Mediation: The Anthropology of Modern Time." *Journal of the Royal Anthropological Institute* 20: 18–20.

Balslev, Anindita Niyogi. *A Study of Time in Indian Philosophy.* Wiesbaden: O. Harrassowitz, 1983.

Bannerjee, Prathama. 2006. *Politics of Time: "Primitives" and History-Writing in a Colonial Society.* Oxford: Oxford University Press.

Benedict, Ruth. 1948. "Anthropology and the Humanities." *American Anthropologist* 50: 585–593.

Benjamin, Walter. 1968. "Theses on the Philosophy of History." In *Illuminations*, edited by Hannah Arendt and translated by Harry Zohn, 253–264. New York: Schocken.

Berger, Karol. 2007. *Bach's Cycle, Mozart's Arrow: An Essay on the Origins of Musical Modernity.* Berkeley: University of California Press.

Bergson, Henri. 2002. *Time and Free Will: An Essay on the Immediate Data of Consciousness.* London: Routledge.

Bevernage, Berber, and Chris Lorenz, eds. 2013. *Breaking up Time: Negotiating the Borders between Present, Past and Future.* Göttingen: Vandenhoeck & Ruprecht.

Bhabha, Homi. 1994. *The Location of Culture.* London: Routledge.

Blacking, John. 1970. "Tonal Organization in the Music of Two Venda Initiation Schools." *Ethnomusicology* 14: 1–56.

Boas, Franz. 2014. *Anthropology and Modern Life.* New York: Routledge.

Born, Georgina. 2015. "Making Time: Temporality, History, and the Cultural Object." *New Literary History* 46: 361–383.

Bohannan, Paul. 1963. *Social Anthropology.* New York: Holt, Rinehart and Winston.

Bryant, Levi. 2014. *Onto-Cartography: An Ontology of Machines and Media.* Edinburgh: Edinburgh University Press.

Chakrabarty, Dipesh. 2000. *Provincializing Europe: Postcolonial Thought and Historical Difference.* Princeton, NJ: Princeton University Press.

Clark, Suzannah, and Alexander Rehding, eds. 2016. *Music in Time: Phenomenology, Perception, Performance.* Cambridge, MA: Harvard University Press.

Delanda, Manuel. 2016. *Assemblage Theory.* Edinburgh: Edinburgh University Press.

Deleuze, Gilles, and Félix Guattari. 1987. *A Thousand Plateaus: Capitalism and Schizophrenia.* Minneapolis: University of Minnesota Press.

Derrida, Jacques. 1982. "Différance." In *Margins of Philosophy*, translated by Alan Bass, 1–28. Chicago: University of Chicago Press.

Edwards, Bill. 1994. "Living the Dreaming." In *Aboriginal Australia: An Introductory Reader in Aboriginal Studies*, edited by Colin Bourke, Eleanor Bourke, and Bill Edwards, 77–99. St. Lucia: University of Queensland Press.

Evans-Pritchard, E. E. 1939. "Nuer Time-Reckoning." *Africa* 12: 189–216.

Fabian, Johannes. 1983. *Time and the Other: How Anthropology Makes Its Object.* New York: Columbia University Press.

Fischer, Wilhelm. 1915. "Zur Entwicklungsgeschichte des Wiener klassischen Stils." *Studien zur Musikwissenschaft* 3: 24–84.

Garfias, Robert. 1964. "Symposium on Transcription and Analysis: A Hukwe Song with Musical Bow. Transcription I." *Ethnomusicology* 8: 233–240.

Gikandi, Simon. 1996. *Maps of Englishness: Writing Identity in the Culture of Colonialism.* New York: Columbia University Press.

Grant, Roger Matthew. 2014. *Beating Time & Measuring Music in the Early Modern Era.* New York: Oxford University Press.

Harman, Graham. 2002. *Tool-Being: Heidegger and the Metaphysics of Objects.* Chicago: University of Chicago Press.

Harris, Marvin. 1968. *The Rise of Anthropological Theory: A History of Theories of Culture.* New York: Thomas Y. Crowell.

Harootunian, Harry. 2005. "Some Thoughts on Comparability and the Space-Time Problem." *Boundary 2* 32 (2): 23–52.

Hasty, Chris. 1997. *Meter as Rhythm.* Oxford: Oxford University Press.

Heidegger, Martin. 2010. *Being and Time.* Translated by Joan Stambaugh. Albany SUNY Press.

Hulse, Brian. 2010. "Thinking Musical Difference: Music Theory as Minor Science." In *Sounding the Virtual: Gilles Deleuze and the Theory and Philosophy of Music,* edited by Brian Hulse and Nick Nesbitt, 23–50. Farnham, Surrey: Ashgate.

Husserl, Edmund. 1973. *The Idea of Phenomenology.* Dordrecht: Springer.

Jameson, Fredric. 2003. "The End of Temporality." *Critical Inquiry* 29: 695–718.

Jones, Arthur M., and L. Kombe. 1952. *The Icila Dance: Old Style.* Roodepoort: African Music Society.

Kirnberger, Johann Phillipp. 1968. *Die Kunst des reinen Satzes in der Musik (1771-1779).* Facsimile edition. Hildesheim: Georg Olms.

Kittler, Friedrich. 1995. "Musik als Medium." In *Wahrnehmung und Geschichte: Markierungen Zur Aisthesis Materialis,* edited by Bernhard Dotzler and Ernst Martin Müller, 83–100. Berlin: Akademie Verlag.

Koetting, James. 1970. "Analysis and Notation of West African Drum Ensemble Music." *Selected Reports in Ethnomusicology* 1: 116–146.

Kramer, Jonathan. 1988. *The Time of Music: New Meanings, New Temporalities, New Listening Strategies.* New York: Schirmer.

Krebs, Harald. 1999. *Fantasy Pieces.* Oxford: Oxford University Press.

Kubik, Gerhard. 1962. "The Phenomenon of Inherent Rhythms in East and Central African Music." *African Music* 3: 33–42.

Kubik, Gerhard. 1972. "Transcription of African Music from Silent Film: Theory and Methods." *African Music* 5: 28–39.

Langer, Susanne. 1959. *Reflections on Art: A Source Book of Writings by Artists, Critics, and Philosophers.* Baltimore: Johns Hopkins Press.

Larkin, Brian. 2008. *Signal and Noise: Media, Infrastructure, and Urban Culture in Nigeria.* Durham, NC: Duke University Press.

Latour, Bruno. 2005. *Reassembling the Social: An Introduction to Actor-Network Theory.* Oxford: Oxford University Press.

Leach, Edmond Ronald. 1961. "Two Essays Concerning the Symbolic Representation of Time." In *Rethinking Anthropology,* edited by Edmond Ronald Leach, 124–136. London: Athlone Press.

Lerdahl, Fred, and Ray Jackendoff. 1983. *A Generative Theory of Tonal Music.* Cambridge, MA: MIT Press.

Lewin, David. 2007. *Musical Form and Transformation: Four Analytic Essays.* New York: Oxford University Press.

Lochhead, Judith Irene. 2015. *Reconceiving Structure in Contemporary Music: New Tools in Music Theory and Analysis.* New York: Routledge.

Locke, David. 2010. "*Yewevu* in the Metric Matrix." *Music Theory Online* 16, no. 4. http://www.mtosmt.org/issues/mto.10.16.4/mto.10.16.4.locke.html.

London, Justin. 2012. *Hearing in Time: Psychological Aspects of Musical Meter.* 2nd edition. New York: Oxford University Press.

MacGaffey, Wyatt. 1972. "The West in Congolese Experience." In *Africa & the West: Intellectual Responses to European Culture*, edited by Philip D. Curtin, 49–74. Madison: University of Wisconsin Press.

MacGaffey, Wyatt. 1978. "African History, Anthropology, and the Rationality of Natives." *History in Africa* 5: 101–120.

Malago Shiro. 2012. "'Muheme' Nyati Group/Wagogo Music in Tanzania." YouTube video. 12:37. Posted on October 30, 2012. https://www.youtube.com/watch?v=lfY1Lbocо-4.

Massumi, Brian. 2002. *Parables of the Virtual: Movement, Affect, Sensation.* Durham, NC: Duke University Press.

Mbembe, Achille. 2001. *On the Postcolony.* Berkeley: University of California Press.

McGraw, Andrew. 2008. "Different Temporalities: The Time of Balinese Gamelan." *Yearbook for Traditional Music* 40: 136–162.

McLuhan, Marshall. 2004. "Visual and Acoustic Space." In *Audioculture: Readings in Modern Music.* Edited by Christoph Cox and Daniel Warner, 67–72. London: Continuum.

Meillassoux, Quentin. 2009. *After Finitude: An Essay on the Necessity of Contingency.* London: Continuum.

Merriam, Alan. 1982. *African Music in Perspective.* New York: Garland.

Mitchell, W. J. T. 2005. *What do Pictures Want? The Lives and Loves of Images.* Chicago: University of Chicago Press.

Mumford, Lewis. 1934. *Technics and Civilization.* New York: Harcourt, Brace, and Co.

Nketia, Kwabena J. H. 1963. *African Music in Ghana.* Evanston, IL: Northwestern University Press.

Osborne, Peter. 1995. *The Politics of Time: Modernity and Avant-Garde.* New York: Verso.

Parry, Benita. 2009. "Aspects of Peripheral Modernisms." *Ariel* 40: 27–55.

Polak, Rainer. 2010. "Rhythmic Feel as Meter: Non-Isochronous Beat Subdivision in Jembe Music from Mali." *Music Theory Online* 16, no. 4. http://www.mtosmt.org/issues/mto.10.16.4/mto.10.16.4.polak.html.

Priestley, Joseph. 1772. *The History and Present State of Discoveries Relating to Vision, Light, and Colours.* London: J. Johnson.

Przybylek, Stephanie. 2016. "What Is Funk Music?" https://study.com/academy/lesson/what-is-funk-music-definition-characteristics.html.

Rosenberg, Daniel, and Anthony Grafton. 2010. *Cartographies of Time.* New York: Princeton Architectural Press.

Schachter, Carl. 1987. "Rhythm and Linear Analysis: Aspects of Meter." *The Music Forum* 6: 1–60.

Scherzinger, Martin. 2010. "Temporal Geometries of an African Music." *Music Theory Online* 16, no. 4. http://www.mtosmt.org/issues/mto.10.16.4/mto.10.16.4.scherzinger.html.

Scherzinger, Martin. 2013. "Enforced Deterritorialization, or the Trouble with Musical Politics." In *Sounding the Virtual: Gilles Deleuze and the Theory and Philosophy of Music*, edited by Brian Hulse and Nick Nesbitt, 103–128. Farnham, Surrey: Ashgate.

Scherzinger, Martin, ed. 2015. *Music in Contemporary Philosophy.* New York: Routledge.

Schopenhauer, Arthur. 1958. *The World as Will and Representation.* Indian Hills, CO: Falcon's Wing Press.

Sedgwick, Eve Kosofsky. 2003. *Touching Feeling: Affect, Pedagogy, Performativity.* Durham, NC: Duke University Press.

Seidel, Wilhelm. 1975. *Über Rhythmustheorien der Neuzeit.* Bern: Franke.

Shouse, Eric. 2005. "Feeling, Emotion, Affect." *Media Culture* 8. http://journal.media-culture.org.au/0512/03-shouse.php.

Simondon, Gilbert. 2017. *On the Mode of Existence of Technical Objects.* Minneapolis: University of Minnesota Press.

Sun Ra. 1972. *Space Is the Place.* Directed by John Coney. DVD. Plexifilm.

Tairako, Tomonaga. 1996. "Time and Temporality from the Japanese Perspective." In *Time and Temporality in Intercultural Perspective*, edited by Douwe Tiemersma and Henk Oosterling, 93–104. Amsterdam: Rodopi.

Temperley, David. 2007. *Music and Probability.* Cambridge, MA: MIT Press.

Tenzer, Michael. 2010. "Africa Stand Up!—and Be Counted Among Others." *Music Theory Online* 16, no. 4. http://www.mtosmt.org/issues/mto.10.16.4/mto.10.16.4.tenzer.html.

Tenzer, Michael. 2011. "Generalized Representations of Musical Time and Periodic Structures." *Ethnomusicology* 55: 369–386.

Thomas, Dominic, ed. 2014. *Afroeuropean Cartographies.* Newcastle upon Tyne: Cambridge Scholars Publishing.

Thrift, Nigel. 2008. *Non-Representational Theory: Space, Politics, Affect.* New York: Routledge.

UNESCO. 2008. *Vimbuza Healing Dance.* DVD. http://www.unesco.org/archives/multimedia/?pg=33&s=films_details&id=3758.

Ward, W. E. 1927. "Music in the Gold Coast." *Gold Coast Review* 3: 199–223.

Waterman, Richard A. 1952. "African Influence on the Music of the Americas." In *Acculturation in the Americas*, edited by Sol Tax, 207–217. Chicago: University of Chicago Press.

Wenzel, Jennifer. 2009. *Bulletproof: Afterlives of Anticolonial Prophecy in South Africa and Beyond.* Chicago: University of Chicago Press.

White, Hayden. 1987. *The Content of the Form: Narrative Discourse and Historical Representation.* Baltimore: Johns Hopkins University Press.

Whitehead, Alfred North. 1929. *Process and Reality: An Essay in Cosmology.* Cambridge: Cambridge University Press.

CHAPTER 11

GROOVE

GUILHERME SCHMIDT CÂMARA
AND ANNE DANIELSEN

INTRODUCTION

GROOVE is a musical term commonly used among musicians, enthusiasts, and music scholars alike. According to the *Merriam Webster Dictionary*, it denotes "a pronounced enjoyable rhythm."[1] Such a definition captures two important aspects of the concept: first, the ways in which the term "groove" is used (as a noun) to describe a characteristic rhythmic pattern typical of a musical style (swing groove, rock groove, funk groove), and, second—as is reflected in the adjective "groovy"—the particular pleasurable quality, as well as the appeal to dance and movement emanating from such patterns when they are performed in the optimal manner.

The earliest references to the term are from the swing-jazz era, when groove, according to R. J. Gold (quoted in Kernfeld 2017), evoked the excellence and/or sophistication of a performance.[2] Likewise, in her ethnographic work on improvisation and interaction between musicians in 1990s jazz combos, Monson (1996, 67–68) found that most musicians tended to use groove as an aesthetic term, although she also observes that groove was used as a synonym for the "rhythm matrix" of a particular style.

In musicology and music theory in recent decades, the expression "groove-based music" has primarily come to be associated with African American musical styles, such as jazz, R&B, soul, funk, disco, and hip-hop, all of which seem to rely on a common set of rhythmic principles (see, for example, Bowman 1995; Burnim and Maultsby 2015; and Danielsen 2006). While groove as an aesthetic/stylistic practice is a prominent feature of many other Afro Diasporic–derived styles as well, such as Afro-Cuban (salsa), Afro-Brazilian (samba), and other forms of Latin American dance music, these traditions tend to use other terms to describe those aspects encompassed by the term "groove" in the African American tradition (examples include "Balanço"/"Suingue" in samba or "Sabor"/"Bomba" in salsa; see Bøhler 2013 and Gerischer 2006). The term "groove" is also not typically used within West African drumming traditions, which likewise display many of the formal aspects of groove-based music (see, for example, Locke 1982; Nketia 1974; and Polak 2010). Groove thus seems to be used, first and foremost, although not exclusively,[3] to describe the foundation and aesthetic qualities of African American rhythmic music.

In what follows, we will first address three distinct general understandings of groove. Then, we will propose a set of typical (rhythmic) features that seem to be common to a wide range of groove-based styles. Finally, we will present some viable analytical approaches to various grooves typical of the African American musical tradition.

Defining the Undefinable: Three Understandings of Groove

We must begin this discussion by remarking upon the highly processual character of groove. Groove happens in the here and now of performance, meaning that groove is, in a sense, ungraspable as such—the very moment one tries to come to terms with a groove experience, one is no longer in the groove (Roholt 2014). Defining groove is thus a challenging task, although the main disciplines involved in groove studies have developed three discrete approaches to it. Each one focuses on particular aspects: (1) groove as pattern and performance; (2) groove as pleasure and appeal to movement; and (3) groove as a state of being.

Groove as Pattern and Performance

As mentioned in the introduction, the word "groove" is often used to denote a particular rhythmic pattern typical of a musical style (a swing groove, a funk groove, and so on). Accordingly, groove has been defined as "a persistently repeated pattern" (Kernfeld 2017). In music-theoretical terms, this pattern equals the basic rhythmic structure that characterizes the style in question. In notation-based analytical traditions, rhythmic structure has commonly been conceptualized as a pattern of onsets in time that aligns with a traditional metric grid of isochronous pulsations at different levels. Seen as such, the structure then becomes what one would transcribe as the groove. The word "groove" itself, of course, directs our attention to some important limitations of this approach. When used to denote stylistic-rhythmic patterns (swing, funk, and so on), groove invariably also encompasses the particular prescribed manner in which these patterns are played, in relation to both the timing and the sound and shape of the rhythmic events.

As Bengtsson, Gabrielsson, and Thorsén (1969) point out, what constitutes this pattern in perception is an open question that might, in fact, be impossible to answer, due to so-called systematic variations—that is, stylistic/idiomatic patterns of microrhythmic features might act as constituents of the norm, or the groove pattern itself. Thus, rather than asserting the traditional divide between structure (notation) and expression (performance) of notation-based music, the metric grid in groove analyses should instead be seen to supply a pragmatic means of measurement of actual locations of rhythmic events—one that leaves open to discussion what the pattern actually is. In any case, the groove is always shaped in relation to perceptual reference structures (Danielsen 2010, 19–20) that perceiver and performer alike rely upon to provide structure to the sound. Metric layers such as pulse and subdivision are obvious reference structures in the perception of groove. The actual location and shape of the pulse, however, can vary and do not need to derive from a series of points in time (Danielsen 2010; Danielsen et al. 2015a). Likewise, the norm for layers of subdivision in a groove does not need to be isochronous. Swing in jazz is one example, and non-isochronous subdivisions are also common in other African-derived musical styles (see, for example, Gerischer 2006 and Haugen 2016 on samba; London et al. 2017, Polak 2010, Polak and London 2014, and Polak et al. 2016 on djembe drumming in Mali; and Câmara 2016 on funk). In addition to pulse and layers of subdivision, the intermediate level of stylistic figure (Danielsen 2006, 47–50) is also an important identifying structural layer in a groove.

What unites pulse, figure, and subdivision as aspects of the rhythmic structure of a groove is that they do not exist as sound per se. Rhythm as experienced always represents an interaction between virtual reference structures and actual sounding rhythmic events.[4] This interaction works in two directions: a groove always generates some form of reference structure, and reference structures are always applied to a groove. It evokes the relationship between meter and rhythm, as described by London (2012), who understands meter as all or some aspects of the structure provided by endogenous processes in the perception of rhythm, and rhythm as the exogenous, sounding aspect of this interaction. Experienced rhythm involves both such aspects of meter and sounding rhythm, and, in what follows, "rhythm" will denote "experienced rhythm," whereas actual sounding rhythm will always be labeled as such.

When one is in the act of producing and/or perceiving a groove, this interaction between sounding rhythm and reference structures usually goes on automatically and imperceptibly. When conducting analytical work on groove, however, the question of pattern and deviation can become hazardous. The absence of a written "template" in oral traditions calls for relevant, well-considered proposals of groove structure. These may be based on actual performances or recordings and should take into account the fact that microrhythmic features, which often elude traditional notation-based representations of rhythmic structure, have a structural impact as well. Deciding on what is systematic variation—that is, intrinsically part of the groove pattern—and what is not is, therefore, crucial for analytical and theoretical accounts of groove.

Last but not least, the pattern (including basic reference structures) may also change along the way, generating always fresh expectations at the micro, meso, and macro levels. The basic pattern of a groove is usually designed to activate an inner dynamic that keeps the listener or dancer constantly sensorimotorically engaged. What should be considered structural in a perceptual sense must always be evaluated on the basis of the preceding events as well (Danielsen 2006, 2010, 2015; Hasty 1997). If we overlook this condition, we risk missing crucial aspects of a groove's structural identity, as well as the critical interaction between this virtual structure and the actual sounds.

Groove as Pleasure and "Wanting to Move"

The word "groove" is also used in a normative manner to judge (in an aesthetic sense) the quality of a groove: a groove is not a groove until it *actually grooves*—that is, it is experienced as groovy. Steven Feld (1988), studying groove from an ethnomusicological perspective, incorporates appealing aspects of groove-based music into its definition: groove is "an unspecifiable but ordered sense of something . . . that is sustained in a distinctive, regular and *attractive way, working to draw the listener in*" (76; our emphasis).

Groove-directed music is also commonly described as music that imparts a feeling of "motion," "vital drive," or "rhythmic propulsion" (Keil and Feld 2005). This aspect of groove is the foundation for recent psychological attempts at establishing an operational definition of groove as "the sensation of wanting to move some part of the body in relation to some aspect of the sound pattern" (Madison 2006, 201). Janata, Tomic, and Haberman (2012) also stress the coupling of groove to dance and motion but regard this urge to move as closely related to groove's pleasure aspect. Based on their survey of 153 undergraduate students' ratings of a variety of preformed descriptive phrases believed to be "associated with the concept of the groove to varying degrees" (informed by music-theoretical definitions of groove and the authors' own intuitions), these researchers concluded that groove is "that aspect of the music that induces a *pleasant* sense of wanting to move along with the music" (Janata et al. 2012, 56; our emphasis). Accordingly, they theorize groove as a "pleasurable drive toward action" that results from sensorimotor coupling—that is, from an "engagement of the brain's motor action systems while listening to music"—and that induces a "positive affective state" (54).[5]

It is important to clarify the fact that, unlike the pleasurable state of more teleological musical forms, groove's pleasurable state derives first and foremost from the process itself. A groove mode of listening or dancing (Danielsen 2006, 177–179) is not directed toward a goal (such as tonic closure); instead, it demands one's presence in the groove's here and now. Put differently, when one is in the participatory mode (Keil 1995), one moves together with the groove—in a sense, co-producing it. Witek (2017) applies a similar perspective to explain the widespread presence of countermetric structures in groove-based musical styles: "When synchronizing our bodies to the beat, we enact parts of the musical structure by filling in the gaps; as long as the syncopations are repeated, we continue to participate, and processual pleasure is prolonged" (Witek 2017, 151). Groove is often characterized by structural tension at the level of figures and/or microrhythm that requires active interpretive participation, such as filling in beats at structurally salient positions that are not explicitly articulated in the sound. As Witek points out, this means that pleasure in groove is not caused by some cognitive-physical stimulation but emerges through one's enactment of aspects of the musical structure and, thus, one's constant engagement, almost as a part of the groove itself.

Groove as a State of Being

Musicians often use the term "groove" to refer to a pleasing state in which the creation of music becomes seemingly effortless (Berliner 1994; Monson 1996; Pressing 2002). Enthusiasts also describe groove as engendering an intense, almost euphoric feeling. This condition is often referred to as "being in the groove" (Danielsen 2006, 11–12, 215; Janata et al. 2012; Roholt 2014, 108). When one is in the state of "being in the groove," one's experience of time is—somewhat paradoxically—not really an experience of time. There is no distancing from the musical events: one is continuously engaged in the co-production of the groove, and, as a consequence, time dissolves. Moreover, despite its highly repetitive character, groove's repetition never becomes repetitive. The distancing required for repetition to be identified as such does not arise (Danielsen 2006, 162).

A striking aspect of groove *experience* (to separate it from groove as a musical-analytical object or psychological construct) is that, when one is in the midst of it, one feels as though it could go on almost forever. To reach this state, however, the interaction of listener/dancer and music has to persist, uninterrupted, for a long time. This condition impacts how a groove is organized in time on both local and larger scales. In a pure groove, there is no song structure in the traditional sense; the musical aspects that create large-scale musical timespans, such as harmony, melody, and larger formal sections, are significantly diminished. Instead of waiting for events to come, one is submerged in what is before one. The focus turns inward, as if one's sensitivity to details, timing inflections, and tiny timbral nuances is inversely proportional to musical variation on a larger scale. When groove is experienced in this way, it ceases to be an object that exists apart from its listener (see also discussion of the music–mind–body cycle in Witek 2017). The relation of subject and object is almost suspended. One operates within a continuous field where the limit between music and musician/listener/dancer is not yet established or has vanished.

Phenomenological reflection highlights the temporal space between immediate "being in time" and understanding this same being. One result of this fundamentally temporal character of experience is that the exchange between "being in the groove" and understanding this state of being is in itself bound to unfold in time. There is no way to attend to one's own groove experience at a distance (see Danielsen 2006, 12). The epistemological consequence of this fundamental hermeneutic premise is that the process of understanding the state of being in the groove necessarily involves a process of distanciation or objectification that implies transforming what is to be understood into something other than what it was. The groove experience as a state of being seems to be especially difficult to grasp. Because of the highly processual character of its meaning, groove is about how things are in "real time"—how the groove unfolds in performance, right then and there (see also Danielsen 2006, chapter 11).

Academic discourses such as cultural-critical discussions or music-analytical investigations often fail to address the phenomenological qualities linked to the experience of music—that is, how things are when they happen. However, the difference between *how groove is* when it happens, in time, and *what it is* in the process of understanding, is impossible to transcend: it cannot be leveled out. Theoretical or analytical accounts of grooves may be aware of this premise, to various extents. Generally, however, experiential aspects of the groove are probably better understood through more holistic descriptions that, in parallel to the notion of groove itself, incorporate all aspects of the groove experience—structural, performative, aesthetic, perceptual/psychological, and phenomenological—rather than treat them as separate domains.

Groove Features

When analyzing and theorizing groove, the relationship between the experience of being in a groove and the rhythmic qualities of that same groove presents a key challenge: what is it in the sounds or their organization that brings the participant into a state of "being in the groove"? In this section, we identify some necessary but not sufficient conditions of groove—that is, common rhythmic properties seemingly present in the majority of styles associated with groove—while remaining very much aware of the fact that groove is a complex matter at its core and is not to be summarily defined as the sum of these parts.

Pulse or Regular Beat

Groove is overwhelmingly associated with music that compels body movement in some form or fashion, and, as such, a regular *beat* is of paramount importance to it. Without a steady beat (also called "pulse" or "tactus") to guide dancers' feet or musicians' fingers, there can be no groove. In psychological research, the beat is often described as corresponding to the most comfortable rate at which one readily "entrains," or synchronizes, to a musical rhythm via body movements such as hand claps or foot taps (Danielsen et al. 2015a; Jones 1976; Large and Jones 1999; London 2012; Merker et al. 2009). In many groove styles, the beat level can often be heard as expressed or externalized by one or more salient instruments in the accompaniment section. For example, in some styles of funk, soul, or hip-hop in 4/4 meter, one frequently observes percussive elements regularly coinciding with all of the (quarter-note) beat locations, either alone or in combination with other elements, the most common example of which being the snare drum and bass drum marking every other beat in tandem (a "back-beat pattern"). However, even in lieu of such explicit and un-ambiguous (near-)isochronicity at the beat level, the sensation of a regular underlying beat scheme may still be reliably induced by longer, cyclically repeating rhythmic patterns (Large et al. 2015). Such "isoperiodic" patterns (Arom 1991) are usually iterated within the span of one or two measures of the meter and, in groove contexts, may be referred to as the "basic unit" (Danielsen 2006, 43). Regardless of whether a clear-cut (external) pulse is evident in the sound or not, an internal sense of beat is vital for understanding or entraining to a groove, in terms of either playing, dancing, or listening. If one fails to catch the "correct" beat reference, the best-case scenario is that one will be unlikely to appreciate the delicate interplay of multilevel rhythms within it; the worst-case scenario is that one will fail to entrain to it at all, resulting in rhythmic disorientation and confusion.

Subdivisions of the Beat

A simple (near-)isochronous pulse alone will not create a sense of groove—few would claim, for example, that the ticking of a metronome would constitute a groove, let alone an instance of music. In addition, the presence of sound events perceived to be oper-ating at faster metrical levels than the level of the beat (such as the eighth- or sixteenth-note levels)[6] is generally considered to be a necessary structural element for most groove styles (Pressing 2002; Stewart 2000). Events at subdivision levels of the beat are often subjectively described as imparting rhythmic "drive" or "motional energy" to grooves (Butterfield 2011); in funk, for example, they are said to evoke the feeling of "double time [within] regular time" (Payne in Milkowski 2007; see also discussion in Danielsen 2006, 74–75). In addition, psychological studies have shown that faster metrical levels tend to facilitate entrainment with the actual beat level itself by providing extra temporal cues (Madison 2014).

One could conceivably distinguish between certain broad styles of groove simply according to the degree of frequency of events on the "density referent" level—that is, the metric level comprising the shortest practical subdivision unit (Nketia 1974). While sixteenth-note events in classic soul and R&B styles generally tend to be sparse, they are exceedingly more commonplace in funk and disco, although they are interwoven into the overall texture of the groove in aesthetically distinct ways. At the same time, the determination of the density referent in groove is not always straightforward, as it depends not only on the onset locations of events but also on their durations. Should an event corresponding to the onset location of a slower met-rical level be shorter in duration than said level, it could be assigned, at least implic-itly, to a faster metrical level. This ambiguity in the "emergent non-fit of subdivision [phrasing] and density referent" (Danielsen 2006, 75) seems to be a typical feature of faster-metrical-level events in many groove styles.

Moreover, the degree to which subdivisions are swung is also an identifying aspect of grooves. The term "swing" has been used to denote a general "feel" engendered by particular rhythmic interactions, usually when speaking within the context of jazz styles. If one extends the term in the direction of the more technical definition of eighth or sixteenth notes divided into unequal durations (either individually or altogether), swing pertains to many groove-based styles outside of jazz as well (see the James Brown funk example in the analytical discussions below). The extent to which a rhythm "swings" can be expressed more objectively via "swing ratios" between on-beat and off-beat notes. In an expanded sense, then, swing may be considered simply one kind of "microrhythmic" feature that emerges from the character of a groove. Overall, what fundamentally contributes to a successful groove is not only the presence of faster-metrical-level events swung to some degree but also the particular manner in which those events are structurally positioned and dynamically articulated within the context of the basic unit, as well as combined with other rhythmic devices, such as syncopation and counter-rhythm.

Syncopation (Local Contradictions of Meter)

One of the rhythmic devices most typically associated with enhancing a groove is syncopation (Sioros et al. 2014; Witek et al. 2014). Several formal music-theoretical definitions and models for quantifying measures of syncopation have been proposed (see Gomez et al. 2007 for an overview). Most, however, seem to share an understanding of syncopation as a form of localized "violation" of a normal metrical expectation scheme (Huron 2006; London 2012; Temperley 1999). Viewed as such, syncopation is contingent upon the notion that meter subjectively affords varying degrees of temporal expectation or strengths of "accent." Slower metrical levels are typically ascribed more weight than faster metrical levels; in music theory derived from the Western art music tradition, the metrical accent pattern of the main beat level in 4/4 meter is "strong–weak–strong–weak." However, in 4/4 meter–based grooves, the beats that are subjectively felt to be stronger or heavier than others may vary from genre to genre, and "phenomenal" accent patterns (Lerdahl and Jackendoff 1983, 17) of actual rhythms can either reinforce or conflict with the metrical accentuation scheme.[7]

Syncopated events are ubiquitous in groove music and frequently interpreted as functioning to momentarily subvert the prevailing beat-accentuation scheme. Because most groove styles feature patterns that are firmly anchored to the beat level and thus evocative of a strong metrical sense that is not easily derailed, local syncopations can be thought to supply lesser degrees of metrical tension to an overall groove, rather than full-on metrical ambiguity. Conversely, in fact, syncopations can even serve to reinforce the meter of grooves by virtue of "pointing out the significant beats of the pulse without accentuating them" (Danielsen 2006, 80). This capacity to indirectly emphasize the meter derives from the fact that, when an expected strong beat fails to materialize following a syncopated event on a weak beat, it makes listeners even more aware of the "missing" beat, consequently strengthening their entrainment to the meter (London 2012, 109; see also discussion in Witek 2017).

Counter-Rhythm (Systematic Tendencies toward Cross-Rhythm and Metrical Ambiguity)

As mentioned, a salient feature of numerous groove styles seems to be the pervasive use of syncopation. However, should a series of syncopations repeat in a systematic and predictable fashion over the course of a basic groove unit, these syncopations may eventually cease to be perceived as local instances of momentary metric displacements, or unexpected accentuations of weak metrical locations, and instead become framed as characteristic "counter-rhythmic" figures in their own right, in some instances even introducing "a tendency towards cross-rhythm" (Danielsen 2006, 62). Cross-rhythm may be defined in formal terms as the result of an overlap of rhythmic streams "whose periodicities ['metrical levels'] are noninteger multiples" (London 2012, 66). Typical examples in 4/4 meter would be when two evenly spaced events are superimposed over three beats (2:3 cross-rhythms) or four events over three or six beats (4:3 or 4:6 cross-rhythms). The *New Harvard Dictionary of Music* describes the effect that cross-rhythm has upon the perception of an established meter: "A rhythm in which the regular pattern of accents of the prevailing meter is contradicted by a conflicting pattern and not merely a momentary displacement that leaves the prevailing meter fundamentally unchallenged" (Randel and Apel 1986, 216).

Cross-rhythm is typically associated with West African drumming traditions (Anku 2000; Burns 2010; Locke 1982; Nketia 1974; Novotny 1998) in which one or more instruments within an ensemble can often be found to prominently accentuate onset locations that are congruent with a competing pulse within the context of multilayered rhythmic textures (that do not always clearly externalize the beat level). These kinds of cross-rhythms tend to elicit a powerful sense of metrical ambiguity, especially if one is unfamiliar with the particular style at hand, often inviting more than one metrical construal upon repeated listening. According to Pressing (2002), this type of "perceptual rivalry and multiplicity" is central to rhythm in many African musical traditions.[8] In groove-based styles, however, such strong cross-rhythm is relatively rare;[9] while cross-rhythmic figures are extremely common, their implementation tends to be limited to durations shorter than the span of a basic unit, and they almost never occur in ambiguous metrical contexts, because the beat level in grooves is usually externalized by some layer of the rhythm section. Furthermore, cross-rhythmic layers in grooves are generally even subtler by virtue of being nestled within figures rife with metrically ambivalent events that simultaneously confirm and contradict the main beat level, depending upon one's frame of reference. In order to distinguish this "lighter" form of cross-rhythm from the West African sort, Danielsen proposes the term "counter-rhythm" to denote momentary instances of cross-rhythm or systematic off-beat rhythm whose ultimate purpose is to destabilize, but not fundamentally challenge, the main pulse (2006, chapter 4; see the Jackie Wilson analytical example below). Such a notion of counter-rhythm recalls Kolinski's (1973) "contrametric" repertoires, or those musical corpora in "which a significant portion of note onsets tend to be non-congruent with the metrical framework" (London et al. 2017, 475–479).

Microrhythm

Groove has also been associated with patterns of microrhythmic deviations from assumed metrical references on an order ranging from tens to hundreds of milliseconds, encompassing sounds that are often implicitly felt more often than heard when they occur on the threshold of auditory perception (see Butterfield 2006; Danielsen 2010; Iyer 2002; Senn et al. 2017; and Mitchell Ohriner's chapter in this book). The assumption is that the presence of such minor deviations from a presumed norm, or so-called participatory discrepancies (Keil 1995; Keil and Feld 2005) between the different musicians, is important for the "dynamic" dimensions of a groove—that is, it is what makes a groove *groove*.[10] In many microtiming studies, the norm has been conceptualized as a metrical grid, which may work well as a starting point for measurements but which, in many styles, becomes less useful if one seeks to identify the reference structures at work in perception. Because of the malleable character of rhythmic structure (it changes with context and may also change during a given performance), there is no guarantee that the pattern one suggests in theory or analysis is representative of the pattern(s) at work in the experience of those same rhythms. Depending on the context, an event onset that is measured to be twenty milliseconds early in relation to the grid, for example, might be heard as an early attack. However, it might also be heard not as a deviation from the grid/norm but rather as *part* of it—that is, as an extended beat event.

Microrhythmic features in grooves involve both temporal (timing and duration) and sonic (intensity and timbre) aspects of rhythmic events. At the micro level of rhythm performance and perception, such temporal and sonic aspects interact (see, for example, Danielsen et al. 2015a; Repp 1996; Tekman 1997; Waadeland 2001). In general, the overall shape of the sound seems crucial to the perception of timing. Sounds with sharp, impulsive attacks, for example, are heard as positioned earlier in time than sounds with slow, rounder attacks, even when their onsets are the same (Danielsen et al. 2015b; Gordon 1987; Rasch 1988; Wright 2008). This means that microrhythm is potentially present even in groove-based music where all the rhythmic events are supposedly located firmly on the grid.

Other related forms of microrhythmic features arise when separate sound events occur asynchronously at similar times—for example, when the bass is positioned slightly ahead of or behind a drummer's beat. Such asynchronies can be participatory discrepancies (Keil 1995; Keil and Feld 2005) produced by musicians or clustered events produced by editing the temporal location of rhythmic events (Brøvig-Hanssen and Danielsen 2016, chapter 6; Danielsen 2010; see also the D'Angelo and Rihanna analytical examples below).

ANALYTICAL EXAMPLES

Swingin' Grooves and Anticipated Beats in James Brown's "Get Up (I Feel Like Being a) Sex Machine"

Groove-based styles tend to present consistent rhythmic relationships at the micro, or "sub-syntactical," level, which is obscured in traditional transcription. In order to more accurately represent grooves, then, one must supplement transcriptions with more fine-grained measurement methods capable of supplying precise temporal information regarding the onset locations and durations of sound events relative to a metrical reference scheme.[11]

As mentioned, two forms of microrhythm in particular have been frequently investigated by scholars: the systematic "asynchrony" between onsets of various instruments and the degree of durational inequality present in note pairings at the same metrical level, the latter commonly referred to as "swing" and expressed as a ratio between durations of on- and off-beat events—or between "(down)beats" and "upbeats". While many microrhythmic empirical studies have been undertaken in recent decades on various jazz styles (see Butterfield 2011 for an overview), only a handful have collected data on the rhythmic styles more typically associated with groove in the modern era, such as funk or hip-hop (Butterfield 2006; Câmara 2016; De Haas 2007; Frane 2017).

Although subdivisions in funk rhythms are generally considered as comparatively "straighter" than those in jazz rhythms,[12] several scholars have noted that sixteenth-note off-beat events in funk seem to be frequently positioned slightly "late" in relation to on-beat locations of the meter (Danielsen 2006), often to such a consistent extent over the course of a basic unit as to imply subtle, yet noticeable degrees of swing (Butterfield 2006; Stewart 2000). In an empirical investigation into the microrhythmic aspects of guitar, bass, and drums in classic funk and jazz-funk recordings, Câmara (2016) observed that, in the majority of samples analyzed (twelve out of thirteen), at least one instrument was found to be swinging its off-beat sixteenth notes at or above a ratio of 1.2:1,[13] either in a consistent fashion throughout the course of a repeated basic unit (presenting a "global swing," on average) or in a fluctuating manner where certain off-beats were swung to either greater or lesser degrees ("local swing"), or a combination of the two. Let us look in more depth at one of these recordings, the iconic funk tune "Get Up (I Feel Like Being a) Sex Machine" by James Brown from 1970, in order to demonstrate potential interactions between microrhythmic swing and macrostructural pattern.

In the A section (verse) of "Sex Machine" (Figure 11.1 and ⊚ Audio Example 11.1) the instruments with the highest to lowest average swing ratios at the sixteenth-note level (shown by the global mean swing ratio values, or GMSR) were the guitar (2.01, SD = 0.16), then the drums (1.60, SD = 0.10), then the bass (1.52, SD = 0.40).[14] The consistency of swing throughout various repetitions of the basic unit, indicated by standard deviation (SD) values, shows that both guitar and drums tend to maintain a slightly

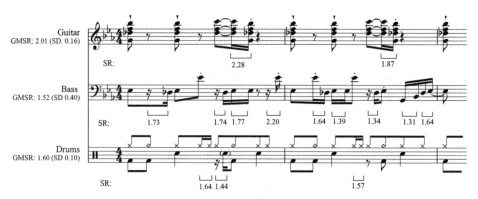

FIGURE 11.1 Two first measures (1× basic unit) of the A section in "Get Up (I Feel Like Being a) Sex Machine" by James Brown (starting about 0:15). SR = Swing Ratio of local pairs of on-beat and off-beat sixteenth notes. GMSR = Global Mean Swing Ratio, that is, mean swing ratio of all sixteenth-note pairs, averaged from about eight basic units in all.

more stable swing ratio than the bass. However, all instruments swing both higher and lower than their mean (as evidenced by the fluctuating swing ratio [SR] values between individual, local sixteenth-note pairs within the basic unit). Overall, the swing in the rhythm section of "Sex Machine" demonstrates what might be typical of the funk formula in general—that of a juxtaposition of subdivision layers swung to varying degrees, from the obvious to the subtle. This may engender different kinds of swing "feel" at any given time depending on whether one chooses to focus on a single instrument, or all of them at once. In addition, certain local, individual notes are occasionally swung with greater or lesser emphasis, and can further modulate the extent to which swing is heard at critical points within the groove.

According to Butterfield (2006, 2011), off-beat subdivisions may be interpreted as imparting various degrees of "motional energy" to events on ensuing on-beat locations when swung. Very high swing ratios (that is, when the distance between the off-beat and the subsequent on-beat approaches zero) tend to generate a halting, choppy feeling rather than a propulsive or driving one (although this can be mitigated by a range of dynamic effects). In "Sex Machine," as Danielsen has observed, drummer John "Jabo" Starks's use of a "few slightly swung sixteenth notes" is experienced not as choppy, but instead as "continuously pushing forward," and indeed this can be corroborated by the fact that the notes display only a moderate swing ratio of 1.60 (2006, 77). The drum pattern's overt swinging character would be further diminished by the fact that the swung notes occur rather sparsely over the course of a basic unit. As Frane and Shams's (2017) study indicates, the lower the "swing density" (amount of swung events) in a rhythm, the higher the "just noticeable difference" threshold for distinguishing swing from straight subdivisions.[15]

The off-beats of Phelps "Catfish" Collins's guitar rhythm, which anticipate every fourth downbeat of the basic unit measure, on the other hand, are swung on average at a high "tied-triplet" ratio of 2.01:1. Because they are syncopations, there are technically no ensuing guitar on-beat events to provide motional energy toward, and thus seemingly no ensuing "downbeat closure" (Butterfield 2011). However, as they are played within the context of an ongoing multilayered groove rather than in isolation, it could be argued that they do in fact "close" either the expected virtual location of an ensuing guitar on-beat or the actual snare hit of the second back-beat sounded by the drums. Regardless of which way one goes here, by the simple virtue of being heavily swung, such off-beat syncopations may be interpreted as heavily emphasizing on-beat locations without directly accentuating them.

A similar perspective, articulated by Danielsen, suggests that when certain local sixteenths are swung to a radical extent, particularly in the form of syncopations, they may be perceived as virtual extensions of the on-beat locations that they precede—that is, as "downbeats in anticipation." Here, a syncopation is heard as the attack of the following "core of the beat ... [which] becomes more a centre of gravity or concentration of energy than a fixed point in a metrical framework" (Danielsen 2006, 79). In "Sex Machine," highly swung off-beat events are regularly positioned less than 90 milliseconds or so from their ensuing on-beats, albeit sparingly. Interestingly, such a value falls just below the limit of short sound event durations likely to be heard as categorical subdivisions in their own right (Butterfield 2006; Efron 1973) and therefore these events could be argued as falling within the groove's "beat bin," that is, occurring within the duration of time in which a listener would expect a beat event to happen (Danielsen 2010). However, funk styles tend to be rather "tight" overall, generally presenting small on-beat onset asynchronies between rhythm section instruments, and thus likely inviting syncopations to be heard just as such—as temporally distinct from the on-beats which they precede. In certain kinds of hip-hop/R&B, on the other hand, where "looser" grooves with larger inter-instrument-onset asynchronies are the norm, it is possible that such large discrepancies may be more readily absorbed by experienced listeners within the applicable beat bin (see the D'Angelo analysis below).

Counter-rhythm: Ambiguous riffs in Jackie Wilson's "(Your Love Keeps Lifting Me) Higher and Higher"

It is rare to find a song described as "groovy" that does not feature some prominent use of off-beat gestures, either within the basic unit of the accompaniment section or in the main melody of a groove. As mentioned previously, when a series of accentuated events repeatedly occurs on "unexpected" off-beat locations within a basic unit, these events may cease to be heard as singular displacements of the main beat and instead be perceived as counter-rhythmic figures that emphasize focal points within the groove that are incongruent with the main meter. In a wide range of groove-based styles, one encounters rhythmic figures that group the eighth- or sixteenth-note subdivisions of the main meter into asymmetrical patterns such as 3+3+2 or 3+3+3+3+2+2, respectively. Such figures can be perceived as allusions to alternative cross-rhythmic pulse layers that function to destabilize, but not usurp, the dominance of the main meter. Counter-rhythms are ubiquitous in African American groove-based styles,[16] especially in funk (see Câmara 2016; Danielsen 2006; and Wilson 1974), but they can also be found in more upbeat, dance-oriented soul tunes such as Jackie Wilson's "(Your Love Keeps Lifting Me) Higher and Higher" from 1967, which we will examine next.

The track begins with a highly driving, drone-like bassline by James Jamerson that is centered on the tonic of the song's D major key and initially accompanied only by tambourine and congas. The latter instruments establish a clear pulse sensation by marking the quintessential "two" and "four" backbeats of the 4/4 meter. The bassline, on the other hand, seems to somewhat simultaneously disturb and reinforce the main pulse, which is subsequently articulated by a steady stream of eighths on the hi-hat cymbals and a further backbeat emphasis on the snare. The bassline soon appears to doggedly insist on subverting the pulse on every repetition of the first basic unit measure: while it starts out firmly ensconced on the first downbeat, it promptly proceeds to accentuate an off-beat on the "two-and" before settling back into the third downbeat. On the "four," then, it accentuates the main pulse once again, but when the duration of this stroke suddenly extends itself beyond the measure boundary by an extra eighth note, a hint of a 3+3+3 grouping emerges, alluding to the possibility of an abiding 4:6 cross-rhythmic layer in action (four dotted quarter notes against six quarter-note beats of the main pulse; see Figure 11.2(a) and ⏵ Audio Example 11.2). However, no fourth event manifests itself to reinforce this impression; instead, an ascending motif of eighth notes starting on the "two" of the second measure returns the bass riff to the main pulse before a final anticipatory pick-up to the "one" kicks off the basic unit all over again.

Taking into account the centripetal force produced by all the tonic D notes in the entire basic unit, coupled with the fact that the syncopation on the "three-and" is located a further dotted quarter note before the 3+3+3 grouped events, one might even begin to hear this D as setting into motion the dotted quarter-note cross-rhythmic layer implied previously, potentially forming a 4:6 counter-rhythm. Alternatively, though, if one considers that the first A in the ascending eighth-note motif of the second measure can be heard as a focal tonal point in its own right (the track, in fact, begins on it), this note and the following two eighth notes may additionally be heard as a grouping of 3. As a result, the bass riff presents no single clear instance of 4:6 cross-rhythm as such but instead implies several potential groupings of three eighth notes that, upon repeated hearings, allude to a layer of dotted-quarter notes atop the main pulse that forms a number of potential counter-rhythmic configurations at any given time depending on one's perspective (see Figure 11.2(b) and ⏵ Audio Example 11.2).

Admittedly, such an interpretation may seem rather tenuous at first; after all, whichever way one sees it, the bass figure always presents salient events that coincide with the main beat locations of the meter. However, as Butler has noted, counter-rhythmic patterns that display complex subdivision groupings "actually tend to *reinforce* important metrical junctures" (Butler 2006, 157), and it is precisely this inherently ambiguous character—belonging to both and neither pulse and counter-rhythm at the same time—that provides the exciting element of rhythmic tension that drives many a successful groove.

FIGURE 11.2 Bass riff in "(Your Love Keeps Lifting Me) Higher and Higher." Potential eighth-note groupings and cross-rhythmic tendencies indicated by brackets and rhythmic notation above the staff, respectively.

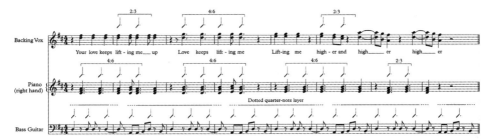

FIGURE 11.3 Cross-rhythmic tendencies in piano, backing vocals, and bass in "(Your Love Keeps Lifting Me) Higher and Higher," indicated by rhythmic notation above the staffs.

During the chorus sections, the piano actually displays counter-rhythms where the tendency toward 4:6 (and related 2:3) cross-rhythms is much more obvious than it is in the bass (see Figure 11.3 and ⓟ Audio Example 11.3). Here, the dotted quarter-note layer frequently manifests itself on the second downbeat of the first measure and ends a quarter note before the second measure ends. (Note that the cross-rhythmic tendency of the bass pattern comes forward as phase shifted in relation to the piano, probably causing the bass rhythm to seem even more ambiguous.) Once one has tuned into these counter-rhythmic motifs, one begins to hear them in several other instruments throughout the track as well, including the backing vocals (also shown in Figure 11.3) as well as the tambourine, guitar, and various combinations of all of them.

Beat Bins: Clustering and Extending Beats through Editing and Processing of Rhythmic Sounds in Contemporary R&B and Neo Soul

The experience of a groove can also be enhanced via manipulation of the shape of the sound. This practice has accelerated as a consequence of new possibilities for editing and/or processing sound. Through the combination of different layers that imply more radically divergent locations of the pulse at the micro level than the onset asynchronies usually found in played styles such as jazz and funk, one can achieve a characteristic feeling of "clustered" beats. Alternatively, one sound can be edited or processed such that its exact rhythmic placement becomes vague. As a consequence, the internal beat changes from a narrower point-like shape (narrow beat bin) to a more saddle-like shape (wide beat bin) with a considerable extension in time (Danielsen 2010; see Figure 11.4). Both these forms of beat-bin meter (Danielsen 2018) yield a very characteristic microrhythmic feel.

Early examples of clustered beats can be found on D'Angelo's *Voodoo* (1999). On several songs on this album, multiple locations of the pulse merge into extended beats at the micro level of the groove. These effects are most likely produced through the displacement of recorded layers of the groove. Measurements in the amplitude/time representation of the groove of "Left & Right" reveal that the "glitch" or discrepancy measured as inter-onset-interval (IOI) between the two rhythmic layers of the song is considerable: approximately 55 milliseconds on the downbeats (beats 1 and 3) of the basic one-bar-long rhythmic pattern (in 4/4 meter), and approximately 80 milliseconds on the offbeats (beats 2 and 4)—that is, between 8 and 12 percent of a quarter note in the song's tempo (92 beats per minute [bpm]; see Figure 11.5 and ⏵ Audio Example 11.4a–c).

Especially on the offbeats, the sharp attack of the syncopated guitar, which structurally strikes a sixteenth note ahead of the beat, is far too close to the equally sharp attack of the snare drum on the beat. Put differently, the virtual or "structural" distance is one sixteenth note, but the actual distance is only one thirty-second note (for detailed analyses, see Danielsen 2010; Danielsen et al. 2015a). This discrepancy produces a very characteristic tilt in the groove. On the track "Untitled (How Does It Feel)" from the same album, the beat bin is even bigger—in fact, generally around 90 milliseconds (see

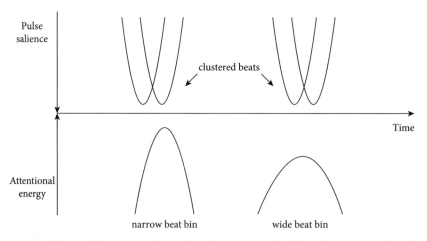

FIGURE 11.4 Clustered beats (actual sound) and narrow and wide beat bin (internal beat shape), respectively.

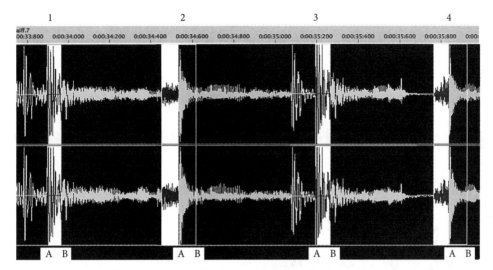

FIGURE 11.5 Waveform of bar 14 of "Left & Right" (amplitude/time). Highlighted areas (in black) mark the IOI (inter-onset-intervals) between bass drum (A) and guitar (B) at beats 1 and 3, syncopated guitar and snare drum (A) at beats 2 and 4. Pulse location B is indicated by a black line that appears a sixteenth note after the attack of the syncopated guitar. The three audio clips in ⊙ Audio Example 11.4 illustrate: (a) an excerpt from the first verse to provide a sense of the overall groove; (b) the bar shown in Figure 11.5; (c) the same bar, slowed down to make the wide beat bins audible.

analysis in Bjerke 2010)—which approaches the threshold for temporal segregation in auditory perception (London 2012, 27–29).

A recent example of the use of sound processing to manipulate the internal pulse of the listener is the synth-pad/kick drum "bins" of Rihanna's "Needed Me" (the third single from her 2016 album *Anti*). A crucial aspect of this song's microrhythmic dynamics derives from the manipulation of the sounds that constitute the groove foundation of the track (see Figure 11.6 and ⊙ Audio Example 11.5).

A reversed sound consisting of a deep, sawtooth-like bass synth and a voice sample/synth pad accelerates toward the bass drum kick, reversing the expected dynamic of a traditional bass drum/bass layer, where the kick usually initiates the more extended sound of the bass. When this motion is reversed, it generates a peculiar rhythmic feel that recalls the much-used side-chain "ducking" effect of electronic dance music and related styles. This is achieved through the use of a kick drum to control a compressor on the main output such that the level of the main output is reduced whenever the kick drum is present. This technique might have been employed to produce the accelerating "reversed" feel of the synth-pad sound in "Needed Me" as well, only that the kick drum stroke on beat 4 initiating this reversed sound is not audible. Microrhythmic manipulation of this kind has become an almost standard part of the groove repertoire in contemporary R&B-based pop music.

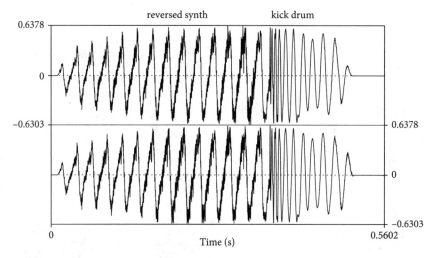

FIGURE 11.6 Reversed sound accelerating toward the kick drum in Rihanna's "Needed Me" (2016). ⓟ Audio Example 11.5(a) provides an entire bar of the song for context 11.5; (b) corresponds to the single beat shown in the figure.

Conclusion

While there is generally little doubt as to whether a groove is "good" or not when one is experiencing it in the moment, what exactly makes it so can be quite challenging to ascertain after the fact. As it occurs in the here and now of performance or perception, the ineffable state of being in the groove is, in fact, impossible to come to terms with; the very act of endeavoring to grasp it a posteriori dissociates one from the immersive groove experience itself. No definition—including those that explicitly aim to capture the elusive processual character of groove—escapes this basic hermeneutic premise. Nonetheless, despite groove's inherently multifarious nature, we have attempted to elucidate a few aspects of it, first by reviewing three general understandings derived from various disciplines concerned with its study (groove as pattern and performance; as pleasure and appeal to movement; as a state of being), then by proposing a non-exhaustive set of features seemingly common to a wide range of groove styles (pulse/beat, subdivisions, syncopation, counter-rhythm, microrhythm), and finally by applying a combination of these outlined approaches to the analysis of a few selected grooves from the African-American musical tradition. As a final note, it should be acknowledged that the impetus toward an academic understanding of groove is a relatively new one, and therefore the theoretical and methodological approaches touched upon in this chapter by no means delimit all possible avenues of exploration. Much like groove itself, our knowledge about groove seems to get better the longer we engage with it, and, as it stands today, the future of analytical groove studies still holds a great deal of promise and potential.

Audio Examples

Audio Example 11.1. Excerpt from A section of "Get Up (I Feel Like Being a) Sex Machine" by James Brown.

Audio Example 11.2. Bass riff in "(Your Love Keeps Lifting Me) Higher and Higher."

Audio Example 11.3. Chorus, "(Your Love Keeps Lifting Me) Higher and Higher."

Audio Example 11.4. Three excerpts from "Left & Right": (a) an excerpt from the first verse to provide a sense of overall groove; (b) the bar shown in Figure 5; (c) the same bar, slowed down to make the wide beat bins more audible.

Audio Example 11.5. Reversed sound accelerating toward the kick drum in Rihanna's "Needed Me" (2016). Audio example (a) provides an entire bar of the song for context; (b) corresponds to the single beat shown in the figure.

Notes

1. *Merriam Webster Dictionary Online, s.v.* "Groove," https://www.merriam-webster.com/dictionary/groove.

2. According to Kernfeld (2017), early examples of the term used in song titles are "In the Groove" (1937, Decca 1621), by Andy Kirk's big band, and Chick Webb's "In the Groove at the Grove" (1939, Decca 2323), with Ella Fitzgerald.

3. It is to be noted that, due to the non-culturally specific nature of certain "groove" definitions (see below), the term has come to be applied to describe aspects of musical genres extending far beyond the confines of its original African American connotation, such as Western classical (Roholt 2014) and Scandinavian folk music (Johansson 2010; Kvifte 2004), among others.

4. This interaction resembles the interaction between syntax and actual speech or writing in linguistics (for linguistic theory that conforms to this theoretical premise, see Bakhtin 1986; Ricoeur 1973). This theoretical premise is today widely accepted in the various strands of research on rhythm (see, e.g., Clarke 1985; Desain and Honing 2003; Iyer 2002; Keil 1995; Kvifte 2004; Pressing 2002).

5. The participants also rated music from various genres. Overall, soul and R&B were rated highest in terms of mean groove rating, compared to jazz (second), rock (third), and folk (fourth) (Janata et al. 2012, 59). However, the differences among the ratings of the other three genres (jazz, rock, folk) were not statistically significant. Moreover, faster tempi resulted in higher groove ratings. Generally, groove rating was strongly positively correlated with how much a person enjoyed the excerpts (59–60).

6. In the tempo ranges typical of most groove styles (90–120 beats per minute), the duration of thirty-second notes approaches or falls below the threshold of human perception of short durations (around 120 milliseconds, according to Efron 1973). Thus, they will tend to be heard as "categorically" subsumed within slower subdivision levels (Clarke 1987) and likely experienced either as ornamentations (grace notes, tremolos, flams, and so on) or as late/early attacks (Butterfield 2006). Interestingly, research has pointed to the potential structural salience of events faster than 100 milliseconds as well (Câmara 2016; Polak 2010).

7. For example, in styles featuring the archetypical "back-beat" pattern, the phenomenal accent pattern can be felt as the opposite of the normal 4/4 metrical accent: weak–strong–weak–strong. This does not imply, however, that back-beat events are felt as "unexpected"

syncopations of the meter, but rather that they form instances of beat-level "hocketing" ("streams of the same basic period ['metrical level'] out of phase" London 2012, 66), that is, the back-beat accents regularly chafe against established metrical accents without displacing them.

8. In the Black Atlantic rhythmic diaspora—including, for example, jazz, blues, gospel, reggae, rock, candomblé, cumbia, and hip-hop—this practice takes the form of syncopation, overlay, displacement, off-beat phrasing, cross-rhythm, and swing (Pressing 2002, 300–301).

9. With perhaps the exception of overtly jazz-influenced styles such as jazz-funk or acid jazz, although even here they tend to be utilized during solo segments rather than within accompaniment-section rhythms.

10. Keil (1995) left the question of norm open, focusing primarily on the relationships among musicians in performance. However, he has been criticized for understating the importance of structure by, among others, Butterfield and Kvifte, who both point to the interaction of structure and microtiming (Butterfield 2006; 2011) or syntax and process (Kvifte 2004) as crucial aspects of groove.

11. The term "onset" has commonly described the beginning of a sound event; it is often formally defined as the location in a waveform graph where an event's amplitude signal crosses a predetermined minimum threshold. The term "attack point" is commonly equated with the maximum amplitude peak. In fact, however, the perceived attack lies somewhere between perceptual onset and the attack point of the sound (see Villing 2010 for an overview of research into the perceptual center of sounds).

12. In jazz, musicians tend to swing pairs of eighth notes at ratios typically ranging between 1:1 ("straight") and 2:1 ("tied-triplet swing," or a quarter triplet note followed by an eighth triplet note), although occasionally up to even higher ratios of 3:1 ("heavy swing," or a dotted eighth note followed by a sixteenth note) and beyond (Friberg and Sundström 2002).

13. Roughly the threshold where subdivisions cease to be categorically heard as straight (even in duration) and instead as swung (uneven in duration), based on conservative heuristics proposed by Friberg and Sundström (2002) and Butterfield (2011).

14. Swing ratios of sixteenth-note pairs were calculated by dividing the duration of an off-beat note by the duration of its preceding on-beat note. This relationship is then represented in either ratio (e.g., 1.2:1) or decimal form (e.g., 1.2). Durations were determined based on inter-onset-intervals (IOIs), that is, the time distance between onsets of successive note events, using instruments' own note onsets as reference points for IOIs, where available. In instances where either the first on-beat sixteenth was unsounded (as is the case with syncopations or pick-up notes) or no third on-beat sixteenth-note or eighth-note event ensued after the second sounded sixteenth-note off-beat, swing ratios were instead calculated relative to the attack onset locations of actual sounded hi-hat cymbal strokes. See Câmara 2016 for further explanation.

15. The difference in thresholds between high and low swing density rhythms was found, however, to be generally higher for non-drummer than drummer subjects.

16. They are also exceedingly common in Afro-Latin and Afro-Caribbean music, particularly the 3+3+2 counter-rhythm, commonly termed the "habanera" (London 2012) or "tresillo" figure (Stover 2012). This figure features prominently in the Cuban "son clave," as well as in countless foundational rhythmic patterns of genres ranging from Brazilian samba to Jamaican dancehall, to name only a few.

WORKS CITED

Anku, Willi. 2000. "Circles and Time: A Theory of Structural Organization of Rhythm in African Music." *Music Theory Online* 6, no. 4. http://www.mtosmt.org/issues/mto.00.6.1/mto.00.6.1. anku_essay.html.

Arom, Simha. 1991. *African Polyphony and Polyrhythm: Musical Structure and Methodology.* Cambridge: Cambridge University Press.

Bakhtin, Mikhail Mikhailovich. 1986. "The Problem of Speech Genres." In *Speech Genres and Other Late Essays*, edited by Caryl Emerson and Michael Holquist, 60–102. Austin: University of Texas Press.

Bengtsson, Ingmar, Alf Gabrielsson, and Stig-Magnus Thorsén. 1969. "Empirisk rytmforskning." *Svensk tidsskrift för musikforskning*, 95–96.

Berliner, Paul. 1994. *Thinking in Jazz: The Infinite Art of Improvisation.* Chicago: University of Chicago Press.

Bjerke, Kristoffer Y. 2010. "Timbral Relationships and Microrhythmic Tension: Shaping the Groove Experience through Sound." In *Musical Rhythm in the Age of Digital Reproduction*, edited by Anne Danielsen, 85–101. Farnham, Surrey: Ashgate/Routledge.

Bowman, Rob. 1995. "The Stax Sound: A Musicological Analysis." *Popular Music* 14: 285–320.

Brown, James. 1970. "Get Up (I Feel Like Being a) Sex Machine." King. 7″ single.

Brøvig-Hanssen, Ragnhild, and Anne Danielsen. 2016. *Digital Signatures: The Impact of Digitization on Popular Music Sound.* Cambridge, MA: MIT Press.

Burnim, Mellonee V., and Portia K. Maultsby, eds. 2015. *African American Music: An Introduction.* 2nd edition. New York: Routledge.

Burns, J. 2010. "Rhythmic Archetypes in Instrumental Music from Africa and the Diaspora." *Music Theory Online* 16, no. 4. http://www.mtosmt.org/issues/mto.10.16.4/mto.10.16.4.burns. html.

Butler, Mark J. 2006. *Unlocking the Groove: Rhythm, Meter and Musical Design in Electronic Dance Music.* Bloomington: Indiana University Press.

Butterfield, Mathew. 2006. "The Power of Anacrusis: Engendered Feeling in Groove-Based Musics." *Music Theory Online* 12, no. 4. http://www.mtosmt.org/issues/mto.06.12.4/mto. 06.12.4.butterfield.html.

Butterfield, Matthew W. 2011. "Why Do Jazz Musicians Swing Their Eighth Notes?" *Music Theory Spectrum* 33: 3–26.

Bøhler, Kjetil Klette. 2013. "Grooves, Pleasures, and Politics in Salsa Cubana: The Musicality of Cuban Politics—and the Politics of Salsa Cubana." PhD diss., University of Oslo.

Câmara, Guilherme Schmidt. 2016. "Swing in Early Funk and Jazz-Funk (1967–1971): Micro-Rhythmic and Macro-Structural Investigations." Master's thesis, University of Oslo.

Clarke, Eric F. 1985. "Structure and Expression in Rhythmic Performance." In *Musical Structure and Cognition*, edited by Peter Howell, Ian Cross, and Robert West, 209–236. London: Academic Press.

Clarke, Eric F. 1987. "Categorical Rhythm Perception: An Ecological Perspective." In *Action and Perception in Rhythm and Music*, edited by Alf Gabrielsson, 19–34. Stockholm: Royal Swedish Academy of Music.

D'Angelo. 2000. "Left & Right." *Voodoo.* Virgin. CD.

Danielsen, Anne. 2006. *Presence and Pleasure: The Funk Grooves of James Brown and Parliament.* Middletown, CT: Wesleyan University Press.

Danielsen, Anne. 2010. "Here, There, and Everywhere: Three Accounts of Pulse in D'Angelo's 'Left and Right.'" In *Musical Rhythm in the Age of Digital Reproduction*, edited by Anne Danielsen, 19–36. Farnham, Surrey: Ashgate/Routledge.

Danielsen, Anne. 2015. "Metrical Ambiguity or Microrhythmic Flexibility? Analysing Groove in 'Nasty Girl' by Destiny's Child." In *Song Interpretation in 21st-Century Pop Music*, edited by Ralf von Appen, André Doehring, and Allan F. Moore, 53–72. Farnham, Surrey: Ashgate.

Danielsen, Anne. 2018. "Pulse as Dynamic Attending. Analysing Beat Bin Metre in Neo Soul Grooves." In *The Routledge Companion to Popular Music Analysis: Expanding Approaches*, edited by Ciro Scotto, Kenneth M. Smith, and John Brackett, 179–189. London: Routledge.

Danielsen, Anne, Mari Romarheim Haugen, and Alexander Refsum Jensenius 2015a. "Moving to the Beat: Studying Entrainment to Micro-Rhythmic Changes in Pulse by Motion Capture." *Timing and Time Perception* 3: 133–154.

Danielsen, Anne, Carl Haakon Waadeland, Henrik. G. Sundt, and Maria. A. G. Witek. 2015b. "Effects of instructed timing and tempo on snare drum sound in drum kit performance," in *Journal of the Acoustical Society of America* 138: 2301–2316.

De Haas, W. Bas. 2007. "The Role of Tempo in Groove and Swing Timing." Master's thesis, Utrecht University.

Desain, Peter, and Henkjan Honing. 2003. "The Formation of Rhythmic Categories and Metric Priming." *Perception* 32: 341–365.

Efron, R. 1973. "An Invariant Characteristic of Perceptual Systems in the Time Domain." In *Attention and Performance IV*, edited by S. Kornblum, 713–736. New York: Academic Press.

Feld, Steven. 1988. "Aesthetics as Iconicity of Style, or 'Lift-Up-Over Sounding': Getting into the Kaluli Groove." *Yearbook for Traditional Music* 20: 74–112.

Frane, Andrew V. 2017. "Swing Rhythm in Classic Drum Breaks From Hip-Hop's Breakbeat Canon." *Music Perception* 34: 291–302.

Frane, Andrew V., and Ladan Shams. 2017. "Effects of Tempo, Swing Density, and Listener's Drumming Experience, on Swing Detection Thresholds for Drum Rhythms." *Journal of the Acoustical Society of America* 141: 4200–4208.

Friberg, Anders, and Andreas Sundström. 2002. "Swing Ratios and Ensemble Timing in Jazz Performance: Evidence for a Common Rhythmic Pattern." *Music Perception: An Interdisciplinary Journal* 19: 333–349.

Gerischer, Christiane. 2006. "*O suingue Baiano*: Rhythmic Feeling and Microrhythmic Phenomena in Brazilian Percussion." *Ethnomusicology* 50: 99–119.

Gómez, Francisco, Eric Thul, and Godfried T. Toussaint. 2007. "An Experimental Comparison of Formal Measures of Rhythmic Syncopation." In *Proceedings of the International Computer Music Conference*, 101–104. Copenhagen.

Gordon, John W. 1987. "The Perceptual Attack Time of Musical Tones." *Journal of the Acoustical Society of America* 82: 88–105.

Hasty, Christopher. 1997. *Meter as Rhythm*. New York: Oxford University Press.

Haugen, Mari Romarheim. 2016. "Music–Dance: Investigating Rhythm Structures in Brazilian Samba and Norwegian Telespringar Performance." PhD diss., University of Oslo.

Huron, David. 2006. *Sweet Anticipation: Music and the Psychology of Expectation*. Cambridge, MA: MIT Press.

Iyer, Vijay. 2002. "Embodied Mind, Situated Cognition, and Expressive Microtiming in African-American Music." *Music Perception* 19: 387–414.

Janata, Petr, Stefan T. Tomic, and Jason M. Haberman. 2012. "Sensorimotor Coupling in Music and the Psychology of the Groove." *Journal of Experimental Psychology: General* 141: 54–75.

Johansson, Mats. 2010. "Rhythm into Style: Studying Asymmetrical Grooves in Norwegian Folk Music." PhD diss., University of Oslo.

Jones, Mari R. 1976. "Time, Our Lost Dimension: Toward a New Theory of Perception, Attention, and Memory." *Psychological Review* 83: 323–355.

Keil, Charles. 1995. "The Theory of Participatory Discrepancies: A Progress Report." *Ethnomusicology* 39: 1–20.

Keil, Charles, and Steven Feld. 2005. *Music Grooves: Essays and Dialogues.* 2nd edition. Tucson, AZ: Fenestra.

Kernfeld, Barry. 2017. "Groove (i)." *The New Grove Dictionary of Jazz.* 2nd edition. *Grove Music Online, Oxford Music Online.* http://www.oxfordmusiconline.com/subscriber/article/grove/music/J582400.

Kolinski, Mieczyslaw. 1973. "A Cross-Cultural Approach to Metro-Rhythmic Patterns." *Ethnomusicology* 17: 494–506.

Kvifte, Tellef. 2004. "Description of Grooves and Syntax/Process Dialectics." *Studia Musicologica Norvegica* 30: 54–77.

Large, Edward W., Jorge A. Herrera, and Marc J. Velasco. 2015. "Neural Networks for Beat Perception in Musical Rhythm." *Frontiers in Systems Neuroscience* 9, no. 11. https://doi.org/10.3389/fnsys.2015.00159.

Large, Edward W., and Mari Riess Jones. 1999. "The Dynamics of Attending: How People Track Time-Varying Events." *Psychological Review* 106: 119–159.

Lerdahl, Fred, and Ray Jackendoff. 1983. *A Generative Theory of Tonal Music.* Cambridge, MA: MIT Press.

Locke, David. 1982. "Principles of Offbeat Timing and Cross-Rhythm in Southern Eυe Dance Drumming." *Ethnomusicology* 26: 217–246.

London, Justin. 2012. *Hearing in Time: Psychological Aspects of Musical Meter.* 2nd edition. New York: Oxford University Press.

London, Justin, Rainer Polak, and Nori Jacoby. 2017. "Rhythm Histograms and Musical Meter: A Corpus Study of Malian Percussion Music." *Psychonomic Bulletin and Review* 24: 474–480.

Madison, Guy. 2006. "Experiencing Groove Induced by Music: Consistency and Phenomenology." *Music Perception* 24: 201–208.

Madison, Guy. 2014. "Sensori-Motor Synchronisation Variability Decreases as the Number of Metrical Levels in the Stimulus Signal Increases." *Acta Psychologica* 147: 10–16.

Merker, Bjorn H., Guy S. Madison, and Patricia Eckerdal. 2009. "On the Role and Origin of Isochrony in Human Rhythmic Entrainment." *Cortex* 45: 4–17.

Milkowski, Bill. 2007. "Professor of Funk Jim Payne Holds Court on the Art of Groove." *Modern Drummer* 31, no. 1: 146–154.

Monson, Ingrid T. 1996. *Saying Something: Jazz Improvisation and Interaction.* Chicago: University of Chicago Press.

Nketia, J. H. Kwabena. 1974. *The Music of Africa.* New York: W. W. Norton.

Novotny, Eugene D. 1998. "The 3:2 Relationship as the Foundation of Timelines in West African Musics." PhD diss., University of Illinois.

Polak, Rainer. 2010. "Rhythmic Feel as Meter: Non-Isochronous Beat Subdivision in Jembe Music from Mali." *Music Theory Online* 16, no. 4. http://www.mtosmt.org/issues/mto.10.16.4/mto.10.16.4.polak.html.

Polak, Rainer, and Justin London. 2014. "Timing and meter in Mande drumming from Mali." *Music Theory Online* 20, no. 1. http://www.mtosmt.org/issues/mto.14.20.1/mto.14.20.1.polak-london.html.

Polak, Rainer, Justin London, and Nori Jacoby. 2016. "Both Isochronous and Non-Isochronous Metrical Subdivision Afford Precise and Stable Ensemble Entrainment: A Corpus Study of Malian Jembe Drumming." *Frontiers in Neuroscience* 10, no. 6. https://doi.org/10.3389/fnins.2016.00285.

Pressing, Jeff. 2002. "Black Atlantic Rhythm: Its Computational and Transcultural Foundations." *Music Perception* 19: 285–310.

Randel, Don Michael, and Willi Apel, eds. 1986. *The New Harvard Dictionary of Music*. Cambridge, MA: Belknap Press of Harvard University Press.

Rasch, Rudolf A. 1988. "Timing and Synchronization in Ensemble Performance." In *Generative Process in Music: The Psychology of Performance, Improvisation, and Composition*, edited by John A. Sloboda, 70–90. Oxford: Clarendon Press.

Repp, Bruno H. 1996. "Patterns of Note Onset Asynchronies in Expressive Piano Performance." *Journal of the Acoustical Society of America* 100: 3917–3932.

Ricoeur, Pierre. 1973. "The Hermeneutical Function of Distanciation." *Philosophy Today* 17: 129–143.

Rihanna. 2016. "Needed Me." *Anti*. Westbury Road/Roc Nation. CD.

Roholt, Tiger C. 2014. *Groove: A Phenomenology of Rhythmic Nuance*. New York: Bloomsbury Academic.

Senn, Olivier, Claudia Bullerjahn, Lorenz Kilchenmann, and Richard von Georgi. 2017. "Rhythmic Density Affects Listeners' Emotional Response to Microtiming." *Frontiers in Psychology* 8, no. 10. https://doi.org/10.3389/fpsyg.2017.01709.

Sioros, George, Marius Miron, Matthew Davies, Fabien Gouyon, and Guy Madison. 2014. "Syncopation Creates the Sensation of Groove in Synthesized Music Examples." *Frontiers in Psychology* 5, no. 9. https://doi.org/10.3389/fpsyg.2014.01036.

Stewart, Alexander. 2000. " 'Funky Drummer': New Orleans, James Brown, and the Rhythmic Transformation of American Popular Music." *Popular Music* 19: 293–318.

Stover, Chris. 2012. "The Clave Matrix: Afro-Cuban Rhythm: Its Principles and Origins (review)." *Latin American Music Review* 33: 131–140.

Tekman, Hasan G. 1997. "Interactions of Perceived Intensity, Duration, and Pitch in Pure Tone Sequences." *Music Perception* 14: 281–294.

Temperley, David. 1999. "Syncopation in Rock: A Perceptual Perspective." *Popular Music* 18: 19–40.

Villing, Rudi. 2010. "Hearing the Moment: Measures and Models of the Perceptual Centre." PhD diss., National University of Ireland, Maynooth.

Waadeland, Carl Haakon 2001. " 'It Don't Mean a Thing If It Ain't Got That Swing'—Simulating Expressive Timing by Modulated Movements." *Journal of New Music Research* 30: 23–37.

Wilson, Jackie. 1967. "(Your Love Keeps Lifting Me) Higher and Higher." Brunswick. 7′ Single.

Wilson, Olly. 1974. "The Significance of the Relationship between Afro-American Music and West African Music." *The Black Perspective in Music* 2: 3–22.

Witek, Maria A. G. 2017. "Filling In: Syncopation, Pleasure and Distributed Embodiment in Groove." *Music Analysis* 36: 138–160.

Witek, Maria A. G., Eric F. Clarke, Mikkel Wallentin, Morten L. Kringelbach, and Peter Vuust. 2014. "Syncopation, Body-Movement and Pleasure in Groove Music." *PLoS ONE* 9, no. 4. https://doi.org/10.1371/journal.pone.0094446.

Wright, Matthew J. 2008. "The Shape of an Instant: Measuring and Modeling Perceptual Attack Time with Probability Density Functions." PhD diss., Stanford University.

CHAPTER 12

....

PHRASE

....

JANET SCHMALFELDT

A BEGINNING, OR WHERE TO BEGIN?
....

"WHAT is a Phrase? What is Phrase Rhythm?" This is the title of William Rothstein's first chapter in his ground-breaking *Phrase Rhythm in Tonal Music* (1989). Rothstein's responses to these questions continue to inspire, and to invite debate, especially among Schenkerian scholars, historians of the eighteenth-century *Satzlehre* tradition, and theorists of tonal form. Rothstein specifically announces that his book addresses "Classic and Romantic music only"; his four case studies focus on music by Haydn, Mendelssohn, Chopin, and Wagner. And yet, if his theory of phrase is relevant to *all* tonal music, as he suggests (1989, vii), then it would also embrace an unlimited range of musical styles flourishing before Haydn and after Wagner, and extending to much folk and popular music in our era. Of course, Rothstein knows this; he opens his study by inviting us to think of the melodic shape of "a popular song, any popular song—from operetta to the latest rock hit to 'America the Beautiful'" (1989, 2).

Might we entertain the possibility that, with certain admittedly striking exceptions, "phrases" can be imagined in many of the world's musics—tonal or otherwise, notated or aurally transmitted, Western or beyond? Indeed, even the music in Robert O. Gjerdingen's fictional land of Bijou would seem to have phrases![1] This speculation runs awry as soon as we acknowledge that there may be as many shades of meaning for the term "phrase" as there are applications of it, ranging from carefully defined to offhand. It should go without saying that any idea of phrase will be contingent upon the nature of the music under consideration—its style, its historical, cultural, and ethnic context, its social functions. Moreover, for scholars of a broad range of musical styles, the concept of phrase is inextricably bound to ideas about musical grammar, syntax, cadence, accent, rhythm, meter, and form. By contrast, performers—music-makers of any status, amateur or professional—are centrally concerned with *phrasing*, the expressive and dynamic act of shaping "phrases."[2] For these musicians, concepts of phrase devised by music theorists, analysts, historical musicologists, and ethnomusicologists may seem foreign, or at least needlessly complex; as well, practitioners within those disparate but related fields often have good reasons for disagreeing with one another. In short, the effort to arrive at a unitary, global definition of phrase is doomed to fail. There may, however, be the possibility of finding a few commonalities among definitions and appropriations of the term; this is what I seek.

Accordingly, I begin with a search for origins, or at least emerging notions, of phrase, and for modern-day applications of the term to some of the oldest notated music in the West.

ORIGINS: TEXT, PUNCTUATION, GROUPING

Those knowledgeable about Western medieval chant will recognize the kinds of music shown in Figure 12.1, and perhaps even their role within the liturgy. *Ecce apparebit Dominus*, in Figure 12.1(a), is an anonymous ninth-century antiphon, a short chant for the season of Advent, to be performed antiphonally by a choir as a frame for the singing of the psalm *Laudate Dominum* in Figure 12.1(b) (only the first two intoned verses of the psalm are shown). The texts, with translations from the Latin—for the antiphon, from the book of the prophet Habbakuk (Hab. 2:3), and for the psalm tone, the opening of the Hebrew Psalm 147—are given in Figure 12.1(c). The entire psalter, a collection of the 150 psalms, would be intoned, as aurally (and orally) memorized by the singers, over weekly cycles of the Divine Office—eight daily hours of prayer within medieval monasteries, cathedrals, and parish churches in the Latin West. Each psalm text was assigned to one of the eight medieval modes ("church modes"); an antiphon with an associated text would be paired with it, to introduce the psalm and then to be repeated upon its completion. For this antiphon and its psalm tone, we have mode 7 (G authentic, or Mixolydian).

In the staff directly above the beginning of *Laudate Dominum* (Figure 12.1(b), first staff), you'll see the formula for psalm tones in the seventh mode. As explained by musicologist Margot Fassler, from whose work I have drawn the example, the formula begins with an "intonation" that moves to the "reciting pitch" of the mode (here D, given a "flex"—a short line, to accommodate long texts). A "mediant," or "middle phrase," reaches a "midpoint cadence" (Fassler's terms). As the text nears its end, it will be fitted into a "termination formula" (*differentia*), in this case the stepwise descent to A; the cadential formula smoothly links the intoned psalm verse to the reprise of the antiphon (Fassler 2014b, 18–19). All three phases (if not phrases)—the opening formula, the middle phrase, and the termination—generate "musical punctuation marks . . . One can think of the *flex* as a kind of comma, whereas the mediant is a semicolon, and the *differentia*, a period" (Fassler 2014a, 64).

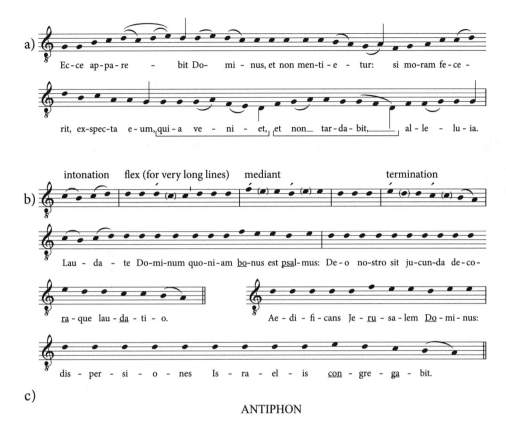

c)

ANTIPHON

Ecce apparebit Dominus, et non mentietur: si moram fecerit, expecta eum, quia veniet, et non tardabit, alleluia.	Behold, the Lord will come; He will not prove false. If He makes a delay, wait for Him; for He will come and not be slow, alleluia.
	Habbakuk 2:3, Douay/Reims Bible

PSALM VERSES 1 and 2

Laudate Dominum quoniam <u>bon</u>us est <u>psal</u>mus: Deo nostro sit jucunda deco<u>ra</u>que lau<u>da</u>tio.	Praise the Lord, because a psalm is good: to our God be joyful and comely praise.
Aedificans Je<u>ru</u>salem <u>Do</u>minus: dispersiones Israelis con<u>gre</u>gabit.	The Lord builds up Jerusalem: He will gather together the dispersed of Israel.
	Psalm 147 (146): 1–2

(Translation from Fassler 2014b, 17–18.)

FIGURE 12.1 Antiphon with the first two intoned psalm verses (ninth century): (a) *Ecce apparebit Dominus;* (b) *Laudate Dominum* (Psalm 147) (Fassler 2014b, 16–18); (c) texts with translations.

In Fassler's words: "The antiphons and the psalm tones formed the backbone of medieval chant. They not only allowed for the memorization and proclamation of the most
important texts for singing from the Bible, but also promoted through the tones a very
successful way of learning music" (2014a, 63).

We can note, first of all, that Fassler freely uses the term "phrase" in her analysis, and
that in each case the length and shape of a musical phrase for her is defined by the textual
phrase or, in some cases, by the single word that it sets—for example, "Ecce apparebit
Dominus," in the antiphon, and "Laudate" at the opening of the psalm tone (2014b, 19–
20).[3] Fassler thus invokes the centuries-old association of "vocal phrase" with text—
music with language, tone with word—in application to music from the very beginning
of the Western notated tradition.[4] In a similar vein, Richard Hoppin speaks of the psalm
tones as "liturgical recitative":

> Quite obviously, musical interest in these tones is entirely subservient to sentence
> structure and word accentuation. We may well agree with Johannes de Grocheo, a
> theorist writing about 1300, when he says that prayer and readings do not concern
> the musician. One might even ask why these texts were sung at all.

But Hoppin has an answer:

> The practice of chanted Biblical readings is, of course, very old, reaching back to the
> Jewish synagogue. Moreover, the combination of song with prayer and storytelling is
> as old as humanity itself and undoubtedly arose from a desire for the most effective
> communication.
>
> (Hoppin 1978, 79–80)

The storytelling continues—in the great sacred and secular choral music from the
Middle Ages to the present; in opera; in Lieder of the eighteenth- and nineteenth-century
traditions; and in popular song. The dependency of phrase upon text extends alongside and well beyond Romantic valorizations in the early nineteenth century of "pure,"
wordless instrumental music as an autonomous art form. Composers and performers of
these vocal genres—singers, conductors, accompanists—tend to be acutely aware of the
demands that a distinct articulation of the text makes upon the shaping of a phrase. For
such performers, phrases will be like Fassler's: short or longer segments of the melodic
line that correspond with textual divisions, as signaled by punctuation signs and often
marked by the need for a breath.

In fact, Fassler directly alludes to theories of "punctuation-form": when the three
phrases of her psalm tone combine to intone the complete psalm verse, they invoke an
analogy with the successive, hierarchically ordered punctuation sequence in written
language of comma, semicolon, and period. More broadly speaking, we needn't remind
ourselves that, faced with a temporal but essentially non-verbal, non-spatial, and non-
pictorial art form, we have shamelessly, and with probable necessity, borrowed so much
of our analytic terminology from the punctuation, grammar, syntax, and rhetoric of

language, itself only understood as it proceeds in time: this includes the word "phrase" itself, of course, but also subject, predicate, clause, sentence, theme, paragraph, period, cadence, prefix, suffix, and even ideas about rhythm and meter borrowed from poetic verse—all of these metaphors persist in discourses about music today.

The theory of musical punctuation achieves its heyday in the mid-to-late eighteenth century, in the proliferation of encyclopedia, lexicon, and dictionary entries about music, and in expositions on "how to compose" (composition treatises by, for example, Mattheson, Riepel, Marpurg, Kirnberger, and Koch, about whom more in due course). That this development parallels a "linguistic fascination" with the subject of punctuation within Enlightenment thought has been amply documented (Vial 2008, 9).[5] But references to punctuation in writings about music have been with us since the dawn of medieval music theory around the mid-ninth century—a fact of which Fassler is clearly aware.

Caleb Mutch gives a comprehensive account of the revival in Western Europe of classical Greek and Roman rhetoric, as advanced by Aristotle and his successors. In his *Rhetorica* of ca. 330 BCE, Aristotle defined the term "period" [*periodos*] as "an *utterance that has its own beginning and end*, and an *easily comprehensible magnitude*. These periods may be made up of shorter *clauses*, called 'colons' ... [pl., *kōla*]."[6] Mutch explains that "at some point in the following two centuries a new, still shorter unit was added to the hierarchy of period and colon. This was the 'comma' ... [*komma*], that is, a 'cutting,' 'incision,' or 'articulation' of the utterance into brief segments" (Mutch 2015, 17, my emphasis). During Antiquity, theorists in the discipline of rhetoric "focused on developing a vocabulary for analyzing speech into its constitutive phrases and sub-phrases, whereas grammarians formulated a system of punctuation marks to assist the parsing of written text. Both of these approaches proved useful to medieval music theorists as they attempted to describe chant melodies in terms of phrases, their component parts, and their conclusions" (2015, 14). Innovative but muddled applications to chant of the rhetorical-punctuational triad *period–colon–comma* (for example, in the *Musica enchiriadis* and in the treatises attributed to Odo) culminate for Mutch in the "substantial theory of musical closure" articulated by John of Affligem in his *De musica* of ca. 1100 (2015, 10). John actually applied the triadic punctuation hierarchy to the text of the then well-known antiphon "Petrus autem servabatur." Figure 12.2 provides

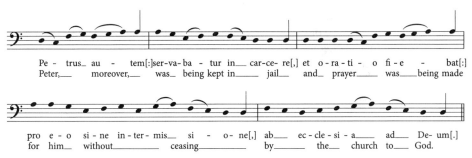

Pe - trus_ au - tem[:]ser-va-ba - tur in__ car-ce- re[,] et o - ra- ti - o fi- e - bat[:]
Peter,__ moreover,__ was_ being kept in____ jail_ and_ prayer____ was__being made

pro e - o si - ne in - ter- mis__ si - o- ne[,] ab__ ec - cle - si - a__ ad__ De- um[.]
for him_ without____ ceasing____ by____ the_ church to__ God.

FIGURE 12.2 "Petrus autem servabatur," antiphon for the feast Vincula Petri (from an early twelfth-century antiphoner) (Mutch 2015, 53).

this antiphon; the chant melody has been supplied by Mutch, who adapts a version from within a contemporaneous twelfth-century antiphoner and adds bar lines to mark John's *distinctiones*—his punctuations—in the syntactic order of colon, comma, colon, comma, and period (2015, 53).[7]

John's *distinctiones* are defined by musical factors: "when a melody rests in a suspended manner (*per suspensionem*) a fourth or a fifth from the final note, it is a colon. When [the melody] is led back to the final note in the middle, it is a comma. When it arrives on the final note at the end, it is a period"[8] (see the stems added by me to tones at the ends of the phrases). Clearly, however, "these musical criteria operate in conjunction with a rhetorical analysis of the text into units of suitable length" (2015, 54). As acknowledged by John, his melodic principles most certainly do not apply to all chants—the stems that I've added to apparent phrase endings within the antiphon in Figure 12.1 show that only four phrases conform with John's rules. Moreover, Mutch reminds us that "our modern concept of a simple sentence does not appear to have a direct correlate in grammatical thought of John's day" (2015, 55).[9] Just the same, John of Affligem's theory shows *where* closure occurs in chant; he "conceives the temporal span of a given chant largely in terms of its verbal text, and defines phrase conclusions in terms of the text's syntactical divisions" (2015, 71). Transmissions of John's doctrine remained of lasting interest to theorists for generations to come.

An entire four and a half centuries later, and now in reference to the high-Renaissance polyphonic music of his preceding generation, we find Gioseffo Zarlino preserving the idea of punctuation in music, while driving home the inseparable connection between "period" in prose or verse and "cadence" in music—terms that for Zarlino seem virtually synonymous. In his greatly influential *Le Istitutioni Harmoniche* from 1558, chapter 53 of Part III, on "The Cadence: Its Nature, Species, and Uses," Zarlino writes:

> The cadence [*cadenza*] is a certain simultaneous progression of all the voices in a composition accompanying a *repose* in the harmony [defined by the translators as "simultaneously moving voices"] or the completion of a meaningful segment of the text upon which the composition is based. We might also say that it is a sort of termination of part of the harmonic flow at a midpoint or at the end, or a separation of the main portions of the text … it should not be used unless the end of a *clause* or *period* of the prose or verse has been reached, that is, only at the end of a section or part of a section. The cadence has a value in music equivalent to the period in prose and could well be called the period of musical composition. It is found also at *resting points* in the harmony, that is, where a section of the harmony terminates, in the same way that we pause in a speech, both at intermediate points and at the end.
>
> (Zarlino 1968, 141–142, my emphasis)

Cadences for Zarlino derive conservatively from the *contrapunctus* tradition, with its individual voice-leading rules, that had come to govern closure in two- to four-voice polyphony as developed over the fourteenth and fifteenth centuries.[10] His many examples, two-part in chapter 53, and then three- to four-part in chapter 61, nicely summarize cadential options, with their relative strengths and the contrapuntal means of achieving them, for polyphonic composers of his time (these options even include how to "evade the cadence"). Indeed, Zarlino refers to "clauses" [*clausule*] in prose, translated as "phrases" in his chapter on "The Rests" (1968, 124). Do "phrases" at "intermediate points" within a "period" thus take "cadences"? For contemporary theorists of form in later music, the question remains in full debate to this day, as we shall see.

Thus far a modest, and perhaps commonplace but irresistible, hypothesis emerges. If the phenomenon of phrase in music has an origin in Western culture, then this arises from the age-old practice of setting words to music. A word or phrase in speech or literature is commonly understood to be a constituent of a sentence, itself usually described as a "complete thought"; in this sense, the meaning of a phrase is dependent upon the grammatical and syntactic role it plays within the sentence, which ends with a period. In our earliest Western vocal music, the setting of a phrase of text tends to become a "musical phrase." The reason why this came about seems clear. The first obligation of medieval composers and singers of plainchant, or, for that matter, of polyphonic composers subsequent to the restrictions on sacred music imposed by the Council of Trent (1543–1565), was to make segments of a multitude of texts and glosses from the scriptures *comprehensible*, in an Aristotelian sense: intelligible and moving.

Ongoing studies in cognitive psychology provide empirical evidence of the innate tendency to parse text or music (or both) into segments, thus suggesting another origin for the idea of phrase, and amplifying explanations about the listening experience proposed by Fred Lerdahl and Ray Jackendoff in 1983: "The process of *grouping* is common to many areas of human cognition. If confronted with a series of elements or a sequence of events, a person spontaneously segments or 'chunks' the elements or events into groups of some kind. The ease or difficulty with which he [*sic*] performs this operation depends on how well the intrinsic organization of the input matches his internal, unconscious principles for constructing groupings" (Lerdahl and Jackendoff 1983, 13, my emphasis).[11] The implication here is that "intrinsic organization" is the province of the composer, who is also a listener, and thus, like all the rest of us, uses grouping structures to create music that is "organized" and communicative. In short, groupings into phrases would seem to be a purposeful, if not predeterminate, activity for composers as well as listeners, in respect to both instrumental and vocal music (Lerdahl and Jackendoff address both).

To be clear, although Lerdahl and Jackendoff's *A Generative Theory of Tonal Music* adopts a linguistic methodology, the authors have no use for "pointing out superficial analogies between music and language," which, "with or without the help of generative grammar, is an old and largely futile game ... Linguistic theory is not simply concerned with the analysis of a set of sentences; rather it considers itself a branch of psychology, concerned with making empirically verifiable claims about one complex aspect of human life: language. Similarly, our ultimate goal is an understanding of musical cognition, a psychological phenomenon" (1983, 5, 6). Grouping structure, independent from but interrelated with metrical structure, plays the central role in the authors' theory; phrases, like motives, themes, periods, theme-groups, sections, and the piece itself, are most fundamentally "musical groups ... heard in a hierarchical fashion" (1983, 13).

Text Interrupted!

Phrase as text setting, cadence as the punctuation of closure, grouping as an innate cognitive activity—with these fundamental ideas now in place, let us consider whether they have relevance to music from a much later era and an entirely different culture, Russian rather than Western European. Figure 12.3 and ⊙ Audio example 12.1 reproduce the celebrated opening—the bride's lament—of Igor Stravinsky's *Les Noces* (*Svádebka*), completed in 1922; the annotation "2nd, expanded phrase" is borrowed from Gretchen Horlacher, whose explanation for this term warrants our full attention.

Horlacher begins by noting the "clear stability of E," as one of only four pitches within the complete vocal passage: the E–D–B trichord (Stravinsky's well-known pc set 3–7 [025]) and the ornamental grace-note F♯. The vocal line departs from and returns to E, now marked as a goal because it takes the longest durational value thus far. Much to her credit, Horlacher does not on this basis alone proclaim an opening "four-bar phrase" without examining its content; she observes "two ordered gestures, an opening neighbor figure E–D–E–(D) and the succeeding ascending gesture B–D–E," with D as a pivot between E and B (Horlacher 2011, 35–36). These gestures give shape to the opening melody, in support of a phrase that would seem to be determined by the text, in both Russian and French.

And yet, what Richard Taruskin has described as an "end-clipping—a device common in the singing of Russian folk music" (Horlacher 2011, 36)—prevents the word "Koca" in the Russian text from being completed. The four-bar phrase ends on the syllable "ko ... "; the overwrought bride is unable to finish the word! For Horlacher, it is "as if she must stop for a gulp of breath! After getting 'stuck' on that word (and on that long E), she must return to the opening of the text in bar five to begin the next phrase of the lament" (2011, 36).[12] This second phrase, now six bars in length, clearly expands upon the content of the first; unimaginatively, we could just say that the second phrase is a "varied repetition," which retroactively delimits and closes the first phrase.[13] Horlacher

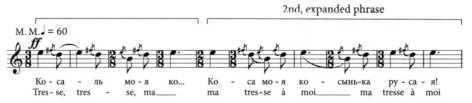

FIGURE 12.3 Stravinsky, *Les Noces* (*Svádebka*), opening: "Bride's Lament" (Horlacher 2011, 35) ⊙ Audio Example 12.1.

goes further: "A reading based on ordered succession characterizes the final six bars ...
as a culmination in length and shape, growing out of the initial four bars. It has three
(instead of two) departures from E, two of which are the fuller versions including B;
moreover, the bride is able to complete the text of her lament ... by returning to her
original E–D–E gesture" (2011, 37–38). Together, the two phrases would be regarded by
Stravinsky commentators as examples of a textural "block" of music—static, iterative,
timeless, and often at the service of ritual. By contrast, Horlacher strives to capture the
ordered, unidirectional *activity* within and through the block itself—a "pull between
repetition and evolution"; "as a fragment is repeated, its pitches become associated with
beginnings, middles, and endings by virtue of their placement within a clearly defined
whole: as a group, the fragment acquires a formal shape (for example, as a phrase)"
(Horlacher 2011, 39, my emphasis).[14]

I highlight Horlacher's analysis of the opening of *Les Noces* for several strong reasons.
First, hers is an exemplary account not only of the criteria by which she defines her
phrases but also of their internal content. Second, she focuses upon an unusual text
setting—one that is put to great dramatic effect, while contravening the tendency in so
much vocal music for only a completed textual phrase to become a coherent "phrase"
in music. Stravinsky's setting is uncommon, but it is by no means unprecedented. For
example, within the opening of his light-hearted, even bawdy villanella "Madonna mia
fame bon'offerta" of 1545, Adrian Willaert, Zarlino's teacher in Venice, breaks off the
completion of the poem's initial verse at the end of his first four-bar "phrase," as shown
at Figure 12.4.

The sense of a phrase ending at m. 4 is reinforced by the notated rest that follows,
but the validity of the unorthodox cadential counterpoint has been contested (note that
the basso and alto parts create tritone clashes against the tenore—a printer's error?).
"Madonna mia famme bon'offerta" translates as "My lady, make me a good offer." Richard
Freedman proposes that the exaggerated cadential dissonances might underscore an
"erotically suggestive" *double entendre*, characteristic of a villanella like this one: the text
of the first phrase now translates as "My lady does" (Freedman 2013, 110).[15] As with the
Stravinsky example, the text starts again and reaches completion over the span of the
second phrase. But in both cases, a distortion of the text's meaning has served as the
basis for the first phrase ending.

Phrase, Temporality, and Cadence

Horlacher's commentary further invokes a time-oriented idea very common to past
and recent characterizations of phrases and phrase-groups; Kofi Agawu has called
this the beginning–middle–end paradigm (Aguwu 1991, ch. 3).[16] Fassler's three
processes within the psalm tone—"opening formula, middle phrase, and termination"—anticipate the paradigm; Aristotle's version (italicized above) is a simplification: a "period" (in rhetoric) is "an utterance that has its own beginning and end";

FIGURE 12.4 Adrian Willaert, "Madonna mia fame bon'offerta," mm. 1–14 (Freedman 2013, 107).

Horlacher would seem to apply the paradigm both to Stravinsky's opening phrase and to her longer two-phrase "block." William Rothstein, for whom "a phrase should be understood as, among other things, a directed motion in time from one tonal entity to another" ("*If there is no tonal motion, there is no phrase*"), interprets both Roger Sessions's and Peter Westergaard's definitions of phrase as describing "a motion with beginning, middle, and end" (Rothstein 1989, 5).[17] Edward T. Cone captures the "rhythmic principle," the "musical energy," within a single phrase with his memorable ball-throwing analogy: "If I throw a ball and you catch it, the completed action must consist of three parts: the throw, the transit, and the catch"; he thus distinguishes "three types of 'strong' points: the initial, the terminal, and the medial" (Cone 1968, 26–27).[18]

Agawu himself initially applies his paradigm not to individual phrases, but rather to rhetorical and structural characteristics of sections within complete sonata movements. For example, with the beginning (main theme) of Beethoven's Violin Sonata op. 12, no. 1, "the [postponed] beginning *itself* has a beginning and an end" (Agawu 1991, 58). In his later study of "Romantic music," Agawu now addresses beginnings, middles, and ends on different structural levels within a complete piece (Mendelssohn's *Song without*

Words in D major, op. 84, no. 4).[19] Preliminary to this analysis, he states: "On the thematic front, for example, we might postulate the imperatives of clear statement or definition at the beginning, fragmentation in the middle, and a restoration of statement at the ending, together with epigonic gestures or effects of reminiscence. In terms of phrase, we might postulate a similar plot: clarity (in the establishment of premises) followed by less clarity (in the creative manipulation of those premises) yields, finally, to a simulated clarity at the end" (Agawu 2009, 54).[20]

By far the most rigorous development of the beginning–middle–end paradigm has been undertaken by William E. Caplin, in reference to classical instrumental music. The paradigm does not directly apply for him to individual phrases, except to the extent that multiple phrases (at a minimum, two) can combine to create a theme: "a complete middleground structural unit" consisting of "a conventional set of initiating, medial, and ending phrase functions," the last of which normally achieves a cadence (Caplin 2004, 54).[21] The many who know Caplin's work will recognize that the key term here is phrase functions. Although the term "phrase" for him "can be used as a functionally neutral term for grouping structure (embracing approximately four measures of music)" (2004, 59), phrases within classical instrumental genres carry specific "formal functions," just as "ideas" (for example, "basic idea," "contrasting idea") are accorded functions within a phrase, and themes and sections fulfill constituent functions within full-movement forms.[22] In 2009, Caplin returned to the foundational concept of his 1998 treatise— formal functionality—toward the goal of clarifying that classical formal functions, by their very nature, themselves project *temporal functions*, or time-spans, on multiple hierarchical levels: formal functions convey beginnings, middles, or endings, as signaled especially by prolongational, sequential, or cadential harmonic progressions, but also by means of parameters such as tonality, grouping, cadence, and, I would add, rhythm as well as meter. The third of Caplin's three tree-like diagrams proposes that the slow introduction, exposition, development, recapitulation, and coda within a sonata-form movement function as the before-the-beginning, beginning, middle, end, and after-the-end. Nested within this overarching hierarchy, the main theme, transition, and subordinate theme-groups provide the beginning, middle, and end of the exposition, with a closing section expressing an after-the-end. When, closer to "the surface," a main theme or subordinate theme takes on the now well-known theme-type that Schoenberg (1967) designated as "sentence" (in Schoenberg's sense, *la frase* in Italian; *la phrase* in French; *der Satz* in German), its internal phrase functions of presentation, continuation, and cadential themselves serve as beginning, middle, and end (2009a, 24–27). Thus, these three temporal functions are operative on all levels of the formal process, and "a given time-span on the musical foreground can be conceived to express multiple temporalities [for instance, 'beginning of the end']—seemingly at the same time, but really at different 'time-spaces'" (Caplin 2009b, 55).

Markus Neuwirth emphasizes the unmistakable association of the beginning– middle–end paradigm with another widespread topos: the view that "classical" music is distinctively "goal-directed" (this is the "ending" aspect of the paradigm). Neuwirth reviews some of the well-worn teleological metaphors analysts have often applied to that music: a "journey" to the goal, a "'trajectory' and 'path' as well as 'departure' and 'arrival.'" For Neuwirth, then, "a musical 'phrase' may be considered the smallest building block expressing goal-directedness, as it articulates a tonal motion toward a final sonority . . . that is usually established by means of a cadential progression. Expressing the tripartite temporal paradigm of a beginning, a middle, and an end, a phrase may thus rightly be regarded as the prototype of form in classical music in general" (Neuwirth 2015, 117).

Phrase as the prototype of classical form—advocates of this view underscore the extraordinary breadth of the topic on which I've embarked. The claim at hand is, of course, not as sweeping as the proposal that in "a general way every piece of music resembles a cadence" (Schoenberg 1967, 16), or that a phrase can be heard as "an upbeat to its own cadence" over the span of the complete composition (Cone 1968; see note 18). Caplin addresses these and comparable outlooks. In Caplin's theory, a cadence marks the end of a process that has had a beginning and usually a middle: "As far as an entire piece being a single cadence, the idea can quickly be dismissed as illogical, for such an overarching cadence could not be construed to end anything other than itself" (Caplin 2004, 57, 60–61). The comparison of phrase to form in general hinges mightily upon the efficacy of the beginning–middle–end paradigm, broadly applied—a model that, not so long ago, was much disparaged as self-evident, too general, overinflated, and thus trivial.[23] Do *individual* phrases tend to have beginnings, middles, and ends? Yes, for Neuwirth, for Cone, and, by implication, for Rothstein; loosely speaking, for Agawu; and not necessarily for Caplin, as clarified above. Surely a much-anticipated question now arises: What constitutes "an ending"?

Nearly all of the writers I've cited, Zarlino included (but Fassler and Horlacher excepted), suggest that the strongest possible ending—the goal, the point of repose—will be achieved by a cadence. But John of Affligem's twelfth-century "period" as a musical and textual punctuation goal, followed so much later by Zarlino's representative sixteenth-century polyphonic cadences, participates within a centuries-long development of theories of cadence, which is surely ongoing, as we shall see.[24] Present-day textbook definitions of cadences and cadential progressions tend to draw empirically upon the practices of tonal (rather than modal) composers, especially within eighteenth- and nineteenth-century repertoires; just the same, and even in respect to earlier and later music, it has generally been accepted that a cadential progression creates the effect of an ending *only* if it completes a musical process that has had a beginning. In current North American parlance, broadly adopted, tonal harmonic progressions that can complete such processes—that is, cadential, rather than prolongational or sequential progressions—yield the following well-known cadence-types: the perfect authentic cadence (PAC), the imperfect authentic cadence (IAC), the half cadence (HC), and the deceptive cadence (DC); in other languages as well as in English, different terms for similar cadence-types have long abounded.[25]

For Caplin and many others, complete cadential progressions in classical forms "confirm a tonal center by bringing the fundamental harmonic functions in this order: (initial) tonic, pre-dominant, dominant, and (final) tonic"; an incomplete (but no less strong) cadential progression "lacks an initial tonic, or a pre-dominant; for example: I^6–V^7–I or II^6–V^7–I (authentic); I–V or II^6–V (half)" (2013, 4–5). Sticking points—obstacles to widespread endorsement—are that in authentic cadential progressions, "both the dominant and final tonic harmonies must be placed in root position," and that the dominant, as goal of the half-cadential progression, "must take the form of a root-position *triad*"— in other words, not V^7 or an inverted dominant (Caplin 2013, 15, 17). The so-called deceptive cadence (DC) has commonly been taught as one in which the cadential progression promises an authentic cadence but "deceives" by replacing its final tonic with a chord on $\hat{6}$ (VI or IV^6); but Daniel Gottlob Türk's *Klavierschule* of 1789 summarizes earlier ideas about *cadenze d'inganno* with examples that show "deceptive cadences" ending on all manner of non-tonic goal harmonies, including I^6, ♭VI, and diminished-seventh chords arriving by leap above or below the cadential dominant in its penultimate position (Türk 1982, 341). Türk's broad outlook on what constitutes a deceptive cadence has largely been adopted. Finally, we have the evaded cadence (EC), which, as the term suggests, is not really a cadence, because the cadence is not achieved: here again, an authentic cadence is promised, but its goal—the final cadential tonic—is withheld; the music that follows strictly belongs to a new group with a new beginning—one that often "backs up" to repeat the approach to closure, in what has been dubbed the "one more time" technique (Schmalfeldt 1992; Caplin 2013, 131).[26]

Rigorous definitions of the kind concerning cadences offered above (note Caplin's "must"s, directed to students within a textbook for the classroom) may point for some readers to the limits of description in music-theoretical language for capturing particular musical experiences, no matter how empirically grounded such terminology may be in relation to actual compositional practice.[27] Moreover, even if we can agree that to describe a phrase calls for determining where it ends, there is simply no consensus within music-theoretical communities as to whether, by definition, a phrase within tonal music needs to end with one of the types of cadences I've described. For example, Caplin's "presentation phrase," which initiates the sentence as theme-type, tends in principle to be tonic-prolongational, rather than cadential; thus, presentation phrases "never close with a cadence," nor is a cadence a requirement in general for phrase endings within Caplin's work (Caplin 1998, 45; 2013, 36). Hepokoski and Darcy acknowledge a "Caplin-Rothstein split," with Rothstein as the "clearest advocate of the necessity of the terminal cadence"; Hepokoski and Darcy side with Rothstein (2006, 68n10).[28] In his most recent work, Carl Schachter says: "Notice that I'm not insisting that the end of every phrase be marked with a cadence. Rather, phrases involve motion from one musical place to another, ending with a feeling of breathing or stopping . . . A formal cadence is the strongest way of conveying that sense of breathing or stopping, but it's not by any means universal in what one would call a phrase" (2016, 195).[29]

In his "The Half Cadence and Other Slippery Events" (2014), Poundie Burstein contests the long-held notion that a half cadence must end with a root-position dominant triad; though he grants that "almost all writers" hold this view, he cites several eighteenth-century theorists (212) and a sampling of excerpts—from Joseph and Michael Haydn, Mozart, Beethoven, Rosetti, and W. F. Bach—in which "phrase endings" feature "HC on V^7" or "HC" on an inverted V or V^7 (215–216). We can note that Burstein must regard these phrase endings as half cadences, because he follows Rothstein, Hepokoski/Darcy, and others on the dictum that a phrase must end with a cadence (203n2). In his sequel article of 2015, Burstein offers a detailed overview of seventeenth- and eighteenth-century theorists who contribute, often vaguely, to the development of the "half cadence concept"; his Table 2 lists hundreds of "examples of half cadences demarcated by inverted V or V^7's in works from around 1750–1825" (Burstein 2015, 100–101).[30]

If phrases must end with cadences, then readers will surely recognize that I've arrived at one of the greatest hurdles in defining phrase, so entirely attached to the idea of closure. If a cadence is required for a phrase ending, then phrases might be as short as four bars (ending, say, with a HC), or as long as the 37 bars that Caplin registers in reference to Rothstein's analysis of Chopin's Mazurka in G# minor, op. 33, no. 1 (Caplin 2004, 59, n.23).[31] It should also be clear by now that a cadence, whatever one holds this to be, will not be the *sole* criterion for a phrase ending. Burstein's two articles are particularly strong on this point: citing Caplin (a cadence "essentially represents the structural *end* of broader harmonic, melodic, and phrase-structural processes" [1998, 43; as quoted in Burstein 2014, 203]), Burstein gives attention, especially in 2015, to the roles, sometimes "noncongruent," of melodic as well as harmonic content, of phrase-structural syntax, and also of such dimensions as texture, hypermeter, surface rhythm, dynamics, and voice leading in contributing to the effect of a phrase ending. In Figure 12.5, I reproduce one of Burstein's examples (it appears in both of his articles)—one not discussed individually by him, but in which the interaction of such extra-harmonic parameters invites our consideration.

My annotated Figure 12.5 (and ⓟ Audio example 12.2), which opens the Andante (second) movement of and Joseph Haydn's "London" Symphony no. 104 (his last, from 1795), places Burstein's example (mm. 1–4) within a larger context—the period, or antecedent/consequent theme-type completed over the span of mm. 1–8 and closing with a PAC in the dominant. We needn't question that a phrase, not to mention an entire movement, begins with the two-bar basic idea (BI) at mm. 1–2; but, having not yet considered how phrases in general tend to open, let's note that this phrase begins not by "opening up" but, rather, by "closing down" (Caplin 1998, 37; 264n14). Unusually, although not without precedent, its opening melody makes a stepwise descent from its starting point, the B♭ as $\hat{3}$, and the deceptive progression I–V^7–vi supports the descent. Here, then, is a cadence-like gesture that cannot create a cadence, because it initiates, rather than closes, a phrase-structural process. Haydn will now want to compensate for the closing effect he suggests, and he does this right away: his melody reaches above the little $\hat{3}-\hat{2}-\hat{1}$ melodic descent, to the *subito, sforzando*-accented E♭ on the offbeat at m. 2, and this mobilizes a contrasting idea (CI, mm. 3–4) that "opens" the melodic line through its stepwise ascent to the C♭ on the downbeat of m. 4—the seventh of Burstein's "HC on V^7."

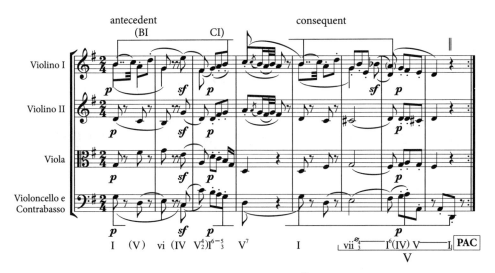

Figure 12.5 Haydn, Symphony no. 104, Andante, mm. 1–8 ⏵ Audio Example 12.2.

Here a straightforward voice-leading consideration would seem to relate to the choice of the "HC on V⁷," with its dissonant seventh in need of resolution. As a varied repetition of the antecedent, the consequent begins at m. 5 (the "repetition ensures closure" of the antecedent), again with $\hat{3}$ as its point of departure. Now the C♯ as seventh in m. 4 resolves to B♮ in m. 5;[32] from the Schenkerian perspective, as proposed by my analytic overlay, the end of the consequent suggests a local interruption on $\hat{2}$.

Has a phrase ended at m. 4? This seems undeniable. Does it really matter whether we call this phrase ending a case of "HC on V⁷," with Burstein, or the non-cadential ending of a compound basic idea (CBI), as Caplin would probably argue? Some may think not; but the *affective* difference between a phrase ending on V⁷ and one that ends on the root-position dominant triad has apparent relevance for Haydn. Within two later returns of the antecedent shown in Figure 12.5, the composer replaces his "HC on V⁷" with the much more common triad on the dominant—no seventh. These moments—at mm. 101 and 125—both arise within the third part of this movement's much expanded large-ternary form, where the rounded-binary first part, the main theme, returns with variation not once but twice. At m. 101, within the *a'*-section of the rounded binary, delicate triplets in flutes and violins embellish the original melody from mm. 3–4, this time treating the C♯ of m. 4 only as an incomplete neighbor within a $\hat{3}-\hat{2}$ descent over root V. However, this first reprise of the main theme wanders harmonically way "off track"— listen to the amazing passage at mm. 105–121—thus calling for another embellished repeat of the *a'*-section, now triumphant and complete. The unalloyed dominant triad returns as the antecedent's HC at m. 125, this time within a *tutti* texture and a *fortissimo* dynamic. Its greater stability as a phrase ending contributes to the exultant character of that final reprise.

INFLUENTIAL NOTIONS
OF PHRASE FROM THE MID- TO
LATE-EIGHTEENTH CENTURY

My comments about Figure 12.5 have attempted to deflect the matter of phrase from its apparent dependency upon notions of cadence—a preoccupation of late, especially among the American theorists whom I cite. It is time now to review what mid-eighteenth-century European theorists and their successors had to say about phrases and cadences. After all, this was the era during which what we today call "phrase structure" became a central concern, even anticipating later notions of the phrase as a microcosm of the complete tonal work.

Here I move into territory that will be all too familiar to historians of music theory, to theorists of form, and especially to the many translators who have brought composition manuals in German, Italian, and French to the light of day for readers in English. Some of the melodies displayed in Figures 12.6 through 12.10 might well be recognized as "household tunes" for scholars who have assiduously studied the writings of the German theorists Joseph Riepel (1709–1782), Johann Philipp Kirnberger (1721–1783), and Heinrich Christoph Koch (1749–1816).

Riepel

I shall focus primarily upon Riepel for the reason that he is now regarded as having "initiated the tradition of phrase-structural analysis" (Caplin 2002, 671). Ample evidence supports the claim that Kirnberger's ideas about phrase were influenced by Riepel's, and both of these theorists influenced Koch, who acknowledged that "*Riepel* was the first (and is also the only theorist yet known to me) who has treated [the matters of length and ending of melodic segments] in detail" (as translated in Hill 2014, 441; see Koch 1983, xviii). All three theorists perpetuate the association of music with language, speech, rhetoric, and the resting points of punctuation; as we shall see, Riepel goes so far as to compare certain types of phrases in music with linguistic equivalents in German-language sentences that manifest implicit or complete syllogisms in logic (called "philosophy" by Riepel).

A few words about Riepel's treatise, before we proceed. The core of his *Anfangsgründe zur musicalischen Setzkunst* ("Foundations of Music Composition") (Riepel 1752–1768) consists of the five chapters published during his lifetime (another two were published posthumously; three remain in manuscript).[33] His first two chapters, on *Rhythmopoeïa*, or *Tactordnung* ("metric order") and on *Tonordnung* ("tonal order"), appeared in 1752 and 1755, respectively; they are now available in a much-welcomed translation with commentary by John Walter Hill (2014). Riepel was well respected during his day, but studies of his work in recent years have included criticism of its inconsistencies and its rambling style[34]—it takes the Fux-like format of an informal dialogue between a good-natured Preceptor (obviously Riepel himself) and his young student the Discantist, a precocious, aspiring composer (who boasts that "yesterday" he "composed fifty minuets" [Hill 2014, 42]). What Riepel's treatise lacks in systematic rigor is compensated for by its entertainment value and its dazzling breadth of subsidiary topics. Instruction on how to create metrically and tonally well-ordered compositions is the Preceptor's pedagogical mission; but on the way toward that goal, the Discantist also learns, for instance, about bass lines; contemporaneous instrumental and vocal genres; tutti and solo entries; performance issues (for example, how to avoid difficult fingerings for violinists and flutists); the individual harmonic roles of diatonic scale-steps within a key, as analogous to the social hierarchy of farm laborers (in descending order of importance, the steward,

FIGURE 12.6 Examples from Joseph Riepel, *Anfangsgründe zur musicalischen Setzkunst* ["Foundations of Music Composition"] (Hill 2014, 235, 233, 236, 248).

foreman, maids, day laborers, errand girl, and so on); and the animal called the sloth in (South) America. We occasionally even receive gossip from the Discantist's hometown, pointing up a droll pedagogical rivalry between the Preceptor and the young man's former teacher, his "lord."

The annotated excerpts at Figure 12.6 arise from deep within Riepel's *Tonordnung* chapter 2, by which time the Discantist has already learned much about *Tactordunung* (in chapter 1). For example, he would know that the excerpt at Figure 12.6(a) begins with a *Vierer* (quaintly translated as "foursome" by Hill)—that is, an *Absatz* (Hill's "comma") of four bars in length.[35] As later with Kirnberger and Koch, the term *Absatz* occasionally refers to both the entire "phrase" itself (Hill does not use this term in his translation) and the type of harmonic/melodic punctuation that marks its ending. Because the initial *Vierer* ends on the tonic, it would be, or lead to, a *Grund-Absatz* ("tonic comma," marked by Riepel with a **black** square). The four-bar unit is comprised in turn of a *Zweyer* ("twosome")—a two-bar *Einschnitt*, or *Abschnitt* ("caesura") at mm. 1–2, and its varied repetition at mm. 3–4. The second four-bar unit (mm. 5–8) responds to the first by leading to a stronger punctuation, the "complete" *Cadenz* in the dominant, as indicated by Riepel at m. 8. Riepel's *Cadenz*, with its $\hat{3}$–$\hat{2}$–$\hat{1}$ melodic closure, can be equated with the perfect authentic cadence (PAC) in modern terminology.

Readers will easily identify the complete excerpt at Figure 12.6(a) as exemplary of a simple minuet: in binary form, with each part of eight bars in length, albeit in this case not repeated. The lack of repeat signs here is the only detail that distinguishes this minuet from all of the many others in Riepel's chapter 1, in which the composition of minuets is his almost exclusive topic. Indeed, the second part of the excerpt begins, just as in the sixteen-bar minuets in his first chapter, with one of Riepel's three well-known harmonic schemata, whose colorful topological names—the *fonte*, the *monte*, and the *ponte*—suggest that he was well acquainted with contemporary Italian music.[36] Here, at mm. 9–12, we have the *fonte*; Riepel's only definition (in Hill 2014, 222n90) is "fountain, to climb down." As a type of sequential harmonic progression, this would be known as a descending-fifths sequence over the following specific path: $[V^7]$–ii; V^7–I. The conclusion of the sequence reaches another "tonic comma," which motivates the last four-bar unit to hasten toward the stronger final *Cadenz*. Presumably because the Discantist, who has "composed" the minuet, labels it with the concerto term "Tutti" and indicates where the "Solo" would enter, he says that he may certainly not call this a minuet. So, "what would this be, then?" In what seems like a complete non sequitur, the Preceptor answers:

> a **complete conclusion** [Syllogism]. Which, as it were, seems to convince us of the following: Any sort of usage is unnecessary to composition (**black**-squared comma) if one cannot know how to give any rule for it (**white**-squared cadence [in the dominant]). Now, one cannot know how to give any rule for compass usage [*Zirkel*, a drawing compass] (**black**-squared comma), therefore compass usage is certainly quite unnecessary to composition (**black**-squared cadence).
>
> (Hill 2014, 235)

Riepel's insertions of commas and cadences within this statement clarify that each of the four "foursomes" plays an ordered role in the completion of the "syllogism." In his essay "*Rhythmopoeïa* and *Melopoeïa*," Hill provides the original German for Riepel's statement and unravels it to show that Riepel's "verbal equivalent" does indeed amount to a "fully fledged syllogism" (2014, 364). Hill's argument is complex, but it nearly convinces. In rough summary, Riepel's first two four-bar units stand for the *major premise*: any usage (of a tool) is unnecessary to composition ("phrase" 1) if one can't give a rule for it ("phrase" 2). The two "foursomes" of the second part stand for the *minor premise* and the *conclusion*: there is no rule for the use of a compass ("phrase" 3); therefore, the compass is unnecessary to composition ("phrase" 4).[37]

To my knowledge, Riepel's remarkable, even radical effort to adopt syllogistic logic in analogies between verbal and musical statements has no precedent in earlier writings about phrase structure.[38] In effect, he is assigning a formal function to each of the four "foursomes" in the minuet. An opening premise is dependent upon the continuation that follows—if I read Hill correctly, this "if" clause in the verbal statement has been reversed in the syllogism; it would usually have come first. Then comes the minor premise (the *fonte* "foursome"), now requiring a conclusion. Even though the instability of the sequential *fonte* does not correspond well (for me) with the "statement of fact" of the minor premise, Riepel strives to prove that music "speaks"—that, in "good" composition, the role of phrases is context-dependent; that the relative strengths of their endings determine a logical order that ultimately leads to the strongest, most conclusive goal. His theory is hardly a theory of form, in the sense that Koch later anticipated in his "nature and arrangement" of short and larger complete compositions. But with this and other demonstrations of logical "metrical and tonal" order in miniature models and short "symphonies," Riepel sets the stage for later ventures into the emerging domain of large-scale form. Finally, we cannot help but be amused that, in his antipathy toward earlier "mathematical" theories of music (Rameau is Riepel's main culprit), his linguistic syllogism features the drawing compass—a tool in mathematics, among other fields, and the object of his disdain.[39]

Riepel precedes his discussion of the "complete" syllogism in Figure 12.6(a) with four shorter examples; these are accompanied by increasingly complex linguistic parallels, all still harping on the uselessness of the drawing compass. The first of the four excerpts, in Figure 12.6(b), is of course a variant of the opening "foursome" in Figure 12.6(a), so I think that we can apply Riepel's commentary to both. The linguistic expression that "the musical notes wanted to speak" in Figure 12.6(b) is not a syllogism, but rather only a relatively simple sentence; in Hill's translation it reads: "Compass and numbers help, perhaps (**white**-squared caesura), the ear to tune the keyboard (**black**-squared comma)." On this linguistic basis, the Preceptor calls the "foursome" itself a *Satz* (bold-faced), translated as "**sentence**" by Hill; in a footnote Riepel adds the term "Proposition" (*propositio*). Hill notes that this four-bar phrase "contains two halves that form a 'call and response,' an implication and a realization, or a subject and a predicate, depending on the preferred metaphor" (359–360). The reference to "call and response" should ring a bell for those knowledgeable about the type of phrase nowadays called a *presentation*: in this case, an initiating two-bar "basic idea" implies the motion of I to V and reaches only a "caesura"; its varied repetition responds with the motion V-to-I and ends with the somewhat stronger "comma." The second "foursome," at mm. 5–8 in Figure 12.6(a), suggests the faster harmonic and rhythmic activity of a continuation, and the resultant eight-bar unit (an "eightsome" for Hill[40]) ends with a *Cadenz*, thus completing the type of eight-bar theme called the sentence (*Satz*) in Schoenberg's sense, as discussed earlier.

We've staggered into a terminological quagmire here: *Satz* ("sentence," or *propositio*[41]) as Riepel's "foursome," versus *Satz* as an eight-bar theme-type for Schoenberg and his followers. I raise this issue because it is symptomatic of the enormous problems that scholars and translators of German treatises face when confronted with what would best translate as "phrase." In an aside, we might note that today's sentential presentation is regarded by Riepel as comparable to a complete unit, both linguistically and musically, though one that closes only with a "comma." This view conforms agreeably with Caplin's "presentation phrase," as discussed above: an initiating, usually tonic-prolonging type of phrase, whose ending does not take a cadence. More important, the model of the Schoenbergian eight-bar sentence in Figure 12.6(a) is just one of the many examples of this theme-type, with its potentially infinite possibilities for content, that appear in Riepel's work as well as (but less so) in the treatises of Kirnberger and Koch.

The Four-Bar Phrase and the Dance

Before turning to Riepel's remaining excerpts in Example 12.6, I pause here to broaden our outlook. First of all, Riepel's term *Absatz*, for the opening four-bar unit (*Vierer*) in Figure 12.6(a), is shared, closely enough, by other eighteenth-century theorists; in English this term, or simply the term *Satz*, is usually translated as "phrase" (Hill provides an exception, with his "foursome"). That is, a "phrase" in translations tends to be of four bars in length, and this becomes the eighteenth-century norm, sustained well beyond the nineteenth century: not only Riepel but Kirnberger, Koch, and their successors regarded the four-bar unit as basic, and they strongly favored even-numbered formal divisions. Here's Riepel, anticipating by more than two hundred years the recent empirical and experiential views of cognitive psychologists about grouping:

> The four, eight, sixteen, and even thirty-two **measures are those which are so deeply ingrained in our nature that it seems difficult to us to listen (with delight) to another structure.** And I say that two successive twosomes are nothing other than a foursome.
>
> (Hill 2014, 43; Riepel's boldface)

Kirnberger follows Riepel in 1776: "The best melodies are always those whose phrases have four measures. A few of two measures may enter in among them, but they must occur in pairs, since they are then heard as phrases of four measures with a caesura in the middle" (Kirnberger 1982, 409). And from Koch in 1787, we have this:

> Most common, and also, on the whole, most useful and most pleasing for our feelings are those basic phrases which are completed in the fourth measure of simple meters. For that reason they are called *four-measure phrases* [*Vierer*]. They may actually appear as four measures in simple meters or in compound meters in the form of only two measures.
>
> (Koch 1983, 11)

What accounts for these preferences? At least one answer seems straightforward. A profound change in musical style marks the emergence within the mid-eighteenth century of what, even in its time, had come to be known as the galant. By the 1770s, it had become commonplace to speak of a serious "strict style," or "strict composition" (*strenger Satz*), in contrast with a lighter "free style," or *freier Satz*, which Kirnberger explicitly identifies as *galant* (1982, 990). Efforts to characterize this new style run the risk of trivializing it, or needlessly defending it: galant as a rejection of Baroque contrapuntal rigor; galant with its simpler, "thinner," homophonic textures, its shorter syntactical units and frequent cadences, its stock, recognizable melodic/harmonic formulae, its greater accessibility, its courtly refinement and sensibility, and yet its appeal to the rising middle classes—all of these ascriptions and many more have been made. Whatever can be said about the galant, it emerges in tandem with the advance of non-texted instrumental music, now competing for prestige with vocal genres; and, most especially, the style becomes associated with music for the dance.[42] To this day, social dance music calls for a steady beat and for regular, predictable, even-numbered phrases; dancers don't want to be tripped up by unexpected "extra" bars.

It is to their great credit that all three eighteenth-century theorists under consideration were attuned to the new music of their era, and that many of their models for composition drew not only upon the minuet but also on other dance types that had survived the *ancien régime*. Both Kirnberger and Koch summarize the definitive meters, tempi, and characters of such dances as the bourrée, the gavotte, the sarabande, the polonaise, and the passepied (with Koch including the contradanse and the march).[43] The increased attention in the eighteenth century to instrumental dance music impels us to expand our notions of sources for the concept of phrase. Language metaphors—music as speech, phrase as a vocal, text-oriented phenomenon, even in textless music—continue to thrive; perhaps these metaphors will always be with us. But just as language is "a complex aspect of human life" (to recall Lerdahl and Jackendoff), dance brings human corporeality to music, and phrases become expressions of measured physical movement. Writing about the nature of meter, Kirnberger has this to say:

> A regular walk has steps of equal length, each of which represents a measure of the melody. However, the steps can consist of more or fewer little movements or *beats* ...
> If a precise uniformity is observed in the steps and small movements, this results

in the measured walk which we can dance, and this is precisely analogous to measured melody. In just the same way as dance expresses or portrays various sentiments merely by motion, melody does it merely by notes. (1982, 382)

Phrase Extensions

Riepel

On the other hand, it would be a huge mistake not to acknowledge that another common thread passing from Riepel to Kirnberger to Koch is the concern for variety in phrase lengths, content, and the ordering of resting points—in other words, a concern for how to counteract or disrupt symmetrical phrase rhythm and the "tyranny of the four-measure phrase" (Cone's coinage, which he rightfully associates more strongly with nineteenth-century music; even then, he argues, composers like Mendelssohn, Chopin, and Schumann knew how to disguise "the problem"; 1968, 74). A "basic" four-bar *Absatz* (Koch's *enger Satz*) can be "extended" (*erweiterter Satz*) or "compounded" (*zusammengeschobener Satz*); two three-bar *Einschnitte* (segments; "caesurae," as above) may occasionally be employed to create a six-bar *Absatz*; and basic *Absätze* of five and seven bars or longer, if self-sufficient in themselves, rather than extended, are also entirely acceptable. Why? Because these theorists *observed* such repetition, extension, and expansion techniques in the music they knew and attempted to describe. Riepel's and Koch's techniques in particular have been widely and richly explored; for example, Elaine Sisman (1982) provides a superb early account of their relevance to analyses of movements by Haydn.[44] I offer a sampling of examples.

Returning to Riepel at Figure 12.6, you'll see that one and the same four-bar "presentation phrase" from Figure 12.6(a) opens (c), (d), and (e), and that each of the excerpts has now been extended to the length of ten bars. At (c), a new continuation completes the Schoenbergian sentence with a *Cadenz* on the tonic at the downbeat of m. 8, as metrically expected; but continued quarter-note motion provides the link into a repetition of the last two bars of the continuation—the cadential idea. This is what Riepel's Preceptor would call a "doubling of the cadence" (*Verdopplung der Cadenz*), which, for Koch, becomes "the multiplication of closing formulas and cadences" (*Vielfältigung der Absatz-formeln und Cadenzen*). At Figure 12.6(d), we see an immediate repetition of the two-bar idea that initiates the continuation function; at (e), the contrasting idea (CI) of the presentation takes an immediate repetition. Without the need for "any philosophy," the Discantist has himself "composed" this series of *Verlängerungen*, about which the Preceptor remarks, in a note: "What a relief that the young man has grown tired of philosophy on his own" (so much for that complete syllogism). The Preceptor regards the Discantist's extensions as nothing more than "a reinforced eightsome" (Hill 2014, 237). Likewise, an extended phrase for Koch takes the value in length of the "basic phrase" from which it departs: for example, "a four-measure phrase, which has been extended to six measures by the repetition of two, is always considered as a four-measure unit with respect to the rhythmic relations of phrases" (Koch 1983, 43).

From this point forward, Riepel's Discantist grows ever wilder with delight about new methods for expansion (*Ausdähnung, Ausdehnung*). The Preceptor introduces him to numerous ways of "doubling the cadences," the last and most audacious instance of which is shown at Figure 12.6(f). My annotations here include Hill's method for the numberings of "foursomes" in his commentary. What we have is a sentential continuation that should have arrived at a *Cadenz* on the downbeat of its fourth bar; here Riepel enacts a genuine *evaded cadence* (EC), motivating a "one-more-time" repetition that "backs up" to the second bar (note the lack of voice-leading resolution from $\hat{2}$ to $\hat{1}$ and the melodic leap back to $\hat{3}$). A true *Cadenz* seems to be achieved on the downbeat of the sixth bar, but it elides with the beginning of the next metric unit, thus effecting what Riepel calls a "cutting away" (*Eintheilung*), to which Koch later applies the term *Tacterstickung* ("suppression, or choking, of the measure"; I represent this elision with <—>). I think that we can infer an imperfect authentic cadence (IAC) at the ninth bar, but then another two-bar repetition seems again to elide with a final three-bar codetta— perhaps an "appendix" (*Anhang*) for Koch. All told, Riepel has created *three* "doublings of the cadence," or even *four*, if we count the last three measures.

Both Riepel and Koch stand firmly on the premise that: " . . . **a minuet**, with respect to execution, is **no different from a concerto, an aria, or a symphony** . . . we want always to begin with something very small and inconsiderable in order later to arrive at something larger and more praiseworthy" (Hill 2014, 6; Riepel's boldface). To demonstrate, Riepel's Preceptor now composes a "quite short and simple Allegro," twenty-four bars long; the Discantist (a proto-Riemannian) reduces the Preceptor's "symphony" to a "miniature" in eight bars; then, bursting with runaway enthusiasm, he expands the "symphony" to sixty-four bars.[45] The resultant larger form can be classified as Hepokoski/ Darcy's "Type 2 sonata": no return of the opening theme in the role of a recapitulation, thus no third "rotation."[46] That small forms for Riepel and Koch serve as the basis for larger, expanded forms cannot be underscored enough. In Sisman's words: "By focusing first on the phrase, the theorist and his student could move from details of its melodic and harmonic construction to the combination and expansion of phrases" (1982). More broadly speaking, Riepel's and Koch's compositional approach places phrase at the absolute center of their enterprise.

Kirnberger

Kirnberger's only substantial discussion of phrase arises within the second volume of *Die Kunst des reinen Satzes* (1776), chapter 4, titled "Tempo, Meter, and Rhythm." As compared with both Riepel's and Koch's treatments of the topic, Kirnberger's is brief and underdeveloped, but it has its strong points. One of these is that, although Kirnberger attends to tempo, meter, and rhythm separately, he stresses from the outset that "none of these elements is sufficient by itself to give melody a precise character; the true expression of the melody is determined only by their synthesis and their interaction" (Kirnberger 1982, 375–376). Riepel's influence can be sensed in Kirnberger's hierarchy of formal divisions, but here a different category takes priority: along with *Einschnitt* ("segment"), *Abschnitt*, or *Rhythmus* (rather than *Absatz*, and translated as "phrase"), we now have *Periode* ("period")—as we know, a term long borrowed from language and speech, and one that will be much more fully expanded by Koch in respect to larger forms. For Kirnberger: "The musical statement that is complete and ends with a formal cadence [defined earlier as a V⁷–I progression, thus 'perfect authentic'] we will call a *section* or *period*; but the incomplete one that ends only with a melodic break or a satisfying harmony we will call a *phrase* or a *rhythmic unit*" [*Rhythmus*] (1982, 405; emphasis original). The implication is that large-scale rhythmic organization is defined for Kirnberger at the level of the phrase, thus the emergence of the concept of phrase rhythm—so central to nineteenth-century theorists, and, early on, especially to Beethoven's friend Anton Reicha.⁴⁷

We might note here that, as earlier for Riepel and later for Koch, a phrase for Kirnberger need not end with a formal cadence: "A phrase is articulated most forcefully by the half cadence; its inversions produce weaker breaks. Inversions of full cadences can also be used for this ... Finally, each new consonant harmony produces a small break [*Cäsur,* 'caesura'] or rest point. Thus, the break or end of a phrase can be made perceptible in all these different ways" (1982, 408). We can assume, moreover, that the four-bar phrase is "basic" for Kirnberger, as explicitly defined by Koch. Kirnberger's conservative streak seems evident in his view that "the ear" can be somewhat offended if the uniformity of equal phrase lengths is broken. Nevertheless, odd-numbered phrases of three, five, seven, nine, "and more measures" are all possible, as long as they are made comprehensible by caesuras, "and, besides, can occur only in short meters" (412). Figure 12.7(a) shows a particularly attractive example of a five-bar unit created by an "insertion"

FIGURE 12.7 Examples from Johann Philipp Kirnberger, *Die Kunst des reinen Satzes* ["The Art of Strict Musical Composition"], Vol. II, Part 1, chapter 4 (Kirnberger 1982, 409, 411, 412).

(Riepel's *Einschiebsel*) within a four-bar phrase that "is not counted, since it is heard as something foreign that attracts the attention in a very special way ... like an echo ... which, because of the text, is very effective." (The text translates as: "I think I hear the sweet hope.")

In only two other instances, however, does Kirnberger speak directly of "extensions" of phrases in the sense of transformations of a four-bar model; in both cases a rhythmic unit of only five bars results. At Figure 12.7(b) we see "the extension of certain principal notes that are to be given a special emphasis" (411). Figure 12.7(c) shows a similar "extension of a few notes," at work to create *three* rhythmic units of five bars each, but they are "perceived as units of four measures" (412). This elementary extension technique—the lengthening of note values within a model four-bar phrase—will be picked up by Koch (1983, 34–35), but it serves as only the beginning of Koch's full-blown discursus on how phrases can be extended, compounded, and expanded into larger forms.

Koch

As the author who "developed the most comprehensive account of phrase structure in eighteenth-century theory" (Caplin 2002, 671), Koch has until now received much more attention than Riepel,[48] with Kirnberger's work better known for its contributions to theories of harmony and meter. Comparisons of Riepel's manual with Koch's *Versuch einer Anleitung zur Composition* (Introductory Essay on Composition) consistently applaud Koch for his far greater systematic rigor and much broader scope, while generally acknowledging Koch's debt to Riepel. Just how enormous that debt should be is the opening topic of Hill's essay on the reception of Riepel's work—the fullest technical comparison to date of Koch's work with Riepel's; on my count, Hill raises more than sixteen "general and specific ways in which Koch depends upon Riepel" (2015, 441). Hill's account begins with a breath-taking eighteen key terms (in German) that Koch "takes over" from Riepel and uses more or less identically (442), many of which I have earlier introduced in reference to both theorists. Koch refines and updates some of these terms, while introducing new ones. For example, Riepel's *Cadenz* becomes Koch's *Schlusssatz*—the "closing phrase" that leads to the conclusive ending of a "melodic section." *Schlusssatz* is contrasted with the "internal" *Grundabsatz* (as for Riepel, closing on tonic harmony) and *Quintabsatz* (Riepel's *Änderungs-Absatz*, closing on V, thus HC). Riepel's "comma" and "*Cadenz*" become Koch's celebrated "resting point of the spirit [or mind]" (*Ruhepunkt des Geistes*)—so eloquent in its suggestion as to how we as listeners might perceive, by "feeling" or cognition, the ending points of segments, phrases, and periods. The latter is newly defined by Koch as a higher level of phrase organization that combines several phrases into, say, the first and second parts of a small binary form, or the *Hauptperiode* of larger forms. I needn't reiterate that Koch's starting point is the same as Riepel's: Koch's four-bar *Absatz*, or "phrase," serves, like Riepel's, as the fundamental point of departure for expansions and extensions. My examples from Koch demonstrate his three main types of phrase extension: (1) the repetition of some part of a basic phrase; (2) the creation of an "appendix" (*Anhang*) to the ending of a cadential formula; and (3) the parenthetical insertion of "incidental" material between segments of a phrase. All three of these techniques were anticipated by Riepel, but now they are given much sharper definition.

At Figure 12.8(a) we see Koch's very first example of a "basic phrase" (from his second volume [1787], Part 2, section 3 [Koch 1983, 4]). Reminding us of Riepel's linguistic "equivalents" and of his allusion to the logic of grammar in speech, Koch describes mm. 1–2 as a "subject," and mm. 3–4 as a "predicate."[49] Readers will recognize this "basic phrase" as comparable to the combination of a basic idea (BI) and a contrasting idea (CI) in current theory. Now the process of extension begins. Six transformations of the phrase lead, in the end, to Figure 12.8(b), where both the "subject" and the "predicate" take immediate repetition. The result sounds very much like a Schoenbergian sentence: a presentation is followed by a continuation, with its faster rate of harmonic change.[50] But of course the "continuation" only consists of a repeated CI, leading to its stronger authentic closure.

In his volume 3, section 4 (1793), Koch reviews his methods for extending and expanding a basic phrase, now within the context of "The Connection of Melodic Sections, or the Structure of Periods." At Figure 12.9, he shows that a "parenthetical" but "complete" segment has been inserted at mm. 5–8 "between a phrase and its repetition" (1983, 161). The inserted four-bar unit clearly bears the characteristics of a continuation, in response to the presentation at mm. 1–4, and so today we would likely hear mm. 5–8 not as an "insertion," but rather as an integral second phrase within a Schoenbergian sentence. Had Koch regarded the HC at m. 8 as the goal of a *Quintabsatz* ("V-phrase"), then the "repetition" that follows might also be heard differently today—as a consequent, in the sense of a varied repetition of an antecedent at mm. 1–8, but one that ends with a stronger cadence (I introduced these terms in reference to Ex. 5). The complete excerpt at Figure 12.9 would be heard, then, as a period—not Koch's *Periode*, but a period in Schoenberg's restricted sense (1967).[51] More precisely, we would have a compound sixteen-bar period, with sentences as antecedent and consequent. But this interpretation hinges entirely upon the "etc." at m. 16: our consequent wants to end with a PAC!

FIGURE 12.8 Examples from Heinrich Christoph Koch, *Versuch einer Anleitung zur Composition* ["Introductory Essay on Composition"], Vol. II, Part 2, section 3, chapter 1 (Koch 1983, 4, 7).

FIGURE 12.9 From Koch, *Versuch*, Vol. III, section 4, chapter 3 (Koch 1983, 161).

FIGURE 12.10 Georg Benda, opening ritornello for the aria "Selbst die glücklichsten der Ehen," from the Singspiel *Walder* (1776); in Koch, *Versuch*, Vol. III, section 4, chapter 4 (Koch 1983, 173).

A genuine eight-bar period arises at Figure 12.10—the opening of an aria in rondo form from the Singspiel *Walder* (1776) by Georg Benda. Koch explains that in an aria of this type the "rondo theme" is first presented as an instrumental ritornello, "and very often an appendix is added to its cadence." His description of the "rondo theme" perfectly accords with modern-day notions of the typical period: a "single melodic section" is "presented first as a V-phrase, but in its immediate repetition is transformed into a closing phrase [*Schlusssatz*]."[52] My annotations adopt current analytical terminology for showing the periodic design of the passage. Koch's "appendix" appears at mm. 9–11—a post-cadential, tonic-prolonging codetta; the singers enter in duet at the upbeat to m. 11, giving an embellished repetition (not shown) of the complete rondo theme. It can further be mentioned that, of the minuets by Haydn displayed by Koch, two open with eight-bar periods in the Schoenbergian sense.[53] This should probably come as no surprise; in the music of such composers as Benda, Haydn, and especially Mozart, eight-bar periods and sentences (as outgrowths of Koch's four-bar model) become stabilized and emerge as the two most pervasive theme-types of the classical repertoire.

BEETHOVEN IN 1795

Do the ideas just surveyed about phrases and their expansions have relevance to music that postdates the writings of Riepel, Kirnberger, Koch, and other mid-to-late-eighteenth-century theorists? Strong cases have been made that the answer is *yes*, at least in respect to the later Haydn and to Mozart. Leopold Mozart owned at least one volume of Riepel's *Anfangsgründe*, and keyboard works by him and his young son have been shown to manifest Riepel's influence.[54] What about Beethoven? It's improbable that he was reading Koch when, just two years after the appearance of Koch's third volume, Beethoven published his first official opus in 1795—the Piano Trio in E♭ Major, op. 1, no. 1. The kinds of expansion techniques that this work explores are, however, Riepelian and Kochian in so many ways. To show what I mean, let's consider the first secondary theme (ST^1) of Beethoven's opening movement, shown as annotated at Figure 12.11. (A recording of this passage can be heard in ⏵ Audio example 12.2.) The greatest expansions within classical sonata forms tend to occur within secondary-theme regions; this early work already provides a vivid demonstration.

A lengthy "standing-on-the-dominant" of the secondary key, B♭ (V)—possibly an "appendix" for Koch to a "V-phrase" (see Koch 1983, 101 and Ex. 256)—ends with "hammer-strokes" (not shown) and a link into the new theme, which begins at m. 33. A quiet four-bar compound basic idea (2:bi. + 2:ci.) now finds its individual charm by shifting upward stepwise from the new tonic to the supertonic (ii) and then pausing on its dominant; a varied repetition, beginning sequentially, moves back to the tonic and ends more firmly with the tonicized HC at m. 40 (here's an *Änderungs-Absatz* for Riepel, and a *Quintabsatz* for Koch; already a *Vierer*, rather than only a *Zweyer*, has been repeated, thus expansion is already under way). The HC at m. 40 makes the claim for the initiating formal function of an eight-bar antecedent at mm. 33–40, so we might expect that a consequent will follow. Sure enough, a richly varied repetition begins at m. 41, with the piano's melody in the upper octave and the violin providing a new eighth-note figuration. But, as with the excerpt from Koch at Figure 12.9, a stronger cadence would be needed to close a genuine consequent; at the moment where this might have occurred— mm. 47–48—only another HC is achieved. Thus, a potential eight-bar consequent has "become" (⇒) simply the repetition of an antecedent, comparable to Riepel's and Koch's immediate phrase repetitions, but on a much broader scale.[55] This eight-bar repetition is only the first of Beethoven's expansions, with more to follow. At mm. 49–50, he repeats the two bars of his cadential idea, much like Riepel's, Kirnberger's, and Koch's "echo-like" insertions.

I'll now reinterpret Beethoven's antecedent and its varied repetition as the case of an immensely extended sixteen-bar presentation within an ever-expanding sentence

FIGURE 12.11 Beethoven, Piano Trio in E♭ Major, op. 1, no. 1, first movement: mm. 31–82 (first secondary theme) ▶ Audio Example 12.3.

whose continuation, if it were to balance the presentation—a characteristic classical tendency—might be expected to close sixteen bars later. This doesn't quite happen. The continuation begins, *fp*, with a new two-bar *cantabile* idea at m. 51 (*Singer* style, à la Riepel; the falling fifth seems to beckon); it is immediately repeated, and so it suggests another sentential presentation. A third repetition, at mm. 55, initiates what becomes a local continuation, with its more active rhythm and a progression that leads to the PAC

FIGURE 12.11 *continued.*

at m. 58. But this sentential continuation has only been eight bars long. To balance his sixteen-bar presentation, Beethoven now repeats the continuation, beginning at m. 59; but then even further expansion gets underway. Just where a cadence might have become imminent, the composer launches at mm. 65–68 into Riepel's *fonte*, [V⁷]–ii; V⁷–I, and then even repeats this at mm. 69–72—a straightforward case of Riepel's and Koch's "parenthesis," which interrupts and delays the approach to a cadence. An "extra" two bars at mm. 72–73 allow the pianist to ascend by step to the climactic high B♭ at m. 74, and then a victorious cadential progression prepares for closure. The expected authentic cadence on the downbeat of m. 76 is, however, *evaded*, and it takes a "one-more-time" repetition finally to achieve the authentic cadential goal at m. 80 (review the excerpt from Riepel at Figure 12.6(f)). An elision (<—>)—*Tacterstickung* in Koch's sense—might well occur in m. 80, permitting the second secondary theme (ST²) to begin at either m. 80 or m. 81. Listeners are free to choose.

I propose that Beethoven's ST¹ might technically have closed so much earlier; had he eliminated the *fonte* interpolation and the "one-more-time" repetition, he might have moved directly from m. 64 to the expanded cadential progression at mm. 76–80. And this is only the young Beethoven in 1795. He will make far more impressive, even monumental expansions throughout his career, and so will his symphonic successors throughout the nineteenth century. It is almost as if the mid-eighteenth-century theorists I have discussed enjoyed a kind of prescience about how European music into the nineteenth century would continue to "expand"; the techniques they described remained vital well beyond their era.

The "Great Nineteenth-Century Rhythm Problem" and the Four-Bar Phrase

If the mid-to-late eighteenth century achieved a kind of "apotheosis of the phrase" in both theory and practice, then, in the view of many, much nineteenth-century music exulted in this achievement but risked leading it toward "dangerous" consequences: "the danger . . . of too unrelievedly duple a hypermetrical pattern, of too consistent and unvarying a phrase structure—the danger, in short, of submitting too complacently to [Cone's] 'tyranny of the four-measure phrase,' not to mention the eight-and-sixteen-measure phrase" (Rothstein 1989, 184–185). The "Great Nineteenth-Century Rhythm Problem" is Rothstein's diagnosis of a symptom that could have resulted in a fatal disease, had it not been for the development of compositional techniques that could camouflage or work against "foursquare" phrase structures. These, often found in early Romantic "character pieces," have ancestors for Rothstein in the "unpretentious dance pieces" and the simple, *volkstümlich* Lieder that proliferated from the end of the eighteenth century and into the nineteenth. Even in the incomparable Lieder of Schubert and in some of the songs of Mendelssohn and Brahms, the "rhythmic squareness and symmetry" associated with the "folk aesthetic" remain in evidence; this goes as well for a host of piano works of the period. Rothstein introduces "the rhythm problem" at the beginning of his chapter on Mendelssohn's *Songs without Words* (*Lieder ohne Worte*)—an explicit case of the Lied's influence on nineteenth-century character pieces, and, for me, an exquisite example of music's ongoing bond with language. For Rothstein, Mendelssohn managed to solve the problem "most of the time" (190), through such techniques as syncopations at the hypermetric level, deceptive recapitulations of opening themes, phrase expansion, metric reinterpretation (via *Tacterstickung*), and parenthetical interpolations. These last three techniques will be familiar from our investigation into the work of Riepel, Kirnberger, and Koch.

Although not highlighted in Rothstein's book, Robert Schumann has been just as aptly implicated as his early nineteenth-century peers in the "problem" of a predilection for four-bar phrases; he seemed "to glory in the *Viertaktigkeit*," as Cone puts it (1968, 79). But Schumann has also been greatly admired for his capacity to undercut "foursquareness" in striking ways. A case in point, shown at Figure 12.12, is the unforgettable opening of his *Kreisleriana*, op. 16—a cycle of eight *Phantasien* from 1838, dedicated to Chopin. *Kreisleriana* is of course the title of a series of musical writings by E. T. A. Hoffmann embedded within his first book (1814–1815); there, Hoffmann introduces the passionate fictional character of Kapellmeister Johannes Kreisler—tormented, unbalanced, and subject to violent outbursts. It's tempting to imagine Kreisler storming onto the stage, in an impulsive, manic mood, as Schumann's first movement begins, *äusserst bewegt* (extremely agitated).

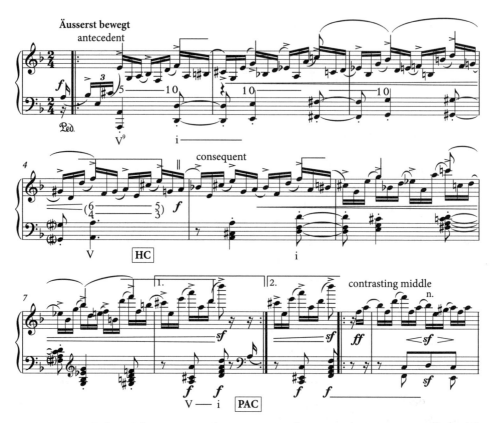

FIGURE 12.12 Robert Schumann, *Kreisleriana*, op. 16, first movement, mm. 1–10. ▶ Audio Example 12.4

If we search beneath the tumultuous surface of mm. 1–8, an unexpanded eight-bar period emerges, but hardly a breath separates the antecedent's barely discernible HC at m. 4 from the beginning of the consequent at m. 5. More disturbing is the bass line's unwillingness to coordinate with the flurry of sixteenth-note triplets in the pianist's right hand: the bass lags behind by one eighth note within the 2/4 meter, thus supporting no notated downbeats whatsoever. From experience, I'll confess that it is *really difficult* to perform the bass in syncopation, as notated (although observing the staccato markings on the bass notes can help); and I venture that it is well-nigh impossible for listeners to avoid hearing strong beats at entrances of the bass, especially because its ascent gives support, partly in tenths, to the fundamental ascent in the upper voice. Our initial hearing might be further complicated by Schumann's off-tonic beginning, on V⁹. Indeed, a metric pattern controlled by the bass allows for the cadential 6/4 at m. 4 to fall, appropriately, on a "downbeat." But it might begin to dawn on us that something has been off-kilter when, at the PAC in m. 8, the cadential tonic lands on an early weak beat, as if racing to the finish with an extra second to spare—"victory!" It is only at the beginning of the contrasting middle section (mm. 9–16) that the "real" downbeat shifts to its

FIGURE 12.13 Schumann, *Kreisleriana*, fifth movement, mm. 1–20. ▶ Audio Example 12.5.

proper place: again, eighth rests in the bass at mm. 9–10 open the passage, but now the *sforzandos* on the neighbor-tone B♭s insist that we hear this second beat within the bar as relatively strong. Here, then, is a special case of metrical conflict—a variant of the technique of conflicting downbeats, as described by Carl Schachter and cited by Rothstein in reference to their frequent occurrences within Mendelssohn's *Songs without Words*

(1989, 199–200). In Schumann's case, the 4 + 4 structure of his period is not completely disguised, but our perception of its metric structure has been seriously undermined.

Those who know the complete *Kreisleriana* might agree with me that, with very few exceptions, phrases within all eight movements and sections therein are rarely extended or expanded beyond the four- or eight-bar length; but Schumann finds ingenious ways of working against his *Viertaktigkeit*. At Figure 12.13, from the beginning of the fifth movement (*Sehr lebhaft*), the quirky *pianissimo* opening phrase reaches a HC on the downbeat of m. 5, but an apparent elision on that downbeat retrospectively reduces the phrase to a four-bar unit.

A new idea begins here, and it continues, through an ascending-3rds sequence (i–III–V–i) with imitation between soprano and bass, to another HC on the downbeat of m. 12, thus at least apparently spanning a regular eight-bar unit (maybe 4 + 4). But the accented D♮ on the second beat of m. 5 pretends to be the *beginning* of this next phrase unit, thus robbing m. 5 of its rightful three beats. I attempt to show in the score that, from this point forward, Schumann might subtly be encouraging us to hear three-beat segments within this eight-bar stretch, thus again, as in Figure 12.12, "relocating" the downbeat. But we are "corrected" on the downbeat of m. 12; here the eighth bar of the eight-bar metric unit again elides at the HC, followed by one of those rare phrase extensions in this oeuvre—a two-bar prolongation of the dominant.

Figure 12.13 includes the opening, at m. 14 (second repeat), of a contrasting middle section, where, unless the downbeat is again elided, a metric unit would seem again to begin on the second beat. Whether yes or no, a four-bar model arises here, to be sequenced and then fragmented over the course of the section. The pensive little cadential gesture at mm. 17–18 clearly marks the end of the model. Dare I suggest that here the four-bar unit really does seem to begin in the middle of m. 14? If so, Schumann has again robbed that measure of its full value and created a metrical shift. The young Martha Argerich's fabulous performance of the movement, heard in ⊙ Audio examples 12.3 and 12.4, invites this hearing. What matters is simply the composer's open-endedness as to where his four-bar phrases begin and end; perhaps the performer needs to make a decision about this, but listeners are left to their own imagination.

Repetitions of at least two or more metric units of the same length create what has been called hypermeasures, a term introduced by Cone, whereby a measure asks to "behave as a single beat" (1968, 79). In comparison with Mendelssohn and Schumann, "the composer who really absorbed, digested, assimilated, and nourished himself on the four-measure concept was Chopin" (80). Regular successions of "four-bar hypermeasures" are a defining feature of Chopin's early waltzes and mazurkas; after all, this is dance music—music that celebrates the dance in the salon. In recorded performances of the mazurkas that have survived since the mid-1920s, pianists can be heard to counterbalance Chopin's phrase symmetry by means of the characteristic "mazurka rubato," and this explains in part why he has been the darling of empirical work on "expressive timing" in the field of performance studies.[56] Even in his other genres and later music, four-bar hypermeasures tend to provide the underpinning. And yet, for many of us, the ease with which this composer, like Schumann, "mitigates the hypermeter without violating it" (Cone 1986, 80) contributes to his music's ineffable elegance and poignancy. In his chapter on Chopin's nocturnes, mazurkas, and études, Rothstein expertly employs Schenkerian graphs and durational reductions of hypermetic passages to demonstrate Chopin's mitigating devices: his astonishing rhythmic variety, his phrase overlaps, with "lead-ins" that blur the boundaries of phrases, his contrapuntal ingenuity, and, most astounding, his long legato slurs over many bar lines, "as if he wishes us not to know that one phrase is ending and another beginning" (1989, 220).

As the nineteenth century wanes, phrases, in the sense of symmetrically occurring "hyper-phrases," grow longer and longer, to the point where, in some music, "metric and hypermetric articulation have gone too far." Cone singles out Franck and Bruckner as cases in point (analysts of music by these composers have since come to their defense), and he finds it not at all surprising that "with Strauss, Mahler, and especially Debussy, a new, looser, sometimes almost anti-metrical principle begins to emerge" (1986, 82). As if Cone's and Rothstein's "Nineteenth-Century Rhythm Problem" were not enough for nineteenth-century composers to confront, this "problem" can, I think, be subsumed within a much broader aesthetic and technical "problem nexus" that Carl Dahlhaus developed in his influential "Issues in Composition" (published in translation in 1980). Whether or not his ideas in that essay have by now lost their freshness, Dahlhaus's arguments have direct relevance to the fate of the phrase in the later nineteenth century, as I shall try to explain.

Dahlhaus searches for the sources of a major change of direction taken by composers "after Beethoven," and especially after the 1840s, with Wagner and Liszt, Brahms and Bruckner as representative. Well into the early 1800s the "thematic technique of classical composers" was one in which "the single [musical] idea was still understood primarily as a corollary of the whole, and not the central sustaining substance"; "the musical 'idea' is the ... process itself" (Dahlhaus 1980, 43).[57] We can think here of some of the classical formal traditions I have discussed—for example, the long-lasting conventions of the Schoenbergian sentence and period, or the larger formal role of a secondary theme, in which each phrase carries a specific formal function—say, beginning, middle, or end. The insistence on "originality," which became well established by the early nineteenth century as "an unquestioned aesthetic doctrine," led to a rejection of composition as a "system of formal relations" (42). Eventually, the musical idea itself and its elaboration, rather than its relation to the whole, became the principal compositional point of departure. As a consequence, the "idea itself" becomes shorter; and so, the "problem" that mid-to-late nineteenth-century composers strove to solve, each in their own way, was how to "annul the discrepancy between the narrow dimensions of thematic ideas and the tendency towards, large, expansive, monumental forms" (48).

Here we can think, as does Dahlhaus, of Wagner's usually short leitmotifs and their vast networks in his music dramas, or of his and Liszt's and Bruckner's massive sequential, rather than periodic, passages, often based on a brief idea, and serving an expositional rather than developmental role (the opening of the Prelude to *Tristan* is the classic example). Neither the leitmotif nor the sequence requires cadential closure, and both "threatened to undermine traditional musical syntax and the regular periodic structure which provided the framework of . . . form conceived of as a large-scale metrical pattern" (53). In fact, Wagner scorned what he called "quadratic compositional construction," cultivating instead his conception of "endless melody" (*unendliche Melodie*)—an aesthetic and technical mode of composition intolerant of cadences and of the "forever breaking off" in Italian opera (55). "Endless melody" is an ideal that was anticipated, for Rothstein, in Chopin's late music (1989, 233–248) and that later became connected with Schoenberg's notion of "musical prose," as opposed to the periodic "verse-like" forms of the classical style. Nietzsche captured the rhythm-dissolving nature of "endless melody" in this way: "While earlier music walked or danced" [remember my quote from Kirnberger], the new music tried to 'float' or 'hover' " (Dahlhaus 1980, 58).

This brings us, finally, to the changing role of harmony in the late nineteenth century: "In Wagnerian harmony, with its reliance on chromatic alteration and its consequent tendency towards 'wandering' or 'floating' tonality . . . the accent falls on harmonic details—on single chords or unusual progressions," in short, on a technique that Dahlhaus characterizes as "the individualization of harmony" (73). As one of several examples, he refers to the leitmotivic role of the "mystic chord" in *Parsifal*; jumping ahead by sixty years, we might summon the "Wir arme Leut' " motive in Alban Berg's *Wozzeck,* whose referential sonority is the "minor-major" seventh chord (pc set 4-19 [0148]), associated leitmotivically with the title character throughout the opera. In his "Issues" essay Dahlhaus's discussion of harmony ends with Wagner, Liszt, and Brahms, but it seems safe to say that, from *Tristan*'s "floating" tonality in 1865 to Berg's modernist "atonal" harmonic language in 1925, all of the characteristics of late nineteenth-century music that Dahlhaus explores, including the abandonment of cadences, "four-bar phrases" and periodic harmonic syntax, converge to contribute toward the abandonment of "common-practice tonality" as well.

My précis of Dahlhaus's essay hardly does justice to its rich content, nor would his argument ever be regarded as the last word on the evolution of European music over the course of the nineteenth century. But Dahlhaus lays bare for us just how strongly some of our notions of phrase, as these arose during its heyday in the eighteenth century, have been dependent upon the elements of periodic classical forms and theme-types, regular harmonic/metric syntax, functional dominant-to-tonic cadences, and, indeed, tonality itself, as it is most commonly understood. What happens to the phrase in the absence of these dimensions?

PHRASE WITHOUT WESTERN TONALITY

Tonal elements were of course not the condition that suggested phrases in the plainchant I've discussed (Figures 12.1 and 12.2), and they did not play a role in Gretchen Horlacher's analysis of the opening of *Les Noces* (Figure 12.3). In that case, as in other music of the twentieth century, what has been called "pitch centricity"—for Stravinsky, E♮ as the focal point—"stood in" for tonal stability; the text, though interrupted, contributed to determining phrase lengths; the second phrase gave closure to the first by dint of an expanded repetition; and a pause, a "resting point," marked the end of each of the two phrases.

p (désolé)

←→

FIGURE 12.14 Opening of "Abîme des oiseaux" (movement 3), for solo clarinet in B♭, from Messiaen's *Quatuor pour la fin du temps.*

Figure 12.14 is a comparable example without text—the opening of the third movement, "Abîme des oiseaux," for solo clarinet in B♭, from Olivier Messiaen's *Quatuor pour la fin du temps* (1941).[58]

Observing the composer's breath mark at the end of the excerpt, Anthony Pople regards the complete excerpt as a single "phrase," falling into "two equal halves, the second of which answers the first" (1998, 42). Messiaen's tempo and character marking, *Lent, expressif et triste*, might, on the other hand, suggest *two slow* "phrases," the second as a varied repetition, with its newly inflected close. Either way, the composer's focal pitch, like Stravinsky's, is the E♮: the point of departure, the tone around which the melody circles in m. 2, the goal of the first metric unit at m. 3, and the goal of the complete excerpt. Like Pople, I hear an elision at m. 3: the long E♮ serves as both a goal and a new beginning. Messiaen's pitch-class matrix here, and generally for the movement as a whole, is his mode 2, the octatonic; unlike Stravinsky, he eschews time signatures altogether, but his bar lines in this opening would seem to delineate phrase segments, while also guiding the performer. Altogether, the phrase structure of Messiaen's opening is remarkably similar to Stravinsky's in *Les Noces*, and not uncommon in other twentieth-century music in which direct, expanded phrase repetition plays a structural and formal role. I think, for example, of the fugal subject at the opening of Béla Bartók's *Music for Strings, Percussion and Celesta* (1936), and of some of his *Mikrokosmos* pieces, many of which draw from his collection of Eastern European folk songs and dances.

Just as we struggle with multiple ideas about phrase, it has been noted that conceptions of tonality—including ideas of tonic, tonicity, and tonicness—remain divergent and problematic (see Steven Rings's chapter in this volume). Just the same, historians and theorists alike have argued that vestiges of tonality, and thus even of phrases as articulated through quasi-tonal techniques, continued to thrive in much Western music over the course of the twentieth century. For example, in his contribution to the recent Norton series *Western Music in Context*, Joseph Auner indexes "uses of," or "allusions to," tonality in music by thirteen of the most prominent twentieth-century composers he discusses (Auner 2013a, A44). Broad, if loosely defined, applications of the term would admit music by many others over the last century; as well, past and present blues, jazz, folk, and pop styles would be included. Auner cites an interview from 1995, in which Philip Glass rejects the notion that atonality should be central in narratives of twentieth-century music. Says Glass: "It now seems to me that the mainstream was tonal music, if you think about Shostakovich, Sibelius, Strauss, and Copland. When we look at the major literature from the perspective of the ninth decade in the twentieth century, it seems that twentieth-century music is tonal music. But there were moments when it didn't appear that way" (Auner 2013a, 289).

Where, then, would we find phrases that are *not* influenced by Western tonality? Glass's comments notwithstanding, the range of possibilities is actually quite vast, thus well beyond the scope of my work. Just two examples will have to suffice, but I trust that these will suggest others, especially in the realms of world music.

Many years ago, I had the privilege of witnessing a live performance of György Ligeti's *Continuum*, for harpsichord, composed in 1968; this piece has held my fascination ever since. Thus it was a pleasure to discover that Auner himself presents a succinct overview of *Continuum* (Auner 2013a, 240, and 2013b, 247–254); I have also gained further understanding of the piece through a study that investigates sound analysis and cognition-based principles of "auditory streaming" to probe how listeners might perceive its compositional process (Cambouropoulos and Tsougras 2009). Neither of these two accounts of *Continuum* focuses on the question of its performance (although Auner does mention that "Ligeti pushes both the mechanism of the instrument and the technique of the harpsichordist to the breaking point" [240]). Truth be told, it is the sheer virtuosity, the spectacular rendition, *prestissimo*, of an unremitting *moto perpetuo* over the composer's required "four minutes or less," that has taken my breath away upon every hearing. For those who don't know the piece, a mere glance at the excerpts presented at Figure 12.15 and ▶ Audio example 12.5 should alert you to the performer's extraordinary challenge.

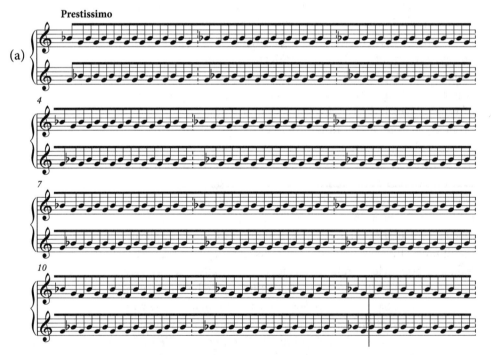

EXAMPLE 12.15 Excerpts from Ligeti, *Continuum*, for harpsichord: (a) Opening, divisions 1–12; (b) Divisions 85–97; (c) Divisions 99–205. ▶ Audio Example 12.6.

SECTION 3

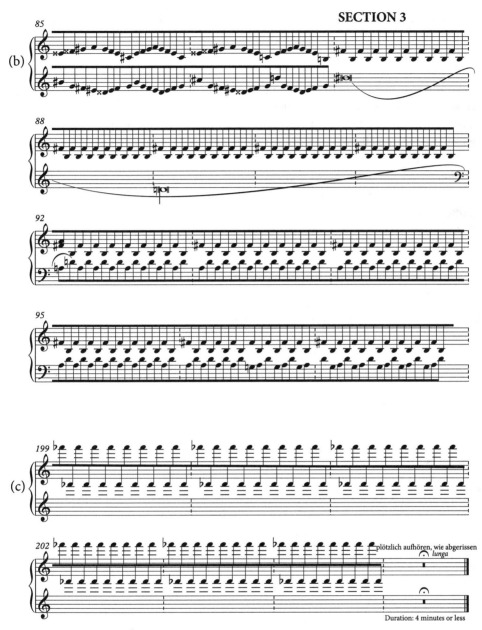

FIGURE 12.15 *continued.*

Ligeti has related *Continuum* to other pieces within his "pattern-meccanico" style—works that reflect his fascination with the ticking of clocks and with other mechanical devices (he came to realize that "a harpsichord was really like some strange machine"; Auner 2013a, 240, citing Clendinning 1993). Auner reports that *Continuum* "was inspired by an experiment Ligeti heard at the Cologne Studio for

Electronic Music demonstrating that a series of pitches played quickly enough would be perceived as a chord" (253). Thus, as shown at Figure 12.15(a), the opening minor-third dyad G♮–B♭ will be played, *prestissimo*, in continuous eighth notes by the right and left hands, and in contrary motion, on two separate manuals, using only the 8-foot stop (normal pitch, no doublings) on the modern harpsichord; the result will sound like one single whirring, buzzing simultaneity. You'll see that the composer uses broken vertical lines after each series of sixteen eighth notes; these are not in any way to be regarded as bar lines indicating beat or meter, and so Auner refers to them as "divisions" (253).

The term "net-structures" (*Netzstrukturen* for Ligeti) has also been applied to *Continuum;* a net-structure is "a continuous web of finely-woven lines or re-peated patterns in a constant, interactive process of transformation of one or more parameters, such as pitch, rhythm, texture, dynamics, or timbre" (Cambouropoulos and Tsougras 2009, 121). In interviews, Ligeti has described his "net-structure micropolyphony" in terms of "interval signals" that gradually get "blurred" when an-other interval signal appears and creates "mistiness": these "signals are neither tonal nor atonal yet somehow, with their purity and clarity, they constitute points of rest" (122). The idea of "resting points" as signals for ends of "phrases" has occurred re-peatedly in my study; but when, after nine divisions (almost ten seconds?) of the initial dyad, the F♮ in division 12 enters as a new "signal," the effect of a "resting point" can hardly be claimed. The harpsichordist must absolutely maintain the *prestissimo* tempo.

On the other hand, a new auditory stream, out of phase with the continuing sound of the dyad, subtly asks for our attention. Additions of new tones, and their eventual deletions, within asynchronous two-handed patterns of up to five tones, and most often in contrary motion, expand or contract the register between lowest and highest tones of the patterns, while creating new streams and new textures. These shifting patterns yield a large-scale form in five sections, displayed with an impressive graph by Jane Piper Clendinning (1993), reproduced both by Auner and by Cambouropoulos and Tsougras. For example, Clendinning's Section 1 (divisions 1–55) takes its definition by means of the systematic expansion of the opening dyad and then its contraction to a major second. At my Figure 12.15(b), we approach the beginning of Section 3 (divisions 87–125), where, as if from out of the blue, a radiant B-major triad emerges from within the texture, as greatly magnified by the sudden pause in the left hand; when this chord shifts to a B-minor sonority, the D♮ that provides that transformation completes the twelve-note chromatic collection over the span of the piece thus far. A climax seems to have been reached—the achievement of a long-range goal—but the greater climax will occur only in the last divisions. A dramatic *subito* engagement of three stops, 16-, 8-, and 4-foot, at the beginning of Section 4 (division 126) greatly increases both the volume and the intensity, all within the widest registral expanse, and the racket of "extra-musical" noise created by the harpsichord's action contributes to the antic-ipation that a goal will soon be reached. But then, suddenly, only the 4-foot stop is left in control of the final passage, which leads to the repetition in the two hands over twelve divisions of a single F♭ in its highest register. And then, as seen in Figure 12.15(c), the music simply *stops*, "as though torn off" ("plötzlich aufhören, wie abgerissen"). In short, this piece has *no ending*.

Does *Continuum* even have "phrases"? I'll contend that only the harpsichordist might need to think so. For an accurate performance of the piece (would this be possible?), I can only imagine the need to annotate the score (in red!), perhaps by numbering the divisions or subdivisions before a pattern changes, and marking "phrases" as concluding and beginning where these occur. The need to parse, to organize our perceptions, leads naturally to an attribution of some sort of phrase structure to almost any passage of music. But in a case like *Continuum*, that impulse might reasonably be resisted. Here *phases* take the place of phrases.

An Ending, or Where to End?

I opened this chapter with the speculation that perhaps phrases can be identified in many of the world's musics. Now would be the time for ethnomusicologist scholars of diverse non-Western cultures to step in and either support or disparage this extravagant claim. I can at least report that ethnomusicologist David Locke, well known for his ethnomusicological studies and performances of the music of Ghana, has expressed enthusiasm for efforts to raise serious questions about such fundamental concepts as phrase, in his field as well as mine. Locke's remarkable website (http://sites.tufts.edu.davidlocke/) hosts two online monographs: critical commentary, transcriptions, and audio files for the Agbadza music of the Ewe people, and a comprehensive presentation on Dagomba dance-drumming. I've focused on the Agbadza collection, where I've learned that Locke freely ascribes the term "phrase" to the essential time-line unit and foundation upon which much West African music is built—the bell phrase (see Locke's website, especially 44–49). This is the internationally known, cyclically recurring rhythmic pattern of twelve pulses, shaped into a pattern of longer and shorter durations: 2 + 2 + 1 + 2 + 2 + 2 + 1. Locke reports that Ewe musicians feel the bell phrase in four. In other words, the time span is $4 \times 3 = 12$, a ternary-quadruple structure is approximate to 12/8-time signature, with the tempo roughly at the dotted quarter = 112.

The bell phrase provides the aural skeleton for all the participants and elements within an Agbadza performance: the song leader and group, in call-and-response antiphony, the dancers, the clapping, the rattle, and the drums, with their own drum language phrases closely shadowing the language and message of the song. Although performers and instructors always say, "Listen to the bell" (31, 44), its sound is often drowned out by the rattles; thus Locke suggests that the bell phrase is as much an abstract musical idea, or "muse," as it is a tangible guide—one that all the performers must internalize. Locke says that the question "Where is ONE?"—that is, where does the bell phrase begin?—is like asking "Where does a circle begin?" Phrases, whether in song melodies or drumming parts, can be set on any moment of the phrase's cycle. Agbazda musical time, then, is circular (32).

The vocal and instrumental contributions to an Agbadza performance also have their own repeated phrases, but these move at different speeds relative to the bell phrase. For example, one of the many phrases of the medium-pitched kidi drum (which responds to the call of the sogo, or leader's drum) plays three times over the span of two bell phrases before it comes around to where it had begun (55). Likewise, the phrases of the instruments and of the songs, usually pentatonic in nature, have their own lengths, metric feels, and individual rhythmic motives, often expressing the duality of two and three. The outcome, Locke suggests, is an extremely complex polymetric, multideterminant, multidimensional "composite phrase" (37) within a "meter as a matrix of different streams of beats." Each part within this matrix competes for our attention, and perceptions of the phrase may undergo "shape-shifting transformations" (31). In contrast with Ligeti's *Continuum*, which stops but does not "end," the Agbadza performance may really *end*: the dancers enact a cadence (27), and a special lead drum theme serves as the ending signal (66–67).

In search of common and new uses of the term "phrase," I've concentrated mainly on that topic in Locke's account of the Ewe Agbadza tradition, so I've not even begun to capture the intricacy and vitality of the music, which I've experienced many times in Locke's own performances with groups at Tufts University. The effort to engage with one musical culture outside of the West gives me the chance, however, to bring a close to my chapter by returning to the concerns I myself expressed about notions of phrase as a potentially universal phenomenon. Song, dance, and drumming play the definitive roles in Agbadza music—another case in support of my position that "phrases" in music have long been associated with language and speech as well as with the rhythms of dance as bodily movement. But every generality has its exceptions—maybe a healthy product of the generalities themselves. For just one example, experimental vocal works by such composers as Berio and Nono in the West strove to *undercut* meaning in language by deconstructing it, extracting phonemes for their sound qualities, and placing the spotlight on pure vocal gesture, even on pre-linguistic expression. The deconstruction of phrases in language eliminates the phrase structures of the vocal music of the past, so dutiful to the text; but "phases," or groupings of gestures, like inhaling and exhaling, remain clearly in evidence. Might we say that, paradoxically, this kind of vocal music engages with language and human utterance on the deepest of levels? Here's another generalization that will elicit exceptions.

There is really no end to the question, what is a phrase? I'm convinced, however, that listeners, analysts, theorists, music historians, and especially performers *need* phrases, as these seem to be implicated, often quite differently, in so much of the music of different styles, eras, and cultures. So, it might be incumbent on all of us, when we write about music or perform it, to ask ourselves: What is the context in which "phrase" means something to me? How shall I adopt this term?

ACKNOWLEDGMENTS

I express profound gratitude to my two colleagues at Tufts University, David Locke and Joseph Auner—to David, for his patience and advice in helping me to gain a grasp of his work on Agbadza music, and to Joe, for his unfailing inspiration and support. I am also grateful to Etha Williams, a doctoral student at Harvard, for her careful preparation of my music examples and audio files.

AUDIO EXAMPLES

Audio Example 12.1. The recorded excerpt is performed by the Philharmonia and the Simon Joy Chorale, Robert Craft, conductor (Koch International Classics 2002; KIC– CD– 7514).

Audio Example 12.2. Haydn, Symphony No. 104, Andante, mm. 1– 8.

Audio Example 12.3. The recorded example is performed by Eugene Istomin, Isaac Stern, and Leonard Rose (Sony Classical 1995; 01--64510-10).

Audio Example 12.4. The audio recording info is missing here. It should serve as the caption for Audio Example 12.4: The recorded excerpt is performed by Martha Argerich (Deutsche Grammophon 1984; 410 653–1).

Audio Example 12.5. The recorded excerpt is performed by Martha Argerich (Deutsche Grammophon 1984; 410 653–1).

Audio Example 12.6. The recorded excerpt of the opening (extended) is performed by Antoinette Vischer (Wergo 1984/1988; WER 60161-50).

NOTES

1. In his chapter on musical grammar in this volume, Gjerdingen creates a fictional world— the land of Bijou—in which, for example, a "first rule states that phrases must end with a musical gesture known as *beryl.*"

2. For an overview of the concept of "phrasing," its emergence within the nineteenth century, and the work of especially Momigny, Lussy, and Tobias Augustus Matthay (1858–1945) in promoting its importance for performers, see Doğantan-Dack 2012.

3. Fassler notes that, in interaction with the psalm tone, the antiphon "has the reciting tone of D as a goal in several of its phrases," and that, twice near its end, the voices descend to D an octave below the reciting tone, creating a kind of musical rhyme between the phrases "quia veniet" and "non tardabit." (I have bracketed these "phrases" in the score for the antiphon; the stem notations in Figure 12.1(a), explained below, are mine.)

4. Fassler's analytic method is representative of long-standing work by musicologists in "the fields of research in monadic music, folk-song scholarship and the study of Christian liturgical chant," as discussed by Harold S. Powers in his landmark "Language Models and Musical Analysis" (1980, 12). Powers critically assesses both the music-and-language analogy and the music-*as*-language metaphor from the perspective of semantics (for example, drum and whistle languages; medieval North Indian systems of melodic types associated with non-musical phenomena), phonology (for instance, correspondences between long and short syllables in classical South Indian texts and in South Indian music), and syntax/grammar (in reference to "new" linguistics-based analyses of music, these having begun to emerge by 1980 in both the Western theoretical and the ethnomusicological traditions). For Powers: "the new literature seems uninterested in older traditions of

language models for musical analysis. Yet those traditions are of value not only in their own right but even more because they have left significant residues in our modern notions of what constitutes musical analysis and even music itself " (1980, 9).

5. See especially Vial's chapter 2. Vial's Appendix B provides a "Chronological Chart of Punctuation References," drawn from sixty-one sources, beginning with Quintilian (ca. 92–95 CE) and ranging through Riemann to Fischer.

6. In a private communication with me (on April 5, 2017), Caleb Mutch has clarified that "Aristotle's use of *periodos* does not refer to a punctuation mark, but rather to a series of words encompassing a complete idea. Whether that series of words is necessarily spoken aloud or can be written is a little less clear." Mutch's sense is that "spoken is the default, but that it also extends to words on the page." From Mutch's dissertation we also have the following: "From the modern reader's perspective, the development of a system of punctuation would seem to have been almost necessary for classical culture. Greek scribes, and Roman scribes from the second century CE onwards, wrote in continuous script (*scriptura continua*), in which all the letters of a text were spaced at roughly equal distances from each other, a practice that gave no indications of distinctions between words, let alone large sense units. In a context like this, scribes could have relied on punctuation as a way to help readers intuit the text's syntactic structure, or even to give aspiring orators indications of appropriate points at which to breathe or to pause form emphasis" (2015, 24).

7. As noted by Mutch (2015, 53n75), Calvin Bower and Harold Powers have presented similar transcriptions of "Petrus autem servabatur," in each case using later sources, thus further in time and distance from John of Affligem; see Powers (1980, 50).

8. John of Affligem, as quoted in translation by Mutch (2015, 51).

9. It can be added that in modern writing, the colon usually precedes (sets up) an explanation or an enumeration—apparently not the case for John's colons; note as well that Margot Fassler avoids the term "colon" in favor of "semicolon."

10. For further discussion of cadence and its relationship to the contrapuntal tradition, see Daniel Harrison's contribution to this volume.

11. A survey of experimental studies in music cognition through the 1990s will be found in David Temperley's *The Cognition of Basic Musical Structures* (2001).

12. Horlacher notes that text interruption also occurs in the French translation (on "ma," which modifies "tresse") ["my braid"]; she clarifies that the translation adapted from the Russian was made by the French-Swiss novelist Charles-Ferdinand Ramuz under Stravinsky's supervision (2011, 36n12).

13. Years ago, I was introduced to the expression "repetition ensures closure," attributed to the great jazz pianist and composer Mel Powell; I have never forgotten this useful maxim. Powell's expression finds an endorsement in Leonard B. Meyer's writings about repetition and closure in his *Explaining Music* (1973): for example, "one of the most effective ways of emphasizing that an event is ended, is to begin it again" (52); and "the closure of the first phrase is emphasized by the fact that the second begins like a repetition" (86).

14. On a related note, the epigraph by Stravinsky at the opening of Horlacher's Preface reads: "*Melody is . . . the musical singing of a cadenced phrase*" (2011, vii). Here's the larger context for this statement: "Melody, *Mélôdia* in Greek, is the intonation of the *melos*, which signifies a fragment, a part of a phrase. It is these parts that strike the ear in such a way as to mark certain accentuations. Melody is thus the musical singing of a cadenced phrase—I use *cadenced* in its general sense, not in the special musical sense" (Stravinsky 1947, 42).

15. The complete score for Willaert's villanella can be found in Freedman (2013, 107–109).

16. Here, Agawu discusses intimations of the paradigm in the writings about oratory and music of Mattheson, in the model of a Schenkerian *Ursatz*, in the work of Wilhelm Fischer and Leonard Ratner, and in Edward Said's ideas about the beginnings of literary works. See also Agawu (2009), chapter 2, 51–61 ("Beginnings, Middles, Endings," about which more below).

17. Also see Sessions (1950, 13): "The phrase is a constant movement toward a goal—the cadence"; and Westergaard (1975, 311).

18. Cone's analogy arises within a much broader context: "musical form, as I conceive it, is basically rhythmic . . . It would be an oversimplification to state, as I have been on the verge of doing, that every tonal composition represents a variation on a single rhythmic form, viz., an extended upbeat followed by its downbeat. Yet the oversimplification would not be a gross one. Just as, in a normal musical period, the antecedent phrase stands in some sense as an upbeat to the consequent, so in larger forms one entire section can stand as an upbeat to the next. And if, as I believe, there is a sense in which a phrase can be heard as an upbeat to its own cadence, larger and larger sections can also be so apprehended. A completely unified composition could then constitute a single, huge rhythmic impulse, completed at the final cadence" (Cone 1968, 25–26). His caveat of oversimplification notwithstanding, Cone's view has been taken at face value and firmly rejected by some, but it has also been defended and amplified in association with "end-accented" and "beginning-accented" phrases in Ng 2012. Doğantan-Dack (2012, 29n87) chides Cone for not having noted a similar ball-throwing analogy in the writings of Dom André Moquereau (1849–1930).

19. In this study, Agawu cites Lewis Rowell's survey of a variety of beginning strategies in music, with Rowell's descriptions of these in terms of "birth, emergence, origins, primal cries, and growth." "Endings, similarly, have elicited metaphors associated with rest and finality, with loss and completion, with consummation and transfiguration, with the cessation of motion and the end of life, and ultimately with death and dying" (2009, 52).

20. Surprisingly, Agawu does not return to the paradigm of beginning–middle–ending until the very end of his study (2009, 318).

21. See also Caplin (2009, 63n9) and (2013, Glossary of Terms, 714) for his definition of the term "theme"; I draw from both of these clarifications.

22. See the Glossary in Caplin 2013, under "phrase function," "idea function," "thematic function," and "section function."

23. See Hepokoski (2009), Webster (2009), and Ng 2012 (51n3).

24. For example, consider Neuwirth and Bergé (2015). See also the Latin names given by Robert Gjerdingen (2007) to bass-line patterns that, in combination with harmonic progressions, define his galant "cadential schemata," or *clausulae*. Danuta Mirka (2010) adopts Gjerdingen's names in her analyses of ending formulas within excerpts from Mozart and Haydn featuring phrase expansion by means of "twisted caesuras" and "overridden caesuras."

25. From L. Poundie Burstein: "Adding to the terminological complications are the multitudinous terms for each cadence type. For instance, half cadences are also known as 'semicadences,' 'imperfect cadences,' 'incomplete cadences,' 'half closes,' and the like. Especially in publications from earlier eras, references to half or authentic cadences (or words that usually are translated into English as such) might not precisely match the modern use of these terms" (2014, 203n2).

26. Caplin regards the deceptive cadence and the evaded cadence as "cadential variants" (1998, 265n39) and, later, "cadential deviations" (2013, 129–132), thus not genuine cadences "in music in the classical style" (1998, 43). A third type of cadential deviation for Caplin is the abandoned cadence—"the failure to realize an implied authentic cadence by eliminating the cadential dominant in root position or by inverting that harmony before its resolution" (2013, 703, 132). L. Poundie Burstein "avoids" the term "evaded cadence," on the grounds that its meaning has "not been standardized … and which often refers to events that do *not* occur at ends of phrases" (2014, 218–219n31). As explained below, Burstein's "phrases" *must* end with cadences; the EC *withholds* a cadential ending (it is not really a cadence!). His Example 18(a) (2014), of a "disrupted ending," from Pleyel, beautifully demonstrates what I've described (in Schmalfeldt 1992) as an "evaded cadence" followed by a "one-more-time" repetition.

27. This is the announcement for a Themed Session titled "Rethinking the Language of Music Theory: Concepts, Objects, History," sponsored by the Society for Music Theory, Music and Philosophy Interest Group, the Royal Musical Association, King's College, London, UK, on July 13–14, 2017:

    Music-analytic language is typically conceived and deployed as a well-oiled machine: the musical terms we use rest on rigorous definitions and operate within clearly marked conceptual territories, so that particular music-theoretical labels correspond necessarily, and often exclusively, with particular concepts in a one-to-one relationship. From such assumptions, it is a short step to ascribing ontological value to music-theoretical language, so that the very nature of musical phenomena (such as "chord," "dominant," or "meter") is regarded as contingent on the dedicated labels attached to them. The essentialist bias informing current music-analytic practice is in need of critical scrutiny: it is one thing to argue that language (as a manifestation of consciousness) provides a privileged path to musical ontologies; quite another to regard those ontologies per se as radically contingent upon language. Accessed online, January 16, 2017.

28. "We regard the normative 'phrase' as a more or less complete musical thought involving motion to a cadence … What Caplin calls a phrase we would often call a subphrase or module—although 'module' is intended to be a flexible term covering any of a number of small building-blocks within a work, ranging from each of Caplin's two smaller ideas, to any slightly larger unit without strong inner contrast, to, at times, a consistent 'phrase' itself" (Hepokoski and Darcy 2006, 69n10).

29. Schachter continues: "Along these lines, I think it is possible to distinguish between a subphrase and a small phrase inside a larger one. A small phrase has a claim to independent existence, whereas a sub-phrase doesn't really cut it by itself" (2016, 195).

30. Burstein's demonstrations of the "HC on V^7" in eighteenth-century music seem in part to be an implicit response, though unacknowledged, to my own "nineteenth-century HC" ("19cHC")—a category of half cadence I introduce in respect to music after 1800, where the tendency to include the seventh within the dominant at a clear half-cadential phrase ending becomes so much more prevalent; see Schmalfeldt (2011, 202–203, passim).

31. Let it be clarified that Rothstein's "large phrase motion" within Chopin's mazurka spans mm. 1–38 (not 37); the large phrase concludes at the end of the first two bars of the recapitulation, where an overarching I–III–VI *Bassbrechung* reaches its completion. Rothstein also identifies "smaller phrases" at mm. 1–12 and at mm. 13–20, and he hears cadences (in III = B

major) at mm. 28 and 36. His main objective is to examine Chopin's purposeful, although apparently "whimsical," slurring articulations as ramifications of the long-range role of Chopin's opening idea, an "old witticism from the Classic period" by which "a cadence—a phrase ending—" serves as "a phrase beginning." See Rothstein (1989, 229–233).

32. Burstein is certainly right to assume that the seventh as C♯ in m. 4 does *not* immediately resolve to the B♮ in that measure; the B♮ serves as a passing tone to A♮, and the unfolding C-to-A prolongs the seventh.

33. See John Walter Hill's Introduction to his translation of Riepel's chapters 1 and 2 (Hill 2014, vii).

34. See Nancy Kovaleff Baker's comments about Riepel in the Introduction to her translation of Koch (Koch 1983, xviii); see also London 1990 and Lester 1992, chapter 10.

35. As noted by Hill (2014, xvi) and others, an example of Riepel's inconsistencies involves the term *Absatz*: in his first chapter, *Absatz* can refer to a two-bar as well as four-bar unit and its harmonic/melodic punctuation; in his chapter 2, the term is restricted to units of four bars, or expansions of these that are reducible to a four-bar segment.

36. See chapters 4 ("The Fonte"), 7 ("The Monte"), and 14 ("The Ponte") in Gjerdingen (2007).

37. For a reminder about syllogisms as a form of deductive reasoning, here's a well-known example: (*major premise*) "All men are mortal"; (*minor premise*) "Socrates is a man"; (*conclusion*) "Therefore, Socrates is mortal."

38. If I'm wrong, I'll welcome the challenge.

39. In his discussion of Riepel's syllogistic "logic," Stefan Eckert (2007) clarifies that the drawing compass was used to geometrically divide the string of the monochord (116n60). For Eckert, the *Zirkel-Harmonisten*, cited in the subtitle of Riepel's first chapter, refer to "theorists in the Pythagorean tradition," involved with ratios and proportion—that is, "speculation" that does not aid composition, which depends upon the "ear" (hearing) and upon musical practice (116–117).

40. For Hill (2014, 384), an "eightsome" that begins with a "caesura-defined" initial "foursome" (2 + 2) "is so completely common in mid-eighteenth-century music that it would probably be preferable to consider it a thing unto itself." Hill then cites Eugene K. Wolf, who calls this construction "a 2+2:4 bar form." The now well-accepted term for this type of "eightsome" is the eight-bar sentence, in Schoenberg's sense.

41. While teaching for a two-week period in October 2016 within the Musicology Department at the University of Pavia, in Cremona, I learned that my students use the term "propositio" for "presentation" in English, that is, the first "phrase" within a Schoenbergian sentence (*la frase* in Italian).

42. Reaching beyond the *galant*, Wagner frequently claimed that "all Classical instrumental music was essentially dance music"; as cited in Rothstein (1989, 279).

43. See Kirnberger (1982, 216) and Koch (1983, 78–83).

44. See also Budday (1983, 52–76); Caplin's concise summary in his article for *The Cambridge History of Western Music Theory* (2002, 670–675); and, as the most comprehensive study of Riepel's expansions, Hill (2014, 369–400).

45. Both Sisman (1982, 450–451) and Lester (1992, 264–265) align the binary first part of the examples that represent this three-stage process; in Hill's translation, these will be found at Ex. 565 (the 8-bar "miniature"), Ex. 561 (twenty-four measures), and Ex. 576 (sixty-four measures). Sisman (456–457) and Lester (291) also both undertake an alignment of Koch's eight-bar "period" and its expansion to thirty-two measures, as drawn from Exx. 361 and 362 in Koch 1983.

46. See Hepokoski and Darcy (2006), chapter 17, "The Type 2 Sonata."

47. Peter M. Landrey, the translator of Reicha's *Traité de mélodie* (1814), clarifies that Reicha "makes a qualitative distinction between 'phrase' (*phrase*) and 'rhythm' (*rythme*), using the former where the thematic content of a unit is primarily concerned, and the latter to describe its rhythmic function" (Reicha 2000, xiii).

48. As a mere sampling of studies concerning Koch, see, for example, Forschner (1984); Budday (1983); Dahlhaus (1989); Baker and Christensen (1995); and Byros (2015), who focuses upon Koch's *Form der Sonate* as a "punctuation form" (*interpunctische Form*).

49. Koch no sooner introduces the linguistic terms "subject" and "predicate" before he abandons them, on the basis that "beginning musicians" seldom have knowledge of grammar in speech (1983, 6n8). Perhaps Koch needs to distance himself here from Riepel's syllogistic "logic"; on the other hand, Riepel himself seems to have disparaged this "philosophy" when he learns that his Discantist can do without it in composing (see above).

50. In Koch (1983), his Ex. 188 does indeed show all the characteristics of the Schoenbergian eight-bar sentence, ending with a HC; here the continuation consists of two distinct segments, the second serving as cadential. In this example, the repetition of the two-bar basic idea is shown to take the same type of "punctuation formula" as the opening idea itself. For Koch: Now "the first phrase ... is made incomplete, and the second phrase, even though complete in itself, is yet necessary to finish the first. By this means, two complete phrases are given the form and the value of a single, integral phrase, that is, they are compounded" (57). In short, the Schoenbergian sentence emerges as one type of compound phrase.

51. Koch's broader notion of *Periode* has continued to flourish well beyond Schoenberg's narrower definition of the term, and it prevails in many contemporary theoretical studies. Rothstein (1989), for example, allowing for a HC to mark the end of a phrase, posits that "the cadence of the second phrase [i.e., the stronger cadence] serves as the cadence for the whole unit (itself a large phrase); this larger unit is called a *period*. Note, however, that the term *period* can refer to any phrase that contains at least two smaller phrases; it is not necessary that any of the smaller phrases end with a half cadence" (17). Like many others, Rothstein reserves the term parallel period for the case where the antecedent ends with a HC and the consequent serves as a varied repetition that closes with a stronger cadence.

52. Koch's association of rondo themes with the present-day period (antecedent-consequent) resonates with the nature of classical rondo themes in general, which most often have the period as their basis.

53. In Koch (1983), see the excerpts by Haydn at Exx. 280 and 283.

54. See Hill's essay "Reception: Leopold and Wolfgang Amadeus Mozart," in Hill (2014); see also, for example, Sisman (1982).

55. For the Hegelian idea of "becoming," as applied to "retrospective formal reinterpretation" in phrase-structural and formal analysis, see Schmalfeldt (2011).

56. In addition to Mitchell Ohriner's contribution to this volume, see Cook (2013, 157–208, passim) and Ohriner (2012).

57. The influence of Theodor W. Adorno on Dahlhaus is much in evidence in Dahlhaus's view about "the idea" as "the process itself." See Schmalfeldt (2011).

58. From Messiaen's Preface, on "Abîme des oiseaux": "The abyss is Time, with its sorrows and its weariness. The birds are the opposite of Time; they are our desire for light, for stars, for rainbows and joyful songs" (translation in Pople 1998, 40).

WORKS CITED

Agawu, Kofi. 1991. *Playing with Signs: A Semiotic Interpretation of Classic Music.* Princeton, NJ: Princeton University Press.

Agawu, Kofi. 2009. *Music as Discourse: Semiotic Adventures in Romantic Music.* New York: Oxford University Press.

Auner, Joseph. 2013a. *Music in the Twentieth and Twenty-First Centuries.* Western Music in Context: A Norton History. New York: W. W. Norton.

Auner, Joseph. 2013b. *Anthology for Music in the Twentieth and Twenty-First Centuries.* New York: W. W. Norton.

Baker, Nancy Kovaleff, and Thomas Christensen, eds. 1995. *Aesthetics and the Art of Musical Composition in the German Enlightenment: Selected Writings of Johann Georg Sulzer and Heinrich Christoph Koch.* Cambridge: Cambridge University Press.

Budday, Wolfgang. 1983. *Grundlagen musikalischer Formen der Wiener Klassik: An Hand der zeitgenössischen Theorie von Joseph Riepel und Heinrich Christoph Koch dargestellt an Menuetten und Sonatensätzen (1750–1790).* Kassel: Bärenreiter.

Burstein, L. Poundie. 2014. "The Half Cadence and Other Slippery Events." *Music Theory Spectrum* 36: 203–227.

Burstein, L. Poundie. 2015. "The Half Cadence and Related Analytic Fictions." In Neuwirth and Bergé 2015, 85–116.

Byros, Vasili. 2015. "*Hauptruhepuncte des Geistes*: Punctuation Schemas and the Late-Eighteenth-Century Sonata." In Neuwirth and Bergé 2015, 215–252.

Cambouropoulos, Emilios, and Costas Tsougras. 2009. "Auditory Streams in Ligeti's Continuum: A Theoretical and Perceptual Approach." *Journal of Interdisciplinary Music Studies* 3: 119–137.

Caplin, William E. 1998. *Classical Form: A Theory of Formal Functions for the Instrumental Music of Haydn, Mozart, and Beethoven.* New York: Oxford University Press.

Caplin, William E. 2002. "Theories of Musical Rhythm in the Eighteenth and Nineteenth Centuries." In *The Cambridge History of Western Music Theory*, edited by Thomas Christensen, 657–694. Cambridge: Cambridge University Press.

Caplin, William E. 2004. "The Classical Cadence: Conceptions and Misconceptions." *Journal of the American Musicological Society* 57: 51–117.

Caplin, William E. 2009a. "What Are Formal Functions?" In *Musical Form, Forms, and Formenlehre: Three Methodological Reflections*, edited by Pieter Bergé, 21–40. Leuven: Leuven University Press.

Caplin, William E. 2009b. "Response to the Comments." In *Musical Form, Forms, and Formenlehre: Three Methodological Reflections*, edited by Pieter Bergé, 51–61. Leuven: Leuven University Press.

Caplin, William E. 2013. *Analyzing Classical Form: An Approach for the Classroom.* New York: Oxford University Press.

Clendinning, Jane Piper. 1993. "The Pattern-Meccanico Compositions of György Ligeti." *Perspectives of New Music* 31: 192–234.

Cone, Edward T. 1968. *Musical Form and Musical Performance.* New York: W. W. Norton.

Cook, Nicholas. 2013. *Beyond the Score: Music as Performance.* New York: Oxford University Press.

Dahlhaus, Carl. 1980. *Between Romanticism and Modernism: Four Studies in the Music of the Later Nineteenth Century.* Translated by Mary Whittall. Berkeley and Los Angeles: University of California Press.

Dahlhaus, Carl. 1989. "Logik, Grammatik und Syntax der Musik bei Heinrich Christoph Koch." In *Die Sprache der Musik: Festschrift Klaus Wolfgang Niemöller*, edited by J. Fricke, 99–109. Regensburg: G. Bosse.

Doğantan-Dack, Mina. 2012. " 'Phrasing—the Very Life of Music': Performing the Music and Nineteenth-Century Performance Theory." *Nineteenth-Century Music Review* 9: 7–30.

Eckert, Stefan. 2007. "*Einschnitt, Absatz*, and *Cadenz*: The Description of Galant Syntax in Joseph Riepel's *Anfangsgründe zur musikalischen Setzkunst*." *Theoria* 14: 93–124.

Fassler, Margot. 2014a. *Music in the Medieval West*. Western Music in Context: A Norton History. New York: W. W. Norton.

Fassler, Margot. 2014b. *Anthology for Music in the Medieval West*. New York: W. W. Norton.

Forschner, Hermann. 1984. *Instrumentalmusik Joseph Haydns aus der Sicht Heinrich Christoph Kochs*. Munich: Musikverlag Emil Katzbichler.

Freedman, Richard. 2013. *Anthology for Music in the Renaissance*. Western Music in Context: A Norton History. New York: W. W. Norton.

Gjerdingen, Robert O. 2007. *Music in the Galant Style*. New York: Oxford University Press.

Hepokoski, James, and Warren Darcy. 2006. *Elements of Sonata Theory: Norms, Types, and Deformations in the Late-Eighteenth-Century Sonata*. New York: Oxford University Press.

Hepokoski, James. 2009. "Comments on William E. Caplin's Essay 'What Are Formal Functions?'" In *Musical Form, Forms, and Formenlehre: Three Methodological Reflections*, edited by Pieter Bergé, 41–45. Leuven: Leuven University Press.

Hill, John Walter. 2014. *Joseph Riepel's Theory of Metric and Tonal Order, Phrase and Form: A Translation of His Anfangsgründe zur musikalischen Setzkunst, Chapters 1 and 2 (1752/54, 1755) with Commentary*. Harmonologia: Studies in Music Theory No. 20. Hillsdale, NY: Pendragon Press.

Hoppin, Richard H. 1978. *Medieval Music*. New York: W. W. Norton.

Horlacher, Gretchen. 2011. *Building Blocks: Repetition and Continuity in the Music of Stravinsky*. New York: Oxford University Press.

Kirnberger, Johann Philipp. 1982. *The Art of Strict Musical Composition*. Translated by David Beach and Jurgen Thym. Introduction and explanatory notes by David Beach. New Haven, CT: Yale University Press.

Koch, Heinrich Christoph. 1983. *Introductory Essay on Composition: The Mechanical Rules of Melody, Sections 3 [1787] and 4 [1793]*. Translated by Nancy Kovaleff Baker. New Haven, CT: Yale University Press.

Lerdahl, Fred, and Ray Jackendoff. 1983. *A Generative Theory of Tonal Music*. Cambridge, MA: MIT Press.

Lester, Joel. 1992. *Compositional Theory in the Eighteenth Century*. Cambridge, MA: Harvard University Press.

London, Justin. 1990. "Riepel and *Absatz*: Poetic and Prosaic Aspects of Phrase Structure in 18th-Century Theory." *Journal of Musicology* 8: 505–519.

Meyer, Leonard B. 1973. *Explaining Music: Essays and Explorations*. Chicago: University of Chicago Press.

Mirka, Danuta. 2010. "Punctuation and Sense in Late-Eighteenth-Century Music." *Journal of Music Theory* 52: 235–282.

Mutch, Caleb Michael. 2015. "Studies in the History of the Cadence." PhD diss., Columbia University.

Neuwirth, Markus. 2015. "*Fuggir la Cadenza*, or the Art of Avoiding Cadential Closure: Physiognomy and Functions of Deceptive Cadences in the Classical Repertoire." In Neuwirth and Bergé 2015, 117–155.

Neuwirth, Markus, and Pieter Bergé, eds. 2015. *What Is a Cadence? Theoretical and Analytical Perspectives on Cadences in the Classical Repertoire.* Leuven: Leuven University Press.

Ng, Samuel. 2012. "Phrase Rhythm in Classical Instrumental Music." *Music Theory Spectrum* 34: 51–77.

Ohriner, Mitchell. 2012. "Grouping Hierarchy and Trajectories of Pacing in Performances of Chopin's Mazurkas." *Music Theory Online* 18, no. 1 http://mtosmt.org/issues/mto.12.18.1/mto.12.18.1.ohriner.php.

Pople, Anthony. 1998. *Messiaen: Quatuor pour la fin du temps.* Cambridge: Cambridge University Press.

Powers, Harold S. 1980. "Language Models and Music Analysis." *Ethnomusicology* 24: 1–60.

Reicha, Anton. 2000. *Treatise on Melody. A Translation of Traité de mélodie* (Paris, 1814, Vienna, 1832) by Peter M. Landey. Harmonologia Series No. 10. Hillsdale, NY: Pendragon Press.

Riepel, Joseph. 1752–1768. *Anfangsgründe zur musikalischen Setzkunst.* 5 vols. Frankfurt: J. J. Lotter.

Rothstein, William. 1989. *Phrase Rhythm in Tonal Music.* New York: Schirmer.

Schachter, Carl. 2016. *The Art of Tonal Analysis: Twelve Lessons in Schenkerian Theory*, edited by Joseph N. Straus. New York: Oxford University Press.

Schmalfeldt, Janet. 1992. "Cadential Processes: The Evaded Cadence and the 'One More Time' Technique." *Journal of Musicological Research* 12: 1–52.

Schmalfeldt, Janet. 2011. *In the Process of Becoming: Analytic and Philosophical Perspectives on Form in Early Nineteenth-Century Music.* Oxford Studies in Music Theory. New York: Oxford University Press.

Schoenberg, Arnold. 1967. *Fundamentals of Musical Composition.* Edited by Gerald Strang and Leonard Stein. London: Faber and Faber.

Sessions, Roger. 1950. *The Musical Experience of Composer, Performer, and Listener.* Princeton, NJ: Princeton University Press.

Sisman, Elaine. 1982. "Small and Expanded Forms: Koch's Model and Haydn's Music." *The Musical Quarterly* 68: 444–475.

Stravinsky, Igor. 1970. *Poetics of Music in the Form of Six Lessons* (1947). Translated by Arthur Knodel and Ingolf Dahl. Cambridge, MA: Harvard University Press.

Temperley, David. 2001. *The Cognition of Basic Musical Structures.* Cambridge, MA: MIT Press.

Türk, Daniel Gottlob. 1982. *Klavierschule.* Leipzig: 1789. Translated by Raymond H. Haggh as *School of Clavier Playing.* Lincoln: University of Nebraska Press.

Vial, Stephanie. 2008. *The Art of Musical Phrasing in the Eighteenth Century: Punctuating the Classical "Period."* Rochester, NY: University of Rochester Press.

Webster, James. 2009. "Comments on William E. Caplin's Essay 'What Are Formal Functions?'" In *Musical Form, Forms, and Formenlehre: Three Methodological Reflections*, edited by Pieter Bergé, 46–50. Leuven: Leuven University Press.

Westergaard, Peter. 1975. *An Introduction to Tonal Theory.* New York: W. W. Norton.

Zarlino, Gioseffo. 1968. *The Art of Counterpoint: Part Three of Le istitutioni harmoniche*, 1558. Translated by Guy A. Marco and Claude V. Palisca. New Haven, CT: Yale University Press.

CHAPTER 13

··

FORM

··

DANIEL M. GRIMLEY

FORM—THE shape, layout, or arrangement of a piece of music—is a basic and foundational category in Western musical thought and practice. Attempting to sketch a more
detailed and precise definition of the term, however, presents one of the most difficult
tasks when writing about music: a challenge Pieter Bergé describes as a "precarious
enterprise" (Bergé 2010, 12). Form is a fugitive concept, but in its casual current-day
usage, it is seemingly commonplace. Invoked with disarming regularity in program
notes, textbooks, and other music literature, form appears predictive and containable.
To identify the form of a particular piece is to imply closure, cohesion, meaning, value,
and design, qualities that in turn support the elevated aesthetic status of the musical
work. Form provides answers to what Edward T. Cone proposes as a "first set of foolish
questions" (Cone 1968, 12) in musical analysis: where does a work begin, and where
does it end? To describe music as "formless," meanwhile, goes beyond a simple negative, and suggests an almost existential sense of emptiness, loss, or incomprehension.
This is one reason why form has historically provoked some of the most sustained and
polarized debates in music theory and aesthetics. Another reason, however, is the relative obscurity and opaqueness of the term. As literary scholar Angela Leighton suggests,
"form can signify both the finished object, the art form in its completion, or the parts
that make up its technical apparatus. It can signify a visionary apparition in the mind,
or the real, physical properties of a work" (Leighton 2007, 3). Discussions of form point
toward music's paradoxical material and immaterial qualities, and its (often contested)
sites of production and reception. Contemplating form hence prompts deeper questions
of musical ontology and epistemology. Form shapes not only how we think about music,
but also what we think music is, and why it sounds meaningful. "In form alone," György
Lukács suggests, "does every antithesis, every trend, become music and necessity"
(Lukács 2009, 38).

Given the complexity of the term, and the breadth and range of its historical reach, the
current chapter cannot offer a comprehensive account of musical form.[1] Neither does the
chapter offer a taxonomy of standard *Formenlehre* types, such as Sonata Form, as they
have typically figured in music textbooks. Rather, it adopts a more pragmatic approach.

The first part of the chapter considers the term's etymological origins, drawing attention to its associated philosophical and aesthetic complexities. The second part of the chapter presents a brief and highly selective series of formal "encounters" in a group of case studies, from Machaut to Miles Davis. The aim is not to suggest any sense of linear continuity or historical convergence. Nevertheless, certain themes and problems emerge recurrently: form's relationship with notions of time and space; issues of authoriality, intention, meaning, and design; and music's richly contingent status as a live event. As ever, the gap between theory and practice cannot be resolved. But abiding in this tension provides one of the most productive ways of thinking about musical form.

DEFINITIONS AND ANXIETIES

Tracing the form's development as a pedagogical or didactic term provides one way of beginning to consider problems of definition and application more closely. Mark Evan Bonds suggests that the use of form as a technical term is a relatively recent phenomenon, and that form appeared "only sporadically in eighteenth-century writings on music and did not become a widely accepted category in its own right until the second half of the nineteenth century" (Bonds 1991, 2). Standard dictionary definitions of form from the latter half of the 1800s frequently adopted a strongly utilitarian tone. John Stainer and William Alexander Barrett's *Dictionary of Musical Terms* (1876), for example, defined form simply as "the shape and order in which musical ideas are presented." C. Hubert Parry's entry in the first edition of *Grove's Dictionary of Music and Musicians* (1879), however, indicates a more ideologically determined view of musical progress. Form, capitalized for Parry, is "the means by which unity and proportion are arrived at in musical works" (Parry 1879, 541).[2] Whereas "the first attempts at Form in music were essentially unconscious and unpremeditated," Parry suggests, later periods gradually developed supposedly more sophisticated notions of musical form culminating in the "real peculiarities and individualities of Beethoven's instrumental compositions." This is the real apotheosis of formal thinking in music, Parry's essay concludes, and "there can be no object in following the development of the system of Form farther than Beethoven, for it can hardly be said that there is anything further to trace" (1879, 549, 552). By the end of the nineteenth century, therefore, form had become a canonizing device, based on highly essentialized notions of gender, race, national identity, and class, in which the sonata allegro became the most emblematic and revered category of musical expression (Burnham 2002, 903–904).

More recent and more critically reflective accounts have sought to avoid the bluntly historicist language adopted by Parry and other late nineteenth-century writers. Arnold Whittall's entry for *The New Grove Dictionary*, written a century after Parry, begins by defining form more cautiously as the "constructive or organizing element in music": a discussion that continues to stress principles of arrangement, balance, and design without invoking the same evolutionary grand narrative propounded nineteenth-century accounts (Whittall 1980, 709). Whittall's concern rather is with exploring shifting theoretical models of form in early twentieth-century writing, particularly the tension between Schoenbergian ideas of motivic logic and developing variation, and Heinrich Schenker's graphic representations of large-scale voice-leading and melodic diminution. Whittall draws in particular from Suzanne Langer's notion of form as a "perceptible, self-identical whole," but even here, his discussion reveals an underlying anxiety about the term's contingency. The first version of Whittall's entry, for example, concludes by proposing that "to conceive an idea is to imagine a form, that particular form which, however remote from the acceptable categories of a particular time or place, will successfully or unsuccessfully animate form itself, *the most protean and omnipresent element of art*" (Whittall 1980, 710, emphasis added). The conclusion of Whittall's entry for the revised edition of the dictionary, published in 2001, however, states more cautiously that form is simply "a factor making for *relative stability* in the *inherently open-ended* process of musical communication" (Whittall 2001, 94, emphasis added). Form, in other words, has shifted from being the animating force that vitalizes all art to being an altogether more provisional phenomenon, subordinate to the wider processes of signification through which the musical work engages its listeners.

The sense of equivocation evident in Whittall's two contrasting definitions points not only toward shifts of disciplinary emphasis, but more deeply to the term's cloudy etymological origins. As Klaus Städtke observes, there is no straightforward classical equivalent of the term that might serve as a suitable basis for comparison (Städtke 2001, 463). On the contrary, tracking form's origins in classical texts points to a more fundamental schism in Western metaphysical thought, whose legacy can be identified in continuing debates about the quality and status of form in music. Hermann Danuser, for example, explains that,

> While Plato differentiates between *morphe* [μορφή] (as the outer shape of things) and *eidos* [εἶδος] (as the inner, ideal, form constituted by its metaphysical, numerical structure), Aristotle distinguishes between *hule* [ὕλη] (as the formless, or shapeless material of all things) and *eidos* (as a teleological *entelechia* [ἐντελέχεια] of things, an ideal status to which all things strive by their inner forces).
>
> (Danuser 2003, 128)

Classical notions of form are already characterized by a series of binary oppositions that fracture and threaten to break apart unitary definitions of the concept: namely, between form as an internal or external property; its abstract or mimetic quality; and its stable or dynamic condition. For Danuser, "it makes little sense to simply speak of 'the' form in singular." Rather, all discussions of form (at least in the Western philosophical tradition) necessarily need to acknowledge its ambiguity, its double meaning as *form* and *forming*. Form refers both to the musical work and to the process of (trans)formation through which it is created. Given the historical contingency of the work concept, Danuser ultimately proposes abandoning the term "form" altogether, and adds that "given its terminological advantages reflecting the temporal, processional dimensions of this art, in music theory and aesthetics the term *formation* proves to be clearly superior over form" (Danuser 2003, 131, emphasis added).

The Oxford English Dictionary similarly dwells on these two basic underlying senses of form. As a noun, derived from the Latin "forma" and Old French "fourme/furme," form can refer to shape, or the arrangement of parts into a whole (consistent with its use in the nineteenth-century dictionary definitions quoted above), but also to appearance, or to the essential quality of an object or thing. To assume a form is to adopt a particular shape or configuration, often as a quality of existence or of being. Hence, form suggests a powerfully generative capacity, an act of creation, invoked, for example, in a familiar passage from the start of the King James Bible (1611): "And the earth was without form, and void, and darkness was upon the face of the deep: and the Spirit of God moved upon the face of the waters" (Gen. 1:2). Form can also indicate modality, species, or typology, as in "forms of knowledge," "formes fixes," or "variation form." The title of Erik Satie's celebrated *Trois morceaux en forme de poire* (1903), for example, puns playfully on this ambiguity, indicating both likeness or resemblance and also shape or configuration, none of which, of course, Satie's work actually supports. In the idea of a formal taxonomy, however, lies a more pernicious definition of form, namely, the shift from the idea of an orderly arrangement of elements or parts toward a set of conventions, routines, or procedures. Form, in this sense, can become legislative and prescriptive: a "form of words" can quickly assume a legal meaning that serves to delineate, divide, order, or exclude, even as it simultaneously permits common understanding, communication, and exchange within an agreed set of parameters. Form, in other words, can refer to social codes and patterns of behavior, and to specific "forms of address" or comportment. Ophelia's despairing cry, as Hamlet abandons "The glass of fashion, the mould of form" (*Hamlet*, 3.1, 156), is a characteristically complex Shakespearian metaphor. Hamlet once seemed perfect, a model of princely virtue and courtly elegance, but has given way to violence and psychological decay (implied by punning on the word "mould"). To be "true to form" suggests regularity and predictability: it is to *conform*. And to be formless, in this context, is to appear threateningly anarchic or destabilizing. Form hence becomes an instrument of discipline, regulation, and containment, whether social or aesthetic. As Caroline Levine notes, "It is the work of form to make order. And this means that forms are the stuff of politics" (2015, 3).

The idea of form as a verb (derived from Latin "formare," Old French "fourmer," or Provençal "formar") is no less complex and opaque. The OED lists the word's different shades of meaning, including to shape, fashion, or mould (precisely the terms listed by Ophelia); to discipline, train, or educate; to order or arrange; or to bring into existence. The King James Bible again offers a symbolically charged example of the use of form in this latter sense, to refer to an act of animation or creation: "And the LORD God formed man of the dust of the ground, & breathed into his nostrils the breath of life; and man became a living soul" (Gen. 2:7). To form, then, is to produce or to compose: in this way, form implies a privileged notion of authoriality that remains stubbornly central to Western ideas of the work concept, which likewise refers both to an object (the musical work) and to the labor or activity involved in its production (even if that labor is concealed by the elevation of the work as a site of aesthetic contemplation). Much recent writing, however, has sought to shift emphasis away from the idea of creation and form as an originary source toward greater attention to the active production and negotiation of meaning. As James Hepokoski has suggested, for example, "perceptions of form are as much a collaborative enterprise of the listener or analyst as they are of the composer" (Hepokoski 2010, 71). Form, in other words, is *performative*: it is a live, temporally contingent event which involves the conscious or unconscious processing of musical data under a set of specific environmental conditions that shape and determine shared perceptions of musical meaning. Form, in this sense, is a dynamic two-way communicative process, which engages both the composer and listener in reciprocal stages of reception and transformation. For Hepokoski, form is hence most properly understood as a ludic, dialogic pattern of exchange, which takes place within prescribed boundaries or formal limits: "the deeper sense of form with which we are concerned here is something to be produced—an engaged act of understanding—through a dialogue with an intricate and subtle network of piece-appropriate norms and guidelines (rules of the game)" (Hepokoski 2010, 71). Form is necessarily both generative and conformational, as Mark Evan Bonds suggests, without which meaningful musical communication could not take place. But it is equally through this double motion, which relies upon a sense of the original and familiar, or of complementary patterns of recognition and surprise, that form opens out the potential for new meanings and interpretations, and through which it is continually able to renew itself.

Hepokoski's dialogic notion of form helpfully highlights both music's suasive qualities, the way in which form moves and affects its listeners, and also the extent to which those listeners form or shape the musical work in return through their own expectations and experience. But such reciprocal models of reception and exchange also pose more challenging and difficult questions of agency and representation. Whose form is heard, and when, and according to which rules are such forms regulated and understood? Listening formally, in other words, is always intrinsically bound up with deeper issues of ethics and responsibility. The Kantian notion of the disinterested subject, for whom musical form is little more than the interplay of shapes or "pleasurable sounds" (Kant 1981, 219), is helpful only as a philosophical abstraction. As both Enlightenment and Romantic thinkers swiftly realized, to try and think through different competing ontologies of musical form is to encounter a crisis of subjectivity whose implications extend far beyond the realm of aesthetics. Such processes immediately decenter and destabilize notions of authority and further complicate the idea of form as a simple two-way process of exchange within closed or stable limits.

FORM'S FORMS

Concerns about the status of form and authorial agency and about the ethics of listening for musical form significantly predate Enlightenment and early Romantic debates. The rondeaux, ballades, and virelais of Guillaume de Machaut, for example, frequently dwell on the rhetorical power and contingency of the authorial voice through works whose musical and literary structures are tightly bounded or assembled. Figure 13.1 shows a particularly exceptional work: Rondeau 14, *Ma fin est mon commencement*. Both Michael Eisenberg and Elizabeth Eva Leach comment on the rondeau's ludic reflectivity, namely the way in which its text and music wind around different kinds of symmetry and inversion (Eisenberg 2007; Leach 2011). Such strong literary and musical patterning already suggests a heightened attention to structure, form, and symbolism, highlighted by the self-consciously performative quality of the text:

Ma fin est mon commencement	My end is my beginning
Et mon commencement ma fin	And my beginning my end
Et teneure vraiement.	And is truly the tenor.
Ma fin est mon commencement.	My end is my beginning.
Mes tiers chans .iii. fois seulement	My third part three times only
Se retrograde et einsi fin.	Moves backwards and thus ends.
Ma fin est mon commencement	My end is my beginning
Et mon commencement ma fin.	And my beginning my end.[3]

FIGURE 13.1 Guillaume de Machaut, R14, *Ma fin est mon commencement*, opening and conclusion, after Eisenberg, "The Mirror of the Text," 89.

As Eisenberg notes, the structural organization of the text is particularly intricate: "not only does the rondeau form return to its beginning, but its opening lines are inverted in a textural palindrome where subject and predicate positions are reversed" (Eisenberg 2007, 91). The musical setting is no less ingenious: the tenor and cantus sing the same melody simultaneously but in opposing directions, so that the melody's beginning and end are heard at the same time both at the opening of the rondeau and at its conclusion. A third voice, the contratenor, sings a second melody twice, once in normal order and once in reverse, creating a further kind of symmetry in which the contratenor's end musically becomes its beginning (and vice versa). Machaut's arrangement of the pitch structure further reinforces the impression of reflectiveness: the wedge-like pattern of the opening tenor and cantus entry is mirrored by the way in which the two parts close together again at the rondeau's end, and the rondeau's midpoint (where the tenor and cantus appear to "swap" roles) is marked by a half-cadence, after which the text restarts "Et mon commencement/Se retrograde et einsi." This is shown in Figure 13.2. Eisenberg writes at greater length both about the allegorical associations between symmetries,

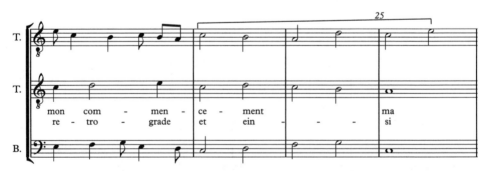

FIGURE 13.2 Guillaume de Machaut, R14, *Ma fin est mon commencement*, middle (mm. 17–25), after Eisenberg (2007, 89).

retrogrades, circles, and labyrinths, and their religious significance within the liturgical calendar (particularly Easter or the vernal equinox), and also about the rondeau's number symbolism (the 54, or $2 \times [3 \times 3 \times 3]$, pitches of the contratenor melody, and the same number of note shapes in the tenor and cantus in their original notation; Eisenberg 2007, 92–95, 106). More significant still is the idea of form as allegory, and the way in which it collapses notions of musical and textual representation. "*Ma fin est mon commencement* requires the audience to unravel its multiple semiotic layers," Eisenberg suggests, "as its text, like the *speculum* of the palindrome, descends into an infinite regress." The rondeau's elusiveness, in other words, stems from its apparent assumption of a strong first-person presence, only for such authority to be compromised by the seemingly redundant symmetry of its self-reflectiveness (Stone 2003, 137). "The ambiguous 'I' is a non-referential 'empty' sign that does not index any reality or objective position and can only obtain a momentary referent in the context of its local utterance," Eisenberg concludes. Machaut's rondeau becomes a "textual mise-en-abîme"; nothing is left but the idea of form (Eisenberg 2007, 108–109). For Leach, in contrast, such symbolic obscurity becomes instead a means of reflecting upon the nature of mortality and the creative voice. Rondeau 14 "replicates the experience of existence" precisely because its symmetry is deceptive: "the end and the beginning do not *sound* the same." Attending to the acoustic dimension of the rondeau, in other words, suggests a subtly different narrative, bound by a more Christian eschatology, in which the work's complex and recursive textural-musical interactions evoke "the wheel of Fortune and of life, whose course can only be borne through the maintenance of Christian Hope, mediated through the cognate female figure of Mary" (Leach 2011, 298).

Ma fin est mon commencement illustrates the complex and contradictory quality of form as it is frequently conceived. In its tightly organized and ordered structure, the rondeau exemplifies the Platonic view of music as an abstract pattern of ratio, symmetry, and proportion. Understood symbolically or allegorically, however, its form immediately challenges Cone's "first set of foolish questions": namely, that sense of precisely where (and how) a piece begins and ends. Rather, in its potentially illimitable recursiveness, *Ma fin* becomes a hall of mirrors whose true form is ultimately unknowable. By thematizing and then collapsing the authorial voice in this way, the form of *Ma fin* offers both a vertiginous glimpse into the abyss, and also a revelatory intimation of the divine.

A similar tension, between form as structure or design and as symbol, allegory, act, or process, is foregrounded by Figure 13.3, another well-known example that has prompted considerable scholarly discussion: Guillaume Dufay's majestic four-part motet *Nuper rosarum flores*. Composed for a specific occasion to commemorate the symbolic presentation of a golden rose by Pope Eugenius IV to the city of Florence on March 25, 1436, at the consecration of the cathedral of Santa Maria del Fiore, Dufay's motet has since gained a canonic place in the repertoire.[4]

Like Machaut's *Ma fin*, Dufay's motet suggests a strong concern with numerical patterning and design: the motet falls into four sections of 2×28 (4×7) breves length. Each section consists of a canonic statement of the first fourteen notes of the plainchant

FIGURE 13.3 Dufay, *Nuper rosarum flores* (mm. 49–56), note values halved.

melody *Terribilis est locus iste* ("Awe-inspiring is this place") in the tenor (at the interval of a fifth), preceded by a lengthy duet between triplum and motetus that becomes increasingly elaborate and florid as the motet proceeds in "majestic series of variations" (Blackburn 1994, 4). The text in the two upper voices similarly consists of four seven-line heptasyllabic verses (the closing line of each verse is octosyllabic). Although the textual and musical structures are not synchronized, the motet occasionally highlights specific words or images—for example, the rising arc in the Triplum at "amplissimum" in mm. 50–51 (Figure 13.3) evokes the lofty interior of the dome, and the extended decoration in the upper parts of the opening syllable of "oratione" intensifies the reflexivity of the first word of the final verse at the start of the third section. A change of mensuration at the start of the four sections, as listed in Table 13.1, indicates that the tenor statements are arranged metrically in the proportion 6:4:2:3 (Blackburn 1994, 4).

Charles Warren first suggested that this ratio, unique among Dufay's isorhythmic compositions, corresponded to the length of the nave, transept, apse, and the height of Brunelleschi's dome at Santa Maria del Fiore (Warren 1973). Dufay's motet thus

Table 13.1. Dufay, *Nuper rosarum flores*: mensural structure.

Section	Sign	Meter	Value
1	O	Perfect	(12 whole notes)
2	C	Imperfect	(8 whole notes)
3	¢	Half imperfect	(4 whole notes)
4	Φ	Half perfect	(6 whole notes)

apparently offered a strikingly early instance of the association between musical form and architectonic structure, seemingly embodying in sound the physical dimensions of the building where its first performance took place.

Warren's analysis has come under sustained critique, most notably from Craig Wright, who suggests that "for any architectural analysis to have validity, it must relate accurately, indeed exactly, to the components of the structure that is being measured, either as that structure presently exists or as it existed earlier in history" (Wright 1994, 402). If the architectonic structure of Dufay's motet fails on these grounds (because it does not, in fact, correspond to the actual proportions of the cathedral), the music nonetheless points symbolically to an appropriate biblical reference: the proportions of King Solomon's Temple (recorded in 1 Kings 6.8 KJB; Wright 1994, 406–407). As Bonnie Blackburn notes, "the Temple took seven years to complete, and the dedication ceremony lasted twice seven days. The Temple of Solomon figures prominently in the liturgy for the dedication of a church, and the consecration of the altar also stresses fourfold and sevenfold actions" (Blackburn 1994, 4). Structure, act, and ritual, in other words, are symbolically combined in the form of the motet as allegory: Dufay's music celebrated the Duomo's recreation of the biblical Temple, rather than sonically realizing the concrete dimensions of the actual building. More recently, however, Marvin Trachtenberg has sought to renew the symbolic associations between the motet and the Duomo, not in terms of the finished building, but rather via the proportions of the cathedral's component parts (including baptistery, campanile, and cupola) as they accumulated over the course of its construction. Reading the building interpretively, alongside the motet, suggests a more complex mode of symbolic representation. "What we may be dealing with here," Trachtenberg suggests, "is not two independent binary relationships—music to building, and music to biblical/exegetical text—but a triadic nexus in which all three factors are densely interrelated" (Trachtenberg 2001, 755). The four broad arching phrases of *Nuper rosarum flores* might, thus, be heard in very different ways. For Wright, the question of the motet's shape and symbolism remains intrinsically linked to the two-fold Classical notion of form:

> As a composition in which a foreground of audible sound is determined by a grand design of inaudible numerical ratios, *Nuper rosarum flores* conforms to an ancient

Platonic ideal—the world as sounding number. Yet its isorhythmic structure of four homologous sections, and sections of sections, is rationally hierarchical in the tradition of the thirteenth-century Aristotelian scholastics. Its textual allusions are those of medieval scriptural exegesis. Its theme is a biblical paradigm: Solomon as precursor of Christ, and Mary as mother of both.

(Wright 1994, 439)

For Trachtenberg, however, the motet's form was more embedded in the symbolic meaning of a particular place, one that was "deeply rooted in Florentine as well as church ideology" (Trachtenberg 2001, 770). Dufay's music, in other words, becomes part of a "multiply referential" nexus in which it is arguably the interlocking relationships between different forms of symbolic representation—physical, allegorical, textual, and chronological—that are meaningful, rather than any privileged sense of one-to-one correspondence between the musical work and the architectural structure of the cathedral. For its contemporary listeners, the complex intertwining form of *Nuper rosarum flores* must have opened up a dazzling array of interpretive possibilities, instead of a single authentic truth, as the music echoed and resounded beneath the soaring vault of Brunelleschi's dome.

Both *Ma fin* and *Nuper rosarum flores* exemplify, in very different ways, the complex and paradoxical quality of musical form and illustrate why it resists easy definition. In either piece, form can be heard as ratio or proportion—the order, patterning, or arrangement of musical events—and as symbol, drawing both upon the works' respective texts but also from wider allegorical systems of representation. Form in *Nuper Rosarum Flores* can be conceived analogically as musical architecture. But this reading alone fails to capture every aspect of the work's form with sufficient care. As David Lewin explains, musical form is necessarily complicated by its experiential quality: "the idea of Form is not adequately conceived as something 'spatial,' something that can be disassociated from the ways in which our impressions build and change during the passage of time for a listener or a performer" (Lewin 2003, 157). Whether understood through scholastic exegesis, Platonic notions of harmony, or through the rhetorical metaphor of oration, in other words, both Machaut's rondeau and Dufay's motet suggest that musical form was fundamentally subject to the contingency of human perception. Far from being a purely abstract category, form is inescapably shaped by rhythm and by the idea of duration, and by the mutability of sound in live performance and in its synoptic comprehension— from the desire to capture and retain the fleeting impression of a whole gained from the active experience of listening to a performance that can only ever have been perceived sequentially.

This dialectical tension between form as a spatial and temporal category becomes increasingly marked in late eighteenth- and early nineteenth-century writing on music. It underpins, for example, the shift from Heinrich Christoph Koch and Jérôme-Joseph de Momigny's concern with phrase structure and periodic rhythm (Burnham 2002, 882– 884) and Anton Reicha's notion of large-scale binary form (the "grande coupe binaire"; Hoyt 1996, 141–142) to A. B. Marx's dynamic notion of linear melodic motion ("Satz" and

"Gang") and Eduard Hanslick's "tönend bewegte Formen" (tonally moving forms): each theoretical model engages, in a different way, the idea of form as a spatial or architectonic category alongside music's complex and reflexive unfolding through time. Form's unstable quality was not merely a philosophical problem, related to deeper concerns about music's ontology; it also had a catalyzing effect upon the shape and design of much late eighteenth-century music. Figure 13.4 shows the well-known finale of Joseph Haydn's Symphony No. 45, "Farewell," composed in 1772 for performance at Esterháza, which, for example, exemplifies particularly urgently this response to form as a mode of creative engagement and invention. Final movements conventionally suggest a more relaxed approach to large-scale form in late eighteenth-century symphonic works: a trend that supports a greater variety of different formal types (variations, binary forms, fugal movements, minuets, and other dance forms) than in opening movements. As James Webster has shown, however, the structural and expressive weight of the finale of the "Farewell" Symphony is already intensified by its placement at the end of a multi-movement work that can be heard as a single through-composed structure on the basis of its common harmonic and thematic materials (Webster 1991, 13–17). In other words, the symphony complicates the relationship between part and whole, or closure and open-endedness, in a way that radically decenters the work's formal articulation. Symmetry and balance are achieved in the symphony's final measures, but in a manner that threatens to collapse the distinction between time and space upon which the idea of musical form relies.

The finale itself is in fact a complex concentric arrangement of three different formal structures. The movement begins with a full-scale sonata form Presto in the tonic minor, a furious duple-time contredanse which modulates to the mediant major, tonicizes the dominant, and then achieves a double return (tonal and thematic) at the reprise. The closing group is dramatically extended, however, so that the Presto finishes on a half cadence rather than with the expected full close. The coda is followed instead by a complete rounded binary Adagio in A major. This is, in effect, a second finale: a slow minuet or round dance, with independent but motivically related first and second themes, cadencing on a structural dominant at its midway point. This is the moment at which instruments begin to leave the ensemble: a poignant pair of fanfares signals the departure of the first oboe and second horn. Haydn inverts the ordering of the Adagio's two themes at the reprise (m. 42), so that final appearance of the second oboe and first horn after the return of the first theme leads straight into a mysterious modulatory transition, dominated by the double bass (Figure 13.4). The finale then concludes with an abbreviated restatement of the Adagio in F♯ major, effectively resolving the imperfect close of the opening Presto and serving as a large-scale tierce de Picardie. This final section itself breaks down into two complementary sections, again marked by the staged disappearance of instruments from the ensemble: the first section is a simple binary form, articulated by the Adagio's two themes, whereas the second simply riffs on the Adagio's second theme, divided by the deceptive cadence in m. 95 and reaching full structural closure at m. 103. The symphony closes famously with a short four-measure codetta for two solo violins, dissolving the sixteenth-note motion of the Adagio into a pair of distant horn calls.

FIGURE 13.4 Haydn, Symphony no. 45 ("Farewell"), Hbk. 1: 45. Final movement, mm. 55–71.

What is so moving and affective about the finale of the "Farewell" Symphony is not only the dramatic coup of the closing measures, but the gradual process of formal concision from which they emerge: the music seemingly contracts telescopically from a complete large-scale sonata structure to a single four-measure sentence. This is sufficient to generate a strong sense of teleology, of movement toward (or away from) a vanishing point or distant horizon, an impression consistent, of course, with the programmatic implications of the slowly departing ensemble. But the sense of subject position involved in this process is itself ambiguous—it is unclear, figuratively, whether it is indeed the ensemble that gradually retreats from the stage or whether it is the listening subject who withdraws (or, more plausibly, both). The movement's spatial dimensions, in those terms, are highly relative, rather than fixed or determined. The sense of temporal progression is similarly ambivalent. The sharp tempo and rhythmic articulation of the Presto suggest an insistent forward momentum, with little scope for retrospection. The Adagio, in contrast, suggests circularity and recurrence, an impression reinforced both by the reverse reprise and also by the melodic profile of its two principal themes, which appear to curve back upon themselves continually. It is the shadowy *ombra* effect of the transition passage that follows, however, which constitutes the finale's most remarkable sequence.[5] The double bass's insistent sixteenth-note pulse and the sighing chromatic appoggiaturas in the upper parts seemingly pull back any sense of progressive temporal motion, suggesting instead a more hypnotic feeling of stasis or suspension. It is this disturbing double-impression, of a clock ticking but of time symbolically standing still, that frames the magical return of the Adagio in the final measures, and which partially explains their curious sense of poise. For Haydn's contemporaries, the impression of balance and symmetry restored, but of an environment entirely transformed in the process, must have been breathtaking. For later nineteenth-century listeners, however, such gestures would have seemed increasingly empty and uncanny: the promise of return to the identical time and place becomes an illusory fiction, and closure is revealed as a utopian desire that can never properly be realized or fulfilled. In that sense, the finale of the "Farewell" Symphony captures the unstable nature of musical form particularly acutely, achieving both wholeness and unity but simultaneously foreshadowing what later writers would recognize as the essential hollowness of the musical subject.

FORM'S MOTION

The strained relationship between form, time, and subjectivity that begins to emerge in Haydn's later work became the recurrent concern for nineteenth-century writers and composers.[6] For Friedrich Schiller, music's "calm clarity" could be achieved "by form alone, not by content, for form affects *universal*, content only *specific* powers" (Schiller 1981, 236). Separating form and content, however, only serves to intensify form's inherent emptiness and re-enacts music's deceptive removal from the physical world. As Daniel Chua explains, musical form in nineteenth-century thought "functions like the kind of political rhetoric that creates a vision without any concrete policy" (Chua 1999, 164). Form thus assumes a utopian character without any capacity to affect real material change. Music becomes abstracted as the highest mode of aesthetic contemplation: pure form = beauty. It is in this sense that music becomes absolute, Chua suggests, since "the formal structure of music can figure a better shape of things to come with a totally contingent content that does not predict the details of history: it creates a formal ending that makes sense of the world, without being in the world" (1999, 64). Musical form is entirely self-generated, reliant upon nothing beyond its own content in order to take shape. For A. B. Marx, it is precisely this inner energy or momentum that becomes the source of music's agency. Marx defines form as "the summation of all the manifold configurations in which the content of music appears before our spirit," and suggests that "gaining shape—form—is nothing other than self-determination, a Being-for-itself apart from the Other" (Marx 1997, 56, 60). Music, in other words, shapes itself through the dynamic motion of the imaginative spirit. And form is the means, immanently conceived, through which content is articulated, realized, and projected through time. Form and content, for Marx, are essentially the same. At one level, therefore, Marx's model is radically liberating, freeing the imagination to play within the seemingly limitless realm of musical shapes and ideas that constitutes form's proper domain. At another level, however, it subjugates authorial freedom to the imperatives demanded by the musical idea. Form, in this sense, emerges through its own self-regulating discipline, its own inviolable set of laws, accountable only to itself.

Marx's idealist account of music as form-in-motion is famously echoed in Eduard Hanslick's 1854 essay *Vom Musikalisch-Schönen* ("On the Musically Beautiful"). Hanslick reverses Marx's formulation, stating that "in music there is no content as opposed to form, because music has no form other than the content" (Hanslick 1986, 80). One consequence of this reordering of terms is to lay greater stress on the question of music's origins: "music consists of tonal sequences, tonal forms; these have no other content than themselves" (1986, 78). Hanslick's reading is in that sense consistent with Marx: aesthetic beauty is "mere form" and hence purposeless, and the beauty of a musical composition is determined by "a specifically musical kind of beauty" that is abstract, self-contained, and "in no need of content from outside itself." The goal of musical form, in other words, is the expression of "musical ideas." But since musical ideas are themselves entirely self-subsistent (*selbständig*), Hanslick explains, music becomes "an end in itself, and it is in no way primarily a medium or material for the representation of feelings or conceptions" (1986, 28). Hanslick's account has been widely criticized for its solipsism, for its apparent insistence on the idea of "the music itself." That is, however, to overlook the philosophical context in which his argument was proposed. To try to ascribe extra-musical meaning to musical works, in Hanslick's terms, would be paradoxical, since music's form and content logically cannot, in fact, be separated. Neither does it imply that Hanslick's ontology of music is in any sense fixed or static. On the contrary, it is music's movement that is meaningful. "Motion is the ingredient which music has in common with emotional states," he suggests, "and which it is able to shape creatively in a thousand shades and contrasts" (1986, 11). This is then the basis on which his most famous dictum should be understood. The statement that "the content of music is tonally moving forms" (even more explicitly stated in its original 1854 formulation: "tonally moving forms are the sole content and subject of music"; Hanslick 1986, 29)[7] points precisely to the sense of temporal and spatial progression that animates musical form, and which underpins its vital and dynamic character.[8] For Hanslick, this becomes the source and motor of music's transformative potential.

Hanslick emerges from this context not as a straightforwardly conservative or reactionary figure, as his reception has frequently implied, but as an active participant in a more complex and dynamic aesthetic discourse in which the definition and status of musical form became increasingly precarious. Notions of formal wholeness, coherence, and unity were challenged in late nineteenth-century thought both by a growing concern with empirically based models of musical perception (advanced, for example, by theorists such as Hugo Riemann) and also by a sense of breach or rupture, an inability to sustain or support idealist models of musical autonomy. At the same time, however, the principle of music's essentially non-representational nature, and of form's blankness, remained a central tenet of modernist musical practice. Indeed, many modernist works rely on precisely this dialectical tension, between the tendency toward abstraction on the one hand, and a seemingly infinite plurality of meanings on the other. Form's ability to contain or enclose, under such conditions, becomes increasingly compromised or fragile. For writers such as Adorno, form operates as a force-field, tenuously holding together a series of disparate musical parameters, each of which threaten to break the musical work apart, rather than maintaining a strict sense of structural integrity (Paddison 1993, 276). This is why form remains central: it acts as music's mode of immanent critique, a mirror of its fractured social contexts and broken vision.

FORMS OF MODERNITY

Few works capture this sense of formal strain more intensively than the third movement of Ruth Crawford Seeger's remarkable String Quartet (1931), shown in Figure 13.5. Written in Berlin and Paris, the quartet is in four compact movements: the Andante is preceded by a mercurial scherzo ("Leggiero") and followed by a scurrying, roguish finale (Allegro possible), but the third movement forms the single most sustained passage in the work, and acts as the quartet's structural and expressive fulcrum. In terms of register and dynamics, the Andante traces an asymmetrical arc. The movement begins silently, with each instrument entering in turn (starting with the viola), and gradually accumulates greater energy through the layered polyphonic transposition of an ascending chromatic melody whose mix of whole and half-tone steps never quite becomes a regular octatonic collection: fourths and fifths tend to serve instead as relatively stable intervals and points of reference.[9] Seeger adds the direction that "bowing should be as little audible as possible throughout" at the start, but the swelling hairpins under each pitch suggest the vibrating amplitude of the string: the whole movement, in fact, can be

FIGURE 13.5 Ruth Crawford, String Quartet, movement 3, climax and breach (mm. 70–76).

heard as an acoustic study in sympathetic frequencies and complex upper partials, the effect similar (in an accurate performance) to a ringing glass or bell. From its low initial base, the ascent up to the movement's high point in mm. 73–74 is a steeply graded curve: the asymptotic rate of dynamic change increases relatively rapidly from m. 53 as the harmonic and registral tension intensifies. The climax itself is marked by the first attainment of what appears to be the movement's pitch ceiling—E3—approached incrementally by the rising contour of the second violin from m. 63. It is at this point, however, that the form breaks down: m. 75 marks a sudden rupture, the ensemble's triple-stopping tearing apart the seamless legato that had prevailed from the start of the movement, followed by three disjointed gestures that fracture any sense of registral and voice-leading cohesiveness. From here, the Andante reverses direction, descending rapidly having punctured the climax's earlier pitch ceiling (starting on F3), and accelerating as it tumbles downward. The coda more-or-less regains the Andante's starting position, "quasi tempo primo," and the movement closes on the same pitch (C♯) as it began, but the viola is shadowed by the cello's dark open C-string: the movement reaches only an uneasy quiet before leading, *attacca*, into the rapidly swirling chromatic figuration of the finale.

The form of Seeger's Andante is unusually plastic (in the sense of being strongly shaped or contoured): the slow ascent up to an angular climax, which is the movement's breaking point, is followed by the swift return to near its point of origin. This impression of dynamic change is also temporal: the complete stasis or immobility of the opening measures gives way to a more fluid sensation of time moving forward as the music gains registral and chromatic momentum, followed by the *accelerando molto* at mm. 79ff that propels the quartet precipitously downward until grinding to an almost complete halt in the final measures. The effect of the climax itself, however, is more ambiguous. The sense of a violently snapped thread at m. 75 suggests that time is suddenly broken apart, any illusion of linear continuity abandoned in a shocking simultaneity. From here, it is difficult to regain sufficient orientation and balance: the coda feels more like a retreat than a resolution, and the pitch symmetry of the conclusion does little to restore the Quartet's expressive equilibrium. The fleeting and ephemeral quality of the finale's retrogrades and inversions,[10] as a consequence, sounds like an escape, a deflection of the deeper anxieties which the formal outline of the Andante cannot fully contain or hold in check.

Seeger's String Quartet exemplifies the condition of form in much twentieth-century modernist music: the desire for unity or wholeness in dialectical tension with a harmonic syntax that pushes in the opposite direction: a form which cannot fully hold or contain. But it also returns to the same issues of agency and authority raised by Machaut's motet: whose voice speaks, whose unity is attained (or lost)? For Ruth Crawford Seeger, such questions were critical (Hisama 2001). But they also have wider implications for understanding form's relationship with history and materiality. As Judith Butler suggests, "form is always in a bind with life, with soul, and with experience; life gives rise to form, but form is understood to distill life; life wrecks the distillation, only to open us to the ideal that form itself seeks to approach, but cannot" (Lukács 2009, Introduction). It is in this way, Butler suggests, that form remains dynamic and unstable. In one sense, this binary motion might be read as a legacy of Romantic aesthetics, of the debates provoked by Marx and Hanslick's notions of musical autonomy. But in another sense, it reflects deeper epistemological problems with the idea of form as process and as object, its double nature as verb and noun, or as pattern and symbol. Seeger's Quartet plays productively with these tensions, between form as socially produced and as a unique property of the musical work in performance, a source of creative energy. It also foregrounds the idea of form as bounded or enclosed, and it is precisely by stretching and ultimately breaking those limits that the Andante leaves its most striking mark.

The climax at the apex of Seeger's Andante might appear to be a negative point of formal articulation—a sudden inability to speak or maintain coherence, a gesture of frustration or rage. But it might also be heard as a site of liberation, the moment at which the movement's form breaks down and uncovers a new set of potentialities, one that could permit the emergence of a different register or voice. As Carole Levine suggests, "binary opposition is just one of a number of powerfully organizing forms, [and] many outcomes follow from other forms, as well as from more mundane, more minor, and more contingent encounters, where different forms are not necessarily related, opposed, or deeply expressive, but simply happen to cross paths at a particular site" (Levine 2015, 19). This indicates how form has been productively reimagined elsewhere in twentieth-century music: as suggesting an alternative sense of space or encounter, another kind of motion or duration. One of the most influential and compelling studies in form as space and time is Miles Davis's groundbreaking 1969 fusion album *In a Silent Way*.[11] Issues of authorial agency are significantly widened here: both the producer, Teo Macero, and the available studio technology were crucially involved in determining the music's final shape, especially through the overdubbing, splicing, and cutting of prerecorded tracks (Burgess 2014, 92). The album's form, in that sense, is explicitly the emergent effect of a distributive process, rather than a single intentional act, realized through multiple layers of technological mediation that supported (and operated in dialogue with) the players' own creative interplay.

Just over four minutes into the album's B-side, the music undergoes a sudden and unexpected change of mood and direction: whereas the opening track (from which the album takes its title) is an ecstatic immersive meditation based on a single modal collection, the new section, "It's About That Time," immediately strikes a tenser and more urgent note. Tony Williams's metronomic cross-stick drumming provides an insistent sense of propulsion and regularity, like the ticking of an atomic clock. But the feeling of anxiety is generated more by the friction between other elements in the musical texture, especially the three-measure chaconne-like chord progression that drives the track's refrain and the more normative four-measure phrase rhythm of the funk riff at the end of each solo. After a short prefatory bridge passage (at 4'15"), which returns at the end of the track, the solos themselves are arranged so as to generate a sense of growing textural intensification (echoing the order of their appearance in "In a Silent Way"): starting with John McLaughlin's guitar, followed by Wayne Shorter's saxophone, and peaking with Davis's trumpet.

McLaughlin's solo is spacious and expansive, consistent with his performance across much of the album, whereas both Shorter's and Davis's solos are more insistent, rhythmically articulated, and compressed. The cumulative effect, as each solo leads into the return of the funk riff, becomes irresistible: the tension between the improvisatory figuration of the solos and the repeated ground bass is increasingly tight, culminating in the third return of the riff (around 13'15"), the only point in which Williams's drumming significantly departs from its cross-stick pattern and where the ensemble threatens to break loose from its relatively subdued dynamic level. This cumulative energy, however, ultimately fades into a looped return of "In a Silent Way," without ever achieving a genuine breakthrough, framing the chaconne's insistent ostinato within music that has no apparent metrical pulse or sense of duration. The impression (both here, and, as Keith Waters notes, elsewhere in Miles Davis's work) is of entirely independent temporal planes that coexist without ever entirely coinciding. Each plane suggests a different rate of motion as well as a different mood or affect, but it is their simultaneity, the productive friction between their individual rhythmic layers, which creates a new sense of formal logic or cohesiveness, and which lends the track its feeling of openness (Waters 2011, 123). No less than Machaut's *Ma Fin*, "It's About That Time" plays with form's boundaries and limits, with the idea of where the piece begins and where it ends, and with the listener's sense of place. And as its title playfully suggests, the track's subject becomes its own ambiguity: *that* time, or that *time*, its underlying syncopation and its pulse.

CONCLUSION

Form's elusiveness cannot be resolved. But the continuing centrality of form, as Levine suggests, lies in its potentiality: the way in which it affords different modes of behavior and relation (Waters 2011, 6–7). Form remains a didactic tool, a textual device, and a system of comportment and behavior. It facilitates meaning and communication, but equally excludes or marginalizes other values or possibilities. It is always exclusive, even when it gathers material, actors, and different voices together. Form's relationship with agency and intention is complex: it can never simply be reduced to a single set of authorial intentions, or to a neutral pattern of organization or arrangement. It moves within both space and time. Even where it appears most inward-looking, form always pushes outward, resisting its limitations or testing its boundaries. In that sense, form is always dynamic and unstable. But form also monumentalizes, regulates, and disciplines. Form's historical agency remains considerable, as does its enduring presence in contemporary debate. In searching for new kinds of formal connection, however, the space for alternative understanding and interpretation becomes possible, and it is precisely through this critical engagement with form, by listening to what lies both outside and within, that its greatest richness can be grasped. That is how form moves.

ACKNOWLEDGEMENTS

I am grateful to the editors of the volume for their patience and care with this text, to Tom Phillips for advice on Classical language, and to Keith Waters, for kindly sharing his work on Miles Davis with me as I prepared my final draft. This chapter is dedicated to Brian Hyer, in admiration and with thanks.

NOTES

1. These are too numerous to list in full, but some significant contributions (largely focusing on late eighteenth- and nineteenth-century music) include Caplin (1998); McClary (2000); Smith (2005); Hepokoski and Darcy (2006); Vande Moortele (2010); and Schmalfeldt (2011).
2. Parry's entry was reprinted unchanged in both the second and third editions of the dictionary (the latter edited by H. C. Colles and published in 1944).
3. Text, translation, and underlay adapted from Leach (2011) and Eisenberg (2007).

4. For a critical discussion of the problematic historiographical canonization of the isorhythmic motet and its implications for reading Dufay's work, see Bent (2008, 121–143).
5. On definitions and uses of *ombra*, see McClelland (2012).
6. For a detailed and illuminating study that discusses the relationship between form and time extensively, see Taylor (2015).
7. The familiar version of Hanslick's text ("Der Inhalt der Musik sind tönend bewegte Formen") was published for the first time in the 1865 edition of his essay. Payzant discusses problems of translation in the appendix of his edition ("Essay: Towards a Revised Reading of Hanslick," 93–102, at 102). The original (1854) draft reads: "Tönend bewegte Formen sind einzig und allein Inhalt und Gegenstand der Musik." See Strauß (1990, 75).
8. The idea of music and movement has been significantly challenged. See, for example, Adlington (2003, 297–318).
9. For a more detailed and systematic analysis of the movement's pitch structure than is possible here, see Hisama (2001, 12–34).
10. On the pitch organization of the fourth movement, see Straus 2007, 33–56, especially 44ff.
11. The material for *In a Silent Way* was recorded on a single day, February 18, 1969, at the CBS studios in New York. Davis and Macero worked extensively on the tracks before release; see Davis with Troupe (1989, 296–297).

WORKS CITED

Adlington, Robert. 2003. "Moving beyond Motion: Metaphors for Changing Sound." *Journal of the Royal Musical Association* 128, no. 2: 297–318.
Bent, Margaret. 2008. "What Is Isorhythm?" In *Quomodo cantabimus canticum? Studies in Honor of Edward H Roesner*, edited by David Butler Cannata, Gabriela Ilnitchi Currie, Rena Charnin Mueller, and John Louis Nádas. Middleton, WI: American Institute of Musicology.
Bergé, Pieter. 2010. "Prologue: Considering Musical Form, Forms and Formenlehre." In *Musical Form, Forms & Formenlehre: Three Methodological Reflections*, edited by Pieter Bergé, 11–18. Leuven: Leuven University Press.
Blackburn, Bonnie J. 1994. "Introduction." In *Guillaume Dufay: Nuper Rosarum Flores*, 3–7. Espoo, Finland: Fazer Music.
Bonds, Mark Evan. 1991. *Wordless Rhetoric: Musical Form and the Metaphor of Musical Oration*. Cambridge, MA: Harvard University Press.
Burgess, Richard James. 2014. *The History of Music Production*. Oxford: Oxford University Press.
Burnham, Scott. 2002. "Form." In *The Cambridge History of Western Music Theory*, edited by Thomas Christensen, 880–906. Cambridge: Cambridge University Press.
Caplin, William E. 1998. *Classical Form: A Theory of Formal Functions*. New York: Oxford University Press.
Chua, Daniel. 1999. *Absolute Music and the Construction of Meaning*. Cambridge: Cambridge University Press.
Cone, Edward T. 1968. *Musical Form and Musical Performance*. New York: Norton.
Danuser, Hermann. 2003. "Form—Formation—Transformation." In *L'Orizzonte filosofico del comporre nel ventesimo secolo/The Philosophical Horizon of Composition in the Twentieth Century*, edited by Gianmario Borio, 127–155. Venice: Fondazione Ugo e Olga Levi.
Davis, Miles, with Quincy Troupe. 1989. *Miles: The Autobiography*. New York: Picador.

Eisenberg, Michael. 2007. "The Mirror of the Text: Reflections in *Ma fin est mon commencement*." In *Canons and Canonic Techniques, 14th–16th Centuries: Theory, Practice, and Reception History*, edited by Katelijne Schiltz and Bonnie J. Blackburn, 83–110. Leuven: Peeters.

Hanslick, Eduard. 1986. *On the Musically Beautiful: A Contribution Towards the Revision of the Aesthetics of Music*. Translated and edited by Geoffrey Payzant. Indianapolis: Hackett.

Hepokoski, James, and Warren Darcy. 2006. *Elements of Sonata Theory: Norms, Types, and Deformations in the Late-Eighteenth-Century Sonata*. New York: Oxford University Press.

Hepokoski, James. 2010. "Sonata Theory and Dialogic Form." In *Musical Form, Forms and Formenlehre: Three Methodological Reflections*, edited by Pieter Bergé, 71–95. Leuven: Leuven University Press.

Hisama, Ellie M. 2001. *Gendering Musical Modernism: The Music of Ruth Crawford, Marion Bauer, and Miriam Gideon*. Cambridge: Cambridge University Press.

Hoyt, Peter A. 1996. "The Concept of *Développement* in the Early Nineteenth Century." In *Music Theory in the Age of Romanticism*, edited by Ian Bent, 141–162. Cambridge: Cambridge University Press.

Kant, Immanuel. 1981. *Kritik der Urteilskraft* [Critique of Judgement] (Berlin, 1790), §14. In *Music and Aesthetics in the Eighteenth and Early-Nineteenth Centuries*, edited by Peter Le Huray and James Day, 214–229. Cambridge: Cambridge University Press.

Leach, Elizabeth Eva. 2011. *Guillaume de Machaut: Secretary, Poet, Musician*. Ithaca, NY: Cornell University Press.

Leighton, Angela. 2007. *On Form: Poetry, Aestheticism, and the Legacy of a Word*. Oxford: Oxford University Press.

Levine, Caroline. 2015. *Forms: Whole, Rhythm, Hierarchy, Network*. Princeton, NJ: Princeton University Press.

Lewin, David. 2003. "The Form of Rhythm, the Rhythm of Form." In *L'Orizzonte filosofico del comporre nel ventesimo secolo/The Philosophical Horizon of Composition in the Twentieth Century*, edited by Gianmario Borio, 157–188. Venice: Fondazione Ugo e Olga Levi.

Lukács, György. 2009. "Platonism, Poetry and Form: Rudolf Kassner." In *Soul and Form*. Translated by Anna Bostock, edited by John T. Sanders and Katie Terezakis, 35–43. New York: Columbia University Press.

Marx, Adolf Bernhard. 1997. "Die Form in der Musik" (1856), §21 and §25. In *A. B. Marx: Musical Form in the Age of Beethoven*. Translated and edited by Scott Burnham. Cambridge: Cambridge University Press.

McClary, Susan. 2000. *Conventional Wisdom: The Content of Musical Form*. Berkeley: University of California Press.

McClelland, Clive. 2012. *Ombra: Music of the Supernatural in the Eighteenth Century*. Lanham, MD: Lexington Books.

Paddison, Max. 1993. *Adorno's Aesthetics of Music*. Cambridge: Cambridge University Press.

Parry, C. Hubert. 1879. "Form." In *A Dictionary of Music and Musicians*, edited by George Grove, 1: 541–555. London: Macmillan.

Schmalfeldt, Janet. 2011. *In the Process of Becoming: Analytic and Philosophic Perspectives on Form in Early Nineteenth-Century Music*. New York: Oxford University Press.

Smith, Peter H. 2005. *Expressive Forms in Brahms's Instrumental Music: Structure and Meaning in his* Werther *Quartet*. Bloomington: Indiana University Press.

Städtke, Klaus. 2001. "Form." In *Ästhetische Grundbegriffe*, edited by Karlheinz Barck, 462–494. Stuttgart und Weimar: J. B. Metzler.

Stainer, John, and William Alexander Barrett. 1876. *Dictionary of Musical Terms*. London: Novello.

Stone, Anne. 2003. "Music, Writing, and Poetic Voice in Machaut: Some remarks on Ballade 12 and Rondeau 14." In *Machaut's Music: New Interpretations*, edited by Elizabeth Eva Leach. Woodbridge, UK: Boydell & Brewer.

Straus, Joseph N. 2007. "Ruth Crawford's Precompositional Strategies." In *Ruth Crawford Seeger's Worlds: Innovation and Tradition in Twentieth-Century American Music*, edited by Ray Allen and Ellie M. Hisama, 33–56. Rochester, NY: University of Rochester Press.

Strauß, Dietmar. 1990. *Eduard Hanslick: Vom Musikalisch-Schönen, Ein Beitrag zur Revision der Ästhetik in der Tonkunst. Teil 1: Historisch-kritisch Ausgabe*. Mainz: Schott.

Taylor, Benedict. 2015. *The Melody of Time: Music and Temporality in the Romantic Era*. New York: Oxford University Press.

Trachtenberg, Marvin. 2001. "Architecture and Music Reunited: A New Reading of Dufay's *Nuper Rosarum Flores* and the Cathedral of Florence." *Renaissance Quarterly* 54: 740–775.

Vande Moortele, Steven. 2010. *Two-Dimension Sonata Form: Form and Cycle in Single-Movement Instrumental Works by Liszt, Strauss, Schoenberg and Zemlinsky*. Leuven: Leuven University Press.

Warren, Charles. 1973. "Brunelleschi's Dome and Dufay's Motet." *The Musical Quarterly* 59: 92–105.

Waters, Keith. 2011. *The Studio Recordings of the Miles Davis Quintet, 1965–68*. New York: Oxford University Press.

Webster, James. 1991. *Haydn's "Farewell" Symphony and the Idea of Classical Style: Through-Composition and Cyclic Integration in His Instrumental Music*. Cambridge: Cambridge University Press.

Whittall, Arnold. 1980. "Form." In *The New Grove Dictionary of Music and Musicians*, vol. 6, edited by Stanley Sadie. London: Macmillan.

Whittall, Arnold. 2001. "Form." In *The New Grove Dictionary of Music and Musicians*, vol. 9, edited by Stanley Sadie and John Tyrrell. Basingstoke: Macmillan.

Wright, Craig. 1994. "Dufay's *Nuper rosarum flores*, King Solomon's Temple, and the Veneration of the Virgin." *Journal of the American Musicological Society* 47: 395–441.

CHAPTER 14

....

EXPRESSIVE TIMING

....

MITCHELL OHRINER

A CURIOUS MOMENT IN CHOPIN'S
E-MAJOR ETUDE

....

FIGURE 14.1 shows a passage approaching the end of the first large section of Frédéric Chopin's Etude in E major, op. 10, no. 3, a piece that has taken on the title "Tristesse" and is considered an exemplar of major-mode sadness. The climax at m. 17 is an arresting moment: an E-major chord with the fifth (B) in the bass, what Robert Hatten calls an "arrival six-four" (1994, 15). William Rothstein points out that Chopin's treatment of this sonority in this instance is virtually unique. In all other cases, the arrival six-four precedes the cadence's dominant, merging into that function. Instead, Chopin treats the sonority as a tonic, initiating a harmonic sequence familiar to listeners of Pachelbel's Canon in D major, thereby delaying the cadence suggested at m. 17 all the way until m. 21. For Rothstein, then, m. 17 is a unique blend of harmonic functions, which almost by definition are distinct: dominant with respect to the anticipation of cadence wrought by the arrival six-four, but tonic with respect to the initiated harmonic sequence (1989, 225).

Measure 17 is also an important moment in the emotional trajectory of the piece. Up until this point, the etude presents a placid series of phrases ending in half and authentic cadences. Only at m. 17 is there a suggestion that all might not be well. Whether the implication of sadness resonates with a listener in part depends on their perception of a phrase ending at m. 17. For if m. 17 is viewed as a moment of cadence, then the arrival six-four might dispel the harmonic tension of the preceding measures. Alternatively, if the suggestions of closure at m. 17 are minimized and that tension remains active until m. 21, then the emotional angst of mm. 15–17 might more assertively support the implications of sadness in the piece.

However one views m. 17, the notes remain the same. Therefore, the way those notes are presented in performance can be decisive. And "the way those notes are presented"

pertains to the research area of expressive timing. "Expressive timing" refers to variation in performed durations among notes represented in a musical score with a single
rhythmic value. While expressive timing touches on the analysis of many different kinds
of musical structures, our understanding of timing at moments of cadence is particularly clear: performers indicate cadences through deceleration. Figure 14.2 plots duration in two different and contrasting performances of the passage. Four levels of points
refer to durations of, from lowest to highest, sixteenth notes, eighth notes, quarter notes,
and half notes. (Note that, on the y-axis, higher means slower.) Except for the highest
level, lines connect durations within a measure.

Immediately striking is the vast difference in duration between two performances of
the same passage. While some passages can elicit greater conformity in duration, this
kind of variation is by no means unique (see, for example, the discussion of performances
of Varèse below). Briefly, James Kwong in Figure 14.2(a) decelerates dramatically during
the bass descent through $\flat\hat{6}$, but begins the harmonic sequence at a faster tempo that is
maintained throughout mm. 18–20. In contrast, Ignacy Jan Paderewski's deceleration in
m. 16 in Figure 14.2(b) continues all the way until the E5 of m. 18. By lengthening m. 16
and starting m. 17 faster, Kwong presents the arrival six-four as precisely that: an arrival
that enables a new phrase to begin less encumbered by the harmonic tension preceding
it. By continuing the deceleration further, Paderewski refuses to relinquish tension,
holding the beginning of the harmonic sequence in the same frame of mind as the arrival six-four. In both cases, I would argue that the individual choices of the performers
not only color the experience of hearing the piece, but might even change how we describe its structural features. This analytical vignette shows two quite different purposes
to the study of expressive timing: it is at once an area that uses empirical measurements
to describe and model how performers convey musical structures to listeners and, at the
same time, a potential source for analysts crafting interpretations of those structures.

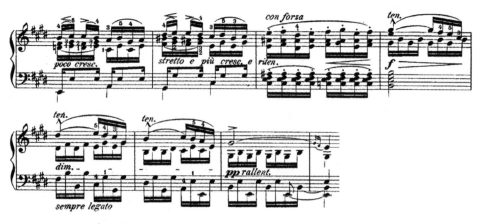

FIGURE 14.1 Etude in E Major, op. 10, no. 3, mm. 14–21.

(a)

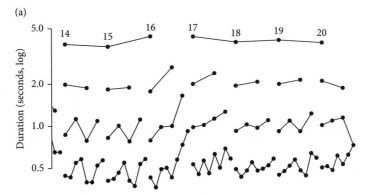

FIGURE 14.2(a) Duration in Chopin, Etude in E Major, op. 10, no. 3, mm. 14–20, in the performance of James Kwong (2008). ▶ Audio Example 14.1

(b)

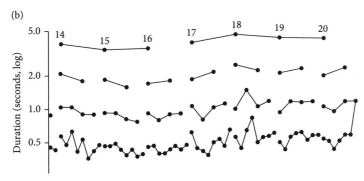

FIGURE 14.2(b) Duration in Chopin, Etude in E Major, op. 10, no. 3, mm. 14–20, in the performance of Ignacy Jan Paderewski (c. 1920/1994). ▶ Audio Example 14.2

EXPRESSIVE TIMING: FROM THE CENTER
TO THE MARGINS

Generally, expressive timing scholarship seeks to relate acceleration and deceleration in a performance or (more often) a group of performances to features of the musical score such as phrase structure, harmonic tension, or rhythmic activity. Although there are precedents for the study of expressive timing in the nineteenth and early twentieth centuries, the area blossomed following two developments.[1] First, advances in recording technology produced an extensive artifactual record of performances of the same piece.

Second, advances in digital signal processing eased the annotation of events in those performances.

These developments supported robust activity in the study of expressive timing in the 1980s and 1990s. In those decades, a group of researchers including Bruno Repp, Nicholas Cook, Neil Todd, Ingmar Bengtsson, Alf Gabrielsson, Peter Desain, and Henkjan Honing established the three principal findings of the field:

1. Performers communicate grouping structure, *à la* Lerdahl and Jackendoff (1983), through a tendency to decelerate at the ends of phrases, a phenomenon termed "phrase final lengthening," itself a term borrowed from research on speech prosody (Pike 1945).[2]
2. Performers communicate metric structure by configuring patterns of relatively long and short beats (Sloboda 1983). Furthermore, the patterns often distinguish genres that share a time signature (e.g., the waltz and the mazurka; see Gabrielsson and Bengtsson 1983).
3. Some (but not all) aspects of expressive timing (e.g., phrase final lengthening) are tempo-invariant (Desain and Honing 1994; Repp 1994).

The continued reliance on this research, evidenced by high citation counts, testifies to the accomplishments of this late twentieth-century research program. Yet it must also be recognized that this scholarship, on the whole, addressed a surprisingly narrow scope of about half a dozen pieces, namely the theme of Mozart's Piano Sonata in A major, K. 331, Beethoven's Six Variations on "Nel coro più non mi sento," WoO 70, Schumann's "Träumerei" from *Scenes from Childhood*, Chopin's Etude in E major, op. 10, no. 3, and various Chopin Mazurkas.[3] While these pieces are somewhat diverse in style, they are far more alike than they are different; all are written for piano between roughly 1775 and 1850 and all have relatively little diversity of phrase types or length.

Because of these commonalities, existing scholarship of expressive timing primarily addresses questions of grouping structure and meter. This limited purview has two flaws. As Nicholas Cook points out, it minimizes the agency of the performer, who is understood as a passive conveyer of the music's meaning and structure (Cook 1999, 243). And as Cohn and Dempster argue, music has a host of different structures—those of group segmentation, yes, but also voice-leading, motivic association, and schemes of meter and/or dance types (1992, 167–168). Tempo changes could (simultaneously) apply to any of these structures, and their contribution to the durational contour of a performance is not easily disentangled. Even within these different parameters, musical structure presents a constellation of possible meanings rather than a fixed signal.[4] All those who interact with the music—performers and listeners alike—must wend a path through those potentialities.

More recent studies of expressive timing have sought to move from the "center" of the repertoire addressed in the core of the literature out to the "margins," to pieces that differ in structure, chronology, or style (e.g., Goodchild, Gingras, and McAdams 2016; Clarke and Doffman 2014). I aim to continue this expansion of the scope of expressive timing scholarship. After reviewing the principal findings of the literature in a bit more detail and discussing the often-vexing challenges of data collection, I will present three case studies of expressive timing, each at a further remove from the kind of music engaged by the core of the literature. These case studies address timing across an entire movement of the Brahms violin concerto, in the unmetered context of Edgard Varèse's *Density 21.5* for solo flute, and in the mechanically regulated tempo of Kendrick Lamar's "Momma" from his album *To Pimp a Butterfly*, a 2015 rap release. While the repertoire varies considerably throughout these studies, the focus remains consistent: I aim to document aspects of timing in irregular phrasing or metric environments. Further, in addition to reporting the average tendency of performers, I also aim show how consensus, or lack thereof, can refine our understandings of musical works.

EXPRESSIVE TIMING AS A TRACE

The term "expressive timing" can obscure what timing expresses. Much of the literature understands grouping structure to be the musical feature expressed by timing. If Lerdahl and Jackendoff's tree structures uncover how composers segment spans of music and relate them to each other, expressive timing research uncovers how performers convey that structure to listeners. As Clarke puts it, "it appears that the amount of timing modification is directly related to the structural significance of a musical segment" (1988, 15).

The relationship between deceleration and phrase structure, however, is clearest when phrase structure itself is clearest. Many early studies address beginnings of Classical and Romantic piano music, which present declamatory thematic statements in four or eight measure phrases ending in clear cadences. This research likely overstates the timing/grouping nexus. As a corrective, recent literature addresses timing in ambiguous or multifaceted phrase structures (Dodson 2008 and 2011; Ohriner 2012). This turn not only expands the scope of research: it also shifts the objective of expressive timing research from supporting existing music analysis toward generating new questions. Furthering this turn, the first case study below addresses timing in non-declamatory statements (e.g., transitions).

While many studies document the communication of musical structures, others frame timing as expressive of performers' identity and life history. Craig Sapp has focused on clustering performances in large datasets to determine the features that drive a given pair of performers toward similarity. Frequently, these clusters contain the trace of lived experience. In a study of thirty-two performances of Chopin's Mazurka in C major, op. 24, no. 2, Sapp found an especially high correlation between a student-teacher pairing (Rieko Nezu and Ewa Pobłocka). Nezu studied with Pobłocka as a post-graduate student, suggesting that the aspects of style captured by expressive timing continue developing in performers rather late (2011, 34). Sapp's work also highlights the resilience or malleability of a performer's style. When a dataset contains a pair of performances by one individual, the pair is usually the most similar in the set (2008, 505). However, performers who defy this trend invite investigation into how particular pieces invite divergent interpretations over the course of a lifetime. Repp (1992b and 1995), for example, shows that students and experts execute timing similarly when considered as groups, but that experts display far more variability within the group, suggesting that experts take the additional step of developing unique readings.

In addition to musical structure and performers' identity, timing also contains the trace of music-cognitive processes related to memory, emotion, and preference. Dowling, Tillmann, and Ayers (2001) show that timing improves short-term musical memory for some listeners, heightening their ability to say if a stimulus is the same as one heard recently. The longer the delay, the more expressive timing aids in memory, especially for subjects with less musical experience.[5] Sloboda and Lehmann, among others, have explored how timing relates to the perception of musical emotion. In particular, deviations from widespread timing practices elicit high emotional responses (2001, 112). Finally, expressive timing also relates to preference. Beyond preferring performances with expressive timing to those without, listeners have developed preferences for the most common expressive profiles. Drawing on data from his seminal studies of timing in Schumann's "Träumerei," Repp abstracted the execution of the end of a phrase to a parabolic function. He then synthesized performances with different variations on that curve. Musically experienced listeners consistently preferred performances most like the typical performance of experts (1992, 273).[6] Ângelo Martingo (2007) has further documented the connection between expressive timing and preference. Using a model based on Fred Lerdahl's Tonal Pitch Space (2001), Martingo presented performances in which expressive features were and were not correlated to Lerdahl's tension and attraction measurements. Those in which timing clarified levels of tension were preferred. The core finding of these studies is that attending to timing in performance can reveal much about the musical structure of a piece, how that structure is conveyed to listeners through performance, and how listeners perceive and come to prefer that structure.

GENERATING DATA FOR STUDIES
OF EXPRESSIVE TIMING

Generally, expressive timing addresses the time intervals between note onsets in performance. The first challenge the would-be scholar of expressive timing confronts is determining these note onsets. A long tradition of expressive timing studies bypasses this challenge through MIDI-equipped instruments that record onsets electronically. While such instruments are extremely useful, they present three disadvantages. First, their expense reduces their accessibility. Second, the MIDI approach favors instruments with widely available controllers, namely pianos. And finally, a MIDI approach necessitates the recruitment of performers as participants. These performers likely study at the institution in which the research is conducted, raising issues similar to the problem of WEIRD subjects—Western, educated, industrialized, rich, and democratic—that underlie social science research (Henrich, Heine, and Norenzayan 2010). By opting instead for recorded artifacts, researchers can address a broader range of performance styles than those encountered in conservatories and universities.

Examining such artifacts highlights a widespread and problematic view of music's temporality voiced by Matthew Wright (2008, 14), that music "consists of independent, distinct events (for example, musical notes)." Although music notation assumes discrete events, and although mental music processing discretizes the sound signal into events (Bregman 1994), many musical scenarios—the violinist's *portamento*, the arpeggiated piano chord, the vocalist's diphthong—belie this partitioning. Even when dealing with easily discretized events (e.g., piano onsets), one must still distinguish between the physical onset of a sound and the "perceptual attack time" (PAT) of a sound—the displacement of the perception of a sound relative to its physical onset. The PAT varies based on the attack envelope of the instrument producing the sound; for example, it is earlier for clarinet than for trumpet (Wright 2008, 91). Complicating the question further, the fundamental frequency may appear later in the attack envelope than other frequencies. This delay may vary over an instrument's range, and listeners may each align the PAT with different stages of the event's attack envelope (Gordon 1987, 94).[7]

In my view, the question that scholars of timing in recorded performances must address is not the exact value of the PAT, but whether the size of the range of potential values impacts a subsequent musical analysis. How accurate and precise must timing measurements be? If one is trying to show a general change in tempo over many events across many performers, measurement imprecisions may be assumed to be unbiased and neutralized through averaging. But some analyses of timing are more sensitive. Figure 14.3 reprints example 4 from Benadon (2006). Here, Benadon shows how Bill Evans creates triple groupings within a duple framework of very fast eighth notes. The first event circled is longer than the immediately previous note by only 10ms. Since shifting the annotated onset of the third note earlier affects both the

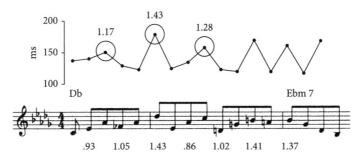

FIGURE 14.3 Duration in Bill Evans, piano, "Love for Sale," from Miles Davis's 58 Sessions, Columbia CK 47835, reprinted from Benadon (2006, 79). "Binary long-short groupings yield even BURs [beat-upbeat ratios] that can be reinterpreted as ternary long-short-short durations."

second and third duration, a change of ~5ms would reverse the relationship between the two. One solution around this issue is to undertake repeated measurements of event onsets, illuminating the range of errors in measurement. Then, researchers can demonstrate that the magnitude of the error is insignificant given the scope of the analysis.

From a practical standpoint, marking note onsets requires software that displays an audio signal and records user annotations. Suitable stand-alone applications include Audacity, Sonic Visualizer, and PRAAT. Audacity and Sonic Visualiser both support Vamp plug-ins for automatic beat and/or onset detection. In my own experience, these algorithms require too much manual correction to be useful. Furthermore, in these software environments one usually chooses between annotating the signal's time-domain representation (i.e., a wave form) or its frequency-domain representation (i.e., a spectrograph); these rarely elicit equivalent annotations.

A final choice a researcher must make is a scheme for visualization. Generally, timing is plotted in a Cartesian space with duration (or tempo, its inverse) on the y-axis and time on the x-axis. This x-axis can either index events or seconds; the latter effectively amplifies the information on the y-axis (Senn, Kilchenmann, and Camp 2009). It can be helpful to visualize durations in several metric levels simultaneously by plotting duration on a logarithmic axis. Finally, for comparing durations or onsets within a recurring metric pattern, a polar plot in which the 360° of the circle represents the measure may be appropriate (Benadon 2007; Grachten, Goebl, Flossmann, and Widmer 2009).

THREE CASE STUDIES OF TIMING IN PERFORMANCE

In the following case studies, I hope to clarify some future directions that studies of expressive timing might take as a more expansive field of inquiry. In particular, I aim to highlight the utility of timing studies in music that differs from underlying, much earlier work, namely uncomplicated phrases of Classical and Romantic piano music.

Variety in Phrase Structure: Brahms, Concerto for Violin in D Minor, op. 77, second movement (Adagio)

In contrast to so many studies that focus on a single phrase, usually at the beginning of the piece, Edward Cross, in his dissertation, addresses tempo changes in thirty-one performances of the second movement of Brahms's Violin Concerto in D major, op. 77, composed in 1878; he has generously shared his data with me to undertake this case study.[8] As a late Romantic movement, the Adagio does not contain the clear phrase structures (e.g., parallel periods) one encounters in the core repertoire discussed above.

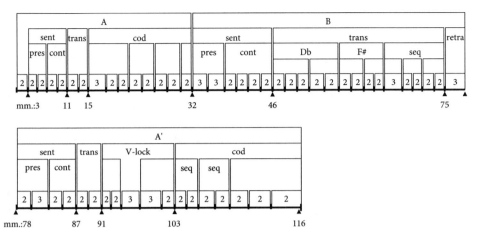

FIGURE 14.4 Brahms, op. 77, second movement, timeline of form (Brahms 1927). After Caplin (1998), sent = sentence, pres = presentation, cont = continuation, trans = transition, cod = codetta, seq = sequence, and retra = retransition. After Hepokoski and Darcy (2006), V-lock = dominant lock or standing on the dominant.

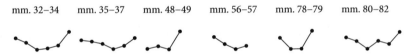

FIGURE 14.5 Tempo curves of two- and three-measure groups that present thematic material (mm. 52–53 are a tutti presentation of a theme and therefore not included in the data). Each point is one beat; higher points are slower. The range of the y-axis is determined by the tempo of the group, but the scale of the y-axis is invariant.

Yet, as a complete movement, it does contain passages of transition, anticipation, and reflection. Figure 14.4 interprets the form of the movement as a large ternary, segmented into two- and three-measure groups, many of which combine into familiar phrase structures and small forms described in Caplin (1998). Besides statements of the main theme beginning in mm. 32, 35, 78, and 80, mm. 48, 52, and 56 present other non-tonic themes. In concordance with previous research, tempo in passages of thematic presentation projects a curve of initial acceleration and a group-final lengthening curve (see Figure 14.5).

Outside of these thematic regions, the movement thrives on continual transition. In these transitional passages, two of which I will address in detail, tempo does not invariably function as a group-final lengthening curve. Figure 14.6 shows a score excerpt and a corresponding plot of measure durations in mm. 35–45, the end of the soloist's initial presentation of the main theme. I have highlighted four measures with asterisks: these measures mark moments of acceleration, each ~6% faster than the preceding measure. A complex of musical features, including note density, predicts acceleration in these

FIGURE 14.6 (a) Brahms, op. 77, second movement, mm. 35–45. An asterisk indicates a measure substantially faster than the preceding measure. (b) Brahms, op. 77, second movement, mm. 35–45, average duration, per measure of thirty-one performers. ▶ Audio Example 14.3.

measures. But the unfolding tonal ambiguity is also predictive. Measures 42 and 43 fall within a descending fifths sequence whose goal is uncertain—the sequence could lead back to tonic or overshoot it, transitioning elsewhere. The acceleration of mm. 42–43 contrasts with the deceleration of m. 44 and thereby clarifies the tonal meaning of m. 44's G^7 harmony as the dominant of the cadence, not just another link in the sequence.

Figure 14.7 shows another transitional passage, approaching the recapitulation of the opening section. Like many development sections of sonata forms, this passage includes

FIGURE 14.7 Brahms, op. 77, second movement, mm. 64–74.

a "point of furthest remove" (Ratner 1980, 225–227), alluding to a cadence in B minor in m. 70, a local tonic an augmented fourth above the global F-major tonic. Tempo in the passage generally accelerates to m. 72 and decelerates thereafter to mm. 77, the measure preceding the return of the main theme and one of the slowest measures of the movement (see Figure 14.8).

But the acceleration from m. 64 through m. 72 is by no means gradual. The duration contour of mm. 69–72 is especially striking. Here, the first beats of each measure are invariably longer. When differences in beat lengths arise, they are often considered emblematic of the meter, as in London (2012) or Gabrielsson and Bengtsson (1983). In this case, however, beat length difference is a function of solo-orchestral interaction. Throughout the passage, the orchestra is more active at the beginning of the measure. While the passage has an overall trend of acceleration, it is the soloist who propels the tempo, seemingly dragging the orchestra further from tonic. The social dynamics of the concerto have recently come under increased scrutiny. While timing has yet to play a role in this discussion, the data from Cross (2014) suggests that differences of tempo between performing forces may also underlie differences of agency.[9]

Finally, the broad historical sweep of Cross's data enables an investigation in to how tempo changes over time. José Bowen (1996) documents historical trends in tempo, in particular a "flattening" of tempo contrasts over the twentieth century, wherein both slow and fast sections of pieces are moving toward more moderate tempos. This compression of tempos would predict an overall acceleration over time. In contrast, as Figure 14.9 (left) shows, the movement is getting slower. But this decrease in tempo is not uniform across the movement. While every group is decreasing in tempo over time, the statistical significance of these decreases contrast starkly by section. Only four groups of the B section are significantly decelerating; only four groups of the A section are not significantly decelerating. The right side of Figure 14.9 plots the correlation between the trend and data on the y-axis, against the change in tempo across the half-century of recordings. The groups that slow the most, and that have the most agreement that slowing is appropriate, cluster within the section of codettas beginning at m. 103. There is a congruency between the tendency to slow after the final cadence of m. 103 and the

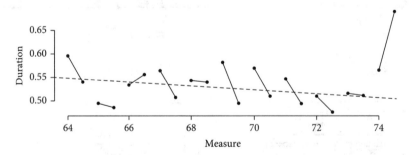

FIGURE 14.8 Brahms, op. 77, second movement, mm. 64–74, beat duration (points connected with lines represent beats within a measure). Dashed line indicates linear regression, excluding m. 74. Linear regression is not statistically significant ($r^2 = .12, p < .13$). ▶ Audio Example 14.4.

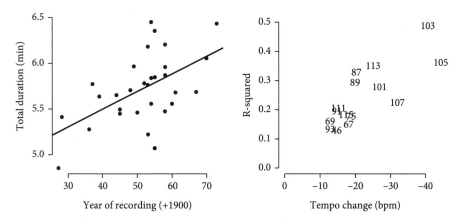

FIGURE 14.9 Total duration of movement (excluding tutti sections), plotted against year of recording, with linear regression ($r^2 = .30$, $p < .002$). (Right) Trends in tempo of two- and three-measure groups in Brahms, op. 77, second movement. Correlation of performances to trend on y-axis, total deceleration across the trend on x-axis. Groups not plotted do not have statistically significant trends over time.

tendency to accelerate on the weak beats of mm. 69–72. In both cases, the push by the soloist away from the tonic and the reassertion of tonic by the orchestra is mapped, respectively, onto acceleration and deceleration. Here too, attending to the dynamics of tempo may reveal the dynamics of soloistic autonomy and orchestral control.

Expressive Timing without Meter: Edgard Varèse, *Density 21.5* for solo flute, mm. 1–14

In the previous discussion of Brahms, as in most scholarship on expressive timing, the comparison of interest is between the durations of nominally equivalent beats. This is a frequent assumption, that the music being studied has a nominally steady pulse, and that can interpret deviations from that periodicity through features of musical structure. In this case study, I will argue that studies of duration can also illuminate music without a constant pulse. Further, attending not only to average durational contours but also to performer consensus in works without meter can reveal correspondences not explicit in the musical score; correspondingly, a lack of consensus highlights moments of ambiguity.

Edgard Varèse's *Density 21.5* for solo flute, like much of his output (Bernard 1987, 133), studiously avoids a constant pulse. Not only is the downbeat rarely articulated, the piece also has an unusually even distribution of event durations (see Figure 14.10). In many pieces of classical music, we would expect Figure 14.10 to include greater frequencies of fewer durations. The avoidance of a clear meter and the variety of rhythms undermines some classical analytic methods for post-tonal rhythm, such as beat-class set analysis

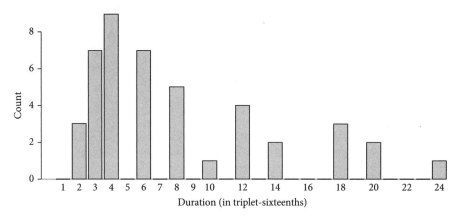

FIGURE 14.10   Varèse, *Density 21.5*, durations of events (as the sum of triplet sixteenths).

(e.g., Cohn 1992). Yet as Elizabeth West Marvin (1991, 74) argues, rhythmic patterning is more consistent in the piece than patterning of pitch-class set or melodic contour. How does timing interact with this rhythmic patterning?

A rhythmic motive of short-short-long pervades these measures. I will call this motive α and formally define it as a segment of three notes without intervening rests (and thus two durations) in which the interval between the first and third notes is a unison or half step and the ratio of the notated durations is between 1:2 and 2:1. I further stipulate that instances of α cannot overlap—if two three-note segments both meet the criteria, the second is removed from the set of α. With these criteria, there are nine instances of α in the first 14 measures—a higher proportion than any other segment of the piece (see Figure 14.11). Note that these α-instances do not share a common pitch-class set, pitch-class set cardinality, notated durations, or metric identity within the beat or measure.

My questions concerning the execution of α-instances are as follows: first, do the durational ratios of the score obtain in performance? If not, why might performers alter the durations of the score? And second, is there a consensus regarding temporal relationships in performance, and what might moments of reduced consensus say about different passages in the opening? In most cases, the notated ratio of the two durations in the short-short-long pattern is 1:1 (e.g., ♪:♪). Figure 14.12 plots these ratios. The bars on the left and right of each pair, respectively, track the notated and performed durational ratios in an average of twenty renditions. In most cases, the two values are similar, but performers as a group make three substantial revisions to notated rhythms, at instances 1, 3, and 6. In each case, the ratio between the two durations is much higher than expected—performers execute the rhythm as closer to long-short-long than the even short-short-long rhythm.

The revisions to instances 1 and 3 make them more rhythmically similar to instance 2 and give a greater rhythmic coherence to the beginning of the piece, now heard (in contrast to the notation) as three statements of the same rhythm. Instance 6—the first instance of the motive since m. 4 with shorter durations—is also revised toward

FIGURE 14.11 Varèse, *Density 21.5*, mm. 1–14. The asterisk indicates instance of α motive.
▶ Audio Example 14.5.

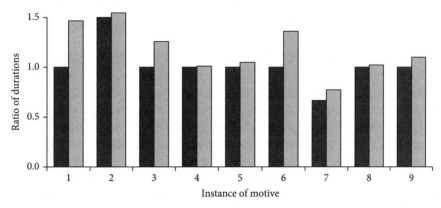

FIGURE 14.12 Varèse, *Density 21.5*, durational ratios in instances of α motive. In each pair of bars, the notated ratio is on the left and the performed ratio is on the right.

the long-short-long rhythm of the beginning. Why might performers as a group revise the rhythm of the motive away from equal durations and toward long-short-long patterning? The answer seems to lie in the introduction of a new pitch. The first fourteen measures introduce eighteen new pitches, and seven of these are introduced as either the first or third note of an instance of α. Shortening the second note of an α-instance causes the third to be perceived as early, and thereby takes on greater salience. In a piece in which the introduction of new pitches seems more important than the replication of pitch motives, it is vital that listeners attend to these expansions of the gamut. In several cases (e.g., the F♯4 of m. 1, the D5 of m. 11, and B♭5 of m. 13), the group action of performers facilitates this attention.

As demonstrated above, treatment of successive durations in the α motive can create correspondences not evident in the score with existing analytical tools. This kind of discovery of correspondence supports the frequent project of music analysts to demonstrate the unity and coherence of musical works. Yet recent analysis has seen a shift in focus toward highlighting disunity and incoherence in musical works.[10] Expressive timing also has a role to play here. In *Density 21.5*, tempo—defined as the relative frequency of events—constantly shifts, even if the score has a metronome marking and an indication to play "always strictly in time." The shifts in tempo affect the perceived pacing of the piece. And while one can read them from the score, the pacing is understood only in the context of a performance. To what extent do performers agree on the relative lengths of events in the opening of the piece?

Figure 14.13 shows a violin plot (Hintze and Nelson 1998; Wickham 2009, 68) of the duration separating the first and third notes in each statement of the motive in the twenty performances. A violin plot is a refinement of the classic box-and-whiskers plot that portrays density distributions of observations (in this case, durations of the first two notes of instances of α in different performances) among variables (instances of α in this case). The durations comprising the density distributions are given as points, with the mean duration of each instance given as a diamond point. These mean durations largely correspond to indicated durations in the notation. But here the averaging obscures the widely different rates of consensus around the proper duration in the motive. Motive instances with tall and narrow distributions show a lack of agreement on the most appropriate way to pace the piece.

This consensus is remarkably strong at α-instance 6, the D♭5 of m. 9. This motive instance introduces a new pitch, with the loudest dynamic marking yet, on the beat. These factors clarify for performers what the tempo ought to be (although it is not the notated tempo of 72). The consensus is weakest in groups 5, 7, and 8. These correspond to moments when oscillations between a pair of pitches—the defining feature of α—extend well beyond the short patterning of the motive (i.e., between B♭ and G in mm. 6–8 and between C and D♭ in mm. 9–10). Disrupting the tendency toward repeating the notes of a dyad for only two or three notes, these passages seem to challenge performers to create a consistent rhythmic structure. By attending to moments of disunity in collections of

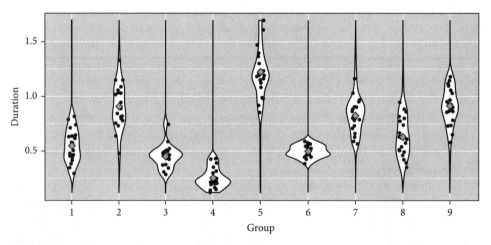

FIGURE 14.13 Duration of instances of α motive.

performances, scholars of expressive timing can support the growing trend that seeks to unsettle (or even disrupt) the notion of the fixed musical work.

Expressive Timing without Tempo Change: Kendrick Lamar, "Momma," verse two

In a final case study, I'd like to examine what analytical meanings can be drawn from durations in a performance of a rap verse, specifically the second verse of Kendrick Lamar's "Momma," from the groundbreaking 2015 release *To Pimp a Butterfly* (Duckworth et al. 2015). Rap music occurs in a metric environment rarely encountered in studies of timing, one in which the durations in some parts of the music are mechanically regulated. Although this scenario is absent in literature on timing, it applies to a wide and growing range of musical performances, especially in popular music genres.

Rap music presents three substantial challenges to the study of expressive timing. First, studies of timing in Western classical music compare durations of a performance to a "ground truth" of a musical score. For Lamar, no such ground truth exists. Second, the ontology of classical musical works enables a comparison among many performances in studies of timing. Because Lamar is the only person to perform the verse, the meaning of his timing cannot be established through such comparisons. Finally, much of the sound signal in "Momma" maintains a steady tempo. Lamar's durations, then, are expressive of neither the score, nor his position in a group of performers, nor ongoing dynamics of tempo. Rather, his durations are expressive of the ongoing dynamics of alignment between his flow and the steady beat of the rhythm section. In what follows, I will show how this varying alignment gives rise to a formal narrative for the verse, one reflected in the text.

Figure 14.14 segments the lyrics of the verse into seven stanzas, mainly according to rhyme and the placement of the verse's refrain, "I know everything." Figure 14.15 transcribes the first stanza, plotting one measure per line. The dashed vertical lines show the sixteenth-note metric grid. There is an upper and lower point for each syllable, showing the actual onset and inferred quantized position, respectively.[11] Solid horizontal lines connect those syllables said within a single breath.

Within this stanza are three lines: "I know everything," "I know everything, know myself," and "I know morality, spirituality, good and bad health." Lamar's level of alignment varies in each line, although the first stanza has the closest alignment of the verse. We can represent this alignment as the average distance between syllable onsets and their quantized positions, expressed in units of sixteenth notes. The three lines are nonaligned by, respectively, .13, .28, and .14 sixteenth notes. What differs between the lines is how this nonalignment can be characterized. In the first line, "I know everything," every syllable except one similarly lags behind its metric position. This suggests to me that Lamar is entrained with the meter and presenting durations that are intelligibly rhythmic (in that they are proportional to the tempo of the music), but also that Lamar is slightly "out of phase" with the meter. In this way, Lamar's delivery relates to

Stanza 1: I know everything, I know everything, know myself, I know morality, spirituality, good and bad health	*Stanza 5:* I know if I'm generous at heart, I don't need recognition. The way I'm rewarded, well, that's God's decision. I know you know that line's from Compton School 　　District. Just give it to the kids, don't gossip about how it's 　　distributed.
Stanza 2: I know fatality might haunt you, I know everything, I know Compton, I know street shit, I know shit that's conscious, I know everything, I know lawyers, advertisement and 　　sponsors I know wisdom, I know bad religion, I know good karma	*Stanza 6:* I know...how people work, I know the price of life I'm knowing how much it's worth.
Stanza 3: I know everything, I know history, I know the universe works mentally, I know the perks of bullshit isn't meant for me,	*Stanza 7:* I know what I know and I know it well not to ever forget, Until I realized I didn't know shit, The day I came home.
Stanza 4: I know everything, I know cars, clothes, hoes and money I know loyalty, I know respect, I know those that's hungry, I know everything, the highs the lows the groupies the junkies	

FIGURE 14.14 Kendrick Lamar, "Momma," verse two, text segmented into seven stanzas.

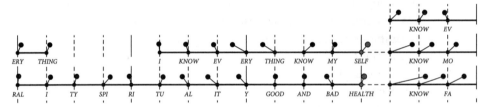

FIGURE 14.15 Kendrick Lamar, "Momma," verse 2, stanza 1. Upper points show syllable onsets, lower points show quantized syllable onsets. Horizontal lines connect syllables uttered in the same breath. ⓫ Audio Example 14.6.

out-of-phase performance practices documented in other Afro-diasporic genres such as Cuban *danzón* (Alén 1995), jazz (Doffman 2009), and funk (McGuiness 2006). The amount by which it is out of phase is the average displacement of the syllables, expressed as a percentage of sixteenth notes, in this case about 10%. If we were to imagine Lamar shifting these syllables back toward the beat by only 17ms, 22% of the nonalignment between syllable onsets and quantized metric positions would be explained.

The second line differs from the first in that it has both syllables ahead of and behind their quantized positions, as if Lamar knows to give the last syllable of "everything" more space. To do so, he rushes the beginning of the phrase and remains behind at the end. Without changing the durational relationships of the phrase, we can imagine "correcting" for this shift in tempo by multiplying by some constant, re-centering the phrase, and measuring the average nonalignment of this tempo-shifted phrase. In this case, rapping 6% faster, coupled with a phase adjustment as described above, would explain 42% of the nonalignment.

The third line, the longest of the stanza, also has substantial nonalignment, nearly as much as the second. The difference is that computing an optimal phase- and tempo-correction for the line—in other words, understanding the onsets through musical rhythm's proportionality—addresses less of this nonalignment. This suggests two different modes of rapping. A music-rhythmic mode of rapping will have less nonalignment, and its nonalignment will be explainable as a shift in phase or tempo (or both). A speech-rhythmic mode of rapping, like that heard in the third line, will have more nonalignment, and this nonalignment will be unexplained by tempo- and phase- adjustment because these adjustments are only responsive to proportional durations.

Figure 14.16 shows the fifth stanza of the verse. Some of these lines, to my ears, sound more like the rhythm of speech than that of music. While the quantization grants each syllable a unique metric position and aligns rhyming syllables within the beat, it implies a great deal of nonalignment, starting the first line of the stanza a sixteenth earlier than it appears in the signal and the third line nearly a sixteenth late. Figure 14.17 compares the average nonalignment and the percent of that nonalignment unexplained as phase or tempo shifts in the seven stanzas of the verse. The first three stanzas each have either moderate asynchrony (i.e., stanzas 2 and 3) or asynchrony that is mostly due to

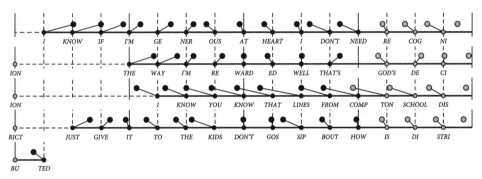

FIGURE 14.16 Kendrick Lamar, "Momma," verse 2, stanza 5.

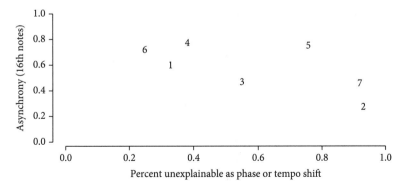

FIGURE 14.17 Average nonalignment (in sixteenth notes) and percent of nonalignment unexplained as phase and tempo shift in the seven stanzas of Kendrick Lamar's "Momma," verse 2. ▶ Audio Example 14.7.

phase and tempo shifts (i.e., stanza 1). The interior stanzas have more asynchrony, but by stanza 6 most of this asynchrony is explainable as phase or tempo shift. The experience of the first six stanzas, then, is an arch beginning and ending with delivery that largely resembles the proportional durations of music, contrasted with a more speech-like interior.

The last stanza of the verse, however, does not fit into this arch-shaped narrative. In that stanza, and particularly in the last line, nonalignment with the beat is relatively high and completely unexplained as a tempo or phase shift, presenting a rhythm much more reminiscent of speech than music. In my own hearing, the ending of the verse is a kind of text painting. Lamar has spent the entire verse assuring us of his competence and wisdom—he "knows" a remarkable amount. Indeed, many other tracks from *To Pimp a Butterfly* evoke a similar braggadocio familiar in rap music. But at the end of this verse, this confidence melts away as Lamar returns home to "realize [he] didn't know shit." The pairing of this text with the speech-like rhythm underlines how Lamar's ability to flow to the beat is tightly entwined with his authenticity as a native son of Compton—when the latter is questioned, the former also falls away.

Music Theory, Interaction, and Expressive Timing

After more than three decades of scholarship in expressive timing, this area of inquiry remains of greater interest to music psychologists than music theorists. Indeed, music theorists face a number of barriers to entry into this discussion. First, studies of expressive timing rely on methods of data collection and statistical analysis absent from most music theorists' graduate training. Second, because of the strong lineage of expressive timing studies in music psychology, the field is often conceived as an inquiry into the motor, perceptual, and cognitive processes of humans, questions more amenable to experimental methods than humanistic inquiry.

Beyond these barriers, the purview of music theory has in recent decades expanded in ways that distance the field from expressive timing. The 1990s saw sustained criticism, from the so-called New Musicology, of music theory's supposedly limited scope on pitch structures of Western classical music. (Such criticisms of music psychology were rarer.) In response, music theory has dramatically diversified the repertoires it addresses toward early music, postmodern music, popular music, and music of non-Western cultures. As traditionally conceived, studies of expressive timing best address repertoires that foreground continual tempo change at the level of the beat, such as soloistic classical performance.

These barriers can be overcome. As the paradigm of "big data" ascends in both the academic and corporate spheres, tutorials in data science become more numerous and accessible.[12] And, as I hope I have shown in this contribution, the range of repertoires that responds well to studies of timing far exceeds those addressed thus far. But the biggest hurdle confronting the integration of music theory and expressive timing is not technical or methodological, but philosophical. In essence, expressive timing is the study of interactions: the interaction of a performer and a musical object, that of a performer and a performance tradition, or that of multiple musicians collaborating in time.[13] While many of music theory's foundational attitudes toward repertoires have shifted, the value placed in the solo author (in both music creation and scholarship) has held steady. This may be the next expansion of the scope of music theory, toward a discipline that values both the isolated genius and the meanings created through group interaction. Such a shift would make music theory more amenable to expressive timing studies. Or, put more actively, studies of expressive timing could well be the agent for enacting such a shift.

AUDIO EXAMPLES

Audio Example 14.1. Chopin, Etude in E Major, op. 10, no. 3, mm. 14–20, performed by James Kwong (2008).

Audio Example 14.2. Chopin, Etude in E Major, op. 10, no. 3, mm. 14–20, performed by Ignacy Jan Paderewski (ca. 1920).

Audio Example 14.3. Brahms, op. 77, second movement, mm. 35–45, recorded in 1974 by Henryk Szeryng and the Royal Concertgebouw Orchestra (Bernard Haitink, conductor).

Audio Example 14.4. Brahms, op. 77, second movement, mm. 64–74, recorded in 1974 by Henryk Szeryng and the Royal Concertgebouw Orchestra (Bernard Haitink, conductor).

Audio Example 14.5. Varèse, Density 21.5, mm. 1–14, recorded in 2013 by Claire Chase.

Audio Example 14.6. Kendrick Lamar, "Momma," verse 2, stanza 1.

Audio Example 14.7. Kendrick Lamar, "Momma," verse 2, stanza 1.

NOTES

1. On historical precedents for studies of expressive timing, two scholars are of especial note: Mathis Lussy (1892), see also Lussy (1900), Doğantan-Dack (2002), and Carl Seashore (1936 and 1938).
2. The finding of phrase-final lengthening in music is established in Seashore (1936) and refined in Todd (1985 and 1989), Cook (1987), and Repp (1990).
3. On Mozart K. 331, see Todd (1985 and 1992), Gabrielsson (1987), and Clarke (1989). On Beethoven WoO 70, see Desain and Honing (1993 and 1994), and Windsor et al. (2006). On Schumann's "Träumerei," see Penel and Drake (1998) and, for example, Repp (1992, 1995, and 1996). (Seven other articles by Repp address "Träumerei.") On the opening of Chopin, op. 10, no. 3, see Repp (1998a and 1998b) and Grindlay and Helmbold (2006). On performances of Chopin's Mazurkas, see Cook (2009), Dodson (2009), Sapp (2007), Rink, Spiro, and Gold (2011), and Ohriner (2012).
4. A similar point is made in Rink, Spiro, and Gold (2011).

5. This finding was confirmed in Tillmann et al. (2013, 424).

6. Nonmusicians did not produce consistent results. Ibid., 270.

7. Errors in estimating the PAT are especially significant in instruments with variable attack envelopes; this may contribute to the overemphasis on piano music in expressive timing studies.

8. Cross (2014) includes a particularly good discussion of the challenge of annotating *portamento* and other non-discrete phenomena of violin playing. His data set includes beat-level annotation of passages of the piece in which the soloist plays and omits the orchestral opening and three other brief *tutti* passages.

9. I would argue that timing could lend support to the kinds of solo-orchestral narratives found in Keefe (1999), Kawabata (2015), and especially McClary (1986).

10. Among many others, see especially the recent contributions to this shift in James Manns (2007) and Fink (1999).

11. By "inferred quantized position," I refer to an automatic quantization I undertook on the onsets of syllables in the verse. Briefly, the algorithm places every syllable on the nearest sixteenth-note position and shifts syllables around within cases where two syllables initially quantized to the same metric position. I manually corrected the output of this algorithm in three instances so rhyming phrases would relate to the beat in the same way.

12. My own preference is the R programming language (www.r-project.org) run through the development environment of RStudio (www.rstudio.com). R continues to gain popularity in the data science community (Cass 2016). For non-programmers, this popularity ensures an active community to answer questions, some excellent book-length introductions on data analysis and visualization (e.g., stackoverflow.com/questions/tagged/r; Lander 2014; Wickham 2009 and 2015), and instant access to the latest developments in statistical methods.

13. In connection to "interaction," scholars of expressive timing might look to frameworks developed in jazz, in which interaction is understood as a central concern. Garrett Michaelsen (2013) provides such a framework.

Works Cited

Alén, Olevo. 1995. "Rhythm as Duration of Sounds in Tumba Francesa." *Ethnomusicology* 39: 55–71.

Benadon, Fernando. 2006. "Slicing the Beat: Jazz Eighth-Notes as Expressive Microrhythm." *Ethnomusicology* 50: 73–98.

Benadon, Fernando. 2007. "A Circular Plot for Rhythm Visualization and Analysis." *Music Theory Online* 13, no. 3. http://www.mtosmt.org/issues/mto.07.13.3/mto.07.13.3.benadon.html.

Bernard, Jonathan. 1987. *The Music of Edgard Varèse*. New Haven, CT: Yale University Press.

Bowen, José. 1996. "Tempo, Duration, and Flexibility: Techniques in the Analysis of Performance." *Journal of Musicological Research* 16: 111–156.

Brahms, Johannes. 1927. Concerto for Violin, op. 77. Arranged for violin and piano by Adolf Busch. Leipzig: Breitkopf and Härtel.

Bregman, Albert S. 1994. *Auditory Scene Analysis: The Perceptual Organization of Sound*. Cambridge, MA: MIT Press.

Caplin, William E. 1998. *Classical Form: A Theory of Formal Functions for the Instrumental Music of Haydn, Mozart, and Beethoven*. New York: Oxford University Press.

Cass, Stephen. 2016. "The 2016 Top Programming Languages." *IEEE Spectrum* (blog post). http://spectrum.ieee.org/computing/software/the-2016-top-programming-languages

Chase, Claire. 2013. *Density*. New Focus Recordings, frc135.

Clarke, Eric. 1988. "Generative Principles in Music Performance." In *Generative Processes in Music*, edited by John Sloboda, 1–26. Oxford: Clarendon Press.

Clarke, Eric. 1989. "Mind the Gap: Formal Structures and Psychological Processes in Music." *Contemporary Music Review* 3: 1–13.

Clarke, Eric, and Mark Doffman. 2014. "Expressive Performance in Contemporary Concert Music." In *Expressiveness in Music Performance: Empirical Approaches across Styles and Cultures*, edited by Dorottya Fabian, Renee Timmers, and Emery Schubert, 98–116. New York: Oxford University Press.

Cohn, Richard. 1992. "Transpositional Combination of Beat-Class Sets in Steve Reich's Phase-Shifting Music." *Perspectives of New Music* 30: 146–177.

Cohn, Richard, and Douglas Dempster. 1992. "Hierarchical Unity, Plural Unities: Toward a Reconciliation." In *Disciplining Music: Musicology and Its Canons*, edited by Katherine Bergeron and Philip V. Bohlman, 156–181. Chicago: University of Chicago Press.

Cook, Nicholas. 1987. "Structure and Performance Timing in Bach's C Major Prelude (WTC I): An Empirical Study." *Music Analysis* 6: 257–272.

Cook, Nicholas. 1999. "Analyzing Performance and Performing Analysis." In *Rethinking Music*, edited by Nicholas Cook and Mark Everist, 239–261. Oxford: Oxford University Press.

Cook, Nicholas. 2009. "Squaring the Circle: Phrase Arching in Recordings of Chopin's Mazurkas." *Musica Humana* 1: 5–28.

Cross, Edward W. 2014. "Musical Timing in the Adagio from Brahms's Violin Concerto, op. 77: An Empirical Study of Rubato in Recorded Performances Dating from 1927–1973." PhD diss., Newcastle University.

Desain, Peter, and Henkjan Honing. 1993. "Tempo Curves Considered Harmful." *Contemporary Music Review* 7: 123–138.

Desain, Peter, and Henkjan Honing. 1994. "Does Expressive Timing in Music Performance Scale Proportionally with Tempo?" *Psychological Research* 56: 285–292.

Dodson, Alan. 2008. "Performance, Grouping and Schenkerian Alternative Readings in Some Passages from Beethoven's 'Lebewohl' Sonata." *Music Analysis* 27: 107–134.

Dodson, Alan. 2009. "Metrical Dissonance and Directed Motion in Paderewski's Recordings of Chopin's Mazurkas." *Journal of Music Theory* 53: 57–94.

Dodson, Alan. 2011. "Expressive Timing in Expanded Phrases: An Empirical Study of Recordings of Three Chopin Preludes." *Music Performance Research* 4: 2–29.

Doffman, Mark. 2009. "Making it Groove! Entrainment, Participation, and Discrepancy in the 'Conversation' of a Jazz Trio." *Language and History* 52: 130–147.

Doğantan-Dack, Mine. 2002. *Mathis Lussy: A Pioneer in Studies of Expressive Performance*. Pietelen, Switzerland: Peter Lang.

Dowling, W. Jay, Barbara Tillmann, and Dan Ayers. 2001. "Memory and the Experience of Hearing Music." *Music Perception* 19: 249–276.

Duckworth, Kendrick, Glen Boothe, Lalah Hathaway, Rahsaan Patterson, Rex Rideout, and Taz Arnold. 2015. "Momma." On *To Pimp a Butterfly* (compact disc), Interscope Records AFTMB002295802CD.

Fink, Robert. 1999. "Going Flat: Post-Hierarchical Music Theory and the Musical Surface." In *Rethinking Music*, edited by Nicholas Cook and Mark Everist, 102–137. New York: Oxford University Press.

Gabrielsson, Alf. 1987. "Once Again: The Theme from Mozart's Piano Sonata in A Major (K. 331)." *Action and Perception in Rhythm and Music* 55: 81–103.

Gabrielsson, Alf, and Ian Bengtsson. 1983. "Performance of Musical Rhythm in 3/4 and 6/8 Meter." *Scandinavian Journal of Psychology* 24: 193–213.

Goodchild, Meghan, Bruno Gingras, and Stephen McAdams. 2016. "Analysis, Performance, and Tension Perception of an Unmeasured Prelude for Harpsichord." *Music Perception* 34: 1–20.

Gordon, John W. 1987. "The Perceptual Attack Time of Musical Tones." *Journal of the Acoustical Society of America* 82: 88–105.

Grachten, Maarten, Werner Goebl, Sebastian Flossmann, and Gerhard Widmer. 2009. "Phase-Plane Representation and Visualization of Gestural Structure in Expressive Timing." *Journal of New Music Research* 38: 183–195.

Grindlay, Graham, and David Helmbold. 2006. "Modeling, Analyzing, and Synthesizing Expressive Piano Performance with Graphical Models." *Machine Learning* 65: 361–387.

Hatten, Robert. 1994. *Musical Meaning in Beethoven.* Bloomington: Indiana University Press.

Henrich, Joseph, Steven Heine, and Ara Norenzayan. 2010. "The Weirdest People in the World?" *Behavioral and Brain Sciences* 33, no. 2–3: 61–83.

Hepokoski, James, and Warren Darcy. 2006. *Elements of Sonata Theory: Norms, Types, and Deformations in the Late-Eighteenth-Century Sonata.* New York: Oxford University Press.

Hintze, Jerry, and Ray Nelson. 1998. "Violin Plots: A Box Plot-Density Trace Synergism." *The American Statistician* 52: 181–184.

Kawabata, Maiko. 2015. "Playing the 'Unplayable': Schoenberg, Heifetz, and the Violin Concerto, Op. 36." *Journal of Musicological Research* 34: 31–50.

Keefe, Simon P. 1999. "Dramatic Dialogue in Mozart's Viennese Piano Concertos: A Study of Competition and Cooperation in Three First Movements." *The Musical Quarterly* 83: 169–204.

Kwong, James. 2008. Performance of Chopin, Op. 10, no. 3. http://www.youtube.com/watch?v=i4RcWdfcoO4.

Lander, Jared. 2014. *R for Everyone: Advanced Analytics and Graphics.* Upper Saddle River, NJ: Pearson Education.

Lerdahl, Fred, and Ray Jackendoff. 1983. *A Generative Theory of Tonal Music.* Cambridge. MA: MIT Press.

Lerdahl, Fred. 2001. *Tonal Pitch Space.* New York: Oxford University Press.

London, Justin. 2012. *Hearing in Time.* 2nd ed. New York: Oxford University Press.

Lussy, Mathis. 1892. *Traité de l'expression musicale.* Paris: Libraire Fischbacher.

Lussy, Mathis. 1900. *Musical Expression, Accents, Nuances, and Tempo, in Vocal and Instrumental Music.* 4th ed. Translated by M. E. von Glehn. London: Novello and Company.

Manns, James. 2007. "The Concept of Unity in Music." In *What Kind of Theory Is Music Theory? Epistemological Exercises in Music Theory and Analysis,* edited by Per Broman and Nora Engebretsen, 107–131. Stockholm: Acta Universitatis Stockhomiensis.

Martingo, Ângelo. 2007. "Making Sense out of Taste: A Study on Listeners' Preferences of Performed Tonal Music." International Symposium on Performance Science, 245–250. Porto, Portugal.

McClary, Susan. 1986. "A Musical Dialectic from the Enlightenment: Mozart's 'Piano Concerto in G Major, K. 453, Movement 2.'" *Cultural Critique* 4: 129–169.

McGuiness, Andrew. 2006. "Groove Microtiming Deviations as Phase Shifts." In *Proceedings of the 9th International Conference on Music Perception & Cognition (ICMPC9)*, University of Bologna, Italy.

Michaelsen, Garrett. 2013. "Analyzing Musical Interaction in Jazz Improvisations of the 1960s." PhD diss., Indiana University.

Ohriner, Mitchell. 2012. "Grouping Hierarchy and Trajectories of Pacing in Performances of Chopin's Mazurkas." *Music Theory Online* 18, no. 1. http://mtosmt.org/issues/mto.12.18.1/mto.12.18.1.ohriner.php.

Paderewski, Ignacy Jan. 1994. *Ignacy Jan Paderewski: Great Pianists of the Twentieth Century*. Germany: Philips Classics 456919.

Penel, Amandine, and Carolyn Drake. 1998. "Sources of Timing Variations in Music Performance: A Psychological Segmentation Model." *Psychological Research* 61: 12–32.

Pike, Kenneth Lee. 1945. *The Intonation of American English*. Ann Arbor: University of Michigan Press.

Ratner, Leonard. 1980. *Classic Music: Expression, Form, and Style*. New York: Schirmer Books.

Repp, Bruno H. 1990. "Patterns of Expressive Timing in Performances of a Beethoven Minuet by Nineteen Famous Pianists." *The Journal of the Acoustical Society of America* 88: 622–641.

Repp, Bruno H. 1992a. "A Constraint on the Expressive Timing of a Melodic Gesture: Evidence from Performance and Aesthetic Judgment." *Music Perception* 10: 221–241.

Repp, Bruno H. 1992b. "Diversity and Commonality in Music Performance: An Analysis of Timing Microstructure in Schumann's 'Träumerei.'" *The Journal of the Acoustical Society of America* 92: 2546–2568.

Repp, Bruno H. 1994. "Relational Invariance of Expressive Microstructure across Global Tempo Changes in Music Performance: An Exploratory Study." *Psychological Research* 56: 269–284.

Repp, Bruno H. 1995. "Expressive Timing in Schumann's 'Träumerei': An Analysis of Performances by Graduate Student Pianists." *Journal of the Acoustical Society of America* 98: 2413–2427.

Repp, Bruno H. 1996. "The Dynamics of Expressive Piano Performance: Schumann's 'Träumerei' Revisited." *The Journal of the Acoustical Society of America* 100: 641–650.

Repp, Bruno H. 1998a. "The Detectability of Local Deviations from a Typical Expressive Timing Pattern." *Music Perception* 15, no. 3: 265–289.

Repp, Bruno H. 1998b. "A Microcosm of Musical Expression: I. Quantitative Analysis of Pianists' Timing in the Initial Measures of Chopin's Etude in E Major." *Journal of the Acoustical Society of America* 104: 1085–1100.

Rink, John, Neta Spiro, and Nicolas Gold. 2011. "Analysis of Performance." In *New Perspectives on Music and Gesture*, edited by Anthony Gritten and Elaine King, 267–292. New York: Routledge.

Rothstein, William. 1989. *Phrase Rhythm in Tonal Music*. New York: Schirmer Books.

Sapp, Craig Stuart. 2007. "Comparative Analysis of Multiple Musical Performances." In *Proceedings of ISMIR*, 497–500. Vienna, Austria.

Sapp, Craig Stuart. 2008. "Hybrid Numeric/Rank Similarity Metrics for Musical Performance Analysis." In *Proceedings of ISMIR*, 501–506. Philadelphia.

Sapp, Craig Stuart. 2011. "Computational Methods for the Analysis of Musical Structure." PhD diss., Stanford University.

Seashore, Carl E., ed. 1936. *Objective Analysis of Musical Performance*. vol. 4. Iowa City: University of Iowa Press.

Seashore, Carl E. 1938. *Psychology of Music*. New York: McGraw-Hill.

Senn, Olivier, Lorenz Kilchenmann, and Marc-Antoine Camp. 2009. "Expressive Timing: Martha Argerich Plays Chopin's Prelude, Op. 28, no. 4 in E minor." In *Proceedings of the 2009 International Symposium on Performance Science*, edited by Aaron Williamon, Sharman Pretty, and Ralph Buck, 107–112. Utrecht, The Netherlands: European Association of Conservatories.

Sloboda, John. 1983. "The Communication of Musical Metre in Piano Performance." *Quarterly Journal of Experimental Psychology* 35: 377–396.

Sloboda, John, and Andreas Lehmann. 2001. "Tracking Performance Correlates of Changes in Perceived Intensity of Emotion During Different Interpretations of a Chopin Piano Prelude." *Music Perception* 19: 87–120.

Szeryng, Henryk, Bernard Haitink, and the Amersterdam Concertgebouw Orchestra. 1974. Johannes Brahms: Violinkonzert D-dur Op. 77. Philips 6500530.

Tillmann, Barbara, W. Jay Dowling, Philip Lalitte, Paul Molin, Katrin Schulze, Bénédicte Poulin-Charronnat, Daniele Schoen, and Emmanuel Bigand. 2013. "Influence of Expressive Versus Mechanical Performance on Short-term Memory for Musical Excerpts." *Music Perception* 30: 419–425.

Todd, Neil P. McAngus. 1985. "A Model of Expressive Timing in Tonal Music." *Music Perception* 3, no. 2: 33–57.

Todd, Neil P. McAngus. 1989. "A Computational Model of Rubato." *Contemporary Music Review* 3: 69–88.

Todd, Neil P. McAngus. 1992. "The Dynamics of Dynamics: A Model of Musical Expression." *The Journal of the Acoustical Society of America* 91: 3540–3550.

West Marvin, Elizabeth. 1991. "Perception of Rhythm in Post-Tonal Music: Rhythmic Contours in the Music of Edgard Varèse." *Music Theory Spectrum* 13: 61–78.

Wickham, Hadley. 2009. *ggplot2: Elegant Graphics for Data Analysis*. New York: Springer-Verlag.

Wickham, Hadley. 2015. *Advanced R*. Boca Raton, FL: CRC Press.

Windsor, W. Luke, Peter Desain, Amandine Penel, and Michiel Borkent. 2006. "A Structurally Guided Method for the Decomposition of Expression in Music Performance." *The Journal of the Acoustical Society of America* 119: 1182–1193.

Wright, Matthew James. 2008. "The Shape of an Instant: Measuring and Modeling Perceptual Attack Time with Probability Density Functions." PhD diss., Stanford University.

PART III

HORIZONTALS AND VERTICALS

CHAPTER 15

···

MELODY

···

DAVID TRIPPETT

It is said, melody is merely a succession of sounds. No doubt. And drawing is only an arrangement of colors. An orator uses ink to write out his compositions: does this mean ink is a very eloquent liquid?

(Jean-Jacques Rousseau [1781]; Rousseau and Herder 1986, 53)

Midas's Judgment

···

In ancient myths of music, melody often takes second place to harmony. The story of Pan's duel with Apollo, the god of music, established this hierarchy through unequal participants, but also planted a seed of doubt through a disagreement over the duel's outcome. After speaking poorly of Apollo's gift, Pan was summoned to a competition between his monophonic pipes and Apollo's multi-stringed lyre. This was to be judged by the old mountain god, Timolus. While Pan's wild melody coaxed and charmed the animals, Apollo's "skillful thumb" brought forth such "sweetness" from his strings that the sound won over all listeners but one (Ovid 2010, 294). King Midas defiantly disagreed with Timolus's judgment, upon which—so the tale goes—Apollo promptly transformed Midas's ears into those of an ass. Figure 15.1 shows Jean Matheus's seventeenth-century engraving, which captures the scene, depicting hands raised, symbolically, in protest and power. While the tale scarcely conceals an official criticism of poetic form in which the bucolic is outranked by the lyric, it also offers license for a dissenting view of melody. For Midas's pleasure in Pan's melody, so shamefully written into his visage, establishes a precedent for defying the hierarchy of a cosmic harmony, for prioritizing melody as an autonomous form.

As a fundamental concept in Western musical thought, melody connotes the form and affective power of successive (typically, single-pitch) sounds in motion, perceived as an aesthetic unity. Within the common practice period, its power of expressive shaping forms the focal point for listeners attuned to the top of a musical texture, that which

FIGURE 15.1 Jean Matheus (1619, 308), engraving "Jugement de Midas."

Warburg Institute.

seizes our attention, and whose character-defining contours most readily hook our sympathies and understanding. As an unfolding linear structure, it is also the compositional parameter that most closely mirrors our experience of finite duration, with all the allusive value this has for the nature of transient experience, sonic decay, expiring breath, and the impermanence of living matter.[1] Given this lofty profile, it is perhaps unsurprising that within the Humanities, melody has enjoyed great currency as a literary metaphor and emblem of attainment. Within music-theoretical writing more specifically, however, the nature and hierarchy of its constitutive, organizing materials remains contested, and has provoked vigorous, occasionally legally consequential, argument. Needless to say, its status as such is high within Western aesthetics.

While melodic material has existed for millennia (and a rich melodic tradition in historical "folk" and vernacular musics must be presumed largely undocumented), this flowering of concept only occurred over the last three centuries, and writing since that time—both specialist and non-specialist—is replete with paeans to melody as the centerpiece of musical experience. The first major Western treatise devoted to melody,

Johann Mattheson's *Kern melodischer Wissenschaft*, set the tone: "the art of composing a good melody encompasses what is most essential in the whole of music" (1737, 29). The sentiment would be echoed in composition treatises later in the century, where J. G. Sulzer declared melody "the most essential element of a piece of music" (1779, 3:219), and Michel Chabanon identifies it more particularly as music's "main driver and most effective agent, that which gives [music] form, movement and life" (1785, 29). By the *Gefühlsästhetik* of the early nineteenth century, Anton Reicha could posit melody as nothing less than "the language of feeling" itself (2000, 13), while E. T. A. Hoffmann, poeticizing melody's affective power, vaunted it as "the primary and most exquisite thing in music, that which grasps human sensibility with wonderful magical power" (1983, 1:452). Within this genealogy of arch-advocates, it fell to Richard Wagner to epitomize a totalizing position whereby the concept becomes synonymous with music's capacity to express. "Music's only form is melody," he argued in *Oper und Drama* (1851), "it is not even conceivable without melody" (Wagner 1911–1914, 7:125).[2] Even at this stage, Wagner's sentiment—like Mattheson's in 1737—set a trend that saw the magnitude of the concept expand further: writing in 1864, the Leipzig Thomaskantor Moritz Hauptmann lauded melody as "the alpha and omega of music," (1892, 2:249) while in 1899, pedagogue Salomon Jadassohn iterated the point to students using the language of the classroom: "To composition there belong three elements: first melody, then again melody, and now finally, for the third time, melody" (cited in Busoni 1956, 48).[3]

There is a certainty about the discursive object in the above accounts. That is to say, each writer is confident in their reference. Ostensibly, then, melody ought to be relatively unambiguous: you know one when you hear one (adapting Augustine's verdict on the concept of "time," or Supreme Court Justice Potter Stewart on "obscenity").[4] To look at the English Hymnal of 1906, or the corpus of Bellinian operas, one would be forgiven for thinking such narrow bands of repertoire would be one way to begin substantiating such a case. The reassurance of common assumption is not borne out in the history of theoretical writing on melody, however. Johann David Heinichen touched on this point in his treatise on figured bass in 1711 when he protested that: "[a] musician is certainly unable to say what melody may be. There is a great difference, though, between entirely grasping something and thoroughly describing it," adding: "[a] confused picture will not do when teaching" (cited in Mattheson 1737, 34n). Heinichen's statement goes to the heart of the matter I want to address: melody has an identity problem.

Perhaps this "confused picture" is just what we receive from that chestnut of theory pedagogy, Prelude no. 1 in C major from J. S. Bach's WTC book 1. Here, the physically comfortable arpeggiation of an underlying bass progression forms, for Joel Lester, the archetypal "pattern-prelude" in which the overall coherence depends not on melodic material, but on "underlying harmonies and [contrapuntal] voice leading" (1999, 27). In such a reading, the improvisational idiom and regular sixteenths conspire to create the very definition of harmonic rhythm, a model accompaniment, and it is indicative that Charles Gounod, composing in an age closer to Hoffmann than Mattheson, was only the first who saw fit to improvise a melody above it, as though one were somehow lacking.[5]

For Ernst Kurth in 1917, Bach's monophonic lines—even in pieces that "appear to consist only in harmonic outlines"—have the goal of "evoking the impression of polyphony" by alluding to accessory voices within the single line (Kurth 1991, 76–77). While such "profoundly concealed subtleties" resist systematic explication, they typically become audible through apex or accented pitches, implied melodic dissonances, and the counterpointing of melodic continuities in distinct registers, often through sequential passagework. Such latent polyphony—later dubbed melodic fission[6]—"suggests an aural comprehension and supplementation of musical procedures," Kurth concludes (1991, 76). Like the famed optical illusions in which a single picture appears as a rabbit or a duck, an old or a young woman, depending on how you look at it, Bach's Prelude might be seen as temporally unfolding *chords* (undoubtedly its chief identity) or as a monophonic *melody* based on a principle of sustained arpeggiation. In light of Gounod's melodic ghosting (wherein no sixteenths are sustained), the sounding effect somehow meets in the middle, and the categorical distinction—melody or chord—becomes punctilious.

As Kurth argues, we may silently hear unwritten melodic lines such as Gounod's, prompted by underlying voice-leading, as a natural consequence of active listening, just as we may supply harmonic coherence for melodies deemed insufficiently harmonized (as Schumann did for Bach's works for solo violin and cello). Such instances of soliciting completion by the auditor arguably emerge from tension between abstract structure and sensuous realization, and merely constitute cases of individuals "recording as composers what they had experienced as unusually active listeners," as Edward T. Cone once suggested (2009, 33).

This is literally the case in an episode from Schumann's *Humoreske* (1839), in which a third stave inserted between the pianist's two hands contains a melodic line that is neither to be played nor specifically imagined during performance. It is embodied in the outer parts "as a kind of after-resonance," observes Charles Rosen. "It has its being within the mind and its existence only through its echo" (Rosen 1999, 8–9). Is Bach's melody missing in quite the manner of Schumann's virtual melody? It is telling that commentators seem unable to decide. "The [Prelude's] melody is not always inscribed recognizably for the eye," Jadassohn chides in 1899, "but the ear feels it. We hear the melody in the peaks of the arpeggiated chords. . . . Every understanding performer would know here to subordinate the accompanying harmony" (1899, 1–2).[7] Figure 15.2 shows the close correlation between Gounod's applied melody and Jadassohn's voice-leading wherein square boxes indicate shared pitches. Given the correlation, this seemingly amounts to the same thing, where Gounod is merely elaborating as a descant the upper line Jadassohn identified, thereby externalizing what Kurth called Bach's curvilinear intensifications [*Kurvensteigerungen*]. Phenomenologically speaking, then, the "melody" is present in the Prelude's structure, but it seemingly relies on external agents for realization, whether listeners or performer.

The same argument might be made for the Largo of Chopin's Sonata op. 58 (1844), given in Figure 15.3. Here—unlike the tradition of sequential harmonic arpeggiation in sonata developments (such as the first movements of Beethoven's op. 58; op. 2, no. 3; and

FIGURE 15.2 J. S. Bach's Prelude No. 1 in C major, from the *Well-Tempered Clavier* (Book 1), mm. 1–12, overlaid with Salomon Jadassohn's illustration of Bach's underlying melody of peak pitches (1899), and with Charles Gounod's descant "Méditation" (1853). Square brackets highlight common pitches in the two accessory melodies.

FIGURE 15.3 Chopin, Piano Sonata no. 3, op. 58, iii (Largo), mm. 29–36.

so on)—a twice-recurring chordal arpeggiation is pregnant with melodic impetus, yet no line emerges to dominate attention. Whereas Schumann supplied an absent melody, Chopin resolutely delineates a tonic arpeggio, as though relishing the absence of melodic focus between the movement's more traditionally melodic outer sections: the RH eighth notes are weighted with calculated metrical accents to project the triad, and the peak pitches gently elaborate an E-major arpeggio (B4–B4–B4–C♯5–B4–G♯4–G♯4–E4–E4–D♯4–C♯4–B3–B3–A3–G♯3) in a texture whose role seemingly is to project E major resonance against momentary inflections.

The above comparison of repertoire in which melody may be actual, implied, or virtual begins to substantiate Heinichen's belief that while musicians cannot say what melody is, they grasp it. To this, I would add a continuation: that they seldom agree on it. It is partly this condition of personal ownership that has undermined attempts to theorize melody beyond narrowly confined bands of repertoire. As successive pedagogical treatises acknowledged, melody turns out to be something of a slippery conceptual problem, forever flitting between definitions and local schemes of taste and identity. By the mid-nineteenth century, the lack of consensus was itself an old story: "Let's leave aside for once the misused, even equivocal expression 'Melody,'" the critic Ludwig Bischoff demurs. "Melody or no melody: we don't want to argue about that" (1858, 300).[8] By the early twentieth century, art historian Oscar Bie simply admitted defeat, confessing that "every definition falsifies" (1916, 402). A durable, strict definition has indeed proven elusive, creating something of a moving target for writers and composers who sought to engage the concept for the purposes of recording or imparting musical knowledge. Even steeled with all the armament of tonal and post-tonal theory, the problem remained intractable well into the twentieth century, it seems. And it is indicative that even after detailed illustration of Mozart's G-minor symphony for CBS in 1962, Leonard Bernstein, asking what melody is, concluded evasively that "melody is exactly what a great composer wants it to be."[9]

DEFINITIONS

One reason for this enduring ambiguity is that the simplest definition of "melody" advanced over the last three centuries—a linear succession of discrete pitches in time—has proven both too broad and too narrow: it could be a definition of music itself, but neglects telling details of style, shape, and patterning, not to mention expression and—since the mid-eighteenth century—putative relations to aesthetics. In other words, all the parameters that concern the phenomenological experience of sounds connected successively in time.

Another reason is that theories of melody inherently refer back to the judgment of a listening subject. This element of particularism, with its focus on unquantifiable factors of individual experience, renders the topic more resistant than most traditional epistemological schemes such as Dahlhaus's three paradigms for the history of music theory, or the broader schema of Foucauldian épistèmes (Dahlhaus 1989, 1:6–9). Approaches to "melody," conceived as an elusive, forever ill-defined concept, thus rely on the elective tracing of common discursive threads, and on historical comparison of nascent methods and their attendant commentaries. In this, though, the concept remains ensnared within a tension Nicholas Cook identifies between theory and epistemic self-awareness: "when theorists are confident of the epistemological status of their work they will say nothing about it, whereas when they *do* talk about it we can deduce they are not quite sure about what they are saying" (2013, 78). The evidence indicates that "melody" remains in permanent transition from the first category to the second, which helps explain why each theorist to write on the subject professed to being the first who dared to do so. Earlier attempts, if known, belonged to a moribund past. "The lack of continuity provokes astonishment when one considers the development of the theory of counterpoint and of harmony," Dahlhaus comments, qualifying that the teaching of harmony "disappoints" in its scope and limitation; that is, its "almost unbroken continuity" is measured unequally to that of melody.[10]

HISTORICAL CHANGES

A brief overview of the historical emergence of the concept of melody as a musical line offers some perspective on the matter. The earliest Western writings on the concept "melos," from Cleonides's account of Aristoxenus to Aristotle and Aristides Quintilianus, differ in their discussion of four species of relative motion between sounds (sequence, succession, repetition, prolongation), but broadly insert the patterning of such motion within a strict musical typology that governs the properties of "melic" movement (ode, dirge, hymn, paean, dithyramb). Here, Plato's definition has come to hold sway: "melos" referred to nothing less than music conceived as a performing art.[11] It centers on the conjoined entity of word, harmony, and tempo/dance/movement that properly characterizes what Aristides Quintilianus calls "perfect melos." In other words, music wherein:

> it is necessary that melody, rhythm, and diction be considered so that the perfection of the song may be produced: in the case of melody, *simply a certain sound*; in case of rhythm, the motion of sound; and in the case of diction, the meter. The things contingent to perfect melos are motion—both of sounds and body—and also chronoi and the rhythms based on these.
>
> (Mathiesen 1999, 25, emphasis added)[12]

Here, melos appears to constitute nothing less than organized sound ("a certain sound"), and, as such, offers a totalizing view of music's organizing matter between the teachings of Aristotle and Aristides Quintilianus (ca. 480 BCE and 300 CE).[13] Writing a hundred years thereafter, St. Augustine arguably engages the issue when he asks: "who can mentally perceive so subtle a thing as to be able to distinguish without great labor how sound may be prior to melody?" He answers: "melody is formed sound ... [and] matter is prior to what is made out of it ... When it is sung, its sound is heard, for there is not first a formless sound that is afterwards formed into a melody" (St. Augustine 1960, 298–299). This critique of Genesis ("the earth was without form and void," Gen. 1:2) sees the matter of sounding as prior in origin to the form of singing, but prior neither in time nor in choice; as such, it adds a philosophical ground for later debates over the identity of melody and its origin as a form.

Despite the vast body of medieval chant that bears witness to the praxis of melodic singing,[14] melody was only defined as a linear pitch structure in the late sixteenth century, amid the prestige and quantitative predominance of sacred polyphony within European cultural centers. In order to differentiate a single voice of successive pitches from a polyphonic texture, Friedrich Beurhusius argued in his *Erotematum musicae* of 1573 that "melodia"—melody's Latin cognate—had two meanings: "cantus conjunctus" was vocal music whose melody flows through several connected hexachords within a system of notation (as when using multiple vocal ranges), and "cantus simplex" was vocal music whose melody moves within the hexachordal range of a single voice.[15]

From this schism, the nascent definition of melody begins to solidify around 1599 with Joachim Burmeister, who posits melodia, still a succession of notes in a single voice, as an integral component of the syntactical structure of *musica poetica*:

> A melody is the bringing about of sounds which follow one another by means of the raising and lowering of successive intervals, constituting a species of harmony, [as

in] a single voice which when sung touches the sense in its own way, so that in a not obviously unmusical person the effects it creates are felt.

(Burmeister 1599, Dd 4 f)[16]

Later, the ordered sequence of pitches is cleanly contradistinguished from harmony, to which melody remains bound during polyphony:

> Melody and harmony are different, in that the latter is a euphony bound together from the melodies of a plurality of voices into a harmony; the former is a product of just one voice.

(Burmeister 1599, C4)[17]

As Markus Bandur has argued, the principle of melodic monophony, perceived as a determinate musical shape, begins to emerge securely by the early seventeenth century (2006, 18–19). In such a conception, "melody" achieved a degree of autonomy as a formal structure, requiring neither text nor harmonic accompaniment. For Christian Bernhard, in his 1660 treatise *Tractatus compositionis augmentatus*: "it can also happen that *notes* by themselves can make a good melody, [but] sound ugly with underlaid text" (Bernhard 1963, 40).[18] During these decades of early codification, the terms tune, song, notes, *Lied, Weise, Thon*, and *Stimme* are used freely and interchangeably in Latin dictionaries to define "Cantus" and "Melodia" in the vernacular.[19] It is indicative of the consequential effect this had on contemporary understanding that Charles Butler could reverse the languages in a discussion of four-part writing that encapsulates the emergent historical category in 1636: "But heere one of dhe upper Partes is necessarily to have a special Melodi aboov the rest: which is called dhe *Cantus* or Tune: such as may delight a Musical ear, dhowgh [though] it bee sung along by it self" (1636, 45). Numerous refinements to this basic position are traceable in French, German and British writings,[20] but it would take a century before the category, in a corresponding definition of melody by J. A. Scheibe, could be proposed as fully independent of harmonic accompaniment: "a natural connectedness of successive simple tones that sound good *with and without harmony*" (1961, 13, emphasis added).[21]

It was at precisely this time, around 1730, that "melody" attains perhaps its most familiar definition as a closed phenomenon, that of a connecting, progressing succession of tones, pitches, sounds, or intervals that ensound an organic, actively unfolding form: "the Progression of a Sound proceeding from one Note to another successively in a single Part," as John Christopher Pepusch put it in his 1737 *Treatise on Harmony* (Pepusch 1976, 3). Arias from canonical operas by Handel, Hasse, and Graun, to name but three contemporaries, would seem to offer ready exemplification of this conception of self-sufficient melody: texted vocal lines in intimate dialogue with, but timbrally and conceptually distinct from the orchestral accompaniment. Yet if we look to the keyboard music of the time, specifically the rich tradition of realizing thorough bass extempore, this image of a self-sufficient "melody" becomes less clear. And this juncture has a claim to be an origin of the identity problem mentioned above.

In his 1711 treatise, Heinichen treats melody as a special form of embellishment: a horizontal outgrowth or decoration of harmonic logic. As Figure 15.4 shows, he offers

(a)

(b)

FIGURE 15.4 (a) J. D. Heinichen's illustration of a weak-sounding, simple accompaniment to be improved by avoiding repetition of the top notes in the right hand. (b) J. D. Heinichen's illustration of an improvement by dividing the accompaniment into two parts per hand.

students a choice on how to realize a simple harmonic accompaniment (in Figure 15.4(a)): (1) divide a rhythmicized accompaniment between the hands as seen in Figure 15.4(b); or (2) take the entire accompanimental harmony in the left hand, leaving the right hand "to invent a particular song or melody on the bass as good as our imagination, taste, and talent will allow," as seen in Figure 15.4(c).[22] Here, Heinichen appears to invest the concept of melody with a degree of autonomy, but locates melodic invention firmly within the grid of a predefined harmonic movement.

We need only look to the Andante of J. S. Bach's Italian Concerto (1735)—a D-minor cantilena (ABA), whose florid, arioso style, above uninterrupted accompanimental eighth notes, decorates two cadences (in VI and I)—to see that without a metrical container or the finitude of a singer's breath, the endless spinning of melodic material relies on a harmonic syntax of prolongation rather than what we might call melodic form, derived

(c)

FIGURE 15.4 *continued.* (c) J. D. Heinichen's illustration of an improvement by taking the full accompaniment in the left hand, and inventing a melody in the right hand (Buelow 1966, 170–173).

from rhythmic periods or phrasal units. For prominent bassists such as Heinichen and Gasparini, such melodies were only warranted during ritornello passages or in solo performance, and C. P. E. Bach warns against obfuscating textures around them.[23] Despite the manifest existence of an operatic repertoire and folksong tradition, then, Scheibe's sense of "successive simple sounds that sound good *with and without harmony*" would seem misleading to the extent the melodic line remains subservient to harmonic function within the epistemology of thorough bass. Historiographically, the standard-bearer for this argument is of course Rameau, who—leaning on the dominant acoustic science of his age—makes this argument most clearly in the opening sentences of his 1722 *Traité*:

> Music is the science of sounds . . . [and] is generally divided into harmony and melody, but we shall show in the following that the latter is merely a part of the former and that a knowledge of harmony is sufficient for a complete understanding of all the properties of music.
>
> (Rameau 1971, 3)

The corollary of this position is made explicit when he proceeds to specify how a composer selects pitches to compose a melody: "once we know the chords each bass note should bear, we may choose any of the sounds in each chord so as to form a melody to our liking" (Rameau 1971, 321).[24]

Melody only exists by implication, then, as a liminal property. If it is merely a halo-effect of harmony, the suspicion that vocal melody could not function "without harmony" raises the question as to whether melody, as a manifest form, ever really existed. Looking back from the mid-nineteenth century, Helmholtz's quasi-ethnographic argument that "finely cultivated music existed for thousands of years without harmony, and still exists today among non-Europeans," echoed A. B. Marx in asserting the historical primacy of melody (Helmholtz 1954, vii; Marx 1841, 16). But this relies on an appreciation of overtones, as we shall see. And with continuing uncertainty about what melody "is," the argument buckles under the weight of its colonialist context.

VOICE: THE CHILDREN OF ROUSSEAU

One of the most effective opponents of the bassists' view, Jean-Jacques Rousseau, is also the figure chiefly responsible for the longevity of melody as a popular concept. For his statements, in both the *Lettre sur la musique française* (1753) and the *Essai sur l'origine des langues* (1781), were widely read—in part because of the journalistic spats to which they gave rise—and bring together the cardinal discourses that would characterize later traumas over melodic theory: nationalism; feeling/expression; nature. It would seem no coincidence that melody emerges secure in an identity contradistinguished from harmony at this juncture; the moment its glassy fragility—as a decorative extension of harmony—is assertively and publicly repudiated.

Unlike thoroughbassists concerned with harmony as a science of applied mathematics, Rousseau begins from the premise that all melody is fundamentally concerned with voice. His rationale is humanist rather than historical: "as soon as vocal signs strike your ear, they announce to you a being like yourself. They are, so to speak, the voice of the soul. If you hear them in the wilderness, they tell you you are not alone" (Rousseau 1986, 63–64). This bond of communication underwrites the innateness of melodic expressivity, for him, carving out the space for a vocal-melodic epistemology untouchable by reasoning based on the overtone series. This innateness of expression is arguably the basis for later claims—hermeneutic and mimetic—for quasi-semantic melodic meaning, from Arthur Schopenhauer, who proselytized about intuitive understandings of a melody "which says a great deal" as a criterion for natural selection,[25] to Reicha, for whom "there are good and bad melodies, that is, those which express something and those that do not" (2000, 3). The derivative critic Max Nordau sums up the basic position: "melody may be said to be an effort of music to say something definite" (1993, 200). Earlier writers had used the term "cantabile" to refer to both melodic shape and a manner of performance, from Zarlino (1558), who refers to "[la] perfettione della Figure cantabili" (1558, 260), to the title page of J. S. Bach's Inventions and Sinfonias (1723), which seeks "eine cantabile Art im Spielen zu erlangen" (Bach 1998, 98). Yet these establish little ground for an ontology of melody. By contrast, Rousseau, writing on a platform of historical linguistics, made the decisive claim in 1781 that melody and voice are intimately linked through the principle of imitation (in vogue among European philosophers, after J. J. Winckelmann's 1764 treatise on Classical art declared it a modern necessity):

> By imitating the inflections of the voice, melody expresses pity, cries of sorrow and joy, threats and groans. All the vocal signs of passion are within its domain. It imitates the tones of language, and the twists produced in every idiom by certain psychic acts ... [I]t has a hundred times the power of speech. This is what gives music its power of representation and song its power over sensitive hearts.
>
> (Rousseau 1986, 57)

Voice is here invested with the authority of centuries of human development; in the *Essai*'s schema, it forms an invisible bond reaching back to the earliest and most natural state of being (where the term *première mélodie* refers to the melodiousness of the very earliest languages), while also witnessing a transition from poetry to prose, figurative to conceptual forms of utterance, states of passion to those mediated by reflection. For this reason, voice, melody, and nature were forged as a crucible of human identity, no less, for the Romantic imagination. This bond also laid the ground for nineteenth-century discourses of *Sprachmelodie* and its compositional outlets, from the satellite genres of melodrama to Schoenberg's *Sprechstimme*. And we need only look to Herbert Spencer's *Origin and Function of Music* (1858) for an evolutionist revision of Rousseau's theory wherein sympathetic physiological response to vocal melodic sounds (most palpably markers of suffering: screams and cries) ensure we understand the intonation of utterances intuitively.

Returning to the Enlightenment, at a local level Rousseau famously invokes Nature in his *querelle* with Rameau to counter similarly lofty claims: that natural laws of acoustic science underpin the *corps sonore*. "Nature inspires songs, not accords," he corrects, "she speaks of melody, not harmony" (Rousseau 1986, 62). But the occasion tapped into a far deeper association with birdsong and folksong, where variegated constructions of the "natural" further complicated the establishment of a lasting theory of melody. Consider the range of historical definitions of melody linked to concepts of nature, from melody as a natural product (Roger North: "a sort of musick ... [that] seems to flow from nature" [1710]; cited in Strahle 2009, 8b), to melody as a more essential part of nature (David Mollison: "this voice of nature" [1798]; Mollison 1798, 17). From here, it is only a small step to the hierarchical division of *Poiesis* into inspiration and human toil, in which agent-less minds of composers become the vessels through which the external authority of nature is channeled. Melody was centrally implicated in the discourse on musical genius in this sense, and Berlioz is representative in declaring it simply: "a gift of nature" (1837, 407a).

At the risk of appearing practical and prosaic, such ideas were unhelpful for theorists engaged in pedagogy. They failed to engage with familiar, more useable concepts (pitch, rhythm, shape, pattern, form, and so on); they failed to identify an organizing material for melody that could be learned, in other words. They also avoided specifying a hierarchy of expressive parameters for students of melody. "Why all these authorities anyway?" asked a frustrated Flodoard Geyer, author of a quickly forgotten treatise on composition in 1862. "For every opinion, even the most absurd, there will always be at least *one* advocate!" (Geyer 1860, 322, emphasis added).[26] One zany skeptic declared A. B. Marx a charlatan for seeking, in his *Compositionslehre*, to grow periodic melodies organically from germinal motifs and scale formulae. "[S]hould [a composer] wish to invent a melody of eight bars, to fit to a long or short meter," the New York critic exhorts, "he will find, at last, that his carefully nursed [motivic] germs will forsake him in the hour of necessity, and he will be thrown back, musically poverty-stricken, upon his barren Marx again. I speak from experience" (Braun 1857, 567). Ensconced in Berlin, Marx did not reply.

As noted above, Rousseau had identified vocal utterance (its imitation and implied heritage) as the organizing material of melodic expression. While later philologists revised his arguments about language, it may be no coincidence that, after the age of the castrato, a celebrated tradition of Italian melodists—Bellini, Donizetti, Leoncavallo, Verdi, Puccini—rested on writing for voice, where new perceptions of operatic realism drew opera closer to the manner of a spoken play, with raw cries and sotto voce, differentiated vocal characters often dovetailing melodic lines in ensemble, cutting in and out of the drama as needed. Bellini's famous conviction for opera links supple poetic forms with an inviolable amalgam of voice and melody in no uncertain terms:

> Carve into your head in adamantine letters: *Opera must make people weep, feel horrified, die through singing.* It's wrong to want to write all the numbers in the same way, but they must all be somehow shaped so as to make the music intelligible through their clarity of expression, at once concise and striking.
>
> (Rosselli 1996, 43)

Perhaps the most prominent melodic theorist of the nineteenth century to cultivate the ground Rousseau (among others) established was German. As I have written elsewhere, Wagner's mid-century theory of melody posited language rather than music-theoretical concepts as its primary material (Trippett 2013, 280–329). Moving beyond the principle of imitation, he drew on emergent philological studies of phonology to explicate melody, qua musical tone, in terms of a vowel-enhanced sounding of poetry that connects concepts through alliterated consonants: "the redemption of the poet's endlessly conditioned thought into a deep-felt consciousness of emotion's highest freedom" (Wagner 1911, 4:142).[27] This idealist definition of melody, at first glance a casually abstract gloss, refers quite deliberately to a rationalization of the process by which modern melodists were to retrieve the communicative power of fossilized units of utterance, whose indivisibility promised—for Sanskritists—the origin of all meaning. The slippage between enunciated vowel and musical tone links the domains of speech and music at the level of sensation, for Wagner, which meant at the level of "truth" and "reality," according to his intellectual mentor Ludwig Feuerbach.

Perhaps because this theory emerged in the same text as Wagner's public evisceration of Rossini as the "murderer" of modern operatic melody, it spawned a bilious debate that saw Wagner labeled as a melodic pretender: a composer who denounced operatic melody hitherto, yet placed melody at the center of his worldview, and was himself unable to compose melody. Criticism that exceeded personal enmity often cited the central role of language as the problem, from skepticism toward *Stabreim* to suspicions of historically retrograde tendencies in opera:

> If opera is indeed to be only a succession of recitatives, without a resting point—a mere musical intoning of the dramatic dialogue, without any specific musical aim and substance ... Wagner is no reformer, but the most violent artistic reactionary, who ignores the progress made since Rameau and Lully, and in a most unpractical way and in place of the cultivated dramatic music we have had for eighty years, wants to re-establish recitative, the exclusive predominance of whose quintessence would form the worst monotony.
>
> (W. M. S. 1858, 437)[28]

While Wagner resisted what we might call linguistic determinism (the idea that a text can be set to music in only one way, according to its constitutive intonation and syntax), the fear that he was vacating established ground by replacing metrically governed, harmonically rounded arias with declamatory recitative secured his temporary role as the poster boy of *Melodielosigkeit*.

If we take a broad view of vocal melodic "composition," it becomes clear that others had made claims in the same direction. We might look to Guido d'Arezzo in the early eleventh century, who developed a formal technique for setting a text to music automatically. Each vowel was assigned a pitch, and the melody resulted from the chain of vowels in the text.[29] Or to Conrad Beissel in the early eighteenth century, who argued that every sentence has a unique pitch structure determined by master and slave words (Blakely 1967). Not to mention the twin impulses of realism and nationalism that fueled an international attraction to the language-melody axis in the nineteenth century, from a predominantly German discourse on *Sprachmelodie*, and the slightly later but no less radical concern for a unified French language—bolstered by Paul Passy's phonetic dictionary in 1897—that explains the conspicuous display of French speech distinguishing contemporary *mélodie* (Bergeron 2010), to Mussorgsky's musical ideal of "the sound of human speech in all its subtlest shadings," and Janáček's claim that "the motifs of every word in *Jenůfa* are close to life."[30]

OBJECTS OF INSTRUMENTAL MELODY

Whether or not melody relates archeologically to voice, of course, not all melodies are actually vocal. Beyond the Rousseauian argument lay the challenge to define an alternative constitutive material or organizing principle for instrumental melody. The concept of an exclusively instrumental melodic line, non-transferable to texted voices, is traceable to the mid-seventeenth century, as noted above. While it would be misleading to claim this led to a consensus around the firming opposition of such categories,[31] Schoenberg's uncontroversial observation that "instrumental melodies admit much more freedom in every respect than vocal" raises the question of how this freedom was to be governed (Schoenberg 1967, 98). It proved a deceptively simple question. Answers differ widely among theorists of the last three centuries, a sampling of which can be summarized under the following categories, conceived both separately and in combination:

- Periods/metrical rhythm (Koch; Reicha).
- Intervals/dyads (Mattheson; Marx).
- Rotation and development of figures or motives (Koch; Riepel; Daube; Reicha; Marx).
- Imitation of models (Daube; Lobe).
- Overtones (Helmholtz; Hindemith).
- Archetype- and pattern-based expectation (Meyer; Narmour).
- Pitch peaks (Koch; Eitan; Jadassohn).
- Contour, and arch shaping, of a phrase (Schoenberg; Dowling; Polansky and Bassein; Huron).

This list, appearing at once comprehensive and motley, needs to be qualified by a countervailing list of caveats—offered by some of the same theorists—about the impossibility of teaching melodic invention itself. In other words, it was possible to articulate the elements of instrumental melodic form, and their functional relationships, but not their genesis as an aesthetic impulse.

Mattheson simply declared such invention the province of Greek melopoeia, referencing the antique authority of Aristides Quintilianus without further explanation (Mattheson 1737, 33). Koch is widely echoed in referencing genius, supported by taste, as the arbiter of melodic judgment, the ability to determine: "if and how [the sections of a work's inner composition] are beautiful in themselves and varied among one another. . . . To give rules for this," he continues, pre-empting Kant's third critique, "according to which one judges the beauty and variety of the [melody], is actually not at all the object of the study of melody, in which we must only observe the outward form of the same" (Koch 1782, 1:12).[32] Philosopher Jean-Paul Richter reinforced this strategy of distancing inner impulse from outer form in 1802, arguing that each melody was its only manifest explanation, that all melodic theory could do was investigate the external structure of pre-existing models, where inner invention is glimpsed fleetingly through "genius of the instant" driven by an inscrutable "blindness and security of instinct" (Richter 1974, 25, 26).[33] Reicha (1814), believing his to be the first genuine melodic treatise, reluctantly accepted prior readings of melody as "the fruit of genius," and cautioned "let no one assume that the aim of my work is to impart a genius for melody to those who do not possess it."[34] But he also offers defiance, arguing that the objects creating meaning from "a succession of tones" are nothing but "scales, intervals, modulations, various note values, the measure, cadences (or resting points), and rhythm" (Reicha 2000, 9). Talent that engages these building blocks is more valuable then genius, he continues, for it can be cultivated through "assiduous, painstaking" endeavor; genius without talent "amounts to little and often comes to nothing" (2000, 6). In this work ethic, he is echoed by numerous later voices, G. Weber, Lobe, and Marx, among them.

Turning from the perspectives of theory to criticism, the temperature rises without student readers to appease; at an extreme, melody conceived as an outpouring of the natural genius could achieve an untouchable status, beyond the reach of theory, and aggressively at odds with reformist aims of public education. To take just one example, the Wagner antagonist Eduard Sobolewski assumed an absolute stance in 1855: "Melody cannot be taught … We may criticize it here and there, but we cannot improve it, or it is no melody" (1855, 45). Leaning on apparent ethnographic evidence, he relates the following tale as proof of concept:

> There lived in Dresden, when I was studying music there, a tall individual with … an expression of pain in his countenance, who desired to be a composer, and was only deficient in one thing—melody. The poor man applied to many persons for advice, but no one could help him. Thereupon he continued to grow more and more melancholy, and, whenever a new composer came to Dresden, he would sell the last thing he had, pay a visit to him, and beg for lessons, under the impression that the stranger would be able to teach him what others could not. … Nothing, however, availed him.
>
> (Sobelewski 1855, 19)

Why the defensive stance, we may wonder? Where, for such a critic, is the desire for a "ghost in the machine" coming from?[35]

One answer is that "melody" is unwittingly presented in criticism as a totalizing phenomenon. This is not limited to the nineteenth century. "[M]usicologists have suffered from vertigo upon realising that melodic theory seems to dissolve into a theory of music as a whole," suggests Jean-Jacques Nattiez (1979, 8). To compose one requires a composite set of skills—inseparable from each other—in harmony, counterpoint, rhythm, control of texture, and expression. Theories of individual parameters excerpted from this holistic totality inevitably fail in the eyes of those seeking to understand their response to a replete musical texture conceived as melodic form. For present purposes, I examine two such excerpted parameters: rhythm and intervals.

Rhythm

A case in point is Anton Reicha's theory of melodic rhythm that sought to balance "resting points" and differing degrees of cadence within periodic forms. While he

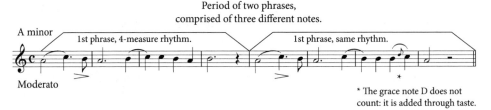

FIGURE 15.5 Anton Reicha's (2000, 171) three-note melody demonstrating a period of two phrases.

[I]n tapping a table or beating some percussive instrument, when an undifferentiated series like this:

is at all developed, it becomes something like this:

or,

FIGURE 15.6 Edmund Gurney's (2011, 132) illustration of the human propensity toward "dual balance" through the beating of an undifferentiated percussion instrument.

addresses matters such as contour, figure, patterning, and rhetoric through fourteen "principles" (explicated by analogy with oratory), a metrical bedrock remains:

> The symmetry and unity of a good melody require that the second rhythm be similar to the first, that it be of equal length, and that the resting points be placed at equal intervals. ... The period is thus the most important part of melody; rhythm and cadences exist in relation to the period; without the period, it is impossible for a good melody to be created. The composer of interesting periods is sure to overcome all difficulties in the art of melody.
>
> (Reicha 2000, 15–16)

Here, as Figure 15.5 shows, the creation of balanced melodic periods with a single figure ("principle two") demonstrates the maximum economy of pitch, resulting in "an interesting melody" of just three notes.

Writing within an evolutionary mind-set, psychologist Edmund Gurney would later identify the principle of rhythmic balance Reicha sought in melody as a human "characteristic of dual balance" that is basic to "the superior musical development of man" (Gurney 2011, 132). As Figure 15.6 shows, Gurney illustrates this propensity toward

melodies with even-numbered measures that alternate rhythmic patterns, a characteristic rooted "in the simple fact of our being made symmetrically with two sides externally alike, which results in alternate motions with each side" (Gurney 1880, 134).
To jump historical periods for a moment, the affinity between these examples and the
minor-mode James Bond theme tune, resting principally on the rhythmically bal-
anced repetition of scale degrees $\hat{1}$, $\hat{2}$, and $\hat{3}$ within a periodic structure, indicates that
responses to such challenges easily transcend Reicha's epoch.

But François-Joseph Fétis, for one, found Reicha's focus wanting. "The author has
considered his topic in only one respect," he chides, "that of rhythm and melodic phra-
seology ... a good treatise on melody is yet to be written" (Fétis 1863, 7:203). Proceeding
to call for more inclusive theories, where "tonality, modulation, harmony, and aesthetics" would be addressed, his attitude exemplifies instances wherein any attempt to
reify melody appears partial, and risks similar criticism.

Beyond Fétis's individual predilection for *tonalité*, this totalizing view of melody
emerged from traditional practices of schooling composers in thorough bass and counterpoint alone (of which Schenker's *Kontrapunkt* of 1922 appears perhaps the most extensive, late instance);[36] here, as G. W. Fink argued, all that one needed to know about
melody was to be found in principles of voice leading. Melody was not an exemplary
object as such—that is, autonomous and capable of imitation—but was an inexpli-
cable part of an overall musical fabric. A. B. Marx notably disagreed, arguing in 1841
that isolated training in separable compositional parameters—melody, form, rhythm,
harmony—was needed for a new generation of composers.[37] By 1911, a draft definition
of melody by Ferruccio Busoni (for his aborted treatise on the topic) indicates just how
multifaceted the concept had become, and hence how many aspects of composition
would be drawn into a putative melodic theory. Written as a footnote in a letter to his
wife, it is one of the most comprehensive definitions of his age:

> Footnote: Attempt at a definition of melody: a row of repeated (1) rising and falling
> (2) intervals, rhythmically (3) articulated and animated, containing latent harmony
> within it (4) and conveying an atmosphere or mood (5); that exists and can exist inde-
> pendently of words of text for expression (6), independent of accompanying voices
> as a form (7); and by whose performance the number of pitches (8) and instruments
> (9) bring about a shift in its essence.
>
> (Busoni 1930, 97)

Reflecting on the tension between melody as a special category and musical totality half
a century later, Abraham and Dahlhaus seize on Busoni's third and fourth points to declare the historical project of melodic theory a failure. "A theory of melody pedagogy,"
they asserted, "in order to avoid dry abstraction, must suspend or involve a theory of
musical rhythm—a contributing factor to melody—and a theory of harmony (in the
original, comprehensive sense of the term: that is, a theory of the ordering of tones). It
thus appears as a summary discipline, concluding the cycle of music theory" (Abraham
and Dahlhaus 1972, 11).[38] The separability of melody from a musical texture remained

an illusion for some in the late twentieth century, in other words, just as it had for Rameauians in the mid-eighteenth century.

Two cases in which theorists frame a progression from empty stave to composed melody serve to illustrate the skills gap between singular theory and summary discipline. Daube presented two "arias by Mozart" as empty staves in 1797, indicating only where melodic figures and their repetition should occur. While the fixed spatial arrangement guards against artificial complexity and enables the substitution of "many changes and figures" vis-à-vis Mozart's unspecified originals, the remaining musical apparatus are glaringly absent (Daube 1797, 24). Likewise, in 1844, in order to demonstrate the formation of melodic ideas, J. C. Lobe reverse-engineered the principal theme of Haydn's Symphony no. 104, leading from eight identical whole notes to progressive specification of melodic rhythm, its harmonic underpinning, and finally, its pitch content (Lobe 1844, 3–4). Such contrived demonstrations implied that melodic composition was not limited to a monophonic line but, by definition, carried a whole musical texture, whose linear pitch content digested a comprehensive understanding of other compositional means.

Unsurprisingly, some of the conceptual ambiguity spills over into terminology. Since the eighteenth century, the term "melody" was subsumed within syntactical categories of theme, idea, period, phrase. All imply the need for sensory unity, although inevitably, change in their usage is traceable. We have only to look at the first edition of Grove's *A Dictionary of Music and Musicians* (1880), where the aspiring English church composer, Charles Hubert Parry, sought to differentiate tune/air from melody, where the former is "constructively and definitely complete" while the latter—perhaps influenced by Wagner's conception of *unendliche Melodie*—"has a more indefinite signification, and need not be a distinct artistic whole" (Parry 1929, 371).

Intervals: Toward a Scientific Paradigm

Beyond theories of rhythm, for those who sought to study melody as an exemplary object, intervals and their character appeared to offer a means of objectifying melodic expression. Dyads sit at the intersection of harmony and melody as separable elements within a musical texture. They are the minimal diachronic units extractable from a melodic line, and can imply a determinable harmonic identity, even without vertical stacking. As such, the various historical attempts to characterize intervals for the purpose of melodic pedagogy typically assume a harmonic context.

In the early twentieth century, the psychologist and comparative musicologist Carl Stumpf widened the remit of such enquiry by asking how humans first began to create transposable, fixed intervallic steps. He suggested two complementary impulses: (1) they took pleasure in the "fusion" [*Verschmelzung*] effect of perfect consonances in our system, and valued the practical benefits of sending vocal signals further that such intervals afforded herdsmen; and (2) at the same time, humans used small incremental steps of equal distance from a given pitch to build stepwise pitch chains, which created the first transposable melodic motives. "If such songs with arbitrarily small steps were temporally prior, which is possible, indeed highly probable," Stumpf judged in 1911, "we would say: the secondary stream has a longer course but it does not hereby become the primary stream" (Stumpf 2012, 49). A cognitive-biological appreciation for perfect consonance is primal, he maintains, and while later psychologists have substantiated Stumpf's position (see Schellenberg and Trehub 1994, 1996), there was almost an organological premonition of his thesis in 1798, when one melodic theorist proposed the invention of an "octave violin," which would have had double strings tuned at different octaves to be played simultaneously in order to increase the sonority of melodic lines (a full century before this became orthodoxy for Puccini's moments of lyric climax; Mollison 1798, 81). That octave-related double courses were long common in a range of non-melodic, plucked string instruments—lutes, vihuelas, baroque guitars—and could seamlessly be transferred to melodic instruments, arguably only underscores the relevance of Stumpf's insight.

Beyond the fundamental intervals, though, there appeared little means to rationalize other melodic steps. Theoretically, the intervallic organization of Greek tetrachords informed the sound of "melos," but the concept of "melic composition" underpinning it did not exist as a topic in its own right. Cleonides defines four musical categories— genus, scale, tonos, and melos—and proceeds to explain types of modulation within each (where modulation in melic composition is a matter of switching from one ethos to another) as well as types of musical gesture in composition. But when it comes to melic composition per se, "it is disappointing that he has almost nothing to say," Thomas Mathiesen explains; it is merely "the use of everything described in the previous sections" (1999, 389). In one sense, this lacuna points to an anachronistic concept of composition—of organically piecing together disparate parts—that is not substantially part of Greek musical thought. But it also asks a question of melodic structure that has proven unanswerable—"How are melodic intervals meaningful?"—one that would dog later investigation.

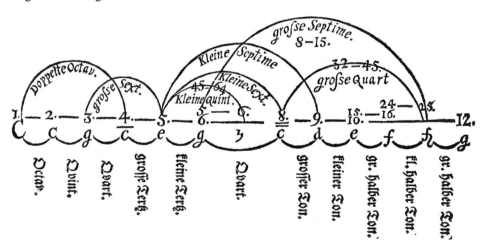

FIGURE 15.7 Johann Mattheson (1737, 11), the derivation of all melodic intervals from the natural harmonic series.

Returning to Mattheson's treatise of 1737, his first chapter, "On the content of sounding intervals" (*Vom Verhalt der klingenden Intervalle*), is devoted to outlining the array of all possible melodic intervals and their derivation, as ratios of each other, from the natural harmonic series. His synoptic illustration, reproduced as Figure 15.7, makes clear his hierarchical elevation of harmony over linear dyad, which he later confirmed in no uncertain terms: "Melody is at root nothing but original, true and simple harmony itself, wherein all intervals follow successively, simultaneously and behind one another" (Mattheson 1737, §6).[39] Within this reconciliation, however, he equivocates between relative harmonic and melodic significance within interval types, citing the augmented and diminished sixths as those that serve a more harmonic than melodic function, while the augmented fifth and fourth "are more common and useable that those above and serve melody and harmony equally" (1737, 35–36).[40] This emphasis on the harmonic derivation of melodic intervals precedes his four species of "good" melodic composition ("simple, sweet, distinct, flowing"), their "rules," and genre-based discussions of melodic type; that is, the authority of a natural harmonic series precedes any consideration of style and taste (1737, 54).

Several later theorists offered typologies of melodic intervals that went beyond appeals to nature. Attempts to order tonal intervals according to degrees of emotional character, implied movement, and so on reveal a tale of discrepancy, however, that undermines claims for a truth coherence. A. B. Marx, whose *Die Kunst des Gesangs* (1826) assigns each tonal interval an apparently inherent emotional character for listeners, was on the cusp of a sematic melodic theory even while his presentation makes clear that each interval presupposes a harmonic context and the effort of human breath.[41] For philosopher Arthur Edwards, one hundred and thirty years later, it is the perception of implied linear movement, or "degree of potential activity," rather than character that is the

Least active

Prime
Octave
Perfect fourth
Perfect fifth
Major sixth
Minor sixth
Major third
Minor third
Major second
Minor seventh
Diminished seventh
Diminished fifth
Augmented fourth
Minor second
Major seventh

Most active

FIGURE 15.8 Arthur Edwards's (1956, 151) order of intervals based on degrees of potential activity implied by the relationship between the pitches.

distinguishing feature; like Marx's characterizations, this is sensed intuitively (Edwards 1956, 151). Figure 15.8 reproduces his list.

Historically, such claims to quantify emotional expression in melody generated significant debate, and, to the extent they concerned the concept of "purely musical" experience, they could be seen as attempting to answer questions motivated philosophically rather than musically. The restless quest for a stable basis for intervallic expression was thus a tributary in search of a river; and historiographically, it can be read as a blip against the more enduring epistemological basis provided by the overtone series.

Helmholtz, writing in 1863, adjured an aesthetics devoid of reason in this sense. To contemplate lofty works of art, he argued, teaches us "to feel that even in the obscure depths of a healthy and harmoniously developed human mind . . . there slumbers a germ of order that is capable of rich intellectual cultivation" (Helmholtz 1954, 367). As is well known, this germ, for him, was scrutable through empirical approaches to the auditory system's physiology in relation to physical overtones. Unlike Rameau, who rooted his theory of harmony in what is calculable with a monochord, Helmholtz regarded *melody* as "the essential basis of music" (1954, vii). As such, he described himself as the first to draw empirically on auditory sensations to investigate the "real reason of the melodic relationship of two tones" (1954, 368).[42] His theory of melodic affinity identified the relational quality of two notes according to the perception of identical partial tones in the corresponding compound tones: "We shall consider musical tones to be related in the first degree which have two identical partial tones; and related in the second degree, when they are both related in the first degree to some third musical tone" (1954, 256). While first-degree relations accounted for perfect consonances, those of the second degree allowed for adjacent pitches in a diatonic scale to be related (his illustration was: C–D, related by the two partials each has in common with G). Pushing the aesthetic envelope, Helmholtz's affinity theory led him to conclude that the major sixth and third were the most beautiful intervals because the weakening overtone relations between their constituent pitches sit "at the limits of clearly intelligible intervals" (1954, 351).

Qualification and criticism of this brilliantly insightful, if seemingly straightforward, theory ensued. Helmholtz readily acknowledged the perception of overtones varies according to timbre, leading him to argue that our memory was crucial, that a listener's recollection of overtone-rich pitches is associated with, and influences, how we hear overtone-poor pitches when we encounter them. But as Benjamin Steege

FIGURE 15.9 Paul Hindemith's (1970, 87) illustration of the "melodic force" generated between harmonic and melodic tension, with his ordering of pitches, Series 2.

reasons, the case of overtoneless melody in organ pipes nevertheless "emerged as a limit case for Helmholtz's melodic theory" (Steege 2012, 134). Others, such as the contemporary American philosopher Xenos Clark, followed Darwin in arguing empirical approaches to the auditory system are not particular to humans, and that the "physical peculiarities of vibrating bodies [that existed] long before any living being came upon the earth, are also the basis of human and . . . extra-human melody" (Clark 1879, 211). Neither the empiricism of human particularity (trained ears) nor appeals to nature (ontic overtones) were impervious to critical revision in the debate over melodic intervals.

With an acoustic epistemology, Paul Hindemith was effectively cultivating the furrow Helmholtz had ploughed when he ordered melodic intervals in his Series 2 according to the combination tones they produced (the difference between the frequencies of the directly struck notes), an order that balanced what he called harmonic and melodic "force," as shown in Figure 15.9. The relational ordering of all twelve chromatic pitches in Series 2 formed a structural device in his penultimate opera, *Die Harmonie der Welt* (1957), which allied concepts to keys based on the strength of their overtone relations to other keys (and allied concepts). It must count as one of the purest applications of Helmholtz's melodic theory to composition: E [1] represents *musica mundana*, the cosmic sonorities sought by the opera's protagonist Johannes Kepler; B♭ [12] the forces most hostile to their attainment on earth.

From a more abstract stance, Hindemith's work highlights the way intervals pivot equivocally between "harmony" and "melody" in the conundrum we encountered earlier in Bach's Prelude: "neither is strong enough to stand alone; each needs the other for its full unfolding . . . [N]o harmonic progression can be made except through melody—that is, by traversing the intervals. Harmony, on the other hand, connects and organizes the waves of melody" (Hindemith 1970, 87). Helmholtz's scientific explanation of the same was characteristic:

> [W]hereas, however, in melodic relationship the equality of the upper partial tones can only be perceived by *remembering* the preceding compound tone, in harmonic relationships it is determined by *immediate sensation*, by the presence or absence of beats.
>
> (Helmholtz 1954, 368)

With this, Helmholtz accounted for harmonic effect as the power of immediate sensation as opposed to a linear experience reliant on recollection and association, with all the cognitive distance this implies.

We glimpse the contradictions between the above-mentioned approaches—aesthetic and scientific—when considering the harmonic tension or character of intervals that occur within a single chord. The postulate that "a rising melody always expresses and excites a growing intensity of feeling . . . whilst a falling one depicts a relaxation . . . from the climax of excitement," as one critic summarized in 1849, does not apply when the intervals occur in a single chord, even in wide leaps, Hindemith explains: "the traversing of this space involves no effort, and it does not produce in the listener the feeling of expectation fulfilled that he gets when the leap is made to a non-chord tone" (Teutonius [pseudonym] 1848, 794; Hindemith 1970, 189). Opinion was divided among earlier composers. A hundred and fifty years previously, William Crotch parroted Rameauian orthodoxy when he categorized "essential and unessential [melodic] notes" as those that "form a part of the harmony" and those that do not, respectively; while Wagner, writing thirty-eight years later, suggested the "ineffectiveness of operatic melody hitherto" resulted from the opposite: the failure to differentiate accompanimental harmony from vocal melody owing to their timbral dissimilarity (Crotch 1812, 74–75; Wagner 1911, 168).[43]

Each approach testifies to the importance of comprehensible expression, which an atomized approach to dyads appeared to offer. Even into the twenty-first century, psychological research into the perception of intervals continues to pursue the goal of determinate expression, but with the caveat that only perceived, rather than innate, expressive values are obtainable. Alf Gabrielsson, building on such milestones as Meyer's *Emotion and Meaning in Music* (1956) and Lehrdahl and Jackendoff's *Generative Theory of Tonal Music* (1983), appears to move little beyond the speculative verbal categories of early nineteenth-century theorists when summarizing referential meanings perceived in different types of melodic motion:

> [S]ome results indicate that large intervals sound more powerful than small ones, the octave is perceived as positive and strong and the minor second as the most sad interval. . . . Stepwise motion may suggest dullness, intervallic leaps excitement; stepwise motion leading to melodic leaps may suggest peacefulness (Thompson and Robitaille 1992). Activity (sense of instability and motion) may be conveyed by a greater occurrence of minor seconds, tritones, and intervals larger than the octave. Potency (vigour and power) may be expressed by a greater occurrence of unisons and octaves.
>
> (Gabrielsson 2011, 144)

The drive to quantify expression in this manner had met with incredulity when it was first suggested in the late eighteenth century, even from theorists hitherto content to bond music with rhetoric. J. A. P. Schulz, for one, poured cold water on the hope that individual intervals or characteristic figures (which, for contemporaries Daube and Riepel, formed the basis of melodic expression) could function as a kind of decipherable language of feelings. "It would be a ridiculous task to want to stipulate to the composer particular formulae or small melodic phrases that truly express every particular emotion, or even to say how he should invent such forms or phrases" (Sulzer 1793, 3:379).[44] One reason, of course, would be that this presupposes a lexicon of "every particular emotion," for which composers would supply the musical counterpart. And the impossibility of itemizing the totality of human experience, specifically an alphabet of human thought, is precisely the reason the project of a universal language failed in the early eighteenth century after it had been promulgated by Descartes and Leibnitz et al.

Wholeness, Shape, and Statistics

What are we to make of these historical efforts and skepticism? One of the arguments made against atomizing melody into its constituent intervals is that "we do not first enjoy one sixth, and then wait and enjoy the next," as Gurney observed in 1880. "It is as impossible to pick out special intervals in a melody, and say they are more attractive than others, as to pick out a certain square inch in a beautiful face, and say the same of it" (Gurney 2011, 148). Gurney's argument that the beauty of an interval or square inch depends upon the whole to which it belongs has a long history. As an aesthetic principle, it dates back at least to Aristotle's *Poetics*, while the perception of the wholeness of a melodic shape was obliquely defended in Rousseau's theory of *unité de mélodie*, and formulated as a fully spatial (*plastisch*) aesthetics in Hegel's words: "the meaning to be expressed in a musical theme is already exhausted in the theme."[45] In either case, the holistic concept feeds into Gurney's crowning principle of "ideal motion" wherein the experience of melodic form and motion "are blended—where form is perceived by continuous advance along it" (Gurney 2011, 164). The concept seeks to account for the paradox of perpetual movement within a fixed structure.

Ironically, the notion of melodic wholeness received its most enduring theoretical treatment outside of music theory. In 1890, philosopher Christian von Ehrenfels found melody to be a good example of what he called "gestalt qualities," that is, a mentally created shape. He pointed out that when a melody is transposed to a different key, it is heard as being identical to the original melody, even though the two are constituted from entirely different pitches. Thus, the perception of a melody is more than the perception of its individual parts, he proposed. A melody is, therefore, a gestalt quality (Ehrenfels 1890).[46] For Stumpf, building on Ehrenfels's ideas, the ability to transpose a melody distinguishes human from avian musical faculties,[47] although the practice of abstracting holistic form from constituent elements is demonstrable among primates, suggesting that a faculty of melodic transposition is merely undeveloped rather than absent in animals. When a dog recognizes its owner at different distances or in different lighting, for example, the visual stimuli received are different from those received when the owner stands directly in front of the dog. Hence the dog "has managed to separate the form mentally from the different circumstances" (Stumpf 2012, 44). The remaining question, for Stumpf, is why birds never transposed songs using the same faculty, after humans had so readily.

Ongoing statistical research into preferences for melodic shape, pattern, or peak pitch indicates that the impulse to study pitch content empirically is unlikely to abate. One of the most comprehensive more recent theories of melody as a note-to-note phenomenon is Eugene Narmour's Implication–Realization (IR) model (1990/1992). "Because science in the past century has demonstrated everywhere nature's obedience to powerful yet parsimoniously structured laws," he explains, echoing Helmholtz:

> a similar kind of natural economy must govern the human perception of artworks. Thus, a few simple laws—perceptual-cognitive ones powerful enough to account

both for the multiplicity of singular experiences and for the variation in perceived
style—probably regulate the art of melody.

(Narmour 1990, 4)

Specifically, contours become foreground structures of "implication and realization"; the
implication of continuation arises through the workings of Gestalt principles of likeness,
proximity, or common direction where consecutive pitches lie relatively close together.
Two consecutive minor seconds establish a "process" wherein we expect another small
interval. That is, proximate pitches imply a continuing pitch direction and interval size.
A large interval, by contrast, implies differentiation, and hence a "reversal" of direction
and size. A falling minor sixth would imply a small interval in the opposite direction,
for instance. Narmour identifies five melodic archetypes, of which "process" and "reversal" are the first two. While this seeks to model musical experience itself, criticism of
IR echoes Fétis's complaint about Reicha, that of partiality or insufficiency: "the influence
of meter and rhythm are neither clearly nor separately ... delineated from the factors
that Narmour purports to demonstrate govern note-to-note succession. ... [Similarly,]
the role of harmony in the theory remains ambiguous" (Cross 1995, 502). In Narmour's
approach, sitting at the midpoint of notated pitches and their cognition as sound, the minimum individual structures of a melodic line must have at least three pitches, he explains;
these are given letter symbols and combine to form anagram abbreviations of ongoing
melodic processes. It is indicative of the taxonomic and combinatorial rationalism such a
theory emotes that Narmour anticipates software using these symbol-string reductions to
manipulate "large amounts of melodic data in 'search and sort' operations. This has the potential," he continues, "for enabling critical analysts, style analysts, and ethnomusicologists
to manage melodic data in new ways" (Narmour 1992, 340).

Picking up this thread of optimism, David Huron asserts that "inferential statistical
approaches [to melody] will help us generate and test much more refined hypotheses
about the precise nature of compositional processes. What indeed are composers doing
when they arrange notes on a page? Are they arranging pitches, or intervals, or scale
degrees, or contours ... or some combination? A systematic statistical approach allows
us to answer such questions" (1999, 257–264). The fruits of such confidence include
Zohar Eitan's combinatorial model of peak pitches in Haydn, Chopin, and Berg, and
Huron's own investigation into melodic arches in folksongs using *Humdrum Toolkit*
software to analyze the 6,251 melodies of the (mostly European) *Essen Folksong
Collection* (Eitan 1997; Huron 1996; see also Schaffrath 1995). The former argues that
"an independent, nonsyntactic, gestural domain [exists] in music," exemplified in the
pitch contour of melody, which Eitan posits as an embodied, primordial dimension
of human utterance in general (Eitan 1997, 152). Cross-stylistic analysis leads to the
conclusion that:

few features tend to be associated with peaks in all three repertories, and some are peculiar to one repertory ([for instance] the tendency to avoid second-inversion chords

at peaks in Haydn) . . . [A]n association of peaks with emphatic or intensifying features, is corroborated for two of the three repertories, Chopin and Berg.

(Eitan 1997, 145)

In Huron's study, each folk melody is coded for pitch and duration information, rests, bar lines, meter, and phrase markings. By quantifying melodies with a given number of pitches (five to fifteen)—ignoring rests and interpreting tied notes as a single pitch— Huron was able to confirm a hypothesis that: "a disproportionate number of musical phrases and melodies tend to exhibit an arch-shaped pitch contour" (Huron 1996, 4). While these are based on average pitch contours within a melody-type of a fixed number of pitches, fewer than half of the melodies actually exhibited an arch shape in their contour, we learn. If we accept the "tendency for ascending and descending phrases to be linked together in pairs" on the basis of such a study, this needs to be qualified by Huron's own caveat against phrasal balance or maintaining tessitura: "What goes up is likely to come down, but what goes down is less likely to come back up," he summarizes (Huron 1996, 12).

(a)

(b)

(c)

(d)

FIGURE 15.10 Eduard Kulke's illustration of the evolution of melodies through a form of cultural inheritance, including from folkdance to symphonic theme: (a) Beethoven's Andante theme from the Symphony in C minor, (b) Kulke's abstraction of a simpler theme, (c) Beethoven's theme presented in simplified form, and (d) Kulke's "Bauerntanz," which he posits as the cultural prototype for Beethoven's theme. From *Über die Umbildung der Melodie*, 4–7.

To be sure, such empirical approaches are a far cry from the recessed creativity celebrated by Jean Paul in 1802, and we might say if aesthetics is the privileged method
of appreciating eighteenth- and nineteenth-century melodic composition, statistical
sampling is the natural complement of algorithmic composition. Such tools as Dirk-Jan
Povel's *Melody Generator* (2010) or Dmitri Kartofelev and Jüri Engelbrecht's "structured
spontaneity" (2013) use Markov chains or fractal geometry to create melodies based on
restrictive programming of overtone properties and predefined stylistic parameters
(Povel 2010; Kartofelev and Engelbrecht 2013). This declarative approach to melodic
data mirrors statistical analysis of the same, and the role of cognition recedes. Not all
algorithmic approaches to melody work in such a directly automatic way, of course. Just
as critic Eduard Kulke—fired by Darwin and Lamarck—believed melodies were subject to evolutionary principles (Kulke 1884, 4–7), and proposed genealogies of melodic
transformations in 1884 as part of a collective cultural memory (of which Figure 15.10
offers an illustration from Beethoven), Francesco Vico's computer system *Melomics*
uses an algorithm that mimics the process of natural selection (http://www.geb.uma.
es/fjv). It first generates random musical fragments, mutates them, and determines
whether they conform to predefined rules (genre-specific, instrument-specific, stylistic). By this process, all fragments are incrementally refined into rule-adhering music.
Under conditions of improvisation, such a process could not be entirely automated, of
course. While evaluation criteria cannot be clearly stated in a programming language,
Interactive Evolutionary Computation allows for interaction between the algorithm
and human participant. One example is John Biles's jazz melody generator *GenJam*,
described as "a genetic algorithm-based model of a novice jazz musician learning to improvise," in which a human mentor gives real-time feedback which is then absorbed by
the program to improve the future generation of melodic patterns—such as in a closed-
loop feedback function (Biles 2007, 2016).

Conclusion

With historiographic spectacles, it is tempting to conclude that the concept "melody"
is perhaps only scrutable in a range of historically specific definitions where each approach reflects the precepts and theories of its context, a verdict that renders the concept
hollow, a means for examining the intellectual environment rather than an object sui
generis.

The trouble with defending the "object" theory is that approaches to melody are
racked between the fixity of notation and phenomenological experience. Forms of
notation, conceived as a closed system, offer "the completeness of the musical 'text'"
in Jean-Jacques Nattiez's sense of what can be said to be immanent (2013, 372). This
supports the comparative study of figures, metrical organization, and intervals
that proliferated in the late eighteenth and early nineteenth centuries. Yet a reception aesthetics, tracing individual responses to heard melodies, betrays an array of

evaluations and their unpredictable psychology between and across cultures. At the end of his study of popular melody, Gino Stefani asks "[w]hy is a melody truly popular? The answer is obvious now: because it is better suited than others for appropriation, in more ways, for more purposes" (1987, 31). This, for Stefani, includes singing, whistling, dancing or marching, and setting to words, all of which constitute forms of arrangement. Perhaps this law of appropriation explains why the postman, recalling an optimistic prediction of Webern's, is not yet whistling his melodies. The retort, from a 1909 interview with Schoenberg, would be that "what a musician and what a non-musician can whistle back are already two very different things," an argument that leads him to qualify that the flipside of (appealing) simplicity is primitiveness: "it follows that our simplicity is different from that of our predecessors, that it is more complex, but also that even this complexity will in turn be regarded one day as primitive" (Auner 2003, 59).

As suggested above, he appears to have been wrong. The history of aesthetics teaches that on the one hand, listeners between the eighteenth and twentieth centuries would expect, by degree, originality and expressivity of thought from a melody, while on the other hand, a certain regularity of syntax. It is a paradox of restriction that pits convention against novelty. For the more "original" a melody, the less it accords to codes of communication that are understood by reference to melodic precedents (over and above the existence of melodic archetypes). Tonal function and modal coherence provide a systematic context for generating a repository of precedents. And here it would be hard to disagree with Dahlhaus's observation that "the harmonic structure of a melody can be thoroughly individual and unrepeatable, and this is not rare in the nineteenth century" (Abraham and Dahlhaus 1972, 16).[48]

The conservative critic Carl Gollmick summarized what was at stake in 1839 when he wrote about melody's capacity to excite or be ineffectual: "the more such successions of pitches [*Tonfolge*] are comprehensible, attractive and enduring to our ear, the more they deserve the name *melody* [*Melodie*]. Thus one says of *compositions* whose pitch successions lack these: they have no *melody*" (Gollmick 1839, 59).[49] After the acerbic debates of the ensuing century, Busoni eyed the problem in historical terms as one of familiarity versus advancing technical means in composition. His statement sums up a certain frustration with attempts to specify what he called the material means of melodic expression:

> It has become a commonplace of music history that the appearance of every new composition is reproached for a *lack of melody*. This complaint greeted *Don Giovanni* on the occasion of its first performance in Berlin, Beethoven's Violin Concerto, Wagner's music dramas etc. etc. Again and again one sets rising technical ingenuity against decreasing melodic invention! It almost seems as though technical mastery can operate more through what is *unfamiliar*, melodic expression only through what is *familiar*. In fact, Mozart was a richer melodist than his forebears; Beethoven broader and more protean than Mozart; Wagner more sumptuous than Beethoven,

if also less noble, less independent, more material; more of a character-smith, less of a psychologist.

(Busoni 1930, 94–95)[50]

Busoni's animating impulse for this complaint was the view that "immateriality is music's very essence, which always resounds in a blossoming and sublime melody" (1930, 95).[51] Whereas voice was self-expressive, carrying the association of soul, pneuma, and hence of primary essence, instrumental sounds were not. So quantifying "expression" for instrumental lines appeared plausible only in the context of alternative schemes of knowledge, such as figures and intervals.

While calls to invest "meaning" in the shaping or physiognomy of a melody have long since receded, Busoni's call appears to be on the wrong side of history, for scrutiny of melodic "material" has grown with growing computational means. From a genealogical perspective, aligning algorithmic composition with statistical analysis arguably highlights what is missing in "material," and latterly, computational approaches to melody: consciousness, that slippery term for organic agency that is self-aware. It may be no coincidence, then, that while certain theorists advocated states of unconsciousness when composing, melody has more commonly been adopted as a metaphor for consciousness itself. Witness Schopenhauer, for whom:

> Only human beings, being endowed with reason, keep looking forwards and backwards over the course of their actual life as well as the countless possibilities, thereby achieving a life course that, in being thoughtful, is a coherent whole: -- correspondingly, only melody is joined up from beginning to end in a way that is full both of purpose and significance. As such, it narrates the story of the will as it is illuminated by thoughtfulness, the will whose imprint in reality is the sequence of its deeds.
>
> (Schopenhauer 2014, 1:287)

In 1905, Edmund Husserl would sharpen this metaphor into a phenomenological insight. He locates reality not in the total sequence of deeds but in the "real now" of immediate perception, which "becomes irreal again and again" as time passes and present moments become past moments (Husserl 1991, 15). The paradox that mental events "are in consciousness successively, but they fall within one and the same total act" (22) of consciousness is exemplified in melody's successive single pitches that give rise to an overall shape. Rather than overlaying discrete perceptual acts—pitches remembered, sensed "now," and anticipated—it is the mind's capacity for simultaneous "primary consciousness, retention and protention" (40) that allows it to comprehend dynamic totalities, whether life events or musical lines. That is, for Husserl, melody becomes an epistemological tool of the mind: a way of conceptualizing our understanding of the consciousness of time. In like vein, Henri Bergson (1910) and Jean-Paul Sartre (1936) both write of the unity of inner consciousness and ego, respectively, as a metaphysical melody.[52] It seems reasonable to read this as a verdict—albeit an inconclusive one—on centuries of debate, in which self-awareness of epistemological schemes, from mimesis to the overtone relation of intervals, falls short of what was needed: an objective confirmation of one's own familiar preference.

NOTES

1. Pan's very instrument, Syrinx, was created from a nymph of the same name who had fatally metamorphosed into reeds to escape his advances.
2. See also Wagner (1995, 3:333).
3. "Zum Komponieren gehören drei Dinge: zuerst Melodie, dann nochmal Melodie und dann nun schließlich zum dritten Male Melodie." All translations by the author unless indicated otherwise.
4. See Stewart's judgment of *Jacobellis vs. Ohio* (1964), in which he spoke about a threshold test for obscenity. This is critiqued in Gewirtz 1996.
5. Gounod's *Méditation sur le Premier Prélude de Piano de S. Bach* (1852) allegedly resulted from his improvisation at the piano, and was notated by his father-in-law, Pierre-Joseph Zimmermann. Copycat descant melodies were applied to this and other "incomplete" Preludes by Carl Kossmaly, Ferdinand Gumbert, Gustav Graben-Hoffmann, Mario Castelnuovo-Tedesco, Ignaz Moscheles, August Gottfried Ritter, and Johann Joseph Abert. On this topic, see Feder (1969).
6. The term is in Piston (1947). See also Dowling (1973).
7. "Nicht immer ist die Melodie für das Auge erkennbar gezeichnet; das Ohr empfindet sie jedoch. Wir hören die Melodie in den Spitzen der arpeggierten Accorde . . . jeder verständige Spieler würde hier die begleitende Harmonie der Melodie . . . unterzuordnen wissen."
8. "Lassen wir einmal den durch Missbrauch allerdings zweideutig gewordenen Ausdruck 'Melodie.' Melodie oder nicht Melodie: darüber wollen wir nicht streiten."
9. Leonard Bernstein gave a series of "Young People's Concerts" for CBS between 1958 and 1972. This comment concludes the 21st broadcast on December 21, 1962. See ArtfulLearning (2011).
10. "Der Mangel an Kontinuität mag Erstaunen hervorrufen, wenn man an die Entwicklung der Kontrapunkttheorie und der Harmonielehre denkt." Abraham and Dahlhaus (1972, 16–17).
11. Plato, *Republic* III: 398 d.
12. Chronoi are units of time that constitute meter.
13. While *melopoeia* (Greek: "song making") refers more specifically, by relation to onomatopoeia, to the melodic line of the verses in Greek tragedy, the later problem of a specific identity is latent here.
14. The body of Western liturgical chant bears witness to the fact that monophonic vocal melody exists in ritualized practice from at least the fourth century CE onward. The extent to which singers and scholars in Benevento or Aquitaine conceived of these chants as autonomous linear pitch structures in parallel to the liturgical texts is unknowable. But applying the label "melody" to them in this sense has arguably less to do with the intentional fallacy than the extent to which they relate to the four-by-two

matrix of modes as a means of organizing the gamut of available tonal space (and the enduring debates over whether such a scheme, codified centuries later, was "real"). See Powers (1973).

15. "What is a simple song? A simple one is one whose melody is inflected through a simple system of one order of voices, or at least transcends 'la' by the space of a second; and it is therefore performed by one order of voices, and the note exceeding 'la' is expressed by 'fa' (as it often is also in conjoined songs). What is a conjoined song? A conjoined one is one whose melody proceeds through a system of conjoined orders; and it is performed by a permutation of widely ranged voices, especially 're' and 'la', through the conjunction of those orders of voices" (Beurhusius 1961).

16. "Melodia est sonorum aliorum post alios pro ratione elevationis & depressionis intervallorum se subsequentium effectio, Harmoniae speciem, videlicet unicam vocem constituens, quae decantata sensum suo modo tangit, ut affectus in homine non planè amuso create sentiantur."

17. "Melodia & harmonia differunt, eo quod haec sit modulamen, explurium vocum Melodiis in harmoniam devinctum; illa unius solum vocis affectio."

18. "Denn es kann sonst geschehen, daß *noten*, so an sich selbst eine gute *Melodie* haben, [aber] durch Unterlegung des *Textes* übel lauten."

19. The earliest example is Fritsche Closener, whose *Glossarum* of 1362 defines melodia as "Licht oder wise," in Kirchert and Klein (1995, 2:892). Further examples include: "Art. Cantus: Citharae Cantus . . . The tune or melody," Cooper (1565, 3b); "Art. Cantus: A song or singer, a tune, sound melodie, or dumpe: a charme, an inchuntment in verses," in Thomas (1587).

20. Michael Praetorius wrote of melody in 1619 as "unicam cantilenae vocem . . . vel Symphonium." And Butler of it in 1636 as "the sweete modulation or tune of each part in it self." See Praetorius (1619, 28); Butler (1636, 44). Thereafter, the identity of melody as an unaccompanied line is traceable across a range of sources, from Jean Rousseau (1687) to Alan Malcolm—"melody is the Effect only of one single Part"—(1721, 414); and Roger North—"Melody is the modulation of one production . . . harmony is of divers"—(1990, 96).

21. "Die *Melodie* aber ist ein natürlicher Zusammenhang aufeinander folgender einfacher Klänge, welche mit und ohne *Harmonie* wohl klinget" (Scheibe 1961, 13). Emphasis added.

22. Johann David Heinichen, *Neu erfundene und gründliche Anweisung . . . zu vollkommener Erlernung des General-Basses* (1711), cited and translated in Buelow (1966, 171).

23. "Gratuitous passage work and bustling noise do not constitute the beauties of accompaniment. In fact, they can easily do harm to the principal part by robbing it of its freedom to introduce variations into repetitions and elsewhere. . . . [The accompanist] need feel no anxiety over his being forgotten if he is not constantly joining in the tumult. No! An understanding listener does not easily miss anything. In his soul's perception melody and harmony are inseparable. Yet, should the opportunity arise and the nature of a piece permit it, when the principal part pauses or performs plain notes the accompanist may open the draft on his dampened fire" (Bach 1949, 367–368).

24. Sevenths need appropriate resolution through voice leading, he continues, indicating that Rameau's principle refers to *consonant* sounds in the first instance.

25. "A significant melody which says a great deal soon makes its way round the entire earth, while one poor in meaning which says nothing straightaway fades and dies" (Schopenhauer 1970, 162).

26. "Ueberhaupt, wozu denn immer Autoritäten? Für jede Meinung, selbst die absurdeste, wird es immer wenigstens einen Gewährsinn geben!"

27. See also Wagner (1995, 2:281).

28. "Soll die Oper nichts sein, als eine Reihe von Recitativen, ohne Ruhepunct,—eine bloße musikalische Betonung der drammatischen Rede, ohne specifisch musikalischen Zweck und Gehalt ... Wagner ist dann kein Reformator, sondern der ärgste Reactionär im Gebiete der Kunst, der die seit Rameau und Lully gemachten Fortschritte mißachtet und, höchst unpractischer Weise, an die Stelle der ausgebildeten dramatischen Musik, wie wir sie seit achtzig Jahren besitzen, das Recitativ wieder herstellen möchte, dessen Alleinherrschaft den Inbegriff ärgster Monotonie bilden würde."

29. See Guido d'Arezzo's treatise, *Micrologus de disciplina artis musicae* (ca. 1025).

30. Mussorgsky to Ludmilla Shestakova, July 30, 1868, cited in Taruskin and Weiss (1984, 395). Janáček's comment is cited in Tyrrell (1988, 292), and in Wingfield (1992, 291).

31. Reicha, for one, asserts, "I do not treat vocal or instrumental melody specifically, but deal with them *in general*, leaving readers free to make applications to the genres of their interest" (2000, 3).

32. "[S]o ist es das Genie, vom Geschmack unterstützt, welches diese Theile so erfindet und wählt, daß sie schön, und gegen einander gehalten mannigfaltig sind. Hierüber Regeln zu geben, nach welchen man die Schönheit und Mannigfaltigkeit derselben beurtheilt, ist eigentlich gar nicht der Gegenstand der Lehre von der Melodie, in welcher wir nur die äusserliche Form derselben betrachten müssen."

33. "Eine Melodistik gibt der Ton- und der Dichtkunst nur der Genius des Augenblicks; was der Ästhetiker dazu liefern kann, ist selber Melodie. ... [D]ie Oberherrschaft eines Organs und einer Kraft, z. B. in Mozart, wirkt alsdann mit der Blindheit und Sicherheit des Instinktes."

34. "For centuries numerous treatises on harmony have been published, but not a single one on melody" (Reicha 2000, 1:4).

35. I refer to Gilbert Ryle's classic description of Cartesian dualism (Ryle 2000, 17).

36. Fétis concludes his 1844 treatise on harmony by asserting the universal governance of tonality as a principle: "I will say that tonality resides in the melodic and harmonic affinities of the notes in the scale, from which results the quality of necessity in their successions and aggregations" (Fétis 2008, 246).

37. In such a reading, it remains uncertain if general music theory should count as the substance of melody or as its ancillary support and regulation. His key statements, in opposition to Gottfried Wilhelm Fink, occur in Marx (1841); selected excerpts are translated in Marx (2006, 17–34). The most comprehensive study of the Marx–Fink debate remains in Eicke (1966).

38. "Denn eine Melodienehre muß, um nicht dürftig abstrakt zu bleiben, eine Theorie des musikalischen Rhythmus—der ein Teilmoment der Melodie ist—und eine 'Harmonielehre' (im ursprünglichen umfassenden Sinne des Wortes: also eine Theorie der Tonordnung) voraussetzen oder einschließen. Sie erscheint demnach als zusammenfassende, den Zyklus der Musiktheorie abschließende Disziplin."

39. "Die Melodie aber ist im Grunde nichts anders, als die ursprüngliche, wahre und einfache Harmonie selbst, darin alle Intervalle nach, auf und hintereinander folgen."

40. "[Die] sind schon üblicher und brauchbarer, als obige Intervalle, und dienen sowol in der Melodie, als Harmonie, mit gutem Nutzen."

41. Marx (1826, 258–259). See also Trippett (2013, 58–60).

42. Others—including Rudolf Hermann Lotze and Eduard Hanslick—had looked to nervous excitation, but rejected the notion that this could ever yield information about melodic expression. I take this reference from Hanslick (1986, 55).

43. See also Wagner (1995, 2:310).

44. "Uebrigens würde es ein lächerliches Unternehmen seyn, dem Tonsetzer besondere Formeln, oder kleine melodische Sätze vorschreiben zu wollen, die für jede Empfindung den wahren Ausdruck haben, oder gar zu sagen, wie er solche erfinden soll." (Schulz wrote the music entries in Sulzer's edition.)

45. Rousseau's *unité de mélodie* appears in the *Lettre sur la musique française*, see Rousseau (1959–1995, 5:289–328, especially 305ff). Hegel (1988, 2:896).

46. See also Mitchell (1995); Gjerdingen (2002); Schultz and Schultz (2000).

47. Stumpf notes that for years, Otto Abraham carried out a number of experiments with parrots aiming at demonstrating a capacity for transposition, but without any luck. See Stumpf 2012, 35–36.

48. "[D]ie harmonische Struktur einer Melodie [kann auch] durchaus individuell und unwiederholber sein, und im 19. Jahnhundert ist sie es nicht selten."

49. "Je mehr solche Tonfolgen verständlich, anziehend und bleibend für unser Ohr sind, desto mehr verdienen sie den Namen *Melodie*. Darum sagt man von *Compositionen*, deren Tonfolgen es nicht sind: sie haben keine *Melodie*."

50. "Es ist zum ständigen Gemeinplatz in der Musikhistorik geworden, jeder neuen kompositorischen Erscheinung *einen Mangel an Melodie* vorzuwerfen. Dieser Vorwurf traf den 'Don Giovanni' annläßlich der ersten Berliner Vorstellung, traf Beethovens Geigenkonzert, die Wagnerschen Musikdramen ___ ___ ___ ___ Und immer wieder setzte man die zunehmende technische Findigkeit gegen die abnehmende melodische Erfindung! Fast scheint es, daß technische Meisterschaft mehr durch das *Ungewohnte,* melodischer Ausdruck nur durch das *Vertraute* wirken könne. In der Tat war aber Mozart ein reicherer Melodiker als seine Vorgänger; Beethoven breiter und vielgestaltiger als Mozart, und Wagner üppiger als Beethoven, wenn auch weniger edel, unselbständiger, materieller; mehr Charakteristiker, weniger Psychologiker."

51. "Immaterialität ist der Musik eigentliches Wesen, das in einer immer blühenderen und erhabeneren Melodik ausklingen wird."

52. Bergson: "Il y a simplement la mélodie continue de notre vie intérieure,—mélodie qui se poursuit et se poursuivra, indivisible, du commencement à la fin de notre existence consciente" (1972, 1384). And Sartre: "If we take a melody, for example, it is useless to presuppose an X which would serve as a support for the different notes. The unity here comes form the absolute indissolubility of the elements which cannot be conceived as separate, save by abstraction. ... For these very reasons, we shall not permit ourselves to see the ego as a sort of X-pole which would be the support of psychic phenomena" (Sartre 1991).

Works Cited

Abraham, Lars Ulrich, and Carl Dahlhaus. 1972. *Melodielehre*. Cologne: Hans Gerig.

ArtfulLearning. 2011. "Leonard Bernstein: Young People's Concerts: What Is Melody? (Part 2 of 4)." YouTube video, 11:19. Posted May 30. https://urldefense.proofpoint.com/v2/url?u=https-3A__ www.youtube.com_watch-3Fv-3DbTmrGbwmX7w&d=DwMFaQ&c=WO-RGvefibhHBZq 3fL85hQ&r=yglbC5td16rZjrWP6Q3j-N6pXKPtAo315CkzeDS9rRg&m=kRRUCKVOMTBk FPbhvNdGpYJS4VFfGbd6ZuioTzK-Wzo&s=9PUwYAjBMBcF74L0pCJNDUu4PEpOnw_ qlKdkrnGkGeM&e=" \t "_blank.

Ash, Mitchell G. 1995. *Gestalt Psychology in German Culture 1890–1967: Holism and the Quest for Objectivity*. Cambridge: Cambridge University Press.

Auner, Joseph, ed. 2003. *A Schoenberg Reader: Documents of a Life*. New Haven, CT: Yale University Press.

Bach, C. P. E. 1949. *Versuch über die wahre Art das Clavier zu spielen*, 2 vols. Translated and edited by William Mitchell. New York: Norton.

Bach, Johann Sebastian. 1998. *New Bach Reader*, edited by Hans David, Arthur Mendel, and Christoph Wolff. New York and London: Norton.

Bandur, Markus. 2006. "Melodia/Melodie." In *Handwörterbuch der musikalischen Terminologie*, edited by Hans Heinrich Eggebrecht and Albrecht Riethmüller. Wiesbaden: Steiner.

Bergeron, Katherine. 2010. *Voice Lessons: French Mélodie in the Belle Epoque*. New York: Oxford University Press.

Bergson, Henri. 1972. "La pensée et le mouvant." In *Oeuvres*, edited by André Robinet, 1251–1484. Paris: Presses Universitaires de France.

Berlioz, Hector. 1837. "De la musique en général I." *Revue et gazette musicale de Paris* 4: 405–409.

Bernhard, Christoph. 1963. *Tractatus compositionis augmentatus: Die Kompositionslehre Heinrich Schützens in der Fassung seines Schülers Christoph Bernhard*, 2nd edition Kassel and New York: Bärenreiter.

Beurhusius, Friedrich. 1961. *Erotematum musicae* (1573), 2nd edition, facsimile. Edited by Walter Thoene. Cologne.

Bie, Oscar. 1916. "Melody." Translated by Theodor Baker. *Musical Quarterly* 2: 402–417.

Biles, John. 2016. "GenJam." *Rochester Institute of Technology*. http://igm.rit.edu/~jabics/GenJam.html. Accessed January 5, 2016.

Biles, John. 2007. "Improvising with Genetic Algorithms." In *Evolutionary Computer Music*, edited by Eduardo Miranda and John Biles, 137–169. London: Springer.

Bischoff, Ludwig. 1858. "Richard Wagner's Lohengrin." In *Niederrheinische Musik-Zeitung* 38: 300.

Blakely, Lloyd George. 1967. "Johann Conrad Beissel and Music of the Ephrata Cloister." *Journal of Research in Music Education* 15: 120–138.

Braun, Max. 1857. "Max versus Marx: Critical Analysis of A. B. Marx's 'Musical Composition' with Additional Commentary on Musical Training." *New York Musical World* 18: 567.

Buelow, George. 1966. *Thorough-Bass Accompaniment According to Johann David Heinichen*. Berkeley and Los Angeles: University of California Press.

Burmeister, Joachim. 1599. *Hypomnematum Musicae Poeticae*. Rostock: Stephani Myliandri.

Busoni, Ferruccio. 1930. "Die Melodie der Zukunft." *Zeitschrift für Musik* 97: 94–95.

Busoni, Ferruccio. 1930. "Über Melodie: nachgelassene Skizzen," edited by F. Schnapp. *Zeitschrift für Musik* 97: 95–101.

Busoni, Ferruccio. 1956. *Wesen und Einheit der Musik*. Berlin: Hesse.

Butler, Charles. 1636. *The Principles of Musik in Singing and Setting*. London: John Haviland.

Chabanon, Michel Paul Guy de. 1785. *De la Musique considérée en elle-même et dans ses rapports avec la parole, les langues, la poésie et le théâtre*. Paris: Pissot.

Clark, Xenos. 1879. "Animal Music, Its Nature and Origin." *The American Naturalist* 24: 209–223.

Cone, Edward T. 2009. *Hearing and Knowing Music*. Edited by Robert Morgan. Princeton, NJ: Princeton University Press.

Cook, Nicholas. 2013. "Epistemologies of Music Theory." In *The Cambridge History of Western Music Theory*. Edited by Thomas Christensen. Cambridge: Cambridge University Press.

Cooper, Thomas. 1565. *Thesaurus Linguae Romanae & Britannicae*. London.

Cross, Ian. 1995. "The Analysis and Cognition of Melodic Complexity: Eugene Narmour." *Music Perception* 12: 486–509.

Crotch, William. 1812. *Elements of Musical Composition*. London: Longman, Hurst, Rees, Orme & Brown.

Dahlhaus, Carl. 1989. *Die Musiktheorie im 18. und 19. Jahrhundert: Grundzüge einer Systematik*. 2 vols. Darmstadt: Wissenschaftliche Buchgesellschaft.

Daube, Johann Friedrich. 1797. *Anleitung zur Erfindung der Melodie*. Vienna: Christian Gottlob Täubel.

Dowling, W. Jay. 1973. "The Perception of Interleaved Melodies." *Cognitive Psychology* 5: 322–337.

Dowling, W. Jay. 1978. "Scale and Contour: The Components of a Theory of Memory for Melodies." *Psychological Review* 85: 341–354.

Edwards, Arthur. 1956. *The Art of Melody*. New York: Philosophical Library.

Ehrenfels, Christian von. 1890. "Über Gestaltqualitäten." *Vierteljahrsschrift für Wissenschaftliche Philosophie* 14: 249–292.

Eicke, Kurt-Erich. 1966. *Der Streit zwischen Adolf Bernhard Marx und Gottfried Wilhelm Fink um die Kompositionslehre*. Regensburg: Gustav Bosse.

Eitan, Zohar. 1997. *Highpoints: A Study of Melodic Peaks*. Philadelphia: University of Pennsylvania Press.

Feder, Georg. 1969. "Gounods Méditation und ihre Folgen." In *Die Ausbreitung des Historismus über die Musik*. Regensburg: Gustav Bosse.

Fétis, François-Joseph. 1863. *Biographie universelle*. Paris: Firmin Didot Frères.

Fétis, François-Joseph. 2008. *Complete Treatise on the Theory and Practice of Harmony*. Translated by Peter Landey. Hillsdale, NY: Pendragon.

Gabrielsson, Alf. 2011. "The Relationship between Musical Structure and Perceived Expression." In *The Oxford Handbook of Music Psychology*. New York: Oxford University Press.

Gewirtz, Paul. 1996. "On 'I Know It When I See It.'" *Yale Law Review* 105: 1023–1047.

Geyer, Flodoard. 1860. "Kann und soll die Melodie gelehrt werden?" *Neue Berliner Musik-Zeitung*. October 10.

Gjerdingen, Robert. 2002. "The Psychology of Music." In *The Cambridge History of Western Music Theory*, edited by Thomas Christensen. Cambridge: Cambridge University Press.

Gollmick, Carl. 1839. *Kritische Terminologie für Musik und Musikfreunde*, 2nd edition. Frankfurt am Main: Johann David Sauerländer.

Gurney, Edmund. 2011. *The Power of Sound* [1880]. Cambridge: Cambridge University Press.

Hanslick, Eduard. 1986. *On the Musically Beautiful: A Contribution Towards the Revision of the Aesthetics of Music*, 8th edition [1892, original 1854]. Translated and edited by Geoffery Payzant. Indianapolis, IN: Hackett.

Hauptmann, Moritz. 1892. *The Letters of a Leipzig Cantor*. Translated by Arthur Duke Coleridge. London: Richard Bentley & Son.

Hegel, Georg W. F. 1988. *Hegel's Aesthetics: Lectures on Fine Arts*, 2 vols. Translated by Thomas Malcolm Knox. Oxford: Clarendon Press.

Helmholtz, Hermann von. 1954. *On the Sensations of Tone*. New York: Dover.

Hindemith, Paul. 1970. *The Craft of Musical Composition*, 4th edition. Translated by Arthur Mendel. Mainz and London: Schott.

Hoffmann, E. T. A. 1983. *Poetische Werke*, 6 vols. Berlin: Aufbau, 1983.

Huron, David. 1996. "The Melodic Arch in Western Folksongs." *Computing in Musicology* 10: 3–23.

Huron, David. 1999. "Highpoints: A Study of Melodic Peaks." *Music Perception* 16: 257–264. http://www.musiccog.ohio-state.edu/Huron/Publications/huron.Eitan.review.html.

Husserl, Edmund. 1991. *On the Phenomenology of the Consciousness of Internal Time* [1893–1917]. Translated by John Barnett Brough. London: Kluwer Academic.

Jadassohn, Salomon. 1899. *Das Wesen der Melodie*. Leipzig: Breitkopf & Härtel.

Kartofelev, Dmitri, and Jüri Engelbrecht. 2013. "Algorithmic Melody Composition Based on Fratal Geometry of Music." Tallinn University of Technology: Department of Cybernetics. http://www.cs.ioc.ee/~dima/fractalmusic.html.

Kirchert, Klaus, and Dorothea Klein, eds. 1995. *Die Vokabulare von Fritsche Closener und Jacob Twinger von Königshofen*. Tübingen: Niemayer.

Koch, Heinrich Christian. 1782. *Versuch einer Anleitung zur Komposition*, 3 vols. Leipzig: Bey A. F. Böhme.

Kulke, Eduard. 1884. *Über die Umbildung der Melodie: Ein Beitrag zur Entwickelungslehre*. Prague: J. G. Calve'sche K. K. Hof- und Univ.-Buchhandlung.

Kurth, Ernst. 1991. *Ernst Kurth: Selected Writings*. Translated and edited by Lee A. Rothfarb. Cambridge: Cambridge University Press.

Lester, Joel. 1999. *Bach's Works for Solo Violin: Style, Structure, Performance*. New York: Oxford University Press.

Lobe, Johann Christian. 1844. *Compositions-Lehre oder umfassende Theorie von der thematischen Arbeit und den modernen Instrumentalformen*. Weimar: Bernhard Friedrich Voigt.

Malcolm, Alan. 1721. *A Treatise of Musick*. Edinburgh: Printed for the author.

Marx, Adolf Bernhard. 1841. *Die alte Musiklehre im Streit in unserer Zeit*. Leipzig: Breitkopf & Härtel.

Marx, Adolf Bernhard. 1826. *Die Kunst des Gesangs: Theoretisch—Praktisch*. Berlin: Schlesinger.

Marx, Adolf Bernhard. 2006. *Musical Form in the Age of Beethoven*. Edited and translated by Scott Burnham. Cambridge: Cambridge University Press.

Matheus, Jean. 1619. *Les Metamorphoses d'Ovide traduites en prose françoise, et de nouveau soigneusement reveues, corrigees en infinis endroits, et enrichies de figures à chacune fable*. Paris: Langelier.

Mathiesen, Thomas J. 1999. *Apollo's Lyre: Greek Music and Music Theory in Antiquity and the Middle Ages*. Lincoln: University of Nebraska Press.

Mattheson, Johann. 1737. *Kern melodischer Wissenschaft*. Hamburg: Christian Herold.

Mollison, David. 1798. *Melody: The Soul of Music*. Glasgow: Courier Office.

Meyer, Leonard. 1961. *Emotion and Meaning in Music*. Chicago: University of Chicago Press.

Narmour, Eugene. 1990. *The Analysis and Cognition of Basic Melodic Structures*. Chicago: University of Chicago Press.

Narmour, Eugene. 1992. *The Analysis and Cognition of Melodic Complexity: The Implication Realization Model*. Chicago: University of Chicago Press.

Nattiez, Jean-Jacques. 1979. "Melodia." In *Enciclopedia Einaudi*, vol. 8, 1042–1067. Turin: Einaudi.

Nattiez, Jean-Jacques. 2013. *Analyses et interprétations de la musique: La mélodie du berger dans le* Tristan et Isolde *de Richard Wagner*. Paris: Vrin.

Nordau, Max. 1993. *Degeneration* [1895], 2nd edition. Lincoln: University of Nebraska Press.

North, Roger. 1990. *The Music Grammarian* [1728]. Cambridge: Cambridge University Press.

Ovid. 2010. *Metamorphoses*. Translated and edited by Charles Martin. New York: Norton.

Parry, Hubert. 1929. "Melody." In *Grove's Dictionary of Music and Musicians*, 3rd edition, edited by Henry Cope Colles. London: MacMillan and Co.

Pepusch, John Christopher. 1976. *A Treatise on Harmony* [1730]. Hildesheim: Georg Olms.

Piston, Walter. 1947. *Counterpoint*. New York: Norton, 1947.

Polansky, Larry, and Richard Bassein. 1992. "Possible and Impossible Melodies: Some Formal Aspects of Contour." *Journal of Music Theory* 36: 259–284.

Povel, Dirk-Jan. 2010. "Melody Generator: A Device for Algorithmic Music Construction." *Journal of Software Engineering and Applications* 3: 683–695.

Powers, Harold. 1973. "Is Mode Real: Pietro Aron, the Octenary System, and Polyphony." *Basler Jahrbuch für historische Musikpraxis* 16: 189–239.

Praetorius, Michael. 1619. *Syntagma musicum*. Volume 3. Wolfenbüttel.

Rameau, Jean-Philippe. 1971. *Treatise on Harmony* [1722]. Translated by Philip Gossett. New York: Dover.

Reicha, Anton. 2000. *Treatise on Melody*. Translated by Peter M. Landey. Hillsdale, NY: Pendragon Press.

Richter, Jean Paul. 1974. *Vorschule der Aesthetik*. Edited by Norbert Miller. Munich: Carl Hanser.

Rosen, Charles. 1999. *The Romantic Generation*. London: Fontana.

Rosselli, John. 1996. *The Life of Bellini*. Cambridge: Cambridge University Press.

Rousseau, Jean. 1687. *Traité de la Viole*. Paris: Christophe Ballard.

Rousseau, Jean-Jacques. 1959–1995. *Oeuvres complètes*, 5 vols. Paris: Gallimard.

Rousseau, Jean-Jacques, and Johann Gottfried Herder. 1986. *On the Origins of Language: Two Essays*. Translated by John H. Moran and Alexander Gode. Chicago: University of Chicago Press.

Ryle, Gilbert. 2000. *The Concept of Mind* [1949]. London: Penguin.

Sartre, Jean-Paul. 1991. *The Transcendence of the Ego*. Translated by Forrest Williams and Robert Kirkpatrick. New York: Hill and Wang.

Schaffrath, Helmut. 1995. *The Essen Folksong Collection in the Humdrum Kern Format*. Edited by David Huron. Menlo Park, CA: Center for Computer Assisted Research in the Humanities.

Scheibe, Johann Adolf. 1961. *Compendium musices theoretico-practicum, das ist Kurzer Begriff derer nötigsten Compositions-Regeln* [1730]. Reprinted as supplement to *Die deutsche Kompositionslehre des 18. Jahrhunderts*, edited by Peter Benary. Wiesbaden: Breitkopf & Härtel.

Schellenberg, E. Glenn, and Sandra E. Trehub. 1994. "Frequency Ratios and the Discrimination of Pure Tone Sequences." *Perception & Psychophysics* 56: 472–478.

Schellenberg, E. Glenn, and Sandra E. Trehub. 1996. "Natural Intervals in Music: A Perspective from Infant Listeners." *Psychological Science* 7: 272–277.

Schoenberg, Arnold. 1967. *Fundamentals of Musical Composition*. Edited by Gerald Strang. London: Faber.

Schopenhauer, Arthur. 1970. *Essays and Aphorisms*. Translated by Ralph J. Hollingdale. London: Penguin.

Schopenhauer, Arthur. 2014. *The World and Will and Representation*. Translated and edited by Judith Norman and Alistair Welchman. Cambridge: Cambridge University Press.

Schultz, Duane P., and Sydney E. Schultz. 2000. *A History of Modern Psychology*, 7th edition. Belmont, CA: Wadsworth, Thomson Learning.

Sobelewski, Eduard. 1855. "Reactionary Letters II." *The Musical World* 33: 45.

St. Augustine. 1960. *The Confessions of St. Augustine*. Translated by John Ryan. New York: Image Books.

Steege, Benjamin. 2012. *Helmholtz and the Modern Listener*. Cambridge: Cambridge University Press.

Stefani, Gino. 1987. "Melody: A Popular Perspective." *Popular Music* 6: 21–35.

Strahle, Graham, ed. 2009. *An Early Music Dictionary*. Cambridge: Cambridge University Press.

Stumpf, Carl. 2012. *The Origins of Music*. Translated and edited by David Trippett. Oxford: Oxford University Press.

Sulzer, Johann Georg. 1779. *Allgemeine Theorie der schönen Künste*. Leipzig: Wiedmann.

Sulzer, Johann Georg. 1793. *Allgemeine Theorie der schönen Künste in Einzeln*, 2nd edition. Leipzig: Weidmannschen.

Taruskin, Richard, and Piero Weiss, eds. 1984. *Music in the Western World*. New York: Schirmer.

Teutonius [pseudonym]. 1848. "Letters to a Music Student: VI. Melody and Melodious Composition." *The Musical World* 50: 794.

Thomas, Thomas. 1587. *Dictionarium Linguae Latinae et Anglicanae*. London.

Trippett, David. 2013. *Wagner's Melodies: Aesthetics and Materialism in German Musical Identity*. Cambridge: Cambridge University Press.

Tyrrell, John. 1988. *Czech Opera*. Cambridge: Cambridge University Press.

Wagner, Richard. 1911. "Oper und Drama." In *Sämtliche Schriften und Dichtungen*, Vol. 4. Leipzig: Breitkopf & Härtel.

Wagner, Richard. 1995. *Prose Works*, 8 vols. Translated by W. Ashton Ellis. Lincoln: University of Nebraska Press.

W. M. S. 1858. "Lohengrin in Wien." *Monatsschrift für Theater und Musik*: 437.

Wingfield, Paul. 1992. "Janáček's Speech-Melody Theory in Concept and Practice." *Cambridge Opera Journal* 4: 281–301.

Zarlino, Gioseffo. 1558. *Le Istitutioni Harmoniche*. Venice.

CHAPTER 16

....

CONSONANCE AND
DISSONANCE

....

ALEXANDER REHDING

WHEN is a dissonance not a dissonance? This question may sound like the beginning of a bad joke, but we can answer this conundrum by listening to ⊙ Audio Example 16.1, taken from the first movement of Haydn's string quartet op. 50, no. 2 in C major, performed here by the Quatuor Zaïde, which features an ear-opening "auditory illusion." The short passage, which forms part of an extended second-subject area, introduces a short new motif: the first violin plays a descending fourth G–D–D, supported in the lower strings with a G-major harmony in first inversion; the three-note motif is repeated with the D chromatically raised to D♯, which turns the harmony into an augmented triad. The cello next moves up by a semitone to C, while the first violin lingers on the D♯ for the duration of the whole measure—as if to savor the dissonant sound of the augmented second between violin and cello. The Quatuor Zaïde underlines the drama of this moment by beginning the passage softly and crescendoing into the chord. The harmonic tension is finally released when the first violin gives up its chromatic passing tone. It lets go of the built-up tension in the most theatrical manner, shooting over the goal to a brief F♯, before it resolves as expected to E, and concludes the phrase with a cadential gesture in G major.

But, as if to make a point, the whole passage is repeated—with a twist. The quartet approaches the augmented triad and continues it exactly as before. When we reach the climactic sustained chord again during the "one-more-time" segment, at [0:09] in ⊙Audio Example 16.1, we think we know what is going to happen next, but this is where we have to clean out our ears. The chromatically altered note in the violin does not resolve as it did before. The harmonic flow stops in its tracks when the chord is tied across the downbeat, as if hovering in mid-air. The Quatuor Zaïde underlines this unsettling effect in performance by tarrying and diminuendoing on this chord. Instead of resolving back to G major as before, the not-quite-resolved triad swerves into a surprising modulation that takes us flatward, briefly tonicizing A♭ major and F minor, before landing on the dominant of G minor. It is not until many measures later that we return just as unexpectedly to G major, after an extended half cadence on D with an augmented sixth chord that is as expressive as it is harmonically judicious.

With this harmonic roller coaster that is introduced by the augmented triad the second time around, it is hard not to think of the many Road Runner cartoons, in which Wile E. Coyote suddenly realizes that he has run off a cliff, and he stops, hovering in the air, to carefully feel around for ground under his feet, while the laws of gravity are momentarily suspended. It is this realization, not the physical loss of the running surface, that causes him to lose the ground beneath his feet and to come crashing down.[1]

How did Haydn achieve this effect? Did he break the rules of voice leading? No. If we study the score closely—rather than listen to a performance of this passage—we notice that Haydn spells the two occurrences slightly differently. As Figure 16.1 shows, the first time around he marks the augmented triad with a D♯ in the first violin, at m. 59, the second time the enharmonic equivalent E♭, at m. 64.

It is the harmonies that follow, marked with arrows in the example, that play a pivotal role in this passage. With this slight enharmonic change, the chord at m. 65 that seemed dissonant when we heard it the first time around, at m. 60, is in every way a consonance. To be sure, it is only with the benefit of hindsight (or hind-audition), after the standard Viennese resolution of the augmented second was emphatically rejected in m. 66, that we realize that that moment—the moment when we lose the ground under our feet—was already in C minor, we *were* already in a flat region, without having been aware of it (especially if we listen to the piece without following the score). What was a chromatic passing tone the first time around, is now a resolution. How is it possible for a dissonance to suddenly be a consonance?

Haydn's acoustical illusion is, in many ways, a textbook example of homophones—acoustical structures that *sound* the same but mean different things (and that may look different in writing). These are much more common in language than in music. A great example of this kind of verbal illusion is: "Time flies like an arrow. Fruit flies like a banana." Without the first iteration, the second one would not be nearly as confusing. The double pivot is on the words "flies" and "like"—in the first case "flies" is a verb and "like" part of an adverbial construction; the second "flies" is a noun in the plural and "like" a finite verb. In both cases, music and language, the illusion works by entraining us to hear (that is, to conceptualize) the phrase in one particular way, the first time we hear it. And the second time it comes around, a phrase that apparently sounds the same has a different meaning. Fruit simply does not fly like a banana, but small drosophila fruit flies do enjoy dipping their proboscis into a tasty banana. While the verbal homophones in this example play with syntactical structures, the musical homophone in Haydn's example expresses these structures by playing with notions of consonance and dissonance.[2] Haydn's two spellings of the sonority seem to subtly underline the literal meaning of consonance and dissonance, as "sounding together" and "sounding apart."

We can parse the notion of consonance and dissonance in this example in at least three different ways. First, in an approach that we may call "consonance/dissonance as event," we could imagine that a quartet may decide to play the two phrases

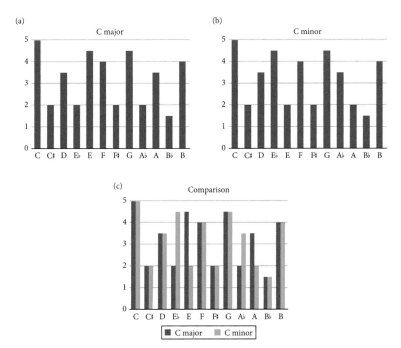

RINGS, CH. 5: TONIC, FIGURE 5.4 David Temperley's (2011) key profiles.

Modified from Krumhansl and Kessler 1982.

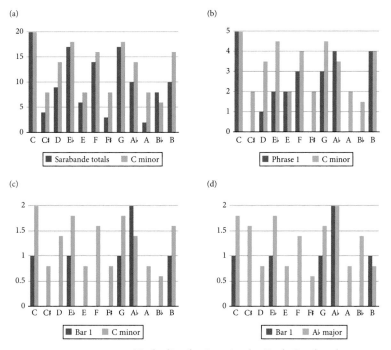

RINGS, CH. 5: TONIC, FIGURE 5.5 Pitch distributions in the Bach Sarabande, compared with key profiles.

Phrase 1

	m.1	m.2	m.3	m.4
C	19.5	23.5	23	25
c	25	22.5	22	27.5
C♯	20	18	17	21.5
c♯	20	18	17	19
D	15	16	20.5	12
d	13.5	15.5	23	13
E♭	23	17	22.5	21
e♭	20.5	18.5	17.5	18
E	21.5	22.5	17	16.5
e	20.5	21.5	19.5	21
F	15.5	19.5	21.5	22
f	20.5	22	22.5	22
F♯	18.5	19	15	17.5
f♯	17	19	16.5	16
G	19.5	20	21.5	20
g	18.5	13.5	19	19
A♭	25	19	20.5	23.5
a♭	25	21.5	20.5	17
A	17	19.5	17.5	13.5
a	19.5	23.5	19	22.5
B♭	16	15.5	19.5	21
b♭	14.5	15.5	14	21
B	20.5	21.5	15.5	17.5
b	16.5	20	19.5	15

Phrase 2

	m.5	m.6	m.7	m.8
C	20.5	17.5	17	12
c	24.5	19	21	27
C♯	23	22	17.5	21
c♯	23	16.5	16	21
D	15	14.5	20	12
d	15	20	21.5	12
E♭	22	20	26	30
e♭	16.5	22.5	23.5	30
E	18	14	15.5	24
e	19.5	13	15.5	24
F	18	23	18	9
f	22	24	17.5	9
F♯	17.5	20.5	17.5	21
f♯	16	17	16.5	12
G	19	16	20	12
g	20.5	21	24	21
A♭	26.5	22	21	27
a♭	21.5	18	21	27
A	16	16	17.5	12
a	18.5	20	17.5	12
B♭	18	24	23	24
b♭	19	21.5	16.5	24
B	17.5	17.5	18	27
b	15	18.5	20.5	12

Phrase 3

	m.9	m.10	m.11	m.12
C	15.5	23.5	22	20
c	18	21	19.5	19
C♯	21	16	23	23.5
c♯	19.5	14.5	21.5	17
D	21	19.5	14.5	13.5
d	22.5	23.5	18.5	22.5
E♭	21	23.5	18.5	21
e♭	18.5	16	15.5	21
E	16.5	15	16.5	17.5
e	16	22.5	18	15
F	16.5	23.5	24	25
f	18	23.5	25.5	27.5
F♯	21	16	18.5	21.5
f♯	18.5	13.5	16	19
G	17.5	22	17	12
g	21.5	23	18	13
A♭	22	21	22	21
a♭	22	21	17	18
A	18.5	13	17	16.5
a	13.5	14.5	21	21
B♭	21	22	20.5	22
b♭	22	17.5	23	22
B	19.5	16	17.5	17.5
b	21	20.5	17.5	16

Phrase 4

	m.13	m.14	m.15	m.16	m.17	m.18	m.19	m.20
C	18	24.5	22.5	23.5	19	22.5	23.5	25.5
c	21.5	24.5	24	23.5	22.5	21.5	26	28
C♯	21	16	20	15.5	19	16.5	17	22
c♯	18.5	13.5	20	15.5	20.5	16.5	14.5	19.5
D	14	21	17	22.5	18.5	20	16.5	12.5
d	18	22	13	18.5	16	21	16	15
E♭	23.5	21.5	19.5	20.5	22	20	20.5	23.5
e♭	22	19	18	18	20.5	19	19.5	16.5
E	18	13.5	18.5	15.5	19.5	19.5	19	14
e	19.5	17.5	21.5	22	23.5	19.5	23	21
F	21	22	18.5	19	17.5	20	18.5	23.5
f	18.5	19	21	17.5	15	21	18.5	15.5
F♯	19.5	16	18.5	17	18	17	19.5	14
f♯	16.5	19	18.5	18.5	17.5	18.5	18	20.5
G	15	24	23.5	27	20.5	21	21.5	22
g	20.5	21.5	21	24.5	23.5	17	18	25.5
A♭	22.5	18	21.5	18	21	18.5	20.5	16.5
a♭	18.5	16.5	19	18	18.5	21	21.5	11.5
A	15	17	16.5	16	16	19.5	14.5	20.5
a	19	21	20	17	17	21	18.5	22.5
B♭	25	22.5	16	19	21	18	19.5	25.5
b♭	16	16	16	15	21	14	18	16.5
B	18.5	15	19	17.5	19	18.5	20.5	21
b	13.5	21.5	19	23	15.5	13.5	19.5	13.5

= best key-profile match(es)

= 2nd-best key-profile match(es)

= preferred key (modulation penalty = −4)

RINGS, CH. 5: TONIC, FIGURE 5.7 Temperley's key-finding algorithm applied to the Bach Sarabande.

GJERDINGEN, CH. 22: MUSICAL GRAMMAR, FIGURE 22.1 Two proper sequences of jewels (rows 1 and 2) and two improper sequences (rows 3 and 4). Sequence 4 violates the rule for a beryl at stage C. The grammatical problem with sequence 3 is unknown.

Image courtesy of the American Gem Trade Association.

GJERDINGEN, CH. 22: MUSICAL GRAMMAR, FIGURE 22.2 Two different grammars for four-jewel sequences. They differ in that sequence 5 goes "sapphire to garnet" while sequence 6 goes "garnet to sapphire."

Image courtesy of the American Gem Trade Association.

GJERDINGEN, CH. 22: MUSICAL GRAMMAR, FIGURE 22.3 Jewels used to represent different sequences of chords. Both beginning and ending chords are the same, but the inner chords have opposite sequences.

Image courtesy of the American Gem Trade Association.

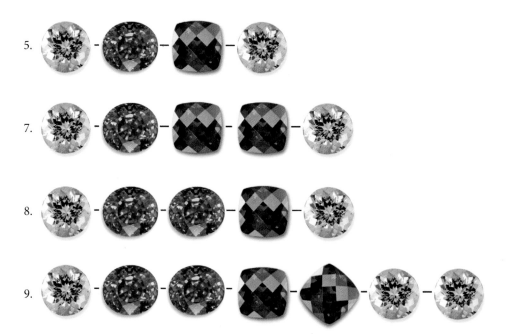

GJERDINGEN, CH. 22: MUSICAL GRAMMAR, FIGURE 22.5 Four versions of one Bijouan sequence: the basic pattern (no. 5), two extensions by repetition (nos. 7 and 8), and a further extension (no. 9) by two repetitions and one slight variation (garnet to altered garnet).

Image courtesy of the American Gem Trade Association.

GJERDINGEN, CH. 22: MUSICAL GRAMMAR, FIGURE 22.6 The subordination of three-jewel sequence 1 to the beryls in four-jewel sequence 5.

Image courtesy of the American Gem Trade Association.

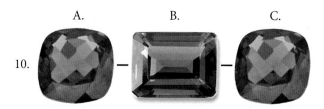

GJERDINGEN, CH. 22: MUSICAL GRAMMAR, FIGURE 22.7 A simple three-jewel sequence of emerald, blue iolite, and emerald. This pattern occurs only in subordinated roles.

Image courtesy of the American Gem Trade Association.

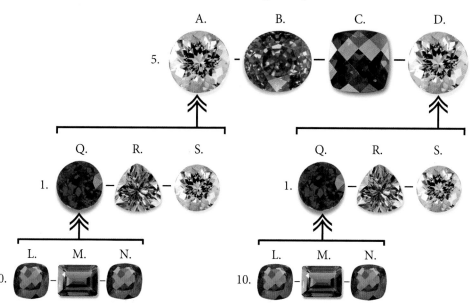

GJERDINGEN, CH. 22: MUSICAL GRAMMAR, FIGURE 22.8 Two levels of subordination. Sequence 10 is subordinated to the rubies in sequence 1, which in turn begin a three-jewel sequence subordinated to the beryls of sequence 5.

Image courtesy of the American Gem Trade Association.

11.

GJERDINGEN, CH. 22: MUSICAL GRAMMAR, FIGURE 22.11 A summary syntax of the bass from Figure 9. The four jewels stand for Romanesca (citrine), Rising Semitones (sapphire), Rising Fifths (garnet), and Cadence (beryl).

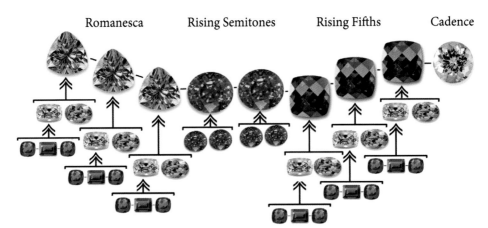

Romanesca   Rising Semitones   Rising Fifths   Cadence

GJERDINGEN, CH. 22: MUSICAL GRAMMAR, FIGURE 22.12 A more detailed look at the syntax of the bass from Figure 9. Coordinate patterns predominate at the high levels (the ascending and descending sequences), but the Romanesca (yellow citrines) and Rising Fifths (garnets) both feature two levels of subordination: pairs of jewels (pink morganite to yellow topaz) can replace single upper-level jewels, and three-jewel neighbor-note figures (emerald to blue iolite to emerald) can replace the first jewel of each middle-level pair.

GJERDINGEN, CH. 22: MUSICAL GRAMMAR, FIGURE 22.13 A first-prize-winning realization of the bass from the harmony contest of 1857 (see Figure 9) by the thirteen-year-old Henri Fissot, a student of François Bazin at the Paris Conservatory. The markings of contrapuntal imitations are original. Jewels have been added for comparison with Figures 11 and 12.

Image courtesy of the American Gem Trade Association.

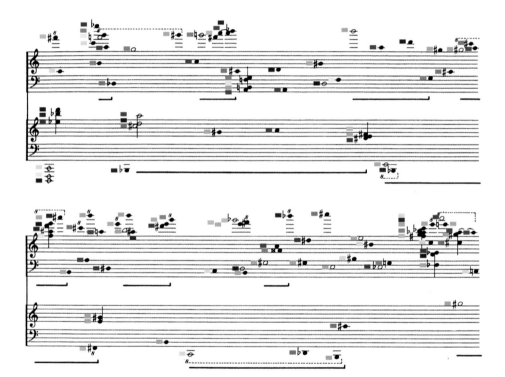

HANNINEN, CH. 24: IMAGES, VISUALIZATION, AND REPRESENTATION, FIGURE 24.4 Cage, *Etudes Australes* VI, opening, with pitch chroma enhancement.

Image from Hanninen 2014, 2.20, Slide 14.

FIGURE 16.1 Joseph Haydn, String Quartet op. 50, no. 2, first movement.

differently, in accordance with their different spelling in the score. They would be emphasizing the comma difference that technically distinguishes D♯ from E♭. This very literal approach would then distinguish between the acoustically rougher sound of the augmented second and the slightly smoother sound of the consonant minor third the second time around. If we are at all concerned about dramatic effect, this maneuver is perhaps not advisable: the effect—the punch line, as it were—of the illusion will be much more startling if we refrain from making a distinction in performance.

Second, in an approach we might call "consonance/dissonance as voice-leading rule," we take the part-writing of the passage as a starting point. The chromatic passing tone in the violin—the deviation from the diatonic D that we simply expect to resolve—is an important part of the explanation here, but it is not the whole story. A good measure of the effect of the illusion is based on the timing of the resolution of the augmented triad, following mm. 59 and 64. We remember the peculiarity of augmented triads and their dizzying range of possible resolutions.[3] When the augmented triad is left the first time around, the resolution in two voices is split up over two measures—the effect of the illusion is created out of the cello's move up to C, which further underlines an expectation for the first violin, which first introduced the chromatic deviation D♯, to complete its ascent to E. The second time, when this final step doesn't occur, the effect is all the more startling: recognizing that the expected resolution won't happen, and accepting the "passing" sonority as a consonance in its own right requires a fair amount of rapid mental reconceptualizing on the part of the listener.

And third, in a model we could call "consonance/dissonance as tension and relaxation," we take all of the syntactical discrepancies into account, with the dissonance emerging as a consequence of the functional harmonies deployed within the phrase. In this explanation, dissonant tension diminishes after the augmented triad, but we learned from our experience the first time around that resolution is not achieved until m. 63, when the "one-more-time" phrase begins. We entrain ourselves to hear the harmony of m. 60 as a partial solution, less dissonant, but not fully consonant within G major. In the second occurrence, the tonal scene has changed around the chord we hear—we have to readjust our tonal hearing toward C minor, a starkly different tonal context in which the E♭ is harmonically and syntactically consonant. The long and leisurely flat section, circling through closely related harmonies, is designed to give the listeners enough time to adjust their hearing to this new harmonic context. The notions of consonance and dissonance employed here are ultimately relative notions, figuring as lesser or greater tension.

These three approaches to the "auditory illusion" of Haydn's op. 50, no. 2 broadly correspond to three major schools of thought in the long history of understanding consonance and dissonance, which we will review in the course of this chapter.[4]

The Haydn example has presupposed that we already have a good practical understanding of what constitutes a consonance and a dissonance. If we try to define the terms, however—beyond the bare fact that they describe the relationships of harmonic or melodic intervals between simultaneous or successive pitches—we soon get into difficult terrain, resorting to psychological or metaphorical dimensions such as unpleasantness and pleasantness, roughness and sweetness, fission and fusion, instability and stability, or tension and release. Outside of specialist discussions, the terms even have a tendency to take on connotations of bad and good, which move freely from the aesthetic to the ethical in ways that are rarely helpful.[5] While every interval is either consonant or dissonant—there is usually no third option[6]—various periods in music history were locked in debate about whether these terms constitute categorical distinctions or a continuum. Each of these decisions has a bearing on how consonance and dissonance are conceptualized—in terms of acoustics, physiology, cognition, aesthetics, or other factors.

Since an intuitive understanding of consonance and dissonance is second nature to musicians, or at least feels this way to most, it is useful to defamiliarize the terms. The vignettes that follow amount neither to a history of the concepts nor to a systematic exploration of its rules. Rather, we will plunge into a variety of scenarios that may at times seem wildly out of the ordinary—they present extreme cases, like Haydn's homophones, in which the concepts of consonance and dissonance are probed and tested, poked and prodded, with the view to gaining a better understanding of the boundaries of these concepts.

Consonance/Dissonance as Event

The question of where to locate the explanation of consonance and dissonance has had musical thinkers scratching their heads since time immemorial. Are the phenomena of consonance/dissonance products of the mind or the senses? Are the two a feature of the soundwave or our auditory apparatus? Physical, physiological, or psychological? This set of questions is typically focused on the phenomenon in isolation, removed from any musical context, and treats consonance and dissonance as an event.

To start, we should do away with the enduring explanation, perpetuated mostly in introductory music theory texts, that the phenomenon of consonance is grounded in the harmonic series, as represented in Figure 16.2. While this illustration is a helpful shortcut, any attempts to justify this music-theoretical concept on the basis of the acoustics of the harmonic series are dubious.[7] The purported foundational role of the harmonic series is easily questioned: why would we leave out the seventh harmonic

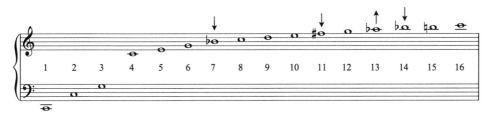

FIGURE 16.2 Representation of the harmonic series, in which each partial is depicted as a note in its own right. The arrows indicate tuning deviations, when the partials do not fully correspond to the pitches as which they are represented.

from consideration? How far up the harmonic series does the natural basis for consonance come to an end? How do we explain the historical and cultural variability of consonances? What are the consequences of treating upper partials as the equivalent of musical notes? Why would our ear accept deviations from the harmonic series, as are common in equal temperament? All that said, the resemblance between the lower parts of the harmonic series and intervals that are generally considered consonant is striking, and it easily invites this kind of thinking. It is best to treat this explanation as a useful fiction. But to get a better sense of the issues in this discussion, we should turn to a different representation of consonant sound.

Among the countless discussions of consonance and dissonance over the centuries, we will zoom in on the philosopher and encyclopedist Johann Georg Sulzer, who chose the phenomenon of consonance as a prime locus for his exploration of pleasure and displeasure, *Theorie der angenehmen und unangenehmen Empfindungen* (1762).[8] While Sulzer is considered a key figure in eighteenth-century aesthetics, his impact on music theory is more complicated; in his most influential work, the aesthetic encyclopedia *Allgemeine Theorie der schönen Künste* (1771–1774), he relied in the more technical musical entries on the support of Johann Philipp Kirnberger and Johann Abraham Peter Schulz (see Christensen and Baker 1995; Riley 2004). But his explanation is useful because he tried to get behind the sounding phenomenon of consonance, to get to what lies beyond the notes, to get to the bottom of what happens when we hear a consonant formation. This unconventional approach, which is focused on mediating between the sensory and the intellectual sides of the argument, presents a perfect scenario to pry apart some of the complexities of the concept.

Sulzer represented a four-voiced C-major triad as shown in Figure 16.3, which he in turn based on the mathematician Leonard Euler's music theory treatise *Tentamen novae theoriae musicae* (1739, 36–38). He chose this example on the assumption that the C-major triad would be universally recognized as a source of pleasure. As is common in music theory, Sulzer made no distinction between the consonance of a two-voiced interval and that of a harmony with more than two voices.[9] In his approach, the four simultaneous sounds are represented as repeated impulses or beats, marked as regular lines of dots spaced out at varying densities along the horizontal axis—bear in mind that

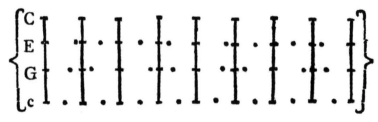

FIGURE 16.3 Johann Sulzer's representation of consonance from *Theorie der angenehmen und unangenehmen Empfindungen* (1762, 97).

the graph reverses the normal order of pitches, placing the lowest note at the top and the highest at the bottom of the figure. Coincidences between the pulsations of multiple pitches are highlighted by vertical lines. Every beat of low C coincides with every other beat of top C—with the effect that the dots marking the pulsation of low C are hidden entirely under vertical lines—with E and G joining them intermittently.

Sulzer's explanation is primarily based on the visual impression that this representation conveys. His general principle of beauty, which can be summarized as ordered complexity (Sulzer 1762, 99), closely matches this situation. Each line of events follows its own regular trajectory and results in its own pitch in the auditory domain, but the patterns that emerge in their interaction between the horizontal rows reveal a certain regularity and symmetry that Sulzer finds pleasing to the eye. At closer inspection, we note that the pattern in this visual representation is repeated, the left half of the figure is identical to the right half. Beyond that, each half is symmetrical around a central axis, located in the third and seventh vertical lines. For Sulzer, it is no surprise that the phenomenon, once translated into the sonic domain, produces the impression of a pleasing consonance.[10]

Sulzer prepares the ground here to make the case that consonance is both a sensuous and intellectual pleasure, as it brings together diversity and regularity, stimulating nerves and imagination in equal measure (Sulzer 1762, 99). To understand better what is going on here, we will have to go back further in intellectual traditions. The ancient Greek school following Pythagoras, mathematician and religious leader from the isle of Samos, captures musical intervals in terms of number. Pythagoreans would explain every worldly phenomenon, from musical consonances all the way up to the entire cosmos, in terms of ratios, ideally low-integer superparticular ratios $(n+1)/n$, such as 2:1, 3:2, and 4:3. Appropriately, the most sacred emblem of their cult was the *tetractys,* an arrangement of ten counting pebbles (or *psephoi*) in an equilateral triangle, laid out in rows of one, two, three, and four pebbles.

To his disciples, the truth of Pythagoras's teachings was confirmed over and over again by the diversity of phenomena that could be explained with reference to these basic ratios. This is why in the Pythagorean worldview, which bequeathed us the medieval quadrivium, music and astronomy go hand in hand, alongside arithmetic and geometry. The practice of measuring sounds by dividing string lengths on the monochord is emblematic of Pythagorean teachings—even though there is no evidence that monochords were around during Pythagoras's purported lifetime (see Creese 2010).

Throughout the ages, Pythagorean thought has reveled in the perfection of numbers in its own right: Gioseffo Zarlino's lengthy encomium to the number six that opens his monumental *Le istitutioni harmoniche* (1558), in true neo-Pythagorean manner, is all that is required to justify the validity of his *senario,* 1:2:3:4:5:6, the construct he introduced to explain his concept of consonance and harmonic generation, as an updated (and secular) kind of *tetractys* that expands the basis of consonances to six, adding the major third at 5:4, and the minor third at 6:5 (Moreno 2004).

In the early modern age, the philosophical worldview based on numbers was still going strong, but its long-lived pre-eminence came to a gradual end during Sulzer's lifetime (Kittler 2005). The eminent seventeenth-century rationalist philosopher Gottfried Leibniz had famously explained music as a "secret arithmetic exercise in which the soul is not aware of its own counting" (Leisinger 1994, 43).[11] More specifically, Sulzer himself was a follower of the philosopher Christian Wolff, who continued Leibniz's rationalism into the eighteenth century. In this worldview, any aspect of beauty was related to numerical elegance. As a consequence, the ear appreciated music not as a sensory sounding phenomenon, but by subconsciously counting vibrations.

With this lengthy excursion into the intellectual traditions informing Sulzer in mind, we can return to his visualization of consonance. Sulzer's decision to represent the C-major chord as a succession of pulsations, marked as dots on the page, underlines this aspect of rationalist music aesthetics. The fleeting resemblance between dots and Pythagorean *psephoi* may be coincidental, but it indicates a fundamentally related approach to music and numbers. Of course, there is nothing inherent in the number of dots (8:10:12:16) in the figure that would necessarily result in four pitches sounding specifically C–E–G–c. Unless we specify the speed at which these events happen in time, we cannot determine the resulting frequencies. Nevertheless, this four-voiced C-major chord symbolizes the simplest and purest harmony known to Western tonal music. What the image suggests is that our mind perceives this harmony, via the ears, by means of the numbers of pulsations—eight for the root, ten for the third, twelve for the fifth, and sixteen for the upper octave—by appreciating, or (*per* Leibniz) unconsciously counting, the ratios between them (4:5:6:8).

But Sulzer also encourages a reading of this image in a more material, empirical way. The pulsations, the dots, can be seen as indicative of how air molecules—that is, pressure changes—move from the sound source to the ear. Each dot signifies the vibration that strikes the eardrum and is translated into sounds. The two cycles we see are representative of any number of these periodic soundwaves that form the material basis of musical sounds. When Sulzer wrote his treatise, to be sure, most of the physiological details about our auditory system had yet to be researched. But when he describes how the pulsations striking the eardrum "stir the nerves without interruption for as long as [the soundwaves] last" (Sulzer 1762, 87), he is right on the mark. The Leibnizian (or, by extension, Wolffian) worldview is marked by the axiom *Natura non facit saltus*, nature doesn't make leaps. In this intellectual framework, the idea that a continuous sensation could be based on a non-continuous stimulus must count as a remarkable scientific observation (Hilgers 2003).

Sulzer explained that his graphic could represent the sound of string instruments, which is entirely possible, but it is a much closer image of another instrument that was widely used in acoustical research, a Savart wheel, as seen in Figure 16.4.[12] In this polyphonic Savart wheel, four cogwheels with different numbers of teeth are rotated with a belt. When stiff paper, such as a playing card or a beer coaster, is held against the rotating wheels, each tooth striking the paper will produce a click sound. Given sufficient rotation speed, the clicks will fuse into pitches corresponding to the click rate. Savart wheels were originally used to test the relationship between frequency and pitch. If we turn Sulzer's image into a cylinder, we have a precise template for the positioning of the teeth

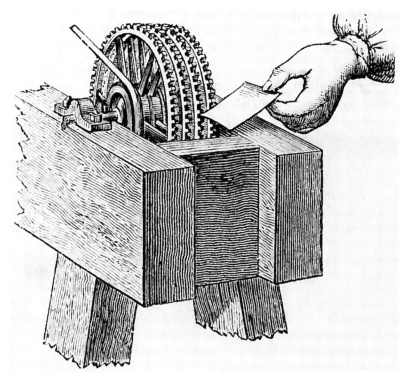

FIGURE 16.4 Illustration of the Savart wheel, from *Harper's Monthly Magazine* 45 (1872, 846). The artist's rendition is sloppy: for full sonic effect each cog wheel should contain a different number of teeth.

in the four wheels. While the four pitches heard will depend on the rotation speed, the intervals between them will remain constant so that a four-voiced harmony with octave doubling will always be sounded in this constellation.

The critical feature of the Savart wheel was the direct connection it made between sound and perception, in a way that went beyond mere counting. It was an instrument that could put Sulzer's idea to the test. In his detailed observations on the consonant impression of the C-major harmony, Sulzer inched toward a reconciliation of the rationalist and the empiricist position. "The soul," he posited in a kind of psychophysical parallelism, "does not have sensations without analogical motion in the nerves or the senses" (Sulzer 1762, 78). The fact that the discontinuous impulses are received as a continuous pleasant sensation is for him the proof of the convergence of mental and sensuous stimuli: "What pleases the soul when presented indistinctly by means of the senses, also pleases it when presented clearly to the spirit" (Sulzer 1762, 99).[13] Hearing and unconscious counting are just two different ways for the perceiving subject to come to terms with the "ordered diversity" that makes up Sulzer's concept of the beautiful.

This neat analogy between nerves and spirit, between sensations and cogitations, could not last long. The rise of acoustics in the nineteenth century made Pythagorean (numerical) principles much harder to uphold, especially as equal temperament became more widely accepted as an inevitable musical reality. A generation after Sulzer, other experimenters found that even when the sequence of stimuli was not exact, when the cogwheels had irregularly spaced teeth, or when the ratios between wheels were tempered, the sensation of consonance remained undisturbed. The applied mathematician and polymath Friedrich Wilhelm Opelt, for one, developed a multiphonic siren in the 1830s that is effectively another realization of Sulzer's abstract design, which he used to test various aspects of music theory.[14] With one important difference: in the mathematical considerations that make up the heart of his work, Opelt eventually opted for 19-tone equal temperament (1852, 52–53). This temperament is distinguished over standard 12-tone equal temperament by the circumstance that there are close neighbors of pure intervals present for the whole chromatic scale, while also enabling full modulatory and transpositional flexibility that allows a certain degree of enharmonic exactitude.

The mistunings are therefore effectively minimized in Opelt's 19-tone equal temperament. For a true Pythagorean, however, this approximation would not be good enough. Far from it—the irrational relationships on which equal temperament relies were strictly banished from this tradition: in a cautionary tale from Pythagorean lore, the mathematician Hippasus was punished for experimenting with irrational numbers by drowning at sea. In the physiological domain, from the perspective of our auditory apparatus, the consonances produced in 19-tone equal temperament (on an Opelt siren, or any other instrument) are virtually indistinguishable from those derived from purely intoned intervals, but music theory can no longer rely on a numerical justification, based on the simplicity of ratios.

In a word, you simply cannot have it both ways. Sulzer's construct trod the fine line between numbers and stimuli, between *ratio* and *sensus*, but the coincidence between both is not foundational. Our current age may be inclined to see the empirical side of Sulzer's thought experiment as more relevant, but we shouldn't rush to conclusions here. There are currently a number of competing empirically grounded theories, and the only thing that seems certain is that no single theory can explain the phenomena of consonance and dissonance, at least not in the free-wheeling sense in which music theorists like to employ the concepts.[15]

The reason for this discrepancy is simple. Music-theoretical conceptions of consonance/dissonance generally start from the note, an abstract category, best understood as a blueprint for a performance, that does not in itself have particular physical properties of tone and is generalizable according to the rules of musical composition.[16] Empirical approaches to consonance and dissonance, by contrast, generally start with the properties of sound.[17] Thus the cognitive music theorist David Huron points out that from a perceptual point of view, the interval of the minor second can sound more consonant than a major third—provided the stimuli are presented in just intonation as pure sine waves, under optimum conditions, as shown in Figure 16.5 and ⏵ Audio Example 16.2.[18] In the first pair of intervals, the vast majority of subjects judged the first interval more pleasing than the second one, just as one would expect, whereas most musicians were taken aback by how "dissonant" the just major third sounded in the second pair. In other words, the specific timbre and the specific register in which the pitches are presented can have a pronounced effect on dissonance perception.

FIGURE 16.5 David Huron's demonstration of consonant and dissonant intervals.

Physiological or acoustical explanations of consonance and dissonance have often been in tension with compositional and intellectual music-theoretical approaches, largely because they are based on different sets of assumptions: the conceptual abstractions with which music-theoretical discourse operates map only in part onto empirical approaches.[19] And conversely, these theoretical constructs are always intersected by cultural and historical factors, which often follow different principles than empirical experimentation. Perhaps the best point that we can make with any certainty in this regard is the observation that habituation plays a major part in our sense of consonance and dissonance.

CONSONANCE/DISSONANCE AS VOICE-LEADING RULE

Although many theorists and musicians have attempted over the centuries to discuss consonance and dissonance as isolated acoustic phenomena—that is, as "events"— as the previous section has shown, these attempts have always been complicated by the rules of counterpoint: dissonances need to resolve into consonances. The two approaches, while historically related to each other, are not fully congruent and can at times cut across one another. The most famous problem is the complicated status of the perfect fourth. Applying Pythagorean principles, the interval is one of the central consonances (4:3), whereas from a voice-leading perspective, the perfect fourth, when formed with the bass, is a dissonant interval that is in need of resolution. René Descartes offers a striking geometric arrangement of those intervals that his age considered consonant, stacked within the compass of the octave (called *diapasson* in the image), as shown in Figure 16.6. Descartes's complementary pairs worked beautifully for most intervals, down to thirds (*ditonus* and *tertia minor*) and sixths (*hexachordon majus* and *minus*) in their major and minor versions.[20] The perfect fifth (*diapente*) and fourth (*diatessaron*) form another complementary, visually appealing arrangement. But conceptually, the fourth was the odd one out. Descartes was reduced to calling it "the unhappiest" of the consonances, introducing it as the "mere shadow" of its complementary interval, the perfect fifth (Descartes 1992, 24). He was awkwardly grasping for an explanation because consonance-as-event treated the fourth differently than dissonance-as-rule.

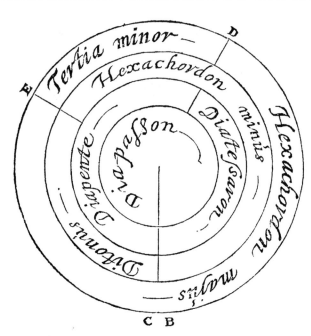

FIGURE 16.6 Descartes's representation of consonant intervals as complementary sectors within concentric rings, from *Compendium musicae* (Descartes 1992, 10).

The classification of certain intervals as "imperfect consonances," which was common during the Middle Ages, speaks to this conflict: a class of intervals (usually comprising thirds, sixths, and tenths) was classified as dissonant when considered in its own right, and acceptable in certain voice-leading contexts. The thirteenth-century music theorist Anonymous IV, for one, didn't mince his words when he called the major sixth in itself a *vilis discordantia*, a vile dissonance, which immediately becomes an *optima concordantia*, the best consonance, if it precedes the octave (Coussemaker 1864, 1:359).[21]

A voice-leading complication that is less well known nowadays, because it has become obsolete in tonal four-part writing, unlike the dissonance treatment of the fourth, concerns the use of consecutive major thirds. The traditional rules of counterpoint hold that successions of major thirds in conjunct motion are not allowed.[22] The German music theorist Johann Mattheson, writing in the mid-eighteenth century, emphatically rejected this rule:

> There used to be a rule that ... two major thirds should not be sounded in succession, but only in alternation [with minor thirds]. Nowadays we have cast off this yoke, though multiple major thirds in succession are rarely encountered.
>
> (Mattheson 1739, 269)[23]

Considerations of "dissonance as event" cannot apply here: if a major third is considered a consonant interval (as it was at least since Zarlino emphatically declared it so in 1558), it should not matter how many times it is sounded. The relevant considerations, rather, concerned the rules of counterpoint, and particularly the relationship between scale and harmonic structure.

The explanation for this age-old prohibition falls under the rubric of *mi-contra-fa*. It is an error *propter relationem non-harmonicam* [*tritoni*], as Matthesons forebear and music-theoretical foil Wolfgang Printz put it at the close of the seventeenth century (Printz 1696, 78, 91).[24] Taken together, two major thirds a whole tone apart would span the range of tritone, traditionally the most dissonant interval, which is to say these two intervals producing false relations could not be accommodated within one hexachord. Mattheson, by contrast, set out to show how this was not a problem: in Figure 16.7, he created contexts in which rising or falling consecutive major thirds could sound good. The numbers 1–2–3 mark the major thirds in each example—it's no surprise that Mattheson also dismisses all diabolical associations of the tritone, considering it instead a "pleasant interval" (Mattheson 1739, 52n).[25] The key to these examples is in the detail: the added barlines guide our imaginary hearing and turn these abstract voice-leading examples into compositional miniatures.[26] The two examples present the parallel voices in a tonal context as cadential gestures in the minor mode, a half cadence in the first place, and a perfect cadence in the second.

Mattheson took a broad approach to false relations. False relations, per his working definition, are "two tones sounded in succession in separate voices that cannot otherwise be brought together without creating an unpleasant sound" (Mattheson 1739, 289).[27] Put differently, he regarded false relations as dissonances laid out over time. In Figure 16.7, he marked the intervals created between B♭ and C♯ in the first half and the diminished fourth between C and F♯ in the second, by diagonal slashes between upper and lower parts—and proceeded to argue that these in fact constitute no problem. The false relations that Mattheson highlights constitute only a sampling of all that are potentially included in these passages: another tritone occurs between B♭ and E in both halves of the example, and the (non-successive) intervals C♮–C♯ from the first half and B♭–F♯ in the second would also fall under Mattheson's broad rubric of false relations.

It would seem that we don't have to look far in the musical literature to find examples of these two figures. Mattheson's figures can be identified as versions of what Robert Gjerdingen (2007) has called the "Prinner" (with $\frac{3\,2\,1\,7}{8\,7\,6\,5}$ in the outer parts) and a

FIGURE 16.7 Johann Mattheson's demonstration that consecutive major thirds are not a problem, from *Der vollkommene Kapellmeister* (Mattheson 1739, 269). The numbers 1–2–3 mark the major thirds in the examples; the diagonal lines highlight two intervals usually considered problematic.

cadencing schema ($^{5\,6\,7\,8}_{3\,4\,5\,1}$) in the *partimento* tradition. And from a more explicitly tonal point of view, the first example can be captured as a half cadence, while the second outlines a i⁶–ii⁶–V–i progression that becomes fairly standard in much eighteenth-century music (with the chromatic twist that the ii chord is not a diminished harmony here but a regular minor one). More specifically, Mattheson's descending Phrygian figure resembles what is sometimes called the "Andalusian cadence." And Domenico Scarlatti's sonata in B♭ major K 47/L 46, in Figure 16.8, shows a good example of such descending thirds sounding over a pedal C.

But one thing is striking: while Mattheson's figures can be found in a range of seventeenth- and eighteenth-century music—especially in passacaglias or chaconnes where the descending fourth is used as a lamento bass—it is relatively rare to find them in this precise configuration, as the examples listed under Figure 16.9 indicate. Monteverdi's expressively dissonant "Lamento della ninfa" from the *Eighth Book of Madrigals* (1638) largely eschews the middle parallel thirds.[28] In the other instances, parallel thirds are avoided by means of suspensions or contrary motion: the example given here singles out two striking iterations among many. Heinrich Biber's Passacaglia for solo violin (1676) consistently alters the parallelism of his figuration for the third interval of this pattern. Note especially the fourth iteration in the example. And Elisabeth-Claude Jacquet de la Guerre's Sonata in D major (1707) introduces melodic figuration that avoids precise parallel thirds.[29]

Mattheson is correct to note that parallel major thirds in succession "are only rarely encountered." In light of these examples, perhaps there is more to Mattheson's point than the explicit authorization to dismiss an archaic rule that had long been ignored in practice. What is interesting about the way in which the examples eschew consecutive major thirds is that it they *don't* avoid the false relations, the implied tritone, as one might expect. In the conception of these pieces—explicit in the laments, implicit in the sonata—it was paramount to preserve the descending bass. It was the upper part, therefore, that had to be modified—even though the offending implied dissonance, *mi-contra-fa*, paradoxically, remained.

In other words, Mattheson's dismissal of the prohibition of consecutive major thirds updated a compositional practice that seemed to adhere to traditional contrapuntal rules without actually paying heed to the problem the rules were designed to avoid. But more momentously, Mattheson's observations indicate a fundamentally changed conception of consonance and dissonance, at the heart of which is an intimate connection to modern conceptions of scale. The old rule was based on the diatonic collections of

FIGURE 16.8 Domenico Scarlatti, Sonata in B♭ major K 47/L 46, mm. 14–15.

FIGURE 16.9 Instances of Mattheson's schema. (a) Claudio Monteverdi, "Lamento della Ninfa" from the Eighth Book of Madrigals, Lament, mm. 33–37. (b) Heinrich Biber, Passacaglia for Violin solo, mm. 1–8. (c) Elisabeth-Claude Jacquart de la Guerre, Sonata no. 1 in D major, first movt, mm. 23–27. All instances demonstrate ways to avoid parallel major thirds.

hexachordal theory, and Mattheson's demonstration to the contrary replaces this under-lying basis with the minor scale in its multiple chromatic variants (merging melodic and natural). Against this new underlying conception of how the tonal material was organ-ized, it should be no surprise that Mattheson considered the old rules of counterpoint an unnecessary and outdated yoke that badly needed to be shaken off.

INTERMISSION: CROSS-CULTURAL CONSONANCES

This is a good moment to pause for an excursion and an outlook into the wider research on consonance and dissonance that goes beyond the confines of the Western tradition. The ground we have covered so far shows that the twin concepts of consonance and dissonance span various dimensions, and that no single approach—numerical, physio-logical, historical—can capture all aspects. It would not be difficult to show, moreover, how cultural variation leads to different attitudes toward consonance and dissonance. In his chapter on Polyphony in this volume, Michael Tenzer discusses a Croatian duet moving predominantly in diminished thirds, which offers a good example of a dif-ferent approach to dissonance treatment. Or take Balinese gamelan, which values the "shimmering" quality of paired instruments that are tuned slightly differently, resulting in beating between upper partials. But these are ultimately different aesthetic evaluations of a phenomenon that can essentially be explained with reference to the physics of the soundwave; as such it is still predicated on a fundamental distinction be-tween consonance and dissonance. Despite all the cultural, historical, and aesthetic vari-ance, a general capacity to discriminate between consonance and dissonance is assumed to be—somehow—universal.

A group of neuroscientists at MIT working with Josh McDermott sent shockwaves around the musical world in 2016, when they cast doubt on this fundamental assump-tion.[30] In a series of experiments, they played simultaneous intervals to subjects from different cultural backgrounds and asked them to rate the pleasantness—which they equated with consonance—of these intervals. This equation may seem problematic, but given the linguistic and cultural complexities of cross-cultural research, this may be a necessary simplification. The researchers made the surprising discovery that the Tsimane', an indigenous people living along the Amazon in lowland Bolivia, largely un-affected by the products of the Western world, are indifferent to consonance and disso-nance. McDermott concluded "that consonance preferences can be absent in cultures sufficiently isolated from Western music, and are thus unlikely to reflect innate biases or exposure to harmonic natural sounds" (McDermott, Schultz, Undurraga, and Gudoy 2016, 547). Do the Tsimane' really not discriminate between consonance and disso-nance? What are the consequences of these findings?

It may be worth probing this startling conclusion a little deeper, from a music-theoretical perspective, as this may lead us to reconsider the ramifications of our thinking about consonance and dissonance. As indicated earlier, music theory has a habit of lumping together separate aspects of the concept that may or may not be related, and to treat them as if they were the same. The case of the Tsimane' offers a rare opportunity to pry apart some of these conflations, or rather to probe whether there is a connection or not. How deep does the concept of consonance reach into the fabric of tonal organization?

Two aspects come into focus here. First, there is additional evidence from the Tsimane', presented in passing but left unexamined by McDermott et al., that may offer interesting insights: Tsimane' singing. McDermott's group includes two recordings of Tsimane' song, reproduced in ⓑ Audio Examples 16.3a and 16.3b. Despite some small fluctuations in intonation, these recordings confirm the findings of the only ethnomusicological study available on Tsimane' music (Riester 1978), which transcribes a range of songs as following the anhemitonic pentatonic scale.

As in the previous example from Mattheson, it is useful to consider the notion of consonance and dissonance in the context of the scale systems within which they are employed. Scales, in the everyday sense that we generally use—which also applies to Tsimane' music—are based on fixed-interval steps, and these must on some level embed interval preferences. In an exhaustive statistical analysis, Huron (1994) showed that the anhemitonic pentatonic scale is unusual: it is *optimally* consonant, that is, it contains more consonant intervals than all other scales of similar size. To be sure, this does not mean that the scale yields exclusively consonances: like all scales, the anhemitonic pentatonic scale is a grab bag of pitches that can be combined in any number of ways, to construct intervals that are consonant or dissonant.[31] Huron grants that cultural inertia and habit may play a part in scale generation, but the generating principle of the anhemitonic pentatonic scale—by means of concatenation of fifths—is intervallic consonance.

Huron is aware of cross-cultural implications, but his statistical methodology is not interested in particulars of various cultures. Thus, an obvious objection presents itself: does this conclusion not in fact beg the question? Are we not presupposing here that the fifth *is* consonant, and concluding—hey presto—that the fifth is consonant (which would obviously be a tautology)? I think not: it doesn't matter so much that we call the specific most abundant interval, the fifth, a consonance, as rather what we do with it. It becomes a question of preference for certain intervals over others, which is, after all, what McDermott et al. were investigating.

We can also ask the other way around: if the Tsimane' showed no preference for consonance at all, for certain intervals over others, is it likely that a fixed scale could have emerged in their culture? On what principles would the scale be constructed? Without a preference for certain intervals over others, how would the Tsimane' have developed a memory for intervals in the first place? As it is, the perfect fifth is the most hierarchically abundant interval in the scale. It is useful to bear in mind that this is not backsliding into some kind of outmoded naturalism. Or put differently: the critical point is not that the anhemitonic pentatonic scale is somehow "based" on perfect fifths, but rather that, absent a preference for certain intervals over others, it is hard to imagine how this scale could have come about in the first place. What exactly are the mechanisms by which a culture makes a scale its own? At this level, the hypothesis seems inescapable that the very structure of the anhemitonic pentatonic scale, and the Tsimane' use of it, would reflect a selection based on a fundamental bias for certain intervals, which we can also call consonances.

And second, McDermott et al. note that the Tsimane' have a monophonic musical culture; so, it is likely that the phenomenon of two different pitches sounding simultaneously is foreign to them. Is it possible that what the Tsimane' registered in these experiments was first and foremost their unfamiliarity with simultaneous pitches? To put this armchair critique in perspective, it is worth acknowledging that cross-cultural cognitive fieldwork is immensely difficult, and the findings that this research yielded are nothing short of impressive. It could be argued that the questions raised here boil down to a problem of definition. Can simultaneous (harmonic) intervals in fact be equated with successive (melodic) ones? The two are generally treated in music-theoretical discourse as though they were interchangeable, which may or may not be justified.[32] The case of Tsimane' dissonance perception opens up a unique scenario in which this common equivocation could be put to the test. If one limits the concepts of consonance and dissonance to harmonic simultaneities and separates them from melodic intervals, then McDermott et al.'s conclusions hold, and this would be the end of the story. But if the Tsimane' have a conception of melodic consonance/dissonance that is separate from its harmonic counterpart, this would complicate the story in interesting ways.

This issue can also be framed as an extension of questions we raised in earlier sections. First, we recognized that cognitive science and music theory (the latter taken here in its conventional definition with its roots in the humanities) take different approaches to the definition of consonance and dissonance. This difference can handily be summarized as percept-vs.-concept. That is to say, whereas we know that music theory typically treats melodic and harmonic intervals as conceptually equivalent, McDermott et al.'s findings raise the possibility that melodic consonances might exist in their own right in the realm of perception.[33] The basis for this assumption—a hypothetical, to be sure—is given in the existence of a stable scale among the Tsimane', which must, by necessity, be based on a form of tonal memory. These questions of memory and the structure of the scale, second, take us back to Mattheson's reconfiguration of consonance in the context of contrapuntal traditions in the early eighteenth century. Mattheson's work was symptomatic of a broader shift in musical thought, which led us further toward more fundamental questions of scales, or rather Tymoczko's macroharmonies, and the sounds we retain in our memory as we encounter new ones.

Ancient Greek music theory offers an interesting point of comparison. Greek musical culture was monophonic, like that of the Tsimane', but discussions of consonance and dissonance, *symphoniai* and *diaphoniai*, were the bread-and-butter topics of their theoretical and philosophical treatises. And the famous scene at the blacksmith's workshop, in which the clanking of the hammers on anvils revealed the secret of consonances based on simple ratios to Pythagoras, enshrines simultaneous intervals at the very heart of musical thought.[34] The endless discussions about how to divide the string of the monochord that makes up a large part of Greek theorizing, by contrast, describes a practice of successive intervals. It was something of a badge of honor for orthodox Pythagoreans to reject dichords, with two strings sounding simultaneously, which would have been much more practical to handle.[35] What can be said, at the very least, is that the Greeks had an implicit understanding of the equivalence between simultaneous and successive intervals, even if they likely employed only one type in their music.

Can this be generalized? Are simultaneous and successive intervals two sides of the same coin? If consonance and dissonance are conceived as harmonic *and* melodic phenomena, the picture among the Tsimane' would become considerably more complex. The musical structures of Tsimane' melodies, and the existence of a stable scale, seem at least to suggest that the Tsimane' might discriminate between consonance and dissonance if these were presented not as simultaneous but as successive intervals, in keeping with their own musical practice. It would be instructive if further empirical testing of Tsimane' preferences for melodic intervals might be carried out. If a preference for certain melodic intervals were confirmed, this would not mean that we should revert to the outmoded position that specific consonances are universal. What it would mean is that each scale system implies a commitment to certain consonant intervals. The special anthropological perspective of Tsimane' music is interesting because it might shed some light on the unsolved question of how consonance is bound up with the construction of scales—that is, how consonances function in some of the most fundamental processes of music. And ultimately, this might give us a fuller understanding of the significance of consonance and dissonance within the organization of musical structures.

CONSONANCE/DISSONANCE AS TENSION AND RELAXATION

In the preceding sections, we have probed, destabilized, shaken up, and reframed the concept of consonance and dissonance. In the context of historical and cultural variability of the term covered so far, we can now return to our starting point, the harmonic series serving as the purported wellspring of consonance and dissonance. Arnold Schoenberg employed this useful fiction to his own ends when he posited in his *Harmonielehre* (1911) that there was no categorical distinction between consonance and dissonance, but rather a gradual journey of discovery.[36] If upper partials form the basis of consonance, as he assumed they did, then even the remoter partials should be taken into account. Even when these remoter partials are inaudible, they still contribute to the "total phenomenon of the tone—tone accepted as euphonious, suitable for art" (Schoenberg 1983, 21), just less perceptibly and more unconsciously. As the ear becomes more familiar with these remoter partials, it learns to accept a greater range of consonances, or rather "what is euphonious, suitable for art," as Schoenberg repeats for added emphasis (1983, 21), deliberately avoiding the charged conventional terminology.

This gradual progression toward an ever-greater number of euphonious sounds, then, has an impact on the evolution of Western music. Music history could effectively be understood, from a technical perspective, as a progressive expansion of the concept of consonance, moving an imaginary slider higher and higher up along the elements of the harmonic series.

There is a certain appealing logic that is also borne out, to a certain extent, by the stations that we have visited over the course of this chapter: from the first four partials, in ancient and early medieval theory, via the first six, in the early modern period. Anything beyond these two instances, however, gets hand-wavey very quickly. Schoenberg sought to extend this progression with the view to getting rid of the categorical distinction between consonance and dissonance altogether, in the service of his own advanced use of harmony. Other than the neat analogy between moving along a chronological time axis and a spatialized axis of upper partials, however, there is little to support this Spencerian idea of an evolution of consonance and dissonance. The whole idea remains a conceptualization, a schematic image, which has the additional advantage of allowing Schoenberg to remove the slider altogether and proclaim the "emancipation of the dissonance."

But Schoenberg succeeded in capturing a phenomenon that was being discussed in his age, although usually within a different conceptual frame. By projecting it onto the harmonic series, Schoenberg's schema externalizes a process that would be better located in the realm of psychology. It is impossible not to think here of the famous opening of Wagner's *Tristan* prelude, that poster child of nineteenth-century chromaticism. After all, early responses were alternately shocked and elated by what they heard or saw in the score. Thus, the conductor Hans von Bülow reported excitedly to his friend, the composer Felix Draeseke, that "not a single pure triad is to be found, not a single one" (Bailey 1985, 13).

Wagner's progressive chromaticism need not, however, lead with inevitable drive toward Schoenberg's emancipation of dissonance. There are at least two distinct ways in which the use of consonance and dissonance has been imagined in this famous operatic passage. The critical point here is not the celebrated, endlessly analyzed sonority of the "Tristan chord" itself, but the conclusion of each of the phrases. The three opening phrases, which are sequences of one another (loose in the third case), end by progressing from sharper to lesser dissonances—or, put differently, by offering partial, incomplete release from tension. One approach has argued that in the terms of Wagner's advanced chromatic language, these dominant seventh chords offer closure equivalent to a triad's capacity to effect closure in a conventional tonal idiom (Bailey 1985, 120). This argument aligns by and large with Schoenberg's view toward an ever-greater acceptance of dissonance that will eventually lead to the emancipation of dissonance. Others have countered, meanwhile, that the concluding dominant sevenths point beyond themselves, toward (unsounded) tonics (see Hyer 1989). While the sounded chords do not offer absolute closure in their own right, they point to a stable tonal center that lies outside of what is sounded.

This second option is best captured by a psychological approach to consonance and dissonance that Hugo Riemann explained in 1882:

If I think to myself of a C-major chord in the context of the key of C major, it is itself the tonic, center, conclusive chord, its mental representation thus contains nothing that opposes its consonance, it appears calm, pure, simple; but if I think to myself of a G-major chord in the context of the key of C major, then I think of it as the *Klang* of the over-fifth of the C-major *Klang*; that is, the C-major chord itself enters the mental representation as the *Klang* by which the significance of the G-major chord is determined as something departing from it—the center of the mental representation, then, lies outside it, so to speak; that is, an element of unrest occurs in it, the desire for a progression to the C-major chord, dissonance.

(Steege 2011, 84)

Riemann presents a striking conception of consonance, in which the tonal center serves as the sole perfect consonance, and any other chordal sonority is measured against this (imagined) tonal center. This psychological conception is built on a notion of tonal memory, and it conceives of consonance and dissonance in terms of tension and relaxation. Riemann may be the first to spell out this general principle built on triadic harmonies, but a comparable psychological conception was already present in Mattheson's example: the outmoded prohibition of consecutive thirds had been based on an underlying conception of tonal memory—or, to be precise, on the *avoidance* of certain sounds in relation to our aural memory. In effect, this conception is nothing more—and nothing less—than the core idea of counterpoint, in which all dissonances must be resolved into consonances.

But if we follow Schoenberg's narrative, the other path outlined above, it is the very need to resolve that is being suspended. The difference between tension and relaxation by means of a tonal hierarchical order is eliminated. The explicitly political metaphor of the emancipation of the dissonance also changes the role of the consonance, which no longer has any power to resolve anything. But this does not mean that tension and resolution have become irrelevant in the fabric of music; what it *does* mean, however, is that other parameters play a more important role. To choose an example from the Schoenberg circle, Figure 16.10 shows the closing measures of Alban Berg's first of the Four Pieces for Clarinet and Piano op. 5 (note that the clarinet part, though without key signature, is a transposing part, written in B♭).

The ample markings in the final measures, which indicate progressive ritardando and diminuendo down to a final *pppp* in the piano, are only the tip of the iceberg. The repeated sonorities in piano and clarinet in decelerating rhythms also contribute to a sense of coming to a gradual standstill, which is carefully set up in the clarinet in m. 9 with a chromatic wedge that leads into the final repeated G♯ (notated A♮). But even the motivic-harmonic figures provide closure: as the notation shows, the upper staff of the piano is divided into two trichords each including a fourth, a tritone, and a major seventh, [016] or 3-5, in Forte's pc-set taxonomy. The lower staff of the piano, together with the clarinet, sounds a third [016] trichord. Only the B♮0 at the bottom end of the piano, the final bass note, is not part of this organization, which instead links up with the low D♯1 in the same register that was sounded earlier in m. 8.

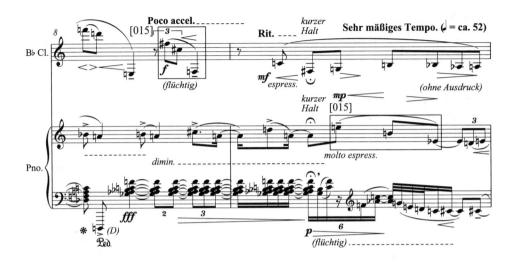

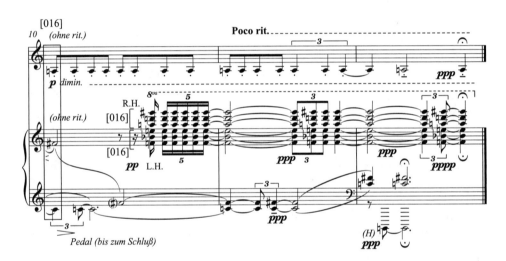

FIGURE 16.10   Alban Berg, Vier Stücke für Klarinette und Klavier op. 5, no. 1, mm. 8–12.

Closure is not created by specific pitches here. Despite its emphatic bass register, the B♭0 cannot be said to function as a tonal center in any relevant way. This function is instead taken over by a particular interval configuration, the [016] trichord that is sounded almost obsessively in these last measures of the piece. These trichords are the equivalent of consonance; they offer repose, release from tension, in the context of this piece. In this, they are deployed in a strategic way, as the graphically suggestive notation underlines. Much of the piece is permeated by a slightly different trichord, [015] or 3–4, right from the three opening notes in the clarinet, A♭4–E♭4–G3 (notated B♭–F♮–A♮), not shown in the example. Our music example shows two prominent instances of this trichord, the descending clarinet figure in the second half of m. 8, E♮4–B♮3–E♭2, echoed in the following measure in the piano, as E♮4–B♮3–E♭3. The [016] trichord, by contrast, is withheld except for very few structurally significant moments. It is employed to demarcate an end, to signify a form of closure, exactly in the way one would expect consonance to function in other musical idioms.

The American experimentalist Henry Cowell once suggested taking Schoenberg's historical model one step further. In the early twentieth century, he envisioned a musical future in which consonance and dissonance would simply invert their roles. Based on his training in Bachian counterpoint, he imagined a topsy-turvy world in which seconds, seventh, and tritones served as foundation intervals, and thirds, fifths, and sixths were only admitted as passing intervals. Octaves, Cowell added, would only be permitted in the most exceptional circumstances (Cowell 1996, 39). Almost a hundred years after Cowell sketched out this musical *Erewhon*, the straightforward inversion of relations is not quite what has happened in Western music. Individual instances can be found, to be sure, in which consonant intervals "resolve" into dissonances.[37] But a sustained effort to fully invert the relationship between intervals that are generally considered consonant and dissonant would be difficult to accomplish. The problem, I imagine, is less any natural barrier that would prohibit such a radical move than the sluggishness of our listening habits, our ears' continued willingness to accommodate the familiar. At the same time, examples such as Berg's clarinet piece—and there are many others—show ways in which patterns of tension and relaxation can be created outside the conventional hierarchies of consonance and dissonance.

CONCLUSION

Let's stay with the systematizing force of pitch-class sets for a little longer. If we turn the possible intervals of the twelve-tone chromatic scale into halftone steps, it is striking that three contiguous interval classes—3, 4, and 5—encompass those intervals that are generally considered consonant in the tonal tradition: minor thirds and major sixths, major thirds and minor sixths, and the perfect fifth. Could this be more than a coincidence? As so often, when neat systematicities seem tantalizingly within reach, the details must disappoint: Descartes's "saddest interval," the perfect fourth, trips us up, as do the perfect octave and the perfect unison, which are not included in this cluster.

The real problem is captured, of course, in the phrasing of "those intervals that are generally considered consonant in the tonal tradition." The idea of treating those intervals in isolation only ever works in the theory classroom—it is a Platonist's dream. In reality, various other factors come into play at any given moment: range and timbre play a vital part when we take our starting point in cognitive or acoustical approaches; historically appropriate notions of style come to the fore in the contrapuntal tradition, and once we step outside the Western modal-tonal tradition, then all the bets are off. Habituation is an important factor, and Berg's example suggests that the combination of secondary parameters (such as tempo, loudness, register) can contribute to a sense of tension and relaxation that is at the heart of consonance and dissonance in its most abstract form.

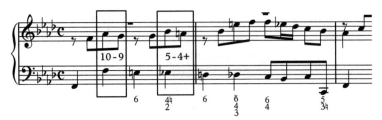

FIGURE 16.11 J. S. Bach, Sinfonia no. 9 in F minor, BWV 795, mm. 1–3.

The notion of consonance and dissonance is so fundamental to the experience of music in the Western tradition, and at the same time the underlying principles are so heterogeneous, that the most instructive examples are those in which two or more regulatory frameworks are in conflict with one another. We saw these competing principles at work in the initial "homophone" from Haydn's String Quartet op. 50 no. 2, which turned the conventions of the Classical style against itself. Mattheson's composed examples presented empirical evidence against the contrapuntal prohibitions of hexachordal music theory. Berg had left behind the tonal idiom, and with it the hierarchies of consonance and dissonance, but the formal articulation of his composition continued in the same tradition of dissonant tension and consonant relaxation within his motivic-harmonic idiom.

Perhaps the best way to conclude, then, is to consider a particularly striking example from J. S. Bach's three-part invention in F minor BWV 795.[38] On the surface, the two-part counterpoint seems to contradict the most basic rules of dissonant treatment: in the opening two-part counterpoint the three-note motive in the right hand strikes a number of consonances that "resolve" by downward step into dissonances: the A♭ on the second beat "resolves" into G forming a ninth against the F in the bass; the B♭ "resolves" into a tritone A♮ against E♭ in the bass. Is this the topsy-turvy world that Henry Cowell imagined?

Not so fast. Closer inspection shows that the strict punctus-contra-punctum framework is deceptive. The bassline outlines a chromatic lamento bass, a descending fourth, not dissimilar from the ones Mattheson invoked in Figure 16.9(a) and (b). This well-known bassline pattern implied a harmonization even when presented solo or, as here, with minimal accompaniment. Against this implied harmonization, indicated in Figure 16.11 with added figured bass annotations, the sharp intervallic dissonances disappear: the G on the second beat is an anticipation of the V_6 that arises when the bass drops to E♮ in the third beat, and the E♭–A tritone can be heard as part of the V_2^4/IV that properly resolves outwards into the sixth D–B♭ in the following measure. When regarded in its proper framework, the apparently faulty voice leading disappears. In this case, too, the question of consonance and dissonance turns out to be a matter of perspective.

There is hardly an area in which music theory has invested as much energy over the centuries as in the formulation of rules for dissonance treatment. This is only understandable, since consonance and dissonance have for the longest time been considered fundamental to our conception of music. But just as music changes, so do the conceptions of (and approaches to) the consonance and dissonance pair. This is why the apparently immutable laws with which music theory's pedagogical wing has traditionally liked to operate are in fact surprisingly liable to change. This does not mean that consonance and dissonance are completely arbitrary. But it does mean that in concrete situations there is considerable wiggle room, which composers—and theorists—have been able exploit in interesting ways. Despite appearances, then, consonance and dissonance are in the beholder's ears.

Audio Examples

Audio Example 16.1. Excerpt from Joseph Haydn, String Quartet op. 50, no. 2, first movement.

Audio Example 16.2. Test intervals from David Huron's demonstration (recorded by Christopher Danforth).

Audio Example 16.3a. A recording of Tsimane' song. (from McDermott et al. 2016).

Audio Example 16.3b. A recording of Tsimane' song. (from McDermott et al. 2016).

Notes

1. I tip my hat here to Brian Hyer, who, as so often, has come up with just the right image to clothe musical experiences in words.

2. One difference between the verbal and the musical homophones are their respective lengths. The verbal joke thrives on the brevity of the two statements, which forces us to reconstruct their syntax in retrospect, whereas Haydn is eager to expand the flat section to give our ears time to adjust.

3. For historical discussions of the augmented triad, see Weitzmann (1853) and Tappert (1868).

4. This chapter makes no claims to terminological comprehensiveness. Beiche (2001), which approaches the long history of the concepts from the perspective of German *Begriffsgeschichte*, is very good at teasing out the terminological subtleties. Conceptual extensions, such as metric dissonance, and sonic extensions, as are found in blues and jazz traditions, also fall outside the scope of this chapter.

5. For an epic example of applying these connotations fancifully, see Kennedy (2014).

6. Among the rare exceptions that introduce a third intermediary category, we find Gerolamo Cardano, Vincenzo Galilei, and Paul Hindemith. James Tenney is quite interested in the phenomenon of this third category; see especially Tenney (1988, 2, 46, and 54–55). For "imperfect consonances" and the special role of the perfect fourth, see the section "Consonance/Dissonance as Voice-Leading Rule."

7. We don't need to go into the even more dubious implications that consonance is somehow given by nature and therefore immutable; see Clark and Rehding (2001).

8. I am grateful to Arne Stollberg, who first pointed out this important example to me.

9. At various points in the history of music theory, different terms were introduced for a consonance of more than two sounds, such as Zarlino's "perfect proper harmony," or Carl Stumpf's "concordance," but these were never widely adopted.

10. The critical word here is *Empfindung*, which is typically translated as "sensation." But in Sulzer's specific usage, *Empfindung* is not necessarily restricted to the sensory realm, as he underlines in the eponymous entry in *Allgemeine Theorie der schönen Künste*.

11. Leibniz's definition is taken from a letter to Christian Goldbach (April 17, 1712). This letter states *animae* (of the soul), whereas the widely read print version changed this word into *animi* (of the spirit).

12. The wheel was initially conceived by the English natural philosopher Robert Hooke in the seventeenth century, but takes its modern name, confusingly, from the early nineteenth-century French physicist Félix Savart, who used it to test human audition.

13. The terms "indistinct" and "clear" should not be taken as value judgments—they describe different qualities of (sensual/intellectual) sensation. The category of intensity cuts across them: the most intense sensation in Sulzer's account, sexual pleasure, clearly belongs to the sensual world.

14. There is no indication that Opelt—who was a tax collector by day—was aware of Sulzer's aesthetics. It is more likely that Euler was Opelt's inspiration, from mathematician to mathematician. For an introduction to Opelt's music theories, see Rehding (forthcoming).

15. David Huron lists no fewer than fourteen distinct approaches (plus an additional two, for good measure) to explain the phenomena of consonance and dissonance: https://music-cog.ohio-state.edu/Music829B/main.theories.html.

16. One could even argue, more specifically, the basis for "consonance/dissonance as event" is pitch, whereas the concept of the note forms the basis of the contrapuntal approach of "consonance/dissonance as voice-leading rule." See also the chapter "Pitch, Tone, and Note" in this volume.

17. Thompson (2015) provides an excellent overview of recent scientific theories.

18. Listen to this sound example with headphones. Conventional computer speakers add too much distortion. The experiment is described on https://music-cog.ohio-state.edu/Music829B/ratios.html.

19. Huron (2016) makes an impressive effort to bridge that divide.

20. The *ditonus* is usually defined as the Pythagorean third $81:64 = (9:8)^2$, whereas Descartes is talking here about the simpler (and slightly larger) just major third $5:4$. Descartes provides no reason for consistently referring to the major third as *ditonus* in this treatise. The letters in his Euclidian diagram (from B–E) refer not to pitch names but to divisions of a line, an imaginary monochord, which Descartes used previously to derive intervals. In turning this line into a circle, he lost one-half of its length, between A and B.

21. The complex history of classifying consonances and dissonances during the period of early polyphony goes beyond the scope of this chapter; suffice it to say that the boundaries were in flux. See Beiche (2001).

22. This rule goes back to early polyphony, in which no identical consonances could be sounded in parallel succession: the prohibition was strict for perfect consonances and

recommended for imperfect consonances. Fétis (1844, 1:17) includes the prohibition of parallel major thirds; Schenker (1910, 202) and (1922, 42–43) also discusses it.

23. The full rule also includes consecutive minor thirds, but Mattheson dismisses this part of the rule without providing any reasons. (Thanks go to Roger Grant for interesting conversations about Mattheson.)

24. The "tritoni" specification is mentioned in the paragraph preceding the example, but should clearly apply in this case, too. Printz has no prohibition for consecutive minor thirds in stepwise motion, only in leaps; see Printz (1696, 83).

25. Strictly speaking, Mattheson is discussing the diminished fifth, not the tritone proper (that is, the augmented fourth), although the reference to the *diabolus in musica* is unmistakable.

26. Mattheson (1739, 269) creates a further example, this time in fashionable galant style, with as many as four major thirds in a row, which essentially expands the second example of Figure 16.7 by inserting a deceptive cadence. For this example, he adds a third voice, to clarify the harmonic context.

27. Needless to say, this working definition is not without problems. Mattheson devotes a whole chapter to false relations (1739, 289–296). He concludes his exploration by arguing that not all false relations are "unbearable," and should be handled accordingly.

28. Consecutive major thirds in the middle of the ostinato are sounded only twice, at mm. 9–10 and 17–18, on "dov'è la fe' / ch'el traditor" and at "ch'io / non mi tormenti." Thanks go to Daniel Harrison, whose insightful comments were particularly helpful for this section.

29. This progression is also frequently found in pop music, such as Zager and Evans's pop hit "In the Year 2525" (1969) or the "Stray Cat Strut" (1981). (With thanks to Yael Meroz for pointing me to the Stray Cats.) These examples are far less concerned about consecutive major thirds.

30. This section emerged out of long discussions with Steven Rings.

31. This conception is close to what Tymoczko (2011) calls "macroharmony." See also Harrison (2017, 94).

32. Michael Beiche (2001, 21–22) pinpoints the conceptual separation of melodic from harmonic intervals in Western musical thought in the eleventh century.

33. There are obvious reasons for this conceptual equivocation. In the analysis of Western music—music theory's main field of application—melodic and harmonic aspects are typically seen as interrelated. Western composers have often used intervals or chordal structures as both melodic motifs and harmonic building blocks. And conversely, discovering chordal configurations laid out in the melodic dimension has often been

considered self-evidently relevant in music analysis. Pitch-class set analysis regards the equation between the melodic and harmonic dimensions as fundamental to its principles.

34. See Barker (1989, 2:256–258). The fact that this story is certainly apocryphal—because Pythagoras's mathematical ratios do not correspond to acoustical reality—is a complicating factor, to be sure, but it does not diminish the central relevance of simultaneous consonances to Greek musical thought.

35. Critical of the two major music-theoretical schools that preceded him, Ptolemy embraces multiphonic *kanones* to test musical intervals. He proposes an eight-stringed *kanon*; see Barker (1989, 2:298–301).

36. Leonard Bernstein (1978) proceeds on a similar evolutionary model in his Norton Lectures, with the significant difference that he comes to a screeching halt when the domain of tonality is reached. Bernstein's dissonance remains unemancipated.

37. Two examples can stand paradigmatically for many more: Wagner's *Walküre* Act ii, scene 4 (at "und *Siegmund* lebe mit ihr"), and Brahms's *Alto Rhapsody* op. 53, m. 43 (at "die Öde verschlingt ihn"), offer extraordinary dissonance treatments.

38. I am grateful to Edward Klorman for pointing me to this example.

Works Cited

Abbott, Jacob. 1872. "The Siren of Science; or, the Mode of Numbering Sonorous Vibrations." *Harper's Monthly Magazine* 45: 844–848.

Bailey, Robert. 1985. *Richard Wagner: Prelude and Transfiguration from Tristan und Isolde.* New York: Norton.

Barker, Andrew. 1989. *Greek Musical Writings.* 2 vols. Cambridge: Cambridge University Press.

Beiche, Michael. 2001. "Consonantia—Dissonantia/Konsonanz—Dissonanz." In *Handwörterbuch der musikalischen Terminologie,* edited by Albrecht Riethmüller, 1–60. Wiesbaden: Steiner.

Bernstein, Leonard. 1978. *The Unanswered Question.* Cambridge, MA: Harvard University Press.

Christensen, Thomas, and Nancy Kovaleff Baker, eds. 1995. *Aesthetics and the Art of Composition in the German Enlightenment: Selected Writings of Johann Georg Sulzer and Heinrich Christoph Koch.* Cambridge: Cambridge University Press.

Clark, Suzannah, and Alexander Rehding, eds. 2001. *Music Theory and Natural Order from the Renaissance to the Early Twentieth Century.* Cambridge: Cambridge University Press.

Coussemaker, Edmond de, ed. 1864–1876. *Scriptores musicae medii aevi.* 4 vols. Paris: Durand.

Cowell, Henry. 1996. *New Musical Resources.* Edited by David Nicholls. Cambridge: Cambridge University Press.

Creese, David. 2010. *The Monochord in Ancient Greek Harmonic Science.* Cambridge: Cambridge University Press.

Descartes, René. 1992. *Compendium musicae: Leitfaden der Musik* [1619/1650]. Edited by Johannes Brockt. Darmstadt: Wissenschaftliche Buchgesellschaft.

Euler, Leonard. 1739. *Tentamen novae theoriae musicae.* St. Petersburg: Academia Scientiarum.

Fétis, François-Joseph. 1844. *Traité complet de la théorie et de la pratique de l'harmonie.* Paris: Schlesinger.

Gjerdingen, Robert. 2007. *Music in the Galant Style*. New York: Oxford University Press.

Harrison, Daniel. 2017. *Pieces of Tradition: An Analysis of Contemporary Tonal Music*. New York: Oxford University Press.

Helmholtz, Hermann von. 1954. *On the Sensation of Tone* [1863]. Edited by Alexander Ellis. New York: Dover.

Hilgers, Philipp von. 2003. "Sirenen: Loslösungen des Klanges vom Körper." *Philosophia Scientia* 7: 85–114.

Huron, David. 1994. "Interval-Class Content in Equally Tempered Pitch-Class Sets: Common Scales Exhibit Optimum Tonal Consonance." *Music Perception* 11, no. 3: 289–305.

Hyer, Brian. 1989. "Tonal Intuitions in Wagner's Tristan." PhD diss., Yale University.

Kennedy, Jay. 2014. *The Plato Code*. London: Simon & Schuster.

Kittler, Friedrich. 2005. "Musik als Medium." In *Wahrnehmung und Geschichte: Markierungen zur Aisthesis materialis*, edited by Bernhard J. Dotzler and Ernst Müller, 83–99. Berlin: De Gruyter.

Leisinger, Ulrich. 1994. *Leibniz-Reflexe in der deutschen Musiktheorie des 18. Jahrhunderts*. Würzburg: Königshausen & Neumann.

Mattheson, Johann. 1739. *Der vollkommene Kapellmeister*. Hamburg: Christian Herold.

McDermott, Josh, Alan F. Schultz, Eduard A. Undurraga, and Ricardo A. Gudoy. 2016. "Indifference to Dissonance in Native Amazonians Reveals Cultural Variation in Music Perception." *Nature* 535: 547–550.

Moreno, Jairo. 2004. *Musical Representations, Subjects and Objects*. Indianapolis: Indiana University Press.

Opelt, Friedrich W. 1852. *Allgemeine Theorie der Musik*. Leipzig: Joh. Ambr. Barth.

Printz, Wolfgang. 1696. *Phrynis Mitilenaeus*. Dresden and Leipzig: Johann Christoph Mieth und Johann Christoph Zimmermann.

Rehding, Alexander. Forthcoming. "Opelt's Siren and the Technologies of Music Theory." In *Testing Hearing*, edited by Viktoria Tkaczyk, Alexandra Hui, and Mara Mills.

Riester, Jürgen. 1978. *Canción y producción en la vida de un pueblo indígena: los Chimane, tribu de la selva oriental*. La Paz: Editorial Los Amigos del Libro.

Riley, Matthew. 2004. *Musical Listening in the German Enlightenment: Attention, Wonder, and Astonishment*. Farnham, UK: Ashgate.

Schenker, Heinrich. 1910. *Kontrapunkt: Erster Halbband*. Vienna: Universal.

Schenker, Heinrich. 1922. *Kontrapunkt: Zweiter Halbband*. Vienna: Universal.

Schoenberg, Arnold. 1983. *Theory of Harmony* [1911]. Edited by Roy E. Carter. Berkeley and Los Angeles: University of California Press.

Steege, Benjamin. 2011. "Hugo Riemann, 'The Nature of Harmony': A Translation and Commentary." In *The Oxford Handbook of Neo-Riemannian Music Theories*, edited by Edward Gollin and Alexander Rehding, 55–91. New York: Oxford University Press.

Sulzer, Johann Georg. 1762. *Theorie der angenehmen und unangenehmen Empfindungen*. Berlin: Friedrich Nicolai.

Sulzer, Johann Georg. 1771–1774. *Allgemeine Theorie der schönen Künste*. 4 vols. Leipzig: Weidmann und Reich.

Tappert, Wilhelm Georg. 1868. "Der übermäßige Dreiklang." In *Musikalische Studien*, 117–144. Berlin: Guttentag.

Tenney, James. 1988. *History of Consonance and Dissonance*. New York: Excelsior.

Thompson, William Forde. 2015. "Intervals and Scales." In *The Psychology of Music*, edited by Diana Deutsch, 108–116. New York: Springer.

Tymoczko, Dmitri. 2011. *A Geometry of Music*. New York: Oxford University Press.

Weitzmann, Carl. 1853. *Der übermäßige Dreiklang*. Berlin: Trautwein.

Zarlino, Giuseffo. 1558. *Le istitutioni harmoniche*. 4 vols. Venice: F. De Franceschi.

CHAPTER 17

··

TONAL HARMONY

··

IAN QUINN

HARMONY AND COUNTERPOINT

THE standard accounts of European tonal harmony promulgated by undergraduate theory textbooks these days, although they differ in many ways, begin with a common set of assumptions:

Chord structure. Chords are built by stacking successive thirds on top of roots. A chord's most important attribute is its root; its most important secondary attribute is its quality, determined by the species of the thirds.

Harmonic partitioning. Every moment of a piece or passage of tonal music belongs to one and only one of a series of discrete time-spans, each of which is governed by a single chord or harmony.

Non-harmonic tones. The chord or harmony exerts its governance by creating a marked class of pitches called non-chord tones or non-harmonic tones.

Surface structure. This distinction between in- and out-groups of notes, in turn, regulates local melodic or voice-leading behavior: chord tones may be approached and left freely, but non-chord tones must appear in one of a small number of acceptable formations, including among others passing tones, neighbor tones, and suspensions.

Tonal theory's strongest predictions concern the question of which chords may follow which others. Tymoczko (2003) makes a useful distinction between three basic approaches to this question: root-motion theories, scale-degree theories, and function theories. Root-motion theories, which can be traced to Jean-Philippe Rameau (1722), are expressed as laws about the intervals by which roots may move: avoid root motion by step, and prefer motion by descending third or fifth to motion by ascending third or fifth. Function theories, which have their source in Rameau's later work and were developed most influentially by Hugo Riemann, may be expressed in terms of groups of chords (tonic I and VI;

dominant V, VII, and III; and subdominant II and IV) that obey the same laws of progression. Scale-degree theories, which originate in the teachings of Abbé Vogler as transmitted by Gottfried Weber, enumerate specific laws of progression for individual chords. Figures 17.1 and 17.2 display two such systems of laws: Walter Piston's "Table of Usual Root Progressions" (1941, 17) and Tymoczko's own node-and-arrow diagram of major-mode tonality (2011, chapter 7) both exemplify this category of model.

From a still more abstract viewpoint, we might reduce the number of categories to two. Function theories and scale-degree theories have in common the principle that a chord's tendencies depend on the scale-degree identity of its members, or at least of its root. Root-motion theories, on the other hand, make predictions based solely on the intervallic structure of a chord. Indeed, the engine of Rameau's originary root-motion theory is the differential resolution of seventh chords and chords of the added sixth, whose patterns of resolution are in principle independent of scale-degree identity. On the basis of this observation, Christensen argues that Rameau "was able to subsume the rules of counterpoint within his theory of the fundamental bass" (1993, 8). Since Rameau's theory, particularly beginning with the *Nouveau système* of 1726, came to include rules about specific scale degrees, it is not strictly a root-motion theory in Tymoczko's sense. Nonetheless, the distinction is useful, and we might profitably

TABLE OF USUAL ROOT PROGRESSIONS

I is followed by IV or V, sometimes VI, less often II or III.
II is followed by V, sometimes VI, less often I, III, or IV.
III is followed by VI, sometimes IV, less often II or V.
IV is followed by V, sometimes I or II, less often III or VI.
V is followed by I, sometimes VI or IV, less often III or II.
VI is followed by II or V, sometimes III or IV, less often I.
VII is followed by III. (VII is rarely used in root position.)

FIGURE 17.1 A scale-degree theory from Walter Piston, *Harmony* (New York: W. W. Norton, 1941), 17.

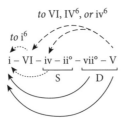

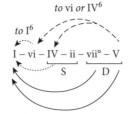

Any major or minor triad can be preceded by an applied dominant.

Any major or minor triad can be preceded by an applied dominant.

Root-position V can be preceded by i$_4^6$

Root-position V can be preceded by I$_4^6$

FIGURE 17.2 A scale-degree theory from Dmitri Tymoczko, *A Geometry of Music*, 2011.

think of Rameauian theory—and the many systems that have been built on Rameau's foundation—as a complex interaction between two kinds of laws:

Contrapuntal laws are those that operate independently of a controlling tonic and can be expressed without recourse to a scale-degree concept. Rameau's laws of chordal dissonance treatment, which drive his theory of chord progression, are in this category.

Harmonic laws are those that describe the ways in which a tonic exerts its control and must be expressed in terms of scale degrees. Rameau's laws of association between chord structures and local tonics are in this category.

What makes a theoretical rule contrapuntal or harmonic, in this account, is the structure of the rule rather than its domain of application: the distinction is not one between lines and chords, or between literal notes and fundamental-bass tones. Thus, many common rules that regulate chord usage would be classified as contrapuntal in this sense, e.g., "resolve chordal sevenths downward by step," "don't double the third of a triad," and "avoid second-inversion chords except under certain conditions." On the other hand, certain rules that govern the formation and interaction of lines are harmonic, particularly those describing the behavior of tendency tones. We might expect that harmonic laws emerged more recently than contrapuntal laws, but two of the more quotable laws of traditional counterpoint theory are harmonic in a sense, even calling attention to their scale-degree specificity through rhyme: *una nota super la / semper est canendum fa* (a basic rule of *musica ficta*) and of course the old saw *mi contra fa / est diabolus in musica*. Although there is no evidence that the latter phrase predates Fux (1725), it is certainly snappier than Guido's original formulation, "quia F cum quarta a se ♮ tritono differente nequibat habere concordiam" (Guido 1955).

Many theoretical systems show a high degree of tension at the interface between contrapuntal laws and harmonic laws. From a history-of-theory perspective, it is often the concepts theorists invent to patch over this interface, plus whatever foundation stories they tell to motivate the concepts, that are the key features of any given theorist's approach. Rameau's concept of the fundamental bass, which lives on today in a wide variety of chord-labeling systems, is deeply contrapuntal, as are the rules for its progression. Yet when it comes to a specific zone in the diatonic scale, $\hat{2}$ and $\hat{1}$, Rameau's contrapuntal rules fail. The common fundamental-bass progressions $\hat{1}-\hat{2}-\hat{5}$ and $\hat{1}-\hat{4}-\hat{5}$ both involve an "illegal" ascending step. Rameau's *deus ex machina* is the theory of *double emploi*, by which both of these progressions are understood to begin as $\hat{1}-\hat{4}$ and end as $\hat{2}-\hat{5}$. This esoteric device, in Rameau's first exposition, is scale-degree specific: a harmonic exception to a contrapuntal rule.

Rameau made great contrapuntal use of a generalized form of *double emploi*, which he termed *supposition* so as to connote both the "sub-posing" of a fundamental bass below the apparent root of a chord and the imaginary nature of this action. *Supposition* allowed Rameau both to develop a network of ideas that Kirnberger would shape into the theory of essential dissonances to unify it with his fundamental-bass framework, but it also started a vogue for asserting conceptual affinities between chords with roots a third apart. A century later, *supposition* resurfaces in harmonic drag as Hugo Riemann's concept of the *Scheinkonsonanz*, a chord whose root is a third lower (or higher) than one of the primary triads I, IV, and V. Among the many unfortunate corollaries of this attempt to use a contrapuntal tool to solve a harmonic problem is the prediction that a mediant triad can serve as a substitute for V, a usage that is vastly less frequent in the corpus of tonal music than those involving the tonic and subdominant *Scheinkonsonanzen*.

A more recent example of the troubled pedagogical relationship between contrapuntal and harmonic laws is the distinction between chord tones and non-chord tones. The primary function of this distinction is to regulate the behavior of tones at the musical surface. The idea is that a melody, line, or voice is only fully free to leap when it moves from chord tone to chord tone, and non-chord tones are restricted to certain formations involving stepwise connections to chord tones. The distinction maps onto the basic distinction between consonance and dissonance that pervaded historical theories of counterpoint: dissonances are bound, and consonances are free. In the chordal context, the distinction becomes complicated when third-stacks grow taller, thanks to the Kirnbergerian concept of essential dissonance. While they are chord tones and thus "essential," the motion of sevenths (and higher extensions) is still bound by intervallic dissonance, and they must resolve downward by step into a change of harmony. Essential dissonance is another example of the frailty of the distinction between chord tones and non-harmonic tones as a way to regulate voice leading, and it became a crucial component of the "chords at all costs" strategy for shoring up pedagogical systems. Arnold Schoenberg's *Harmonielehre* shows an awareness of the tension: "To prove the existence of the ninth chord, apart from its occurrence as a suspension, it should really be enough to mention the dominant-seventh-ninth chords with major or minor ninth, chords that are not disputed by anyone." He continues with the observation that applied dominant ninths can be used on any scale degree, "even if all cannot be used immediately and unconditionally as diatonic chords" (Schoenberg 1978, 347–348).

There are problems even in the supposedly secure domain of chord tones. Bret Aarden and Paul von Hippel (2004) compared rules for triadic doubling in a number of modern pedagogical systems against the practice of triadic doubling in a corpus of Bach chorales and string quartets by Mozart and Haydn. They note a great diversity in the way rules for doubling are expressed among the forty textbooks they studied. Most rules are cast in terms of chord members, e.g., "don't double the third of a triad," and would be classified as contrapuntal for our purposes. The only harmonic rule that appears in textbooks is universal: avoid doubling the leading tone. Textbooks differ widely in terms of rules given: some give different rules for different inversions, many rule systems differ when it comes to chordal fifths, and some systems condition doubling rules on chord quality. Aarden and von Hippel's empirical study led the authors to conclude, however, that contrapuntal (chord-member) rules are generally not supported by musical evidence: instead, after controlling for chord frequency, they found that $\hat{1}$, $\hat{4}$, $\hat{5}$, and $\hat{6}$ are the scale degrees most likely to be doubled, with $\hat{2}$ and $\hat{3}$ lagging behind; $\hat{7}$ and any chromatically inflected note were unlikely to be doubled. In other words, doubling practice seems to have a significant harmonic component—even though the concept of the triad itself is contrapuntal.

One conclusion that might be drawn from the foregoing examples, and the countless similar antinomies that pervade traditional pedagogical systems for tonal harmony, is that chords and roots, as contrapuntal constructs, are not the proper instruments for explaining harmonic phenomena. Yet since the mid–eighteenth century establishment of the concept of the rooted tertian entity, music theorists have universally come to a different conclusion. They work hard to stabilize the concept of the chord in the face of conflict between harmony and counterpoint: chords at all costs. Rules are expressed in terms of chord members and root progressions, and while exceptions are often enumerated, it is typical for systems of tonal harmony to make predictions that are overly general on some matters and too limiting in others. Schoenberg takes up these issues in his Chapter 17, whose title is " 'Non-Harmonic' Tones," complete with scare quotes. It is only three-quarters of the way through the chapter that Schoenberg gets around to the usual exposition of dissonance treatment; the bulk of the chapter is devoted to a thoroughgoing critique of the coherence of the very idea of "non-harmonic" tones. As a devotee of third-stacking, however, Schoenberg frames much of his argument in terms of emancipating taller chords and their inversions, an idea whose currency has waned in contemporary academic treatments of tonal harmony.

My aim in this chapter is to offer proof of the concept that a strict distinction between a tonic-agnostic contrapuntal domain and a tonic-dependent harmonic domain, together with an acknowledgment of the limits of the chord concept and the chord-tone/non-chord tone distinction, enables a substantially richer explanation of the connections between these two domains, the expressive complexity of their interaction, and the history of European tonality.

A MODEL SYSTEM

The corpus of J. S. Bach's chorales has been a touchstone for European-American music theory pedagogy for a century. It has also been very important for theorists constructing formal or computational models of tonality. The importance of this corpus for both projects is attributable to many of the same factors. The corpus is large enough to seem pedagogically inexhaustible; from a computational perspective, the size of the corpus is just sufficient to produce statistically robust analyses. It is also unusually stylistically consistent, showing much less variation at the surface than almost any other single-composer, single-genre corpus of music that is generally agreed to be tonal. But it is the character of the genre's compositional constraints, and their unusual power over the surface structure, that make this corpus so useful as a model system. With rare exceptions, every moment of every chorale has four distinguishable sounding voices. The rhythm is regular. Each part moves mainly in quarter notes, with a healthy dose of half notes and eighth notes, but vastly fewer shorter or longer notes. The harmonic rhythm is also typically at the quarter-note level, a feature that combines with voice-leading constraints to greatly limit figuration.

Allen Irvine McHose's 1947 textbook *The Contrapuntal-Harmonic Technique of the Eighteenth Century* is not only "an exposition of the traditional material of harmony: triads, non-harmonic tones, seventh chords, and altered chords," in the words of a contemporary reviewer. McHose also secures his exposition to an empirical footing: "The manner in which Bach treated this material is deduced from analysis of root movements, and principles are established by determining the frequency with which these movements occur. That the statistical method is carried out with exactness may be seen in the statement that Bach uses diatonic triads 83.7% of the time" (Parrish 1947). Four years earlier, Helen Budge had published a doctoral dissertation that enumerated chord frequencies in Bach chorales and a number of other repertoires (Budge 1943). More recently, Rohrmeier and Cross (2008) and Tymoczko (2011) have made more theoretically sophisticated computer-assisted studies of harmony in the chorales. All four studies are bursting with the precise percentages that impressed Parrish, but the exactness of a statistical method alone does not guarantee the validity and generality of its conclusions. The devil is in the details of what counts as a chord; all four studies agree that, as Rohrmeier and Cross put it, "[empirical] analyses of harmony face the problem of identifying the actual chords from the musical surface structure which also contains all kinds of voice-leading phenomena" (2). This is only a problem, of course, if one believes that "the actual chords" are something other than the notes actually present, and it can be solved only if "voice-leading phenomena" can be either isolated from the chords themselves or fully explained in terms of chord members.

The Bach family, which stayed up to date on Rameau's theoretical project, maintained a clear position on the aforementioned problem. "You may proclaim that my and my deceased father's principles are contrary to Rameau's," C. P. E. Bach wrote in a letter to Kirnberger quoted in the latter's *Kunst des reinen Satzes* (Kirnberger 1982). Bach and Rameau differed most notably on the question of what counts as a chord. In the introduction to his translation of Bach's *Versuch*, William J. Mitchell (1949) notes that Bach's interest in chord behavior rather than abstract origins leads him not only to classify chords differently than Rameau but to treat chords that Rameau would not bother to include in the scope of his theory. Bach's category of chords with sevenths, for example, includes not only the seven-five-three chord, but also the seven-six chord, the seven-four chord, and the seven-four-two chord. Only the first of these falls in the purview of Rameau's theory, and where Rameau's theory is organized around inversional equivalence, Bach (in keeping with the pedagogical traditions of the thoroughbass community) treats each of the inversions of this chord separately, under the heading of chords with sixths. Bach's more exotic formations contain what most modern analysts would consider to be non-chord tones. The seven-six chord and its variant with an added fourth, for example, are described by Bach as a seventh chord with suspensions; he is able to detail the requirements for preparing the suspensions and to show by numerous examples that this typically happens only over $\hat{5}$ in the bass. Yet where Rameau would worry that the sixth and the seventh can only be in the same chord if a third is sub-posed beneath the apparent fundamental bass to make it a ninth chord, Bach is unconcerned with a distinction between notes that can and cannot be organized into a stack of thirds. He is instead interested in showing how such a chord arises and how it continues. His failure to distinguish between chord tones and non-chord tones does not seem to hinder him even slightly from making an accurate account of chord behavior; indeed, his account arguably makes more accurate predictions about musical surfaces than any of the root-oriented theories that followed. What it lacks is the explanatory allure of generality.

Daniel Harrison's theory of chords as "scale-degree assemblies" (Harrison 1994) circumnavigates the question of non-harmonic tones in a framework that is, in contrast to Bach's, highly general: "in this regime, harmonic function resides in the scale degrees that make up chords," a program that he admits "might seem seditious and perversely ironic" (42–43). For Harrison, the conditions of late nineteenth-century chromaticism were such that identifying roots of chords in the process of analysis can be a tedious exercise with diminishing returns. Seeking to preserve the notion of Riemannian function in this environment, Harrison constructs an analytic system in which function accrues to a chord through the interaction of its constituent scale degrees, whatever they are. The only chords with roots, thirds, and fifths are the primary triads; in the process of abstraction the scale degrees occupying these positions become functional *bases, agents,* and *associates,* even when they appear in configurations other than the primary triads. By effacing boundaries between chords and thus the principle of harmonic partitioning, Harrison is able to treat the musical surface as a supple and dynamic playing field of harmonic tendencies governed by shifting alliances and confederations of scale degrees accumulating and discharging functional potentials.

To make the case that Harrison's idea is equally productive for understanding tonal harmony at the opposite end of the "common practice," we will need to make another empirical excursion into the Bach chorales. This time, however, we will take a radical approach to the problem of non-chord tones by defining it out of existence: any simultaneously sounding collection of scale degrees is a chord. A corpus of 186 chorales was prepared for analysis in several steps. First, each chorale was divided into successive sonorities using the method of "salami slicing" (Quinn 2010), in which any change in any voice causes a new sonority to be recorded, comprising all sounding pitches after the change; 186 chorales yielded 18,951 chords. Second, a distributional key-finding algorithm (White and Quinn 2016) was used to divide each chorale into passages that are unambiguously in a single key; 142 tonally ambiguous passages containing 651 chords, or 3.4% of the corpus, were omitted from the study. Finally, each passage was transposed to the key of C, allowing pitch class to stand for scale degree.

The analysis of the corpus was focused on a simple question: Given three successive sonorities (s_0, s_1, s_2) and knowledge of mode (major or minor), how much does the fact that s_0 contains a particular dyad affect the likelihood of a given pitch class p occurring in s_2? (We are looking at two slices because the median slice duration is an eighth note and the typical harmonic rhythm of Bach's chorales is at the quarter-note level.)

In order to answer the question about scale-degree succession, we need to know the "background probability" of each degree occurring in each mode. Figure 17.3 compares the distributions of scale degrees in any s_2 that follows an s_0 equal to $(\hat{7}, \hat{2})$ with these background probabilities. What we are interested in is how the background probability distribution is distorted by the presence of a given pair of notes. In this case, it can be easily read from the bar graph that the $(\hat{7}, \hat{2})$ dyad is associated with increased likelihood of scale degrees $\hat{1}$, $\hat{3}$, and $\hat{5}$, and suppression of $\hat{2}$, $\hat{4}$, and $\hat{6}$, with no significant change in the likelihood of $\hat{7}$. The difference between the background distribution and the distribution following a dyad can be made more perspicuous by subtracting the logarithms (base 2) of the two probabilities. A result of 1 means that a dyad makes a scale degree twice as likely as it would be otherwise, and a result of -1 means that it is half as likely. Figure 17.4 recapitulates Figure 17.3 from this perspective; here we can see more clearly a tendency for $(\hat{7}, \hat{2})$ to suppress chromatic scale degrees, with the exception of $\flat\hat{6}$, which is neutralized in the same manner as $\hat{7}$. For the sake of simplicity, we will set aside the admittedly intriguing observations about chromaticism this approach engenders and consider only diatonic scale degrees.

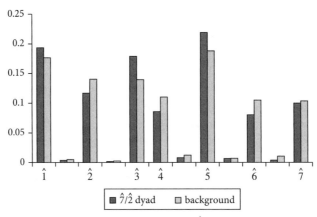

FIGURE 17.3 Scale-degree likelihoods following a $(\hat{7}, \hat{2})$ dyad (black) viewed against the background "key profile" of overall scale-degree likelihood (gray).

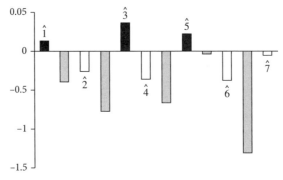

FIGURE 17.4 Isolating the effect of the $(\hat{7}, \hat{2})$ dyad by subtracting log likelihoods (base 2).

The aggregate results of the study appear in Figure 17.5. Each bar graph corresponds to a particular diatonic dyad, indicated by the two gray bars in each graph. Space does not permit a full investigation of these data here, but a few systemic sources of variance in the data will provide plenty of fodder for the theorizing that follows. Sevenths and fifths tend to make contrapuntal predictions about what scale degrees will follow. In a seventh, the root of the interval is predicted to stay in place, while the seventh is suppressed in the following chords; the note below the seventh is predicted to take its place. In general, the notes of the triad having a root a fifth above the root of the seventh are also suppressed in favor of the notes of the triad a fifth below. These tendencies seem to be fairly independent of the particular scale degrees involved, which is what makes them contrapuntal, although the interaction between harmony and counterpoint creates exceptional cases like the $(\hat{7}, \hat{6})$ seventh (see "Harmonic Function without Dualism," below). A similar situation obtains for fifths, which generally increase the likelihood of their roots staying around, and either suppress or neutralize the fifth. Thirds, by contrast, evidently follow a harmonic pattern of distributions: each of the two dyads of a Riemannian primary triad seem to make the same predictions. In particular, $(\hat{1}, \hat{3})$ and $(\hat{3}, \hat{5})$ both increase the likelihood of a IV chord, $(\hat{4}, \hat{6})$ and $(\hat{6}, \hat{1})$ encourage the arrival of a VII chord, and $(\hat{5}, \hat{7})$ and $(\hat{7}, \hat{2})$ predict a resolution to I. For the primary triads, at least, descending-fifths root motion appears to be the order of the day, and judging from these findings alone, the only *double emploi* required is between VII (qua destination of the IV chord) and V (qua predictor of the I chord). It is not obvious, however, how to account for the $(\hat{2}, \hat{4})$ dyad, which belongs to no primary triad and has the unique tendency to neutralize four out of the seven diatonic scale degrees.

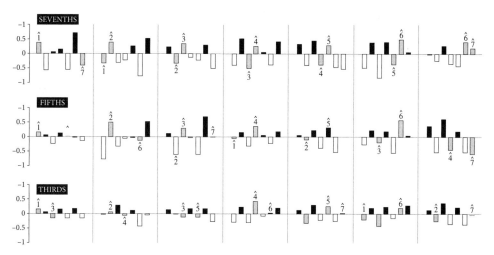

FIGURE 17.5 Overall effect of each dyad in major-mode sections of the Bach chorales, organized by generic interval class. Gray bars and scale-degree numbers mark the effective dyad in each bar graph. Otherwise, black (and white) bars mark scale degrees more (and less) likely to follow the dyad than they are to appear in a general context.

The remainder of this chapter develops an explanatory framework for these data that builds on Harrison's approach. Rather than treating a chord as a confederation of individual scale degrees, we will consider a chord's tendencies to be the sum of the tendencies of its constituent dyads, since those dyads seem to have very clear tendencies. Although the framework does not postulate a special role for triads and seventh chords, it still robustly predicts all of the familiar behaviors of those chords. Moreover, it provides an explanation for these behaviors that does not involve exceptions to its surprisingly small base of rules, or appeals to the metaphysics of consonance and dissonance.

A MINIMALIST THEORETICAL FRAMEWORK

Carl Dahlhaus's *Studies on the Origin of Harmonic Tonality* (1990) returns nearly twenty times to the idea that a key is a "closed society of scale degrees," borrowing the term from Handschin. Sometimes he means the scale degrees themselves, sometimes he means chords built on the scale degrees, and sometimes he means the keys of the scale degrees. The distinction maps on to a series of stages in his account of tonality's relationship to the diatonic scale, which goes something like this: sixteenth- and seventeenth-century composers burst the pipes of an ancient modal theory that was never meant to handle polyphony, setting the stage for the "emancipation" of the diatonic scale. Scale-degree consciousness arises in the seventeenth century as a result of the diatonic scale's new transposability, and a key is now a closed society of scale degrees qua notes. As chords spring up from their roots in the scale degrees, a key becomes a society of chords. Theorists begin to derive the scale from three primary triads, a striking break from the tradition of requiring that conceptual ontogeny recapitulate historical phylogeny. Nineteenth-century developments in chromaticism have a profound effect on the structure of the society of scale degrees, which no longer needs the diatonic scale to hold it together. As the major and minor modes collapse on each other in a decisive consolidation of the parallel key system's power over the relative system, the diatonic scale becomes fully vestigial. A key becomes, finally, a society of subsidiary keys, each with chords of their own, organized according to a modern grid system measured out in chromatically specific intervals rather than the quirky generic intervals of the diatonic scale. The ease of navigating the grid at the level of the diatonic neighborhood belies the strange complexity that arises on longer chromatic journeys. That complexity inspired generations of composers to invent ever-newer harmonic effects. More recently it has been the subject of a good deal of attention from music theorists interested in tonality and inclined to system-building, including, for example, Lerdahl (2001), Tymoczko (2011), Rings (2011), Cohn (2012), Chew (2014), and the various contributors to *The Oxford Handbook of Neo-Riemannian Music Theories* (Gollin and Rehding 2011).

The Bach chorales date from a crucial moment earlier in this story. The old modes have (mostly) withered away, replaced by a system of relative major and minor keys that has almost solidified, strung along the expanding line of fifths. The parallel system is just coming into focus as major and minor modes begin to mirror each other, a necessary final step in developing a scale-degree consciousness that draws an identity between, say, $\hat{3}$ in a major mode and $\hat{3}$ in a minor mode. (Under the relative system alone, $\hat{3}$ in major is identified with $\hat{5}$ in minor.) The historical stage is set for the story of so-called common-practice tonality, where Dahlhaus sees a gradual victory of chord over scale. And although this music is generally believed to be governed by the same tonal laws that underwrite the "common practice," Bach and his chorales are already on stage when the curtain rises. Only then does Rameau enter from the wings to introduce the notion that every triad has a root. A model of the tonality of the Bach chorales that does not depend on this idea can thus claim a historicist edge over one that does. Perhaps it can even serve as the basis for a clearer understanding than Dahlhaus offers of the diatonic regime that was overturned by emerging chromatic forces in the mid-nineteenth-century phase of his drama. This diatonic regime, which is continuous with Baroque and galant practices, has variously been characterized in terms of a "first practice" of tonality (Kinderman and Krebs 1996) and a "first nature" of the triad (Cohn 2012), although the titles of their books highlight the fact that the majority of recent music-theoretic work on tonality has focused on the second phase. Robert Gjerdingen's influential work on galant schemata, which verges on a construction grammar for music of the first phase, is a notable exception to this principle (Gjerdingen 2007; Gjerdingen and Bourne 2015).

The model I propose begins with very few assumptions, essentially those of a continuo player at the turn of the eighteenth century with well-developed scale-degree consciousness improvising at the keyboard. First, a key is understood as a closed society of seven scale degrees; we will not concern ourselves with modulation here. Second, a chord is understood loosely as anything that might be notated in a basso continuo part, even one that errs on the side of specifying ornamentation. Third is a general preference for smooth voice leading (although certain exceptions are made for the bass line). Finally, the model assumes what is by now the dominant psychological theory of meter, Dynamic Attending Theory (Jones and Boltz 1989; London 2012), which views meter as regulating attention toward metrically stronger moments in musical time. Since attention is required for our imaginary continuo player to make decisions about where to move her fingers, we will assume the principles elaborated below apply with a force that increases under conditions of metrical accent, and with less urgency otherwise.

If a key is a society in this model, then a chord is an encounter between members of that society. In such a small society, these encounters quickly become routine, so most notes leave the encounter with a clear idea of what to do next. The options are limited to two: **mobilize**, or move to a neighboring scale degree, and **stabilize**, or stand fast as a common tone. Although this stabilization or mobilization is an emergent property of the encounter as a whole, we will model it in terms of pairwise interactions of individual notes. This seems to capture most of the structure we need while keeping things relatively simple.

A chord, then, is held to be the sum of its dyads, and we will classify dyads by their generic interval class. Each interval class is named after its member that is traditionally labeled by an odd number: sixths will be called **thirds**, fourths will be called **fifths**, and seconds are **sevenths**. Each dyad has a **root**, defined as the lower note of the interval as it is named, and the other note is the **antiroot**. I intend for the familiarity of these nominalist terminological moves to serve only as a digestive aid for the substantial theoretical meal to come. Readers who share my skepticism for metaphysical explanations of tonal phenomena may separate the term from its psychoacoustical baggage. The distinction between roots and antiroots is identical in all but name from the distinction between stabilized and mobilized notes, as will shortly become clear.

Although triadic formations in general are not axiomatic to this system, it is easy to see that naming interval classes after the first three multiples of thirds will productively align the notes of a tertian structure when it comes to the root/antiroot duality: a triad's root is the root of both of its dyadic interactions, its third is the root of one and the antiroot of another, and its fifth is the antiroot of both of its dyads. The analysis of seventh chords proceeds along similar lines. Under this framework, any triad or seventh chord, when conceptualized as a stack of thirds, is polarized from bottom to top along a root/antiroot axis. Figure 17.6(a) shows all of the dyads in a seventh chord, with black noteheads for roots and gray noteheads for antiroots; each note of the chord belongs to three dyads. The root of the seventh chord is the root of all three of its dyads, and the chordal seventh is the antiroot of its dyads. The intermediate notes occupy intermediate positions along the root/antiroot gradient. The remainder of Figure 17.6 demonstrates that this tidy alignment of stacked thirds is unique in this system: neither of the other two dyad classes is able to form a coherent root/antiroot gradient.

Most of the main ideas introduced so far—the idea that a chord is a locus of scale-degree interaction, the motivating forces of mobilization and stabilization, the root concept for dyads, and the foregoing observations about tertian structures' alignment of root/antiroot polarity—are **contrapuntal** in the sense I have been using it here: they

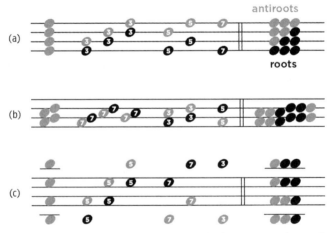

FIGURE 17.6 Each interval has a root and an antiroot. (a) The root/antiroot gradient of a seventh chord. (b, c) Neither of the other two generic interval classes creates such a gradient when cycled.

depend on scale-degree interval rather than scale-degree identity. The final postulate of this framework is scale-degree specific and thus **harmonic**. It asserts two special collections of scale degrees, the two primary triads: **tonic** $(\hat{1}, \hat{3}, \hat{5})$ and **dominant** $(\hat{5}, \hat{7}, \hat{2})$. We may derive from these two other entities consisting of their complements: the **antitonic** collection $(\hat{7}, \hat{2}, \hat{4}, \hat{6})$ and the **antidominant** collection $(\hat{4}, \hat{6}, \hat{1}, \hat{3})$. The "missing" subdominant is a feature, not a bug: my claim is that what we think of as subdominant function, at least at this early stage of tonality's consolidation, is an emergent property of the complex interaction between tonic/antitonic and dominant/antidominant.

In what follows, I will develop the argument that under this framework, just two laws of dyadic interaction are sufficient to create a powerfully predictive account of the dynamics of the "society of scale degrees" and the chord progressions it tends to produce.

(LC) **Law of Counterpoint.** A seventh or fifth stabilizes its root and mobilizes its antiroot. A seventh mobilizes its antiroot downward. The motivating forces of the seventh are stronger than those of the fifth.

(LH) **Law of Harmony.** A third belonging entirely to the tonic or dominant triad, or to the antitonic or antidominant collection, mobilizes both of its notes.

We will study the effects of the two laws individually before studying their interaction. Although this theory is based on major-mode data of Figure 17.5, the laws are parallel between the major mode and the minor mode as represented by the harmonic minor scale. (The effect of varying $\hat{6}$ and $\hat{7}$ in the minor mode will be treated separately.) To keep the exposition clean, Roman numerals used to identify triads and seventh chords will all be capitalized, since mode interacts with scale degree to generate two distinct orders of chord quality, delineating the major scale and harmonic minor scale, respectively.

THE LAW OF COUNTERPOINT

The Law of Counterpoint (LC), which covers fifths and sevenths, unifies a number of important rules in the traditional pedagogy of counterpoint, most obviously those touching on parallel fifths and suspensions. By predicting a differential motivation of scale degrees a fifth apart, LC indirectly makes stepwise parallel motion by fifths unlikely. This is both more general than the traditional proscription of parallel fifths in that it makes stepwise parallel motion by fourths equally unlikely, and less general in that it has little to say about the possibility of two voices moving in parallel fifths or fourths by a larger interval. This is one of many cases we will encounter where this novel pair of laws makes predictions that resemble axiomatic rules of standard formulations of tonal theory, but limits the scope of these predictions in ways that forestall the need for additional rules patching over inconsistencies such as those discussed in the first and second parts of this chapter.

LC's treatment of sevenths most closely resembles the various rules for syncopes in historical theories of counterpoint, brought together by Diruta (1597) and given the lasting rubric "fourth species" by Fux (1725); incidentally, *Gradus ad parnassum* is the one book that bears an ownership mark in Bach's hand (Wolff 2001). The differential mobilization of root and antiroot in the seventh, particularly in metrically accented positions, is again both more and less general than the traditional bundle of rules. It matches the fourth-species rules of 7–6 and 2–3 suspensions. It directly conflicts with the fourth-species rule of 9–8 suspensions, although Fux himself admits this is a different kind of suspension, since it cannot be chained along a stepwise descending cantus firmus as the first two can, and it also seems to conflict with Fux's fourth class of suspensions, the 4–3. These apparent inconsistencies highlight the sense in which LC is more general than the rule-base of species counterpoint—in this case, quite deeply. The dyadic interaction framework makes no a priori distinction between consonance and dissonance, which at the very least relieves us from worrying about whether the fourth is a dissonance or not, perhaps the most vexed question in the history of music theory. The force that motivates notes in traditional counterpoint theory, the drive to resolve dissonance, appears in a more general guise in this framework as a motivating **contrapuntal force** polarized along the stabilization/mobilization axis. In the chordal encounter, scale degrees confer the force on each other, polarizing each other along this axis through dyadic interactions regulated by the twin laws of harmony and counterpoint. Since these laws depend on the intervallic character of dyads (size and root polarity), it is by studying the interactions of sevenths in various chordal contexts that we can compare the framework's predictions to standard views of dissonance treatment.

Figure 17.7 shows the basic types of three-note chord that result from joining a fifth with a seventh via a common tone. This is the simplest setting in which we may observe the interaction of the two contrapuntal laws. The figure uses a visual language that we will develop throughout the remainder of this chapter. A scale-degree assembly being analyzed appears in gray noteheads, followed by a representation of each dyadic interaction. Dyads interacting contrapuntally are shown in black noteheads: round noteheads indicate stabilized notes, and diamond-shaped noteheads indicate mobilized notes. Often the dyads will be followed by a barline and a representation of notes projected or implied by the first scale-degree assembly. A four-line staff provides some helpful defamiliarization and serves as a reminder that the objects represented by the noteheads are not pitches or pitch classes but scale degrees. In this case, the staff is clefless, since Figure 17.7 depicts a strictly contrapuntal situation and the noteheads thus represent something still more abstract.

At the top of Figure 17.7 are the cases where the remainder interval (i.e., the two notes that are not the common tone) is a third. These happen to be precisely the two ways of omitting a note from a seventh chord without yielding a triad. At (a) the common tone is the root of the seventh chord; it is stabilized by virtue of being the root of both fifth and seventh, which, as antiroots, are mobilized in turn. The situation reverses at (b), where

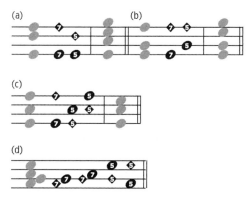

FIGURE 17.7 Interactions between fifths and sevenths under the Law of Counterpoint.

the common tone is the seventh of the chord and the antiroot of the chord's root and third. Here again, the chordal seventh is mobilized, the chordal root is stabilized, and the middle note is motivated in the same way as its partner in the remainder interval of a third. In both cases, the dyadic interactions reinforce each other, since the common tone between two dyads receives the same charge from both interactions. While the predicted destination chord is slightly different in each case, they have two out of three common tones, and the difference amounts to which one of the two Rameau-approved intervals would appear in a fundamental-bass analysis: a fifth or third descending.

Lest we think a chordal encounter is always so agreeable, a counterexample appears at (c) in Figure 17.7, where a seventh is divided into two fifths (manifesting as fourths). Each of the three interactions works against the other two in this case. The result is a three-note chord where each note is mobilized by one of the others and stabilized by the third. The standoff is only broken by LC's provision that gives sevenths more weight in a chordal encounter, and while the seventh mobilizes its antiroot and stabilizes its root, the third note is neutralized as its two fifth-interactions cancel each other out. The chord as a whole ends up resolving in the manner of a 4–3 suspension within a consonant triad. This was one of the suspensions that turned up missing in our initial exploration of the relationship between LC and fourth-species rules, because it emerges only from the interaction of sevenths and fifths. The other "missing" suspension, 9–8, appears in a typical contrapuntal context at (d), if only to delay the matter by suggesting that the contrapuntal conflicts in this chord mostly cancel each other out, and it is the Law of Harmony that must provide a resolution in this case.

Figure 17.8 depicts a consequential aspect of the interaction of contrapuntal laws in this theory when it comes to seventh chords. We have seen how sevenths and fifths, when arranged compactly on the line of thirds, collaborate to align the root/antiroot gradient of the stack of thirds (recall Figure 17.6) with a stabilization/mobilization gradient. The resulting **tertian gradient** will encourage a three-story stack of thirds to collapse in on itself in one of several specific ways, as the middle level is squeezed between a mobilized upper story and a stabilized ground level. This is equivalent to saying that a seventh chord (all other things being equal) creates in itself the desire to move to

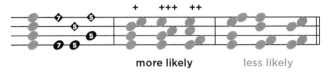

more likely   less likely

FIGURE 17.8 The Law of Counterpoint acting on a seventh chord.

another seventh chord via root motion by descending fifth. The most likely other contrapuntal outcomes are seventh chords by descending third or seventh, or triads sharing a root with any of these seventh chords. The small crosses in Figure 17.8 roughly describe the relative likelihood of the outcomes, with more crosses indicating higher probability. Even in the absence of harmonic tendencies, or with notes missing from a seventh chord, the coordinated action of the Law of Counterpoint on third-stacks makes it easy for a scale-degree assembly to find their way into this pattern of grooves worn into the diatonic landscape. The core of this pattern, depicted in Figure 17.9, is typically taught to undergraduates as an inverted variant of the seventh-chord variant of the descending-fifths sequence, yet, in this framework, it falls decisively in the center of the realm of counterpoint.

Tymoczko (2011) has made an extensive study of the contrapuntal relationships between triads and seventh chords. Beginning with the observation that tonal harmony tends to privilege descending-third root motion and its small multiples, he notes that triads tend to exhibit smooth ascending voice leading under these conditions and seventh chords tend to exhibit smooth descending voice leading. The top and bottom staves in Figure 17.10 show how this works. With triads, the characteristic 5–6 move (an important propulsive technique in Schenkerian theory) is equivalent to descending-third root motion. Descending fifths, as compound descending thirds (indicated by arrows in Figure 17.10), involve two stepwise ascents, and descending sevenths cause all three voices to move by ascending step. A four-voiced descending analogue to this pattern governs seventh chords. While Tymoczko's interest is in the deep voice-leading complexities of this situation, the Law of Counterpoint suggests a simple and fully contrapuntal explanation of why tonal music tends to flow through these grooves: (1) roots of fifths and sevenths are stabilized, (2) antiroots of these intervals are mobilized in particular ways, and (3) stacks of thirds self-reinforce each other's motivations. The Law of Harmony, in turn, distorts the landscape into which the grooves are worn in ways that make it easier to slip into and out of the sequence at some points than others.

THE LAW OF HARMONY

The second basic motivating force of tonal harmony is illustrated at (a) in Figure 17.11. Members of the tonic triad mobilize each other to move to a neighboring tone, which is in the antitonic collection. This chord, which is known to Roman-numeral analysts

FIGURE 17.9 The Law of Counterpoint and the descending-fifths sequence.

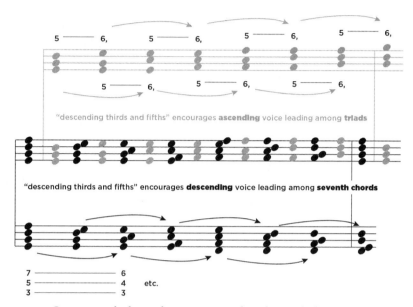

FIGURE 17.10 Contrapuntal relationships among triads and seventh chords in Tymoczko (2011).

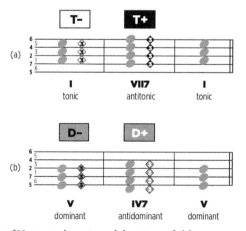

FIGURE 17.11 The Law of Harmony's tonic and dominant fields.

as VII7, is not among the more common simultaneities in seventeenth- and eighteenth-century music, particularly in the major mode. Its function in this framework is not as a simultaneity, but as an abstraction, a locus of destinations to which members of the tonic triad move when motivated by a kind of negatively charged tonic force. In turn, members of the antitonic collection mobilize each other with a positively charged tonic force, to move back into the tonic triad. These motivating forces, which scale degrees experience in the presence of a **tonic field**, are the product of a kind of harmonic charge that is generated in the chordal encounter. (This concept, and its dominant counterpart, play a crucial role in tonal phrase structure, which will be clarified in the next section of this chapter.) Like an electrical charge, the tonic charge has two poles: **protonic charge** (T+) mobilizes scale degrees into the tonic triad, and **contratonic charge** (T–) mobilizes them out of it. Because scale degrees pick up harmonic charge in the chordal encounter, it only arises in the presence of multiple members of either the tonic triad or its complement. Five of the seven possible thirds will generate tonic charge of some kind, but the dyads $(\hat{5}, \hat{7})$ and $(\hat{6}, \hat{1})$ will not, because they contain one tonic and one antitonic scale degree.

The basic dyadic actions of this tonic-antitonic-tonic motion underwrite a healthy majority of the schemata that, as Gjerdingen (2007) has shown, form a repertoire of stock phrases out of which galant musicians typically began their compositions. Many of these schemata have four stages, unfolded at a metrically regular pace; the standard pattern for piece-opening phrases is for the stages to form tonic-antitonic, antitonic-tonic pairs. Figure 17.12 illustrates the two-voice frameworks of some standard opening gambits at (a), and at (b) shows some standard piece-internal schemata whose stages articulate parallel pairs rather than contrasting pairs: antitonic-tonic, antitonic-tonic (or the reverse). The Prinner in particular, a ubiquitous eighteenth-century schema, is worth a closer look: in its prototypical form, its opening antitonic dyad $(\hat{4}, \hat{6})$ descends into the tonic dyad $(\hat{3}, \hat{5})$, continuing its downward trajectory through antitonic $(\hat{2}, \hat{4})$ and tonic $(\hat{1}, \hat{3})$. Each step is motivated by a kind of alternating current that moves these dyads downward through the tonic field. Some of these schemata begin with a duplication of $\hat{1}$ rather than a $(\hat{1}, \hat{3})$ dyad; although this trivial dyad generates no motivation on its own, it is safe to assume that a continuo player will literally or mentally add $\hat{3}$ above the bass in such cases, and that this third dyad will generate the contratonic charge postulated here.

The tension between contratonic and protonic charges produces effects that traditional approaches to harmony associate with dominant and subdominant function. Because the tonic field is symmetric around $\hat{3}$, it equally predicts both the downward protonic motion of $(\hat{4}, \hat{6})$ to $(\hat{3}, \hat{5})$ and the upward protonic motion of $(\hat{7}, \hat{2})$ to $(\hat{1}, \hat{3})$, as well as the reverse moves, brought about as a way to leave the tonic triad. Riemann and his dualist followers, including Oettingen and Hauptmann, made much of this symmetry, building outward a symmetric theory of harmonic functions organized around an upward/downward duality. Although many of the excesses of dualism have been tempered by the strong influence of Schenker, who recognized that the corpus of tonal music does not exhibit this type of symmetry in any meaningful way, dualist terminology still pervades the everyday musical vocabulary, and the concept of harmonic function is alive and well after a century of Schenkerian attacks.

One might interpret Schenker's concept of the *Ursatz* as expressing the idea that the genesis of a tonal composition is accompanied by (or is identical with) a breaking of

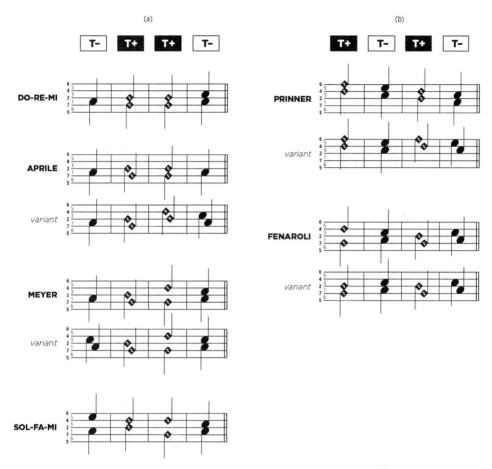

FIGURE 17.12 Some schemata from Gjerdingen (2007) that show "alternating current" in the tonic field, including (a) opening gambits and (b) piece-internal schemata.

the fundamental symmetry of the tonic force by introducing two competing forces: a contrapuntal force represented by the *Urlinie* and what Brown (2004) calls the "middleground transformations"; and a projection of the tonic force a fifth upward, represented by the *Baßbrechung*. It can be difficult to see the depth of this idea through the aestheticist excrescences that surround the *Ursatz* in the context of Schenker's writings as a whole: the cult of the masterwork, the organicist ideology, and a questionable belief in deep recursion, just to name a few. But the idea is separable from all that, as Benjamin (1981) has shown, and in the dyadic interaction framework, these three forces—counterpoint, tonic, and dominant—are separable from one another too. Each is simple on its own, but their interaction creates a dynamic system over the diatonic scale whose complexity provides a richly expressive medium for composers and improvisers.

As Figure 17.11 shows at (b), the **dominant field** is structurally identical to the tonic field, but is transposed up a fifth, so its axis of symmetry is $\hat{7}$ rather than $\hat{3}$. The force experienced by a scale degree in this field depends on its polarity with respect to the dominant force, which accrues to scale degrees in the chordal encounter just as the tonic force does. Dyads in the antidominant collection mobilize each other with a **prodominant charge (D+)**, and dyads in the dominant triad mobilize each other with a **contradominant charge (D–)**. Figure 17.13 displays some additional piece-internal schemata from Gjerdingen's account of galant music. The first is the modulating version of the Prinner, which begins on the $(\hat{1}, \hat{3})$ dyad common to the tonic and antidominant collections, then moves downward through the dominant field propelled by the same kind of alternating current we observed in the prototypical Prinner. The Indugio, which we will examine in closer detail a bit later in this section, begins with the antitonic $(\hat{2}, \hat{4})$ dyad that represents a decisive phrasal move away from the tonic. The scale degrees are subsequently captured by the dominant field that typically drives the approach to a cadential dominant, and they outline a framework of antidominant scale degrees that generates a prodominant collapse onto $(\hat{5}, \hat{7})$.

The interaction between the tonic and dominant fields is schematized in Figures 17.14 and 17.15. Figure 17.14 enumerates the seven thirds of the diatonic scale, indicating the polarity of tonic and dominant force (if any) generated by each charged dyad in the chordal encounter. Every third generates at least one type of harmonic force. Three dyads in particular—$(\hat{1}, \hat{3})$, $(\hat{4}, \hat{6})$, and $(\hat{7}, \hat{2})$—are mobilized by both forces, each with a unique combination of polarities. The four possible combinations are enumerated in Figure 17.15, which also details the systemic interactions of the tonic and dominant forces. Since the harmonic mobilization of a scale degree is equivalent to stabilizing its neighbors, the figure shows the distribution of each harmonic force over all seven scale degrees, with diamond-shaped noteheads denoting mobilization and round noteheads signifying stabilization.

The combination of contratonic and prodominant charge appears at Figure 17.15(a). The two forces are aligned with respect to mobilizing $(\hat{1}, \hat{3})$ and stabilizing $(\hat{7}, \hat{2})$. Scale degrees $\hat{4}$, $\hat{5}$, and $\hat{6}$ show a kind of destructive interference between tonic and dominant forces. We might think of the result as a kind of "unmotivation" or **neutralization** of those scale degrees, which are mobilized by one force and stabilized by the other. A change in the balance of the two harmonic forces might sway these neutralized scale degrees toward a mild motivation, but since the contrapuntal force is generally stronger

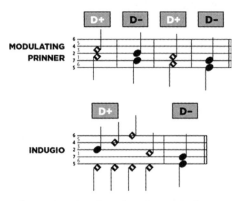

FIGURE 17.13 Dominant alternations in other piece-internal schemata.

dyad (third)		charge	
		tonic	dominant
3̂	5̂	T–	
1̂	3̂	T–	D+
6̂	1̂		D+
4̂	6̂	T+	D+
2̂	4̂	T+	
7̂	2̂	T+	D–
5̂	7̂		D–

FIGURE 17.14 Interaction between the tonic and dominant fields in thirds.

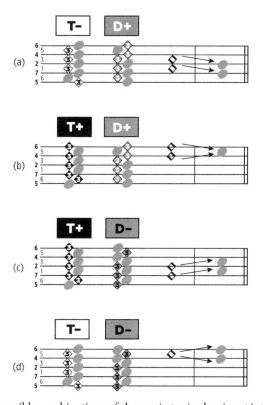

FIGURE 17.15 Four possible combinations of charges in tonic-dominant interaction.

than the harmonic forces, the Law of Counterpoint is likely to be responsible for any motion of neutralized scale degrees.

Continuing on to (b) in Figure 17.15, which reverses the polarity of the tonic force but not the dominant, we now see constructive interference for just three scale degrees and destructive interference for the remaining four. In this case, the (4̂, 6̂) dyad is mobilized and the scale degree between them, $\hat{5}$, is stabilized, encouraging convergence of the mobilized dyad while also enabling parallel motion of $(\hat{4}, \hat{6})$ upward or downward. At (c) the protonic charge of (b) is retained while reversing the polarity of the dominant force to contradominant. As at (a), which also showed opposite charges in the two harmonic forces, constructive interference motivates four scale degrees while neutralizing three. Because the overall effect of the protonic–contradominant combination is precisely the reverse of the contratonic–prodominant combination, the voice-leading drives simply reverse: this combination is characterized by a preference for mobilized $(\hat{7}, \hat{2})$ to move upward to stabilized $(\hat{1}, \hat{3})$. The last remaining combination appears at (d), which is the inverse of (b). As we will see shortly, the contratonic-contradominant combination is not a significant component of tonal harmony—after all, where else is there to go?

HARMONIC FUNCTION WITHOUT DUALISM

We began our study of interacting harmonic forces with the observation that there are three third-dyads that are acted on by both tonic and dominant forces. The particular identity of these dyads, as the reader may have begun to suspect, is highly suggestive of the three Riemannian harmonic functions: $(\hat{1}, \hat{3})$ as tonic, $(\hat{4}, \hat{6})$ as subdominant, and $(\hat{7}, \hat{2})$ as dominant. Figure 17.16 explores this notion further, by reorganizing the material of Figure 17.15 and adding representations of the fourteen diatonic triads and seventh chords. Each chord appears on a staff corresponding to the particular pairing of forces and charges generated in the chordal encounter. The chords themselves are represented using an extension of the notation in Figure 17.15: diamond noteheads and round noteheads, respectively, for scale degrees mobilized and stabilized jointly by tonic and dominant forces, plus a squiggly *quilisma* shape for scale degrees neutralized by destructive interference between tonic and dominant forces. Asterisks mark four seventh-chord formations that are associated with two overlapping pairs of forces/charges. The left-to-right ordering of chords matches that of Figure 17.10, the directed voice-leading schema for triads and seventh chords under the influence of the contrapuntal force.

As the figure makes clear, the first three combinations of harmonic forces and charges map more or less perfectly onto the usual equivalence classes of chords under function-oriented theories:

Chords with **tonic function** are motivated by contratonic and prodominant forces that motivate $\hat{1}$ and $\hat{3}$ to move by step, most likely downward;

Chords with **subdominant function** are motivated by prodominant and protonic forces that motivate $\hat{4}$ and $\hat{6}$ to move by step; and

Chords with **dominant function** are motivated by protonic and contradominant forces that motivate $\hat{7}$ and $\hat{2}$ to move by step, most likely upward.

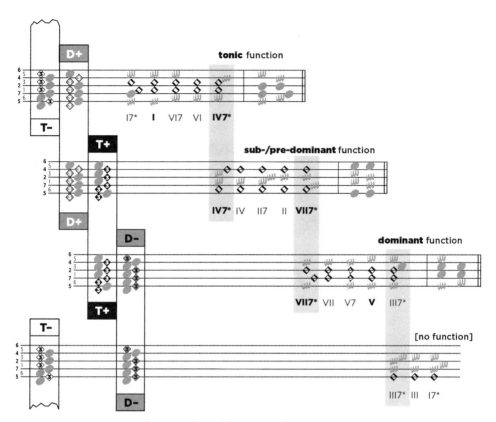

FIGURE 17.16 Harmonic function derived from tonic-dominant interaction.

Readers skeptical of the appearance of IV⁷ not just in the subdominant category, but also in the tonic category, are directed to Figure 17.17, which shows just a few examples of a distinctly tonic usage of IV⁷ in the Bach chorale corpus. (All excerpts have been transposed to C major to facilitate comparison.) Modern analysts accustomed to the usual distinction between chord tones and non-chord tones might dismiss $\hat{4}$ and $\hat{6}$ in these cases as mere passing tones. But in this framework, we take a page out of Schoenberg's book and treat these notes as equal players in the local functional environment: they are part of a passing motion that begins with a contratonic drive for $\hat{3}$ and $\hat{5}$ to move upward to $\hat{4}$ and $\hat{6}$; the resulting dyad is compelled another step upward by its own prodominant charge. In the other two voices, $\hat{1}$ and $\hat{3}$ fulfill their contratonic and prodominant drive in one fell swoop. The sense in which the chord has tonic function in these contexts is that it combines contratonic and prodominant forces, which are emphasized musically in these cases through meter and voice leading. By contrast, more typical subdominant usages of IV⁷, such as the common case (illustrated in Figure 17.18) where the chord results from a passing motion between IV and V or VII, involves a different configuration of forces. In this case the tonic field first motivates the protonic attraction of $\hat{4}$ to $\hat{3}$,

FIGURE 17.17 Examples of a tonic usage of the IV^7 chord in the Bach chorales.

at which point the powerful contradominant charge of the complete antidominant collection activates the dominant field and pulls the notes of IV^7 toward $\hat{5}$, $\hat{7}$, and $\hat{2}$. A similar line of argument shows that there is little to recommend the notion that VI preceding a dominant harmony has subdominant function, since its dynamics are contratonic rather than protonic, as evidenced by the unlikeliness of a motion from VI to I.

The Indugio schema, which made a brief appearance in Figure 17.13, will help us explore how the concept of subdominant function is expressed in this framework. Gjerdingen avoids the anachronistic term *subdominant*, introducing the Indugio as "a schema for extending and focusing on the first type of sonority" among those mentioned in the title of Daube's *General-Bass in drey Accorden* (1756)—that is, the six-three or six-five chord over $\hat{4}$ in the bass. Later in the book, Gjerdingen describes the Indugio as "a teasing delay of the approach to a converging cadence" (464). This description emphasizes the phrasal position of the Indugio in particular and the subdominant in general. From the perspective of the Law of Harmony, each phrase of tonal music has three zones with different dynamics: an initial zone characterized by protonic/contratonic polarity, a medial zone in which the dominant field overtakes the tonic field, and a cadential zone in which the dominant

FIGURE 17.18 Example of the standard subdominant usage of the IV⁷ chord.

field achieves (however temporarily) a prodominant arrival on the V triad. Figure 17.19 shows a common elaborated variant of the Indugio characterized by outer voices twining around between $(\hat{4}, \hat{2})$ and $(\hat{6}, \hat{4})$ while an inner voice holds $\hat{1}$. This is driven by the same kind of alternating current in the tonic field that enables the Prinner; this section of the schema may be repeated. As the dominant field gains in power, the relationship between scale degrees shifts: $\hat{1}$ and $\hat{3}$, which were initially motivated by a contratonic drive, are now reoriented as prodominants; and $\hat{4}$ and $\hat{6}$, which have opposite polarity to $\hat{1}$ and $\hat{3}$ in the tonic field, now reinforce $\hat{1}$ and $\hat{3}$'s prodominant tendencies, and they make a coordinated arrival on the phrasal dominant. The dominant field can gain so much strength that it reorganizes the diatonic scale around itself, which simply moves antidominant $\hat{4}$ to $\sharp\hat{4}$ (as a projection upward of antitonic $\hat{7}$).

By tracking the positively charged ("pro-") forces mentioned in the functional descriptions above, it becomes clear that chords with tonic function are motivated to become chords with dominant function and vice versa. Chords with subdominant function are evidently motivated to become chords with either tonic or dominant function, thanks to the dual antitonic/antidominant nature of $\hat{4}$ and $\hat{6}$. This model of functional progression under the Law of Harmony is illustrated at (a) in Figure 17.20. A dashed line demarcates an axis of symmetry about the tonic/dominant opposition, which also places the subdominant function at the center of the symmetry. This is a fundamentally different symmetry than the one promulgated by Riemann and the dualists, which places tonic function, and a dominant/subdominant opposition, at the center.

Since the general effect of the contrapuntal force in isolation is to motivate scale-degree assemblies to reconfigure themselves in ways that tend to move them rightward through the schema in Figures 17.10 and 17.16, it follows that chords adhering solely to the Law of Counterpoint would most likely move through the more familiar cycle of functions at (b) in Figure 17.20. In other words, from a contrapuntal perspective the functions have a rotational symmetry rather than a reflective one. Finally, (c) overlays the two node-and-arrow diagrams on top of one another to show a combined model of chord progression under both harmonic and contrapuntal forces.

Tonic harmonies move to subdominant harmonies by contrapuntal tendencies illustrated in Figures 17.10 and 17.16, which move $\hat{3}$ and $\hat{5}$ to $\hat{4}$ and $\hat{6}$; they may

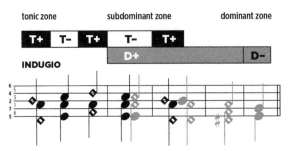

FIGURE 17.19 The three zones of a standard tonal phrase expressing a dominant-tonic interaction.

also move directly to dominant harmonies as contratonic and prodominant tendencies collaborate to displace $\hat{1}$ and $\hat{3}$ in favor of $\hat{7}$ and $\hat{2}$. The situation is quite different for dominant harmonies, in which harmonic and contrapuntal forces align to create a unified protonic drive even in the V triad. The presence of scale degrees $\hat{4}$ or $\hat{6}$ further strengthens this drive, especially when they are mobilized as antiroots of sevenths. The $(\hat{5}, \hat{4})$ seventh shows this effect most clearly: its root is stabilized by the tonic and dominant fields and by its contrapuntal interaction with the antiroot, and the antiroot is mobilized by all three forces. Less unity is seen in a dominant chordal encounter involving the $(\hat{7}, \hat{6})$ seventh, whose root has opposite polarity in the two harmonic fields; the reader may recall the statistical anomalies around this dyad in Bach's corpus, discussed above in connection with Figure 17.5.

Subdominant harmonies have a characteristic combination of protonic and prodominant charge, and the Law of Harmony on its own thus encourages motion to either tonic or dominant. Contrapuntal pressures, however, tend to stabilize $\hat{7}$ and thus encourage motion to the dominant when $\hat{2}$ is included, since $\hat{2}$ motivates both $\hat{6}$ and $\hat{1}$ contrapuntally (as its fifth and seventh, respectively). Purely harmonic protonic motion is only possible in subdominant harmonies containing neither $\hat{2}$ nor a $(\hat{4}, \hat{3})$ seventh: that is, the only subdominant harmony that this theory predicts can move to tonic is the IV triad.

Harmonic functions as modeled here are not general-purpose concepts; they specifically make predictions about phrase structure. (A more extensive discussion of the phrasal role of harmonic function may be found in White and Quinn 2018.) To summarize the predictions discussed above: A default phrase involves a motion from the tonic field at the beginning of the phrase to the dominant field at the end. The cadential dominant (be it a half or authentic cadence) is the goal of the phrase, and is most stable when the scale degrees in play are those having contradominant charge, i.e., the V triad. The **tonic zone** of a phrase is characterized by a play of tonic/antitonic oppositions, and while chords with $\hat{7}$, $\hat{1}$, and $\hat{4}$ are common in this zone, their function is as bearers of

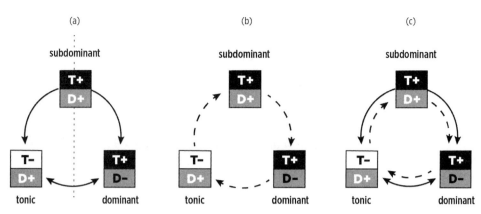

FIGURE 17.20 (a) Harmonic function under the Law of Harmony alone. (b) Harmonic function under the Law of Counterpoint alone. (c) Harmonic function under the interaction of harmony and counterpoint.

protonic charge, and these chords therefore have a distinctly different configuration of qualia than their counterparts in the dominant zone. (See Huron 2006 and Rings 2011 for more on scale-degree qualia.) The **subdominant zone** occupies the transition from the tonic field to the dominant field, and we have seen above how the IV triad occupies a unique position that balances it precisely between these two fields in a way that enables the phrase to end with a failure to cross into the third zone, the sphere of dominant influence.

The **dominant zone** is the goal of the phrase, and is where prodominant forces produce the cadential dominant. At times, the dominant field can strengthen to the point that it bends the diatonic scale around itself, moving $\hat{4}$ to $\sharp\hat{4}$. Once it is achieved, the cadential dominant engages three forces that align as they do in no other zone: contrapuntal, contradominant, and protonic forces come together to powerfully stabilize the notes of the tonic triad and mobilize the others. This framework helps us understand why III and III7 chords are so unusual in this music: the contrapuntal pathways depicted in Figure 17.10 are most heavily deformed by the unique confluence of harmonic forces in the dominant region. In other words, the theory predicts that harmonic forces make III and III7 difficult to get to, thanks to a powerful curvature of scale-degree space in their vicinity. That same distortion prevents the scale degrees involved in these chords from generating much harmonic force, since most of them are neutralized by destructive interference between contratonic and contradominant charges. It is only when harmonic forces are muted, as they are in sequential passages, that this chord turns up, and in the absence of harmonic forces its constituent tones have little scale-degree identity.

Toward a Theory
of Thoroughbass Tonality

The dyadic interaction framework developed above, as we have seen, has great explanatory power when it comes to harmonic progression at the phrase level in tonal music written under the thoroughbass regime that encompasses Baroque and galant practices. Its explanatory scope roughly coincides with that of seventeenth- and eighteenth-century thoroughbass manuals. But where theorists in the thoroughbass tradition preferred to treat the behavior of chords on an individual basis, often running into hundreds of pages, this framework reveals that a surprisingly simple set of principles govern all of these behaviors. There is good reason to think the internalized knowledge of a skilled continuo player takes something like this form. The dyadic analysis of the Bach chorales shows that these principles are clearly learnable from the experience of playing large quantities of this music. Continuo players immersed in related repertories of Baroque and galant music likely developed their internalized knowledge in just this way, as Robert Gjerdingen has argued, particularly since they are physically instantiated in the player's motor involvement with the geography of the keyboard.

Aspects of musical structure beyond the phrase level are outside the explanatory scope of this theory. There is no reason to think, as Schenker did, that the local and global levels of structure in musical works are governed by the same cognitive principles. Gjerdingen has recently begun to propose that his schema-based theory is a kind of construction grammar for music, analogous to a linguistic approach to sentence structure that strings stock expressions together rather than generating them from a deep structure through Chomsky-style rules. This framework is offered as a morphosyntactic infrastructure that generates and constrains the schemata that constitute such a construction grammar.

A fuller account of what we might call "thoroughbass tonality," to distinguish it from the tonality of the triad's "second nature," must include a theory of diatonic modulation, modeled as a system for relocating harmonic fields in scale-degree space. (Agmon 2013 introduces some formalizations that may be useful, although his theory is quite different from mine in its basic commitments.) We have seen a hint of how this works in the case of modulations to the dominant, brought about by a characteristic chromatic alteration ($\sharp\hat{4}$). Other modulations are likewise connected to specific alterations: in the minor mode, where the harmonic-minor scale is the default, $\flat\hat{7}$ is often sufficient to bring about modulation to the relative major. Because of the particular way in which diatonic scales and harmonic minor scales relate to each other (see Tymoczko 2011), the reverse journey is not so simple.

The second theoretical component needed to integrate this framework into a comprehensive account of thoroughbass tonality is a model of diminution that predicts the musical surface directly. A simple law that regulates leaps on the basis of the stabilization or mobilization of the scale degrees involved is likely to explain a great many well-formed surfaces without generating the kind of malapropisms that undergraduates often generate by applying non-harmonic ornamentations to triadic progressions. A complementary low-level construction grammar of schemata for figuration may enable this theory to serve as the basis for a model-composition engine, which would provide the ultimate test of the theory's predictive power: after all, the proof of the pudding is in the tasting.

In the spirit of pudding, I proffer a digestif to conclude our study of tonal harmony: an analysis of the dynamics of the cadential six-four chord within the dyadic interaction framework. In general, bass lines prefer to leap only to and from stabilized scale degrees. Because chordal fifths are mobilized contrapuntally as antiroots, six-four chords tend to show up in stepwise bass contexts. The Indugio variant shown in Figure 17.18 provides a standard example in which six-four chords are obligatory during the tonic zone. They arise in the tonic phase of the tonic/antitonic alternation typical of the tonic zone, and thus are conceptualized as stable with respect to the tonic field. A cadential six-four occurs in the subdominant or dominant zones. In this case, $\hat{5}$ is mobilized contrapuntally as the fifth of a triad, but it is also heavily stabilized by the dominant field. In the chordal encounter, the contratonic charge of $\hat{1}$ and $\hat{3}$ is reinforced by their prodominant charge in the looming dominant field. Especially under conditions of metric accent, this dyad is propelled downward to $\hat{7}$ and $\hat{2}$ through the coordinated action of the two harmonic fields, which also stabilize $\hat{5}$ throughout the process. The cadential six-four, then, involves a completely different configuration of qualia over its constituent scale degrees than the very same chord generates for itself in the tonic zone of a phrase. This framework provides a characteristically nuanced answer to the question of how a "tonic six-four" chord functions: it depends on the context.

Acknowledgments

An earlier version of this material was presented at the University of British Columbia in November 2016. For stimulating questions, comments, and colloquy, I am grateful to Angharad Davis, Dan Harrison, Liam Hynes, Steve Rings, Joe Salem, Chris White, and one anonymous referee for this volume.

Works Cited

Aarden, Bret, and Paul von Hippel. 2004. "Rules for Chord Doubling (and Spacing): Which Ones Do We Need?" *Music Theory Online* 10, no. 2. Available at: http://www.mtosmt.org/issues/mto.04.10.2/mto.04.10.2.aarden_hippel.php.

Agmon, Eytan. 2013. *The Languages of Western Tonality*. Heidelberg: Springer.

Benjamin, William E. 1981. "Pitch-Class Counterpoint in Tonal Music." In *Music Theory: Special Topics*, edited by R. Browne, 1–32. Orlando, FL: Academic Press.

Brown, Matthew. 2004. *Explaining Tonality: Schenkerian Theory and Beyond*. Rochester, NY: University of Rochester Press.

Budge, Helen. 1943. *A Study of Chord Frequencies: Based on the Music of Representative Composers of the Eighteenth and Nineteenth Centuries*. New York: Teachers College.

Chew, Elaine. *Mathematical and Computational Modeling of Tonality: Theory and Applications*. New York: Springer.

Christensen, Thomas. 1993. *Rameau and Musical Thought in the Enlightenment*. Cambridge: Cambridge University Press.

Cohn, Richard. 2012. *Audacious Euphony: Chromatic Harmony and the Triad's Second Nature*. New York: Oxford University Press.

Dahlhaus, Carl. 1990. *Studies on the Origin of Harmonic Tonality*. Translated by Robert O. Gjerdingen. Princeton, NJ: Princeton University Press.

Daube, Johann Friedrich. 1756. *General-Bass in drey Accorden*. Frankfurt: André.

Diruta, Girolamo. 1957. *Il transilvano*. Venice: Vicenti.

Fux, Johann Joseph. 1725. *Gradus ad parnassum*. Vienna: van Ghelen.

Gjerdingen, Robert O. 2007. *Music in the Galant Style*. New York: Oxford University Press.

Gjerdingen, Robert O., and Janet Bourne. 2015. "Schema Theory as a Construction Grammar." *Music Theory Online* 21, no. 2. http://www.mtosmt.org/issues/mto.15.21.2/mto.15.21.2.gjerdingen_bourne.html.

Gollin, Edward, and Alexander Rehding. 2011. *Oxford Handbook of Neo-Riemannian Music Theories*. New York: Oxford University Press.

Guido Aretinus. 1955. *Micrologus* [1026]. In *Corpus Scriptorum de Musica 4*, edited by Joseph Smits van Waesberghe. Rome: American Institute of Musicology.

Harrison, Daniel. 1944. *Harmonic Function in Chromatic Music: A Renewed Dualist Theory and an Account of Its Precedents*. Chicago: University of Chicago Press.

Huron, David. 2006. *Sweet Anticipation: Music and the Psychology of Expectation*. Cambridge, MA: MIT Press.

Jones, Mari Riess, and Boltz, Marilyn. 1989. "Dynamic Attending and Responses to Time." *Psychological Review* 96, no. 3: 459–491.

Kinderman, William, and Harald Krebs, eds. 1996. *The Second Practice of Nineteenth-Century Tonality*. Lincoln: University of Nebraska Press.

Kirnberger, Johann Philipp. 1982. *The Art of Strict Musical Composition (1771–1779)*. Edited and translated by David W. Beach and Jürgen Thym. New Haven, CT: Yale University Press.

Lerdahl, Fred. 2001. *Tonal Pitch Space*. New York: Oxford University Press.

London, Justin. 2012. *Hearing in Time*, 2nd ed. New York: Oxford University Press.

McHose, Allen Irvine. 1947. *The Contrapuntal-Harmonic Technique of the 18th Century*. New York: Appleton-Century-Crofts.

Mitchell, William J. 1949. "Introduction." In *C.P. E. Bach: Essay on The True Art of Playing Keyboard Instruments*, edited and translated by William J. Mitchell, 1–23. New York: Norton.

Parrish, Carl. 1947. Review of McHose 1947. *Notes* 4: 342–343.

Piston, Walter. 1941. *Harmony*, 1st ed. New York: Norton.

Quinn, Ian. 2010. "Are Pitch-Class Profiles Really 'Key for Key'?" *Zeitschrift der Gesellschaft für Musiktheorie* 7: 151–163.

Rameau, Jean-Philippe. 1971. *Treatise on Harmony* (1722). Translated by Philip Gossett. New York: Dover.

Rameau, Jean-Philippe. 1726. *Nouveau systême de musique theorique, où l'on découvre le principe de toutes les regles necessaires à la pratique, pour servir d'introduction au Traité de l'harmonie*. Paris: Ballard.

Rings, Steven. 2011. *Tonality and Transformation*. New York: Oxford University Press.

Rohrmeier, Martin, and Ian Cross. 2008. "Statistical Properties of Harmony in Bach's Chorales." *Proceedings of the 10th International Conference on Music Perception and Cognition*, edited by Ken'ichi Mayazaki, 619–627. Sapporo: ICMPC.

Schoenberg, Arnold. 1978. *Theory of Harmony* [1911]. Translated by Roy E. Carter. Berkeley: University of California Press.

Tymoczko, Dmitri. 2003. "Progressions fondamentales, fonctions, degrés: une grammaire de l'harmonie tonale élémentaire." *Musurgia* 10, nos.: 35–64.

Tymoczko, Dmitri. 2011. *A Geometry of Music: Harmony and Counterpoint in the Extended Common Practice*. New York: Oxford University Press.

White, Christopher W., and Ian Quinn. 2016. "The Yale–Classical Archives Corpus." *Empirical Musicology Review* 11: 50–58.

White, Christopher W., and Ian Quinn. 2018. "Chord Context and Harmonic Function in Tonal Music." *Music Theory Spectrum* 40, no. 2: 314–335.

Wolff, Christoph. 2001. *Johann Sebastian Bach: The Learned Musician*. New York: Norton.

CHAPTER 18

··

KEY AND MODULATION

··

SUZANNAH CLARK

THE hallmark of tonal music is that it is written in one of twenty-four keys; that is, one of either twelve major or twelve minor keys. Yet, when we say that a work or a movement of a work is in a particular key—say, in C major or C minor—we do not mean that it articulates that key throughout. It will venture to numerous others, which are attained through various means of modulation. New keys may be articulated for various lengths of time and with various gradations of certitude, often reflecting the conventions of musical form. The briefest encounters with a new key are known as tonicizations, though the precise point at which tonicization becomes modulation is often a matter of interpretation and debate. In apparently well-behaved musical structures, modulations serve at once to negate the sense of the overarching or home key (as it is often called) in order to create variety, yet at the same time they reinforce it by remaining closely related. What harmonic features, then, are invoked when a work or a passage within a work is said to be in a particular key? And how is that careful balance maintained between introducing modulations that reinforce the home key and those that supplant it altogether?

In tackling these questions, this chapter begins with an analysis of the song "Im wunderschönen Monat Mai" that opens Schumann's song-cycle *Dichterliebe*. This song withholds many key-defining features, which allows us to come up with some rules of thumb about what features are present when keys are clearly articulated. As we shall see, one feature that is often relied upon in determining whether or not a key has been fully articulated is the presence or absence of a final cadence. This observation raises an important issue, which permeates this chapter, namely the tension between contents and cadences—a tension that arises when the content of a passage or work offers clear signals of a key's identity, only for the cadence to be missing; or the content may offer signals of one key, only for the cadence to articulate another one. Over the course of the chapter, we shall examine a range of scenarios of such tension, and we shall trace how different theorists and analysts have weighted the relative importance of content versus cadence.

If the first part of the chapter identifies the criteria for identifying keys, the rest explores what strategies composers employ to move from one key to another and what kinds of key relations they choose. While rehearsing each of the conventional ways of modulating is beyond the scope of a chapter of this length, I devote much of my attention in the section

"The Art of Modulation" to new theoretical insights on common-tone modulation. The chapter then returns once again to the issue of content versus cadence in the determination of degrees of certainty about the establishment of new internal keys, as well as definitions of tonicization versus modulation. It ends by touching on how key relations have been defined over time and shaped into various configurations known as tonal spaces.

Key Fragments: Content Versus Cadence

Perhaps counterintuitively, a good way to grasp how a home key is established is to turn to an example where its standard-bearer features are deliberately withheld. As indicated above, such an example is the first song from Schumann's song-cycle *Dichterliebe*, "Im wunderschönen Monat Mai." This song also exemplifies modulations that vie for equal status as tonic defining, perhaps even overshadowing the ostensible home key altogether.

"Im wunderschönen Monat Mai" begins in medias res, which an observer of the score (see Figure 18.1) can immediately tell because the key signature of three sharps suggests the tonic key is either A major or F♯ minor yet the opening harmony is B minor. Moreover, B minor is in the first-inversion position, which further undermines any sense of an emphatic beginning. It can serve either as ii^6 of A major or iv^6 of F♯ minor, making it a useful predominant in either key—a harmonic feature that will prove crucial in the art of modulation in this song.[1] Once the second measure moves to V^7 of F♯ minor, it becomes clear that the latter key is in play. The progression f♯: iv^6–V^7 turns out to be the full sum of the harmonic material in the piano prelude, as well as on its return as an interlude in mm. 12–15 and postlude in mm. 23–26 (albeit with a tiny adjustment to the B-minor harmony to turn it into a root position chord—f♯: iv—since a root-position D major chord—D: I—was just heard at the beginning of measures 12 and 23, respectively).[2] The piano's pre-, inter-, and postludes embody the sense of longing expressed in the poetry ("Sehnen und Verlangen"); they sound inconclusive. This feeling is especially poignant at the very end of the song, which is poised on V^7 of F♯ minor, held on by a fermata as the sound of the keyboard dies away and further dwindles on release of the pedal.

The harmony that convention invites us to yearn for after the fermata is F♯ minor, the would-be tonic of the two-measure progression iv^6–V^7 set up in mm. 1–2 and repeated no fewer than five times in mm. 3–4, 12^4–13, 14–15, 23^4–24, and 25–26. Indeed, a V^7 chord is the strongest indicator of a key, other than the tonic itself. As such, the desire for a conventional resolution to F♯ minor is so powerful—and the tutored ear is so trained to supply it—that Schumann even wrote "Schluß" (end) above the fermata in his sketch of the song as a kind of note-to-self lest he forget that he intended to compose a cliffhanger.[3] Had Schumann obliged our ears by providing the tonic after the fermata in a hypothetical m. 27, we would have no trouble identifying F♯ minor as the key of "Im wunderschönen Monat Mai"—no matter how quietly or briefly it might have sounded.

FIGURE 18.1 Schumann, "Im wunderschönen Monat Mai," *Dichterliebe*, op. 48, no. 1.

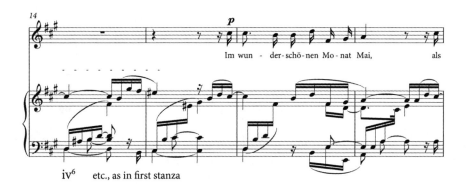

Im wun - der-schö-nen Mo - nat Mai,   als

iv^6 etc., as in first stanza

al - le Vö - gel san - gen,   da hab' ich ihr ge - stan - den   mein

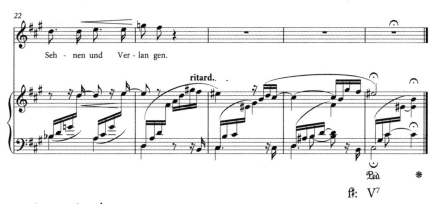

Seh - nen und Ver - lan gen.

ritard.

f#: V^7

FIGURE 18.1 *continued*

But without the tonic actually sounding, we cannot say that the key of F♯ minor is unequivocally established.[4]

It may seem like an overreaction to suggest that withholding the tonic itself constitutes a dereliction of duty when defining a key. For, as we have witnessed, all harmonic functions in the piano solo sections point indubitably to F♯ minor as tonic. Moreover, these sections appear at both the beginning and ending of the song, where the territory of a home key is typically charted. Surely we ought instead to marvel at how the fragmentary nature of Schumann's song hinges on the creation of a harmonic fabric that is frayed at the edges. And what better way to design such a fragment than to provide a solid middle of a highly familiar harmonic progression and to leave its edges unbegun and unfinished. Instead of presenting the key-defining phrase structure T–PD–D–T, Schumann provides the internal segment PD–D.[5] Put this way, the key of the song is just as clear as the reason why it epitomizes the Romantic fragment.[6]

The ambiguity of key for which this song is so famous comes not so much from the lapse in providing an opening and closing F♯-minor triad as from other complementary factors, which, together with the absence of F♯ minor, mark A major as another contender for the key of the song.[7] To hear this case, we must press on to the entry of the voice in the upbeat to m. 5. Earlier was mentioned that the opening harmony, B minor, could serve as a predominant to either F♯ minor or A major. Significantly, the vocal line takes off from this same harmony, however it pivots to A major instead of F♯ minor. This time, A major is articulated with a perfect authentic cadence (PAC), and, just like in the prelude, the phrase is immediately repeated in mm. 7–8. The segment of T–PD–D–T, while still fragmentary, is more complete: A: ii^6–V^7–I, or PD–D–T. Although the beginning of each phrase is missing its tonic, endings—that is, cadences—matter emphatically more than beginnings when it comes to the articulation of key. There is nothing more tonic affirming than a PAC, which is defined by the root position V–I motion, with a closed $\hat{1}$ in the uppermost voice of the tonic harmony. One can immediately compare its conclusive effect to the less conclusive impression left by the two ensuing cadences in mm. 9–10 and 11–12, which are imperfect authentic cadences (IAC). Here, the IACs are characterized by an appoggiatura leading to $\hat{3}$ over their tonics.[8] The idea that A major is articulated by a PAC, whereas the other two cadences in B minor and D major, respectively, are IACs, virtually clinches the argument that A major is a contender for the key of the song.

I say "virtually" because, while it is the only key in the song that is fully established with a PAC, what divests A major of home-key status is its position within the formal structure of the song as the first cadence in the voice. In its favor is the fact that, from a formal point of view, the vocal material in a vocal work—and especially in Lieder—is often taken to be the substance of the musical form, lending the piano's material the non-structural role of "before the beginning," "between the stanzas," and "after the ending."[9] From this perspective, A major qualifies emphatically as the tonic—or home key—of the song. However, from another perspective, we once more come up against the condition that endings matter more than beginnings when defining a key. The stanza ends in D major. Why can we not say that the song is in D major, articulating a global D: iii–V–(vi)–I incomplete arpeggiation? We could, except for the fact that D major does not achieve "complete harmonic and melodic closure" because of the IAC.[10] We might also refer back to the key signature, which does not signal D major—a piece of testimony that is perhaps especially relevant in Schumann's oeuvre because we know him to have been fascinated by keys and key relations, particularly with respect to the overarching design of the tonics of the songs in *Dichterliebe* (Hallmark 1977, 125).

In sum, if either the piano postlude had ended with a PAC in F♯ minor or the stanzaic material had been bounded by A major instead of only beginning with it, then we would have a winner. Given the absence of emphatic endings, we can only say that Schumann's song hovers between F♯ minor and A major. We have therefore a genuine case of the ambiguity of key.[11]

DETERMINANTS OF KEY: THE SENSE OF AN ENDING

We are also now in a position to list some rules of thumb for how musical structures unfold when their composer states a key unambiguously. The tonic announced at the opening of the structure and asserted at the end will be identical, and it will correspond to either the major or minor key denoted by the signature. Clear opening tonics launch the musical structure incisively with a tonic-functioning harmony, starting from the first downbeat. Additionally, the opening tonic pronouncement will be confirmed by a cadence early on in the structure, preferably a PAC but an interim IAC will do, especially as the latter lends a sense of continuity and flow to the music. Final tonics are not so much asserted by their reprise after other internal keys have been explored than by their final cadence, which must categorically be a PAC. The moment that qualifies as the "final cadence" need not be the final sounds heard in the piece, for the formal issue of the identity of the end of the structural essence and the beginning of closing material or a coda may come into play. The coda is an addendum that does not have the same obligations of closure as the main structural close (it might end with a whimper rather than a bang), although classically it is the space in which the closure is further asserted—with, indeed, repeated PACs, usually *forte*.

Once again, this truism may be exemplified by turning to exceptions that prove the rule. Instead of ending on $\hat{1}$ / I, pieces that end on either $\hat{5}$ / I or $\hat{3}$ / I sound distinctly unsettling, although not, of course, to the extent of undermining the identity of the key itself. For example, the final stanza of Brahms's "Von ewiger Liebe," op. 43, no. 1 ends with $\hat{1}$ / I; however, the piano's postlude ends with $\hat{3}$ / I (see Figure 18.2). In this song, the woman asserts that, while iron and steel can be melted down and recast, the love between her and her beloved must last forever ("unsere Liebe muß ewig bestehen"). To mark the strength of her conviction, her vocal line roars to a PAC close. The piano postlude afterwards evokes the everlasting sense of their love by being open-ended on $\hat{3}$ / I—or perhaps it provides a doubt.[12] Performers of this song sometimes underplay the third in the uppermost voice to provide a greater sense of closure than the composer indicates in the score. Compare

FIGURE 18.2 Brahms, "Von ewiger Liebe," op. 43, no. 1, mm. 111–21.

the recordings of Kathleen Ferrier and Bruno Walter or Dietrich Fischer-Dieskau and Günther Weißenborn, which downplay the $\hat{3}$, versus Brigitte Fassbaender and Irwin Gage or Jessye Norman and Geoffrey Parsons, in which it is more audible.

Similarly, Schubert's "Schwanengesang" (D. 744) ends with a clear PAC in mm. 17–18, just as the narrator reports that the dying swan expels its last breath (Figure 18.3).[13] For all intents and purposes, this cadence draws this modified stanzaic song to a conclusion. Yet, a brief glance ahead shows that the singer has one more line to deliver: extraordinarily, the voice sings during the piano's postlude in mm. 19–23, which is otherwise a repetition of the piano's prelude mm. 1–4 (not shown in the example). Aptly, the words in the postlude are a reflection on the song's meaning: "das bedeutet des Schwanen Gesang" ("that is the meaning of the swansong"). Much like the musical structure of a coda or, here, piano postlude, these words are structurally outside of the main song, which comprises a stanza of the swan's song, followed by a second modified stanza in the voice of a narrator reporting on the swan's final song and moment of death. After the PAC, the ensuing material continues the quest for closure and, much like Schumann's "Im wunderschönen Monat Mai," the piano's first attempt at closure is cut short, with a fermata over a dominant in m. 18. The tonic after the pregnant pause is not cadential (observe some robust Schenkerian analysis in this assessment), but rather is a "retaking" or reprise of the piano's prelude.[14] Though serving as a coda, it does not reinforce the expected closure, for there is no confirmation of the tonic with a final PAC in either the voice or piano. Instead, as if to suggest the spirit of the swan lives on or is journeying

FIGURE 18.3 Schubert, "Schwanengesang" (D. 744), mm. 17–23.

into the afterworld, $\hat{5}$ haunts the voice's final rumination and the open-ended IAC of the piano. Like the similar tactic in Brahms's "Von ewiger Liebe," not all pianists make the effect obvious: compare Graham Johnson's rendition with Brigitte Fassbaender, where the $\hat{5}$ is clear, and Rudolf Jansen's with Robert Holl, where it is downplayed.

While the endings on $\hat{3}$ and $\hat{5}$ may seem like small details, they have the powerful effect of destabilizing the final tonic, while not undermining the identity of key itself. As we shall see later in the sections on "The Art of Modulation" and "Modulations and Tonicizations," when it comes to internal keys, these kinds of details in the presentation of cadences—as well as whether cadences are present or not—determine the structural hierarchies of their keys within a musical form.

A BRIEF HISTORY OF THE ROLE OF CLOSURE IN THE DEFINITION OF KEY

The idea that endings are more powerful than beginnings in defining a key has its origins in modal theory, specifically in its ninth-century incarnation. The eight church modes (also commonly referred to as the Gregorian modes, based on the Carolingian reform) were mainly defined by their ambitus (authentic or plagal) and by their finals, the principal cadence point and final resting place of a chant. Each mode also had subsidiary cadential or resting points, most commonly the tenor or cofinal and the mediant. Since all modes contained the same pitches—the white notes on the piano—it was their range and the behavior of their subsidiary cadences, together with how they ended—their final—that distinguished them.

An important step in the transition from church modes to modern keys was the divorce between finals and transposition. For instance, the mode with the final pitch G and a signature of one flat is a transposition of the Dorian mode, which is characterized by the final D and no signature. In such cases, D-Dorian would always have been considered the original mode and G-Dorian its transpositional derivative. With modern keys, the same major or minor scale has twelve transpositions but no one key is considered the original one from which all others are transpositions, even if C major and A minor appear to be default keys or starting points because they have no sharps or flats. Although it was some time before all twenty-four keys were recognized both in practice and by theorists, in the new tonal system each major and minor key is identical in scalar structure (notwithstanding the amorphous sixth and seventh degrees of the minor scale), and distinguished only by signature and final.[15]

While we might nowadays casually explain that the tonic note of a major or minor key may be found by looking for the first note of its scale and the tonic triad may be built by adding scale degrees $\hat{3}$ and $\hat{5}$, early tonal theorists understood the tonic in musical practice to be the final pitch. In a detailed study of the intense theoretical maneuvers that occurred during the transition from modes to keys during the late sixteenth and seventeenth centuries, Joel Lester identified Monsieur de Saint Lambert as an important pioneer: he was the first to differentiate between key and mode in the modern sense.[16] According to Saint Lambert, the final pitch in the bass was the means through which the key was identified and the mode (i.e., major or minor) was identified through the ambulation of the melody and chordal unfolding, which was known as "modulation"—a meaning of the term that died out in the first decades of the nineteenth century.[17]

In the chapter on "Des Tons, des Modes, et de la Transposition" in his *Nouveau traité de l'accompagnement du clavecin, de l'orgue, et des autres instruments* (1707), Monsieur de Saint Lambert makes these principles clear:

> Every air or piece of music is composed in a certain key and in a certain mode.
>
> The key of an air is the note on which it ends, and that note is also called the *final*.
>
> If the final of an air is a C, we say that the air is in *C Sol Ut* (this is the label). If it is a D, it is in *D La Ré* etc.
>
> When an air has several parts, the parts (including the one we call the *subject*) sometimes end on another note than the principal final of the air. But with regards to the bass—whether it is the subject of the air or whether it is not—it always ends on the principal final. So when we would like to know in which key an air is composed, it is the final of the bass that one should look at. This final is always the fundamental note of an air, and for that reason is called the *tonic* note.

Mode is the determination of the path that the melody of an air should take, as well as those of its parts, should there be any—all of which relates to the final note. It is this that constitutes the species of each interval; it is the particular system on which a piece of music is built.

(Saint Lambert 1707, 26–27)[18]

Given this emphasis on finals, it is perhaps no coincidence that Rameau famously encapsulated harmonic motion in the cadence V^7–I. Musical motion falls to its localized final, its point of (momentary) rest. The modern imagination of a work that opens up from a beginning tonic and returns to it at the end is a later conception. This thinking was influenced by such models as Riemann's phrase structure, T–S–D–T, encountered earlier in its modern equivalent, T–PD–D–T. It shows a closed structure, where both Ts are presumed to represent the same key. The first T is the most expansive and can therefore extend over a long time, while the final three elements in this model are often cadential and happen in short succession (the Americanized nomenclature T–PD–D–T makes this harmonic scenario clearer).[19] Or, the idea of a lengthy opening tonic, followed by V–I cadential closure is wonderfully captured by Schenker's *Bassbrechung*: first it seeks the rising fifth, in consort with nature's overtone series and in order to open up tonal space ("der Tonraum"), then it seeks closure with a PAC—no less—that brings the *Urlinie* to a close,o $\hat{2}-\hat{1}$ over V–I (Schenker 1979, 10–16, Figs. 2–7). To be sure, for Riemann, Schenker, and others, the supreme importance of endings in the definition of key took on the additional burden of goal-orientedness. However, as we have seen, the preoccupation with endings cannot be considered a modern phenomenon, attributable to the nineteenth-century zest for teleology, even if it certainly aligns nicely with their ideology. Rather the emphasis on endings as mode- or key-defining has long been embedded within the Western tradition.

Indeed, the emphasis on cadence can sometimes lead to analytical errors: witness a sample fugue provided in a textbook by George Oldroyd first published in 1948, where the subject cadences in G major but is clearly in C major and Oldroyd has given the key signature as G major. As such, this academic fugue ends in the wrong key.[20] Moreover, advice on composing "academic" or "examination fugues" (as they are sometimes called) very much centers on producing cadences at the end of subjects, even if short codettas then require insertion before the answer enters (as in the fugue sample just cited). However, stylistic study of historical fugues of the Baroque shows that, while cadences were certainly important, they held less sway than in the academic fugue (Bullivant 1971, 40).

The emphasis on endings also explains important analytical decisions when identifying the keys of passages or even complete works that begin in one key and end in another. Witness, for example, the second theme in the first movement of Brahms's Cello Sonata in F major, op. 99 (see Figure 18.4). It begins with a C-major harmony in m. 34, the expected dominant of the home key. Despite its promising harmonic start, the second theme cannot be said to be "in the key of C major." This is not because it quickly veers off but because it emphatically concludes with a PAC in A minor in m. 60. The

FIGURE 18.4 Brahms, Cello Sonata in F major, op. 99, first mvt., mm. 30–65.

FIGURE 18.4 *continued*

time spent in A minor is minimal, yet the theme is said to be "in A minor." Schenker captured this in *Free Composition*, Fig. 110d, the graph of which is reproduced in Figure 18.5(a). Observe the arrow pointing to A minor—an indication that this portion of the structure is driving towards its cadence. Using his theory of "incomplete structures," Schenker argues that mm. 34–60 (which any formalist would agree is the second theme) comprises a middleground arpeggiation, a: III–V–i. The key and harmonic content are defined by the endpoint.[21]

Roger Graybill (1988) sought to reinterpret the function of these harmonies in order to re-anoint C major with what he saw as its rightful status of dominant. To do so, he had to downplay the PAC in A minor as an endpoint and argue instead that the repetition of the exposition produces the arpeggiation F: V–iii–I. In his view, A minor is a midpoint. A purist (nay, a stickler) would say that Graybill's revised arpeggiation is flawed because the arrival on F major is not effected through a PAC but rather a reprise of the first theme's opening tonic. To be sure, in this respect, Schenker's analysis of the Cello Sonata is more traditional. It also represents a kind of thinking applicable to numerous other non-tonic openings of thematic units, as well as to so-called double-tonic complexes.[22]

As an example of the former, take, for instance, the first theme of the first movement of Brahms's String Quartet in A minor, op. 51, no. 2, which sets out from D minor. Observe

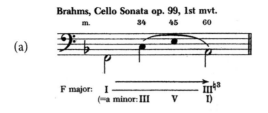

FIGURE 18.5 (a) Analysis of the exposition of Brahms, Cello Sonata in F major, op. 99, first mvt., from Schenker, *Free Composition* (Fig. 110d) and (b) Analysis of mm. 1–8 of Schumann, "Im wunderschönen Monat Mai," *Dichterliebe* op. 48, no. 1 from Schenker, *Free Composition* (Fig. 110c.2).

in Figure 18.6 how quietly the arrival of A minor sounds in m. 20, with the tonic only represented by the tonic pitch in the violin and cello (that is, there is no third or fifth). The PAC takes emphatic structural care of the harmonic whisper. Despite spending plenty of time elsewhere harmonically, this first theme is "in A minor."

Schenker's notion of the "incomplete structure" can also make tidy work of whole movements or even whole pieces that begin and end in one key. Notably, it always ensures that what might hit the listener as a tonic at the opening is reinterpreted in light of the final key. Schenker's theory is well suited to this axiom, and indeed *Free Composition* contains graphs of non-tonic openings for virtually all imaginable diatonic starting points. Schenker's Figures 110–111, of which two are reproduced in Figure 18.5 here, illustrate how such structures are imagined to be missing their opening tonic. They are understood to begin in medias res and to unfold an *Ursatz* from their sounding starting points.[23]

In the wake of Robert Bailey's contributions on double-tonic complexes, such structures were re-analyzed as having two tonics.[24] Although often associated with late nineteenth-century practice, particularly of opera, such structures were relatively common in the eighteenth century, especially in vocal repertories, notably Lieder. While Bailey and others cast their theoretical agenda and analyses as a resistance to the concept of monotonality expressed by the likes of Schenker and Schoenberg, from a historical point of view their most radical claim was actually the elevation of the opening harmony to the status of tonic.

In so doing, they achieved what theorists before them had wished for, but they had been unable to come up with a formula that caught on. Indeed, as far back as 1640, Giovanni Battista Doni (1640, 237) expressed frustration with the principle of defining a

FIGURE 18.6 Brahms, String Quartet in A minor, op. 51, no. 2, first mvt., mm. 1–20.

whole musical structure based on its final. Writing at that time about mode, he ridiculed those who were stumped by pieces that lack a final, although he left implied that the opening or main body of a piece could be key-defining (also observe, again, that the defunct meaning of the word "modulation" is used in this passage):

> Pray, this is one of the strange things of the world; it really amounts to saying that in order to distinguish a lion from a horse, it is necessary to look at his tail; and if by any means the poor animal should happen to have that cut off, it would no longer be possible to recognize him or to tell of what species he might be. So if in a modulation [piece of music][25] that last note happens to be wanting, it will be impossible to determine in what key ("*modo*") it was written!
>
> (Weber 1841, 126) [26]

If we apply this to the missing triad at the end of Schumann's "Im wunderschönen Monat Mai," we might wonder what all the fuss regarding key identification has been about. As long ago as the seventeenth century, Doni was saying that a missing final ought not to be off-putting. Doni's yarn was repeated and glossed in 1817 by Gottfried Weber, who was not only a contemporary of Schumann's but whose treatise was also read by Schumann (Hoeckner 2006, 71). Weber was reappropriating what Doni had said about mode and applied it to tonal keys. Nonetheless, the translation of Doni's reference to "modo" as "key" is an intervention by Weber's English translator, James Warner. However, conveniently for our present discussion, Weber's invocation of a theorist from over two centuries earlier together with Warner's editorial translation from mode to key emphasizes the continuity of thought regarding finals in the age of both modal and tonal theory.

In his treatise, Weber calls for a more holistic view of the determination of a key than focusing on how pieces end. Additionally, he points to how fragile the definition of key by its final can be since not all pieces end in the tonic in which they begin, although the examples given of such works seem fairly tame:

> Equally fallacious [as using key signatures to determine keys] is the method of ascertaining the key and scale from *the last note* or *the last harmony* of the piece. For, in the first place, it is far from being true that every piece of music ends with the tonic harmony. It not unfrequently [*sic*] happens, on the contrary, that a piece, even though it terminates with a regular close and that too with a tonic harmony, yet does not terminate with the harmony of that tonic which was the tonic of the piece, as a whole, but with some other; as e.g. pieces in the minor mode sometimes close with the common chord of the tonic of *the major* key. In the second place, many pieces terminate wholly without any regular musical close, and in such cases it could not be ascertained at all, in what key the music is, nor in what key this or that division of a piece may be. This case is quite aptly hit by a humorous exclamation of old *Doni*: "Pray, this is one of the strange things of the world . . . ."
>
> (Weber 1841, 126; see above for the rest of the quotation)[27]

Significantly, this passage appears in one of Weber's "remarks" ("Anmerkung"), which are lengthy asides sprinkled throughout the *Versuch* in which Weber challenges common wisdom. While Weber echoes Doni in mocking narrow definitions of key, another contemporary composer—namely Brahms—challenged a growing expectation that pieces will begin and end in a single key. As Brahms's composition pupil Gustav Jenner reported, Brahms expressed the following opinion:

> How often, when listening to songs, particularly modern songs, must one wonder why a certain song has to end in A-flat major and find no answer except that it began in A-flat major? Here the composer, who appears to move so freely in his modulations, has actually become the slave of an idea whose true meaning he does not seem to grasp. He would be much more consistent in his arbitrariness if he ended in some other key into which he had been led just as his text was coming to its conclusion.[28]

Indeed, Brahms may have been speaking his own mind but also, it is worth noting, he owned a copy of Weber's popular treatise. To be sure, owning a book is not the same as cracking it open (and we have no direct evidence that Brahms read the treatise), but the sentiments expressed by both men are two sides of the same coin.

As these statements from the seventeenth to the nineteenth centuries attest, neither composers nor theorists felt the necessity to remain confined to a single key for a whole movement, nor necessarily bound to definitions of key through cadences or finals. Indeed, twentieth-century attitudes were more conservative thanks in large part to Schoenberg and Schenker, who developed separate theoretical systems but shared the insistence on monotonality, whereby all keys—no matter how distantly related—would be reckoned according to a single tonic, defined as the final tonic. Clearly, the loosening of monotonal definitions of key by Bailey and others revisits the propositions of earlier theorists.

THE ART OF MODULATION

Thus far, we have twice encountered the now-defunct sense of the term "modulation." An emblematic definition of the old sense, which held sway until the beginning of the nineteenth century (see n. 17), may be found in Jean-Jacques Rousseau's dictionary:

> [Modulation] is, properly speaking, the manner of establishing and treating the mode; but this word is more commonly taken today to be the art of steering the harmony and melody successively through several modes in a manner agreeable to the ear and that conforms to the rules.

> If the mode is produced by the harmony, it is also from it that the laws of *modulation* are born. These laws are easy to imagine but difficult to observe. The following explains of what they consist.

To modulate well within a single key, one must first go through all of its sounds with
a beautiful melody, striking fairly regularly the essential chords and holding onto
them for longer: that is to say, the dominant seventh and tonic chords must be used
frequently, but in different guises and through different routes to avoid monotony.
Secondly, [one must] not establish cadences or resting points on harmonies other
than these two, except, at most, on the subdominant. Thirdly and finally, never alter
any notes of the mode; because one cannot—without exiting the key—sound a sharp
or flat that doesn't belong to it or remove any of those that belong.

But, to move from one key to another, one must think of the analogy: be attentive
to the relationship between tonics and the quality of the chords that are common to
both keys.

(Rousseau 1768, 298)[29]

This older sense of "modulating within a key" focuses on both content and cadence.
As Rousseau points out, the melody and harmony should be confined to pitches diatonic
to the mode. The essential diatonic harmonies—especially the dominant seventh and
tonic—should be exploited to ground the key. Observe that Rousseau mentions the use
of the dominant seventh and tonic in that order, which echoes Rameau's newly minted
theory of harmonic progression. Clearly Rousseau does not rely only on cadences to
define the key. Rather he emphasizes which harmonies best serve as resting or cadence
points to establish the sense of key: namely, the tonic and dominant, and under certain
circumstances the subdominant.

This older sense of modulation adds some additional features to our rules of thumb
mentioned earlier, which focused on finding the identity of the key through its cadence
over content, which can—as was hinted at—lead to some contradictions. Insofar as
modulation within a key considers the treatment of melody, the harmonic and melodic
progression through the key, as well as cadences, it espouses a kind of in-the-moment
analysis or listening process, rather than an analysis or hearing by hindsight. As we
shall see again later, content and cadence do not always align, and thus the eighteenth-
century emphasis on the unfolding of a key, rather than overly focusing on its cadential
point of articulation, becomes an important listening, analytical, and theoretical tool.

The current sense of the term "modulation" refers to the process of changing from
one key to another. There are a variety of generally recognized methods of modulation,
many of which are known by multiple names: (1) pivot—or common-chord modulation, (2) chromatic modulation, (3) enharmonic modulation, (4) sequential or chain
modulation, (5) direct, abrupt, or phrase modulation, which in the context of popular song has recently also been coined the "truck driver's modulation" (Everett 2009,
283), and (6) common-tone modulation. Perhaps the easiest way to draw a distinction
among all these is to group together those that occur while a phrase or passage of music
is underway (1–4) and those that occur between phrases or sections (5–6), although
in a certain sense (4) also belongs in this latter category. A taxonomy of modulatory
schemes such as the list above rather than their formal function is very much the stuff
of modern textbooks. The distinction, for example, between a pivot-chord, chromatic,

and enharmonic modulation is helpful when gradually rolling out chords, harmonic functions, or key relations for students to learn. But, in effect, modulations within a phrase all employ similar techniques but differ in whether they involve major and minor harmonies, false relations, diminished chords, augmented sixth chords, or closely related versus distantly related keys. The same may be said for modulations between sections.

I will not rehearse here all the technical details associated with each method of modulation, which in any case can be found in any textbook. Rather, I shall launch into an analysis of a song by Schubert in which many of these types of modulation can be heard in action, namely the common chord, sequential, and common tone modulations. Schubert's "Selige Welt" (D. 743), shown in Figure 18.7, begins in A♭ major, although the

FIGURE 18.7 Schubert, "Selige Welt" (D. 743).

FIGURE 18.7 *continued*

first A♭-major root-position chord appears at the end of the piano prelude with the emphatic PAC—again illustrating that endings are often stronger than beginnings. The first two lines of the first stanza are squarely in A♭ major. The harmonic move that prepares the ear for the first modulation appears in m. 7, where there is a mode change to A♭

minor—suitably on the words "hin und her," meaning "back and forth." The shift to A♭ minor is not considered a modulation (or a tonicization) because parallel moves share the same tonic and are therefore considered merely changes of color—or going back and forth between modes. However, the introduction of the pitch $\hat{C}♭$ that brings about the mode change signals the direction of the new key.[30] C♭ major is established with a PAC in mm. 8–9. The A section of the ABA′ form of this song would therefore be called a modulating A section. The new key is brought about through a pivot-chord modulation. Although the D♭-minor pivot is chromatic in relation to the overall tonic of the song, it is diatonic to the more local A♭ minor. Therefore the modulation itself is a straightforward diatonic one. The pivot chord serves as a predominant, which offers the smoothest possible method of modulation: the chord is iv⁶ in A♭ minor and ii⁶ in C♭ major.

Schubert maintains the key of C♭ major at the opening of the B section of the song and in so doing confirms the new key. The words of the first line of the second stanza are repeated, with an undulating I–V, V–I phrase pattern in C♭ major.[31] Given the length of the song as a whole, this harmonic stability feels remarkable. However, it is soon interrupted when a sequential modulation kicks in. A series of dominant-seventh-to-tonic gestures unfurl in a sequence of thirds G: V⁷–I, e: V⁷–i, c: V⁷–i.

There are a number of things to observe about this sequential modulation, some of which are fairly conventional, others of which theorists have argued over for generations. Observe that the sequence contains a model plus two repetitions or three utterances altogether. It is often said that more than three or four utterances in a sequence creates boredom (in fact, some theorists have cautioned against using sequences altogether, arguing that this compositional technique shows a chronic paucity of imagination on the part of the composer).[32] In practice, the third entity in the sequence usually brings about variety, again for reasons of interest but also to offer the listener a sense of punctuation or a kind of foretelling that a potentially never-ending sequence is indeed drawing to a close: in "Selige Welt," the voice drops out for the third iteration.

Intense theoretical debate circulates over whether or not Roman numerals should be applied throughout a sequence, as I have done in Figure 18.7. One of Schubert's contemporaries—none other than Gottfried Weber—would say unequivocally yes. He analyzes a number of sequences in his treatise and each harmony is assigned a Roman numeral. Importantly, if any harmony in the sequence is not a member of the fundamental harmonies of the overall major or minor key of the sequence, then, for Weber, the sequence experiences a brief internal modulation. He indicates this using another convention he invented and which features in my Figure 18.7. A new key is denoted by introducing a new letter-name of the key, followed by a colon, followed by the Roman numeral of the major, minor, diminished or seventh chords according to the scale degree on which they occurred. Indeed, to invoke Weber, who invented a method by which every chord and every hint of a new key could be notated analytically, is to invoke a zealous analytical annotator. Many modern theorists, by contrast, advocate the suspension of Roman numeral analysis for sequences, preferring instead to identify only the endpoints and to determine whether a sequence is "tonal" or "real" and what root motion drives it.[33]

Much like entries in a fugue, in tonal sequences changes are made to each utterance to accommodate an overall sense of key, to keep the sequence diatonic. By contrast, a real sequence repeats the material exactly and often replicates it at equal intervals between roots. Sequences are not always strictly in one or other category; they may mix tonal and real statements. Additionally, there can be melodic sequences where the harmony changes underneath. Broadly speaking, by this definition, the sequence of thirds in "Selige Welt" would seem to be "tonal" because it moves by a minor and then a major third between the articulations of G major, E minor, and C minor. The adjustments within each component are quite simple in this case because the only difference between each entity is whether the dominant seventh chord prepares a major or minor tonic. However, what prevailing key does it articulate? The roots of the tonics outline a C major triad, but the destination tonic is C minor, producing a kind of reverse *tierce de Picardie*, for the landing ought to be C major. Since Schubert could so easily have picked C major, the question is: why did he opt for C minor? C major is not diatonic to the next event Schubert is trying to set up: the return of the A section in A♭ major. That is not to say, however, that ending the B section in C minor is harmonically expedient or even convenient, for it means there is a shift of a third back to the prevailing tonic of the song. The return is hardly set up in a typical fashion, although third-related returns are not uncommon in ternary forms either. Schubert deploys another of his party tricks, a kind of modulation that he had become adept at by the time this song was written and published in 1823. He uses a common-tone modulation.

There are two tones shared by C minor and A♭ major: $\hat{C}$ and $\hat{E}♭$. Indeed, if Schubert had landed on a C-major triad in m. 17, he could still have linked C and A♭ majors with the common tone $\hat{C}$. However, the $\hat{E}♭$ common tone has considerable advantages over the $\hat{C}$. First and foremost, it is $\hat{5}$ of A♭ or, in other words, can serve as a single-tone dominant to the return of A♭ major. In so doing, Schubert introduces the new key by sneaking in the barest thread of its own dominant. Moreover, the melody begins with a $\hat{5}$ upbeat, going to $\hat{3}$ (the other common tone), so the return of the melody demands no re-writing, which it would if Schubert had used $\hat{C}$ as the common tone.

This last observation about how Schubert pivots from one key to the next by deploying the dominant pitch of the new key within an otherwise third-related common-tone modulation deserves a theoretical excursus, for it separates out different tonal qualities in such modulatory strategies. There are a multitude of keys available in common-tone modulations. A. B. Marx attempted to theorize them.[34] Figure 18.8a contains, as it were, the launch pad to the material in Figures 18.8b–c. The lead-up to the G major triad provides a V^7–I cadence, with a single tone that serves as a kind of "caesura fill" (Hepokoski and Darcy, 2006). It is also, as Marx explains, only one of the three possible pitches in the triad that may generate a common-tone modulation. Figure 18.8b shows the even wider array of keys that may be attained by arriving on dominant seventh and ninth chords that contain the

FIGURE 18.8 Examples from Marx, *Theory and Practice of Musical Composition* (*Die Lehre von der musikalischen Komposition*), pp. 207–208. (a) Cadence in G major at end of phrase or section with common tone $\hat{G}$ as link to next phrase or section; (b) array of keys attained by resolving seventh or ninth chords that contain common tone $\hat{G}$; (c) list of possible modulations from cadence in G major with $\hat{G}$, $\hat{B}$, and $\hat{D}$ as common tone.

pitch G and then resolving them. Figure 18.8c shows all possible major and minor triads that share $\hat{G}$, $\hat{B}$, and $\hat{D}$, respectively. As this example shows, there are twelve possible modulations. A full theoretical account must, however, cater also for the arrival of a minor triad at the end of Figure 18.8a, even if a major triad is more likely since it mimics the end of a transition. Adapting Marx (and setting aside for the moment dominant sevenths and dominant ninths as vehicles to modulations further afield), the following principle may be stated: from any given major or minor triad, there are twelve other triads that will share either the root, third, or fifth of the initial triad. The calculation may be made by taking the six major and minor triads around each of the three pitches of the triad and then eliminating the overlapping triads. A visualization using the PLR tonal space makes this easy to grasp. As shown in Figure 18.9, the PLR cycles that exhibit the $\hat{C}$, $\hat{E}$, $\hat{G}$ common tones of the C-major triad include the C, a, F, f, Ab, and c triads around $\hat{C}$, the C, e, E, c♯, A, and a triads around $\hat{E}$, and the C, e, G, g, Eb, and c triads around $\hat{G}$. Once the overlapping triads are eliminated, the conglomerate of possibilities around C major are: c, Ab, a, A, Eb, e, E, F, f, G, g, and c♯. As shown in Figure 18.9, the C minor triad shares the same set of triads around $\hat{C}$ and $\hat{G}$ but includes c, Ab, ab, Cb, eb, and Eb around $\hat{E}$b. Again, once overlapping triads are eliminated, the list of possibilities around C minor is: C, a, Ab, ab, Eb, eb, e, F, f, G, g, and Cb.[35]

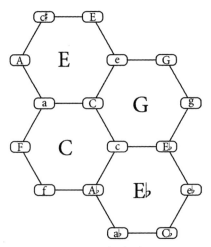

FIGURE 18.9 Conglomerate of triads sharing $\hat{C}$, $\hat{E}$, $\hat{G}$ common tones with the C-major triad and $\hat{C}$, $\hat{E}\flat$, $\hat{G}$ common tones with the C-minor triad.

Yet not all of these constitute "modulations," nor do all of them operate under the rubric of a "common-tone modulation." As mentioned above, a move from C major to C minor or vice versa does not constitute a modulation; rather, it is a modal shift. So our count of common-tone modulations must discount these, leaving eleven possible modulations. Although fifth-related modulations clearly possess a common tone, they do not generally go by that name. Rather, it is those that involve third-related moves that are most commonly associated with the rubric. SLIDE is another possibility (C to c♯ or c to C♭), though relatively rare. In all of these cases, however, there is an important detail to add to our definition of common-tone modulations: they are only labeled as such when the common tone is exposed in the texture—that is, the common tone must be rhetorically or gesturally deployed in an obvious way, as in the return to the A section in "Selige Welt." Without such an exposed thread in the textural fabric, they are mere juxtapositions, usually of a phrase or section ending in one key and the next phrase or section beginning in another, which is the hallmark of "direct" or "abrupt" modulations. In such cases, the presence or absence of common tones is an incidental trait and has more to do with assessing the level of proximity of a direct modulation. For instance, C major to B minor (with no common tones) is farther than C major to E major (with one).

The example in "Selige Welt" is thus a classic third-related modulation employing the common tone, although the essentially diatonic move was not as prized in the nineteenth century as chromatic mediants. Aldwell and Schachter (2003, 597) include a classic chromatic example in their textbook from "Widmung" from Schumann's *Myrthen*, op. 25. As shown in Figure 18.10, the common tone is held over in the voice, where it sets out as $\hat{A}\flat$ of A♭ major and becomes $\hat{G}\sharp$ of E major as the new harmony enters. In neo-Riemannian terms, it is a PL transformation; the one in "Selige Welt" is L. Indeed, as William Rothstein (2008) has illustrated, the pattern in "Widmung" is typical fare in Italian opera, which is where he argues such neo-Riemannian moves most

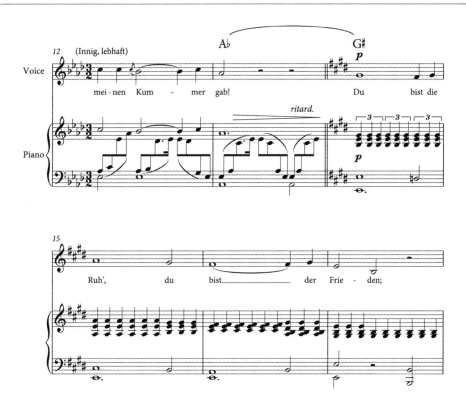

FIGURE 18.10 Schumann, "Widmung," *Myrthen*, op. 25, no. 1, mm. 12–17.

likely originated and gained their aural allure, rather than with German composers with which they have come to be most associated.

There is, however, another important distinction between the move in "Selige Welt" and the one in "Widmung," a distinction that has received little critical attention but is vital to the sensibility of the different incarnations of third relations. As already observed, the two harmonies in the L transformation in "Selige Welt" allow for the held-over common tone to serve as a dominant to the new key. This feature is only available in the minor to major direction of L. In other words, there is no common tone in the direction A♭ major to C minor that would allow for such a maneuver. PL from a major triad (as in A♭ major to E major in "Widmung") also contains no such common tone; nor does its reverse LP. This phenomenon may be theorized: of all the possible common-tone relations listed above, those in Figure 18.11 have this voice-leading potential (the example centers on the common tone D).

From any given major triad, the transformations R and RP produce third relations with a dominant-functioning common tone to the new key (and, to complete the list, P, DOM, and DOM(P) do too), while from any given minor triad, the transformations L and LP produce third relations with a dominant-functioning common tone to the new key (and to complete the list P, DOM, and DOM(P) do too).[36]

Of course, composers can choose to exploit or camouflage such dominant-preparation potential, depending on the effect they are after. In, for example, Schubert's "Die Berge"

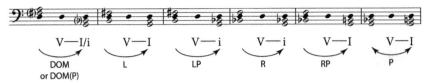

FIGURE 18.11 Directional flow of triadic transformations containing a common tone that exhibits the property of being a dominant-functioning tone in relation to the destination triad. This phenomenon is modeled here using the common tone $\hat{D}$ as example.

FIGURE 18.12 Schubert, "Die Berge" (D. 634), mm. 45–50.

D. 634, the common-tone modulation from B minor to G major is an L transformation. As shown in Figure 18.12, Schubert elects to emphasize the $\hat{B}$ in m. 47, rather than the $\hat{D}$. He elects, in other words, to highlight the pitch other than the dominant-functioning pitch within G major, creating a different effect than had he chosen the other pitch. By comparison, the famous move in the exposition of the "Unfinished" Symphony, which involves the same harmonies, deploys the $\hat{D}$ in the medial caesura-fill rather than the $\hat{B}$. This is undoubtedly motivated by a desire to hint at the conventional role of the transition to the new theme, which prepares the new key with its own dominant—much like the return to the tonic in "Selige Welt." In the "Unfinished", the preparation that was not included in the transition (TR) because it landed back on the overall tonic of B minor is given over to the caesura-fill, where the $\hat{D}$ serves such a purpose in the modulation to the new key. For this reason, identical key relations—or neo-Riemannian transformations—can have vastly different aural effects depending on their surface presentation.

MODULATION VERSUS TONICIZATION

The difference between a modulation and tonicization—and the gradations in between—may be best captured by an analogy. Imagine someone is sitting comfortably at home and decides to go to her neighbor's house. She rises from her sofa, goes to her neighbor's front door, rings the doorbell, and waits for an answer. There is no answer, so she returns home. That is like a tonicization: moving from a home key and reaching the threshold of a new key, but not actually going in. In fact, she could even have started to head home after there was no answer, only to wonder if the bell had rung and return to the doorstep to ring again, only to receive no answer. She might even double-check a couple of times. That would still be tonicization. Modulation, therefore, is the equivalent to her neighbor answering the door and going beyond chatting to her on the doorstep—he must invite her in. Crucially, she needs to remain at her neighbor's for a bit, for if she was invited in, only to make a quick exit, that would merely constitute the equivalent of a slightly extended tonicization. For many theorists, there would even be a critical difference between her lingering in her neighbor's hallway to chat versus going in the living room and plonking herself on the sofa. That is, by lingering in the hallway, she is merely in the new house, hovering about, which is the equivalent to being in the new key without fully establishing it. In contrast, by going into the living room and sitting on the sofa, she has performed the equivalent of establishing the new key by cadencing there, PAC style.

In short, then, a tonicization is generally defined as a brief cadence articulating a harmonic station that is otherwise unexplored. A passage of music may tonicize a particular key multiple times in a row—like our neighbor who keeps checking whether she actually pushed the doorbell and whether her neighbor actually heard it. A modulation is generally agreed to have occurred when meaningful time is spent in the new key; typically, the key persists after the PAC.

There are, however, no hard and fast definitions, and often the scale of the musical form in which the key change occurs can also be a factor in whether something counts as a tonicization or a modulation. In short pieces, a brief sojourn in a key may constitute a modulation, while more emphasis on the new key will be expected in longer pieces. The countless examples of modulating A sections in rounded binary form often end in the dominant but they become modulations proper if, for example, they extend into a new phrase in the dominant (as in the minuet in Mozart's Piano Sonata K. 331) or if the material immediately after the repeat remains in the same key. Donald Francis Tovey also made the useful distinction between arrivals "on" and "in" the dominant. The former articulate the dominant with a HC, the latter with a PAC, a distinction that can apply to numerous other formal junctures.[37]

Using pieces already mentioned in this chapter, we can identify the keys of A major, B minor, and D major in "Im wunderschönen Monat Mai" as a series of tonicizations.[38] Each is articulated by either a PAC or IAC—and heralded by a trusty pivot chord. The observant reader might protest that, after each cadence, the new key persists. Ah, yes, but these are mere repeats; the material must be different—a further composing-out of the key is required. The difference between the modulations and tonicizations in "Selige Welt" is clear: C♭ major is a modulation, for after the modulating A section, the B section continues in the same key, before a series of tonicizations occur through the use of secondary dominants in a sequence. The common-tone modulation brings about the return of A♭ major, a key established by virtue of being extended for the whole section, albeit curtailed compared with the opening A section.

The belief that a proper modulation to a new key is only achieved once a cadence has occurred in that key, followed (usually) by more material in that key, leads to some paradoxical scenarios. In some cases, a key area may be operating for a while but not confirmed by a cadence, and in others, a key area may be nebulous but confirmed by a cadence. Therefore, definitions involving cadences do not necessarily correspond to how strongly a key may be sensed for the entirety of a passage. Witness once more examples referenced above where the tonal content of the melody of a fugue and its final cadence may lead to uncertainty in the identity of the key, a phenomenon that typically arises in so-called modulating subjects.[39] Let's also illustrate the point through some secondary key areas in nineteenth-century sonata forms. Witness Brahms's Cello Sonata in F Major, studied earlier. The end of the theme is articulated by an unmistakable, strong perfect authentic cadence. The time spent in A minor is minimal. However, the theme would be said to be "in A minor," and it is unequivocally established by the ensuing closing in the same key. Take also the strikingly similar case of Schubert's Quartet in G Major (D. 887), whose secondary theme meanders around harmonically and also ends with a brief cadence in the expected key of D major (the theme is then repeated a further three times, in D major again, followed by B♭ major and then D major, each time with a PAC). Unlike Brahms's Cello Sonata, however, the moment the cadence occurs the music embarks on a transition. Only the fourth time is the key of the cadence established by closing material in the same key. In many ways, the expectation of form helps define these as modulations. After a medial caesura, a new tonic is expected. If it is delayed or thwarted, then a PAC (specifically marking the essential expositional closure) will suffice. The closing material may be in a different key from the secondary theme, as is the case for three-keyed expositions.

Compare the two scenarios just explored with the second theme of Schubert's String Quintet in C major (D. 956). After the I:HC arrival that announces the medial caesura, the caesura fill sinks into E♭ major, rather than the expected G major. E♭ major is never confirmed by a PAC. Instead, in m. 71 C major receives a cadence, although it is in the wrong place within the thematic unit; no analyst would conclude that the second theme is "in C major," though they invariably mark the moment as significant because of the cadence. However, without a PAC in E♭ major, the secondary theme cannot be said to be "in E♭ major." It is therefore considered by some to be a "gigantic floating pivot chord" (Webster 1978, 29), while Rosen (1988, 257) declares it to be "not . . . an established opposing tonality to C, but a contrast in color"—not least because of the C-major cadence that appears in m. 71; that is, part way through the secondary theme.

As in social cues, so in music certain gestures point to the intention to stick around or not. To return to our anecdote above, the lyrical melody in the String Quintet has all the hallmarks of a second theme in a new key—but it is equivalent to our neighbor being invited in and, like the British comedian Ken Platt, saying "I won't take my coat off, I'm not stopping!" only—surprisingly—to overstay her welcome ("surprisingly"—because keeping one's coat on signals a brief visit). Schubert's theme similarly never offers the proper cues that the new key is here to stay.

KEY AND MODULATION   525

KEY RELATIONS

The first diagram explicitly designed to measure the distance amongst keys was Gottfried Weber's "table of the relationships of keys" (see Figure 18.13). His method of calculating those distances is often misrepresented in descriptions of this diagram. What is not commonly appreciated is that the distance between each node on the grid is measured by comparing the differences in pitch between the scales represented by each key. The more pitches they have in common, the more closely they are related. Moreover, it is vital to recognize that, for Weber, the minor mode was represented exclusively by the harmonic minor scale, not the natural minor scale. Therefore, the circle of fifths that runs in the vertical direction is not the traditional model whereby the major and minor relative keys share the same key signature. While the difference between adjacent fifths in the major mode is an incremental sharp or flat—F becomes F♯ between the scales representing the keys of C major and G major, for instance—the difference between fifths in the minor is three pitches. For example, between A harmonic minor and E harmonic minor, F becomes F♯, G♯ becomes G♮, and D becomes D♯. This method of calculating also

TABLE OF THE RELATIONSHIPS OF KEYS.

C	a	A	f♯	F♯	d♯	D♯	b♯	B♯	g×
F	d	D	b	B	g♯	G♯	e♯	E♯	c×
B♭	g	G	e	E	c♯	C♯	a♯	A♯	f×
E♭	c	C	a	A	f♯	F'♯	d♯	D♯	b♯
A♭	f	F	d	D	b	B	g♯	G♯	e♯
D♭	b♭	B♭	g	G	e	E	c♯	C♯	a♯
G♭	e♭	E♭	c	C	a	A	f♯	F'♯	d♯
C♭	a♭	A♭	f	F	d	D	b	B	g♯
F♭	d♭	D♭	b♭	B♭	g	G	e	E	c♯
B♭♭	g♭	G♭	e♭	E♭	c	C	a	A	f♯
E♭♭	c♭	C♭	a♭	A♭	f	F'	d	D	b
A♭♭	f♭	F♭	d♭	D♭	b♭	B♭	g	G	e
D♭♭	b♭♭	B♭♭	g♭	G♭	e♭	E♭	c	C	a

FIGURE 18.13 Table of the relationships of keys from Gottfried Weber, *Theory of Musical Composition* (1817–1821, 1:320).

means the other keys adjacent to C major and A minor—the two keys at the center of the grid from which Weber measures all others—are not related in the manner we might expect. Between the relative pair C major and A harmonic minor, there is a single semitone displacement or SSD (to use a neo-Riemannian term): G becomes G♯.[40] Between the parallel keys C major and C minor or A minor and A major, there are two: respectively, E becomes E♭ and A becomes A♭ or C becomes C♯ and F becomes F♯.

The key relations outlined so far are the "first grade of relations," as shown in Figure 18.14 (Weber 1851, 313). In sum, they represent four—not three—distinct relations: (1) the major-key fifth relation (in the dominant and subdominant directions), (2) the minor-key fifth relation (in the dominant and subdominant directions), (3) the relative (R), and (4) the parallel (P). Following the calculation of displaced tones just outlined, the major-key fifths and the relative are equidistant from C major and both the closest relations, parallel is next, and the minor fifths are the most distantly related keys within the first grade of relations. This is not how we would reckon these distances nowadays. If we hark back to the circle of fifths and calculate these distances using major and natural minor scales, then R would be the closest relation, major- and minor-key fifths the next, and P the farthest. Similarly, if we measured the displacements in neo-Riemannian transformations—based therefore on major and minor triads, not scales—then P would be the closest with one SSD, R the next with a tone displacement (or two SSD), and major and minor fifths the farthest with one SSD and one tone displacement. Such differences ought perhaps to put a question mark over the idea that any one reading of tonal space is necessarily correct. Instead, any such reading is a trace of a history of perception.

We can generalize: just as Weber's space allows for multiple plausible readings, so the history of theory is also filled with a variety of tonal spaces. Among the most popular in modern analyses are the (neo-)Riemannian *Tonnetz*, the hexatonic cycle, and the PLR group. These highlight different adjacent keys and are suited to tracing different harmonic schemes in musical works. As Richard Cohn (1999, 213–214) so powerfully pointed out, these tonal spaces have the capacity to illuminate the logic of concomitant harmonic passages that would otherwise appear baffling. The exploration of new tonal spaces is simultaneously a quest for an explanation of harmonic succession in music and of the beauty of harmonic and voice-leading properties in the abstract. Nonetheless, most textbooks continue to teach key relations based on key signatures. According to this traditional method, closely related keys either share a signature or

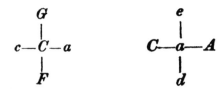

FIGURE 18.14 First grade of relations around C major and A minor from Weber, *Theory of Musical Composition* (1817–1821, 1:313).

are plus or minus a sharp or flat from each other: for C major, A minor shares the signature, G major and E minor add a sharp, and F major and D minor add a flat.

Given this history, how might one understand Weber's investment in the harmonic minor scale, which undermines the measurement of the proximity of relations by key signature? It makes sense in the context of the history of musical styles and forms. The Baroque may be said to be an era dominated by counterpoint. In fugues, the dominant answer to a minor tonic subject was also in the minor dominant. To be sure, it was motivated by maintaining the integrity of the subject's melody but it ensured that the dominant minor was understood as the diatonic harmony. Even block forms, such as the binary forms in suites or the ritornelli in concertos, tended to maintain the modally matched dominant (and subdominants). Exceptions prove the rule: in Bach's *Well-Tempered Clavier*, Book 2, Fugue 6 in D minor, the entry in m. 21 is in A major rather than A minor. However, observe how the integrity of the melody is intact: the minor third of the subject's first three notes, $\hat{1} - \hat{2} - \hat{3}$, in D minor is shifted to $\hat{3} - \hat{4} - \hat{5}$ of A major, which therefore maintains the overall intervallic pattern. It is the accompanying material of the melody beginning C♯–D–E that transforms this entry into A major. By the beginning of the nineteenth century and in the wake of the Classical style in which the melody and accompaniment texture was pervasive, theorists began to regard the major form of the dominant as the one that was the intrinsic harmony on the fifth degree of the minor mode. Concomitantly, the raised seventh was equally intrinsic to the mode in their view.

Whatever the methods of measuring distances of key, the fact remains that the same set of keys were regarded as closely related and theorists proffered the virtues of their usage. Nonetheless, perhaps one of the greatest myths regarding key and modulation is that it took theorists a long time to acknowledge the respectability of chromaticism or distantly related keys. In fact, composition treatises tend to be conservative, seeing as they are often guides to amateur composers, but more speculative harmony treatises always celebrated the full range of available modulations, even if they advised those who made use of them to proceed with caution, or to use dramatic effects wisely, and not to overdo it.

While numerous theorists explored all possible key relations, the following insight, which Brahms shared with Jenner, reminds us that even the commonest harmonic moves and methods of modulation still have plenty of musical mileage left in them:

> With regard to the overall course of the modulation, with the exception of individual divergences, the guiding principle was: The straight path is the best path. In specific instances, too, as he corrected me, I often thought of the saying: "Do you want to wander farther and farther away? Look, the good things are so near." And precisely these nearby, good things—how often they are overlooked because our vision has been obscured by the force of a hastily conceived idea and we have neglected the essential things in favor of inessential ones, so that we can't see the forest through the trees![41]

This explains the continued appeal of tonality both in so-called conservative art music, as well as vernacular idioms in our own century. To be sure, the vocabulary of harmonies that define keys may be manipulated in ever more adventurous ways or may modulate (in the old meaning of the word) through different voice-leading principles highlighted in different tonal spaces. At the same time, the most diatonic maneuvers, the most familiar key relations, and the most well-traveled modulations may exude renewed beauty even today.

NOTES

1. For a particularly striking visual analysis of the changing functional meaning of the pivot chord B minor as it brings about each key region in this song, see Cohn (2011, 331).
2. Upper- and lowercase letters and Roman numerals refer to major and minor keys and harmonies respectively, a system developed by Gottfried Weber (1817, 258), although he did not include inversions, as I have and as has become convention.
3. For a facsimile and transcription of this sketch, see Hallmark (1977, 128 and 113).
4. Observe that there is an F♯ major (sic) sonority in mm. 9 and 20, but it does not function as a tonic; rather, it is a dominant seventh to another key.
5. The nomenclature T–PD–D–T derives from T–S–D–T. The latter is from Riemann's function theory (1893), and the former is a pervasive Americanization that emphasizes the predominant (PD) nature of the subdominant (S) function.
6. Rosen (1995, 48) remarked that "Im wunderschönen Monat Mai" is "the perfect fragment." For an excellent overview of attitudes towards Romantic fragments (including Rosen's), see Perrey (2002, 162–177).
7. Many have remarked on this ambiguity, including Hoeckner (2006, 70), Lerdahl (2004, 138), Neumeyer (1982, 95), and Tunbridge (2010, 14–15). However, Rosen (1995, 47) asserts that F♯ minor is the tonic, while insisting that the "controversy" over the identity of the key is "largely misguided." By contrast, Komar (1971, 67–69), who takes a Schenkerian approach, asserts the tonic is A major, largely thanks to considerations about the overarching structure of the song cycle as a whole. Yonatan Malin (2006, 302) argues that A major is an "illusion of stability."
8. Alternatively, an IAC could land on $\hat{1}$ in the upper voice but use inversions in the bassline.
9. Caplin (1998, 15) distinguishes introductions and codas as outside the main structure with "before-the-beginning" and "after-the-end" functions. Schenker (1979, 129–130) has a similar notion, called the "initial ascent" ("Anstieg") and coda. Here I add "between the stanzas," which seems a logical extension of these widely accepted concepts of form.
10. Caplin (1998, 51). For the same theoretical phenomenon addressed within the context of art song, see Schachter (1999a, 23).
11. Genuine cases of ambiguity are rare. As Agawu (1994, 86) astutely proclaimed, "Once a context is taken into account—and by 'context' I mean a series of additional texts—ambiguity dissolves into clarity." Here, the key is neither completely one, nor the other. Lerdahl (2004, 138) captures this by saying "the first song, 'Im wunderschönen Monat Mai,' is ambiguous between prolonging **V/f♯** and **I/A**." (The boldface is in the original; it denotes key regions.)

12. For an elegant Schenkerian analysis and hermeneutic reading of this song, see Dunsby (2004, 35–56). My analysis above places the $\hat{G}$ in m. 117 at the end of the vocal material; Dunsby places the closure of the *Urlinie*'s $\hat{G}$ during the postlude in m. 119 even though it is not supported by a tonic harmony.

13. This song is an 1824 setting of words by Johann Chrysostomus Senn, rather than its namesake, the more famous song cycle D. 957.

14. Schenker (1979, 36) famously argues that the return to the tonic at the point of recapitulation or reprise does not make a cadence with the dominant at the end of a retransition but rather comprises an interruption and retaking of the *Urlinie*.

15. For a detailed narrative of the transition from modes to keys, see Lester (1978, 78). Lester argues that Tomáš Baltazar Janovka (1701) was one of the first theorists to identify all twenty-four keys and to dispense altogether with explanations of church modes. Moreover, Lester points out (1978, 78) that Janovka represents the first wave of theorists to recognize keys not only by their tonic triad or final, but also by their scale, which for minor was the natural minor scale. For an argument that the inclusion of scale in the definition of mode is anachronistic, see the chapters "Mode" and "Scale" in this volume.

16. Given that Lester refers to Saint Lambert as a pioneer, it is important to note that Saint Lambert's observations first emerged even a few years earlier than Lester reports. Lester (1978, 95) refers to the Amsterdam pirated edition of Saint Lambert's treatise, which he dates to ca. 1710 (the edition is undated). The original edition was published in Paris by Christophe Ballard in 1707. For a clarifying discussion over the confusion of these editions and their purported precursors, see Harris-Warrick (1984, viii–ix). Misunderstanding has also occurred over Saint Lambert's name. Identified as Monsieur de Saint Lambert in both of his extant treatises, he has often been given the first name Michel (as Lester gives him). Harris-Warrick (ix) traces this to a confusion dating back to eighteenth-century biographical lexicons, where Mʳ de Saint Lambert is confused with Michel Lambert, the *maître de la musique de la chambre du Roi* in the age of Louis XIV and Lully. These are two different men.

17. See, for instance, Gottfried Weber (1851, 326), who sets out his chapter on modulation by distinguishing between modulation "in the key" versus "out of the key" ("leitergleiche Modulation" versus "ausweichende Modulation"). However, he ends that paragraph by indicating that the latter meaning has become the norm: "I will here remark, in passing, that according to the usage of many musical writers, the word *modulation* is synonymous with what is here called *digressive modulation*, or *modulation out of the key*, and that the latter species alone is called *modulation*; and thus, with these writers, *to modulate* is *to pass out of the key*" (italics in original).

18. "Tout Air ou Piece de Musique est composée sur un certain ton, & dans un certain mode. Le ton d'un Air est la note sur laquelle il se termine; & cette note s'appelle aussi la *finale*. Si la finale d'un Air est un *Ut*, on dit que l'Air est composé en *C Sol Ut*. (c'est le terme) Si elle est un *Ré*, il est en *D La Ré*, &c. Lorsqu'un Air a plusieurs parties, les parties, (même celle qu'on appelle le *Sujet*,) se terminent quelquefois sur une autre note que la finale essentielle de l'Air; Mais pour la Basse, soit qu'elle soit le sujet de l'Air, ou qu'elle ne le soit pas, elle se termine toûjours sur la finale essentielle. Ainsi quand on veut sçavoir sur quel ton un Air est composé, c'est à la finale de la Basse qu'il faut regarder. Cette finale est toûjours la note fondamentale de l'Air, & pour ainsi dire la note *Tonique*. Le Mode est la détermination du chemin que doit tenir le chant d'un Air, & celui de ses parties, quand il en a, le tout par rapport à la note finale. C'est ce qui constituë l'espece de chaque intervalle; C'est le sistême

particulier sur lequel une Piece de Musique est bâtie." The original orthography of the French is preserved here. In Ballard it appears on pp. 26–27; in Amsterdam it is pp. 51–52. I present a more complete citation of this passage, which is abbreviated in Lester (1989, 100–101).

19. For a notable example where the predominant is expanded, after a normative presentation of an expanded opening tonic followed by cadential material, see mm. 309–329 of the fourth movement of Mozart, String Quartet, K. 499. The example is analyzed in Schachter (1999a, 106).

20. For this observation on Oldroyd (1967, 215), see Bullivant (1971, 182). Bullivant also cites other subjects with, as he diagnoses it, "misleading melodic tonalities," whereby conflicts in the tonal markers of the contents and cadence lead to uncertainty.

21. Schenker, (1979, 88–90, Figs. 110–11). Such a view is not unique to Schenker. Hepokoski and Darcy (2006) would arrive at the same conclusion because the cadence in A minor is the "essential expositional closure" (EEC). Observe too in Figure 18.5b how Schenker deployed the same idea to incorporate the dominant of F♯ minor into the key of A major for the opening of "Im wunderschönen Monat Mai." The PAC cadence in A major thus ends up subsuming the unarticulated tonic of F♯ minor because the latter's dominant becomes III♯ of A major.

22. The bibliography on double tonics is extensive. The origins and popularity of the concept are especially owed to Bailey (1985) and Krebs (1980) and (1985).

23. An extension of these structures to the full chromatic gamut of possible key relations need only add sharps or flats to these starting points—and add VI and ♭VI for completeness— while modifying the analysis of the counterpoint to absorb them into the structure, as Schenker so frequently does for chromaticisms. For the reasons the VI and ♭VI are missing from Schenker's account and the chromatic extension of the material in *Free Composition*, see Clark (2011, 218).

24. Bailey (1985). The subsequent bibliography is too extensive to mention here but see Kinderman and Krebs (1996) for a critical juncture on this topic.

25. This bracketed clarification that "modulation" is the old meaning and refers to the harmonic profile of the whole "piece of music" is an editorial addition by the translator James Warner (Weber 1841, 126). It does not appear in later translations by Warner (Weber 1846, 374; 1851, 373).

26. The passage appears in the first edition of Weber's treatise (Weber 1817, 318). He identified its source as "dell'inutile osservanza dei Tuoni hodierni, p. 237," which is the (incomplete) title of the section in which the passage appears. The complete title from Doni (1640) is "Discorso primo Dell'inutile Osservanza De'Tuoni, ò Modi hodierni."

27. This context is common to all editions, except the English translation (Weber 1846, 374).

28. Quoted in Daverio (1993, 84) and Dunsby (2004, 50). Translation from Jenner (2009, 402).

29. "C'est proprement la manière d'établir & traiter le Mode; mais ce mot se prend plus communément aujourd'hui pour l'art de conduire l'Harmonie & le Chant successivement dans plusieurs Modes d'une manière agréable à l'oreille & conforme aux règles. Si le Mode est produit par l'Harmonie, c'est d'elle aussi que naissent les lois de la *Modulation*. Ces loix sont simples à concevoir, mais difficiles à bien observer. Voici en quoi elles consistent. Pour bien moduler dans un même Ton, il faut, 1° en parcourir tous les Sons avec un beau Chant, en rebattant plus souvent les Cordes essenciales [*sic*] & s'y appuyant d'advantage: c'est-à-dire, que l'Accord sensible, & l'Accord de la Tonique doivent s'y remonter fréquemment, mais sous différentes faces & par différentes routes pour prévenir la monotonie. 2° N'établir de Cadences ou de repos que sur ces deux Accords, ou tout au plus sur celui de la

sous-Dominante. 3° Enfin n'altérer jamais aucun des Sons du Mode; car on ne peut, sans le quitter, faire entendre un Dièse ou un Bémol qui ne lui appartienne pas, ou en retrancher quelqu'un qui lui appartienne. Mais pour passer d'un Ton à un autre, il faut consulter l'analogie, avoir égard au rapport des Toniques, & à la quantité des Cordes communes aux deux Tons."

30. I minted the analytical notation whereby note names with a caret indicate a tone in Clark (2011). For a more extensive analysis of "Selige Welt," comparing Schenkerian and neo-Riemannian approaches, see Clark (2011, 67–76).

31. The treatment of C♭ major is a good example of the distinction between tonicization and modulation. I will return to this moment in "Selige Welt" in the next section of this chapter.

32. For a detailed view of changing attitudes to sequences, see Bass (1996).

33. See for instance Laitz (2012). For more on different theoretical perspectives and analytical strategies regarding sequences, see Naomi Waltham-Smith's essay in this volume.

34. For an excellent discussion of this aspect of Marx's theory, see Kopp (2002, 49–51).

35. This is a modified view—through the lens of the PLR cycle—of the theory of common-tone relations by David Kopp, whose theory is encapsulated by a table of relations in Kopp (2002, 2). My reason for using the PLR chicken-wire tonal space instead is that the triads in each cycle within the chicken-wire revolve around a single common tone, which make them easy to visualize.

36. For a deeper exploration of this phenomenon, see Clark (2016). The DOM transformation is the descending fifth.

37. Tovey was fond of pointing out this distinction but here is a sample of one of his more succinct observations about it: "An analyst who imputes the key of A major to bars 19–24 of the first movement of Beethoven's G major Sonata, op. 14, no. 2, *when he hears them in their context*, should not attempt to discuss key-relationship until he can discriminate between a passage *on* the dominant and a passage *in* the dominant" (italics in original); see Tovey (1944, 59–60).

38. Cohn (2011, 330) concurs.

39. See note 20 above.

40. The terminology and initialism for SSD ("single semitone displacement") arose in the context of neo-Riemannian theory. The importance of SSD in the privileging of the hexatonic cycle is explained in Cohn (2012, 17–18). The same principle of parsimony—but measured between scales, not triads—motivated Weber's commitment to the harmonic minor scale.

41. Cited in Dunsby (2004, 50).

Works Cited

Agawu, Kofi. 1994. "Ambiguity in Tonal Music: A Preliminary Study." In *Theory, Analysis and Meaning in Music*, edited by Anthony Pople, 86–107. Cambridge: Cambridge University Press.

Aldwell, Edward and Carl Schachter, with Allen Cadwallader. 2003. *Harmony and Voice Leading*, 3rd edition. Belmont, CA: Schirmer; Thompson Learning.

Bailey, Robert, ed. 1985. *Richard Wagner: Prelude and Transfiguration from Tristan and Isolde*. Norton Critical Scores. New York: W. W. Norton.

Bass, Richard. 1996. "From Gretchen to Tristan: The Changing Role of Harmonic Sequences in the Nineteenth Century." *19th-Century Music* 19: 263–285.

Beach, David. 1993. "Schubert's Experiments with Sonata Form: Formal-Tonal Design versus Underlying Structure." *Music Theory Spectrum* 15: 1–18.

Bullivant, Roger. 1971. *Fugue*. London: Hutchinson & Co Ltd.

Caplin, William E. 1998. *Classical Form: A Theory of Formal Functions for the Instrumental Music of Haydn, Mozart, and Beethoven.* Oxford: Oxford University Press.

Clark, Suzannah. 2011. *Analyzing Schubert.* Cambridge: Cambridge University Press.

Clark, Suzannah. 2016. "A Gift to Goethe: The Aesthetics of the Intermediate Dominant in Schubert's Music and Early Nineteenth-Century Theoretical Thought." *Nineteenth-Century Music Review* 13: 39–70.

Cohn, Richard. 1999. "As Wonderful as Star Clusters: Instruments for Gazing at Tonality in Schubert." *19th-Century Music* 22: 213–232.

Cohn, Richard. 2011. "Tonal Pitch Space and the (Neo-)Riemannian *Tonnetz*." In *The Oxford Handbook of Neo-Riemannian Music Theories*, edited by Edward Gollin and Alexander Rehding, 322–348. New York: Oxford University Press.

Cohn, Richard. 2012. *Audacious Euphony: Chromaticism and the Consonant Triad's Nature.* New York: Oxford University Press.

Daverio, John. 1993. "The *Wechsel der Töne* in Brahms's *Schicksalslied*." *Journal of the American Musicological Society* 46: 84–113.

Doni, Giovanni Battista. 1640. *Annotazioni sopra il compendio de'Generie de'Modi della Musica.* Rome: D'Andrea Fei.

Dunsby, Jonathan. 2004. *Making Words Sing: Nineteenth- and Twentieth-Century Song.* Cambridge: Cambridge University Press.

Everett, Walter. 2009. *The Foundations of Rock: From "Blue Suede Shoes" to "Suite: Judy Blue Eyes."* New York: Oxford University Press.

Finson, Jon W. 2007. *Robert Schumann: The Book of Songs.* Cambridge, MA: Harvard University Press.

Graybill, Roger. 1988. "Harmonic Circularity in Brahms's F Major Cello Sonata: An Alternative to Schenker's Reading in *Free Composition*." *Music Theory Spectrum* 10: 43–55.

Hallmark, Rufus. 1977. "The Sketches for *Dichterliebe*." *19th-Century Music* 1: 110–136.

Harris-Warrick, Rebecca. 1984. *Principles of the Harpsichord by Monsieur de Saint Lambert.* Cambridge: Cambridge University Press.

Hepokoski, James, and Warren Darcy. 2006. *Elements of Sonata Theory: Norms, Types, and Deformations in the Late Eighteenth-Century Sonata.* New York: Oxford University Press.

Hoeckner, Berthold. 2006. "Paths through *Dichterliebe*." *19th-Century Music* 31: 65–80.

Janovka, Tomáš Baltazar. 1701. *Clavis ad thesaurum magnae artis musicae.* Prague: Impensis Authoris.

Jenner, Gustav. 2009. "Johannes Brahms as Man, Teacher, and Artist," translated by Susan Gillespie and Kaestner Elisabeth. In *Brahms and His World*, edited by Walter Frisch and Kevin C. Karnes, revised edition, 381–423. Princeton, NJ: Princeton University Press.

Kinderman, William, and Harald Krebs, eds. 1996. *The Second Practice of Nineteenth-Century Tonality.* Lincoln: University of Nebraska Press.

Komar, Arthur, ed. 1971. *Robert Schumann: Dichterliebe.* Norton Critical Scores. New York: Norton.

Kopp, David. 2002. *Chromatic Transformations in Nineteenth-Century Music.* Cambridge: Cambridge University Press.

Krebs, Harald. 1980. "Third Relation and Dominant in Late 18th- and Early 19th-Century Music," 2 vols. PhD diss., Yale University.

Krebs, Harald. 1985. "The Background Level in Some Tonally Deviating Works of Franz Schubert." *In Theory Only* 8, no. 8: 5–18.

Laitz, Steven. 2012. *The Complete Musician: An Integrated Approach to Theory, Analysis, and Listening*, 3rd ed. New York: Oxford University Press.

Lerdahl, Fred. 2004. *Tonal Pitch Space*. New York: Oxford University Press.

Lester, Joel. 1977. "Major-Minor Concepts and Modal Theory in Germany: 1592–1680." *Journal of the American Musicological Society* 30: 208–253.

Lester, Joel. 1978. "The Recognition of Major and Minor Keys in German Theory: 1680–1730." *Journal of Music Theory* 22: 65–103.

Lester, Joel. 1989. *Between Modes and Keys: German Theory, 1592–1802*. Harmonologia Series, no. 3. Stuyvesant, NY: Pendragon Press.

Malin, Yonatan. 2006. Review of *Schumann's "Dichterliebe" and Early Romantic Poetics: Fragmentation of Desire*, by Beate Julia Perrey. *Music Theory Spectrum* 28: 299–310.

Marx, Adolph Bernhard. 1837–1847. *Die Lehre von der musikalischen Komposition, praktisch-theoretisch*, 4 vols. Leipzig: Breitkopf & Härtel.

Marx, Adolph Bernhard. 1851. *Theory and Practice of Musical Composition*. Translated and edited from the third German edition by Hermann S. Saroni, with Appendix and Notes by Emilius Girac. Fifth American edition. New York: Mason Brothers.

Neumeyer, David. 1982. "Organic Structure and the Song Cycle: Another Look at Schumann's *Dichterliebe*." *Music Theory Spectrum* 4: 92–105.

Oldroyd, George. 1967. *The Technique and Spirit of Fugue*. London: Oxford University Press.

Perrey, Beate Julia. 2002. *Schumann's Dichterliebe and Early Romantic Poetics: Fragmentation of Desire*. Cambridge Studies in Music Theory and Analysis. Cambridge: Cambridge University Press.

Riemann, Hugo. 1893. *Vereinfachte Harmonielehre, oder die Lehre von den tonalen Funktionen der Akkorde*. London, Augener.

Rosen, Charles. 1988. *Sonata Forms*. Revised edition. New York: Norton.

Rosen, Charles. 1995. *The Romantic Generation*. Cambridge, MA: Harvard University Press.

Rothstein, William. 2008. "Common-tone Tonality in Italian Romantic Opera: An Introduction." *Music Theory Online* 14, no. 1. Available at http://www.mtosmt.org/issues/mto.08.14.1/mto.08.14.1.rothstein.html.

Rousseau, Jean-Jacques. 1768. *Dictionnaire de musique*. Paris: Duchesne.

Saint Lambert, [no name] de. 1707. *Nouveau traité de l'accompagnement du clavecin, de l'orgue et des autres instruments*. Paris: Christophe Ballard; pirated edition, 1710. Amsterdam: Estienne Roger.

Schachter, Carl, 1983. "Motive and Text in Four Schubert Songs." In *Aspects of Schenkerian Theory*, edited by David Beach, 61–76. New Haven, CT: Yale University Press.

Schachter, Carl. 1999a. "Rhythm and Linear Analysis: A Preliminary Study; Durational Reduction; Aspects of Meter." In *Unfoldings: Essays in Schenkerian Theory and Analysis*, edited by Joseph N. Strauss, 17–117. Oxford: Oxford University Press.

Schachter, Carl. 1999b. "Analysis by Key: Another Look at Modulation." In *Unfoldings: Essays in Schenkerian Theory and Analysis*, edited by Joseph N. Strauss, 134–160. Oxford: Oxford University Press.

Schenker, Heinrich. 1956. *Der freie Satz*. [1935] 2nd edition. Edited by Oswald Jonas. Vienna: Universal Edition.

Schenker, Heinrich. 1979. *Free Composition*. Translated and edited by Ernst Oster. New York: Longman.

Tovey, Donald Francis. 1944. "Harmony." In *Musical Articles from the Encyclopædia Britannica*, 44–71. London: Oxford University Press.

Tunbridge, Laura. 2010. *The Song Cycle*, Cambridge Introductions to Music. Cambridge: Cambridge University Press.

Weber, Gottfried, 1841. *General Music Teacher: Adapted to Self-Instruction, both for Teachers and Learners*. Translated from the third German edition by James F. Warner. Boston: J. H. Wilkins & R. B. Carter.

Weber, Gottfried. 1817–1821. *Versuch einer geordneten Theorie der Tonsetzkunst*, 3 vols. Mainz: B. Schott.

Weber, Gottfried. 1846. *Theory of Musical Composition*. Translated by James F. Warner. Boston: Wilkins, Carter, and Co.

Weber, Gottfried. 1851. *Theory of Musical Composition, Treated with a View to a Naturally Consecutive Arrangement of Topics*. Translated from the third German edition by James F. Warner and edited by John Bishop, vol. 1. London: Robert Cocks and co.

Webster, James. 1978. "Schubert's Sonata Form and Brahms's First Maturity: Part I." *19th-Century Music* 2: 18–35.

CHAPTER 19

··

CADENCE

··

DANIEL HARRISON

How music starts and stops is one of the first things students learn. Of the two, stopping—including pausing, articulating, and other related effects—is the more conventional and therefore the easier to name and thence to categorize. Most students recognize and appropriately perform stopping conventions well before they learn their names, let alone any categories they belong to, though these are among the first items learned in elementary theory and composition. Some names seem self-explanatory, such as the "fade-out" used in many popular song recordings, and perhaps are never really taught but learned quickly by example. Others, particularly those in the Western art tradition, have medieval sources that remained influential long afterwards. These are the focus of this essay.

The approach is historical, with particular interest in the sixteenth through eighteenth centuries—the period in which the concept and its associated terms were shaped into their textbook forms. Readers eager for illustrations involving later music will find a few, but other means of articulating musical flow were tried out in the nineteenth century and have been increasingly employed since then—certainly proliferating in the twentieth. These, I submit, should fall under another heading, e.g., "closure," which may well deserve its own handbook chapter.

In this one, "cadence" is a creature of counterpoint—its first and chief schema, in fact. We will follow its historical formation in medieval polyphony, its growth and consolidation under the strict technique of sixteenth- and seventeenth-century composition, and its ultimate adaptation (reduced in number and variety) into the semiotic system associated with Classical form. This journey will bring readers both to familiar territory of terms, types, and uses (but through explanation rather than textbook definition) as well as to some unfamiliar territory of disused terms and apparently obsolete ideas. My usual habit is to try such things out again, testing for unrealized potential or new, adaptive uses. Readers interested in Baroque music—especially in imitative genres like fugue—should find here very useful analytic instruments made from refurbished parts.

THE CONTRAPUNTAL BACKGROUND

Taken together, the stopping conventions in Western art music are described as types of "cadence" (Ger. *Schluß*; It. *cadenza*; Fr. *cadence*). In strict counterpoint, the most rudimentary polyphonic procedure, they are defined as a mandatory pair of ending intervals, illustrated in Figure 19.1, which shows situations in which the given part ("cantus firmus") descends by step to the tonic—in the influential practice of Gioseffo Zarlino and Johann Joseph Fux.

Because these successions work under invertible counterpoint at the octave, it is immediately apparent that they could apply to cases in which counterpoint is made below the cantus firmus, in the bass, making the succession m3 to P1. This property will prove consequential in what follows. For now and for the sake of simplicity, most of the remaining illustrations use the model at (a) to cover general cases, with important exceptions noted as needed.

While it's usual to begin work in composition and theory with this kind of axiomatic beginning—given: three cadence types (a), (b), (c)—putting these into a long historical and theoretical context repays effort.[1] We discover that stopping is as conventional as it is because of the influence of metaphysical ideas about the nature of ultimate things, which cadences are understood to enact and perform. These ideas turn out to limit and shape the pitch structures available as polyphonic density increases beyond a2, creating even more recognizably conventional stopping structures. Working out analytic consequences of these results leads us to uncover sensitive analytic instruments especially suited for nonstandard repertory. Concerning this last point, if this essay has a desired effect, it is to increase the repertorial range of any "theory of cadence" and thereby (hopefully) encourage less compression of the topic in future textbooks and treatises.

Initial bearing is taken from the observation that the models in Figure 19.1 musically enact medieval ideas about completion, finality, closure, and perfection. These have permanently settled into the nomenclature of intervals, in which the perfect consonances reflect their symbolic value—defined classically by monochord arithmetic and later explained by acoustics and psychology—as the best possible ending sonorities. The

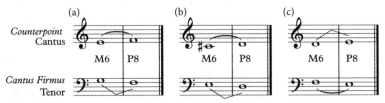

FIGURE 19.1 With counterpoint above the cantus firmus, mandatory ending of major sixth to perfect octave in strict counterpoint a2. Curved lines mark semitones; angled lines mark whole tones. (a) applies to cases where a diatonic semitone is below the tonic. It's transposable to a final on C. (b) shows a case with no diatonic semitone below the tonic; a chromatic one is used instead. It's transposable to A and G. (c) shows an instance where a diatonic semitone is above the tonic in the cantus firmus, necessitating a whole tone approach to final in the cantus.

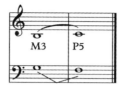

FIGURE 19.2 Motion into perfect fifth, a possible cadence a2 between ca. 1330–1430.

basic structure of Figure 19.1, then, is a symbolic ending sonority (the perfect octave or unison) preceded by an imperfect one a step away in each voice. Moreover, steps are taken in contrary directions, underscoring the difference between the two sonorities. That is, in the change from one to the other, neither voice remains the same, and neither voice moves the same way. Contrary motion maximizes difference and distinctness and also symbolizes the unity-of-opposites that is the ideological basis of harmony.

The models in Figure 19.1 are what remain of quite a large range of cadential possibilities in late medieval music. Figure 19.2 shows one type, also using a semitone and whole tone in contrary motion.[2]

Adding a third voice to the contrapuntal texture permits new possibilities. Those shown in Figure 19.3 reconcile the requirements of approaching a concluding perfection with some kind of differentiated motion.[3]

These characterize widely used formations, named by modern scholars and still learned by specialists in the repertory. In light of illustrations (b) and (c), the requirement of a perfect sonority at the conclusion overrules the preference for proximate voice-leading in all parts—leading to leaping basses in both. By the later standards of strict counterpoint, illustrations (a) and (b) are noncompliant and thus not useful as models going forward. Illustration (c), as its more familiar name suggests, remains relevant.

This is so, I argue, not because it is innately superior to (a) or (b)—though the leaping octave is indeed difficult to perform—but because it scales up perfectly with an increase

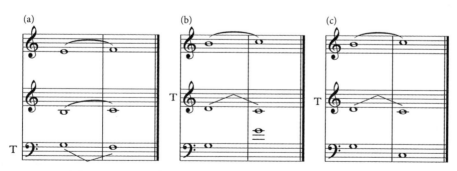

FIGURE 19.3 Schematic approaches to concluding perfect consonance a3, mid-fourteenth century. "T" = tenor. (a) the "double leading tone" combines stepwise approaches of Figs. 19.1 and 19.2; (b) the "leaping octave" in the bass crosses the tenor, making perfect fifths on either side of it; (c) the "authentic" has no fifth in the final sonority.

FIGURE 19.4 Schematic of formal cadence a4; a fifth (quintus) part can diverge from either the alto or tenor stream to reach a harmonic triad. In strict a4 settings, only one of the paths can be traced, taken by either the alto or the tenor.

in default texture from three to four voices, which is the scaffolding for polyphonic art music from the sixteenth through the nineteenth centuries. In particular, between the tenor and soprano is room for a contratenor alto on G4, which eliminates the need for a leaping octave and introduces oblique motion into the mixture. Figure 19.4 shows all this (and more).

Leaving aside the *quintus* line (which we will abbreviate Q) for a moment, we should pause to appreciate how lines in the basic SATB framework move by every motion type except parallel: contrary between S and T/B, oblique between A and other voices, and similar between T and B. In terms of individual activity, S and T move by step, B moves by leap, and A holds its place. Unity-in-diversity, *harmony*, is fully encoded into this structure.

Figure 19.5 shows a typical example from a model repertory at (a), a beautifully elaborated close of a mass movement by Ockeghem, in which all parts lock in for the cadence on the last quarter of the penultimate measure and then proceed according to rule. The same can be said of (b), a studied bit of sonorous "antiquing" by Mozart that brilliantly underscores the solemnity of the movement.

Hereinafter, I call this kind of cadence—strict SATB a4 as modeled in Figure 19.4 and exemplified in Figure 19.5—the All-Perfect Authentic Cadence (APAC). Taste for this structure changed over the course of centuries—from being a staple of Ockeghem's and even Dufay's technique, to becoming an increasingly disused (and therefore old-fashioned) option in the later *ars perfecta*, to becoming a special effect in Mozart's practice. These differences notwithstanding, the intuition of finality predicated on the all-perfect final sonority can, I think, be located in well-tuned performances in which spectral overlap fuses the individual tones nearly into a single timbre. Brass ensembles, barbershop quartets, and good early music groups can make this happen during sustained final chords. Thirds being comparatively difficult to locate (because of conflicting intonational ideals), their absence in an all-perfect chord makes perfect fusion possible.

FIGURE 19.5 (a) Johannes Ockeghem, *Missa L'Homme Armé*; conclusion of first "Kyrie."
(b) W. A. Mozart; Requiem; conclusion of "Kyrie."

To listen intently to such a sound, especially if under a fermata, is to hear the techniques
of spectralism *avant la lettre*.

Of greater interest in Figure 19.4 is the quintus staff and its additional voice leadings
emanating from the alto and tenor parts, respectively: A_Q and T_Q. These lines target an
imperfect third spotted near the middle of the space marked by the tenor and alto finals.
In SAQTB a5, the final chord is a familiar *complete* harmonic triad. In keeping with
values enacted in the other parts, A_Q and T_Q reach their final by closest approach. Doing
so is an easy upward step for T, but A requests (but not requires) the services of a dissonant passing half note to smooth its way.

The arrangement of the *two* alternate A and T voice-leadings into a single notional
part is significant. It's a claim that five-part texture—SATB plus one from Q—is required at minimum to ensure a cadence from one complete harmonic triad to another.
Another way of putting this is claiming that a5 is the textural "sweet spot" of all-triadic
progression under parsimonious voice-leading in general, and it is especially suited for
cadences in particular. Jean Philippe Rameau's well-known illustration, revoiced and
adapted in Figure 19.6, repays reflection on this point (1971, 63ff).

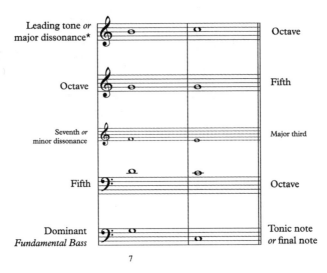

*The major dissonance is formed by the major third of the dominant.

FIGURE 19.6 Adapted from Rameau (1971), Ex. II.1; illustration of perfect cadence. The original voicing has the Seventh and the Octave lines transposed up an octave. This adaptation has reshuffled the lines into regular order.

The final chord is a complete triad a5, with the telltale trace of A_Q—the minor seventh dissonance—leading the way. The disposition of perfect intervals over the lowest voice is clearly of importance to Rameau, as is identifying the essential imperfect note of the penultimate chord as the "leading tone." Rameau's bass line is precisely that which works contrapuntally, as we have seen, but what distinguishes it from the others is the labeling as scale degrees instead of by interval membership. This points the way towards Roman-numeral chord analysis, generalizing the contents of a fundamental bass line determined by cadential activity in upper parts.

While using both Q lines is certainly possible for a6, it is not a favored part-writing choice. The imperfect third is doubled thereby, loudened as a result, and likely unwanted as noise in the signal broadcast by perfect intervals at cadential sign-off. Moreover, at and beyond a6, homophonic writing becomes increasingly difficult under laws of strict counterpoint. All conjunct pathways are taken, and prohibitions against parallel perfect intervals prevent any increase in their capacity. Options narrow upon highly disjunct lines that leap from one consonance to another, similar to the characteristics of a (fundamental) bass line. (This can all be verified in upcoming examples involving a8 and a10 textures, Figures 19.16 and 19.24.) In conditions of even greater density, changing chords according to rule is a monumental task, and the natural result is very slow harmonic rhythm underneath surfaces decorated with voice exchanges of one kind or another. The homophonic sections of Thomas Tallis's *Spem in Alium*, a tour-de-force a40, bear study on this point.[4]

In contrast, composing triadically in a thinner, a4 texture seems easier. Yet it cannot be in full compliance with the ideal laws of strict counterpoint, and working out the resulting compromises involves good taste and judgment. The issue can be quickly grasped by considering the two a4 adaptations of Figure 19.4 that maintain the SB outer-voice frame but swap in a Q line for either T or A. One option, SA_QTB is attractive, because its passing dissonance takes over the role previously performed by imperfect consonance in the penultimate chord of the strict setting (M6 over T), thus reinscribing the general rule of succeeding from a less to a more perfect sonority when making a cadence. Yet the cost for this is a decidedly imperfected final sonority, missing a P5 over T—that is, no G, one E4, and a tripled C3,4,5. Strictly speaking, it's not even a triad, but thanks to powers of resonance, it's not hard mentally to supply a fifth in order to adjust actual input to the templated requirements, which is why a term like "incomplete triad" is not seriously contested.

The other option, SAT_QB, permits A to hold station at the fifth, but the ersatz T declines to descend properly to the tonic and is deflected upward into the third instead. The final chord is thus complete (i.e., one G4, one E4, and a doubled C3,5), but at the cost of the foundational (one might say primordial) contributions of T to the cadence. The counterpoint is strict, but the originary line is tampered with to make it so. In sum: with A_Q, a chord tone goes conspicuously missing; with T_Q, the founding voice part is forced off track.

These kinds of solutions to composing triadically a4 are precisely those that shape the "free" counterpoint of the eighteenth century, distinguishing it from the "strict" observance illustrated thus far. They are schemes of arrangement from the point of view of the art of rhetoric, but more typically described as "exceptions" or "licenses" in counterpoint, giving the impression that things aren't so strict after all. They are better understood as the enacted compromises between linear motion in regular order and properly if not perfectly built harmonic triads. We shall encounter a few more of these below. For now, let us restart with five-part SAQTB and note that it models no longer an All-, but a (Mostly) Perfect Authentic Cadence, which I'm happy to abbreviate as PAC. This familiar textbook construct is the polestar that guides the rest of this work. To reconnoiter the terrain ahead, we now zoom out from the cadential moment—the final and its penult—and survey the approaches and exits.

EVENTS

Figure 19.7 plots a timeline by placing the cadential semibreve-and-breve pair of Figure 19.4 in an extended metric flow, symbolized by the filled noteheads on the solid centerline of the figure. These noteheads stand for chords. The presentation so far has not shown any chords after a cadence, and this condition is registered with the double bar after the breve. By introducing the possibility of cadences having potential "afterwards," we attempt to expand its purview from "stop" alone to include "pause" as well. Much more of consequence results from this expansion than can be covered immediately in the explanation of this figure; a later section, on rhetoric, will occasion a return to the topic. For now, let "before and after" be simply modeled as integers on a line of action points, set according to a cadential endtime, C. These action points number the chords according to distance from final. Up to now, we have been concerned solely with chords −1 (semibreve) and C (breve).

Between chords are the voice-leading pathways that connect their constituent lines in succession. These are sets of melodic intervals and are labeled *i* in the figure. For example, the cadential mandate for cadence a2—the succession M6 to P8 in upper-voice descant—makes these intervals the elements of *i* between −1 and C. For short, we'll refer to them as *i*C, though when analytic interests suggest, the synonym −1*i* might be employed.

Figure 19.7 suggests ways in which musicians understand cadence more comprehensively than merely the final *i*C move. Contrapuntal convention requires that parts have to be voice-led into position at the head of their final pathways to C, a process that takes time depending on how distant the voices are when summoned for cadential duty. When that occurs, a certain freedom that characterizes musical flow in midphrase is noticeably lost as voice parts make their way toward −1 so as to discharge the final, mandated duty, *i*C. While this duty defines the general situation at C and −1, it also affects the structures available at −2 to a large degree, −3 to a lesser degree, and even points earlier in some cases.[5] The cadential moment is thus the predicate of antecedent objects and moves, chords and pathways, arranged syntactically to terminate at C.[6]

This apparatus allows us to analyze the context around the cadence, which work is begun in Figure 19.8 with a survey of possible pathways from −2 to −1.[7] This survey assumes conjunct motion or even repetition in the cantus firmus tenor, as befits its status as originary melody. In short, disjunct approach to −1 for the tenor is disallowed (Schenker 1987, 1:103–4). The survey also introduces a suspended soprano, a highly conventional diminution in this style and the impetus for trills and other characteristic cadential ornaments. Because of the suspension, the other parts arrive at their stations before S. When S arrives, −1 is fully realized and notated. But the influence of the other parts allows −1 to be fractioned into the two action points as shown.

The requirements for preparing the suspension at −1½ sort the possibilities for −2 into two functional categories: (a) Tonic and (b) Subdominant.

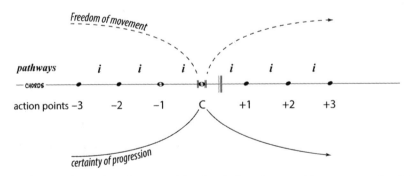

FIGURE 19.7 Time plot of a cadence. C is the chord of resolution, with contrapuntal activity before and after shown as numbered "action points."

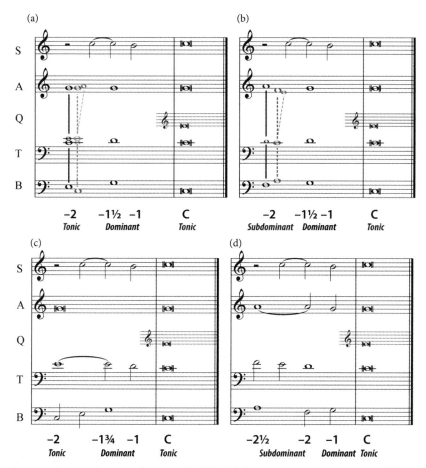

FIGURE 19.8 Approaches to cadence a5 SAQTB. (a) Soprano suspension prepared from Tonic; (b) Soprano suspension prepared from Subdominant. (c) A particular soprano and tenor suspension creating cadential six-four chord. (d) Soprano and alto suspension creating six-five chord.

If the alto, tenor, and bass parts are in regular order underneath the soprano as they approach C from −1, each category has a few options for the chord at −2. At (a), the tenor moves by step to −1 on D3, either up or down, and those two possibilities result in chords connected with solid and dotted lines, respectively. The bass approach from E3, responsible for the solid-line chord, is the most proximate non-conjunct motion available, and it fixes the alto firmly at its G4 final station, awaiting other parts to arrive at theirs. The tenor provides perfect-consonance coordination for the soprano suspension and alto by stepping up into −1, though the direct approach with the bass is inelegant in strict settings. Perhaps better, though with imperfect coordination with the soprano and alto, is a contrary-motion step down to −1 from E4, shown with a smaller notehead for contrast.

The bass approach from C3, associated with the dotted-line chords, works best with this step down from E4, providing contrary motion into −1. (The tenor may also step up from C4, but the direct motion with bass—involving two perfect consonances, to boot—is even more inelegant.) The C3 bass also permits A4 in the alto, as the dotted-line shunt to it indicates, which provides some variety for that static line. Either alto note can fit with either tenor note, though the complete harmonic triad with the tenor E4 seems reasonable as a default.

At (b) are the results of exploring more counterpoints for the alto A4. As before, the solid-line chord has the close, conjunct approach in the bass. The tenor cannot prepare the suspension properly as other options are strictly not available. This responsibility passes to the bass and alto. Under the circumstances, the tenor can do no better than fasten onto −1 and wait for the other parts to arrive. (A more compliant setting requires the tenor to be loosened from its approach restrictions, leaping by third into −1 from F4, not shown in the figure.) An easier and more varied approach is shown in the dotted-line chord, with A3 in the bass. This permits conjunct motion in all parts to −1, and also gives the alto a leaping option.

Figure 19.8(c) further elaborates (a) by suspending the tenor along with the soprano and diminuting the bass into its two possible pitches. Elaborating multiple parts like this allows for a certain amount of "chord reification" in the analysis. Here, −1¾ is the point at which bass has reached −1 but crucial others have not. The result is the familiar cadential six-four. (Recall that suspending the fourth alone is event −1½.) The same urge to decorate is tried out on the Subdominant approach at Figure 19.8(d). Here, the alto's A is suspended in parallel with the soprano at −2, and an additional elaboration is worked into the bass, which opens a descending stepwise passage for the tenor. The result at −1½ is a familiar six-five chord over $\hat{4}$. Additional elaborations and diminutions along these lines can easily be imagined, culminating in a mixture of white- and black-note values in all parts, which the reader is invited to explore.[8]

As the cadential time plot in Figure 19.7 suggests, the situation prior to −2 becomes difficult to predict because the general entropy of musical activity increases with distance from C. The same can be said for activity after C, but for different reasons, which we'll cover below. For now, we note the invitation to more rigorous statistical analysis of these larger contexts and resume focus on the cadential moment by detailing more of its contrapuntal opportunities.

Cadence and Clausula

We can make an important connection from strict composition to thoroughbass harmony by way of invertible counterpoint. The connection was identified as early as Viadana's time (ca. 1602), but a crucial transformational development was undertaken by Andreas Werckmeister in 1702 (2013, 301).[9] The basics are quickly grasped in Figure 19.9, an adaptation of his original diagram.

The top staff names four characteristic cadential moves, by now familiar from our previous study of pathways from −2 through C. Werckmeister's choice—apparently conventional—to describe these as verbals makes for no less awkward renderings in English than in German.[10] But the idea that, at a cadence, the soprano "discantusizes," the tenor "tenorizes," and so forth, is clear enough and is the basis for the annotations

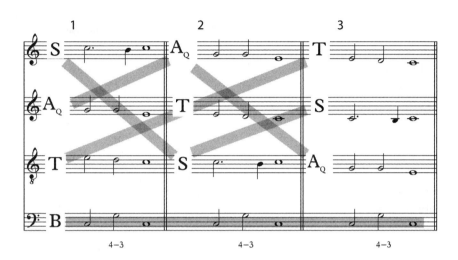

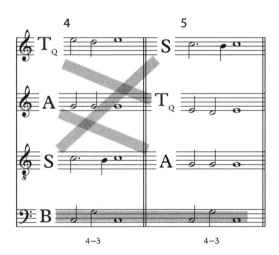

FIGURE 19.9 Annotated adaptation from Werckmeister (2013, 301).

added to the original: the voice-leadings of S, A_Q, T, and B (with A_Q declining its opportunity for a dissonant passing tone).

Werckmeister intends his adjectives to describe cases in which a cadence is made, but the upper parts are not in their regularly ordered slots. Holding the bass constant—in order to maintain the formality of the cadence—he shows five examples, all related through a triple-counterpoint permutational subgroup transforming the upper parts. (Follow the grey bars in the figure.) Example 1 is familiar from previous figures, especially Figure 19.8(a). Example 2, however, shows an "altoized" cadence—the soprano moves like an alto.[11] Example 3, likewise with the tenor. In Examples 4 and 5, Werckmeister has the tenor take the Q part from the alto, which then can revert to its original course as A. He begins to demonstrate the relevant permutational structure, but breaks off without comment before having to show an altoized arrangement that would result from transforming Example 5 into an "Example 6" along the lines of transforming Example 2 into Example 3.

Of the five arrangements Werckmeister does show, those in Examples 1, 3, and 5 correspond to current definitions of the PAC—top and bottom voices both conclude on the tonic scale degree, harmonically related by perfect fifteenth (octave, *vel sim.*). This relation between the exposed outer voices is missing in Examples 2 and 4, where Q overtops S and the outer-voice interval is a tenth. These two are, sensibly enough, tokens of the Imperfect Authentic Cadence (IAC). As just noted, Werckmeister is unclear about whether A can overtop S at a cadence—the missing "Example 6." If it cannot, the IAC is specifically "quintusized," concluding with a (mandatory) outer-voice imperfect tenth instead of perfect fifteenth. In these terms, an altoized cadence presents difficulties. It would conclude with a perfect twelfth, so it shouldn't belong to any category with "imperfect" in its title. Yet it is noticeably less effective than any PAC and even than a quintusized IAC on account of the melodically inert alto being exposed in the top voice. Nevertheless, it seems prudent to conform to current doctrine by using IAC to cover either case, $\hat{3}$ or $\hat{5}$ in the soprano.

More consequential is the observation that the PAC has two types of approaches: (1) a *regular* setting with S in its customary top-voice register, and (2) a *cantional* setting with a *tenorized* top voice.[12] Each of these has subarrangements involving transformations of inner parts. All this can be grasped in Figure 19.10, which shows the situation with the comparatively simpler APAC (that is, without the complication of the two Q parts). The bass is contrived to move contrary to the top voice—falling fifth for regular, and rising fourth for cantional.

The compositional differences between regular and cantional settings are significant. In the former, a structural tenor can be counterpointed both above and below, building texture from within. In the latter, the primordial melodic structure (cantus firmus) is featured at the top, and texture is built up from outside in.[13] Momentarily extending our purview beyond cadence, we can observe the distinction in approaches to polyphonic composition in general, as suggested in Figure 19.11, two arrangements of a famous psalm tune. In the regular setting (a), the tune is in the tenor, and three out of the four cadences are made with voices in their proper slots (at the end of mm. 1, 2, and 4). The last is an APAC, and the previous two are PACs, made by swapping T_Q for T in m. 1, and likewise with A_Q in m. 2. The cadence in m. 3 is quintusized, with S sent to the T register and both A and B staying their regular course.

The cantional setting at (b) can be analyzed in much the same way. Even in m. 2, where the phrase ends at −1 instead of C (i.e., a half cadence, to be discussed below), we can describe tenorizing "in progress," with S and A being displaced downward by one slot and

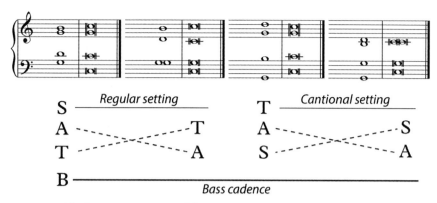

FIGURE 19.10 The four arrangements of the APAC.

FIGURE 19.11 Two settings of "Old Hundredth." (a) A regular by setting W. Parsons, 1563. #1 in Havergal (1854, 54). (b) A cantional thoroughbass setting by C. Müller, 1703; transposed, rebarred, and inner parts realized. #13 in Havergal (1854, 58). Rhythmic variance in the last phrase is original.

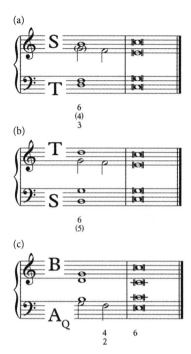

FIGURE 19.12 Three clausulas, with only the outer voices labeled. (a) Tenor clausula with regular S. (b) Soprano clausula with cantional T. (c) Quintus clausula with bass in descant.

B holding station. All things considered, the difference in harmonic progression—an increase in tonal directionality—is quite noticeable in the cantional setting.

So far, Werckmeister's invertible counterpoint procedures have described one new cadential type, the IAC, and they have also distinguished suggestively between the regular and cantional PAC. Extending these procedures to the bass—sending it to other parts, in effect—results in a significant decrease in stopping power. The relevant arrangements can be reasonably styled "inverted cadences," but even retaining the term "cadence" may overstate the similarity. Three of these are shown in Figure 19.12, with thoroughbass signatures and marked outer voices.

Adapting a rhetorical term used by Werckmeister and his contemporaries, who used it as something of a synonym for cadence, we'll refer to these as examples of clausula—a "little close" instead of the "bigger," more formal kind with a regular bass.[14] Following established precedent, a clausula will be named according to the part in the lowest voice, though we can thankfully dispense with the awkward verbal form (e.g., tenorized) and revert to a more natural adjective-noun pair (e.g., "tenor clausula").

The tenor and soprano clausulas at (a) and (b), respectively, conclude with the outer-voice octave perfection that characterizes the PAC. The former, topped with S, is sufficiently standardized that some authors name it "clausula vera" (Gjerdingen 2007, 164–167).[15] The latter is something of a cantional counterpart of (a), but differences in inner parts are telling. Tenor clausulas cannot properly support B and A lines at −1 because of the fourths they make with the lowest voice. A can tolerate a deflection onto a third, which explains the F3 at −1 in (a). At the final chord, it reacquires its position on

G3. Eighteenth-century thoroughbass authors recognize and rationalize attempts that would make G a chord tone at −1, but the simultaneous presence of its "deflected third," F in this case, was required for it to work.[16]

The soprano clausula at (b) has none of these difficulties in supporting other lines. A and A_Q both work as shown, and in a5 texture, T_Q does as well. Even so, there's something enervated about the soprano clausula compared with the tenor variety. Placing S at its opposite extreme in register may be partly responsible, and in the perfect cantional setting here, the pedant's disdain for *ottava battuta*—outer voices compressing onto a perfect octave—might reasonably be shared. The soprano clausula seems better suited to imperfection, with Q or A at the top of the texture instead of T or B (though the latter truly bashes into its octave). In this form it was adapted and commonly used, but as an opening schema, with S suspended in the bass and A_Q on top. As we have seen, this suspension illuminates cadential pathways from C back through −2. Options for using the soprano clausula in opening moves narrow onto well-known four-chord strings, of which the locus classicus is Bach's C-major Prelude from WTC 1: (1) initial tonic at −3; (2) same bass supporting a four-two, five-two, or six-four-two chord at −2; (3) A_Q taking over the maintenance of dissonance at −1, a V six-five chord; (4) close accomplished, with imperfect outer voices ready for continued action at +1 and beyond.

With respect to the A_Q clausula at (c), little needs to be noted save that it is the best opportunity for the bass to sound at the top of the texture, perfectly supported at −1. The bass then contributes its considerable portion of stopping power by leaping onto tonic, supported imperfectly and even restlessly by the lowest voice.

At this point, as the proliferation of cadence and clausula arrangements threatens to become overly detailed, Figure 19.13 collects and sorts them according to a reasonable order of precedence based on their power to conclude musical flow—more simply put, their strength.

Under the general heading of authentic cadence, our exclusive focus so far, the APAC sets the strictest standard, rarely met after the seventeenth century, during which the PAC acquired all of its formal authority. The right side of the figure attempts to make finer and possibly arguable distinctions, such as giving regular settings precedence over cantional ones. Stepping down into the weaker IAC, we bring along Werckmeister's preference for Q in the top voice over A.

As suggested above, moving B out of the lowest voice results in a decline in strength noticeable enough for us to draw a line and create a subcategory called "clausula." The first is the so-called clausula vera, abbreviated as T//S, which is the mandatory cadence a2 in strict counterpoint.[17] A weaker alternative is T//Q, which is associated with what Robert O. Gjerdingen has called the Prinner, a common four-event (−3 through C) riposte concluding with $T//A_Q$ (Gjerdingen 2007, 46).[18]

Previous comments about the S// and A_Q// clausulas shown in Figure 19.12 have suggested their placement in the current scheme of Figure 19.13. Gjerdingen (2007, 155–156) finds $S//A_Q$ significant enough to name it a "comma," suggesting that it is a default, normative arrangement. The singling-out of A_Q in this way argues for putting it next in line, below the S// in precedence. At this rank, C is no longer a root-position chord in its various perfections, but inverted, imperfect, and mobile. The $A_Q//B$ clausula is able to expose the distinctively cadential B in the upper voice, as shown in Figure 19.12(c),

Authentic

All Perfect	APAC	⎫
		⎬ Regular > Cantional
Perfect	PAC	⎭

| Imperfect | IAC | Q > A(?) |

— — — — — — — — — — — —

Clausula

Tenor	T//	S (*clausula vera*) > Q (*Prinner*, A_Q)
Soprano	S//	T > Q (*comma*, A_Q) > A
Alto *Quintus*	A_Q//	B > S > T > A
Tenor *Quintus*	T_Q//	?

FIGURE 19.13 An Order of Precedence for authentic cadences and clausulas; abbreviations in middle column, potential top-voice accompaniments on the right. Double slashes in the abbreviations (//) show nonadjacent, outer-voice pathways, lowest voice first. (When useful to track inner voices, single slashes separate adjacent pathways.)

but power wanes considerably after that, such that while the final entry, T_Q//, is systemically possible, it's difficult to recognize any meaningful connections to ideas of pausing, closing, stopping, concluding, ending, etc. Making further distinctions at this point appears pointless.

These concerns are far outweighed by new opportunities to analyze compositional structure and form, which we will take advantage of in the next section. But important insights are available from addressing them, and even putting them under some stress. For one thing, not only have categories proliferated, but (turning towards actual, composed music) so have occasions for them to be applied in vastly different circumstances. In one concrete example, is every succession of, say VII⁶–I, necessarily a tenor clausula, or V–I a PAC? These questions were familiar to Rameau and his descendants, who had few scruples about noting "micro-cadences" in textbook examples.

The current approach cuts this problem off with a dashed line in Figure 19.13. Above the line are (bass-regular) cadences that normally conclude *formal* units of music, from phrases, sentences, and periods through ever larger sections. These and their formal responsibilities are very familiar to students of the so-called new *Formenlehre*. Below the line, clausulas conclude a single cycle of a traditionally conceived T–S–D–T functional progression. That is, they terminate a *tonal* unit, something that has both an orienting reference point (tonic) and some variation in aspect (mode), which two features are the basis of *key*. Any clausula in a composition, therefore, momentarily fastens it onto some underlying key like a finish nail through molding, pinning it to tonal structure. In this way, the order of precedence presented in Figure 19.13 is something of a sizing guide, ranging from little clausulas suitable for easy, straight, corner-to-corner installations to large cadences needed to terminate these runs, which must reach the framing members of compositional form.

BACH, SINFONIA NO. 1

The dashed line of Figure 19.13 that separates formal cadences from tonal clausulas is correctly placed for galant music and its fashionable descendants, a repertory known for clearly defined expressive roles of melody and accompaniment. In contrast, this approach to composition doesn't lend itself to the kind of contrapuntal artifice with inversion that Werckmeister, for one, was interested in. This other approach has more use for a "melody" that could appear in any register, and its accompaniment likewise—its members are perhaps better styled as subject and countersubject.

In either case, a melody/subject concludes by aligning onto a cadential pathway and choosing one of the a5 options at iC. If it ends "like a soprano," it may be used in that voice in a form-defining PAC. In the bottom voice, however, it does not have the same effect. The same is true if the melody/subject ends "like a tenor" (a cantional setting), though it is marginally less conclusive than a regular one. Other compositional difficulties attend any melody/subject that ends "like a bass," which could not help but create a cadence whenever it is placed in the lowest voice and perhaps elsewhere. Ending "like an alto" is most difficult, since the line is immobile and moreover implies an impermissible perfect fourth (eleventh) above at C. Targeting the third from either Q approach, however, leaves easy continuations. When in the top voice, the subject ending could be as strong as an IAC, and when in the lowest voice, it creates an A_Q clausula ($A_Q//$). Both are attractive choices for the beginning contrapuntist.

This presumably was one of the lessons J. S. Bach intended to teach his pupils in the C-major Sinfonia BWV 787, a3. Formally, the lesson appears to be about using clausulas instead of cadences to harmonize the ending of a subject. In this way, constantly spinning sixteenth notes maintain momentum without apparent articulation until the only PAC in the piece, which happens at the very end.

Figure 19.14(a) gives an introduction to the technique by analyzing the first seven measures.[19] Underneath the score are two rhythmic reductions. The middle one has thoroughbass signatures and is meant as a loose "accompaniment" to the original piece, its "imaginary accompaniment" or *thoroughbassis*, if you will.[20] The lower staff group adapts the structure to strict counterpoint, where the clausulas are marked.

Let's start at the ending, mm. 6–7, which concludes the opening section in C major, thanks to a tenor clausula vera, with S the top: T//S. To show a middle voice, in this case A_Q, the slashes can be redeployed: T/A_Q/S. Most analytic circumstances won't call for this level of detail, but this one is worth a moment's pause. The upper-voice trill calls attention to the "all-but" regular setting of a PAC, missing only the bass to complete it. Lacking that, it's a clausula, but it is an extremely strong one that sensibly articulates a formal span of the piece. The dashed line in Figure 19.13 might be shifted to accommodate it.

Shifting focus to mm. 1–2, we encounter a weaker clausula, S//A_Q deployed in a familiar opening move, nailing the subject to tonic at its conclusion. Then a stronger T//S into G

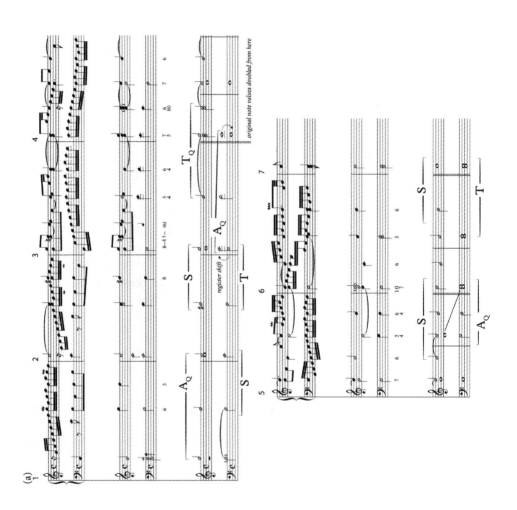

(b)

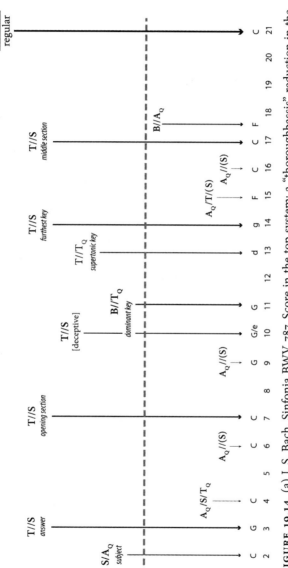

FIGURE 19.14 (a) J. S. Bach, Sinfonia BWV 787. Score in the top system; a "thoroughbassis" reduction in the middle; and an adaptation to strict counterpoint in the bottom system. (b) Location of the cadence and of several clausulas in BWV 787. Clausulas above the dashed line conclude formal units as identified, and those below mark tonal and modulatory developments.

major, finishing the middle voice's tonal answer. After that, the subject goes to the lowest voice, and finishes as $A_Q//$. Complications in the piece make the upper voice difficult to identify, but the activities in mm. 5–6 are clear, with the suspended S a noteworthy touch.

Of the clausulas marked in the figure, the dotted line in 19.13 could be moved not only to acknowledge the T//S that concludes the opening section, but the S//A_Q that concludes the subject (surely, an object of form) and the more powerful T//S in the dominant key, G major, that concludes the tonal answer. For various reasons, the $A_Q//$ clausulas of mm. 3–6 can remain below the line—not implicated in a formal design, but rather resetting the tonality into C after a strong swerve to G at m. 3, effectively setting up the form-functional clausula vera of m. 7 as the consequence of a descending cantus firmus in the lowest voice.

The strict counterpoint representation gets at certain underlying processes, but can oversimplify the surface if some schemes of arrangement aren't invoked to show how contact underneath is maintained. For example, a voice overlapping happens in m. 4, where a new upper voice is slipped in over the suspension, creating the illusion that the suspension resolves *upwards* to E5 instead of resolving, normatively, to C5. A similar example is showing a register shift—a leap of octave or seventh in the "closed-note" counterpoint of the thoroughbassis—as a simultaneous event in "open-note" counterpoint, as in mm. 3–4. Another adaptation undoes the doubling of harmonic-rhythm tempo that occurs in m. 3 by notating traditional and characteristic diminutions in their "open note" versions, doubling the original note values. Finally along these lines, rendering the first measure in strict counterpoint is surprisingly interesting, leading to the rather odd off-tonic solution. Keeping A_Q in second species requires a single "semibreve" for them to be set against, and the choice is between C4 and B3. The latter reflects Bach's thinking in m. 3, where the subject does indeed enter on the dominant. But since convention dictates a tonic downbeat, Bach supplies one in the bass C3, overwriting the hypothetical non-tonic B. (The urgency of this move is suggested by the imagined tonic-chord arpeggio supplied in the thoroughbassis.)

Most of the rest of the thoroughbassis transcription is self-explanatory, but an astute observer could wonder why the top-voice eighth notes in m. 3 aren't passing through A_Q while the lowest executes a filled in B move—why, in other words, is this event not marked as a clausula? In response, we note that the metric situation neither suggests nor supports this suggestion, and trying to claim something about conclusion at the very moment surface activity picks up is inopportune. This too-fast and metrically wrong-footed move doesn't need to be registered as a clausula. Neither, for that matter, does a similar event in the next measure, the top voice this time rushing down the same A_Q channel in even faster sixteenth notes. At that point, as the thoroughbassis shows, chord rhythm picks up as suspensions are applied to quarter notes rather than half notes. (This is where the strict counterpoint transcription goes to doubled note values.)

Moving away from tedious detail, Figure 19.14(b) zooms out to the entire piece, calibrates the dashed line to register the formally significant clausulas just discussed, and marks the location of these as well as any occurring below the line. Formal significance is briefly noted, and best understood as the answer to the question "What is being ended?"

The prevalence of T//S clausulas, variously figured, is particularly striking. Those at mm. 14 and 17 are recognized by unfigured S and A_Q beneath it in standard figuration, and a very light and quick touch on T as the last sixteenth note of the measure. The

T//T$_Q$ in m. 13, while lesser in precedence because of its imperfect upper voice, is here presented very clearly a3 as a kind of clausula vera with a descant: diverging T and S move in unhurried eighth note beneath a typically figurated Q.

New to the theoretical development underway is the possibility of a "bass clausula," and the two marked here (m. 11 and m. 17, third beat) show the two ways they can come about. The B// in m. 11 fills the regular B leap from dominant to tonic with a quick scale run, which obscures B's most outstanding characteristic. In this case, however, the D3 dominant is strongly predicated on the downbeat and then restruck on the second beat, so the figuration clearly depends upon it. The situation in m. 17 is different. The bass line is similarly predicated and reinforced (with two restrikings of the dominant C4) before executing its regular leap to tonic, F3. Above is A$_Q$ in quarter notes with T beneath it, weakened by suspensions. Formally, this clausula is just below the dashed line, since it doesn't conclude any relevant unit. On the other hand, it does suggest an opening into a coda of some kind, as B♭ contends with B♮ from this point on (and as foreshadowed in m. 15), indicating a move into Subdominant regions where codas are conventionally sited. Developing this idea further, we may retroactively brevet the tenor clausula on the downbeat of that measure to higher precedence; may it be that it overwrites a normative PAC (in regular setting, as in m. 7), a cadence that would be the essential structural close of the piece? This perhaps is a (dashed) line too far. Those interested in moving it are free to do so, which is surely a benefit of this style of analysis.

To leave the confines of this remarkable piece and to discover more about cadences, we should turn our attention to ways of adjusting the strength of cadential effect besides inverting its lines into imperfections and clausulas. Some of these are clearly in evidence in Figure 19.14(a) and have already been cited informally—suspensions that stagger the movement of voices through their pathways, for example, or figurations that cover underlying structure. The parenthesized notes in the thoroughbassis also belong here, as pathways pointedly broken off before their known ends. When relevant to clausulas, these show up in Figure 19.14(b) as parenthesized part abbreviations (for example, m. 6). Techniques of this kind—including the "deceptive" T// at m. 10—belong to the art of rhetoric, and further development of cadence in general can take place under its auspices.

CADENTIAL SCHEMES AND TROPES

Some familiar textbook cadences haven't figured into the narrative so far. That's because none of these—with the partial exception of plagal—have much new in the way of contrapuntal technique. They are, for the most part, rhetorically affected (inflected) authentic cadences and clausulas. To be sure, this is not a standard line about these structures, and rather than support it immediately and in general, I'll show specific cases, starting from the most obvious one, and letting the general show itself by degrees as more nuanced ones are engaged.

Half Cadence. Although examples of phrases and sections ending with intentionally inconclusive progressions can be found certainly in music of the sixteenth century,[21] these could not be recognized as cadences per se before the middle of the seventeenth, when the theorist Conradus Matthaei noted that the process that leads to some perfect final product, C, could be contrived by various means to "conceal" that product in some way, by withholding C, misdirecting iC, and similar unexpected events. Mutch (2015b, 152–153) recognizes this as the first proposal for an "entirely new meaning for the familiar imperfect-perfect binary," mentioning but not inferring anything from Matthaei's own use of vernacular rather than Latin terms (*unvollkommene* vs. *imperfecta*).[22] We will take a hint and from here on reserve the vocabulary of perfection for harmonic intervals and chords, and use vernacular for processes that fall short of their goal.

The most familiar scheme stops a cadence at −1 by contriving to shift it into a position where C would normally be expected. This so-called "half" or "semi cadence" is, in short, an authentic cadence that stops prematurely, making −1 = C. Matthaei did, in fact, seem to recognize this unfinished ending as a cadence, and given the subsequent history of the term and its structural importance in later music, it's imprudent to call it anything else. But "cadence" is under no small pressure here as a sign of completion. This is perhaps why it has tentative and (as Burstein 2014 puts it) "slippery" qualities, which evidently underwrote the prepending of "so-called" to its name in the eighteenth century (Burstein 2015, 90). Admitting it to the set of cadences is to enlarge the meaning of cadence to cover generalized harmonic punctuation, not just the mark that ends the musical equivalent of clauses. As punctuation, the half cadence is more semicolon than period, question mark than comma. Even so, it is fully derived from authentic-cadence counterpoint and intended as a rhetorical device that plays off authentic stopping power, the purpose of which can be nothing other than to create expectation for more music that in some way responds, answers, or—in the case of the classical period—repeats and successfully completes the process.

Because C is located at −1, we can identify an important yet underappreciated feature of textbook definitions of the half cadence: it does not have a single mandatory progression to the goal like the authentic dominant to tonic. Unlike iC, $i-1$ has two tributaries, (a) from Tonic, and (b) from Subdominant. (A look back at Figure 19.8 will refresh the details.) This greater degree of freedom is responsible for the many and diverse approaches half cadences can take in the literature. As its possibilities were explored during the eighteenth century—reflecting "the increasingly important role of midsection rhetorical articulations in music of the era" (Burstein 2015, 92)—some of these achieved schematic status as conventions in their own right. As a result, the half cadence has recently been the object of remarkable attention in studies of galant music, a style in which it perhaps achieved its definitive expressions (Caplin 2004; Gjerdingen 2007, 153–154, 160–162; Burstein 2014, 2015).

Deceptive cadence. In addition to sanctioning half cadences, Matthaei also illustrated cases in which C is markedly different than expected—what we have come to call a deceptive cadence. In its simplest form—that is, the easiest to execute—the leaping bass in a typical SA_QTB cadence is deflected at iC into an ascending step. The expected tonic chord is overwritten by a submediant one—different not only in chord root, but also in quality (minor, if tonic is major). Drilling further down, we can appreciate how this particular chord transformation neatly "reverses" the perfection of all the important final chord tones. That is to say, were the cadence to come off as expected, in regular order, C would have perfect intervals between bass, tenor, and soprano, with A_Q sounding the imperfect third; with the deception, the bass makes an imperfect third with tenor and soprano, while the formerly imperfect final of A_Q is promoted to perfect fifth.

Conventional theory has claimed this just-described transformation as *the* deceptive cadence, which is unfortunate though perhaps statistically justified. A wider definition, adopted here, extends the idea over a class of rhetorical effects that make C any unexpectedly different chord.[23] Two excerpts from Mozart's sacred music show what is caught analytically by this approach.

A remarkable passage from K. 321 is shown in Figure 19.15, which demonstrates that much more can happen in iC than a single nudge on the bass line. The chord delivered on the downbeat of m. 11 is not I but II♯ (alias V/V), a jolt of a jest in the context of the regular SAT_QB cadence being set up from Subdominant −2. A quick loop back to the second half of m. 9 sets up another try, which comes out perfectly in m. 12.

More awesome is Mozart's cadential rhetoric in "Qui Tollis" from the C-minor Mass, K. 427. A dotted-rhythm, G-minor Largo for double choirs a4, this movement stands out in Mozart's output for the dreadful, dramatic solemnity of its slow-moving rotations, grounded at the start by the venerable lament bass (descending fourth, chromaticized). The respective middles of each rotation vary slightly according to text, but all are chromatically dense, involve both choirs for thick, a8 texture, and relentlessly increase dramatic pressure for a cadence. Figure 19.16 shows the situation the first time a cadence is approached in the piece, at a climactic downbeat.

As in the previous excerpt, Mozart puts all the lines into regular order by m. 328, where a texture that had been consistently merging voices since the third beat of the previous measure reaches a4. Rather than spring the deception at C, Mozart signals it at −1 by deflecting S downward from its leading tone while the other parts proceed regularly (though subtly thickened to a6 during a *subito piano* at that point). This deflection dashes hopes for C, and the affirmative, relative major so powerfully predicated by the events from −2 is overwritten by an unstable seventh chord. (Or is it an augmented sixth? An eventual cadence in D minor wouldn't be out of the question in this very tonally unstable environment.)

One feature that this excerpt shares with the textbook deceptive cadence is that iC has only one change compared to regular order. In this case, it's S that's deflected downwards; in the textbook version, it's B that's deflected upwards. Minimal pathway alteration like this can be experienced by performers in ways most listeners don't notice. This happens when iC is altered in a way that does not change the identity of C but does change its expected voicing by swapping in pitches from another part. This is common in four-part cantional settings in which a complete triad at C is desired but −1 is not set up to deliver one. Figure 19.17 shows paradigm cases in which S—inverted into the interior of a chord—has its leading tone "sprung" from its proper pathway and into that of another part. In the first illustration, S takes a short jump into A, and top-voice T covers the pitch that was originally targeted. In the second, parts are set up for an APAC, and S jumps—farther and more noticeably—into Q in order to provide a chordal third.[24]

The identity of C is unaffected by these changes in iC; indeed, C is sonorously strengthened by them. And yet performers assigned to a sprung line certainly experience

FIGURE 19.15 W. A. Mozart, *Vesperae de Dominica*, K. 321, "Magnificat." Chorus and continuo of mm. 8–12.

the characteristic disruption associated with a deceptive cadence, and all the more so in these two cases since the leading tone is involved—a mandatory element of the originary cadence. Both of these are schemes of arrangement to adapt an ideal a5 setting, where regular order and fully built chords can be obtained, into a4 texture. The first, springing S to A, is especially effective when cantional T is close by, as in the example. The obligation of S to resolve the leading tone is—to everyone but S—perfectly satisfied.

Evaded cadence. If outer-voice lines are sprung at C, the result is a different chord than expected, like a deceptive cadence—but different in degree rather than kind, since the

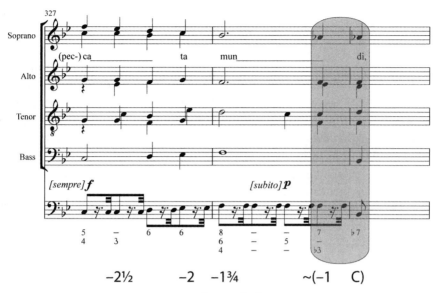

FIGURE 19.16 W. A. Mozart, Mass, K. 427, "Qui Tollis," mm. 327–29. Two choirs a4 condensed onto four staves, with continuo.

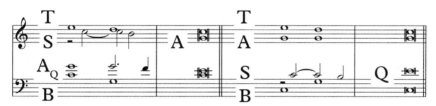

FIGURE 19.17 Sprung PACs. S in cantional cadence jumps down to the A position in m. 2, and jumps up to Q in m. 4.

expected chord root is present. This is precisely where clausulas previously entered the narrative, as imperfected cadences. But "evasion" clues us about the rhetorical technique at work—that an option to convert a cadence-in-formation into a clausula is taken unexpectedly. Two simple but suggestive contrapuntal frameworks are shown in Figure 19.18.

At (a), B springs downward to Q while regular order is maintained elsewhere.[25] The result is an inverted tonic chord overwriting the expected perfect tonic. This technique is a basis for what Janet Schmalfeldt (1992) has called the "one more time" routine, which can be deployed into elaborate cadential deferrals and multiple looped-back approaches that abound in galant music.[26] A more dramatic instance is shown at (b), where both outer voices are sprung in contrary motion.

All techniques detailed so far fall under a larger heading as schemes of continuation. A cadence is predicted and indeed has begun to form, but the process in some way falls short or fails to deliver. More music is expected at least to remedy the fault—and possibly much more than that, as when a concerto cadenza, for example, pointedly stops all lines at −1¾ and then elaborately explores the way towards −1.

The most versatile continuation scheme is "staggered arrival," in which C doesn't materialize immediately on account of suspensions, anticipations, or other figurations that execute the moves of *iC* over time rather than simultaneously.[27] In the simplest version—suspension(s) at the final chord of a piece, movement, large section, or some other case of subsequent "dead air"—the expectation for more music shrinks onto the completion of all lines and their ornaments. More widely applicable are techniques that delay the arrival of some lines while moving others into +1 and following positions. Bach's Sinfonia in C has several of these. In the score shown in Figure 19.14(a), the $A_Q//$ on the downbeat of m. 4 has two upper-voice suspensions (figured seven-five in the thoroughbassis); when these resolve on beat 2 (though with some licenses shown in the figure), B has moved on from its clausula final to a different bass note (though keeping a common chord root) and then continues to move towards the next clausula, leaving the upper voices rushing to catch up.

A stronger effect blurs through a cadence by changing the chord root before all lines have arrived. In the Sinfonia, this happens with the remarkable "bass clausula" in F major in the middle of m. 17, discussed previously. The middle voice, T, suspends a ninth over the F bass on the third beat, with A_Q moving on time in the top voice. By the time the ninth resolves in the next beat, the bass has changed from F to D, and an F-major tonic chord expected fully to materialize there gives way to a D minor chord on its way to something else instead. The rest of the below-the-line clausulas identified in Figure 19.14(b) are similarly staggered, and some have other complicating effects as well, such as the sprung S at the $A_Q//$ in m. 6, which skips downwards to A. Staggered arrival can also be applied, of course, to any cadential event—meaning that half, deceptive, and evaded cadences can be given this treatment.

Finally, *elision* is a technique of phrase joinery whereby C not only finishes correctly but also starts something new—and thus music continues, thanks to this ironic reversal of meaning from "completion" to "initiation." C becomes the zero point of the next phrase. Unlike the previous cases of continuation, an elided cadence has adequate power to close the previous musical unit and thus does not stand in need of any continuation, remedial or otherwise. Instead, the overlapping of a phrase beginning onto C emphasizes it by an instantaneous re-energizing of musical flow, an emphasis that is forward-looking and leaves the just-achieved cadence behind as the composition continues into new areas.

In sum, schemes of continuation enable additional music after a cadence is contrived to fail in some way—stopping short, ending irregularly, being late to finish, ironically undermined. Figure 19.19 summarizes those discussed so far and places them underneath the time plot of Figure 19.7, showing where and on what objects the various schemes work.

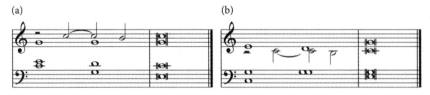

FIGURE 19.18 Evaded cadences as sprung outer voices. Both (a) and (b) spring B to A_Q; (b) also springs T to A.

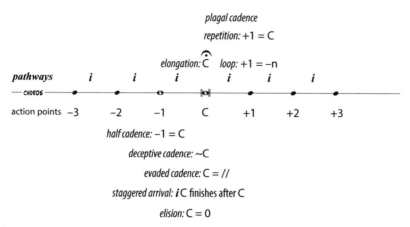

FIGURE 19.19 Cadential time plot showing schemes of continuation (below) and schemes of emphasis (above).

Above the time plot are several schemes of emphasis. Elision, in fact, could be considered one of them, since a satisfying arrival at C is accented by simultaneous take-off towards a new series of events. Accenting, highlighting, underscoring, and the like are the hallmarks of the schemes of emphasis. Unlike continuation schemes, which produce music after the cadence in order to make up for some loss of stopping power (or on override, in the case of elision), those adding emphasis produce postcadential music that dissipate kinetic energy built up over a stretch of music leading up to the cadence, extending the point of cadential resolution into a temporal area.

The simplest technique is elongation, symbolized by a fermata, in which C is markedly longer than the preceding chords, a length that may well be extended beyond what the notation suggests by a preceding *rallentando*. Elongation of this kind is, of course, most suitable for final cadences, where it signals an ultimate finality.[28]

Another signal of similar function is (multiple) repetition of the final chord, a technique that became a commonplace in galant music and was developed to extraordinary lengths by some later nineteenth-century composers. To illustrate the former, a practically random search yielded the end of the first movement of Mozart's "Linz" Symphony, excerpted in Figure 19.20 and short-scored for ease of inspection. As admirers of this movement know, the excerpt comes well after its essential structural close at m. 233 and after several succeeding cadences. It shows only the last one, at m. 285, which simply repeats the chord at C, extending its duration (like a fermata) for two more measures while figurating it as a set of hammered chords. The excerpt also provides a fine example of an evaded cadence at m. 283. S is in regular position, but B runs up to Q, and T jumps away as well.

Illustrating this kind of repetition in nineteenth-century music is not worth the space of an example. Beethoven's Ninth Symphony, for instance, ends with twenty measures of repeated C, variously figured. Tchaikovsky's 1812 Overture, op. 49, for another, has thirteen measures of repetition. The last movement of Bruckner's Fourth Symphony has only nine measures, but they take up about thirty seconds at tempo.

The "loop" emphasizes the cadence by rearticulating it. Minimally it goes back to −1 and repeats the mandatory progression, resulting in another V–I progression. Multiple

FIGURE 19.20 W. A. Mozart, Symphony no. 36 in C major, K.425, I, mm. 281–287. Condensed score.

loops of this kind (+1 = −1) are perhaps even more common than simple repetition in galant music. In earlier music, the loop may start at some greater remove. Figure 19.21 shows a typical case of Corelli's practice, in which an approach to a cantional *cadenza doppia* in m. 20 is repeated more softly, with +1 looping back to −3.[29]

Loops may not involve literal repetition, as is the case here, but instead use different chords and arrangements when reapproaching, as is seen in the conclusion of a Telemann sonata, shown in Figure 19.22, a relatively lengthy excerpt that can also serve summarily to illustrate various rhetorical techniques discussed so far in combination.

Five cadential modules are identified, terminating in mm. 35, 38, 39, 40, and 41. All but the last receive schematic treatment, with evasion the leading technique, often accompanied by a sprung top line. The passage begins with sprung clausulas that set the C-minor key. After a final S//T_Q in m. 33, a rising bass sends notification of an upcoming cadence, the approach to which can be identified as early as −6. In m. 35 the cadence is evaded, T is sprung upwards, and the approach re-initiated from −6. The chord at action point −3 is extended in such a way that −1 shows up unambiguously on the downbeat of m. 38, out of phase with its regular place in a weak beat. A trill on the top-voice figure all but commands C to appear on the second, weak beat. A "clausula option" is taken so C is A_Q//S, and then normal metric position is subtly restored on the third beat with S//A_Q, staggered in order to take some perfection off the goal chord. One last evasion and reapproach from −6 occurs in m. 39, with a satisfactory cantional PAC finally occurring in the middle of the next measure. For emphasis, a loop back to −4 provides space to absorb the impact of the previous evasions and allows the next and final C to receive a regular setting, higher in precedence.

FIGURE 19.21 Arcangelo Corelli, Chamber Sonata, op. 4, no. 2, Allemanda, mm. 18–22, showing cadential loop in m. 21.

Plagal Cadence. Yet higher still in precedence is a technique of emphasis that is "oddly controversial" despite being a well-known textbook verity (Mutch 2015a, 69). The plagal cadence is not a routine choice because its perfection dares to invoke divine sanction, and few occasions are appropriate for this. Being the conventional setting for "Amen," its association with sacred music is so strong that the influential music theorist A. B. Marx (1846, 299) called it the "church cadence" [*Kirchenschluß*], a term that persists in German discourse to this day.[30] In this way, it is a declaration of ultimate conclusion, ne plus ultra. It is therefore eminently suited to close strophic forms, like hymns. More significantly, it can also be a topic that references spirituality, transcendence, and similar sites of religious awe (Amon 2005, 100). This is certainly the meaning of its deployment in secular genres of the nineteenth century by composers of as different aesthetics and techniques as Wagner (e.g., the endings of *Tristan* and *Parsifal*) and Brahms (e.g., the endings of the second movements of the First and Third Symphonies).[31]

The plagal cadence cannot be satisfactorily explained contrapuntally, as might be hoped, as a kind of retrogression of the authentic cadence from C to −1. This move entails reversing the idea of imperfect-to-perfect motion that underwrites the operations of cadence to begin with, which brings hard questions in its wake. Instead, the plagal cadence can be set up as the harmonic and contrapuntal dual of the authentic, illustrated in Figure 19.23 in the style of a5 open-score arrangements encountered in previous examples.[32]

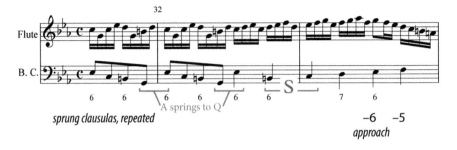

FIGURE 19.22 G. P. Telemann, *Sonata metodica* (1732) TWV41:c3, III, analysis of cadential rhetoric.

In place of the major dominant chord at −1, the plagal employs a minor subdominant chord—dualizing both mode and function. S and B each preserve their characteristic motions—semitone and fifth leap, respectively—though their directions are reversed. The pathways associated with A and T are exchanged, so that T maintains a common tone while A moves stepwise. The Q pathways into the final chordal third are dualized as well, with the superior perfection of the major triad compared to the minor permitting a major (Picardy) third at C.

As always with dualism, versions of the derived entity—in this case, the paths and lines of the plagal cadence—need to show up in literature if analytic value is to be cashed out. A particularly clear example—thanks to ten-part texture—is offered in Figure 19.24, the conclusion of a motet, "Hodie Christus Natus est," by Giovanni Gabrieli.[33]

The passage begins after a regular-setting PAC on an A-major chord, which places S on the pitch A5. As the minor subdominant chord is elaborated in the following measures, the voices move into position to discharge in regular plagal order, with pitches poised on every path. Although the thick texture means extensive pitch doubling and crossing, the layout generally conforms to regular arrangement: S and B are at the extremes, T is over B, A_Q is over T, and A is over T_Q. A few details deserve note. The second tenor, on F3 in the penultimate measure and thus doubling S, has to be sprung to A3 to avoid parallel octaves with regular S. A particularly masterful touch is the staggered arrival for baritone 2, who steps rather than springs from T up to A.

One of the pertinent features of the plagal cadence is that it uses an immediately preceding authentic cadence to take off most effectively, as in the Gabrieli excerpt. Outside of Phrygian-mode harmonizations—an increasingly rarefied need during the period covered in this study—a plagal cadence generally did not close pieces on its own until nineteenth-century aesthetics made increasing room for them in secular musical genres.[34] The normal dependence of the plagal upon the authentic is what sanctions the discussion of it here as a rhetorical scheme that emphasizes finality and perfection. Compared with other schemes, the plagal cadence involves new, dualized counterpoint and harmony, and thus requires time and space for lines at authentic C to slot into those needed for plagal C.

FIGURE 19.23 Plagal pathways derived as contrapuntal duals of the authentic.

FIGURE 19.24 Giovanni Gabrieli, "Hodie Christus natus est," C. 40 (1597), plagal cadence at conclusion. Two choirs (SSATB and ATBBB) have been interleaved by register in a single-system score. Original choirs 1 or 2 indicated.

A hypothetical a5 arrangement of the complete, four-stage scheme is shown in Figure 19.25.

The contrapuntal outlines of many codas, both short and lengthy, are easily discerned here, and even more can be brought into view if invertible counterpoint brings other lines to the top—T_Q to expose the ascending passing tone, for example, or T for a cantional pedal point, as in a clichéd yet always effective chromatic plagal tag shown in Figure 19.26.

Because of the special conventions around the plagal cadence, it does not regularly exhibit the same kind of clausula derivatives as the authentic. As in the previous example, the pedal point in the lowest part—putting the subdominant into six-four position—may have the strongest claim for being recognized as a plagal tenor clausula, but going beyond that isn't yet warranted by any obvious analytic need.

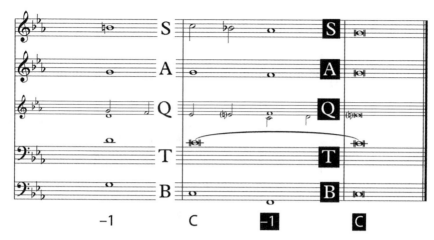

FIGURE 19.25 Plagal cadence fused onto a preceding authentic cadence.

FIGURE 19.26 Chromatic plagal "tag" a5, following cantional PAC.

CONTEMPORARY DEVELOPMENTS

The contrapuntal basis developed so far, along with its suite of rhetorical transformations, supports most conventional closing moves in Western art music up through the early part of the nineteenth century. As the century went on, convention was in danger of being critically reassessed as cliché, and the authentic cadence came under pressure to freshen its sound while maintaining contact with traditional practice. One noteworthy effect—associated with Chopin's style but by no means limited to him—deforms the standard approach by altering the order of part movement through the pathways. Figure 19.27 shows the basics, with detailed action point information; (a) shows the well-established eighteenth-century cantional norm and (b) the nineteenth-century "Chopin style" transformation.

The most prominent change from earlier to later is the delayed descent of T to tonic, which happens only after A_Q moves into its passing seventh. Thus, at −1¼ two harmonic sevenths dissonate noticeably: the normal minor seventh from bass G to passing F, and the deformational major seventh from F to delayed E.[35] This so-called dominant thirteenth resulting from the combination of the two sevenths was durable enough to be used even into the last decade of the century, as the excerpt from Mahler's Symphony no. 2 shown in Figure 19.28 illustrates at action points −1¼.

The cadential thirteenth chord is a small but telling piece of evidence for a general increase in nontonic dissonance throughout the nineteenth century. In

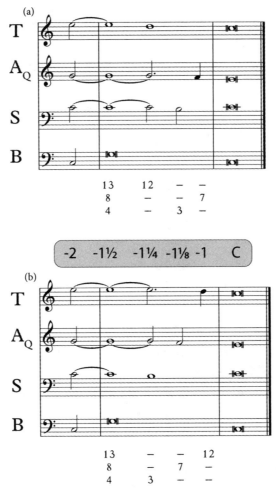

FIGURE 19.27 Two PACs in cantional settings. (a) normal order of part movement in eighteenth century (grand cadence); (b) possible order in nineteenth century ("Chopin style").

cadential situations, other signs of this increase include freely mixing authentic and plagal pathways to create functionally mixed chords at −1, one example of which is illustrated in Figure 19.29.[36]

In general over the course of the century, as harmonic variety and richness increased (and periodicity as a formal norm decreased), contrapuntal cadential approaches became harder to detect before −1. This can be quickly apprehended in the later examples collected in Casella and Rubbra (1964), in which cadences can come on very suddenly. One is reproduced in Figure 19.30, from about halfway through the first movement of Florent Schmitt's estimable Piano Quintet of 1908. Although −1 is a traditional dominant seventh (in a regular setting, to boot), it is completely unpredicated by the preceding harmonic activity, with −2 being a nontraditional passing verticality and the chords before giving no hint about an upcoming cadence in G♭.[37]

A similar kind of surprise cadence from later in the twentieth century is found in the final measures of Hindemith's Sonata no. 3 for organ, excerpted in Figure 19.31.

FIGURE 19.28 Gustav Mahler, Symphony no. 2, V, Rehearsal 48–4; reduction.

FIGURE 19.29 Functionally mixed cadence.

A dominant pedal point prolongs proceedings towards −1 on the downbeat of m. 61. A modified plagal cadence then takes over from −3 moving through conjunct plagal pathways toward the Neapolitan sixth (= *Leittonwechsel* of the minor subdominant), located at −1, producing nontraditional, pentatonically inflected passing sonorities on the way.

By the late nineteenth century, the increased importance of secondary parameters in shaping musical process and structure permitted new forms of articulation that did not rely on the traditional cadence and its clausula derivatives. Leonard B. Meyer was loath to admit that structural closure could be effected by such means, since "music based on them can cease, or end, but cannot *close*," adding in a footnote that "termination created by secondary parameters will be referred to as *cessation* to distinguish it from closure."[38] Such effects can be heard in Debussy's music and in that of other impressionists. Similarly, the "emancipation of the dissonance" made any distinctions nugatory between a priori imperfect and perfect sonorities, necessitating innovative contextual forms of articulation and ending. Casella and Rubbra's collection documents these developments quite clearly. Some theorists could want to extend the franchise of cadence to them, but I am reluctant to do so. Instead, I aver that cadence was a shared convention of many musical styles—born from counterpoint, schematized in harmony, and deployed according to rhetorical need. Developed in the Middle Ages from venerable ideas about perfection, it proved to be extraordinarily durable yet possessed remarkable transformational elasticity. It is perhaps the longest-lived convention of Western musical composition, but it is not a transcendent category. It is finite, and its pathways of development do, in the end, find their end.

FIGURE 19.30 Florent Schmitt, Piano Quintet, op. 51, i, condensed. (Casella and Rubbra 1964, ex. LXVIII, extended by one and a half measures).

FIGURE 19.31 Paul Hindemith, Organ Sonata iii, no. 3, final cadence.

NOTES

1. Valuable guidance for this effort was provided in Moll (1998), Cohen (2001), Bain (2003), Taruskin (2005, vol. 1), Schwind (2009), Neuwirth and Bergé (2015), Mutch (2015b), and Zayaruznaya (2018, ch. 2), with Schenker (1987) acting as a consultant. For this chapter, conversations with James Hepokoski, William Caplin, and Liam Hynes were influential, as were the perceptive questions of many undergraduate counterpoint students.

2. The (extravagant) range of possible moves to perfect consonances in early contrapuntal theory is shown in Coussemaker (1931, 3:72–73). Figure 19.2 is adapted from illustration 72.1.

3. See Mutch (2015b, ch. 2), for further background on the theoretical development of cadence for polyphonic textures.

4. Schubert (2018) is an important contribution in this direction, imaginatively related to Thomas Campion's counterpoint treatise of 1613.

5. In music with regularized, deep metric hierarchies, cadential anticipation can be triggered via hypermeter and thus rises in direct proportion to phrase length, starting from chord +1 after the previous cadence.

6. The opportunities for statistical analysis are abundantly clear yet not sufficiently developed to be incorporated in this chapter.

7. Eberlein and Fricke (1992, 70–71) draw a similar picture, but at a lower level of generality and theoretical detail.

8. The way toward complex cadential elaborations, such as the *cadenza doppia* of the partimentists (Menke 2011), should be clear from this point.

9. Arnold (1965, 1:12–14) details the differences between Viadona and Werckmeister. Mutch (2015b, 142–143) notes that the basis for this move can be traced to the "Cologne school" theorists of the sixteenth century. Werckmeister's illustration and its usefulness in analyzing Bach's music (especially fugal subjects) are discussed in Deppert (1993, 73ff.). See also Byros (2015, ex. 4).

10. Mutch (2015b, 167) points out that Werckmeister inherited this style of vocabulary, citing Johann Andreas Herbst (*Musica Poetica*, 1643) and Conrad Matthaei (*Kurtzer Bericht*, 1658).

11. This is just one way to compose the effect. That is, giving singers on a particular part (in this case, the soprano) moves that properly belong to another (in this case, the alto). It can also be done with voice crossing, in which case the singers keep their moves but in another part's register, taking over its space.

12. Cantional is a term originally associated with sixteenth-century Lutheran hymn settings, which have the tune in the top voice instead of the (interior) tenor.

13. The observation that Schenker's *Ursatz* is thoroughly cantional is pertinent in this connection. The disqualification of regular-setting upper-voice structures may be related to his rejection of other "outmoded" concepts like the "church modes," but this is entirely conjectural. But every Schenkerian analyst has encountered the unfolding of $\hat{2}$ to $\hat{7}$ at the cadence (also in reverse, though less often), a move that helpfully enlists the discharge vectors of both the tenor and soprano lines to tighten the close.

14. Confusingly, clausula can also refer to the earliest, medieval efforts at note-against-note strict counterpoint, including specific procedures/genres such as the substitute clausula.

15. Gjerdingen (2007, 490–491n21) points out that this seemingly archaic phrase is perhaps of nineteenth-century vintage.

16. See, for example, Bach (1949, 228–229).

17. This abbreviation is best rendered in speech as "TS clausula."

18. Gjerdingen's Example 3.1 shows how Prinner himself transformed a T//S clausula into the eponymous arrangement by invertible counterpoint.

19. The analytic interests here, developed independently, are entirely consonant with those propounded at greater length and detail in Byros (2015).

20. Rothstein (1991) developed the basis for this move and demonstrated its analytic potential.

21. See, for example, the extraordinary chord progression that marks the conclusion of an uninterrupted span, mm. 1–45, in Thomas Tallis's "Dum transisset sabbatum." A simplistic analysis could label it a deceptive cadence with a Picardy third, but the effect is rather more ineffable than that description suggests. A more conventional-sounding half cadence marks the conclusion of the following, shorter section, mm. 45–58. The final cadence of the piece sounds almost equally inconclusive, though an obscured plagal basis can be uncovered analytically. Burns (1994, 47–50) discusses sixteenth-century theories about such "irregular endings."

22. Burstein (2015), following Burns (1994), cites Johann Andreas Herbst (*Musicae Poëtica*, 1643) for first illustrating an irregular ending with a half cadence constructed as an incomplete authentic cadence. (See Burns 1994, 51, ex. 3.)

23. This suggestion agrees with the general program of Neuwirth (2015).

24. J. S. Bach's chorale settings provide multiple instances of both treatments, with the first being more common. For examples of the second, see no. 3 (Ach Gott, vom Himmel sieh' darein) at m. 4, and no. 179 (Wachet auf, ruft uns die Stimme) at m. 5.

25. It's common for B to follow the example of A_Q and fill the space with a passing tone.

26. Her examples 1c and 7a (both from Mozart's music) clearly illustrate this technique.

27. The presence or absence of suspensions in cadences gave rise early on to a variety of descriptors, helpfully summarized in Neuwirth (2015, 126). However, these are concerned only with the situation at −1, not at C, which is where the suspension scheme is applied in the current development.

28. A related scheme of understatement is occasionally deployed for effect: the final chord is remarkably and perhaps even uncomfortably short—an ironic inversion of the norm. J. S. Bach's music has a number of examples in which final chords last only an eighth note: the E-minor fugue from WTC 1, BWV 855.2; B-minor organ prelude, BWV 544.1.

29. The particular form of this *cadenza doppia* is found in Menke (2011, ex. 5, col. 3, row j).

30. See also Louis and Thuille (1913, 12), and Amon (2005, 220). On other authors' views of the association of the plagal cadence with church music, see Mutch (2015a, 69).

31. See Meyer (1989, 285–291) for more examples and discussion of nineteenth-century usage. Meyer notes that the plagal cadence "is not a substitute for strong syntactic closure but a

sign *confirming* prior closure" (286). One might turn the terms around and claim that a plagal cadence performs stronger syntactic closure after the closure proposed by a prior authentic cadence.

32. The following presentation derives from and develops ideas in Harrison (1994, 27–34). Eberlein and Fricke (1992, 63) also informally propose the plagal as the dual of the authentic.

33. The plagal cadence here sets the word "Alleluia," which preceding music had also set. Even so, the association of the plagal cadence with "Amen" is so strong—and executed normally in many of Gabrieli's other works—that it is easily legible underneath the festive "Alleluia." A perhaps easy-to-recall example of the same effect is the conclusion of Handel's "Hallelujah Chorus" from *Messiah*.

34. Mutch (2015a) expertly analyzes a mid-eighteenth-century attempt to theorize the plagal cadence, emphasizing its links to Phrygian modality. Burns (1995, 43–50) discusses in detail plagal effects in Bach's chorales. Meyer's views on nineteenth-century plagal cadences have already been cited in n. 31 above.

35. See Narmour (1991, 98–111) for discussion and background on Chopin's use of this sonority, though not necessarily in cadential settings. Liszt, among others, favored it; see, for example, *Sonetto 123 del Petrarca*, m. 74.

36. This particular formation is disassembled and analyzed in Harrison (1994, 64–68), illustrated with examples from Richard Strauss and Max Reger. Unlike the dominant thirteenth, which is a particularly nineteenth-century innovation, functionally mixed cadences can be found throughout the common-practice era. See, for example, the conclusion of J. S. Bach's E-major Prelude from WTC 1.

37. The surprise effect of this cadence contrasts with the much more traditional cadential effect at Rehearsal 9, the seam between the slow introduction and the main body of the movement.

38. Meyer (1989, 209–209n184).

WORKS CITED

Amon, Reinhard. 2005. *Lexikon der Harmonielehre: Nachschlagewerk zur durmolltonalen Harmonik mit Analysechiffren für Funktionen, Stufen und Jazz-Akkorde*. Vienna: Doblinger.

Arnold, F. T. 1965. *The Art of Accompaniment from a Thorough-bass, as Practised in the XVIIth & XVIIIth Centuries*. 2 vols. New York: Dover Publications.

Bach, Carl Ph. E. 1949. *Essay on the True Art of Playing Keyboard Instruments* [1762]. Translated and edited by William J. Mitchell. New York: W. W. Norton.

Bain, Jennifer. 2003. "Theorizing the Cadence in the Music of Machaut." *Journal of Music Theory* 47: 325–362.

Burns, Lori. 1994. "Modal Identity and Irregular Endings in Two Chorale Harmonizations by J. S. Bach." *Journal of Music Theory* 38: 43–77.

Burns, Lori. 1995. *Bach's Modal Chorales*. Stuyvesant, NY: Pendragon Press.

Burstein, L. Poundie. 2014. "The Half Cadence and Other Such Slippery Events." *Music Theory Spectrum* 36: 203–227.

Burstein, L. Poundie. 2015. "The Half Cadence and Related Analytic Fictions." In *What Is a Cadence? Theoretical and Analytical Perspectives on Cadences in the Classical Repertoire*, edited by Markus Neuwirth and Pieter Bergé, 86–116. Leuven: Leuven University Press.

Byros, Vasili. 2015. "Prelude on a Partimento: Invention in the Compositional Pedagogy of the German States in the Time of J. S. Bach." *Music Theory Online* 21, no. 3. http://www.mtosmt. org/issues/mto.15.21.3/mto.15.21.3.byros.html.

Caplin, William E. 2004. "The Classical Cadence: Conceptions and Misconceptions." *Journal of the American Musicological Society* 57: 51–118.

Casella, Alfredo, and Edmund Rubbra. 1964. *The Evolution of Music Throughout the History of the Perfect Cadence* [1924]. 2nd edition. London: J. & W. Chester.

Cohen, David E. 2001. "'The Imperfect Seeks Its Perfection': Harmonic Progression, Directed Motion, and Aristotelian Physics." *Music Theory Spectrum* 23: 139–169.

Coussemaker, Charles Edmond Henri de. 1931. *Scriptorum de musica medii aevi: Novam seriem a Gerbertina alteram collegit nunque primum edidit E. de Coussemaker.* 4 vols. Milan: Bollettino bibliografica musicale.

Deppert, Heinrich. 1993. *Kadenz und Klausel in der Musik von J.S. Bach: Studien zu Harmonie und Tonart.* Tutzing: H. Schneider.

Eberlein, Roland, and Jobst Peter Fricke. 1992. *Kadenzwahrnehmung und Kadenzgeschichte: Ein Beitrag zu einer Grammatik der Musik.* Frankfurt am Main: Peter Lang.

Gjerdingen, Robert O. 2007. *Music in the Galant Style.* New York: Oxford University Press.

Harrison, Daniel. 1994. *Harmonic Function in Chromatic Music: A Renewed Dualist Theory and an Account of Its Precedents.* Chicago: University of Chicago Press.

Havergal, W. H. 1854. *A History of the Old Hundredth Psalm Tune: With Specimens.* New York: Mason Bros.

Louis, Rudolf, and Ludwig Thuille. 1913. *Harmonielehre.* 4th edition. Stuttgart: Carl Grüninger.

Marx, Adolf Bernhard. 1846. *Die Lehre von der musikalischen Komposition, praktisch theoretisch.* 3rd edition. Leipzig: Breitkopf & Härtel.

Menke, Johannes. 2011. "Die Familie der Cadenza Doppia." *Zeitschrift der Gesellschaft für Musiktheorie* 8: 389–405.

Meyer, Leonard B. 1989. *Style and Music: Theory, History, and Ideology.* Philadelphia: University of Pennsylvania Press.

Moll, Kevin N. 1998. "Voice Function, Sonority, and Contrapuntal Procedure in Late Medieval Polyphony." *Current Musicology* 64: 26–72.

Mutch, Caleb. 2015a. "Blainville's New Mode, or How the Plagal Cadence Came to Be 'Plagal.'" *Eighteenth-Century Music* 12: 69–90.

Mutch, Caleb. 2015b. "Studies in the History of the Cadence." PhD diss., Columbia University.

Narmour, Eugene. 1991. "Melodic Structuring of Harmonic Dissonance: A Method for Analyzing Chopin's Contribution to the Development of Harmony." In *Chopin Studies*, edited by Jim Samson, 77–114. Cambridge: Cambridge University Press.

Neuwirth, Markus. 2015. "*Fuggir la Cadenza*, or the Art of Avoiding Cadential Closure." In *What Is a Cadence? Theoretical and Analytical Perspectives on Cadences in the Classical Repertoire*, edited by Markus Neuwirth and Pieter Bergé, 117–155. Leuven: Leuven University Press.

Neuwirth, Markus, and Pieter Bergé. 2015. *What Is a Cadence? Theoretical and Analytical Perspectives on Cadences in the Classical Repertoire.* Leuven: Leuven University Press.

Rameau, Jean-Philippe. 1971. *Treatise on Harmony* [1722]. Translated by Philip Gossett. New York: Dover Publications.

Rothstein, William. 1991. "On Implied Tones." *Music Analysis* 10: 289–328.

Schenker, Heinrich. 1987. *Counterpoint.* Translated by John Rothgeb and Jürgen Thym. 2 vols. New York: Schirmer Books.

Schmalfeldt, Janet. 1992. "Cadential Processes: The Evaded Cadence and the 'One More Time' Technique." *Journal of Musicological Research* 12: 1–52.

Schubert, Peter N. 2018. "Thomas Campion's 'Chordal Counterpoint' and Tallis's Famous Forty-Part Motet." *Music Theory Online* 24, no. 1. http://mtosmt.org/issues/mto.18.24.1/mto.18.24.1.schubert.html

Schwind, Elisabeth. 2009. *Kadenz und Kontrapunkt: Zur Kompositionslehre der klassischen Vokalpolyphonie.* Hildesheim: Olms.

Taruskin, Richard. 2005. *The Oxford History of Western Music.* 6 vols. New York: Oxford University Press.

Werckmeister, Andreas. 2013. *Harmonologia Musica* [1702]. Translated and annotated by Casey Mongoven as *Andreas Werckmeister's Cribrum Musicum (1700) and Harmonologia Musica (1702): The Original German Treatises with Parallel, Annotated English Translations.* New York: Pendragon Press.

Zayaruznaya, Anna. 2018. *Upper-voice Structures and Compositional Process in the Ars Nova Motet.* Royal Musical Association Monographs, no. 32. London and New York: Routledge.

....

CHAPTER 20

SEQUENCE

....

NAOMI WALTHAM-SMITH

THE SEQUENCE BETWEEN IDENTITY
AND DIFFERENCE

....

A sequence is a bipolar machine for transforming identity into difference and difference into identity. At first blush, this seems a somewhat baffling, and perhaps unnec-
essarily complicated, way to describe a common harmonic-melodic phenomenon
of tonal music. An example from Schubert's *Gretchen am Spinnrade* (Figure 20.1(a))
indicates why it might be useful. A traditional definition would focus on two constitutive moments of the sequence: (1) a fragment of musical material that is to be repeated at
different pitch levels and (2) a pitch-based schema that determines the relationship between successive statements of the material. The material to be repeated is readily identifiable as a rising, stepwise dyad, embellished with an upper neighbor to the second
note, harmonized by an applied dominant seventh resolving to the root-position triad
it tonicizes. The schema dictating the trajectory of transposition is less easy to pinpoint,
because the quality of the intervals within and between each melodic statement varies
so as to adapt to the diatonic context. In this way, intervallic differences are needed to
achieve a diatonic sameness, at least melodically. Preserving identity between the melodic material repeated, however, precipitates a discrepancy between the melodic and
harmonic dimensions. The rising melodic tetrachord A–B♭–C–D, which is entirely diatonic in F major, could have been harmonized by exclusively diatonic focal harmonies
with A minor supporting the C, but this would have entailed the insertion of a melodic
chromatic passing note B♮ to be harmonized by the applied dominant. Schubert's solution is to harmonize the melodic C with the nondiatonic A♭ major, thus privileging
melodic over harmonic diatonicism, while allowing the harmonic dimension to determine the irregular projection with its mixture of half and whole steps together with the
modal inflection of the second step (see the reduction in Figure 20.1(b)). This passage

FIGURE 20.1 (a) Schubert, *Gretchen am Spinnrade*, mm. 54–60. (b) Reduction of same.

exemplifies the way in which sequences commonly contend with negotiating between identity and difference across various parameters and structural levels.

There are, of course, other phenomena in tonal music taking place at various structural levels, from local detail to global form, which could be said to convert identity into difference or difference into identity. For the most part, however, these various processes have as their primary task the *subordination* of one to the other, thereby privileging *either* identity *or* difference. The hallmark of the sequence, by comparison, is that it is traversed by a double movement such that it produces *both* identity *and* difference at one and the same time and holds them in tension. That is not to say that particular uses of this musical process in the context of specific pieces do not tend toward one pole or the other (which they almost always do). Rather, not only can the trace of the countermovement not be entirely eliminated, but this double traversal is constitutive of the sequence: the sequence depends for its musical effect upon two simultaneous processes of transformation that cut across one another. As this essay explores, the play of identity

and difference manifests itself in a number of dimensions: as a tension rhetorically between parataxis and hypotaxis and stylistically between Baroque and Classical, and as a
function of temporality, between diachrony and synchrony. Finally, as the last section of
this essay demonstrates, it is both *different* from, even *disruptive* of, other harmonic, melodic, and formal principles in tonal music and a *prototype* for the operation of tonality
more widely.

In this way, my description of the sequence seeks to capture not only its technical
internal workings, but also the position it occupies within theories of tonality: the sequence tends both toward coinciding with the definition of tonality (most obviously in
the theory of Jean-Philippe Rameau, for example) and toward diverging from normative patterns of tonality's functioning, even to the point of enjoying an exceptional status
(as in the theories of François-Joseph Fétis and Hugo Riemann). This interplay of identity and difference within tonal theories can be seen to replicate itself at a higher level
if one surveys the body of theoretical discourse on this topic from the seventeenth to
twentieth centuries. One of the difficulties in providing a definition of the sequence is
the sheer proliferation of terminologies and theoretical models generated by thinking
about this seemingly straightforward little device, and with it the risk that the definition will be so diluted in order to cover all these positions that it would extend to any
vi–ii–V–I progression. For this reason, the sequence provides a fruitful vantage point
from which to grasp the differentiation of various theoretical traditions, from which to
divide figured-bass from fundamental bass models, French from German schools, melodic from harmonic conceptions.[1]

The sequence provides an exemplary lens, for instance, through which to highlight a
particular fracture in the history of theory: in a certain strand of nineteenth-century harmonic thought, the idea that figured-bass theories do not adequately acknowledge the
hierarchical nature of relationships within the tonal system gains currency. By leveling
out the differences between the scale degrees or harmonic functions upon which the hierarchy of the tonal system is constructed, the sequence effects a temporary suspension
of this system. Fétis describes, for example, how "the mind, absorbed in the contemplation of the progressive series, momentarily loses the feeling of tonality and regains it
only at the final cadence, where the normal order is reestablished" (2008, 27). Riemann
adopts much of this line of thinking, crediting Fétis with realizing that the sequence is
an essentially melodic formation that consists in the suspension of harmonic movement
throughout its duration (1896, 122). Riemann, though, effectively misrepresents Fétis
in attempting to assimilate Fétis's assessment of the sequence to his own functional-
harmonic perspective. Riemann's theory eschews any of Fétis's arguments about the
relative instability of the diatonic scale and instead consolidates chords into three primary perceptual categories of tonic, dominant, and subdominant. Unlike Rameau, who
sees the diatonic sequence as paradigmatic for tonality as a whole insofar as it projects
the cadential movement from dominant to tonic across a descending-fifth progression,
Riemann denies the sequence the status of harmonic prototype because the D–T relation of the model is not strictly replicated at each step. Riemann in fact requires a more
substantial T–S–D–T to express tonality fully.

Nothwithstanding these divergences, it is possible to discern the emergence of a common thread among these various theoretical traditions: the multiple discussions of the sequence converge upon a single anxiety that sequences are too static, too monotonous; in short, they present too much of the *same*. Hence the advice found in modern and historical texts to limit the number of repetitions, often to no more than the optimal three. Heinrich Christian Koch's dismissal of the melodic sequence is typical of concerns in Germany during the later eighteenth century: he claims that these types of transposition of a phrase segment are "obsolete" and "are to be avoided … unless they appear in a new form" (1983, 45). Koch's worry that the sequence exhibits insufficient innovation is echoed by what Jairo Moreno describes as "an oddly assorted, transhistoric jury loudly proclaiming the lackluster qualities of sequential repetition in a variety of contexts" (2000, 127–28). Moreno's jury includes figures as diverse as Beethoven, Wagner, Charles Burney, Heinrich Schenker, Theodor W. Adorno, and Richard Taruskin. Particular condemnation is reserved for what came to be known as *rosalia* after the Italian popular song "Rosalia, mia cara" (see Figure 20.2). Christian Friedrich Daniel Schubart, for `example, disparages these stepwise rising melodic sequences for sounding out-of-date by the late eighteenth century; they are best suited to the incessant repetitions of *Trinklieder* in the beer halls or to empty virtuosic displays, provided that the musician's hands are on display so that the dizzying visual display of the approach toward the end of the fingerboard might compensate for the boredom induced by the sonic repetition (1812, 1:220–26). Burney (1775, 2:329) had lamented the "tediousness" of the *rosalia* and, in words penned by Adorno, Thomas Mann's *Doktor Faustus* condemns them as "cheap" (Mann 1948, 60). Beethoven was even said to have poked fun at the "*Schusterfleck*" or cobbler's patch in the theme he later used in the Diabelli Variations (see Figure 20.3; Anton Schindler reports Beethoven's words in Forbes 1957, 856n). In other words, theoretical discourse moves toward identity precisely in its anxiety about the sequence's tendency toward identity.

As if to underscore the point that the sequence—in both its internal workings and its theoretical elaboration—is always marked by a double movement of identity toward difference and difference toward identity, there is, as Moreno (2000) notes, an important exception to this otherwise univocal condemnation. Chief among the dissenting minority are Adolf Bernhard Marx and Anton Reicha, whose theories detach the sequence from notions of monotony and stasis by associating sequential repetition with a dynamic process of generating melodic content. As Moreno argues, this change in view can be situated within the context of a broader shift from the rhetoric-inspired *Satzlehre* of the later eighteenth century to the *Melodielehre* of the early nineteenth century; while the former considers how preformed and self-contained melodic units are repeated and added in a block-like fashion to preexisting phrases for the purposes of expansion, the

FIGURE 20.2 *"Rosalia, mia cara."*

FIGURE 20.3 Beethoven, Theme from Diabelli Variations for Piano in C major op. 120, mm. 1–32.

latter thinks of these melodic units themselves as both capable of being decomposed into smaller components and also containing an intrinsic demand for transformation and expansion through repetition. From the perspective of *Satzlehre*, musical material is subjected to an external process of repetition, while for *Melodielehre* the material itself necessitates the repetition and thereby generates further melodic content. This emphasis on a mutable dynamic process as opposed to the subsequent spatial layout of preexisting blocks firmly inserts the sequence into the temporal realm. In turn it becomes possible, as discussed in the third part of this chapter, to think of the sequence as a means for producing different representations of time.

Types of Sequence

Perhaps the strongest argument, however, against the notion that the sequence is a means of producing identity and boredom is the fact that as a category, the sequence resists reduction to a single, self-identical musical phenomenon. Instead, any attempt to pin down the sequence with a narrow definition is met by a wealth of self-differentiation. Examining these differences provides a summary of the various issues and debates in the history of music theory's engagement with the sequence. These differences fall on either side of the binary division inherent within the standard definition of the sequence, between the material to be repeated and the logic governing the trajectory of its repetition. One immediate source of differentiation in the category of the sequence lies in the variety of musical materials and combinations of materials that may be subject to sequential repetition. This has led to a lack of terminological consistency in describing the primary material of a sequence. In his recent theory of formal functions in the classical style, William Caplin (1998, 77) uses the term "model-sequence," which no doubt derives from Reicha's terminology, but Moreno (1996) prefers the more processual implications that come with "repetend." More frequent is the term "pattern" (e.g., Bass 1996; Harrison 2003; Aldwell and Schachter 2010), although the potential difficulty here is that pattern can connote not only a model designed for imitation, but also a regular design itself formed through repetition.

This terminological inconsistency reflects the difficulty in defining what type of material is capable of being repeated sequentially. The use of the word "pattern" suggests that the primary unit of material itself has a recognizable form of its own; indeed, some theorists exclude the possibility of a sequence where the repeated component has fewer than two states, so that there is always an internal relation within the unit to be repeated (two different inversions or a triad and a seventh chord would be admissible, but not a chain of $^6_3$ chords, for example).[2] This makes sense if the unit of repetition is considered in terms of vertical simultaneities, because the transposed repetition of a single chord requires careful revoicing to avoid excessive parallel motion, if not actually parallel fifths or octaves. Moreno is content to consider a series of $^6_3$ simultaneities as a sequence mainly because it allows him to forge connections between different theorizations of scale-degree steps, but notes that the requirements of good voice-leading often yield pairs of voice-leading patterns in any case (Moreno 1996, 41). One such example is the embellishment of the successive $^6_3$ chords with local suspensions (see Figure 20.4). The term "pattern" thus foregrounds the idea that a sequence consists of the repetition of a particular contrapuntal fragment; this notion has its roots in the figured-bass tradition, for which the sequence is the repetition of an intervallic progression above the bass, and is taken up in more recent Schenkerian theorizations with the notion of a linear intervallic pattern (Forte and Gilbert 1982, 83). An alternative thread of theoretical discourse sees a melodic or motivic fragment as the object of sequential repetition.

Daniel Harrison (2003), for instance, conceives of the *rosalia* as a primarily melodic procedure of transposition either up or down a step, but his interest in this process lies not simply in the fact that it presents a counterpoint to harmonic or intervallic sequences, but, more significantly, in the way in which the appropriation of this device enables him to trace the fusion of melodic and intervallic elements in the practice of Arcangelo Corelli, his contemporaries, and his descendants. Specifically, Corelli's

FIGURE 20.4 Mozart, Piano Sonata in G, K. 283, i, mm. 112–18.

sequences exploit a kinship between serial transpositions of thematic patterns and the chains of consonant syncopes and dissonant suspensions in fourth-species counterpoint. Conversely, the plurality of basic materials capable of being subjected to sequential repetition also opens up the possibility of disconnecting melodic, harmonic, and intervallic components such that only one is subject to strict transposition, while others are reworked more freely. Figure 20.5 shows a purely melodic sequence in which the harmony does not follow the same transpositional scheme as the melody.

This separation of melodic from harmonic or intervallic material is just one of the ways in which the sequence may escape uniformity in its repetition phase. Besides the possibility of subjecting different components of the original material to different processes, there is considerable diversity of theoretical opinion on what kind of musical object or principle may govern these trajectories of repetition. Variously described as a "projection" (Bass 1996, 266) or a "vector" by modern theorists (Harrison 2003, 226), the tradition largely agrees that the logic of repetition is pitch based. It is far from clear, however, that this will always be conceived primarily as a transpositional schema (rising or falling by a certain interval with each restatement). In many cases, sequential repetition is determined not by replicating a fixed interval of transposition, but by motion through scale-degree steps. Other theoretical models dispense with the requirement for a linear-melodic schema to privilege instead the underlying harmonic progression or cycle as generative of the sequence: harmonic sequences frequently elaborate the circle of fifths (a descending-fifth progression) or other common root motions such as ascending or descending seconds or thirds.

That the vector of sequential repetition may be governed by scalic or harmonic arrays has led to one of the important and frequent distinctions in theories of the sequence, between those that are based on exact transpositional schemas and those that retain the number, but not consistently the quality, of the interval of transposition. The first type is typically described as *real* and the latter as *tonal*, but a further distinction between

FIGURE 20.5 Mozart, Piano Concerto no. 21 in C, K. 467, ii, mm. 45–50.

modulating and *nonmodulating* sequences has led to a degree of terminological inconsistency. The two systems of classification do not coincide exactly, especially when analyzing sequences in nineteenth-century repertoires. Real sequences are often taken to be modulating, in contrast to tonal sequences, in which the interval is modified precisely for the purpose of maintaining the prevailing tonic.

It is precisely the capacity of the real sequence to resist confinement within a hierarchical framework of the scale that grants it a certain utility within tonal music. The real sequence produces this tonal difference at the level of the entire progression, though, only by reproducing the very same intervallic relation between each of its individual steps. In other words, the real sequence can be said to be a machine for producing global difference out of local identity. The local relations between each step of a sequence governed by a circle of perfect fifths, for instance, coincide with one another, while the gap between the tonal centers at the beginning and end of the sequence marks a higher-order noncoincidence. The tonal sequence, by contrast, produces a higher-order identity out of local difference; a slight modification to the vector (e.g., contracting one of the steps into a diminished fifth) allows what would have been a modulating progression to function instead as a prolongation. The local disjunction is thus subordinated to global sameness.

It is equally possible, however, that a tonal sequence might modulate and that its intervallic modifications might be performed with this goal in view. A further distinction then suggests itself: sequences might be tonal without being strictly diatonic. Richard Bass (1996, 267) uses the term "tonal anchor" to describe an overall tonal framework through which local tonicizations at various junctures of the sequence might be united. In his model, the tonal sequence's subordination of local difference to global identity is maintained. These tonal anchors also operate on various structural levels such that local anchors may be subordinated to a larger-scale movement in a modulating sequence from an initial to a closing tonal anchor. Here, it seems as if the equivalence of local tonicizations (each is the same insofar as it has the status of a tonic) is secondary to the higher-order difference produced through the modulation as a whole. The securing of identity may simply be deferred here by subordinating the sequence to a tonic prolongation on a yet larger scale. But what is interesting about the case of the modulating tonal sequence is how it demonstrates that otherness is not simply to be found in the real sequence's apparent suspension of tonality, but is fundamentally constitutive of tonality's own elaboration and articulation. This disruptive potential of the sequence within the tonal framework is discussed in greater detail in the final section of this essay.

Whereas the typical usage defines tonal sequences as those that subordinate their local harmonic progressions to the larger-scale prolongation that sustains the prevailing key, Bass groups together under this category all progressions whose transpositional schemas are modified by the presence of tonal anchors, or what might therefore be described as tonal magnets to explain how their attractive force is able to make the transpositional vector veer off course. To this extent, the tonal sequence could be said to be defined by its local difference in contrast to the real sequence's local identity. This discussion shows, however, that there is little consensus about whether a sequential vector should be classified from a local or global perspective: while the real sequence is typically defined by its local consistency rather than the global effect of modulation, the tonal sequence is constituted by the interaction between a set of tonal forces that operate across a spectrum from local to global tonicizations. If the theoretical tradition is right to express some anxiety about the tendency of the sequence to produce sameness, it is significant that this identity manifests itself in a diversity of ways—local and global, melodic and harmonic—whose combination resists straightforward classification.

If real sequences are, by contrast, not subject to any tonal influence, Bass nonetheless argues that this category is not selfsame either: "Nineteenth-century harmonic practice . . . admits alterations to the patterns and projections of real sequences" (1996, 270). At the same time, apparently tonal sequences in nineteenth-century music may be modified for reasons other than the influence of a tonal anchor. In this way nineteenth-century examples of sequential repetition dismantle the binary opposition between tonal and real sequences. It is not simply that those sequences that are not real are tonal and those that are not tonal are real, for within the category of real sequences there are those that are not-real (which Bass calls "unreal") and within the category of tonal sequences those that are not-tonal (insofar as the modifications are not exclusively determined by tonal anchors). This is to say that, while real sequences may frequently be modified at their end to provide a more coherent transition to the subsequent harmonic progression, others, especially in nineteenth-century practice, contain modifications that are not attributable to tonal concerns, but rather to larger-scale motivic or harmonic processes. For instance, a local modification within the sequence may serve to ensure an exact echo of a thematic reference point at an earlier juncture of the overall form, thereby sacrificing local difference for higher-order identity. This kind of "unreal" sequence reverses the common assumption that it is the sequence's real element that harbors a disruptive impulse, capable of unraveling tonal articulations; rather, it is sometimes tonal considerations at the level of the overall form that disrupt the exact transpositional schemas of the local sequence. The next two sections of this chapter consider interactions between the sequence's disruptive potential and questions of larger-scale form.

It is possible to analyze many sequences as containing a mixture of real and tonal elements, but only on the condition that one also recognizes that each of these categories is marked by internal difference.[3] Recall how the example from *Gretchen am Spinnrade* shown in Figure 20.1(a) illustrates that it is not always possible to preserve diatonicism within melodic and harmonic dimensions at the same time. Such examples act as a prism, which refracts the classification of "tonal" sequences along parametic grounds, distinguishing between sequences that are tonal by one criterion but not by another; the effect is to introduce a subset of sequences that are neither wholly tonal nor straightforwardly not-tonal (i.e., real), but might be described as "not-not-tonal." In certain situations it becomes difficult to discern between this category and the corresponding one of the "not-not-real." This tendency of sequences to produce identity or difference at one structural level or within one parameter, while producing the other in another dimension, is what motivates the description of a double traversal or bipolar operation, in which one movement is never fully subsumed into the other.

THE TEMPORALITY OF THE SEQUENCE

This double movement is also what explains the sequence's distinctive and fascinating capacity to produce an experience of music's *temporal* unfolding. The theoretical tradition has long grasped intuitively that sequences participate in the construction of musical time, as both anxieties about their monotony and alternative theories of their role in melodic development testify. The exact mechanism by which sequences build a representation of time, however, has not yet been rigorously theorized. Across the body of theoretical writings on the sequence there nonetheless exists a certain ambivalence about whether the sequence tends toward stasis or dynamism, toward space or time. Similarly, it is unclear whether to attribute the spatial impulse to the mechanical repetition of melodic fragments, as opposed to the inherently dynamic logic of dissonance-resolution in the suspension chain (as in Harrison's example of the cross-fertilization of the *rosalia* tradition with fourth-species counterpoint), or the harmonic progression that governs the transposition can itself be the agent of stasis. The sequential episode that interrupts the flow of variations in the second movement of Beethoven's Piano Sonata op. 111 illustrates these difficulties (see Figure 20.6). For Charles Rosen (1997, 445–446), the "greatest master of musical time" here succeeds in freezing time altogether. It is not so much that Beethoven suspends the temporality of harmonic succession from without through the imposition of a rhythmic or textural brake, but rather that the descending-fifth progression realizes its potential to suspend its own movement when it appears as a diatonic sequence:

> The mastery lies in Beethoven's understanding that a sequence does not move, that a diatonic circle of descending fifths within classical tonality does not exist on a plane of real action, so that the long series of tiny harmonic movements that prolong this immense inner expansion serve only as a harmonic pulse and in no sense as a gesture. (1997, 447)

This suspension of time—a treadmill-like display of pseudo-labor without a goal—is possible precisely because the circle of fifths that governs this sequence contains within it a double temporal potential.[4] The overall effect in this example is the absolute subjection of time to space. And yet it is upon this same harmonic trajectory that the dynamic linear propulsion of Corelli's suspension chains would be founded. This then raises the question of how the sequence is simultaneously capable of freezing time and of being the source of forward momentum. This duality lies at the heart of Rameau's

FIGURE 20.6 Beethoven, Piano Sonata op. 111, ii, mm. 106–30.

theory of the sequence. If the cadential movement from dominant to tonic is paradigmatic of harmonic progression more broadly, the sequence becomes an ideal expression of the tonal system by projecting a cadential progression onto every degree of the
scale via the fundamental bass's motion through descending fifth. The succession from
one chord to another in the sequence, as in the cadence, is motivated by the presence,
sounding or implied (*sous-entendu*), of a dissonant seventh above the bass that compels

the dominant to resolve to the tonic. In a descending-fifth sequence, "the progressions of harmony are nothing but a chain of tonic notes and dominants, and we should know the derivatives of these notes well, so as to make sure that a chord always dominates the chord which follows it" (Rameau 1971, 288).

As Moreno notes, however, all the chords in the sequence, with the exception of the cadential goal, enjoy a certain sameness by virtue of the fact that none can claim a hierarchical superiority. The result is that, cut off from its closing progression, the sequence "reduces harmonic content, particularly function, to pure motion" (Moreno 2004, 118). Without any relation to an origin or end, the motion itself appears static. The absence of hierarchy between scale degrees in Rameau's system at this point and the preference for a single local relation between *dominante-tonique* and *tonique* remove the differential on account of which one might perceive movement. To this extent, it is possible to think of the interplay of identity and difference in expressly temporal terms: the diachronic or moment-to-moment perception of each local progression is leveled out as each of these moments is collapsed into a single moment of synchronous perception. The real sequence, by contrast, starts from a local synchrony (the identity of each local progression to the next), out of which it produces a global diachrony (the opposed initial and closing tonics).

What makes the sequence a representation of time, however, is that it resists the twin possibilities of pure synchrony or pure diachrony. While the effect of the nonmodulating tonal sequence is to subordinate the sequential progression to a second-order tonic prolongation, it is unable to produce this synchrony without there being a trace of residual diachrony at the level of local relations between steps of the cycle. This stain of first-order difference consists of the introduction of the diminished fifth into the progression of otherwise perfect fifths, in the trace of the Pythagorean comma that prevents the tonal system from coinciding with itself. This residue of noncoincidence is what permits an experience of time. If there were pure synchrony, there would be no sense of time unfolding from moment to moment, but rather the collapse into an eternal present in which every moment has always-already taken place. Pure diachrony would equally destroy all sense of time's passing, because each new moment would be completely unrelated to any prior moment and would always be experienced as a never-before. Only with a differential margin between diachrony and synchrony—only with a residue of one forestalling the other's totalization—does it become possible to grasp the passage of time.

A fascinating example of the way sequences participate in small- and larger-scale temporal representations occurs in the slow movement of Beethoven's String Quartet op. 131. Here the sequence interacts with a formal process, with which it shares a repetitive impulse. Like the sequence, variation has often been maligned by comparison with thematic *Entwicklung* for its propensity to repeat the basic substance of its melodic and harmonic materials. More sophisticated analyses of variation forms, however, tend to recognize that the process is marked by a double traversal similar to that of the sequence. The process of variation seeks difference in repetition; each successive variation repeats the theme only insofar as it marks its own distance and transformation from its original statement. In the slow movement of op. 131, the fulfillment of a real sequence in the final variation produces a pair of unusually striking interruptions of the form, marked by two outbreaks of trills, thus highlighting the sequence's potential for formal disruption.

The local origin of the trills can be traced back to the introduction of the ornament in the second half of the third variation, *Andante moderato e lusinghiero*. Here, the trill functions in a fairly conventional way, as the decoration proper to a cadential flourish. It is then taken up in imitation across the four parts (mm. 113 onward), but what is more important is that the imitation actually cuts across the division of the template binary form. With the exception of the second half of the fifth variation, this set contains written-out repeats throughout, but instead of simply repeating each half of the form with supplementary ornamentation, Beethoven redoubles and accelerates the momentum of variation by internalizing the process *within* each variation. Here the cello's entry in the second half of m. 113 is an echo of the cadential figure with which the repeat of the A section culminated. In this way, the trill introduces a zone of indistinction between A and B sections, between inside and outside.

This structure gives rise, in the final variation, to two outbreaks of trills where one would expect the written-out repeat: the first at m. 228 and the second at m. 250, an octave higher (see Figures 20.7a and Figures 20.7b, respectively). In both cases, the trill moves up from B to C♯ underpinned by a V_{4-3}^{6-5} progression, only to fall unexpectedly with a modal inflection to C♮ so as to produce an A-minor chord before the bass rises to reharmonize the C♮ with IV in C major. At this point the two passages part ways. The first time, in m. 231, the bass rises again by a step to G to form a V_{4-3}^{6-5} progression, which resolves in m. 235 before it is deflected back to A major via A minor. When the trills return for the second time, the F-major chord is instead reinterpreted as a tonic in m. 254, and the common tone $\hat{3}$ in A provides the glue to bind this interlude to an abridged reworking of the theme's second half at m. 264.

In this way, this variation set thematicizes the way in which return necessarily coincides with transformation, identity with difference. A significant digression becomes the occasion for structural return. While the expected return to the tonic is denied at the end of the first eight measures of the final variation, the thematic return is not entirely absent, even if it is held back by the trills for four measures. When it does arrive, this is a return, not simply within the context of the variation, but across the entire set, for the material at mm. 231 and 250 reprises the theme in its original, rather than varied, form, albeit in the wrong key. A tonal and thematic return of the variation's opening phrase is postponed until m. 243, where the trills from the interruption are absorbed into a varied repeat.

The eruption of trills in the final variation of op. 131 appears as a moment of synchrony when it is seen, not as the production of tonal identity, but as the completion of a real sequence. This large-scale sequential process can be traced in reverse: a search for a precedent for the C♮ trill yields a chromatic upper neighbor to B in m. 137 in the fourth variation, which scarcely seems significant enough or early enough in the movement to provoke the later disruption. Here it functions as part of a 7–3 linear intervallic pattern (see Figure 20.7(c)) and is to that extent perfectly predictable: the C♮ corresponds exactly to the E and

FIGURE 20.7 (a) Beethoven, String Quartet op. 131, iv, mm. 225–35. (b) Beethoven, String Quartet op. 131, iv, mm. 250–264. (c) Linear intervallic pattern in op. 131, iv, mm. 136–137.

D♮ earlier in the sequence. It is the D♯ in the bass that breaks with the real sequence in order to maintain the local tonic by means of a half cadence (an exact sequence would have demanded a D♮). In the final chord of the sequence in m. 137, the B alone is synchronous.

The sequence originates in mm. 6–8 of the theme (see Figure 20.8(a)), where it again begins as a nondiatonic sequence until the fourth harmony, which introduces a D♯ in the viola (see Figure 20.8(b)). In both the theme and the fourth variation, this D♯ moves to a G♯ harmonized as E major, thus ending the progression of fifths. The theme, however,

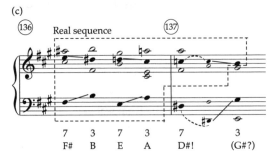

FIGURE 20.7C *continued.*

(b)

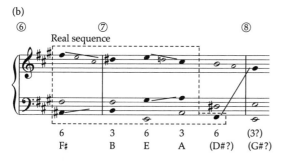

FIGURE 20.8 (a) Beethoven, String Quartet op. 131, iv, mm. 5–9. (b) Linear intervallic pattern in op. 131, iv, mm. 6–8.

disguises the projected course of the sequence, misconstruing the relation between the final two chords and the sequence that precedes them by misaligning the melodic and harmonic sequences. The point of imitation between the violins implies that the falling third from B to G♯ in the second violin is a sequential repetition of the first violin's fall from E to C♯ and, by extension, of the slightly more embellished falling third F♯ to D♯ earlier in the second violin. It might seem that the sequence has skipped two steps, but the viola's D♯ suggests otherwise. It is this note, in fact, and not the second violin's imitative figure, that continues the 6–3 linear intervallic pattern, but the expected B is absent on the downbeat of m. 8.

The turn back to the repeat of the phrase seeks to iron out this wrinkle: the first violin takes up the point of imitation again, beginning from the top with a descent from F♯ to D♯, but in order to effect the return to the tonic, the second violin counters with a falling dyad (D♯ to B). This tiny detail "corrects" two "errors" in the measures beforehand that disrupt the sequence's local synchrony: the B completes the foreshortened melodic sequence, while the D♮, the real continuation of the harmonic sequence, contradicts the erroneous D♯. In the 7–3 pattern in the fourth variation, real and diatonic components of the sequence coincide. Whereas the continuation of the melodic sequence is already distorted into a D♯, the penultimate step of the sequence in m. 137 is both synchronous and diachronous, insofar as the C♮ allows one to hear the continuation of the pattern, while the D♯ subverts it. Further, the doubled third in the final E-major chord with a doubled third hints that it should have been a chord on G♯.

The unexpected intrusion in this final variation dramatizes the indissoluble residue that inheres in the tonal sequence by enabling the sequence finally to coincide with itself through an exact transpositional schema only in a moment of seemingly absolute diachrony. The final variation as it were "corrects" the theme by providing a model version of the real sequence at whose possibility the earlier incarnations only hint (see Figure 20.9). This final variation adopts the 7–3 linear intervallic pattern from the fourth variation, but where one now expects a D♯ at the end of m. 226, the cello moves down a perfect fifth from A to D. But this is only the first inkling of what is to come. The C♮ that is part of the real sequence does not come immediately, but is approached via a pair of lower and upper neighbor notes, the rise to C♯ surely playing with expectations about the continuation. The bass persists with the continuation of the real sequence, rising to a G with the return of the original thematic material. The C♮ is reinterpreted as a fourth above the bass and then resolves to B to form the third of V in C major. The return of the theme thus completes the hitherto unfulfilled step of the sequence.

The intrusion that breaks through in m. 250 then advances the real sequence by another step. This time the C♮, transposed up an octave, is not reharmonized when the theme returns, but continues to be supported by F major. When it does fall, it moves to a B♭, picking up where the previous descending chromatic line left off in m. 232. This in turn steps down to A to complete the descent. The F in the bass thus reveals itself as a continuation of the descending-fifth progression passing through the D in m. 226, the G in m. 231, and the C in m. 235. In this way the sequence finally becomes real, seemingly purifying itself of the diachronous residue that had haunted its previous occurrences, precisely at the moment at which it abandons the synchrony of variation procedure, introducing a higher-order formal diachrony.

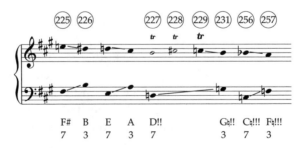

FIGURE 20.9 Linear intervallic pattern in Beethoven, String Quartet op. 131, iv, mm. 225–57.

SEQUENCE AS DISRUPTION

The realization of the sequence in op. 131 exemplifies *in nuce* the disruptive potential of sequences, especially real ones. In other cases, the disruption is contained as a local interruption of the form, but has much more wide-ranging ramifications for the overall form and for the attainment of global tonal goals. The theoretical tradition has variously conceptualized the sequence as an agent of tonal and formal disturbance.[5] I first look in more detail at those nineteenth-century harmonic theories that see the sequence as an obstacle to tonal articulation and its theorization. Unlike Rameau, for whom the sequence is prototypical of tonal harmony in general, both Fétis and Riemann find that the sequence sits at odds with their models of harmonic progression and tonality. I then consider how the sequence's association with harmonic instability begets the idea that this type of progression fulfills its proper function within certain looser parts of formal constructions, both within the phrase and as larger-scale agents of formal expansion.

For Fétis, the sequence's repetition and sameness lead to a temporary loss of the sense of tonality: "The mind suspends any idea of tonality and conclusion until the final cadence, so that the degrees of the scale lose their tonal character, the ear being preoccupied only with the similarity of movement" (2008, 252). In contrast with Rameau's theory of implied or supplementary dissonances, which give the sequence's harmonic progression its forward momentum, [6] Fétis maintains that not all triads can be thought of as unstable and in need of resolution. This is because Fétis argues for a correlation between notes of the scale and the kinds of chords that may be built upon each scale degree. If the scale itself is hierarchically structured around the pair of tendency tones $\hat{7}$ (resolving to $\hat{8}$) and $\hat{4}$ (resolving to $\hat{3}$), the chords built upon each degree must reflect the varying degrees of stability of the scale, such that only triads may be constructed on $\hat{1}, \hat{4}, \hat{5}$ *and* $\hat{6}$, while $\hat{2}, \hat{3}$, and $\hat{7}$ support inversions only.

Sequences threaten this hierarchy of stability by putting triads over every degree of the scale and in this way forget the way in which the law of *tonalité*, grounded in the scale's relations of attraction, depends on differentiation. The suspension of tonality thus comes about precisely through an inattention to differences between degrees of the scale, which are instead supplanted by a notion of pure identity. Fétis in this way objects to the idea that every step in the sequence is a local temporary tonic. Sequences undermine the set of relations between scale degrees through which Fétis conceptualizes the system of tonality, because they are too symmetrical.

Riemann's analysis of the sequence, discussed above, also questions whether the sequence is not, in fact, better explained as a melodic rather than harmonic formation (1896, 122). He argues that the sequence as a whole has no functional-harmonic significance, but only makes sense if we hear each pair of simultaneities as an autonomous fragment with a caesura between each fragment. In much the same way that the mind of Fétis's listener is absorbed in the similarity of the movement, it is only the process of repetition that forges a connection between these pairs of harmonies and that gives the sequence a measure of coherence.

More recently, espousing a mixture of *Stufen-* and *Funktionstheorie*, William Caplin's theory of formal functions in late eighteenth-century music retains the idea that the sequence is a locus, if not of outright tonal suspension, then of heightened harmonic instability. Whereas Riemann sees melodic process as taking priority, Caplin argues that "although some sequential progressions exhibit a degree of harmonic functionality among their constituent chords, this aspect of the progression is secondary to the fundamental purposes they are meant to serve" (1998, 29–30).[7] While this is mainly for the purpose of modulation, sequences are also "especially suitable for destabilizing harmonic activity in a given key." Caplin then categorizes sequences not only according to their underlying linear intervallic pattern, but also by the degree of harmonic functionality they express; even the descending-fifth progression, in which this functionality is most prominent, "nevertheless promotes a weakening of the harmonic-tonal environment."

This observation leads Caplin to develop a tripartite model that maps harmonic progressions onto formal functions: if cadential progressions form natural endings and prolongations tend to open up beginnings, model-sequence technique is most closely associated with middle-type functions and specifically with the continuation phrase of a sentence, which works in combination with other destabilizing effects such as fragmentation of structural units and increased rhythmic activity. In a broader view, sequential repetition finds its proper place in those thematic constructions and formal regions that Caplin defines as "loose" as opposed to "tight-knit." Loose insofar as "the individual links in the sequential chain are harmonically nonfunctional," the sequence sits alongside other modulatory processes, asymmetrical grouping structures, motivic diversity, and unconventional formal types as a means of destabilizing formal organization. Hence, looser constructions and sequences in particular are associated with transitions, developments, and, within the second half of a sonata exposition, expansion strategies aimed at postponing cadential closure in the new key.

The capacity for sequential repetition to disrupt the attainment of cadential goals in sonata form is exemplified in a remarkable fashion in Beethoven's *Grosse Fuge* op. 133, originally composed as a finale for the String Quartet op. 130. After an introduction in which a forceful opening statement of the fugue subject is followed by a snippet of a contrasting *piano* Meno mosso, a lengthy opening fugue in the tonic of B♭ gets underway before collapsing into an expansive version of the Meno mosso material in G♭ to give a brief period of calm. Roughly midway through an ensuing Allegro molto e con brio in 6/8 that fragments the fugue subject, the extraordinary descending-fifth sequence begins. Taking the tail of the subject as its motivic material, the sequence initially passes its model imitatively between the two violins before descending into the lower parts. The exchange produces a series of half-step dyads aligned with the descending-fifth progression so that the focal pitches form a 10–10 linear intervallic pattern with the bass. The repetition of the melodic patterning at four-measure intervals gradually dissolves into fragments of the fugue subject, scattered across a drawn-out extension of the harmonic sequence.

What is most striking, however, is how this sequence takes the logic of repetition and sameness to extreme lengths, with the final result that it produces a tonal rupture in complete violation of normative formal expectations. The sequence holds to an exact transpositional schema throughout its dizzying six cycles of repetition, plummeting flatward through the circle of fifths without any tonal correction, and the real harmonic sequence even extends beyond where the melodic pattern of repetition dissolves, until it reaches what is technically B♭♭ (see Figure 20.10). The enharmonic reinterpretation from m. 331, staggered across the four parts, seems like a matter of purely notational expediency rather than a decisive shift across this harmonic seam. The result of this extended sequence, then, is that in holding to an exact (real) transpositional schema, the closing tonic is technically not B♭, but C♭♭: from a harmonic-functional perspective, not a tonic, but the end of a lengthy chain of nested subdominant functions. As David Lewin (1984) has demonstrated elegantly, such harmonic sequences illuminate the conflict between *Stufen* and Riemannian space and show how the sequence assumes an important role in mediating between these two theoretical constructions of tonality.

This outcome is all the more remarkable when one considers that the fugue is, if not exactly a sonata structure itself, a rewriting of the first movement's own peculiar sonata deformation. The extended sequence is a retracing of a similar descending-fifth progression in the first movement's development, confirming the association of model-sequence technique with loosening impulses. That the fugue repeats the unusual choice of ♭VI for a second contrasting thematic area cements the connection to the first movement; any sonata background structure that may be implied in the fugue is filtered through this relation. In the first movement, however, the enharmonic reinterpretation takes place before, rather than midway through, the sequence at the juncture between exposition and development and is given greater rhetorical weight, taking place across a gap of silence. The enharmonic shift here also seems less like a matter of notational convenience, because it straddles an important thematic contrast from the movement's opening, separating material from the Adagio introduction from the motivic content of the main Allegro body of the exposition and thereby suggesting a repositioning from outside the frame to inside. Unlike in the fugue, the real sequence descends from D major down a whole step to C and then a further whole step to B♭ and thus provides a more convincing return to the tonic.

In any case, the first movement's sequence is normalizing, correcting an unexpected sharpward turn, rather than disruptive, because the unsettling sleight of hand of enharmonic equivalence lies outside its scope. The effect of the fugue's sequence, though, is to destabilize the large-scale tonal resolutions that articulate the form. The first movement's recapitulation transposes the second group down a fifth to D♭ major, thereby maintaining the typical transpositional relation if not the strict tonic reprise. In the fugue, by contrast, the sequence yields a reprise of its Meno mosso in A♭ (notated) or B♭♭ (by diachronic listening), eschewing the usual mechanics of recapitulatory transposition while also aurally projecting a type of $\hat{1}$ precisely at the moment when the tonic is expected. In this way, Beethoven's sequence forms a quasi-essay on the sequence's

FIGURE 20.10 Reduction of Beethoven, *Grosse Fuge* op. 133, mm. 325–453.

capacity to drive wedges between theoretical systems and even to unsettle their internal construction, but also at the same time to provide a passage or a means of transitioning between one mode of tonal hearing to another. This example also demonstrates how the sequence may precipitate *formal* destabilization: the fugue's sequence is instrumental in derailing a crucial juncture in the articulation of sonata form, not only displacing tonal expectations for the reprise of the second group, but also suppressing the return of first-group material by allowing the overgrown sequence to extend beyond and blur the essential structural boundary between development and recapitulation.

This example also suggests another facet to the sequence's disruptive potential. If the theorists of the late eighteenth century found sequential repetition stylistically outdated, this reflects the possibility that sequences may generate interstylistic conflict. In its fusion of fugal and sonata processes, the *Grosse Fuge* presents a way of dramatizing the tension between Baroque *Fortspinnung* and the Classical style's rhythm-punctuation model. While the Baroque aesthetic is premised on the interminable forward momentum of the cycle of fifths and relegates cadences to the status of momentary deflections, the Classical style elevates the cadence into the governing form of harmonic progression and the primary determinant for the comprehension of form. In the latter style, the music is divided by a series of endpoints of varying degrees of closure into a gridlike structure; the idea of periodicity allows the hierarchy of cadences to project the local metrical patterns onto increasingly higher hierarchical levels, such that a global cadence may subsume an entire span of music under its concept. This idea is central to sonata form, whose structure is generated through this projection of closing function from local to global. It is also this mechanism that permits a certain predictability, insofar as the listener is able to form a synoptic view of the whole and thereby to foresee what might happen next.

Beethoven's *Grosse Fuge* stages a confrontation between these two stylistic worlds, attempting to contain within the boundaries of sonata form the untrammeled momentum of the Baroque fugue with its abundance of sequential processes. Just as Johann

Georg Sulzer observed a shift in rhetoric from the old-fashioned, list-type construction of parataxis to the contemporary hypotactic practice that groups clauses together under a conceptual unity, music undergoes a similar change. Baroque *Fortspinnung*, exemplified above all by sequential repetition, exhibits the successive quality of paratactic construction, while the Classical sonata form, with its strongly articulated formal divisions and cadential goals, typifies the synoptic character of hypotaxis. This contrast replicates and separates out the two strands of the sequence's double traversal: the Classical style tends toward collapsing local difference into global identity through its hierarchy of rhythmic grouping and punctuation, while the Baroque *Fortspinnung* works by producing differences out of identical or similar musical materials, be they motivic units, linear patterns, or harmonic progressions. The interstylistic tension thus plays out the double movement toward synchrony and diachrony inherent in the sequence. At the same time, through this stylistic transformation from Baroque to Classical, the status of the sequence also shifts from being prototypical of tonal operations in general to becoming a disruptive exception to tonal and formal norms. Far from being an inert mechanism at risk of inducing boredom, it is in fact the sequence's repetitive character that enables it to become an agent of stylistic change and a driving force in the transformation of tonal processes and their theorization across the common practice era.

NOTES

1. This is the premise of Moreno (1996), which uses shifting conceptions of the sequence to parse the theoretical traditions into a series of broad paradigms. Within this framework, Moreno nonetheless notes a considerable degree of cross-fertilization between and even fusion of paradigms that threaten any paradigm's claim to self-identity.
2. See, for example, Schoenberg (1978, 283).
3. An alternative approach, which instead emphasizes the common origin of real and diatonic sequences in patterns in generic pitch space (i.e., indifferent to exact interval sizes and qualities), is found in Julian Hook and Adam Ricci's use of a combination of diatonic set theory and transformation theory (Hook 2014 and Ricci 2004).
4. For a discussion of this twofold temporal character, see Berger (2008, 10).
5. Two recent articles on sequences have focused on this disruptive possibility: Bass (1996), which looks at the tension between real sequences and their tonal context, and Ricci (2011), which examines simultaneous melodic sequences with different intervals of transposition.
6. The translation of *sous-entendu* as "implied," with the psychological intentionality this suggests, is contentious and arguably reflects an anachronistic preoccupation of more reflective Anglophone theory. The nuance of the French is perhaps better captured in the idea of "hearing-as-understanding." Rameau also describes these dissonances as *ajoutées*, whence Brian Hyer's (1994) bid to capture the deconstructive impulse here with his notion of "supplementary dissonances."
7. Caplin explicitly rejects a melodic definition of sequence, insisting that the presence of a harmonic sequential progression is essential.

BIBLIOGRAPHY

Aldwell, Edward, and Carl Schachter, with Allen Cadwallader. 2010. *Harmony and Voice Leading*. New York: Cengage.

Bass, Richard. 1996. "From Gretchen to Tristan: The Changing Role of Harmonic Sequences in the Nineteenth Century." *19th-Century Music* 19: 263–85.

Berger, Karol. 2008. *Bach's Cycle, Mozart's Arrow: An Essay on the Origins of Musical Modernity*. Berkeley: University of California Press.

Burney, Charles. 1775. *The Present State of Music in Germany, the Netherlands, and the United Provinces*. London: Printed for T. Beckett and co.

Caplin, William. 1998. *Classical Form: A Theory of Formal Functions for the Instrumental Music of Haydn, Mozart, and Beethoven*. New York: Oxford University Press.

Fétis, François-Joseph. 2008. *Complete Treatise on the Theory and Practice of Harmony*. Translated by Peter M. Lanley. Hillsdale, NY: Pendragon.

Forbes, Elliot. ed. 1967. *Thayer's Life of Beethoven*. Princeton, NJ: Princeton University Press.

Forte, Allen, and Steven Gilbert. 1982. *Introduction to Schenkerian Analysis*. New York: Norton.

Harrison, Daniel. 2003. "Rosalia, Aloysius, and Arcangelo: A Genealogy of the Sequence." *Journal of Music Theory* 47: 225–72.

Hook, Julian. 2014. "Generic Sequences and the Generic Tonnetz." In *Oxford Handbooks Online* (October). doi: 10.1093/oxfordhb/9780199935321.013.003.

Hyer, Brian. 1994. " 'Sighing Branches': Prosopopoeia in Rameau's *Pigmalion*." *Music Analysis* 13: 7–50.

Koch, Heinrich Christian. 1983. *Introductory Essay in Composition*. Translated by Nancy Baker. New Haven, CT: Yale University Press.

Lewin, David. 1984. "Amfortas's Prayer to Titurel and the Role of D in Parsifal: The Tonal Spaces of the Drama and the Enharmonic C♭/B." *19th-Century Music* 7: 336–49.

Mann, Thomas. 1948. *Doctor Faustus*. Translated by Helen Tracy Lowe-Porter. New York: Vintage Books.

Moreno, Jairo. 1996. "Theoretical Reception of the Sequence and Its Conceptual Implications." PhD diss., Yale University.

Moreno, Jairo. 2000. "Challenging Views of Sequential Repetition: From 'Satzlehre' to 'Melodielehre.' " *Journal of Music Theory* 44: 127–69.

Moreno, Jairo. 2004. *Musical Representations, Subjects, and Objects: The Construction of Musical Thought in Zarlino, Descartes, Rameau, and Weber*. Bloomington: Indiana University Press.

Pfannkuch, Wilhelm. 1994. "Sequenz (Satztechnischer Begriff)." In *Die Musik in Geschichte und Gegenwart*, edited by Friedrich Blume and Ludwig Finscher. Kassel: Bärenreiter.

Rameau, Jean-Philippe. 1971. *Treatise on Harmony*. Translated by Philip Gossett. New York: Dover.

Ricci, Adam. 2004. "A Theory of the Harmonic Sequence." PhD diss., University of Rochester.

Ricci, Adam. 2011. "Non-Coinciding Sequences." *Music Theory Spectrum* 33: 124–45.

Riemann, Hugo. 1896. *Harmony Simplified or the Theory of the Harmonic Functions of Chords*. Translated by Henry Bewerunge. London: Augener.

Rosen, Charles. 1997. *The Classical Style: Haydn, Mozart, Beethoven*. London: Faber and Faber.

Schoenberg, Arnold. 1978. *Theory of Harmony*. Translated by Roy E. Carter. Berkeley: University of California Press.

Schubart, Christian Friedrich Daniel. 1812. "Von der Rosalien." In *Vermischte Schriften* 1:220–26. Zurich: Gessner.

Sprick, Jan Philipp. 2010. "Die Sequenz in der deutschen Musiktheorie um 1900." PhD diss., Humboldt-Universität zu Berlin.

Yust, Jason. 2015. "Distorted Continuity: Chromatic Harmony, Uniform Sequences, and Quantized Voice Leadings." *Music Theory Spectrum* 37: 120–43.

CHAPTER 21

....

POLYPHONY

....

MICHAEL TENZER

THIS chapter explores basic concepts pertinent to studying the worldwide realm of musical polyphony. The premise portends a very far reach, whose limits we don't know, but let us take the term at face value and say that polyphony is any music with two or more sounds at a time. For now there is nothing for it except to dive into some music headlong, and resolve to tame the vastness, once a concrete example gives us a sense of what is at stake and at issue. So where in the world? I strategically choose two bizarre— and when you hear them you will know why I say so—vocal duets from opposite sides of the planet that sound uncannily (more like unbelievably) similar. Is their seeming siblingship coincidence? To use biology-speak, are they homologous (sharing an origin) or analogous (sharing a sociobiological function)? Can we deepen our feel for their odd similarity or will we expose it as a facade? What are the relevant factors? And how can they guide us in seeing polyphony writ large?

A POLYPHONIC HOMONYM

....

The first duet was recorded off the Istrian peninsula, on the island of Krk in the Adriatic Sea, now part of Croatia. In an oral tradition genre called *kanat*, it uses the so-called *Istrian* scale.[1] Marušić (2007, 188) writes the scale as [G𝄪, A♯, B, C, D♭, E♭♭, F♭], but I hear no "F♭" in this tune. Figure 21.1 is my transcription of the song, titled *Otrgnem rožicu ruman cvet* (Tear off the Ruddy Rose, ⊙ Audio Example 21.1). As is often the case in ethnomusicological transcription, the pitch names are approximations; here the scalar intervals are a bit smaller than tempered half-steps, but the orthography conveys the effect well enough.[2]

The duet is arresting for its narrow intervals, restricted both horizontally and vertically. Even in this region of the world, where related musical dialects abound, few are so intense in this way. Though pulsation does not seem strongly emphasized the singers harmonize, breathe, and move together as if one; indeed in this tradition the most

FIGURE 21.1 *Otrgnem Rožicu Ruman Cvet*, Krk, Croatia.

Performers and recording details unknown.

appreciated singers typically pair for life (Bonifačić 1991, 55). The phrases are of uneven length and notated as eight, ten, and seven beats, a total of twenty-five; the text but not the music changes during the repetition.

Essentially there are only two kinds of sonority present—the unison and a psychoacoustically rough interval that sounds like a neutral second (almost but less than a whole step), except that the constituent tones span a third on the scale because there is a degree in between. The singers alternate between these two kinds of sound rather like inhaling and exhaling on a harmonica, the lower voice often parallel to but adding a few more diminutions than the upper. The combined range nestles within a perfect fourth. The interrupted succession of unisons (these numbered beats are circled) create a triptych of stepwise descents from

1. B to A♯ in the first phrase (beats 4–5)
2. E♭ to A♯—a wider fall—in the second phrase, but skipping the B (beats 11, 12, 14, 17)
3. C to B in the last phrase (beats 22–23), which is a transposition up one step of the B to A♯ move in the first phrase.

The longer middle phrase has a developmental character and spotlights the B by withholding it, thus drawing attention to it as the first unison of the initial phrase, and the agogic conclusion of the last phrase, where it lasts two full beats. Is the B a tonal center of some kind?

At beats 6–8 and 17–18, the A♯ unison splits in contrary motion, but at 23–25 the B holds until the other voice moves up obliquely. Offsetting the parallelism between the unisons of phrases one and three, this parallel move is between phrases one and two, setting up the last phrase for a fresh-sounding finish. The song's other non-unisons progress stepwise, except for something special at the beginning of the last phrase: a big leap from beats 19–20, where the lower tone of the first interval and the upper tone of the latter frame the whole gamut from G𝄪 to E♭ in a nutshell for the first and only time. They then head down for the long B. It's an exceptional moment effective at different levels.[3] The song's structure is efficient and concise, and, with that extra twist, dramatic.

The second song is from the arid isle of Flores in southeastern Indonesia. It is in a genre few non-Floresians have ever heard. Other than scattered earlier examples, recordings of Flores's varied vocal traditions only became widely available in 1995 on the Smithsonian/ Folkways *Music of Indonesia* series (Yampolsky 1995a, b). Ethnomusicologist Dana Rappoport subsequently recorded this song, *Najan,* among Lamoholot speakers in Waiklibang village in 2010 (Rappoport 2010, 2011). It is sung at dawn on a rice-harvesting day, one of a series of *najan* songs integral to a ritual agricultural cycle that is still practiced.

The Flores and Krk polyphonies have strong qualities of being musical homonyms, which, considering the 12,000 kilometers between their cultural homes together with their utter distinctiveness as a pair, is exceedingly strange. This was noticed some time ago. Early ethnomusicologist Jaap Kunst visited Flores in the 1920s in search of music, and regardless of whether he knew of Krk, specifically, he had heard Istrian singing (Messner 1989). He was overwhelmed by the resemblance and wrote that "it was not only a matter of a certain similarity or parallelism [between them], but now and then of complete identity" (Kunst 1954, 3, in Messner 1989, 5).[4] The existence of two such distant bedfellows deeply baffled him and, unable to refrain from explanation, he attributed the kinship to an ancient eastward migration from Europe. To any prudent modern ethno-musicologist, that is a preposterous rush to judgment, but Kunst's bewilderment is ours, too. Here, some comparative analysis can at least partly part the painted curtain of the similarity.

Najan's pitch collection sounds like Krk's, but the logic of its polyphonic interrelationships is obscure.[5] Figure 21.2 (▶ Audio Example 21.2) shows two periods of eighteen beats, but within each, where the Krk duet was clearly switching to and from unisons and generating contrasting sonorities, the vocal lines of *Najan* seem bound by a common pulse but not much else. There are no discernible breaths or contrasts dividing the periods into smaller segments, as the Krk song did in its twenty-five beats. The only points of articulation are the second voice's brief imitation of the first's initial four pitches in the first period—but not at all in the same rhythm—and the fact that the second period begins on the same pitch as the first did. Each voice makes an 18-beat beeline for the ends of the phrases, seemingly caring for little else than sustaining the intensity of the harmony. The voices cross repeatedly, and the mix of rhythmic independence, vertical intervals, and unisons feels haphazard. One may speculate that they are

FIGURE 21.2 *Najan,* sung by Bapak Lego and Bapak Dagan. ▶ Audio Example 21.2.

Recorded in Waiklibang, Flores, Indonesia, by Dana Rappoport.

not thinking in terms of a scale or tune at all, but instead of certain kinds of motion and a sustained level of harmonic intensity. Nonetheless, the fact that they end the first period together shows their synchrony and the presence of a shared sound image, and that the second period is the same length as the first shows that there must be an operative concept of form.

Figure 21.3 removes the focus on pitch to juxtapose the songs' rhythms, and, above the staves, morphs these into contour lines. We see that the Krk voices move in parallel: bending in to touch at the unisons and vertically aligned elsewhere, they never cross. *Najan*'s are like two skeins patternlessly entangled. We appreciate now how much latent difference is belied by the psychoacoustic similarity that so struck us and Jaap Kunst. They are distinct enough to tip the scales of the evidence (as if such was needed) against Kunst's conjecture of homology.

As for the similarities and any analogous sociobiological functions such a narrow pitch and scale bandwidth might imply, we may well wonder why a culture would evolve such an anomalous sound-world. These musics are not sung as a presentation to a passive listening audience—they do collective kinds of cultural work. It has been suggested that the energizing stimulus singing acoustically rough polyphony provides may be a very ancient practice, extant now only in small pockets of the globe, which intensified awareness, enhanced group cohesion, and once upon a time served to intimidate enemies or predators (Jordania 2011, 98–104, 107–110).[6] Rappoport writes of the emotional qualities of ritual time in Flores, and explains that singers, just like those in Krk, bond deeply and form exclusive singing partnerships (2014). Could this commonality be due to the focus needed to sustain this kind of polyphonic interaction? Both genres

FIGURE 21.3 Krk and Flores songs compared.

are intrinsic to group identity and old ways, but more ethnography is needed before we can claim deeper insight.

It's unlikely that musical features we described would be conceived in similar or analogous ways by culture bearers; we'd have to bridge different systems of knowledge to find out. But is the songs' commonality coincidence? We have some evidence that they are functionally similar, but they must have developed separately. So yes, quite literally: they are coincident in the world, and they stand out because—different *and* similar as we now see them to be—they are global outliers, to say the least. Their separate emergence is something that could not have been predicted even by a whole think tank of music cognition researchers because they do not light up the brain's supposed cognitive preferences for scalar intervals distributed with maximal evenness in the octave. Nor do they satisfy the supposed wish for fifths and other simple ratios which cognitive science asserts to be an innate human affinity. They're black sheep in the big family of traditional music that only a cognitive scientist's mother could love.[7] We profit from being drawn to them in the ways celebrated neurologist Oliver Sacks was drawn to study weird brain lesions—for their potential to shed light more largely—and we should not see them as aberrations but as windows opening on to the enormous scope of polyphony.

Fundamentals of Polyphony?

The lesson of the Flores and Krk comparison is that anything is possible in polyphonies of the world, and to receive surprises in wait, we had best not be blinkered even by principles cognitivists assert, until they have been tested exhaustively. Removing blinders and questioning the fundamentals will let us gradually enlarge to a synoptic view of polyphonic music and music traditions.

Putting sound under the microscope, the guiding question is: what constitutes *difference* between two sounds? The answer is not at all obvious and depends on how "difference" is understood in music systems, in cultures, by performers, and by listeners. These can surely diverge. But if tones are heard as different, we want to know which combinations can go together or not, and in which situations. Any proscriptions would imply something like a concept of dissonance, possibly of different kinds or strengths. As pairs of sounds develop into lines with separate continuities, we will be curious about how far and much the lines can stray from each other, or from their individual starting points, and how to measure the distance. Are they equal or in a leader-follower relationship?

In the Krk song, for example, a new, outside listener hears difference between the parts. We have understood the unison and non-unison combinations as polyphonic, traced their paths of departure and return, and noticed a compositional logic. Yet, given all the parallelism between the voices, it could also be that the singers conceive them as a timbrally intensified (or elaborated, or enriched—however one puts it) single melody. In other words for the singers, the mere presence of another scale-tone and singing partner might not mean *categorical* difference at all (and certainly needn't imply dissonance). This might well strike one as absurd, since if there are two different tones coming out of two singers' mouths, then *obviously,* mustn't it be polyphony? But not so fast: what if the singers see themselves as if in the singular, and perhaps have some special conception of what a *tone* is? Etically (that is, for the outsider) it is multi-part; emically (for the insider), well—what is it then?[8] Yet even with all the ethnographic research one could do to find out, if we follow the implications of these problems to their inexorable end we could *never really get to the bottom* of whether a music is polyphonic or not.

One reason for this has to do with the way language shapes knowledge. *Polyphonia* (πολυφωνία), a term of Greek origin shared by European languages, has specific connotations for Western art music that must be unlearned because they cannot always be made to align with other cultures' conceptions. On the other hand, for consistency and to compare one music with another—unless we desire a purely mathematical formalism—we have to make do with English-language terminology. This is the devil's bargain one makes to do comparative musicology because it suppresses vital aspects of other musics as lived in their webs of significance.[9] There is no "polyphony" if one's language has no equivalent word for it. But the payoff of relaxing that hardline stance is that of an enlightening panorama gradually coming into view.

Another reason is that difference is intrinsic to sound itself. To remind oneself why, do the thought experiment of imagining a single sound played on any timbrally rich instrument. Zoom way in until you are immersed, slow time down, and attend to the flow of overtones and their attack-sustain-decay curves, which change independently. Tone is multiple and paradoxically contains its own difference.[10] Sound is temporal and never static; only a sine tone is pure, and perhaps only if heard (and if then) by a meditating monk in the stillness of a vacuum. The monk would tell us that existence is synonymous with change. Thus, however good a rule of thumb it seems that polyphony needs *two* instruments or people or musical lines, that is the case only so long as we keep our observations at a certain order of magnitude and do not overly obsess about monks or Krk singers.

Here we arrive from two directions at the status of polyphony's *ontology*—its essence—and find it to be, like all essences of matter or energy, hard to pin down. We may as well get used to this kind of uncertainty because we will meet it again in different forms all the way up the line, but we have to be practical. We can let tones just be tones and not intrinsically micropolyphonic vortices,[11] and we can set up categories of how they combine, and test them to see how they work in musical contexts. And, speaking English, we can observe "polyphony" of all kinds and later adjust as we learn more about other perspectives.

Two Typologies

Continuing a bit more in this abstract and pre-musical realm, consider that a single tone can float unmoored in time, whereas polyphonic tones are in temporal relationship.

Here we broach music's innate time dimension. This prompts us to conceive of various such relationships, so we can ask: how many ways can two sounds (or groups of sounds) be oriented with respect to one another in time? We can respond with a *typology*, a classification of all possible kinds of things specified within a certain *parameter*, possessing a particular *trait*, and sorted by a consistent *criterion*. We consider now two classical typologies, that is, ones striving to be conceptually pure without category overlap or mix. The first considers only individual pairs of tones, and the other considers longer groups or successions of tones. We will see right away that, helpful as the categories they provide are for thinking about polyphony, they cannot escape ambiguity and mixture, despite an intention to be pure.

Figure 21.4 gives Robert Morris's (2010, 346) typology in which the parameter is that of two tones, the trait is the ordering of their beginning and end points with respect to one another, and the criterion is that the ordering be expressed in terms of the elemental time relations before-ness, simultaneity, and after-ness (as opposed to a quantity like numbers of seconds or beats, which would yield an unhelpful infinity of categories). Of the seven ways shown, numbers three through seven involve simultaneity during some or all of their duration, hence are irreducibly polyphonic.[12] But the first two ways compel us to imagine actual sounds to decide if they represent polyphony. They could be construed as *monophonic*, that is, as two sounds from the same source played one-at-a-time, as if detached, like the first way, or abutting, like the second. But if one sound is played low on a tuba or *didjeridu* and the other high on a piccolo or set of *crotales*, or if two similar sounds are heard as emanating from opposite directions, or any of a number of other possible distinguishing factors, we might predict them to be independent agents, hence polyphonic. Thus, as soon as the categories hit the real world, the shackles of abstraction start to buckle.[13]

Morris's seventh way shows tones that begin and end together, which will seem more polyphonic if they have differentiated timbre or range (the didjeridu and piccolo again) than if they blend and stay in a narrow band, like the Krk singers do. Either way suggests a block-like texture, which is one of several textures the Western tradition groups under the label *homophony*—most coming under the wide rubric

FIGURE 21.4 Robert Morris's typology of temporal relationships between two tones (2010).

of melody-and-accompaniment, in which one part is primary and others give support. We can pause here to observe that the common Western typology of musical textures—the monophonic, the homophonic, and the polyphonic—relies on a criterion of rhythmic *independence* for its category construction. Monophony lacks it, homophony regulates it (either by granting independence only to pitch and keeping the block-like homorhythm, or by making one part more prominent, as in melody-and-accompaniment), and "true" polyphony exhibits independence, ideally to the point of full equality among the parts. This scheme has a dimension of cultural judgment, because the high exemplar of Western polyphonic independence, the fugue, is enshrined as a peak achievement. Parochially projecting that onto musics of the world would be a pyrrhic victory for fugues, and burden us with the assumption that others value that sort of "independence" too. Indeed, we will prefer the more neutral term "homorhythm" for Morris's seventh way, just to (try in good faith to) avoid bias. It is an open question as to whether Morris's before/simultaneous/after criterion, or that of the typology about to be discussed, *actually is* objective. Perhaps the most we can say is that their categories aim to be irreducible.

Figure 21.5 shows the second typology (Arom et al. 2007), which is not as abstract as Morris's, but distills and sorts its categories from a large inventory of recorded examples of oral tradition musics of the world.[14] Referenced in the article's discography, these sources are dispersed and hard to find separately, so I illustrate below with tracks from the CD-set *Les Voix du Monde,* a survey-compilation of world vocal expressions produced by a team of French ethnomusicologists. The third CD of the set is in fact organized as a sampler of polyphonies of the world, and there is some overlap of the selections or their genres with the article corpus (CNRS–Musée de l'Homme 1996; see the endnote for links to the recordings and superb accompanying booklet).[15] The columns of Figure 21.6 list the 30 track titles, their geocultural origins, briefly describe the music of each drawing on the CD notes, and indicate which of Figure 21.5's categories are applicable to it.

The parameter for this typology is that of two voices (one could also say lines, sound sources, or auditory streams) and the criterion is simply that the lines differ so as to be polyphonic—which the authors define by negation as everything that is not monophonic. The selected trait is "systematic organization on the vertical axis," connoting consistent kinds of time relationships between the polyphonic parts (Arom et al. 2007, 1088; and Macchiarella 2012, 10, formulates this similarly). All of this reminds us of the previous typology, but at the higher level of successive groups of tones (or phrases, or passages) rather than pairs of individual tones. The authors find seven categories— *tiling (tuilage* in the original French), *drone* (Fr. *bourdon), homorhythm, counterpoint, imitation, hocket (hoquet),* and *polyrhythm.* For completeness they precede these with one more, *heterophony,* which requires exceptional membership status because it is temporally *un*systematic, but neither can it be excluded, because it is not monophony. This alerts us to a chink in the typology's armor, in that the selected trait (systematic organization) is not universally present. There are others *within* the seven: are tiling and hocket the same thing but at different speeds or densities? Speed was not

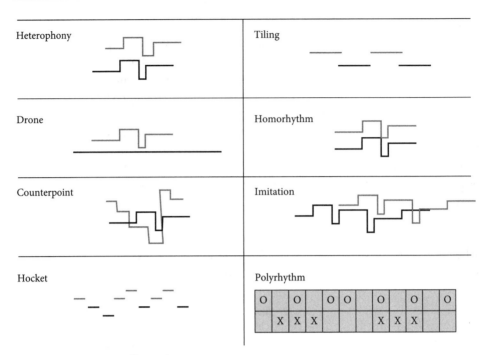

FIGURE 21.5   Arom et al.'s typology.

the typology's selected trait, hence should not be a basis for distinguishing categories. Imitation could be a subcategory of counterpoint in which the parts are the same but displaced in time; and polyrhythm could be counterpoint with pitch suppressed. Neither similarity of parts nor the mere presence of pitch was the selected trait either. What about homorhythm—is imitation merely its temporally displaced cousin? Frustratingly, the categories do not always hold water, but neither is it clear how they could be any purer.

Nevertheless, we are dealing with a practical collection of types of ways that oral traditions have been invented to combine polyphonic lines in time, a teeming canvas to be sure. Because the scale and combinatorial possibilities of the parameter are so enormous, what the categories specify will necessarily be quite general, and we need hardly note that Figure 21.5's stick-figure schemata merely shadow the diverse sonic details they purport to represent. Yet as visual models they clarify and stimulate us to test their applicability to actual music. The rewards outweigh the flaws.

In the typology, *heterophony* lies in between monophony and systematic polyphony. Brinner (1995, 192–194) shows how multifarious heterophony actually is in the world: it comes in rhythmically congruent, independent, overlapping, echoing, and many other styles. Most instances of it on the *Voix du Monde* CD are probably the result of cultural tolerance (or preference) for rhythm or pitch looseness in singing a unison melody or parallel harmony (tracks 1, 2, 4, 9, 30). It is worth reflecting that the whole concept of being "together" or "in tune" hinges upon concept and purpose. Is the goal communal

Track Number/Title	Origin	Brief description	Polyphony type(s) per figure 5
1. Grande Danse - Ahidus	Morocco (Berber)	Large group of singers in a loosely coordinated homorhythm plus frame drums playing a 5-beat pattern. The vocal phrase lasts 6 drum cycles.	Heterophony Homorhythm Polyrhythm
2. Choeur De Femmes - Ujaj	Ecuador (Shuar)	Many overlapping female voices, some maintaining a constant pitch, some imitating others	Heterophony Drone Imitation
3. Chant - Heyalo	Papua Nugini (Kaluli)	Two women singing overlapping, imitative call and response, phrases pulsed with irregular pauses between them	Imitation
4. Chant - Yangango	Senegal (Bedik)	Groups of men and women sing a set of 4 antiphonal, lightly heterophonic phrases, then the whole thing repeated 4 times, making a long cycle.	Heterophony Tiling
5. Danse Pour Appeler La Pluie	Indonesia (East Timor)	Mixed chorus sings loosely pulsed heterophony and cyclic melody with some small changes on the repetitions.	Tiling Drone Homorhythm
6. Choeur D'Hommes - Pasi But But	Taiwan (Bunun)	8 men's voices organized in 4 parts, 2 on a part, the effect is of constant upward glissando. The CD notes say there's a "rhythmic formula" heard eight times.	Drone (moving) Homorhythm Imitation
7. Choeur D'Hommes - Manimbong	Indonesia (Toraja of Sulawesi)	Male chorus (drone), with soloist often at the interval of a quasi-2nd; a sustained, unmeasured first part, followed by second part with short durations and clapped pulse.	Drone Homorhythm
8. Chant - Përmetarçe	Albania (Tosk)	A series of 3 call-response pairs between 2 male soloists, with drone sounding. Then it all repeats as a cycle starting 1:03 and 2:06.	Drone
9. Chant De La Fête - Guéréwol	Niger (Peul)	Chorus divided among drone and heterophonic melody, plus claps entering at 1:08; when the claps come in they organize the loose upper parts into brief quasi-cycles	Heterophony Drone Homorhythm Polyrhythm
10. Chant De Rite De Passage	Ethiopia (Guji)	Chorus with most voices on an ostinato part, plus a soloist. The ostinato organizes the music into a 4-beat cycle	Counterpoint
11. Chant - Oniugu	Gabon (Bateke)	Lamellophone, percussion, claps, several layers of voices (some interlocking), clearly regulated into a cycle of 6 fast beats.	Counterpoint Hocket Polyrhythm
12. Musique De Fête	Eritrea (Rashaida)	Voices in loose parallel quasi-4^{ths} plus drums; a cycle of 18 beats repeated almost verbatim 23 times.	Homorhythm Polyrhythm
13. Chant De Deux Fillettes Et Choeur	Ivory Coast (Baule)	Girls and women in call and response, plus scraping percussion Each call or response is 20 beats (40 per cycle) each subdivided in three; the percussion cycle is 4 beats.	Tiling Homorhythm Polyrhythm
14. Chant De Labour Des Femmes	Ivory Coast (Gere)	Mixed group singing. Some sections use overlapping counterpoint, others homorhythm. Starting around 1:45 clear 8 beat cycle emerges.	Homorhythm Counterpoint
15. Chant Pour La Pluie - Dodole	Macedonia	Two women mostly in parallel quasi-2nds; one phrase in cyclic repetition.	Heterophony Homorhythm
16. Chant De Travail Alterne - Xi	Vietnam (Nung an)	Two men veering from drone unison to various intervals of a fifth or less. Un- or weakly pulsed but the phrase repeats cyclically.	Drone Homorhythm
17. Chant D'Hommes - Tenore	Sardinia	Four men, two or three in homorhythm, with intense triadic composite. The fourth solos and sometimes one of the first three breaks out counterpoint. A 3-beat ostinato cycle sets the frame for the soloist(s).	Drone Homorhythm Counterpoint
18. Choeur De La Semaine Sainte	Sardinia	Four men in homorhythm; unmeasured and through-composed	Homorhythm
19. Chant - Paghiella	Corsica	Three men in mixed chordal texture; loosely pulsed with three separate, similar phrases	Homorhythm Counterpoint
20. Chant Funeraire D'Hommes - Zär	Georgia (Svaneti)	Male voices in harmony; unmeasured and through-composed	Drone Homorhythm
21. Lamentation Funebre - Aamamata	Solomon Islands (Are'are)	2 female voices in counterpoint; 6-beat ostinato cycle in one voice. The other voice's phrase is twice as long but varies more.	Counterpoint Imitation
22. Chant De Sarclage - Miololot Alaliu	Taiwan (Amis)	Men's and women's voices, responsorial solo-and-chorus. Cyclic strophic form; varied repetitions within strophes.	Tiling Counterpoint
23. Chant De Table - Supruli	Georgia (Guria)	Three men's voices. An introduction followed by a cycle (countable as 24 beats) that repeats with variants	Homorhythm Counterpoint
24. Chant - Trallallero	Italy (Genoa)	Mixed chorus, triadic harmony; partly through-composed structure without enough internal repetition to qualify as cyclic.	Drone Homorhythm Counterpoint
25. Chant - Himarioçe	Albania (Lab)	Men's choir; sustained pitches are un-pulsed. A cycle is heard three times, with variation in text at the beginning of each repetition.	Drone Homorhythm
26. Musique De Divination - Bondo	Central African Republic (Aka)	Mixed chorus with rhythmic accompaniment (hand clapping, two drums, two pairs of clashed metal blades, rattle and jingles), in an 8-beat cycle, 3 subdivisions per beat	Counterpoint Polyrhythm
27. Choeur Imitant Des Trompes	Central African Republic (Banda Linda)	Chorus of ten men imitating an orchestra of horns in a 4-beat cycle with 3 subdivisions per beat	Counterpoint Hocket
28. Chant - Edho	Ethiopia (Dorze)	Multiple parts organized in a 6-beat cycle. Includes a chorus in several parts and, several solo voices.	Counterpoint
29. Chant De Danse Rituel - Suahongi	Solomon Isls. (Bellona)	Two separate songs with contrasting forms are performed simultaneously: *huatanga* by ten men (left channel) and *pese* by two men (right channel). The scales, rhythms, tempos, and texts are different, coordination not occurring until the end of the cycle, which is repeated three times. (Abridged from the CD notes)	Counterpoint
30. Chant Individuel - Dit	Indonesia, Irian Jaya (Elpo)	Girls singing together freely without attempt to coordinate, while weaving.	Heterophony Counterpoint

FIGURE 21.6 *Les Voix du Monde,* disc 3 (see note 15).

or ritual efficacy, passing time pleasurably or easing work, aesthetic refinement, or a combination? When aesthetics serve an independent purpose, more attention can be devoted to tonal and rhythmic precision, although looseness/roughness may also be desired.

Other heterophony issues from idiomatic ornaments that cause two or more musicians to briefly diverge from a unison (track 15). The latter is characteristic of Central and South Asian traditions such as Indian classical music that features a monophonic solo melody flexibly tracked by a secondary instrument. But much traditional music, in East and Southeast Asia especially, has been called heterophonic in the very different sense of having simultaneous *systematic* variant parts that all trace to a "core" monophony, sometimes stated and sometimes implied. Later we will touch on Balinese gamelan and Japanese gagaku, both examples of this.

As for the seven systematic polyphony types:

- *Tiling* refers to antiphonal and call-and-response situations in which individuals or groups alternate, and sometimes overlap (tracks 4, 5, 13, 22).
- *Drone* polyphony may utilize a sole sustained drone note virtually all of the time (tracks 7, 8, 9, 16, 25). Drones may be articulated or interrupted (track 2, 17, 20, 24), or slowly change or alternate tones (track 5, 17, 20). The frontier separating slowly changing drone from melody is indistinct.
- *Homorhythm* is most often in parallel motion in this collection (tracks 1, 5, 9, 17, 20, 24), or mixed motion (track 19), or it may converge and diverge from unison (track 7, 16, 25). Track 6 is a unique case and features slow, continuous, harmonized upward glissandi.
- *Counterpoint* supposes two or more parts with some rhythmic independence. It is distinguished here from polyrhythm, which is assumed to involve non-pitched percussion. Among the most common contrapuntal designs are varieties of melody-and-accompaniment format, such as melody plus homorhythmic ostinato (tracks 10, 11 14 [starting at 1:45], 17), quasi-homorhythm (19, 24). Fuller independence (tracks 21, 26, 27, 28) nonetheless relies on brief periodicities or ostinato. There are also examples of *polymusic,* the superposition of separate musics whether coordinated (track 29) or not (30).[16]
- *Imitation* comes in brief motivic bursts of "you do this, then I will too" (tracks 3, 6) suggesting phase asynchrony or echo, or it may be embedded in longer melodies (track 21).[17] Through-composed, measured canon is not represented here.
- *Hocket* (track 11, 27), vocal in this corpus, is created by the "interweaving, overlapping, and interlocking of several rhythmic figures located on different pitch levels in a specific scalar system" (Arom 1991, 307). Track 27 is a choral rendition of a hocketing music that is also played by an ensemble of antelope and hollowed tree root horns (ibid., 309).[18] (Examples of instrumental interlocking will be introduced in the next subsection.)
- *Polyrhythm* in the form of percussion ostinatos may be achieved through accents built-in to a monorhythmic pattern that is juxtaposed to pitched parts (tracks 1, 9,

12, 13), or with a percussion ensemble playing multiple interwoven rhythms (tracks 11, 26), which are polyrhythmic internally as well as combined with pitched parts.

A glance at the right-hand column of Figure 21.6 reaffirms that the categories are ideals, because most music presents them in mixture.[19] Figure 21.7(a)–(d) illustrates incipits of tracks 1, 8, 13, and 21, respectively, so we can observe how this does (or doesn't) occur. In 7(a), from an outdoor ritual in Morocco, a choir sings a blended heterophonic and homorhythmic phrase in three sub-phrases of equal length, in AAB format. They are accompanied polyrhythmically by a drum ostinato that repeats six times for each iteration of the whole. The onsets of sub-phrases are reinforced by the first, third, and fifth drum patterns, but the second, fourth, and sixth are syncopated to the vocals. Figure 7(b), a song of praise to the Albanian communist party, is a simple drone setting, but there is a hint of tiling in the exchange between two singers in the lead part. The lead melody eventually converges to the drone note. Figure 7(c), from Ivory Coast, is a 48-pulse homorhythmic song sung for fun, tiling between a girls duet and a chorus an octave lower for a total of 96 pulses before the full repeat; the antiphony is nearly precise (but see the added harmony at the arrow). Percussion sets up a 12-pulse ostinato all the while.

Figure 7(d), a lamentation from the Solomon Islands, presents a two-voice counterpoint of 12-beat phrases using an anhemitonic pentatonic scale. Each 12-beat phrase divides in half, as the brackets show. The second voice enters five beats after the first. The upper part is an ostinato, with diminutions of some notes as it repeats. The first half of the pattern descends an octave for the third iteration, the switch between head and chest voice providing additional timbral contrast. The second voice is not an ostinato but the sub-phrases are grounded by alternating G♯ and B as their initial tones. The dotted ovals show imitation between second sub-phrases of each. We can observe the apparently free treatment of vertical intervals and the lack of strong tonal opposition available in the pitch collection, but this is also true of the heptatonic 7(c).

Figure 21.7 is synoptic of other rhythm features that organize polyphony in the corpus. One is the prevalence of repetition and ostinato in (a), (c), and (d). The CD notes tell us that there is dance for 7(a), social play in 7(c), and 7(d) is for death rites—in short, the functional and quotidian. Ostinato is a technology of time regulation available to dancing, musicking, entraining bodies, and regular periodicity a principal way of keeping musical time in traditional cultures—as well as something to observe in nature that can help track time in general. Figure 7(b)'s rhythm offers a contrasting way: it is aperiodic, regulated by the breath and the text's narrative, and suggests an arc-like trajectory of thought, embodied, but differently.

It is fitting to have considered voice and unpitched percussion music since these are, of course, humanity's oldest and most universal music instrument technologies. They nonetheless give relatively narrow access to the range of pitch, speed and precision of rhythm, band of dynamic and timbre, and varieties of attack, sustain, and release that are available in the sound spectrum, and that our ears readily perceive. The muscles of

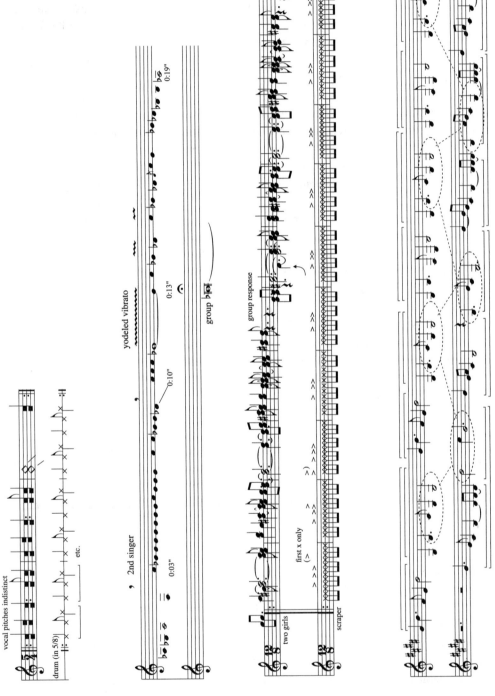

FIGURE 21.7 *Les Voix du Monde*, disc 3, tracks 1, 8, 13, and 21 (see note 15).

the arm and hand fire more rapidly than those of the lips and throat. Wood, gut, metal, and other materials can be transformed to sound a wider range of pitches than the oral cavity does. Compared to the larynx, nature's materials can respond faster and require less energy expenditure when they are struck, bowed, plucked, blown, amplified, or made to electronically synthesize.

Consequently, while assimilating the foregoing typological focus, we ought to give more consideration to music for instruments, and embrace technology (in the broadest sense) as a theme. This is as much for its potential to cast a wider net as for the historical perspective it can bring. The long arc of evolving technologies of time measurement, instruments (organology), and writing (music notation) loop in feedback with imagination and cognitive and physical capacities, driving polyphony's efflorescence.

INTERLUDE: SECOND HOMONYM

Hocket is all over the world: Inuit throat games, Andean panpipes, early French polyphony, Balinese and Javanese gamelan, the Central African musics discussed above, among many more, all partake in one form or another, using voices and many types of instruments. It is collaborative and musically demanding—two or more parts making similar tones on similar instruments must deftly interlock to form a composite—and a technique so omnipresent and rooted that surely it is very ancient. Although the separate parts in some hocketing overlap or coincide as well as fill in each other's gaps, there exist types in which one partner plays only when the other is silent, and vice versa, with the resultant forming a one-note-at-a-time single stream of equal durations (such as shown in Figure 21.5). This suggests a hocketer's paradox: when two players' lines fuse seamlessly into one, are there then one or two lines?

However, music logic and cognition see no issue here, since we easily integrate multiple sound streams if their sources are near each other and similar in register and timbre, but language logic fails to help us decide whether this is in fact polyphony, or maybe monophony after all. Perhaps it is the former in the production and the latter in the reception, or maybe it is a counterintuitive "collaborative monophony." There is no reason to dwell on this because ambiguity of this kind is not news . . . except perhaps in the expanded sense that the following case study conveys. In the homonym illustrated in Figures 21.8 and 21.9 and ⏵ Audio Examples 21.3 and 21.4(a)–21.4(b), the hocket parts, structured similarly, connect very differently to the fuller dimensions of the music, so that what one hears suggests twin masks concealing very different things.

The two patterns, respectively from the repertoire of Balinese *gamelan gong kebyar,* and the *amadinda* tradition of the former Buganda court in Uganda, are played with hard mallets on keyed idiophones in the one-note-at-a-time way. The instrument keys—ten bronze ones in the first case, and twelve wooden ones in the second—are

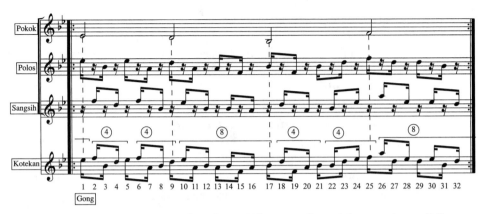

FIGURE 21.8 *Jaya Semara,* Gamelan Gong Kebyar, performed by members of Sanggar Çudamani, Pengosekan, Bali.

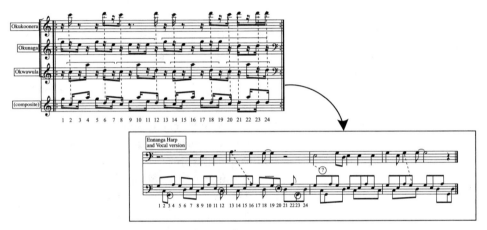

FIGURE 21.9 *Olutalo olw'e nsinsi* (The Battle of Nsinsi), Amadinda and Ennanga versions, Evaristo Muyinda and Group.

Recorded by Gerhard Kubik.

responsive and permit a clean, loud, sharp attack with but a flick of the wrist, and offer an ambitus of two full octaves of five-tone scales (plus a further two tones in *amadinda).* No singer represented in Figure 21.6 ranges that widely, and no voices could possibly interlock with the combined speed and precision these materials permit. Since the interlock is so fast each player depends on a vivid mental representation of the composite and confirms the rhythmic evenness at every moment by crosschecking internal and external listening.

The gamelan excerpt is from an early twentieth-century composition called *Jaya Semara* (The Triumphant God of Love) calling for two dozen performers, many on other parts not shown here.[20] ⊙ Audio Example 21.3 is a pedagogical recording isolating the hocketed parts before recombining them; the tempo is kept artificially slow until near the end. The scale, *pélog*, is approximated from the recording as D–E♭–F–A–B♭.[21] The middle staves show the separate lines of the hocket, in Balinese terms the on-the-beat *polos* and the off-the-beat *sangsih;* in the lowest staff the composite *kotekan*. Eight players are assigned to it, two each on *polos* and *sangsih* in this register, and the same an octave above (not shown). The hard wood sounding the bronze produces a thick, overtone-rich timbre. The *kotekan* is one of many kinds of patterns that could be generated from the slower melody, known as the *pokok* (basis or core, in Balinese), shown in the top staff. The *pokok* is projected in its register by a pair of keyed instruments, struck with softer mallets, whose limpid sustain and timbre give it acoustic prominence on a par with the *kotekan* in the full ensemble texture.

The *pokok* is inherently instrumental, an insistent ostinato of a type associated with old rituals and the placating of autochthonous unseen forces. Its rhythm provides a slow regulative beat. The dotted lines show how the *polos* matches the scale degree of each *pokok* tone, a vertical convergence characteristic of much gamelan. Simultaneous, systematically related versions of a single tune like this account for the music having been called heterophonic, but there is much to say in favor of it being heard as polyphony too. True, the *kotekan* is fungible, lacking a "real" existence other than as the *pokok*'s progeny, and musicians think of it this way. But they also understand that the *kotekan* lives on a stratified plane with its own timbre and rhythm idiom, and the grouping structures of its pitch organization give it a robust profile. Above its staff brackets and numbers show the sixteenth-note duration of pitch sequences, which, in Balinese hearing, are end-accented and lead *to* strong beats. Those of four pulses project a quicker motion than those of eight, which hiccup on the neighbor note figures at 11–14 and 27–30. During the seven-step ascent from nadir to apex at 19–26, the immediately repeated B♭ at 21–22 is a slippage further tripping up the motion, and the apex, despite landing at the beginning of a group, is a strong expressive counter-accent. The passage trespasses on the boundaries of the pitch sequences and imparts compositional flair. All of this enlivens an indelible polyphonic relationship between *kotekan* and *pokok*.

The *amadinda* composition illustrated in Figure 21.9 and ⓟ Audio Example 21.4(a)–21.4(b) is *Olutalo olwé nsinsi* (The Battle of Nsinsi); the tones C–D–E–G–A represent the scale. The instrument has twelve logs of the *lusambya* tree for keys and is played by three people. Two of them commandeer the lower ten logs. They sit facing each other and play their interlocking parts with two mallets each, in parallel octaves (the *okunaga* and *okwawula,* middle two staves; as with Figure 21.8 the upper octave is not shown). The third musician's part (*okukoonera,* top stave) uses only the piercing top two notes of the instrument, playing them when and only when they appear anywhere in the composite of the lower parts; the dotted lines in Figure 21.9 show these alignments. The irregular rhythm thus created stands out, because those pitches are heard in that extra upper octave. No other instruments are present (Kubik 2010, chapters 1, 4).

It is striking how difficult it is to aurally segment the composite (bottom stave) into smaller chunks. Due to the speed and the constant swirling of the five tones, the component parts dissolve in the mix. This is so despite their individual clarity: the *okunaga* comprises two six-note halves whose first three tones (G–E–G) are identical, and the last three different (E–E–E vs. G–D–D), while the *okwawula* is merely four iterations of the particle C–A–D; and in the composite tones 1–6 repeat at 13–18. Yet the composite's elusive logic makes for fertile listening to what Kubik calls *inherent patterns:* "the inner dimensions of the composition . . . are so manifold that they cannot be perceived all at once . . . [one must listen] in the same way as one looks at an object from different sides" (2010, 79). The ear extracting various inherent patterns tunes in to the music's polyphonic potential.

Olutalo olw'e nsinsi, however, like other items in this repertoire, is not inherently instrumental or part of any collection of compositions exclusive to the *amadinda*. Its origins lie in song melody and text, and as transformed for playing on *amadinda* it should be considered "instrumentalized song" (Cooke 1970, 68). Having generated sonically diverse, stand-alone representations on drums, several kinds of xylophones, and string instruments, with and without vocals too, it is better understood as a mental representation that can be adapted to different media. In a version on the *ennanga* harp, shown in the boxed system and available online as ⊙ Audio Example 21.4(b), the composite is split between the hands—not in an *amadinda*-like one-to-one interlocking (is a hocket for one still a hocket?)—but instead between two registers: three upper notes (A, G, E, stems up) for one hand balanced by three lower ones (D, C, and a new lowest note, G, stems down) for the other, so as to keep fingers from colliding. The circled notes at positions 3, 12, 20, and 23 are the few deviations in pitch from the amadinda version.

Harpists' fingers can pluck faster than percussionists' wrists can strike, so even greater speed is attainable. The harpist sings a melody in which most tones align in unison with the harp, but, as shown with dotted lines, a few are displaced, and in this excerpt one— the vocal E at the beginning of the harp repetition (indicated with a question mark)— is unaccounted for. As the performance continues, the harp repeats verbatim but the singer produces many other counterpoints in a similar way. The differing timbres and rhythms of voice and harp, the melody-and-accompaniment texture, and the contrast between harp ostinato and sung text unfolding over many repetitions linearize the music and highlight its polyphonic potential.

The Balinese and Bugandan hockets seem at first like kin but are conceptually very different: *kotekan* is the dependent child straining for polyphonic release from the immutable *pokok,* but without which it would never be heard, while *amadinda* is one of many mature and freestanding polyphonies birthed from song and encoded in musicians' minds. The instruments that play these musics catalyze the imaginations of their inventors in utterly distinctive ways, and neither music could have been invented without them.

HOMAGE TO HAROLD POWERS

Starting here, we scan the trajectory of vocal and instrumental polyphony in Western art music over the long arc of a near-millennium, from its near-beginnings to the near-present. It will be a supersonic trip in which the speed and height bring their own perspectives. The closer study of polyphony in Western music is open to all via the most copious and venerated musicological corpus that there is. It ranges from the 9th century anonymous *Musica Enchiriadis* and Guido d'Arezzo's *Micrologus* (c. 1025), through myriad others such as Johannes Tinctoris's *Liber de arte contrapuncti* of 1477, Fux's 1725 *Gradus ad Parnassum*, Ebenezer Prout's 1891 *Fugue*, and the proliferating contributions of the last century—didactic, historical, and theoretical as they are by turns. And this is only the realm of "Talmudic" commentary on the entire corpus of published compositions since the days of illuminated manuscripts and the dawn of the print era, astronomical in number and surely dwarfing all documentation of all non-Western music put together (although perhaps now no match for recorded, mass-culture popular music). These mentions must suffice as tribute, for to be comparative in an essay like this we cannot afford to relinquish the long view for too long—although we run out of fuel if we don't alight, as we have and will, on at least *some* examples. But it is our lot to feign comprehensiveness.

The question of how much prominence to give Western music in this ostensibly universal discussion hangs in the air. Harold Powers, a scholar with impeccable integrity, who thought deeply about many kinds of music, argued for:

> privileging the teaching and study of the historical canon of European music . . . based on two very simple features of that music: (1) its abstracted complexity, which it shares with canonical musics of other cultures; [and] (2) the profusion of its interpretable documentation over centuries of change—and there it stands alone.
>
> (Powers 2000, 51)

> The particular value of the European musical language as an object of historical study is the continuously documentable depth over a continuous stretch of a millennium of a number of its dialects, through the survival of readable musical notations. That much cannot be said of any other surviving canonical music. Some other cultures do have notated musical documents, but they are of limited use for the historical study of how the workings of their complex canonical musics may have changed over time.
>
> (ibid., 55)

Among authoritative studies such as Powers's "Mode" (1980), Sachs and Dahlhaus's "Counterpoint" (also 1980), Blum's "Composition," and Frobenius et al.'s "Polyphony" (both 2001), all in *The New Grove Dictionary of Music and Musicians* (2001),[22] Blum and Powers especially deal with non-Western traditions in a depth unprecedented for their publication dates. All the same, they hew to Powers's doctrine—and so will we, in light of the following.[23] Western music's prestige has been inseparable from, and at times an instrument of, its society's history of power, which is not innocent. While Western musicians are nearly always eager to expand their canon via curiosity about the music of others, the expansion bears witness to the receding voices of traditional musicians in the wake of modernity's blunt potency. This is not to say that Western hegemony is generalizable or a simple condition, or to overlook how popular musics can revitalize oral traditions. Nor is it within the West's power to marshal the historical forces it unleashes, one of the best of which is literacy itself. Musicology trying to do right by all of this from within its own little vortex is like the tail trying to wag the dog.

Powers is outwardly indifferent to this complex tableau, opting instead for an ivory tower ethic that eschews "endless questions of [the music's] value" (2000, 52). Possessing a credible historical narrative for Western music may be an ivory tower blessing, but it lopsidedly mitigates against comparing the world's musics dispassionately. I cannot offer much to right the balance except for the idea that we should keep all of this in mind, and sometimes try to view music as a whole from ever-greater distance, posing the most basic questions we can devise. We can also reflect on how different the music of the past is from that of the present, so a visit to the past is much like a visit to elsewhere.[24]

Polyphony and Technology in the West

"What constitutes difference between two sounds?" was the parent question we explored using a typological approach. A historical and cultural tack suggests a sister question: how does the *perception* of difference between sounds change *over time*? The "time" intended is a broadly historical one, and the response will be to develop the idea that changing musical practice is tied to technological advance.[25] The scope of polyphony broadens when musicians adapt technology to their purposes, and society embraces the changes they propose. A thousand years ago, the inventory of polyphonic possibilities in what came to be known as Western art music numbered a quite modest infinity, but today it is a much vaster one. How did we get from there to here?

Technology's primary function is to develop tools and concepts allowing us to more precisely measure, manipulate, and explain the environment. A corollary and equally important function is the invention of tools that disseminate these explanations. In music, examples of the first kind of tool include musical instruments, temperaments, and time measurement devices like clocks or metronomes, all of which lead to more finely calibrated access to the perceptible spectra of pitches, rhythms, and timbres.[26] Examples of the second include music notation, the printing press, and recording machines that communicate and preserve music. In the absence of these, our technologies are those of our physical selves, and what we can hear, remember, and reproduce unaided.

A depiction of Western music as if from afar can show that polyphony prospered, and composers' options continually increased, because of a rising confluence of these very kinds of material and technological conditions. Their combined functions stimulate musical change and creativity. Technologies of measurement and explanation awaken sensual-perceptual capacities, enabling the body and mind to experience musical elements more acutely. Preservation tools like notation exteriorize music and make it more accessible as an object of conscious contemplation. This is a sea change from how it is when unwritten in the minds of the oral tradition collective, since the constraints of both cyclical repetition and adherence to text—two of the most pervasive ways of structuring oral-tradition music—become choices rather than necessities. Nevertheless, over the course of Western music history, oral tradition recedes but does not disappear. It persists to enable a hugely expanded set of possibilities—analogous to how, in the past few decades, computers and virtual technologies have become adjuncts to our minds and bodies.

Let us consider five "growth areas" that have expanded the reach of Western polyphony since the time of its first flourishing at Notre Dame cathedral: (1) extension of pitch range; (2) diversification of timbre; (3) development of scales, temperament, and harmony; (4) counterpoint (and harmony); and (5) elaboration of rhythm. Their intertwined paths of change activated music cognition powers theretofore latent or embryonic, though some of them may have always been necessary for our sensitivity to sound in the natural world. As indicated, we'll do this in fly-over fashion to survey the forest, but we will loop back to look at a few trees (and leaves).

Range. Although the limits of human hearing stretch from about 20 Hz to 20 kHz, above 5 kHz, the distinct qualities of pitch thin out, losing what Huron (2001, 7) calls "toneness." Due mainly to improvements in musical instrument construction, the percentage of the 20 Hz–5 kHz range in active musical use has steadily increased since the tenth century. Pitch norms and nomenclatures varied over time and throughout Europe; and the 1711 invention of the tuning fork, a milestone in pitch measurement, was one factor leading to the A440 standard for equal temperament proposed in the nineteenth century. But regardless of both the variability and eventual standardization, the full frequency continuum accessible to the ears steadily became more available for composers to exploit.[27]

Vocal range capacity is a given, but usage is another matter. In individual Gregorian chants, the ambitus was a seventh or an octave (rarely, a ninth); across the repertoire, it spanned a thirteenth, from A3 to F5 (Hiley 2009, 169). In an organum such as Perotin's *Viderunt Omnes* from the late twelfth century, the widest space between voices was a tenth; by the fourteenth century, the lowest note across the repertoire was D2 and the highest remained F5—a range of three octaves and a minor 3rd.[28] Bass range hasn't gone lower since then, and although sopranos have edged up to the coveted high C6, coloraturas stake out the F a fourth above.

As for instruments, we take keyboards and strings as samples. Early fourteenth-century clavichords spanned about an octave (Remnant 1989, 80). Harpsichords, spinets, and virginals in the sixteenth to eighteenth centuries eventually stretched to four octaves, and of course Cristofori's modern pianoforte covers seven and a third of them, producing tones with fundamentals from 27.5 Hz to 4186 Hz. The idea of combining ensembles of viols into consorts arose in the fourteenth century, but the first such groups combined instruments of similar size playing arrangements of vocal music. It wasn't until the late sixteenth century that "large double-basses as well as small trebles" were combined to expand the range (Woodfield 1984, 186). The modern violin with its arched bridge came into being around 1550, and the first string quartets a century later (Hull 1929). If in a quiet texture and playing an artificial harmonic, the violin can sound E8 above the piano's (and the piccolo's) C8 apex. Unless scordatura is used, though, not even a contrabass with a C extension can match the modern piano's low A. No other orchestral instruments exceed the piano at either end, although pushing the extremes is a trivial matter for electronics and digital synthesis.

Endnote 13 touches on the so-called interleaving effect. This describes the aural fusion one experiences when timbrally similar polyphonic parts lie in the selfsame register, and the proportionally growing independence resulting when registral space widens. So-called compound melodies, in which a single (usually instrumental) part cuts back and forth between two registers separated by some significant intervallic distance, evoking the presence of two or more independent lines, are an example of this.

Timbre. Timbre is sometimes defined, by a kind of subtraction, as the difference between two tones that remains when their pitch, loudness, and attack-decay profile are the same (Erickson 1975, 4; Sethares 2005, 28). Timbral difference without these other kinds of difference—that is, between tones at the unison, or perhaps octave or fifth—is insufficient to produce polyphonic separation. This is because the ear can fuse multiple timbres to perceive a single sound, particularly when the upper partials of the two constituent sounds are related by the whole-number frequency ratios of the harmonic spectrum. On the other hand, timbral difference *strengthens* polyphonic sensation when combined with the other kinds of difference, and even more so when the partials are inharmonic. However, if two timbres can fuse, the polyphony they create when in motion through different pitches and rhythms will feel perceptually integrated and unified, with the different parts flowing in distinct yet coordinated auditory streams. Strongly contrasting or inharmonic timbres, when in polyphonic motion, may tend toward disintegration and create sensations of separate, stratified musical planes (Huron 2001, 32–35).

The variety of timbres in use has grown, just as pitch range has widened. Percussion, string, and wind instruments have been in use since pre-antiquity, but until the Renaissance, sacred music was mainly choral and instruments reserved for secular song accompaniment. Combining instruments into multi-timbral ensembles became more common in the late fifteenth century, on the heels of the emergence of a public sphere wherein new contexts arose for making music, and the benefits of advancing craft and commerce in instruments, notation, publication, and distribution gradually came available. Coupled with the long-range development of scientific thought defining the era, what emerged for composers was curiosity about sounds themselves, their physical components and potential expressive combinations, and eventually their perception and aesthetic qualities—all of which comprise a line of inquiry at the core of Western musical values. The idea can be traced backwards to dawning awareness of different intervals' qualities in *Musica Enchiriadis*, and forward to today's digitally liberated control of sound for sound's sake.

The symphony orchestra enlarged in size and internal diversity from its origins in the seventeenth-century opera orchestra. At first, its dominant color was of strings, but it included winds and sometimes brass in support. These instrument sections were soon used in novel ways, such as in the late eighteenth century with the Mannheim orchestra's fanfare-like bursts of chord and color. Haydn, Berlioz, and their contemporaries developed orchestration as an independent musical element in the nineteenth century (Dolan 2012) and the orchestra absorbed more and different kinds of instruments—tuba, and harp, for example. The twentieth-century orchestra reached an apotheosis of size and color in Mahler's symphonies, Stravinsky's *Sacre du Printemps,* and Schoenberg's *Gurrelieder,* but spun off into a plethora of smaller combinations, some common and many one-offs, such as a 1962 *Sextet* for violin, clarinet, trumpet, cello, harp, and piano by Stefan Wolpe. Even in standard and timbrally unified chamber combinations such as the string quartet, the search was on for color: witness the progression from gentle pizzicato in Beethoven's op. 74 Harp Quartet, to the *thwack* of Bartok's snap pizzicato in his quartets a century later, to the collection of smacking and striking sounds in Helmut Lachenmann's *Gran Torso,* finished in 1988. Composers disencumbered timbre of pitch so it stood apart.

Scale, Temperament, Harmony. Timbres lie along a continuum that eludes quantification, and range is a fairly crude property of groups of tones. Therefore these dimensions provide only rough data for assessing polyphonic difference. Pitches arranged in scales, on the other hand, are something more precise. Each dyad drawn from a scale is (1) a member of the scale's limited set of interval classes; and (2) an instance of one of those classes at a specific pitch level. In a 12-tone system there are 11 non-unison directed pitch-class intervals and 66 dyads with unique pitch-class content. (Compare this to 6 and 21 for a 7-tone scale, and 4 and 10 for a pentatonic one.)[29] Hearkening back to the typologies presented earlier, we can conceptualize a polyphonic system in terms of the seven ways (see Figure 21.4) that each of the 66 (or 21, or 10) dyads can be ordered in time. Musical grammar constrains how successions of such pairs could move in the kinds of musical contexts sketched in Figure 21.5, but the inventory of possibilities has, as with range and timbre, vastly increased over the centuries. Today, scales and constraints on succession still take many forms from which composers may choose.

Early sacred polyphony at first functioned with the simple ratios of Pythagorean temperament, comfortable for the singing voice. The conundrum of chromaticism—gremlin in the machine—sparked the centuries-long transformation from diatonic to the twelve-tone chromatic/harmonic system. Medieval musicians altered by semitone the dreaded tritone that could result when transposing modal tetrachords. By the fourteenth century, era of Machaut and *musica ficta,* chromatic alterations were standard in many contrapuntal contexts and had become like an addictive substance craved by every cadential impulse. Pythagorean gave way to mean tone and just (and many other) intonations in an effort to domesticate tuning commas and discordant interval ratios resulting from such alterations. The rise of fixed-pitch instruments catalyzed experimentation with temperaments that could keep chromatic intervals in tune relative to one another on the same keyboard or fretboard.

Twelve-tone equal temperament (TET) was a mathematical and musical achievement arrived at by theorists and composers in the seventeenth century. All interval ratios except the 2:1 octave were compromised so that the value in Hz of each next-highest semitone was the product of the previous one and $\sqrt[12]{2}$. The consistency made possible the system of twenty-four networked major and minor keys and reinforced the striking dualism of tonal opposition between tonic and dominant harmonies in each one. These features were the basis for far-reaching innovations in musical form and function, normalizing previously inaccessible and thus jarring and dramatic tonal regions. The pitch structures TET allowed became "the glory of European art music," and could "excavate channels of connection and continuity" in an abstract relational space of unprecedented dimension, unique in musics of the world (Benjamin 2006, 334, 374).

Glorious indeed, and captivating to this day, yet, from a bird's-eye perspective, the system was a phase, not a destination, and it yielded to modern splitting of the tradition into rivulets with diverse premises.[30] This may have been innate to the implications of TET tonality itself but was equally due to technologically driven historical forces: increased commerce, migration, and broader communication had broadened and upped cross-cultural musical interaction. TET solved the problem of temperament for a while, but hindsight shows that temperament wasn't the problem in the first place, it was more of a symptom. What the "problem" actually *was* can be proposed later on, but, meanwhile, note that just as composers let timbre shirk pitch, they unburdened pitch of tonality.

Counterpoint and Harmony.   This is the moment to concisely acknowledge what could easily have been the default focus throughout: the practice of contrapuntal voice leading between the sixteenth and nineteenth centuries. This is the realm of:

1. *Melodic motion:* step, skip, gap-fill, passing and neighbor tones
2. *Relative motion:* oblique, similar, parallel, contrary
3. *Permutation:* repetition, embellishment, reduction, extension, truncation, transposition, augmentation, diminution, inversion, retrograde, etc.

Which are typological features not specific to the materials of Western music, although they are the stuff of discourse about it. But features particular to it include:

4. *Consonant and dissonant intervals:* perfect, imperfect, major, minor, augmented, diminished

5. *Dissonance process:* suspension, appoggiatura, anticipation, cambiata, no preparation

6. *Melodic structure:* theme, subject, motive, sequence, transition, cadence

7. *Interpart relations:* idiom (rhythm species), dissonance approach and resolution, outer- and inner-voice treatment, chord voicing, imitation and stretto, free counterpoint

Of these, the most consequential for our purposes are the consonant and dissonant interval types, for as their classification changed, the other features felt the impact. The technological forces driving the evolution of scale, temperament, and harmony are operative here too. Over the centuries, the realm of consonance gradually engulfed and finally swallowed dissonance, dissolving the distinction between them and revealing both as constructs.

In plainchant, everything but the unison and octave was understood as dissonant, in organum, the perfect fifth was accepted, and later, as tuning and temperament allowed, so were the imperfect thirds and sixths. (Fourths were in and out of the club.) For seconds, sevenths, and tritones to no longer be treated as unstable dissonances took centuries on a zigzag course, toward the eventual advent of atonality. Of course, we find instances of scofflaw dissonance embedded in compositions of all eras, many only explainable as artistic necessity, delight in transgression, conceptual thinking, mystic prescience—whatever one calls it. They are everywhere—Gesualdo's bolts of chromatic harmony *(Beltà poi che t'assenti),* a dodecaphonic subject in J. S. Bach (the B-minor fugue in Book I of the WTC), free-floating tritones in Haydn (Largo, Symphony no. 64), poignant hanging sevenths in Chopin (B-minor and F-major Preludes), richly crunchy chords in Schumann *(Vogel als Prophet,* from the op. 82 piano set *Waldscenen)*—to touch only the tip of the tip of the iceberg. In modern jazz, tonal harmony and a thoroughly free approach to interval combinations became the bread and butter of the idiom; for artists like Thelonious Monk and Charles Mingus, all interval combinations were fair game. And with digital synthesis, not just TET but scale itself became optional. Just as timbre and pitch became free agents, intervallic dissonance was cut adrift.

We cannot neglect the perspective that tonality in some form is a permanent, embodied human percept transcending the perturbations of history and culture. Cognition research shows that human capacity to parse tonal pitch hierarchies is a power evolved precisely for that purpose and no other (Lerdahl and Jackendoff 2006). But these authors insinuate that Western art music tonality is more—let's not mince words—worthy:

> Traditional Western tonality has sought a greater convergence between sensory and musical factors than have many cultures . . . Huron (2001) demonstrates this for the conventional rules of Western counterpoint. For example, parallel octaves and fifths are avoided because parallel motion between such consonant intervals tends to fuse two voices into

one, contradicting the ideal in Western counterpoint of independent polyphonic voices. (Melodies sung in parallel fifths have a "medieval" sound to modern Western ears.) Parallel thirds and sixths, common in harmonization of modern Western melodies, are acceptable because these intervals are sufficiently dissonant to discourage fusion yet not so dissonant as to cause roughness. Cultures that do not seek a polyphonic ideal, however, have no need to incorporate such syntactic features into their musical idioms.

(Lerdahl and Jackendoff 2006, 48–49).

This recalls Jean-Phillipe Rameau in the eighteenth century, who, because the strongest harmonic overtones sounded a major triad, insisted upon tonality's naturalness—yet struggled to explain the minor triad. But unlike Lerdahl and Jackendoff, Rameau had no empirical meta-perspective on world traditions to speak of, although he made (usually erroneous) assertions about Chinese, Egyptian, and ancient Greek music based on travelers' reports and the like.[31] One response to Lerdahl and Jackendoff and Rameau is to say that tonality is no function of consonance and dissonance, but mere assertion of a basic tonal structure by any means at hand (often by repetition)—as the blues, minimalist composition, and other traditions show. There is no conflict once we disarticulate "Western" from "tonality," and do not confuse the vehicle with the engine.

How then to assess consonance and dissonance in cross-cultural perspective? A striking fact is that from Leonin to Webern (an apt antipode to Leonin), Western art music is irreducibly multi-voice. Heinrich Schenker showed that common practice tonality cannot be reduced to less than two contrapuntal voices: a scalar melodic descent, and a dominant-tonic resolution in the bass. More research is needed, but it would seem that many polyphonic traditions in contiguous geographic regions (Sardinia, the Balkans, Georgia, Russia, and more), while constituted with different principles, are multi-voiced also.[32] Whereas in some East and Southeast Asian musics, as mentioned when heterophony was discussed earlier, polyphonies may reduce to monophonic tunes, sometimes explicitly stated, sometimes implicit. Might it be beneficial to think about polyphony around the world in terms of this distinction?

Perlman (2004, 63) offers the term *divergence* to describe moments in Javanese gamelan music where multiple polyphonic parts align on different pitches "at a cadential point," only to reach their expected convergences at the unison with the core melodic structure afterward, and often at different times. Perhaps convergence and divergence, which have an air of neutrality and minimal baggage, are useful for thinking about consonance and dissonance as well. Divergence is the elemental polyphonic force par excellence in all of these traditions, and a key dimension of what we have been calling *difference* within them.

Rhythm. In one sense, Western rhythm has not been a "growth area" in the same way range, timbre, and pitch have, that is, by always accruing new resources over the centuries and never retrenching. Instead, for most of the millennium under consideration, we observe rhythm—perhaps the signature feature of musical style—oscillating between more and less complex patternings, through historical phases of innovation and consolidation, and varying among regional European idioms. Speech-based articulations of biblical Latin guided plainchant rhythm until early polyphony introduced the patterns of rhythmic modes, which were shortly upturned by intricate rhythm calculations of the *ars nova* in fourteenth-century France, a style refined through Palestrina's *ars perfecta* two centuries later. That conservatism yielded to the ornateness of the later Baroque and *Empfindsamkeit,* and settled in the eighteenth century on the transparent periodicity and tuneful dance rhythms of the classic style. In due course, they fragmented and swelled in the Romantic generations... and so on. With each phase, rhythm acquired possibilities but shed others.

In another way, actually in two ways, rhythm *has* always been on the march. Early polyphonic rhythms were limited to elemental divisions of the *tactus* into twos and threes, their notation was largely contextual to each piece, and polyphony was written in separate part books, limiting the manner of coordination among performers. Oral tradition enriched practice, but in the fourteenth century, music was transformed by discoveries in mathematics, a sister subject in the education quadrivium. New formulations explored multiplication exponents beyond those observable in the real world, i.e., squares and cubes, and revealed how species of *prolation,* or subdivision, could enlarge the rhythmic palette (Berger 1993). Musicians thenceforth began to conceive musical rhythm analogously, as a hierarchy of multiples of a fixed temporal reference unit, which notation was adapted to express (Taruskin 2010a, 248–252). This was a watershed after which notation eclipsed orality and fed back continuously into composers' imaginations, allowing them to see rhythm reflected off the page, and imagine larger and larger structures in a "bold leap of imagination" (Rowell 1994, 420). Eventually, they wrote music on scores in Cartesian grid format, and played multiple polyphonic parts on the peerless ergonomic compositional tool (prior to the computer), the keyboard.

The other way that rhythm grew, especially after the eighteenth century, was through emerging historical consciousness that resuscitated materials from its own past. The ascendance of the secular concert meant that more music was heard, and music publishing afforded better access to scores, inspiring composers to study and deploy prior styles expressively thenceforth. After 1900, the search for rhythm resources went global, and eventually virtual, and even further into the imagination. Technology was always there to make it happen.

In speaking of polyphony as a universal, what kinds of rhythm relationships do we find, distinct from those described in the Morris and Arom typologies? Rhythm is manifest in, and the vehicle for, movement of pitch and other dimensions. Rhythms have properties of *tempo* and *density* (number of events per unit of time), variety of *durations,* presence (or not) of *pulsation,* alignment (or not) of durations to pulsation, and articulation into segments or sections—by meter, by grouping of durations, or a mix of the two. There can be polyrhythm or homorhythm. Complementary or clashing, polyrhythms can differ even when they don't, as for example in hocket or imitation where identical rhythms start at different times.

Can one essentialize Western rhythm in terms of how it wields these properties? Not without pretending that history didn't happen. It is, however, a curious irony that, alongside J. S. Bach's, the jewel in the crown of the tradition is widely held to be the music of the First Viennese School. It is often described as a musical reflection of the age of clockmakers, enlightened reason, and Isaac Newton. Music was then in a simplification phase, and had incorporated the rhythms of dance and the public sphere with their regular, metric periodicities and clear melodic profiles. Granted, the way that style can enrich and subvert regularity is more to the point of classic music's idiosyncratic genius. But the foot-tapping regularity is *sui generis* and a striking exception among the succession of styles through which the tradition evolved. In the main, because of the intellectual resources devoted to refining notation and its pervasive effect, Western music could revel in overlapping contrapuntal lines and eschew regular periodicity and repetition. Whereas, in many traditions outside the West, they were manna.

Two Sets of Synonyms

To illustrate this millennium-long panorama with actual score analysis, which we will now do, is to cure vertigo with a skydive. Dizziness or nausea may result from rapid loss of altitude, but the air is not so thin at ground level, and the spinning sensation will slow. Yet one would have to be clueless to seek a meaningful chronology of examples showing successive increases in range, timbral variety, etc., as spied from on high, because life doesn't tidy that way. Those are tendencies building up statistically over centuries—pantries to stock, not recipes for dishes. Individual works cannot be expected to wear tendencies like badges. Compositions can differ as much or more from their contemporaries as they can from their future or past brethren because composers work in multiple genres, use varied techniques, and express many things. How then to choose? By limiting the variables and seeking difference amid similarity.

At the beginning and in the interlude about hocket (and once more to come) we introduced musical homonyms, juxtaposing polyphonies from contrasting traditions that sound superficially similar. Here we select a pair and a quartet of synonyms—different sounding but related in meaning—within Western art music. In each set, the similarity is anchored in a canonical shared tune, a fixed orientation bringing differences in polyphonic treatment into relief. The tunes are the anonymous secular chanson *L'Homme Armé* (The Man at Arms) in the pair, and the Lutheran chorale melody *Es ist genug* (It is enough) in the quartet. The composers as a group dwelled in every century from the fifteenth to twenty-first, from Antoine Busnoys (c. 1430–1492), Giovanni Pierluigi da Palestrina (1525–1594), Johann Rudolf Ahle, (1625–1673), and Johann Sebastian Bach (1685–1750), to Alban Berg (1885–1935) and Magnus Lindberg (1958–).

Two L'Homme Armé Masses. The careers of Busnoys and Palestrina bookend the era during which many composers used *L'Homme Armé* as a cantus firmus in settings of

FIGURE 21.10 Busnoys, *Kyrie Eleison, Missa L'Homme Armé.*

FIGURE 21.11 Palestrina, *Kyrie Eleison, Missa Quarta.*

the mass. The century that elapsed between them was a time of stylistic consolidation. We don't know the precise year of Busnoys's *Missa L'Homme Armé* but it was probably first heard in the years after 1460 (Taruskin 1986; Wegman 1999). We consider the latter of two *L'Homme Armé* masses that Palestrina wrote, titled simply *Missa Quarta* (fourth in order) in the 1584 folio of seven, *Missarum liber quartus* (fourth book of masses), published in Venice. This one, and that of 1572, were among the last *L'Homme Armé* masses overall, in fact his *ars perfecta* style marks dusk in the era of modal contrapuntal composition. Palestrina was a conservative whose tonal vocabulary is not much different than Busnoys's. Thus, their masses share not just a tune but a genre, norms of dissonance treatment, the vocal timbre, and because we will look only at the *Kyrie eleison* in each, a melismatically set text. Accordingly, we can narrow the focus: range will not be an issue, nor timbre, nor dissonance treatment, nor text-setting. With all of those similarities, the differences that point to real stylistic change are subtle and pregnant. We will consider the bass and its role in shaping harmony and cadence, and rhythm.[33]

The *Kyries* are shown in Figures 21.10 and 21.11. The tune (or at least the first part of it—the rest comes in subsequent portions of the mass) is quoted verbatim in Busnoys's tenor, its durations augmented fourfold with respect to the original. In the Palestrina, the tune comes in distorted and even briefer form, in imitation between the outer voices at a distance of four bars.

The bass: In Busnoys's *Kyrie* there are nineteen measures in triple meter and G-Dorian mode; in ten of them, the tonic G sounds in the lowest-sounding voice (usually bass, sometimes tenor) on the first beat. This happens five times in a row beginning at measure 10. D, the fifth scale degree, occupies this position only three times, at measures 8 and 9, but only at 16 does it do so as if to suggest, albeit weakly, harmonic arrival and muscular contrast with G. This moment is slightly reinforced by the chromatic neighbor E♭ in the previous measure, but the leading tone F♯ only arrives at the end of measure 18. Of the remaining modal tones in the bass, B♭, C, and E occur, respectively, thrice, twice and once at measure beginnings; A and F never do. There is scarce sense of a patterned meting out of tonal resources, and G so overwhelms the tonal quality throughout that one is tempted to invoke the idea of drone. The last four bars offer some contrast. Each has a different tone on the first beat, creating momentum to cadence.

Palestrina's seventeen-bar *Kyrie* is in duple meter and we always find a tone change at the first and third beats of the lowest voice, except at phrase beginnings and at the end. The long bass A at mm. 15–16 supports a clear dominant triad with a suspension in the alto yielding to a leading tone, and resolving to a bright tonic major third at m. 17.[34] The bass A is reached through a full octave step-descent starting in the middle of m. 11, leaping from C to A at the nadir to accentuate the following B♭'s strong subdominant aura. The equivalent E♭ at the same spot in the Busnoys has less oomph because it doesn't last as long, and harmony is weaker overall. Palestrina gives every Dorian scale tone a chance to shine on a strong bass beat, plus that B♭, reserved for its special use.

Rhythm: In a first impression, Busnoys's rhythm is nimble and the parts individuated and independent. He uses ten different durational values of ¼, ½, 1, 1½, 2, 3, 4, 6, 8, or 12 quarters— a 48:1 ratio between fastest and slowest. The faster ones are in play much of the time, in at least one voice. Palestrina uses six values, of 1, 2, 3, 4, 6, or 8 quarters, an 8:1 ratio; his inventory of durations is austere by comparison, and the lines are independent but similarly paced.

The composition of lines and the textures they collaboratively make strengthen the contrasts between the *Kyries*. Busnoys's has spontaneity and generates a roiling texture of changing contours. Except for the quasi-imitation and longer durations at the very beginning, foreshadowing *L'Homme Armé* in the tenor, lines zig and zag, and there is scant motivic relation among parts. As if to divine compositional momentum where harmony and melody give little help, the noteheads get blacker and blacker in all voices but the tenor near the end.

Palestrina's texture is sleek but unexciting by comparison. *L'Homme Armé*'s own contour, in the outer voices, already satisfies the composer's predilection for leaps up followed by long descents. Meanwhile the inner voices cohere around a stepwise ascent of a fifth that comes in the alto at measures 2, 9, and 15, and in the tenor, in slower rhythm, at measures 2–3 (with a small kink) and 5–6. The dramatic octave leap in the altus at m. 11 launches a sinuous descent pervading the second half. Expunging Busnoyesque complication for a restrained surface rhythm, something mysterious begins to come into focus. That of course would be harmonic tonality, an image on the horizon just starting to resolve. Palestrina could only have suspected, and Rameau was a century ahead.

FIGURE 21.12 (a) J. R. Ahle, *Es ist genug*. (b) J. S. Bach, *Es ist genug*. (c) Alban Berg, from Violin Concerto.

It Is Enough. Johann Sebastian Bach, the West's paragon of excellence and expression in the composition of polyphony, is here represented with but a tiny and concentrated sample. With the particular reverence one feels for Bach, not affording a wider berth to his music is a fraught musicological choice. The melody of *Es ist genug*, moreover, was actually composed by Johann Rudolf Ahle in 1662.[35] The opening measures of his, Bach's, and Alban Berg's arrangements are illustrated in Figure 21.12(a)–(c). The opening of Finnish composer Magnus Lindberg's orchestral version of 2002 is shown in short score in Figure 21.12(d). Ahle's melody, in B♭ major, begins with a powerful agent (bracketed in the figures): four whole-tone scale steps spanning B♭–C–D–E, the diabolical tritone, the tradition's most potent intervallic force for change and mark of difference.[36]

Detested in medieval times, and gradually domesticated via experiments in temperament during the Renaissance, by Bach's day, the tritone was both unstable and natural. Its voices moving by semitone in opposite directions yielded a minor sixth (or major third when inverted), whose consonance was in permanent tension with the tritone's dissonance. The tritone slices the octave exactly in half, and in TET that symmetry gave each tritone an enharmonic equivalent native to the key a tritone away: F–B folds out to the minor sixth E–C, confirming C major as tonic, but its homonym B–E♯ folds out to A♯–F♯, confirming F♯.[37] Structures such as augmented sixth and diminished seventh chords, major-minor modal mixtures, octatonicism, omnibus progressions, and a variety of others are all in one way or another a dimensional reflection of this symmetry, and their implosive effect on the tonal system accrued and accrued.[38] It is glib to equate the tritone's growing impact with a progress-oriented dialectical view of the tradition's history, but it's no exaggeration to say that its evolution was implicit in TET. It would have been inconceivable for its implications *not* to have been discovered and exploited.

The smooth accessibility of all tonalities gradually chipped away at tonal hierarchy itself, and led to atonality, a horizon that could not be unattained once attained. It is enough, says *Es ist genug*'s text, to live a life of suffering and be embraced by the Lord at its end; and it is enough, says the Western tradition, to have passed centuries in unstable relationship to a certain dissonance, only to finally embrace it without judgment, to neutralize our perception of its dissonance and change its status to that of one sound different than, but equal among, others.

Ahle's version treats the high E as the raised fourth degree of the B♭-major scale and harmonizes it with a C-major triad—the applied dominant of F, B♭'s own dominant. The exposed E, and the melodic tritone it tops, were deeply expressive for listeners of the era, but Ahle goes only so far to paint the text. The phrase has textbook voice-leading balance: the soprano moves in similar motion with the alto, oblique with the tenor, and contrary with the bass. The harmonies used in measure 1 are only V and I. The C-major chord coming next suggests a Lydian mode, or mild uncertainty about what the tonic is.

Bach's approach to these four chords, and painting the text, is audacious. We are at a loss to situate the bass line at first. Its first through third notes, B♭–A–B♮, complete a chromatic trichord that may as well be atonal. The second through fourth bass notes form a whole tone trichord, and are in canon at the minor ninth below with the soprano. When we hear the second chord, a first inversion dominant to the initial B♭, we are all right. But the third chord is an inverted G major triad which, heard as a pair with the previous chord, could mean IV–V to an impending C major tonic—which would be right out of the style. The parallelism with the F triad is only possible because alto and tenor voices have switched places at the third chord to avoid parallel fifths with the soprano; we are distracted from noticing by the ruse of the alto's E♭–D appoggiatura. The parallel fifths are still evoked, though, as the fifth between soprano and alto on chord four seems to confirm, and if Bach didn't intend as much he could certainly have done differently. That chord, supporting the crowning note of the melody's tritone, is also parallel to the previous two, which leaves our ears with one, thankfully correct, option: to hear the bass whole tones as steps 5–6–7 in an ascending D melodic minor. But before one knows this, when one is poised between chords three and four, an expressive chasm gapes. The D-minor resolution comes at measure 3, and the rest of the phrase punctures the intensity (it could hardly have been increased). The B♭–E soprano tritone never does resolve to F major, as it should and does in Ahle, but hangs there, while the one that does, C♯ to G in the bass and tenor of chord four, brings in D minor through a rear door.

Berg's decision to incorporate *Es ist genug* into the Violin Concerto, his final complete composition, bespeaks historical consciousness. It is a twelve-tone work often extolled and analyzed in part because of its overt gestures to the past. The first nine notes of Berg's row suggest dovetailed G-minor, D-major, A-minor, and E-major triads, while the last four are a whole-tone tetrachord like *Es ist genug*'s (see the lower left corner of Figure 21.12). Berg

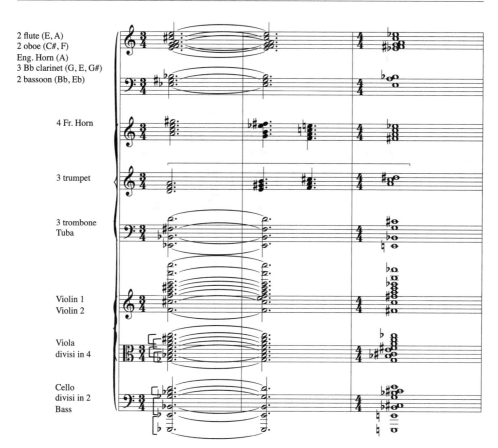

FIGURE 21.12D Magnus Lindberg, *Chorale*, mm. 1–3.

exploited these features, and sketch studies show that he fully investigated them in advance (Headlam 1993, 163); tonal analyses of the piece have been attempted (Pople 1991).[39] The blend of tonality and atonality powerfully symbolizes the inevitable outcome of the past that Berg (and Schoenberg and Webern) felt their music to be. I preface my remarks about the Concerto this way to acknowledge this aspect of the music's character, although to the listening ear, there is little about the *Es ist genug* quotation at measures 135–142 of the second movement that exudes tonality in the warp and weft of the polyphony, whatever the composer may have intended there or elsewhere.

In the passage cited, *Es ist genug* first appears in canon at the fifth between viola and violin, beginning with the viola E♭ in measure 134. The viola changes roles at 136 but the violin solo floats atop, playing Ahle's melody accompanied by active polyphony for viola and contrabassoon (handing off to bassoon). Three occurrences of the row are outlined and each labeled with order numbers 1–12; the first begins with the low F♯ in 136, the next with the viola B♭ in 138, and the last, in retrograde inversion, with the violin E in 140. The arpeggiation built into the row makes the first easy to hear despite the E marked * in the middle of measure 138, which is extraneous to the row (the viola F does duty). If this was an error on Berg's part we know not, but the row contour, already familiar by now, carries the day. Contour also makes the retrograde version easy to parse, although perhaps not until measure 141, where it settles in the bassoon. The second occurrence is veiled because the contour is shuffled. Some notes come out of order or piled up—including the initial B♭. Elsewhere, there are touches of heterophony, in the shared pitches of viola and bassoon beginning in m. 137, as well as many notes not accounted for at all in this short depiction. One is struck too by the dusky, murmuring timbre of strings and bassoon in close counterpoint, and by how the tessitura begins wide, narrows with the first bassoon arpeggio, and partly reopens with the second one.

The row has melodic and rhythmic force as used here, and provides harmonic color especially in a passage like mm. 141–142, where there are no extraneous tones (the viola onsets double the bassoon's). It is however no casting of aspersions on Berg or his method to say that even adept listeners hear mainly polyphonic independence, and little that is analogous to vertical constraints of tonal consonance and dissonance. Unlike with most tonal harmonies, moreover, the row is dissociated from the meter and pulsation. This suppresses periodicity, a key aspect of tonal rhythm. Berg's polyphony refers to Bach, but its dissonance is emancipated in many ways.

Saluting Berg, Bach, and Ahle, Magnus Lindberg's *Chorale* uses *Es ist genug* yet again, here, at the opening, perched in the upper voice of a trumpet trio.[40] But although the melody projects through, it is mainly bathing in an orchestral pool of glistening harmonies covering a more-than-six-octave range. In measures 1 and 3, the chords contain ten of the twelve pitch classes, while the chords in measure 2 fill in bar 1's missing G and B. There is felt harmonic motion, to be sure, strengthened by the change in bass from E♭ to E♮, the inverse of this in the top wind and string notes, and the wedge-shaped motion of the horns and trumpets toward one another. Such orchestration, with meticulous attention to doublings and spacing, is the star. (The woodwind voicing in the first chord is specified to the left of the staff, and the low strings' double stops are bracketed.) Ahle's tritone has lost its tonal moorings and is subservient to the timbre.

Seen through these four examples, the tritone's biography from 1662–2002 is a *Bildungsroman* of how it evolved from being a tonic-confirmer (Ahle), to a mischief-maker (Bach), to an office of full TET equality (Berg), to membership in a spectrum of sound for sound's sake (Lindberg). Fully emblematic of the notion of dissonance in Western polyphony, its story is indicative of the "problem" Western art music been investigating with its huge expansion of possibilities: namely, what exactly is dissonance? What processes inhere to all Western polyphony after we have accounted for the irregular paths of stylistic and technological changes? We have seen the possibilities for *difference* increase exponentially, with corresponding lessening of the impulse to experience dissonance as conflict or tension. Dissonance and consonance meld. As students of world music traditions deepen their perspectives, we will have opportunities to compare the West's to other histories of dissonance and difference.

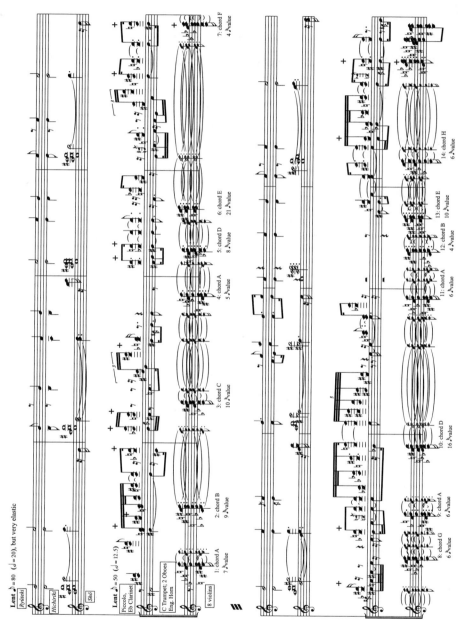

FIGURE 21.13 Gagaku *Etenraku* (adapted from Terauchi 2011, 32), aligned above Olivier Messiaen's "Gagaku" from *Sept Haïkaï*.

FINAL HOMONYM

We have considered oral tradition polyphonies and those of the European past, but what about when those worlds collide? The two previous homonym pairs were from Krk/Flores and Uganda/Bali, places whose people, even today, would be unlikely to meet or hear each other's music. In contrast, the members of this pair were parties to an actual encounter. Figure 21.13 juxtaposes the first complete melodic phrase of the composition *Etenraku* (music from heaven, ⊙ Audio Example 21.5), from the repertoire of the ancient Japanese court ensemble *gagaku,* with the first eight measures of "Gagaku," the fourth movement of French composer Olivier Messiaen's 1962 composition *Sept Haïkaï* (Seven Haiku). After a trip to Japan, during which he heard *gagaku,* Messiaen (1908–1992) chose to compose a homonym in homage, but in his idiolect. His distinctive compositional language proved up to the task, for heard side-by-side, and despite the very different instrumentation, the pieces are uncannily evocative of one another. Yet, on paper, the notations reveal no correspondence: Messiaen went in with surgical precision and produced something complex to both eye and ear; *Etenraku* is simple in concept and looks that way on paper, but doesn't sound that way. To account for the sonic resemblance we are advised to look behind the notes at traditions of performance practice. Just as in the West, Japanese music has accommodated changing perceptions of difference over time.

Gagaku has several repertoires; *Etenraku* is an example of *togaku,* music with origins in China. From the seventh century, it was heard only in the Imperial Palace or the homes of aristocrats; only very recently has it migrated to new, often educational contexts. The lead melody instruments are the double reed *hichiriki* and transverse flute *ryûteki,* plus the seventeen-pipe bamboo mouth organ *shô,* playing slow thick chords called *aitake.* Not shown in the figure are the plucked string instruments *koto* and *biwa* that punctuate strong beats with clipped arpeggio patterns, and a small battery of gongs and drums that play a repeating rhythm cycle. The music is understood to be in a mode called *hyô-jô,* akin to a Dorian mode on E. The wind instrument parts are written almost entirely in parallel octaves, while the lowest *shô* tone in each *aitake* matches the winds' note at the beginning of each measure. Only four scale tones come at measure beginnings—D (mm. 1 and 5), E (mm. 3, 4, 7, and 8), B (m. 2), and F♯ (m. 6)— hence there are only four *aitake* in this passage, sometimes differing in voice-leading details, but with the same notes stacked the same way. Terauchi (2011) explains that this way of arranging the music into a score, based on a variety of tablature and other sources dating in some cases as far back as the eighth century, reflects the musicians' conception that all parts reduce to a single basic melody, given in its simplest form by the lowest *shô* notes.

But while the music barely looks polyphonic on the page, the pungent pitch divergences we hear reflect sedimented, idiomatic changes in *hichiriki* and *ryûteki* fingering and embouchure that have become standardized over the centuries. This causes them to veer to and from one another in waves of pitch and dynamic divergence.[41] For pitch, this is especially prominent in measure 5 where the counterpoint has chromatic bite. At other moments, the higher *ryuteki* blends but its piercing, sliding tone enriches the *hichiriki* as if by the addition of inharmonic upper partials. The *shô* player's fingers, meanwhile, gently open or stop selected pipes, bringing chordal inner voices to the fore, one by one, each creating a distinctive intervallic relation to the *hichiriki* and *ryûteki*.

Neither does rhythm sound as it looks. Although tempi were apparently faster in the past, in current practice the music is slow, and in wild flux during performance. Each instrument in the timbrally diverse ensemble is a soloist, and has a distinctive attack-decay profile. The percussion's rhythmic cycle, *haya yo hyôshi*, tumbles. It lasts four measures, but the small *kakko* drum plays a few different kinds of roll whose strokes change speed very quickly. One cannot tap a steady beat. The elasticity is such that responsibility for leading and coordinating the ensemble falls to the musician whose part at any given instant most strongly delineates the beat as the musicians have learned to embody it, and who that is continually changes, as much as once per beat (Terauchi 2011, 34). All of these features combined imbue the perception of *gagaku* with an inner life of polyphonic difference, even if the music is monophonic in concept.

Messiaen assigned an octet of violins to the *shô* role, a duo of piccolo and E♭ clarinet playing in varied intervals to the *ryûteki,* and a quartet of C trumpet, two oboes, and English horn playing in unison to the *hichiriki.* I have lettered the octet chords A to H below the staff; like the *aitake,* they are limited in number and repeat irregularly.[42] In measure 1, the lowest note of the first two chords (G♯/A♭) even matches the quartet's G♯ on beat 3, just as the *shô* would. The quartet's stately melody focuses, quasi-modally, on only a few pitches, especially at first: F♯, G♯, and E dominate in the first half, then D to C♯ in measures 4–5, and high E for the remainder. The duo's part is skittish and much more chromatic than the quartet's, but I place a + at each moment where it aligns with a quartet onset. This happens more at the beginning than the end of the passage, but often at points of articulation, before or after pauses. This loosely synchronizes the duo and quartet strands, similar to how the *hichiriki* and *ryûteki* interact. I have also placed a + above the octet at the two places where it aligns with both other parts. This divides the whole passage nearly exactly in half.

Other than this mild coordination, Messiaen's rhythms float in durational layers so divergent that pulsation and periodicity are virtually flat-lined. The durations of the string chords (and those of percussion parts, not shown) vary according to arithmetically derived permutation schemes characteristic of the composer's work (see Sawatzky 2013, 131–132). The contrast in density between the strings and winds/brass radically stratifies them as orchestral sections, their planes askew. But the aural result is surprisingly Japanese. In this way, Messiaen mimicked a rhythm style achieved collectively and without notation by the *gagaku* players.

That the homonym succeeds aurally owes much to Messiaen's refined mind and ear, but we should put that explanation in a social context. The music reflects the empowering wealth, personal freedom, and education that cultivated Messiaen's very desire for the encounter. It relies on the technology he could wield—of notation, agile instruments, of recordings that exposed him to *gagaku,* and (worth pointing out even if mundane) transportation that allowed him to visit for direct exposure and inspiration. A Catholic mystic, Messiaen also appreciated the slow ritual qualities of Japanese *gagaku* and saw in them the timeless realm he strove to create in many works with layered rhythm permutations, a fully chromatic pitch idiom eschewing tonal oppositions, and by evoking birdsong. There is thus an aesthetic confluence.[43]

Should we have called this pair a synonym rather than a homonym since they both reference the same tradition? Reasonable people could disagree—this is music, after all, and meaning is more negotiable than in language. But consider that: (1) in concept *Etenraku* is monophonic and Messiaen's *Gagaku* is irreducibly polyphonic; and (2) *Etenraku,* though archived in notation, is a collective practice, whereas Messiaen's is an individual's concept. It comes to life only when an autocrat (the conductor) leads others who follow written parts and have less musical agency than the Japanese musicians, who do not perform from notation, and share the leadership. That the composer *intended* the musics to sound similar is only one of many factors in play, and the aural resemblance is only one dimension of what they signify, just as with language homonyms. To facilely conflate their meanings would be to undervalue the long traditions on whose shoulders they stand.

DIFFERENCE UNBOUND

We saw at the outset that for the deepest of listeners, difference emanates from within virtually all sound-in-time, and is innate to time's passage. But in ordinary experience it is the social and historical construction of difference between discrete tones that regulates the realm of the polyphonic. Musical syntaxes emerge from the splitting of different kinds of difference into those that are permitted to coexist without restriction (the convergent, the consonant) and those that must yield (the divergent, the dissonant). In the West, these categories have been unstable and led to their own dissolution. In *gagaku,* we observe a related kind of evolution where the psychoacoustic frequencies of the two wind instruments oscillate between divergence and convergence in modern performance, although they are founded on a quite ancient equivalence throughout, that is, of playing the same modal degree. Theory and practice cleaved polyphonically, and difference proliferated.

Figure 21.14 (⊙ Audio Example 21.6), a passage of twenty-first-century Balinese gamelan music, can be compared with *Jaya Semara,* discussed in Figure 21.8. In this, a snippet from the composer Dewa Ketut Alit's 2000 work *Geregel,* features of the earlier example such as the slow, steady core melody and the vertical unisons that came at every strong beat, are absent. In *Geregel,* three of the four parts meet at the scale-degree unison at the outset, and at beat 19, while all four parts converge just once in the middle. But these alignments are as if happenstance. Instead what unifies and clarifies

FIGURE 21.14 From *Geregel* (2000) by Dewa Ketut Alit.

Performed by members of Sanggar Çudamani, Pengosekan, Bali. Recorded by Michael Tenzer.

the counterpoint are the four-tone pitch collection (shown as E–F♯–G♯–B), the careful rhythmic and registral stratification of the parts, the independence of their melodic material, their shared periodicity of 20 beats, and their emphasis through repetition. What happened to Balinese music in the near-century that elapsed between the composition of these two pieces? The answer is simple: technology and travel brought Balinese into close contact with music from everywhere else; composers' imaginations did the rest. Alit's style is not typical, but it is exemplary.

To characterize the Western, Japanese, and Balinese examples of accumulating tolerance for difference as a norm or universal would be a rush to judgment on a par with Jaap Kunst's proposal of homologies between Eastern Europe and Eastern Indonesia that our initial homonym refuted. More conservative traditions can restrict or resist notions of difference, Palestrina-like, in the spirit of preservation or fealty to a time-honored social and musical practice. They may not change much or at all. Indeed, to view polyphony from as great a distance as we could, we have juxtaposed worlds of oral tradition and "classical" musics, emphasized sonic output and technical means, and only sometimes considered social practice. In a study focused on multi-part music-making in older, smaller societies, Macchiarella issues a plea to regard polyphony in such terms, and its "deep essence as a human action" (2012, 22). Humanity's many specific polyphonic practices are strongly rooted in their own times and places.

But if we leave the realm of the classical and oral and focus for these last few words on what is global and of our time, it would seem that in music, sounds with difference now can coexist and move with complete freedom. Accelerated, contemporary cross-cultural mixing and idiolectic choice are social practices too, even as the music made in that way jostles the old and the oral-traditional, the unmediated and the culturally bounded, the under-the-radar and the ungoogleable—to the margins. Digitally wired studio producers can juxtapose samples from the entire world library of recorded, acoustic, and synthetic sound. Composers can be the prophets they always were, now with that same omnibus access. If music does not, as some say, predict the future, it is at least a hopeful field reflecting present idealism, and dreams of the future. Would that these impulses bear fruit in a future of polyphonic politics and social relations.

Audio Examples

Audio Example 21.1. *Otrgnem Rožicu Ruman Cvet.* (Performers and recording unknown.)

Audio Example 21.2. *Najan.* Waiklibang, Flores, Indonesia. Performers: Bapak Lego and Bapak Dagan (Recorded by Dana Rappoport, 2005, used with permission.)

Audio Example 21.3. Excerpt from *Jaya Semara.* Perfomers: members of Sanggar Çudamani; Pengosekan, Bali. (Recorded by Lisa Gold, 2003, used with permission.)

Audio Example 21.4. *Olutalo olwè nsinsi* (The Battle of Nsinsi), Amadinda version. Performers: Albert Sempeke and group. (Recorded by Gerhard Kubik, 1962, used with permission.)

Audio Example 21.5. Etenraku, Nokorigaku Sanben (Hyojo). Performed by the Imperial Court Ensemble. (Excerpted from Track 2 of *Gagaku: Ancient Japanese Court and Dance Music.* Legacy CD 402. 1994.)

Audio Example 21.6. Excerpt from *Geregel.* Perfomers: members of Sanggar Çudamani; Pengosekan, Bali. (Recorded by the author, 2003.)

Notes

1. The scale was first described by Austro-Hungarian composer Ivan Ronjgov (1880–1960).

2. Regional variants of the song can be very different in tune, scale, title, and text; see for example https://www.youtube.com/watch?v=gnVD5Dwx9EY (personal communication, Josko Caleta, Institute of Folklore and Ethnology, Zagreb, June 27, 2016).

3. Coming at the end, it is uncannily like the two-voice concluding phrase of the first movement of Bartók's *Music for Strings Percussion and Celesta*, which sums up the entire fugue in just a few notes—and Bartók did know this music. More generally, the modal transformation of the chromatic fugue subject to a diatonic tune in the last movement of that piece reminds one of the link between this song and its more conventional tonal variants (see note 2).

4. Messner (1989) investigates music from three Floresian villages, contemplates Kunst's legacy of Flores research, and reports on the astonishment of both Floresian and Bulgarian villagers to whom he played recordings of each other's songs.

5. An inset in Rappoport's transcription of *Najan* (2011, 121), specifies her use of the five-tone collection B, C, D, E♭, F, but there are also instances of A and G in the transcription itself. I hear six pitches (some indistinct, it is true) and have rewritten the music with the same notes used in the Krk song for ease of comparison. Also, alignment between systems in Rappoport's transcription does not bring out the periodicity of eighteen beats, which I show in my reworking.

6. See also Jordania (2006), a remarkable survey of polyphonic music throughout the world. Jordania is associated with http://polyphony.ge/en/home-2/, a research center in Tbilisi founded in 2003 after UNESCO added traditional Georgian polyphony to its roster of world intangible cultural heritages. The center holds biannual conferences on traditional polyphonies of the world and issues numerous publications.

7. For a concise summary of research about cognitive constraints on music perception, see Lerdahl (1992, 102–115). Research continues to support the idea that harmonic consonance, traditionally defined, is an innate preference (see for example McDermott et al. 2010 or Cousineau et al. 2012).

8. Bonifačić (1991), an experienced Croatian researcher, investigated this very question with extensive interviews and reached inconclusive results, as her article candidly describes. The quest for musicians' conceptions of their own music is an important aspect of ethnomusicology research, and can rely on informants' verbalizations, descriptive metaphors, and inferences at various levels of overt awareness. But intersubjective communication about such elusive topics is always problematic, especially cross-culturally.

9. See Savage and Brown (2013) for optimistic assessment of new prospects for this longstanding but often troubled (for the reasons given here) research stream.

10. The elaboration of "difference" as an inherent property of something, independent of a distinct other, is important to the philosophy of Gilles Deleuze. He articulated the full independence of difference from "identity," as opposed to the more conventional usage of the two terms in a relation of complementarity (Deleuze 1994). As for music—critical

to his thought in general—the implications of Deleuzian difference for the concept of "tone" extend beyond the timbral and polyphonic unfolding that I emphasize. Hulse, for example, in an essay on Delueze and music theory, writes of pure duration: "Duration is the repetition of tone unfolding its difference, insisting and consisting in time" (2010, 32).

11. "Micropolyphony" is used with apologies to and differently than the composer György Ligeti did. He used it to describe the chromatically clustered, closely intertwined, multiple parts of some instrumental textures in his music of the 1960s and 1970s.

12. Morris's original typology was *only* intended to categorize the "ways two tones of equal or different duration can succeed each other," and did not address polyphony. My version is a truncation of his original thirteen categories, which continued on with number 8 flipping the upper and lower bars of number 6, and so on for 9 and 5, 10, and 4, 11 and 3, 12 and 2, and 13 and 1. For the purposes of his discussion of musical time, he wished to conceptually prioritize the sounds' independent identities, hence the inclusion of their inverted forms.

13. Cognition researchers have investigated factors affecting whether or not a stream of individual sounds (whether detached or connected) are perceived as polyphonic. Strong contrasts in volume, pitch, timbre, and spatial origin accentuate difference. Dowling's 1973 experiment on interleaving, for example, alternates tones of *Frère Jacques* and *Twinkle Twinkle* one-by-one in the same register and key. Listening subjects recognize neither tune but hear instead a new, long sequence of the two shuffled tunes. But when one of the tunes is shifted up an octave in the same rhythm positions, the two melodies are heard in a distinctly polyphonic way (Dowling and Harwood 1986, 125; Bey and McAdams 2003). We ought to also keep the effect of time scale in mind. Any of Morris's seven ways, if rendered extremely slow or fast, would confound memory or perception. Our bodies have a hard time correlating two tones sufficiently far apart in time or space, or so close in microseconds that they can no longer be distinguished.

14. The authors do cite some examples from Western art music repertoire. But they state their purpose thus: "Encompassing non-written musics, the typology draws upon traits that any music lover can perceive by simple listening" (Arom et al. 2007, 1088). *("S'agissant de musiques non écrites, la typologie prend appui sur des traits que toute mélomane averti peut déceler à la simple écoute.")*

15. The CDs are out of print but permanently accessible at CREM, Paris (Centre de Recherche en Ethnomusicologie): http://archives.crem-cnrs.fr/archives/collections/CNRSMH_E_ 1996_013_001/. On the web page, the CD tracks are numbered as 003–001 to 003–030 just to the right of the track titles in the Title column. Space limitations prevent including more information here on these selections and those in the other two CDs in the set (devoted to different kinds of vocal "techniques"). A great deal of valuable research is summarized in the extensive booklet, downloadable at http://archives.crem-cnrs.fr/archives/collections/ CNRSMH_E_1996_013_001/related/5/view/.

16. Polymusic can be thought of as meta-polyphony. From Charles Ives's youthful memories of multiple marching bands converging on the town square in New England to rituals throughout Southeast Asia, it is common for multiple ensembles/choruses/groups to make music separately but together in a large open space, increasing the power, effect, and copiousness of the activity (see Rappoport 2013, on Indonesian types).

17. See Feld (1988, 80), for description of the Kaluli "lift-up-over-sounding" aesthetic of the imitation in track 3.

18. See Arom (1991, 451–507).

19. Yampolsky 2015, a comparative study of music in Eastern Indonesia and Timor, uses Arom et al.'s categories to formulate sub-categories useful for more finely classifying polyphonies of the region. For example, tiling is broken down into contrastive and iterative antiphony; hocket into instrumental and vocal; homorhythm into occasional, parallel, assigned harmonies, mixed intervals, and divergent motion; counterpoint into that with homorhythmic tendencies (plural ostinati), descant over chorus, and rhythmic independence, etc. (Yampolsky 2015, 179). I make some similar distinctions describing the *Voix du Monde* CD below.

20. Audio Example 21.3 is a condensed, edited amalgam of tracks 19 and 20 from the CD accompanying Gold (2004). See Tenzer (2000, 327–331), for a full transcription of this piece, and that book's CD2, track 3, for a recording.

21. *Pélog* is a Javanese term that has become standard. The local term is *saih lima*, series of five.

22. Available in 29 book volumes or online at www.oxfordmusiconline.com, subscription only.

23. Despite a great deal of space devoted to a comparative view of the topic, fully fifty percent (6,583 out of 13,115 words) of Blum's brilliant essay is consecrated to a historically based presentation of composition in Western art music. Powers's 1980 "Mode" article, influential and pathbreaking for its deep treatment of mode in several cultures, was nonetheless even more disproportionate in that way.

24. Powers quotes L. P. Hartley's novel *The Go-Between*: "The past is a foreign country: they do things differently there" (2000, 55).

25. This is not to imply in any way that music advances in value, although it surely does advance in technique and precision. For discussion of this issue see Meyer 1994 and, on why the arts do not develop by "supersession" of new works over previous ones and "progression toward greater truth," see Meyer (2000, 24). And of course a focus on technology is merely one of several others (political, social, aesthetic, etc.) that would be needed for a fuller portrait.

26. Music itself can be considered a technology, if one does not consider it instead an evolutionary adaptation on a par with language, or if one is skeptical that human evolution and the technologies humans invent are in fact separable. For a summary of the debate on this issue see Lawson (2014).

27. Standard references include Ellis and Mendel (1968) and Mendel (1978).

28. My gratitude goes to Michael Cuthbert for searching his database of 3,000 fourteenth-century works at my request. See post to the Ars Nova Facebook Group, July 26, 2016: https://www.facebook.com/groups/128983113783974/.

29. The number of interval classes multiplied by n where n is the cardinality of the scale gives the number of distinct dyads. This is also calculated with the formula for the binomial coefficient, or "n-choose-k": where $n = 12, 7,$ or $5,$ and $k = 2$.

30. This statement alludes to atonality, electronic sound synthesis, and other post-1900 accretions to Western music's language, but is not intended to suggest, as some did, that they were historically inevitable or desirable (though technology made them conceivable and, following the culture's spirit of invention, probable). Nevertheless, once they came into existence they could no longer be unavailable. Many felt these changes to be a flat-out mistake (Levi-Strauss 1969); and some held that spurning pure intervals was itself fatal (Partch 1974).

31. See Christensen (1993, 272), for discussion of Rameau's strategies to encompass the minor triad within his theory and ibid., 294–296, for sources of his remarks on Chinese and Egyptian music theories.

32. In the *Voix du Monde* collection introduced in note 15, Sardinia and Corsica are heard on tracks 17–19, and Georgia on 20 and 23. Balkan musics in this collection (Macedonia and Albania on tracks 15 and 25) are drone-based, and nothing from Russia is included.

33. Many movements in Busnoys's mass are packed with structural mathematics and rhythmic permutations that bear the stamp of the previous century's *ars nova*, but not the *Kyrie*. See Taruskin (1986).

34. No claim is made that this is a norm. In four-voice Palestrina compositions, "the proportion of perfect cadences which omit the third is very high, probably about fifty percent" (Boyd 1973, 8).

35. Ahle was organist at St. Blasius church in Mühlhausen. His son Johann Georg succeeded him, and J. S. Bach in turn succeeded him, in 1707 (Buelow 2004, 228).

36. In its setting at the end of Bach's cantata *O Ewigkeit, du Donnerwort*, BWV 60, *Es ist genug* is given in A major, but I have transposed it to B♭ to match both Ahle and Berg. Lindberg writes the melody a semitone lower, as if in A, where I have left it.

37. One of the voices moving by whole step yields a minor third, and minor tonality.

38. See Cohn (2012) for additional chromatic harmony constructs, and Schoenberg (1983) for a catalog of ways to construct modulations between remote keys.

39. Some passages are overtly triadic, albeit constrained by the rigors of twelve-tone writing. The G-minor–D-major–A-minor–E-major progression at measures 11–15 in the first movement are often cited as tonal, although they should be read in reverse to make sense as a tonal progression (Taruskin 2010b, 715).

40. Hear the Lindberg *Chorale* at https://www.youtube.com/watch?v=UBrQjIZw1lA.

41. The passage shown in Figure 21.13 is usually repeated, and the first time through only the *ryûteki* and percussion play for the first five measures. The ensemble then enters at measure 6.

42. Irlandini (2010), 202, analyzes this passage and comes up with a slightly different result; I believe he has erred on the eighth chord, which he may have omitted.

43. Irlandini (2010) discusses these matters in more detail.

WORKS CITED

Arom, Simha. 1991. *African Polyphony and Polyrhythm: Musical Structure and Methodology.* Cambridge: Cambridge University Press.

Arom, Simha, Nathalie Fernando Fernando, Susanne Fürniss, Fabrice Marandola, et al. 2007. "Typologie des Techniques Polyphoniques." In *Musiques: Une encyclopédie pour le XXIe siècle*, volume 5, edited by Jean-Jacques Nattiez, 1088–1109. Arles and Paris: Actes Sud/Cité de la Musique.

Benjamin, William. 2006. "Mozart: Piano Concerto No. 17 in G Major, K. 453, Movement 1." In *Analytical Studies in World Music*, edited by Michael Tenzer, 332–376. New York: Oxford University Press.

Berger, Anna Maria Busse. 1993. *Mensuration and Proportion Signs: Origin and Evolution.* Oxford: Clarendon Press.

Bey, Caroline, and Stephen McAdams. 2003. "Postrecognition of Interleaved Melodies as an Indirect Measure of Auditory Stream Formation." *Journal of Experimental Psychology: Human Perception and Performance* 29: 267–279.

Blum, Stephen. 2001. "Composition." In *The New Grove Dictionary of Music and Musicians*, edited by S. Sadie and J. Tyrell. New York: Oxford University Press.

Bonifačić, Ruža. 1991. "Mi Cemo Zak'antat Glason Od Slavića: Koncepclje Izvodača o Tradicijskom Pjevanju u Puntu Na Otoku Krku." ("We Will Sing with the Voice of the Nightingale: Conceptions of Traditional Singing Held by Performers on the Island of Krk.") *Narodna umjetnost: hrvatski časopis za etnologiju i folkloristiku (Croatian Journal of Ethnology and Folklore Research)* 28: 49–84.

Boyd, Malcolm. 1973. *Palestrina's Style: A Practical Introduction.* London: Oxford University Press.

Brinner, Benjamin. 1995. *Knowing Music, Making Music: Javanese Gamelan and the Theory of Musical Competence and Interaction.* Chicago: University of Chicago Press.

Buelow, George. 2004. *A History of Baroque Music.* Bloomington: University of Indiana Press.

Christensen, Thomas. 1993. *Rameau and Musical Thought in the Enlightenment.* Cambridge: Cambridge University Press.

CNRS/Musée de l'Homme. 1996. *Les Voix du Monde.* Conception and realization Hugo Zemp, Bernard Lortat-Jacob, and Gilles Léothaud. Le Chant du Monde CMX 374 1010.12.

Cohn, Richard. 2012. *Audacious Euphony: Chromatic Harmony and the Triad's Second Nature.* New York: Oxford University Press.

Cooke, Peter. 1970. "Ganda Xylophone Music: Another Approach." *African Music* 4: 62–80, 95.

Cousineau, Marion, Josh McDermott, and Isabelle Peretz. 2012. "The Basis of Musical Consonance as Revealed by Congenital Amusia." *Proceedings of the National Academy of Sciences USA* 109 (48): 19858–19863.

Deleuze, Gilles. 1994. *Difference and Repetition.* Translated by Paul R. Patton. New York: Columbia University Press.

Dolan, Emily. 2012. *The Orchestral Revolution: Haydn and the Technologies of Timbre.* Cambridge: Cambridge University Press.

Dowling, W. Jay. 1973. "The Perception of Interleaved Melodies." *Cognitive Psychology* 5: 322–337.

Dowling, W. Jay, and Dane Harwood. 1986. *Music Cognition.* Orlando, FL: Academic Press.

Ellis, Alexander, and Arthur Mendel. 1968. *Studies in the History of Musical Pitch.* Amsterdam: Frits Knuf.

Erickson, Robert. 1975. *Sound Structure in Music.* Berkeley: University of California Press.

Feld, Steven. 1988. "Aesthetics as Iconicity of Style, or 'Lift-up-over Sounding': Getting into the Kaluli Groove." *Yearbook for Traditional Music* 20: 74–113.

Frobenius, Wolf, Peter Cooke, Caroline Bithell, and Italy Zemtsovsky. 2001. "Polyphony." In *The New Grove Dictionary of Music and Musicians*, edited by Stanley Sadie and John Tyrell. New York: Oxford University Press.

Fux, Johann Joseph. 1971. *Gradus ad Parnassum* [1725]. Translated by Alfred Mann under the title *The Study of Counterpoint.* New York and London: Norton.

Gold, Lisa. 2004. *Music in Bali: Experiencing Music, Expressing Culture.* New York: Oxford University Press.

Hartley, L. P. 2000. *The Go-Between.* London: Penguin.

Headlam, Dave. 1993. "Sketch Study and Analysis: Berg's Twelve-Tone Music." *College Music Symposium* 33/34: 155–171.

Hiley, David. 2009. *Gregorian Chant.* Cambridge: Cambridge University Press.

Hull, A. Eaglefield, and Allegri Gregorio. 1929. "The Earliest Known String-Quartet." *The Musical Quarterly* 15: 72–76.

Hulse, Brian. 2010. "Thinking Musical Difference: Music Theory as Minor Science." In *Sounding the Virtual: Gilles Deleuze and the Theory and Philosophy of Music: Gilles Deleuze and the Theory and Philosophy of Music*, edited by Nick Nesbit and Brian Hulse, 23–50. Surrey: Ashgate Publishing.

Huron, David. 2001. "Tone and Voice: A Derivation of the Rules of Voice Leading from Perceptual Principles." *Music Perception* 19: 1–64.

Irlandini, Luigi Antonio. 2010. "Messiaen's *Gagaku.*" *Perspectives of New Music* 48: 193–207.

Jordania, Joseph. 2006. *Who Asked the First Question? The Origins of Human Choral Singing, Intelligence, Language and Speech*. International Research Centre of Traditional Polyphony: University of Melbourne.

Jordania, Joseph. 2011. *Why do People Sing? International Research Center for Traditional Polyphony*: University of Melbourne.

Kubik, Gerhard. 2010. *Theory of African Music*, Vol. 1. Chicago: University of Chicago Press.

Kunst, Jaap. 1960. *Cultural Relations between the Balkans and Indonesia*, 2nd edition, enlarged. Mededeling 107, Afdeling Culturele en Physische Anthropologie 47. Amsterdam: Royal Tropical Institute [Koninklijk Instituut voor de Tropen].

Lawson, Francesca R. Sborgi. 2014. "Is Music an Adaptation or a Technology? Ethnomusicological Perspectives from the Analysis of Chinese Shuochang." *Ethnomusicology Forum* 23: 3–26.

Lerdahl, Fred. 1992. "Cognitive Constraints on Compositional Systems." *Contemporary Music Review* 6: 97–121.

Lerdahl, Fred, and Ray Jackendoff. 2006. "The Capacity for Music: What Is It, and What's Special About It?" *Cognition* 100: 33–72.

Lévi-Strauss, Claude. 1969. *The Raw and the Cooked*. New York: Harper & Row.

Liber de arte contrapunti, 1477. Translated by Albert Seay. Rome: Musicological Studies and Documents 5.

Macchiarella, Ignazio, ed. 2012. *Multipart Music. A Specific Mode of Musical Thinking, Expressive Behavior and Sound*. Udine: Nota/International Council for Traditional Music (ICTM).

Marušić, Dario. 2007. "Reception of Istrian Musical Traditions." *Музикологија* (Musicology) 7: 185–198.

McDermott, Josh, Andriana Lehr, and Andrew Oxenheim. 2010. "Individual Differences Reveal the Basis of Consonance." *Current Biology* 20: 1035–1041.

Mendel, Arthur, 1978. "Pitch in Western Music since 1500: A Re-Examination." *Acta Musicologica* 50: 1–93.

Messner, Gerald. 1989. "Jaap Kunst Revisited. Multipart Singing in Three East Florinese Villages Fifty Years Later: A Preliminary Investigation." *The World of Music* 31: 3–51.

Meyer, Leonard. 1994. *Music, the Arts, and Ideas* [1967]. Chicago: University of Chicago Press.

Meyer, Leonard. 2000. *The Spheres of Music: A Gathering of Essays*. Chicago: University of Chicago Press.

Morris, Robert. 2010. *The Whistling Blackbird*. Rochester, NY: University of Rochester Press.

Partch, Harry. 1974. *Genesis of a Music* [1946]. New York: Da Capo.

Perlman, Marc. 2004. *Unplayed Melodies: Javanese Gamelan and the Genesis of Music Theory*. Berkeley: University of California Press.

Pople, Anthony. 1991. *Berg: Violin Concerto*. Cambridge: Cambridge University Press.

Powers, Harold. 2000. "The Western Historical Canon as Exotic Music." In *La storia della musica: Prospettive del secolo XXI Convegno inernazionale di studi, Bologna, 17–18 novembre 2000. Il Saggiatore Musicale* 8: 51–61.

Powers. Harold, 2001. "Mode," [1980]. In *The New Grove Dictionary of Music and Musicians*, edited by Stanley Sadie and John Tyrell. New York: Oxford University Press.

Prout, Ebenezer. 1891. *Fugue*. London: Augener and Co.

Rappoport, Dana. 2010. *Indonesia: Songs from the islands of Flores and Solor*. Geneva: Archives Internationales de Musique Populaire, 1 CD, VDE-CD-1304.

Rappoport, Dana. 2011. "To Sing the Rice in Tanjung Bunga (Eastern Flores), Indonesia." In *Austronesian Soundscapes: Performing Arts in Oceania and Southeast Asia*, edited by Birgit Abels, 103–133. Amsterdam: Amsterdam University Press.

Rappoport, Dana. 2013. "Space and Time in Indonesian Polymusic." *Archipel* 86: 9–42.

Rappoport, Dana. 2014. "Songs and Sorrow in Tanjung Bunga: Music and the Myth of the Origin of Rice (Lamaholot, Flores, Indonesia)." In *Bijdragen tot de Taal-, Land- en Volkenkunde* 170: 215–249.

Remnant, Mary. 1989. *Musical Instruments: An Illustrated History from Antiquity to the Present*. London: B.T. Batsford.

Rowell, Lewis. 1994. "Music: Western." In *The Encyclopedia of Time*, edited by Samuel L. Macey, 419–424. New York: Garland.

Sachs, Klaus-Jürgen, and Carl Dahlhaus. 2001. "Counterpoint" (1980). In *The New Grove Dictionary of Music and Musicians*, edited by S. Sadie and J. Tyrell. New York: Oxford University Press.

Savage, Pat, and Steven Brown. 2013. "Toward a New Comparative Musicology." *Approaches to the Analysis of World Music* 2 (2): 1–14.

Sawatzky, Grant. 2013. "Olivier Messiaen's Permutations Symétriques in Theory and Practice." M.A. thesis, University of British Columbia.

Schoenberg, Arnold. 1983. *Theory of Harmony* [1911]. Berkeley: University of California Press.

Sethares, William. 2005. *Tuning, Timbre, Spectrum, Scale*, 2nd edition. London: Springer-Verlag.

Taruskin, Richard. 1986. "Antoine Busnoys and the L'Homme Armé Tradition." *Journal of the American Musicological Society* 39: 255–293.

Taruskin, Richard. 2010a. *Music from the Earliest Notations to the Sixteenth Century*. New York: Oxford University Press.

Taruskin, Richard. 2010b. *Music in the Early Twentieth Century*. New York: Oxford University Press.

Tenzer, Michael. 2000. *Gamelan Gong Kebyar: The Art of Twentieth Century Balinese Music*. Chicago: University of Chicago Press.

Terauchi, Naoko. 2011. "Surface and Deep Structure in the *Togaku* Ensemble of Japanese Court Music *(Gagaku)*." In *Analytical and Cross-Cultural Studies in World Music*, edited by Michael Tenzer and John Roeder, 19–55. New York: Oxford University Press.

Wegman, Rob. 1999. "Mensural Intertextuality in the Sacred Music of Antoine Busnoys." In *Antoine Busnoys: Method, Meaning and Context in Late Medieval Music*, edited by Paula Higgins, 175–214. New York: Oxford University Press.

Woodfield, Ian. 1984. *The Early History of the Viol*. Cambridge: Cambridge University Press.

Yampolsky, Philip. 1995a. *Vocal and Instrumental Music from East and Central Flores*. Washington, DC: Smithsonian/Folkways CD 40424.

Yampolsky, Philip. 1995b. *Vocal Music from Central and West Flores*. Washington, DC: Smithsonian/Folkways CD 40425.

Yampolsky, Philip. "Is Eastern Insulindia a Distinct Musical Area?" *Archipel* 90 (2015): 153–187.

PART IV

THE BIG PICTURE

CHAPTER 22

···

MUSICAL GRAMMAR

···

ROBERT O. GJERDINGEN

Music has been called the "universal language." That might be true within areas that share similar musical traditions. A Norwegian, for instance, could enjoy Italian instrumental music without the need for any kind of translation. But were a French military band to provide the music for a traditional Bedouin ceremony in Qatar, the limits of music's universality would quickly become apparent. Even within a single family, teenagers might enjoy listening to things that the parents or grandparents totally reject as being music. Given this diversity it seems wise not to discuss musical grammar solely in terms of any one style. True statements about heavy metal in 1980s Los Angeles might be false for Latin masses in 1680s Rome. A great deal of the following discussion thus concerns a rare and beautiful kind of music that is foreign to everyone.

MUSICAL GRAMMAR IN BIJOU

Let us begin by imagining how music works in the fictional land of Bijou. Like many real musics, the music of Bijou is highly prized for its beauty and emotional power. Brides insist on it for their weddings, bereaved families want it for a dignified funeral, and even everyday entertainments seem more entertaining when accompanied by it. The styles of this music are famously complex, with elaborate melodies and subtle rhythms that have developed over the centuries. The musicians of Bijou nevertheless manage the complexity through a unique system known as the "Rules of the Jewels," and musicians think of these rules as summarizing the grammar of Bijouan music.

The first rule states that phrases must end with a musical gesture known as *beryl*, after the pale yellow-green jewel. Gemstones are so abundant in Bijou that musicians teach the rules by aligning jewels in rows, with a left-to-right arrangement representing order in time. Four such rows are shown in Figure 22.1. (Color versions of all figures in this chapter are found in the color insert.) Rows 1 and 2 show popular three-jewel sequences. Rows 3 and 4, flagged with asterisks, show sequences that sound wrong and are actually

FIGURE 22.1 Two proper sequences of jewels (rows 1 and 2) and two improper sequences (rows 3 and 4). Sequence 4 violates the rule for a beryl at stage C. The grammatical problem with sequence 3 is unknown. (A color version of this figure can be found in the color insert.)

Image courtesy of the American Gem Trade Association.

offensive to local musicians. Though we are outsiders to Bijou, we can still guess that sequence 4 is wrong because it ends with a blue sapphire, violating the first rule. Sequence 3, however, *does* follow the rule, so its problem is more of a mystery. Maybe a ruby at stage B is forbidden, or perhaps a pink morganite at stage A signals an entirely different sequence. How could we make educated guesses to explain the problem with sequence 3?

Many music lovers, in the long history of music in Bijou, have asked similar questions. The explanations given them by teachers and scholars have varied widely over the ages. In early times appeals were made to religious and cultural ideals. Thus sequence 1 was said to be especially fine because the jewels moved "toward the light," "becoming ever brighter." Those ideals did not, however, fit sequence 2 nearly as well, even though it was a favorite of musicians and audiences. In the era of its first natural scientists, the Bijouan Academy of Science considered a theory that the proper sequence of jewels should exhibit an increasing index of refraction. But again, the approach from physics made distinctions between sequences that did not fully match the behaviors and preferences of the best musicians. More recently, Bijouan scholars have begun to wonder if better explanations might come from studies in psychology and learning.

An Experiment

At this point in our discussion curiosity about music in Bijou happens to align with curiosity about music in the real world of the twenty-first century. In 2008, for instance, three North American researchers—Psyche Loui, David Wessel, and Carla Hudson Kam—began to seek a new way to study how listeners learn a musical grammar. They wanted to start with a clean slate, but any real musical style that they chose would already be known by some people. So instead they created a completely new kind of music unfamiliar to everyone. It has a radically different kind of scale that is not used by any ethnic or social group in the real world (the notes are stretched apart so that the scale becomes strangely wider). One version of the so-called "Bohlen-Pierce" scale can be heard in ⓹ Audio Example 22.1.

The grammar invented for this music is not unlike musical grammar in Bijou, so we can use patterns of jewels to explain it. The four-jewel patterns shown in Figure 22.2 have the same beginnings and endings: beryls. The only difference is that for sequence 5 the middle jewels are "sapphire, garnet" while for 6 they are "garnet, sapphire." Each jewel represents a different "chord" of three tones from the scale. A grammatically correct melody sounds two tones chosen from each of the jewels for a total of eight tones. As a melody progresses through each jewel, left to right, it can sound two different tones or the same tone twice. Depending on which chord tones are chosen, the first beryl, for example, may not sound the same as the last one.

A melody from sequence 5, one used in the experiment, can be heard in ⓹ Audio Example 22.2. A test melody from sequence 6 can also be heard in ⓹ Audio Example 22.3.

In a controlled experiment reported in the journal *Music Perception* (Loui, Wessel, and Hudson Kam 2010), our researchers asked each participant to listen to 400 different melodies that conformed to one but not the other sequence of jewels. It took about 30 minutes to listen to all the melodies. Afterward participants were first tested to see if they could recognize the melodies that they had already heard; they were about 65% accurate, which is very good for having heard 400 different short melodies just once. Then participants were played several pairs of new melodies, where for each pair one melody followed the grammar of sequence 5 and one followed sequence 6. They were asked to choose which melody was more familiar and like the ones they had learned. Because

FIGURE 22.2 Two different grammars for four-jewel sequences. They differ in that sequence 5 goes "sapphire to garnet" while sequence 6 goes "garnet to sapphire." (A color version of this figure may be found in the color insert.)

Image courtesy of the American Gem Trade Association.

each participant had listened to melodies from only one sequence, this was like distinguishing proper tunes in a recently learned style from tunes that were somewhat similar but not quite right. In effect, the choice was between grammatically correct and incorrect melodies. Participants made the correct choice about 75% of the time.

To most people, the two sample melodies provided here sound a little strange and may seem more alike than different. Certainly neither one is easy to hum or whistle. So how were people able to tell a new sapphire-to-garnet melody from a garnet-to-sapphire one? Every physical aspect of the melodies was balanced between the two sequences, and the participants were unlikely to have cultural preferences that might bear on such unusual tunes. One is left with the likelihood that "statistical" learning is the best explanation. Students trained on sequence 5 learned the regularities in its patterns of tones (the statistics or probabilities of what followed what). Later, when tested, they remembered the gist of the patterns learned earlier and were able to generalize their learning so that they could identify new melodies that followed the same "rules." Participants trained on sequence 6 did the same thing, and each group later heard the other group's melodies as sounding wrong or at least not quite right. It all came down to a learned sensitivity to usage, whichever usage the participants had chanced to learn.

Usage ≈ Rules

Think back now to the problem of sequence 3 (see Figure 22.1). If we knew more rules (more grammar), we might be able to explain why the sequence is wrong. But where would the extra rules have come from? Notice that the prior sentence ended with a proposition—"from." For centuries now many teachers of English grammar have proclaimed such usage ungrammatical. The topic was raised in an influential eighteenth-century grammar book by Robert Lowth.

> The Preposition is often separated from the Relative which it governs, and joined to the Verb at the end of the Sentence, or some member of it: as, "Horace is an author, *whom* I am much delighted *with*." "The world is too well bred to shock authors with a truth, *which* generally their booksellers are the first that inform them *of*" [a quote from Alexander Pope]. This is an Idiom which our language is strongly inclined to; it prevails in common conversation, and suits very well with the familiar style in writing; but the placing of the Preposition before the Relative is more graceful, as well as more perspicuous; and agrees much better with the solemn and elevated Style. (1763, 141)

Lowth (1710–1787), a high churchman and Oxford professor, was the very sort of person who might have been expected to issue strict rules like "Thou shall not dangle Prepositions!" Yet instead he treats usage as the deciding factor—he believes the idiom is fine for all but the more formal styles. If usage determines rules, then rules are like small stories told about usage. Even if Bijouan musicians pronounced a rule that applied to the problem of sequence 3, it is likely that the rule would itself be a generalization derived from many individual musical utterances that shared similar patterns of usage. In fact, if we could examine the statistics of enough patterns of jewels, or learn those statistics implicitly through years of training and performance under the guidance of Bijouan master musicians, we might find explicit rules to be needless oversimplifications.

THE LAWS OF HARMONY

Today many musicians are uncomfortable with the suggestion that the rules of a music—its grammar—are just the norms of its usage or that mastering a music's grammar is much the same as developing a sensitivity to those norms. They may ask, "What about the laws of harmony?" or "Doesn't the overtone series determine how tones go together?" Questions like these often confuse correlation with causation. It is true, for instance, that faint higher pitches—"overtones"—are produced when a string is plucked or when a narrow column of air is set vibrating. It is also true that most of the world's musics contain intervals of a fourth, fifth, or octave that match, in their simple frequency ratios, the ratios among the strongest of those overtones. But the art of those musics is no more determined by that coincidence than are automobile drivers in the northern hemisphere forced to drive northward because of the influence of the magnetic pole on the iron in their vehicles. As Isaac Newton revealed long ago, the earth and the automobiles do attract each other, but that fact of physics does little to determine patterns of driving.

Some of the assumed "laws of harmony" come from the period when Europe was beginning to industrialize. Images of machines with their fixed actions and reactions may have inspired musicians to transform their knowledge of normal successions of chords into a more rigid and mechanistically prescriptive "chord grammar," with attendant "part-writing rules." Especially in Protestant lands during the Victorian era, the connections were only too obvious between the strictures set up for a "proper" musical grammar and the strictures of propriety in "good society." Not surprisingly, a better fit to such a grammar was to be found in earnest, upright hymns than in sensuous art songs, virtuoso chamber music, or scandalous opera. More esoteric ideas about harmony came from a somewhat later time when European scientists were discovering all sorts of new and unseen phenomena. The early discoveries of overtones and principles of electromagnetism were followed by even more unexpected phenomena like radio waves, invisible gases like helium, and secret worlds within the atom. Musicians began to wonder if tones and chords could also have fundamental, previously unrecognized "functions" (Riemann 1877), spiritual "wills" (Schenker 1979), or dynamic "energies" (Kurth 1917) that could explain the underlying causes of music's observable surface. In hindsight, it now seems apparent that these writers were transferring their deep feelings about music into beliefs about deep, incorporeal causes, thereby mistaking causes for effects.

The Principle of Chordal Inversion

Jean-Philippe Rameau (1683–1764), one of the greatest composers to have ever written about musical grammar, embarked on a conscious attempt to uncover the "natural principles" of music just as Newton had done for physics (Rameau 1971). Rameau tried for decades to bring his new theory of harmony into line with what working musicians of his day called the "Rule of the Octave" (a practical guide to which chord to play on each step of the ascending and descending scale), never quite getting the two to match. In the course of writing several books on harmony, he popularized the notion of chordal inversion, whereby a chord retains the same grammatical meaning whichever of its several tones happens to be the lowest one. His contemporary J. S. Bach, according to the testimony of Bach's son Emanuel, did not believe this was true, but later generations of music students have nonetheless taken the principle of chordal inversion to be a verified rule of musical grammar.

Let us take two patterns of Bijouan music and reinterpret them in terms of chords from styles of music in Europe and America. As shown in Figure 22.3, the jewel sequences 5 and 6 imply that the beginning and ending chords are always the same but that the middle chords reverse their order. If the theory of inversion is correct, any note of a "sapphire" chord could serve as the lowest tone, as could any note of a "garnet" chord, without changing the grammar. That is, merely switching the octaves in which we place any chord's tones should not change the identity of the sequence or cause a grammatical mistake.

A.   B.   C.   D.

5.

6.

FIGURE 22.3 Jewels used to represent different sequences of chords. Both beginning and ending chords are the same, but the inner chords have opposite sequences. (A color version of this figure may be found in the color insert.)

Image courtesy of the American Gem Trade Association.

The music notation shown in Figure 22.4 represents six variants of a small cadence, all of which can be heard in ⊙ Audio Example 22.4.

Let us arbitrarily assign cadence 1 to the first four-jewel pattern, the "sapphire-to-garnet" order of sequence 5 (see Figure 22.3). Cadence 1 is the most classical sounding, with its introduction and "preparation" at stage A of a treble G that will become dissonant over an F chord at stage B (see the arrow on Figure 22.4) and then resolve downward by step during stage C on its way to a final consonance at stage D (⊙ Audio Example 22.5). For the grammarian Lowth, this would be the "graceful and perspicuous" usage appropriate for "the solemn and elevated Style." From innumerable cadences like this we get the "rule" that "sapphire progresses to garnet and garnet progresses to beryl," though this is better known as "IV progresses to V, and V progresses to I." The roman numerals stand for the scale steps of the major scale viewed as "roots" of chords.

Cadence 2 is more casual in doing away with the niceties of preparation and resolution, though it still sounds like a "sapphire-to-garnet" sequence. Lowth might say that it "suits very well with the familiar style," especially where, as indicated by the arrow, it adds a jazzy seventh (a B) to the final chord (⊙ Audio Example 22.6). Note that this chord of closure and resolution is acoustically the most dissonant of the whole progression, suggesting that dissonance and consonance are not the most important factors in this grammar. Cadence 3 takes the principle of inversion literally and places the seventh of the C chord in the bass. The asterisk on Figure 22.3 marks an ungrammatical utterance: this low B sounds like a wrong note, whatever the theory of inversion might claim (⊙ Audio Example 22.7).

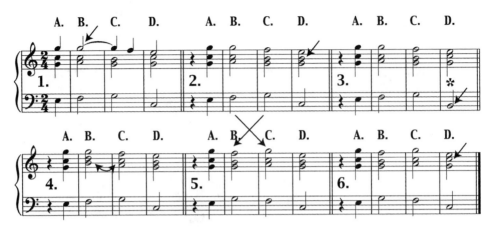

FIGURE 22.4 Four-chord progressions like the jewels of Figure 22.3. The text describes points of interest (marked by arrows) for each of these six small cadences.

Cadence 4 again sounds somewhat like the "sapphire-to-garnet" patterns of cadences 1 and 2 (▶ Audio Example 22.8). Yet observe that cadence 4 switches the inner voices of stages B and C. In cadences 1 and 2, the second stage had the notes F–A–C–G and the third stage had G–G–B–F. Now, in cadence 4, the second stage has the notes G–B–D–F and the third stage has F–A–C–G. These combinations of notes have reversed ("sapphire" becomes "garnet" and IV becomes V), but the perceived grammar has *not* changed. The important outer voices stayed the same as in cadences 1 and 2, and listeners familiar with styles of popular music in the later 1970s and 1980s (e.g., Steely Dan) know how to interpret the upper voices (consonant among themselves) as a collective dissonance that, like the simpler dissonance of cadence 1, will ultimately resolve downward as the cadence concludes. If simple enumerations of note-name aggregates adequately defined the grammar of chords, then cadence 4 should not sound at all like the other "sapphire-to-garnet" cadences because its collections of tones objectively read "garnet to sapphire."

Cadence 5 completely reverses the middle stages of cadence 2. It does sound different from prior cadences and could be said to match sequence 6—beryl, garnet, sapphire, beryl (▶ Audio Example 22.9). Stylistically, the "garnet-to-sapphire," V-to-IV progression is a better match to the usage of some cadences in light popular styles from the 1950s and 1960s, especially those influenced by African American genres like the blues. The seventh in the chord at stage D is, however, uncommon in that usage, so replacing the seventh with the plain tonic (a C) at the last stage of cadence 6 better aligns the choice of sonority ("chord morphology") with the associated genres and their norms of usage (▶Audio Example 22.10).

Are the C-major chords—the beryls—that begin and end all these cadences interchangeable, as would be expected from the theory of inversion? The answer is "Partially but not fully." Concluding a cadence with the third of the chord in the bass (the low E in stage A replacing the low C in stage D) was perceived in the time of Mozart as an "imperfect" kind of ending, while beginning a cadence with the low C in the bass was less common than with the low E.

In sum, the theory of inversion is not very successful as a theory of chord morphology, leaving aside its broad dissemination in pedagogy. Without a workable theory of inversion, the putative laws of harmony applied to art music quickly devolve into observations about usage, observations that of necessity must include factors like melody, rhythm, and counterpoint. That is hardly surprising since European art music was founded on the coordinated movements of two or more voices—a counterpoint of melodies. In early European art music, chords were less like primary elements of the musical grammar and more like secondary phenomena—byproducts of a contrapuntal and melodic grammar. These resultant sonorities might appear with similar shapes (e.g., C-major triads) when actually caused by different melodic and contrapuntal designs.

The dependency of harmony on melody and counterpoint did not end with Bach and Handel. Even in the early twentieth century the French composer Vincent d'Indy (1851–1931), a master of harmony, declared that "Musically, *chords* do not exist, and harmony is not the *science of chords*. The study of chords *per se* is, from a musical point of view, completely in error esthetically, for harmony comes from melody and ought never to be separated from it in practice" (1903, 91). His polemical statement, influenced perhaps by his location in the upper echelons of European art music, may seem extreme. His opinions would not, for instance, be shared by guitarists in many folk-music traditions. D'Indy's view, nevertheless, serves as a useful caution against thinking of the laws of harmony as being *solely* about chords.

The Many Meanings of *Grammar*

In reference to language, the term *grammar* covers a variety of usages. There are informal meanings in everyday speech and highly formal meanings with special vocabularies in linguistics or computer programming. The meanings of *musical grammar* inherit this range of usage and extend from the general sense of "correctness" to the highly specialized and technical meanings of advanced music analysis.

Informally, *musical grammar* can mean "the basics of the art" just as *grammar school* refers to the place where one learns the basics of literacy and numeracy. Young performers are expected to learn scales, arpeggios, simple chords, and cadences, and how to read basic notation or, in the case of jazz, chord symbols. These skills are often referred to as "fundamentals." In this domain of musical grammar, rules predominate and the focus is on the prescriptive and proscriptive—"do this, and don't do that!" As with language, the clarity of such rules does not always conform to the realities of usage. Many music students, for instance, believe the "natural minor" scale must in some sense be natural or fundamental, when in reality it is rare and artificial within the European classical tradition.

Chord grammar refers on the one hand to the proper spelling of chords ("chord morphology") and, on the other hand, to the arrangement of chords in series ("chordal syntax"). Theoretically, chord morphology depends on chordal syntax in the sense that a particular musical grammar can determine whether a tone is "in" or "out" of a chord. Practically speaking, a small number of "rules of thumb" operate within each musical tradition, and such rules may be quite rigid. In the music of nineteenth-century Europe, chords were treated as simple "stacks of thirds" like C–E–G or C–E–G–B. One could, in theory, continue this stacking to eventually include every note of the scale. In practice, however, triads and some seventh chords were treated as unitary chordal objects, whereas other sevenths, and all ninths and elevenths above a "root," were treated as "nonharmonic" (i.e., extraneous to the chord). By contrast, in twentieth-century jazz and popular traditions the categories of harmonic objects included many note combinations that the art-music tradition would view as composites of harmonic and nonharmonic tones. In this sense the chord morphology in the classical tradition was more theoretically driven and prescriptive while that of jazz and popular traditions was more descriptive and inclusive.

The informal grammars just mentioned have a practical orientation toward reading music notation or discussing basic musical objects. One could learn these things well but still know very little of the art of music. So music scholars have pursued the creation of formal grammars that offer more insight into how a music might be created or how one could describe all the interrelationships of its tones, rhythms, and phrases. In his 1977 book *Early Downhome Blues,* the ethnomusicologist Jeff Todd Titon outlined a "song-producing model" for that style. He described his model as a "generative grammar," referring to the work of the linguist Noam Chomsky. A grammar is "generative" if it is capable of producing a large set of correct utterances and no incorrect ones. Titon's work coincided with the high-water mark of Chomsky's influence on music studies. There were "generative" studies of Indian ragas (Cooper 1977) and of the European art-music tradition (Keiler 1977; Lerdahl and Jackendoff 1977), culminating in Lerdahl and Jackendoff's 1983 book *A Generative Theory of Tonal Music,* one of the most complete grammars of classical European music ever published. Its only competitor in that regard would be Heinrich Schenker's 1935 *Free Composition*, which analyzes entire movements of symphonies and other large works as a complex hierarchy of various contrapuntal combinations.

While Noam Chomsky (1928–) is without doubt the most famous linguistic theorist of the past fifty years, his highly abstract theories have long been opposed by important "functionalists," which is to say linguists who see language as rooted in the real situations of human communication and social interaction. Over the decades, data from experiments in psycholinguistics and statistics from computer analyses of large collections of texts or speech have been increasingly favoring the functionalists, as have studies in child development. In Chomskyan linguistics, it was argued that children could never learn a grammar solely from exposure to the speech of adults. The so-called "argument from the poverty of the stimulus" held that sequences of syllables do not provide sufficient information from which to infer a grammar. Hence certain aspects of language must be innate.

Functionalists have argued to the contrary that children have much more information available to them than just a sequence of syllables (Tomasello 2003). "More-ap-ple-sauce?" when viewed as four abstract sounds may seem like an impoverished stimulus. But for a hungry baby looking at a spoon of tasty food held by a smiling mother who raises her eyebrows as she intones "More-ap-ple-sauce?" with a rising inflection, the stimulus is rather rich and inferentially productive, especially when quickly reinforced by the reward of applesauce. Even without all the helpful cues provided by human interactions, it has been experimentally confirmed that infants can learn words based solely on the statistics of the order of syllables (Saffran 2001). Infants are amazing learners; the similarities among the grammars of the world's many languages may have less to do with any special genes for grammar and more to do with our genes for general learning. And in the absence of any known genes for music, it seems likely that the similarities that exist across all the world's musics may be attributable to similarities in how we learn, compare, and remember sounds.

THE OPERATIONS OF SYNTAX

What linguists call *coordination* is the linking of similar items, often by conjunctions (common words like "and"). In music, simple repetition serves as a cue to coordinate one statement of a pattern with its restatement. The same scheme works for a statement and a subsequent minor variation. Figure 22.5 shows a now-familiar Bijouan pattern and three longer versions of it. For musicians in Bijou, all four sequences are said to have the same structure: a basic form (no. 5), an extended form with repeated garnets (no. 9), a different extension with repeated sapphires (no. 10), and the longest version (no. 11) with repeated sapphires, varied garnets, and repeated beryls.

Simple coordination of similar items is quite limiting in language (e.g., "He and she went here or there"). One of the hallmarks of a developed human grammar is the ability to coordinate hierarchical relationships among different items. This typically involves understanding how small patterns fit within and modify the meaning of larger patterns. Linguists call this *subordination*. In English, the basic subject–verb–object pattern ("The boy kicked the ball") is easily elaborated and modified by subordinate adjectives ("The young boy kicked the big red ball") or by subordinate phrases ("The boy who mows the Smiths' lawn kicked the ball that he found behind their garage").

The American music theorist Leonard B. Meyer (1973) made the distinction between features of music that can be used to construct a syntax and those that cannot (or at least are not presently so used). Examples of the former would be distinct tones (not sirens or noises) and distinct durations (times that we can compare, as in "this is twice as long as that"). Examples of nonsyntactic features would be tone color, loudness, or texture. Meyer's ideas suggest that syntax in music is easiest to create and perceive when it involves things we can remember as distinct, countable objects (a melody goes "up two

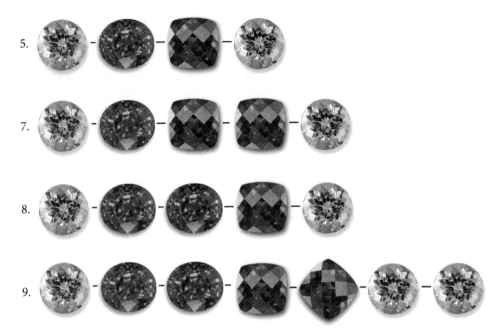

FIGURE 22.5 Four versions of one Bijouan sequence: the basic pattern (no. 5), two extensions by repetition (nos. 7 and 8), and a further extension (no. 9) by two repetitions and one slight variation (garnet to altered garnet). (A color version of this figure may be found in the color insert.)

Image courtesy of the American Gem Trade Association.

steps and then down one step") or relate to clear reference points (the trumpet's licks "always start on the downbeat").

By using simple patterns of scale tones and durations, Bijouan musicians are able to create a syntax that subordinates smaller patterns within larger ones. In particular, the grammar allows for the subordination of three-jewel sequences into longer patterns of four-jewel sequences. We already know that many three-jewel sequences end with a beryl (e.g., nos. 1, 2) and that many four-jewel sequences begin and end with a beryl (nos. 5, 6, 7, 8, and 9). So the jewel-pattern diagram shown in Figure 22.6, while more complex than anything shown previously, is still considered grammatical in Bijou. Musicians, of course, do not perform diagrams. When they perform this structure, they play the jewels in the order "Q–R–S–B–C–Q–R–S," with the subordinated patterns replacing beryls A and D.

Some patterns of jewels only occur at lower levels of subordination. For example, sequence 10 shown in Figure 22.7 is never a top-level pattern. Its simple scheme of an emerald, a blue iolite, and a second emerald is always associated with embellishing a ruby.

Since rubies can form the first jewel in a three-jewel pattern, and since three-jewel patterns can be subordinated in four-jewel patterns, the result can be a three-level hierarchy (see Figure 22.8). When performed, this structure will produce the long sequence of jewels "L–M–N–R–S–B–C–L–M–N–R–S." Here the "Qs" of Figure 22.5 have been

FIGURE 22.6 The subordination of three-jewel sequence 1 to the beryls in four-jewel sequence 5. (A color version of this figure may be found in the color insert.)

Image courtesy of the American Gem Trade Association.

FIGURE 22.7 A simple three-jewel sequence of emerald, blue iolite, and emerald. This pattern occurs only in subordinated roles. (A color version of this figure may be found in the color insert.)

Image courtesy of the American Gem Trade Association.

replaced by the "L–M–N" pattern of sequence 10. And due to the two levels of subordination, the top-level A has now been replaced by five jewels—L–M–N–R–S—as has the top-level D.

Sapphires and garnets in a top-level pattern (e.g., sequence 5) could be repeated and/or varied. They also have their own traditions of subordinate patterns, so very elaborate structures can easily be constructed. Music of this complexity is typical of performances at the royal court of Bijou, where young girls train intensively for a decade or more before they attempt to perform any of the courtly genres. In lighter genres of urban entertainment music or rural folk music, this degree of complexity is generally avoided. Music for children often uses little or no subordination, while art music for Bijouan connoisseurs revels in it.

With graphs of the type shown above in Figure 22.8, one could create hierarchies of any degree of complexity. The eye sees the whole picture of how the brackets and arrows

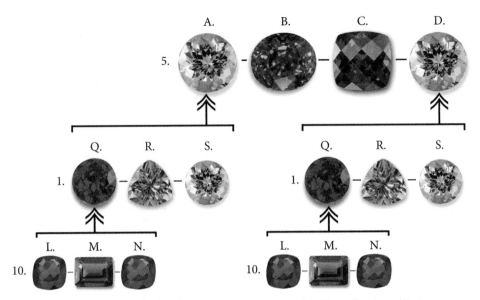

FIGURE 22.8 Two levels of subordination. Sequence 10 is subordinated to the rubies in sequence 1, which in turn begin a three-jewel sequence subordinated to the beryls of sequence 5. (A color version of this figure may be found in the color insert.)

Image courtesy of the American Gem Trade Association.

relate subordinate patterns to a top-level sequence. When patterns are not visual but aural, humans have some limitations because we only hear one "jewel" at a time. Take language, for instance. When we hear a sentence being read or spoken we must construct for ourselves an idea of the meaning as the sentence unfolds. Many languages help us to do this by giving us words or special word forms that give us clues to the intended structure. In the sentence presented earlier to illustrate subordination—"The boy who mows the Smiths' lawn kicked the ball that he found behind their garage"— helpful cues are provided by "who," "Smiths," "that," "behind," and "their." The presence of such cues—"predictive dependencies" (Saffran 2003)—facilitates statistical learning. If one leaves out too many cues, a listener may be "led down the garden path," meaning led to a wrong conclusion about sentence structure. A "garden path sentence" like "The old man the boat" is intended to mean something like "The boat is manned by the old people." But when we hear or read "the old man" we tend to assume that an "old man" is the subject of what comes next (which is false).

To illustrate aurally the limitations but also the potential of musical hierarchy, we first turn the graph of Figure 22.8 into a very simple type of Bijouan music with obvious cues for subordination. We can translate jewels into single tones on the Bohlen-Pierce scale, and we can translate subordination into duration, with higher-level jewels having longer durations. For the top-level sequence 5 played alone, listen to ⏵ Audio Example 22.11. Notice that the beryls are the same pitch, the sapphire is higher, and the garnet is lower. In ⏵ Audio Example 22.12 we hear the middle-level sequence 1 played alone as a rising sequence of pitches. In ⏵ Audio Example 22.13, sequence 1 is subordinated to the top-level sequence 5 by fitting into the time allotted for each beryl. Finally, in ⏵ Audio Example 22.14, a further level of subordination is added by the neighbor-tone pattern of sequence 7 played rapidly as an ornamentation of the first tone (the ruby) of sequence 1.

The structure of this simple type of Bijouan music was aided at every turn by "outsider-friendly" choices and clear cues to the syntax. The contours of each component pattern were simple and easy to comprehend. The direct translation of the level of subordination into duration made it possible to hear the full version as a straightforward enriching and ornamentation of a largely unchanged top-level pattern.

If we instead adopt outsider-*un*friendly choices, our ability as outsiders to hear the intended structure can be greatly diminished. In ⏵ Audio Example 22.15 we hear the same structure shown in Figure 22.5. The top-level sequence 5, however, is now realized as a series of 10-note melodies, one per jewel. Each component melody is significant to Bijouan musicians because it replicates a theme from the sacred repertory. The subordinated sequence 1 is played as a nine-note melody, three tones per jewel, interleaved between the tones of the melodies for the beryls of top-level sequence 5, and the doubly subordinated sequence 7 is performed as a three-tone pattern that sounds simultaneously with the tones of the ruby from sequence 1. Comprehension of this performance is difficult for outsiders because we lack the memories of Bijouan musicians and because most of us are not used to subordination working in quite these ways. We may get the overall form, where rapid events from the beginning reoccur near the end, but we are likely oblivious to the details and the intended content (Bijouans, by contrast, hear this as a lament). Were more levels of subordination added, and were more complex components devised, we could quickly lose any connection between the structure intended and the structure perceived. The syntax of a musical grammar may in principle allow for unlimited complexity, but listeners *do* have limits. The composer and music theorist Fred Lerdahl described this situation as reflecting "cognitive constraints on compositional systems" (1992).

THE IMPORTANCE OF MEMORY

As mentioned, ideas about technology have often had an effect on ideas about grammar, whether in language or in music. In the late 1950s, when Chomsky published his first book on language and Meyer his first book on music, the "artificial intelligence" of room-sized computers depended on elaborate programs—algorithms—because such machines had almost no memory. The first Apple computers sold in the 1980s still could store only a few pages of text in active memory. Today, by contrast, an ordinary home computer can store and almost instantaneously access the equivalent of a whole library, and the Internet collectively constitutes a digital memory of unfathomable depth.

Over the same decades the estimated storage capacity of the human brain has grown enormously. Psychologists once thought that information in the brain had to be reduced to a small essence before it could be squeezed into our limited long-term memories.

Today researchers strongly suspect that there is no practical limit to the capacity of human long-term memory.

The shift from algorithms to memory has major implications for thinking about grammar. The "generative" or "transformational" grammars of Chomsky and his many brilliant students had strong similarities to algorithms, both in their mathematical formalisms and in their reliance on "processing." Functionalist accounts of grammar, by contrast, assume relatively little processing but a huge reliance on massive memories of individual utterances, grouped by similarity. In recent formulations, often called "usage-based grammars" or "construction grammars" (Bybee 2006; Goldberg 2006), the statistics of usage determine much of the grammar. Those statistics identify "constructions," which act as matchmakers between incoming sounds and stored meanings. Instead of having an abstract syntax acting on a separate lexicon (i.e., looking up words in a mental dictionary), construction grammars create dynamic combinations of words and word patterns that function like holistic gestalts or schemas.

A usage-based grammar treats language as it is, without fixed notions about what the grammar ought to be. Imagine hearing for the first time a construction like "That's *so* '90s!" (Wee and Tan 2008). In terms of anything Robert Lowth might have imagined in the 1700s, the phrase is ungrammatical. Yet today a large percentage of English speakers know that it means "That [thing in view] is so [characteristic and sadly reminiscent of similar things once common in] the 1990s." Construction grammars assume that a contextually important meaning is learned along with the syntactical form. One could look up each individual word of "That's *so* '90s!" and never find out that the phrase is often used disparagingly. Yet people who have learned the construction know this meaning and will use the construction accordingly. In construction grammars, idioms like "That's *so* '90s!" are fully part of the grammar, not strange exceptions.

The idea of constructions recognizes the fact that learning and memory affect perception and expectation. If we hear someone say "That's *so* . . . " we will already have matched those sounds to the beginning of the appropriate construction, and we will be expecting a date or other word associated with style to fill the missing slot. This is a very efficient way to navigate an ever-changing world of language, and it resembles in many ways the strategies used to teach music in the old conservatories of Europe.

Teaching and Learning a Musical Grammar

In Europe during the 1700s and 1800s, music was a trade like carpentry or jewelry making. Young children were apprenticed to masters who taught them to imitate the proper shapes and designs of their trade. For carpentry we can look at the pattern books used by apprentices. For music, we can look at workbooks and exercises. Few of these documents survive from individual apprenticeships, but, first in Naples and later in Paris, hundreds of young apprentices were gathered in large urban conservatories. Many documents survive from these institutions, and their pages tell a story about how a musical grammar was learned (Gjerdingen 2007; Sanguinetti 2012).

In Naples, students first learned some basic "rules," although the manuscripts from that period (1730s–1790s) reveal that the rules were really musical exemplars—small encapsulations of real music. The Rule of the Octave, for instance, was a scale harmonized in a certain way. The children learned the way it was done. They did not learn verbal rules explaining why. The great Neapolitan master Francesco Durante, whose music was once copied by J. S. Bach, is reputed to have told his students, "My dears, do it this way because this is the way it is done."

After learning a few exemplars, the students learned to play them at the keyboard in response to the matching patterns in basses called *partimenti*. A partimento bass would mix cues for the recently learned patterns with cues for cadences, and it would modulate to various keys in the course of an exercise. Unlike thorough-bass, usually intended for the role of harmonic background in an ensemble, partimenti were meant to be self-standing improvisations where a student's evolving repertory of constructions was rehearsed and refined.

The Paris Conservatory (1795–) chose the Italian tradition as the classic model for its instruction. The young students in Paris were taught Italian exemplars and practiced them by playing "realizations" of partimenti. Unique to conservatory life in Paris were annual contests in harmony and counterpoint. For the contest in harmony, the students were given an unfigured bass before being sent to small cubicles where, in a few hours and without a keyboard, they were expected to add three more melodically elegant parts to the bass, parts that would employ imitative counterpoint and collectively conform to the approved usage of each construction. This was not composition in the sense of a unique artistic expression. This was more like the presentation of a "masterpiece" to a craft guild, where the masters of the trade would inspect the journeyman's product for any defects or failures to understand the approved methods.

Figure 22.9 presents the first sixteen measures of the bass given to contestants for the harmony contest of 1857. Listen to ⊙ Audio Example 22.16 to hear this bass.

This excerpt from the complete bass contains thirty-three tones and thirty-two intervals. The more skilled contestants would see through that forest of tones and recognize a simpler scheme: the cadence in measures 15 and 16 is preceded by just three constructions. The student contestants had previously been taught to memorize a large repertory of constructions, all written out in four parts, with indications of where there were opportunities for imitative counterpoint. The four constructions shown in Figure 22.10 come from the treatise of François Bazin (1857), a harmony teacher at the conservatory. They can be heard in ⊙ Audio Example 22.17. Bazin taught many variations of each construction, but the four exemplars of Figure 22.10 would have been sufficient to guide a four-voice realization of the contest bass of Figure 22.9.

The first of these, construction "A," treats a neighbor-tone figure in the bass (⊙ Audio Example 22.18). The second, B, presents the bass of Pachelbel's Canon, sometimes called

FIGURE 22.9 Measures 1 through 16 of the unfigured bass (*basse donnée*) given to contestants in the harmony contest of 1857 at the Paris Conservatory.

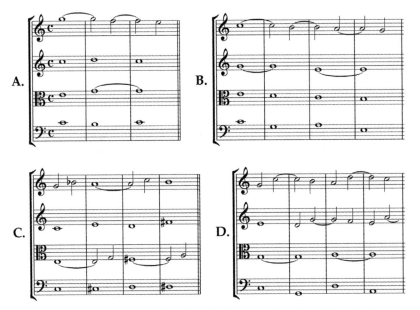

FIGURE 22.10 Four constructions taken from the harmony treatise of 1857 by François Bazin, harmony teacher at the Paris Conservatory.

a Romanesca bass (▶ Audio Example 22.19). The third, C, involves rising semitones in the bass (▶ Audio Example 22.20), and the fourth, D, has a sequence of falling fourths and rising fifths (▶ Audio Example 22.21). For each of these basses the upper voices indicate preferred counterpoints. Both C and D, for example, have a pair of upper voices in canon with each other (tenor and soprano for C; alto and soprano for D). To say that these constructions are chord progressions is to oversimplify what was being taught and learned.

One can diagram the basic syntax of the contest's bass with a simple pattern of jewels. As shown by sequence 11 (see Figure 22.11), a beryl can stand for the cadence, and the three jewels to the left of it can stand for the three constructions: Romanesca (citrine), Rising Semitones or Monte (sapphire), and Rising Fifths (garnet). The Monte construction was named in the eighteenth century by Joseph Riepel (1755), who associated its ascending sequence with climbing a mountain (Italian: *monte*).

This simple syntax of coordination (Romanesca *and* Rising Semitones *and* Rising Fifths) is made more complex by levels of subordination. As shown in Figure 22.12, each jewel of Figure 22.11 summarizes sequential transpositions. Each of these is in turn a composite of two bass notes, the first of which can be replaced by a subordinated neighbor-note construction. These neighbor notes (emerald–iolite–emerald) act like the "predictive dependencies" in language by aurally marking each stage of the two longest constructions.

Two technical points about Figure 22.12 are worth noting. First, component jewels for each separate stage of the Romanesca and Rising Fifths constructions could involve identical note names (two bass tones, the second one being a fourth lower or a fifth higher). For that reason Gjerdingen (2007) named the Rising Fifths construction a *Monte Romanesca*. Yet because the two constructions differ in their successive transpositions and their associated counterpoints, they sound quite different. It is the whole pattern that counts. Second, if the jewel pattern of Figure 22.12 were a legitimate sequence of Bijouan music, we could now explain why sequence 3 (see Figure 22.1) was wrong; from the six identical exemplars of Figure 22.12 we could say with some confidence that a morganite leads to a topaz and not, as in Figure 22.1, to a ruby. Sequence 3 was thus ungrammatical based on the statistics of Bijouan usage and the expectations that were formed from experiencing that usage.

The patterns of Figure 22.12 are so simple to grasp that they could legitimately be called "child's play," especially because one of the actual winners of the contest of 1857, Henri Fissot, was only thirteen years old (see Figure 22.13). Listen to ⊙ Audio Example 22.22 to hear his realization of the contest bass, complete with its many approved patterns of imitation. It is worth noting that this thoroughly contrapuntal and quite sophisticated realization was something a student was expected to complete *before* entering the class on counterpoint. At the Paris Conservatory even the work specifically

FIGURE 22.11 A summary syntax of the bass from Figure 22.9. The four jewels stand for Romanesca (citrine), Rising Semitones (sapphire), Rising Fifths (garnet), and Cadence (beryl). (A color version of this figure may be found in the color insert.)

Image courtesy of the American Gem Trade Association.

Romanesca   Rising Semitones   Rising Fifths   Cadence

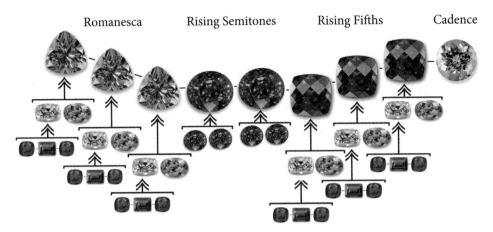

FIGURE 22.12 A more detailed look at the syntax of the bass from Figure 22.9. Coordinate patterns predominate at the high levels (the ascending and descending sequences), but the Romanesca (yellow citrines) and Rising Fifths (garnets) both feature two levels of subordination: pairs of jewels (pink morganite to yellow topaz) can replace single upper-level jewels, and three-jewel neighbor-note figures (emerald to blue iolite to emerald) can replace the first jewel of each middle-level pair. (A color version of this figure may be found in the color insert.)

Image courtesy of the American Gem Trade Association.

focused on harmony was primarily concerned with the coordination of independent melodic lines.

Summary

A musical grammar describes regularities in a particular musical style. Those regularities are largely determined by the behaviors of musicians and the preferences of their audiences. Nonmusicians can learn a musical grammar from mere exposure to music, though it helps if the exposure occurs in situations (concerts, dances, movies, theater, songs with lyrics) where additional cues add meaning to the patterns of sound. Musicians learn a large repertory of constructions that help them organize and conceptually simplify the complex patterns that they will need to perform or compose. In the past, conservatories managed this learning through partimenti and textbooks designed to guide the imitation and improvisation of a repertory of constructions. Today, in homes and garages, young musicians in popular genres accomplish much the same thing through the careful imitation of recordings and participation in improvisational "jam sessions." The physics of sound plays a limited role in shaping a musical grammar. The biggest factors are the psychological abilities and constraints that determine what humans can learn, remember, and reproduce. As we learn new works and experience new patterns, we relate them to previous experiences and update our ideas about usage. Each evolving hunch about usage—a part of our personal musical grammar—guides

FIGURE 22.13 A first-prize-winning realization of the bass from the harmony contest of 1857 (see Figure 22.9) by the thirteen-year-old Henri Fissot, a student of François Bazin at the Paris Conservatory. The markings of contrapuntal imitations are original. Jewels have been added for comparison with Figures 22.11 and 22.12. (A color version of this figure may be found in the color insert.)

Image courtesy of the American Gem Trade Association.

our future expectations and helps to make our next musical experience just a little bit richer.

Audio Examples

A complete list of audio examples for this chapter is available with the recordings on the companion website.

REFERENCES

Bazin, François. 1857. *Cours d'harmonie théorique et pratique*. Paris: Escudier.

Bybee, Joan. 2006. "From Usage to Grammar: The Mind's Response to Repetition." *Language* 82: 711–733.

Cooper, Robin. 1977. "Abstract Structure and the Indian Rāga System." *Ethnomusicology* 21: 1–32.

d'Indy, Vincent. 1903. *Cour de composition musicale*. Paris: Durand.

Gjerdingen, Robert. 2007. *Music in the Galant Style*. New York: Oxford University Press.

Goldberg, Adele. 2006. *Constructions at Work: The Nature of Generalization in Language*. Oxford: Oxford University Press.

Keiler, Allan. 1977. "The Syntax of Prolongation (I)." *In Theory Only* 3, no. 5: 3–27.

Kurth, Ernst. 1917. *Grundlagen des linearen Kontrapunkts: Einführung in Stil und Technik von Bachs melodischer Polyphonie*. Bern: M. Drechsel.

Lerdahl, Fred, and Ray Jackendoff. 1977. "Toward a Formal Theory of Tonal Music." *Journal of Music Theory* 21: 111–171.

Lerdahl, Fred, and Ray Jackendoff. 1983. *A Generative Theory of Tonal Music*. Cambridge, MA: MIT Press.

Lerdahl, Fred, and Ray Jackendoff. 1992. "Cognitive Constraints on Compositional Systems." *Contemporary Music Review* 6: 97–121.

Loui, Psyche, David Wessel, and Carla Hudson Kam. 2010. "Humans Rapidly Learn Grammatical Structure in a New Musical Scale." *Music Perception* 27: 377–388.

Lowth, Robert. 1763. *A Short Introduction to English Grammar: With Critical Notes*, 2nd edition. London: Millar and Dodsley.

Meyer, Leonard B. 1973. *Explaining Music: Essays and Explorations*. Berkeley: University of California Press.

Rameau, Jean-Philippe. 1971. *Treatise on Harmony* [1722]. Translated by Philipp Gossett. New York: Dover.

Riemann, Hugo. 1877. *Musikalische Syntaxis: Grundriss einer harmonischen Satzbildungslehre*. Leipzig: Breitkopf and Härtel.

Riepel, Joseph. 1755. *Grundregeln zur Tonordnung insgemein*. Frankfurt and Leipzig.

Saffran, Jenny R. 2001. "Words in a Sea of Sounds: The Output of Statistical Learning." *Cognition* 81: 149–169.

Saffran, Jenny R. 2003. "Statistical Language Learning: Mechanisms and Constraints." *Current Directions in Psychological Science* 12, no. 4: 110–114.

Sanguinetti, Giorgio. 2012. *The Art of Partimento: History, Theory, and Practice*. New York: Oxford University Press.

Schenker, Heinrich. 1979. *Free Composition* [1935]. Translated and edited by Ernst Oster. New York: Longman.

Titon, Jeff Todd. 1977. *Early Downhome Blues: A Musical and Cultural Analysis*. Urbana: University of Illinois Press.

Tomasello, Michael. 2003. *Constructing a Language: A Usage-Based Theory of Language Acquisition*. Cambridge, MA: Harvard University Press.

Wee, Lionel, and Ying Tan. 2008. "That's So Last Year! Constructions in a Socio-Cultural Context." *Journal of Pragmatics* 40: 2100–2113.

CHAPTER 23

....

ANALYTICAL RELATIONSHIPS

....

MARION A. GUCK

ONE might expect, given the title, that this paper will address the relationships that analysts identify between entities in musical works. It does not. The relationships referred to are those between some music and the person analyzing that music. Relationships with music vary widely, from the purely musical to those that transform music into stories and dramas. E. M. Forster portrays an array of relationships in a well-known passage from *Howards End*, in which he describes four characters listening to a performance of Beethoven's Fifth Symphony: Mrs. Munt taps her foot "when the tunes come"; Helen imagines "heroes and shipwrecks in the music's flood"; Margaret "can only see the music"; and Tibby "is profoundly versed in counterpoint, and holds the full score open on his knee" (Kivy 1990, vi).[1] We tend to think that music analysis results from the kind of "purely musical" relationship Tibby has. But Mrs. Munt's toe-tapping hints at the physical responses analysts feel and may integrate in our texts. Helen's imaginings, at the opposite pole from Tibby's informed attention, are fanciful—distractingly so—but they allude to possibilities of musical activity that an analyst might hear and report in the Beethoven symphony.

Analysts, then, have many different relationships with music, relationships usually evident only through what we write about it. Such writing will be my sources in exploring analytical relationships. I will begin with purely musical relationships and expand my purview from that center. I will extend my consideration of analytical relationships to the imaginings and responses the sounds might elicit in an analyst. I will consider two very general types of imagined qualities: one centered on movement and the other on tension. I will close with an analysis of Brahms's song "Meerfahrt," op. 96, no. 4, that illustrates my own analytical relationship with the song.

APPRECIATION OF MUSIC AS SOUND

....

Tibby's knowledge, Peter Kivy says, "causes pleasure *in* the perceiving and the being aware" (Kivy 1990, 41). This working among the sounds is what I mean by a "purely musical relationship." The inclination to form such a relationship is evident in such descriptions as Roland Jordan's account of the opening of the *Adagio* of Mozart's A-major Piano Concerto, K. 488, in which he writes of "the difficulty of [the music's] unfolding, the evasive, rejected move toward A major, the diversionary turn to the Neapolitan, the shifting pitches in measure eight" (Jordan, 1991, 8–9).[2] Even where appreciation for the play of sounds is not the dominant mode of interaction, it is a critical part of involvement for many music lovers, whether professional musicians or amateurs.

As with any artwork, indeed, with any valued object, an appreciator takes pleasure in the qualities of the thing itself. You might say that she has a feeling for the object. Thus, I might appreciate the color scheme of my Iranian carpet, the saturation of its colors, the peculiar shapes of its figures and their density, the softness and fineness of the wool, and many more features and qualities. I like to be in its presence and feel affection for it. Caring about it, I have also spent time contemplating it, noticing what I am responding to in it. Awareness of these things has enhanced my pleasure. In the same way, I might appreciate other objects, both more mundane and more exalted. Such relationships are to be found everywhere in life, and they are based on a connection with the perceptible qualities of the object, beyond any cultural meaning it might also have.

Many music analysts take pleasure principally in immersing ourselves in the interplay of sounds that is the musical process. We find our musical meanings among the sounds and in appreciation of the musical process. For example, Kendall L. Walton, describing music analysts' appreciation of music, suggests that, if one is surprised by a modulation due to "certain rhythmic features of the passage in question," or if one recognizes that "one passage [is] an elaboration of another" due to "accents or dynamic qualities," one might "relish or admire the elegant manner in which the surprise or the recognition is effected" (Walton 2015, 206–207). Walton is addressing the appreciation that music analysts experience, but his account can extend both to musically educated amateurs like Tibby and to others, like Tibby's companions, who are entranced by the music, even if they do not have the musical concepts that might allow them to articulate what so captivates them.

I would be surprised if anyone who loves music is not sometimes, or from some angles, interested in music purely for its own sake, for its "intrinsic nature."[3] When music analysts articulate this relationship, I will call us "observationalists."[4] The senses of "observation" that I wish to invoke are noticing and paying attention; these are the virtues of the purely musical type of engagement with music.

Most analyses might be thought of as paeans to beloved or esteemed works. As I did in my description of the carpet, we identify some of the aspects of the music that contribute to the feeling for it, a recitation that recalls the captivation of listening and might lead to a new awareness of musical features, thus to heightened appreciation. One might say it is a kind of contemplation of a beloved object for its own sake, and for the appreciator's enrichment as well.

Among the strictest observationalists is Milton Babbitt, who resorts only occasionally even to a mention of musical motion (of a line). It is perhaps no surprise that he accomplishes this when writing about post-tonal music, where a verbal style has developed that avoids animism; however, he manages it also when writing about tonal music.

And yet he enacts his personal involvement with musical works in his brief analyses of two Bach chorales found in one of the lectures published in *Words about Music* (Babbitt 1987, 124–143). The style is lively and Babbitt's fascination with the piece is infectious, as he leads his audience through a thought process, as if composing the chorale setting. He stimulates his audience to imagine Bach's compositional acts by asking: how would *you* harmonize this note in the melody? What connections does *your* choice create with other notes, other harmonies? He encourages audience members to imagine being the composer and creates a fantasy in which his audience imagines writing the chorales. This point of view makes perfect sense in a composer, for whom it is especially vivid that musical works result from the composer's acts.

Analysts often pursue a superficially similar variant of this strategy. The analyst asks "what was the composer thinking when he wrote this?" She tries to "reverse engineer" the composer's intellectual process, sometimes described in terms of (musical) logic, using the music to read the composer's mind. It is a curious strategy: it seems both vestigial, left over from a time when musical analysis was done primarily by composers like Babbitt, and at the same time persistent in viewing music primarily as acts of the imagined composer.

I can advance two possible reasons for an analyst to invoke a work's composer. The first is entirely practical: sentences require subjects and in describing what music does it can be very convenient to construct them in such a way that the music's actions are motivated by the composer.[5] Musical activities, articulated as verbs, take the composer as subject. Thus, Mozart sometimes figures as the actor in William Rothstein's analysis of the D-major Rondo: "In m. 39, Mozart arpeggiates a diminished triad . . . Mozart models m. 42 after m. 27 . . . but he reverses the melodic motion across the bar line . . . Mozart could easily have written a [perfect authentic cadence] here, effectively ending the section . . . Instead he begins the theme in the left hand" (Rothstein 2005, 208).

The second possibility is more personal: if analyses are appreciations of the works for which analysts have the strongest feelings, then through the work they may also try to make contact with its composer, an often nearly sacred figure, and this contact may be expressed by representing the composer in the analytical text. Heinrich Schenker is a principal exemplar of this attitude. Introducing his analyses of two of Chopin's Etudes, he writes:

> The skill of his voice-leading ranks him among the greatest masters of music, the sheer expansiveness of his unfolding progressions [*Auswicklungszüge*] derives from a compositional power beyond compare! . . . Where is there a voice-exchange as bold as that in bars 21–33 of the [E♭ minor etude]? Where is there a passing-note progression executed in so masterly a fashion as that in bars 21–41 of the G♭ major etude? But then every work of Chopin's teems with such unfoldings—unfoldings that far outstrip the acuity of any ordinary ear.
>
> (Schenker 1994, 81)[6]

For these two reasons, and doubtless others, musical acts are often represented as human acts through the intervention of their composers.

Doubtless, from this habit Edward T. Cone derived the concepts of the composer's persona and, more influential, musical agency, in *The Composer's Voice*.[7] He defines a plethora of personae and agents. These concepts live on in subsequent writers' robust use of the notion of agency and in studies of the concept. The plethora of musical entities culminates in "one controlling persona, which is in turn the projection of one creative human consciousness—that of the composer" (Cone 1974, 114).[8] The work is therefore the "musical utterance" of the composer's persona.

Musical "utterance" is "the gestural aspect . . . that is simulated, and symbolized, by music" (Cone 1974, 164). Cone's elaboration of this idea might be congenial to the observationalist at least as much as the associative listener, since it includes: "direct actions . . . pauses . . . startings and stoppings, . . . rises and falls . . . tenseness and slackness . . . accentuations" (Cone 1974, 164). Many observationalists do hear such things as harmonies and lines moving. They sense that dissonant and tendency tones have particular qualities and that these qualities call to mind the future in the form of their resolutions. That is to say that the observationalist is constantly interpreting the sounds and might imagine their ongoing continuity as movements. The strict observationalist is rare; Babbitt comes close. Even for observationalists, for whom music represents a primarily aural-mental process, the composer infuses music with a human presence.

Viewing a musical work as the "utterance" of a composer's persona might provide a meeting point between those observationalists who hear music in terms of composers' acts, and what I will call "associationalists."[9] By "associationalists" I mean listeners who imagine in music's sounds the qualities of everyday movement or action and of tension or affect.

HUMAN EXPERIENCES

Stanley Cavell captures the involvement of music lovers, including analysts, whether observationalist or associationalist:

> [O]bjects of art not merely interest and absorb, they move us; we are not merely involved with them, but concerned with them, and care about them; we treat them in special ways, invest them with a value which normal people otherwise reserve only for other people.
>
> (Cavell 1976, 197–198)[10]

Often "treating [musical works] in special ways" is associated with hearing musical versions of human behavior in the qualities and continuities of musical sounds. The relationships engaged in, when we do this, constitute human–music intersubjectivity. Two aspects of human experience that are widely invoked by music analysts are movement and tension. Movement is an aspect of behavior that is outward, visible to those around us, while tension and related states are inward, seemingly noticeable only to ourselves. Both play a role in the experience of affect, broadly speaking.

The remainder of this paper will examine facets of human–music intersubjective experience. Two caveats are necessary here: this examination is limited to analysis of Western concert music, principally tonal music; and, while I claim that many people very often invest music with human qualities, these are not the only possibilities. Indeed, even movement and tension need not be human.

MOVEMENT AND ACTION

It is commonplace to speak of musical lines moving, of leaps and steps, and of other relatively neutral and general kinds of musical movement. Most listeners hear, in a melody or chord progression, a movement through the pitches rather than a mere succession from one to the next. An impression of movement is, as I have said, nearly unavoidable, and ubiquitous in the analyses even of most observationalists. As in everyday life, musical movement is related to action and gesture, as well as a multitude of more specific qualities of these.

Exploring these claims, I will consider the ideas of Roger Sessions and Fred Everett Maus. Maus's formulation engages the notion of musical agency, and this will entail further consideration of Cone.[11] All three have contributed importantly to this area of music-philosophical thought, and, while my ideas are often closely related to theirs, they also differ significantly on subtle but important points.

Sessions has given us an excellent account of ways in which music enacts the behavioral manner of an emotion as the emotion is felt in oneself or sensed in another.[12] Such qualities of movement are directly interpretable as musical qualities, as Sessions says. However, music, he thinks, cannot express emotion.

He writes, in *The Musical Experience of Composer, Performer, Listener*, that "music embodies the attitudes and gestures behind feelings—the movements . . . of our inner being, which animate our emotions and give them their dynamic content" (Sessions 1950, 26). Contributing to musical movement are "rhythm, tempo, pitch, accent, dynamic shading, tone quality, and [other elements] sometimes even more subtle" (Sessions 1950, 25). More explicitly, he writes that "in embodying movement, in the most subtle and most delicate manner possible, [music] communicates the *attitudes* inherent in, and implied by, that movement; its speed, its energy, its elan or impulse, its tenseness or relaxation, its agitation or its tranquility, its decisiveness or its hesitation. It communicates in a marvelously vivid and exact way the dynamics and the abstract qualities of emotion" (Sessions 1950, 23, italics added). Emotions, if one wishes, can be inferred from such qualities.

He provides examples in the paragraph quoted below in which each of several emotions (bold, added) is paired with several qualities, usually of movement (double underline, added), and, occasionally, with the means by which the movement quality is heard in the musical sounds (single underline, added):

> Music cannot express **fear** . . . . But its <u>movement</u>, in <u>tones, accents, and rhythmic design</u>, can be <u>restless, sharply agitated, violent</u>, and even <u>suspenseful</u>. Music cannot express **love**, but its <u>movement</u> can be <u>gentle, tempestuous, quiet</u>, and <u>insistent</u>, with an inexhaustible variety of nuance. It cannot express **joy** or **exultation**, but its <u>movement</u> can be <u>decisive</u> and <u>fast</u>; it can <u>accelerate</u>, its <u>register can be high</u>, its <u>range wide</u> and its <u>texture compact</u>. It cannot express **despair**, but it can <u>move</u> <u>slowly</u>, in a prevailingly <u>downward</u> direction; its <u>texture</u> can become <u>heavy</u> and, as we are wont to say, <u>dark</u>—or it can <u>vanish</u> entirely.
>
> (Sessions 1970, 44)

Most of the specific qualities mentioned in this quotation are manners of moving or behaving, what Sessions calls "attitudes." The attitudes he associates with each emotion are, of course, not emotions, but they are qualities of affect. An action having any of these attitudes is an action felt in a certain way: it is affect-tinged. The feeling is conveyed to others in the action. This is what I mean by "affect, broadly speaking."[13]

In "Music as Drama" Fred Everett Maus proposes that listeners understand music "by drawing on the skills that allow understanding commonplace human action in everyday life" (Maus 1988, 65–66).[14] In transferring these skills from the human to the musical situation, some are "relatively unchanged, while other habits of thought must be changed to fit the new context" (66). Actions are intended—not accidental or random. This means that usually they are done by a sentient being, although Maus does not identify the composer or any other determinate agent as that being.[15]

Maus's proposal differentiates actions on the one side, evident in the human or musical behavior, and their causal psychological states on the other. This formulation lines up well with Sessions's position. Actions are motivated or explained by the being's psychological state. In the case of people:

> The explanatory psychological states can be divided roughly into epistemic states (beliefs and the like) and motivational states (desires and the like). Ascriptions of psychological states are constrained by the need for the agent to shape up as an intelligible person: fairly coherent, consistent, rational, and so on. Besides beliefs and desires, one important class of explanatory states includes character traits, moods, and emotions. These function in a variety of ways: they can affect epistemic and motivational states, and they sometimes help to explain failures of consistency or rationality.
>
> (Maus 1988, 66)[16]

In this paragraph, Maus groups psychological states into what I'll call intellectual states and feeling states. The intellectual states are epistemic, "beliefs and the like," and motivational states, "desires and the like." Since, in music, there is no one to have intentions, there is no one to have epistemic or motivational states. Imputing these states to music reflects a sense we have, a feeling of mutual engagement between ourselves and music. What such imputations can do is to provide a way to imagine or describe a cluster of musical actions together as "shaping up" in such a way as to seem reasonable. "Character traits," as well as "moods, and emotions," are affects. Their function is to modify the more intellectual epistemic and motivational states, sometimes causing a flaw in the performance of the primary state and the resulting action.

Maus exemplifies and explains his proposals through an analysis of the opening of the first movement of Beethoven's String Quartet, op. 95, that "mingles" musical actions described in everyday language and more typical technical terms. In the opening measures, there are three phases of action: an "abrupt outburst" to which he ascribes "clumsiness" (Maus 1988, 60), followed by a second outburst that is "aggressive," "repetitious," and "frustratingly halting" (63), and concluding with a "passage that is long and continuous, continually purposeful, neither abrupt nor repetitious" (64).

Examining the second phase, a response to the first, Maus explains how the music's actions are motivated by the types of psychological states he has identified: "one can identify beliefs—'There was something vague about the harmony at the opening; a straightforward alternation of tonic and dominant would be much clearer'—and a desire—'I want to replace the sound of the opening with something clearer'—combining to give a reason for acting" (67). However, he doesn't merely describe an "alternation" between tonic and dominant, he says that "the passage *harps on* the dominant" (67) and this more colorful description "further suggests that the same *mood* or *character trait* that led to the initial outburst continues to operate, infecting the response with a certain clumsiness" (67).

The illustration of explanation in terms of belief and desire is, I think, problematic for three reasons. First, although I agree that the acts of the Beethoven seem intended, they do not seem like a series of thoughts that proceed coherently, even if not perfectly coherently. Second, and perhaps more importantly, the portrayed process of evaluating and planning distracts attention from the music by portraying it as proceeding through a carefully reasoned, step-by-step logical process. Third, in doing so, this narrative comes too close to reifying a determinate intelligence, not the composer, but, as Maus suggests, a "consistent, rational" person.

This might be a matter of personal interpretive inclinations, of course. However, if I wanted to tell a story about the passage, I'd say that I hear an argument. In the first phase, I hear an irritated complaint and in the second, an angry rejoinder—it sounds like yelling about the first utterance. The third phase begins by repeating the first phase, although modified, quickly calming down. It goes on in a calm, agreeable vein for some time, but eventually gets worked up again. In my story, there is no judicious stopping to think about the shortcomings of the first utterance and how to mitigate its effect. There is a succession of acts and they make sense by analogy with person-to-person interactions. They reflect my sense of how the contrasting and discontinuous events of the passage "shape up."

On the other hand, the descriptions of the actions characterize the passages well and reflect the flow of the music. They describe the drama that is the opening of op. 95, and they tell me what the music sounds like to Maus in quite particular ways. The first two phases are "outbursts," both are "abrupt." Both have an excessive aspect about them: not mere utterance but "loud, aggressive, astonishingly brief" utterance (Maus 1988, 60); not repeating the dominant but "harping on the dominant triad" (63), which is not simple reiteration but reiteration that is "repetitious and perhaps a little out of control," inferably obsessive (67).

Both outbursts might be described as actions with attitudes or particular manners, as I mentioned earlier, and such actions with attitude or manner are typical of both human behaviors and musical actions. Although I have pointed out that there is an utterance that is aggressive, I do not think that there is an action separate from its manner—no physical act separate from the psychological state. There is no utterance plus loudness, aggressiveness, and brevity—no adding the expression—there is only the outburst; there is no reiteration plus being out of control, there is only the harping. The obsessiveness is in the act. Behavior and psychological state (affective state) are fused. As Gilbert Ryle points out: "the styles and procedures of people's activities *are* the way their minds work" (Ryle 2002, 58).[17] There is no hidden emotion behind the act; an act is emotive in its execution.[18]

Many of the affective attributes listeners ascribe to music can be understood as styles of action. Walton lists a miscellany of qualities he considers it essential not to miss in music.[19] Several of the listed attributes are musical actions familiar to music analysts, including rising and falling, motion and rest, leaps, skips, and stepwise progression, statement and answer, tension and release. Many of these are also everyday movements. The remainder are largely affective states: exuberant, agitated, serene, timid, calm, determined, nervous, wistful, resign[ed], resolve[d], impetuous, sprightly, witty, majestic, tender, arrogant, peevish, spirited, yearning, chilly. But what do we think of as exuberance? Lively, energetic, upbeat, perhaps extravagant gestural behavior. To be timid is to behave in a hesitant, cautious, fearful way. To be calm is to behave in a quiet, poised, and collected—an evenly balanced—way. So it goes for many of the attributes Walton identifies.

Maus's model is explicit about how a listener can use human experience to understand a musical passage. It is apparently tacit, however, about how a listener responds to or is involved with the music, which is perfectly normal. However, if op. 95 were a person, one might infer that Maus is somewhat impatient or frustrated with this clumsy, aggressive individual. His response to the musical work op. 95 is more complex. He might respond with appreciation to the frustration-and-impatience-inspiring musical behavior of this work with which he is clearly fascinated (as he might also respond appreciatively to an actor in a drama who portrays these qualities). Music can inspire aesthetic appreciation of qualities that, in everyday life, would be merely exasperating.

In order to continue examining how an analyst's characterizations of a passage might imply a response, I will for the moment consider a musical relationship that is not intersubjective. Disagreeing with Cone's insistence on human agency, some years ago

I characterized the intensifying activity of the second theme of the *Waldstein* sonata's first movement in terms of a rising hurricane. I felt that the piece has no concern for me and overwhelms me, hence it seems like a natural force (Guck 1989, 6–16). The movement and action that I hear feels beyond my control. The opening chorale-like passage is, over time, stripped of character as it becomes increasingly generic arpeggiations, while the durations become shorter and shorter. The music engages me with the chorale and then, unless I consciously push it away, it captures me and I become increasingly excited in synchrony with it. It controls me without my willing participation and eventually overwhelms me.

In the *Waldstein* analysis, the hurricane plays the role of a determinate agent and I would not typically imagine the music in this way. As I have said, it indicates my response to the passage. It is a vehicle—a subject for sentences—in whose terms I describe how I hear the musical actions. It provides force and a shape or trajectory that organize the musical events without suggesting the mutuality of any interpersonal narrative. This seems similar to the role that I have proposed that epistemic and motivational states play in Maus's psychological formulation.

Granting this organizing function, it is the actions that are crucial. Ultimately, despite my *Waldstein* analysis, I do not tend to reify agents but rather interpret musical continuities in terms of musical movement and action. I agree with Maus, who, by contrast with Cone, proposes that the agents of musical actions are indeterminate, as illustrated by his analysis.[20] He points out that "the first sentence [of his analysis] mentions an outburst, an awareness of something and an effort, without identifying anyone other than the music to whom these thoughts and actions belong" (Maus 1988, 68). He thus elides any agent "other than the music." Sometimes instruments, lines, etc., are mentioned but they are not identified as agents. They are vehicles, not framing images that determine a domain of actions. Being inconspicuous, they maintain attention on the actions. Indeed, because they arise and disappear in the musical texture without clear sustained extents, they are ephemeral. They dissolve, leaving the actions. Aristotle's comments on tragedy, cited by Maus (1988, 72), are suggestive: "the most important of all is the structure of the incidents. For Tragedy is an imitation, not of men, but of an action and of life . . . Dramatic action, therefore, is not with a view to the representation of character: character comes in as subsidiary to the action, and of the agents mainly with a view to the action" (Aristotle 1961, 62–63).[21]

Movement and action are ubiquitously ascribed to musical passages. We can hear music move and act directly, without the mediation of composers' personae or heroes and ships. Even most analysts who might be considered observationalists hear music as moving and acting. Doing so requires both observation and imaginatively joining succeeding events into an overarching flow. Moreover, many analysts hear particular qualities of movement or action and choose adverbial verbs and other qualifiers that articulate them more precisely. Frequently, our characterizations are affectively tinged and reflect the ways in which we hear music as adapting in suitably musical ways the manners and attitudes of human movement and action. In such characterizations movement and action fuse with tension and affect.

TENSION AND AFFECT

Tension is a relatively general property ascribed to music, a property, like movement, that is capable of more precise specification. Also like movement, tension and its partner relaxation or release fluctuate in intensity throughout a passage or complete work. Some music scholars have considered it essential.

Sessions, for example, considers tension "absolutely fundamental" to music. He cites the tonal phrase, as many others do, describing everything leading to the cadence as an upbeat and tensing, while the final accent, downbeat, is a "moment of relaxation." Sessions continues, "The principle of tension and relaxation is perhaps the most important single principle of musical rhythm, and its bearing on all questions of musical expression and interpretation cannot be overestimated" (Sessions 1951, 84).[22] Fred Lerdahl relates tension and relaxation to stability and instability.[23] In Leonard Meyer's early thinking about expectation and delay, musical events create expectations that, if unfulfilled, cause tension and instability, calling for goal-directed motion toward events that can, by satisfying expectations, resolve the tension and instability.[24] In all three writers, tension and relaxation figure as central musical qualities.

Tension and relaxation nevertheless engender discomfort in some analysts. They seem more expressive, vaguer, less directly observable than movement. There are reasons for these concerns. Consider, first, human tension. While movement in other people is known by outward behavior, tension and relaxation seem to have no outward expression. They are qualities of feeling, both somatic and psychological. We sense them in ourselves and, somehow, we infer them in others, although how we infer them is often not consciously known and may therefore seem mysterious.

Furthermore, the relation between tension and related qualities is more complicated than that between movement and its types. Movement's many types (leaping, clambering, trudging), often characterized by qualifiers (clumsy, sprightly, undulating), are clearly ways of moving. Similarly, some types of tension, such as being coiled tightly or stretched, are recognized as types of tension. For example, if I am holding a spring that is tightly wound, I know that it's tense because I can feel myself restraining it until I let go and it unwinds. If I think another person is "tightly wound," I know what I mean by analogy with the spring, although I may not be aware of how I know.

Affects, on the other hand, are not types of tension and relaxation, although they involve tension and relaxation in crucial ways. It may be difficult to notice the involvement of tension and relaxation in affect because the former are usually thought of as primarily somatic, whereas the latter are thought of as psychological. However, both affects and the feelings of tension and relaxation are both somatic and psychological. They are also outwardly physical, recognized in others through the bodily disposition, tone of voice, and style of movement or action of others. They are recognized in ourselves through proprioceptive awareness of such things as our muscles expanding and contracting, sensations of balance, visceral states, and muscle tone. We can imagine these internal states in others, as I will explain below.

It may seem that one just senses tension or uneasiness in another, whether human or musical, because the outward expressions of tension and affectual states are subtle and may not be noticed consciously. However, I might, subliminally, see that another individual is moving haltingly, in small steps, eyes watchfully darting around, and I might say that he is timid. Or I might see that someone is smiling and also, subliminally, see her broad, well-defined, direct gestures, and wide-open eyes, and I might say she is exuberant.

In ourselves, we may recognize tension, relaxation, and affects, perhaps subliminally, in our somatic states. If I feel timid, it is not because I notice timidity's outward expressions but because I sense such things as my chest hunched and drawn in, my face turned a bit downward but my eyes darting all around, my jaw tight, my leg muscles contracted in order to step lightly, and perhaps my digestive organs pinched and distressed. Or I might feel myself exuberant if my torso, especially my chest, is expanded, my arms are freely extended by stretched muscles and gesturing broadly, my leg muscles are energized, and my mouth stretches in a grin.

Music, as I have said, does not literally move. It is also incapable of tension and affect. The intersubjectivity we feel in relation to it is provided by us in imagination, based on interpersonal experience. This imagined mutuality draws on human empathy, understood as psychological resonance with another, and sympathy, understood as psychological response to another. Walton provides a persuasive formulation of empathy in two papers, "Empathy, Imagination, and Phenomenal Concepts," which considers human empathy, and "Projectivism, Empathy, and Musical Tension," which considers both human and musical empathy.[25]

In "Empathy, Imagination, and Phenomenal Concepts" (Walton 2015, 5–15), Walton proposes that empathy results when someone either imagines how she would feel if she were in another person's current situation, or she relives a "memory trace" of an earlier experience of her own in order to sense what another is currently feeling. Either might serve as a "sample" of what she imagines the other is experiencing. She might say "he feels like *this*," where "feels like" could be either psychological or physical and "*this*" is either the speaker's present feeling or a memory trace of a feeling, not a verbal description of it. Walton also distinguishes "*sort-of* empathy," in which one "recollects" but does not "re-live" a previous experience; I will call this "empathy," as well, although I am inclined to speak of empathy proper inducing such things as tension and to speak of sort-of empathy as only recognizing what, in the other, might elicit it.

When the empathizer experiences something like the other's feelings, Walton speaks of "contagion" or "infection." I'll continue to rely on "empathy" or substitute "resonance." The latter suggests more strongly the possibility of two entities coming to behavioral or somatic accord without implying the disagreeable aspects of illness.[26]

Transferred to music, one might use one's experiences of feeling tense to hear that the music "feels like *this*," where "*this*" is one's first-person experience of everyday tension, whether present or past. It would be perfectly normal to think that one is hearing the tension directly in the music, recognizing one's use of oneself only subliminally, as—Walton argues—is often the case in person-to-person empathy. An important difference between musical empathy and person-to-person empathy is the location of the tension or affect. In music, unlike in people, although "listeners experience [tension and relaxation] as intrinsic properties of passages of music," Walton doubts that we hear "*actual* tension" in music, "if this implies that the sounds themselves are literally tense" (Walton 2015, 122).[27]

"Motor mimicry" (Walton 2015, 133) of another person's behavior can elicit one's past or present experiences of tension, effecting its attribution to that other.[28] In music, the rhythms and other qualities of a passage can also elicit motor mimicry, effecting attribution of tension to that passage. Walton provides examples of tension-inducing rhythms, pointing out: "the unpredictable syncopations in Stravinsky's *Rite of Spring*," "steady, relentless, entirely predictable, driving rhythms, characteristic of Beethoven," and "rapidly repeating sixteenth note accompaniment figures common in baroque string music" (Walton 2015, 120–121).

The examples of rhythmic unpredictability and predictability hint at the further important point that tension can be ascribed to widely differing musical qualities and passages. It can be heard in such contradictory circumstances as: a passage that extends a single harmony, for example a dominant, for several measures without moving; and, on the other hand, a passage that accelerates, grows louder, and expands in registral space as it moves toward a climactic point. In the first case, delay induces tension and, in the second, intensification in various dimensions induces tension. The first might induce increasing impatience and the second, excitement.

To illustrate how he understands human empathy, Walton tells a brief story about his response to Nellie, who "is fidgeting nervously. I find myself fidgeting and feeling nervous also, when in her company … My fidgeting is unwitting mimicry, motor mimicry, of Nellie's fidgeting, which results in my feeling nervous. I may then judge Nellie to be nervous" (Walton 2015, 134).

Empathetic resonance is affected through Nellie's fidgeting, which Walton observes, probably subliminally, resulting in (possibly inward) mimicry. He may mimic her nervous behavior subliminally and, becoming nervous himself, think that Nellie feels like he does, or he might attribute his reflected nervousness back to Nellie without realizing that he has become nervous. Or, based on his trace memory of fidgeting nervously, he may recognize Nellie's nervousness without becoming nervous himself.

Like Nellie's nervousness, tension and related qualities are attributed to a musical passage due to musical behaviors that may elicit them in a listener. Many Beethoven passages that liquidate a melody or motive, shortening it and speeding up generally, perhaps adding instruments, growing louder—generally intensifying—may excite their listeners and may be designed to get them worked up, as I think the *Waldstein* is. They may be designed to create resonance, even entrainment.

In a second example, Walton addresses how empathy may occur in relation with non-representational aspects of artworks by considering how he senses uneasiness while viewing Vincent van Gogh's *Portrait de l'artiste*. In the case of the painting, tension is induced by purely medium-specific effects which do not resemble the means by which tension is expressed by people. The painting makes Walton "feel, if not nervous, at least somewhat uneasy or tense." This results from "producing the affect in the spectator" through "[f]eatures of the work" other than the representation of van Gogh himself. These include "the busy brushwork in the background and on the jacket, the choppiness of the strokes on the face and beard." Walton nevertheless thinks of his "response as an empathetic response to the person in the picture" (Walton 2015, 144).

Several additional features of the background brushwork contribute to the uneasiness experienced. The brushwork is also heavy and the swirling background is particularly active, irregular in its patterns, and chaotic. Van Gogh, by contrast, seems still and dejected, as shown by his downward-sloping shoulders, grim, impassive expression, collapsed torso, and generally dark coloring (both of figure and clothing). In the non-depictive features, I think I see how van Gogh experiences the world around him, or his own state of mind, or how his state of mind might influence his experience of the world around him—distracted, chaotic, restless, and, yes, uneasy. I see also by the depictive features of his posture that he is unhappy and weighed down.

The non-depictive, medium-specific qualities of paint and brushstroke are intense, energetic, scattered—in a word, chaotic. They are not like chaotic human behavior—flailing one's arms, erratically moving this way and that, etc. They nevertheless perform the role of human behaviors in eliciting empathy and awareness of van Gogh's inner psychological state.

In music, medium-specific features of musical sound also create effects that a listener can experience and, through empathy, interpret as feeling qualities. They need not be mediated through an implicit human agent. Walton identifies musical features that are interpreted or experienced as tense, features that do not require the mediation of human behavior: "Dissonant harmonies, dense musical textures, and modulations to new keys needn't be understood to be or to represent [human] behavioral or physical manifestations of tension at all … [T]hey work simply by producing in appreciators an experience of tension felt as an infection from without" (Walton 2015, 150).[29] The familiar notion of "tonal tension" recognizes the fact that many listeners experience tension directly through the inherent harmonic and relational conventions of common-practice tonality.

Finally, while I might empathize with Nellie, the depiction of van Gogh, or a musical work, I might instead respond with sympathy. Sensing Nellie's nervousness, I might want to calm her with soothing words and gestures. Sensing how uncomfortable van Gogh must have been in his whirling world, I might not imagine empathy with the painting, but feel pity instead. A passage of delicate, sad music might evoke in me concern and the desire to care for it. I might reach toward it—its sounds—outwardly leaning toward its source or inwardly feeling my muscles preparing as if to reach out to its source. Such a feeling might induce me to analyze such a passage, acting to give it the care and attention that it seems to ask for. Or I might respond less sympathetically, as I have fantasized that Maus might feel frustration at op. 95's clumsy outbursts or as I have felt overwhelmed by the arousal the *Waldstein* provokes. These might be called reactions rather than responses.

Whether through resonance, response, or reaction, music and listener are bound together in a process to which both contribute and a third entity, the experienced music, is formed. Investing in imagining tension or movement in the sounds of music no doubt facilitates this fusion.[30]

An Analytical Relationship with a Brahms Passage

I sense that the introduction of Brahms's song "Meerfahrt," op. 96, no. 4, is unsettled (the score can be found in the Appendix at the end of this chapter). I feel apprehensive when I hear it. The text of the song, by Heine, portrays a relationship in decline:

Meerfahrt	Sea Journey[31]
Mein Liebchen, wir saßen beisammen	My darling, we sat together,
Traulich im leichten Kahn.	Snugly in a light boat.
Die Nacht war still, und wir schwammen	The night was still, and we floated
Auf weiter Wasserbahn.	On the broad waterway.
Die Geisterinsel, die schöne,	The ghostly island, the beautiful,
Lag dämm'rig im Mondenglanz;	Lay duskily in the moonlight;
Dort klangen liebe Töne	There sounded lovely tones,
Dort wogte der Nebeltanz.	There waved the dancing mists.
Dort klang es lieb und lieber,	There it sounded lovely and lovelier,
Und wogt' es hin und her;	And waved here and there;
Wir aber schwammen vorüber,	But we floated past,
Trostlos auf weitem Meer.	Desolate on the wide sea.

The voice and piano express different psychological states. The voice alone seems almost cheerfully tuneful as it begins to sing, turning darker and more dramatic later in the stanza (m. 27). That mood does not last, as the second stanza again begins cheerfully, this time becoming hectic as it depicts the sound and movement of the dance (beginning at m. 43, beat 3). But in the last stanza, the voice sings in increasingly passionate desolation.

The piano is subtly and pervasively unsettled almost from the opening, and it is this quality of the introduction that I will consider briefly, since it establishes the voice's environment. The regular barcarolle figure in the left hand musically depicts the gentle undulating movement of the boat and water. The pleasant regularity of the figure carries the music on but is also disturbed by its harmonies and by the melody flowing more slowly above. The opening promise of A minor is supported by the right hand's E, but E moves to F♯ (m. 3), forcefully struck and held before E returns, while the left hand rolls on without change. A minor fades a bit and E minor becomes a possibility. The opening is thus already drifting between tonalities and between the tonic and pre-dominant of a harmonic phrase.

As the A-minor chord continues to ripple in the left hand, the right hand falls to A, then rises first from C to E, and then to G♯ (m. 6). The major quality of the third that G♯ creates with the left hand's E is unexpectedly bright. G♯'s forceful resolution to A on the next downbeat is immediately upset by the A triad's major sonority. The right hand's correction to A minor in the middle of the next beat has already been upset by the left hand's F♯, and this leads to a brief, more explicit passage toward E minor. Although the progression might be ii^7–V^7–I, the conjunction of bass B with A on the downbeat of m. 8, held over in the right hand from m. 7, suggests that the span of V might rather support a suspended seventh, decorated through a falling third, and resolving to G as the bass moves to E. In other words, the music suggests a harmonic and a contrapuntal interpretation that are just slightly in conflict with each other. Then the figure from mm. 7–8 is foreshortened, shifted a half measure, and repeated with harmonic modifications that hint at D minor, so that the repetition increasingly diverges from the earlier measures.

Activity accelerates through the next measure until V$^6_4$ initiates the dominant of A minor (m. 11), but before reaching V$^5_3$, the two hands pass through an inner-voice line whose A moves to a jarring A♭ (not G♯) that moves on to G before rising to V's G♯. The inner, passing, chords hint at F minor, a chromaticized vi, distant in relation to A minor. The melody of these two measures is repeated (mm. 13–14), although a more conventional cadential progression masks the repetition.

One could view this passage as a single phrase in which the right hand rises from $\hat{5}$ to $\hat{8}$ and then falls again to $\hat{5}$ within the melodic minor scale while the harmony moves from an extended tonic toward iv in m. 10 to reach V, which is extended from m. 11 to m. 14. However, the passage is characterized by the unsettled moves outlined above and these color the experience, throwing into doubt the voice's simple tunefulness when it enters.

The music repeatedly undercuts its A minor, and I can never quite rely on its behavior: I feel uneasy. If the song represents a single individual, it is as if the voice represents conscious beliefs while the piano portrays the individual's discomfort with his relationship, a discomfort that is unconscious until voice and right hand begin to trace the same lines, briefly at "wogte der Nebeltanz" and decisively when they join on the F♯ to E of the neighbor motive in m. 54. In some respects, it is like the van Gogh painting, externalizing the singer's mental state through the swirling background, or like any normal human interaction in which behavioral cues are subliminally noted and interpreted in the course of conversation. I hear the singer's state of mind through the accompaniment's behavior before he begins to sing, as I see a friend's state of mind in her walk as she approaches before she even greets me.

While I am encouraged to hear the qualities I have ascribed to the piano as the psychological state of the couple because of the text, in a purely instrumental work I could hear the discrepancies between the accompanimental pattern and right-hand melody as well as the instabilities and distances implied by the harmonies as disquieting in themselves— no singer or text is needed. In response to this song (or a purely instrumental work) I may be empathetically unsettled by the music, resonating with its undermining ways, or I might respond to its disturbance with sympathetic apprehension.

Either way, I interpret and resonate or respond to the music's events and continuities, as they are illuminated by the movement-affect qualities I impute to the music as well as by my involvement with it. The music-analytical observations, the characterizations of the music, and my involvement with it are all appropriately part of this narrative of my personal and analytical relationship with the Brahms passage.

CONCLUSION

There are many kinds of music with which people have relationships, and there are many relationships that a person might have with music. Analytical relationships are, among these, specialized and intensive. There is a great deal that might be said about analytical relationships, and I have, of course, found it necessary to impose limits. There is much more to be said and other viewpoints to take.

I have concentrated on the content of analytical texts as a source of information about analytical relationships, principally those that portray intersubjective relationships between the analyst and the music, relationships that attribute human qualities to music. I have focused on two widely accepted domains that connect musical experience to everyday experience: movement/action and tension/affect. In coordination with the examination of musical experiences of movement, tension, etc., I have distinguished analytical relationships that I have called observationalist, for those who prefer to focus their attention on musical events as such, and associationalist, for those who integrate imaginings about movement/action or tension/affect with attention to musical events.

Movement/action and tension/affect are rich sources of musical imagining and analysis. In human experience, movement and action are both our own and those of others, visible to us. The ways in which they are verbally articulated frequently go beyond the bare generic notion of movement to characterize the quality of movement or action. Very often, such characterizations incorporate the affect expressed in the movement. Tension and release, their more specific types and affectual relatives, are inner visceral and proprioceptive—first-person—physical and psychological experiences. They are also visible physical movements and actions.

Thus, movement and affect are not distinct from each other in human experience. Nor are they in music. An intensification to a climax might be heard as rushing forward or as increasing excitement. An analyst might experience or think in terms of movement/action or tension/affect and, as a result, might notice or emphasize different musical details. Whatever the preference, however, analysis calls for interpreting what she hears and experiences, not in human but in musical terms.

Observationalists, I have said, are analysts who experience music aurally and intellectually, and who, reflecting that relationship, describe musical processes and events in music-observational terms. However, observation, defined as paying close attention, noticing, is fundamental to any analytical relationship. It reveals our shared devotion and fascination with music itself. Music analysts are all observationalists.

All associationalists infuse listening and the analytical relationship with imaginings based on interpretation of music-specific qualities, processes, and patterns. But I have distinguished two types of associationalist: movement-oriented associationalists and affect-oriented associationalists. It is a fragile distinction because movements tend to have an affective attitude.

The movement-oriented associationalist is, of course, also an observationalist because her analysis "mixes" musical and everyday vocabularies. Her associational approach also maintains a trace of the observational stance in its engagement with the outward aspect of human experience. The analyst follows the music's movements and actions as if it is "out there" moving about, not quite touching the analyst (or inside her, as the sounds are).

Affect-oriented assocationalists involve themselves with the internal aspect of human experience, using their own feelings in aid of their musical imaginings. They are also observationalists, attending to the interactions of musical events. They are necessarily movement-associationalists, since feeling the affect in the music's movements is crucial to the imagined experience. They feel the flux of musical intensities in the musical events and movements as their own, possibly merging with the music.

Affect associationalists might have any of three types of musical involvement. They might resonate or empathize with the music, feeling what they imagine it feels and providing it with that feeling. They might respond or sympathize with the music, providing it with an affectual character but feeling an answering affect that complements the music's. Or they might react in a less complementary or affirmative way to the music, providing it with an affectual character but involving themselves more dispassionately.

Finally, a few words about the analyst's presence in the text. There are many analyses in which the author's persona seems absent. Allen Forte might provide good examples. However, his style of writing reveals a distinctive analytical persona with well-defined musical inclinations. As illustrated in my consideration of Maus, sometimes the authorial persona's attitude toward the musical work might be suggested (speculatively) through the qualities ascribed to the music. In my own analysis, my authorial persona appears explicitly in order to explain features of my account of musical events, to identify the elicited qualities that are attributed to the music, and to express the personal feelings that result.

The various distinctions just summarized are, however, artificial as a matter of analytical practice. As I have been considering varieties of movement and tension, I have been addressing them as individual predicates. That is not usually how we encounter them. Rather we write analyses about passages and complete pieces—scenarios that incorporate all sorts of descriptions of the music, depending on what we notice and what it elicits in us: observations about the music, musical movements and actions, and the music-intensive and music-affectual qualities heard and felt. Analytical relationships are thus complex and varied, responsive to and reflective of the manifold and diverse experiences that a musical work gives the analyst.

Acknowledgment

I am grateful to an anonymous reviewer for a sensitive reading of my paper, resulting in very useful suggestions about how it might be improved.

APPENDIX

4. Meerfahrt
H. Heine

FIGURE 23.1 Brahms, "Meerfahrt," op. 96, no. 4.

FIGURE 23.1 *continued*

FIGURE 23.1 *continued*

FIGURE 23.1 *continued*

Notes

1. The quotation from Forster appears in Kivy (1990, vi). The material Kivy cites is at the beginning of Chapter 5 of Forster (1999, 28).
2. Jordan is quoted more fully in Guck (1997, 350).
3. The phrase is used by Scruton (1993, 200). He is in the process of considering the interplay of interest in music's intrinsic nature with "sympathetic response" to it. See 198–201.
4. I have not chosen "observer" because I think that it suggests a more distanced, uninvolved, and objective relationship than that which analysts have.
5. I made this point about the need for a sentential subject in Guck (1994, 217–230), where I also consider the role of the composer in analytical texts.
6. Schenker was not a pure observationalist (as most Schenkerian analysts also are not). The attribution of psychological states to a musical passage or a responding listener can be found in various analyses.
7. A recent example is Monahan (2013), which organizes the notion of agency in four "classes."
8. See Cone (1974, 2–3). As a source of the notion of authorial persona, Cone cites Booth (1956).
9. Unlike "observationalist," choosing a term for a more imagination-oriented analytical relationship is difficult. A term derived from expression emphasizes what is heard in the music rather than what the analyst does. One derived from interpretation denies that observation-oriented analysis is interpretive. There is some appeal for a term derived from imagination, but that might suggest—incorrectly—that such analysts are excessively fanciful or subjective. Association is clear about connecting musical experience with other aspects of life, and this seems desirable.
10. My thanks to Joseph Dubiel for bringing the quotation to my attention.
11. Sessions, Cone, and Maus are intellectually related. Sessions taught Cone, who taught Maus. This is evident in the relationships among their ideas.
12. Sessions also associates music with gesture, especially when he considers performers, the actual humans who realize music's vitality through physical activity. Discussing two performances of a Webern cantata, he criticizes one because singers could so effortlessly produce a wide interval. In this performance he asserts that a listener could not sense "the connection and relationship between the notes" and he associates these with *the quality and character of the musical gesture*" (1970, 65).
13. Although music does not convey some of the so-called canonical emotions (for example, disgust), it certainly conveys others: joy can be heard in joyful musical behavior, as can sadness or anger.
14. See also Maus (1991).
15. Maus (1995, 3 and 4) describes musical behaviors (and agents) as fictional. He is, at that point, summarizing and endorsing Jerrold Levinson's proposal that "expressive music is heard *as if it were* an alternate, audible but sui generis mode of behaviorally manifesting psychological states." See Levinson (1990, 338).
16. Maus's footnote 19 (1988, 66) follows: "For careful and influential explorations of the point, see [Davidson (1980)]. My account draws largely on Davidson's views. Along with Davidson's work, [Anscombe (1957)] was crucial in establishing the study of action as a central preoccupation of current analytic philosophy. Sophisticated, engaging, recent work includes [Dennett (1978), Peacocke (1979), Morton (1980), and Hornsby (1980)]."

17. See Ryle (2002, 58). Ryle typically addresses the cognitive aspect of actions, but his point here denies the mind-body split. He may deny the existence of mental events more absolutely than I am inclined to. The quote is drawn from chapter 2, "Knowing How and Knowing That"; chapter 4, "Emotion," more directly addresses matters of emotion evident in action. An example of the point from that chapter is: "on hearing that a man is vain we expect him, in the first instance, to behave in certain ways, namely to talk a lot about himself, to cleave to the society of the eminent, to reject criticisms, to seek the footlights and to disengage himself from conversations about the merits of others . . . . To be vain is to tend to act in these and innumerable other kindred ways" (86). In conclusion he writes that "I find out your inclinations and your moods more directly" than by "inferences to occult inner states or processes" because "I hear and understand your conversational avowals, your interjections and your tones of voice; I see and understand your gestures and facial expressions" (115). Finally, "interjections, tones of voice, gestures and grimaces are modes of communication" (115). Ryle considers what verbs like "outburst" do in "Thinking and Reflecting" (1971). He calls such verbs "adverbial verbs."

18. The notion that a given emotion is displayed in a style of action is advocated by a number of current researchers in neuroscience and psychoanalysis, including Damasio (1994), who also views the mind-body split as mistaken, Stern (2002), and Gallagher (2005).

19. See Walton (2015, 157). Walton writes that "we call passages of music exuberant, agitated, serene, timid, calm, determined, nervous. We speak of rising and falling melodies, of wistful melodies and hurried rhythms, of motion and rest, of leaps, skips, and stepwise progression, of statements and answering phrases, tension and release, resignation and resolve, struggle, uncertainty, and arrival. Music can be impetuous, powerful, delicate, sprightly, witty, majestic, tender, arrogant, peevish, spirited, yearning, chilly."

20. Maus (1988, 66) nevertheless acknowledges the influence of Cone (1974) on his ideas about agency.

21. Maus has written about music as drama and as narrative. His articles on these subjects suggest that he thinks that music is more like drama than like narrative. I too prefer the analogy of music as drama, that is, of music as enactment rather than telling about enactment. It is verbal accounts of music, including analyses, that are narratives. In addition to Maus (1988) and (1991) cited above, see Maus (1997).

22. Sessions (1951, 84, italics in original). I was led to this quotation by a mention in Walton (2015, 119); Walton also considers Zuckerkandl's notion of "force" to be a way to speak of tension.

23. See Lerdahl (2001), especially chapter 4, "Tonal Tension and Attraction."

24. See Meyer (1956). Meyer invariably maintains this level of schematic abstraction, converting notions of stability, goal, and expectation virtually into a formulaic vocabulary tending away from a psychological account and toward a more observationalist perspective. In later works, expectation is replaced by implication, a logical operator replacing a mental state.

25. See Walton (2015, 5–15 and 118–150). Walton's explication of empathy is complex and I am simplifying it in some respects. I am, of course, responsible for any misconceptions in my summary.

26. "Resonance" was suggested by Cozolino (2006). He describes "*resonance behaviors,*" which are also associated with mirror neuron systems, as "the reflexive imitation responses we make when interacting with others," such as yawning when others do (59). However, these behaviors can be voluntary and, with imitation and empathy, are important to interpersonal understanding and group coherence (200–204).

27. Walton's views about empathy as he extends it to music are extracted from a larger argument (in Walton 2015, 118–150). His consideration of several important points is omitted from my summary: Walton concludes that more specific types of tension such as musical emotion "are optional layers of 'meaning' built on top of such fundamental properties as those of musical tension and relaxation" (150). He makes this claim based on arguing that it is indeterminate whether one associates a particular instance of musical tension and release to an animate or inanimate entity and whether it is physical or psychological. He considers physical tension to include both that of objects, such as coiled springs, and that of muscles. (I distinguish physical tensions in inanimate entities from physical tensions in people.) I am grateful to Fred Everett Maus for allowing me to read his excellent Maus (2007), which corrected misconceptions I had about Walton (2015). Maus also presented Maus (2007) at the conference "Bodies in Motion: Explorations in Perception and Performance," Florida Atlantic University, Boca Raton, December 4, 2008.

28. Recent research suggests that some sort of imitative capacity underlies our understanding of other people beginning in the first hours of life, perhaps through the mechanism of so-called "mirror" neurons. Mimicry is the foundation of Arnie Cox's theory of engagement with music in Cox (2016). Although there are some significant overlaps between Cox's terminology and Walton's, their ideas are very different. For the purposes of this paper, I find Walton's more persuasive.

29. Jenefer Robinson takes a similar view in some circumstances. In Robinson (1994) she suggests that a feeling that some music induces in us is the same feeling expressed by the music: "Music that disturbs and unsettles us is disturbing, unsettling music. Modulations that surprise us are surprising. Melodies that soothe us are soothing. Furthermore, unexpected harmonic shifts excite us and are exciting; a protracted stay in a harmonic area distant from the home key makes us uneasy and produces uneasy music ... And so on" (19).

30. In Guck (1994, 224–228) I discuss the permeability of the boundary between music and listener (analyst) as exemplified in Schachter (1983, 55–68). Robinson plausibly suggests that the feeling of intimacy with music considered by Walton (2015, 151–174) is the result of physiological effects, such as changes in heart rate, that music has on its listeners. See Robinson (2005, 376). The difficulty of maintaining a separation between music and self is also addressed in Walton (2015, 208–247).

31. Trans. Emily Ezust, in *The Lied, Art Song, and Choral Texts Archive*, http://www.lieder.net. (The translation has been modified to make it more literal than the published form is.)

WORKS CITED

Anscombe, G. E. M. 1957. *Intention*. Ithaca, NY: Cornell University Press.

Aristotle. 1961. *Poetics*. Translated by Samuel H. Butcher. New York: Hill and Wang.

Babbitt, Milton. 1987. "Professional Theorists and Their Influence." In *Words about Music*, edited by Stephen Dembski and Joseph N. Straus. Madison: University of Wisconsin Press.

Booth, Wayne C. 1956. *The Rhetoric of Fiction*. Chicago: University of Chicago Press.

Cavell, Stanley. 1976. "Music Discomposed." In *Must We Mean What We Say?*, 180–212. Cambridge: Cambridge University Press.

Cone, Edward T. 1974. *The Composer's Voice*. Berkeley: University of California Press.

Cox, Arnie. 2016. *Music and Embodied Cognition: Listening, Moving, Feeling, and Thinking.* Bloomington: Indiana University Press.

Cozolino, Louis. 2006. *The Neuroscience of Human Relationships: Attachment and the Developing Social Brain.* New York: W. W. Norton.

Damasio, Antonio R. 1994. *Descartes' Error: Emotion, Reason, and the Human Brain.* New York: G. P. Putnam's Sons.

Davidson, Donald. 1980. *Essays on Actions and Events.* New York: Oxford University Press.

Dennett, Daniel. 1978. *Brainstorms.* Montgomery, VT: Bradford Books.

Forster, E. M. 1999. *Howards End.* New York: The Modern Library of Random House, Inc.

Gallagher, Shaun. 2005. *How the Body Shapes the Mind.* Oxford: Clarendon Press.

Guck, Marion A. 1989. "Beethoven as Dramatist." *College Music Symposium* 29: 8–18.

Guck, Marion A. 1994. "Analytical Fictions." *Music Theory Spectrum* 16: 217–230.

Guck, Marion A. 1997. "Music Loving, or the Relationship with the Piece." *Journal of Musicology* 15: 343–352.

Hornsby, Jennifer. 1980. *Actions.* Boston: Routledge & Kegan Paul.

Jordan, Roland. 1991. "How Does the Tune Go?" Paper read at the Society for Music Theory Fourteenth Annual Meeting, Cincinnati, OH.

Kivy, Peter. 1990. *Music Alone.* Ithaca, NY: Cornell University Press.

Lerdahl, Fred. 2001. *Tonal Pitch Space.* New York: Oxford University Press.

Levinson, Jerrold. 1990. "Hope in *The Hebrides.*" In *Music, Art, and Metaphysics: Essays in Philosophical Aesthetics,* 336–375. Ithaca, NY: Cornell University Press.

Maus, Fred Everett. 1988. "Music as Drama." *Music Theory Spectrum* 10: 56–73.

Maus, Fred Everett. 1991. "Music as Narrative." *Indiana Theory Review* 12: 1–34.

Maus, Fred Everett. 1995. "Imagining Emotions and Actions in Music." Paper read at the Joint Meetings of the American Musicological Society, the Center for Black Music Research, and the Society for Music Theory, New York, November.

Maus, Fred Everett. 1997. "Narrative, Drama, and Emotion in Instrumental Music." *The Journal of Aesthetics and Art Criticism* 55: 293–303.

Maus, Fred Everett. 2007. "Tension and Narrative." Paper read at the Congress of the International Musicological Society, Zurich, Switzerland, July 12.

Meyer, Leonard B. 1956. *Emotion and Meaning in Music.* Chicago: University of Chicago Press.

Monahan, Seth. 2013. "Action and Agency Revisited." *Journal of Music Theory* 57: 321–371.

Morton, Adam. 1980. *Frames of Mind.* New York: Oxford University Press.

Peacocke, Christopher. 1979. *Holistic Explanation.* New York: Oxford University Press.

Robinson, Jenefer. 1994. "The Expression and Arousal of Emotion in Music." *The Journal of Aesthetics and Art Criticism* 52: 13–22.

Robinson, Jenefer. 2005. *Deeper than Reason: Emotion and its Role in Literature, Music, and Art.* New York: Oxford University Press.

Rothstein, William. 2005. "Playing with Forms: Mozart's Rondo in D Major, K. 485." In *Engaging Music: Essays in Musical Analysis,* edited by Deborah Stein, 202–214. New York: Oxford University Press.

Ryle, Gilbert. 2002. *The Concept of Mind* [1949]. Chicago: University of Chicago Press.

Ryle, Gilbert. 2009. "Thinking and Reflecting" [1971]. In *Collected Essays 1929–1968: Collected Papers Volume 2,* 479–493. New York: Routledge.

Schachter, Carl. 1983. "The First Movement of Brahms's Second Symphony: The First Theme and its Consequences." *Music Analysis* 2: 55–68.

Schenker, Heinrich. (1925) 1994. "Chopin: Etude in E♭ minor, Op. 10, No. 6." In *The Masterwork in Music: A Yearbook, Volume. 1*, edited by William Drabkin and translated by Ian Bent, 81–89. Cambridge: Cambridge University Press.

Scruton, Roger. 1993. "Notes on the Meaning of Music." In *The Interpretation of Music: Philosophical Essays*, edited by Michael Krausz, 193–202. Oxford: Clarendon Press.

Sessions, Roger. 1950. *The Musical Experience of Composer, Performer, Listener*. Princeton, NJ: Princeton University Press.

Sessions, Roger. 1951. *Harmonic Practice*. New York: Harcourt, Brace & World, Inc.

Sessions, Roger. 1970. *Questions about Music*. New York: W. W. Norton & Co., Inc.

Stern, Daniel N. [1985] 2002. *The Interpersonal World of the Infant: A View from Psychoanalysis and Developmental Psychology*. New York: Basic Books, Inc.

Walton, Kendall L. 2015. *In Other Shoes: Music, Metaphor, Empathy, Existence*. New York: Oxford University Press.

CHAPTER 24

....

IMAGES, VISUALIZATION, AND REPRESENTATION

....

DORA A. HANNINEN

BROWSE or scroll through the pages of a scholarly book or article in music theory and you will likely encounter a number of visual images. Along with musical examples—whether in the form of scores, annotated scores, transcriptions, or recordings—you may find tables, plates, line or bar graphs, matrices, network graphs, digraphs, schematic diagrams, voice-leading sketches, and other visual displays of musical information and ideas. Compared to musicology, writings in music theory and analysis tend to use many more types of visual images. They also tend to use images differently. Whereas musicologists generally provide scores, photographs, and tables as primary documents, for reference, or as accompanying illustrations, theorists often present images as evidence or employ them as a mode of argument. They use images to visualize the invisible (e.g., mathematical relations, musical spaces, or sound itself); to fix and objectify transient and often subjective phenomena and music perceptions; and to present theoretical models and analytical interpretations in a concise, easily apprehensible form.

The multimodality of text and images in contemporary music theory extends to the very formation and development of ideas. With advances in music notation and graphics software, our discourse has become increasingly visual, prompting questions about the properties and potential of visual images, their intended meaning, and their use. How do images differ from words as a mode of expression? What conceptual work do they do? Are all aspects of an image iconic, or are some of them non-iconic, incidental artifacts of visualization or non-propositional elements of graphic design? As readers and creators of these images, do we know which are which?

With visual images now often seen as essential, not ancillary, to contemporary music theory and analysis, we would do well to understand how they work. Part I of this chapter begins by establishing the concept of mode, focusing on the different affordances and demands of visual images versus verbal text. Drawing on a substantial relevant literature in science and technology studies, cartography, information visualization, and visual studies, I outline how images can be used to reason, present information, offer an interpretation, and advance an argument, whether by explicit claim or implicit suggestion of avowed content, or through aesthetic or rhetorical features.

In Part II, I draw a conceptual distinction between two functions of visual images in music-theoretic discourse: visualization (to render information in visual form that is otherwise invisible) and representation (to convey a specific analytic interpretation of what is shown). At the risk of oversimplification, these roughly correspond to "show" and "tell," respectively. After discussing these two functions in some detail, I proceed to a series of illustrations, drawn from work in music theory and analysis.

I close the chapter with some thoughts on elements of graphic design and on relations between visual images and accompanying verbal text—a large subject (and, indeed, the subject of another study).

Mode, Images, and Reasoning

Visual studies scholar Gunther Kress defines *mode* as "a socially shaped and culturally given resource for making meaning. *Image, writing, layout, music, gesture, speech, moving image, soundtrack,* are examples of modes used in representation and communication" (2014, 60). Each mode affords the user a particular set of communicative resources and entails a certain set of commitments. Visual images use spatial location, size, shape, and other variables; music uses pitch, loudness, and temporal position; words engage a lexicon, grammar, and shades of meaning accessible to a community of speakers. No indifferent, translucent window on meaning, mode—whether an image or words—does not just convey meaning, but "fixes" it: the communicative resources, limitations, and entailments of the mode affect meaning, with implications for the ontology, properties, and relationships attributed to—or read from—what is depicted.[1]

Scholars in visual studies recognize multimodality as both a practice and a field of inquiry. Theo van Leeuwen defines multimodality as (a) the "integrated use of different communicative resources such as language, image, sound, and music in multimodal texts and communicative events"; and (b) a "field of study investigating the common properties of the different modes in the multimodal mix and the way they integrate in multimodal texts and communicative events" (2011, 549). Much as the different lexicons, grammars, and cultural associations of English and Chinese frustrate any attempt at complete and literal translation, so do the different communicative resources, limitations, and entailments of two modes, such as words and images.[2] When words and images are used together, then, how do they interrelate? Do the images largely replicate what is said in words? Or do words and images say and do different things? What can images do that words cannot?

The workings of visual images have received little attention in music theory, but they are an important subject in the relatively young and growing interdisciplinary fields of visual studies and science and technology studies.[3] Scientific discourse is typically multimodal, moving freely among words, mathematical expressions, and all sorts of visual images, from tables, graphs, and schematic diagrams to data visualizations, enhanced photographs, artists' renderings, and animations. As Michael Lynch, Luc Pauwels, and many others have pointed out, this multimodality is intrinsic to the content and, historically, even to the progress of science.[4] Visualizations of large and complex data sets enable scientists to perceive patterns that they would not be able to detect from numeric data alone (Irving 2011, 775–776, 780). Visual images also perform essential conceptual work: scientists use images to develop theories, present them, and advance arguments.[5] In some fields, such as cartography, data visualization, and visual social science, images are the primary means to formulate and express ideas, stabilized and interpreted with a few critical words in the form of captions, labels, and footnotes.[6]

What are some of the key differences between visual and verbal modes of expression? What can images do that words cannot?[7]

In *The Semiology of Graphics*, an early and influential text in the theory of graphics, Jacques Bertin contrasts words, music, and other "linear systems" with images as "spatial" systems (1983, 3). Words, both written and spoken, unfold in time in a linear sequence; visual images have spatial extension and are presented to us as simultaneities. Regarding the different "logics" of words and images, Kress notes that for words, "*sequence in time* is a fundamental organizing principle" (2014, 62). Words come in a distinct order. That order carries meaning, whether in the form of grammatical function (e.g., as in English, an SVO, or subject–verb–object, language) or emphasis (as in Finnish, and to a lesser extent in English). But in a visual image, disparate elements are presented simultaneously. It is the arrangement or "*relation of the simultaneously present elements* in that space [that provides] the underlying 'semiotic logic'" (Kress 2014, 62).

Two points here warrant elaboration, regarding space and the apparent simultaneity of visual images. First, while we move in a three-dimensional (3D) world, the retinal image is two-dimensional (2D). Visual perception is somewhere in between, sometimes described as 2.5D (but more like 2.05D), to reflect the fact that a stationary observer receives much less information about the depth dimension than about the horizontal or vertical one (Ware 2008, 45). The visual image is always a projection—a viewpoint on a scene—not a comprehensive and fully objective depiction. Second, "simultaneity" refers to the presentation of visual images. But we cannot actually access images in this way. Although our experience of visual images seems continuous, in fact it is punctuated and intermittent. The brain constructs the apparent constancy of the visual image from a series of saccades (rapid eye fixations) that focus on, and successively attend to, different points in the image. The points of fixation and attention are ordered, but that order is not determined solely by the image. However, the center and flow of attention around an image can be channeled strongly by elements of graphic design such as object placement, perspective, color, and weight, as well as by cognitive search tasks.

As Colin Ware points out, the logics of words and visual images differ in other ways, too. "Language," he writes, "is a socially developed system of shared symbols, together with a grammar" (Ware 2008, 131). It is "full of qualifiers such as 'if,' 'and,' 'but,' 'otherwise,' 'nevertheless,' and 'while.' This is not formal mathematical logic, but it does allow for a kind of abstract reasoning" (132). Visual images partake of a different logic, the perception of basic spatial relationships such as inside/outside, apart-from/connected-to, and part/whole (145). Whereas words allow us to express conjunctions, subordination, and contingencies between abstract and complex ideas packaged as a series of clauses, visual images cast relations between ideas in the same spatial terms that we use to navigate and interact with the world.

Richness, or continuity, is another important difference between the visual and verbal modes. Vision is our dominant sense and richest source of information; it involves, or stimulates activity in, roughly half the brain, directly or indirectly. Ware observes that "the visual system will always be the highest bandwidth sense by far" (Ware 2008, 182). But we do not cognize all that we see, nor can we express all our thoughts in words. Words are created to be used more than once; they tend to filter and fragment the continuity of experience into recognizable chunks, associated with reusable concepts. Psychologist Zenon Pylyshyn goes so far as to say that "*most* of the properties of the object I am seeing and which can enter into my thoughts *cannot* be expressed, linguistically or otherwise" (Pylyshyn 2003, 432; emphasis added).[8] More fine-grained than thought, and much more fine-grained and attuned to particularity than individual words, visual experience can have unconceptualized contents that not only *are not,* but *cannot,* be expressed easily in words.[9] These include subtle gradations and continuous or coordinated change in size, distance, hue, value, thickness, and texture, as well as all sorts of topological relationships.[10]

All these differences between the verbal and visual modes—sequential versus simultaneous presentation, their different logics of word order and spatial arrangement, and the relative sparseness and discontinuity of language and individual words, compared to the richness and continuity of visual images—are meaningful differences that impose themselves upon and shape the content conveyed. In J. J. Gibson's terms, each mode comes with a set of "affordances"—features that enable or facilitate certain actions or perceptions by a subject, including the potential for communication.[11] But modes also have exigencies; they make demands.

Kress calls these demands the "epistemological commitments" of mode (2003, 3).[12] He gives the example that the English language requires every sentence or clause to have a verb, which expresses a commitment with regard to action or relation: "I cannot get around the fact that I have to name the relation, and refer to either a state or an action, even if I do not want to do so at all" (Kress 2003, 3). On the other hand, the visual mode requires a commitment regarding spatial location and object size, whether or not these are part of the intended meaning.[13]

Similarly, while it is easy to specify a range of values in numerals or words (a purple coneflower can have ten to twenty rays; hydrangeas come in all shades ranging from white through pink, purple, and blue), that is not the case for visual images. One can use a visual image of an individual to stand for the general case, but expression in the visual mode forces a commitment to a particular number of rays or a color. Even if the commitment is insignificant, no more than an artifact, it can still be misleading.[14]

Multimodal texts provide an opportunity for cross-modal checks and commentary that can distinguish significant, intended meaning from insignificant artifacts of modal exigency. What is conveyed in an image or in words by choice rather than necessity likely carries an intended meaning. Cross-modal elucidation or duplication by choice is available as a form of emphasis.

Affordances and exigencies of mode extend beyond the visual image or verbal text to the thought process behind it. The choice of mode can shape thought. In the earliest stages of writing, I am especially sensitive to the pressure that typing straight, line-by-line text in a uniform font on a computer screen exerts on inchoate ideas.[15] To avoid this, I revert to pencil and paper in landscape orientation, which supports a more fluid, hybrid (proto-?) mode of expression, in which words combine with spatial placement, brackets of different sizes, color, letter size, angle, and arrows. An easy slippage between visual and verbal modes is better suited to work at this stage, where the goal is not to transcribe ideas but to formulate and start organizing them.[16] Intermingling words with the spatial affordances of images occurs in some finished forms of writing as well, such as computer programs, where spacing articulates a logical structure; and poetry, in which the arrangement of words on the page can suggest intonation or the timing of vocal delivery.[17]

Affordances and exigencies of the visual mode support thought in other ways too. It is well known, for example, that visual images can facilitate problem-solving. Presenting a problem visually—or attempting to—tends to focus attention in a certain way, enabling certain thought patterns and foregrounding certain kinds of questions. As Pylyshyn puts it, "when we think in terms of spatial layouts we tend to think about different things and represent the problem in different ways than when we think in terms of abstract properties" (2003, 462). We "*think different thoughts*" (Pylyshyn 2003, 467; emphasis added). Used in this way, images serve not only to illustrate the result of a thought process, but as a means for information processing and a stimulus to reason.[18] Just as we use language as a medium for thought, so we can literally "use images to think" (Card, Mackinlay, and Shneiderman 1999, 1)—not just to communicate ideas, but to create them.[19]

How, then, do images help us think? To represent a problem visually, we must first identify and externalize its basic components; this itself can be illuminating. Images can also transform how we represent, access, and use information. An image can serve as an external memory store: it effectively expands both working memory and long-term storage. Through images, we can take advantage of properties of the visual medium, including its high information density and continuity. We also enlist the particular strengths of human visual perception, which include the rapid parallel processing of early vision for features such as color, shape, and orientation; immediate recognition and quick comparisons of object features, relative distances, multiple pathways, or potential groupings; and the use of visual schemata to read off values, trends, and other relationships.[20] When we represent a problem visually, we map abstract relationships onto spatial ones, transforming challenging tasks for cognition and recall into much easier—even automatic—ones for visual perception and recognition. The image allows us to offload work from memory and cognition to visual perception, and it also can function as a form of external cognition.[21]

In an oft-cited 1987 study, Jill Larkin and Herbert Simon explore some of the particular advantages that diagrams have over verbal text for problem-solving. After drawing a distinction between "internal representations" (in the brain) and "external representations" (recorded on paper, electronically, or by other means outside the brain), they define two types of external representations, sentential and diagrammatic. "*Sentential* representations are sequential, like the propositions in a text" (Larkin and Simon 1987, 65). They can be formulated in words, mathematical expressions, or symbolic logic.[22] "*Diagrammatic* representations are indexed by location in a plane" (65) and include "information about relations with adjacent loci" (66).

For problem-solving, diagrammatic representations have several important advantages. First, they reduce the need to search for and compile information. All the information about a given element is attached to the same point in space, which effectively cross-indexes different kinds of information by location (e.g., a topographic map of Mt. Rainier shows at a glance that the summit is at 14,410 feet, inaccessible by road or even an established hiking trail, and covered by glaciers). Related elements and their accompanying information tend to be located nearby or are picked out easily by the visual system on the basis of similar size, color, orientation, and other elements. A diagrammatic representation also "preserves explicitly the information about the topological and geometric relations among the components of the problem, while the sentential representation does not" (Larkin and Simon 1987, 66).[23] Overall, "diagrams automatically support a large number of perceptual inferences, which are extremely easy for humans" (Larkin and Simon 1987, 98).[24]

Along with the diagram proper, the very process of its creation can be valuable. According to Pylyshyn, diagrams can not only facilitate reasoning, but also elicit information held subconsciously: "Diagrams drawn from memory can allow you to make explicit what you knew implicitly" (2003, 455); they enable you to "*see the relationships that are entailed by what you recalled,* however sparse the set of explicitly encoded (i.e., 'noticed') relationships might be" (458, emphasis added).[25]

Visual images are most effective as supports for reasoning when they have just enough detail, but not too much. Research shows that schematic diagrams, lacking extraneous detail, are best.[26] A series of diagrams is often more effective than photographs or a video to convey a sequence of simple actions because it removes extraneous detail and focuses on the task at hand, expressed as a series of cognitive steps and physical actions.[27] However, even if extraneous detail can be a distraction for reasoning (Pauwels 2006, 10; and 2015, 293), it can still have aesthetic or rhetorical value, and serve to advance an argument in those terms.[28] Indeed, in our field, as in general, images can persuade not only through their avowed content but also through more subtle forms of representation.

VISUALIZATION AND REPRESENTATION

Once we recognize that ideas can be formulated and developed in visual terms, and that images can themselves be intellectual contributions that facilitate reasoning and advance an argument, we are in a position to consider what sort of work each image (or part of an image) does. In this discussion, I will use *image* as a broad, neutral term for a visual display of information or ideas—a graphic.[29] An image does not necessarily entail any ontic, phenomenal, or interpretive commitment (although in the context of music analysis, at least a phenomenal commitment is usually implied). Within this broad category, I distinguish two basic functions of images, their composite parts, or various graphic attributes: visualization and representation. By extension, these terms can also be used to refer to the corresponding images or parts of images, or to the process by which these images are created—to object and activity, product and process.

Visualization denotes an intermodal translation whereby data, objects, or relationships—i.e., information—in a non-visual mode such as sound or words comes to be rendered in visual form. Alternatively, visualization can involve projection from a higher- to a lower-dimensional space (as when a digital camera captures an image of the 3D world in two dimensions).[30] When we visualize information, we exchange the properties, logic, affordances, and exigencies of one mode for another. Moving from words to images, for example, we go from sequential expression and a mode that is relatively sparse and discontinuous, even categorical, to simultaneous presentation in a medium that is more dense and continuous. In so doing, we aim to maximally preserve the information content of the original and to avoid or minimize introducing new content including—most notably for our purposes—a specific analytic interpretation of that content. Visualization focuses attention on the particular musical attributes, objects, and relations shown, but once the initial parameters are set and a means for iconic or symbolic translation established, the process itself is fairly systematic, even algorithmic. Thoughtful and consistent translation, perhaps outlined in accompanying text, can largely prevent misreadings, in which a reader ascribes iconic significance to what is only an artifact of the visualization process.

Although visualization is essentially an act of translation—and imperfect translation at that—its effective power and value for music analysis should not be underestimated. Music, whether sounding vibration or aural imagery, resides in the aural mode; it is inherently temporal and ephemeral. To visualize music is not only to translate and depict, but to fix, and in a sense to create, musical objects for contemplation: we visualize not music itself, in its totality, but music filtered through a certain musical ontology (for instance, pitches, duration ratios, articulations, character designations, or actions).[31]

Musical scores are, for the most part, visualizations. Their primary function is to record musical ideas in visual form and transmit them for subsequent performance. Recognizing the ontological and evocative import of musical notation, John Cage, George Crumb, Morton Feldman, Joji Yuasa, and other composers active from the 1950s through the 1970s deconstructed and reconstructed music notation in various ways to align the image of the score with the new sound worlds that they imagined (see, e.g., Cage 1969; Karkoschka 1972; Sauer 2009).[32]

The fact that intermodal translation, like literary or interlingual translation, is necessarily imperfect poses a constant challenge. But this imperfection can also be a virtue, which can be put to good use. As most music analysts will have observed, some musical patterns are easier to hear than to see on the page (e.g., in an orchestral score, cleffing, the various key signatures associated with transposing instruments, and the convention of grouping parts by instrumental family rather than register can frustrate pattern recognition). Other musical patterns may be easier to locate first in visualizations, or through the practice of making or using visualizations that serve as supports to focus aural attention accordingly.[33] In addition to its ontological significance in the abstract, visualization can have direct perceptual significance: it can become a point of access to the musical phenomena that we recognize as objects in analysis.

In contrast to visualization, a *visual representation* (or *representation,* as context permits) expresses an interpretation, whether explicit and claimed by the analyst as such, or implicit and tacit. Whereas the primary function of visualization is to show, that of representation is to tell. The distinction between the functions of visualization and representation might be drawn in two ways, by content and use. James Elkins (1999, 39–40) casts the relevant distinction in the terms of content and logical argument: Some images, or particular parts of an image, are non-propositional (they visualize); others are propositional (they serve to represent, in our terms, an analytic interpretation).[34] Bas van Fraassen focuses instead on use: "The use is what bestows the relevant role or function on the term used" (2008, 23).

Either way, the basic concept is supramodal; representations can be expressed in images, words, sounds, mathematical expressions, or even physical movements. Whereas the primary function of a visualization is intermodal translation—a re-presentation of information in the visual mode—representation adds a second layer. A representation does not only show, but makes a statement *about* what is shown: it *tells,* using graphic elements not only iconically (or symbolically) but propositionally, to convey not only informational content, but a particular analytic interpretation of that content.

Representation has been a hot topic in philosophy of science for over thirty years.[35] For Steven Woolgar, it is "the practice that lies at the very heart of science" (1988, 11).[36] But representation and its practices are not exclusive to science. Woolgar deems representation to be "axiomatic not just to science but to all practices which trade upon an objectivist epistemology, in short, to all activities which claim to capture some feature beyond the activity itself" (1988, 30). The extent to which work in music theory and analysis does, or should, "trade upon an objectivist epistemology" is a provocative question (and one outside our scope), but I think that we can agree that it assumes at least an intersubjective epistemology with regard to musical phenomena. On that basis, we proceed.

At the heart of the idea of representation, according to van Fraassen, is intentionality. A representation is "about" something; one represents something *as* something else. Visualization has two significant terms: non-visual information in the source mode and its intermodal translation into the visual mode. Representation has three: it adds an interpretation of the basic content as a significant component.[37] In van Fraassen's words, "There is no representation except in the sense that some things are *used, made, or taken, to represent* some things *as* thus or so" (2008, 23; emphasis added). "Our full locution must in the general case be *at least* of the form "X represents Y as F" (20). As van Fraassen points out, representation is asymmetric.[38] It also requires elucidation by context—here embedded in F—which can include reference to other events, similar cases, and a supporting theory, developed and recognized as functionally independent of the example at hand.[39]

In music theory and analysis, a representation indicates a particular way of hearing—a "hearing as," whereby a listener transforms a psychoacoustic event into a musical phenomenon, perceived through or in terms of its relations (or potential for relations) with other musical events or framing ideas.[40] Visualizations focus attention on the sonic attributes and events shown. Representations proffer specific ways to hear them; they situate and saturate individual events with musical relations and contexts that can involve events near or far in the composition, works by other composers, extramusical ideas, and functionally independent music theories.

Like visualization, representation is not only a product but a process—there is a practice of representation. To represent is not just to illustrate, but to inscribe, or even to create, phenomena and objects in light of specific ways of perceiving them. Philosopher of science Steven Woolgar calls this formative relationship between representation and object "reversing the arrow." "The idea of reversing the arrow," he says, "is to suggest that objects are constituted in virtue of representation" (Woolgar 1988, 56).[41] Construed in this strong sense, interpretation is not only *of*, but *that*—a specific perception that one attaches to, and through which one perceives the phenomenon.

Visualization and representation practices are as much a part of music theory and analysis as they are of science. Too often, however, the representational practices at work in music analysis are elided out of discussion, with images presented prima facie, as if they constituted evidence for an argument rather than propositions in an argument presented in visual form. As in science, the practices of visual representation in music analysis extend to the very creation and definition of phenomena—here, musical objects. The analyst, or listener, segments the sound flow, plucks out events of interest, and endows these with clear boundaries and an appearance of permanence that neither they nor music in fact have.[42] Using what may appear only to be notational practices, the analyst can create an ontological universe in which the analysis moves.

The distinction that I have drawn between visualization and visual representation is conceptual: it identifies two primary functions of visual images in music analysis. But the component parts of an image, or even various attributes of a single part, can function differently: while some parts, or attributes (e.g., size, color), visualize, others can represent. Unless accompanying text or some larger context (e.g., a standard, widely accepted practice for reading similar images) provides clarification, the primary function of individual parts or attributes can also be ambiguous. This plurality or ambiguity of function complicates the reading of images. It also frustrates attempts to identify kinds or classes of images, such as scores, transformation graphs, or the like, exclusively and consistently with visualization or with representation.[43] So although the conceptual distinction between visualization and representation and primary functions of images is fairly clear, when applied to individual images, it starts to look like more of a continuum.

Images are aggregates of graphic elements that can differ in function. Considered in the aggregate, some images work more like visualizations; others, more like representations. Some visualize and represent in roughly equal measure, as representations of musical ideas are coupled with, or overlaid upon, visualizations. As a general principle, we can say that reading a representation usually requires two layers of image analysis—one to determine whether the individual component images and graphic elements involved in visualization are iconic or non-iconic (symbolic or non-symbolic), and another to assess whether they are propositional or non-propositional with respect to an analytical interpretation.[44]

Visualizations have a long history in Western music theory. They are especially prevalent in speculative, and later mathematical, music theory concerned with the conceptualization of musical space. The Guidonian hand, a medieval solmization system and mnemonic device that mapped the pitches of the gamut onto points on the hand, was used to visualize the modal system and the progress of individual melodies using drawings and a kind of digital choreography performed on the hand. In 1728, Johann David Heinichen introduced his "musical circle," in Figure 24.1(a), an early visualization of diatonic key relationships later separated by David Kellner in 1737 into two nested circles of keys related by fifths, an outer circle of major keys and an inner circle of minor keys, with relative major–minor pairs aligned, as seen in Figure 24.1(b). Similar visualizations of diatonic key relationships appear in tonal theory textbooks today.

Nineteenth-century visualizations of musical space include the 2D matrices of fifths and thirds known as *Tonnetze*, associated most closely with the theorist Hugo Riemann. As Edward Gollin (2011) has shown, as Riemann's thinking about tones, intervals, and musical space changed, so did the visual presentation of his ideas.[45] Figure 24.2(a) shows an excerpt from the comprehensive *Tonbestimmungstabelle* that appeared in the fourth edition of the *Musik-Lexikon* (1894). Interval derivations and precise acoustic ratios (as string lengths) are shown at up to five decimal places for intervals from C to various tunings of C♯ and D♭, up to D in a 53-tone, equal-division tuning. As Riemann's thinking gradually moved away from acoustics and the mathematics of tuning and temperament and toward a psychology of tonal relationships, the communicative image changed from a table that tallies the precise locations of pitch points to a theoretically unbounded 2D space laced with intervallic pathways—the *Tonnetz* that appears in Riemann's "Ideen zu einer 'Lehre von den Tonvorstellungen'" (1914–1915), shown in Figure 24.2(b).

When Riemann's work was revived in the late twentieth century with the rise of neo-Riemannian theory, it was reinterpreted and presented in the context of twelve-tone equal temperament. Accordingly, the visualization changed again, from Riemann's

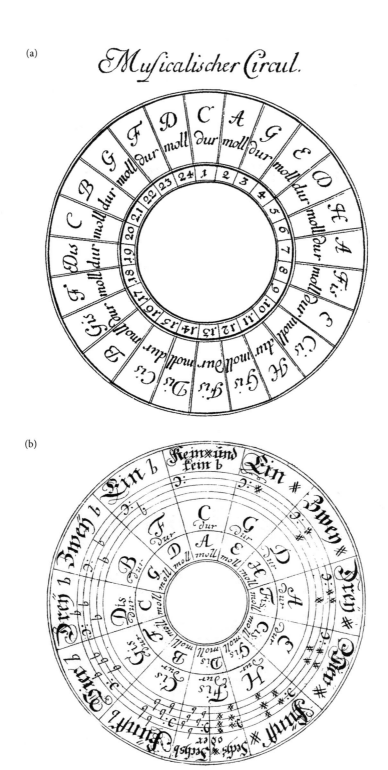

FIGURE 24.1 (a) Heinichen, Musical Circle from *Der Generalbass in der Composition* (1728).
(b) Kellner, Musical Circle from *Treulicher Unterricht im General-Baß* (1737).

SYNOPSIS
OF THE MOST IMPORTANT DETERMINATIONS OF TONE.

Tone.	Degree of Relationship.*	String Lengths.	In Decimals.	In Logarithms on basis 10.	In Logarithms on basis 2.	System of 53 degrees. In Logarithms on basis 2.	System of 12 degrees of equal temperament.	In Logarithms on basis $\sqrt[12]{2}$
					Relative Vibration Number.			
c	Prime	1/1	1,00000	0,00000	0,00000	0,00000	0,00000	0,00000
B♯	T 8 Q / 5 O	32768/32805	1,0012	0,00049	0,00162	Schisma		0,01953
d♭♭	3 O / 2 T 4 Q	2025/2048	1,0114	0,00490	0,01629			0,19552
c	4 Q / T 3 O	80/81	1,0125	0,00539	0,01792	Comma syntonum ..0,01886		0,21506
B♯	12 Q / 7 O	524288/531441	1,0136	0,00588	0,01954	Comma of Pythagoras		0,23460
d♭♭	O / 3 T	125/128	1,024	0,01030	0,03421	Diesis minor		0,41058
c	8 Q / 2 T 4 O	6400/6561	1,0252	0,01079	0,03584	..0,03773		0,43012
c♯	3 T 2 O / 5 Q	243/250	1,0288	0,01233	0,04097	..0,05660		0,49166
c♯	2 T / Q	24/25	1,04165	0,01772	0,05889	Minor Chroma		0,70672
d♭	3 O / 5 Q	243/256	1,05351	0,02263	0,07519	..0,07547		0,90224
c♯	T 3 Q / 2 O	128/135	1,05470	0,02312	0,07681	Major Chroma	0,083333	0,92178 ..1,00000
* c♯ (d♭)	17th Overtone	16/17	1,0625	0,02632	0,08746			1,04912
d♭	O / T Q	15/16	1,06666	0,02802	0,09311	Leading Tone Step ..0,09433		1,11732
c♯	7 Q / 4 O	2048/2187	1,06785	0,02851	0,09473			1,13685
e♭♭	4 O / 5 Q 3 T	30375/32768	1,0788	0,03293	0,10940			1,31288
d♭	3 Q / 2 T O	25/27	1,08	0,03342	0,11103	..0,11320		1,33237

(b)

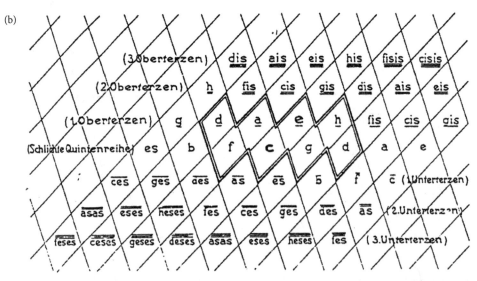

FIGURE 24.2 (a) Riemann, Tonbestimmungstabelle from *Musik-Lexikon*, 4th edition. (b) Riemann, *Tonnetz* from "Ideen zu einer 'Lehre von den Tonvorstellungen'" (1914–15) (from Hyer 1995, 102).

theoretically infinite plane to the surface of a (bounded) three-dimensional torus, which suggests greater freedom of movement and continuous pathways throughout the space (Gollin 2011, 288).

In contrast to both the Riemannian and neo-Riemannian *Tonnetze*, which depict intervals as relations between individual pcs, Robert Morris's "Riemann Wreath" renders the intervals explicitly (Figure 24.3). The wreath takes the form of a literal two-partition graph that interweaves four strands of pc sets: three for the ics 3, 4, and 5 associated with the intervallic content of major and minor triads (these correspond to the edges of triangles that one can flip on the *Tonnetz* to model the L, R, and P relations, respectively), together with a fourth comprised of the twelve individual pcs.[46] Dyadic nodes are

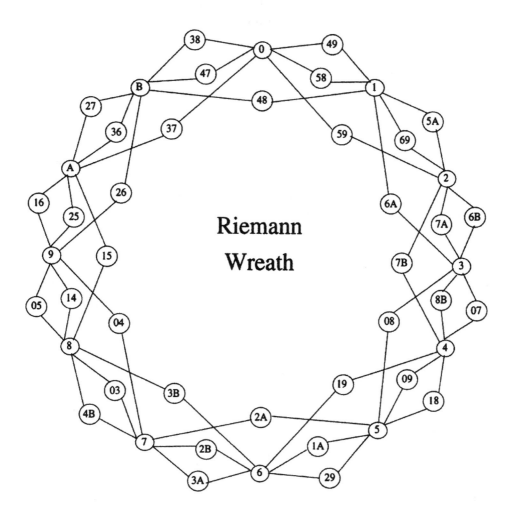

The content of any two connected nodes is a member of set-class 3-11[037].

FIGURE 24.3 Morris, Riemann Wreath from "Voice-Leading Spaces" (1998).

connected by edges to single-pc nodes, which serve as links to forge chains of major and minor triads linked by common tones. While the graph appears to contain edge crossings (which may seem to suggest that it is a projection from a higher-dimensional space), it is in fact planar (i.e., it can be drawn in two dimensions without edge crossings).[47]

The Wreath presents the same basic information as the neo-Riemannian *Tonnetz,* but it shifts the focus from individual pcs and triads to the composition of pitch-class sets and the pathways that they define. This change reflects the Wreath's affiliation with numerous other compositional spaces that Morris has devised or visualized, and his orientation as a composer with an active practical interest in partitioning and navigating diverse musical spaces. Despite the change in perspective, however, the Wreath remains a visualization, not a representation. Comprehensive and systematic, it re-presents the pitch-class and voice-leading relations associated with the neo-Riemannian *Tonnetz* without further comment.[48]

In recent years, theorists have enlisted or developed their own algorithms and software to visualize and explore the geometries of three-, four-, and higher-dimensional musical spaces populated by chords, voice-leadings, and scales. Clifton Callender, Ian Quinn, and Dmitri Tymoczko (2008) present numerous visualizations of various musical geometries, including contrasting views of the space given by four-note chord types (in planar projection).[49] As Julian Hook (2006), Dmitri Tymoczko (2011), and others have shown, still or animated visualizations of complex musical spaces can be valuable tools for music analysis. By tracing the path that a piece or passage takes through a harmonic or voice-leading space, the analyst can identify areas of relative continuity, as well as discontinuities such as sharp turns, reversals, or leaps; these may elicit musical perceptions that were previously unattended to.

The fact that the analyst can use such images to develop an interpretation does not, however, mean that the image itself presents one. Only when the music, due to symmetries or skeins of transformations between a pair of nodes, requires the analyst to choose which transformations to show as part of the path does the visualization venture into the realm of representation. Still, such visualizations can influence how analysts and readers think about and hear music. When we visualize music as inhabiting or moving through a larger musical space, we affirm not only the path taken, but the surrounding space and the many paths *not* taken; the music seems to unfold in relation to a backdrop of possibilities it does not pursue.

Paradoxically, harmonies or voice-leadings that do not have correlates in the music under discussion may appear more real and relevant, simply because they are shown, than events that actually do occur but involve other parameters (e.g., timbre) that are not shown or discussed. Even inert parts of images can command visual attention and influence music perceptions. Once again, accompanying text can clarify and provide appropriate balance.

Even basic visualizations can stimulate new musical perceptions and analytical observations. In an analysis of the opening of Cage's *Etudes Australes* VI, I experimented with a simple visual enhancement of the score: adding swatches of color that render pitch-class chroma literally (Hanninen 2014, 2.20, Slide 14; see also Figure 24.4). The

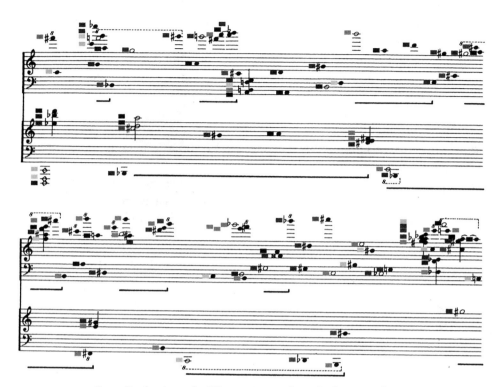

FIGURE 24.4 Cage, *Etudes Australes* VI, opening, with pitch chroma enhancement. (A color version of this figure is included in the color insert.)

Image from Hanninen 2014, 2.20, Slide 14.

use of color is iconic (or symbolic), but it is not propositional. Taking advantage of the rapid, effortless processing of color in early vision, this visualization focuses attention on a specific psychoacoustic attribute—pitch-class equivalence—that is notated in the published score (but harder to glean and compile from it at a glance), but it does not add any information content.

Listeners (including analysts) can use this image in at least four ways: to track pitch-class repetitions among registers, to track motions around the pitch-class spectrum within a register, to monitor changes in the distribution of the twelve pitch classes per unit time (the score is in proportional notation), and even to track some harmonic changes, such as where chromatic set classes dominate (i.e., the associated color swatches are concentrated in a small part of the spectrum) and where they give way to mostly diatonic sets or more varied harmonic content. One could also redraw the image, extracting only its pitch-class content over time and dispensing with music notation altogether: the twelve-color pitch-class spectrum could be laid out vertically at the start of each system, with intermittent swatches running horizontally to indicate the presence or absence of each pitch-class per unit time and gradations of saturation or brightness to indicate pitch-class duplications across registers. Such visualizations are valuable primarily as working documents that motivate listeners and analysts to focus their attention in a particular way and to investigate the musical implications and consequences of doing so.

Unlike scores, which visualize psychoacoustic phenomena such as pitch, calibrated durations, and loudness, spectrograms visualize the acoustic information associated with particular musical performances. Within music studies, they are most often found in analyses of timbre in contemporary music and of microtiming or intonation in performance.[50] Because they rely on technology and algorithmic computation to translate acoustic information into visual images, spectrographs may seem to endow music analysis with an air of scientific objectivity. While one might well question whether objectivity should be a goal of music analysis, I want to look at another way in which this sort of appeal is, quite simply, wrong: visualization practices in the sciences are far more nuanced and interactive, less strictly "objective," than one might think.[51]

In science and technology studies, a substantial literature has developed around how scientific visualizations are created and used in research.[52] There is no clean, bright line between the scientist and the phenomenon visualized, or between the observer and what is observed. The purpose and audience for which a particular image is created affect what is shown and how, which in turn affect what is available for observation and what scientists, based on observation, then may postulate to exist. Choices made in the process of visualization, which at least appear to reside in the realm of epistemology, can translate into statements about *ontology*—about *what is*, the objects and phenomena that constitute our world. In an ethnographic study of the visualization practices of scientists on the Mars Rover team, sociologist of science Janet Vertesi (2015) puts this point in the strongest terms.[53] Framing scientific visualization as a kind of "drawing as," which recalls Ludwig Wittgenstein's "seeing as," she writes: "*drawing as* makes epistemology look like ontology. It conflates our interpretative work in the world with the objects we encounter there and draws them accordingly" (Vertesi 2015, 103).[54]

Recognizing the fluidity between epistemology and ontology in scientific visualization transforms what was at first a problematic appeal to the sciences into a productive one. This sort of interplay between imaging practices and purported phenomena or objects is common in music analysis, even when a reliance on technology, algorithmic computation, and automation may seem to suggest that the visualizations constitute objective evidence of musical phenomena. Spectrograms, as well as their use in music analysis, are a case in point.

To create the spectrograms for his 1984 book *New Images of Musical Sound,* Robert Cogan used a fast-Fourier transform instrument, a scan control unit, and two tube displays (Yuatt 2012, 8–9). The process was labor intensive, requiring multiple steps, interventions, and choices to produce each image, as well as some framing choices, such as the recordings selected and the temporal scale represented.[55] By running more recent software such as Sonic Visualiser under default settings, the process of creating spectrograms from audio files can now be largely automated. But relegating the process of visualization to the software and its default settings may be more convenient than illuminating. Default settings, most likely conceived by the software developer as the best compromise among a wide range of applications, are unlikely to serve the analyst's

reasons for creating a particular image, as well as some experimentation with the resolution or display mode for frequency (for instance, bandwidth in octaves, linear or
logarithmic scale), time (sample length, temporal resolution, beat-tracker), or amplitude (color, brightness). A change of settings can reveal, amplify, mute, or mask particular features of the acoustic data and their perceptual correlates and call attention to
those properties of the sound and musical perceptions in which the analyst is most interested.[56] The analyst who takes advantage of the software's capabilities engages in her
own practice of "drawing as." What looks like an instrument of epistemology morphs
into a way to design an ontology, and even to create or recommend phenomena to perceive or consider. [57]

As analysts who seek to investigate and convey the delicate perceptions that constitute musical experience, we must acknowledge and recognize that the relationship
between epistemology and ontology in music analysis can be uncomfortably intimate,
and that the visualizations that we create have both creative and destructive potential.
Music is transient. Musical experience is fleeting, and our musical perceptions fragile,
subject to reconstruction and overwriting by the apparent veracity of visual images.
Because spectrograms are often used to investigate, document, or "reveal" subtle, non-
categorical musical phenomena, such as details in timbre, timing, or intonation for
which we lack the language that might otherwise have helped to stabilize and support
fragile perceptions against visualizations that seem to provide conflicting "evidence,"
they must be used and read with special care. In spectrograms, some clear musical
perceptions recede into the background. Others have no visual correlates at all—for instance, the enharmonic reinterpretation of a diminished seventh chord set in two different tonal contexts.

Although spectrograms can be used to focus attention on details that we hear, or can
learn to hear, they cannot, in and of themselves, provide evidence that conclusively
confirms or disconfirms a musical perception or interpretation that we wish to advance.[58] In our eagerness to visualize what we hear, we must remain vigilant and true to
our perceptions, lest we come to hear only what we can see. The purpose of visualization
is intermodal translation, not substitution; the visualizations that we create should support and enrich our musical experience, not replace it.

With software for high-quality computer graphics now readily available, computer-
assisted visualizations are becoming increasingly common in music theory and analysis. As new theoretical approaches and lines of inquiry develop in this environment,
the visual mode is becoming more prominent in our discourse and the images more
diverse, requiring careful attention to what, exactly, each one might show or represent.
The various affordances of the visual mode (for instance, rapid and simultaneous processing of multiple graphic features, the logic of spatial placement, continuity and richness) are especially well suited to corpus studies, which require an efficient, rich means
to work with, and present results deduced from, large data sets.

In a recent study of style change, Christopher White (2014, 247) presents a visualization of broad stylistic similarities and dissimilarities among nineteen composers
from Byrd to Debussy, based on the results of a clustering algorithm that groups them

according to the frequency of various trigrams (sequences of three simultaneities) within a corpus of selected works (2014, 247), reproduced in Figure 24.5(a). The image might be seen as a 2D projection of a 3D mobile, in which all horizontal arms swing freely in the transverse plane. At the highest level of structure, the mobile shows three groupings: (a) eighteenth-century Baroque (shown in alphabetical order—Bach, Handel, Telemann, and Vivaldi); (b) late eighteenth- and nineteenth-century Classical and Romantic (in two groups—the first Germanic, from Beethoven to Wagner, and the second, continental non-Germanic, comprised of Chopin, Tchaikovsky, Saint-Saëns, and Liszt); and (c) three outliers (Byrd, Debussy, and Scarlatti). The vertical scale ("Height") indicates that similarity is calibrated (for instance, Telemann and Vivaldi are more like Handel than they are like Bach). But the order of composers from left to right, the even spacing between them, and the length of the swing arms in the horizontal dimension are all non-iconic artifacts of conventions used in the visualization.[59]

As White explains in accompanying text, Byrd, Debussy, and Scarlatti cluster together by default: they have little in common other than the fact that each has little in common with the other composers in the study. But the visual impression that they form a significant group remains: clustered together in the upper-right corner, they seem suspended, separated by a channel of white space from the main action on the continent that proceeds along the bottom margin. Although the visualization represents the data accurately, it must be read in conjunction with White's description, which elaborates upon and unplugs some of its apparent implications.

One of the intriguing things about visualizations in corpus studies is that the results that we can see at a glance (and investigate later in depth) are deduced bottom-up, rather

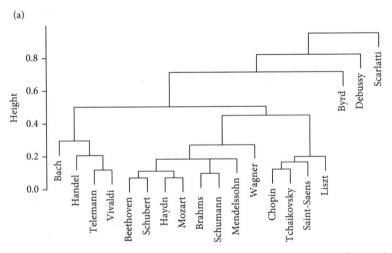

(a)

FIGURE 24.5(a) White, cluster analysis of composers' trigram frequencies (from White 2014, 247, Fig. 2).

than top-down. Ian Quinn and Christopher White's (2018) "persimmon" is a transition graph that shows thirteen harmonic functions distilled from a corpus of rock music by an algorithm that uses the relative frequencies of event successions to define a specified number of harmonic functions (Figure 24.5(b), center).

Although I will concentrate on global aspects of the persimmon rather than its details and the many individual statements that these suggest, some explanation of the symbols is in order:

- Uppercase T, D, and P denote "tonic," "dominant," and "predominant," not as specific triads but as baskets of simultaneities (identified in the corresponding pie graphs) of analogous function.
- Superscript x indicates an auxiliary ("secondary" or "applied") function (e.g., D^x includes V/V); + indicates an added tone (e.g., D$^+$ includes V^7).
- Spatial placement indicates progression strength: the two "strong cadential progressions" T–D and T–P–D lie on the persimmon's perimeter; "precedential progressions" (e.g., T–T$^+$–p–d) are near the center.

(b)

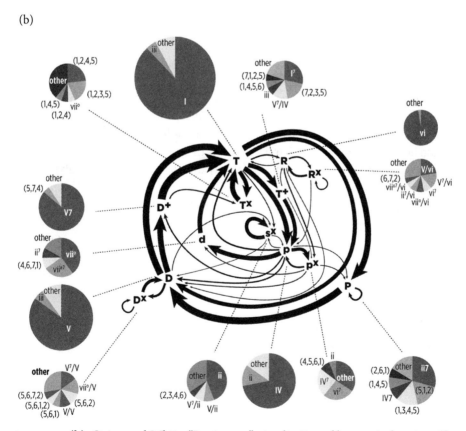

FIGURE 24.5(b) Quinn and White, "Persimmon" visualization of harmonic functions (from Quinn and White 2018).

- Line weight denotes the relative frequency of each transition: the thicker the line, the more common the progression.

Once this visual language was established, much of the symbolic content was determined by output from the algorithm—for instance, which pairs of nodes are connected by an edge, which lines are thicker or thinner. But judgment calls were also necessary—for instance, the number of gradations in line weight and their relative thicknesses, and the precise spatial placement of symbols within the image. For example, lowercase *p* and *d* appear about halfway from the perimeter to the center, likely for ease of reading, as the distance along the radius is not calibrated; and this is similarly the case for the placement of R and Rˣ at the upper right. The persimmon might also be read as iconic in another way. The energetic curves, stark contrast between thick, muscular lines and tangled filigree (the latter being an artifact of visualization in two dimensions that could be untangled in three), and asymmetrical placement of symbols on the page give the impression of a swirl of activity—a reading that, although more poetic, conforms with the idea of harmonic motion.

Visualizations like White's mobile and Quinn and White's persimmon are not only informative, but stimulating, and not only for the recipient who reads them thoughtfully and deeply, translating their visual implications back into statements to test against his or her own experience, but for the theorist and analyst who creates and uses them. Automating the process of data collection, computation, and compilation provides a limited claim to objectivity. But important decisions remain, including the corpus selected, other input data, and algorithm design. Far more valuable than this limited claim to objectivity, however, is what the automation allows the analyst to do. Using automation, the analyst can study large data sets, run multiple experiments, and quickly ascertain how changing different variables affects the results.

These results (in the plural, which is relatively uncommon in music analysis) can be seen as a set of windows into how "objectivity" looks (or sounds) from different vantage points, and against which the analyst's own interpretations, interventions, and creative impulses—including the creation of new theory—play. An intriguing tangential question is what actually is visualized in such a corpus study. For example, does Quinn and White's persimmon visualize a body of data, the authors' analysis of the data, or a developing theory of rock harmony? Can clear lines be drawn between these elements in corpus studies, where new theory is emerging from comprehensive, algorithmic, and experimental music analysis?

Visualization involves thought and choice on the part of the creator, but its primary function is intermodal translation. Images that are largely, or even exclusively, visualizations can be used to support work in music analysis, but they do not, in and of themselves, convey musical interpretations. Images that function primarily as representations do. Representations do not only show—they also tell.

With their emphasis on formal relations among abstract musical objects, transformation networks may look a lot like small patches taken from a musical or compositional space, such as the *Tonnetz* shown in Figure 24.2(b) or the "Riemann Wreath" in Figure

24.3. Indeed, if the nodes are occupied by pc sets from a single set class that has no in-variance, connected by arrows labeled with transformations from the standard group of forty-eight serial operators ($R \pm Tn \pm I$), the connecting transformations are determined once the nodes are filled and arrows drawn. In this respect, there is no room for the analyst to develop and convey an interpretation.

Of course, the pc sets included in a transformational network need not all come from the same set class, nor need the transformations be limited to functions. The nodes included, or excluded, are also up to the analyst.[60] But even under the strictest constraints, there is a critical difference between musical or compositional spaces, which are inherently abstract, and transformation networks, which are relatively concrete and specific to a given musical situation. Transformation networks not only visualize formal relations, but also have the potential to represent musical interpretations through the use of space, individual graphic elements, and aesthetic or rhetorical aspects of graphic design.

A transformation network can present the viewer with much more than its explicit formal content, which we might define as the topology of the underlying graph (which nodes are connected by edges) plus the specific content of the nodes and labels for edges. That explicit formal content is coupled with a specific visual representation—a particular arrangement of nodes and edges on the page. One graph (or network) can have many formally or isomorphically equivalent representations. Tree structures, for example, can be shown with diagonal branches or straight parallel and perpendicular lines (as in a cladogram); with the root at the top, bottom, right, or left; radially, with uniform symmetry or in a fisheye view; or as a tree map, a large rectangle partitioned into smaller, successively nested rectangles (Johnson and Shneiderman 1991). In any graph (or network), distances can be altered, lines curved, and nodes rearranged from left to right, all without affecting the explicit formal content. But the use of space, an element of graphic design (along with font, line weight, and shape), can influence what one sees in, or reads into, an image. Although layout is not part of a graph's explicit formal content, it can be iconic or propositional: space and the arrangement of explicit formal content in space are important resources that analysts can use to represent and convey musical interpretations.

In a substantive and highly suggestive discussion of precedence and layout in node/arrow systems, David Lewin (1987, 209–216) shows how network layout can highlight conflicts between network-formal and music-chronological precedence and how it can be used to represent specific musical perceptions and interpretations. Figure 24.6 reproduces Figure 9.14 from his *Generalized Musical Intervals and Transformations (GMIT)*. Part (a) shows what Lewin, after Jeanne Bamberger (1986), calls a "figural" layout, in which the placement of nodes from left to right on the page represents score chronology. Part (b) is topologically identical to part (a), except for the addition of a [START] node that designates the Db node at the top as the network's entrance point. But instead of emphasizing the chord-to-chord chronology of the passage (which can still be read from top to bottom if one collapses the white space from left to right), the rearranged layout places the two Gb chords that Lewin refers to as "carriage returns" at the left margin, drawing attention to *"precisely those moments in the listening chronology*

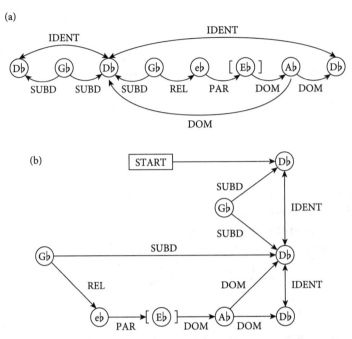

FIGURE 24.6 Lewin, figural and formal layout of Beethoven, Piano Sonata No. 23 in F Minor, II, opening, from *Generalized Musical Intervals and Transformations* (1987), Figs. 9.14a and b.

at which that chronology violates precedence ordering" (Lewin 1987, 215). In this way, Lewin inscribes a subtle quality of his musical perception—a specific way of hearing the two Gb chords—into the network's image as an overt feature of its graphic representation. In so doing, he objectifies and amplifies the perception through visual reinforcement of his verbal description.

Many of Lewin's formal innovations were quickly recognized as important, even inspiring the new subfield of transformational music theory, but the import of this particular passage in *GMIT* seemed to attract little attention until relatively recently. In *Tonality and Transformation*, Steven Rings (2011, 140–144) takes up the issue of the graphic representation of transformational networks in a succinct and thoughtful discussion of "figural" and "formal," or "event" and "spatial," networks.[61] Figure 24.7 reproduces Rings's Figure 3.24, parts (a) and (b), which represent the network topology of the subject from Bach's E-major fugue from the *Well-Tempered Clavier*, Book II, first as an event network (a), and then as a spatial network (b).

While the explicit formal content of the two images is identical and both representations use layout in a logical way, the visual impressions and musical intelligibility of the two images are very different. In the event network (a), the use of space is iconic: time proceeds from left to right and pitch height from low to high, as in a musical score. The image clearly represents the pitch contour and the embedded pitch symmetry as significant musical features of the subject. These elements are all but lost in

(a)   (b)

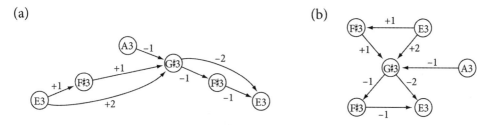

FIGURE 24.7 Rings, event and spatial networks for subject from J. S. Bach WTC II, E major fugue, from *Tonality and Transformation* (2011), Figs. 3.24a and b.

(b), a spatial network in which the use of space is non-iconic (and non-propositional).[62] Here space represents intervallic symmetry rather than temporal progress or pitch contour. The image is compact and symmetric, but it has little to do with visually or aurally salient features of the score. Indeed, one might ask—as Rings does—in what sense the spatial network in (b) actually represents the fugue subject: that is, what musical perceptions is it supposed to convey or suggest? Looking at (b), we may know what to think, but it's hard to figure out what we are supposed to hear.

With association graphs, details of graphic representation are a central consideration. An association graph is a visual representation of an associative set in which segments occupy nodes and edges of varying line weights indicate associative adjacency or degrees of associative proximity between pairs of segments (Hanninen 2012, 119, 485).[63] Significantly, temporal adjacency (or proximity) and associative adjacency (proximity) need not coincide; they can even operate at a considerable remove from one another.[64] An association graph shows an analyst's interpretation of associative adjacencies (the structure of the underlying graph), filtered through the lens of a graphic design that represents a particular hearing. Using space, analysts can convey conceptual proximity or grouping, parallelisms at various levels, and other idiosyncratic aspects of musical form.

Figure 24.8 shows an association digraph of sixteen segments from an associative set *A*, taken from the first half (mm. 1–16) of Dallapiccola's "Simbolo," from the *Quaderno musicale di Annalibera*. The segments are fully notated and named for the set (*A*) and measure numbers in which they occur. Edges connect pairs of segments that, in the analyst's view, associate with one another by criteria that are stronger than those used to define set *A* as a whole; arrows highlight associations that are also direct temporal successions.[65] (Segment names also encode score chronology, but in a less obvious way.)

Figures 24.9(a) and 24.9(b) show two representations of an association digraph for the second half of the piece (mm. 17–36). This time, segments are identified only by name rather than notated. The layout of the first graph, in Figure 24.9(a), brings out a parallelism between the associative organization of two pairs of segments (*A*17–20, *A*21–24, and *A*29–32, *A*33–36, represented by parallel pairs of edges in the box at the lower left) and a temporally embedded quartet of segments (*A*25, *A*26 and *A*27, *A*28, represented by an isographic box with different line weights at the upper right). The second graph, shown in Figure 24.9(b), preserves the configuration of nodes and edges in Figure 24.9(a), as well as their corresponding line weights, but it rearranges nodes on

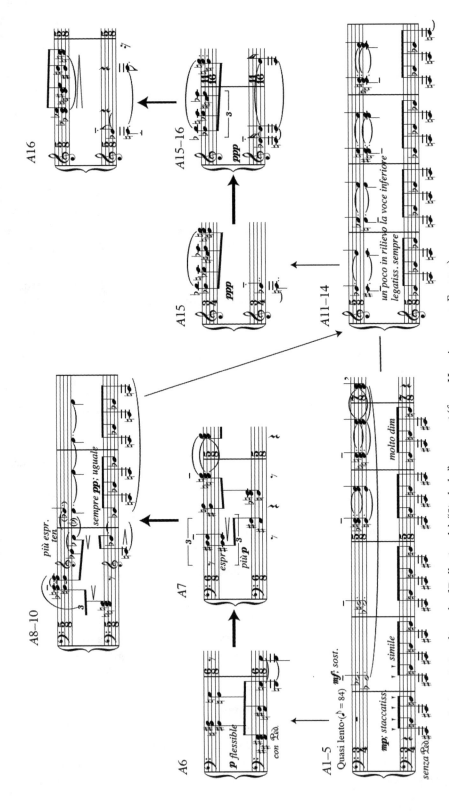

FIGURE 24.8 Association digraph of Dallapiccola's "Simbolo," mm. 1–16 (from Hanninen 2012, Ex. 10.2).

the page so that left–right and bottom–top placements bring out the associative path that conforms with score chronology, from A17–20 through A21–24, A25, and A26–A27. The digraph in Figure 24.9(b) brings out a different resonance than that in 24.9(a)—with Lewin's transformational network of the same passage (1993, 13, Fig. 1.5), and between the first and second half of the piece, as modeled and discussed by Lewin in detail.[66] The question is not which representation, Figure 24.9(a) or 24.9(b), is correct, but what each one proposes we attend to and how we might hear it. The two digraphs present two different interpretations of musical form.

The question of whether (or the extent to which) spatial placement and white space are iconic or propositional in a particular representation is not always clear. Certainly, spatial arrangement is often influenced by exigencies of the publication medium, such as the dimensions of the printed page or screen. But questions can arise in other contexts where the use of space may appear to be iconic, or even propositional with respect to a particular way of hearing.

Consider, for example, Richard Cohn's (1996, 17) arrangement of the four hexatonic systems as the vertices of a parallelogram. Each system is identified with a compass point, from "northern," at the top, moving clockwise through "eastern, southern, and western" at the right, bottom, and left. Placing the "northern system," which includes pc o, at the top conforms with a graphic convention of the mod-12 pc "clock," but it is

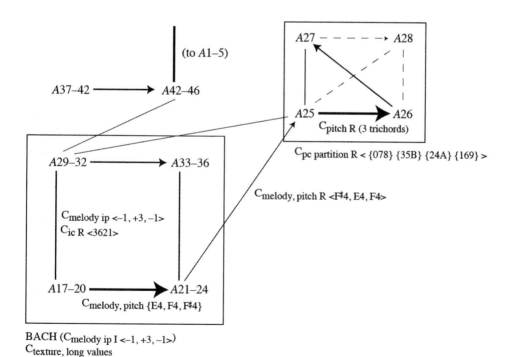

FIGURE 24.9(a) Representation 1 of association digraph of Dallapiccola's "Simbolo," mm. 17–36 (from Hanninen 2012, Ex. 10.3b).

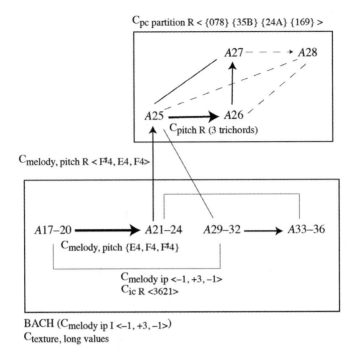

FIGURE 24.9(b) Representation 2 of association digraph of Dallapiccola's "Simbolo," mm. 17–36 (from Hanninen 2012, Fig. 10.4).

otherwise insignificant: in practice, the hexatonic systems operate in a movable-do system, which reflects the primary transposition level (if any) in a particular musical passage. So even though text references to "northern, eastern, southern, [and] western" reinforce the spatial designations, the spatial arrangement is non-iconic and non-propositional with regard to the underlying structure, and it may even contradict its application to the specific transposition levels within a particular musical piece or passage.[67] What the graphic and accompanying references to compass points in the text present is a nomenclature, not an iconic visualization of basic content—and much less a proposition for how we should, in all cases, orient ourselves in this musical space.

Along with the use of space, the aesthetics and rhetoric of visual representations in music analysis warrant consideration. Explicit formal content is one thing; aesthetic and rhetorical features, another. But these are integrated in visual representations, where ideas take form and form has communicative force. As visual researcher Darren Newbury puts it, "the aesthetic cannot be neatly divided from the intellectual . . . There is meaning in form, and in the form of presentation. Images are not ideas in disguise, but are themselves intellectual propositions" (2011, 652).

Those intellectual propositions can include implicit claims to objectivity and credibility, expressed graphically as a neutral professionalism as opposed to conspicuous artistry, through page composition and image design (uncluttered and balanced); typeface (serif, sans-serif, script, display), font (standard, bold, italic), size, and spacing; the relative sizes of type and music notation; and line weights (neither too heavy nor too light, with gradations easily distinguished). Writing about the use of images in the sciences, Pauwels (2006, xv) cautions that readers should not mistake production quality for basic content: "A professional-looking execution by a skilled craftsman gives the visual representation greater credibility and appeal, irrespective of whether it is scientifically sound."[68]

Even such seemingly innocuous things as straight lines and arrangements of objects in parallel and perpendicular grids, inherited from the limitations of print technology, can function not only aesthetically, but rhetorically. As the most direct route between two points, a straight line can be read as a default visualization for a connection between two points that suggests no more than the explicit formal content connoted by an edge in a graph.

But why draw the line at all? Including the line in the graph may represent analytical interpretation. As a grapheme, it may suggest only a formal relationship, unmediated by analytical individual interpretation. But it may have another, subtle psychological purpose: to suggest an unadorned, uninterpreted view. Layout in parallel and perpendicular grids can be used similarly, to create an impression of objectivity. In contrast, indirect routes—whether zigzags, broad curves, or wiggly lines—and idiosyncratic layouts, through their geometric inefficiency, immediately suggest a contribution by the individual analyst, whether a propositional representation of a musical interpretation, non-propositional artistic license, or something else (Tversky, Zacks, Lee, and Heiser 2000, 222).

Aesthetics and visual rhetoric are a quiet but persistent force in music analysis, as various communities have developed and perpetuated different representational traditions over time. One of the contributions of David Lewin's *GMIT* was its codification of the visual representations of two graphic tools—the transformation graph and transformation network. Transformation graphs and networks did not originate with *GMIT*. With his background in mathematics (of which graph theory is a part), graphs were a natural resource for Lewin—one that he had used to represent explicit formal content at least since the early 1980s (see, for instance, Lewin 1982a and 1982b). But the standardization of a visual style that occurred as a by-product of monograph publication (as opposed to the differences in house styles of different journals) likely helped to promote these images as tools in the field's evolving and increasingly visual discourse.

During the 1990s, transformation graphs and networks became the image of a whole new way of thinking about voice-leading and music analysis—one that presented compact networks of one-dimensional (1D) pitch-class relations as relatively neutral readings of messier, multidimensional musical surfaces.[69] Over time, the graphs and networks themselves came to serve not only an expository purpose—presenting content—but also a rhetorical one, an attempt to persuade, as if the very presence of these images conferred a kind of authority upon, or constituted evidence for, the analyst's viewpoint.

Informed by Schenker's own background in music performance and composition (disciplines in which interpretation and artistry are traditional values) and a tradition of private tutelage, Schenkerian analysis has developed a different aesthetic.[70] Deriving its graphic language from standard Western music notation, Schenkerian analysis repurposes certain symbols to express analytical interpretations of musical structure. Instead of indicating duration, open and closed noteheads represent structural weight; instead of articulation, slurs represent prolongation and contingency. Schenkerian sketches are full of slurs and other curves that lend grace and flow to the image.[71] Indeed, within the Schenkerian community, it is not uncommon to hear a sketch described as "beautiful," referring not only to the graph's explicit formal content, but also the calligraphy and artistry of its visual representation.

With the rise of personal computers in the 1980s and the move to computer graphics in the 1990s and since 2000, authors no longer rely on publishers for the graphic "performance" of their ideas. As more and more publishers require authors to submit camera-ready images, the aesthetics and rhetoric of visual representation increasingly revert to individual authors (subject, of course, to editorial oversight). It will be interesting to see to what extent authors choose to maintain disciplinary traditions or take strategic advantage of this new environment and the potential for more individuality and idiosyncrasy in the visual presentation of their ideas.

As noted earlier, the images found in music analysis need not function as visualizations or representations in entirety. One part—or even one aspect—of an image can visualize (be iconic but non-propositional), while another can represent (be iconic and propositional). A Schenkerian voice-leading sketch is a good example of an image in which some aspects function non-propositionally, to visualize, while others function propositionally, to represent. Vertical placement on the staff usually visualizes the pitch height of an abstract tone; horizontal placement indicates temporal succession.[72] But the duration symbol associated with the very same note generally serves to represent: it expresses an interpretation of structural weight.[73]

Slurs and beams in the sketch also represent, expressing an analytical interpretation of contingency and connection among tones. Roman numerals, which music theory students too often use solely to visualize triadic roots, here represent the analyst's interpretation of bass *Stufen*. Although some aspects of the sketch visualize and others represent, overall the sketch functions primarily as a representation: pitch and temporal succession are visualized *in order to be able to represent* an interpretation of relative structural weight among events.

Lerdahl and Jackendoff's (1983) time-span reductions and prolongational reductions bear a superficial resemblance to Schenkerian sketches, in that they too display hierarchies of pitch events. In fact, however, if we take Lerdahl and Jackendoff at their word, prolongational reductions are visualizations: they are supposed to model a listener's "intuitions" about a passage, which can be ascertained by following the various well-formedness and preference rules that comprise the authors' theory of tonal cognition through their complex and sometimes contradictory interactions to a normalized result (what "the listener" hears.)[74]

It's important to note that the distinction between reductions that function primarily as visualizations and those that serve to represent can be clarified or further clouded by accompanying text. Casting representation in the rhetoric of visualization, a Schenkerian analyst may claim to show *the* underlying structure. Conversely, while Lerdahl and Jackendoff describe their prolongational reductions in terms indicating that they are to be construed as visualizations, in fact the need for analytical intervention in determining the relative weights of conflicting preference rules means that the images also function, at least in part, as representations.

Evolutions of association graphs are another kind of image in which some aspects visualize while others represent (Hanninen 2012, 151–157). An evolution is an ordered set of association subgraphs that shows the order in which nodes (which correspond to individual musical segments) enter the graph.[75] Usually, but not necessarily, this reflects the temporal order in which segments appear in the composition. The evolution can be presented as a series of still images—what Edward Tufte (1990) calls "small multiples"— or as an animation.

Figure 24.10 shows an evolution of eight segments from an associative set *J* in mm. 1–7 of Schoenberg's *Klavierstück* op. 23, no. 3. Whether still or animated, the evolution demonstrates a division of function by layers. The underlying association graph is a representation: the analyst decides what segments to include in the graph, how closely these are related to one another, and how segments are arranged on the page. The evolution proper, however, is a visualization, showing the temporal order in which segments appear in the composition.

Whether an image, or a certain part or aspect of an image, functions primarily as a visualization or a representation can be ambiguous. The potential for confusion associated with individual glyphs such as lines or arrows, layout, and other aspects of graphic design is a persistent problem in music analysis.[76] We've already seen how something so ostensibly neutral as a straight line can subtly serve another purpose. Whether a particular line does or not can be an open question. Arrows take the potential for ambiguity to another level. At the most basic level, an arrow shows "a relationship, a link" and "direction of the asymmetry" (Tversky 2012, 230). But arrows can function in many ways, including to "label or focus attention; to convey sequence; to indicate temporal or causal relations; to show motion or forces; and more" (Tversky 2011, 521).[77] In music theory and analysis, we might fine-tune some of these a bit and add others in order to speak of implication, causality, precedence, and becoming. Without elucidation by accompanying text or a larger context, exactly what a particular arrow is supposed to mean can be unclear.[78]

Or consider the depiction of musical space in a swatch from a *Tonnetz* or another voice-leading space that an analyst might offer as a model of musical relations in a passage. Does the uniform distribution of nodes in space, and the resulting pattern of edges and the angles between them, signify, or is it insignificant and incidental, an artifact of modal exigency? Of course, strictly speaking, the lines and edges in the graph denote only an underlying configuration of objects and pairwise relations between them. The arrangement of nodes and edges in space, whether edges are straight or curved, and whether the overall musical space appears uniform or warped, is not part of that configuration. But it does make a visual impression. Absolute regularity in

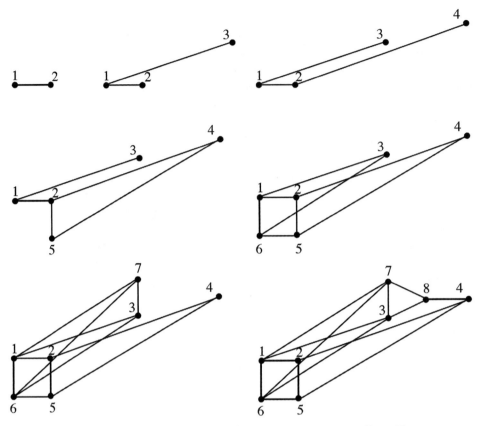

FIGURE 24.10 Evolution of eight segments from an associative set *J* (from Hanninen 2012, Ex. 3.36a).

the geometry of the graph's visual presentation seems to suggest that musical distance is external to us, as listeners; it renders musical distance as a phenomenon rather than phenomenological.

On the other hand, if musical distance is phenomenological, why assume, and show, musical space as being uniform? Our lived experience of space and time is context dependent: a half-mile walk in a botanical garden feels very different than one between gates in an airport; the trip between two gates on the outbound flight can feel much longer or shorter than on the return flight. Locations and events of interest, including musical ones, tend to distort the psychological sense of space around them—a feature that analysts might well incorporate into their visual representations of musical phenomena.

To decide whether a particular image, or part of an image, serves primarily to visualize or to represent, or whether it is a visual artifact or an element of graphic design, can require an appeal to another, elucidating mode in which the aspects in question are not a modal exigency. Here, verbal text can be an essential accompaniment for the effective use of visual images. Used strategically, it can complement and clarify, or duplicate and underline. Because words do not *require* the author to comment on, say, the spatial placement of nodes in a transformation graph, they can *provide an opportunity* to do so—to confirm or deny what, if any, iconic or propositional significance the given spatial placement might have. If redundancy in the elucidating mode (in this case, verbal text) explicitly affirms significance when no commitment is required, or even implicitly duplicates it, the ambiguity with regard to primary function (visualization, representation, or neither) can be resolved, or at least significantly reduced.

The same applies if the elucidating mode explicitly denies that significance. But if the supposedly "elucidating" mode clearly contradicts the ascription of significance without the author's acknowledging that this is so, or only implicitly denies it, the original question is posed again, but reformulated: when image and text disagree, which takes precedence? In such cases, all that we have learned from the "elucidating" mode is that the question is real, and where, exactly, our uncertainty regarding the image's intended content lies.

Still, that is something, and more than one might think. Identifying sources of confusion in reading images can lay a path to clarity in creating and using them. The question as to whether particular images, or parts of images used in music theory and analysis, serve primarily to visualize or to represent, or whether they are artifacts or elements of graphic design, does not always have a clear answer. That is precisely what makes it so interesting and valuable for those of us who create and use these images in our daily work.

Notes

1. Kress notes, "It matters which mode is used to 'fix' meaning. Scientific conceptions, as much as 'common sense,' are shaped by that choice … *Modal fixing* provides the fundamental epistemological and ontological basis for representation and communication" (2014, 71).

2. "In my opinion, semiotic modalities (e.g., language, depiction) are essentially incommensurable: no verbal text can construct the same meaning as a picture, no mathematical graph carries the same meaning as an equation, no verbal description makes the same sense as an action performed" (Lemke 1998, 110).

3. Isaacson (2005) offers a fine, compact discussion of visualization and visual images in music theory and analysis. In a comparative analysis of iconic visual models, Michael Fitzpatrick includes this insightful observation: "Even though iconic models pervade music theory literature, we encounter few comprehensive analyses of music theory models that describe how they work as models per se and how they relate to their subjects" (2011, 20).

4. "A characteristic feature of scientific activity is the production of visual displays of objects, processes, relationships, and theoretical constructs" (Lynch 1985, 37). "Visual representations are not to be considered mere *add-ons* or ways to popularize a complex reasoning; they are an essential part of scientific discourse" (Pauwels 2006, vii; and 2015, 281). See also, e.g., Amann and Knorr Cetina (1990), Cambrosio et al. (2006), Frankel and Whitesides (1997), Giere (1996), Lynch (2006a, 2006b), Ruse (1996), and Vertesi (2015).

5. Lemke (1998, 87) considers many scientific concepts to be "semiotic hybrids," which he traces to the fact that many of the phenomena that scientists work with are effectively invisible (e.g., they lie outside the visual spectrum or are too small, too big, or too far away), exist only as patterns in numeric data, or are postulated rather than observed; and to the centrality of theoretic models that have no visual correlate in scientific discourse. "Science is not done, is not communicated, through verbal language alone. It *cannot* be. The 'concepts' of science are . . . semiotic *hybrids*, simultaneously and essentially verbal, mathematical, visual–graphical, and actional–operational."

6. The idea that maps do not only depict but argue, presenting information from a particular point of view through editorial selection and graphic design, attracted a good deal of attention in the late 1980s and early 1990s. See, e.g., Harley (2011), MacEachren (1995), and Wood and Fels (2011). On the principles and process of information visualization, and for a striking array of graphics, see Tufte (1990, 2006), Lima (2011), and Börner and Polley (2014). In addition, Pauwels (2015) provides a thoughtful discussion of the prospects of a visual social science.

7. Because my subject is visual images in music theory and analysis, I will focus on their properties, affordances, exigencies, and use, highlighting points of contrast with verbal language. This should not be taken to suggest that I privilege the visual over the verbal mode, or that I find it more trustworthy in general. Both modes can be used for expository or artistic purposes, and to convey information, persuade, or mislead (intentionally or unintentionally), whether individually or in combination.

8. Pylyshyn gives the example of color recognition. While we can say that "this" paint swatch is "the same" color as "that" one, we cannot say exactly what color that is, nor can we identify the two swatches other than with the indexicals *this* and *that*.

9. "Some thoughts . . . can contain *unconceptualized contents*. . . . the grain of thoughts, or the possible distinctions between their contents, is even finer than that of one's potential linguistic vocabulary" (Pylyshyn 2003, 432).

10. Summarizing the different strengths of words and images, Lemke says that whereas language is good at "formulation of difference and relationship, for the making of categorical distinctions, [it] is much poorer (though hardly bankrupt) in resources for formulating degree, quantity, gradation, continuous change, continuous co-variation, non-integer ratios, varying proportionality, complex topological relations of relative nearness or connectedness, or nonlinear relations and dynamical emergence (which I refer to collectively as the *topological* dimensions of meaning . . .)" (1998, 87).

11. The affordance is a central concept in Gibson's ecological theory of visual perception: "The *affordances* of the environment are what it *offers* the animal, what it *provides* or *furnishes*, either for good or ill" (Gibson 1979, 127). "An affordance is neither an objective property nor a subjective property . . . . [It] cuts across the dichotomy of subjective–objective. . . . It is equally a fact of the environment and a fact of behavior" (129).

12. Bezemer and Kress (2008, 176) describe these "epistemological commitments" as an "unavoidable affordance" of mode.

13. Unsworth and Cléirigh (2014, 179) give the example of the physical distance between two characters, as in a play: "In the visual mode the artist or designer is obliged to show the distance between two characters (and other spatial relativities) which are not obligatory in a verbal description of the scene."

14. "Verbally, for instance, one can state that a certain bird species may have three to seven spots on its wings. However, when producing a visual representation, one inevitably must draw a definite number of spots" (Pauwels 2006, 14; and 2015, 297).

15. Tufte (2003) offers a sharp critique of Microsoft PowerPoint and its adverse effect on the formation and the quality of ideas. Ware (2008, 136) suggests that PowerPoint slides "should be primarily devoted to images and diagrams," with minimal text, such as for labels and captions.

16. "There is little doubt of the importance of spatial constructs in organizing our thoughts, including at the highly abstract levels" (Pylyshyn 2003, 453).

17. Boretz (1979) and Randall (1975) are literary texts in music theory and analysis that exemplify the poetic use of space and typography.

18. "The graphic is no longer only the 'representation' of a final simplification, it is a point of departure for the discovery of these simplifications and the means for their justification. The graphic has become, by its manageability, an instrument for information processing" (Bertin 1983, 3).

19. "We are so close to language (it is us; we are it), we can't understand it. We are in language as a fish is in water: for the fish there's no such thing as water; water is just the way things are; it's the medium for being. Language is that for us" (Fischer 2016, 94).

20. "Certain properties of the visual system . . . can be exploited to facilitate reasoning" (Pylyshyn 2003, 441).

21. "As cognitive tools, graphics facilitate reasoning, both by externalizing, thus offloading memory and processing, and by mapping abstract reasoning onto spatial comparisons and transformations" (Tversky 2012, 232). Card, Mackinlay, and Shneiderman (1999, 16) identify six main ways that information visualization "amplifies cognition." In their view, graphics can serve as a form of external cognition, which recognizes the "role of the external world in thought and reasoning" (1). Other examples of external cognition include longhand multiplication and division, navigation charts, and the slide rule (1–3).

22. "The expressions form a sequence corresponding, on a one-to-one basis, to the sentences in a natural-language description of the problem" (Larkin and Simon 1987, 66).

23. Larkin and Simon continue: "A sentential representation may, of course, preserve other kinds of relations, for example, temporal or logical sequence. An outline may reflect hierarchical relations" (1987, 66).

24. Citing Larkin and Simon, Barbara Tversky (2012) distinguishes two kinds of inferences that can be drawn from diagrams: structural and functional. Structural inferences are "about qualities of parts and the relations among them" (227). "Distance, direction, size, and other spatial qualities and properties can be 'read off' a diagram (Larkin & Simon 1987)" (227). "Functional inferences about the behavior of entities cannot be readily made from inspection of a diagram [alone]" (Tversky 2012, 227–228); they require "linking perceptual information to conceptual information" (228).

25. Pylyshyn (2003, 459) notes that mental images are self-limiting in this regard: "Visual percepts and imagined pictures are very different from physical drawings. When we imagine carrying out certain operations on mental images . . . what we 'see' happening in our mind's eye is just what we believe would happen . . . . we cannot rely on discovering something by observing what actually happens."

26. Summarizing their research, Hegarty and Stull make two points: "The representations that are most functional in reasoning are very schematic, without visual detail" (2012, 620); and although "people prefer displays that simulate the real world with greater fidelity . . . they are often better served by simpler, more abstract displays" (621).

27. Ware (2008, 142–144) cites a 2004 study in which Tversky and her team found a sequence of assembly diagrams to be the most effective way to convey instructions for assembling prefabricated furniture.

28. Citing Meyers's 1988 critique of E. O. Wilson's use of photographs in *Sociobiology*, Alan MacEachren (1995, 454) says that "while the detail carries no 'relevant' information, it has an important function in making the illustration 'seem to be a document recording an unmediated perception of a particular piece of nature'" (contains a quote from Meyers 1988, 238).

29. For instance, see James Elkin's *The Domain of Images*, where the central word *image* serves as a broad term (1999, ix), a "placeholder" (82) that takes in both art and nonart visual artifacts. Elsewhere, with Maja Naef, Elkins notes that the term *image* is often taken as a given in art production, art history, and visual studies (Elkins and Naef 2011). Nonetheless, what constitutes an image remains a topic of theorizing and active discussion; for example, see Elkins and Naef (2011).

30. Ware defines visualization as a product: "a graphical representation of some data or concepts . . . tools for visual thinking" (2008, 20). Visual studies scholar Luc Pauwels focuses on the process: "[V]isualization in science basically involves the complex processes through which scientists develop or produce (and communicate with) imagery, schemes, and graphical representations, computer renderings, or the like, using various means" (2006, 1). In science and information visualization, the term often more specifically connotes the use of computers or automation. Card, Mackinlay, and Shneiderman (1999) trace this usage to *Visualization in Scientific Computing* (McCormick, DeFanti, and Brown 1987), a report supported by the National Science Foundation that is associated with the genesis of the field. By 1995, *scientific visualization* had largely taken on this "narrower meaning of advanced computer technology to facilitate 'making visible' scientific data and concepts" (MacEachren 1995, 355), a meaning that is also evident in Card, Mackinlay, and Shneiderman's equally specific definition of the more general term *visualization* as "the use of computer-supported, interactive, visual representations of data to amplify cognition" (6).

31. For a fascinating discussion of the epistemological and ontological import of visualization associated with the Mars Rover mission, see Vertesi (2015, chapter 3, "Image Processing").

32. Regarding the complexity of music notation as a semiotic system and changes in music notation associated with changing compositional practices in the twentieth century, see Morris (2016). Yuasa summarizes the relationship between musical notation and ontologies as follows: "'Musical ideas' and 'notation' are separated as a matter of convenience. They are actually interdependent—inseparable" (Cage 1969, 30. The pages are unnumbered; Yuasa's words appear opposite the score excerpt from Arthur Bliss's "Swallows.")

33. "The purpose of visualization is insight," with the goals of "discovery, decision making, and explanation" (Card, Mackinlay, and Shneiderman 1999, 6).

34. "James Griesemer, Ruse, and others have argued that pictures in science can work both propositionally and nonpropositionally: Sometimes they illustrate or propose theories; other times they merely *exist,* taking a certain place in the chain of written discourse and modifying it in ways that are difficult to describe" (Elkins 1999, 39).

35. See, e.g., Woolgar (1988); Lynch and Woolgar (1990a, 1990b); van Fraassen (2008); Coopmans et al. (2014); and Vertesi (2015).

36. Luc Pauwels (2006, vii; and 2015, 280–281) agrees: "The issue of *representation* touches upon the very essence of all scientific activity. What is known and passed on as *science* is the result of a series of representational practices. Visual, verbal, numeric, and other types of representations are used in all sciences and in various types of scientific discourses." Woolgar (1988, 36) goes further, however, saying that the very "discourse of science . . . is organized to reinforce the ideology of representations." Since the 1980s, growing interest

in the practices, sociology, and ideology of representation in the sciences has given rise to a new field: science and technology studies.

37. Throughout this chapter, I use *interpretation* not in the broad sense that it is used in hermeneutics, but in the narrower sense that the term is often used in science and music analysis. In the latter fields, one "interprets" data or events in light of other cases, contexts, or a supporting theory (explicitly or tacitly). As shorthand for *analytic interpretation,* it is somewhat like *explanation* in the sciences, in that it often invokes a conceptual system or "theory" developed apart from, and considered functionally independent of, the data set or musical passage at hand.

38. "There is an asymmetry in representation that resemblance does not have" (van Fraassen 2008, 17); and "resemblance must go both ways ... [it] is both reflexive and symmetric, while representation is neither" (18).

39. "Whether or not A represents B, and whether or not it represents the represented item as C, depends largely, and sometimes only, *on the way in which A is being used*" (van Fraassen 2008, 23).

40. "Hearing as" invokes Ludwig Wittgenstein's idea of "seeing as," which is, roughly, "to see an object according to an interpretation" (Wittgenstein 2002, 171). Here, as in much of my work, I construe "hearing as" largely in terms of the complex workings of contextual criteria, theorized as in Hanninen (2012). In contrast, Lawrence Kramer's implementation of "hearing as" (as in Kramer 2012, 2016) is expressly culturally situated, emphasizing larger-scale and more diffuse connections with ideas, events, or other artworks outside the work at hand.

41. Michael Lynch (2014, 325) notes the separation between representation and what is represented, urging attention to the practice of representation in science: "[W]ords do more and other than refer, pictures do more and other than depict, and representations do more and other than correspond to objects and/or ideas. The point of emphasizing practice is ... that their practical uses establish *what* they do, *how* they mean, and what is done *with* them."

42. Christopher Hasty makes a similar point with regard to representation: "[M]usic theory has embraced representation as a way of fixing the musical object" (2010, 4).

43. For example, I noted earlier in this article that most musical scores function primarily as visualizations. But there are numerous exceptions. Rainer Wehinger's "aural score" for Ligeti's *Artikulation* (1958) for electronic tape is a highly selective visual representation that uses color and size to call attention to and objectify some sonic attributes and events, while effectively silencing others in white space (Ligeti 1970). The score for Karlheinz Stockhausen's *Kontakte* (1959–1960) is a hybrid, in which the fully notated piano and percussion parts are visualizations (albeit in different ways), while the tape part is a selective representation of salient events (along with minute/second timings, which visualize their locations in the flow of time).

44. Cf. Pauwels: "Every *representational* process involves a translation or conversion of some kind; a process of inscription, transcription, and/or fabrication whereby the initial source (phenomenon, concept) is captured, transformed, or even (re)-created through a chain of decisions.... This complex process of meaning-making has an important impact on what can be known and how, on what is revealed or obscured, and what is included or excluded" (Pauwels 2006, 4–5; 2015, 288).

45. Although I have reproduced the graphics from other sources, the choice of examples, surrounding argument, observations, and background, are Gollin's (2011, 282–289).

46. A literal two-partition graph shows how pc-sets combine or partition into harmonies; an abstract two-partition graph shows how set classes do. Morris's Babbitt network is an example of the latter (1995, 341); it shows how the twelve trichords combine to create the six all-combinatorial hexachords.

47. To see this, flip every other one of the innermost nodes (for pc dyads 04, 2A, 08, etc.) out to the periphery of the graph, while maintaining all node–edge connections.

48. Indeed, it *cannot* comment if it is to serve its purpose as a compositional space—a realm of possibilities, rather than a representation of specific choices made.

49. These are shown in Figures S5L–M in the online supplement to the print version of Callender, Quinn, and Tymoczko (2008).

50. Spectrograms have been used widely in fields ranging from speech pathology, speech recognition, and linguistics to ornithology and zoomusicology. In music studies, pitch is a psychoacoustic phenomenon that involves the fusion of harmonic partials (or frequencies within a very narrow bandwidth) into a single perceptual event. Loudness refers to perceived amplitude, which varies over the frequency spectrum according to the Fletcher-Munson or other equal-amplitude curves.

51. For that matter, what constitutes scientific objectivity has itself changed over time, as Daston and Galison (2007) detail in a fascinating and wide-ranging history of the idea and associated imaging practices. They trace a path from an ideal of "truth-to-nature" (roughly, the late eighteenth to early to mid-nineteenth centuries) to "visually grounded mechanical objectivity" (late nineteenth century) (121), to structural objectivity grounded in logic and mathematics (early twentieth century), and, more recently, to a revitalized recognition of the role of trained observers and image-makers (late twentieth century and on).

52. W. J. T. Mitchell, a humanist whose work has focused on images, pictures, and visual culture, notes the present lack of a science of images and expresses his interest in developing one that centers not around practices in the so-called soft sciences, such as political science or economics, but around those in what he calls "hard sciences—mathematics, physics, and biology" (2015, 26–27).

53. Vertesi's study devotes special attention to digital image processing and the particular disciplinary interests and scientific purposes that individual images were created to serve.

54. Vertesi's use of the word *interpretative* can be confusing in the present context. Her denotation is broader than mine—closer to that in hermeneutics, which embraces not only scientific explanation or analytical interpretation that references theory (which I identify with representation), but also the interplay between researcher and imaging technology (which I consider part of visualization). Here, I read her use of "interpretative work in" to mean something like "imaging practices," which can focus the viewer's attention on specific "existing distinctions in the data," but do not offer explanations (or "interpretations," in the strong sense that I use the term) for what is shown (Vertesi 2015, 95). They show, but they do not tell about what is shown.

55. "The spectrum photos are the result of an accumulation of human choices in the design and use of analytic and display instrumentation . . . . Even more important than technical limitations are the choices that have been made in performing and photographing the analyses—for example, the choice of time scale" (Cogan 1984, 14).

56. Norman Adams advocates tailoring the process of creating spectrographic visualizations to what one wants to show: "In generating time-frequency images, care must be taken in setting image parameters such as frame size and colormap to visually emphasize the important aspects of the sound" (2006, 27).

57. Sonic Visualiser also allows a user to add annotations, which music analysts use. However, these add a new dimension to the image. As Vertesi points out, annotations represent interpretations; they do not visualize information already available in the data. "The colors depict 'information' that is 'contain[ed]' *in* the image, not glossed onto it in interpretive annotations. This is important to team members, who distinguish between annotations as interpretations ... versus image-processing work that presents existing distinctions in the data" (2015, 95).

58. Here, I use *musical perception* in the rich sense advocated by David Lewin (1986), and in contrast to simpler aural perceptions.

59. On the horizontal axis, composers are listed alphabetically (not chronologically or stylistically) within the lowest-level cluster that includes all of them and evenly spaced, for visual balance. If we imagine translating the 2D visualization into a 3D mobile, the swing arm that supports Byrd could rotate, allowing us to position him to the left of Bach, his successor. To bring Scarlatti back toward the eighteenth-Century Baroque cluster, we would need to extend his horizontal swing bar and rotate it. But this can be done without distorting the visualization: the length of the horizontal swing bars appears to be determined not by patterns in the data, but by the convention for ordering composers on the horizontal axis.

60. Lewin makes this point and discusses his criteria for including nodes at the start of his analysis of Stockhausen's *Klavierstück III* (1993, 19–22).

61. Lewin (1993) adopts the terms *figural* and *formal* from Jeanne Bamberger. Rings uses the equivalent terms *event* and *spatial* from Roeder (2009). An event network is a "left-to-right temporal" network; a spatial network is a "spatial, temporally indeterminate" network (Rings 2011, 140).

62. This noniconic use of space reflects a choice, not a necessity: the use of space can be iconic for spatial networks, for parameters other than time (which defines the event network).

63. An associative set is a set of musical segments interrelated by contextual criteria. An association graph represents an analyst's interpretation of associative adjacency, proximity, or distance, among segments and perhaps among formal features.

64. The degree of alignment or disparity between temporal and associative proximity for segments within one or more associative sets is essentially a basis for a generalized view of musical form.

65. An association digraph replaces one or more of the edges with arrows in order to indicate succession of some kind, whether by score chronology (chronological order in the music, as in Figures 24.8 or 24.9) or associative chronology (associative derivation, or order of recognition and entry into an associative set). As with temporal and associative adjacency, score and associative chronology need not coincide.

66. For a more detailed discussion of the comparison and its graphic re-presentation, see Hanninen (2012, 406–414).

67. That is, compass points are fixed, but in analytic practice, the hexatonic systems may be relabeled in a movable-do system that assigns priority to the primary transpositions or transformations at work within each specific composition.

68. Alan MacEachren notes the semiotic significance of visual aesthetics and rhetoric, describing maps produced by the U.S. Geological Survey as "highly detailed, unadorned, visually unassuming maps to connote accuracy, impartiality, [and] authority [and] thereby creating an impression that U.S. Geological Survey maps have no point of view" (1995, 335).

69. Albeit sometimes, and unfortunately, without the nuance and sensitivity to musical detail that informed Lewin's own analyses.

70. On the title page to the 1906 *Harmonielehre,* the first volume of the *Neue Musikalische Theorien und Fantasien* that culminated in *Der Freie Satz* (1935), Schenker identifies himself as "ein Künstler" (an artist).

71. In Felix Salzer's *Structural Hearing* (1962), some of the slurs are replaced with straight lines and brackets, perhaps representing a more modernist aesthetic that finds resonance in his expanded choice of repertoire.

72. In some cases, actual pitch registers in the score are normalized, which indicates a move toward representation.

73. Although Schenker's own analytic and representation practices varied over the course of his career, by the time of *Der freie Satz* (1935), durational symbols largely indicate structural weight, as they now do in Schenkerian analysis in general (durational reductions aside) (Schenker 1979).

74. "Some readers may feel uneasy with the complexity of the apparatus we have introduced to *describe* musical intuition, particularly that used to *derive* prolongational structure. Beyond the *sheer empirical power of the theory to describe* the characteristics of specific pieces and of tonal music in general, we offer three arguments that support this complexity. First, we have been careful to relate every step in our development of musical grammar to musical intuition . . . . Second, anyone who has thought about musical structure in any depth ought to expect it to be this complex . . . . A third justification for the complexity of the grammar is its *status as a theory of musical cognition*—what the experienced listener knows that enables him to comprehend music" (Lerdahl and Jackendoff 1983, 248–249; emphasis added). However, whether the reductions actually visualize the result of Lerdahl and Jackendoff's theory of music cognition or represent how the authors themselves interpreted and settled various ambiguities and conflicts among specific well-formedness rules (WFRs), and especially preference rules (PRs), along the way remains an open question.

75. "An *evolution* of an association graph, EVOL(*AG*), is an ordered set of association subgraphs $<SAG_m, \ldots SAG_n>$, where n is the number of nodes in N(*AG*), m is a number of nodes from 1 to $n-1$, and each *SAG* in the sequence is a subgraph of its immediate successor, which adds at least one node and some number of edges (perhaps zero)" (Hanninen, 2012, 152).

76. A *glyph* is "a specific kind of symbol . . . [examples include] simple features like points, lines, blobs, and arrows, which derive their meanings from their geometric or gestalt properties in context. Glyphs are especially important in diagrams because they allow visual means of expressing common concepts that are not easily conveyed by likenesses" (Tversky 2011, 515).

77. Various scholars associate arrows with anywhere from seven basic meanings to dozens of meanings (Tversky 2011, 521).

78. For a critique of the inclusion and interpretation of arrows in Klumpenhouwer networks, see Buchler (2007). Janet Schmalfeldt's (2011, 9) definition of the double-edged arrow to indicate "becoming" is notably articulate.

Works Cited

Adams, Norman. 2006. "Visualization of Musical Signals." In *Analytical Methods of Electroacoustic Music,* edited by Mary Simoni, 13–28. New York: Taylor & Francis.

Amann, K., and K. Knorr Cetina. 1990. "The Fixation of (Visual) Evidence." In *Representation in Scientific Practice*, edited by Michael Lynch and Steve Woolgar, 85–121. Cambridge, MA: MIT Press.

Bamberger, Jeanne. 1986. "Cognitive Issues in the Development of Musically Gifted Children." In *Conceptions of Giftedness*, edited by Robert J. Sternberg and Janet E. Davidson, 388–413. Cambridge: Cambridge University Press.

Bertin, Jacques. 1983. *Semiology of Graphics: Diagrams, Networks, Maps*. Translated by William J. Berg. Madison: University of Wisconsin Press.

Bezemer, Jeff, and Gunther Kress. 2008. "Written Communication in Multimodal Texts: A Social Semiotic Account of Designs for Learning." *Written Communication* 25: 166–195.

Boretz, Benjamin. 1979. "Language, as a Music: Six Marginal Pretexts for Composition." *Perspectives of New Music* 17: 131–195. Reprinted in *Being About Music. Vol. 2, Textworks*. Red Hook, NY: Open Space. 2003. Recorded by the author on Open Space CD 10.

Börner, Katy, and Davie E. Polley. 2014. *Visual Insights: A Practical Guide to Making Sense of Data*. Cambridge, MA: MIT Press.

Buchler, Michael. 2007. "Reconsidering Klumpenhouwer Networks." *Music Theory Online* 13, no. 2. Available at http://www.mtosmt.org/issues/mto.07.13.2/mto.07.13.2.buchler.html.

Cage, John. 1969. *Notations*. New York: Something Else Press.

Callender, Clifton, Ian Quinn, and Dmitri Tymoczko. 2008. "Generalized Voice-Leading Spaces." *Science* 320 (April 18): 346–348.

Cambrosio, Alberto, Daniel Jacobi, and Peter Keating. 2006. "Arguing with Images: Pauling's Theory of Antibody Formation." In *Visual Cultures of Science: Rethinking Representational Practices in Knowledge Building and Science Communication*, edited by Luc Pauwels, 120–152. Hanover, NH: Dartmouth College Press.

Card, Stuart K., Jock D. Mackinlay, and Ben Shneiderman. 1999. *Readings in Information Visualization: Using Vision to Think*. San Francisco: Moran Kaufmann Publishers.

Cogan, Robert. 1984. *New Images of Musical Sound*. Cambridge, MA: Harvard University Press.

Cohn, Richard. 1996. "Maximally Smooth Cycles, Hexatonic Systems, and the Analysis of Late-Romantic Triadic Progressions." *Music Analysis* 15: 9–40.

Coopmans, Catelijne, Janet Vertesi, Michael E. Lynch, and Steve Woolgar. 2014. *Representation in Scientific Practice Revisited*. Cambridge, MA: MIT Press.

Daston, Lorraine, and Peter Galison. 2007. *Objectivity*. New York: Zone Books.

Elkins, James. 1999. *The Domain of Images*. Ithaca, NY: Cornell University Press.

Elkins, James, and Maja Naef, eds. 2011. *What Is an Image?* University Park: Pennsylvania State University Press.

Fischer, Norman. 2016. *Experience: Thinking, Writing, Language, and Religion*. Tuscaloosa: University of Alabama Press.

Fitzpatrick, Michael. 2011. "Models and Music Theory: Reconsidering David Lewin's Graph of the 3–2 Cohn Cycle." *Music Theory Online* 17, no. 1. Available at http://www.mtosmt.org/issues/mto.11.17.1/mto.11.17.1.fitzpatrick.html.

Frankel, Felice, and George M. Whitesides. 1997. *On the Surface of Things: Images of the Extraordinary in Science*. San Francisco: Chronicle Books.

Gibson, James J. 1979. *The Ecological Approach to Visual Perception*. Hillsdale: Lawrence Erlbaum.

Giere, Ronald N. 1996. "Visual Models and Scientific Judgment." In *Picturing Knowledge: Historical and Philosophical Problems Concerning the Use of Art in Science*, edited by Brian S. Baigrie, 269–302. Toronto: University of Toronto Press.

Gollin, Edward. 2011. "From Matrix to Map: Tonbestimmung, the Tonnetz, and Riemann's Combinatorial Conception of Interval." In *Oxford Handbook of Neo-Riemannian Music Theories*, edited by Edward Gollin and Alexander Rehding, 271–293. New York: Oxford University Press.

Hanninen, Dora A. 2012. *A Theory of Music Analysis: On Segmentation and Associative Organization*. Rochester, NY: University of Rochester Press.

Hanninen, Dora A. 2014. "Asking Questions/Making Music." *Music Theory Online*. 20, no. 2. Available at http://www.mtosmt.org/issues/mto.14.20.2/mto.14.20.2.hanninen-intro.html.

Harley, J. B. 2011. "Deconstructing the Map." In *Classics on Cartography: Reflections on Influential Articles from* Cartographica, edited by Martin Dodge, 273–294. New York: John Wiley & Sons.

Hasty, Christopher. 2010. "The Image of Thought and Ideas of Music." In *Sounding the Virtual: Gilles Deleuze and the Theory and Philosophy of Music*, edited by Brian Hulse and Nick Nesbitt, 1–22. Burlington, VT: Ashgate.

Hegarty, Mary, and Andrew T. Stull. 2012. "Visuospatial Thinking." In *Oxford Handbook of Thinking and Reasoning*, edited by Keith J. Holyoak and Robert G. Morrison, 606–630. New York: Oxford University Press.

Heinichen, Johann David. 1994. *Der Generalbass in der Composition*. Hildesheim: G. Olms.

Hook, Julian. 2006. "Exploring Musical Space." *Science* 313 (July 7): 49–50.

Hyer, Brian. 1995. "Reimag(in)ing Riemann." *Journal of Music Theory* 36/1: 101–138.

Irving, Zachary C. 2011. "Style, but Substance: An Epistemology of Visual Versus Numerical Presentation in Scientific Practice." *Philosophy of Science* 78: 774–787.

Isaacson, Eric. 2005. "What You See Is What You Get: On Visualizing Music." *ISMIR Proceedings of the 6th International Conference on Music Information Retrieval*, London, 389–395.

Johnson, B., and B. Shneiderman. 1991. "Tree-Maps: A Space-Filling Approach to the Visualization of Hierarchical Information Structures." *Proceedings of the 2nd International IEEE Visualization Conference*, San Diego, October, 284–291.

Karkoshka, Erhard. 1972. *Notation in New Music: A Critical Guide to Interpretation and Realization*, translated by Ruth Koenig. New York: Praeger Publishers.

Kellner, David. 1985. *Treulicher Unterricht im General-Bass. Nebst einer Vorrede von Georg Philipp Telemann*, edited by Eitelfriedrich Thom. Blankenburg: Kultur- und Forschungsstätte Michaelstein.

Kramer, Lawrence. 2012. *Expression and Truth*. Berkeley: University of California Press.

Kramer, Lawrence. 2016. *The Thought of Music*. Berkeley: University of California Press.

Kress, Gunther. 2003. *Literacy in the New Media Age*. London: Routledge.

Kress, Gunther. 2014. "What Is Mode?" In *Routledge Handbook of Multimodal Analysis*, edited by Carey Jewitt, 60–75. New York: Routledge.

Larkin, Jill H., and Herbert A. Simon. 1987. "Why a Diagram Is (Sometimes) Worth Ten Thousand Words." *Cognitive Science* 11: 65–99.

Lemke, Jay. 1998. "Multiplying Meaning: Visual and Verbal Semiotics in Scientific Text." In *Reading Science: Critical and Functional Perspectives on Discourses of Science*, edited by Jonathan R. Martin and Robert Veel, 87–113. New York: Routledge.

Lerdahl, Fred, and Ray Jackendoff. 1983. *A Generative Theory of Tonal Music*. Cambridge, MA: MIT Press.

Lewin, David. 1982a. "A Formal Theory of Generalized Tonal Functions." *Journal of Music Theory* 26: 23–60.

Lewin, David. 1982b. "Transformational Techniques in Atonal and Other Music Theories." *Perspectives of New Music* 21: 312–371.

Lewin, David. 1986. "Music Theory, Phenomenology, and Modes of Perception." *Music Perception* 3: 327–392.

Lewin, David. 1987. *Generalized Musical Intervals and Transformations*. New Haven, CT: Yale University Press.

Lewin, David. 1993. *Musical Form and Transformation: Four Analytic Essays*. New Haven, CT: Yale University Press.

Ligeti, György. 1970. *Artikulation: Elektronische Musik. Eine Hörpartitur von Rainer Wehinger*. Mainz: Schott.

Lima, Manuel. 2011. *Visual Complexity: Mapping Patterns of Information*. New York: Princeton Architectural Press.

Lynch, Michael. 1985. "Discipline and the Material Form of Images: An Analysis of Scientific Visibility." *Social Studies of Science* 15: 37–66.

Lynch, Michael. 2006a. "Discipline and the Material Form of Images: An Analysis of Scientific Visibility." In *Visual Cultures of Science: Rethinking Representational Practices in Knowledge Building and Science Communication*, edited by Luc Pauwels, 195–221. Hanover, NH: Dartmouth College Press.

Lynch, Michael. 2006b. "The Production of Scientific Images: Vision and Re-Vision in the History, Philosophy, and Sociology of Science." In *Visual Cultures of Science: Rethinking Representational Practices in Knowledge Building and Science Communication*, edited by Luc Pauwels, 26–40. Hanover, NH: Dartmouth College Press.

Lynch, Michael. 2014. "Representation in Formation." In *Representation in Scientific Practice Revisited*, edited by Catelijne Coopmans, Janet Vertesi, Michael Lynch, and Steve Woolgar, 323–328. Cambridge, MA: MIT Press.

Lynch, Michael, and Steve Woolgar. 1990a. "Introduction: Sociological Orientation to Representational Practice in Science." In *Representation in Scientific Practice*, edited by Michael Lynch and Steve Woolgar, 1–18. Cambridge, MA: MIT Press.

Lynch, Michael, and Steve Woolgar, eds. 1990b. *Representation in Scientific Practice*. Cambridge, MA: MIT Press.

MacEachren, Alan M. 1995. *How Maps Work: Representation, Visualization, and Design*. New York: Guilford Press.

McCormick, Bruce H., Thomas A. DeFanti, and Maxine D. Brown. 1987. *Visualization in Scientific Computing. Computer Graphis* 21, no. 6.

Meyers, Greg. 1988. "Every Picture Tells a Story: Illustrations in E. O. Wilson's *Sociobiology*." In *Representation in Scientific Practice*, edited by Michael Lynch and Steve Woolgar, 231–265. Cambridge, MA: MIT Press.

Mitchell, W. J. T. 2015. *Image Science: Iconology, Visual Culture, and Media Aesthetics*. Chicago: University of Chicago Press.

Morris, Robert D. 1995. "Compositional Spaces and Other Territories." *Perspectives of New Music* 33: 328–359.

Morris, Robert D. 1998. "Voice-Leading Spaces." *Music Theory Spectrum* 20: 175–208.

Morris, Robert D. 2016. "Notation's One Thing, Analysis Another, Musical Experience a Third: What Can They Have to Do with One Another?" In *Music in Time: Phenomenology, Perception, Performance: Essays in Honor of Christopher Hasty*, edited by Suzannah Clark and Alexander Rehding, 71–107. Cambridge, MA: Harvard University Press.

Newbury, Darren. 2011. "Making Arguments with Images: Visual Scholarship and Academic Publishing." In *SAGE Handbook of Visual Research Methods*, edited by Eric Margolis and Luc Pauwels, 561–664. Los Angeles: SAGE Publications.

Pauwels, Luc. 2006. *Visual Cultures of Science: Rethinking Representational Practices in Knowledge Building and Science Communication*. Hanover, NH: Dartmouth College Press.

Pauwels, Luc. 2015. *Reframing Visual Social Science: Toward a More Visual Sociology and Anthropology*. Cambridge: Cambridge University Press.

Pylyshyn, Zenon. 2003. *Seeing and Visualizing: It's Not What You Think*. Cambridge, MA: MIT Press.

Quinn, Ian, and Christopher White. 2018. "Chord Context and Harmonic Function in Tonal Music." *Music Theory Spectrum* 40: 314–335.

Randall, J. K. 1975. "A Soundscroll." *Perspectives of New Music* 13: 126–149. [Reprinted in *Being About Music. Vol. 1, Textworks*. Red Hook, NY: Open Space. 2003.]

Rings, Steven. 2011. *Tonality and Transformation*. New York: Oxford University Press.

Roeder, John. 2009. "Constructing Transformational Signification: Gesture and Agency in Bartók's Scherzo, op. 14, no. 2, measures 1–32." *Music Theory Online* 15, no. 1. Available at http://www.mtosmt.org/issues/mto.09.15.1/mto.09.15.1.roeder_signification.html.

Ruse, Michael. 1996. "Are Pictures Really Necessary? The Case of Sewall Wright's 'Adaptive Landscapes.'" In *Picturing Knowledge: Historical and Philosophical Problems Concerning the Use of Art in Science*, edited by Brian S. Baigrie, 303–338. Toronto: University of Toronto Press.

Sauer, Theresa. 2009. *Notations 21*. New York: Mark Batty.

Salzer, Felix. 1962. *Structural Hearing*. New York: Dover.

Schenker, Heinrich. 1979. *Free Composition*. 2 vols. Translated and edited by Ernst Oster. New York: Longman.

Schmalfeldt, Janet. 2011. *In the Process of Becoming: Analytic and Philosophical Perspectives on Form in Early Nineteenth-Century Music*. New York: Oxford University Press.

Tufte, Edward Rolf. 1990. *Envisioning Information*. Cheshire, CT: Graphics Press.

Tufte, Edward Rolf. 2003. *The Cognitive Style of PowerPoint*. Cheshire, CT: Graphics Press.

Tufte, Edward Rolf. 2006. *Beautiful Evidence*. Cheshire, CT: Graphics Press.

Tversky, Barbara. 2011. "Visualizing Thought." *Topics in Cognitive Science* 3: 499–535.

Tversky, Barbara. 2012. "Visuospatial Reasoning." In *Cambridge Handbook of Thinking and Reasoning*, edited by Keith J. Holyoak and Robert G. Morrison, 209–240. New York: Cambridge University Press.

Tversky, Barbara, Jeff Zacks, Paul Lee, and Julie Heiser. 2000. "Lines, Blobs, Crosses, and Arrows: Diagrammatic Communication with Schematic Figures." In *Diagrams 2000— Theory and Application of Diagrams—First International Conference September 1-3, 2000, Edinburgh*, 221–230. Available at http://link.springer.de/link/service/series/0558/bibs/1889/1889o221.htm.

Tymoczko, Dmitri. 2001. *The Geometry of Music*. New York: Oxford University Press.

Unsworth, Len, and Chris Cléirigh. 2014. "Multimodality and Reading: The Construction of Meaning Through Image-Text Interaction." In *Routledge Handbook of Multimodal Analysis*, edited by Carey Jewitt, 176–188. New York: Routledge.

Van Fraassen, Bas. 2008. *Scientific Representation: Paradoxes of Perspective*. New York: Oxford University Press.

Van Leeuwen, Theo. 2011. "Multimodality and Multimodal Research." *SAGE Handbook of Visual Research Methods*, edited by Eric Margolis and Luc Pauwels, 549–569. Los Angeles: SAGE Publications.

Vertesi, Janet. 2015. *Seeing Like a Rover: How Robots, Teams, and Images Craft Knowledge of Mars*. Chicago: University of Chicago Press.

Ware, Colin. 2008. *Visual Thinking for Design*. Burlington, MA: Morgan Kaufmann Publishers, Elsevier.

White, Christopher. 2014. "Changing Styles, Changing Corpora, Changing Tonal Models." *Music Perception* 31: 244–253.

Wittgenstein, Ludwig. 2002. *Philosophical Investigations: The German Text, with a Revised English Translation*. Translated by G. E. M. Anscombe. Malden: Blackwell Publishing.

Wood, Denis, and John Fels. 2011. "Designs on Signs/Myth and Meaning in Maps." In *Classics on Cartography: Reflections on Influential Articles from* Cartographica, edited by Martin Dodge, 209–260. New York: John Wiley & Sons.

Woolgar, Steve. 1988. *Science: The Very Idea*. New York: Tavistock Publications.

Yuatt, Andrew Pierce. 2012. "Analyzing Edgard Varese's Ionisation Using Digital Spectral Analysis." MM diss., University of Arizona.

CHAPTER 25

....

WHAT IS MUSIC, ANYWAY?

....

ANDREW BOWIE

DEFINITIONS

FACED with any object of study, the obvious demand would seem to be that one define the key term in that study. However, anyone now expecting a definition of music is about to be disappointed. Indeed, part of what I want to say is that seeking to arrive at a definition of music may actually get in the way of comprehending music. The *Cambridge Dictionary* does its definitional duty with the following: "a pattern of sounds made by musical instruments, voices, or computers, or a combination of these, intended to give pleasure to people listening to it." So no *4'33"*, no natural sounds like birdsong, no avantgarde that ensures that you can't get any immediate sensuous or melodic pleasure from the music. *The Oxford English Dictionary* probably does a bit better, always assuming that what is "produce[d]" can be alternatives and are not all necessary for "music": "The art or science of combining vocal or instrumental sounds to produce beauty of form, harmony, melody, rhythm, expressive content, etc.; musical composition, performance, analysis, etc., as a subject of study; the occupation or profession of musicians."

It is not that these characterizations are of *no* use: general terms for designating things, however vague, play a vital role in everyday life. In this respect, one can see music in terms of what Ludwig Wittgenstein calls "family resemblance," where nothing is identical among different cases of what is at issue, but the cases are linked by overlapping similarities. Definitions, in contrast, have to be able to set boundaries of inclusion and exclusion that establish the scope of a concept. Such boundaries may be notoriously unstable, though; indeed, the history of Western music in particular can be characterized precisely by the ways in which the boundaries of the musical and the non-musical shift. The Greek "art of the Muses," *mousike* (μουσική), included much more than just patterns of sounds, involving poetry and drama, for example, so the restrictions in the dictionary definitions are themselves historical developments. The Greek notion of *poiesis* (creative production), which the early German Romantics adopted for their idea of Poesie (which involved all the arts), led the Romantics to suggest that we should appreciate how the arts interact and may affect each other's borders. But where does that leave one in terms of contemporary attempts to characterize music as an object of study? In what follows, I shall concentrate on the issues as they appear in the Western traditions, although I hope that some of what I say will be relevant to other traditions.

The way out here might seem to be to historicize the concept of music, tracing how its boundaries have shifted and what might have occasioned those shifts. This can make us aware of how differently the concept has been used at different times and in different places, and so alter our perspective on our own uses of the term. However, just describing such shifts may not do justice to the way in which the tensions inherent in a concept like music reveal things that are hidden from a historicist approach. Merely detailing how the term "music" has been used in various contexts risks making the issue seem not to matter much, when disputes about whether something is music clearly do matter a lot in many contexts. Otherwise, why would the Taliban and other religious extremists ban it?

So far, we have touched on approaches that seek to establish music's nature in discursive terms. But one of the reasons that there has been such extensive reflection about the nature of music is that music, especially in the modern period, can itself be understood to pose questions about exclusive reliance on discursive means. The failure to define music, in that case, may tell us more about music than attempts at defining it.

FORM AND CONTENT

If what music is "saying" is supposed to be "unsayable," success in verbally articulating what it says would make the music itself superfluous. At the same time, verbal articulation of the content of music can reveal things that would not have been manifest without the verbal accounts. Otherwise, much of the study of music would be redundant. One can see here the source of conflicts in the contemporary study of music that emerge, for example, in relation to the New Musicology's attempts to interpret music by locating it in historical, ideological, gender, and other contexts, in a manner analogous to the interpretation of literary and other texts.

A denial that such an approach tells us anything about the music in question is implausible, but the desire to semanticize music in new musicology has to take account of the objection that music's resistance to semanticization can be as important as its being understood through verbal articulation. Why this can be the case involves the difference between observation of music as an object of study like any other, and participation in music as a practice that can change our relationships with the world. The former has tended to dominate reflection on the status of music, often at the expense of the latter. The other aspect of resistance to semanticization relates in the modern period to the need for forms of expression that can articulate what dominant cultural forms obscure. Why this is the case will become apparent in a moment.

Musical formalism, of the kind that derives from Eduard Hanslick's 1854 *On the Musically Beautiful,* is one version of an anti-semanticizing approach. Mark Evan Bonds (2006, 108) suggests why this is:

> Hanslick's treatise soon became . . . the rallying point for all those who sought to protect instrumental music—above all, Beethoven's symphonies—against encroachments from the world of politics. The musical work, by this line of thought, is autonomous and nonreferential; while it may be susceptible to differing interpretations, these perceptions have nothing to do with the work's true essence.

In relation to such opposed concepts as the hermeneutic approaches in the New Musicology and some versions of formalism, does one come down on one side or the other with respect to music's autonomy, in the name of establishing a true theory? Or is there an alternative that does not lead to adopting contradictory positions, and thus to incoherence?

Bonds's point, that what is at stake in formalism is also political, indicates one reason why music resists any attempt to define it as an object by characterizing its inherent properties.[1] The formalist attempt to insist that music does not refer beyond itself is occasioned not least by a need for a sphere of value outside the social and political antagonisms of a nineteenth-century world, where modern capitalism increasingly makes value a solely quantitative matter. Formalism, therefore, actually depends on something beyond the music itself, even as it seeks to make music self-sufficient. The still-contested reception of Beethoven makes this evident: as Toscanini reportedly said of the *Eroica Symphony:* "To some it's Napoleon, to some it's philosophical struggle, to me it's allegro con brio."

The desire for music to be self-sufficient is also echoed in the changes in listening during Hanslick's period, when, as Heinrich Besseler and others have noted, musical listening can become "mystical immersion in the work" (Besseler 1978, 153), and concerts of so-called art music often become the preserve of certain sections of bourgeois society. However, in a reversal characteristic of many historical responses to music, the anti-political stance in some formalist conceptions subsequently helps give rise to counterreactions, epitomized by twentieth-century attempts to semanticize music in the name of racial or political ideologies, which took their most extreme form in Nazi Germany and the Soviet Union.

Why one might balk at such uses of music is itself part of the question of how to characterize music: there are, after all, cases where we may think that music is aptly employed for ideological and political purposes. The role of jazz in the Civil Rights Movement suggests that music can be a force for achieving positive social and political change. Importantly, this case does not rely on the explicit semanticization of music, for reasons having to do with the connection between music and freedom, considered later in this chapter.

At the same time, none of these connections to politics is necessarily an objection to what can be learned from focusing on music in "formalist" terms—that is, those concerned with structural, harmonic, rhythmic, melodic, and other features, rather than on music as primarily a social practice linked to politics, institutions, social/sexual roles, etc. Some of the political mobilization of music in the Soviet Union, while condemning "formalism," still relied on evaluations that made sense only if they also related to formal aspects of the music in question. Moreover, musical performance without some analysis of formal issues is likely to make little sense, as Adorno (1982) shows.

So, can the contradictions here be resolved by showing how music can be self-sufficient and yet can also have ideological and other significance? In one sense, this is unobjectionable: music, like most cultural phenomena, can function in ways that might seem contradictory at first, because a different context will change the significance of the phenomenon. However, that fact offers few resources for getting at why music can divide people to the point where lives are at risk because they see it in conflicting terms. Just saying that the Soviet authorities were mistaken because they did not realize that, qua object of analysis, music involves an inherent formal autonomy does not explain very much.

Essentialism and Normativity

Arguably, all this returns us to the initial definitional problem because it can seem hard even to agree on what "music" is at all, which can be precisely what leads to author-itarian stipulations. Furthermore, radical sonic innovation is often accompanied by people insisting, "That's not music," when reacting to late Beethoven, Stravinsky's *Sacre du printemps*, Ornette Coleman, John Cage, rap, etc. So, does each person just have her or his own idea of what music is, there being no specifiable common ground referred to by the term? If that were the case, though, there could not even be any debate about the problem of the content of the term. As Schleiermacher puts it: "Disagreement per se presupposes the acknowledgement of the sameness of an object, as well as there being the relationship of thinking to being at all" (1998, 132). People talk about music, and what they talk about exists, but the question is how to negotiate the further fact that they differ over what they think it is.

Trying to establish what music is gives rise to a series of theoretical questions that form the preserve of significant parts of modern philosophy. Kant denies that there are real definitions, apart from axioms in mathematics: "[M]y explanation [of a concept] can better be termed a declaration (of my project) than a definition of an object" (Kant 1968a, B757, A729). He therefore prefers to use the term "exposition" when dealing with empirical concepts. So what would an "exposition" of the concept of music look like? Here, a further methodological point emerges—namely, the very fact that, particularly in the modern period, radical innovation in music often proceeds in terms of what was regarded as extra-musical becoming intra-musical and precludes any exposition that seeks to map out the final scope, even of a dynamically conceived concept of music.

A resolution of questions about essence seems unlikely anyway, given what we know from the history of philosophy. Important strands of modern philosophy, like pragmatism, actually seek to circumvent questions of essence by replacing them with questions about how the content of concepts is established by the social use of terms. From the latter perspective, the question of music becomes "normative," where use of the term is something to be justified in what Robert Brandom calls the "game of giving reasons" (see Brandom 1994). What complicates the issue, as it does throughout the history of modern aesthetics, is that debate about the norms relevant to music also concerns subjective affects—without which the thing in question loses a vital part of its content—but seeks justifications that have claims to objectivity. Even if we drop the idea of music having an essence at all, in order not to get entangled in an apparently endless philosophical debate, we are left with normative disagreements.

Is "music," then, best approached from a normative standpoint? Histories of music can be written in terms of norms and their transgressions and transformations, such that many kinds of music become possible only through their opposition to previous instantiations of musical norms. This already suggests problems with an essentialist conception. The fact that the Council of Trent laid down restrictions to prevent virtuoso organists embellishing sacred music can be read in terms of the ideological/religious aims of the Counter-Reformation, thus involving something extramusical. However, it can also be seen as offering new challenges to composers and players to make intramusical sense while adhering to the restrictions.

Something analogous takes place in relation to late European Romantic music with the emergence of the movements in neoclassicism known as "Neue Sachlichkeit," and "Gebrauchsmusik," against what are seen as overblown, worn-out, or reactionary forms of expression. The new norms in both cases are closely linked to other ideological domains, and the point at which the issue becomes "purely musical" is hard, if not impossible, to establish, because the very status of "music" is itself once again in question.

The complexity of the political implications of twentieth-century moves against Romantic expressivism rules out any straightforward links between the musical and the political. However, there is no denying that the new kinds of composition and performance would not have become what they were, had economic, social, and political pressures not demanded new kinds of symbolic response. Denying that World War I and its aftermath had a major effect on Western music is as indefensible as denying its effects on philosophy, theology, or the other arts.

NEGATION

An instructive point does emerge here that has been implicit in what was said previously: music can be said to be constituted by differing kinds of negation, both in its immanent development, where one stylistic or technical norm is replaced or altered by another that is opposed to it, and in its ontological status, where what was extra-musical can become intra-musical. In the modern period, a link between philosophical reflection on negation and music becomes manifest, which underlines in another way how the sense of music is inseparable from its contexts.

In a conception that becomes crucial for Georg Wilhelm Friedrich Hegel and German idealism, Baruch Spinoza saw negation as what makes things determinate. Particular things are identifiable by *their not* being other things: only the whole is positive, because parts inherently lack completion. When applied to the internal workings of music, this means that the notes or sounds in a piece of music gain their identity in terms of their relations to the notes or sounds that they are *not*—either because they are of a different pitch, duration, intensity, or volume, or because they occur at different times within the piece.

Adequate production and understanding of music depend on how these negations are integrated into a totality that makes sense. When notes in a piece are wrong, because they make no sense in the context in which they occur, they can make us aware of what being right is.[2] In isolation, relations between notes—for example, those in the minor key involving the interval of a minor third (which is determinate by not being a second, major third, etc.)—are just discrete data with no aesthetic significance. In the context of Beethoven's Fifth or Bruckner's Eighth Symphony, the resolution of the tension generated by the use of the minor key at the beginning of the symphony, as well as by the use of the major third in the coda of the finale, creates a kind of sense that is in one respect specific to music.

Adorno argues, though, that in the Beethoven of the heroic period, this kind of cumulative linking of negations into a culminating resolution is paralleled in Hegel's philosophical system, where "the true is the whole," because isolated negative elements make proper sense only when integrated into a dynamic, philosophically articulated totality. This link between music and philosophy might seem like stretching an analogy, but the conjunction of a specific kind of dynamic music, epitomized by Beethoven's technique of "developing variation," and a philosophy that seeks to understand the logic of change, in which what things are shifts in relation to their contexts and the movement of history, is more than coincidental.

At a time when, in the wake of the French Revolution, political and social orders are transformed, conceptual and expressive forms become dynamized in new ways, leading to some of the most important music there is. At the same time, reducing the music just to this parallel would involve semanticization of the kind questioned in the previous discussion. So how are we to keep a degree of autonomy for music at the same time as we sustain its evident connections to the world in which it emerges—connections without which the cultural importance of music in the modern period would be hard to understand? In Ernst Cassirer's terms, music is a "symbolic form" (Cassirer 1994), whose nature depends on what it articulates that other symbolic forms do not. By attending to where and how discriminations are made between music and non-music, it is possible to give a sense of what music means that both has a degree of conceptual determinacy and leaves space for the specific non-discursive sense that emerges from music.

Music and Language

It is here that the questionability of philosophical attempts to concentrate, in the manner of analytical philosophy, on conceptual analysis of "music" becomes most apparent. In the period from around the middle of the eighteenth century in Europe, there is a widespread change in thinking, whose effects make it clear that seeking the essence of music is likely to obscure the extent to which what music *is* depends on changing relationships between forms of expression and articulation, and on changes in the relationship of humankind to nature. When later, more radical approaches to music in the avant-garde emerge—such as that of John Cage, exemplified in his claim that "one may give up the desire to control sound, clear his mind of music, and set about discovering means to let sounds be themselves rather than vehicles for man-made theories or expressions of human sentiments" (Cage 1973, 10)—the fluidity of the concept of music that starts to develop in the eighteenth century becomes very apparent. The underlying changes that lead in this direction are perhaps best approached in terms of changes in conceptions of language in the eighteenth century, whose implications have, as Charles Taylor has argued (Taylor 2016), yet to be fully grasped, even in much contemporary philosophy.

Underlying these changes is a widespread shift away from the idea of what Hilary Putnam has termed a "ready-made world," that is, a world with a pre-existing, perhaps divinely bestowed essence, and toward a sense that what the world is also depends on what we think and do. The "world" need not be thought of solely as the object of knowledge of the natural sciences, but can instead, in the manner of Heidegger, be thought of as the changing context in which things mean something. This context is prior to the objective knowledge sought by the sciences because things have to show up in the world as needing to be explained before we can start to develop theories with which to explain them. The point about the shift from a "ready-made world" is that it is not just the product of theoretical deliberation, but instead occurs in ways which we cannot fully describe in theoretical form, not least because our ways of theorizing about it are themselves in part a product of what has occurred.

Something analogous applies to language itself, which, so to speak, happens to us, and which, although it can be changed by creative initiative, also both normatively restricts how it may be used and changes in ways that are beyond individual initiative. In both language and music, the basic repertoire of sounds and words is often not radically altered (rather, it is usually the manner in which the material is combined that is altered), but what it means is altered. Two related phenomena can help explain what is at issue here: the change in the relationship of people in Europe to wild nature in the eighteenth century and the moves against the idea that language is essentially a means of representing a world whose essence is immanent within it.

In the former case, a world that had been seen predominantly in terms of the relationship of humankind to the divine, where the natural world was significant in relation to religious and other concerns, comes to be seen as valuable in itself, independent of human instrumental goals. The emergence of landscape painting, which no longer makes the human figure or a religious or historical scene the main object, is one sign of this, as is the rapid musical development of "autonomous" musical forms, like the sonata, out of forms which had a social or religious function.

The crucial point here in relation to the changing status of music is that value comes to be seen in what is not expressible in verbal language—hence also the emergence of interest in the sublime and its frequent connection to music by E. T. A. Hoffmann and others from the eighteenth century onward (see Bowie 2003). From being a reflection of the mathematically ordered structure of the universe, as it is in the traditions deriving from Pythagoras and Plato, music can now be an expression of new forms of connection to nature that see nature neither in theological terms nor as an object to be measured and controlled.

In the case of language, the moves, on the part of Johann Gottfried Herder, Johann Georg Hamann, Friedrich D. E. Schleiermacher, Wilhelm von Humboldt, and others, away from what Charles Taylor (2016) terms "designative" theories, in which language is primarily a means of designating pre-existing objects, toward an "expressive" view, in which language is part of what constitutes what the world is, raise in a new way the relationship of language to music. This move puts in question any fixed division between the two, to the point where neither can be given a discrete unified sense, because the musical is part of the linguistic, and the linguistic part of the musical, both of which belong to the interconnected repertoire of forms in which human existence is expressed. Rhythm, tone, gesture, timing, etc., all play a role in the sense of both linguistic and musical articulation and expression.[3]

It is therefore unsurprising that the emergence of these theories of language is accompanied by changes in the way that music is regarded, moving from largely being seen as a subordinate art that accompanies social activity or religious observance, to being seen by some as the highest art—especially in its textless form—an idea later reflected in Walter Pater's dictum that "All art constantly aspires toward the condition of music" (see Dahlhaus 1978; Bowie 2003, 2007). A shift as radical as this, where something non-conceptual comes to be seen as more significant than what can be rendered in conceptual form, is a sign of a new kind of relationship between humankind and nature. The object of study in music cannot be isolated in the form of a work, a score, or a performance, without much of the sense that emerges from music being obscured. Research in acoustics, psychology, biology, and other sciences contributes to the understanding of music by conceptualizing it in more differentiated ways, but failure to consider the most fundamental ways in which music makes sense can mean that those forms of objectifying research lose sight of what first makes music an object of research at all. If this is right, music poses a challenge to the scientistic view present in much contemporary culture.

MUSIC AND FREEDOM

The idea that music is "auditory cheesecake," proposed by evolutionary biologist Steven Pinker, because "the direct effect of music is sheer, pointless pleasure," blocks any possibility of understanding the complexity of the history of music. It also makes it impossible to see how music itself may enable us to understand and inhabit the world as a context of meaning, which scientific research, seeking causal laws governing particulars, cannot explain. The metaphysical assumption on the part of Pinker is that what meaningful things, like music, really are can be reduced to an interaction between the brain and the world that psychology can describe in terms of biological laws, such as those which govern phenomena like the pleasure caused by auditory stimuli.

But in that case, as German philosopher Albrecht Wellmer, a pupil of Adorno who has written extensively about music, argues, there is no way of accounting for the need for novelty, which fuels not only artistic production, but also new scientific descriptions, where "something new comes into the world, whose necessary conditions can admittedly be researched in the form of previous knowledge, of ways of looking at problems, of social constellations, psychic dispositions or biographical preconditions, but which cannot be causally reduced to such conditions" (Wellmer 2009, 224). He maintains that there is a link between art and freedom that does not depend on the metaphysical debate about the existence or non-existence of free will: "That the new happens shows that the scope of freedom of the human mind is not exhausted by that of the free will; rather, the freedom of the will presupposes this other space of freedom, which is bound to language. The latter manifests itself not least in the sphere of art" (ibid.). How does this apply to music?

As we saw in the previous discussion, one way of approaching music is expressed in normative terms: without some way of judging or just feeling what "getting it right" means, claims that something is or is not music make no sense; similarly, language depends on fulfilling normative demands to be language. At the same time, the dominant norms in music and language can become fetters on expression, leading to them ceasing to "say" anything, and thus to the need for liberation from those norms. Such liberation cannot itself function in terms of existing norms, which means that the result has to be new, in the sense indicated by Wellmer, going beyond existing norms of expression. In this respect, music can function as a kind of seismograph that registers social developments before they become explicit within a society. The Second Viennese School's radical reform of compositional norms opened up space for more adequate responses to the new psychological, social, and political uncertainties of the early twentieth century in Europe. The School showed that the limits of what could make musical sense could be transcended in the name of an open-ended revision of the ways that sonic material can be organized to encompass extreme states and situations. For instance, jazz's intensification of rhythm, incorporation of expressive vocal techniques into instrumental playing, and extension of the possibilities of improvisatory freedom act as a counter to rigid and repressive cultural and political norms. In both cases, the resistance that such music encounters is a sign of how it challenges received assumptions about what can make sense, opening up a new sense that can change how the world is seen and experienced.

Underlying this is a further aspect of changes in modernity, illustrated by the following remark about an influential philosopher writing in the period of Beethoven. Dieter Henrich (1987, 61) has suggested:

> Fichte was the first to arrive at the conviction that all previous philosophy had remained at a distance from the life and self-consciousness of humankind. It had had ontological categories dictated to it which were taken from the language in which we communicate about things, their qualities and their changes. With these categories philosophy had then investigated powers and capacities of the human soul. It was therefore fundamentally unable to reach the experiences of this soul, the processes of consciousness, the structure and flow of its experiences and thoughts.

Music's non-propositional status allows it to be in touch with impulses, affects, and moods that are repressed or inadequately expressed in other forms of social expression and articulation. Indeed, music can influence the nature of moods and feelings, transforming emotions like sadness or anger by incorporating their expression into forms that transcend them. Music can therefore embody a particular kind of freedom that acknowledges negativity while seeking to transcend it. Nietzsche's *The Birth of Tragedy out of the Spirit of Music*, which ponders why drama based on the worst things that one can imagine in a community, from matricide to incest, formed the basis of a successful culture in Greece, sums up the way in which music often thrives on the transformation of negativity—Schubert reportedly said that there was no joyful music. One does not have to feel sad listening to sad music (although one can); rather, this music changes how we can relate to sadness by imbuing it with a particular kind of sense.

Despite its questionable aspects, for example, with respect to jazz, Adorno's criticisms of the "culture industry" and its reduction of expressive resources to a series of preformed patterns, in a manner related to the way that objects in modern capitalism can become just exchangeable commodities, suggest the need for significant art to respond critically to social circumstances. Expressive novelty involves a "space of freedom" in which existing norms can be transformed. As Wellmer suggests, freedom in this sense precedes the issue of freedom of the will. Without the pre-existing normative content of expressive freedom within real social contexts, that motivates people to respond to their world, there would be nothing at stake in freedom of the will. The exercise of the will would be a random doing of one thing rather than another, either because of a causal history or because one can choose, even though what is chosen does not actually matter (see Bowie 2013, chapter 5). Norms have to be anchored in concrete motivations that make things matter, so that exercise of the will generates sense in the social and psychological context in which it takes place.

In challenging existing musical norms and establishing new ones in the name of something that cannot be fully explained in conceptual terms, music manifests a freedom that cannot be conjured away by seeking to show, in the manner of Pinker, that it actually depends on something else. Where norms can be conceptually explicit, as they are for instance in politics, the sense of freedom as self-determination, which is central to modern conceptions of freedom since Rousseau and Kant, can be deceptive because adherence to norms may be a result of unconscious social influences.

Conceptually explicit norms routinely generate dissent among members of a society; music, in contrast, sometimes offers space where people who disagree on explicit ideas can still find common ground beyond what is verbally articulated (Barenboim and Said 2004). Ideological pressure for conformity evidently also often plays a role in music—hence the idea of the culture industry—but music can still advert to possibilities of freedom that result from liberation from convention, as well as the creation of new forms of sense out of what in other respects may resist having sense made of it. These forms can be shared by those who do not share political, philosophical, or social views.

The investment in seeking not to be bound by the cultural given that is present in creative musical production testifies to an idea of freedom, of the kind characterized by Schelling (see Bowie 1993, 2015). This acknowledges that freedom is empty unless it has a basis that it opposes in order to realize itself: one can become aware of freedom only by being aware of being inhibited by something that one is driven to overcome. Even at the level of seeking technical mastery of an instrument or vocal technique, this freedom plays a role: the effort made in gaining that mastery is in the name of transcending limitations that inhibit the capacity for expression.

In modern Western music, there is a recurrent awareness that reliance on what has already been done in music involves a failure to fulfill the potential generated by the decline of traditional authority and the emergence of modern individualism. The technical and expressive development of Western classical music, particularly from Bach onward, which is then echoed in the rapid way in which the history of jazz unfolds, depends on forms of social causality that are vital objects of musicological research, but the sense made by that music cannot be grasped wholly in such terms, as its continuing appeal makes clear.

Rhythm, Nature, and Culture

Instead of thinking of music as an object—a score, a performance, or a recording can be described in objective terms, but that is not what makes it music—music is better understood in terms that incorporate the internal movement of musical events, the historical movement of inclusion and exclusion of types of sound (and silence), and the mobile relationships between performers, listeners, and the world which are involved in music.

The borders between the musical and the non-musical play an essential role in the workings of human culture. Human responses to music, however, do not just testify to the development of more complex forms of signification than are present in the animal kingdom; they also reveal a darker underside to the motivations associated with music. This darker side relates to the danger of forms of non-conceptual expression that can be used to generate uncritical collective assent, for example, in military music or music associated with reactionary and authoritarian social movements. Such worries are sometimes also, for example, expressed in relation to certain pieces by Beethoven, such as the last movement of the Seventh Symphony, with its links to French Revolutionary music. The need to establish an appropriate understanding of the relationship between critical conceptual analysis of music and the acknowledgment of music's power, both positive and negative, which is based on its lack of dependence on conceptuality, remains unfulfilled in many areas of the study of music. Music poses questions about our nature that are not answered by scientific analysis of that nature; this is because what is "natural" for us can be made sense of only in relation to what is "cultural."

Take the natural phenomenon of birdsong: it is not produced as music, because music is a cultural product dependent on social intercourse. But a bird's song can be heard as music and used in music in widely differing ways. Whatever the full biological function of birdsong is, it is only when it is incorporated into a cultural context that it definitely makes sense to call it music, because the meaning of music evidently goes beyond a biologically given stimulus and response. At the same time, the element of imitation and improvisation present in some birdsong, or the exchange of playful sonic signs and gestures among higher mammals, suggests that the borderline between the merely mechanical and natural, and what exceeds this in the direction of what becomes cultural communication and creation, may not be straightforward.

The debate over whether any non-human animals can be said to have language further indicates the complexity of the issues here. The scope of the term "language," as Wittgenstein shows in his later work, should clearly extend beyond words, to gestures and to music, and thus to any symbolic articulation that can change our relationships to the world and other living beings. Whatever is really the case concerning language—and a definitive answer would have to deal with Wittgenstein's claim that one "cannot describe the essence of language in language" (Wittgenstein 1999 3, 30)—the continuity between the natural phenomenon of birdsong and the cultural phenomenon of music indicates something significant.

The question of what this continuity means, however, is a difficult one. Hindemith and others claimed that biological features of hearing and mathematical relations between pitches meant that tonality itself is a natural phenomenon. However, this view fails to account for the historicality of norms that determine which pitch relations can be musical pitch relations. Tonality, or the lack of it, is not always decisive anyway because certain kinds of music for percussion, where pitch is irrelevant in some respects, clearly count as music in many contexts. If one is seeking links between the shifting domains of the natural and the cultural with respect to music, they are best found with respect to rhythm.

John Dewey maintains, "What is not so generally perceived is that every uniformity and regularity of change in nature is a rhythm. The terms 'natural law' and 'natural rhythm' are synonymous" (Dewey 1980, 149). The underlying issue, here again, involves a major philosophical issue—namely, how things can be identified at all. A random phenomenon, like a noise that could occur as an element of a rhythmic beat, can recur over time without generating any significance: this changes if it becomes a rhythm. Schelling therefore maintains that rhythm is "introduction of unity into multiplicity" and "transformation of a succession which is in itself meaningless into a significant one," and that it constitutes "the music in music" because music depends on sense emerging from successions of sounds becoming linked (Schelling, 1856–1861, I/5, all 492).

Such significance also depends on there being something—a subject—that apprehends the succession as unified, which therefore must itself remain the same. On the one hand, then, rhythm relies on a subject that apprehends patterns (often unconsciously) as involving meaningful identities between temporally separate phenomena. On the other hand, without the occurrence of uniformity and regularity in nature itself, including the subject's own nature (its heartbeat, breathing, and other functions that work according to natural necessity), there would be nothing for it to apprehend as rhythm and be able to develop in new ways.

Conceptual sense consists of the production of identity from difference, enabling things to be classified, taken as true, manipulated, etc. Musical sense, which is based on rhythm of all kinds—any form of meaningful repetition is a kind of rhythm, as Dewey's and Schelling's remarks suggest—involves the apprehension of identities, but these do not have to be assigned a determinate significance, as repeated moves in a game do not, because the sense that they make occurs in the actual playing of the game.

Something similar applies to metaphors in verbal language, especially in poetry, where what counts is the play of what the metaphor can bring to light, which does not equate to literal meaning. The effects of rhythm are also somatic: the body, as we have seen, has its own rhythms, and behavior based on rhythmic play is essential to childhood development. Rhythm can locate us in a world by structuring time in ways that give pleasure, in which we can become absorbed, and which give coherence to experience through the play of anticipation and fulfillment. This can go to the point of rhythm involving suspension of certain aspects of conscious awareness.

Phenomena relating to rhythm, because they cannot definitively be said to lie either side of the line between the cultural and the natural, suggest how music poses questions about understanding humankind's place in nature. The kind of sense that music articulates precedes the conceptual sense that fixes aspects of how nature is understood in an objective manner, and this helps to understand the relative ease with which music can be appreciated in cross-cultural contexts. The historical dynamic between the concepts of "culture" and "nature" involves the idea that conceptual ordering is vital to human existence, because of the need to control nature. But the division can, as claimed by Nietzsche, and Horkheimer and Adorno in *Dialectic of Enlightenment*, also become a form of repression.

These issues suggest why music takes on a new elevated status in the work of the Romantics, the early (and sometimes the later) Nietzsche, and others at the same time as wild nature is also revalued as a counter to the growth of the technological capacity to gain control of natural processes. The new kinds of objectifying relationships to nature that lead to modern technology and new forms of regimented industrial labor can damage other forms of contact with both external and internal nature. Music's connection to emotional life, and to our impulses and aspects of our somatic existence, opens

up and keeps open dimensions of sense that are not reducible to how we verbally articulate these dimensions, and thus can oppose some of the reifying aspects of modernity.

Identifying and analyzing emotions in psychological and other research is clearly
an important way to come to greater self-understanding. The expressive possibilities
in music, however, can enable us to experience emotions that did not exist before the
music that discloses them. That is a reason why in modernity—where, even as it also
depends on collective symbolic forms, new sense, as suggested in the remark by Henrich
on Fichte cited previously, tends to be generated at the level of the individual subject—
the drive for new expressive resources exemplified by innovation in music is often more
emphatic than in the pre-modern era.

Once these new expressive resources emerge, they can become the object of empirical research, but without the prior level of sense that they embody, there would be no
motivation to try to objectify them. This prior level of sense is most evident in the difference we have discussed, between analytical and other observations of music as objects
of research, and participation in the performance or reception of music.[4] The fact that
the latter cannot be wholly replaced by the former, even though elements of each are
involved in the other (see Bowie 2013, chapter 5), can give rise to questions concerning
how we conceive of the very nature of thought.

THE PHILOSOPHY OF MUSIC

The core issue here is the sense that music is understood as conveying, as well as how
it is conveyed. Often, the fact that music is capable of only a small degree of the representation of the objective world characteristic of verbal language frames the judgment on that sense. In Thomas Mann's novel *The Magic Mountain* (1923), the extremist
Enlightenment believer in rational progress, Settembrini, famously contends that
music is "politically suspect" because it has no clear meaning and is linked to aspects
of human existence that escape rational control. Similarly, in Hegel's *Aesthetics*, music
without words is assigned an inferior status because of its lack of determinate meaning.
For Hegel, purely "musical music" has to free itself from the "determinacy of the word,"
but instrumental, wordless music will appeal only to experts, who will enjoy it because
they can compare the music that they hear with "rules and laws [they are] familiar with"
(Hegel 1965, 322). This point, of course, does not do justice to Hegel's view of music (for a
full discussion, see Bowie 2003, 2007).

Such views point in the direction of a philosophy of music in the "objective genitive," where music is the object of philosophical and other explanation and is very often
regarded as a mystery, or as inferior in sense, rather than as something that may convey
sense that concepts do not (see Bowie 2007). What can be termed the philosophy of
music in the "subjective genitive," in contrast, looks at the idea that philosophy may
emerge from music itself. Rather than being a mystery whose solution is delegated to
philosophy, music is an expressive resource that brings its own kind of sense into the

world. It is clear from the inseparability of the musical element from verbal language, that sense in the latter depends on elements of the former, but also that the sense of the former can be augmented by the ways in which it is talked about.

Music can be used in this respect to interrogate some prevalent directions in contemporary philosophy. In the wake of the orientation of such philosophy toward the methods of the natural sciences, analytical philosophers very often make conceptual clarity the overriding philosophical virtue. Now, it evidently makes no sense to advocate lack of clarity in areas where clarity can be attained and may be lacking. The aim of philosophical clarity, however, is not matched by philosophy's actually arriving at definitive theories that eliminate indeterminacy; indeed, we have already been observing this with respect to "music" itself in this chapter.

The mistake, as Carl Dahlhaus points out with respect to music, is to assume that its indeterminacy constitutes an inherent failing: "Indeterminacy through lack of an object and determinacy in the sense of differentiation do not exclude each other at all; and one might even maintain that musical expression gains in connotations what it loses in denotations" (Dahlhaus 1988, 333). Dahlhaus is proposing something analogous to what Kant means by an "aesthetic idea" (which had a significant influence on how music was discussed in the Romantic era, see Neubauer 1986): "by an aesthetic idea I mean that representation of the imagination which gives much cause for thought without any determinate thought, i.e. concept, being able to be adequate to it, which consequently no language can completely attain and make comprehensible" (Kant 1968b: B190, A193). Kant sees this issue mainly in cognitive terms—aesthetic ideas allow the cognitive faculty to play with different judgments without having to assent to them—but the scope for a philosophy of music in the subjective genitive is wider than is contained in the notion of an aesthetic idea. This takes us back to the issue of observation and participation.

Heinrich Besseler, who was a pupil of Heidegger and helped establish the idea of *Gebrauchsmusik*, asserts, "The musical originally becomes accessible to us as a manner/melody [in the original: *Weise*, which combines the older sense of 'melody' with the more general idea of 'way' or 'manner'—one might translate this as 'mode'] of human existence [*des menschlichen Daseins*]" (Besseler 1978, 45). Besseler is referring here to Heidegger's use of the term *Dasein*, which aims to circumvent the history of philosophical and anthropological attempts to establish the essence of what man is. Rather than having a definable essence, *Dasein* is "that entity which in its being is concerned with its being" (Heidegger 1979, 12).

The open-endedness and indeterminacy of Heidegger's characterization of *Dasein* is precisely the point: we approach a future whose nature cannot be determined in advance, because, at least in some respects, we make it, as it matters to us. Besseler therefore makes music, like verbal language, part of what we are, suspending the dualistic views that place us apart from music as an object of investigation, in order to capture the way in which our existence is partly constituted by the musical. This can be exemplified in the kind of understanding that is achieved in reflective participation in music. Conductors who convey how they want something to go by a gesture or a look, rather than words, are understood when they get the result that they are striving for, and they themselves may understand what they want only by the action that they feel impelled to carry out in order to get it.

There is here a striving for a kind of sense whose possibility is testified to when we fail to achieve it. Indeed, as in Artur Schnabel's remark that there is some music that is better than it can be played, rightness can be a regulative ideal—something that motivates us to strive for it while never being actually present. Getting it right in the most important sense, then, is not meeting a preconceived, conceptually articulated standard, but rather making something happen that makes maximal intersubjective sense.

In this context, Adorno characterizes music (and other art) as "judgementless synthesis" (Adorno 2009, 327)—that is, the creation of sense that cannot be converted into judgment, even though it involves something akin to what takes place in cognition (and can have effects on cognition). This occurs in all the arts, but music's relative lack of representational content and direct link to somatic and affective existence, as well as to the mobile nature of self-consciousness, have meant that it is associated most readily with dimensions that are often underplayed in philosophy. There is no standard for getting it right external to engagement with the practice of the art itself, but this does not make things arbitrary or "subjective," as too many views would have it. Music generates cultures of evaluation that are inseparable from participation in the practice of music itself. Norms and assessments constantly change in these cultures, but the music that sustains itself through such changes, retaining its power to affect people, tells us something vital by the way in which it renews its significance in different contexts.

In this respect, music has its own kind of truth, which is akin to what Heidegger adverts to in his discussions of truth and world disclosure (Wrathall 2011). Anything that is apprehended as music by a listener makes some kind of sense—however questionable that sense may be—but the sense disclosed by great music has a significance that can be termed "philosophical" because the world manifests itself substantially differently in its light, revealing aspects that would not emerge otherwise.

One way of suggesting how this is the case is to question certain versions of how cognition is conceived. Anthony Cascardi suggests: "Feeling nonetheless remains cognitive in a deeper sense; affect possesses what Heidegger would describe . . . as 'world-disclosive' power" (Cascardi 1999, 50–51). Music should not, though, be seen exclusively in relation to its emotional power: its combination of structural, somatic, mathematical, and other aspects with its expressive possibilities offers both affective and other patterns of sense that enable people to inhabit the world more meaningfully.

Music is a legitimate object of the game of giving reasons, but limiting how we understand music to the attempt to explain it in objective terms can obscure some of the ways that it engages so many people in so many different situations. The lack of consensus about music in philosophy is part of the general lack of consensus about major issues in philosophy. As a participatory practice, however, music can make sense of the world in ways that philosophy sometimes does not, offering forms of communication that can bring people together where argument and assertion divide them. At the same time, though, music can also give rise to serious divisions between people, akin to those that arise over religious and ideological matters.

This ambivalence lies at the heart of why music resists definitive characterizations. Daniel Barenboim talks of music, which "is so clearly able to teach you so many things," being also able to "serve as a means of escape from precisely those things" (Barenboim and Said 2004, 122). This dialectical remark captures the idea that thinking about music inherently involves contradictions.

I have mainly used thinkers from the German tradition to try to illustrate this point, but I hope that my remarks can help make sense of music of the most widely varying kinds, from jazz, to folk music, to rock, to so-called classical music. Music can enable one to cope with the world by incorporating and transforming precisely what can make the world so painful. By the same token, it can seduce one away from the world when analytical attention to the world may be what is demanded.

What makes the former so important is precisely what makes the latter possible; but the latter does not mean that music cannot play a role in rationally based transformation in the world by keeping open channels of communication and making sense where other means of making sense may be lacking. Rather than seeking a definitive objective characterization, then, engagement with music in both theoretical and participatory terms should respond to the ways in which the contradictory nature of music shapes our understanding of ourselves and the world.

ACKNOWLEDGMENTS

This article was written with the support of a Leverhulme Foundation Major Research Fellowship.

NOTES

1. The idea of music's properties dominates much discussion in the analytical philosophy of music (see, for instance, Kivy 1993, 1997, 2002).
2. What counts as wrong is subject to massive historical transformation: jazz history can be written in terms of making wrong notes in one style sound right in another.
3. It is remarkable how much the focus on language in much analytical philosophy is exclusively on the semantic dimension, when the social significance and effect of actual utterances and linguistic performances depend to a considerable extent on aspects of language connected to music.
4. The current debates over performance as research indicate how this difference is vital to reflection on how music is studied.

WORKS CITED

Adorno, Theodor W. 2009. *Ästhetik* [1958/9]. Frankfurt: Suhrkamp.
Adorno, Theodor W. 1982. "On the Problem of Musical Analysis." Translated by Max Paddison. *Music Analysis* 1: 169–187.

Barenboim, Daniel, and Edward Said. 2004. *Parallels and Paradoxes*. London: Bloomsbury.

Besseler, Heinrich. 1978. *Aufsätze zur Musikästhetik und Musikgeschichte*. Leipzig: Reclam.

Bonds, Mark Evan. 2006. *Music as Thought: Listening to the Symphony in the Age of Beethoven*. Princeton, NJ: Princeton University Press.

Bowie, Andrew. 1993. *Schelling and Modern European Philosophy*, London: Routledge.

Bowie, Andrew. 2003. *Aesthetics and Subjectivity: From Kant to Nietzsche*. Manchester: Manchester University Press.

Bowie, Andrew. 2007. *Music, Philosophy, and Modernity*. Cambridge: Cambridge University Press.

Bowie, Andrew. 2013. *Adorno and the Ends of Philosophy*. Cambridge: Polity Press.

Bowie, Andrew. 2015. "Nature and Freedom in Schelling and Adorno." In *Interpreting Schelling*, edited by Lara Ostaric, 180–199. Cambridge: Cambridge University Press.

Brandom, Robert. 1994. *Making It Explicit*. Cambridge, MA: Harvard University Press.

Cage, John. 1973. *Silence: Lectures and Writings*. Middletown, CT: Wesleyan University Press.

Cascardi, Anthony J. 1999. *Consequences of Enlightenment*. Cambridge: Cambridge University Press.

Cassirer, Ernst. 1994. *Philosophie der symbolischen Formen*. Darmstadt: Wissenschaftliche Buchgesellschaft.

Dewey, John. 1980. *Art as Experience*. New York: Perigee.

Dahlhaus, Carl. 1978. *Die Idee der absoluten Musik*. Munich and Kassel: dtv.

Dahlhaus, Carl. 1988. *Klassische und romantische Musikästhetik*. Laaber: Laaber.

Hegel, Georg Wilhelm Friedrich. 1965. *Ästhetik*. Edited by Friedrich Bassenge. 2 vols. Berlin and Weimar: Aufbau.

Heidegger, Martin. 1979. *Sein und Zeit*. Tübingen: Niemeyer.

Henrich, Dieter. 1987. *Konzepte*. Frankfurt am Main: Suhrkamp.

Kant, Immanuel. 1968a *Kritik der reinen Vernunft*. Werkausgabe III and IV. Frankfurt am Main: Suhrkamp.

Kant, Immanuel. 1968b *Kritik der Urteilskraft*. Werkausgabe X. Frankfurt am Main: Suhrkamp.

Kivy, Peter. 1993. *The Fine Art of Repetition*. Cambridge: Cambridge University Press.

Kivy, Peter. 1997. *Philosophies of Arts: An Essay in Differences*. Cambridge: Cambridge University Press.

Kivy, Peter. 2002. *Introduction to a Philosophy of Music*. Oxford: Clarendon Press.

Neubauer, John. 1986. *The Emancipation of Music from Language: Departure from Mimesis in Eighteenth-Century Aesthetics*. New Haven, CT: Yale University Press.

Schelling, Friedrich Wilhelm Joseph. 1856–1861. *Sämmtliche Werke*. Edited by Karl F. A. Schelling. II Abtheilung Bde. 1–4. Stuttgart: Cotta.

Schleiermacher, Friedrich. 1998. *"Hermeneutics and Criticism" and Other Writings*. Translated by Andrew Bowie. Cambridge: Cambridge University Press.

Taylor, Charles. 2016. *The Language Animal*. Cambridge, MA: Harvard University Press.

Wellmer, Albrecht. 2009. "On Spirit as a Part of Nature." *Constellations* 16: 213–226.

Wittgenstein, Ludwig. 1999. *Wiener Ausgabe*. Vienna and New York: Springer.

Wrathall, Mark A. 2011. *Heidegger and Unconcealment*. Cambridge: Cambridge University Press.

CHAPTER 26

BENEATH IMPROVISATION

VIJAY IYER

IN music studies, the instability of music as a category should be obvious to us by now. We need look no further back than April 2018, when Kendrick Lamar received the Pulitzer Prize in composition, and was met with a sadly predictable chorus of spiteful howls from the predominantly non-black "new music" circles, coalescing around the central claim that hip-hop (or "rap" as it tended to be called in these responses) is "not music."[1] These critics didn't merely say that it was uninteresting music, or music that lacked their preferred formal concerns or didn't align with their compositional values; they hurled it all the way outside of this vast, seemingly bottomless category. It could not be accepted as music within the laws of this universe. One "music scientist" described "the electronic processing" on the recording as "neurologically divergent from music."[2]

This litany also rehearsed the also-sad and too-obvious alignment between music and the category of the human. For we could ask: What kinds of human behaviors are not musical behaviors? The opposite of music, presumably, is noise. It is the appearance of disorder, chaos, incoherence, disunity, disorganization, or meaningless sound. As it happens, hip-hop,[3] early jazz,[4] and the musical practices of enslaved Africans[5] are lumped together in the historical archive of the Euro-American collective memory under the name "noise"—that is, disorder, the unthought, the unplanned, the unwelcome, marked by the apparent absence of the human capacity for reason—and we can be certain that this is the work of the white gaze, in that peculiar zone where the visual and the aural collide: the realm of racialized sound.

The ongoing ejection of Black musics from the category of music aligns directly with the historic and ongoing dehumanization of Black people, the kind that was used to rationalize and justify enslavement, imperialism, plunder, and genocide on the timescale of the past half millennium—what Frank Wilderson (2016) called "the time of the paradigm," the historical frame that we think of as the age of reason and of global capitalism. As scholars like Cedric Robinson (2000), Gayatri Spivak (1999), Achille Mbembe (2017), Sylvia Wynter (2003), and Lisa Lowe (2015) have carefully outlined, we must rethink these historical frames of Reason in terms of Black and Postcolonial reason, capitalism as Racial Capitalism. What is meant by these maneuvers is not that Black and indigenous peoples have their own special, essentially different forms of reason or trade. Rather, it is that the systems of knowledge and exchange that operate in the West, and that influence thought, freedom, power, and wealth distribution around the planet, are constituted from the very beginning by a massive investment in the concepts of race and racial difference. Mbembe's *Critique of Black Reason* (2017) highlights that Reason as you know it is built around a central "vertiginous assemblage" (2) of Blackness in particular and race in general:

> a collection of voices, pronouncements, discourses, forms of knowledge, commentary, and nonsense, whose object is things or people "of African origin". . . From the beginning, its primary activity was fantasizing. . . A range of intermediaries and institutions . . . contributed to the development of this reason and its transformation into common sense and a habitus. . . . its function was to codify the conditions for the appearance and the manifestation of the *racial subject* that would be called the Black Man (*le Nègre*) and, later, within colonialism, the Native (*L'indigène*). . . . [The] goal was to produce the Black Man as a racial subject and site of savage exteriority, who was therefore set up for moral disqualification and practical instrumentalization. We can call this founding narrative the *Western consciousness of Blackness*. In seeking to answer the question "Who is he?" the narrative seeks to name a reality exterior to it and to situate that reality in relationship to an *I* considered to be the center of all meaning. From this perspective, anything that is not identical to that *I* is abnormal. (27–28)

So Black reason is then a name for this central fact about Western thought, namely that it constitutes itself around and in terms of its racial Others; Western consciousness is none other than Western consciousness *of* Blackness.

As the above examples suggest, we have to recognize in our current framework—this convulsive half-millennium of history—that the underlying category of music begins and ends with the category of the human; and, as many scholars, notably Sylvia Wynter (2003; see also Wynter and McKittrick 2015), have pointed out, the category of the human has been primarily organized around enlightened Western rational Man, in relation to which, again, anything that is not identical is abnormal.

Given all of this, I want to apply similar pressure to the category known as improvisation. We might take improvisation to denote that semi-transparent, multi-staged, multi-leveled process through which we sense, perceive, think, decide, and act in real time. But this notion then encompasses such a broad range of behaviors that it becomes difficult to draw a boundary around it, let alone to definitively prove its presence or absence in a given situation. We cannot "know" whether an action is improvised just by observing it in a vacuum. What we seem to be doing, instead of precisely identifying improvisation according to some intrinsic attribute, is allowing cultural and contextual factors to regulate its presence or absence. That is, we "perceive" improvisation through systems of difference.

Improvisation occupies a strange and unstable position in Western music, as if it were the source of an anxiety. Neither "composition" nor "performance," improvisation is rarely mentioned by name—not because it is actually rare in culture, but indeed perhaps because it is dangerously omnipresent.[6] By the twentieth century it had become one of Western music's principal Others: constructed as a kind of epistemological antithesis to composition, improvisation enjoys a status of literally zero value in the Western economy of musical "works."[7] Not coincidentally, improvisation plays a foundational role in Black culture and aesthetics. (And we can't help but read this as one link in a chain of avoidance, repression, or concealment of improvisation: evidence of a kind of centrifugal force in Eurocentric discourse.)

These key oppositional traits—ubiquity and unknowability, zero value and maximum influence—set up a complex field of signifying relations around the concept of improvisation. This chapter maps out the terrain across which that line of inquiry has led me; it summarizes this ongoing attempt not to master the category but to undo it, to look, as it were, beneath it.

I first found myself in this game as a kind of willing shill for one of my mentors, composer and scholar George Lewis, whose influence in the realms of music studies and music-making cannot be measured, and who, it could fairly be said, engendered the "meta-field" known today as critical improvisation studies (Lewis 1996, 2004, 2009, 2014, 2019). Taking up Lewis's project, many scholars have sought to scour every corner of the humanities, arts, and sciences for traces of this untraceable quality (Nettl and Russell 1998; Solis and Nettl 2009; Heble and Wallace 2013; Fischlin et al. 2013; Heble and Caines 2014; Siddall and Waterman 2016; Lewis and Piekut 2016; Born et al. 2017). Music theory has enthusiastically joined the fray; a colloquy under the heading "Theorizing Improvisation (Musically)" was collected in the journal *Music Theory Online* (19.2, 2013) by Paul Steinbeck, one of Lewis's graduate students, with a critical response from Lewis himself (2013).

I would argue that such efforts to theorize improvisation over the last two decades must be understood as historically inextricable from concurrent efforts to theorize embodiment (Iyer 1998, 2002, 2004, 2014; Cox 2016; Godøy and Leman 2010; Leman et al. 2018), temporality (Hasty 1997; Clark and Rehding 2016; Iyer, forthcoming), and affect (Thompson and Biddle 2013) in music. Rather than treat each movement as yet another proverbial "turn" in the field, we can accept that all of these lines of inquiry have, in a shared post-post-structuralist moment, similarly addressed questions of ephemerality, the limits of textual and score-based analysis, and the crucial roles of bodies, intersubjectivity, and sociality in perception, cognition, and meaning-making.

However, the more closely I have tried to study the perspectives on improvisation resulting from the aforementioned efforts, the less they have cohered into a unified concept. It would seem to me that the notion of improvisation must be viewed as a historically sedimented assemblage of mechanisms, relations, desires, and omissions. But meanwhile, sometime in the last decade I noticed with increasing alarm an accumulation of almost entrepreneurial investment in the term "improvisation." The neo-disciplinary zeal apparent in the institutional coalescence around the term, with its institutes, festival-*cum*-conferences, journals, edited volumes, and other stabilizing gestures[8] dedicated to this most unstable topic, felt out of step with a certain constellation of ethical concerns. How is it that a certain class of events, one already established to have zero value before the law, and already aligned with Blackness, indigeneity, and other forms of alterity, could become the site of such newfound academic value? It started to fit the pattern of a rehabilitative gesture, a vindication, a hollow, performative rescue of that which society has deemed abject. Mbembe writes:

> [T]he reaffirmation of a human identity denied by others is part of a discourse of refutation and rehabilitation. But if the discourse of rehabilitation seeks to confirm the *cobelonging* of Black people to humanity in general, it does not—except in a few rare cases—set aside the fiction of a racial subject or of *race in general*. In fact, it embraces the fiction. (2017, 89)

As I read on, and also found myself delivering talks at various conferences in the field, I couldn't help but notice that in the busy new-construction zone of critical improvisation studies, hardly any Black scholars were ever cited. Despite the epistemological revolution of the last half-century in Black studies, postcolonial thought, feminist theory, indigeneity, queer theory, and their intersections, it was rare to find much of it in the bibliographies of critical improvisation studies. There was a severe lack of engagement with Black studies, in particular. The one author I would find repeatedly, the single tolerated exception, was our beloved progenitor George Lewis. This is not his fault; it is the fault of others who failed to follow up on the implications of his crucial (1996) intervention, "Improvised Music after 1950: Afrological and Eurological Forms." That one essay has appeared in so many otherwise-non-Black syllabi and anthologies that it has apparently functioned for music studies as a kind of permanent stopgap measure. It's an example of what Stuart Hall called "the incorporation of the kind of difference that doesn't make a difference of any kind" (1998, 23).

Juxtaposed against this were the very real histories of violence that coincide with capital-D difference, the violent, constitutive difference that give rise to Afrological forms in the first place. I'm talking about global anti-Blackness, in the history of enslavement and its afterlife. Saidiya Hartman 1997 is one of the foremost scholars excavating the lives of the enslaved from their obscure, fleeting traces in the physical archive of transactions and accounts of their oppressors. But there is much articulated about the afterlife of enslavement in the present. Christina Sharpe, in her book *In the Wake: On Blackness and Being* (2016), details the case of the girl who wrote "Hi."

> She comes to us from the front pages of the *New York Times* ... Writing is discovered on a school gym bathroom wall. Two students are accused of vandalism: 12-year-old Mikia Hutchings, who is Black, and her (unnamed in the article) white girlfriend. .. As part of an agreement with the state to have the charges dismissed in juvenile court, Mikia admitted to the allegations of criminal trespassing. Mikia ... spent her

summer on probation, under a 7pm curfew, and had to complete 16 hours of community service. . . Her friend, who is white, was let go after her parents paid restitution.

(Vega 2014, quoted in Sharpe 2016, 121)

I chose this example—I could just as easily have used any number of recent news stories from 2018 such as the Philadelphia Starbucks incident, or the case of the eleven-year-old African American girl tased by a policeman for suspected shoplifting, or any one of the thousands of tragic, traumatic examples of the removal of Black life in an ordinary encounter gone wrong. What I hope to indicate is that such clearly improvisative moments that are contiguous with everyday life—events of extremely minor import, the innocuous actions of innocents—are systemically suspected, abhorred, criminalized, punished. So this kind of systemic struggle is what I wanted to study: the very unequal distribution of experience itself, the differential ways that the world "shows up" for different populations, in the real-time, improvisative flow of everyday life. Because if we can't even agree on that, then what do we mean when we speak of improvisation in music? In whose music? Improvisation for whom, and compared to what?

> [I]t is not the specifics of any one event or set of events that are endlessly repeatable and repeated, but the totality of the environments in which we struggle; the machines in which we live; what I am calling the weather.
>
> Living as I have argued we do in the wake of slavery, in spaces where we were never meant to survive, or have been punished for surviving and for daring to claim or make spaces of something like freedom, we yet reimagine and transform spaces for and practices of an ethics of care (as in repair, maintenance, attention), an ethics of seeing, and of being in the wake as consciousness.
>
> (Sharpe 2016, 111 and 130–131)

To get beneath improvisation, I sought a scientifically informed humanism, one that could face the instabilities of truth, knowledge, and power with rigor and care. What I wanted from science was a rigorous understanding of the limits of any species-wide claim; what I wanted from the humanities was an acknowledgment of the limits of categories like "music" and "the human." But for decades, what I tended to find at the intersection of science and the music humanities was a reinscription of those categories; provincial claims to universality; the pervasive tendency to let aspects of nineteenth-century Western tonal music stand for human music; a skepticism of rhythm, improvisation, or creativity in performance; a facile equation of all forms of musical "training"; an unquestioning belief in the measurability of music; a persistent circularity in claims like "music makes us human." Music was invariably treated as an object, a substance, clearly identifiable, ready to be received and "liked" by human beings, as if it came to us, rather than from us.

Several years ago I found myself gravitating to the work of historical musicologist and evolutionary biologist Gary Tomlinson, in particular his remarkable book *A Million Years of Music: The Emergence of Human Modernity* (2015a). It seemed as though he might make some significant headway in reconsidering the scientific components of musicality as a capacity, musicking as a social practice, musicmaking as a creative (as in, constructive) embodied action, by looking at nothing less than the fossil record. I found myself highlighting a potential point of contact among what Tomlinson calls "cultural archives" (2015a, 38), Foucault's "archive," and Bourdieu's "habitus"—different views on how an accumulation and hardening of past cultural information shapes sociality, behavior, and interaction in the (co-)present. For Tomlinson, what is generally thought of as a cultural archive is at one with biology, as expressed in his term "biocultural evolution." His succinct, non-essentialist definition of culture—"the transmission to future generations of learning acquired during a lifetime" (42)—allows for emergence, situatedness, local and generational specificity, and historical change. Yet I can't help but notice how it neither mentions nor rules out difference or power.

Tomlinson does address difference more explicitly in a short essay titled "Beneath Difference" (2015b), in which he offers a corrective to what he identifies as two common "mistakes" in evolutionary considerations of music. "The first," he writes, "misjudges what is being recognized as universally human. It is not *difference* that the best new evolutionary work judges to be innate, but *similarity*, and as I have suggested," he continues, "the fascination with alterity in the recent humanities has always been tacitly predicated on this more general human community" (370). In other words, our theorizations of difference are founded upon an epistemological assumption of species-wide sameness. The second mistake is "to presume that universal features [of the species] will be narrowly deterministic of human behavior" (371): that, for example, the selective pressures that gave rise to our aural capacities led inevitably to an association between a major triad and happiness. In a key passage, Tomlinson responds to that common error, by describing the human production of difference as if it were a kind of situated improvisation: "The foremost innate similarity of all humans is the capacity to respond flexibly to circumstances and so to produce difference through complex social, cultural, and environmental action. . . *We are all humanly the same, most deeply, because we are all programmed to generate difference*" (371, emphasis added). He goes on to describe this particularly human flexibility as "very special indeed" and "unprecedented in the history of life on earth," and he highlights "the *inevitability* that that [biological] sameness, given its phylogenetic history, would burgeon into that [cultural] difference." This is the benign, celebratory view of sociality and difference that we have come to recognize not only in the sciences, but also in critical improvisation studies. There is nothing particularly wrong with it, but it manages to put the realities of cultural difference rather mildly. How are we to understand the last five hundred years of violence, suffering, and loss as merely the result of a proliferation of difference in the human species? That is why I found it necessary to turn to some far more trenchant perspectives on this "capacity."

If cultural difference is inevitable, then perhaps so too is the differential distribution of difference, or the differential distribution of power. But I am reminded of another quite singular attribute of the human species. Among mammals, only three species will form arbitrary alliances, to then gang up on and murder each another: wolves, chimpanzees, and humans (Wrangham 1999). Humankind's doomed pair of capacities—arbitrary alliances (or "communities"), and mutual murder—was perhaps also selected for in some deep past; but whether that places these behaviors in the realm of aesthetics alongside musicality is simply too barbaric to contemplate. But it does place our species squarely in the condition of an endless precarity: the condition, identified with the current neoliberal economic moment but probably predating and outlasting it, in which the most powerful among us take advantage of the most vulnerable. Judith Butler defines precarity as the condition of "differential distribution of precariousness" (2015, 33).

The discourse of critical improvisation studies is full of warm assurances about community. But if we understand that humans can also improvise murderous alliances, we might think twice about this banal category, with its implications for race, nation, and kinship, and its use as a premise for war, hyperpolicing, and other blood rites. More benignly, we might hypothesize that even as bland a formation as community emerges in relation to other such potential or actual aggregates; we gather for safety, to consolidate power and resources, and to share work and its fruits, and it is in these relational contexts—families, caves, tribes, villages, cities, each one situated among many—that musicking emerges.

In invoking what lurks "beneath improvisation," I borrow from Tomlinson's essay "Beneath Difference," even if my agenda would seem somewhat at cross-purposes from his. If beneath cultural difference is some kind of biological sameness, it is also the case that beneath any presumed unity or "sameness" of improvisation from a bodily, evolutionary, or cognitive perspective lies a differential distribution of possibility, an incommensurate difference. Simply put, we don't all enjoy the same freedoms. Indeed, "Freedom" will turn out to be the master trope, the devil at the end of this conversation, who'll be tricking us all along the way.

So, finally, to the core of this chapter. "Beneath" improvisation, I piece together an aggregate of verbs involving varying degrees of volition:

- Being
- Doing
- Sensing
- Feeling
- Thinking
- Speaking
- Acting
- Moving

which maps directly, one-to-one, onto this constellation of recognizable nouns:

- Subjectivity
- Practice
- Phenomenology
- Affect
- Cognition

- Discourse
- Agency
- Migration

We will stroll through a few of these topics, each one a sprawling network of conceptual complexity and scholarly intrigue, and each of direct relevance to the theorizing of improvisation. But also, I want to condition each one with one or more of the following:

- while Black/Brown/indigenous
- while non-male
- while queer
- while colonized
- while undocumented
- while seeking refuge
- while disabled

Practice is a term for how we "do" everyday life. Pierre Bourdieu (1977) developed the idea of the habitus as a generative field in culture, the "durably installed generative system of regulated improvisations"—that is, a self-sustaining and continuously evolving relational system of social understandings of how one should act: how we do what we're supposed to do, and how those suppositions come to be. Though never one to shy away from questions of power, Bourdieu only occasionally addresses structural difference:

> [H]abitus could be considered as a subjective but not individual system of internalized structures, schemes of perception, conception, and action common to all members of the same group or class ... *each individual system of dispositions* may be seen as a *structural variant* of all the other group or class habitus, expressing the difference between trajectories and positions inside or outside the class. (1977, 86)

That is to say that culture hosts not one but many interpenetrating, overlaid versions of what we call practice, different ways of doing everyday life, which we understand to represent different sociopolitical vantages: what social scientists describe as different structural positions.

Against this again rather benign account of class difference, we can look at Saidiya Hartman's (1997) theorization of practice in the context of enslavement. She invokes De Certeau in describing Black practice while in bondage as

> "a way of operating" defined by "the non-autonomy of its field of action," internal manipulations of the established order, and ephemeral victories. The tactics that comprise the everyday practices of the dominated have neither the means to secure a territory outside the space of domination nor the power to keep or maintain what it [has] won in fleeting, surreptitious, and necessarily incomplete victories. . . .

These efforts generally focused on the object status and castigated personhood of the slave, the pained and ravished body, severed affiliations and natal alienation, and the assertion of denied needs. Practice is not simply a way of naming these efforts but rather a way of thinking about the character of resistance, the precariousness of the assaults waged against domination, the fragmentary character of these efforts and the transient battles won, and the characteristics of a politics without a proper locus. (50–51)

The term "phenomenology" puts us in the realm of embodied experience. Elsewhere I have posited (2004) a correspondence between experience and improvisation, in the suggestion that everything we do is improvisative, consisting of moment-to-moment sensory-guided action. The philosopher Alva Noë describes experience as a "temporally extended pattern of exploratory activity" (2000, 128). This could serve as a definition of improvisation: the real-time interaction with the structure of one's environment. As with improvisation, it is not a passive interaction, for the perceiver/improvisor is engaged in sensorimotor activity, skillfully probing the world at will. This process of embodied action situates the perceiver within the environment; so the perceiver must interact with her embodied self as well.

Phenomenology already offers what is called an embodied view of cognition—the idea that mental processes are grounded in bodily experience. Eleanor Rosch, one of the authors of the influential 1991 treatise *The Embodied Mind*, writes in her introduction to the book's second edition (2017) about what her co-author Evan Thompson calls "enaction," a particular formulation of embodied cognition:

The core idea of enaction is that the living body is a self-organizing system. This is in contrast to viewing it as a machine that happens to be made of meat rather than silicon. Mechanisms act and change their state only because of input and programming from sources outside of themselves, whereas the living body continuously reorganizes itself to survive and maintain its own homeostasis. (Notice how this alone is a radical departure from the dominant view of the body in present research.) Survival means that the organism must preserve the integrity of its boundaries while having constant interchange with the environment. Even the simplest one-celled organism exchanges materials through the semi-permeable membrane of its cell walls and performs overt actions relevant to its self maintenance, such as swimming towards a detectable food source or away from insupportable temperatures. Actions of the organism are thus purposive and have been said by enactivists to be the embryonic forms of cognition, of mind, and even of values. (xxxviii)

There is a tendency, when talking about phenomenology and cognition, to direct research questions to the self, to the solitary body-mind system, to inner experience, and not to our relationships to others—not to the social. Scientists and philosophers imagine human existence to be more solitary than we could possibly ever be. But here, in Rosch's invocation of a term like "values," we start to hear faint traces of the social. "The mind in the body in the world," it must constantly be stressed, only exists among other such bodies and minds; basic cognitive skills like language are acquired from others, in relation to others, in the presence of others, and serve primarily to connect us to others.

In the last twenty years, the discovery of mirror neurons allowed scientists to imagine a possible neural basis for "empathy" in embodied cognition (Gallese et al. 1996; Kohler et al. 2002; Rizzolatti and Sinigaglia 2010; Gallese et al. 2011). To see or hear someone move was shown to activate the networks in one's own brain involved in an analogous motion. This is what neuroscientists call "action understanding"—to see or hear someone do something with their body is to imagine or fantasize doing it oneself. However, in a study at the University of Toronto, this neuronal empathy was shown, chillingly, to fail across racial categories; test subjects (all white Canadians) were shown to display far less mirror neuron activation when shown, say, a video of a black person picking up a coffee cup, than they would when shown a video of a white person performing the same motion (Gutsell and Inzlicht 2010). So a top-down belief in racial difference seems to have the power to override what is otherwise described as a bottom-up neural response; the most basic forms of empathy seem to be constrained by belief in racial difference. This extends to higher levels of cognition; a search for the term "racial empathy gap" produces a depressing mountain of research revealing, for example, that doctors prescribe less pain medication to black people (Silverstein 2013). We have an abundance of such scientific findings about dehumanizing systemic interactions across differentials of power and privilege.

We don't need to go too far down the murky and controversial road of mirror neurons, but we can consider the function of such systems in light of the following assertion: what we call music perception begins with an aural action of understanding (Iyer 2014). In the embodied music cognition framework (Iyer 1998), to hear music is to hear the actions of others. The now-conventional thinking about mirror neurons as a system that generates simulations of actions and mental states of another—what has perhaps abusively been called empathy—has been challenged by Maria Brincker (2012), who essentially asks us to rethink what constitutes the social:

> In terms of social cognition I question the traditional focus on hidden mental states. I suggest that the motor contribution might have more to do with understanding the process of how others choose their actions, navigate the world and relate to others than with simulating specific actual actions or mental states. (159)

This isn't mere mental mimesis of another person's actions, but rather a process of tracking the way that person improvises in the here and now, in relation to what's at hand. How is this person making choices and taking action in real time? Brincker suggests recasting it as affordance understanding, invoking J. J. Gibson's term for how our bodies make use of what's at hand: "In terms of social cognition 'mirror' circuits might thus help us understand not only the intentional actions others are actually performing—but also what they could have done, did not do and might do shortly" (Brincker 2015, 18).

Again, scientists have a way of glossing over difference, but we now know that when individual armed state actors somehow "mis-track" a Black person's intentional actions—Philando Castile, Tamir Rice, and on down the ghastly list—the gruesome consequences are, in the vast majority of cases, tolerated and sanctioned by the state. So where do we find ourselves, along this interface of sameness, difference, and power?

Agency—the socially mediated capacity to act (Ahearn 2001)—seems to overlap significantly with what we mean by improvisation. It does not function in a vacuum; agency forms part of a dyad with what's called structure, the social systems that do the mediating (Emirbayer and Mische 1998). Much ink has been spilled on questions of agency, most recently in a special colloquy in *Music Theory Online* (Montague 2018), and it's especially often used to condescendingly heroicize the oppressed: agency as resistance. The historian Walter Johnson, in his essay "On Agency," cautions against "a teleology . . . which ultimately reproduces the idea of a liberal agent as the universal subject of history" (2003, 117). He warns that framing every act under the rubric of "agency" has the effect of "obscuring important questions about both the way in which enslaved people theorized their own actions and the practical process through which those actions provided the predicate for new ways of thinking about slavery and resistance" (2003, 118).

Regarding *subjectivity*, or the sense of autonomous selfhood, we can look at a century of rethinking of the subject—including twentieth-century challenges to the notion of the unified self. Marx, Nietzsche, Freud, and Saussure revealed economic, ethical, psychological, and linguistic underpinnings of contemporary subjectivity; however, as Moten (2003) points out, none of these four thought very much about the subjectivities of those who are not conferred a basic status of personhood, despite the fact that these thinkers, like all of us, lived within a historical framework characterized by the large-scale revoking of personhood. Accordingly, what we learn from centuries of African diasporic writing is that the privilege of subjectivity cannot be taken for granted. Writers and theorists from Zora Neale Hurston ([1933] 1999) to Houston Baker (1984) and Henry Louis Gates (1989) have identified and catalogued improvisative tendencies in African American culture. These projects form a counterpoint with the trenchant interventions of Black Feminist theorists like Hortense Spillers (1987), Sylvia Wynter (1994), Audre Lorde ([1979] 2007), Saidiya Hartman (1997), and Christina Sharpe (2010), who seek, by training the critical tools of literary analysis on the archive itself, to destabilize and topple the conceit of Western Man as the idealized, transcendental subject. Their efforts lead us to construe subjectivity as relational; the self must be understood in terms of its position in the realm of the social, which is to say, in a network of power relations with other subjects. There is not one subjectivity, but many. There is no transcendent subjectivity; there is only intersubjectivity. Quoting Fred Moten's influential introductory chapter, "The Resistance of the Object," from his book *In the Break: The Aesthetics of the Black Radical Tradition,* in rethinking Black subjectivity from the condition of the person-as-property:

> The animative materiality—the aesthetic, political, sexual, and racial force—of the ensemble of objects that we might call black performances, black history, blackness, is a real problem and a real chance for the philosophy of the human being (which would necessarily bear and be irreducible to what is called, or what somebody might hope to someday call, subjectivity). (2003, 7–8)

Crucially, this line of thought leads us to construe *diaspora* as a form of improvisation: collective movement in relation to power. Diaspora is not only a state of displacement, but also an ongoing navigation of social difference. It is a condition of having to perceive, decide, and act under the watchful gaze of a suspicious and distrustful host culture, particularly intensified by the hypervisibility associated with racial difference. Diaspora is, we might unremarkably observe, improvisation within constraints. Franz Fanon described the experience of colonial occupation (which has often been a precondition and impetus for diasporic movement) in a similar way:

> There is not occupation of territory, on the one hand, and independence of persons on the other. It is the country as a whole, its history, its daily pulsation that are contested, disfigured . . . under these conditions, the individual's breathing is an observed breathing. It is a combat breathing. ([1959] 1967, 50)

This brings to mind the case of Eric Garner, whose gruesome public strangulation by a New York City police officer was documented on a bystander's cell phone. The officers involved were not indicted. Similarly we think of Ferguson, Missouri's Michael Brown, an African American teenager whose supposed crime of jaywalking led to him being shot at a dozen times by white police officer Darren Wilson, and his dead body left out on the street for hours; of unarmed Black teenager Trayvon Martin, pursued and killed by a vigilante, who deemed him a trespasser in his own Florida neighborhood and was later acquitted of all charges; and many thousands more. The condition of Blackness is one in which basic bodily acts—walking and breathing—attract extreme, state-sanctioned violence and terror. Improvisation here takes on radically different meanings for privileged actors and for their victims, for those who move with power and those who simply seek to move across it.

Improvisation could be therefore accurately described as movement in relation to power; or since power is omnipresent, we could just call it *movement in relation*. Here I invoke Relation in the sense employed by the late Martinican poet and theorist Edouard Glissant, in *The Poetics of Relation* ([1990] 1997). In an interview with Mantha Diawara, Glissant explained,

> Relation is made up of all the differences in the world and that we shouldn't forget a single one of them, even the smallest. If you forget the tiniest difference in the world, well, Relation is no longer Relation. Now, what do we do when we believe this? We call into question, in a formal manner, the idea of the universal. The universal is a sublimation, an abstraction that enables us to forget small differences; we drift upon the universal and forget these small differences, and Relation is wonderful because it doesn't allow us to do that.
>
> (Diawara 2011, 9)

One of the universals that we drift upon, that Glissant and others seem to be referring to, is the concept of *freedom*. One of the most potent signifiers in Western discourse, freedom may well be heard as improvisation's master trope. Yet freedom, as scholars like Orlando Patterson (1985) and Mimi Thi Nguyen (2012) have observed, can only be thoroughly understood in relation to its opposites: unfreedom, subjection, incarceration, bare life. The concept of freedom as we know it scarcely exists outside of histories of enslavement and domination.

This was illuminated in a recent talk by Hortense Spillers (2014) about Thomas Jefferson's personal enslaved concubine, Sally Hemings. It's well known that many of the U.S.'s so-called founding fathers were slaveowners. What's truly strange is that the rhetoric of freedom that was used to usher in the birth of the nation was authored by such men in the immediate presence of its complete opposite. Jefferson's phrase "All men are created equal," which appears in his famous preamble to the Declaration of Independence, is starkly contradicted by his own and his country's dependence on the enslavement of others. In the 1780s Jefferson became minister to France, where he discussed the revolutionary ideals of *liberté, égalité, fraternité* with the Marquis de Lafayette, advising him on his Declaration of the Rights of Man and of the Citizen. Jefferson brought slaves with him to France, including Sally Hemings, a black woman born into bondage who was the biological daughter of Jefferson's father-in-law, and who gave birth to many of Jefferson's own "illegitimate" children: Sally Hemings, one of the most unfree human beings imaginable, was literally standing in the same room with Jefferson and Lafayette as the two statesmen discussed freedom and the rights of man.

This wrenching contradiction embedded in the very authoring of the notion of freedom affects every one of us. We are all caught up in and benefiting from not just the business of music, but the business of enslavement. In an interview in 2014, Patterson offered the following:

> The idea of freedom is seen as "inherent"—so there is nothing to explain . . . [The idea is that] "Everybody wants to be free because it is part of the human condition." That's nonsense. Freedom as a value, as a cherished part of one's culture, as something to strive for and die for, is unusual in human history. You can't just take it for granted. So the question turns into, how did freedom become important? My explanation is that freedom emerged as the antithesis to the social death of slavery.
>
> (Lambert 2014, 46)

Under slavery, he explains, there were three groups of people: masters, slaves, and non-slaves.

> All three come to discover this thing we call freedom through their relationships. For the master, freedom is being able to do what you please with another person: freedom as power. For the slave—well, what does a slave yearn for? To be emancipated, to get rid of the social death that is slavery . . . The third group, the non-slaves or freemen, look at the slaves and say, "We are not them. We are born free." Suddenly, being born free becomes important, in a way it never could be for

slaves. Freemen have a different status in society, one that does not depend on their socioeconomic class. (ibid.)

In the horrific context of slavery and its afterlife, freedom is then best understood not as something that Black people have, but something that they must get. The phrase "get free" is a familiar one; it is a goal in Black music and a dream in Black life. It is in his reading of a moment in Frederick Douglass's (1845) classic narrative of his enslavement that Fred Moten notes "the freedom drive that animates black performances" (2003, 12). Today when we talk about freedom in Black music, or freedom for Black people, we are still talking about something closer to *fugitivity*: escape.

Today it seems that we are gripped by questions of freedom—of movement, of speech, of assembly—in our cities and towns, on our campuses, in our presses, in our public restrooms and our elementary schools. We are also witness to the endangered passage of unprecedented numbers of people across the earth, within, outside, and across the political borders of the state. How do our troubled core concepts of freedom give rise to the expressions of empire, as expressed in theaters of war with their code names, Operation Iraqi Freedom and Operation Enduring Freedom, and the massive flows of refugees that they might engender? Mimi Thi Nguyen, a scholar of Critical Refugee Studies, asks this question in *The Gift of Freedom: War, Debt, and Other Refugee Passages* (2012). She argues, "the gift of freedom is not simply a ruse for liberal war but its core proposition, and a particularly apt name for its operations of violence and power."

* * *

I could have continued, pointing out disparities between, say, "affect" as it is routinely theorized (e.g., Massumi 2002) and, say, "refugee affect" (Harney 2013), or "temporality" (Bowker 2015) and "queer futurity" (Muñoz 2009)—but by now the pattern is clear enough. The most we can say at this point is that the transparency of the machineries beneath improvisation—being/doing/acting/sensing/feeling/etc.—cannot be taken for granted while Black/non-male/queer/undocumented/disabled/precarious. These mechanisms' theoretical manifestations—subjectivity, practice, agency, phenomenology, affect, and so forth—seem not to operate equally in the universe of constrained affordances and potentialities that characterize non-normative, othered bodies. Even "relationality" falls short in accounting for these incommensurabilities (Feldman 2016).

If music theory asks us to consider formal analysis in the abstract, or musical experience in general, or music cognition on the scale of the human species, then we will always inevitably find ourselves up against multiple incommensurabilities and differential relationships to the assumed freedoms underlying these disciplinary quests. We cannot theorize improvisation uniformly across incommensurate domains of experience, without accounting (endlessly) for freedom itself. Indeed, the presumed separability of the humanities was always a consequence of humanity's massively unequal distribution of freedom—the separations and differentiations imposed by humanity on itself. We are left with a handful of inconclusive phrases:

response to necessity
movement in relation
(co)Presence while (un)free

Or, quoting Moten (2016):

> The paradox is all about what it is to want to escape the history of freedom, or the history of the struggle for freedom.

Notes

1. The Twitter account @NewMusicDrama aggregated many such responses in real time in the days following the Pulitzer announcement. See, for example, https://twitter.com/NewMusicDrama/status/986672029758836736 and https://twitter.com/NewMusicDrama/status/986672031092617222, accessed December 10, 2018.
2. https://twitter.com/NewMusicDrama/status/985984043731898370/, accessed September 7, 2018.
3. Evolutionary biologist Steven Pinker listed "rap music" as an example of "not-quite-music" (1997, 534–535). Rose 2008 observed that the "blanket rejection of the creativity in hip hop is categorical for some critics [who insist that] hip hop is not music, the rhymes are not poetic, and everything about it is simple and requires no special talent" (218). Despite the fact that a team of data scientists (Mauch et al. 2015) recently reported, upon surveying a vast corpus of recorded music, that hip-hop was the single biggest influence on popular music in the last half-century, it seems that there remains a persistent and powerful minority who refuse to confer on hip-hop the ontological status of music.
4. Kettlewell (2018) outlines a number of such positions: "'Does Jazz Put The Sin In Syncopation?' asked Anne Shaw Faulkner in a 1921 issue of *The Ladies' Home Journal*. She quoted the opinion of Dr. Henry Van Dyke, a Presbyterian clergyman and professor at Princeton, that jazz 'is not music at all.' Sigmund Spaeth took the same position in his piece for *Forum* in 1928, which was flatly entitled 'Jazz Is Not Music.' Mr. Spaeth, who would later become well-known as radio's Tune Detective, heard the music of the golden age of early Louis Armstrong, Duke Ellington, Bix Beiderbecke, and the rest as 'merely a raucous and inarticulate shouting of hoarse-throated instruments, with each player trying to outdo his fellows, in fantastic cacophony.'" The American modernist critic Paul Rosenfeld began an essay with the sentence: "American music is not jazz. Jazz is not music" (1969, 221). *The New York Times*, on November 14, 1924, quoted concert pianist Ashley Pettis: "Jazz is nothing more or less than the distortion of every esthetic principle" (see Kettlewell 2018).
5. Quoting Jeffrey Robert Young's (2007) review of *The Sounds of Slavery* (2006) by Shane and Graham White:

> In ritualized celebrations such as the Pinkster holiday that emerged in the New York region and the Jonkonnu festival celebrated in North Carolina, the singing and joyful sounding of African American voices worked in tandem with the instruments and drums wielded by black musicians to create a sensory experience that clearly belonged to the slaves themselves. White witnesses to these performances sometimes marveled at them and sometimes bemoaned what they deemed the alien noises emanating from the African

American participants, but in either case, whites were acknowledging that they stood outside the cultural space forged through African American sounds.

6. The centrality of improvisation in Western music history is still mentioned often (usually emblemized in the claim that "Bach/Mozart/Beethoven/Bartók/Messiaen was a master improviser"). However, improvisation itself does not appear as a prominent feature of contemporary European or European-American glosses on "classical music."

7. Copyright law confers value (as intellectual property) to fixed compositions, and improvisation is taken to denote the absence of fixity. For a case study, see Sheridan (2002).

8. The Oxford University Press webpage for the Lewis and Piekut (2016) edited volumes describes critical improvisation studies as "one of the fastest growing areas of scholarly inquiry." https://global.oup.com/academic/product/the-oxford-handbook-of-critical-improvisation-studies-volume-1-9780195370935.

WORKS CITED

Ahearn, Laura M. 2001. "Language and Agency." *Annual Review of Anthropology* 30: 109–137.

Baker, Houston A. 1984. *Blues, Ideology & Afro-American Literature*. Chicago: University of Chicago Press.

Born, Georgina, Eric Lewis, and Will Straw, eds. 2017. *Improvisation and Social Aesthetics*. Durham, NC: Duke University Press.

Bourdieu, Pierre. 1977. *Outline of a Theory of Practice*. Cambridge: Cambridge University Press.

Bowker, Geoffrey. 2015. "Temporality." Theorizing the Contemporary, *Fieldsights*. September 24. https://culanth.org/fieldsights/temporality.

Brincker, Maria. 2012. "If the Motor System is No Mirror." In *Connected Minds: Cognition and Interaction in the Social World*, edited by Nicolas Payette and Benoît Hardy-Vallee, 158–182. Newcastle-upon-Tyne: Cambridge Scholars Publishing.

Brincker, Maria. 2015. "Beyond Sensorimotor Segregation: On Mirror Neurons and Social Affordance Space Tracking." *Cognitive Systems Research* 34–35: 18–34.

Butler, Judith. 2015. *Notes Toward a Performative Theory of Assembly*. Cambridge, MA: Harvard University Press.

Clark, Suzannah, and Alexander Rehding, eds. 2016. *Music in Time: Phenomenology, Perception, Performance: Essays in Honor of Christopher F. Hasty*. Cambridge, MA: Harvard University Press.

Cox, Arnie. 2016. *Music and Embodied Cognition: Listening, Moving, Feeling, and Thinking*. Bloomington: Indiana University Press.

Diawara, Manthia, 2011. "One World in Relation: Édouard Glissant in Conversation with Manthia Diawara." *Nka Journal of Contemporary African Art* 28: 4–19.

Douglass, Frederick. 1845. *Narrative of the Life of Frederick Douglass, An American Slave*. Boston: Anti-Slavery Office.

Emirbayer, Mustafa, and Ann Mische. 1998. "What Is Agency?" *American Journal of Sociology* 103: 962–1023.

Fanon, Frantz. 1967. *A Dying Colonialism* [1959]. New York: Grove Press.

Feldman, Keith. 2016. "On Relationality, On Blackness: A Listening Post." *Comparative Literature* 68: 107–115.

Fischlin, Daniel, Ajay Heble, and George Lipsitz, eds. 2013. *The Fierce Urgency of Now: Improvisation, Rights, and the Ethics of Cocreation*. Durham, NC: Duke University Press.

Gallese, Vittorio, Luciano Fadiga, Leonardo Fogassi, and Giacomo Rizzolatti. 1996. "Action Recognition in the Premotor Cortex." *Brain* 119: 593–609.

Gallese, Vittorio, Morton Ann Gernsbacher, Cecilia Heyes, Gregory Hickok, and Marco Iacoboni. 2011. "Mirror Neuron Forum." *Perspectives on Psychological Science* 6: 369–407.

Gates, Henry Louis. 1989. *The Signifying Monkey: A Theory of Afro-American Literary Criticism.* New York: Oxford University Press.

Glissant, Édouard. 1999. *The Poetics of Relation* [1990]. Ann Arbor: University of Michigan Press.

Godøy, Rolf Inge, and Leman, Marc, eds. 2010. *Musical Gestures: Sound, Movement, and Meaning.* New York: Routledge.

Gutsell, Jennifer N., and Michael Inzlicht. 2010. "Empathy Constrained: Prejudice Predicts Reduced Mental Simulation of Actions during Observation of Outgroups." *Journal of Experimental Social Psychology* 46: 841–845.

Hall, Stuart. 1998. "What Is This 'Black' in Black Popular Culture?" In *Black Popular Culture*, edited by Gina Dent, 21–33. New York: New Press.

Harney, Nicholas D. 2013. "Precarity, Affect and Problem Solving with Mobile Phones by Asylum Seekers, Refugees and Migrants in Naples, Italy." *Journal of Refugee Studies* 26: 541–557.

Hartman, Saidiya. 1997. *Scenes of Subjection: Terror, Slavery, and Self-Making in Nineteenth-Century America.* New York: Oxford University Press.

Hasty, Christopher. 1997. *Meter as Rhythm.* New York: Oxford University Press.

Heble, Ajay. 2018. "About ICASP." Accessed September 7. http://www.improvcommunity.ca/about.

Heble, Ajay, and Rebecca Caines, eds. 2014. *The Improvisation Studies Reader: Spontaneous Acts.* New York: Routledge.

Heble, Ajay, and Rob Wallace, eds. 2013. *People Get Ready: The Future of Jazz Is Now!* Durham, NC: Duke University Press.

Hurston, Zora Neale. 1999. "Characteristics of Negro Expression [1933]." In *Signifyin(g), Sanctifyin', & Slam Dunking: A Reader in African American Expressive Culture*, edited by Gina Dagel Caponi, 293–308. Amherst: University of Massachusetts Press.

Iyer, Vijay. 1998. "Microstructures of Feel, Macrostructures of Sound: Embodied Cognition in West African and African-American Musics." PhD diss., University of California, Berkeley.

Iyer, Vijay. 2002. "Embodied Mind, Situated Cognition, and Expressive Microtiming in African-American Music." *Music Perception* 19: 387–414.

Iyer, Vijay. 2004. "Improvisation, Temporality, and Embodied Experience." *Journal of Consciousness Studies* 11, nos. 3–4: 159–173.

Iyer, Vijay. 2014. "Improvisation, Action Understanding, and Music Cognition With and Without Bodies." In *The Oxford Handbook of Critical Improvisation Studies*, edited by George E. Lewis and Benjamin Piekut. New York: Oxford University Press.

Iyer, Vijay. Forthcoming. "Reassembling the Temporal." In *The Oxford Handbook of Time in Music*, edited by Mark Doffman. New York: Oxford University Press.

Johnson, Walter. 2003. "On Agency." *Journal of Social History* 37: 113–124.

Kettlewell, Ben. 2018. "Growing Pains: Reflecting on the Social Climate During the Early Days of Jazz." Accessed September 7. http://www.alternatemusicpress.com/features/features1.html.

King, Martin Luther. 2016. Program Notes for 1964 Berlin Jazz Festival. Republished by JazzTimes. Accessed May 23. http://jazztimes.com/articles/24223-dr-martin-luther-king-jr-from-1964-berlin-jazz-festival-program.

Kohler, Evelyne, Christian Keysers, M. Alessandra Umiltà, Leonardo Fogassi, Vittorio Gallese, and Giacomo Rizzolatti. 2002. "Hearing Sounds, Understanding Actions: Action Representation in Mirror Neurons." *Science* 297: 846–848.

Lambert, Craig. 2014. "The Caribbean Zola." *Harvard* Magazine, November–December.

Leman, Marc, Pieter-Jan Maes, Luc Nijs, and Edith Van Dyck. 2018. "What Is Embodied Music Cognition?" In *Springer Handbook of Systematic Musicology*, edited by Rolf Bader, 747–760. Springer, Berlin, Heidelberg

Lewis, George E. 1996. "Improvised Music after 1950: Afrological and Eurological Forms." *Black Music Research Journal* 16: 91–122.

Lewis, George E. 2004. "Gittin' to Know Y'all: Improvised Music, Interculturalism and the Racial Imagination." *Critical Studies in Improvisation* 1, ISSN 1712-0624, www.criticalimprov.com.

Lewis, George E. 2009. Interactivity and Improvisation. In *The Oxford Handbook of Computer Music*, edited by Roger T. Dean, 457–466. New York and Oxford: Oxford University Press.

Lewis, George E. 2013. "Critical Responses to 'Theorizing Improvisation (Musically)." *Music Theory Online* 19.2. http://mtosmt.org/issues/mto.13.19.2/mto.13.19.2.lewis.php.

Lewis, George E. 2014. "Improvisation." In *The Grove Dictionary of American Music,* edited by Charles Hiroshi Garrett, 311–318. New York: Oxford University Press.

Lewis, George E. 2019. "Listening for Freedom with Arnold Davidson." *Critical Inquiry* 45: 434–447.

Lewis, George, and Ben Piekut, eds. 2016. *The Oxford Handbook of Critical Improvisation Studies*, 2 vols. New York: Oxford University Press.

Lorde, Audre. 2007. "The Master's Tools Will Never Dismantle the Master's House." In *Sister Outsider: Essays & Speeches by Audre Lorde*, 110–114. Minnetonka, MN: Crossings Press.

Lowe, Lisa. 2015. *The Intimacies of Four Continents*. Durham, NC: Duke University Press.

Massumi, Brian. 2002. *Parables for the Virtual: Movement, Affect, Sensation*. Durham, NC: Duke University Press.

Mauch, Matthias, Robert MacCallum, Mark Levy, and Armand M. Leroi. 2015 "The Evolution of Popular Music: USA 1960–2010." *Royal Society Open Science* 2, no. 5. DOI: 10.1098/rsos.150081.

Mbembe, Achille. 2017. *Critique of Black Reason*. Durham, NC: Duke University Press.

Montague, Eugene, ed. 2018. "Agency and Musical Performance." *Music Theory Online* 24, no. 3. Available at http://www.mtosmt.org/issues/mto.18.24.3/toc.24.3.html.

Moten, Fred. 2003. *In the Break: The Aesthetics of the Black Radical Tradition*. Minneapolis: University of Minnesota Press.

Moten, Fred. 2016. *Creative Music Convergences* (Program notes, Fromm Players Concerts). April 7–8, Harvard University.

Muñoz, José Esteban. 2009. *Cruising Utopia: The There and Then of Queer Futurity* New York: NYU Press.

Nettl, Bruno, and Melinda Russell, eds., 1998. *In the Course of Performance: Studies in the World of Musical Improvisation*. Chicago: University of Chicago Press.

Nguyen, Mimi Thi. 2012. *The Gift of Freedom: War, Debt, and Other Refugee Passages*. Durham, NC: Duke University Press.

Noë, Alva. 2000. "Experience and Experiment in Art." *Journal of Consciousness Studies* 7, nos. 8–9: 123–136.

Patterson, Orlando. 1985. *Slavery and Social Death: A Comparative Study*. Cambridge, MA: Harvard University Press.

Pinker, Steven. 1997. *How the Mind Works*. New York: W. W. Norton.

Rizzolatti, Giacomo, and Corrado Sinigaglia. 2010. "The Functional Role of the Parieto-frontal Mirror Circuit: Interpretations and Misinterpretations." *Nature Reviews Neuroscience* 11: 264–274.

Robinson, Cedric. 2000. *Black Marxism: The Making of the Black Radical Tradition.* 2nd edition. Chapel Hill: University of North Carolina Press.

Rosch, Eleanor, 2017. "Introduction to the Revised Edition." In *The Embodied Mind: Cognitive Science and Human Experience,* edited by Francisco J. Varela, Evan T. Thompson, and Eleanor Rosch, xxxv–lv. 2nd edition. Cambridge, MA: MIT Press.

Rose, Tricia. 2008. *The Hip Hop Wars: What We Talk About When We Talk About Hip Hop and Why It Matters.* Philadelphia: Basic Books.

Rosenfeld, Paul. 1969. *Musical Impressions: Selections from Paul Rosenfeld's Criticism.* New York: Hill and Wang.

Sharpe, Christina, 2010. *Monstrous Intimacies: Making Post-Slavery Subjects.* Durham, NC: Duke University Press.

Sharpe, Christina. 2016. *In the Wake: On Blackness and Being.* Durham, NC: Duke University Press.

Sheridan, Molly. 2002. "When Stealing Is Not a Crime: James Newton vs. the Beastie Boys." *New Music Box* (blog). https://nmbx.newmusicusa.org/when-stealing-is-not-a-crime-james-newton-vs-the-beastie-boys/.

Siddall, Gillian and Ellen Waterman, eds. 2016. *Negotiated Moments: Improvisation, Sound, and Subjectivity.* Durham, NC: Duke University Press.

Silverstein, Jason. 2013. "I Don't Feel Your Pain." Slate, June 27. http://www.slate.com/articles/health_and_science/science/2013/06/racial_empathy_gap_people_don_t_perceive_pain_in_other_races.html.

Solis, Gabriel, and Bruno Nettl, eds. 2009. *Musical Improvisation: Art, Education, and Society.* Champaign: University of Illinois Press.

Spillers, Hortense. 1987. "Mama's Baby, Papa's Maybe: An American Grammar Book." *Diacritics* 17: 64–81.

Spillers, Hortense. 2014. "Women and the Early Republics: Revolution, Sentiment, and Sorrow." Du Bois Lecture, Harvard University, October 14. http://hutchinscenter.fas.harvard.edu/hortense-spillers-w-e-b-du-bois-lecture-series-part-1-3.

Spivak, Gayatri Chakravorty. 1999. *A Critique of Postcolonial Reason: Toward a History of the Vanishing Present.* Cambridge, MA: Harvard University Press.

Thompson, Marie, and Ian D. Biddle, eds. 2013. *Sound, Music, Affect: Theorizing Sonic Experience.* London: Bloomsbury.

Tomlinson, Gary. 2015a. *A Million Years of Music: The Emergence of Human Modernity.* New York: Zone Books.

Tomlinson, Gary. 2015b. "Beneath Difference." In *Rethinking Difference in Music Scholarship,* edited by Olivia Bloechl, Melanie Lowe, and Jeffrey Kallberg, 366–381. Cambridge: Cambridge University Press.

Vega, Tanzina. 2014. "Disciplining of Girls Differs Among and Within Races." *The New York Times,* December 11, New York edition, A21.

White, Shane, and Graham White. 2006. *The Sounds of Slavery: Discovering African American History through Songs, Sermons, and Speech.* Boston: Beacon Press.

Wilderson, Frank B. III. 2016. "Doing Time in the (Psychic) Commons." In *Time, Temporality and Violence in International Relations: (De) fatalizing the Present, Forging*

Radical Alternatives, edited by Anna M. Agathangelou and Kyle D. Killian, 87–103. New York: Routledge.

Wrangham, Richard. 1999. "Evolution of Coalitionary Killing." *Yearbook of Physical Anthropology* 42: 1–30.

Wynter, Sylvia. 1994. "'No Humans Involved': An Open Letter to My Colleagues." *Forum N.H.I.: Knowledge for the 21st Century* 1, no. 1: 42–73.

Wynter, Sylvia. 2003. "Unsettling the Coloniality of Being/Power/Truth/Freedom: Towards the Human, After Man, Its Overrepresentation—An Argument." *CR: The New Centennial Review* 3, 257–337.

Wynter, Sylvia, and Katherine McKittrick. 2015. "Unparalleled Catastrophe for our Species? Or, to Give Humanness a Different Future: Conversations." In *Sylvia Wynter: On Being Human as Praxis*, edited by Katherine McKittrick, 9–89. Durham, NC: Duke University Press.

Young, Jeffrey Robert 2007. "Listening to the Evidence of the African-American Slave Experience." *Common-Place* 7, no. 2. http://www.common-place-archives.org/vol-07/no-02/reviews/young.shtml.

Index

Quartet in G major, D. 887, ii, 124, 125 (figs. 5.11–12)

"Schwanengesang," D. 744 [not the song cycle], 504–505 (fig. 18.3)

"Selige Welt," D. 743, 515–520 (fig. 18.7), 523

"Unfinished" Symphony, 522

Schulz, Johann Abraham Peter, 421, 442

Schumann, Robert

accompaniments to Bach's solo violin and cello works, 400

read Gottfried Weber, 512

style, 208, 316, 716 (fig. 24.5a)

compositions in general, 325, 503

Dichterliebe esp. "Im wunderschönen Monat Mai," 499–503 (fig. 18.1), 510 (fig. 18.5b), 523

Fantasie for Piano, op. 17, 225, 226 (fig. 9.9)

Humoreske (1839), 400

Kreisleriana, op. 16, 325–328 (figs. 12.12–13)

"Träumerei" from *Scenes from Childhood*, 372, 374

Waldscenen, op. 82, "Vogel als Prophet," 625

"Widmung" from *Myrthen*, op. 25, 520–521 (fig. 18.10)

schwa (vowel sound), 148

Schwartz, Stephen—*Wicked*, "For Good," 179

science and music, 84

science and technology studies, 714

Scientific Pitch Notation, 44–45

secondary dominant, 193, 523

secondary parameters (Meyer), 137, 150, 459, 570

not named as such, 187–188, 189, 457, 661

Sedgwick, Eve Kosofsky, 240

Sélincourt, Basil de, 238

semantic saturation, 195

semiotics (general)

of graphics, 701

Peircean semiotics, 178

semiotics of music, 175, 176, 178, 179, 180, 353

historic meter signatures, 213

senario (Zarlino), 443, 456

senses of vision and touch, 174, 179

sensorimotor engagement, 273, 274

sensus, 446

sentence (Schoenberg) as phrase type, 193, 305, 313, 314, 316, 319, 321, 322, 329, 359, 596

expectation of balanced presentation and continuation, 323–324

terms in French, German, or Italian, 305

sequence, *See also under* tonality

aesthetic, critical appraisal, 517, 580, 598; "cobbler's patch, " 580

agent of stylistic change, 599

as interplay of identity and difference, 577

as lens on various theoretical traditions, 579, 595–596

as site of stylistic tension between Baroque and Classical, 579, 598, 599

diatonic, 577, 585

enlarged, expositional role in Wagner, Liszt, Bruckner, 329

governing logic, 583

melodic, 518

rule of three, suggested limits on repetition, 517, 580

sequential progressions in Classical harmony, 305, 312, 313

stasis and dynamism, 587

terminology—"model-sequence," 517, 582, 596; "pattern, " 582; "repetend, " 582

theoretical categories of real, tonal, modulating, nonmodulating, "unreal" (Bass), "not-not-tonal" and "not-not-real" (Waltham-Smith), 518, 583, 586

Tristan Prelude and, 329, 456

types—ascending fifths sequence, 668 (fig. 12.10d); ascending thirds sequence, 328; descending fifths sequence, 379, 583, 587, 588–589, 591, 594, 596, *See also related* six-three chords in parallel stepwise motion; descending thirds sequence, 370, 517; like Pachelbel Canon in D major, 369, 667; *rosalia*, 580, 582

serial composition, serialism, serial theory, 51, 719, *See also* tone row; twelve-tone technique

Sessions, Roger—writings, 304, 677–678, 682

seventh chords, 468, 470, 660

diminished seventh chord, 631, 715

incomplete, 480

minor-major, 330

Severy, Melvin L., 25

sforzando, 189, 308, 327